The Modern Theologians

SECOND EDITION

The Modern Theologians

*An introduction to Christian theology
in the twentieth century*

SECOND EDITION

Edited by
David F. Ford
University of Cambridge

 BLACKWELL
Publishers

Copyright © Blackwell Publishers Ltd, 1997

First published 1997

2 4 6 8 10 9 7 5 3 1

Blackwell Publishers Inc.
238 Main Street
Cambridge, Massachusetts 02142
USA

Blackwell Publishers Ltd
108 Cowley Road
Oxford OX4 1JF
UK

Library of Congress Cataloging-in-Publication Data
The modern theologians : an introduction to Christian theology in the
  twentieth century / edited by David F. Ford. — 2nd ed.
    p. cm.
  Includes bibliographical references and index.
  ISBN 0–631–19591–2 (hardcover : alk. paper). — ISBN 0–631–19592–0
(pbk. : alk. paper)
    1. Theology, Doctrinal—History—20th century. I. Ford, David,
  1948– .
  BT28.M59 1996
  230′.09′04—dc20   96–16024
                                           CIP

British Library Cataloguing in Publication Data
A CIP catalogue record for this book is available from the British Library.

Commissioning Editor: Alison Mudditt
Desk Editor: Sandra Raphael
Production/Controller: Lisa Eaton
Text Designer: Lisa Eaton
Indexer: Zeb Korycinska

Typeset in 10/12pt Galliard by Graphicraft Typesetters Ltd, Hong Kong
Printed in Great Britain by T.J. Press Ltd, Padstow, Cornwall

This book is printed on acid-free paper

Contents

Preface

The main aim of this volume is to introduce the thought of most leading twentieth-century Christian theologians and movements in theology. The period for our purposes begins with the First World War, 1914–18. Two criteria of selection were that the theologians should have written constructively on a broad range of theological issues, and that they should be widely studied at present, especially in universities, seminaries, and by others at the third level. There were also the more controversial criteria of quality and significance, and in some cases these have been decisive for inclusion.

The contributors are mostly based in Europe or North America and come from a wide range of institutions, denominational backgrounds, and countries. Most are themselves constructively engaged in modern theology, and their purpose has been both to produce a scholarly account of their subject and also to carry further the theological dialogue in each case. So the aim has been partly "historical theology" but also the sort of engaged discussion that comes from those who are practitioners in the field. I have been acutely aware of the impossibility of trying to look at this vast field from every angle and of the limitations in my chosen way of trying to do some justice to it.

The chapters try to help readers to think in a way appropriate to a theologian or movement while also encouraging dialogue and argument. The only way this can happen adequately is by close study of a theologian's writings, and it is to these above all that we aim to introduce readers. The main intended use of this volume is therefore to prepare for, accompany, and aid reflection on the study of texts. Yet few will be able to read all these theologies, so the complementary intention is to give some grasp of the rest of the field.

There is a common pattern followed by most of the contributors: introduction, survey, content (concentrating on the main issues of a theology, or on particular members of movements), the debate about the content, an assessment of the theology's influence, achievement, and agenda for the future, and a short bibliography. In addition, each part and section of a part has a brief introduction. At the end of the volume there is a list of important dates and a glossary of key words and phrases which a student entering the field might not have met already.

The grouping of theologians and movements into parts and sections should not have too much read into it. The arrangement has not been arrived at easily, because other schemes had almost equal advantages. My brief introductions try to explain the selections, but the overriding concern has been for the particularity of each theology as understood by another theologian.

Part I is about major figures in continental European theology. Among them are the most likely candidates for "classic" status in this type of theology this century: Barth, Bonhoeffer, Bultmann, Tillich, Rahner, and Balthasar. The coherence of Part I revolves around Protestant and Roman Catholic theologies which were largely centered in German-speaking Europe, though of the Roman Catholics included only Rahner is actually German. That German-language tradition of academic theology perhaps deserves its large share of this volume because, for all its problems and peculiarities, it is, as my Introduction explains, the most sustained and intensive example of engagement in the enterprise of modern theology in the nineteenth and twentieth centuries. To know that tradition is to be acquainted with a range of paradigmatic attempts to tackle key issues of modernity and religion in theology. It is not by any means all-inclusive, but it has the diversity, the coherence, and the thinkers of genius that make it educationally the best single tradition through which to be introduced to what it means to do Christian theology in intelligent engagement with modern disciplines, societies, churches, and traumatic events.

Parts II, III, and IV cover further areas defined geographically: Britain, the United States of America, Latin America, Africa, and Asia. Part V on Evangelical and Orthodox Theologies covers a few thinkers from traditions to which hundreds of millions of Christians belong but which are often underrepresented in academic discussion.

Parts VI, VII, and VIII approach theology from different angles. Biblical and Hermeneutical Theology, Ecumenical Theology, Theology of Mission, Feminist Theology, Postmodern Theology, Theology of Religions, and Theology and the Arts and Sciences all, in diverse ways, cut across geographical and church divisions. Many of the theologians treated in earlier chapters contribute to the topics of these chapters too, but I have considered it worthwhile to recognize the importance of these distinctive theological enterprises.

In studying these 35 chapters one can glimpse the global scope of Christian theology, its diversity amounting often to fragmentation, and the immense intellectual energy with which it has accompanied or challenged or been knitted into major Christian, interreligious, and secular movements. At every point I have been painfully aware of having to omit theologies which would, given more space, have merited inclusion. Whole regions with rich theological traditions have been passed over. The Pentecostal churches have not had their complex, lively, and influential theologies discussed. Each of the major world religions (and why not other more local religions too?) would ideally receive the individual treatment that only Judaism has in this volume. The scope for further "Theology and . . ." studies is limitless – some leading candidates for separate chapters in future editions are psychology, information technology, economics, management, social anthropology, medicine, education, criminology, film, and architecture.

Nevertheless, I hope that the changes in this volume are an improvement on the first edition. They are in large part a response to many comments from readers and from fellow academics whose courses require an expanded coverage. For those accustomed to the first edition I will list the main differences. There are new chapters on French Theology, Theology and Society in Britain, Black, Hispanic, and Native American Theologies in the US, Feminist and Womanist Theologies in the US, African Theology, South African Theology, Biblical and Hermeneutical Theology, Theology of Mission, Postmodern Theology, Judaism and Christian Theology, Theology and the Natural Sciences, Theology and the Arts, and Theology and the Social Sciences. There are new authors for the chapters on Bonhoeffer, Balthasar (a joint author), Theological Ethics in the US, Asian Theology, and Ecumenical Theology. There are no longer separate chapters on Lonergan, T. F. Torrance (who is treated both under British Theology through Philosophy and Theology and the Natural Sciences) and Process Theology (which is included under Revisionists and Liberals in the US). Many chapters whose titles and authors remain the same have undergone substantial revision since the first edition.

Finally, in my Epilogue I risk giving a view of Christian Theology at the Turn of the Millennium, in particular suggesting what I consider to be the most important questions facing those who work in this field.

David F. Ford
Cambridge
April 1996

Acknowledgements

During the three years of editing this second edition of *The Modern Theologians* I have been immensely grateful to many who have given assistance. The debts of gratitude acknowledged in the first edition all still stand, and some have continued to increase during the preparation of this edition: to my wife Deborah, my mother Phyllis Ford, Dan and Perrin Hardy, and Micheal O'Siadhail. In addition, Alison Mudditt of Blackwells has been most supportive and accommodating, and many friends in the Society for the Study of Theology and the American Academy of Religion have been generous consultants. I am deeply grateful to each of the contributors who have given so much thought, time, and energy to this project. Above all, Ben Quash has worked hard on updating the Glossary and Table of Dates, as well as helping with proofreading and co-authoring the revised chapter on Balthasar; and Anna Marina has given invaluable and patient secretarial assistance.

Since editing the first edition I have moved from Birmingham to Cambridge. I have greatly appreciated crucial pieces of advice about this edition from my colleague Nicholas Lash. I also frequently look back on 15 years in the Department of Theology in the University of Birmingham with intense thankfulness. The first edition was dedicated to the memory of Hans W. Frei, teacher and friend to me and many others. He had given his Edward Cadbury Lectures, on which the typology in my Introduction draws, in the University of Birmingham the year before his death. The debt that so many of us owe to him increases over the years, as his life and thought continue to be fruitful. This second edition is dedicated to Frances Young, the present Edward Cadbury Professor of Theology and Dean of the Faculty of Arts in the University of Birmingham. Her continuing friendship is a source of great joy and encouragement to me and to Deborah. I am more grateful than I say for our years together as colleagues and co-authors in Birmingham. Not least, I have been inspired by her dedication to the more hidden, institutional side of building up universities and the discipline of theology. Above all it is her passionate, scholarly, and imaginative theological questioning, which continually accompanies my own thinking and that of many others, that make it deeply appropriate to offer this edition to her.

David F. Ford

Notes on Contributors

Ray S. Anderson is Professor of Theology and Ministry, Fuller Theological Seminary, Pasadena, California. He was born in the United States and educated there and at the University of Edinburgh. His publications include *Historical Transcendence and the Reality of God* (London and Grand Rapids, MI, 1976); *On Being Human* (Grand Rapids, MI, 1982); *Theology, Death, and Dying* (Oxford, 1986); *Christians Who Counsel* (Grand Rapids, MI, 1990); and *Self Care: A theology of personal wholeness and spiritual healing* (Wheaton, IL, 1995).

Richard Bauckham is Professor of New Testament Studies at the University of St Andrews, Scotland. He was born and educated in England. His publications include *Tudor Apocalypse* (Appleford, 1978); *Jude, 2 Peter* (Word Biblical Commentary, vol. 50; Waco, TX, 1983); *Moltmann: Messianic theology in the Making* (Basingstoke, 1987); *The Bible in Politics: How to read the Bible politically* (London, 1989, and Philadelphia, 1990); *Jude and the Relatives of Jesus in the Early Church* (Edinburgh, 1990); *The Theology of the Book of Revelation* (Cambridge, 1993); *The Climax of Prophecy: Studies on the Book of Revelation* (Cambridge, 1993); and *The Theology of Jürgen Moltmann* (Edinburgh, 1995).

Kwame Bediako is Director of the Akrofi-Christaller Memorial Centre for Mission Research and Applied Theology, Akropong-Akuapem, Ghana, and Visiting African Theology Lecturer in the Centre for the Study of Christianity in the Non-Western World, New College, University of Edinburgh. His publications include *Theology and Identity: The impact of culture upon Christian thought in the second century and modern Africa* (Oxford, 1992) and *Christianity in Africa: The renewal of a non-Western religion* (Edinburgh and New York, 1995).

Jeremy Begbie is Vice-Principal and Tutor in Doctrine at Ridley Hall, Cambridge, and lectures in theology at the Faculty of Divinity in the University of Cambridge. He was educated at the Universities of Edinburgh and Aberdeen. His publications include *Voicing Creation's Praise* (Edinburgh, 1981); *Music in God's Purposes* (Edinburgh, 1988); and *The Sound of God: Resonances between theology and music* (forthcoming).

James J. Buckley is Professor of Theology at Loyola College, Baltimore, Maryland. He was born and educated in the United States. He has written *Seeking the Humanity of God: Practices, doctrines, and Catholic* *theology* (Collegeville, MN, 1992), as well as articles on contemporary theology; he is also co-editor of *Modern Theology* and *Blackwell Readings in Modern Theology*.

Rebecca S. Chopp is Professor in Theology and Dean of Faculty and Academic Affairs at the Candler School of Theology, Emory University, Atlanta, Georgia. She was born and educated in the United States. Her publications include *The Praxis of Suffering* (New York, 1986); *The Power to Speak* (New York, 1989); and *Saving Work* (Louisville, KY, 1995).

M. Shawn Copeland is Associate Professor of Theology at Marquette University, Milwaukee, Wisconsin. She was born and educated in the United States. She is the author of more than 30 book chapters and journal articles and co-editor, with Professor Elisabeth Schüssler Fiorenza, of the feminist theology series for the international theological journal *Concilium*.

Gavin D'Costa is Senior Lecturer in Theology in the Department of Theology and Religious Studies at the University of Bristol. He is an Indian Roman Catholic who was educated at the Universities of Birmingham and Cambridge. His publications include *Theology and Religious Pluralism* (Oxford and New York, 1986) and *John Hick's Theology of Religions* (London and New York, 1987) and he has edited *Christian Uniqueness Reconsidered* (New York, 1990). He is involved in interfaith dialogue and is an advisor to the Catholic Bishops of England and Wales and a consultant to the Pontifical Commission for Interreligious Dialogue. He is currently writing a book on the trinity and religious pluralism.

John de Gruchy is the Robert Selby Taylor Professor of Christian Studies at the University of Cape Town, South Africa. A native South African, he is an ordained minister of the United Congregational Church of Southern Africa. He studied at the University of Cape Town, Rhodes University, Chicago Theological Seminary, and the University of South Africa. His doctoral dissertation was on the ecclesiology of Karl Barth and Dietrich Bonhoeffer. Having served as minister of several congregations (1961–8), he was Director of Communications and Studies at the South African Council of Churches (1968–73) before joining the faculty at the University of Cape Town in 1973.

J. A. Di Noia, OP, serves as Executive Director of the Secretariat for Doctrine and Pastoral Practices of the National Conference of Catholic Bishops in Washington, DC. He continues as Professor of Systematic Theology at the Dominican House of Studies, as well as serving as Adjunct Professor in the John Paul II Institute for Marriage and Family Studies, and as Editor-in-Chief of the *Thomist*. He was born in New York City, and was educated in the general studia of the Dominican Order and at Yale. His publications include *The Diversity of Religions: A Christian perspective* (Washington, 1982), and articles on the trinity, theological method, and the theology of religions.

David F. Ford is Regius Professor of Divinity in the University of Cambridge and chairs the Management Committee of the Centre for Advanced Religious and Theological Studies. He was born in Dublin and studied classics at Trinity College Dublin and theology at the Universities of Cambridge, Yale, and Tübingen. His publications include *Barth and God's Story: Biblical narrative and the theological method of Karl Barth in the Church Dogmatics* (Frankfurt, Berne, and New York, 1981; 2nd edn, 1985); *Jubilate: Theology in praise*, with Daniel W. Hardy (London, 1984), US title *Praising and Knowing God* (Philadelphia, 1985); *Meaning and Truth in 2 Corinthians*, with Frances M. Young (London,

1987, Grand Rapids, MI, 1988); *A Long Rumour of Wisdom: Redescribing theology* (Cambridge, 1992); and, with Dennis L. Stamps, he edited *Essentials of Christian Community* (Edinburgh, 1996).

George Gispert-Sauch, SJ, is from Catalonia in Spain. He arrived in India in 1949, joining the Society of Jesus, and has lived and taught in India ever since. After taking a first-class MA honours degree in Sanskrit and Pali at the University of Bombay (1955), he followed it with a PhD in Hindu religious thought at the Institut Catholique in Paris (1963). He has just retired from the post of Professor of Indian and Systematic Theology at Vidyajyoti College of Theology, the Jesuit theologate in Delhi, and is now Librarian of the College. He is a member of numerous ecumenical and other societies (including EATWOT), and has published and lectured widely in India and abroad on Indian thought, inter-religious encounter, and the theology of religions.

Daniel W. Hardy was born in the United States, lives in Cambridge, England, and is a member of the Faculty of Divinity at the University of Cambridge. Until 1995 he was Director of the Center of Theological Inquiry at Princeton, and before that he was Van Mildert Professor of Divinity at the University of Durham and Senior Lecturer in Theology at the University of Birmingham. His publications include *Jubilate: Theology in praise*, with David F. Ford (London, 1984), US title *Praising and Knowing God* (Philadelphia, 1985), and *God's Ways with the World* (Edinburgh, 1996).

Graham Howes is Staff Tutor in Social and Political Science at the University of Cambridge Board of Continuing Education and a Fellow of Trinity Hall. He was born in Norfolk. His publications include articles on religious art and religious experience, ritual, and religion and aesthetics in Victorian England. He is a trustee of ACE (Art and Christian Enquiry) and the Centre for the Study of Implicit Religion.

Werner G. Jeanrond is Professor of Systematic Theology at the Faculty of Theology at the University of Lund, Sweden. He was born in Germany and studied at the Universities of Saarbrücken, Regensburg, and Chicago. He previously taught theology at Trinity College, University of Dublin. His publications include *Text and Interpretation as Categories of Theological Thinking* (Dublin and New York, 1988; German original, 1986); and *Theological Hermeneutics* (London and New York, 1991 and 1994), and *Call and Response: The challenge of Christian life* (Dublin and New York, 1995).

Robert W. Jenson is Professor of Religion at St Olaf College, Northfield, Minnesota, Associate Director of the Center for Catholic and Evangelical Theology, and co-founder and co-editor of the journal *Pro Ecclesia*. He was born in the United States, and educated there and in the Universities of Heidelberg and Basel. He has written on topics ranging across the spectrum of theology, perhaps especially on the doctrine of God. His most recent books are *Unbaptized God: The basic flaw in ecumenical theology* (Minneapolis, 1992) and *Essays in the Theory of Culture* (Grand Rapids, MI, 1995).

David H. Kelsey is Luther A. Weigle Professor of Theology at Yale Divinity School, New Haven, Connecticut. He was born in Egypt and educated in the United States at Haverford College and Yale University. His publications include *The Fabric of Paul Tillich's Theology* (New Haven, 1967); *The Uses of Scripture in Recent Theology* (Philadelphia, 1975); *To Understand God Truly: What's theological about a theological school?* (Louisville, KY, 1992); and *Between Athens and Berlin: The theological education debate* (Grand Rapids, MI, 1993).

Fergus Kerr, OP, is Prior of the Dominican house in Edinburgh and Honorary Senior Lecturer in the Department of Theology and Religious Studies at the University of Edinburgh. He has published *Theology after Wittgenstein* (Oxford, 1986).

Ann Loades is Professor of Divinity at the University of Durham. She was born in England and educated there and at McMaster University, Canada. Her past research and publication was largely concerned with theodicy. An invitation to give the Scott Holland Lectures resulted in *Searching for Lost Coins* (London, 1987) and *Feminist Theology: A reader* (London and Louisville, KY, 1990). Most recently she has edited, with David Brown, *The Sense of the Sacramental: Movement and measure in art and music, place and time* (London, 1995) and *Christ the Sacramental Word: Incarnation, sacrament and poetry* (London, 1996), both of which indicate her current and future research field.

Charles Marsh is associate Professor of Theology at Loyola College, Baltimore, Maryland, and Director of Theological Horizons, a nonprofit organization which supports theological research and education. He was born and educated in the United States. His publications include *Reclaiming Dietrich Bonhoeffer: The promise of his theology* (New York, 1994) and, together with Wayne Whitson Floyd, Jr, he edited *Theology and the Practice of Responsibility* (Valley Forge, PA, 1994).

Robert Morgan is University Lecturer in Theology and Fellow of Linacre College, Oxford. He was born in Wales and educated at the Universities of Cambridge, Durham, and Tübingen. His publications include *The Nature of New Testament Theology* (London, 1973); with Michael Pye, *Ernst Troeltsch: Writings on theology and religion* (London, 1977); with John Barton, *Biblical Interpretation* (Oxford, 1988); and

Romans (Sheffield, 1995). He also edited *The Religion of the Incarnation* (Bristol, 1989).

Peter Ochs is Wallerstein Professor of Jewish Studies at Drew University, Madison, New Jersey. He was born and educated in the United States. He edits the *Postmodern Jewish Philosophy Network*, and his publications include *Reading Peirce's Pragmatism: Philosophy, theology, and the logic of Scripture* (Cambridge, 1997); *Reviewing the Covenant: Eugene Borowitz and the postmodern renewal of theology*, with Eugene Borowitz (New York, 1996), and the edited collections *The Return to Scripture in Judaism and Christianity* (New York, 1993) and *Understanding the Rabbinic Mind* (Atlanta, GA, 1990).

Ted Peters is Professor of Systematic Theology at Pacific Lutheran Seminary and the Graduate Theological Union in Berkeley, California. He is a research associate at the Center for Theology and the Natural Sciences. He is author of *GOD – The World's Future: Systematic theology for a postmodern era* (Minneapolis, 1992); *GOD as Trinity: Relationality and temporality in divine life* (Louisville, KY, 1993); and editor of *Cosmos as Creation: Theology and science in consonance* (Nashville, TN, 1989).

William C. Placher is Professor and Chair in the Department of Philosophy and Religion at Wabash College, Indiana. He was born and educated in the United States. His publications include *A History of Christian Theology* (Philadelphia, 1983); *Unapologetic Theology* (Louisville, KY, 1989); *Narratives of a Vulnerable God* (Louisville, KY, 1994); and *The Domestication of Transcendence* (Louisville, KY, 1996).

Ben Quash is Tutor in Systematic Theology, Wesley House, and Chaplain of Fitzwilliam College, University of Cambridge. He was born in England and educated at the University of Cambridge. He is working on "A Critique of Hans Urs von Balthasar's Use of Drama in the Theo-logy of *Theo-Drama*," and has contributed to *Modern Theology*.

John Riches is Professor of Divinity and Biblical Criticism at the University of Glasgow. He was born in England and studied there and in Germany. His publications include *Jesus and the Transformation of Judaism* (London, 1980); and *The World of Jesus: First-century Judaism in crisis* (Cambridge, 1990); and he edited *The Analogy of Beauty* (Edinburgh, 1986) and the English translation of Hans Urs von Balthasar, *The Glory of the Lord* (Edinburgh, 1982–91). He currently edits *Studies of the New Testament and its World* (Edinburgh, 1981–   ).

Richard Roberts is Professor of Religious Studies in the University of Lancaster. Before that he was Professor of Divinity and founding Director of the Institute for Religion and the Human Sciences in the University of St Andrews; M. B. Reckitt Research Fellow in the University of Lancaster; and Lecturer in Theology in the University of Durham. He was educated at the Universities of Lancaster, Cambridge, Edinburgh, and Tübingen. He has published books on Karl Barth and edited, with J. M. M. Good, *The Recovery of Rhetoric: Persuasive discourse and disciplinarity in the human sciences* (Bristol, 1993).

Michael Root is Research Professor and Director of the Institute for Ecumenical Research, Strasbourg, France. He was born in the United States and studied at Yale University. He earlier taught systematic theology at Lutheran Southern Seminary, South Carolina. He is the author of numerous essays on ecumenism and other theological topics, and is editor and translator (with W. G. Rusch) of *Justification by Faith* (New York, forthcoming).

Lamin Sanneh was educated on four continents. He went to school in the Gambia, West Africa, then went to the United States to read history. After graduating he spent several years studying classical Arabic and Islam, including a stint in the Middle East, and working with churches in Africa and international organizations concerned with interreligious issues. He received his PhD in Islamic history at the University of London. He was a professor at Harvard University for eight years before moving to Yale in 1989 as the D. Willis James Professor of Missions and World Christianity, with a concurrent courtesy appointment as Professor of History at Yale College. He is an editor-at-large of the ecumenical weekly, the *Christian Century*. He is the author of over a hundred articles on religious and historical subjects, and of several books, including *The Jakhande Muslim Clerics: A religious and historical study of Islam in Senegambia*; *West African Christianity: The religious impact*; *Translating the Message: The missionary impact on culture* (now in its sixth printing); *Encountering the West: Christianity and the global cultural process*; *The Crown and the Turban: Muslims and West African pluralism*; and *Piety and Power: Muslims and Christians in West Africa*. For his academic work he was made Commandeur de l'Ordre National du Lion, Senegal's highest national honor.

Robert J. Schreiter, CPPS, is Professor of Theology at the Catholic Theological Union in Chicago. He was born in the United States and studied there and under Edward Schillebeeckx at the University of Nijmegen, the Netherlands. His publications include *Constructing Local Theologies* (New York and London, 1985); *In Water and in Blood: A spirituality of solidarity and hope* (New York, 1988); with M. C. Hilkert, *The Praxis of Christian Experience: An orientation to Schillebeeckx* (San Francisco, 1989); and *Reconciliation* (New York, 1992). He also edited *The Schillebeeckx*

Reader (New York, 1984, and Edinburgh, 1988).

Christoph Schwöbel is Professor of Systematic Theology and Director of the Institute for Systematic Theology and Social Ethics at the University of Kiel. He was born and educated in Germany. From 1986 to 1993 he was Lecturer in Systematic Theology at King's College, London. He has written *Martin Rade* (Gütersloh, 1980) and *God, Action, and Revelation* (Kampen, 1992); and he has edited *Karl Barth–Martin Rade. Ein Briefwechsel* (Gütersloh, 1981); *Martin Rade. Ausgewählte Schriften*, volumes I–III (Gütersloh, 1983–8); and, with Colin Gunton, *Persons – Divine and Human* (Edinburgh, 1991) and *Trinitarian Theology Today* (Edinburgh, 1995).

Peter Sedgwick works at the Board for Social Responsibility of the Church of England in London. He was Vice-Principal of Westcott House, Cambridge, and Lecturer in Theology at the Universities of Hull and Birmingham. He was born in Glasgow and educated at the Universities of Cambridge and Durham. His publications include *The Enterprise Culture* (London, 1992) and several edited volumes.

S. W. Sykes is the Bishop of Ely, formerly Regius Professor of Divinity in the University of Cambridge and Van Mildert Professor of Divinity in the University of Durham. He was born in England and educated at the Universities of Cambridge and Harvard. His publications include *Christian Theology Today* (London, 1971, 1983); *The Integrity of Anglicanism* (London, 1978); *The Identity of Christianity* (London, 1984); *Unashamed Anglicanism* (London, 1995); and numerous edited volumes.

Anthony C. Thiselton is Professor of Christian Theology and Head of the Department of Theology in the University of Nottingham, and also Canon Theologian

of Leicester Cathedral. He was born in Surrey and is a graduate of the Universities of London, Sheffield, and Durham. His publications include *The Two Horizons: New Testament hermeneutics and philosophical description* (Exeter and Grand Rapids, MI, 1980; Korean translation, Seoul, 1990); *New Horizons in Hermeneutics* (London and Grand Rapids, MI, 1992); and *Interpreting God and the Postmodern Self* (Edinburgh and Grand Rapids, MI, 1995).

Graham Ward is Dean of Peterhouse, Cambridge, where he teaches theology and philosophy. He is the author of *Barth, Derrida and the Language of Theology* (Cambridge, 1995) and *Theology and Contemporary Critical Theory* (London, 1996). He is the editor of the journal *Literature and Theology*.

John B. Webster is Lady Margaret Professor of Divinity, Christ Church, University of Oxford. Until 1995 he was Ramsay Armitage Professor of Systematic Theology at Wycliffe College, University of Toronto. He was born and educated in England. His publications include *God is Here* (London, 1983); *Eberhard Jüngel: An introduction to his theology* (Cambridge, 1986); and *Barth's Ethics of Reconciliation* (Cambridge, 1995). He has also translated two volumes of Jüngel's *Theological Essays* (Edinburgh, 1989–95) and edited *The Possibilities of Theology: Studies in the theology of Eberhard Jüngel in his sixtieth year* (Edinburgh, 1994).

William Werpehowski is Associate Professor of Theology and Religious Studies at Villanova University, Pennsylvania. He was born and educated in the United States. His publications include *The Love Commandments: Essays in Christian ethics and moral philosophy*, edited with Edmund N. Santurri (Washington, DC, 1992) and *The Essential Paul Ramsey*, edited with Stephen Crocco (New Haven and London, 1994).

Rowan Williams is the Bishop of Monmouth. He was formerly Lady Margaret Professor of Divinity, Christ Church, University of Oxford. He was born in Wales and educated at the Universities of Cambridge and Oxford. His publications include *The Wound of Knowledge* (London, 1969); *Resurrection: Interpreting the Easter Gospel* (London, 1982); *Arius: Heresy and tradition* (London, 1987); and *Open to Judgement* (London, 1994).

Introduction to Modern
Christian Theology

David F. Ford

Christian theology in this century has been immensely varied. This has not just been a matter of diverse approaches and conclusions, but also of fundamental differences about what theology is, what modernity is, and what Christianity is, and which questions within these areas are to be given priority. This makes an overview difficult, all the more so because many of the theologians are still alive and producing new works, and some of the movements are still young. This introduction attempts to give, not an integrating picture, but sufficient background and general understanding of the field to help readers approaching it for the first time to find their bearings, and to assist more experienced readers to explore it further. The Epilogue gives a more forward-looking assessment of the field at the turn of the millennium.

What Sort of Subject is Modern Christian Theology?

Between the European Middle Ages and the end of the nineteenth century there were many major events and transformations of life and thought, often originating in Europe but with global consequences. Chief among these have been the Renaissance and Reformation, the colonization of the Americas, the Enlightenment, the American and French Revolutions, the rise of nationalism, the Industrial Revolution, and the development of the natural sciences, technologies, medical science, and the human sciences. There has also been the combined impact of bureaucracies, constitutional democracy, new means of warfare and of communication, mass education and public health programs, and new movements in the arts and in philosophy and religion.

Theologians have been members of societies, churches, and academic institutions through this innovative, traumatic period, and their theology has inevitably been influenced by it. That is how, in a minimal sense, their theology is modern: by taking account of such developments, even if sometimes in order to dismiss, criticize, or try to reverse them.

Some may wish to repeat a past theology, but this is not possible. The context has changed, and what is actually communicated and understood today can be very far from the original meaning. Yet Christian theology always requires some continuity with the past, so the question is how there can be appropriate continuity without simple repetition.

What is the significance of modernity for the content and method of theology? What is the importance of Christianity for a proper appreciation and response to modernity? And might it be that a religion with the discontinuity of the crucifixion at its heart enables a creative way of coping with the novelty and disruption of modernity? Such questions, which are broadly in the area of interpretation or hermeneutics, are inextricable from others about the nature of Christianity and of theology. All the theologians treated in these volumes have to handle them, and it might be helpful to note some of the main strategies they use. Imagine a line punctuated by five types[1] of theology. At one end, the first type is simply the attempt to repeat a traditional theology or version of Christianity and see all reality in its own terms, with no recognition of the significance for it of other perspectives or of all that has happened in recent centuries. At the other extreme, the fifth type gives complete priority to some modern secular philosophy or worldview, and Christianity in its own terms is only valid in so far as it fits in with that. So, for this fifth type, parts of Christian faith and practice may be found true or acceptable, but the assessment is always made according to criteria which are external to faith and which claim superiority to it. Neither of these extremes is represented among the theologians studied in this book, the first because it is hardly modern in the sense intended, the fifth because it is hardly Christian.

That leaves three types in between. Type two gives priority to the self-description of the Christian community (which is, of course, by no means uncontroversial) and might be characterized by Anselm of Canterbury's motto, "faith seeking understanding." It insists that Christian identity is primary and that all other reality needs to be construed in relation to it, but also that Christianity itself needs continually to be rethought and that theology must engage seriously with the modern world in its quest for understanding. Karl Barth is a leading representative of this approach, though this type-casting by no means exhausts his theology – and the same is true of attempts to pigeonhole most of the other theologians. Robert Jenson's essay (chapter 1) takes as its leading theme how Barth responded to Enlightenment and later thinkers by refusing their terms and developing his own framework through Jesus Christ and the Trinity. Further examples of this type are Bonhoeffer (though some would dispute this, especially as regards his latest letters and papers), Jüngel, Congar, de Lubac, Balthasar, MacKinnon, the postliberals, those called conservative postmoderns in chapter 30, and some Evangelicals and Eastern Orthodox theologians. Peter Ochs in chapter 31 produces an original analysis of how this and other types relate to Judaism and Jewish theologies. Type three comes exactly at the middle of the line. It is a theology of correlation. It brings traditional Christian faith and understanding into dialogue with modernity, and tries to correlate the two in a wide variety of ways. It does not claim any overarching integration of Christianity and modernity – neither one that would subsume modernity within Christian terms nor one that would exhaustively present Christianity in specifically modern terms. In its classic modern representative, Paul Tillich, it takes the form of the basic questions raised in contemporary life and thought being correlated with answers developed through interpretation of key Christian symbols. In a period of fragmentation and pluralism the method of correlation is especially attractive as a way of keeping going a range of open dialogues. It is a component in most theologies and is particularly important in Schillebeeckx, Küng, and many of those in both Britain and North America who could be called revisionist. James Buckley in chapter 17 defines revisionists as those "devoted to shaping Christian practices and teachings in dialogue with . . . modern philosophies, cultures and social practices."

The fourth type uses a particular (or sometimes more than one) modern philosophy, conceptuality, or problem as a way of integrating Christianity with an understanding of modernity. It wants to do justice to both and sees the best way of doing this to be the consistent reinterpretation of Christianity in terms of some contemporary idiom or concern. Robert Morgan (chapter 4) sees Rudolf Bultmann in these terms, using existentialism as the key to interpreting the New Testament. Morgan's critical comments suggest that Bultmann's position would benefit by being opened up to the approach of the third type. Other examples of this fourth type might be Pannenberg, those Buckley describes as liberals, and some leading representatives of theologies which propose issues of gender, race, political liberation, or interreligious dialogue as the decisive integrators.

Such a scheme is too neat to fit the whole of any major theology, but it helps in mapping some of the main possibilities in relation to a central and unavoidable matter, the interaction of Christianity with modernity. It also enables us to notice some theologians in whom apparently no one type is dominant. Karl Rahner, as interpreted by Joseph Di Noia (chapter 7), is irreducibly pluralist, even though many standard readings of him make him seem, in his use of a particular philosophical anthropology, to fit the fourth type. It can be immensely significant for a theologian's reputation and reception to liberate him or her from inadequate typing, and when a particular theology seems to fit well into one type there must be a special effort to discern the ways in which the type is also transcended. Christoph Schwöbel's description of Pannenberg in chapter 11 does this for him. It may also be that, whatever one's own preferred type, the quality of one's theology is still linked to the depth of engagement with those who might be categorized under other types. Hans Frei, who developed this typology, saw himself doing theology between the second and third types, while intellectually and aesthetically participating in all five.

This leads into a final observation that many of the deepest differences about important matters, and even whole ways of doing theology, cut across the above types. This applies, for example, to the role of practice or of decision in Christianity, and to some conceptions of human freedom, divine action, the shape of the church and much else. There is no substitute for engaging with issues of content, and often in the intensive grappling with key questions the rather formal and abstract concern about mapping the types is swallowed up in the adventure of a particular intellectual, spiritual, and practical journey.

Key Modern Issues

What have been the main issues in twentieth-century theology? The following five sections explore what has been characteristic: the continuing importance of the inherited agenda of doctrines, the problem of how to integrate a theology, the recovery and criticism of the past, the special significance of the nineteenth century, and the conditioning of theologies by their contexts and interests.

The systematic agenda

The traditional topics of what is variously called systematic theology, Christian doctrine, dogmatic theology, or constructive theology are: God and revelation, predestination (or election), creation and providence, human being, sin and evil, Jesus Christ, atonement (or redemption or salvation), the Holy Spirit (or grace), and Christian living (including justification, sanctification, vocation, and ethics), the church, ministry and sacraments, and eschatology. These doctrines (or dogmas or loci) can be seen as a concentration of the main events and issues in the Christian overarching story from before creation until after the consummation of history. They continue to be important for modern theology, and even when a theologian has a very different framework the questions raised by these doctrines will have to be answered. Among those topics, there have been some characteristic modern emphases. At least until the 1960s the distinctive contributions of twentieth-century thinkers were in the areas of God (especially the reconception of the Trinity and the relationship of suffering to God), revelation (very different approaches, represented for example by Barth, Bultmann, Tillich, Rahner, and Pannenberg), Jesus Christ and salvation in history (closely tied to the previous two issues), human being, and eschatology.

Eschatology deserves special mention. The century opened with the rediscovery by academic theology of its importance in the New Testament. Secular eschatologies (of progress, socialist revolution, empire, or race) have had immense influence in modern times, but mainstream Christianity had largely ignored the eschatological dimension of its own origins. When it was widely recognized, partly under the pressure of secular alternatives and the crisis of European culture and society manifest in the First World War, then it gave a new standpoint for thinking through Christianity. There was a great variety of eschatologies, and the unavoidability of the question has been one of the distinctive marks of twentieth-century in contrast with nineteenth-century theology.

It becomes increasingly difficult to generalize or have any adequate perspective on more recent years. Certainly any neglect of sin and evil (especially in the aftermath of the Holocaust, the Gulag, and Hiroshima) is being corrected in recent theology. As the Pentecostal movement has spread, not only in new independent churches but also through millions in the traditional denominations, the Holy Spirit has also been a major topic, though some would see this as a variation on the typically modern preoccupation with subjectivity and immediate experience. Christian living and the church have also had increasing attention, in line with emphases on praxis and community. And the earlier concern with eschatology has been somewhat overshadowed by a (not unrelated) focus on creation and ecological matters.

Integrations

How is a theologian to relate these various topics to each other? One tendency (corresponding to the second type described above) is to see Christianity having a certain coherence in itself. The doctrines together are the intellectual description of this. So Lindbcck (see chapter 18) compares doctrines to the statement of the basic grammar or rules showing how a language or culture hangs together. This makes the Christian community the main home of Christian theology (cf. Barth's *Church Dogmatics*) and asserts the priority of a distinctive Christian identity, as expressed above all in the Bible. The way theology is integrated in such an approach is through something internal to the tradition, usually the Bible or one or more key doctrines. Other worldviews and disciplines are discussed and may contribute, but not as equals or superiors.

Other theologians (in the third and fourth types) see integration with modernity as more important and even as essential to a modern theology. Typical concerns are to work out a theological method comparable with other disciplines, often trying to show that theology can justify its claims to rationality and knowledge (see Pannenberg, revisionists and liberals, and many participants in the debates about theology and the natural and human sciences outlined in chapters 33 and 35), or to affirm the relevance of Christian faith by reinterpreting it in relation to a modern philosophy (existentialism, process thought) or urgent issues (oppression, gender, race, nuclear war, ecology, relations between religions).

Overall, these theologies display a tension between the identity of Christianity and its relevance to modernity. At the international and institutional levels this has in the twentieth century been dramatized most publicly in ecumenical theology, as described by Michael Root (chapter 27), and it has been built into the World Council of Churches' twin focus on "Faith and Order" and "Life and Work." But Christianity in the twentieth century has also added hundreds of millions to its numbers in many parts of the world, and here the tensions of identity and relevance are often extreme. Theology of mission (chapter 28) is a direct attempt to cope with these issues.

Recovering and criticizing the past

A major feature of modernity has been its concern with history. Underlying this is a heightened awareness of change and innovation. The tools that have served this are new methods of research and new criteria for historical reliability. These, together with the greatly increased scale of historical work, have had the most obvious effects on theology. The Bible and the rest of the Christian heritage have been examined afresh and traditional opinions often challenged. But that has been just one manifestation of a more comprehensive problem.

Modern historical consciousness recognizes that meaning is closely bound up with changing contexts and that today we are also conditioned by many factors as we try to understand the past. Is the whole enterprise of "true" interpretation possible? For Christian theologians it has seemed unavoidable to attempt it, and the most fundamental reason for this is that Christianity (and it is not alone in this) cannot do without the authority of the past in some form. So a great deal of attention has been paid to what is often called hermeneutics, the art and theory of interpretation (chapter 26). How do we cope with the "hermeneutical circle," the problem that in understanding the past we tend to draw conclusions based on our own presuppositions, interests, and involvements? Is the meaning or truth of a text such as a gospel necessarily bound up with its being historically factual? There are very broad questions about language and self in relation to reality (there has been a great deal of reflection on metaphor, narrative, objectivity, and subjectivity), and other questions about genre, the intention of the author, or the relative roles of disciplines such as philology, literary criticism, sociology, psychology, comparative religion, philosophy, and history. And often there is a divergence between those who see much of the Christian past as on the whole worth recovering, and others who see it more as something from which liberation is needed and who use a "hermeneutic of suspicion" to do so.

The themes of suspicion, doubt, and radical critique are constantly present in modern thought, raising most sharply the issues of authority and reliability. For many the very discipline of theology has disintegrated and lost its intellectual integrity in the face of all this. So most theologians discussed in these volumes are engaged in a recovery of Christianity in the face of unprecedently devastating, sophisticated and widely disseminated dismissals of both Christianity and theology. That, at least, is the situation in the West and in those influenced by it. But some, such as Latin American liberation theologies (chapter 21), try to redefine the concerns and context of theology so that the confrontation with doubt, agnosticism, atheism, and the intellectual world of the modern West takes second place to serving a praxis of liberation.

In addition (and sometimes, as with Marx, accompanying a fundamental strategy of suspicion) there has been the challenge from modern overviews of history as alternatives to the much-criticized traditional Christian story stretching from creation to consummation. Does Christian theology need a renewed overarching conception of history? Pannenberg and Rahner would say so, but Bultmann would see such an idea as dangerously mythological, and many others too have serious reservations.

That and all the issues mentioned thus far can be seen as aspects of a pivotal modern theological concern: the relationship of faith and history. In continental European Protestant theology this was a fundamental matter dividing Barth and Bultmann. When they were found wanting by successors such as Pannenberg and Moltmann it was again this issue that was central. It has likewise been a dominant concern in much British, North American and Evangelical theology, and many new challenges in theology also focus on it in their own ways. It is perhaps in Roman Catholic theology that the implications of modern thinking about faith and history are most sharply underlined. This is partly because it was only in the third quarter of the twentieth century that Roman Catholic theologians could use modern historical methods without official disapproval. So since the Second World War there has been a hectic period of assimilation, reinterpretation, and controversy. It is symbolized in Schillebeeckx's journey from a tradition in which philosophy, not history, was the main partner of doctrine, through *ressourcement* and hermeneutics to a massive and controversial treatment of the main topic in the nineteenth- and twentieth-century debate about faith and history: Jesus Christ.

The nineteenth century: creativity and crisis

In the recovery and criticism of the past a theologian frequently gives a special place to particular periods or contributions. It is often more true to say that a theologian seems gripped in this way, and is immersed in texts and debates which have an authority that permeates his or her theology. The Bible is most widely treated in this way, and the patristic period is likewise usually privileged. The other two main reference points before the modern period are medieval theology and the Reformation. Periods, traditions, and theologies interanimate each other in subtle ways, and it is often crude to draw clear lines of influence. Yet it remains important to understand with whom a theologian finds dialogue most worthwhile.

One period, however, stands out as the most helpful in understanding what it means for twentieth-century theology to be specifically modern: the nineteenth century. That was the century in which the issues of modernity were tackled comprehensively for the first time, and most of the main Christian responses to them explored. So it is not surprising that the main dialogue partners for twentieth-century theologians outside their own period tend to be either nineteenth-century figures or movements of thought which were shaped then. Even though most theologies are, of course, deeply indebted to other periods as well, in their understanding of them the philosophical and historical habits of nineteenth-century thought are usually very influential. Barth, for example, who wanted to break with much of what he saw as characteristic of nineteenth-century theology, was steeped in it and has to be understood in relationship to it. The cost of ignoring the nineteenth century is often paid in energetically repeating the exploration of options which were developed and thoroughly discussed then, and most twentieth-century theologians know this.

It is therefore worth surveying the nineteenth century in its importance for this volume. The brevity of this can best be expanded through two capable treatments of this field, one by Claude Welch and the other edited by Ninian Smart and others.[2] There were three thrusts in nineteenth-century thought which especially need to be appreciated in relation to twentieth-century theologians. The first was the rethinking of knowledge and rationality, and the accompanying need to reconceive theology. This will be treated below through Kant, Schleiermacher, and Hegel. The second was the development of a new historical consciousness joined with the application of critical historical methods to religion. This will be traced through Hegel and Strauss. The third was the challenge of alternative explanations of religion, as seen in Feuerbach, Marx, Durkheim, and others. In the middle comes the awkward figure of Kierkegaard, and at the end the summing up of all the issues in Troeltsch.

Immanuel Kant (1724–1804) died just inside the nineteenth century and is the crucial figure linking it to the eighteenth century, especially its rationalist tradition. He offered an account of knowledge, and especially of the human knower in interaction with the object of knowledge, according to which claims to knowledge by both "natural theology" and "revelation" were disallowed. In place of his denial of knowledge he affirmed a faith which was practical and moral rather than theoretical, and which was not especially religious. The central notion is that of freedom. Its reality cannot be either proved or disproved by "pure reason," but it is reasonable to postulate it in order to make sense of human action and morality. This is the realm of "practical reason," through which Kant argues for the rationality not only of freedom but also of God and immortality. His own main theological work, *Religion within the Limits of Reason Alone*,[3] is a thorough "moralization" of religion, and in its pruning of Christianity to fit his philosophy is a good example of the fifth type of theology described above. Yet he is decisively theistic, with an austere conception of God as the "unconditioned" or "absolute," whose reality is beyond all knowledge or experience but is mediated through our sense of moral obligation. We see in Kant the most influential statement of the modern tendency to distinguish fact (pure reason) from value (practical reason) and to categorize religion and morality together under the latter. We see also the emphasis, typical of so many modern theologies, on the practical or ethical content of Christianity, especially the centrality of freedom. Sometimes this is developed focusing on personal freedom and intersubjectivity, as in existentialism's concern for encounter and decision. In others, such as Moltmann and liberation theologies, the practicality takes a social and political form and is more affected by post-Kantian ideas of history and society.

It is worth reflecting on why Kant's stress on the ethical, practical, and intersubjective in religion continued to be attractive. Partly it is because Kant shared common roots with many theologians in a Lutheran faith constituted by a dynamic interactive relationship between the believer and God. For those who came later it also represented an appealing response to the most dangerous threats which modernity posed, not only to theology but also to the whole realm of value, ethics, and the personal. These were the challenges of naturalistic and other "reductionist" explanations of religion, morality, and humanity which by the end of the century had been built up to massive proportions by such figures as Strauss (critical history), Feuerbach (philosophy), Marx (politics and economics), Durkheim and Weber (sociology), Frazer (comparative religion), William James (psychology), Darwin (evolutionary biology), and Nietzsche (philosophy). These have decisively shaped the "common sense" of many twentieth-century educated Western people about religion, and in the face of them the claim of Kant that the realm of freedom and practicality could not be reduced to any "objective" explanation offered theologians something which was both widely appealing beyond Christianity and a medium through which to express Christianity.

Kant's ethical interpretation was challenged by two major alternative ways of conceiving Christianity and theology in the early nineteenth century, those of Hegel and Schleiermacher. Friedrich Schleiermacher (1768–1834) is usually regarded as the outstanding theologian of the century. At the root of his achievement was a reconception of religion. For him it is primarily neither morality nor belief (knowledge) but is an immediate self-consciousness or feeling of absolute dependence on God. So the roots of faith are pre-moral and pre-cognitive, and this religious consciousness is common to all people, though very variously recognized and expressed. While in Kant God (the absolute or unconditioned) is present through our sense of moral obligation, in Schleiermacher God is present in an immediate dynamic relationship that grasps our whole being. Christianity is the specific form of this

God-consciousness shaped through Jesus Christ and the community of faith in him. This was a view of religion which had an integrity of its own in the subjective realm of feeling or consciousness, but which yet could be reflected upon and discussed intellectually in theology and could inform the whole of practical living. It offered an idiom through which all of Christian doctrine could be expressed afresh. *The Christian Faith*[4] is his culminating work, offering a method of theology which relates it to other disciplines and working out the content of faith with central reference to Jesus Christ and the experience of those with faith in him.

Schleiermacher's influence has been immense (see Jenson's essay on Barth, chapter 1). Besides his powerful account of religion's validity rooted in the dynamics of awareness of God, he pioneered modern hermeneutics; he maintained the importance of aesthetics in theology; he offered a "noninterventionist" account of God's relation to the world, which included a critique of religious language; he suggested a restructuring of the whole theological enterprise which was, due to his advocacy, partly embodied in the new University of Berlin; and in his public ecclesiastical, cultural, and political life he represented a lively and effective integration of modernity and Christian faith. All this was seen by him as in continuity with the Protestant Reformation and its evangelical tradition.

The post-First World War twentieth century began with a reaction against him led by Barth, who yet always acknowledged his greatness. Schleiermacher is the grandfather of those who attempt to correlate or integrate faith with modernity, and particularly of those who see the point of contact in human interiority – Tillich's "ultimate concern." He is the principal creative sponsor of the whole revisionist and liberal enterprise, but he himself constantly eludes simple categories: in those used above he seems, according to interpretation, to oscillate between the third and fourth types.

The second major early nineteenth-century challenge to Kant came from G. W. F. Hegel (1770–1831). He criticized both Kant and Schleiermacher for having an inadequate notion of rationality. Both of them had left the concept of God (the absolute, or unconditioned) relatively untouched. Hegel developed a system in which the absolute was conceived as rational and dynamic, realizing itself through a dialectical process in history. He saw the Trinity as the supreme reality, in which God differentiates himself and becomes actual in Jesus Christ and enters into suffering and death on the way to the ultimate reconciliation of all in the Spirit. The system thus had a dialectical logic embracing history with its developments and conflicts, and Hegel surveyed all of history, including the religions, in order to show the basic forms of life, society, and religion in their evolution. He also saw himself as a Christian, Lutheran philosopher recovering the truth of the basic doctrines of Trinity, creation, fall, incarnation, reconciliation, and the Holy Spirit. For him Christianity was religion in its absolute expression, but, while its content could not be surpassed, philosophy could give a more adequate conceptual expression of it as truth, uniting it with all other truth.

The nineteenth-century shift toward more historical, process-oriented ways of understanding reality was profoundly affected by Hegel. Kant had separated the self from other reality: Hegel offered a comprehensive, historical integration of subjectivity and objectivity in which reason and even logic took on dynamic form, and

Kant's restriction of theoretical reason in knowing God was overcome. Hegel daringly reconceived the idea of God and his involvement with the world (sometimes described as a type of "panentheism"); he placed the issue of truth, not religion, at the top of the agenda; and he encouraged rational and historical reconsideration of key doctrines.

The twentieth-century theologians who have wrestled most thoroughly with Hegel have often emerged deeply ambiguous about him as a Christian thinker – this is true in various ways of Barth, Jüngel, Rahner, Pannenberg, Balthasar, and Küng. One reason may be that, in so far as he can be related to our types, he, like Schleiermacher, oscillates according to the interpretation. But with him it is between the fourth and fifth types: some see him offering an appropriate modern conception of Christianity, others as absorbing it into his system on his own alien terms. But both by setting an agenda and in his contribution on specific issues (a way of conceiving the integration of history in the Trinity in Barth, Rahner, Pannenberg, and Moltmann; the death of God in Jüngel and Moltmann; Rahner's way of affirming reality as rational; Pannenberg's concepts of rationality and universal history; Küng's approach to incarnation) he is still shaping theological debate.

In addition, the reactions provoked by Hegel resonate through the rest of the nineteenth century and into our own. One of the most passionate, that of the Dane Søren Kierkegaard (1813–58), went virtually unnoticed in his own time, but exploded in early twentieth-century existentialism and especially influenced Barth, Bultmann and Tillich. Kierkegaard rejected Hegel's rational integration, accusing him especially of failing to take account of the existing, deciding individual, and he put forward a radical concept of Christian subjectivity which was not dependent on rational or historical justification. We live life forwards, with no neutral or overarching standpoints. We are faced with decisions and have to choose without any guarantees that we are right. We are constituted by such decisions and through them become different in ourselves. All ethical and religious existence is participated in in such self-involving and self-transforming ways. The gospel faces us with the most radical decision of all, which probes us to the depths and challenges us to go the paradoxical way of the cross. In this Kierkegaard is expanding the practical side of Kant and giving it more full-blooded Christian content. He denies both Kant's and Hegel's versions of how reason relates to faith and sees instead the paradoxical reality of incarnation and cross eliciting the leap of radical faith.

More typical of the nineteenth century was the development of Hegel's stress on history, but rejecting his tendency to give ideas and concepts primacy over empirical research. David Friedrich Strauss (1808–74) was the most controversial figure in this. He applied historical critical methods to the accounts of the life of Jesus, found a great deal that he called "mythical" (that is, religious ideas given in the form of historical accounts) and decided that there was little reliable factual information about Jesus.

The issue of the historical Jesus in relation to the Christ of faith was now firmly on the theological agenda. The rest of the nineteenth century saw many other developments in historical study which are part of the essential background to the twentieth century, especially in the fields of history of dogma and (more widely) historical theology (outstanding figures being Ferdinand Christian Baur and Adolf von Harnack), but the controversial center of the field remained the figure of Jesus, a focus which has been a legacy to many theologians treated in this volume. British scholarship (especially after the volume *Essays and Reviews* in 1860) also increasingly joined in the research and discussion, beginning the tradition described by Stephen Sykes in chapter 13.

The middle third of the nineteenth century saw many attempts to rethink and restore orthodox Christianity in Germany, Britain, the United States and elsewhere, and many of these have continued to be influential, generally within particular churches or traditions (for example, biblical fundamentalism, Anglo-Catholicism, various types of confessionalism). It was also the time when new critiques of religion, such as those proposed by Ludwig Feuerbach (1804–72), began to be developed. They multiplied as the century went on, as religion was scrutinized through the disciplines of history, literature, philosophy, geology, biology, physics, psychology, sociology, politics, economics, and comparative religion. These, as mentioned above, were to help cause a major intellectual and cultural crisis in Western Christianity in the twentieth century, but they have also been engaged in a variety of ways by theologians, and the critical dialogues with them are a major theme running through theologies in the late nineteenth and twentieth centuries – for example, Bonhoeffer with sociology; Tillich with socialism, depth psychology, and much else; Balthasar with aesthetics and drama; Pannenberg, Moltmann, Küng, and Tracy with almost every area; Teilhard de Chardin and process thought with evolutionary biology; Moltmann and liberation theologies with Marxism; Torrance and others with physics; postmodern theology with Nietzsche; and theology of religions with comparative religion.

Finally, overlapping the two centuries is Ernst Troeltsch (1865–1923), who in many ways summed up the nineteenth century and is the indispensable background for the twentieth. He saw the Enlightenment, not the Reformation, as the genesis of modernity, and the main nineteenth-century development as that of a comprehensive historical consciousness. So, while constantly in dialogue with the theology of Schleiermacher and the philosophies of Kant and Hegel, he saw them all as needing to be criticized through a more thoroughly historical method. He was immersed in late nineteenth-century history of religions and sociology, and wrestled with the enduring problems raised by them, such as the absoluteness of Christianity, the role of the historical Jesus in Christian faith, and the inseparability of all religion from its social and historical context. He arrived at a complex critical and constructive position: resisting naturalistic, reductionist explanations of religion; emphasizing Christianity's distinctive values worked out through the centuries in interaction with different situations, and calling for a fresh, creative social embodiment of those values in twentieth-century Europe; and stressing the ambiguities of both Christianity and modernity. After the First World War, the dialectical theologians, especially Barth, tended to see Troeltsch's main achievement as negative, showing the cul-de-sac arrived at when theology tries to move from human experience, history, and religion to God. But Troeltsch has also been continually influential, as in Bultmann's historical critical approach to the Bible, the later Tillich's method in dealing with historical patterns and the world religions, Pannenberg's conception of a theology that is consistently and critically historical, North American attempts to work out a practical and sociologically aware theology in a pluralist society, the widespread move to take local contexts more fully into account in doing theology, and the discussion in theology of religions about the uniqueness of Christianity.

The above account of the nineteenth century as it has affected twentieth-century theologians has been largely centered on Germany and oriented more toward the theologians discussed in Part I and toward others who have been in dialogue with them and their forebears. This is because that German tradition, while having many limitations, is the most sustained and intensive example of engagement in the enterprise of modern theology, as already defined, and is the most direct way of introducing historically the typical problems of modernity, such as knowledge and rationality, historical consciousness, and alternative explanations of religion. Other parts of this volume portray traditions which often approach theology very differently and in some cases are in critical confrontation with the methods and habits of the German academy.

Contexts and interests

The nineteenth- and twentieth-century historical and sociological insights urge theologians to take fuller account of the situation in which theology is done and for whom and by whom it is done. The history of ideas is not enough. Theology needs to be seen in relation to many forces and events helping to shape it through the centuries. The twentieth century has added its own conditioning, such as the Holocaust and concentration camps; the unprecedented scale of mass killing of fellow human beings in wars; the Russian, Chinese, and Iranian revolutions; the emergence of new, postcolonial societies; the collapse of Soviet and European Communism; the spread of mass communications, business corporations, technology, and science of many sorts; an unprecedented dialectic of the local and the global, especially in economics and culture; struggles against Fascism, racism, and sexism; the ecological crisis; and a vast expansion of professions and academic disciplines and institutions. More specific to religion have been the Pentecostal movement, Christian and interreligious ecumenism, the World Council of Churches, the Second Vatican Council, the spread of Islam and Christianity (especially in Africa), many armed conflicts with significant religious elements, an immense amount of religious persecution and martyrdom, new religious movements outside the main world religions, the multiplication of "basic communities," liturgical reforms in Christian churches, and new translations of the Bible. Most of these feature in the theologies of this volume, though many are only implicit, or are ignored by theologians in ways that call for more explicit recognition.

More narrowly, there is the significance of the social and institutional context in which theology is produced. All of the nineteenth-century theologies mentioned above and most of the theologies in this volume, as well as the essays on them, were written in universities or, to a lesser extent, seminaries. They are therefore at home in an academic, largely middle-class "high culture," which, in its main centers in continental Europe, Britain, and the United States, has been remarkably stable through a century of traumas. One of the main tensions in Christian theology has been between its participation in this wider academic culture and its relationship to the Christian community. That has been sharpened by the growing professionalization of the clergy. In German-speaking countries academic theology and clergy education has long been integrated in state-financed universities, so that theology has been drawn both toward being an academic discipline on a par with others and toward serving the needs of a profession. These two easily conflict, and the results for theology are symbolized in the debate about the Jesus of history (academic emphasis) and the Christ of faith (clerical requirement).[5]

In Britain similar tensions developed, and, as Sykes describes in chapter 13, there was an attempt to separate institutionally the more "academic" from the more contentiously "ecclesiastical" subjects. In the United States the separation of church and state tied theology more exclusively to seminaries and divinity schools and therefore to the clerical profession. This has tended to polarize "theology" and "religious studies," often in different institutions. It has also contributed to the present situation in which religion is widely practiced and influential but theology tends to be seen as a specialized professional discipline and is marginal within both academic and wider culture.

The marginalizing of theology has also happened in varying degrees in Britain, Germany, and elsewhere. It poses a problem for most of the traditions of theology dealt with in this volume: given the largely academic setting together with the academic marginalization of theology, what sort of academic discipline is it? The main temptation within academic life is clearly to become increasingly specialized and allied with other specialized disciplines. That is just the temptation to which the sort of theology covered in this volume cannot completely succumb, because it is about major issues and their interrelation, and inevitably crosses disciplines. But if theology does not fragment into specialties or become absorbed into other disciplines, how does it understand itself? Other related hard questions follow. What is theology's relation to religious communities and their need not only for professional training but also for critical and constructive thinking? How should it handle its own "ideological" tendency to serve the interests of a particular group, culture, class, religion, or profession? Does theology abandon or compromise or fulfill its academic commitments by fuller involvement in practical social and political matters, whether radical, moderate, or conservative?

Another way of looking at such questions is to ask how theology relates to its three main "publics": the academy, the churches, and society.[6] Most of the theologians who are the subjects of this volume are members of all three but concentrate mainly on addressing two of them, usually academy and church. Yet many (especially among the new additions since the first edition)[7] question this in favor of more attention to addressing and changing society. But such an overview needs to be made more complex by noting major contemporary features of each public. The academy has become more pluralist and self-critical and, at the same time (especially in the West), more subject to pressures to serve the economy in short-term and direct ways. The pluralism of methods appropriate to different disciplines and the increasing awareness by other disciplines of their own often ideological character have somewhat undermined the self-confident positivism and secularism that contributed to theology being marginalized; while economic and political pressures have put many other disciplines in both humanities and sciences in a marginal position, especially in Britain.

As for the public in the mainstream churches, there has been more corporate social and political controversy and involvement this century, especially in liberal and radical causes – two major instances are the World Council of Churches and post-Vatican II Roman Catholicism. In this context it has become harder for a "church" theologian to cover the major areas of Christian thought without grappling with social and political issues. For the "public," that is society around the world, matters of religion or quasi-religion have been (often tragically) prominent this century, so that it has become less easy with integrity to privatize or cordon off religion and reduce its public significance. It has likewise become in some ways easier to make the case for the need for high quality public discourse within religions as well as about them.

The theologians treated in *The Modern Theologians* try to provide such discourse. They have worked at the leading edge of this century's Christianity and contributed to the making of its history. They are of interest both as a "religious study" of twentieth-century Christian thought and also as examples and partners for those who follow them in their discipline. The coverage is not complete; but even including the omissions mentioned in the Preface it is worth remembering that the field of such theology is even wider. A great deal of theology is done by those who write little or who may not write it down at all. A lifetime's theological wisdom may be channelled into teaching or other activity, or may issue in one powerful book. That sort of theology cannot be treated directly here, but it helps to keep the whole enterprise in perspective to remember that at the origins of the two traditions most influential on the theologies of these volumes are Socrates and Jesus, neither of whom left us any writings.

Notes

1 The typology that follows is drawn from the work of Hans W. Frei. In the first edition of *The Modern Theologians* I referred to his Edward Cadbury Lectures, in which he had partly developed it. A version of those lectures, together with other related material, has now been published posthumously in Hans W. Frei, *Types of Christian Theology*, ed. George Hunsinger and William C. Placher (New Haven and London, 1992). In the first edition the types are numbered in reverse order to that in *Types of Christian Theology*, and for the sake of consistency I have here kept my first edition's order. For a brief account and discussion of Frei's typology, see my review article, "On Being Theologically Hospitable to Jesus Christ: Hans Frei's Achievement" in *Journal of Theological Studies*, NS 46 (October 1995), pp. 532–46.

2 C. Welch, *Protestant Thought in the Nineteenth Century*, 2 vols. (New Haven and London, 1972–85) and N. Smart et al., *Nineteenth Century Religious Thought in the West*, 3 vols. (Cambridge, 1985).

3 New York, 1960. First published 1793.

4 Edinburgh, 1928; New York, 1948.

5 Cf. Hans W. Frei, *Types of Christian Theology*.

6 See David Tracy, *The Analogical Imagination* (New York, 1981; London, 1982), ch. 1.

7 See Preface above, p. x.

Bibliography

Primary

Cunliffe-Jones, H., *A History of Christian Doctrine* (Edinburgh, 1978).

Farley, E., *The Fragility of Knowledge: Theological Education in the Church and the University* (Philadelphia, 1988).

Gruchy, J. De (general ed.), *The Making of Modern Theology: Nineteenth and twentieth century theological texts* [on Schleiermacher, Bultmann, Tillich, Bonhoeffer, Barth, Harnack, Reinhold Niebuhr, Rahner] (8 vols, London, 1988–9).

Frei, Hans W., *Types of Christian Theology*, ed. George Hunsinger and William C. Placher (New Haven and London, 1992).

Heron, A. I. C., *A Century of Protestant Theology* (Cambridge, 1980).

Hodgson, P. and King. R. H., *Christian Theology: An introduction to its traditions and tasks* (London, 1983).

Kelsey, David H., *To Understand God Truly: What's theological about a theological school?* (Louisville, KY, 1992).

—— *Between Athens and Jerusalem: The theological education debate* (Grand Rapids, MI, 1993).

Küng, Hans, *Great Christian Thinkers* (London, 1994).

—— *Theology for the Third Millennium: An ecumenical view* (New York, 1988; London, 1991).

Macquarrie, J., *Twentieth Century Religious Thought*, 4th edn (London, 1988).

Nicholls, W., *Pelican Guide to Modern Theology*, Vol. 3. *Systematic and Philosophical Theology* (London, 1971).

Pelikan, Jaroslav, *The Christian Tradition: A history of the development of doctrine*, 5 vols, (Chicago, 1989).

Schoof, T. M., *A Survey of Catholic Theology 1800–1970* (New York, 1970).

Smart, N., Clayton, J., Katz, S., and Sherry, P. (eds), *Nineteenth Century Religious Thought in the West*, 3 vols (Cambridge, 1985).

Welch, C., *Protestant Thought in the Nineteenth Century*, 2 vols (New Haven and London, 1972–85).

Secondary

Ebeling, G., *The Study of Theology* (London, 1979).

Feuerbach, L., *The Essence of Christianity* (New York, 1957).

Kant, I., *Religion within the Limits of Reason Alone* (New York, 1960).

Lindbeck, G., *The Nature of Doctrine: Religion and theology in a postliberal age* (Philadelphia, London, 1994).

Lonergan, B., *Method in Theology* (New York, London, 1972).

Moltmann, J., *Theology Today* (London, 1988).

Schleiermacher, F., *Brief Outline on the Study of Theology* (Richmond, 1966, first published 1810; 2nd edn, 1830).

Sykes, S. W., *The Identity of Christianity* (London, 1984).

Tracy, D., *The Analogical Imagination* (New York, 1981; London, 1982).

Troeltsch, E., *Protestantism and Progress: The significance of Protestantism for the rise of the modern world* (Philadelphia, 1986; first published 1912).

Continental European Theologies

Corresponding to Revelation

The First World War (1914–18) brought about a major crisis in European culture and society. This was the context for Karl Barth's *The Epistle to the Romans* and the explosion of dialectical theology, followed by Barth's attempt to rethink the whole enterprise of modern theology.

Robert Jenson argues that, far from being a conservative revival of premodern theology, Barth's theology takes full account of modernity and could even be seen as going beyond it into "postmodernism." Barth transforms the human autonomy of the Enlightenment by identifying Jesus Christ as the one with true autonomy; he intensifies the modern critique of religion; and he offers a God-centered account of reality in place of a mechanistic, atheist universe. Jenson follows Barth through *The Epistle to the Romans* to his recognition in Anselm of the form of rationality appropriate to Christian theology. He then gives a survey of the *Church Dogmatics*, including an explanation of its structure and approach, before concentrating on two main aspects: its christological description of reality, which puts the life history of Jesus in the place often occupied by an abstract concept of God; and the Trinity as the self-revealed God. The debate makes two sharp points about Barth on election and the Trinity, and the agenda suggests lessons to be learned, especially in Britain and North America.

Charles Marsh shows Bonhoeffer's theology to be in close but not uncritical relation to Barth's. His life and theology are described in their remarkable coherence of belief, action, and thought, culminating in martyrdom. His main works are summarized and discussed, and the remarkable story of his wide and varied posthumous influence is traced. Bonhoeffer, his works often in fragments, his life intensely involved with contemporary events and ethically ambiguous to many critics, is a "classic" in a sense more typically late- or even postmodern than others in Part I.

Eberhard Jüngel's is a post-Second World War theology strongly influenced by Barth, but also deeply engaged with Bultmann. In line with Barth, he has what John Webster describes as a "rigorous" and "highly developed" theological realism, often focusing on the relation of divine to human action. Webster describes his distinctive contributions to the relating of theology and philosophy, to christology, to the doctrine of God, to anthropology, to natural theology, to religious language, and to the church, sacraments, and worship. There is a nuanced probing of Jüngel's lively, passionate thinking in its strengths and weaknesses, and a recognition of his major contribution in offering a rich reconception of classical Christian faith in attentive and critical dialogue with some of the leading philosophers in recent centuries. If one of Jüngel's themes is to be singled out it should perhaps be his concept of God as "the mystery of the world" who in coming to the world makes it "interesting in new ways," renewing and transforming it.

The Scottish theologian Thomas Torrance, treated below in chapters 14 and 33, was included in this section in the first edition, and he adds another strand of Barth-influenced theological realism to those of Bonhoeffer and Jüngel. Torrance attempts, as none of the others in this section do, a theoretical account of theological epistemology in dialogue with modern natural science. All four theologians share the concern that, above all, theology should rationally and faithfully "correspond" to revelation, whose givenness, graciousness, and objectivity are emphasized in various ways.

Karl Barth

Robert W. Jenson

Introduction: Personal

In the summer of 1911 a 25-year-old clergyman become pastor of Safenwil, a small industrial city in his native Switzerland. Karl Barth was born in Basel to a churchly and academic family; he first studied in Berne, then escaped to the grander academic theological world of Germany. In Berlin he studied under Adolf von Harnack and in Marburg under Wilhelm Herrmann, masters of the properly so called liberal theology in its last and greatest efflorescence. The pastorate at Safenwil was expected to season him for a conventional scholarly career; instead it threw him into spiritual and intellectual crisis.

Barth went to Safenwil as a professional of the Christian religion. He supposed it was a pastor's task to cultivate this particular tradition of humankind's quest for unity with the divine. Pastoral work, and perhaps specifically pastoral work among the victims of undisciplined capitalism, broke this conception of his calling. Barth's radicalization came from several sides but made a single experience.

The young pastor had regularly to preach from appointed texts. Trying to fulfill this obligation, he found himself driven to read the Bible differently from the way his education had equipped him to do. He perceived that the Bible is not about our religion or morality or history, but about something called the Kingdom of God. What that might be, he could not make out, but he saw that it could not be what liberal interpretation presumed it was: the success of our historical moral and religious endeavor. If the Bible was about religion or morality or history, it seemed if anything to be about *God's* religion and morality and history. Indeed, Barth discovered in the Bible an entire "strange new world": a reality one could understand only by *inhabiting* it, a world in which everything goes crossways to our apparent world, a world unified not by our relation to the divine but by a specific God's relation to us, the world – he said in amazement – "*of*" God.

As Barth saw the oppression that distorted the lives of his working-class parishioners, he had to acknowledge that cultivation of their religious experience was hardly the first among their necessities. He came to think of the service for which he had been trained as inessential under the actual circumstances. Why *should* the workers of Safenwil use their day off to hear him? The coming of the Bible's Kingdom of God – whatever it might turn out to be – began to seem much more to the point, and that precisely the economic and political point.

And then the Great War began, and Barth had to witness the suicide of the European bourgeois culture for which liberal theology had provided an ideology. From neutral Switzerland he watched with horror as the liberally cultivated European nations slaughtered one another, with little reason and with a barbarity unknown for centuries. He read the "Declaration of German Intellectuals," including his revered teachers, calling for loyalty above all to *Kaiser* and *Vaterland*. How could this happen?

Thus Barth became a theological questioner, a religious outsider, and a political left-winger. As nevertheless a proper intellectual, he did his struggling in print, producing lectures and papers[1] and two successive attempts at a commentary on Paul's letter to the Romans. The second of these, *The Epistle to the Romans* of 1922, achieved instant celebrity, and became the rallying point of a new generation of German-speaking Protestantism's pastors and teachers.

Already in 1921, Barth's reputation was such that without a doctorate he was called to a teaching post at Göttingen – to teach "Reformed" confessional theology, about which he confessed he knew very little. Then he was called to Münster and in 1930 to Bonn. There events again overtook him and he became a theological leader of the "confessing" resistance to Hitler's attempt to appropriate the German evangelical church, and chief drafter of the confessing movement's defiant "Barmen Declaration." In consequence he was in 1935 banned from teaching in Germany.

He returned to Switzerland, to a post opened for him in the University of Basel, and remained there the rest of his life, writing the *Church Dogmatics* and playing with relish the role of the world's most famous – or notorious – theologian. On the morning of December 10, 1968, his wife of 55 years tried to awaken him with the beloved music of Mozart, and failed.

Introduction: Historical

Barth's key position in the development of twentieth-century theology means that a description of influences on his thinking must amount almost to a short history of modern theology. And Barth's theology indeed belongs to that history. Nothing could be more precisely mistaken than many English and American writers' assumption that Barth was a theological reactionary, who tried to save the faith from the acids of modernity by retreating to premodern habits of thought.

Barth's theology is determined in its structure and warrants by the Western church's continuing effort to come to terms with the eighteenth-century Enlightenment, that is, with modernity's founding event. Indeed, if there is such a thing as "postmodernism," Barth is its only major theological representative so far, for his work is an attempt not only to transcend the Enlightenment but to transcend nineteenth-century Protestantism's way of doing the same.

The Enlightenment created a new intellectuality to replace that inherited from "the ancients." By the turn of the eighteenth and nineteenth centuries, this new way of thinking had nearly undone Christianity among the elites of Europe and North America. It has been the effort to overcome this loss, without denying the truth the Enlightenment represented, that has determined the goals and boundaries of all typically modern theology. For present purposes only, two slogans will sufficiently evoke the Enlightenment's spirit; and to neither aspect of that spirit does Barth's theology have an undialectically antagonistic relation.

The first such slogan is provided by Barth himself, in his *Protestant Theology in the Nineteenth Century*: the Enlightenment, he said, was the emergence of a specific sort of *Mensch*, of human person. This is the "absolutist" person, who "discovers his own power, his own ability, the potential that slumbers in his . . . humanity simply as such, and who understands this as something . . . in itself justified and mighty, and who therefore sets this potential in . . . motion in every direction."[2] The Enlightenment was the human subject's declaration of independence from every limitation but faithfulness to him- or herself. Obviously, independence from the authority of revelation and church had to be central to this project.

What the Enlightenment thus thought of as human freedom is what Christianity means by "sin." And Barth's revival of classical teaching about sin is most of what English-speaking "neo-orthodoxy" took from him. The would-be autonomous subject, hostile to everything by which his or her intentions or judgment might be relativized, is precisely the person "curved in on self" of the Reformation's hamartiology. Barth in the *Church Dogmatics* would define sin as the desire to be "the judge of good and evil . . . to be one's own helper."[3]

And yet Barth's condemnation of the Enlightenment's *Mensch* is far from unequivocal – among his examples of its typical personalities is none other than his idolized Mozart. It could be argued that Barth's objection to the Enlightenment's passion for human autonomy is not so much to the ideal itself as to the Enlightenment's statement of who the autonomous human is. For the *Church Dogmatics* can be read as one long description of a human person in whom being the human he is and being lord and judge do indeed coincide, who truly is his own savior; and moreover it teaches our ontological identity with and in this Jesus.

The second slogan is one made definitive for the movement by its perfecter, Immanuel Kant: Enlightenment is the intellectual policy of "critique," of suspicion of all "appearances" of truth. We know reality in that it presents itself to us, but if we are to be autonomous we cannot be content with such impositions. We will instead say: I know that is how the matter appears, but I must myself find out what it is *really* like.

The paradigm of the critique of appearances was, of course, provided by Copernicus and Galileo: it certainly appears that the sun goes around the earth; the great triumph was to ask, and persist in asking, "But does it really?" Through the seventeenth century, in which "modern science" first triumphed, this intellectual policy produced an unprecedented accession of good and useful knowledge about external nature. When the record of success could be reflected upon, the hope inevitable arose of applying the same policy to the intractable problems of humanity's own life. That hope constituted the Enlightenment.

The first target of the Enlightenment's critical enterprise had to be established religion. And as unfortunate history had left the matter, it was precisely those elements of European and American religion that made it Christian – the worship of God as Trinity, confession of "original" sin, and reliance on God's unmerited grace in Christ – which seemed most vulnerable to critique and which most offended the passion for autonomy. For the tradition had divided the West's religious substance between "natural' doctrines and practices – which were in fact simply those inherited from pagan antiquity – and doctrines and practices based on "revelation" – that is, on the Scriptures and the theological experience of the church. The Enlightenment found its lever of critique in this division, judging "revealed" religion by the standard of "natural" religion. The outcome was an elite theology and worship purged of specifically Christian character.

The critique of religion was interrupted by Friedrich Schleiermacher – to whom we are coming – and the main line of nineteenth-century theologians. But it was taken up with increased intensity by a line of outsiders from Feuerbach to Marx to Strauss through Nietzsche to Overbeck. And these have had few such enthusiastic readers as Barth in the days of his radicalization. Indeed, one could almost summarize Barth's whole achievement by saying that he carried the Enlightenment's critique of religion to its conclusion, ending "natural" religion's exemption and subjecting *all* religion to a standard external to it, to that strange and contingent message called "the gospel."

Barth did not of course confront the Enlightenment directly. Between him and it lay his more immediate resource and *bête noire*, the German "neo-Protestant" theology of the nineteenth century. We can, indeed, narrow this down. Christianity's nineteenth-century theological recovery, by which it astonished its turn-of-the-century gravediggers, had been very much the work of one man, with whom Barth had a lifelong fascination.

Friedrich Schleiermacher was a figure in the general flowering of German culture between, let us say, 1780 and 1850. Central to this great German time was a new vision of humanity, nurtured through the last decades of the eighteenth century by such *litterati* as Lessing, Herder, and Goethe. This was a vision of the human person as her or his own work of art: of the person formed through life into something like a classical sonata-movement, in which the greatest possible diversity is held together in a transcendent temporal unity.

In the book that launched Schleiermacher's fame and the following century's theology, the *Speeches on Religion to Its Cultured Despisers* of 1799, he argued: If indeed you want to fulfill the Goethean vision in your own personhood, if you seek both great and various experience and the unity of your experience in itself and with all reality, then you must cultivate your religious life. For it is only in religion that the multiplicities of a human life come together.

The *Speeches* made Schleiermacher "the church father of the nineteenth century." They did not do so by virtue of their specific positions – for example, the famous definition of religion as "feeling" – but by virtue of their general pattern of analysis and argument. Schleiermacher begins with an analysis of human existence, showing that "religion" is a necessary component of complete personal life and is, moreover, the aspect in which other aspects come together. There follows an analysis of religion's possible modes and varieties. Then comes stipulation of Christianity's specific character among the religions, by reference to the person of Christ. And finally there is an argument that of all the religions, Christianity best fills religion's place in life. Along the way, a conceptional creation occurs: of the concept *religion* itself as we all now use it.

Barth's theology would have been as impossible without Schleiermacher as any other theology of the nineteenth or early twentieth centuries would have been. Barth fully adopts Schleiermacher's concept of religion as the inescapable and necessary project of making final sense of our lives. What Barth did was turn Schleiermacher's pattern around. Instead of interpreting Christianity by the general character and function of religion, he interprets religion, including Christian religion, by Christianity's differentiating specificity. Instead of analyzing human existence, in order then to inquire after Christ's contribution to its religious aspect, he analyzes Christ's existence, in order then to inquire after our religion's place therein.

There was of course a century between Barth and Schleiermacher, in which Schleiermacher's pattern of theological procedure was most variously filled in: The initial analysis of human existence could be derived in different ways; the material specifications of religion and its relation to other aspects of life were diversely perceived; and argument for the superiority of Christianity could be conducted by various kinds of warrants. Barth's most immediate context and target was one – the last – of such movements: the "liberal" theology.

Liberal theology was the dominant movement at the turn of the nineteenth and twentieth centuries. Typically, liberal theologians derived their analysis of human existence and the location therein of religion from Immanuel Kant: Religion was understood as the interior presupposition of moral action, and religious doctrines as "value judgments," which only in their naive form seem to be statements of fact. Definitive for the movement was, however, the particular way in which Christ was thought to fit into religious existence: as the "historical Jesus."

The shared supposition of all neo-Protestant theologies was that Christianity is the deepening and shaping of religious life by contact with Christ. But, said the liberals, Christ is a historical phenomenon or he is nothing at all. Here we must note a motif of the German Enlightenment not previously emphasized: its historicism, its understanding of human life as essentially worked out through time.

Moreover, since the liberals interpreted confession of Jesus' resurrection as a value judgment rather than a statement of fact, they had at least initially to regard Christ as a phenomenon of *past* history. So their question had to be: How do we come into relation with the past Jesus, to be affected by him? Their answer defined their movement: We have to do with the past Jesus just as we have to do with other figures of the past, by reconstructing his historical figure from the documentary evidence. Thus for liberal theology, historical scholarship was something like a chief sacrament: We come into contact with Jesus by historical study of Scripture, and in fellowship with him we are sanctified.

Barth came to see liberal theology as a betrayal of the faith. Yet here again his relation to his antecedents was no mere contradiction. Liberal theology was a radically christocentric theology. If all assertions about God – metaphysical propositions in their apparent form – are in fact meaningful only as value judgments, and if Christians make their value judgments in converse with Jesus, then it is only in converse with Jesus that Christians can speak meaningfully about God. Barth learned this argument from Wilhelm Herrmann, and retained its conclusion even as he modified its premises.

Perhaps the one aspect of Barth's early theology that has been generally known in English-speaking scholarship is his polemic against "natural theology." Although Barth came to see the liberal theology as especially addicted to this vice, his polemic was initially a straightforward *continuation* of liberalism's polemic against "metaphysics," that is, against claims for theological assertions' meaningfulness outside of a religious relation to Christ.

Moreover, that to speak of persons, whether God or us, is to speak of history, was as foundational for Barth as it ever was for the liberals from whom he learned it. He came to reject the liberal view that the only history is that reconstructed by research. But he wavered only for a moment in the principle that in talking of Christ and ourselves in God we are talking of genuine events arrayed before and after; it is that moment to which we now must turn.

Survey: to the *Church Dogmatics*

The Epistle to the Romans was the step between two stages of Barth's life and thinking. It also made the break between the nineteenth and twentieth theological centuries.

The thinking of *Romans* was rightly labelled "dialectical" by foe and friend. Barth deliberately repristinated the Socratic dialectic that he learned from passionate reading of Plato and Søren Kierkegaard. As Socrates had invented ever new contradictions to break down Athenians' claim to possession of justice, of any direct line from what justice was in Athens to what justice could mean in itself, so Barth generated contradictions to break down Christendom's possession of holiness, of any direct line from what virtue and faith are in human religion to what they mean in the gospel.

Romans is a direct assault on the reader. It seeks not to inform but to transform. When we read it, the chief thing is to *experience* the spin of paradoxes and counter-questions, to be made uneasy in our religion – and so be freed to hear from Paul about *God*.

Religion, Barth agrees with Schleiermacher, is the highest possibility of humanity, our quest for that beyond ourselves in which alone we can be fulfilled. Just so it is our attempt to use what is beyond us for our own purposes, and so the betrayal of its object. Christ is then the savior as the one who betrays this betrayal, in whom religion reaches its goal by being given up, "who bridges over the distance between God and man – in that he tears it open."[4] "The No that meets us is *God's* No. What we lack is just what helps us . . . What cancels all the truth of the world is just what founds it. Exactly because God's No is complete, it is also his Yes."[5]

Trying to say what *Romans* is about is a treacherous undertaking. But Barth did write in the foreword to a second edition, "If I have a system, it consists in what Kierkegaard called 'the infinite qualitative difference' between time and eternity."[6] And of the many images with which Barth evokes the relation of time and eternity, one is clearest. Time is touched by eternity, Barth said, as a circle is touched by a tangent line. The line does touch the circle, yet there is no part of the circle that belongs to the line or part of the line that belongs to the circle. Beings who lived on the circle and moved around it would be stopped when they came to the point of tangency, but could not experience or grasp their impediment itself. Just so are we stopped at "the line of death" where eternity touches time. Christ is savior in that he occupies that line perfectly.

A tight inner group rallied around *Romans*, declaring its unity by publishing its own journal, *Zwischen den Zeiten*. The group endured only a decade; we may date its end by the journal's demise in 1933. Some of its members went on to become great names in their own rights: Rudolf Bultmann, Emil Brunner, Friedrich Gogarten, and – a bit on the fringes – Paul Tillich.

The breakup of the dialectical theology was inevitable, for the theology of *Romans* could be no more than a polemic moment. How would you *preach* by its lights? Having once said, "All your religion is but a grasping after God, who will not be grasped," what do you say next? The dialectical theology, like its liberal forebear, was a christocentric theology, but was crippled in its ability to speak of Christ. Christ was said to be savior as perfect occupant of the line of death; in consequence the dialectical theology remarkably mimicked its liberal antagonist in being unable to speak materially of the *risen* Christ. But it did not have liberalism's alternative; it could not proclaim the historical Jesus, since this would identify God's salvation with a particular stretch of time.

Thus the dialectical theology could be only the *break* with previous theology. When the dialectical theologians were compelled to say what they *affirmed*, they found they were no longer united. None recanted their shared negations, except perhaps Paul Tillich, if he ever held them. Each found his own way to constructive thought; and the ways they found have provided many of the options of twentieth-century theology.

Barth's own search is documented in papers and lectures and two books: the strange book about Anselm of Canterbury, *Fides Quaerens Intellectum,* and the first volume of a *Christian Dogmatics* of which the second never appeared. The path he found may be characterized in two ways.

A short formula for traditional theology's problem in modernity is that Enlightenment critique undid theology's claim to rationality, undid the "natural" warrants by which it had vindicated the plausibility of its assertions. Schleiermacher had provided a new kind of warrant, in humanity's intrinsic religiosity. But *Romans'* renewal of religious critique, now in the name of the gospel itself, undid this in turn while providing no replacement, thereby sawing off the limb on which it too sat. The rationality of *Romans'* discourse is thus always precarious.

Barth found his way by seeing that also in this matter modernity's proceedings could be simply reversed. Why should faith find the warrants of its rationality in analyses conducted outside faith? Why should discourse about the Kingdom seek cognitive plausibility by attaching itself to the world's discourse? *Why not the other way around?*

The assertions of faith, he argued, have their own internal coherence with one another, and demonstration of theology's rationality consists in tracing the spiderweb of their connections. Nor is this the coherence of an arbitrarily invented system, since the whole which thus obtains is a single witness to an event outside itself, the event of Christ. Moreover, such knowledge, if it is knowledge at all, must be the decisive knowledge also about the world, for if faith is true then all things find their truth in Christ.

Thus we are led to the second, christological way of describing Barth's move. The achievements of the dialectical theology are not to be abandoned; the dialectical assault on religion is to be maintained. The question is, how to maintain it within a constructive theology? Barth's move was to transpose the dialectic of time and eternity into christology. Time and eternity join without joining, draw the line of death along their tangency, not at a general border between God and creatures but as the determinants of one creature's existence. It is as the life, death, and resurrection of Jesus that time and eternity meet without merging. And just so the "infinite qualitative difference" of God and creature encompasses our lives also. The *Church Dogmatics* is all christology; and as it traces the connections and movements of Christ's being, the lineaments of *Romans* are faithfully revealed.

Survey: The *Church Dogmatics*

The volumes of the *Church Dogmatics* appeared from 1932 to 1967. In this section I will sketch the overall structure of the massive work. In the following section I will seek more material access to it. The choice of topics for the latter exercise must be somewhat arbitrary; there is no intrinsically favored entry.

The *Church Dogmatics* is structured as a series of "volumes," each of which is in fact a multivolumed part of the work. Volume I, in two sub-volumes, deals with the possibility of theology, with what modern theologies often call "Prolegomena"; this is, in Barth's understanding, constituted as a doctrine of the Word of God. Volume II, again in two sub-volumes, contains that part of the doctrine of God not treated in volume I. Volume III, in no less than four sub-volumes, treats of creation – Barth's wind is increasing even from its previous majestic capacity. Volume IV occupies three completed sub-volumes, of which the third had again to be subdivided, and breaks off with a fragment of an intended fourth sub-volume; it holds the doctrine of reconciliation, that is, of christology and atonement. Volume V was to have brought the eschatology; Barth did not live to create it.

The work is ferociously systematic, in the particular sense which Barth thought appropriate for Christian theology: It is just such a web of mutually demanded insights as Barth postulated in the Anselm book. But it is not a deductive system. Rather, the work marches to the pattern of the old method of loci, in which each topic develops a whole theology organized around a major theme. Thus with each volume, and indeed with some sub-volumes and chapters, Barth begins his reflections anew. It is therefore possible to begin reading at the beginning of any major section; none absolutely requires its predecessors to be understood. We should also note the role of the passages in small print: These are everything from what would in other books be footnotes to chapter-length excurses. They are some of the most interesting bits, but on a first reading may be skipped if desired.

I may begin description of volume I with a final hint to new readers: always pay careful attention to the lead-propositions which Barth sets at the head of each numbered "paragraph." Thus §1, on the "task" of dogmatics, has as its lead proposition: "The theological discipline of dogmatics is the Christian church's scholarly self-examination, with respect to the contents of its distinctive speech about God."[7] That the church *does* speak about God is a fact. That she *can* speak about God is a claim either believed or rejected. The prolegomenal question for Barth can only be: *How does it happen* that the church does and so can speak about God?

To that question, Barth answers: The church can speak about God because he is the particular God that he is. Thus following a relatively brief discussion of theology's formal characteristics, volume I/1 proceeds immediately to the doctrine by which the gospel's God is *identified*: the doctrine of Trinity. This occupies the bulk of a chapter on the Revelation of God, a second segment of which is a complete christology – the first of several – and the third a consideration of the anthropological possibility of revelation, which for Barth is a doctrine of the Spirit. Only after all this can Barth return to more conventionally prolegomenal matters.

The beginning of volume II on God traces the same ground anew, now under the rubric of our *knowledge* of God. How can we know God? Because he is the God who makes himself known, and for no other reason; because he in unpredictable fact makes himself the object of our in itself all too "natural," that is, self-serving and so idolatrous, theology.

Then three mighty chapters discourse of God himself. The first invokes the "reality" of God: his being and his attributes. The first lead proposition in this chapter states the whole: "God is, who he is in the act of his revelation. God seeks and creates communion between himself and us, and so he loves us. But he is this Loving One, as Father, Son and Holy Spirit, also without us, in the freedom of the Lord who lives from himself."[8]

The next chapter brings the doctrine of election, which will be discussed in the next section of this essay. Here I note two points only. First, the doctrine comes at this point because election is, according to Barth, the *actuality* of God's being, of his love-that-is-freedom and freedom-that-is-love. Second, Barth's treatment has made a revolution of this doctrine, making it explicitly what it always should have been, a doctrine about God's will for us in *Christ*. A third chapter ends the doctrine of God by telling of his "commandment." It is a principle of Barth's theology that ethics are integral to dogmatics; each volume ends with its specific ethics.

Many of Barth's critics thought that he could have little to say about creation; and the relative brevity of III/1 – only 488 pages! – was taken to confirm this. But in fact this volume is a key to all Barth's thinking and has become perhaps the most influential of all. It develops one of the most famous or infamous of Barthian slogans: The creation is the outer basis of the covenant and the covenant is the inner basis of the creation. This structure will be more fully discussed in my next section.

The following sub-volumes of III make up for earlier brevity. III/2 develops, at exhausting length, a christological anthropology, in which at each step knowledge of humanity is enabled by knowledge of the one human Jesus. III/3 is a miscellany of topics embraced by the notion of creation: providence, evil, and angels. The latter two, unexpectedly to moderns, are among the most conceptually revolutionary and sheerly interesting of Barth's discussions. Finally, III/4 brings nearly 800 more pages of ethics, the ethics of human freedom.

In volume IV, on reconciliation, Barth performs a *tour de force*. He carries out what had heretofore been only an unfulfilled postulate of Reformation theology: that christology and soteriology should be identical. To achieve this, Barth melts the doctrine of Christ's person with the doctrine of his "states." Thus in IV/1 the *deity* of Christ and the *descent* of Christ are one, under the title "The Lord as Servant"; in IV/2 the *humanity* of Christ and our *elevation* to God are one, under the title "The Servant as Lord"; and in IV/3 the hypostatic union of deity and humanity in Christ is identified with the event of the proclamation of these two movements, under the title "Jesus Christ, the True Witness." Even to suggest the multifarious problems and possibilities posed in this volume would burst the bounds of this essay.

Content

We can only select some themes from the offerings of the *Church Dogmatics*. The selection is brutal, but not perhaps entirely at random. A first selection may be entitled "christological metaphysics."

Why did God create the world? We may generally suppose that God's motives are obscure. Or we may suppose that a moral description is adequate: that God desires peace and justice and such good things generally, and creates in order to have persons to exercise these virtues. Barth's christological reversal prohibits both agnosticism and general answers. God, he teaches, needs creatures in order that there shall be the one creature Jesus Christ, just as this person is concrete in his actual history.

"Creation," Barth defines, "is the . . . external basis of the covenant." That is, "It prepares . . . the sphere in which the institution and history of the covenant take place."[9] If God is to make loving covenant beyond the triune fellowship he himself is, there must be others than God; *therefore* and only therefore God creates. Moreover, the covenant that is the goal of God's creating is precisely the covenant that actually then occurs, of reconciliation with sinners in the crucifixion and resurrection of Christ.

Thus the content of God's eternal choice is the incarnation of the Son on behalf of fallen creatures. The eternal decree is a "double" predestination, though in a sense very different from that of classical Calvinism. For all eternity God chose that he would live for us and we for him. Since we are chosen precisely as we are fallen, God chose to lose that we might gain, to be himself burdened with sin and evil in order that we might be blessed.

God eternally chose to be one with sinful man in the personal existence, just as it occurs, of Jesus; and it is this choice that is the beginning of all God's ways. "In the beginning . . . in God's decree that precedes the existence and possibility . . . of all his creatures, the primary element is the decision whose carrying out . . . is Jesus Christ."[10] All his works are done to accomplish this decree; thus the Incarnation is its own exclusive reason, it "knows no Wherefore? It is an absolute Therefore."[11]

This doctrine of election is the heart of the christological reversal performed by the *Church Dogmatics*. But the reversal is complete only in a further consequence.

According to Barth, the event of God's choice to be one with us in Jesus Christ must itself be a prevenient reality of Jesus Christ in God's eternity. This is so because God's choice to be one with us is in itself a self-determination of God to unity with us, and just so is itself the chosen state of affairs; and Jesus Christ *is* the chosen state of affairs. Thus Jesus Christ, the God-*man*, happens in eternity before all time, as the reality of the choice by God to be God with this man.

The clarification of such initially bizarre propositions occurs as Barth develops the doctrine of God. All theology that is not *merely* natural theology must stem from trust in the final veracity of God's self-revelation in Christ, trust that God is not himself different than he is among us as this man. But in Christ we have to do with a *life*, not with a static first Being but with a complex sequenced event. Therefore we must acknowledge God's being as in itself *event and action*. For Barth, this is the same as to say that God is perfectly *person*.

The perfection of his personhood must mean that he himself chooses what he is; thus we must even say that God is his own *decision*. And since what God actually chooses is to be one with humanity as Jesus Christ, the pre-happening of the God-man Jesus Christ is itself "the living act in which [God] . . . posits himself and everything that is."[12] If we want to understand the basis in God of his own nature and of all other reality than himself, "We must look to where the eternal God not only foresees and predestines [Jesus Christ], but as the presupposition of this person's revelation in time *is* this person."[13]

Thus in Barth's interpretation of reality, the life-history of one human person has taken the place held in the West's traditional metaphysics by – to use perhaps familiar language – the Ground of Being. The *Church Dogmatics* is the first grand system of Western metaphysics since the collapse of Hegelianism, but a thoroughly revisionary one. It casts a vision of reality founded in a particular temporal entity, the Crucified and Reason.

It is a fixed axiom of the West's inherited metaphysics, deriving from their furthest origin as the theology of Olympian religion, that the Ground of Being can be reached only by abstracting from time and its particularities, that even God can be the Ground of Being only sublimated as "the Divine," and that assuredly no temporal entity can have the role. But why should we obey this rule, if it is not Olympian deity we worship? Barth defied the rule, to construct through the successive volumes of the *Church Dogmatics* an encompassing, flexible, and drastically coherent christological interpretation of all reality.

A second selection must be Barth's revivification of the doctrine of Trinity. The doctrine of Trinity, in the classic tradition as in Barth, is interpretation of God under rigorous obedience to the rule: God is in himself precisely what he is in the history between Jesus, and the one he called "Father," and us in their mutual Spirit. It is from Barth that twentieth-century theology has relearned that this doctrine has and must have explanatory and regulatory use in the whole of theology, that it is not a separate puzzle to be solved but the framework within which all theology's puzzles are to be solved.

Even the doctrine's location within the *Church Dogmatics* is arresting: As we have seen, it comes at the beginning, as part of the prolegomenal description of the theological enterprise. For the first thing we must lay down, to know how theology as a discipline works, is which God we intend to talk about. The "question which the doctrine of the Trinity is to answer" is "*Who* is God?"[14]

By *beginning* with Trinity, Barth reverses the order not merely of nineteenth-century theology but of Western theology since the high Middle Ages. Theology had begun with what we could say about God in methodological abstraction from his actuality in the saving history between Jesus and his Father in their Spirit, and only thereafter invoked that history. Thus a space opened for the intrusion of alien identifications of God, responding to other warrants than those of the biblical narrative. Barth gave the Trinity doctrine the systematic location appropriate to its function: Only *after* identifying God as Father, Son and Spirit does he inquire after God's being and attributes, by analyzing what God must be like to be triune.

The basic identification of God, according to Barth, is that he is whoever "has revealed himself in Jesus Christ." The doctrine of Trinity is analysis of the concept of this revelation, analysis of the way in which Scripture describes the particular historical event Jesus Christ as in fact the revelation of God.

The "root" of the Trinity doctrine, as Barth develops it, is the way in which the scriptural witness to revelation poses three questions. This witness, according to Barth, asks us: *Who* reveals himself? It poses this question in that it will not let revelation be understood otherwise than from its agent; it must not be our religious concern to know God that shapes our reflection. And Scripture thus elicits also the answer: *God* reveals himself.

But revelation demands to be ultimate also as the sheer factual event, and so Scripture's witness to revelation asks: *What* does God *do* to reveal himself? And again the answer can only be: He exists among us as *God*, and so is revealed to us. And finally, this witness asks: What *results* among us from this event? And again the only answer allowed is: The result is *God* with us and in us.

Barth's summary of these analyses became notorious: "*God* reveals himself. He reveals himself *through himself*. He reveals *himself*."[15] God is not only himself, he is also his act of revelation; and he is not only himself, but what he does among us by revealing himself.

Our answers to each of the three questions must repeat our answer to the other two because otherwise our identification of God will merely reflect our religious quest. If the event of revelation and the effect of revelation are not each God himself again, then our knowledge of God's identity must be the result of reasoning *back* to God from revealed data at hand; and then our identifying of God is a religious projection even if the source of the enabling data is the Bible or the historical Jesus or an experience of the risen Christ. Therefore if the gospel so reveals God as to thwart our religious quest – and this is of course Barth's founding insight – then we must answer the three questions posed by revelation "God," "God," and "God."

Yet neither can we reduce the three questions to one question. And the reason is exactly the same: The structure of God's revealing act would not then be taken seriously as the shape of God's own reality, so we would be back with the religious quest for a "real" God behind revelation.

As Barth then develops the three questions and their one answer into a developed doctrine, it is not the resultant formal doctrine of Trinity that is most interesting, for this turns out to be a fairly standard Augustinian doctrine. It is rather the pattern of his arguments. Barth's move is always the same: from the formal structure, the *plot* of historical revelation to the content of that revelation, that is, to God. Or rather, his move is that he refuses to separate form and content at all. What God reveals about himself is that he is Lord; but that he is Lord means that he can reveal himself in the way Scripture describes. *What* is revealed is no more or less than that revelation *does occur* and therefore *can* occur.

What is revealed is that revelation can happen. But the revelation whose possibility is thus grasped as the reality of God himself, is not just any event that might be called a revelation. The revelation that is itself God is the specific event of which Scripture speaks as revelation – it is in order to insure that this is not burked that Barth puts the doctrine of Trinity at the beginning. This event that the Scripture calls revelation has a plot: It is the sequential and coherent event of Jesus' birth, work, crucifixion, and resurrection. That what God reveals about himself is that he can reveal himself as he in fact has revealed himself, means concretely that God is a life with this plot and no other. Barth's derivation and use of the doctrine of Trinity identify God as the one whose being is the occurrence among and for us of Jesus' death and resurrection. It is with this material content that the doctrine then functions as the hermeneutical key for all the developments and new starts and conceptual windings of the *Church Dogmatics*.

Debate

Until quite recently, most English and American discussion of Barth's work rested on at best superficial acquaintance with his actual writing and attacked or – less often – defended a nonexistent "Barth." I will not list the caricatures thus promulgated and debated – except for the oxymoronic idea that Barth is a "christomonist," or the notion that this most amiable of teachers was a gloomy and forbidding blast from the Swiss mountains. I will instead simply refer readers to the appended bibliography. In the listed monographs they will find reliable information, over against what they may encounter in the public prints or even still in their survey courses. This situation is changing for the better, as may be seen from the names, countries of publication, and dates on that list.

Two debates are serious. One centers on his doctrine of the eternal decree, the other on his doctrine of the Spirit.

As we have seen, the whole history of salvation is, according to Barth, actual in God's eternal decision "before all time." It has often been argued that he thereby strips the decisions' temporal realization of salvific efficacy. In German discussions, Barth has even been accused of "gnosticism," of casting a vision of reality in which all the action occurs within a divine pretemporal pleroma, merely to be acted out in time.

There is surely something to worry about here. Barth did deny, throughout the *Church Dogmatics*, that any temporal event, even those of the saving history or those that constitute the church, could be "eschatological"; their force could only be cognitive, only revelatory. But then of course, if we remember Barth's dialectics, "only" is oddly predicated of revelation, since what is revealed is always that revelation can and does happen. In eternity salvation is decided, and this is "merely" revealed in time; but *what* is decided is that there shall be this revelation. The critique that tries to seize Barth by any one turn of this dialectic may find it cannot hold him.

The problem about Barth's doctrine of the Spirit is perhaps less dialectically treacherous. When Barth *uses* the doctrine of Trinity to solve theological problems, what actually appears and functions is regularly a doctrine rather of binity. Many instances could be cited. But here we may for brevity's sake invoke an explicit general statement of principle. The "inner-divine" fellowship of Father and Son in the Spirit is, Barth directly asserts, merely "two-sided," since the Spirit is the fellowship itself. Precisely this merely two-sided fellowship is then the eternal ground for there being fellowship between God and humanity,[16] first between God and the Son Jesus and then between God in Jesus and Jesus' sisters and brothers. But that is to say that this merely two-sided fellowship is the eternal ground of all salvation history, which is what we were afraid Barth meant.

Almost certainly, these two problems in Barth's thinking – if they are problems – depend on a single deeper problem. When Barth refers to God's own eternity, to the eternity of the choice that he is, he regularly and decisively qualifies this as "before all time." Why is it never "after all time"? It must be said: The *eschatological* character of God's reality and work, so clear in Scripture, does not determine the structure of Barth's vision as it should.

Agenda

What then should English-speaking theology, now decades after Barth's death, finally learn from him? I suggest that it is not so much that we need to adopt his theological results – though we could usually do much worse – as that we need to be brought through the overturnings and reversals he experienced and made.

The standard theology of England and North America has never gone through the shock that elsewhere initiated specifically twentieth-century theology. Our theology has a decidedly museal air; "new" and "radical" theologies among us regularly repristinate some nineteenth-century German bright idea. We will not be able so to continue. As confidence in bourgeois culture dissipates among us also, our anachronistic neo-Protestantism becomes ever more obviously a play of illusions. It does not, of course, matter *how* we catch up with the twentieth century, but it might well be by way of Barth.

A decisive element of specifically post-nineteenth-century theology is the critique of religion: It is not at all clear that by the gospel's lights religion is a good thing. Of course Christianity is indeed a religion, but one of its specificities as a religion is that it is suspicious of itself in this capacity. Again it need not be Barth who teaches us this, but no one could do it better.

When Barth reversed the neo-Protestant pattern, inquiring not into Jesus' place in our story but into our place in his, he created the first Western christological vision of universal reality equal to such Eastern visions as those of Gregory Nazianzus or Maximus Confessor. The *Church Dogmatics* is a single-minded doctrine of being, which offends against the whole previous tradition of Western metaphysics by putting a particular, the risen Jesus, at the ground of reality. One need not approve all aspects of this system to find it exemplary. English-language theology can hardly much longer survive its supine acceptance of whatever version of Enlightenment scientism fashion happens from time to time to propose.

Finally, Barth incorporates all these dynamics in a drastically trinitarian theology, after centuries in which the doctrine of Trinity was in Western thinking a problem rather than a resource. The doctrine of Trinity is Christianity's founding doctrine, its starting identification of its God. As Christendom continues to disintegrate, we cannot assume that everyone knows which God the gospel means; surely we cannot make that assumption with the naive sheltered confidence of mainline American and English theology. Again, it need not be Barth from whom we learn better, but why not from the pioneer?

Notes

1 Many of the key essays are available in the translation collection, *The Word of God and the Word of Man.*
2 *Die Protestantische Theologie im 19. Jahrhundert* (Zürich, 1952), p. 19.
3 *Kirchliche Dogmatik* (Zürich, 1932–67), IV/1, p. 395.
4 *Der Römerbrief*, p. 7.
5 Ibid., p. 16.
6 Ibid., p. xiii.
7 *Kirchliche Dogmatik*, I/1, p. 1.
8 Ibid., II/1, p. 288.
9 Ibid., III/1, p. 107.
10 Ibid., II/22, p. 171.
11 Ibid., II/2, p. 20.
12 II/1, pp. 661–2.
13 Ibid., II/2, p. 116.
14 Ibid., I/1, pp. 316–17.
15 I/1, p. 315.
16 Ibid., I/1, p. 504.

Bibliography

Primary

Barth, Karl, *The Word of God and the Word of Man* (Weston, WV, 1928).
—— *The Epistle to the Romans* (London, 1933).
—— *Church Dogmatics* (New York and Edinburgh, 1936–69).
—— *Community, Church, and State* (Garden City, NY, 1960).
—— *Fides Quaerens Intellectum: Anselm's proof of the existence of God in the context of his theological scheme* (Richmond, VA, 1960).
—— *The Humanity of God* (Richmond, VA, 1960).
—— *The German Church Conflict* (London, 1965).
—— *Wolfgang Amadeus Mozart* (Grand Rapids, MI, 1986).

Secondary

Balthasar, Hans Urs von, *The Theology of Karl Barth* (New York, 1971).
Bloesch, Donald G., *Jesus is Victor! Karl Barth's Doctrine of Salvation* (Nashville, TN, 1976).
Bouillard, Henri, *Karl Barth* (Paris, 1957).
Busch, Eberhard, *Karl Barth: His life from letters and autobiographical texts* (Philadelphia, 1976).
Ford, David F., *Barth and God's Story: Biblical narrative and the theological method of Karl Barth in the church* (New York, 1981).
Gunton, Colin E., *Becoming and Being: The doctrine of God in Charles Hartshorne and Karl Barth* (Oxford, 1978).
Hunsinger, George, *How to Read Karl Barth: The shape of his theology* (New York, 1991).

Jenson, Robert W., *God after God: The God of the past and the God of the future, seen in the work of Karl Barth* (Indianapolis, 1969).

Jüngel, Eberhard, *Karl Barth: A theological legacy* (Philadelphia, 1986).

McCormack, Bruce L., *Karl Barth's Critically Realistic Dialectical Theology: Its genesis and development 1910–1936* (Oxford, 1995).

Torrance, Thomas F., *Karl Barth, Biblical and Evangelical Theologian* (Edinburgh, 1990).

Webb, Stephen H., *Re-Configuring Theology: The rhetoric of Karl Barth* (Albany, NY, 1991).

Webster, John, *Barth's Ethics of Reconciliation* (Cambridge, 1995).

Dietrich Bonhoeffer

Charles Marsh

Introduction: Life and Influences

Unlike many other Protestant theologians of the twentieth century, Bonhoeffer was not the son of a minister, nor were his parents given to expressions of piety. Bonhoeffer was born on 4 February, 1906, in Breslau, into a family that held high intellectual standards and preferred to spend religious holidays with relatives rather than attend church services. In 1912 Karl Bonhoeffer, Dietrich's father, was appointed professor of psychiatry and neurology at the University of Berlin, where he developed a reputation as a harsh critic of Freud and Jung. Dietrich's mother, Paula Bonhoeffer, loved the arts, held liberal views about politics, and presided over a domestic staff of at least five servants. Although she kept religious customs alive in the Bonhoeffer home, she did not push church involvement on her children. On Christmas Eve it was her custom to read from St Luke's Christmas narrative, and on New Year's eve Psalm 90. On many occasions, Karl Bonhoeffer responded to the biblical text by saying, "I understand nothing of that."

Bonhoeffer's parents did not expect him to choose theology as his main course of study, and they were not particularly thrilled when he did, though they did not interfere with his decision. They expected him to pursue a career in music (possibly becoming a concert pianist) or one of the professions of his brothers – law or science. When his older brothers heard of his decision, they tried to convince him that he was moving in full intellectual retreat and that the church to which he planned to devote his life was "a poor, feeble, boring, petty bourgeois institution."[1] Dietrich's answer was calm and confident: "In that case, I shall reform it."

Bonhoeffer spent his first two university terms at Tübingen in 1923–24. Despite his general discontent with life in Schwabia, he made the best of his time at this prestigious school. He especially enjoyed his courses on logic, the history of contemporary philosophy, and Kant's first critique. Bonhoeffer transferred to Berlin in the following year, where he studied with many of the finest theological minds in Europe – Reinhold Seeberg, Karl Holl, Adolf Deissmann, and Adolf von Harnack – and continued to read philosophy in seminars on epistemology and German idealism. He received his doctorate in 1927. After a post-doctoral year at Union Theological Seminary in New York (1930–31), he returned to the University of Berlin as a lecturer in systematic theology. He was well positioned toward a promising academic career, when ominous political events caused him to reconsider his vocation.

On 7 April, 1933, a policy called the "Aryan Clause" was passed by the German Reichstag, calling for the exclusion of all Jews and persons with Jewish parents or grandparents from government service. Soon thereafter, the German Reich Church adopted the Aryan Clause as a condition for employment in the ministry. Bonhoeffer responded swiftly with two public statements. In "The Church and the Jewish Question," written in late April, Bonhoeffer declared that in the prevailing political climate the church is compelled not simply to "bandage the victims under the wheel, but to jam the spoke in the wheel itself." Rather than bowing down to the idols of National Socialism, the church has an "unconditional obligation" to the victims of society, regardless of whether the victims are Christian or not.

In *The Bethel Confession*, drafted for the "Pastors' Emergency League" in August 1933, Bonhoeffer criticized the Nazi theologians' "disinheritance theory," which promoted the world mission of a master race to replace the Jewish people, who in rejecting the identity of Jesus as the messiah forfeited their divine election. Bonhoeffer insisted that the divine election of Israel remains unretracted. He said, "[God] continues to preserve a 'holy remnant' of Israel after the flesh, which can be neither absorbed into another nation by emancipation and assimilation . . . nor be exterminated by Pharaoh-like measures. This 'holy remnant' bears the indelible stamp of the chosen people . . . No nation can ever be commissioned to avenge on the Jews the murder at Golgotha . . . We oppose the attempt to deprive the German Evangelical Church of its promise by the attempt to change it into a national church of Christians by Aryan descent."[2] Bonhoeffer's condemnation of newly sanctioned anti-Jewish doctrines in *The Bethel Confession* was followed immediately by a declaration calling for the repeal of the Aryan Clause.

In numerous public pronouncements, Bonhoeffer referred to Hitler as an Anti-Christ without the slightest hint of exaggeration. Until his arrest by the Gestapo in 1943, Bonhoeffer actively opposed the Nazi regime both through church reform and political resistance. In 1935, he helped form the seminary in Finkenwalde for the purpose of training ministers in the "Confessing Church" – the church created at Barmen in 1934 in opposition to the German Reich Church's adoption of the Aryan Clause. After 1939, Bonhoeffer worked as a civilian member in the counter-intelligence agency the *Abwehr*, taking part in the July 20, 1944 assassination attempt against Hitler as well as various coverups of resistance activities. Bonhoeffer was arrested on 5 April, 1943 and executed on 9 April, 1945 at Flossenburg prison, one week before the camp was liberated by Allied forces.

Theological Influences

Bonhoeffer's greatest theological influence was Karl Barth. He read Barth's *The Word of God and the Word of Man* in the summer of 1925 as he was beginning work on his doctoral dissertation, *Sanctorum Communio*. Before his encounter with Barth,

Bonhoeffer was very much the student of the liberal Berlin school. Reading Barth was "like a liberation," Bonhoeffer's biographer and friend Eberhard Bethge wrote. In Barth's theology, Bonhoeffer discovered a theological freedom and courage that well suited his own independence and intellectual temperament. Although Bonhoeffer was never Barth's student, he did visit Barth's seminar in Bonn during the summer of 1931, after which he wrote in a letter to his parents, "I was even more impressed by his conversation than by his writings and lectures. In his conversation the whole of him is present. I have not met anything like it before."[3]

A narrative of the theological relationship between Bonhoeffer and Barth includes four episodes. The first is Bonhoeffer's reading of Barth's early so-called dialectical theology. The description "dialectical" refers to the paradoxical character of this theology, its incapacity to give unambiguous answers to questions about God and culture, its attempt to enact rhetorically the crisis of God's revelation in human history. In the dialectical theology, Barth brings God's radical otherness and freedom to hyper expression; there always agitates a "pathos of distance" or an "infinite qualitative distinction" between human experience and God's incomprehensible mystery. Barth says, "Without prejudice to and yet without dependence upon His relationship to what is event, act and life outside Him, God is in Himself free event, free act and free life."[4]

In his doctoral dissertation, *Sanctorum Communio* (1927), and in various theological essays of the middle 1920s, Bonhoeffer wrote sympathetically of dialectical theology. However, in his habilitation dissertation, *Act and Being* (1930), Bonhoeffer found Barth's dialectical conception of God problematic. Most troubling was his belief that if we think of revelation strictly in terms of God's act or crisis, then it becomes difficult to locate the continuities between God and the world, as well as the continuities within human experience. When Barth describes the new I in Christ as the non-being of the I in Adam – "By faith we are what we are not" – he creates a kind of "theological schizophrenia" that impedes the continuity of the whole historical person. Bonhoeffer accuses Barth of "overdetermining" his ideas of grace and freedom such that the person as socially and historically located becomes unthinkable. He argues that revelation described dialectically short-circuits the full meaning of God's incarnation in Jesus Christ and, as a result, splinters the self and community into discrete moments of divine encounter. Bonhoeffer concludes, "In revelation it is a question less of God's freedom on the far side from us, i.e., his eternal isolation and aseity, than of his stepping-out-of-himself in his *given* Word . . . and his freedom as it is most strongly attested in his having freely bound himself to historical humanity."[5] God's act must be balanced by God's being in a fully developed conception of the God who becomes incarnate in Jesus Christ.

The second episode in the Barth–Bonhoeffer narrative begins with Barth's thinking of the relation between God and human understanding which appeared in his little book on Anselm's *Prologion*, entitled *Fides Quaerens Intellectum* (1931). It is debatable whether the Anselm book marks a new theme in Barth's theology or simply the coming into focus of a theme already present.[6] What is certain, however, is that in his thinking through Anselm's prayerful meditation on God's name, Barth discovered a bridge from dialectical or actualistic conceptions of God to the idea of God as faithfully present in those words of the Christian tradition in which God's story is inscribed. Theology, in turn, becomes a *Nachdenken*, a "thinking after," or a thinking along the path of thought that is opened up in the words of the church. Anselm's naming of God as "that than which nothing greater can be conceived" must not be considered a proof of God's existence, but a meditation or prayer unfolded on the presupposition of faith. Nevertheless, on the basis of this presupposition, descriptions of God's being, or ontological descriptions, are able to acquire a certain appropriateness; for in the words of this name we are given a path for thinking God's thoughts after him – to think propositionally and truthfully about God, though not exhaustively.

Barth's axiom, "God's being is in his act," explicated in the *Church Dogmatics*, II/1, offers even richer material for resolving the conflict between act and being, which Bonhoeffer had rightly detected. Barth is not advancing a general ontological description of the divine being. All ontological statements about God and humanity have as their presupposition the specific story of the God who has revealed himself in Jesus Christ. God's being is not a property or mode of human experience, but is particular to his trinitarian self-relations as Father, Son, and Holy Spirit. Barth emphasizes in exquisite detail the fact that these self-relations should be understood as the originary acts of God's being. No longer ought God to be conceived as totally other (*totaliter aliter*), and thus transcendent of human history; rather human history must be properly construed as a predicate of God's own saving history. God's being is in God's act.

The third episode of the Bonhoeffer/Barth narrative is set in Tegel prison. Bonhoeffer continued to think about the significance of Barth's theology as well as his own uneasiness with certain themes in Barth's developing dogmatics. As helpful as his discussion on Anselm and on "God's being in God's act" may have been, Bonhoeffer suspected that Barth had overdefined the relation of the Word to world, that his doctrine of revelation was monistic or totalistic, diminishing the world's inner sense, its logic and meaning – its genuine worldliness. In a letter written 5 May, 1944, Bonhoeffer conjectured that even though Barth's theology abolished the claims of "religion" – the view that God could be understood on the basis of human experience in some form – he replaced religion with a "positivism of revelation," which says to the believer, "Like it or lump it": virgin birth, Trinity, or all the rest. Put more precisely, the church replaces religion (or nature) as the presupposition of faith. As a result, in the course of the developing dogmatics, the worldliness of revelation loses its integrity. The world, and the whole range of human experience beyond the church, is left theologically undepicted. Bonhoeffer thinks Barth is too readily inclined to interpret worldly experience or particular social and political situations from the perspective of God's sovereignty; his theology is overly confident, or at least prematurely confident. In response, Bonhoeffer wants to account for the worldliness of the world in a more detailed, indigenous, and nuanced way, by balancing God's majesty with his humility and his glory in the resurrected Jesus with his agony on the cross, and thus by attending to the full expanse of the Incarnation's consequence.

Bonhoeffer's criticism of Barth on this point may appear thin and careless. For in *Church Dogmatics*, II/1, Barth insisted that God in his *opus ad extra* does indeed encounter his creation in a reciprocity of recognition and affirmation. Even earlier in the *Church Dogmatics*, I/2, Barth argued that human history and temporality are not exhausted by revelation, but conserved in Jesus Christ. What do we then make of Bonhoeffer's prison criticisms? The general sense is that in Barth's theology God overwhelms the world. The more specific sense is that Barth has still not freed himself from the conceptual repertoire of nineteenth-century German theology. Although Barth rejects the turn to the human subject as the archimedean point of knowledge of God, world, and self, his alternative formulation of conceiving God as the divine knowing subject operates within a similar framework and is vulnerable to the same problems. Barth said repeatedly that the Cartesian epigram *cogito ergo sum* ("I think, therefore, I am") should be revised theologically to read *cogitor ergo sum* ("I am thought [by God], therefore, I am"). But wanting to avoid the legacy of the nineteenth century, wherein God is held to be in and over the world only to "a higher degree of the movement which we know well enough as our own,"[7] the description of God as the knowing subject of the world, in turn leads to the domination of the world by the divine subject. In taking this a step further, Bonhoeffer seeks a way to think the two thoughts of God's prevenient grace *and* the world's freedom to be other than God: He celebrates the Incarnation as the event which brings these two thoughts to unity. Bonhoeffer writes, "Whoever professes to believe in the reality of Jesus Christ, as the revelation of God, must in the same breath profess his faith in both the reality of God and the reality of the world; for in Christ he finds God and the world reconciled."[8]

The final episode includes Barth's two epistolary responses to Bonhoeffer's prison criticism. Barth is puzzled by the criticisms, and he tries to sort through them. But in the end, he confesses that the "positivism of revelation" charge and "all those catchy phrases" make no sense to him. Yet it is interesting that Barth's treatment of "secular parables" in the *Church Dogmatics*, IV/3, takes up the substance of Bonhoeffer's prison comments in great detail. Barth's description of "secular parables" offers a compelling response to Bonhoeffer's worries about the integrity of the world. Barth shows that certain "worldly lights" which ostensibly have no specific relation to the story of Jesus Christ (these worldly lights could take the form of compassionate acts, good people, aesthetic beauty, and the like) can become parables of grace and in their particularity and distinctiveness illustrate the goodness of God. Again, this is not a concession to natural theology, which both Barth and Bonhoeffer rejected as a grave theological error. Jesus Christ remains the sole criterion of the truth of experience, even in those special cases in which secular realities are empowered to become "children to Abraham." Barth's reflection on secular parables demonstrates a significant point in his developed theology of creation – perhaps the clearest point of intersection between Barth and Bonhoeffer's projects – namely, that the created order possesses an inner teleology. This inner teleology always and everywhere witnesses to the divine mystery within which "it is concealed." The world does not contain its own ground; however, it is not for this reason without distinctive meaning.

At the conclusion of our narrative, the question must be asked of the basic difference between Bonhoeffer and Barth. The best way to make clear the theological relationship of the two theologians is to distinguish between the primary and secondary objectivity of God. When we speak of God in his primary objectivity, we speak of him in triune life as such; further, when we speak of God in his secondary objectivity, we speak of him as he reveals himself in Jesus Christ. The distinction emphasizes that God's aseity is prior to his promeity. In this manner, Bonhoeffer's theology is best understood as an extended meditation on, or amplification of, the secondary objectivity of God, which by no means disregards Barth's epochal account of God's aseity. In fact, within the framework of this account, Bonhoeffer's exploration of the depths of God's worldly presence comes to its most meaningful expression. Whether in the end Bonhoeffer leaves the circumference of Barth's thought is a question deserving further consideration.

Survey and Content of the Works

The whole of Bonhoeffer's theology can be understood as an account of the continuities of God's identity, as well as human identities, interpreted through the reconciling work of Jesus Christ. Bonhoeffer was convinced that the pre-eminence of the thinking self or subject in modernity has invidious consequences for the task of understanding Jesus Christ, community, and selfhood. Theologically, it tends to endanger revelation's authority and priority. In social existence, it tends to consume the other into the individual ego. Bonhoeffer's formulations, "Christ existing as community," "Christ the center," "Christ as reality," and "Jesus as the one for others" are all ways of demonstrating how a christological description of human sociality affirms genuine relationship and offers a rich alternative to conceptions of self and other which are grounded in a world-constitutive subject.

In 1927 Bonhoeffer completed his doctoral dissertation under Reinhold Seeberg at the University of Berlin. Bonhoeffer describes the purpose of the dissertation, entitled *Sanctorum Communio: A dogmatic inquiry into the sociology of the church*, as an attempt to place "social philosophy and sociology in the service of dogmatics," to understand the social character of the revelation of Jesus Christ. He holds that all dogmatic propositions contain a social intention, which is not to say that they are reducible to social functions. "[The] history of the Christian community proves to be defined by an inner history,"[9] he writes. This inner history or inner sense of Christian community – the new sociality created by revelation – allows room for non-theological sources like philosophy, sociology, or phenomenology to contribute to the theological task helpful amplifications and illustrations of its own central concerns.

Essential to Bonhoeffer's argument in *Sanctorum Communio* is the avoidance of "the idealist goal of totality" in conceiving the relation between God and the world and the self and others. He calls for a "non-synthetic" description of the I and Thou, by which he means a description that preserves the dialectical tension of the relation and thus the constitutive difference of I and Thou. His description is based on the fundamental otherness or prevenience of grace; thus, the non-synthetic description of God's self-relation to the world in Jesus Christ illustrates the shape of genuine relationship. In making his argument, Bonhoeffer draws on the philosophy of dialogue, which was an intellectually fashionable trend in the second and third decades of the century. In opposition to the "epistemological sphere," wherein all knowledge of God and the world is a modification of self-relation and self-mediation, is the "ethical sphere," in which the I's attempts to master the world are always arrested by the dialogical encounter with the other person. In dialogical or ethical encounter, the individual person recognizes that the other is "not the idealist's reasoning self or personified mind, but a particular living person."[10]

The dissertation's failure is a result of the inability of a non-synthetic description of I and Thou to give an adequate account of the continuities which exist in God's relation to the world and within Christian community. While such language avoids totalistic conceptions of I and Thou, it makes difficult, if not impossible, the task of showing how "structurally separate" persons can also come together in real communion in Christian fellowship. To be sure, Bonhoeffer tries to resolve the conflict christologically. He writes, "In Christ this tension between being isolated and being bound to others is really abolished."[11] In Christ, God no longer confronts humankind with the claim of the divine Thou – in "demands and summons" – but God, as Bonhoeffer says, "gives himself as an I, opening his heart."[12] In turn, the person in Christian community "no longer sees the other members of the community essentially as a claim, but as a gift, as a revelation of his love, that is, of God's love, and of his heart, that is, of God's heart, so that the Thou is to the I no longer law but gospel, and hence an object of love."[13] Thus, without any cancellation of the difference between the I and the other, in the church of Jesus Christ there can be real openness for the other. However, Bonhoeffer's use of the philosophy of dialogue to account for community's inner relational logic forfeits the possibility of a richer conception of life together, based on this promising but undeveloped suggestion of God's I becoming concrete in Christ. It remains to be seen how Bonhoeffer will bring to unity the acting of God in dialogical relation with the being of God in the worldly presence of Christian community.

Bonhoeffer's habilitation dissertation, *Act and Being*, written in the summer and winter of 1929, is a complex theological exercise that seeks to work out this unresolved matter. The book is packed with philosophical references; Bonhoeffer provides "typological sketches" of Hermann Cohen, Paul Natorp, Friedrich Brunstäd, Edmund Husserl, Max Scheler, Martin Heidegger, and Erich Przywara. Readers looking for detailed theological analyses of these seminal thinkers will be disappointed. Bonhoeffer's purposes are to locate philosophical themes which can be applied to the theological project of reconciling concepts of act and being in a Christian reflection on God and revelation, and to show how philosophy can be taken into the service of explicating the secondary objectivity of God. Bonhoeffer's general purpose in the book is to follow the logic of the formula, "Christ existing as community" ("Christus als Gemeinde existierend") with a view to resolving the tension between an understanding of God as act (God's character as revealing event) and as being (God's character as incarnate presence).

Bonhoeffer asks, how can God be conceived as both other than the world (as different; as act) and yet concrete subject in experience (as identity; as being)? This new conception becomes possible if revelation is the event for which God is the active subject; if God is the subject of the knowing of revelation and is thereby understood as the divine I who at once *stands against* and *embraces* the human subject in the prevenience of his knowing. Bonhoeffer writes provocatively in *Act and Being*, "God is in revelation only in the act of understanding himself."[14] The *subject* of the act of the divine knowing is God Himself revealed in Jesus Christ; the *originary location* of this revelation is the story of Jesus of Nazareth narrated in the biblical texts; the *real place* wherein Jesus is present and the story celebrated in proclamation, forgiveness, and fellowship is the gathering of the Christian community. Our knowledge of God is then bound up with whether God has known us in Christ. Bonhoeffer writes, "There is therefore no prescriptive method for acquiring knowledge of God; the person cannot transplant himself into the kind of existential situation that enables him to speak of God; for the person is unable to place himself into truth."[15] As a result, attempts to describe God in terms of his identity with the world are inadequate because they ignore the character of revelation of decision and event. At the same time, attempts to describe God in terms of his difference from the world are inadequate because they obscure the basic truth of the Gospel proclamation that God is always a God with and for humanity.

Thus, the unifying theme of the habilitation dissertation is that the freedom of God "has bound itself into the personal communion," and it is precisely this binding "that demonstrates itself as God's freedom – that God should bind Himself to humanity."[16] The identity of Jesus Christ as God is at the same time his being *pro me*. God's overabounding love in Jesus Christ transforms the individual person from a self turned in on itself (Luther's *cor curvum in se*) to a self open for others. In this most academic of all Bonhoeffer's writings, the argument returns in the end to the level of lived Christianity and responsible action in the world.

While teaching in the theology department at Berlin during the years 1931–33, Bonhoeffer wrote numerous lectures, essays, and occasional pieces in philosophical and systematic theology. Several of these important texts are untranslated, including *Dietrich Bonhoeffers Hegel-Seminar 1933*,[17] "Die Geschichte der systematischen Theologie des 20. Jahrhunderts" 1931/32,[18] "Jüngste Theologie" 1932/1933[19] and "Probleme einer theologische Anthropologie," 1932/1933.[20] The two well-known writings of the period which have been translated and widely read are *Creation and Fall* and the christology lectures (*Christology* (UK) and *Christ the Center* (US)). These books are based on lectures given at the University of Berlin in the winter terms of 1932 and the summer term of 1933 respectively.

Creation and Fall is a theological meditation on Genesis 1–3, similar in hermeneutical style to Karl Barth's commentary on the *Epistle to the Romans*. The exegesis is theologically daring, uninhibited by the conventions of critical biblical studies. Bonhoeffer read Genesis unapologetically as a book of the church, drawing the questions addressed to the text from the distinctive discourse of the Christian community. *Creation and Fall* also illustrates Bonhoeffer's ongoing attempt to understand the continuities of divine and human identity, and thus to think theologically in a way that avoids conflating God and the world (in identity or being) or disconnecting God and the world (in difference or act). He stresses the creative freedom of God as the source of humanity's own freedom. The free God creates humanity in his own image; thus, humanity is free in a sense analogous to its creator. He sees a beautiful analogy. However, this analogy exists because God's being is a being-in-relation, witnessed paradigmatically in his self-relation to the world in Jesus. The analogy, then, that is proper to divine revelation is an analogy of relation (*analogia relationis*) not an analogy of being (*analogia entis*). The relation of God to humanity never lends itself to general ontological descriptions, or to the notion that God and the world share substantive qualities in their respective places along the chain of being; the *analogia relationis* is always particular to the story of Jesus Christ. As such, God's being himself in his relation to the world in Jesus Christ attests to the fact that "being free means being for the other." Bonhoeffer finds in his reading of the creation story the message of the Gospel, that God has not chosen to remove himself from history, but to relate himself freely to humanity as partners in a common history. Thus, only in relationship with the other is the person free.

The 1933 christology lectures (*Christology* (UK) and *Christ the Center* (US)), are an uneven but vigorous and uncompromising explication of Christ as mediator of all reality. While the German Church had begun to sell out to Nazi ideology and theology, identifying Christ with the Aryan ideals of blood, soil, and nationhood, Bonhoeffer insisted on thinking of Christ at the boundary and hidden center of reality. Bonhoeffer seeks to shift the basic christological question from the "How," that is, from the question, "How can Jesus Christ be both God and human," to the "Who," "Who is he?" this one who encounters us in the person of Jesus Christ in the church. Christology does not proceed from abstract notions like logos or Being, but from the historical Jesus of Nazareth, crucified and resurrected from the dead, present in the church. It is important that this Jesus who confronts us in the church with the question "Who am I?" turns the individual away from narcissistic presumptions of self-mastery and praise (nowhere more grotesquely witnessed than in the Nazis' obsessions with racial purity and social order) and toward life for others. Because Christ, in his being Christ, is "being for me," "the core of the person himself is the *pro me*."[21] God's being is in God's becoming for us in Jesus Christ; in this way, God's aseity and otherness are interpreted by God's promeity and his presence in the church.

Although Bonhoeffer left his teaching post at the end of the 1933 summer term in response to the urgency of the church crisis, his next three books are continuous thematically, though not methodologically or rhetorically, with his writings of the academic period. In fact, *The Cost of Discipleship*, *Life Together*, and *Ethics* can be read as a kind of trilogy in which Bonhoeffer's consideration of divine and human identities in Jesus Christ finds articulation in a fresh theological language. This language is at once straightforward and multi-leveled, attentive both to the discourse of the church (and the church crisis) and to the same set of theological issues addressed in his previous writings.

The Cost of Discipleship originated as a series of lectures given at Finkenwalde, a seminary of the Confessing Church where Bonhoeffer served as spiritual director and teacher from 1935 until 1937 (when the school was closed by the Gestapo). The German title, *Nachfolge*, means simply "following after." In his *Church Dogmatics* IV/2, Barth remarked that on the matter of a theology of discipleship, he was tempted to simply reproduce long passages from Bonhoeffer's book and let the matter stand there. Taken as a whole, *The Cost of Discipleship* is a diatribe against any faith that cheapens grace. "Cheap grace means grace sold on the market like cheapjacks' wares." In opposition to cheap grace, Bonhoeffer describes a costly grace, which lives "under the sign of the cross." Costly grace is not governed primarily by doctrine, ethical principle, or religious ritual, but by the call of Jesus Christ to follow after. At the same time, costly grace has pervasive iconoclastic consequences, waging war against the idols and against all competing claims on the disciple.

To dramatically demonstrate this point in *Nachfolge*, Bonhoeffer emphasized the immediacy of the call to discipleship. "For Christ has delivered [people] from immediacy with the world, and brought them into immediacy with himself."[22] Reading the story in Mark's Gospel of Levi's decision to follow Jesus (Mark 2: 14), Bonhoeffer says that the only claim made about discipleship is its immediacy.[23] The response of following after is "void of all content." An "abstract Christology," a christology concerned with the "how" or "what" of Jesus, must give way to concrete discipleship bound to Christ. Knowing Christ *is* following Christ – it *is* obedience. Bonhoeffer asks, "And what does the text inform us about the content of discipleship? It is nothing else than bondage to Jesus Christ alone, completely breaking through every programme, every ideal, every set of laws. No other significance is possible, since Jesus is the only significance."[24] The severity of Bonhoeffer's language, the harshness of his description of discipleship, has a special if not a specific historical purpose: The demands for loyalty and obeisance to the idols of National Socialist ideology are subverted by the immediacy of the call of Jesus – "the One beyond any Other."

Life Together, like *The Cost of Discipleship*, grew out of Bonhoeffer's experience at Finkenwalde. *Life Together* can be read as a theological manual on Christian community, and fits nicely in the genre of devotional literature that has its origins in Benedict's *Rule*. At the same time, the book enriches the theme of divine and human identities considered in Jesus Christ. The theme of the immediacy of the call and the disciple's following recedes into the background. In its place we find again the theme of mediation: Christ as mediator between God and humanity, and other people as mediator of the Christ's worldly presence in the church. Bonhoeffer describes the person's self-relation and relation to others as mediated and opened up solely through the person of Jesus Christ. He says, "Now Christians can live with one another in peace; they can love and serve one another; they can become one."[25] Much as he had done in *Sanctorum Communio*, Bonhoeffer wants to explicate the distinctive sociality of "Christ existing as community." In the church, Christ opens up the way to the other person by pulling the individual out of self-imprisonment into fellowship with others. Without Christ's personal mediation, the other person cannot be known in his or her integrity, but is always consumed or dominated in some form by the ego. What "human love" cannot achieve inasmuch as it inclines toward manipulation (even in heroic or charitable acts), "spiritual love," animated by the transforming love of the Mediator, does: Spiritual love releases the other people from the self's unending and coercive demands, enabling people to live together in common history with God. Bonhoeffer writes, "Because Christ stands between me and others, I dare not desire direct fellowship with them . . . This means that I must release the other person from every attempt of mine to regulate, coerce, and dominate him with my love . . . Because Christ has long since acted decisively for my brother, before I could begin to act, I must leave him his freedom to be Christ's; I must meet him only as the person that he already is in Christ's eyes."[26] Who is the other person? According to Bonhoeffer, the other is not an abstract notion, not simply my neighbor, family member, or compatriot, but the neglected, weak, oppressed, and despised – "the seemingly useless people."

Bonhoeffer's *Ethics* is an unfinished text, posthumously collected and edited by Eberhard Bethge. Bonhoeffer worked on the manuscript from 1940 to 1943, during his years of participation in the resistance movement. There has been lengthy scholarly discussion on the proper arrangement of the fragments;[27] nonetheless, the theological concerns of the unfinished work are coherent, even in their fragmentariness. Above all else, Bonhoeffer seeks to understand the cosmic and worldly efficacy of God's being in the world in Jesus Christ. Whereas in *Nachfolge* the world appeared sinister and idolatrous, in *Ethics* Bonhoeffer renews his early task of thinking about Jesus Christ as the overcoming of divisions like church and world, act and being, or spiritual and material. Of central importance is the section in *Ethics*, "Christ, Reality and the Good." Here Bonhoeffer considers the Incarnation as the event that transforms the total structures of the world. The created order in all its exquisite diversity is part of the detailed integration of this transformation. Therefore the Incarnation of God in the flesh makes it hereafter unacceptable to speak of God and the world "in terms of two spheres." "There are not two realities, but only one reality, and that is the reality of God, which has become manifest in Christ in the reality of the world."[28] In the Incarnation, humanity is accepted by God, and the world is reconciled with him. The whole reality of the world is taken up into Christ and "bound together in Him" such that human history becomes now the "divergence" and "convergence" in relation to this new center. As a result, the church should not define itself in terms of militant opposition against the world, for the church is the visible place where the reign of Jesus Christ over the whole world is "evidenced and proclaimed."[29] Being in Christ compels men and women into full engagement with the challenges and responsibilities of the age.

Bonhoeffer's final book, *The Letters and Papers from Prison*, illustrates not only textual but theological fragmentariness as well. Yet the power of the book lies precisely in its "trial combinations" and "lightning flashes" of theological insight.[30] It is as though Bonhoeffer's lifelong protest against self-constituting systems of thought finds concrete embodiment in the broken texture of the prison writings. From his cell in Tegel prison, Bonhoeffer surveyed the story of modernity with a view toward the identities of God and the self. He concluded that history had reached a point where "God as a working hypothesis" is no longer required – certainly not a necessary hypothesis for science, politics, or morality (even philosophy and religion) to carry out their proper tasks. What then shall the "anxious souls" do, Bonhoeffer asks? His reply is that we cannot get back home, back to a time when religious authority laid claim to the totality of life in the world. What is required instead is "ultimate honesty," the sober recognition that we must live in the world as mature men and women, *etsi deus non daretur* – as though God were not given. Living in view of this recognition is not a concession to "the godlessness of the world"; rather, it enacts a faithfulness to the cross that seems appropriate to the time beyond modernity. The "godlessness of the world" is not concealed, but "exposed to an unexpected light."[31]

The prison writings' widely discussed phrase, "the world come of age" is best understood as a way of talking about Christ's taking form in all the complexities of our constitutive worldliness. Hence Bonhoeffer writes in his letter of 5 December, 1943, "My thoughts and feelings seem to be getting more and more like the Old

Testament, and in recent months I have been reading the Old Testament much more than the New."[32] In prison he discovered again what he had described in his earliest theological writings, namely an indefatigable love of the earth, that "it is only when one loves life and the world so much that without them everything would be gone, that one can believe in the resurrection and a new world."[33] The Christian "must drink the earthly cup to the dregs, and only in his doing so is the crucified and risen Lord with him, and he crucified and risen with Christ."[34] In Jesus Christ God has said Yes and Amen to all creation, and the divine Yes and Amen is "the firm ground on which we stand."[35]

Debate and Influence

Although *Letters and Papers from Prison* was published in an English translation in 1953, it was not until the appearance of John A. T. Robinson's *Honest to God* in 1963 that Bonhoeffer's theology gained wide currency in academic and popular religious debate. As one of the theological inspirations of the Anglo-American death of God movement, the prison writings offered seductive fragments toward a theology of human autonomy and secularity, evoking the idea of what Thomas J. J. Altizer later called, "the self-embodiment of God" into the "total presence" of the world. Although death of God theology stimulated exciting and widespread conversation in universities and churches, its highly speculative appropriation of a few passages from the prison writings led to distorted interpretations of Bonhoeffer's thought as a whole. Still, the death of God theologians believed they were working in the spirit of his "new" theology, asking questions about Christ, history, and culture with "ultimate honesty." The death of God thinkers brought to theological inquiry an exceptional intensity and passion; they might be forgiven their excesses.

In response to the death of God movement, Bonhoeffer scholars in the 1970s and 1980s tried to broaden the interpretative picture by detailing the continuities of his thought and by reconstructing its political and ecclesial context. Scholars also set out in search of the historical Dietrich; and they have been largely successful in providing better texts, with helpful editorial notes and marginalia. The appearance of the 16-volume critical edition of Bonhoeffer's complete writings, the *Dietrich Bonhoeffer Werke* (with a planned English translation) is evidence of the necessity of this task. However, the importance of Bonhoeffer for contemporary theological debate diminished during these two decades, in large part because influential conversations in the academy were ignored.

In recent years, there have been signs of renewed interest in Bonhoeffer's legacy. Among the fresh interpretative initiatives are theological critiques of modernity (Eberhard Jüngel, Wolfgang Huber), social analysis (John W. De Gruchy, Gustavo Gutierrez), political theory (Jean Bethke Elshtain, Larry Rasmussen), onto-theology and philosophical theology (Robert Scharlemann, Klaus-Michael Kodalle), and Christian–Jewish dialogue (Victoria Barnett, Christian Gremmels, Irving Greenberg). A reconsideration of Bonhoeffer's early academic writings accounts for part of this renewal. Undoubtedly, the greater source is the power of his theology to extend beyond its historical context (without deserting it) into new intellectual regions.

The unresolved theological question related to the central theme of understanding the continuities of divine and human identities in Jesus Christ is whether Bonhoeffer's thoroughgoing christological account wears thin. That is, does his christological account of divine and human identity not require richer trinitarian description? Does his conception of the divine promeity, the self for others, and Christian community need fuller trinitarian explication? It would seem to be the case that a theological description of divine and human identities ultimately depends on an understanding of God's inner-trinitarian and extra-trinitarian relations (respectively, God in his triune identity as Father, Son, and Holy Spirit and God as he reveals himself to humanity). How do we position Bonhoeffer's theology with regard to this task?

As the survey of Bonhoeffer's writings makes clear, his project is that of exploring the depths of revelation's worldly objectivity with regard to the event of God's being for the world in the concrete presence of Jesus Christ. This project is not at all incompatible with Barth's explication of the trinitarian identity of God. Bonhoeffer said in his doctoral dissertation *Sanctorum Communio* that only from the proposition "God comes from God" can the proposition "God comes to humanity" proceed. God is the movement from origin to goal within the everlasting identity of God's being God. Therefore, God's being for the world is at the same time an expression of God's being God; who God is is God's being himself and being with the world. Bonhoeffer's thinking through the christological meaning of the world is a way of thinking through the depths of God's being God. It does not indicate a rejection of the trinitarian task, but is an ingredient of that task. Bonhoeffer's theology should be regarded as complementary with Barth's rejuvenation of the doctrine of the Trinity, although with varying nuances and emphases, yet still sharing the common concern of understanding the self-witness of the living God in Jesus of Nazareth and the relationship of humanity to that self-witness – of thinking after the God who has given himself to humanity as an expression of his own loving character.

Bonhoeffer's unfinished project requires fuller articulation of this conception. The promise of a trinitarian articulation of selfhood lies in its capacity to illustrate a conception of life with others that originates in the identity of the subject (God the Father, the Son, and the Holy Spirit as integral persons) and yet requires the movement of and to the other in order to achieve its completed end (the perfect communion of the three). The movement of the subject from self-constitution to self-becoming in fellowship with others can then be modeled on the inner-relationality of the perichoretic mystery of the triune God – God the Father, the Son, and God the Holy Spirit being themselves persons in perfect communion with each other. Of course, Bonhoeffer's rich legacy continues to inspire many other theological and social ventures as well.

Notes

1 Cited in Eberhard Bethge, *Dietrich Bonhoeffer: Theologian, Christian, contemporary* (New York, 1970), p. 22.

2 Dietrich Bonhoeffer, "The Barmen Confession," in *A Testament to Freedom: The essential writings of Dietrich Bonhoeffer*, ed.

Geffrey B. Kelly and F. Burton Nelson (San Francisco, 1990), p. 143.

3 Bonhoeffer cited in Bethge, *Dietrich Bonhoeffer*, p. 132.
4 Karl Barth, *Church Dogmatics*, II/1 (Edinburgh, 1957), p. 264.
5 Bonhoeffer, *Act and Being* (New York, 1961; London, 1962), p. 90.
6 Bruce McCormack argues that the decisive methodological change took place not in 1931 with the Anselm study, but in 1924, with Barth's lectures on dogmatics at the University of Göttingen (Bruce McCormack, *Karl Barth's Critically Realistic Dialectical Theology* (Oxford, 1995)).
7 Karl Barth, *Church Dogmatics*, II/1, p. 270.
8 Bonhoeffer, *Ethics* (London, 1964; New York, 1965), p. 201.
9 Bonhoeffer, *Sanctorum Communio* (London, 1963), p. 38.
10 Ibid.
11 Ibid., p. 106.
12 Ibid., p. 106.
13 Ibid., p. 119.
14 Bonhoeffer, *Act and Being*, p. 92.
15 Ibid., p. 93.
16 Ibid., p. 109.
17 *Bonhoeffers Hegel-Seminar 1933*, ed. Ilse Tödt (Munich, 1988).
18 *Gesammelte Schriften*, vol. 5, ed. Eberhard Bethge (Munich, 1972), pp. 181–226.

19 Ibid., pp. 300–39.
20 Ibid., pp. 340–58.
21 Bonhoeffer, *Christology* (London, 1978), p. 47.
22 Bonhoeffer, *The Cost of Discipleship* (New York, 1963; London, 1964), p. 106.
23 Ibid., p. 62.
24 Ibid., p. 62.
25 Bonhoeffer, *Life Together* (London and New York, 1954), p. 24.
26 Ibid., p. 36.
27 See Clifford J. Green, "The text of Bonhoeffer's Ethics," in *New Studies in Bonhoeffer's Ethics*, ed. William J. Peck (Lewiston, ME, 1987), pp. 3–66.
28 Bonhoeffer, *Ethics*, p. 197.
29 Ibid., p. 202.
30 Wayne Whitson Floyd, Jr., "Style and the critique of metaphysics: The letter as form in Bonhoeffer and Adorno," *Theology and the Practice of Responsibility: Essays on Dietrich Bonhoeffer*, ed. Wayne Whitson Floyd, Jr. and Charles Marsh (Valley Forge, PA, 1994), p. 241.
31 Bonhoeffer, *Letters and Papers from Prison* (London, 1971; New York, 1972), p. 362.
32 Ibid., p. 157.
33 Ibid., p. 157.
34 Ibid., p. 337.
35 Ibid., p. 391.

Bibliography

Primary

Bonhoeffer, Dietrich, *Life Together* (London and New York, 1954).
—— *Act and Being* (New York, 1961; London, 1962).
—— *The Cost of Discipleship* (New York, 1963; London, 1964).
—— *Sanctorum Communio* (London, 1963); US title *The Communion of Saints* (New York, 1963).
—— *Ethics*, rev. edn (London, 1964; New York, 1965).
—— *No Rusty Swords: Letters, lectures and notes, 1928–1936, from the Collected Works* (New York, 1965).

—— *Creation and Fall. Temptation* (London and New York, 1966).
—— *Letters and Papers from Prison*, enlarged edn, ed. Eberhard Bethge (London, 1971; New York, 1972).
—— *Christology* (London, 1978); US title *Christ the Center* (New York, 1978).
—— *True Patriotism: Letters, lectures and notes, 1930–1945, from the Collected Works* (New York, 1973).
—— *Fiction from Prison*, ed. Renate and Eberhard Bethge, with Clifford Green (Philadelphia, 1981).
—— *Love Letters from Cell 92*, ed. Ruth-Alice von Bismarck and Ulrich Kabitz (Nashville, TN, 1995).

Secondary

Bethge, Eberhard, *Dietrich Bonhoeffer: Theologian, Christian, contemporary* (New York, 1970).

De Gruchy, John W., *Bonhoeffer and South Africa* (Grand Rapids, MI, 1984).

Dumas, André, *Dietrich Bonhoeffer: Theologian of reality* (New York, 1971).

Feil, Ernst, *The Theology of Dietrich Bonhoeffer* (Philadelphia, 1985).

Floyd, Wayne Whitson, Jr. and Charles Marsh (eds), *Theology and the Practice of Responsibility: Essays on Dietrich Bonhoeffer* (Valley Forge, PA, 1994).

Godsey, John D., *The Theology of Dietrich Bonhoeffer* (Philadelphia, 1960).

Green, Clifford J., *The Sociality of Christ and Humanity: Dietrich Bonhoeffer's early theology, 1927–1933* (Missoula, MO, 1972).

Lovin, Robin W., *Christian Faith and Public Choices: The social ethics of Barth, Brunner, and Bonhoeffer* (Philadelphia, 1984).

Marsh, Charles, *Reclaiming Dietrich Bonhoeffer: The promise of his theology* (New York, 1994).

Ott, Heinrich, *Reality and Faith* (Philadelphia, 1972).

Rasmussen, Larry, *Dietrich Bonhoeffer: Reality and resistance* (Nashville, TN, 1972).

Eberhard Jüngel

John B. Webster

Introduction

Eberhard Jüngel (1934–) is generally recognized as one of the most significant contemporary German systematicians and philosophers of religion. He has an established reputation both as a severely professional theologian whose academic writing makes the greatest demands of its readers, and as a lively and often controversial commentator on issues of religion and politics. Brought up in the gray Stalinist culture of the German Democratic Republic, he studied with some of the leading figures in German-language theology in the 1950s – Barth, Fuchs, Ebeling, Vogel, Stammler, and others. His experiences under East German socialism not only gave him a permanent interest in atheism but also led him to think of the church "as the one place within a Stalinist society where one could speak the truth without being penalized."[1] Jüngel began his teaching career at the *Kirchliche Hochschule* in East Berlin, moving from there to Zürich in 1966 before taking up his present post in 1969 as professor of systematic theology and philosophy of religion in the Protestant faculty in Tübingen, where he is also dean of the *Stift*.

From his earliest work, Jüngel has not given exclusive allegiance to any one particular theological school. The territory of German Protestant theology in the 1950s was largely divided up between Barth and Bultmann. Jüngel straddled both camps: He studied with Barth as well as with Bultmann's pupil Ernst Fuchs, and one of the main concerns of his early writings was to demonstrate affinities and correlations between Barth's theology of revelation and Bultmann's theology of Christian existence. Bultmann and those of his school certainly shaped Jüngel's reading of the New Testament. Like them, he rejects "historicizing" or "objectifying" interpretation, espouses a fairly radical style of historical and literary criticism (though tempered by the interest shown by the "New Quest of the Historical Jesus" in the content of Jesus' proclamation of the Kingdom of God), and retains a strong interest in the subjective dynamics of the existence of faith as it is encountered by God. Unlike some other students of Bultmann, however, Jüngel stresses the theocentric character of Bultmann's account of the New Testament *kerygma*, and reads his "demythologizing" in a more objective way, not as a covert atheism but as a repudiation of abstract "onto-theology." If Bultmann is thereby brought closer to Barth, the rapprochement was furthered through Jüngel's study with Fuchs, a New Testament theologian of legendary obscurity under whom Jüngel wrote his doctorate. Fuchs offered an interpretation of the New Testament which extended Bultmann's understanding of the *kerygma* as saving event by emphasizing the linguistic character of the *kerygma*. Fuchs took much from the later Heidegger's rejection of "instrumental" theories of language which regard words as mere external signs of prelinguistic ideas. For Fuchs, core New Testament language (such as Jesus' parables) is a "speech event" which is the self-presentation of the reality of God's Kingdom. Jüngel seized on the kinship between Fuchs's theory of language and Barth's theology of revelation, and even after the decline of Jüngel's interest in the hermeneutical debates of the 1950s and 1960s, the influence of Fuchs is pervasive in his mature work.

Jüngel's account of Christianity is also deeply influenced by Barth's dogmatic work. He is one of the very best contemporary interpreters of Barth, thoroughly acquainted with the texts, painstaking in his exposition, and alert to both the resourcefulness and the seductive potential of Barth's extraordinarily compelling description of the Christian faith. Jüngel has assimilated into his own dogmatic work the christological direction of the *Church Dogmatics*, developing this particularly in the areas of the doctrine of God and of Christian anthropology. More generally, he has taken from Barth a rigorous theological realism – a sense, that is, of the antecedence, graciousness, and sheer weightiness of the realities with which the theologian is concerned. "I saw that I had encountered in Barth the thought of someone who truly believed in his subject matter."[2]

A further contemporary of importance in Jüngel's development is Gerhard Ebeling, who not only reinforced Jüngel's interest in existential hermeneutics but also introduced him to Luther. It is Luther's work, alongside that of Barth, which has shaped his approach to many issues in dogmatics, and Ebeling's reading of Luther is crucial for him, especially in his concentration on the anthropological corollaries of the doctrine of justification and the passivity of faith as the essence of Christian life and action. Along with others in his generation (notably Moltmann), Jüngel was deeply impressed by the revival of Luther's theology of the cross (as found in the work of H.-J. Iwand, for example), and its fruitfulness for the development of trinitarian doctrine.

Luther also functions as something of a key figure in Jüngel's reading of the history of the Western philosophical tradition. Luther's critique of Aristotle's ontology and its influence on Western Christian teaching about God and humanity is for Jüngel a paradigmatic instance of theological critique of the misalliance between Christianity and metaphysics. Moreover, Jüngel found similar critical resources in key figures in the philosophical tradition itself. Hegel, he suggests, understood the centrality of incarnation and cross for the Christian doctrine of God better than mainline Protestant theology. Above all, Jüngel has made his own Heidegger's critical account of the history of Western metaphysics. He shares Heidegger's conviction about the fundamental significance of the Pre-Socratic philosophers, offers a similar critique of Plato and Aristotle, and is especially responsive to Heidegger's account of the self-destruction of the subject-oriented traditions of modernity – Descartes, Kant, later German idealism, and their critics in Feuerbach and Nietzsche. Jüngel's major study *God as the Mystery of the World*, indeed, is in part a theological history of modernity which is decisively influenced by Heidegger's repudiation of the metaphysical traditions of the West.

Jüngel's mind is shaped by thinkers, both theological and philosophical, of classical depth and breadth, and his intellectual world is filled with texts of deep resonance in the Western tradition. Accordingly, his best work often takes the form of close conversation with such texts. There are, of course, intellectual traditions which suffer comparative neglect in his published work. There is little detailed discussion of patristic writers (of whom he can be rather brusquely dismissive), of medievals apart from Aquinas, of Calvin, of modern "masters of suspicion" like Marx and Freud and their heirs in critical theory and feminism, of social theory, of the analytical traditions of modern philosophy. Nevertheless, Jüngel's accumulated inheritance has given him enviable command of a wide range of theological and philosophical idioms, and a unique vantage point from which to survey the territory of contemporary continental Protestant thought.

Survey

It is not easy to characterize Jüngel's chief preoccupations in a straightforward manner. Partly this is because he has written extensively in a number of fields – dogmatics, New Testament studies, philosophy, the theory of language, ethics – as well as engaging in a good deal of editorial work (notably of Bultmann's early lectures and of parts of the Barth *Gesamtausgabe*). Partly, too, it is because much of his best work takes the form of shorter studies, densely argued and requiring close familiarity with the texts with which he is interacting. Works of smaller compass, such as those collected in *Unterwegs zur Sache*, *Entsprechungen*, and *Wertlose Wahrheit*, suit him better than the comprehensive surveys of theological topics to which many established German theologians devote their energies. For all this, however, a brief chronological survey indicates how a number of interlocking themes have pervaded his theological development.

His earliest publications focused on hermeneutical issues, and in particular on appropriate ways of understanding the language of the New Testament. His doctoral dissertation *Paulus und Jesus* sought to define the relation between the synoptic parables and the Pauline doctrine of justification. Over against dominant models of that relation which focused on tradition-history or the history of religions, Jüngel found their coherence in their character as "speech events," the "real presence" in the language of the realities to which language refers. However rash its exegesis and uncritical its indebtedness to Fuchs, the work was greeted as something of a *tour de force*, already demonstrating Jüngel's considerable skills in dissecting theological and philosophical argument, as well as his forcefulness in constructing his own position. The centrality of the category of "the Word" is evident here and throughout his early writings. It functions partly as a shorthand term for convictions about the origin of certain traditions of Christian language in divine revelation. But it also acts as a focal metaphor in establishing the coherence of exegesis and dogmatics (a central concern in German language Protestant theology in the 1950s and 1960s, when biblical scholarship and systematic theology seemed to be tugging in different directions). Exegesis and dogmatics cohere in their concern with the divine Word as it "captures" human language, though they have different tasks with regard to the traditions of language of which revelation takes hold.

Jüngel himself first made the move to dogmatics through commentary on Barth, of which the most important expression was the fine early book *Gottes Sein ist im Werden* (translated as *The Doctrine of the Trinity*), a remarkably acute analysis of Barth's doctrine of God. This study laid the ground for much of Jüngel's future work in trinitarian theology. In essence, he took up Barth's affirmation that God's "being-for-himself" and his "being-for-us" are identical. Jüngel developed this theme through applying it to questions of our knowledge and speech of God, but most of all by trying to develop an account of how it is that God can suffer without collapsing into contingency and finitude. This last theme was worked at by Jüngel with increasing frequency in the 1960s in a series of highly-charged reflections on the cross of Christ as the "death of God."

Towards the end of the 1960s, Jüngel began to publish on the metaphysical and anthropological dimensions of the doctrine of justification by faith, as Luther came to occupy an increasingly significant place in the circle of his theological authorities. From this time on, his anthropology gained a sharper dogmatic profile, and to some degree moved out of the idiom of existential anthropology. Jüngel's essays from this first decade of theological activity were collected together as *Unterwegs zur Sache*. At the same time, his work moved out in a number of different directions. The publication of Barth's mature thinking on Christian baptism in *Church Dogmatics* IV/4 stimulated wide debate in German church and academic circles. Jüngel's contributions to that frequently acrimonious debate were especially important in interpreting Barth's strategy, but also in furthering his interpretation of the notion of sacrament and in stimulating a greater concentration upon anthropological issues. His book *Death*, published in 1971, formed the centerpiece of a number of studies of the relation between the cross and the resurrection, and of the nature of eternal life. More important, his work on language acquired increasing sophistication, inquiring more closely into the operations of a variety of types of language. Alongside this, Jüngel became increasingly absorbed in issues of theological anthropology, ethics, and natural theology. In his writings in these areas (many of which are collected together in *Entsprechungen*) Jüngel expressed a strong interest in characterizing divine grace in such a way that it is supportive of the freedom and agency of the human creation. Among these writings, Jüngel continued to produce a steady stream of interpretative studies of Barth (collected as *Barth-Studien*, partially translated as *Karl Barth: A theological legacy*), Luther and Heidegger, as well as a large number of published sermons and other occasional pieces.

Many of these preoccupations found their way into his study *God as the Mystery of the World*, first published in 1977. This – from some perspectives rather diffuse – book is best read as a series of prolegomena studies to a contemporary Protestant doctrine of God. One of the chief agendas of the book was to trace the fate of Christian thought and speech about God since Descartes, who represents for Jüngel the attempt to base certainty of God on certainty of the self-conscious knower. Its main counter-proposal is twofold. At the level of fundamental theology, it recommends a "realist" account of our knowledge of God, in which human thinking about God is brought about not so much by human inventiveness as by an initiative beyond itself. That initiative is primarily articulated in the form of language "transformed" by the coming of God to the world. "Thinking" follows this astonished transformation of our language by the "advent" of God in Christ. At the level of dogmatic substance, the book argues through some themes first identified in the 1960s, notably the freedom of God as a trinitarian act of suffering focused on the cross of Jesus, and attempts to show the persuasiveness of this account of God over against both "traditional" theism and its atheistic shadow.

In the nearly 20 years since the appearance of *God as the Mystery of the World*, Jüngel has published no major new treatise. He has continued to produce nuanced and suggestive studies of classic texts in theology and philosophy (Luther, Barth, Schleiermacher, Kierkegaard, Heidegger), and consolidated and extended his interpretations of justification (especially its political ramifications), Christian anthropology, and the doctrine of God. During the 1980s he turned with renewed interest to questions of sacramental theology, and explored the significance of the centrality of prayer for ecclesiology and Christian ethics. His essays from this period are collected as *Wertlose Wahrheit*. Over the course of this decade. Jüngel's work began to find an audience beyond Europe, as some of his best work was translated into English, and as English-language theologians (especially in North America) began to move with greater ease among the traditions of continental philosophy with which Jüngel is closely familiar.

Content

From these apparently diverse exegetical, dogmatic, and philosophical interests, a number of themes have particular importance in tracing the direction of Jüngel's theology.

First, from his earliest writings such as the reflections on time and eschatology in *Paulus und Jesus* to his mature analysis of metaphysical texts, he has devoted much time to exploring the borders between theology and philosophy, though he has offered no systematic account of their relation. Philosophy of religion, he proposes, cannot be divorced from "positive religion," from the specific beliefs of the Christian community. Philosophy, that is, does not play a foundational role in theology, since it is neither critical investigation of the possibility of faith nor a means of determining the conditions under which Christian beliefs can plausibly be explicated or defended. Indeed, Jüngel is critical of the hold which these apologetic strategies have exercised in modern theology, notably in its focus on human self-consciousness as a primary route to reflection on God. By contrast, Jüngel espouses a twofold use of philosophy by theologians. First, philosophy has an occasional, subordinate, and instrumental role in theological explication of the faith, furnishing arguments or concepts which help clarify the Christian confession. In expounding justification by faith, for example, Jüngel makes frequent use of Heideggerian philosophical categories –

truth as interruption, the ontological primacy of possibility, self-realization as secondary to hearing – which help in constructing a conceptual depiction of what the positive language of Scripture and confession expresses less systematically. Second, because the history of modern theology is inextricably bound up with that of modern metaphysics, attention to philosophy is a central *critical* task for theology. *God as the Mystery of the World*, as well as numerous shorter studies, furnish close readings of major philosophical texts whose usefulness is judged by whether they are compatible with or subversive of the primacy of God's self-manifestation in Christ.

Thus, although Jüngel rejects the assumption that "one must cease to be a philosopher if one believes in the God who only comes to speech in the gospel,"[3] it is indeed the gospel – God's self-announcement in Jesus – which is theologically normative. Revelation, the word of the gospel, defines theology's task and provides its norms and sources. "[E]vangelical theology only exists in scholarly service to the one Word which we are to hear and which we are to trust and obey in life and in death. Evangelical theology only exists in scholarly service to the Word which the church has to proclaim and against which, therefore, the church has to be measured critically."[4] Theology is therefore biblical and ecclesial. Its matter is mediated through the Scriptural texts, read not as means of access to intentions behind the text but as revelatory events in which God "comes to speech"; its locus is the community's hearing and confessing of the Word of God. Jüngel's firm sense of the sheer reality of divine revelation is one of the key elements in the cogency of his writing, as well as a primary reason for his attraction to thinkers like Luther and Barth.

Second, christology is fundamental to his entire theology, in both its formal and its material aspects: It is from christology that "theological thinking has to let it be said what may properly be called God and man."[5] Because he has not published a systematic treatment of the doctrine, what he has to say here has often to be gleaned from occasional pieces or from observing the way in which he uses it as an explanatory key for other parts of Christian teaching. His christology shares the basic framework of Bultmann's kerygmatic interpretation of Jesus, refined by Fuchs's interpretation of Jesus' proclamation, in that Jesus is understood through his preaching, with little attention given to the overall scope or dramatic shape of Jesus' life as a pattern of historical action. Accordingly, for Jüngel, as for Bultmann, the primary christological question is: How does Jesus the proclaimer become the proclaimed Christ? Jüngel's answer is developed by a particular reading of Jesus' proclamation (especially the parables). Jesus' preaching defined him: His being is "a being in the act of the Word of the *Kingdom of God*."[6] The "Word of the Kingdom" is interpreted as an eschatological utterance, a speech-act of decisive authority which effects a complete re-ordering of the hearer's apprehension of reality by presenting that which is utterly new. In this way, it is a revelatory word, an "*elemental interruption*" of absolute and divine effectiveness.[7]

How does this reading of the synoptic presentation of Jesus' preaching of God's rule enable Jüngel to move on to theological affirmations about Jesus' person and his relation to God? Analysis of Jesus' self-understanding shows that he is determined without residue by God's Kingdom which he proclaims: "the kingdom of God, God himself in the event of his kingdom, conditions the existence of Jesus thoroughly and totally... *Jesus is not himself apart from God*."[8] To spell this out,

Jüngel makes use of the concept of relation. Jesus' divinity means that "[w]e must think God in relation to this human person, and think this relation itself as divine being: specifically, as the being of the Son of God. We have to think Jesus in his relation to God, and think this relation itself as the inseparable unity of the humanity of Jesus Christ with the Son of God."[9] Despite his unease with substance ontology, what Jüngel says here is similar to patristic incarnational christology, as can be seen in his appeal to the language of "anhypostasia" and "enhypostasia." Jesus' existence, as presented in the gospels, is "anhypostatic," in that it has no center in itself. This existence is revealed at the resurrection to be "enhypostatic" – to have its center in the Word of God. Jesus' existence is thus "*ontologically* grounded in the fact that his humanity is enhypostatic in the mode of being of the Logos."[10] A closely allied cluster of notions concerns identity and identification. Jüngel turns to this in speaking about the resurrection, which he understands not as the temporal continuance of Jesus' career beyond Calvary but as the manifestation of Calvary as the event of God's identification with the crucified; and so "the meaning of the death of Jesus, which is revealed in the resurrection of Jesus Christ, comes to speech in the identity of God with the crucified man Jesus."[11] It is important here to note, first, that Jüngel envisages Calvary as the central moment of the incarnation, and second, that language about the resurrection points backward, qualifying Jesus' past by disclosing its ontological grounds in God's relation to or identity with Jesus.

In light of God's relation to him, what is the saving significance of Jesus? "God and humanity . . . are to be *distinguished* in such a way that God and humanity can *be together in an unrestricted way*."[12] It is as if the existence of Jesus in relation to God effects the ontological definition of humanity; his "saving" work is thus spoken of more in ontological than in soteriological or moral terms, since what he effects is not so much humanity's reconciliation as its definition. Once again, Jesus is understood primarily as revealer; only minimal attention is given to saving historical action, and salvation becomes primarily a message rather than a drama.

Third, the doctrine of God. Jüngel's handling of this area is markedly impressed by his conviction that authentic Christian theology is christologically determined. The point is most tellingly seen in his thorough dissatisfaction with received "theistic" accounts of divine transcendence, immutability, and impassibility. In a characteristically unqualified statement, he proposes that "the crucified is as it were the material definition of what is meant by 'God'."[13] In constructing its doctrine of God, that is, Christian theology does not presuppose a generally agreed notion of the character of divinity, but rather, taking its rise from reflection upon God's self-identification with the death of Jesus, seeks to fashion an account of what God is like if Jesus is the place of God's self-manifestation. For much of his career Jüngel has sought to clarify a number of issues here, often by thinking through the meaning of the "death of God." *God as the Mystery of the World* offers an extensive review of possible meanings, focusing especially on Hegel, and arguing that in theological usage the "death of God" ought not to refer to an event in cultural history such as the displacement of God as a significant explanatory factor in metaphysics or cosmology. Rather, it seeks to specify God's being by reference to the godforsakenness of the cross. Jüngel's theology is thus in one sense richly theopaschite, affirming that God suffers. However, he has his own particular emphasis to bring to bear upon the discussion. Much postwar German Protestant writing about Calvary was directed by apologetic concerns: defending the Christian faith against atheistic critique, and developing the theme of God's suffering as a new path in theodicy. While Jüngel shares some of these concerns (*God as the Mystery of the World* contains lengthy debates with representative modern Western atheist texts), he is equally concerned to work out the *ontological* dimensions of the issues, to try to state how language about God's suffering and death contains "a deep insight into the peculiar ontological character of the divine being."[14]

Jüngel is distinctly uneasy with much language about impassibility and transcendence because it appears to run counter to the conviction that God *expresses* rather than *denies* his being at the cross. But this does not lead him to jettison the notions of God as self-caused and as absolutely free: "God's self-surrender is not his self-abandonment."[15] Here Jüngel is generally guided by Barth's recasting of the notion of divine sovereignty as the inner possibility of loving action – a theme presented with rare penetration in *Gottes Sein ist im Werden*. God's aseity is his freedom to love and spend himself in identification with the crucified Jesus. Language about God's freedom, therefore, does not propose some putative capacity in God to be other than he is in Jesus Christ. It speaks of God's capacity to suffer death in such a way that it can be a mode of his life and not the occasion of his collapse. Jüngel has worked hard to construct ontological categories to state this identity between God's self-affirmation and his self-surrender. Such categories include the notions of God's presence-in-absence, of God's involvement in transience as "the struggle between being and non-being,"[16] and above all of God as "the unity of life and death in favour of life."[17]

This last category is bound up with trinitarian language about God. Jüngel makes use of such language in trying to state what must be true of God as he makes himself known through Bethlehem and Calvary: The doctrine of the trinity recasts the gospel narratives in conceptual form. More particularly, the concept of God as trinity is closely allied to the further notion that God is love, since both attempt to state how God's unity embraces differentiation. For "love is structurally to be defined as – in the midst of ever greater self-relatedness – even greater selflessness, that is, as self-relation going beyond itself, flowing beyond itself and giving itself."[18] Love is neither negative, uncreative self-loss nor pure self-positing; it is self-fulfillment in a freely chosen act of self-renunciation. To say that God is love is thus to affirm that as a triune being he embraces freedom and self-surrender. While the unformed state of Jüngel's theology of the Spirit means that it is not always clear how this issues in language about a *three*fold differentiation within the being of God, Jüngel is appealing to the doctrine of the trinity to state that it is of the essence of God *a se in nihilum ek-sistere*, to exist from himself in nothingness.[19] The basic setting here again owes much to Barth; but an equally pervasive if less easily detected influence is that of Hegel. In their different ways, both offer a means of stating how God is supremely himself in giving himself as the *human* God.

Fourth, anthropology. "We can conceive what God intends for humankind only by reflecting on the one human being . . . Jesus Christ."[20] Christian anthropology, that is, takes its orientation from the humanity of Jesus Christ, which is able to function as a determination of true humanness because it is God's humanity. Such an approach clearly raises a host of issues, not simply about the place of the human sciences in human self-understanding but also about the dignity and freedom of human persons. Does the grounding of our humanity in the humanity of the one man Jesus Christ reduce us to functions or extensions of a prior divine reality? Jüngel is keenly aware of the force of this question in modernity, in its philosophical, political, and ethical dimensions, and it has evoked some of his most passionate writing.

He insists uncompromisingly on the definition of human persons from outside, by the gracious being and activity of God. Here he again frequently makes use of the category of "the Word," this time understood as God's revelatory interruption of the settled continuity of human identity, the "justifying Word," which "recognizes" the person and creates value independent of the person's acts. This sharp distinction between person and works draws upon classical Lutheran discussions of the nature of justifying grace and its relation to sanctification, merit, and the ethical life. But behind this also lies a deeper discussion of the metaphysical background of how we are to think of our actions and their significance. The discussion focuses on Aristotle and Luther. Aristotle, Jüngel argues, understands the human act as that which realizes the person: A just person is called "just" because he or she does just deeds. This is tightly bound up with the "ontological priority of actuality," which, because being is realized in action, "accords an unsurpassable significance to the act."[21] In Luther, by contrast, Jüngel finds an affirmation that human existence is not self-realized but is properly "existence out of the creative power of the God who justifies."[22] This creative power of God effects what Jüngel calls the "possibilities" of the human persons, granted by God in Christ. These possibilities are more primary than any human self-realization, definitive of the human person in a way which exceeds our self-conscious projects of self-determination.

All this constitutes a vigorous affirmation that Christian – and, indeed, human – existence is properly a matter of "living out of righteousness."[23] Jüngel is nevertheless aware that such affirmations may corrode the substance of the human self and its acts, and balances his stress on justification with some significantly different statements. The balance derives from Barth, in part in his theology of covenant in which human partnership with God as his fellow worker is stressed, but above all in the fragmentary ethics of reconciliation at the end of *Church Dogmatics*, in which Barth laid stress on the responsive human action evoked by God's grace. Jüngel has written widely in commentary upon Barth here, focusing especially on the notion of the "correspondence" (*Entsprechung*) between God's act and the venture of human agency. Here in the late Barth, he writes, "the human person is already in the picture as an agent who corresponds to the God who acts."[24] In effect, then, two rather different accounts of christology in relation to anthropology are found alongside one another in Jüngel's writings. One, derived primarily from Luther, highlights Christ as substitute and emphasizes imputed righteousness and the centrality of faith over against human self-realization. In polemic against the primacy of practical reason in modern culture, as well as in much contemporary "political theology," Jüngel appeals to this model as intrinsic to any responsible theology of grace. The second account, taking its cue from Barth, allows more space to human action, and implies an understanding of the history of Jesus as evocative and exemplary as well as substitutionary.

Fifth, natural theology, which was a particular interest in the 1970s. Like his anthropological writing, Jüngel's interest in this topic shows how wide of the mark are wholesale characterizations of Barth's pupils as hostile to the natural order. His work here starts from a critique of natural theology conceived as the search for evidence of God in the natural order which can be discerned without the aid of revelation. Such a search (of which Pannenberg is for Jüngel the most distinguished contemporary representative) is criticized because it compromises the particularity of the Christian revelation, making it a specific instance of a more generally available knowledge. But more important, it leaves the created order undisturbed: In searching the fixed structures of creation for signs of God, it lacks alertness to the creation's capacity for renewal, to what under God it might *become*. Jüngel, by contrast, envisages natural theology as concerned, not with a universal basis for Christian assertions but with the universal implications of the highly specific event of revelation. In effect, his natural theology is a "theology of nature," and does not locate itself in the area of foundations, apologetics, or the justification of belief.

Once again, the distinction between "actuality" and "possibility" surfaces. The model of natural theology which Jüngel canvasses is not oriented to the actuality of nature or human experience, but to their possibilities, to the gift of enhanced meaning through the self-revelation of God. "Revelation" is a "critical comparative"; it discloses a world of new possibilities, which call into question the self-evident actuality of the world and demonstrate its capacity for enhancement. It "brings that which is hitherto self-evident into a new light."[25] Because of this, human experience is not a second source of knowledge of God beyond revelation; rather, revelation brings about an "experience with experience," a critical appraisal and renewal of human experience of self and world. What is most important here is the underlying dogmatic scheme: God and creation are not irreconcilably opposed (as, on some readings, they are in Barth), nor are they points on a continuum (as Jüngel believes they threaten to become in some accounts of natural theology). Rather, each is substantial in its own right, with the natural order becoming newly interesting through the event of revelation.

Sixth, religious language. His approach tends to be prescriptive rather than descriptive, preoccupied less with observation of actual linguistic usage and more with dogmatic concerns. If language is important, it is because it furnishes the basic model through which God, the world, and humanity are understood. Unlike contemporary theologians who have invested heavily in, for example, secular experience, universal history, human morality, or cosmology as a framework for expounding Christian doctrine, Jüngel makes language the interpretative key to reality.

Like his anthropology, his theology of language moves from an insistence on the disjunction between God and creation toward a sense of differentiation in relation. Earlier work appealed to the notion of God's "coming-to-speech" in a highly eschatological manner: Language about the reality of God remains tangential to worldly language. His interpretation of the parables in *Paulus und Jesus*, for example, presents those narratives as strange intrusions upon the world's language. On this basis, language about God becomes a miracle, going against the grain of our natural linguistic resources, its possibility resting wholly in the event of divine intervention. Later work, especially some important essays on metaphor and anthropomorphism and the treatment of analogy in *God as the Mystery of the World*, softens this eschatological contradiction into a distinction in relation. Language about God is just that – *language*, a structured system which as a human project has to be understood with reference to the speaker and his or her world, and not simply thought of as something created immediately by God. The most crucial development is in Jüngel's refinement of his account of "tropic" language (such as metaphor and analogy). He is attracted to these language forms because of the way in which they embrace two systems of reference: one system of their regular usage, and a new system to which they refer as that habitual usage is extended without being displaced. Metaphor and analogy testify to what might be called the "historicality" of language – to the fact that language is a process of becoming rather than a fixed set of referential relations. Certain fundamental kinds of language refer to more than "actual" states of affairs; in this way they articulate that which is possible. And so, for instance, the parables of Jesus refer both to ordinary worldly states of affairs and at the same time, without abolishing that ordinariness, also refer to the Kingdom of God which "comes to speech" in them.

All of this is undergirded by a dogmatic conviction that God's coming to the world does not dispossess the world of its reality but grants it further possibilities. As the one who makes us and our world "interesting in new ways," God is the "mystery of the world." By "mystery" here, Jüngel does not mean a mute reality which will not yield to inquiry, but an "open secret" – the hidden reality of God made manifest in Jesus Christ. A mystery is that which communicates itself and so makes it possible for us to speak of it. God is the mystery "of the world" because his self-communication is that which brings about the renewal of that world by disclosing its possibilities. Like his whole theology, Jüngel's theology of language is about the conversion of created reality, recalling our attention to the way in which the event of God's self-manifestation transforms the world and so is to be spoken of in a language which itself bears the marks of convertedness.

Seventh, Jüngel turned his attention in the 1980s to topics in the doctrine of the church, sacraments, and worship. Like his earlier explorations in sacramental theology from the 1960s, this later work – in common with his writing on other issues – turns on the interrelation of divine and human action. He insists that a Protestant theology of worship should be focused on the Word, in that it is rooted in the christological-soteriological principle *solo verbo, sola fide*. This emphasis secures the primacy of divine self-communication as well as the passivity of faith which corresponds to revelation. From here he presses repeatedly for the restriction of the term "sacrament" to Jesus, since "the decisive point is that in the sacrament, *the gracious God himself is the one who acts.*"[26] Partly this is characteristic Protestant reserve about sacramental and ecclesial mediation of divine grace; it is this which makes Jüngel highly receptive to Barth's critique of the sacramental status of baptism, and also unfashionably wary about the description of the church as sacrament in recent ecumenical theology. But it is also an assertion that, as the primary action of the church, worship is what he calls "receptive action":[27] Worship is that "human service of God which lets *God perform his work.*"[28] As such, worship is morally paradigmatic, the church's "first and fundamental answer to the question: what should we do?"[29] He explores this theme in a number of essays from the period concerned with the relationship between worship and ethics, which clearly tie in closely with his grace-centered anthropology and its relativization of the significance of historical action.

Influence, Achievement, and Agenda

Jüngel is a significant but rather tangential voice in current theology, partly because he has distanced himself from theological fashion, partly because he has not sought to establish and defend a "position." Moreover, the dominant features of his intellectual landscape – the classical texts of Western philosophy, Heidegger, Barth – are increasingly unfamiliar in much contemporary theology in which experience has a considerably higher profile. Jüngel is a "classicist" thinker, in that he proceeds from a conviction that God's reality precedes our apprehension of it, and is from and for itself even as it relates to us. To this highly developed realism is wedded a "positive" theological manner, one which emerges from a sense that the given language of Christian confession truly depicts what is the case and is therefore irreducible to something more generic. Once again, these commitments isolate him from many contemporaries, though there are signs that some philosophers and theologians are now inclined to share Jüngel's dispute with the culture of modernity. Indeed, one of his most significant achievements has been to show that the alliance between theology and metaphysics in modernity introduced some basic distortions into the way in which Christians talk of God, and to urge that part of theology's vocation is not to improve its apologetic arsenal but to practice authentically Christian discursive habits. Further, his philosophical interests make Jüngel a more congenial heir to Barth than those of Barth's school with a much more restricted range of conversation partners. His work on the ontology of possibility, however much it may need refinement and clarification, is perhaps the best example of his attempt to spell out the metaphysical dimensions of Christian belief without subsuming Christianity under an external scheme.

Much of Jüngel's best work is suggestive but underdeveloped. Because his preferred idiom is the essay or the textual commentary, he rarely undertakes fundamental investigation even of those topics where he is brilliantly evocative: the doctrine of God, the nature of language, anthropology and ethics, truth, possibility and actuality, and a host of others. The problem is compounded by a certain resistance to conceptual analysis. Though Jüngel can dissect the thinking of others with exquisite care, his own primary concepts often stand in need of much closer definition. One reason for this is that when he expounds his basic convictions, he often does so in a strongly prescriptive tone, and by extensive use of the language of Scripture and confession. Like other descriptive thinkers, he is reluctant to engage in second-order analysis. He shares this problem with Barth, though Barth compensates by the extraordinary depth and breadth of his portrayal of Christianity, establishing the meaning of his terms not so much by definition as by extensive use. Lacking Barth's luxuriant style, Jüngel needs more thorough and explicit discussion of his basic convictions than he has so far offered.

Many readers of Jüngel also find him excessively abstract, even idealist, in his creation of a world of discourse only loosely related to non-theological observations of how the world is. This is particularly true of his theory of language. There is a narrowness in its construal of authentic Christian speech: focusing on "tropic" language, it gives little space to other forms of language (discursive, propositional, hortatory) or to non-linguistic communication such as ritual. Furthermore, for all his emphasis on the worldly horizon from which the language of faith is drawn, Jüngel has undertaken very little close analysis of the sociopolitical context of Christian speech, and the relation of discourse to structures of power. It is language as revelation, not language as culture or social practice, which is his near-exclusive concern.

Something of the same can be found in his anthropology, which again operates prescriptively with little depiction of the human scene. Even when Jüngel does attempt phenomenological analysis of the nature of love, what he has to say is largely a-historical.[30] When this abstraction is added to the powerful presence of theological categories like justification, faith, or being in Christ, then the danger is that it leaves the operations of human life mysterious, and can threaten by its lack of description and exemplification to detach theological language about humanity from historical experience.

It may be that Jüngel does not feel the pressure to undertake such descriptions because for him the locus of God's relation to humanity is not experience but language. Here, however, some dogmatic questions can be raised. Like Bultmann and his heirs, Jüngel conceives that the space between God and the human world is bridged by "the Word": kerygmatic language is the point at which God encounters humanity. In dogmatic terms, this – highly Lutheran – emphasis leaves two large areas unexplored. One is the doctrine of creation. A second is the present reality and activity of God in Christ, which classical Reformed dogmatics articulated through its theology of the resurrection and the Holy Spirit, as well as in its ecclesiology and sacramental theology. Most tellingly, Barth responded to Bultmann's theology of the *kerygma* by an extensive recovery of the prophetic office of Christ, that is, of Jesus' self-presentation in the power of the Spirit to the Christian community and the world. Jüngel is prevented from this by strong attachment to the idea of the "word event," which tends to compress God's presence into punctilliar acts of speaking, by the slenderness of his christology, whose focus is Jesus' preaching as a word of revelation, and by a thin theology of the resurrection. At this point, Jüngel's trinitarian theology, and especially his pneumatology, stands in need of development.

Jüngel's major contribution, however, is not likely to be as dogmatician, but as one who has sought to relate the theology of revelation and the history of modern philosophy. Any reflection on God concerned to engage in serious conversation with its cultural and intellectual milieu needs both sufficient confidence in its own language and ideas so that it can marshal them with fluency, vigor, and imagination, and also genuine attentiveness to its conversation partners. Jüngel has amply fulfilled both those conditions, and it is there that his real strength lies.

Notes

1 Eberhard Jüngel, Toward the heart of the matter. *Christian Century*, 108 (1991), pp. 228–33 at p. 229.

2 Ibid., p. 231.

3 Jüngel, *Gottes Sein ist im Werden*, 3rd edn (Tübingen, 1975), p. 126.

4 Jüngel, *Christ, Justice and Peace* (Edinburgh, 1992), pp. 7f.

5 Jüngel, *God as the Mystery of the World* (Edinburgh, 1983), p. 231.

6 Jüngel, "Jesu Wort und Jesus als Wort Gottes," in *Unterwegs zur Sache* (Munich, 1972), pp. 126–44 at p. 129.

7 Jüngel, "The dogmatic significance· of the question of the historical Jesus," in *Theological Essays II* (Edinburgh, 1995), pp. 82–119 at p. 89.

8 Ibid., p. 102.

9 Ibid., p. 115.

10 Jüngel, "Jesu Wort und Jesus als Wort Gottes," p. 129.

11 Jüngel, "Das Sein Jesu Christi als Ereignis der Versöhnung Gottes mit einer gottlosen Welt: Die Hingabe des Gekreuzigten," in *Entsprechungen* (Munich, 1980), pp. 276–84 at p. 282.

12 Jüngel, "The dogmatic significance of the question of the historical Jesus," p. 117.

13 Jüngel, *God as the Mystery of the World*, p. 13.

14 Ibid., p. 62.

15 Jüngel, "Säkularisierung. Theologische Bemerkungen zum Begriff einer weltlichen Welt," in *Entsprechungen*, pp. 285–9 at p. 289.

16 Jüngel, *God as the Mystery of the World*, p. 217.

17 Ibid., p. 299.

18 Jüngel, "Das Verhältnis vom 'ökonomischer' und 'immanenter' Trinität," in *Entsprechungen*, pp. 265–75 at p. 270.

19 Jüngel, *God as the Mystery of the World*, p. 233.

20 Jüngel, "The·royal man," in *Karl Barth – A theological legacy* (Philadelphia, 1986), p. 128.

21 Jüngel, "The world as possibility and actuality," in *Theological Essays* (Edinburgh, 1989), pp. 95–123 at p. 100.

22 Ibid., p. 109.

23 Jüngel, "The sacrifice of Jesus Christ as sacrament and example," in *Theological Essays II* (Edinburgh, 1995), pp. 163–90.

24 Jüngel, "Invocation of God as the ethical ground of Christian action," in *Theological Essays*, pp. 154–72 at p. 161.

25 Jüngel, "*Extra Christum nulla salus* – a principle of natural theology?" in *Theological Essays*, pp. 173–88 at p. 183.

26 Jüngel, "The church as sacrament?" in *Theological Essays*, pp. 189–213 at p. 195.

27 Ibid., p. 202.

28 Jüngel, "Der evangelisch verstandene Gottesdienst," in *Wertlose Wahrheit* (Munich, 1989), pp. 283–310 at p. 289.

29 Jüngel, "The sacrifice of Jesus Christ," p. 183.

30 Jüngel, *God as the Mystery of the World*, pp. 314–26.

Bibliography

Primary

Jüngel, E., *Paulus und Jesus* (Tübingen, 1962).
—— *Unterwegs zur Sache* (Munich, 1972).
—— *Death* (Edinburgh, 1975).
—— *The Doctrine of the Trinity* (Edinburgh, 1976).
—— *Entsprechungen* (Munich, 1980).
—— *Barth-Studien* (Gütersloh, 1982).
—— *God as the Mystery of the World* (Edinburgh, 1983).
—— *Karl Barth – A theological legacy* (Philadelphia, 1986).
—— *The Freedom of a Christian* (Minneapolis, 1988).
—— *Theological Essays* (Edinburgh, 1989).
—— *Wertlose Wahrheit* (Munich, 1990).
—— *Christ, Justice and Peace* (Edinburgh, 1992).
—— *Theological Essays II* (Edinburgh, 1995).

Secondary

Aerts, L., *Gottesherrschaft als Gleichnis?* (Frankfurt am Main, 1990).
Dalferth, I. U., God and the mystery of words. *Journal of the American Academy of Religion*, 60 (1992), 79–104.
Paulus, E., *Liebe – das Geheimnis der Welt* (Würzburg, 1990).
Rolnick, T. A., *Analogical Possibilities* (Atlanta, GA, 1993).

Spjuth, R. J., *Creation, Contingency and Divine Presence* (Lund, 1995).

Webster, J. B., *Eberhard Jüngel: An introduction to his theology* (Cambridge, 1991).

Webster, J. B. (ed.), *The Possibilities of Theology: Studies in the theology of Eberhard Jüngel in his sixtieth year* (Edinburgh, 1994).

Zimany, R. D., *Vehicle for God* (Macon, GA, 1994).

Existentialism and Correlation

Rudolf Bultmann is unusual in being a major New Testament scholar as well as a modern theologian. His context within biblical and hermeneutical theology is discussed in chapter 26. Robert Morgan pays close attention to his biblical scholarship and his constructive theology, and explores Bultmann's relationship to Luther, Barth, nineteenth-century theology, and, above all, existentialism. Since the twentieth-century rediscovery of the Danish Christian thinker Søren Kierkegaard, existentialism has stimulated a remarkably wide range of theologians, philosophers, poets, novelists, and psychotherapists. In particular, it has been a significant influence on leading atheist (e.g., Jean-Paul Sartre, Martin Heidegger) and Christian thinkers, and Bultmann's engagement with Heidegger has tried to make this theologically productive. Morgan weaves in a critical dialogue with Bultmann and concludes with a constructive suggestion designed to open a way for Bultmann's theology to continue to be fruitful.

Paul Tillich's theology is also existentialist, though less dominantly so than Bultmann's. David Kelsey describes Bultmann's lifelong concern for Christianity and culture, and his method of correlating the two. His systematic style is a striking contrast to Bultmann's New Testament interpretation, and Kelsey shows both the conceptual coherence of the *Systematic Theology* and also its method's flexibility and openness. In the final section Kelsey brings up to date the story of the extraordinarily wide and varied influence that Tillich has had.

In terms of the typology suggested in the introduction to this volume Bultmann probably comes under the fourth, with existentialism as the philosophy through which Christianity is both articulated and criticized. Yet the non-systematic mode of his theology, with its intensive engagement with the particularity of texts, helps him to elude easy classification. Tillich is perhaps the modern classic of the third type, and the breadth, dynamism, and subtlety of the correlations he made between Christian theology and many issues and disciplines repeatedly draw him into contemporary debates. In Section C below, the theologies of Schillebeeckx and Küng display many features of the same type.

Rudolf Bultmann

Robert Morgan

Introduction: Life and Theological Development

Rudolf Karl Bultmann (1884–1976) was born near Bremen in northwest Germany, the eldest son of a Lutheran pastor.[1] As with all German theologians, before specializing and earning the right to teach in a university, Bultmann had first to receive a thorough grounding in the different disciplines that the subject requires. His studies at Tübingen, Berlin, and Marburg therefore involved philosophy and history as well as theology. His teachers included at Berlin Hermann Gunkel for Old Testament and Adolf Harnack for history of doctrine, at Marburg Adolf Jülicher and Johannes Weiss for New Testament and Wilhelm Herrmann for systematic theology.

This impressive list associates Bultmann with several different strands of liberal Protestantism. His theology was shaped above all by the pious neo-Kantianism of his teacher Herrmann (1846–1922), a devout follower of Ritschl (1822–89). But most of his biblical teachers came from the opposite wing of Ritschlianism, known as the "history of religions school," whose radical historical criticism had undermined that modern churchman's theology. Bultmann always suspected their representative, Troeltsch, of reducing religion to a human phenomenon, but his biblical scholarship was decisively influenced by this group of young scholars who had qualified in Göttingen around 1890.

This was a high-water mark of the historical critical movement within Protestant theology. In his attempt to resolve the tension between Christian faith and historical reason Ritschl had turned against the radical historical criticism of Baur. Some of his last pupils reacted against this residual biblicism and supernaturalism, and became key figures in twentieth-century biblical study. Gunkel (1862–1932) advanced history of religions research on the New as well as the Old Testament before pioneering a history of traditions approach to the latter and becoming the father of form criticism.[2] There was also William Wrede (1859–1906) and William Bousset (1865–1920) whose work on the history of traditions and the history of religions was particularly important for Bultmann. Johannes Weiss (1863–1914) rediscovered the centrality of eschatology in *Jesus' Preaching Concerning the Kingdom of God* (1892) and Wilhelm Heitmüller (1869–1926) investigated the Hellenistic antecedents of baptism and the Lord's Supper.

All these giants were more consistent historians of intertestamental Judaism and early Christianity than Ritschl. But they seemed barely to be doing *theology* at all. Their application of critical historical methods to the New Testament provided a more secure knowledge of the human past. Whether it also contributed to a knowledge of God was less clear. This question of faith and history has now haunted Christian theology for more than 200 years. It provides the central focus of all Bultmann's work.

One answer is that modern rational methods, including historical research, cannot themselves provide a knowledge of God. They can contribute to this only when associated with some religious, theological, or philosophical framework which licenses talk of God. Without that, history is theologically dumb. Liberal Protestants saw that the traditional religious and metaphysical framework within which the Bible had once been studied conflicted with their new scientific and historical knowledge. Convinced that all truth is of God, and that the Bible must be understood with the help of the best available rational methods, they adopted alternative philosophical theories of religion and reality, and combined their historical research with moral and religious reflection on the Absolute or divine Spirit in history. This idealist terminology was not quite how the Bible spoke of God, but the ancient and the modern ideas seemed broadly compatible. The main philosophical alternatives (materialism and positivism) were clearly unacceptable to the religious mind.

The liberals' metaphysical foundations were looking shaky by the turn of the century, and the theology constructed upon them decidedly weak. Two letters written by Bultmann in 1904 comment on the religious poverty of Bousset's *Jesus* (1903), and show that even as a student he was concerned about the sad state of contemporary theological liberalism. He subsequently studied Schleiermacher, and Otto's *The Idea of the Holy* (1917). His slow maturation as a theologian can be traced in private letters, reviews, and articles, through some 25 years of discussion with the theology of his teachers and contemporaries. The decisive breakthrough came in 1922, when he accepted, with reservations, Barth's critique of liberal Protestantism and his Kierkegaardian interpretation of Paul.[3] The confidence with which Bultmann developed his own theology over the next five years suggests that it had only needed this catalyst.

Barth's *Epistle to the Romans* offered a new solution to the problem of speaking of God in the modern world. The old metaphysics had succumbed to the criticisms of Hume and Kant, and the nineteenth-century idealist alternatives seemed bankrupt in the conflagration of Europe. Barth spoke of God's judgment and grace by interpreting Paul. He aimed to speak *with* Paul, as Calvin had done, only in a new cultural situation. This "hermeneutical" style of theology – theology through the interpretation of texts – corresponded to Bultmann's aim: to do theology as a New Testament scholar. He accepted Barth's theological criticism of the liberals' historical exegesis, and was soon arguing that the main thrust of the neo-Reformation "theology of the Word" was true to the New Testament itself.[4] That was different from what as a loyal follower of the history of religions school he had written in 1920. The same historical scholarship was arranged in new configurations.[5]

But Bultmann's association with Barth and Gogarten in the "dialectical theology" of the 1920s did not involve any sharp break with his past. He saw Barth, like Schleiermacher and Otto, as attempting to preserve the independence and absoluteness of religion. What Barth and Paul called "faith" was what Herrmann and Schleiermacher had called "religion." In his own way Herrmann had preserved the "otherness" of God too. His metaphysical agnosticism prepared Bultmann for Barth's theological modernism, which put God off the cognitive map. But the concept of "religion" had opened the door to a cosy cultural Protestantism whose day was past. Bultmann was therefore willing to accept Barth's subversion of the liberals' talk of "religion" by a new Pauline emphasis upon revelation through the Word proclaimed (the kerygma) and accepted in faith.

What Bultmann gained from Barth's theological interpretation of Paul was the impulse to develop a kerygmatic theology which would do better justice to the "subject matter" or *Sache* of the New Testament than the historical exegesis of his teachers had done. He could learn from Barth, but not imitate him. In speaking *with* Paul, Barth had failed to recognize that this fallible human author may not always have given adequate expression to the theological *Sache*. In Bultmann's opinion *Sachexegese* (theological exegesis) would have to include *Sachkritik*, or theological criticism, challenging particular formulations in the light of one's understanding of what they were getting at.

This initial reservation marked the limits of their agreement, and a parting of the ways in modern theology. Barth's attempt to speak of God by speaking *with* the biblical author demanded "utter loyalty" and led to a *Church Dogmatics*. Bultmann refused to identify the Word of God with the words of Scripture, and sought to express the theological content of the New Testament in other ways. The five years 1922–27 were decisive for his integration of theological conviction and biblical scholarship. The synthesis preserved Herrmann's stress upon the non-objectifiability of God. It agreed with Barth that "the subject of theology is God," and added with Luther that it "speaks of God because it speaks of man as he stands before God. That is, theology speaks out of faith."[6] For Bultmann, "speaking of God . . . is only possible as talk of ourselves."[7]

Bultmann oriented his historical scholarship and theology to human existence through a theory of both history and human existence drawn first from Herrmann's proto-existentialist theology, then clarified by reading Dilthey and Graf Yorck, and perfected in long discussions with Heidegger. It first surfaces clearly in "The Problem of a Theological Exegesis of the New Testament" (1925)[8] and the introduction to *Jesus and the Word* (1926). The theory is that historical sources are not merely data for reconstructing accounts of the past. These voices from the past challenge modern hearers and may transform our understanding of ourselves. They mediate an encounter with reality in a way that is structurally similar to the effects of Christian proclamation. This is surely more plausible as a theory of literature than of history, but it allowed Bultmann to see historical study as a theological task, and so to contribute to the 1920s debates about both the intellectual integrity of theology, and the methods of the humanities or *Geisteswissenschaften*.

Twentieth-century biblical scholars rarely mature as theologians before 40, if ever, because they have so much else to learn. From 1907 Bultmann's time was mainly spent establishing himself professionally. He completed his doctoral dissertation on *The Style of the Pauline Cynic-Stoic Diatribe* in 1910 under Heitmüller, and his second qualifying book, on *The Exegesis of Theodore of Mopsuestia* (1912) also reveals the theological scholar rather than the creative modern theologian. A physical handicap made military service impossible and in 1916 he became assistant professor for New Testament at Breslau. Recognized as the standard-bearer for the history of religions school in the new generation, he became in 1920 Bousset's successor at Giessen and in 1921 succeeded Heitmüller at Marburg, where he taught until his retirement in 1951. He died in 1976: A street was named after him in 1984.

Survey

The appropriate introduction to Bultmann the theologian is through his New Testament scholarship. But these two sides to his work cannot really be separated. Though a consummate biblical scholar in a period when the ruling paradigm in this discipline was consistently historical, he engaged in historical research for the sake of theological understanding. Though well informed on philosophy, history of doctrine, and dogmatics, he did his own twentieth-century theology as "New Testament theology," not as systematics.

Accepting that traditional phrase, and resisting Wrede's attempt to reduce New Testament theology to the history of early Christian religion and theology, Bultmann combined the critical heritage of liberal Protestantism with "the latest theological movement." His own theology is therefore best distilled from his accounts of the theologies of his two favorite New Testament writers. But these reflect his historical and exegetical judgments, as well as his theological perceptions, or pre-understanding of the subject matter. No exegesis is without presuppositions, but the biblical scholar's critical judgments are (or should be) relatively independent of theological preferences. It is therefore appropriate to begin this survey with some account of the linguistic, literary, and historical research with which his own theology is fused in a theological interpretation of the New Testament.

Bultmann's direction and stature as a New Testament scholar were made plain in 1921 with the publication of *The History of the Synoptic Tradition*. Together with Dibelius's *From Tradition to Gospel* (1919) this remains the classical form-critical analysis of the synoptic gospels.[9] It was foreshadowed in the gospel criticism of Wrede and Wellhausen and stimulated by Gunkel's form-critical analyses of Genesis and the Psalms. Gunkel had been driven to investigate the pre-literary history of the Old Testament traditions in his efforts to understand the history of Israelite religion, and Bultmann also combined the two operations, drawing upon rabbinic and other analogous material to illuminate the synoptic tradition.

This double-headed historical approach has dominated most twentieth-century New Testament research. But whereas that is now frequently pursued for its own sake, out of a purely historical interest, Bultmann found a theological relevance in history of traditions work, as his liberal teachers, with their interest in religion, had seen theological relevance in their history of religions research. His form criticism lacks the Lutheran kerygmatic emphasis upon preaching which colors Dibelius's book, but when shortly afterwards he espoused the new Pauline-Lutheran "theology of the Word" advocated by Barth and Gogarten, it made a neat fit with his earlier synoptic criticism. The evangelists and their predecessors were evidently interpreting the tradition as they transmitted it, and doing so in order to enable their hearers and readers to hear the gospel or Word of God through their proclamation. What the New Testament scholar described, the New Testament theologian was himself doing.

The same double-headed historical approach guided Bultmann's next scholarly step as he undertook the preparatory work for his monumental commentary on *The Gospel of John* (1941). The history of religions head was more prominent here, but it was its combination with history of traditions hypotheses which again made possible a link with Bultmann's own kerygmatic theology.

Although the history of religions school began by illuminating the Jewish context of the New Testament, it is best remembered for drawing upon hellenistic and oriental parallel material. Bultmann followed Reitzenstein and Bousset in their search for a pre-Christian gnostic redeemer myth which might explain the Fourth Gospel's peculiar religious language. He recognized that Jewish Wisdom speculation lies behind the Prologue[10] but shortly afterwards emphasized "the significance of the newly discovered Manichaean and Mandaean sources"[11] for understanding this gospel.

However, the Fourth Evangelist was no gnostic, in Bultmann's view. He interpreted his gnostic source in a Christian direction, historicizing it and transforming its metaphysical dualism into a dualism of decision. He also interpreted the earlier Christian tradition, making its mythical eschatology speak more directly of the human existence of the individual believer. Bultmann was thus able to argue later that the evangelist "demythologized" his tradition and anticipated his own existential interpretation of the New Testament. It now seems unlikely that the later gnostic documents used by Bultmann justify the hypothesis of a pre-Christian gnostic redeemer myth. There are certainly some connections between Johannine Christianity and emerging gnosticism, but the Fourth Gospel probably represents a stage in the development of that myth, rather than a reaction to it. Neither the sources of the gospel, nor its subsequent editing into its present canonical shape by a supposed "ecclesiastical redactor" can be established beyond doubt, and Bultmann's hypotheses are contested. But history of traditions research does show the evangelist interpreting his tradition critically. It is this general point which endorses Bultmann's way of doing theology, not the details of his reconstruction.

The "theological exegesis" or interpretation of the New Testament, which flowered in Bultmann's masterpiece *The Gospel of John* (1941), came to final fruition in *The Theology of the New Testament* (1948–53). What followed, during a long and active retirement and in posthumous publications, drew upon work done earlier in an extremely productive professorial career. Thus his 1955 Gifford Lectures, *History and Eschatology: The presence of eternity* (1957), which expound a Dilthey–Collingwood theory of history, are present *in nuce* in the very important introduction to *Jesus and the Word* (1926). The Meyer commentary on *The Johannine Epistles* (1967) builds on essays published in 1927 and 1951, and the torso on 2 Corinthians (1976) on an article from 1947. Most interesting of all, his *Theological Encyclopedia* (1984), a mapping of theological study, was mostly written between 1926 and 1936. Also important for any study of Bultmann's thought are his essays on "The Problem of

Hermeneutics" (1950)[12] and his later essays relating to "demythologizing" and to the "new quest" of the historical Jesus (see below).

The Theology of the New Testament, like the commentary on John, has its roots in decisions made by Bultmann in the 1920s. Even its innovatory interpretations of Paul's theology had been published in outline form in 1930 (*Existence and Faith*), and the opening decision to relegate the teaching of the historical Jesus to the presuppositions rather than to the content of New Testament theology was implicit in several earlier writings. The brilliant Johannine section summarizes and systematizes the interpretation worked out in the 1941 commentary: The incarnation is understood in the Kierkegaardian language of paradox as both historical and eschatological event; and in the language of gnosticism (modified and corrected by the Pauline-Reformation emphases of the dialectical theology) the Revealer confronts the world, calling for the decision of faith.

Bultmann's own theology is surely closer to John's than to Paul's. His fusion of first- and twentieth-century horizons is therefore more convincing historically at that point. But a hand is more in evidence where the glove fits less well. When measured against some recent interpretations of the data, Bultmann's Lutheran-existentialist interpretation of Paul looks historically most questionable where it is theologically most profound. But that throws Bultmann's own emphases into clearer relief and makes this the best key to the "content" of his theology.

Content

When Bultmann writes of "content" (*Sache*, better translated as "subject matter"), it is not the content of his own theology that he has in mind, but the essential theological subject matter of the New Testament: the saving act of God in Christ that Paul calls the gospel of or from God. This "event" has a point of contact with past history, for Jesus was crucified under Pontius Pilate, but Paul's emphasis falls on the theological interpretation of that history, namely God's inauguration of the new age. This in turn throws the emphasis upon the present actualization of the "Christ event" in Christian proclamation, and on the faith-response to the "kerygma."

As a good Lutheran, Bultmann follows the verbal "proclamation and response" emphasis in Paul and John, in which revelation "happens" (when and where God wills) as the gospel or Word is preached through Scripture (or early Christian traditions) being interpreted. It is therefore more appropriate to focus on this hermeneutical "form" of his kerygmatic theology, i.e., his actual existentialist interpretation of the New Testament, than on its doctrinal "content." Bultmann is interested in faith and understanding, not in a system of truths about God and the world. As he explains in the appendix to *The Theology of the New Testament*, volume II:

> *Theological propositions* – even those of the New Testament – can never be the object of faith; they can only be the *explication* of the understanding which is inherent in faith itself... But the most important thing is that basic insight that the theological thoughts of the New Testament are the unfolding of faith itself growing out of that new understanding of God, the world, and man which is conferred in and by faith – or, as it can also be phrased: out of one's new self-understanding.[13]

This account of faith and theology reflects the pastoral concern which also motivated the demythologizing essays. Only if theological statements are interpreted in a way that clarifies their understanding of human existence will they offer to new hearers the possibility of understanding themselves in the same new way. This takes place in obedient response to God's Word proclaimed today on the basis of the biblical witness. New Testament theology is not identified with preaching, and Bultmann is more detached and analytic than Barth, but his theological interpretation of the Bible is equally concerned to guide and direct actual preaching. Hence the importance of grasping its hermeneutical form.

Some important methodological discussions aside, Bultmann's theological concerns are most apparent in his interpretations of Paul and the Fourth Evangelist. As an exegete and a historian of early Christianity he wrote more extensively, and theology is never far from the surface, but his concentration on these two authors is significant.

It is also at first sight puzzling. A "Theology of the New Testament" must surely offer an interpretation of *all* the writers or writings, if not of Jesus himself. It is arguable that modern historical reconstructions of Jesus' life and teaching do not belong within this genre, however important they may be for Christianity. But all 27 writings of the New Testament should surely be interpreted.

Bultmann's point, however, is that only Paul and "John" count as *theologians*, because only they (in the New Testament) explicate faith's self-understanding. "Matthew," Mark, Luke, John of Patmos, the authors of Hebrews, the catholic, and the deutero-pauline epistles, are all discussed by Bultmann the biblical scholar. But they do not provide a model or criterion for the modern theologian. Unlike Luke[14] and Cullmann,[15] who think in terms of "salvation history," enlightened Protestant theologians must articulate their existential faith in Christ, through a theological understanding of human existence, not assent to some ideology about history which idolizes the visible church.

All Christian theology relates to human existence. Bultmann's is "existential" in the further sense of being exclusively oriented in this direction, and "existential*ist*" in the specific philosophical conceptuality it uses. Heidegger was in Marburg from 1923 to 1928, and *Being and Time* appeared in 1927. By 1930 Bultmann is having to defend his use of Heidegger's conceptuality, especially in his essay on "The Eschatology of the Gospel of John" (1928).[16] But the true father of Bultmann's existentialist theology, echoed throughout the all-important 1925 essay on theological exegesis,[17] is Herrmann, who (like Kierkegaard) responded to the collapse of classical metaphysics with new philosophical reflections on human existence. Herrmann not only took critical account of Kant's epistemology and ethics. He was also impressed by the epistemology of his Marburg neo-Kantian colleagues, Cohen and Natorp, and constructed an original philosophical framework for theology based on what he called the "historical" character of human existence.

Bultmann accepted Herrmann's contrast between the past history researched by historians, and a personal, inner, existential "history" (*Geschichte*), which is said to be the locus of faith, genuine religion, and human meaning. This implied lack of religious interest in the social, historical world, and its concentration in ethics on the individual subject rather than on institutions and cultural values, is why many theologians today prefer Troeltsch to Herrmann, and are uneasy about Bultmann. But even Troeltsch, Lagarde, and Overbeck found their religion in a private inner world. Unlike the scholars Lagarde and Overbeck (and many others), theologians such as Herrmann, Troeltsch, and Bultmann all tried to relate this piety to *Wissenschaft*. But they did so in very different ways, Troeltsch through idealist metaphysics, Herrmann and Bultmann in an anti-metaphysical account of faith, which echoes Luther's hostility to scholastic theology and tends to hold the inner realm of religion separate from the natural, social, and historical world.

The adequacy of this modern theological proposal is clearly open to question. But it provided Bultmann with a framework through which to offer penetrating, profound, and above all *theological* interpretations of Paul and John. They can be challenged by criticism of their philosophico-theological framework, and perhaps falsified by further historical and exegetical argument. But unlike a New Testament scholarship which resists philosophical and theological reflection, they represent a serious attempt to express what Christians claim to be the essential subject matter of these writings: God.

Bultmann's claim that "John" provides a theological interpretation of human existence is not self-evident. The Fourth Gospel seems to contain more christology than anthropology. But it retells the story of Jesus in a remarkable way, to assert that the Word was made flesh, and "to the evangelist these stories taken from tradition are symbolic pictures which indicate that the believer feels himself searched and known by God, and that his own existence is exposed by the encounter with the revealer."[18] Jesus reveals nothing about himself except that he is the Revealer. The point is not *what* is revealed but *that* the hearer is challenged by the Word to understand himself (or herself) in a new way, no longer dependent upon the world for security, but dependent upon God. The historical event of Jesus is preached as the eschatological event in which God reveals himself to individuals. Both the evangelist and his modern interpreter call for the decision of faith, in which true "life" or authentic existence is found. All the key Johannine concepts are shown to refer to human existence, understood in relation to God's eschatological self-revelation in Jesus. For example, the "true light" of the Prologue is "the state of having one's existence illumined, an illumination in and by which a person understands himself, achieves a self-understanding, which opens up his 'way' to him, guides all his conduct, and gives him clarity and assurance."[19]

Bultmann has rearranged and edited the text to give it a higher degree of consistency than it possesses in its canonical form. But he can claim to have gone to the heart of what the evangelist is getting at. One defense of Bultmann's own theological position is that if some such critical reduction to bare essentials was good enough for the Fourth Evangelist, why should it not suffice a modern Christian?

The orthodox reply would be that John alone, especially John as reconstructed by Bultmann's elimination of what he considers later additions by an "ecclesiastical redactor," or even John plus Paul, will not provide an adequate account of Christianity. The synoptic gospels certainly, and perhaps even (despite Luther in 1523) all the rest of the New Testament, contribute something essential to a true understanding of Christianity. Neither Bultmann's "canon within the canon" (to borrow an unfortunate slogan of his pupil Käsemann), nor Barth's "biblicism," or rationally indefensible overvaluation of the canon is satisfactory. A theology based on an understanding and amalgam of two biblical authors has both systematic attraction and historical and doctrinal weaknesses. These are clearest where the textual glove fits less well – in Bultmann's interpretation of Paul.

Abstracting Bultmann's own theology from his account of Paul's is possible because "doing theology as scriptural interpretation" (following Barth's *Epistle to the Romans*) allows Bultmann to identify with the biblical author and speak *with* Paul. But in disagreement with Barth, Bultmann insists on the theologian's duty to engage in occasional theological criticism (*Sachkritik*) of Paul, where the latter fails to say what he really meant (or what he should have meant – there is some ambiguity here).

What Bultmann finds in Paul and John corresponds to his own convictions, as one might expect in a Protestant theologian finally dependent on Scripture alone. But what he finds is also inevitably the result of an act of interpretation, and this is justified by a theory of interpretation. The theory owes much to Schleiermacher and Dilthey, who thought it possible to understand an author better than he understood himself. In Bultmann's practice the theological *Sachkritik*, justified by appeal to Luther and the Fourth Evangelist, is as important as the hermeneutical "preunderstanding" (*Vorverständnis*) for which he is better known.

All interpretation (says Bultmann) presupposes some prior understanding by the interpreter of the subject matter of the text. This *Vorverständnis* is then confirmed or challenged in the course of reading. That account of the "hermeneutical circle," which also involves reading a part in the light of the whole and vice versa, is surely correct. So is Bultmann's claim that interpreters can sometimes detect where authors fail to say what they mean and may correct what is said in the light of what is meant.

But Bultmann's prior understanding of what Paul is getting at is not derived purely from reading Paul. It is derived from his own understanding of the Christian gospel, which depends partly on Paul but partly also on other sources, all fused in the crucible of his own experience. Bultmann does not only correct Paul in the light of Paul, as he claims he is doing in *The Theology of the New Testament*, volume I. He also understands Paul in the light of his own understanding of Paul's *Sache*, which is derived in part from other sources. He in effect distills and *corrects* Paul, as the Fourth Evangelist corrected his sources where (in his view) they failed to express the gospel adequately. This is the *Sachkritik* that caused Barth to protest.

It may well be that, like allegory, all theological interpretation does this. Bultmann's response was that Barth also engages in *Sachkritik* of Paul, only without admitting it. But the question remains whether the combination of the interpreter's *Vorverständnis* of the *Sache*, with the right to *criticize* the biblical author for failing to express the *Sache* satisfactorily, gives the interpreter too much power. Does it leave the text with sufficient power to challenge the interpreter's *Vorverständnis*? Will not any such challenge be dismissed by the interpreter as failure to do justice to the *Sache*? Even if Bultmann's basic axiom, that talk of God has to be understood at the same time as talk of human existence, is accepted, there is a danger that Bultmann's prior understanding of the structures of human existence will determine what he can hear the New Testament saying.

Whether Bultmann's theory of interpretation leads to distortion in practice is the critical question in considering *The Theology of the New Testament*, volume I, pp. 187–352. Bultmann here interprets Paul's concepts in two long chapters entitled respectively "Man prior to the revelation of faith" and "Man under faith." In other words, Paul's whole theology is set out in terms of human existence. That does not mean that the revelation of God in Christ, which is decisive for Paul, is any less decisive for Bultmann. Both theologians find that event actualized in the Christian proclamation which confronts the hearer and calls for the obedience of faith. The "kerygma" (Paul's word for preaching) brings a new self-understanding and thus bisects the hearer's human existence. Paul himself contrasts these two alternative self-understandings in ways that allow them to be analyzed in terms of his anthropological and soteriological concepts.

This new mapping-out of Pauline theology gives prominence to several concepts which are clearly important in the epistles. Paul is the one New Testament writer who may be said to have a theological anthropology, since the concepts of flesh, body, conscience, heart, sin, world, and death are clearly important for him. Again, much of Paul's theology is unfolded in soteriological images and concepts which describe redeemed human existence. But if Bultmann's presentation of Paul's theology as a "doctrine of man" is guided by his judgment about which of Paul's concepts are theologically important, that judgment is itself shaped by a prior decision about what theology is.

The controlling theory that theological statements concern human existence is stated with admirable clarity at the outset of Bultmann's interpretation of Paul's theology: "Every assertion about God is simultaneously an assertion about man and vice versa. For this reason and in this sense Paul's theology is at the same time anthropology."[20] The same applies to christology. Paul does not speculate about the "natures," but "speaks of him as the one through whom God is working for the salvation of the world and man. Thus, every assertion about Christ is also an assertion about man and vice versa; and Paul's christology is simultaneously soteriology."[21]

Bultmann is surely correct to connect both theology with anthropology, and christology with soteriology. But despite his "vice versa" there is some reduction of one to the other. There is surely more to theology than anthropology, and more to christology than soteriology, important though it is to ground them in the reality of human existence. "Existential interpretation" of the New Testament rightly aims to address the hearer personally, and "existential*ist*" terminology may be an appropriate vehicle. But reducing everything to this procrustean bed is likely to eliminate much that is essential to Christianity. That is the main criticism of Bultmann which surfaced in the demythologizing controversy. Before considering some other problems about Bultmann's theology which are visible in his account of Paul, we turn to the word with which Bultmann is most indelibly associated.

Debate

Early skirmishes aside, the wider discussion of Bultmann's theology begins with the demythologizing controversy initiated by his lecture on "The New Testament and

Mythology" (1941). The word "myth" was deliberately provocative, intended to draw attention to the "hermeneutical" problem of interpreting the Christian gospel meaning of the New Testament, in an age which no longer accepts the pre-scientific picture of the world it presupposes.

This problem had been faced by earlier liberal Protestants, but Bultmann objected to the loss of the kerygma in their elimination of myth. Like Barth, he insisted on theological interpretation of Scripture, including its mythological elements. Given his pre-understanding of God-talk, that meant existential interpretation. It also meant (as we have seen) *critical* interpretation (*Sachkritik*). Bultmann again expounds this in terms of the distinction between what a text *says*, and what it *means*. The formulations of the biblical writers can be criticized in the light of what, according to Bultmann's pre-understanding (to be confirmed in his exegesis), they were getting at. The mythological formulations *must* be criticized, lest modern readers misunderstand their existential message as information about God and the world.

The "*de-*" (*ent-*) of "demythologizing" thus implies the removal or elimination of myth in the act of interpreting, i.e., understanding and communicating, the essential meaning of the Bible. The gospel, Bultmann insisted, is not myth – and does not require mythical expression. In the modern world that is inevitably misleading.

The ensuing controversy ranged widely over the nature of Christianity, modernity, and myth. By posing the hermeneutical problem so provocatively, Bultmann drew attention to the general issues. But his essay was largely a summary of his own theology, oriented as this was to the hermeneutical problem. If his specific solution was widely misunderstood, the reason is that not many of those who responded were familiar with Bultmann's philosophical and theological assumptions. The controversy was sometimes perceived as simply another round of the conservative–liberal dispute between supernaturalism and anti-supernaturalism. Despite Bultmann's rejection of the liberals' simple elimination of myth (and with it what this had enshrined), his negative-sounding slogan concealed the positive intention of his critical existential interpretation.

For much of the present century Bultmann was seen by religious conservatives as the bogey-man whose form criticism had denied the historicity of the gospels and whose demythologizing reduced the doctrinal content of Christianity to an arbitrary and subjective decision of faith. The hermeneutical form of his theology hindered its discussion by doctrinal theologians accustomed to more systematic forms of elucidating their faith. Even Karl Barth's contribution, "Rudolf Bultmann, an attempt to understand him" (1952), was uncomprehending, though in his *Church Dogmatics* he also provided some more penetrating discussion. Anyone who gave doctrinal statements more than just existential meaning and value was bound to find Bultmann's approach reductive. Other theologians, who remained convinced about the possibility of metaphysics and its necessity for theology, were inevitably impatient with a Reformation-inspired theology that dispensed with this, and those for whom the hermeneutical question was peripheral had little time for a theology which seemed interested in nothing else.

Less biblically-based theologians still think that, despite his rejection of Barth's uncritical loyalty to Scripture, and his remarkably bold treatment of even Paul and John, Bultmann's own dependence on the New Testament is itself biblicistic, that is, it accords to these human documents more authority than is rationally justifiable. Bultmann would reply with Barth that as a Christian he does not have to apologize for supposing that the Bible mediates a revelation of God not accessible to human reason alone. That is part of the self-definition of Christianity. But they go further, claiming that rightly understood and received in faith, the Bible mediates a revelation of God not accessible to purely rational historical investigation (such as Pannenberg's) of even the Bible itself. There is something miraculous about revelation as understood by kerygmatic theologians, and that is why theological rationalists dislike it, even though the concept of miracle involved does not involve breaking laws of nature.

The underlying issue here, the main divide in modern theology, is *where* knowledge of God is to be found. Bultmann sides with confessional theologies since Schleiermacher, and against the rationalism of Enlightenment and liberal philosophical theology. Like traditional Catholicism and Protestantism, he locates saving truth in the religious community responding with heart and mind to a foundational revelation event whose power is experienced in the present. The New Testament is central to Christian theology on account of its roles in protecting and mediating that decisive event to which it bears witness. Any study of the Bible as nothing but a collection of historical sources is destructive of Christian faith in God because historical research alone cannot provide what Christians have always found in it: support and clarification of their religious community's faith in God in Christ. They have brought their own experience to the respected text, and understood each in the light of the other. This is *theological* interpretation because it is guided by the question of God, which has already received an answer in the community, but must constantly be reappropriated and purged of error.

The rationalist temper in theology is rightly suspicious of finding truth behind the closed doors of a specific religious community. Theology is committed to the truth, not to providing ideological support for special interest-groups; and truth must be available to all, on the basis of reason.

"A religion which rashly declares war on reason will not be able to hold out in the long run against it," wrote Kant in 1794, and even if the counter-evidence is strong, theologians must by definition and in faith and hope agree. Their first loyalty to truth includes a commitment to rationality. However, forms of reasoning are partly relative to particular cultures, and there is in any case more to human life than reason. Some truths and values may only become accessible by living within a moral community and sharing its discourse. So long as the doors of the community are open to all knowledge, and due weight is given to the self-critical role of reason within it, confessional styles of theology are rationally defensible. They are also demanded if knowledge of God is located in the appropriation of some contingent historical revelation, such as the Torah, the incarnation, or the Qu'ran. In objecting to finding revelation in a contingent historical event interpreted by a specific community, European rationalism parts company with that "foolishness to the Greeks" which has always been the heart of Christianity. As a fairly orthodox Christian theologian, Bultmann (like Schleiermacher) parts company at this point with the European rationalism he in other respects shares.

In the polemical situation of the 1920s and 1930s he made this break without doing justice to other religious traditions, even Judaism. It is not necessary to deny all other claims to revelation in order to affirm one's own. It is impossible to *affirm* them without participating in their respective religious traditions and communities, and any opinion of their claims will naturally be made from the standpoint of one's own knowledge of God. But it is apparently possible to affirm the reality and nature of God only from within a religious system; and doing so involves claiming a kind of absoluteness for the revelation through which God is known (though not for any particular account of it). But it is impossible to deny the existence and value of other religious systems. It is also impossible to judge them all from some superior rational standpoint, since stepping outside one's own religious practice would be to lose the relationship to God which this mediates. Bultmann's confessional stance is therefore legitimate, but does not exclude a more positive attitude to other traditions, and to the social scientific study of religion. Troeltsch, for example, could appreciate the believer's and confessional theologian's talk of authority, revelation, and miracle, without which Christianity would fade, and yet insist on the preliminary philosophical tasks which Barth affected to despise.

Bultmann sided with the new confessionalism without abandoning the rational methods of his liberal teachers, or denying the importance of philosophy for theology. Unlike Barth he stressed the importance of the "natural theology" task[22] of making talk of God intelligible in the modern world. But he did not mistake this "permanent accompaniment of dogmatic work"[23] for the properly theological task of explicating the understanding contained in faith itself. Christian theology begins with the kerygma, and that means within the religious community, wide though its doors are open to knowledge from any quarter.

Christian talk of God has always been the "property" of the Christian community which draws on a specific tradition and lives within its system of symbols. Its claim to truth about the all-encompassing reality of God requires that this be related to all known truth; and as this changes, theology develops. But the gospel it seeks to clarify and communicate is prior to any theology and inseparable from the scriptural witness, and the justification for doing "theology as the interpretation of scripture" is this dependence on a specific and contingent revelation. The gospel gives rise to thought, including rational analysis of the foundational texts. But Christians are, as a matter of self-definition, those who find the decisive self-revelation of God in Jesus. To abandon that claim, even to substitute his divine teaching for the crucified and risen Lord of faith, is to part company with what from the beginning has constituted Christian identity.

The christological heart of Christianity is thus the justification for this confessional biblical style of theology. It even requires *critical* theological interpretation of the Bible, as Luther insisted when doubting whether the Epistle of James preaches Christ. But Bultmann's negative reading of the Old Testament[24] takes this to extremes, and we have already questioned his particular attempt to hold the balance between loyalty to the traditional text and openness to contemporary experience.

His proposals, however, can be challenged from within his own frame of reference. The most intensive discussion of this theology took place among those who shared its approach. If its weaknesses could be (or can be) corrected from within, using the methods he himself advocated, that should provide the strongest support for the soundness of this whole approach. This contemporary theological debate is simply a part of the Christian community's ongoing conversation with its Scripture. It struggles to become clearer about the meaning of the gospel today while preserving the strong continuity with past expressions of Christianity, which is intrinsic to any claim that a unique, decisive, and (so far as we are concerned) final revelation of God has been given in Jesus, normatively witnessed to in Scripture, and preserved (however imperfectly) in the church. Bultmann and his closest theological relations reintroduced a direct theological interest into New Testament scholarship, addressing the expectations of a religious community that lives from the theological interpretation of its Scriptures. They shared an interest in the religious (including theological) *use* of the Bible today, but disagreed about the master's carrying through of his program.

Those of Bultmann's pupils who had also learned from Barth the centrality of christology and had experienced the trans-subjective power of evil in Nazi Germany were uncomfortable with the certainly one-sided and probably reductive anthropological or existential orientation of his theology, its individualism, and its detachment from the real world. These elements in the New Testament had been heightened in Lutheranism (including Kierkegaard), and given an epistemological twist by Kant and Herrmann. Bultmann radicalized them in his existential theological interpretation.

But the felt needs of the present century point to other emphases, also present in the New Testament. Since it was to this that Bultmann appealed, he could best be challenged on that common ground. For a short period in the 1950s and 1960s the most stimulating Protestant theology was done by New Testament scholars. It seemed possible to dispense with systematic theology, along with metaphysics, and simply do theology as hermeneutics of the Christian tradition. Bultmann's actual interpretation of the New Testament, and so his understanding of Christianity, was challenged, but challenged in its own terms by pupils and colleagues who shared his way of doing theology.

Criticism centered on Bultmann's reduction of christology to a contentless "kerygma." Whereas most theologians would remedy this defective doctrine of God, and of God's relation to the world, by metaphysics, Bultmann's pupils sought a corrective within biblical interpretation by reopening in various ways the quest for the historical Jesus. Clearly Jesus is of central importance for the New Testament writers, and some at least of these had recourse to the historical traditions by which he could be identified. It was neither historically true to the New Testament, nor theologically true to Christianity, to reduce interest in the historical figure of Jesus to a mathematical point – the "mere that" of his historical existence and crucifixion.

Several different motives and standpoints ran through this debate and the issues have never been fully resolved. The historical portrait of Jesus remains disputed, and Bultmann's placing him firmly within Judaism is now receiving strong non-theological support, whereas Käsemann's seeing him in the light of Paul appears most questionable in the matter of his attitude to the Jewish law. But the value of this recourse to the historical Jesus in christology remains disputed. Some of Bultmann's disciples, notably Schubert Ogden, were critical of his retention of any such link. Ever since the christological debate was driven by historical criticism into thinking in terms of a contrast between the "historical Jesus" and the "Christ of faith," or kerygmatic

Christ, attempts to reunite these terms by talk of continuity and discontinuity have proved unsatisfactory. This is an area where the terms of the whole discussion need revising.[25]

Bultmann's critics were more successful in challenging his Pauline interpretation and with it those aspects of his theology which largely depended on that. The opposition was divided, and neither Käsemann's emphasis upon "apocalyptic" nor his interpretation of "the righteousness of God" in Paul were widely endorsed. But they pinpointed the weaknesses of Bultmann's individualistic interpretation of Paul. This is now widely agreed to under-emphasize the importance of the historical church, sacraments, salvation history, and the future hope. It is thus arguably more Johannine and certainly more Bultmannian than the historical Paul. "Body" (*sōma*) is suggestively referred to the whole person ("man does not *have* a *sōma*, he is *sōma*"), but when this is specified as a person's "being able to make himself the object of his own action . . . as having a relationship to himself,"[26] the influence of Heidegger has led Bultmann beyond what is historically persuasive; the interpreter's attempt to link ancient and modern thought fails. Other interpreters rightly see in 1 Corinthians 6 evidence that *sōma* for Paul is more physical than Bultmann claims.

Underlying this exegetical implausibility is Bultmann's own philosophical account of human "historical" existence (learned from Herrmann before Heidegger) as essentially detached from the physical world. It was to oppose this residual idealism that Käsemann interpreted Paul's *sōma* as referring to humanity as "a bit of world." The same distance from the world is evident when Bultmann understands Christian freedom in terms of the "as if not" (*hōs mē*) of 1 Corinthians 7: 29–31. Paul's eschatology is interpreted in terms of detachment from the world.

Käsemann responds by stressing Paul's insistence on concrete obedience to a living Lord in everyday life, and by taking more seriously Paul's cosmological statements, which Bultmann's existential interpretation had dismissed as myth. No doubt they are mythological in form, but they are saying something about the Creator coming to his *world* which cannot be reduced to a matter of self-understanding without damaging consequences for ethics.

It is important to recognize that within these historical and exegetical arguments over the interpretation of Paul a modern theological argument about the correct understanding of Christianity today was taking place. The texts acknowledged by both sides as authoritative provided an arena. Generalized objections to Bultmann's use of a particular philosophy were answered with the retort that Heidegger simply provides conceptual clarification for what the New Testament (or part of it) is saying. Only specific challenges to his reading of Paul and John could meet him on his own ground. Because he put all his theological eggs in this basket, exegetical defeat could in theory dispose of his theology.

But that suggests that there is something wrong with the theory. Bultmann's theological interpretations of Paul and John remain illuminating even when successfully challenged exegetically. That implies there is more to this hermeneutical activity than unearthing the authors' historical situation and message. The ongoing conversation of the church with its Scripture, mediating the reality of God in Christ, may be more like the moral reflection generated by a national community's ongoing reading of its classic literature.

One inadequacy of the inner-Bultmannian discussion has been that critics such as Käsemann and Bornkamm themselves share in what to non-Lutherans is most problematic about Bultmann's theology, namely its punctiliar and decisionistic view of faith. Faith comes from hearing the Word preached, and that requires some understanding of what is said. But Bultmann's "act" of faith is not a reasoned judgment, and sounds suspiciously fideistic. On the other hand, those who criticize it on these grounds seem so out of tune with Bultmann's whole project of combining theology with exegesis, and are also so unrealistic in their own expectations of natural theology, that there has been little fruitful engagement. Bultmann's disciples and his theological and philosophical critics have needed each other; in isolation neither has contributed much to the discussion of his "biblical theology" since the 1960s. This has been continued by those who maintain the centrality of the Bible for contemporary Christianity without artificially limiting the roles of reason and tradition: Roman Catholics who have rediscovered the Bible, and evangelicals who have learned to value biblical criticism.

The loss of Bultmann's legacy by his more natural heirs is explicable in terms of the vulnerability of any theology which borrows from the prevailing culture in order to make the biblical message intelligible. What illuminated the experience of a generation in the 1920s, and remained persuasive through the 1950s, no longer addressed the concerns of a new generation: 1967–68 was the year in which Bultmann's hermeneutical theology lost the dominant position it had held in the liberal wing of German Protestant theology since the demythologizing controversy. Existentialism faded and a new generation, hoping to change society, briefly found more help in the Marxist tradition, until economic pressures restored power and influence to ecclesiastical conservatism.

Bultmann's theology was most avidly discussed in the 1950s and early 1960s by students who still broadly identified with it. The issues which were not resolved have continued to receive attention, and for twentieth-century theology Bultmann's positions still function as markers. But they do so now as part of the history of modern theology, a resource from which many different constructions draw, rather than providing the focus for a school. Bultmannian ghosts still haunt a few theological faculties, but religious and theological vitality is to be found elsewhere. The way in which theological liberalism might recover and be renewed by its Bultmannian legacy is the subject of our final section.

Achievement and Agenda

The immense prestige of Bultmann within New Testament scholarship today is not focused where he would have wished. Though second to none in exacting scholarly standards, these for him served a theological aim. But it is this dimension of his work (like Baur's) which has proved most vulnerable to a changing cultural climate. His achievement was and is a theological synthesis relative to its mid-twentieth-century European cultural base. If the theology which emerged from this combination of history, literary criticism, and philosophy is in some respects flawed and in other respects dated, it nevertheless recalls the church to an agenda that confronts it afresh in every generation: to interpret its scriptures in ways that communicate its gospel message.

The hermeneutical task of interpreting Scripture theologically is crucially important for the religious community. But it cannot provide everything the community needs. Freed from its unrealistic expectations of replacing systematic theology, it can be developed in new ways. The most interesting question, in rethinking Bultmann's heritage two generations on, is whether this might be developed by loosening its attachment to the historical paradigm which guided his New Testament scholarship.

The notion of "interpretation" belongs more within a literary than a historical frame of reference. Historical methods are normally directed toward reconstruction. Bultmann combined his theological interpretation with the historical paradigm which still dominates biblical scholarship by appealing to an "existentialist" theory of history that saw the historian's task as grasping a text's understanding of human existence. He also engaged in the more usual historical task of trying to reconstruct the development of early Christianity. Even his interpretations of Paul and John involve ordinary historical scholarship. But here his main interest was in the existential interpretation in which "history" and theology coincided.

Recent New Testament scholarship has abandoned Bultmann's theological synthesis, taking from him only history of traditions and history of religions research. But theologians who value existential interpretation have their own agenda. If Bultmann's interpretations of Paul and John are read as literary criticism, i.e., as brilliant modern interpretations of classical texts, they can survive the modern biblical historians' loss of interest in philosophy and theology.

The theological interpreter who identifies with the literary critic can also afford to make a less strong claim to reflect the author's intentions. But here Christian theologians would be unwise to follow, since they must (on account of the given revelation fundament) maintain a strong continuity with the classic expressions of Christianity. They require some continuity of meaning, and this is best preserved by maintaining the importance of authorial intention. They also look for agreed or shared interpretations of their community's normative texts and these can best be achieved if authorial intention is preserved as an ideal norm or critical control for rejecting arbitrary and implausible interpretations. Accepting a literary paradigm for New Testament studies need not involve a particular literary theory that advocates total textual indeterminacy – i.e., interpretative anarchy.

This respect for authorial intention, so far as it can be known, means that even when working as literary critics, theological interpreters of the New Testament still have to be schooled in linguistic and historical methods. But they will be free to introduce whatever philosophical and theological perspectives are needed to articulate the texts' theological meanings in a new age. That is to preserve Bultmann's approach, which is that of all the great theological interpreters, without being committed to a conceptuality which seems inadequate to the theological and ethical tasks confronting a later generation. When Kierkegaard is supplemented by Marx, and Heidegger by Freud and Bloch, Bultmann's framework will allow theology's concern with human existence to include a more positive relationship to real history and society.

Notes

1 Cf. Rudolf Bultmann, "Autobiographical Reflections" (1956), in *Existence and Faith*, p. 335.

2 All the scholars mentioned here, including Bultmann, are discussed at greater length in R. Morgan with J. Barton, *Biblical Interpretation* (Oxford, 1988).

3 A translation of his 1922 review article appeared in J. M. Robinson (ed.), *The Beginnings of Dialectial Theology 1920–1926* and is excerpted in R. Johnson, *Rudolf Bultmann: Interpreting faith for the modern era*.

4 See Rudolf Bultmann, "The Concept of Revelation in the New Testament" (1929), in *Existence and Faith*; "The Concept of the Word of God in the New Testament" (1933), in *Faith and Understanding*.

5 Contrast Rudolf Bultmann, "Ethical and Mystical Religion in Early Christianity" (1920), in Robinson, *The Beginnings of Dialectical Theology*, with the essays in *Faith and Understanding*.

6 Cf. Rudolf Bultmann, "Liberal Theology and the Latest Theological Movement" (1924), in *Faith and Understanding*, pp. 29, 52; "The Significance of 'Dialectical Theology' for the Scientific Study of the New Testament" (1928) and other essays in *Faith and Understanding*.

7 Bultmann, *Faith and Understanding*, p. 61.

8 Robinson, *The Beginnings of Dialectical Theology*, excerpted in Johnson, *Rudolf Bultmann*.

9 It is conveniently explained in Rudolf Bultmann, "The New Approach to the Synoptic Problem" (1926), in *Existence and Faith*.

10 Rudolf Bultmann, "The History of Religions Background of the Prologue to the Gospel of John" (1923), in J. Ashton (ed.), *The Interpretation of John* (London, 1986).

11 The untranslated essay of this title appeared in 1925 and was reprinted in *Exegetica* (1967).

12 New English translation in Rudolf Bultmann, *New Testament and Mythology and Other Basic Writings*, ed. S. M. Ogden.

13 Rudolf Bultmann, *The Theology of the New Testament*, vol. II, pp. 237ff., 239.

14 Ibid., pp. 116ff., 126.

15 Bultmann, *Existence and Faith*, pp. 268–84.

16 English translation in Bultmann, *Faith and Understanding*.

17 In Robinson, *The Beginnings of Dialectical Theology*, and Johnson, *Rudolf Bultmann*.

18 Bultmann, *Theology of the New Testament*.

19 Ibid., vol. II, p. 18.

20 Ibid., vol. I, p. 191.

21 Ibid.

22 Rudolf Bultmann, "The Problem of 'Natural Theology'" (1933), in *Faith and Understanding*.

23 Ibid., p. 330.

24 "The Significance of the Old Testament for Christian Faith," in B. W. Anderson (ed.), *The Old Testament and Christian Faith* (London, 1964).

25 See G. Ebeling, *Theology and Proclamation* (London, 1966, first published 1962); C. E. Braaten and R. A. Harrisville (eds), *The Historical Jesus and the Kerygmatic Christ* (New York, 1964). Also my contribution to the memorial volume for G. B. Caird, *The Glory of Christ in the New Testament*, ed. L. D. Hurst and N. T. Wright (Oxford, 1987).

26 Bultmann, *Theology of the New Testament*, vol. I, p. 195.

Bibliography

Primary

Bultmann, R., *Jesus and the Word* (New York, 1934; London, 1958; first published 1926).
—— *The Theology of the New Testament*, 2 vols (London, 1952–55, first published 1948–53).
—— *Kerygma and Myth*, 2 vols, ed. H. W. Bartsch (London, 1953–62).
—— *Essays Philosophical and Theological* (London, 1955, first published 1931–55).

—— *History and Eschatology* (Edinburgh, 1957).

—— *Jesus Christ and Mythology* (New York, 1958).

—— *Primitive Christianity in its Contemporary Setting* (London, 1960, first published 1949).

—— *Existence and Faith*, ed. S. Ogden (London, 1961, 1964).

—— *The History of the Synoptic Tradition* (Oxford, 1963, first published 1921; 2nd edn 1931).

—— *Faith and Understanding* (London, 1969, first published 1924–33).

—— *The Gospel of John* (Oxford, 1971, first published 1941).

—— *The Johannine Epistles* (Philadelphia, 1973, first published 1967).

—— *New Testament and Mythology and other Basic Writings*, ed. S. Ogden (London, 1985, first published 1941–61).

Kittel, G. and Friedrich, G. (eds), *Theological Dictionary of the New Testament* (Grand Rapids, MI, 1964–76), including 27 articles by Bultmann.

Jaspert, B. (ed.), *Karl Barth–Rudolf Bultmann: Letters 1922–66* (Grand Rapids, MI, 1981).

Robinson, J. M. (ed.), *The Beginnings of Dialectial Theology 1920–1926* (Memphis, TN, 1968).

Secondary

Braaten, C. E. and Harrisville, R. A. (eds), *Kerygma and History* (Nashville, TN, 1962).

Hobbs, E. C. (ed.), *Bultmann, Retrospect and Prospect* (Philadelphia, 1985).

Johnson, R. A., *The Origins of Demythologizing* (Leyden, 1974).

—— *Rudolf Bultmann: Interpreting faith for the modern era* (London, 1987).

Kay, J. F., *Christus Praesens: A Reconsideration of Rudolf Bultmann's christology* (Grand Rapids, MI, 1994).

Kegley, C. W. (ed.), *The Theology of Rudolf Bultmann* (London, 1966).

Macquarrie, J., *The Scope of Demythologizing: Bultmann and his critics* (London, 1960).

—— *An Existentialist Theology: A comparison of Heidegger and Bultmann* (London, 1970).

Malet, A., *The Thought of Bultmann* (Dublin, 1969, first published 1962).

Morgan, R., *The Nature of New Testament Theology* (London, 1973).

Ogden, S., *Christ without Myth* (London, 1962).

Painter, J., *Theology as Hermeneutics* (Sheffield, 1987).

Schmithals, W., *An Introduction to the Theology of Rudolf Bultmann* (London, 1968).

Thiselton, A. C., *The Two Horizons* (Exeter, 1980).

Paul Tillich

David H. Kelsey

Introduction: Life

Paul Tillich's principal goal was to make Christianity understandable and persuasive to religiously skeptical people, modern in culture and secular in sensibility. He came to be extraordinarily effective in that role; getting there involved two wrenching turns in his life.

The first was the First World War. When he entered the German Army in 1914 as a chaplain Tillich's life had been fairly sheltered and his views, except in theology, were conventionally conservative. Born in 1886, he was raised in a conservative Lutheran pastor's home. He studied at the Universities of Berlin, Tübingen, and Halle. In 1910 he received a PhD from the University of Breslau for a thesis on the nineteenth-century philosopher Friedrich Schelling, whose thought was to remain deeply influential on Tillich. He was then ordained and served a few years as an assistant pastor. However, four years spent sharing the carnage and suffering of war with working-class men utterly transformed him. As his biographers, Wilhelm and Marion Pauck put it, by the time he left the army in 1918, "the traditional monarchist had become a religious socialist, the Christian believer a cultural pessimist, and the repressed puritanical boy a 'wild man.' These years represented *the* turning point in Paul Tillich's life."[1] Tillich believed the change in himself reflected a change in Western civilization.

That experience gave focus to his vocation. The title of his first public lecture in Berlin named the topic that was to remain central to his theology for the rest of his life: "On the idea of a Theology of Culture." The Berlin to which he returned in 1919 to begin his academic career was a major center for radical politics and avant-garde art. His fairly chaotic personal life there while teaching theology at the University of Berlin was deeply involved in a bohemian world of artists and political agitators. Thereafter, with the exception of three apparently unhappy terms at the University of Marburg (1924–25), Tillich's appointments were not to theological faculties but to "religious studies" (at the Dresden Institute of Technology, 1925–33) or in philosophy (at the University of Frankfurt, 1929–33). In both cases he rejoiced at being "on the boundary," at the point of intersection between a religious tradition and major movements in secular culture. In his years at Frankfurt Tillich became nationally known in German academic circles. There, at the height of his powers, a second wrenching turn was forced on to his life.

In 1933 the Nazi authorities suspended Tillich from his academic position at Frankfurt because his book *The Socialist Decision* attacked Nazi ideology. When it became clear that Tillich had to flee Germany, American friends arranged an appointment to the faculty of Union Theological Seminary in New York City. In the fall of 1933, at the age of 47, Tillich began a second academic career in a culture and language with which he was entirely unfamiliar.

For the next 15 years Tillich taught at Union in relative obscurity, which was not much dispelled by the publication in 1936 of autobiographical reflections, *On the Boundary*. He was widely respected within small circles of academic theologians, but few of his writings were available in English. He came to write effectively in English, but he spoke in so heavy an accent that he was difficult to understand. Then, in 1948 a small volume of sermons he had preached in the Seminary chapel was published as *The Shaking of the Foundations* and, against all expectations, it became a bestseller. Three years later the first volume of his *Systematic Theology* was published. It immediately became the subject of vigorous discussion in both academic and church circles. The press gave him considerable coverage, and suddenly this relentlessly complex Germanic thinker became something of an intellectual superstar in America. Tillich retired from Union in 1955, accepting the post of University Professor at Harvard University. There he published the second volume of the *Systematic Theology* in 1957. In 1962 he accepted a second post-retirement appointment at the University of Chicago, where the third volume of the *Systematic Theology* was published in 1963. Tillich died in 1965, perhaps the most widely known theologian in American history. In the years since his death there has also been a vigorous rediscovery of Tillich in German theological circles.

Survey: Work, Approach, and Themes

Of more than 500 works in Tillich's bibliography, the writings available in English fall into four rough groups: (i) the three volumes of his *Systematic Theology*; (ii) writings outside the system dealing with individual theological topics that are also discussed within the system, notably *Biblical Religion and the Search for Ultimate Reality*; *Love, Power, and Justice*; *The Protestant Era*; and *Theology of Culture*; (iii) three volumes of sermons, *The Shaking of the Foundations*; *The New Being*; *The Eternal Now*; and (iv) essays in the philosophy of religion, notably *The Courage to Be*. In our discussion of Tillich's theology we shall focus on his *Systematic Theology*.

All of these writings may be viewed as variations on the same approach in theology: to *mediate* between contemporary culture and historical Christianity, to show that faith need not be unacceptable to contemporary culture and that contemporary culture need not be unacceptable to faith. That is, they are all exercises in the theology of culture. For Tillich, that means that making a case for Christianity ("apologetics") is not a specialized branch of theology but rather is one dimension of every subsection of theology.[2]

In his *Systematic Theology* Tillich undertakes this mediating task by exhibiting a *correlation* between religion and culture.[3] The relation between the two, he suggests, is like the correlation between "questioning" and "answering" in a conversation. Or it is like the correlation between "form" and "content" (or "substance") in a work of art. Indeed, it is possible to correlate them because in concrete reality "religion" and "culture" are always a single whole of which "the form of religion is culture and the substance of culture is religion."

Tillich suggests that the human condition always raises fundamental questions which human cultures express in various ways in the dominant styles of their works of art, and to which religious traditions offer answers expressed in religious symbols. Accordingly he organizes his *Systematic Theology* in five parts. In each part a major biblical religious symbol is correlated as "answer" with a major human question as expressed by modern culture. Part I correlates the symbol "Logos" with modern culture's form of the skeptical question: How can we know with certainty any humanly important truth? Part II correlates the symbol "God as Creator" with modern culture's expressions of the question of finitude: How can we withstand the destructive forces that threaten to disintegrate our lives? Part III correlates the symbol "Jesus as the Christ" with modern culture's secular expressions of the question of estrangement: How can we heal the alienation we experience from ourselves and from our neighbors? Part IV correlates the symbol "Spirit" with modern culture's expressions of the question of ambiguity: How can our lives be authentic when our morality, religious practices, and cultural self-expression are so thoroughly ambiguous? And Part V correlates the symbol "Kingdom of God" with the question: Has history any meaning?

Content: Essential Nature, Existential Disruption, and Actuality

These five pairs of correlated questions and answers are the main themes in Tillich's theology. They resolve into three major subdivisions that deal with what he abstractly calls, respectively, the "essential nature," the "existential disruption," and the "actuality" of our lives and of every reality. We will follow this trinitarian structure in our discussion of the content of Tillich's theology.

Essential nature

The first two parts of the system deal with questions concerning our "essential nature." "Essence" refers to what something most fundamentally *is*. In Tillich's view, anything whatever that is actual (as opposed to merely ideal) exhibits three very general features: (i) it is itself an integral whole, perhaps we might say, a "system"; (ii) it is part of more inclusive wholes with whose other members it is engaged in various kinds of transactions; (iii) it is "finite," that is, inherently vulnerable to disintegration of itself and to separation from the whole to which it belongs. Tillich analyzes these three features of our essential nature in considerable detail at a high level of abstraction. Part I deals with our essential nature as "knowers." Part

II deals with our essential nature as "creatures." It may make his analysis clearer if we take the parts in reverse order.

Part II of the system addresses the question raised by experience of the threatenedness of our lives. Incidentally, taking this as his central focus, and drawing here on Kierkegaard and Nietzsche, earned him the label of "existentialist." There are moments when we experience our lives on the edge of being overwhelmed by meaninglessness, guilt, and death. Put abstractly, "being" is threatened by "non-being."[4] What is equally important for Tillich is that we also have the experience of continually resisting this threat. Put abstractly, we experience the presence of the "power of being." Out of this rises the question, "Whence comes the power to resist the threat of non-being?" The answer is provided by the Christian symbol "God as Creator."

Before we can get clear about that, Tillich thinks, we need to ask what it is about us that leaves us so vulnerable to the threat of "non-being." Here we encounter Tillich's celebrated ontology.[5] "Ontology" is thought [in Greek: *logos*] about what is is to *be* [in Greek: *on*, gen. *ontos*]. It is a topic many philosophers have taken up. Tillich borrows from a great many of them and was perhaps especially influenced by Heidegger. Note that while some philosophers hold that from a careful analysis of what it is "to be" one can demonstrate the reality of God, Tillich is not among them. His ontological analysis is confined to showing our *finitude*, i.e., that we are inherently threatened by non-being and that we are not ourselves the source of the power of being which resists the threat. Tillich suggests that all our interactions with the world exhibit the same basic structure. The structure consists of three pairs of "polar elements." In every transaction with the world we have to strike a balance between "individualization" and "participation," between preserving and nurturing our own individuality and sharing in a community and communion with others. The balance is not a given. We have to strike it again and again, and it is always possible that we shall fail. Obviously, many psychological and social problems can be understood as situations in which these two poles have come into conflict with each other. In every transaction, secondly, we have to keep a balance between "dynamics" and "form." Without rules (form), interactions become unreliable and chaotic. But without creativity and novelty (dynamics), they become rigid. Many political revolutions may be understood as situations in which these two poles have come into conflict with one another. Finally, in every transacton we have to keep "freedom" and "destiny" balanced. At the moment of any transaction with the world we are deeply conditioned by the immediate situation and by the entire history of what we have done and undergone to that point. That is our "destiny," determining who we are at that moment and setting us on a certain trajectory into the future. At the same time we must exercise our freedom, deciding what to do and taking responsibility for it. On this analysis, then, to *be* is necessarily to be *finite*. It is to be inherently, not just accidentally vulnerable to interactions with the world in which individualization separates from participation, dynamics separates from form, destiny separates from freedom.

Yet we never totally fall apart. Whence comes the power to resist the threats of non-being? That is the question about our "ultimate concern." Now, says Tillich, whatever concerns us ultimately is our "god." So this is a question about god. The answer is provided by Christian symbols of God.[6] They are images and stories about God, especially as Creator, that express the experience of the presence of the power of being in a specially appropriate way. "Creator" does not name a theory about the origin of things. Rather, "God is creator" expresses an experience of a state of affairs: The power of being is present actively ("God lives"), continuously ("God sustains"), grounding our being in the very midst of the threat of non-being ("God creates out of chaos"). At the same time the symbol is nuanced to express another feature of the experience: The presence of the power is experienced as "inexplicable and uncanny" ("God is holy"). As the ontological analysis has confirmed, this power is not an element in the structure of being. Nor is it just another name for the structure of being taken as a whole, i.e., the structure consisting of the tensed polarities individualization/participation, dynamics/form, destiny/freedom. Tillich rejects that as a form of pantheism. Nor can this power be a "supreme being"; for by definition *any* being is finite. Hence Tillich refuses to speak of the "existence" of God. No, the power of being or "ground of being" is "being-itself," utterly unconditioned by anything else while being present to everything ("God is Lord").

Part I of the system applies this same pattern of analysis to one type of transaction with the world – cognition. It addresses the skeptical question raised by our persistent frustrations in trying to know humanly important truth. Tillich adopts a very rich concept of knowledge.[7] Knowing covers every type of transaction with the world in which we both grasp and shape it. Our capacity to do this is the structure of the mind, which Tillich calls "ontological reason." It is much richer than mere "technical reason," or problem-solving capacities. We constantly find our efforts to grasp and shape reality threatened either with meaninglessness or with uncertainty. And yet we do know enough to live on. The question is, "How can it be that the threat is overcome?" The answer is provided by the Christian symbol "Logos."

We need to ask *why* our efforts to know are threatened before we can get clear about how "Logos" addresses our skepticism. Our rational efforts are threatened, of course, because ontological reason is finite. Three pairs of polar elements must be kept in balance in our grasping and shaping of reality, and they threaten to conflict. Rational grasp of reality involves both formal and emotional dimensions. However, the formal and emotional roles of our cognitive transactions with the world threaten to conflict and we yearn for some kind of knowing in which they are united. Rational grasp of reality must also hold static and dynamic aspects in balance. These aspects constantly threaten to conflict. Stress on static principles looks from the other perspective like conservative "absolutism"; stress on concrete changes looks from the other perspective like rootless "relativism." The tension between "absolutists" and "relativists" is common enough. We yearn for some kind of knowing in which absolute and concrete are held together.

There is a third tension in reason that makes it inherently vulnerable to skepticism. We experience a conflict between relying on our selves as the final authority in cognition ("autonomy": self [Greek: *autos*] as law [Greek: *nomos*]) and relying on another, perhaps a tradition or an established "authority figure" ("heteronomy": other [Greek: *heteros*] as law [Greek: *nomos*]). The conflict is rooted in a polarity between what Tillich calls the "structure" and the "depth" of reason. The "structure" of reason is that which makes it possible for us to grasp and shape reality. But grasping and shaping always involve making judgments about what is more (or less) true, good, or beautiful than something else. In making such judgments we employ standards. Furthermore, Tillich holds (borrowing, he thinks, from Plato)[8] we must all, at least implicitly and unselfconsciously, rely on the same ultimate standards or we should never be able to agree. The "depth" of reason refers to the fact that we engage in rational transactions in the light of those standards even when we are unaware of doing so. The presence of these ultimate standards ("truth-itself"; "beauty-itself"; "goodness-itself") to reason *is* the presence of the power of being ("being-itself") to the mind. Because we are unaware of its presence, however, we alternate between relying on something outside us (a tradition or a powerful personality) and relying on ourselves. Neither is adequate and we yearn for some kind of knowing in which the standards are not simply dependent on our own opinion and yet are not imposed on us as something alien to us. In short, the very possibility of there being reliable meaning to our lives seems to depend on a type of knowing which is at once formal and emotional, absolute and concrete, and in which the structure and depth of reason are united. Where do we ever know in that way?

That, says Tillich, is a question about "revelation." The answer to be correlated with it is the Christian symbol, Jesus as "the Logos."[9] It is a question about revelation because it is a question about disclosure of our ultimate concern: that which grounds meaning in life. The disclosure is a revelatory event with two sides. The "receiving" side is a group of persons who are totally grasped by the event, emotions and intellect united in an integral wholeness. To be in this state is to be in "faith."[9] Tillich also calls it "ecstasy." It is a state in which reason transcends itself in a *self-conscious* grasp of the depth of reason, the ground of meaning. The "giving" side of a revelatory event Tillich calls "miracle." It is some particular concrete object, event, or person that functions as a sign-event or religious symbol *through which* the ground of meaning in life makes itself present to persons. In the world's religions various sorts of things have filled the role of medium. For Jesus' disciples it was Jesus himself who was "miracle" or symbol mediating the ground of meaning to the disciples who received it in their ecstasy. That was what Tillich calls an "original" revelatory event. The disciples *expressed* the fact that it had occurred by using a variety of stories and verbal images for Jesus which are preserved in New Testament writings. Central to them is the image "Jesus is the Logos." "Logos" (Greek: reason, word) expresses Jesus' function as concrete instantiation of the presence of the ground of meaning in life.

But just what is known in a revelatory event? Ontological analysis of finite reason has shown independently that the ground of meaning is *constantly* present to all human reason as its "depth," just as the ground of being is constantly present to every life as its "power of being." Just as the ground of being is not simply one more item in the world which it "grounds," so the ground of meaning is not one more object to be known. It transcends the structure of finite reason. It is inherently "mystery." It cannot cease to be mystery even in revelation. What then can be known of it through Jesus? Tillich stresses that, while the ground of meaning may be present to reason constantly, in fact we are not aware of it apart from revelation. The concreteness of the medium (for Christians, the man Jesus) makes self-consciousness possible about the presence of the absolute or unconditioned ground of meaning. It is crucially important that the mystery whose presence is mediated not be confused with the finite medium itself. To confuse them is idolatry, treating something finite as though is were itself ultimate. We may rank the central symbols of various religions with respect to how clearly they make this distinction. Tillich holds that on such a scale Jesus is "final revelation," the standard by which all others must be measured, because central to Jesus' functioning as mediator of the ground of meaning is his absolute transparency to the unconditioned. His total self-emptying, as expressed in the crucifixion, is a built-in reminder that he is not what is to be known, but only its medium. What is known of mystery through Jesus is, first, its reality and, second, in the midst of our unawareness, that we are indeed related to it. In short, the revelatory event in which the man Jesus is "the Logos" is a "knowing" that answers our skeptical question. It is awareness of the unity of the structure and depth of reason that overcomes the tension between autonomy and heteronomy. In its receiving side, or faith, the emotional and formal are united, overcoming their tension. In its giving side, or miracle, the concrete and absolute are united without being confused, thereby overcoming the tension between relativism and absolutism.

Existential disruption

Part II of the system deals with the questions arising from our "existential disruption." Existence means "standing out" of non-being. For Tillich the "non-being" out of which each of us stands is our potentiality which, until it is realized, is simply a possibility. It is our essential nature. To exist is to be distanced, standing out from our essence. Hence for Tillich "existence" and "existential" usually have the sense of "estranged from essence."[10] Our existential situation is a state of estrangement from ourselves, others, and the power of being. Ontological analysis of our essential nature shows why we are inherently threatened by non-being. Description of our existential situation shows that the threat is actively being actualized. Estranged from the power of being, we are in fact unable to hold individualization and participation, dynamics and form, destiny and freedom in balance in our transactions with our world. As a result, our transactions or relations with others break down and our "world" becomes progressively chaotic. At the same time, our relations with ourselves are disrupted and we become progressively disintegrated.

We experience all of this as deep guilt, loneliness, and meaninglessness. The Christian symbols for this situation are "Fall" and "Sin." The story of the "Fall" of Adam and Eve is not an account of an event long ago. Rather it expresses how the transition from essential nature to existential disruption is a result of our freedom and our destiny. On the one hand the transition is not a natural or rational development. It is an absurd discontinuity, an inexplicable leap which freedom makes possible. It is actualized by each individual person. "Sin" is the religious symbol that expresses this personal responsibility for estrangement. On the other hand, each person does this as a participant in a society of persons who are already estranged. Fallenness is our destiny. Out of this rises the question, "Where can we find power for new being?" The Christian symbol for this "where" is "Messiah" or "Christ" (both mean "the anointed one"). These symbols express the filling of a *function*; the one who functions to represent or manifest the power of being to finite human essential nature in the midst of its estrangement. The question about the power of new being is a question about the "Christ."

The answer to be correlated with this question is expressed by the Christian symbol "Jesus the Christ as the power of New Being." Here Tillich develops his christology.[11] Explanation of who Jesus is follows from explanation of what he did to "save" us.[12] Furthermore, "salvation" and "revelation" name two aspects of the same reality.[13] "Salvation" means "healing." Healing of existential estrangement comes by reconciliation with the power of being and, along with that, reconciliation with others and oneself. That is precisely what happens in a revelatory situation. The power of meaning that is given through Jesus as Logos is, of course, none other than the power of being.

As the ontological analysis showed, the presence of the power of being is inexplicable. It is gift or "grace." It is the presence of the power of New Being in the midst of our estrangement from it: God participates *in* our existential situation of disruption. The power of New Being is supremely present in Jesus precisely because Jesus' crucifixion concretely manifests the presence of this power in the midst of an event of the most profound estrangement of persons from one another and from God. Jesus' death is not substitutionary punishment of human sin in the name of divine justice but rather a manifestation of divine love. Divine removal of our guilt and punishment is not accomplished by overlooking their depth but by entering into them in love so deeply as to transform us.

Our reception, in faith, of the power of New Being is a moment of insight in which one experiences one's unity with the depth of reason, that is, with the unconditioned mystery that is ground of being and meaning. As in the moment of therapeutic insight in psychoanalysis, in that insight one is healed of one's ontological disintegratedness. It is only a momentary event, fragmentary and ambiguous. It does not eliminate the situation of existential disruptions. What is mediated through Jesus is the power of New Being in the midst of continuing estrangement. The event of mediation always needs to be repeated. But for that moment of the event it is genuine. Participation in the power of New Being is "new birth" or "regeneration." In one way this is our being accepted by the power of being ("God") despite or in the midst of our estrangement, or "justification"; in another way this is our transformation by the power of being, or "sanctification." These are simply different aspects of reconciliation with "God," or "atonement" (that is, at-one-ment; reunion).

Who Jesus is follows from what he did. What traditional christology expressed by talking about the human and the divine "natures" of Jesus Christ needs, in Tillich's view, to be reformulated today in order to make basically the same points but in less misleading ways. To say that Jesus is "human" is to say that the entire analysis of "essential nature" applies to him too, including vulnerability to disintegration and its underlying estrangement. To say that Jesus is "divine" is to say that the power of being which is constantly present to all persons is mediated to others through him as the power of New Being in the midst of estrangement from essential nature. To say that they are one in Jesus is to say that this one life actualized without existential disruption (i.e., "without sin") the eternal God-man-unity which characterizes our essential nature too (recall the ontological analysis exhibition of the inexplicable but universal presence of the power of being to finite lives; recall the analysis of reason's unity of "structure" and "depth"). Faith thus has a large stake in the historical facticity of Jesus' life. Only if existential disruption is overcome in *one* point – a personal life, representing existence as a whole – is it conquered in principle, which means in "beginning and in power."[14] Our question about where we can find the power to heal our existential disruption is answered by pointing to the particular man Jesus who actualized essential human nature but without existential disruption and hence can mediate to us the power of New Being that heals or saves.

Actuality

The final two parts of the system deal with questions concerning our "actuality." "Actuality" is Tillich's technical ontological concept of concrete life – "life is the 'actuality of being'." "Essence" designates one main qualification of being, taken in abstraction from any particular life in its concreteness. "Existence" designated the other main qualification, also taken in abstraction. "Actuality" refers to your life precisely *in* its concrete uniting of "essence" and "existence."[15] This is a key point. "Uniting" is a *process*, the process of actualizing potentiality or "essential nature" (here Tillich borrows from Aristotle). It is the dynamic process-character of "actuality" that makes it alive, *a* life. Beyond its organic and inorganic dimensions, human life has the dimension of "spirit." The word "spirit" denotes "the unity of life-power and life in meanings."[16] In addition to sheer vitality ("life-power"), human life involves capacities to regulate ourselves according to ideas, purposes, and plans ("meanings") which we intensely love and freely choose for ourselves. The spiritual dimension of human actuality includes not only reason but also "eros, passions, imagination."[17]

With this brace of observations in place, Tillich can offer an ontological analysis of the process that constitutes life with a spiritual dimension. Such life has three functions. Your life process involves *self-integration*, a circular movement out from what you have been into new experience and back to integrate them into your centered self. You engage in self-integration in "moral" life. Here "moral" is not used in contrast to "immoral." Rather, it is used to stress the fact that as self-integrating you are inescapably morally accountable both for integrating yourself as "centered" and for your choice of norms and goals to guide your interactions with others. However, the moral life is thoroughly ambiguous. No matter how "moral" an act may seem in some respects, we are aware that it cost the sacrifice of other acts through which we might have been more richly integrated, and that it involved some loss to some other person. Because our lives inherently drive toward self-integration, we ask whether there is any way to achieve it through unambiguous morality.

Second, your life process involves *self-creation*, a horizontal movement through time as you constantly make yourself up and deeply change. We engage in self-creation in work that produces the meaningful artifacts, symbols, and styles of both art and behavior which comprise a culture and are significant because they express "meanings" in which a human life "participates." However, we experience ambiguity in all elements of culture, from individual artifacts to the way a society is organized and led, finding them both nurturing new life and oppressing it. Because our lives inherently drive toward self-creation, we ask whether there is any way to achieve it through an ambiguous culture.

Finally, your life process involves *self-transcendence*, a vertical movement in which one is "driving toward the sublime."[18] You engage in self-transcendence in religious activity. This function intersects and unites the other two. It is always moral and culturally creative lives that self-transcend. Hence, there is a religious dimension inherent in all moral and cultural acts. However, the ways in which the drive for self-transcendence expresses itself in ritual, myth, and institutional structures are inherently ambiguous. They are all finite things functioning religiously to express the unconditioned, that toward which one "transcends" oneself. At the same time, they invite for themselves the ultimate concern appropriate only to the unconditioned. Thereby they become "demonic," powerfully destructive of the life trying to "transcend" itself. Because our lives inherently drive toward self-transcendence, we ask whether there is any way to achieve self-transcendence through unambiguous religion.

The answers to be correlated with the questions about unambiguous morality, culture, and religion are expressed in two Christian symbols. In Part IV Tillich correlates the symbol "Spiritual Presence" with the question of the ambiguity of every society synchronically. In Part V he correlates the symbol "Kingdom of God" with the question of ambiguity diachronically in the entire history of morality, culture, and religion.[19]

In Part IV "Spiritual Presence" is the Christian symbol expressive of the "revelatory experience of 'God present'"[20] in precisely spiritual (human) life. "Spirit" (with upper-case S) is the most completely adequate symbol for the unconditioned, because it expresses that the unconditioned is *living*. "God as creator" expresses the presence of the unconditioned power of being to us in regard to our essential finitude, and "Jesus the Christ as the power of New Being" expresses its presence to us in our existential estrangement, but "Spirit" expresses its presence to us precisely in our concrete reality as spiritual (lower-case s) lives actualizing our potentiality. In our self-transcendence we reach for this presence. But we cannot grasp it, unless we are first grasped by it. When it does grasp us, we are drawn into its "transcendent unity of unambiguous life" and it creates unambiguous life in us.[21]

In this experience of "the reunion of essential and existential being, ambiguous life is raised above itself to a transcendence that it could not achieve by its own power."[22] Tillich stresses that such experiences are always social and fragmentary. To be sure, they have a subjective dimension which Tillich calls "mystical."[23] As the state of being *grasped by* the "transcendent unity of an ambiguous life," it is called the state of "faith." As the state of being *taken into* that transcendent unit, it is called the state of "love." However, this always occurs in a communal setting, creating what Tillich calls a "Spiritual Community."[24] It is not identical with the Christian churches. The Spiritual Community is not one group beside others. It is "a power and a structure inherent" in some groups, making them religious groups.[25] Spiritual Community is real but immanent in many "secular" communities outside the church and it is manifest sometimes in the churches.[26] Now, given the ontological analysis of life, this means that when Spiritual Community "happens" the ambiguity of our religious enactments of self-transcending has been overcome. Because the ambiguity of self-integration and self-creation follows from the ambiguity of self-transcendence, this means that the experience symbolized by "Spiritual Presence" is also a moment of unambiguous cultural self-creativity and unambiguous moral self-integration.[27] In those moments cultural and moral activity themselves become self-transcending, that is, religious. Here Tillich's theology of culture has its theological center and context. Tillich calls such moments "theonomous"[28] – living social moments whose norm (*nomos*) comes, not from ourselves nor from an alien "other," but from the "transcendent unity of unambiguous life" (*theos*) which precisely in its transcendence is none the less immediately present to us. "Spiritual Presence" expresses those moments when our questions about the possibility of unambiguous religion, culture, and morality are answered. Tillich insists that such moments in social life are fragmentary and paradoxical, but actually do occur in all societies. His favorite examples come from medieval European culture.

"Kingdom of God" is the religious symbol expressive of Christian answers to the question central to Part V about the possibility of unambiguous life in this historical rather than social dimension: Is there any meaning to history?[29] In Tillich's view groups, not individuals, are the bearers of history.[30] The three movements comprising any life comprise history also: History drives self-integratingly toward the centeredness of groups in a harmony of justice and power, self-creatively toward the creation of new and unambiguous states of affairs, and self-transcendingly toward unambiguous fulfillment of the potential of being.[31] "Kingdom of God" expresses the occurrence of this in two ways: as something inner-historical and as something trans-historical.[32]

In one way, "Kingdom of God" expresses that occurrence *in* the life of any one group which is the decisive and normative instance of "Spiritual Presence" in the group's history. It is the event which serves the group as the "center of history," the one particular point in history which is of universal significance for all groups at all times because it is the *most* adequate overcoming of the ambiguities of human life.[33] In its inner-historical sense, the symbol "Kingdom of God" expresses the occurrence of this event. Tillich[34] calls such a moment the *kairos* (Greek: "fulfillment of time"). In such moments a group's experience of *un*ambiguous self-integration, self-creativity, and self-transcendence in a *kairos*, is its experience of the meaning, the point of history.

"Kingdom of God" also expresses a trans-historical actualization of unambiguous historical life. Here it correlates with the question, "Is there anything of permanent value or meaning in the flow of history?" The same question is often expressed personally as a question about immortality: "Will anything of me survive this life?" Ontologically, this is a question about the relation of time to eternity. "Kingdom of God" expresses how the "inner aim" of created time is the elevating of the finite into the eternal.[35] Thus there are two distinct themes in Tillich's explication of the trans-historical sense of the symbol "Kingdom of God." For the creature, the symbol expresses the insight that "nothing which has been created in history is lost, but it is liberated from the negative element with which it is entangled within its existence."[36] Following Schelling, Tillich calls this "essentialization."[37] It amounts to an unambiguous and *permanent* participation of finite life in the very life of Divine Spirit, for which the Christian symbol is "Eternal Life."[38] Tillich says that this is not a datable temporal event but rather what is going on all the time.[39] On the other hand, viewed as it were from God's perspective, the symbol gives expression to a cosmic process. Tillich calls that process "eschatological pan-en-theism."[40] In it Divine Life realizes itself by a movement through self-alienation and engagement in creaturely existential disruption and then back to self-reconciliation, bringing the creaturely realm with it so that, fully reconciled, the creaturely realm is at the end ("eschatologically") wholly "within" the Divine Life (*pan* – "everything" – *en theos* – "within God").

Controversy and Consequences

Tillich has influenced subsequent theology in two ways. He has had direct influence on a number of theologians whose own writings in one way or another follow "Tillichian" themes and trajectories. And, even when his work has been controversial and many theologians explicitly disagreed with him, he has succeeded in defining the terms of the debate.

Particularly influential in direct ways has been Tillich's way of mediating between the Christian tradition and modern culture in a theology of culture. Perhaps his influence is shown to be most pervasive in widespread understandings of the words "religion" and "religious." It has become commonplace to say that any human activity (e.g., works of art, institutions, broadly shared moral standards, various practices) that exhibits an "ultimate concern" is *for that reason* "religious." Indeed, in coining the expression "ultimate concern" Tillich suceeded in introducing a new religious term into the English language. Tillich's way of identifying a religious dimension to all ordinary experience has been influential in two very different cultural situations. Very influential in the intellectual culture of the 1960s was the secularization thesis. It pictured Western industrial civilization as undergoing an inevitable and relentless process of secularization in which "religion" and "religious experiences" would fade away. Some theologians, notably Harvey Cox in *The Secular City*, influenced by the last writings of Dietrich Bonhoeffer, argued that the secularization of culture was, from a theological point of view, a good thing. Others argued that it effectively meant that Tillich's claim that "religion is the substance of culture and culture is the substance of religion" had been empirically disproved by cultural developments. However, others, especially Langdon Gilkey,[41] developed Tillich's analysis of the notion of the "religious" to argue that even "secular" culture continues to have a genuinely "religious" dimension to it. A quarter of a century later American culture, far from being secular, appears religiously speaking to be riotously polymorphous. Now the challenge is to explain just how all the enormous variety of forms of "religion" are nonetheless genuinely "religious." Here too, in the presence of a plethora rather than a poverty of the religious, Tillich's interpretation of "the religious" dimension of culture continues to be influential.

A closely related feature of Tillich's theology of culture that continues to be influential is his theory of symbols, and religious symbols in particular.[42] Often writers will characterize as "religious symbols" not only visual images, ritual practices, saintly personages, and scriptural metaphors and stories, but also Christian concepts and doctrines. This is done in a move to show how the concepts are intelligible and the doctrines are true without construing them "literally." When such writers explain what they mean by "symbol," and "religious symbol" in particular, what they say very often either repeats what Tillich says on the subject in *The Dynamics of Faith* and in *Systematic Theology*, volume. I, or bears a close family resemblance to it. There has been considerable controversy whether "religious symbol," as Tillich understands it, has cognitive import.[43]

Perhaps as a result of the impact of his theory of symbols, Tillich has been very influential on efforts to think theologically about the arts. Tillich himself was especially interested in what he took to be the theological substance of modern painting, as evidenced by several published essays on the subject.[44] His strong influence can be seen in the notable work of John Dillenberger[45] on theology and the visual arts. Tillich's theology of culture has also been the theoretical basis for theological analysis of modern literature, notably in the work of the literary critic Nathan Scott.[46]

While he taught and wrote in Germany, Tillich's focus on the theology of culture led him to reflect theologically on social theory and politics. He also acted on these reflections, taking part in a splinter party of religious socialists. This side of his early thought has generated scholarly interest in a time when liberationist and political theologies are vital movements.[47]

Tillich's way of doing theology of culture has been directly influential in another direction. The way in which he explicated "sin" and "redemption" dynamically in terms of "estrangement" and "reconciliation" has suggested the possibility of integrating theology with various types of dynamic psychology that have deeply shaped modern culture. Especially in the United States, this side of Tillich's theology has deeply stamped theological reflection on pastoral care, with its yearning to combine the Christian message and the techniques of secular counseling. Controversy turns on the question whether Tillich's doctrine of redemption truly yields a correlation of theology and psychology or only offers a pious language in which to make entirely naturalistic psychological remarks.

Alongside his theology of culture, Tillich's doctrine of God has been directly influential on theologians who otherwise may differ deeply. It has also been extremely controversial, and Tillich's position dictates the terms of the controversy. For example, Tillich emphatically holds that God is not a "person." A vigorous case can be made for the view that, on the contrary, a Christian understanding of God shaped by Scripture requires the notion of God "acting" in history. On the other side, theologians like Gilkey and Schubert Ogden,[48] who believe it to be impossible to make sense of the idea of God "acting," tend to turn to Tillich as a guide in formulating alternative doctrines of God.

Perhaps because of his serious effort to think theological and philosophical lines of thought into each other, Tillich's theology has been of special interest to Roman Catholic theologians.[49] It is not uncritical attention, and it would be difficult to show any broad "Tillichian" influence on Roman Catholic theology. Nonetheless, he has been found a fruitful subject of study especially in regard to the nature of the church,[50] and in regard to his relation to both the Thomist[51] and the Franciscan[52] traditions of philosophical theology.

Tillich's christology has been controversial. A major objection[53] has been that the structure of Tillich's argument makes the historical facticity of Jesus largely irrelevant to theological claims about his significance. This is one point at which Tillich has not succeeded in defining the terms of debate. The focus of christological debates has shifted, and it is not clear that Tillich's approach has much influence currently.

Tillich's method of correlation has been another very controversial feature of his work; at the same time, it continues to influence many theologians directly. Tillich's intent was to mediate between faith and culture.[54] Controversy turns on whether such "correlation" does not finally result in translating the content of Christian faith without remainder into the deepest convictions of the secular culture it attempts to address. Karl Barth, Tillich's polar opposite in this matter, insisted that revelation does not answer questions; it poses them. Instead, he insisted, the question/answer scheme is inherently misleading. Revelation brings unheard-of news which totally changes the way everything looks, so that what had looked like important questions now appear relatively trivial or deceptive. However, many theologians are persuaded that Tillich was right to think Barth's route led to the isolation of Christian thought from the intellectual and cultural life of our time. Hence several current theological proposals employ some variant of Tillich's method either implicitly or explicitly, as do David Tracy[55] and Gilkey.

Notes

1 Wilhelm and Marion Pauck, *Paul Tillich: His life and thought* (Chicago, 1956), vol. I, p. 41.
2 Paul Tillich, *Systematic Theology* (Chicago, 1951), vol. I, pp. 59–66.
3 Ibid., pp. 1–6, 66–8.
4 Ibid., pp. 63–8.
5 Ibid., pp. 168–86.
6 Ibid., pp. 211–89.
7 Ibid., pp. 71–100.
8 *Theology of Culture* (New York, 1959), pp. 10–30.
9 *Systematic Theology* (Chicago, 1957), vol. II, pp. 106–59.
10 Ibid., pp. 97–180.
11 Ibid.
12 Ibid., p. 150.
13 Ibid., p. 166; see also vol. I, pp. 144–6.
14 *Systematic Theology*, vol. II, p. 98; cf. p. 114.
15 *Systematic Theology* (Chicago, 1963), vol. III, pp. 11–12; also vol. II, p. 28.
16 *Systematic Theology*, vol. III, p. 22.
17 Ibid., p. 24.
18 Ibid., p. 31.
19 Ibid., pp. 107–10.
20 Ibid., p. 111.
21 Ibid., p. 112.
22 Ibid., p. 129.
23 Ibid., p. 242.
24 Ibid., pp. 149ff.
25 Ibid., p. 162.
26 Ibid., pp. 152ff.
27 Ibid., p. 157.
28 Ibid., p. 266.
29 Ibid., p. 349.
30 Ibid., p. 312.
31 Ibid., p. 332.
32 Ibid., p. 357.
33 Ibid., p. 367.
34 Ibid., p. 369.
35 Ibid., pp. 397, 399.
36 Ibid., p. 397.
37 Ibid., p. 400.
38 Ibid., p. 401.
39 Ibid., pp. 399–400.

40 Ibid., pp. 421–2.
41 Langdon Gilkey, *Naming the Whirlwind* (Indianapolis, 1969) and *Reaping the Whirlwind* (New York, 1976).
42 William Rowe, *Religious Symbols and God* (Chicago, 1976).
43 Sidney Hook (ed.), *Religious Experience and Truth* (New York, 1961).
44 Tillich, *On Art and Architecture* (New York, 1986).
45 John Dillenberger, *A Theology of Aesthetic Sensibility* (New York, 1986).
46 Nathan Scott, *The Tragic Vision and the Christian Faith* (New York, 1957).
47 Ronald P. Stone, *Paul Tillich's Radical Social Thought* (Atlanta, GA, 1980); A. James Reimer, *The Emmanuel Hirsch and Paul Tillich Debate* (Lewiston, ME, 1989).

48 Schubert Ogden, *The Point of Christology* (New York, 1982).
49 Monica Hellwig (ed.), *Paul Tillich* (Collegeville, PA, 1994).
50 Ronald Modres, *Paul Tillich's Theology of the Church* (Detroit, 1976).
51 Robert Barron, *A Study of the De Potentia of Thomas Aquinas in the Light of the Dogmatik of Paul Tillich* (San Francisco, 1993).
52 John P. Dourley, *Paul Tillich and Bonaventure* (Leiden, 1975).
53 John P. Clayton and Robert Morgan, *Christ, Faith and History* (Cambridge, 1972); David Kelsey, *The Fabric of Paul Tillich's Theology* (New Haven, 1967).
54 John P. Clayton, *The Concept of Correlation* (Berlin, 1980).
55 David Tracy, *Blessed Rage for Order* (New York, 1988).

Bibliography

Primary

Tillich, Paul, *The Shaking of the Foundations* (New York, 1948).
—— *The Protestant Era* (Chicago, 1948).
—— *Systematic Theology*. Vol. I (Chicago, 1951).
—— *Love, Power and Justice* (New York, 1954).
—— *The New Being* (New York, 1955).
—— *Biblical Religion and the Search for Ultimate Reality* (Chicago, 1956).
—— *Eternal Now* (New York, 1956).
—— *Systematic Theology*. Vol. II (Chicago, 1957).
—— *Dynamics of Faith* (New York, 1957).
—— *Theology of Culture* (New York, 1959).
—— *Systematic Theology*. Vol. III (Chicago, 1963).
—— *On Art and Architecture* (New York, 1986).

Secondary

Barron, Robert, *A Study of the De Potentia of Thomas Aquinas in the light of the Dogmatik of Paul Tillich* (San Francisco, 1993).
Clayton, John P., *The Concept of Correlation* (Berlin, 1980).
Clayton, John P. and Morgan, Robert, *Christ, Faith and History* (Cambridge, 1972).
Cox, Harvey, *The Secular City* (New York, 1965).

Dillenberger, John, *A Theology of Aesthetic Sensibility* (New York, 1986).
Dourley, John P., *Paul Tillich and Bonaventure* (Leiden, 1975).
Gilkey, Langdon, *Gilkey on Tillich* (New York, 1990).
—— *Naming the Whirlwind* (Indianapolis, 1969).
—— *Reaping the Whirlwind* (New York, 1976).
Hellwig, Monica (ed.), *Paul Tillich: A new Roman Catholic assessment* (Collegeville, PA, 1994).
Hook, Sidney (ed.), *Religious Experience and Truth* (New York, 1961).
Kelsey, David, *The Fabric of Paul Tillich's Theology* (New Haven, 1967).
McKelway, Alexander, *The Systematic Theology of Paul Tillich* (Detroit, 1964).
Modres, Ronald, *Paul Tillich's Theology of the Church: A Catholic appraisal* (Detroit, 1976).
Ogden, Schubert, *The Point of Christology* (New York, 1982).
Pauck, Wilhelm and Pauck, Marion, *Paul Tillich: His life and thought*. Vol I (Chicago, 1956).
Reimer, A. James, *The Emmanuel Hirsch and Paul Tillich Debate: A study in the political ramifications of theology* (Lewiston, ME, 1989).
Rowe, William, *Religious Symbols and God* (Chicago, 1976).

Scott, Nathan, *The Tragic Vision and the Christian Faith* (New York, 1957).
—— *The Broken Center: Studies in the theological horizon of modern literature* (New Haven, 1966).

Stone, Ronald P., *Paul Tillich's Radical Social Thought* (Atlanta, GA, 1980).
Tracy, David, *Blessed Rage for Order* (New York, 1988).

Reconceiving Roman Catholic Theology

The Second Vatican Council (1962–5) has probably been the single most important ecclesial event of the twentieth century, with implications far beyond the Roman Catholic Church. All the theologians in this section were involved in preparing the way for it and in participating in the debates surrounding and following it.

Because of his role in *ressourcement* (return to sources), which was a hallmark of Vatican II, and his initiatives in the accompanying ecumenism between Catholics, Protestants, and Orthodox, Yves Congar may well have had more influence on church history than any other theologian in this volume. He was a courageous reformer dedicated to tradition and its fresh interpretation. Very much a church theologian, and not either systematic or philosophical, his historical sensitivity and vast learning were the medium for a wisdom which helped to change the sensibility of the Roman Catholic Church and informed many of the documents of Vatican II. Fergus Kerr sets him and Henri de Lubac in their complex church and political settings and indicates the scope of their achievement by describing the forces whose theologies and ideologies they challenged. De Lubac's achievements are described: his retrieval of the richness of Catholicism before the Counter-Reformation; his restoration of an understanding of the church focused through the eucharist; his deep appreciation of pre-modern biblical interpretation in all its spiritual, intellectual, moral, and imaginative richness; and above all his deconstruction of the dualism between grace and nature deeply embedded in Roman Catholicism in recent centuries. Kerr's exploration of de Lubac's advocacy of "graced nature" shows the many dimensions (personal, ecclesial, political, eschatological) of relevance in what might seem a somewhat technical theological controversy.

Karl Rahner also contributed to the debate about nature and grace, though with a more philosophical thrust than de Lubac. Rahner is sometimes called a "transcendental Thomist." He found official theology dominated by Thomas Aquinas as understood through the scholastic theologians, who continued his tradition, and their modern successors the "neoscholastics." Rahner broke with neoscholasticism, and tried to integrate the theology and philosophy of Aquinas with post-Enlightenment thought, especially Kant's "transcendental" idealist philosophy. That was so called because of Kant's attempt to identify, beyond any particular experiencing, knowing, and willing, the "transcendental" conditions and limitations under which each person can experience or know or will at all. So "transcendental" here points to the most general and fundamental features of human existence without which we would not be human at all. J. A. Di Noia describes Rahner's attempts to show how God and revelation cohere with the basic dynamics of the human mind and will. His interpretation of Rahner is distinctive in two respects: his stress on the pluralist, nonsystematic nature of Rahner's theology, and his insistence on Rahner's continuity with Aquinas. Rahner emerges as above all a theologian of the gracious mystery of God and salvation, who offers a model for the continuing creative recovery of the Christian tradition in new contexts.

Hans Urs von Balthasar offers a church theology of massive proportions. It is rooted in meditation and prayer, draws widely on European culture and literature, is deeply influenced by his friendship with the mystic Adrienne von Speyr, is committed to the nurturing of lay vocations in the world, and is pervasively expository and biblical. John Riches and Ben Quash describe it mainly under the headings of analogy, beauty, drama, and the Trinity, and show it in debate with Barth, Bultmann, and Rahner. Its pivotal point is found in the "three days" embraced by the crucifixion and resurrection of Jesus, and a range of sharp questions are addressed to it.

Robert Schreiter identifies the interrelation of church and world as the leading theme in the theology of Edward Schillebeeckx. Schillebeeckx developed it by both a critical recovery of historical sources (he was a student of Congar) and engagement with modern thought and life, especially in its problematical aspects. In order to prepare himself for his works on Jesus Christ, Schillebeeckx underwent something like a reeducation in modern historical critical study of the New Testament. Schillebeeckx was influenced by existentialism, but the later thrust of his work was more social and political, and he carries out much of the program suggested by Robert Morgan at the end of chapter 4 on Bultmann.

Hans Küng is, as Werner Jeanrond says, the most widely read, controversial, and wide-ranging of twentieth-century theologians. Jeanrond describes Küng's successive concentrations: on the church; on the main articles of Christian faith; on method, interreligious dialogue, and the relation of religion to modern culture; and, most recently, on global responsibility and the religious situation of our time. His method is seen as one of mutually critical correlation between Christian sources, especially the Bible, and the wealth of human experiences in our world. He and Schillebeeckx also represent some of the serious problems posed by modern theology within the Roman Catholic Church, and Jeanrond gives a concise account of the conflict between Küng and his church authorities.

French Theology: Yves Congar and Henri de Lubac

Fergus Kerr, OP

Introduction

The great influence of a remarkable generation of French theologians on the Roman Catholic Church, particularly through the Second Vatican Council (1962–5), needs to be placed against the background of the bitter struggle that dominated politics in France in the later nineteenth and early twentieth centuries between supporters of the Third Republic, with their increasingly anti-clerical "laicism," as it was called, and adherents of traditional Catholicism, with their monarchist nostalgia and ultramontanist inclinations. The conflict was centered on the education system, with one side fearing that church schools were not forming children in loyalty to the Republic while the other side regarded state schools as seedbeds of atheism. In wider theological terms, the problem was concerned with how to respect the autonomy and intrinsic value of the world without reducing the church to the sphere of purely private religion.

The story no doubt begins with the French Revolution; but, more immediately, in the aftermath of the humiliating defeat of France by Bismarck's Germany in 1871, and the apparent triumph of the papalists at the Vatican Council (1870–1), the mutual suspicion between republicans and Catholics developed into open conflict. The Jesuits, for example, who ran many schools, were banned in 1880. Religious instruction was forbidden in state schools in 1882. The Dreyfus case split the country deeply in the 1890s, with many Catholics displaying obsessive hatred of Jews and Freemasons.

In 1898 the periodical and movement known as *Action française* came into existence, devoted to opposing anticlericalism and republicanism and hoping to restore the monarchy. Charles Maurras (1868–1952), the leader of the movement, was an agnostic for most of his life. Essentially, it was a political movement based on a purely naturalist-positivist view of human nature and society with religion regarded as an indispensable social control. Several of Maurras's books were placed on the Roman *Index* in 1926, as the Vatican became increasingly suspicious of the movement. But many of the clergy believed that his personal doubts about religion and the reality of the supernatural did not prevent his conception of the natural order from being both accurate and indeed in harmony with Catholic social teaching. Many theologians of the time managed to find their neo-Thomism perfectly compatible with right-wing, incipiently fascist politics.

Diplomatic relations between France and the Vatican were broken off in 1904. Legislation was passed in 1905 to embody the separation of church and state in constitutional law. The Catholic Church was deprived of support from public funds, church buildings became the property of the state, parish finances were subject to civil supervision, and so on. Since the religious orders and congregations needed to be licensed by the state, they chose exile, often in England.

The German invasion of Belgium in 1914 united France, at least for the duration of the war. While the politicians were mostly republican, the generals were often devout Catholics. But the majority of Catholics and their clergy kept their distance from the Third Republic right into the upheavals of the 1930s. In 1940, after France collapsed, the Third Republic was voted out of existence by the National Assembly at Vichy and replaced by a state which, initially at least, with its triple ideal of "Work, Family and Country," and its generous support of church institutions, had a great deal of appeal for many Catholics.

Yves Congar and *Ressourcement*

Much more might be said about the background. The important thing for us to note, however, is that, without exception, theologians like the Dominican Yves Congar (1904–95) and the Jesuit Henri de Lubac (1896–1991), who were to become so influential in French theology, were never among supporters of the Vichy state. Congar, a military chaplain, was taken prisoner and spent most of the war in Colditz. De Lubac, who took a leading part in denouncing the anti-Christian character of Nazi neo-paganism and anti-semitism, spent six months in hiding in 1943, when the Gestapo was looking for him. In both cases, as we shall see, their theologies had from the outset immunized them against the attractions of the Vichy state.

Although it was 1938 before the Dominicans brought their library and study house back from Belgium to Paris, most of this brilliant generation of young scholars had already returned to France and their first books had started to appear. Congar joined the Dominicans, then in Belgium, in 1925. De Lubac joined the French Jesuits, then in England, in 1913, was soon interrupted by war service in France (being seriously wounded), and returned to complete his training as a Jesuit in England. When they, and many others like them, burst on the theological scene in the 1930s it was as if the years of exile had prepared them to return home with a wholly new vision of the priorities for theology, and irrepressible energy to put their ideas into practice.

Of course, Congar and de Lubac were only two, if no doubt the two greatest, of the French theologians of the generation that returned from exile with the vision and the scholarship to transform Roman Catholic theology. In effect, their work was to bring the Roman Catholic Church out of the anti-modern and anti-Protestant position adopted at the Council of Trent (1545–63) and reaffirmed at the Vatican

Council (1869–70). Under the heading of *ressourcement*, this generation of theologians, supported by the immediately preceding one, engaged in a great deal of fresh study of the source texts of Christianity.

For example, the French Dominicans founded the École Biblique in Jerusalem in 1890. Over the years, with scholars like M. J. Lagrange and R. de Vaux, they prepared the way for the Jerusalem Bible, the version most widely used by Catholics in the English-speaking as well as the French-speaking world now. In the field of philosophy, the two Jesuits Pierre Rousselot (killed 1915) and Joseph Maréchal sought to show that Kant's transcendental critique may not be as incompatible with Catholic theology and philosophy of religion as had been supposed. Led by Dominicans such as M.-D. Chenu, a much more historical approach to medieval theology, particularly that of Aquinas, helped in another way to release Catholic theology from its Counter-Reformation rigidity. In a series of great multivolume encyclopedias, the *Dictionnaire de théologie catholique* (1903 onwards), the *Dictionnaire d'archéologie chrétienne et de liturgie* (1907 onwards), and the *Dictionnaire de spiritualité* (1932 onwards), with book-length monographs on major topics, theology was placed on an entirely new scholarly basis. While J. P. Migne (1800–75), a diocesan priest, had made patristic texts available with his Latin and Greek patrologies, an astonishing feat of publication, an entirely new series entitled *Sources chrétiennes*, planned years earlier, started to appear in 1942, on the initiative of the Jesuits Jean Daniélou and Henri de Lubac, meeting standards of critical scholarship undreamed of by Migne. This series opened up the Greek patristic texts in particular to Orthodox scholars (as they have said) as well as to Western theologians, Protestant and Catholic.

One of the best ways to counteract anti-Protestant narrowness, then, was research into the literature and liturgies of the ancient church, particularly as it was increasingly conducted in an ecumenical way. With *Chrétiens désunis: principes d'un "oecuménisme" catholique* (1937, translated as *Divided Christendom*, 1939) Yves Congar sought, by surveying the different conceptions of the Church and its unity among Protestants, Anglicans, and the Orthodox, to work out a viable Roman Catholic way of participating in ecumenism. In *Vraie et fausse réforme dans l'Église* (1950, untranslated), a book which many Catholics at the time found deeply shocking, Congar distinguished the senses in which the Church must be holy (thanks to her divine origination) yet could be sinful (owing to her human composition), pleading for reform not of abuses (for there were few) but of the structures of the Church, because of their perceived lack of relevance in the world to which she preaches. In his next major book, *Jalons pour une théologie du laïcat* (1953, translated as *Lay People in the Church*, 1957), Congar strove to develop a theology of the laity, to whom the ministry of mediating between church and world primarily belongs. They are not simply objects of the ministrations of the clergy, as was customarily supposed, but are, in virtue of their baptism and confirmation, agents in their own right in Christ's threefold office as priest, prophet, and king. The contribution of his research to the massive shift in Roman Catholic ecclesiological self-understanding at Vatican II cannot be overestimated. In no way a speculative or systematic thinker, as he would have acknowledged, his work magnificently demonstrates the value of historical research and documentation for renewing theology and reforming church structures and ways of worship and devotion. Finally, in *Je crois en l'Esprit Saint*

(1978–80), his last great work, he offered a full-scale doctrine of the Holy Spirit in three volumes, going from the witness to the Spirit in Scripture to an attempt to resolve the problem of the "*Filioque*," concluding with a picture of church life as a prolonged *epiclesis*, or prayer for the coming of the Spirit.

Created a Cardinal in 1994 by Pope John Paul II, Yves Congar's immense achievement in retrieving and disseminating an understanding of the Church that far transcends the narrowly "Tridentine" Roman Catholicism which he inherited is at present nevertheless generally somewhat neglected. But that might be said also of the work of Henri de Lubac, who may be seen in retrospect as the greatest of all this generation of French theologians.

Henri de Lubac

Henri de Lubac, nominated a Cardinal by Pope John Paul II in 1983, suffered a great deal more harassment than Yves Congar, entirely from his fellow theologians (he was never summoned to explain any of his views in Rome). It was at the insistence of his friend Congar that he wrote *Catholicisme: les aspects sociaux du dogme* (1938, translated as *Catholicism: Christ and the Common Destiny of Man*, 1950), his first major publication.

It already included what was to become his most characteristic, if also most controversial thesis – the vision of God is a free gift, and yet the desire for it is at the root of every soul. The background and implications of this apparently harmless assertion will be the main topic of discussion here (see the next section).

The main purpose of the book was to correct what seemed to de Lubac an extremely individualistic and privatized religious sensibility by reminding Catholics of the inherently social nature of Christianity. Or rather, he saw a double failure on the part of his co-religionists. On the one hand, they were too often satisfied with a purely conventional religion, which was little more than the socially useful "religion for the people" that Maurras admired. On the other hand, in Renan's phrase, many people both inside and outside the Church seemed to regard Christianity as "a religion made for the interior consolation of a few chosen souls." To counter these apparently antithetical deviations from Christian faith, de Lubac sought to show, by a wealth of quotations from patristic and medieval literature, that "Catholicism" means, precisely, that the Church addresses all aspects of human life, the social and historical as well as the personal and spiritual. Against those both inside and outside the Church who saw Christ as having promised salvation not to communities but to individuals, he insisted on the contrary that "Judaism passed on to Christianity its concept of salvation as essentially social." Or rather, again, he sought to overcome the supposed antithesis. In a chapter entitled "Person and Society" he insisted that, unlike many modern theories, the Catholic understanding refuses to sacrifice the individual to the community or vice versa. The key to understanding the infinite value of a person is to recognize that he or she is created in the image of God. That is why a person has a freedom over against all totalitarian claims. But it also means that being the image of God is not something extra added on from outside to a life lived in accordance with natural or secular principles. That secular humanist view of human life, de Lubac discovered, was largely the creation of a certain dualistic theology.

In a brilliant chapter on the effects of doing theology against others – "we have learned our catechism too much against Luther" – de Lubac homes in on what would be the topic of *Surnaturel*, his third great book, in the following words:

> for about three centuries, faced by the naturalist trends of modern thought on the one hand and the confusions of a bastard Augustinianism on the other, many could see salvation only in a complete severance between the natural and the supernatural. Such a policy ran doubly counter to the end which they had in view . . . the super-natural, deprived of its organic links with nature, tended to be understood by some as a mere "super-nature", a "double" of nature. Furthermore, after such a complete separation what misgivings could the supernatural cause to naturalism? For the latter no longer found it at any point in its path, and could shut itself up in a corresponding isolation, with the added advantage that it claimed to be complete . . . Such a dualism, just when it imagined that it was most successfully opposing the negations of naturalism, was most strongly influenced by it, and the transcendence in which it hoped to preserve the supernatural with such jealous care was, in fact, a banishment. The most confirmed secularists found in it, in spite of itself, an ally.

Thus, what de Lubac was already claiming, in *Catholicisme*, was that, as historical research would show, the anticlerical laicism of the Third Republic was simply the mirror image of a supernaturalist religion that was either the empty shell of cultic practice and external observance or individual retreat into a spirituality of private interiority – either way, isolating faith from effective engagement with the real world. Indeed, more challengingly than that, de Lubac was to suggest in his *Surnaturel* that the grace/nature dualism in Catholic theology, invented to protect nature against Lutheranism and grace against Enlightenment humanism, was itself the creator of deism and atheism.

With the Occupation of France in 1940, it was the fourth revised and expanded version of *Catholicisme* (1947) which had greater impact on the theological scene. In the meantime, however, de Lubac had exploded two more highly controversial books. With *Corpus Mysticum: L'Eucharistie et l'Église au moyen âge* (1944), his second major book, he challenged the prevailing interpretation of the eucharist as primarily the miracle of transubstantiation. Working simply as a historian of doctrine, he traced the movement in the Middle Ages "from symbolism to dialectic." By this he meant the shift in the self-understanding of theology from the spiritual under-standing of the faith characteristic of the Fathers – "those geniuses of ontological symbolism" – to the "Christian rationalism" first observable in Berengar of Tours (ca. 1010–88), developed by Abelard (1079–1142) and Anselm (ca. 1033–1109), resisted in vain by Bonaventure (ca. 1217–74), but triumphant in Thomas Aquinas (ca. 1225–74). Given the dominance of neo-Thomism in Roman Catholic theology at the time, it is not hard to see why de Lubac's book was so shocking, although wartime conditions saved him from the harassment of too many hostile reviews.

The zest for new questions, as theology moved from the monasteries to the universities, revealed "a renewed, transformed ardour oriented quite differently than the religious contemplation of mysteries." While accepting the new orientation as inevitable, de Lubac did not hide his regret about what was lost when "symbolic inclusions" became "dialectical antitheses." In particular, the profound change in theological sensibility that occurred about the end of the twelfth century in Western theology altered the relationship between the eucharist and the Church. Whereas the eucharist had been regarded as the mystical body of Christ (*corpus mysticum*), the expression was gradually transferred to the Church – and the original term for the Church, namely the true body of Christ (*corpus verum*), migrated to the eucharist. The Church as people of God and community of believers had been regarded as the "real" body of Christ while his "mystical" body was his body in the eucharist. Essentially, de Lubac showed that the adjective "mystical" with reference to the eucharist dropped out in reaction against Berengar of Tours. For some time both the eucharist and the Church were referred to as *corpus Christi*, with the adjective *mysticum* floating between the two. In the second half of the twelfth century, in order to distinguish the ecclesial from the eucharistic body of Christ, the Church came to be qualified as *corpus mysticum*.

But a new eucharistic piety had developed, along with a new set of theological questions. The transfer of *mysticum* from eucharist to Church reflected increasingly individualistic devotion to the Blessed Sacrament (the consecrated bread), as well as increased theological speculation about transubstantiation. The real presence of Christ came to be located, not in Christ's people, particularly at worship, but in the eucharist, particularly in the consecrated elements.

It might seem an arcane matter, of little relevance in modern theology. But in fact it is a fine example of the importance of explorations in the history of doctrine, often in long neglected and forgotten texts, precisely to understand what needs to be corrected or deepened in theology now. De Lubac's point was that the shift in terminology altered the "center of gravity" of the doctrine of the eucharist. If the emphasis falls on the *corpus* which is understood as *verum*, as it naturally must, then when the term is applied solely to the eucharist, so de Lubac feared, the existence of the Church becomes peripheral. In the earlier tradition, with the Church as *corpus verum*, the eucharist was seen as existing to edify the Church. Historically, from being the source of the Church as the sacrament of Christ's sacrifice, the eucharist becomes an end in itself. Alternative descriptions of the Church begin to emerge, with the first treatise on the Church at the beginning of the fourteenth century preferring the metaphor of the Kingdom of God (James of Viterbo's *De regimine christiano*), to be followed by increasingly juridicist and sociological definitions of the Church as the division of Western Christendom loomed.

It was necessary, de Lubac argued, for Catholics to rethink the relationship between the eucharist and the Church. Whereas the eucharist seemed "the miracle of faith," and the Church an increasingly sociological reality, he sought to reinstate the Church as the "marvel" and to understand the eucharist as "the mystical principle, permanently active," realizing it. "The Church and the eucharist make each other, every day, each by the other." Some 50 years later, it is possible to see that de Lubac's study of this great shift in the history of the understanding of the eucharist opened the way to the eucharistic ecclesiology, the eucharist-centered understanding of the nature of the Church, with which Catholics in ecumenical dialogue, especially with the Orthodox, have recently had to come to terms.

Surnaturel (1946), de Lubac's third and perhaps most significant book, gave rise to the controversy with which we shall mainly be concerned in this discussion (see below). What was again the result of painstaking historical research in often long neglected texts, dating back to the 1920s, had emerged more openly as a demand for the retrieval of the biblical-patristic power of the doctrine of the image of God – retrieved precisely to defend the religious or sacred character of human nature – of all human life.

In *De la connaissance de Dieu* (1945, greatly expanded as *Sur les chemins de Dieu*, 1956, translated as *The Discovery of God*, 1960), one of his few works that carry a light burden of historical documentation, de Lubac sought to move back beyond proofs for the existence of God to an original experience underlying them, thus linking the search for God with the deepest springs of human inquiry and effort. Obviously, in a climate dominated by neo-Thomism and still fearful of modernism, this attempt to place (or, as he would have said, replace) reasoning about God in the context of believing in ourselves as created in the image of God was bound to provoke opposition. Here again, as in *Surnaturel*, de Lubac seeks to overcome the dualism which he had identified in neo-Thomism, where the relationship between nature and grace was regarded as merely extrinsic and tangential – mediated by way of reason (proofs) and formal ecclesiastical authority (identified miracles).

But we shall return to this dualistic theology in the next section. It may be said, in concluding this brief survey of his work, that de Lubac illuminated everything he touched. Consider, finally, his work on biblical exegesis. By the 1960s, in Roman Catholic biblical scholarship, the triumphs of the critical-historical method had led to the discrediting of traditional allegorical interpretation of Scripture. With *Histoire et Esprit* (1950, untranslated), a study of Origen, but particularly in the four massive volumes of *Exégèse mediévale* (1959–64, untranslated), de Lubac, while certainly not despising the historical-critical method, sought to recover something of the hermeneutical richness of traditional pre-Enlightenment exegesis. Unlike some more recent critics, de Lubac never doubted the legitimacy and fruitfulness of historical-critical exegesis; but he also recognized its limitations, as well as the questionable presuppositions with which it had operated from the outset. He even retrieves the phrase "separated science" which Andrew of St Victor (died 1175) applied to biblical exegesis, finding something disquieting about the way that this twelfth-century exegete anticipates the split between fideist-fundamentalist isolation on the one hand and methodological exclusion of faith on the other. In effect, once again, de Lubac's worry is with the dichotomy between the order of pure natural reason and the dispensation of divine revelation.

Henri de Lubac published much else in his long life, including books on Buddhism, on atheism, and on the contentious work of his friend and fellow Jesuit Pierre Teilhard de Chardin (1881–1955). But his four main achievements lie in (1) his retrieval of a much richer and more rounded pre-Tridentine Catholicism; (2) his restoration of a eucharistic ecclesiology; (3) his defense of pre-modern biblical hermeneutics; and (4), above all and most controversially, his deconstruction of grace/nature dualism in post-Tridentine Roman Catholic theology – the subject now to be explored.

Debate: The Nature/Grace Controversy

Surnaturel appeared in 1946. The book was immediately attacked by Jesuit theologians but especially by Dominicans.

The Dominicans were as divided among themselves as the Jesuits. One of the greatest difficulties was over the place of historical study in theology. Marie-Dominique Chenu's book, *Une École de théologie: Le Saulchoir*, published in 1937, outlining a program of theological studies with a firm basis in historical research, had been withdrawn from circulation in 1942 under pressure from his fellow Dominican and former teacher Reginald Garrigou-Lagrange (1877–1964), one of the most influential theologians in Rome for almost 50 years (he supervised the future Pope John Paul II's doctoral work on St John of the Cross). The program was judged by neo-Thomists like Garrigou-Lagrange to be "relativist," and thus verging on modernism, in the sense that concern with the meaning of doctrine in its historical context would inevitably override acknowledgement of its permanent truth value as Catholic dogma.

Garrigou-Lagrange was among the first to attack *Surnaturel*. Although remaining in his university post in Rome during the war, he did not conceal his support for the Vichy regime nor his longstanding sympathies with *Action française*. He was a close associate of the Vichy ambassador to the Vatican, who assured his government in a notorious dispatch that the Holy See had no objections to the Vichy anti-Jewish legislation, even providing supporting citations from Aquinas which de Lubac at least believed to have been contributed by "Thomists." But Garrigou-Lagrange was only one of de Lubac's opponents, and de Lubac was by no means the only theologian under attack. The opposition of neo-Thomists like Garrigou-Lagrange to theologians such as Congar, Chenu, and de Lubac, with their emphasis on the necessity of historical research, did not arise solely from the (not entirely unjustifiable) fear that historical research in theology could easily slip into positivism and relativism. There does not seem much doubt that the conflict over ways of doing theology among these French theologians reflected an even deeper conflict over the relationship between the Church and the world. The Vichy state, in its traditionally Catholic isolation, must have seemed as effective a way of making time stand still as the time-transcending system of the neo-Thomists. For theologians such as de Lubac, on the other hand, theology without historical research was only one more symptom of a church out of touch with the world.

In a nutshell, *Surnaturel* debunks the neo-Thomist hypothesis of a "state of pure nature," in which human beings could live in purely natural happiness without reference to a supernatural end. That hypothesis was not quite as abstract as it might seem. For one thing, it could illuminate the deeply troubling question of the fate of infants who died unbaptized, as well as the question of the salvation of unbelievers. The souls of unbaptized infants in limbo, it would have been claimed by some in the jargon of the day, although excluded from the full blessedness of the beatific vision, might yet enjoy full natural happiness – supposedly a consoling thought for their grieving parents, who might otherwise fear that their children were damned. More contentiously, however, at least for the neo-Thomists, de Lubac maintained that they had misread Aquinas. At one level, then, the conflict was over how to read the text of Aquinas. At another, in de Lubac's terminology, it was about a dualist or separatist theology of nature and grace introduced in the sixteenth century, which fed on the neo-Thomist misreading. Far from being an arcane matter, this nature/ grace dichotomy had both generated modern secular humanism and legitimized the introverted, otherworldly, and world-rejecting Catholicism which succumbed so easily to the illusions of the Vichy state.

The central thesis of *Surnaturel*, positively put, is that in the whole Catholic tradition until the sixteenth century the idea of humanity as the image of God had prevailed. Neither in patristic nor in medieval theology, and certainly not in Thomas Aquinas, was the hypothesis entertained of a purely natural destiny for human beings, something less than the supernatural and eschatological vision of God. There is only this world, the world in which our nature has been created for a supernatural destiny. Historically, there never was a graceless nature, or a world outside the Christian dispensation.

De Lubac was not a philosopher. But he once invited theologians to stop seeing in the human soul a nature that was closed in the same way that material objects are. He asked for a philosophical renewal which would affirm the dynamic orientation of the human spirit to self-transcendence. His noting (in 1934) of the temptation to reify the soul on the model of a material object is astonishingly reminiscent of similar remarks made about the same time by Heidegger and, again quite independently, by Wittgenstein.

As a historian of theology, de Lubac showed that, in the sixteenth century, a new conception of the relationship of grace to human nature began to appear. That is his thesis, illustrated with the results of many years of research in often somewhat obscure and forgotten authors who are nevertheless symptomatic of a wider and ultimately deeply damaging trend. The traditional conception of human nature as always destined for grace-given union with God fell apart between attempts on the one hand to secure the sheer gratuitousness of the economy of grace over against the naturalist anthropologies of Renaissance humanism, and resistance on the other hand to what was perceived by Catholics in the Tridentine period as the Protestant doctrine of the total corruption of human nature by original sin.

The Catholic theologians who sought to protect the supernatural by separating it conceptually from the merely natural facilitated the development of the humanism which flowered at the Enlightenment into deism, agnosticism, and ultimately atheism. The split between Catholic faith and agnosticism in France, and finally between church and state, was not so much the work of the rationalist philosophers of the Enlightenment but, more profoundly, that of theologians themselves. The conception of the autonomous individual for which the philosophers of the Age of Reason were most bitterly criticized by devout Catholics was, de Lubac suggested, first invented by theologians. The philosophies which broke free of supernaturalist Christianity to develop their own naturalist and deist theologies, had roots in the anti-Protestant and anti-Renaissance scholasticism of the late sixteenth and early seventeenth centuries.

The key question, bitterly dividing French students of Aquinas in the 1930s, was about what he meant when he wrote of "natural desire for the beatific vision." Thomas de Vio (1469–1534), better known as Cajetan, the Dominican with whom Martin Luther had a fateful dispute in 1518, argued that, when Aquinas spoke of a natural desire to see God face to face, he meant human nature as actually raised up by God to a supernatural destiny and enlightened by revelation. As a philosopher, so Cajetan held, Aquinas knew that human beings could have a properly natural desire only for a destiny within their own natural possibilities. When he spoke of natural desire for God, then, he was wearing his theologian's hat, and meant human beings who had, by the miracle of grace, already received the gift of union with God. In effect, Aquinas would have meant that our natural desire to see God was always already supernatural. As a philosopher, he would have been able to entertain the possibility of a purely natural happiness as the destiny of human beings in the state of pure nature. As a theologian, on the other hand, he could not have conceived of a desire on the part of human nature for transcendence of that nature which was not already a supernatural desire.

Cajetan needed a distinction between human nature as such and human nature as called to union with God in Christ, partly, no doubt, to maintain the rights of (Aristotelian) philosophy over against (Lutheran) theology, but mainly to defend the order of creation over against what seemed obliteration by Protestant exaltation of the dispensation of grace. This might have seemed to continue the insistence in Aquinas himself against what he saw as an exaltation of divine sovereignty by the theologians of Islam that reduced creatures, human beings included, to puppets.

For de Lubac, Cajetan's interpretation meant that Aquinas had abandoned the traditional patristic doctrine of human nature as created in the image of God and therefore open to divine grace – *capax gratiae* in the Latin jargon. It may seem odd that a controversy over a sixteenth-century interpretation of a thirteenth-century text should have become so important, not to mention so acrimonious, in the 1940s. But Cajetan's interpretation of Aquinas (though regarded by many at the time as an innovation, as de Lubac shows) had become received Thomist wisdom, and neo-Thomism was widely regarded as the only correct Roman Catholic theology. To challenge it, as de Lubac did in his *Surnaturel*, was obviously provocative. Theologians do not like being told that they are wrong – particularly by historians.

The implications of de Lubac's analysis of the textual evidence were very much wider in significance. He was actually suggesting that modern Roman Catholic theology had betrayed the patristic-medieval conception of the unity of nature and grace in the divine plan. At one level, the controversy stirred up by his historical investigations was over whether Thomas Aquinas, writing in the thirteenth century, held that the human person was created for supernatural communion with God – although of course incapable of enjoying such communion except as a gift from God and in no way a due to be exacted. According to Cajetan and his followers, Aquinas meant that the life offered by divine grace so exceeds human nature's possibilities that desire for it could never really be "natural" – the only destiny that human beings could naturally desire would be one commensurate with their natural powers. But is that what is meant by remarks such as the following, of which there are many examples throughout Aquinas' work:

> The beatific vision and knowledge are in one way above the nature of the rational soul, inasmuch as it cannot reach them by its own power; but in another way they are in accordance with its nature, inasmuch as it is capable of them by nature, having been made in the image of God. (*Summa Theologiae*, 3a 9, 2 ad 3)

In other words, the nature of a human being, created in the image of God and thus open to the possibility of face-to-face vision with God, is directed beyond itself to a supernatural destiny – which so transcends its natural possibilities, however, that it cannot achieve this destiny by its natural powers. Aquinas, in such texts, recognizes only one destiny, a supernatural one, for the human being. With the whole patristic and earlier medieval tradition, he is looking at the one and only world in which nature and grace, though totally different, are yet intimately related, in the sense that nature exists for the sake of grace, is subordinate to it, and has its ultimate destiny in it. For Aquinas, there is no ultimate happiness for the human soul that brackets out an eschatological vision of God. He never considered the perfection of the rational creature, to cite his jargon, as consisting only in fulfilling what belongs to it in respect of its nature – rather, that perfection consists also, and principally, in that which the creature receives through grace-given participation in the divine life (cf. *Summa Theologiae*, 2a 2ae 2, 3).

For de Lubac, these explorations in the history of doctrine were directly relevant to exposing and explaining deep distortions in ordinary Catholic morals and piety in his own day. Far from saving the supernatural and grace-gifted character of human destiny, modern Roman Catholic theology had introduced a distinction between nature and grace that ruined the pre-modern understanding of the inner orientation of the human spirit to the beatific vision. Philosophy could now proceed without taking any account of the longing for God that had hitherto been taken to be natural to the human creature. Endless, complicated speculations about the hypothetical status of human nature prior to or apart from grace gradually led to the emergence of totally secularized conceptions of humanity and indeed to the appearance of human beings without any desire for God.

On the other hand, much more serious for Catholicism internally, the loss of the patristic-medieval sense of the internal relationship between the order of creation and the dispensation of grace led to a conception of grace as something so totally extraneous and alien to human nature that anything and everything natural and human was downgraded and demeaned. In particular, when questions about politics or sexuality (say) were detached from the traditional unitary theology of grace as fulfilling nature, it would not be surprising (de Lubac would have thought) if politics were treated with cynicism and sexuality with suspicion and disgust. When the dispensation of divine grace was no longer assumed to have resonance and even roots in some kind of natural desire for God, human nature – and that means reason, feeling, and the body – became temptingly easy to dismiss. When grace is conceived as wholly extrinsic to human nature, so de Lubac thought, there is a temptation toward a dualist and ultimately Manichaean kind of asceticism and piety. It would not be surprising either if theologians, as the experts on divine revelation, kept everyone else out of the conversation – nor if the clergy, as ministers of grace in the sacramental system, maintained an extremely hierarchical and authoritarian Church.

Influence, Achievement, and Agenda

If the Roman Catholic Church may be said to have come out "into the world" at the Second Vatican Council (1962–5), acknowledging the presence of grace in the "signs of the times," there can be no doubt that theologians like Yves Congar and Henri de Lubac, summoned to take part at an early stage, exercised a decisive influence in the composition of the conciliar texts. There was an unexpected and irreversible opening to ecumenical dialogue and to recognizing the ecclesial reality of other churches. There was repentance for anti-semitism. There was an opening toward non-Christian faiths and religions. In particular, in the pastoral constitution "Gaudium et spes," "the holy synod proclaims the noble calling of humanity and the existence within it of a divine seed, and offers the human race the sincere cooperation of the church in working for that universal community of sisters and brothers which is the response to humanity's calling" (see previous section). That certainly sounds like a reaffirmation of the pre-modern understanding of the internal and quasi-organic relationship of nature and grace in the actual historical order, which must have delighted Henri de Lubac (even if he did not draft it!).

Karl Barth, as he explains in his memoir *Ad Limina Apostolorum*, was too unwell to accept the invitation to take part in the Vatican Council, but he spent the summer studying the texts before visiting Rome in 1966 for lengthy discussions with theologians representing diverse views of its achievements. Five out of the seven general questions that Barth raised with his hosts deal with what he regarded as the menace of a subjugation of the Church by the world. In reaction against the experience of the Church as self-isolated and hostile toward the modern world, so he feared, Catholics seemed tempted toward endorsing whatever movements in culture and society seemed most promising for natural flourishing. "Is it so certain that dialogue with the world is to be placed ahead of proclamation to the world?" Is the "thorough optimism" of the Constitution "Gaudium et spes" over the possibilities of the development of the world really in tune with New Testament expectations?

Although Henri de Lubac believed that the conciliar texts register the pre-modern vision of graced nature, it has to be said that he too, certainly by 1967, was deeply troubled by what he could not but regard as rampant secularism in the Catholic Church, particularly in France. He continued to insist that he did not reject the rightful autonomy of lay activity in dealing with affairs of this world, or the doctrine of the image of God and thus the openness for divine grace in every human being. What he rejected was the secularism, or immanentism, which divided the natural and supernatural orders in order to exalt the former at the expense of the latter. The Church that had been introvertedly supernaturalist was now in danger of becoming worldly. In *The Mystery of the Supernatural* (1965, translated 1967), he justified his return to the theme – concerned now, however, to insist on the distinction between nature and grace, each with its own integrity, whereas his earlier emphasis was on the continuity between them. The Council's call for "openness to the world," instead of rediscovering the pre-modern patristic confidence in the order of creation within the dispensation of grace, was being understood in practice (de Lubac feared) as an acceptance of secular humanism. He believed that the clergy, trained in one-sidedly supernaturalist theology in the 1940s, were the ones most to be blamed for going to the other extreme in the 1960s. That was only further proof, if any were needed, of the continuing power and deleterious effects of the neo-Thomist theology of the relationship of grace to nature.

In France in particular, as de Lubac was aware, the spread of what he called secularism among Catholics was accompanied by a politically right-wing and nation-alistic minority, led by Archbishop Marcel Lefebvre, who completely rejected the decrees of Vatican II on the grounds that they were founded on the principles of the French Revolution. Less extreme, and much more widespread, even among young people, there was a feeling that the Catholic Church had lost much of its distinctiveness.

That only shows how difficult it is to get the right balance between the world and the Gospel, creation and salvation, nature and grace. It also shows that, far from being a merely academic and somewhat abstruse problem, the theological under-standing of the relationship between nature and grace has a deep effect on the spirituality and liturgical experience available to the ordinary believer.

Although Congar and de Lubac were prolific writers, no one in their generation in French theology attempted to produce a systematic theology comparable with the work of great Protestant theologians such as Karl Barth or Paul Tillich. Their col-lected works are certainly very distinctive – Congar's writing is quite different from de Lubac's – and each corpus is self-consistent in development and homogeneous. Yet, for whatever reason, perhaps one to be sought in early exile from France or in cultural and educational contingencies and ecclesiastical vicissitudes, neither Congar nor de Lubac ever went far beyond historical research. They undoubtedly showed how effective their indefatigable study of often neglected and tedious authors was for understanding the background to present interests and assumptions. De Lubac's range was much wider than Congar's, but for both it was predominantly Christian writing from about the year 200 onwards that occupied their attention. Neither saw Scripture as a source for theology independently of patristic and medieval writers. Neither had any great interest in incorporating or employing the thought of any single philosopher, ancient or modern. As their work suggests, they were apparently content to go on reading and making notes on every text that they found in Migne or on the shelves of some well-stocked old seminary library – expecting much dross, but confident that, sooner or later, their card indexes would generate new insights into ancient controversies and, above all, into unexamined current prejudices.

Bibliography

Primary

Congar, Yves, *Divided Christendom* (London, 1939).
—— *Lay People in the Church* (London, 1957).
—— *After Nine Hundred Years* (New York, 1959).
—— *The Mystery of the Church* (London, 1960).
—— *The Mystery of the Temple* (London, 1965).
—— *Tradition and Traditions* (London, 1966).
—— *I Believe in the Holy Spirit* (London, 1983).
Lubac, Henri de, *The Mystery of the Supernatu-ral* (London, 1967).
—— *Augustinianism and Modern Theology* (London, 1969).

Secondary

Duffy, Stephen J., *The Graced Horizon: Nature and Grace in Modern Catholic Thought* (Col-legeville, MN, 1992).
Jossua, J.-P., *Yves Congar: Theology in the service of God's people* (Chicago, 1968).
Nichols, Aidan J., *Yves Congar* (London, 1989).
McPartlan, Paul, *The Eucharist makes the Church: Henri de Lubac and John Zizioulas in dia-logue* (Edinburgh, 1993).

Karl Rahner

J. A. Di Noia, OP

Karl Rahner was fond of describing himself as an "amateur theologian." This piece of self-effacing modesty on the part of the most influential and widely-read Catholic theologian of the twentieth century affords an illuminating perspective on his work.

Introduction

Naturally, there was nothing amateurish about Karl Rahner in any conventional sense. He was a scholar of the first rank, in full command of the tools of his craft and with interests ranging across the whole field of theology.

Karl Rahner earned his living, so to speak, as a professional theologian. He was a professor of theology for most of his life. Except for the war years, Rahner was first a teacher of Jesuit seminarians and then a member of the faculty of theology at the University of Innsbruck from 1937 to 1964. In addition to teaching and writing, he served as editor, lecturer, retreat master, and preacher. His success in these activities gained him the attention of church leaders. In 1962 Rahner became an official theological consultant (*peritus*) to the Second Vatican Council and in 1969 he was named to the Papal Theological Commission. Then, after holding appointments briefly at both the Universities of Munich and Munster, Rahner retired from teaching in 1971. By this time he was a theologian of international reputation. During the last 20 years of his life he was the recipient of many academic honors, including several of British and American provenance. He continued to be active almost until the day of his death at Innsbruck on March 30 1984.

Rahner's preparation for his professional career was typical for Jesuits of his generation. Born in Freiburg im Breisgau in 1904, he joined the Society of Jesus in 1922. He pursued the standard Jesuit course of philosophical and theological studies until 1932, when he was ordained a priest. The Society's plan that he earn a doctorate in philosophy in order to teach the subject in its schools was thwarted when, after two years of work at the University of Freiburg, Rahner failed to win his director's approval for his completed dissertation. Instead, he went on to secure a doctorate in theology in 1936 at the University of Innsbruck, where he began teaching the next year.

A crucial influence on Rahner's approach to theology was exerted by the spiritual and intellectual formation which he received in the Society of Jesus. His interior life was shaped by the *Spiritual Exercises* of the founder of the Jesuits, St Ignatius Loyola (1495–1556). The mystical bent of Rahner's theology can in part be traced to his appropriation of the spiritual lessons of the *Exercises*, with its emphasis upon meditative introspection and direct encounter with Christ in long periods of Scripture reading and private prayer. The soul's experience of God in prayer served as a kind of paradigm for Rahner's theological account of the Christian mystery.

His membership in a Catholic religious order helped to give Rahner's theology its characteristic spiritual and churchly orientation. Despite the university setting in which Rahner pursued his professional career, he always practiced theology with a view to its impact upon the church's life, its spiritual progress, and its pastoral and social engagements.

Rahner was educated during the period between the two world wars, when the mood of modern Christian theology was one of reaffirmation in the face of the challenges of modernity. A variety of theological programs emerged to replace the failed accommodationist strategies associated with Protestant liberalism and Catholic modernism. Efforts to reaffirm Christian identity gave added impetus to the revival of the study of the classical sources of Christian thought underway in Catholic circles since the mid-nineteenth century. Renewed study of St Thomas Aquinas (1225–74) and of medieval scholastic thought continued to be an important aspect of this revival. In combination with both favorable and critical readings of modern philosophers, this revival spawned a variety of vigorous neo-Thomistic and neoscholastic movements in Catholic philosophy and theology.

Undertaken in this climate, Rahner's philosophical and theological education favored the development of the ingenious fusion of scholasticism with German idealism and existentialism that is characteristic of his thought. A broadly Augustinian construal of Aquinas, partly dependent upon his reading of St Bonaventure (1217–74), served to confirm the mystical direction of Rahner's thought. The primacy accorded to metaphysics and theory of knowledge (over natural philosophy, logic, and rational psychology) in Rahner's theological appropriation of Aquinas' philosophy was typical of traditions of interpretation initated by the great Jesuit scholastic, Francisco de Suarez (1548–1617). Rahner came under the influence of the Kantian construal of Aquinas' philosophy – "transcendental Thomism," as it has come to be called – advanced in the writings of the two Jesuit philosophers, Pierre Rousselot (1878–1915) and Joseph Maréchal (1878–1944). Then, while studying at Freiburg, Rahner became familiar at first hand with the developing project of existential philosophy through seminars conducted by Martin Heidegger. Under the influence of such diverse factors, Rahner's own transcendental theology gradually took shape.

Along with his brother Hugo Rahner, SJ, and many other theologians of their generation, Rahner was also swept up in the movement to revive the study of prescholastic sources of Christian doctrines and theology. In addition to furnishing resources for renewed Christian affirmation, this *ressourcement* (as the movement came to be called) equipped progressive theologians of this period for battle on another front.

The scholastic revival, while largely beneficial for Catholic thought, had also generated a spate of fairly reiterative and defensive seminary manuals that seemed to block creative developments in Catholic thought. By recovering and exhibiting the diversity of theological expression typical of the classical sources, progressive theologians sought to shake the dominance of derivative and unimaginative forms of neoscholasticism in Catholic theology. Such theologians welcomed the application of new critical and historical methods to the study of the Scriptures, the liturgical sources, and the Fathers of the Church. Rahner himself undertook a considerable amount of scholarly work along these lines. As a result, his own constructive theology came to be profoundly influenced by patristic sources, especially the writings of St Augustine and the Greek Fathers.

Survey

These diverse influences helped to foster the relatively unsystematic approach that would become one of the hallmarks of Rahner's theology. This approach to theological topics could be characterized as at once mystical, philosophical, dogmatic, scholastic, pastoral, apologetic, transcendental, anthropological, and ecclesial. Rahner referred to himself as an amateur theologian in part to signal the unsystematic nature of his work.

In Rahner's writings various conceptual frameworks and theological interests intersect. His approach is experimental, exploratory, even non-technical. His essays represent a series of brilliant experiments, intended to advance the state of discussion of particular Christian doctrines by pressing at the boundaries of prevailing neoscholastic formulations. The internal coherence of Rahner's theology rests less on his espousal of a unitary system or methodology than on a vision of the human reality as being completely embraced and irreversibly transformed by divine grace.

Rahner preferred the essay as a vehicle for theological construction. His essays were published over a 30-year period (1954–84) in 16 volumes, modestly entitled *Schriften zur Theologie* or "writings in theology" (23 volumes in the English edition, *Theological Investigations*). Similar in form are the more extended essays he wrote or co-authored in the theological series, *Quaestiones Disputatae* (1958ff.), which he founded and edited.

No single volume presents Rahner's entire theological project in a comprehensive fashion. Like his essays and monographs, his three most significant book-length publications furnish only elements of that project, the substance of his contribution to foundational theology. The two earliest of these works – *Spirit in the World* (*Geist im Welt*, 1939) and *Hearers of the Word* (*Hörer des Wörtes*, 1941) – together comprise a complex, extended argument in philosophical theology. The more recent *Foundations of Christian Faith* (*Grundkurs des Glaubens*, 1976) surveys the rational warrants or foundations for central Christian doctrines.

In addition to writing numerous shorter works on various topics, Rahner accepted partial or complete editorial responsibility for several major reference works: the

Lexikon für Theologie und Kirche (1955–67), the *Handbuch der Pastoraltheologie* (1964–72), and the theological encyclopedia, *Sacramentum Mundi* (1967–9). These collaborative efforts bear the mark of Rahner's distinctive theological perspectives and, like the single-volume *Dictionary of Theology* (*Kleine Theologische Wörterbuch*, 10th edition with Herbert Vorgrimler, SJ, 1976), hint at the outlines of the systematic theology that he never wrote.

Rahner's immense output embodies a coherent theological program in the service of an encompassing vision of the Christian faith. He was continually in search of conceptual tools equal to the task of depicting this vision. Moving across the whole range of individual theological topics, Rahner at each point sought to articulate a vision of concrete Christian and human existence in the world as embraced by God the holy Mystery. In the modality of self-communication, this holy Mystery presents an inexhaustibly rich object for human contemplation and engagement in knowledge, freedom, and love. Grace enters human reality as something gratuitous though not alien, as something for which the ground is already prepared by creation in the very structure of the human spirit in the world. While faithful to traditional formulations, Rahner sought to express this vision in conceptualities congenial to modernity – the present context of historical human experience in which the divine self-communication takes concrete form.

Content

By referring to himself as an amateur, this highly accomplished theologian maintained a friendly though critical distance from prevailing practices within his craft. Rahner sought alternatives to reigning approaches and conceptions in theology in order to bring his vision of the Christian reality into sharper relief. Still, many of his significant theological proposals about individual Christian doctrines are more nearly intelligible when set in their traditional, usually neoscholastic, contexts. The continuities that obtain between these proposals and the neoscholastic formulations which he sought to correct are as crucial to understanding and appraising his theological program as are the discontinuities.

Rahner's endeavor to recover the vitality and relevance of Christian faith impelled him to probe almost every element of Christian belief and practice. Three topics invite extended consideration here as illustrative of his theological program at work on particular doctrines: the nature and method of theology, the doctrine of God, and theological anthropology.

Rahner's approach to methodological issues shares in common with classical Catholic theology a set of basic convictions about the nature and method of theology. Philosophical analysis and construction play a prominent role in his theological program, particularly as they help to advance the truth claims conveyed by Christian beliefs. In this his work stands firmly within the Catholic theological tradition. Although he exploits modern conceptualities in his articulation of the Christian faith, he resists any tendency to mute the realism of theological affirmation under the pressure of modern philosophical critiques of religion. On this score and despite their contrasting positions on other issues, Rahner's work is akin to Karl Barth's.

Rahner's methodological convictions are likewise typically Catholic in giving primacy to standard Christian idiom in the practice of theology. For Rahner, the proclamation of the kerygma – shaped as it is by Scripture, tradition, liturgy, doctrine, and ecclesial magisterium – provides the original setting for theological inquiry and construction.[1]

A distinctive mark of Rahner's conception and practice of theology is his effort to display the inner unity and intelligibility of the Christian proclamation in its simplicity and richness. His pursuit of this objective led to his rejection of certain neoscholastic theological procedures.

Neoscholastic theologians had of course inherited the intellectual ideal of a unified, comprehensive vision of the Christian faith from their study of the *Summa Theologiae* of St Thomas Aquinas. Indeed, they routinely invoked its authority at many points in their own works. But with rare exceptions the practice and literary forms of neoscholastic theology prevented the realization of this ideal for at least two reasons. First, in order to do justice both to the range of materials requiring explication and to the demands of the theological curriculum, the various topics of theology were distributed over a series of loosely connected treatises for manageable presentation in textbook form. The unity and coherence of the Christian faith were presupposed but not exhibited by this division of labor and materials. Second, given the cumulative character of scholastic dialectics, the exposition was saddled with highly compressed reviews of traditional scholastic debates. Relevant modern views could only receive cursory attention. Such expository procedures were unfavorable to the development of an understanding of fundamental issues in theology or of a comprehensive theological vision of the Christian faith. At the same time, the sweeping repudiation of modernity implied by a dismissive and defensive treatment of modern conceptualities inevitably fostered an isolation of the Christian faith and its expositors from the discourse of educated people of the twentieth century.

Rahner saw these deficiencies of textbook theology with clarity and determined to overcome them. In the end, his alternative methods generated a sustained program of largely coherent theological construction, intended to rescue fundamental Christian doctrines and an integral vision of the Christian mystery from the thicket of standard neoscholastic exposition.

A prominent aspect of Rahner's methodology in developing this theological program was his employment of transcendental arguments.

A transcendental argument is a regressive argument, one that moves backward, logically speaking, "from an unquestionable feature of experience to a stronger thesis as the condition of its possibility."[2] Rahner put such arguments to many ingenious theological uses. Since many of the central elements of the Christian faith are known by divine revelation alone, only God possesses an insider's knowledge, so to speak, of the conditions of their possibility. But theologians and ordinary believers can explore the reasons why Christian doctrines are true and coherent. Aquinas made this point by saying that, although theology could seek the inner intelligibility of revealed truths, it could never supply strict demonstrations for them.

Transcendental arguments function in an analogous manner in Rahner's exposition of individual Christian doctrines. The particular sort of intelligibility that Rahner pursues is that which reveals how the structures of human existence as transformed by grace are the necessary conditions for the experience of Christian faith and life, and, indeed, of human life itself as understood and interpreted by Christian revelation. What is more, by linking individual Christian truths – for example, about purgatory or the sacraments – with a unifying vision of God's personal presence to human beings in grace, such arguments also fulfill a chief objective of Rahner's theological program.[3]

Within the Rahnerian corpus, perhaps the best place to observe the functioning of transcendental arguments is in connection with his exposition of the doctrine of God.

Rahner's numerous essays on the doctrine of God illustrate both his ties with and his departures from standard neoscholastic theology. As a whole, Rahner's theological program is typical of Catholic dogmatic theology in placing God firmly at the center of the enterprise.[4] A fundamental concern for him is that theology do justice to the realism of the Christian confession of the universal personal presence of God and of his absolute claim on human minds and hearts. Rahner is impatient with neoscholastic theological accounts of God that give prominence to metaphysical speculation at the expense of explicating the fundamental experience of the presence of God at the very center of human existence. While he does not repudiate any portion of the classical theology of God, neither does he show much inclination to discuss it in detail. He deploys an extended transcendental argument to disclose in the human experience of God the grounds for explicit belief in him and thus for classical arguments for the existence of God.

This transcendental argument is elaborated sequentially in *Spirit in the World* and *Hearers of the Word*. The argument moves beyond philosophical theology into the domain of fundamental theology in that it considers not only the conditions for the possibility of human knowledge of God's existence but also the conditions of human receptivity to a possible divine revelation. Insofar as this includes receptivity to individual doctrines as well, the project begun in these two early works extends into the more recent *Foundations of Christian Faith*.

Classical arguments for the existence of God take for their starting points regular or persistent features of the natural order like motion, perishability, design, finality, and so on. The arguments are then elaborated, usually in connection with some metaphysical scheme, in order to demonstrate that the whole natural order exhibiting such features is brought into existence and preserved in existence by God. Rahner's philosophical theology does not contest the validity of the classical arguments, but rather advances a transcendental argument for their possibility. Its starting point is not some observable or generalizable feature of the natural order, but the structure of human knowledge itself.

In Rahner's philosophical theology, the Kantian cognitional a priori is transformed into a metaphysical a priori. According to this account, beyond the transcendental structures of reason which Kant argued make it possible for sense perception to become knowledge, there is the readiness to affirm being which serves as a kind of precondition for the knowledge of anything at all. For Rahner's transcendental theology, this observation is of fundamental importance.

Rahner insists that ordinary knowledge of particular objects of experience presupposes a prior readiness to affirm their existence – the readiness to affirm the being of things. But there is always more to "being" than can be contained in any particular being. A transcendental analysis of this readiness to affirm the being of beings and its inexhaustibility discloses that the human mind is structurally oriented to a horizon or backdrop of being (Rahner's notion of the *Vorgriff auf esse*). Beings appear, as it were, on a backdrop of being. The horizon of being appears as limitless, unrestricted, or Absolute Being, and finally as Absolute Mystery.

Rahner argues that this orientation to Absolute Mystery in knowledge is in fact an orientation to God. Thus the experience that supplies the starting point for this argument is a transcendental one. It begins, not with observations and generalizations about the world, but with a reflexive analysis of the structures of knowledge itself. Furthermore, the argument advanced on the basis of this experience is a transcendental one. Rahner argues that a prior experience of God in knowledge is the condition for the possibility of classical arguments for the existence of God that appeal to features of our sense experience of the world. Despite the technical difficulty of this argument, it is not hard to see what Rahner has in mind here.

But the move from Absolute Being to God as Absolute Mystery seems to represent something of a leap, facilitated by a broadly Hegelian conception of Absolute Being as unrestricted. Since in this conceptuality the causal dependence of beings upon Absolute Being is expressed in terms of differentiation rather than creation, the transition from beings to Absolute Being is a relatively smooth one, despite the complexity of the transcendental argument advanced to show this. Aquinas thought that the uses of the concept of "being" in describing the many varieties of entities we encounter in experience – not to mention entities that transcend our ordinary experience – turn out to be irreducibly distinct, and he proposed a theory of analogy to account for the legitimacy of these extended uses. On Aquinas' view of the matter, arguments for the existence of God possess an inferential rather than transcendental structure. In contrast, since Rahner's metaphysics clearly supposes that the concept of being in its various uses has a more nearly univocal sense, the way is clear in his philosophical theology for the extended transcendental argument sketched above.

In its next phase, Rahner's argument undertakes to disclose the grounds for the revelation affirmed by Christianity to have occurred. The Absolute Mystery to which all knowledge is oriented and which could have remained silent has in fact spoken. Rahner's argument here is a transcendental one. It answers the question: Given that Christians confess by faith that revelation has occurred, what must be true about the structures of human knowledge for such a revelation to be recognized and received? The message of revelation – the divine self-communication – travels airwaves, so to speak, which are already in place. Revelation does not invade human reality as something utterly alien but as something to which human beings are already in some sense attuned.

Rahner's emphasis on the incomprehensibility of God reaffirms a traditional Christian theme in the terms of modern German philosophy. God is the Absolute Subject (not, it should be noticed, "substance"), the absolutely transcendent "elusive I" whose self-communication beckons the human spirit. God is incomprehensible in the sense of being never fully comprehensible, endlessly knowable, endlessly interesting; always elusive because always surpassing human spiritual capacities; great enough, in the Augustinian sense, to satisfy the longings of the human heart, and greater still. In Rahner's view, the extended transcendental argument sketched above – indeed any argument or discourse about God – can only begin to hint at the immensity of the Mystery that surrounds us.[5]

Generally speaking, Rahner's proposals in theological anthropology are best interpreted in the light of the mystical or relational character of his theological program, so clear in his essays concerning God's incomprehensibility and mystery. This is especially evident in his proposals concerning the relationship of nature and grace, or the natural and the supernatural orders. Again, the state of discussion within neoscholastic theology provides the context for Rahner's position on these issues. It can be argued that Rahner endeavored to break the mid-twentieth-century stalemate between neoscholastic and progressive theologians by recovering and reappropriating Aquinas' fundamental insight about the true character of the supernatural order of grace.

In popular parlance, the term "supernatural" usually refers to other-worldly realms and their inhabitants, or to phenomena for which no "natural" or scientific explanation can be given. But in the Christian theological tradition, "supernatural" refers to a divinely caused transformation of the natural possibilities and capacities of created persons that permit them to participate in the life of the triune God. Throughout Christian history, there has been a lively debate about precisely how to conceive of the relationship of nature and grace, or the natural and the supernatural orders, and thus how to express the divinely engendered transformation of the human reality.

Augustinian conceptions of the relation of the natural and the supernatural orders decisively shaped Western theological positions on this topic.[6] According to these conceptions, two elements define the specific character of the supernatural. In the first place, whatever is supernatural, properly speaking, surpasses in possibility the innate and acquired capacities of any entity in its natural condition. The supernatural order is thus transcendent. In addition, whatever is supernatural enters the natural order as an unmerited gift. That human beings can have a share in the divine life, for example, and that they begin to enjoy an ultimate communion in the present that will only be fully realized in eternity are utterly free gifts bestowed by God. This is the sense of saying that the supernatural is gratuitous.

Aquinas amplified the classical Augustinian conceptions by subordinating these senses of the supernatural – transcendence and gratuity – to what he took to be the most precise or formal property of the supernatural: that it involves a participation in the divine life itself. Properly speaking, the supernatural order involves living life at a new level, a life lived in charity with God and with other persons in God. On this account, transcendence and gratuity are seen as functions of divinization.

For various reasons, Reformation and post-Reformation controversial theology on all sides tended to revert to earlier Augustinian conceptions in framing the issues in doctrinal dispute. To the extent that controversial theology prevailed in standard neoscholastic formulations, the significance of the advance represented by the theology of Aquinas was often lost or obscured – even where theology was supposedly being practiced under the guidance of his thought. In the climate of post-Reformation polemics, reversion to a definition of the supernatural chiefly in terms of transcendence and gratuity tended to accentuate the discontinuity between nature and grace. "Nature" came to be conceived as something that de facto exists almost in its own right, independently of the divine intention to draw human persons into the communion of trinitarian life. Aquinas' vision of the concrete order of things as an order of grace and salvation was eclipsed in much neoscholastic theology. The natural and supernatural orders were viewed as coexisting, parallel orders of reality that only subsequently come to be related (the "extrinsicism" which Rahner deplores). The reaction to the dualism of these conceptions in some twentieth-century progressive theology (the *nouvelle théologie* as it was tagged) risked a conflation of nature and grace.[7]

In this situation, Rahner strove to recover a genuinely Thomistic position on these issues by stressing the participational or relational character of the supernatural order, and therefore the continuity between human nature as divinely constituted in creation and human being transformed by grace. Rahner proposed the much contested category of the supernatural existential as an antidote to both extrinsicism and its contemporary alternatives. The supernatural existential confirms the orientation of the human being to the supernatural transformation that God's intention to confer grace presupposes.

Rahner and Aquinas are congruent here in striving to do justice to the concrete order of salvation. The "nature" of human persons is understood properly only when subsumed as an inner moment within the order of grace. Neither Aquinas nor Rahner take "nature" to be an independent order which at any time exists outside or beyond the order of grace. A key difference between Rahner and Aquinas at this point is that, with the introduction of the supernatural existential conceived in terms of transcendental philosophy of mind and metaphysics, Rahner cannot provide a description or analysis of the natural order at the theoretical level that is not dependent upon the supernatural order. Despite his emphasis on the unity of the two orders in the concrete working out of the plan of salvation, Aquinas can supply such a description and thinks that it is important for certain purposes to do so.

Rahner's proposals about nature and grace afford an insight into the coherence of his theological program. He is at every point concerned to display the continuities between the human order and the divine purposes and activity in its regard, without subverting the confession of their utter gratuity and transcendence as pure grace. The divine purposes and activities are not alien to human well-being, even though surpassing possibilities and merits utterly.

Debate

Rahner strove to recover the best elements of the Catholic doctrinal and theological tradition, while avoiding some of the obscurities into which it had fallen in some popular conceptions. As might be expected, his theological proposals have provoked controversy on various fronts.

On the one hand, there are broad issues of interpretation. The sheer variety and volume of Rahner's essays, reference work entries, monographs, and books have fueled the search for some overarching conception under which to organize his entire output. "Divine self-communication," "holy mystery," "theological anthropology," and "transcendental method" have all been advanced as likely candidates. Another strategy has been to treat the book-length works, individually or en bloc, as supplying the interpretative key to his writings as a whole. In this connection, there has been substantive debate about the role of transcendental philosophy in Rahner's thought, and the extent to which interpretation of his theological proposals depends upon his philosophical works. Naturally, his more plainly philosophical works afford a perspective on his theology. But it seems preferable to assess the theological essays on their own merits as contributions to particular traditional debates rather than to view them as offshoots of the project adumbrated in Rahner's philosophical and foundational proposals.

In addition to these and other questions of interpretation, there has been controversy about particular aspects of the content of Rahner's theology. Two topics illustrate typical issues raised by his overall theological program: his trinitarian theology, and the universalism of his theology of revelation and grace.

Rahner was sharply critical of a twofold disjunction in standard neoscholastic theology of the Trinity: a disjunction between the doctrine of God and the doctrine of the Trinity, and another within the doctrine of the Trinity itself. In Rahner's view, this twofold disjunction underlay the practical unitarianism of average Christian thought and piety. He advocated strategies to overcome this disjunction which, despite their advantages, posed difficulties that have generated considerable debate.

One aspect of the disjunction which Rahner perceived in standard trinitarian theology was that between God's being as one and God's being as triune. Following Aquinas and in accord with Western theological traditions generally, standard neoscholastic theological accounts of the doctrine of God addressed the existence and nature of God prior to addressing the processions, relations, and persons in God. But neoscholastic imitators of Aquinas in fact often failed to preserve the integration and the scriptural context which characterize his treatment of these issues in the *Summa Theologiae*. Rahner argued that, as a result of this disjunction, the Trinity came increasingly to be viewed as a kind of mysterious (in the sense of merely puzzling) appendage to the doctrine of God conceived primarily along metaphysical lines. Standard theology thus failed to do justice both to Christian revelation about the Trinity and to the distinctively Christian content of the doctrine of God.

In order to correct this first disjunction in standard trinitarian theology, Rahner advocated a recovery of the Greek patristic account of the divine nature, which he took to be better warranted by scriptural usage. In this account, the divine existence and attributes are given a strictly trinitarian setting in the discussion of the doctrine of God the Father. This view was understood by Rahner to respect the biblical account of God according to which the term "God" (*ò theos*) normally refers to God the Father. A theological procedure along these lines, in Rahner's view, would accord full weight to the distinctive Christian confession of God as trinitarian in his very being.[8]

But against Rahner's construal and use of the scriptural evidence, it could be argued that the strongly monotheistic logic underlying biblical usage is better respected by the traditional approach of Western theologians following Aquinas. In such broadly Thomistic positions, the discussion of the divine nature is constructed in such a way as to address those features of the life of the divine Trinity that are shared equally by the divine persons insofar as together they are the one God. Rahner was right to deplore the covert unitarianism fostered by trinitarian theologies that divorce the doctrine of divine existence and nature, and the doctrine of the Trinity. It was entirely apppropriate for Rahner to appeal to the Scriptures in order to support his larger argument, but misleading to suggest that the Scriptures rule out alternative accounts. Appeal to the biblical evidence is not likely to settle this old battle in favor of one approach over the other.

More crucial than the biblical evidence here is the long-recognized systematic disadvantage in treating the divine nature as an aspect of the doctrine of God the Father. Lurking in this approach is the danger of subordinationism. This danger can only be offset by a vigorous subsequent defense of the substantial divinity of the Son and the Spirit against the suggestion that they are only derivatively divine. In any case, it is not clear that a creative recovery of Greek patristic trinitarian theology would necessarily facilitate a spiritual or pastoral retrieval of what might be called trinitarian realism. The sometimes unperceived, although always undesired, tendency toward subordinationism in some Greek trinitarian theology was to a certain extent surpassed by subsequent developments in the doctrine of the Trinity as elaborated in Western theology by St Augustine and others. Something is to be gained in intelligibility and breadth by theological accounts (like Aquinas's) that link the biblical revelation of the divine being and identity as trinitarian with philosophical reflection about the kind of life which is enjoyed by the one, transcendent cause of the world whom Christians know and worship as Father, Son, and Holy Spirit.

Debate has also been generated by Rahner's strategy for dealing with a second disjunction in some standard trinitarian theology. This strategy gave rise to the central axiom of Rahner's theology of the Trinity: the identity of the economic and the immanent Trinity. The axiom is susceptible of a perfectly non-controversial reading. The God who in the activities of salvation appears as triune (the economic Trinity) is triune in himself (the immanent Trinity). Father, Son, and Holy Spirit are not roles which God assumes for the purposes of engagement in the economy of salvation. Father, Son and Holy Spirit are God in himself. The external missions of the Son and the Holy Spirit are extensions of the internal processions in God himself. The Trinity is not a culture-bound manifestation of the hidden God whom we never know in himself and who employs a number of impersonations. Being the Trinity is being God.

Solidly within the Christian mainstream, Rahner wanted to argue that Christ's revelation of the nature, identity, and intentions of the triune God is definitive and complete. Although, given the limitations of human knowledge and the utter transcendence of the divine mystery, God is never fully comprehensible, God's trinitarian self-description is confessed by Christians to provide the most intimate possible knowledge of God's being. Rahner's axiom should be construed as a strong reaffirmation of this traditional understanding of the doctrine of the Trinity. Rahner advanced this axiom to offset a disjunction between the economic and the immanent Trinity latent in some neoscholastic accounts which neglect the trinitarian structure of the divine activity in salvation.[9]

But the conceptuality which Rahner employed to express the identity of the economic and the immanent Trinity has provoked controversy because it involves too tight an identification of the missions and the processions. In this conceptuality, the trinitarian processions and missions are explicated in terms of the concepts of self-expression and self-possession. This conceptuality can suggest that the Trinity really could not be fully itself independently of the orders of creation and redemption.

Central here is Rahner's conception of the nature of symbols which he employed in various contexts in his theological program (e.g., trinitarian theology, christology, ecclesiology, sacramental theology, and exegesis).[10] Rahner's "ontology of the symbol" entails the view that a "real symbol" not only expresses something: it does something. A commonplace example may help us to see what Rahner is getting at here: promising obedience equals committing oneself to the performance of particular actions. Generalized and extended to account for symbols, the point would be, not simply that certain actions performed by an agent are symbolic, but that the agent (and events and things as well) is by nature symbolic. An entity becomes itself (does something) in expressing itself (in saying something).

Rahner applied the ontology of the symbol to his trinitarian theology. The Father expresses himself in the Son in order to possess himself in the Spirit. The processions of the Son and Spirit are thus processions of self-expression and self-possession. Rahner insisted on the tradition that the external missions of the Trinity are extensions of the processions. But in traditional theology, these missions were understood as freely chosen actions, described in terms of efficient causality. Given a description of the processions in terms of the ontology of the symbol in combination with an insistence on the strict identity of the economic and the immanent Trinity, Rahner's trinitarian theology risked a pattern of explanation in which the free actions of creation, incarnation, and grace could be seen as necessary extensions of God's inner self-expression and self-possession.[11]

This tendency also appeared in Rahner's christology. The ontology of the symbol enabled Rahner to make a strong case for the Second Person of the Trinity being the only one who could become incarnate, since only the Son is the self-expression of the Father.[12] The incarnation was for Rahner the supreme instance of the ontology of the symobol. There is no doubt about the great explanatory power of this conceptuality, as can be seen in Rahner's theology of the church and the sacraments.[13] But in Rahner's christology, as in his trinitarian theology generally, it raised the specter of a necessitarian account of divine action.

Another major source of debate concerning Rahner's theology is the universalism of his theology of grace and revelation. To be sure, Rahner was above all else a Catholic dogmatic theologian who, in asking about the conditions for the possibility of this or that aspect of the Christian mystery, endeavored to display the continuities between the natural and the supernatural orders. Rahner's characteristic treatment of these innerly Christian dogmatic issues afforded new perspectives on universal features of religious experience and wisdom. For the most part, these perspectives arose as corollaries of Rahner's central theological proposals. But when either critics or defenders of Rahner's theology reverse the priorities here, they applaud or censure his theological program for its subordination of innerly Christian doctrinal concerns to another explicandum, the universal presence of grace. Rahner's theology of revelation provides an excellent illustration of this controversy.

The doctrine of revelation constituted a major focus of attention for Catholic and Protestant theologians throughout Rahner's lifetime. Progressive theologians during this period sought to correct what they saw as the extreme propositionalism of some accounts of revelation which had arisen in response to the seeming subjectivism of liberal and modernist accounts of the doctrine. Progressive positions on the doctrine of revelation favored categories of interpersonal relation and in particular the notion of self-revelation. According to such positions, God provides in revelation not just information about objective states of affairs, but offers personal communion with himself. Revelation invites a response of faith – not just as an intellectual assent, but as a complete personal commitment to God.[14]

Rahner was one of many Catholic theologians who sought to correct standard neoscholastic theology by arguing along these lines. His characteristic contribution to this discussion was to give an account of the conditions for the possibility in human knowledge of a recognition and reception of divine revelation. Typically, then, Rahner strove to disclose the structure of the Christian revelation by advancing a transcendental argument which appealed to the general states of human beings who are all embraced in the concrete plan of salvation.

Rahner's proposal concerning the doctrine of revelation parallels his conception of a universal divine self-communication which as uncreated grace transforms the horizon of all knowledge and willing. Since the divine self-communication is universal, revelation is in an important sense universal: It has a history that coincides with the whole history of humankind (the "universal transcendental history of revelation"). Throughout this history human beings have striven to give expression to their acknowledgement of this universal revelation in a variety of symbols, actions, and forms of life, some of which have been explicitly religious and many of which have not been. Hence it is possible to speak of a history of revelation in a second sense, also coextensive with the history of humankind, as the history of the expressions of original and universal revelation (the "universal categorical history of revelation"). The Old Testament and Christianity have a special place in this history of expressions of revelation. In both cases God manifested himself in a more direct way and furnished the means by which all human beings could respond to him (the "special categorical history of revelation"). But the place of Christianity is unique because in Jesus Christ both the divine revelation and the human response to it are perfect and definitive ("the unsurpassable climax of revelation").[15]

Rahner posits transcendental revelation in order to explain the structure of special Christian revelation. By extension, this provides the basis for an account of non-Christian religious experience and wisdom. Classical theology fielded the notion of general revelation – identifiable as a possibility only from special revelation – for similar reasons.[16] But, given its identification of transcendental revelation with general revelation, Rahner's argument seems to reverse the order of the classical view. The transcendental argument he advances can be misconstrued to imply that the categorical revelation entrusted to the Christian community is merely an instance, along with other more or less valid instances of general revelation.[17] Rahner's notorious designation of these extra-Christian possibilities as "anonymous Christianity" confounds the difficulties here. Although the work of some of his popularizers merits it, the inevitable charge that his theology subverts the traditional claim of the

Christian community to be in possession of a definitive revelation seems unjust when pressed against Rahner himself. Perhaps such a misunderstanding of Rahner's theology of revelation is unavoidable, given the subtlety and difficulty of the transcendental argumentation in which it is framed.

Influence, Achievement, and Agenda

Rahner's influence and achievements help to define the continuing agenda to which his theological proposals gave rise. He successfully challenged the hegemony of a narrow and defensive neoscholasticism in early twentieth-century Catholic theology. With stunning and refreshing originality, he broadened the standard treatments of one doctrine after another, exposing anew the depths of intelligibility in the Christian faith and unleashing its power to shape and transform human life and society. Despite its relatively unsystematic character, Rahner's theology will undoubtedly stand the test of time and guarantee him a permanent place as an authoritative teacher in the Catholic tradition and beyond.

These accomplishments define an agenda for further research. Commentators have devoted considerable attention to questions of the validity of the transcendental reading of Aquinas espoused by Rahner and others. But Rahner's links with scholastic movements in all their diversity have yet to be fully explored. The objective of such study would be to expose the continuities that obtain between Rahner's proposals and typical neoscholastic formulations in order to define more precisely his place in the history of classical and modern Catholic theology.

On a broader front, Rahner's theological program turned out to have a forceful and effective apologetic edge. His presentation of the Christian faith restored its appeal for many who had been swayed by modernity's critique of religion. In the face of this challenge, Rahner's writings embody a strong affirmation of the central elements of the Christian tradition. The requirements of an emerging world church in dialogue with large religious and non-religious movements increasingly attracted his attention in his later essays. But he reaffirmed the importance of communal commitments in the practice of Christian faith. While critical, his theology remained firmly loyal to the traditions and authority of the Christian community. Through many spiritual writings, Rahner stressed the importance of the interior life for modern men and women, and thus clearly drew many to practices of prayer and meditation.

But Rahner's enthusiastic, if critical, embrace of modernity entwines the fortunes of his theological program with those of specific modern conceptualities which are themselves under attack. It was Rahner's contention that Catholic theology must appropriate the transcendental, anthropological and subjective turns characteristic of modern thought. Thus, in an intellectual climate in which philosophers and theologians are increasingly critical of precisely these elements of modern thought, Rahner's theological program will seem to be wedded to outmoded interests and conceptions. Such a view of Rahner is fostered by disciples and popularizers who typically construe the entire Rahnerian corpus in terms of its foundational segments – commending precisely the modern strategies in retreat elsewhere. An important question is whether a relatively unsystematic reading of his works will help to insure the continued appeal and viability of his theological program in an intellectual climate alert to the deficiencies of modern philosophy.[18]

Rahner was introduced to the English-speaking world in 1961 with the translation of the first volume of *Theological Investigations*. Since then, and particularly after the Second Vatican Council, Rahner has had a powerful influence on English-speaking theology, especially in America. His theology swept into the vacuum created by the collapse of the neoscholastic synthesis in American Catholic theology after the council.[19] This appropriation of Rahner's thought has in some circles fostered the emergence of a "Rahnerian" orthodoxy to replace the neoscholastic orthodoxy that Rahner strove to unseat. In all likelihood, this form of uncritical Rahnerian theology will yield to more eclectic appropriations of his program under the pressure of postmodern developments in Anglo-American philosophy and theology. The deeply traditional and scholastic character of Rahner's thought, and the recognition that he cannot be properly assessed apart from the achievements of classical theology, will presumably encourage a more balanced appropriation of his theology.

Generally speaking, Rahner's essays furnish a model for recovering the tradition in new contexts. Although the style of these essays is famously dense, their format is admirably free of the technical apparatus that sometimes encumbers academic writing. Surely this was deliberate. Despite their convoluted prose, Rahner's essays are accessible precisely because of the directness and inventiveness with which they approach classical theological themes. While steeped in the scholastic tradition, the essays are remarkably free of its trappings.

Perhaps the greatest achievement of the program of this lifelong "amateur" theologian was its unfailing witness to the mystery to which the Christian tradition bears witness. The absence of system in Rahner's theological program finds its final explanation in the nature of this mystery. "The true system of thought really is the knowledge that humanity is finally directed precisely not toward what it can control in knowledge but toward the absolute mystery as such; that mystery is ... the blessed goal of knowledge which comes to itself when it is with the incomprehensible one ... In other words, then, the system is the system of what cannot be systematized."[20]

Notes

1   Karl Rahner, *Theological Investigations* (New York, 1974), vol. 11.
2   Charles Taylor, *Philosophical Arguments* (Cambridge, 1995), p. 21.
3   Rahner, *Theological Investigations* (New York, 1972), vol. 9, pp. 28–45.
4   Ibid., pp. 127–44.
5   Rahner, *Theological Investigations* (New York, 1966), vol. 4, pp. 36–73.
6   Henri Rondet, *The Grace of Christ* (Westminster, MD, 1966), pp. 275–348.
7   Rahner, *Theological Investigations* (Baltimore, MD, 1961), vol. 1, pp. 287–346.
8   Ibid., pp. 79–148.
9   Rahner, *The Trinity* (New York, 1970).
10 Rahner, *Theological Investigations*, vol. 4, pp. 221–52.
11 William J. Hill, *The Three-Personed God* (Washington, DC, 1982), pp. 130–45.
12 Rahner, *Theological Investigations*, vol. 4, pp. 105–20.

13 Rahner, *The Church and the Sacraments* (New York, 1963).

14 Avery Dulles, *Models of Revelation* (Garden City, NJ, 1982).

15 Rahner, *Foundations of Christian Faith* (New York, 1978), pp. 138–75.

16 Rahner, *Theological Investigations* (Baltimore, MD, 1966), vol. 5, pp. 115–34.

17 J. A. Di Noia, "Implicit faith, general revelation, and the state of non-Christians," *Thomist*, 47 (1983), pp. 115–34.

18 Fergus Kerr, *Theology after Wittgenstein* (Oxford, 1986).

19 Philip Gleason, *Keeping the Faith* (Notre Dame, IN, 1987), pp. 136–77.

20 Paul Imhof and Hubert Biallowons (eds), *Karl Rahner in Dialogue* (New York, 1986), pp. 196–7.

Bibliography

Primary

Karl Rahner, *Foundations of Christian Faith*, trans. William Dych (New York, 1978).

—— *Hearers of the Word*, trans. Michael Richards (New York, 1969).

—— *The Practice of Faith: A handbook of contemporary spirituality*, ed. Karl Lehmann and Karl Raffelt (New York, 1984).

—— *Spirit in the World*, trans. William Dych (New York, 1968).

—— *Theological Investigations*, 23 vols (Baltimore, MD, 1961–9; New York, 1971–92).

Secondary

James J. Buckley, "Karl Rahner as a dogmatic theologian," *Thomist*, 47 (1983), pp. 364–94.

William V. Dych, *Karl Rahner* (Collegeville, MN, 1992).

William J. Hill, "Uncreated grace: A critique of Karl Rahner," *Thomist*, 27 (1963), pp. 333–56.

Gerald A. McCool (ed.), *A Rahner Reader* (New York, 1975).

Leo J. O'Donovan, "A journey into time: The legacy of Karl Rahner's last years," *Theological Studies*, 46 (1985), pp. 621–46.

C. J. Pedley, "An English bibliographical aid to Karl Rahner," *Heythrop Journal*, 24 (1984), pp. 319–65.

Herbert Vorgrimler, *Understanding Karl Rahner* (New York, 1986).

Hans Urs von Balthasar

John Riches and Ben Quash

Introduction and Survey

Hans Urs von Balthasar's is not strictly an academic theology. He never held a university post; the circle which surrounded him was drawn as much from the Church and the literary world as from that of academia. The most important influence on him during his active life was, in his own view, that of a medical doctor and mystic, Adrienne von Speyr. His own time, since 1948, was divided between running a publishing house, writing, translating and editing, and being chaplain to a new form of religious order, a secular institute, which he founded with Adrienne. His is above all a theology which springs from a sense of his own commission (*Auftrag*) which has linked him to the development of new forms of life in the Church with their roots in the Johannine/Ignatian tradition of spirituality.

Born in 1905 in Lucerne, Balthasar was educated first by the Benedictines at Engelberg, then by the Jesuits in Feldkirch. In 1923 he enrolled in the University of Zürich. His studies in philosophy and German literature led him to Vienna and Berlin and culminated in his doctoral work on German idealism, subsequently published in three volumes as *Apokalypse der deutschen Seele* (1937–9). At this point, 1929, he entered the Society of Jesus. Three years' philosophy at Pullach near Munich brought him into contact with Erich Przywara, whose work on *analogia entis* (the analogy of being) had a foundational influence on him. For his theological studies he went to the Jesuit school at Lyons. Here he encountered Daniélou, Fessard, and Henri de Lubac, who gave him his enduring love of the Fathers, which was to lead to his studies of Maximus, *Kosmische Liturgie* (1941) and Gregory of Nyssa, *Présence et Pensée* (1942). It was here too that he met the French Catholic poet Paul Claudel, whose works he was to translate into German. Lyons was the centre of the *nouvelle théologie* which raised deep questions about the Thomist doctrine of grace and nature, with its suggestion that human nature could be conceived of in isolation from its relation to the vision of God. Hence the appeal to the Fathers with their conviction that communion with God is of the essence of humanity. Hence too Balthasar's own conviction that nowhere is humanity ever wholly bereft of the grace of God – and his lifetime search for the fruits of such openness in the works of philosophers and poets outside the Christian tradition, notably in the grand tradition of classical antiquity.

After his studies at Lyons he was briefly in Munich as editor of *Stimmen der Zeit*. There then followed a period of eight years as student chaplain at Basel, which shaped the pattern of the rest of his life. Here he met Adrienne von Speyr and received her into the Catholic Church. Together they conceived the idea of a new form of religious order whose members would continue to exercise their normal professions and occupations in the world. It was on the occasion of the first retreat which Balthasar conducted for this *Johannes-Gemeinschaft* that Adrienne experienced the first of the visions which were to accompany her for the rest of her life and provide the central themes of Balthasar's own writing (documented in *First Glance at Adrienne von Speyr* and in many published transcripts of her meditations and experiences, which Balthasar himself made). And it was in Basel that Balthasar turned his attention to the work of Karl Barth, which gave him "the vision of a comprehensive biblical theology."[1] His relationship with Barth, at first enthusiastic and friendly, may have cooled, but Barth's theology remained for Balthasar one of the fixed points by which he set the course of his own work.

In 1950 Balthasar left the Society of Jesus, which would not allow him to remain a member while he was developing his work with the secular institutes. For long he was in the ecclesiastical wilderness, yet it was during this period of isolation and disfavor that his major writings were produced or conceived. He published important studies of literary figures – Bernanos, Schneider; of the saints Thérèse of Lisieux and Elisabeth of Dijon; and it was at this time that the first volumes of his great trilogy began to appear. His restoration to favor came in the wake of Vatican II. In 1967 he was appointed to the Papal Theological Commission and began to gain the reputation of a conservative theologian, not least for his pronouncements on the ordination of women and on his fellow Swiss, Hans Küng. However inadequate such a tag may be, there was nevertheless a growing rift between Balthasar and the circles around Rahner, Küng, and Schillebeeckx which came to the front in Balthasar's attack on Rahner's notion of "anonymous Christians" in *Cordula* (1966) and his own establishment of a rival periodical to *Concilium* entitled *Communio*. To this day his work remains a foreign body in the corpus of progressive Catholic theology, yet there is much that each could learn from the other.

Balthasar died in 1988, a few days before he was due to become a cardinal.

Content

Analogy

Balthasar outlines his approach in the following terms: faithfulness to Christ must be at the center of all theological endeavor, but this "Christian 'exclusivity' demands precisely the inclusion of all human thinking." Human thinking, on this account, is "a presupposition for God's speaking ('revelation') and being understood ('theology')." Human nature, similarly, "in all its forms is understood as the essential language of the *Logos*."[2] Here, initially, we catch sight of the deep concern in Balthasar's thought to sustain an openness to the world. Such concern arises from a commitment, formed along with de Lubac, to raze the bastions of fear which had kept the Church isolated from its cultural and philosophical environment, and had thereby prevented it from engaging freely and redemptively with the world. Balthasar sets out with the bold and consciously "catholic" desire to embrace "all human thinking," and to trace "human nature" through the diverse forms in which it comes to expression.

Nevertheless, there is an important qualification which Balthasar is keen to make – and this qualification comes increasingly to reflect his anxiety over developments in progressive Roman Catholic circles where openness to the world, the readiness to baptize secular and religious movements outside the Church as examples of "anonymous Christianity," can lead to a loss of identity, of consciousness of the specifically Christian call and witness. For Balthasar, there are definite terms on which "the inclusion of all human thinking" by "the Christian 'exclusivity' " can take place. Human thinking is included "as something judged (*gerichtetes*) . . . 'broken,' realigned, and reset (*ab- aus-, und eingerichtet*)."[3]

Already, the guiding concerns of Balthasar's theology are before us. There is (i) a respect for the way that human nature finds expression in a great variety of *forms*. There is (ii) a desire to see theology treating these forms with seriousness, as having some conceivable *relation* to the revelation centered in Christ. Alongside this desire, at every stage, there is (iii) a belief that the relation is grounded not straightforwardly in similarity, but simultaneously in *dissimilarity*: that this dissimilarity has the power to judge and to break worldly forms. And yet beyond this judgment there is (iv) the suggestion of a new (perhaps "supra-") form, in which, as we shall see, some kind of "reset" *harmony* between the divine and the human can be intuited by the faithful believer; a "supra-form" which is the free gift of God and quite underivable from its worldly analogues.[4]

Thus we find Balthasar situated somewhere between a Thomist tradition and the position of Karl Barth. On the one hand, we find a continued concern with the themes which have given form and continuity to Western metaphysics (the perception of unity in diversity; of beauty, goodness, and truth) as proper to our "natural" knowledge of the order which God has created. In support of this, Balthasar stresses a common ground between God and the world which is founded in creation and cannot entirely be destroyed: "Every real 'contra' presupposes a constantly to be understood relationship and thus at least a minimal community in order to be really a 'contra' and not a totally unrelated 'other.' "[5] On the other hand, he holds fast to the belief that it is only in Jesus Christ that this relation is established, brought to its perfection, and truly revealed to the eyes of faith. The order of creation may only be interpreted properly when it is interpreted in its union with the order of salvation, which shows that community with God (that which is common both to God and to the creature) is pure gift, undeserved and impossible to predict in advance (however much convergence on the form of Christ we may see with hindsight in the ancients, in the Old Testament, in literature, and in the metaphysical tradition).

This presents Balthasar with the challenge of how properly to relate the many competing movements of the human spirit to the central "revelation-figure" of

Christ. How to do justice to the unity and diversity not only of the Christian tradition, with its various mediations of the glory at its christological center, but also of the richness of perceptions of beauty, goodness, and truth which are to be met with outside that tradition, in the poets, the philosophers, and the myth-makers? How to avoid reducing the originality and freshness of such perceptions simply to inadequate copies of the Christian revelation itself? Such concerns characterize Balthasar's engagement with Barth throughout the first part of his trilogy, *The Glory of the Lord*, and his standpoint finds articulation in summary form in *Love Alone*. What emerges (and what binds the three panels of Balthasar's great theological triptych together) is a distinctive form of analogical thinking, which owes its character both to Przywára's thought and to the debates Balthasar had with Barth.

Balthasar's use of analogy is not so much a method (it is too ambiguous and ad hoc to be that), as a broad, guiding principle. It continues to leave room for fascination with and insights from outside a narrowly defined Christian tradition, at the same time as it stresses the transcendence of the Christian revelation. It is, for Balthasar, a means of recognizing the relation within difference, and the similarity within ever greater dissimilarity (*maior dissimilitudo*), of human nature/thought and the divine revelation. The touchstone for Balthasar here (as for Przywara) is the famous text from the Fourth Lateran Council (1215): "As great as may be the similarity, so much greater must the dissimilarity between creator and creature be preserved." Whether operating between aesthetic beauty and revealed glory, between human drama and the all-encompassing Theo-Drama, or between the enquiries of philosophy and the obedient reflection of prayerful faith, analogy works to achieve the mediation upon which Balthasar's theology depends. It does so because of its built-in inconclusiveness and dynamism: the space it leaves open for receptivity in all forms of human thought and activity, and its insistence on the impossibility of drawing definite conclusions about the adequacy of such forms as analogues of what is proper to God. There is an ever-greater distance between the world and God. Admittedly, for Balthasar, the world is related to God because it "is" – it has creaturely "being" which owes itself to (and is analogous to) the "being" of God. Yet the "being" of God is self-subsistent, impossible to relativize or deconstruct. So there can be no approximation of finite being to God's being; every degree of correspondence opens up an increased intensity of differentiation (dissimilarity). This has a number of effects, the most important of which is that the finite is confirmed as finite – indeed, as a *given* plurality of forms, and of manifold relations-in-difference. The givenness of the finite both keeps it in its place (it cannot aspire to being non-relative or "absolute") and becomes its own proper glory. The forms which human thought and experience take are endowed with dignity precisely *as* open-ended and receptive. They are of genuine interest because of the way they point beyond themselves to a fulfillment that can only come as a gift (as a revealed "supra-form"). This permits a certain "positivity" to the finite, in all its uniqueness and concrete character. The theologian is permitted to explore these worlds of what is concrete and distinctive (indeed, "all human thinking" can profitably become his concern) because this proliferation, when contemplated aright, is an expression of the greater dissimilarity on which all created distinctions are founded: "Every comparison and relatedness of the creature has therefore its measure in a converse relatedness of God to the creature."[6]

Out of this vision of analogical relation, in which similarity between the creaturely form and the divine revelation is suspended but preserved in ever-greater dissimilarity, Balthasar's contemplative, eclectic, and enormously wide-ranging theology is born. In each part of his trilogy he contemplates particular forms of human expression and experience: in *The Glory of the Lord*, the forms of beauty and its perception; in *Theo-Drama*, the forms of human action as depicted and interpreted in literary drama; in *Theo-Logik*, the forms of philosophical insight. The very fact that the trilogy is constructed so as to answer the ancient concern with beauty, goodness, and truth as manifested in all Being shows Balthasar's respect for the "form" which metaphysical reflection has traditionally taken. Balthasar's theology seeks to attend to such worldly forms in a way that will draw on a christologically centered and ecclesially learned "sensorium" for the revelation form (the *Gestalt Christi* or "form of Christ") in which all other forms find their true center and ground.[7]

Of course, the tension between similarity and dissimilarity, form and supra-form, is a difficult one to sustain, and this difficulty in Balthasar's thought will become more apparent as we proceed.

Beauty and the glory of God

Because of his caveat, that in no circumstances can human thought by means of its own capacities lay hold on the absolutely transcendent reality of God, Balthasar's approach is freed from concentration on human subjectivity to examine the way that human experience is encountered by reality from beyond itself. This object of faith – which is the *Gestalt Christi* – gains in importance in the proportion that preoccupation with the conditions of human subjectivity decreases. The conditions for the perception of this object are given with and in the object. It is self-disclosing and enrapturing.

Balthasar's approach here is contemplative as opposed to critical; it is concrete rather than abstract. Much of Balthasar's work in the first volume of *The Glory of the Lord* is concerned with the notion of the light of faith, with the way of perceiving its object which is peculiar to faith. The biblical writers, Paul and John at least, speak of faith, not simply in terms of modifications of the believers' own self-understanding but as a particular mode of apprehending and entering into relationship with the object of faith: God in Christ. In polemical terms this brings Balthasar into sharp conflict with all those who have turned away from contemplation of the object of theological reflection, God in his self-revelation, to a consideration of the conditions of human subjectivity and the manner of our apprehension of that revelation. And this distinguishes his approach as much from Bultmann's program of existential interpretation as from Catholic transcendental theology. What Balthasar particularly singles out in Bultmann is the combination of critical historical study with an anthropological reduction of faith to the moment of decision. For Balthasar, Bultmann's demythologization and reductive explanations of the origins of mythological concepts in the biblical texts, together with his existential interpretation of those texts, both serve equally to dispel the object of faith, leaving only an existential moralism.[8] And there is a recurring polemic throughout Balthasar's writings against those who choose reductive explanations, historical, psychological, or whatever, and thereby fail to do justice to the object of their study.[9]

It is in defense of this concentration on the object in *The Glory of the Lord* that we find Balthasar making a characteristic use of analogy. He turns to analogies from the world of aesthetic appreciation to demonstrate that there too the object of perception has priority. For Balthasar, to perceive beauty is to perceive the manner of manifestation of a thing as it reveals its being, its reality. (This approach owes much to the aesthetics of Goethe, for whom "[i]t is precisely in the living form that life is found.")[10] To be sure, where a work of art is concerned, we may profit from an understanding of its constituent parts, of the influences and circumstances of the artist, of preliminary sketches, and of contemporary developments in the medium; but none of that will of itself bring understanding unless it enables us to see the work as a whole, to perceive, as Hopkins would have said, its "inscape."[11] Understanding of this kind comes with practiced contemplation, a cultivation of one's appreciation in the course of which youthful enthusiasm gives way to a more mature enjoyment of the work.

On another front, Balthasar rejects, quite rightly, the charge that such a concern with form and beauty is Platonist. It is not that he wishes to penetrate behind the appearances of things to the enduring, eternal ideas of which they are manifestations only. His whole theological endeavor is directed toward learning to see things as they are in themselves, whole and entire (though finite), and in so seeing to perceive the reality of Being in all its variety and concreteness.

Such cultivation is analogous to the contemplative discipline of the saints, who act as a model for our own reception of the form which comes to us (volumes 2 and 3 of *The Glory of the Lord* are given over to studies of saints and contemplative theologians, clerical and lay). Such saints rekindle in an all too functionalist world our sense of the graciousness of things as they give themselves for our beholding. Balthasar's debt here is to Ignatius, whose *Spiritual Exercises* he conducted some hundred times, to the Society of Jesus, and to his own *Johannes-Gemeinschaft*; above all to Adrienne, "who showed the way in which Ignatius is fulfilled by John, and therewith laid the basis for most of what I have published since 1940. Her work and mine are neither psychologically nor philologically to be separated: two halves of a single whole, which has at its centre a unique foundation."[12] The work and insights of contemplative sanctity stand over against those Western theological and philosophical developments (largely post-Reformation, says Balthasar)[13] which have lost sight of the revelation-figure in which the divine glory is seen.[14] Theology of such a kind can listen only to the echoes of the divine word in its own self-consciousness; it loses its power to attract and to convince; it ceases to be concrete and concerns itself with the abstract, that which is perceived as the condition of the possibility of any perception at all. By contrast, the example of the saints – and, indeed, of Balthasar's theological aesthetics as a whole (influenced as it is by Adrienne) – recalls us to the nurture of our perception and understanding in the face of God's glory.

In the concluding volumes of *The Glory of the Lord* (on the Old and New Covenants), it becomes clear that for Balthasar all worldly forms, words, and thoughts – those of the Old Testament included – are measured by that which they exist to serve: the christological *deus dixit* (God has spoken) which is presented to us in the underlying unity of the scriptural *Gestalt*. It is to Barth that Balthasar owes this vision of a comprehensive biblical theology (and it is in these terms that he would ultimately wish his work to be judged). The biblical Word – the Word of grace and promise – has its own unique *Gestalt* or form, in which human words and concepts are given their true sense as they are pressed into the service of the "new" creation in Christ. No demythologization of the New Testament is required by this, but rather a discovery of how all myths have been rescued and transformed in the witness of the Word to itself.

Thus far, the outline of the analogical framework (with its *maior dissimilitudo*) is apparent. Beauty is not strictly the same thing as glory. The "glorious" form of Christ is marred as well as beautiful: the supra-form embraces the Cross and the un-form of Hell. But contemplative perception of the beautiful nevertheless finds itself preserved as an analogue of our infinitely rich contemplation of God's glory, which only the approach of that glory (reinforcing its sovereign distinctiveness and freedom by its very approach) makes possible.

In one sense, this appears to protect Balthasar from the charge that his is a form of natural theology, developed to support his dogmatic claims. It is, of course, apologetic, in the sense that it seeks to convince by its obedient evocation of the form of glory at the heart of the Christian tradition. Once one has shown the way in which the human and created world is taken up into the service of the divine and now mediates the divine glory, what other proof is needed? This was precisely the apologetic strategy of the *nouveaux théologiens* and indeed of the worker priests with whom they were associated. But in another sense Balthasar does begin to develop something closer to a form of natural theology, as can be seen most clearly in his volumes on *The Realm of Metaphysics*. Although that which is grasped of the beauty of Being in the myths, the poets, and the philosophers awaits its fulfillment in God's self-revelation of his freedom and grace, yet at the same time that which is grasped *is* grasped and thus affirmation is made of the continuing value of philosophy as a discipline formally and adequately distinct from theology.

Drama and the Christ-event

As the Church's obedient receptivity gives birth to discipleship and mission, so *The Glory of the Lord* gives birth to *Theo-Drama*. It is out of believers' obedience to the one divine Word that the richness and diversity of the many forms of the Christian tradition are born. Hence the lives of the saints and the classical Christian theologians are not to be seen as pale copies which obstruct our view of the unchangeable reality of the biblical Word. Rather, because it is in the nature of the Word to generate new forms of life insofar as people are obedient and faithful to it, so too we may learn in the study of such lives and theologies to catch sight of the divine glory as it has transformed their lives and in so doing discipline ourselves in the same obedience. The saints – and most of all Mary as (for Balthasar) the archetype of the believing Church – constellate around the form of Christ which their lives represent and mediate, and this ecclesial constellation thereby participates in the fullness of the *Gestalt Christi*. Put another way, the forms of life which take shape in the Church (in response to the generative Word) participate in an overall event of revelation.

And for Balthasar, this event of revelation has all the dimensions of an actual drama between God and his creatures.

Drama, then, is the field of analogy which informs *Theo-Drama*. And, in characteristic fashion, Balthasar refuses to contemplate the specifically ecclesial experiences and representations of the drama between God and his creatures in isolation from all the analogous dramatic representations which are available for contemplation in literature and the theater. Just as *The Glory of the Lord* began with a consideration of the experience of beauty (and related theories of aesthetic apprehension), so *Theo-Drama* begins with a consideration of a great (though almost exclusively Western) tradition of drama. Balthasar shows his continued openness to the insights that are to be found outside a narrowly theological tradition by drawing on Hegel's typology of poetic genre at the culmination of his *Aesthetics* – a *locus classicus* for the discussion of drama. He takes from Hegel the view that drama is the consummation of other perspectives, combining and enhancing the insights of epic and lyric styles in order to do full justice to acting subjects, their freedom, and their interrelations.[15] Drama is the medium in which human beings address questions about agency and event at the widest level, and it is therefore a medium taken seriously by Balthasar in the belief that all human drama, whether consciously or unconsciously, in fact opens onto the drama of God himself. Drama, from Aeschylus to Brecht and Ionesco, represents a cavalcade of human self-interpretation, and its value for Balthasar, following the pattern of *The Glory of the Lord*, is linked to the degree to which it looks to a meaning which transcends (judges, breaks, and resets) its own particularity.

The transcendent meaning is, of course, a christological one. Balthasar's assumption is that all drama points to a Christian horizon on which is situated the ultimately dramatic (the theodramatic), which is to say that which safeguards but transforms the humanly dramatic. Starting with the christological reflections of *Heart of the World*, and running via his reflections on the *triduum mortis* (Good Friday, Holy Saturday, Easter Sunday) in *Mysterium Paschale*, Balthasar presses on toward his sustained meditation in *Theo-Drama* on the central mystery of the Christian faith: the drama of the passion of the eternal Son (with the cry from the cross sounding at its heart); the Son's subsequent descent into Hell; and his entry into resurrection life.

Vital things come to light here about Balthasar's doctrine of the person and work of Christ, and the way that his dramatic perspective recasts and re-enlivens them. Like Barth, Balthasar asserts an identity between christology and soteriology: They are not to be separated. In drama, characters are associated with their roles in the overall movement of the play, but there is always a residual distance which persists between the actor and the role. (This is true for Balthasar at a more general level, too, in society and in social "role-playing.") The theological analogue of the notion of role, which overcomes this residual distance, is the notion of "mission" (*Sendung*). And it is in *Christ's* mission, in which human beings have the possibility of sharing, that there is a perfect coincidence of person and work. Christ's person is wholly invested in his work. It is in the nature of the work – which involves the bearing of the totality of the world's sin in order to initiate and maintain the New Covenant between God and humanity – that it cannot be undertaken unless a "person" is offered in and with the task: The person of Christ alone can accomplish this. Thus

Balthasar is prevented from lapsing into "the kind of purely extrahistorical, static, 'essence' christology that sees itself as a complete and rounded 'part one,' smoothly unfolding into a soteriological 'part two' . . . the question of [Christ's] work implies the question of his person: Who *must* he be, to behave and act in this way?"[16]

Jesus (comes the answer) is the "Beloved Son" (Matthew 3: 17 and par). In other words, he is the actively obedient one, the perfection of whose obedience is the expression and ground of his personal and immediate relation to the Father, as well as of his human faithfulness. Being the Son is not being in a static state; it is being engaged in a personal relationship. Admittedly, in the terms of human life, this personal relationship will mean a certain " 'economic' ignorance" on the part of the Son,[17] which gives the precise outcome of the task over to the Father. But this will not shake (in fact, it emphasizes) the full dimensions of the Son's trinitarian personhood precisely as the one who is at *every* level perfect in his active obedience. He entrusts everything to the one who gives him his mission. "Every worldly dramatic production," says Balthasar, "must take its bearings from, and be judged by, the ideal nature of this [christological] coincidence of freedom and obedience or of self-being and consciously acknowledged dependence."[18]

In soteriological terms, this means that the Sinless One is able to "change places" with sinners; he does so through his own self-giving, in accordance with the Father's will. Human beings are set free by this (ransomed, redeemed, released), and they are included thereby in the divine life of the Trinity itself. Once again, dramatic concerns enliven the picture. It is the saving *action* of God, and not just revelation of his saving will or nature, that counts here. And again, in a way that continues to be true to dramatic insights, it is something inescapably *personal* that is going on. God's loving work is not *behind* but *in* the personal. It is as the person he is that Jesus has the mission he has, with its soteriological goal and eschatological reach. And it is as the person he is that his saving work can continue to take effect in the present, because he continues to be operative in the personal mode in the *Spirit*, still encountering others and drawing them into dramatic relationship with him. Thus the drama is transposed into the life of the Church, within which – and in relation to which – human beings find themselves challenged to have their lives shaped after the pattern of Christ.

On Balthasar's account, the great inclusive drama of Christ's work (whose full ramifications are only to be worked out eschatologically, in the Battle of the Logos)[19] reveals that the yardstick of all truly dramatic action lies in the supra-drama of the trinitarian God of love. But Balthasar's insistence on the fact and continued possibility of transposition shows his conviction that the supra-drama respects the value of the ordinary dramas of human encounter which can point to it, and Balthasar is anxious to hold on to this. The outline of the supra-drama, the measure of all drama, can be traced by the eyes of faith in any giving and rendering back of freedom (of love and obedience; generosity and surrender) between a "Thou" and an "I".

> [The Christian's] faith teaches him to see within the most seemingly unimportant interpersonal relation the making present and the "sacrament" of the eternal I–Thou relation which is the ground of the free Creation and again the reason why God the Father yields His Son to the death of darkness for the salvation of every Thou.[20]

We should pause at this point to consider Balthasar's treatment of the "death of darkness" as signaled in this quotation, because it provides the core of his most original theological reflection. The Son descends into Hell, into the absolute God-forsakenness of the dead. He takes upon himself the fate (not only the substance but the condition) of sinful humanity, drinks its cup to the lees, and so embraces that which is wholly opposed to God – and yet remains God. The exploration of this theological motif, which has rarely attracted much attention, proves surprisingly fruitful. It is a very distinctive development of the concerns of kenotic christology. The kenosis of the Son, for Balthasar, finds its fullest expression precisely in his willingness to take upon himself the whole condition of sinful human nature, in order to "live it round." The full meaning of the burden which he assumes is glimpsed only when we realize that it means the bearing, not only of the pains of dying but of the state of being dead itself. Balthasar draws here on the tradition of Virgil and Dante, more closely on the mystical experience of Adrienne. The passing into the realm of the dead is a passing into the place which is cut off from God, which is beyond hope, where the dead are confronted with the reality of that which is wholly opposed to God. This is the measure then of the Son's obedience to the Father: that he goes into the realm of that which is at enmity with him in order to bring it back under his rule.

And yet it is *God* who enters into the realm of that which is opposed to himself – and he remains God. Such presence of the divine in the God-forsakenness of Hell is possible only on the basis of the trinitarian distinction between the Father and the Son.

> This opposition between God, the creative origin (the "Father"), and the man who, faithful to the mission of the origin, ventures on into ultimate perdition (the "Son"), this bond stretched to breaking point does not break because the same Spirit of absolute love (the "Spirit") informs both the one who sends and the one sent. God causes God to go into abandonment by God while accompanying him on the way with his Spirit.[21]

Balthasar has managed, like Moltmann, to recast the traditional doctrine of the immutability of God in a way that brings out the full trinitarian implications of the death of the Son. But he does not make the doctrine of the divine immutability the object of sustained criticism as a result. This is not his main concern or focus. Rather, as we have seen, he stresses those aspects of the divine sending and the divine obedience which are the loving, inner-trinitarian *supra*-conditions within God's freedom for the suffering into which the Son enters. Christ's action, as Balthasar says, indicates "a drama in the very heart of God."[22] "The dramatic dimension that is part of the definition of the person of Jesus does not belong exclusively to the worldly side of his being: its ultimate presuppositions lie in the divine life itself."[23] So there is not a relation of straightforward similarity between the divine activity and passion and ordinary human change and suffering. The "incomprehensible and unique 'separation' of God from himself" is a supra-event that "*includes* and grounds every other separation – be it never so dark and bitter."[24] It is the highest pitch of the "eternal, absolute self-surrender"[25] which is between Father and Son in the Holy Spirit, and which belongs to God's absolute love.

How is Balthasar's use of analogy at work in all of this? Well, the relation of all human action to the supra-drama of the Christian God is a relation of similarity suspended in ever-greater dissimilarity. Worldly dramas can, of course, give insight into the constitutive receptivity and relationality of human life. But the perfect generosity and perfect obedience (or self-abandonment) which are revealed to us in Jesus Christ speak of a trinitarian self-giving and yet perpetual fullness which are beyond our grasp. No one worldly drama can be adequate to the representation of this truth.

Nevertheless, as we have seen, Balthasar *is* prepared to allow a privileged form of participative, mediating representation of this truth to take shape in the Church, and above all in Mary, in whose will there is no tension with regard to the theodramatic *telos*, no resistance. Her own self-abandonment, though formally dependent on Christ's, is the quality which the human participants in the Theo-Drama are most encouraged to emulate.[26] Her receptivity brings about her fulfillment.

However – as with his position in relation to the status of natural theology in *The Glory of the Lord* – there are ambiguities in Balthasar's thought here. Noel O'Donoghue has pointed out that Balthasar is suspended between conceiving the obedience of faith as pure passivity ("Barthian 'monergism'") and as a creative response to the enabling divine grace (the synergic theology of Scheeben, Adam, Guardini, and Przywara).[27] As Balthasar characterizes it, the response of Mary, the type of the human believer, wavers between these poles, and Balthasar's particular applications of dramatic metaphor do not resolve the ambiguities in any decisive way.

Debate

Balthasar's theology, as we have seen, is biblical and expository. Much of it has been done in and through a sustained engagement with others' work, among them many of his contemporaries in Protestant as well as Catholic theology.

We have seen, for instance, how Balthasar's position is carefully sited between Barth's "*Offenbarungs-positivismus*" (positivism of revelation) on the one hand and traditional Thomist apologetics on the other, especially in relation to Catholic debates about grace and nature. Although Balthasar's desire is not to construct a philosophical or natural theology as a framework around which to erect a "revealed" theology (his position is not grounded in a prior understanding of truth and Being), nevertheless he does not wish to deny all validity to the long history of human search for truth and life outside the Christian faith. His distinctive argument is that the revealed Word is the "apex" inserted into the world *from above*, such that "the revelation of God in Christ and its proclamation is not derivable from the 'base' of cosmic and human nature but can be what it is only as the apex of the base."[28] This is an argument grounded in belief in the identity of the revealed Word and the Creator. Precisely because of this identity, Balthasar maintains, the revelation does not simply cut across the world's attempts to come at the truth but both judges and fulfills them.

Barth was never entirely convinced by this, nor happy with Balthasar's claim, in the preface to the second edition of *The Theology of Karl Barth*, that the dispute between them had been resolved. He remained deeply suspicious of the dangers of a natural theology which would ultimately control a theology of revelation, a suspicion greatly fueled by his battles with theologians like Brunner and Althaus who advocated a doctrine of orders of creation.

Yet Balthasar himself was fully alive to such dangers in the debates he conducted elsewhere. He was to live to see the way in which the opening up of the Church to the world which he and others had fought for could easily lead to the erosion of that which was distinctively Christian. Hence his fierce reaction, notably in *Cordula*,[29] to Rahner's development of the notion of "anonymous Christians." What Balthasar attacked in *Cordula* was Rahner's emphasis on the sense in which men and women are by virtue of their own inherent spiritual dynamism capable of apprehending the divine, of believing, hoping, and loving. If elsewhere Balthasar was sympathetic to Blondel's *méthode de l'immanence*, which attempted to demonstrate from a study of human dynamism the need for divine revelation, he saw in Rahner's identification of such natural spiritual dynamism with the life of faith a fatal blurring of the distinction between men's and women's apprehension of the divine and the divine self-revelation. To speak thus was, in Balthasar's terms, to confuse the natural searching of men and women for the truth with that ultimate vision of God which both fulfills and transcends those intimations of the divine which he had himself treated so sensitively in *The Glory of the Lord: The realm of metaphysics*. It was above all to lose sight of the way in which true Christian belief flourishes as a response to the encounter with the revelation *Gestalt* of Christ. Hence his emphasis on the place of martyrdom and witness in the Christian life.

As Rowan Williams has argued,[30] this debate has deep roots and can be traced back to Balthasar's review of Rahner's much earlier work *Spirit in the World*. There Balthasar warns against the attempt to build a theology simply on a study of the human spirit's transcendence of experience in its judgments and actions. Such a move effectively short-circuits all attempts to perceive the nature of the divine freedom by contemplation of the world of objects. Should we not rather begin by contemplation of the natural tendency of Being to take *form*, by attending, that is, to the way in which the wonderful diversity of created things speaks of the sheer creativity of Being and points us to a source of creativity and freedom beyond Being itself which is God? It is this that kindled the wondering attention, the *thaumazein*, of the myth-makers and the philosophers of antiquity. Analogously, it is as believers contemplate the divine form of the revelation in Christ that their eyes are opened to the grace and majesty of God, and that grace generates new forms of life as it is perceived and obeyed.

It is because of this generative power of Being, as it takes form and is contemplated, that Balthasar insists on the particularity of Christian discipleship and witness, this against Rahner's baptizing of other forms of spiritual life as "anonymous Christianity." Too ready an equation of such forms of life with Christian discipleship would be to lose sight of the heart of the Christian experience of grace, of "being changed into his likeness from one degree of glory to another." Such insistence is not, it should be emphasized, a denial of the spiritual worth or reality of other religious traditions. Nevertheless, Balthasar's emphasis on the dialectic between grace and judgment also obliges him to emphasize the normative character of the revelation form, the sense in which, in its light, all other forms of spirituality are not only affirmed but judged.

In a different field of debate – that of biblical theology and its proper method – it is this same stress on the revelation form and its normative power that makes Balthasar's approach so distinct from that of Bultmann. As we noticed, Balthasar objected first to Bultmann's reduction of the christological and soteriological elements in the New Testament to their sources in first-century mythology, and second to his anthropological reduction of faith to the sightless decision whereby "my" existence is transformed. The combined result of these reductions is that the Christ of faith becomes an incognito Christ grasped only in the *pro me* of "the process of the upturning of all man's natural aims in life."[31] They are two very different kinds of reduction. In the first case we have an *explanatory* reduction whereby, true to the program of the History of Religions School, religious beliefs are explained "out of," that is to say in terms of, their sources in other contemporary – or near contemporary – religious beliefs and systems. In the second we have a *conceptual* reduction: What is being affirmed is that what may have been thought of as statements about the manner of God's action in the world, in certain events in human history, *are really* statements about the manner in which I may experience a change in my existence.

Now it is perfectly true that there is a neat fit between these two reductionisms in Bultmann's historical and theological method. Nevertheless there is a less than adequate acknowledgement in his work of the sense in which he passes from historical exposition of, say, John's Gospel to rational, theological reconstruction of it. What Balthasar wants to affirm is equally two things. First, it is that a proper exposition of such texts must pay due attention, not only to the historical sources of particular doctrines but to the integrity of the synthesis which is achieved by the author when he or she puts such ideas to work. This seems to be a wholly necessary corrective to much of the work which, directly or indirectly, stems from the History of Religions School. The second point is quite different: It is that in reading such texts we should be attempting to see the way in which they mediate to us the revelation-*Gestalt*, in which that is to say there appears in them the divine glory for those who have eyes to see. This is properly contentious. Indeed it is an open question as to whether Bultmann is right in his claim that the only way in which we can understand such texts is insofar as they confront us with an existential decision. He might even be right to rejoin that there is no conceptual reduction involved in reading them in this way; that this was indeed how they were meant to be understood by Paul and John.

To whatever degree Balthasar's *Gestalt* theology is seen as a valuable corrective in the area of biblical study, there remains a question about whether this same *Gestalt* theology can be used too overbearingly by Balthasar to suppress the crucial role of the *maior dissimilitudo* in the context of his analogical framework. Is the *maior dissimilitudo* always strong enough to prevent supra-form or supra-drama from becoming just very large and very comprehensive versions of worldly form and worldly drama? For where similarity is not properly suspended in dissimilarity, seeing things whole can sometimes appear to entail the excessive tidying up of loose ends. In relation to his theological aesthetics, Balthasar's intermittent reliance on metaphors of *harmony* and interweaving *concord*, though qualified, is often read by his interpreters as the unqualified key to his theological vision, and Balthasar himself often fails to take the necessary precautions to defend against such interpretation. Similarly, in relation to his theological dramatic theory, the "shape" which Balthasar imputes to Theo-Drama can seem insufficiently distinct from the famously "shaped" model of drama presented in the dramatic theory of Hegel (whose influence on Balthasar in this area is profound). Balthasar's emphasis on the integrating power of dramatic form (even a theodramatic supra-form) makes it hard for him to distance himself from Hegel's belief that achieving a clear resolution is the one thing of overriding importance in a drama, and that, if necessary, the "pathos" of each individual protagonist must be sacrificed to this end. The theological question that needs to be put both to an aesthetics that is inclined to speak in terms of harmony and a dramatics that is inclined to look for clear resolution, is whether it is proper for any disciple of the Crucified to intuit such things too readily.[32]

The inclination to see clear resolution is linked with the Marian dimension of Balthasar's theology. Balthasar writes that "[t]o the extent that the Church is Marian, she is a pure form which is immediately legible and comprehensible."[33] This Marian form of the Church, which includes the ecclesial constellation of saints and their exemplary interrelations,[34] seems to intrude into the area of the *maior dissimilitudo* by means of a privileged mediation of the supra-form. Marian self-abandonment (echoing the Hegelian call for a sacrifice of the individual "pathos") stands as the analogical counterpart of divine self-giving or kenosis, and archetypally represents the human role in Theo-Drama. But does this analogy (between Marian self-abandonment and divine self-giving) become too uncritical and too unreserved a mediation between divine and creaturely action? If the unbridgeable difference between human forms of action (in this case, primarily, obedience) and the divine "forms" of which they are analogues is to be *maintained* as unbridgeable, then the divine presence in the drama must be depicted as having the power to judge and to break any attempt to pattern (or find a still center for) the divine–human relation, even when it is Mary alone who occupies this place. The relation is necessarily contingent (which is to say, dependent only upon the sovereign freedom of the God who approaches). All analogical apprehensions of this relation are strictly provisional. This is a question about the legitimacy of a theology of what Balthasar calls the *Ecclesia Immaculata*, as focused in Mary, and is another manifestation of the Barthian challenge to analogy.

Despite any such challenge, Balthasar rests a lot of theological weight on the analogy between Marian receptivity and divine kenosis, and one realizes that beneath this analogy there lies a further (and equally suspect) typology of what constitutes the male–female relation, whose suitability as an analogue of the Creator–creature relation may need more critical caution to be applied than is apparently the case. Here, too, a notion of "form" plays too readily into the hands of an over-resolved patterning of "types," which suppresses the provisionality that ought to accompany our sense of the *maior dissimilitudo*, as when Balthasar states that "the active potency of the bearing, giving birth, and nourishing female organism . . . makes the creature as such appear essentially female over against the creating God."[35]

Meanwhile, Balthasar orders a more extended typology of saints around the Marian archetype, in which, for instance, John (with Mary) represents "love," Peter "office," and Paul and James alongside them make up a fourfold structure on which the Church and its theology rest.[36] While consonant with the trends of Balthasar's more general approach to Scripture, this is a manifestation of *Gestalt* theology which depends on some decidedly idiosyncratic interpretations of biblical passages. The fact, for example, that Peter and John run together to the tomb of Jesus is taken as evidence of the birth of "a Church with two poles: the Church of office and the Church of love, with a harmonious [!] tension between them."[37]

It must be acknowledged that Balthasar attempts to counterbalance his theology of the *Ecclesia Immaculata* with a powerful recognition of the marred and sinful aspects of the Church: the wound of the Reformation, the division from Israel, the atrocities and corruptions of the Church's history.[38] This more tragic vision should not be underestimated in his theology. In conjunction with his theology of Holy Saturday, it expresses an acute sensitivity to the concrete reality of death, of betrayal, and of the weight and consequence of sin. Balthasar clearly resists anything like a Barthian doctrine of the unreality of evil.[39] His outlook owes itself at least in part to the contribution that Adrienne von Speyr's mystical experience of Hell (documented most notably in *Kreuz und Hölle*) has made to his theology. Indeed, it can be argued that his distinctive development of the theology of divine kenosis (as found in the witness of Paul and, even more notably, John) to include a concentrated meditation on Hell is undertaken precisely to emphasize the fact that, unless the divine act of salvation embraces the reality of Hell, there remains that of human evil which is for ever past redemption.

This emphasis helps explain Donald MacKinnon's admiration for Balthasar. MacKinnon wrote that it is a test of any contemporary theology that it should refuse to turn aside from the overwhelming, pervasive reality of evil, which was manifested in the deliberate murder of six million Jews in the years between 1933 and 1945. In Balthasar's meditations on Holy Saturday, and also on the Stations of the Cross,[40] he wrestles with the enormity of that history and the ultimate question of its redemption. Balthasar, for MacKinnon, shows signs of that "remorseless emphasis on the concrete"[41] which resists all harmonious and systematizing visions of worldly relationship to the divine purpose.

Yet subsequent commentators have questioned quite how remorseless this emphasis on the concrete really is. For Balthasar's emphasis on the *triduum mortis* (three days of death) and specifically the *descensus* (descent into Hell) is most concrete at the point at which it is also most mythological. It seems to divert attention from the struggles and sufferings that characterize the social and material aspects of human history, and to demonstrate an avoidance of the structural and political aspects of sin, in favor of a realm in which the trinitarian relations are acted out for us and for our salvation *beyond* or *outside* historical time. This has led Gerard O'Hanlon to remark that "[f]rom one who is so conscious of the reality of evil there is a curious lack of engagement with the great modern structural evils."[42]

Achievement and Agenda

Balthasar seeks less to analyze and to systematize his theology on the basis of rational, natural theological argument than to give creative, imaginative expression to Christian truth. The task he has set himself is to articulate a vision of the Christian mystery which draws on the great riches of the Christian tradition as it comes again to life in the meditations of Adrienne, but which above all is rooted and grounded in the language and imagery of the Bible. His achievement is to hold together his love of European culture and letters, his searching study of Scripture and tradition, his debt to Adrienne's mysticism, and his own sense of vocation in developing with Adrienne the work of the secular institute, and to make of them something that is without doubt church theology. The intellectual rigor of his work is joined to the fact that his is self-confessedly a theology done "kneeling":[43] a theology with its roots in meditation and prayer.

Balthasar's comprehensive vision of the Christian mystery bequeathes to those who come after him the perennial task of any church theology: How, as someone who is set in a particular time and culture, to create a theology which is truly catholic, truly universal? Balthasar's context is clearly a fundamental influence in his theology, though it is a context very different from that of the church theologians in Latin America, southern Africa, and elsewhere; and different again from the academic context to which much Western theology has had to answer. Yet Balthasar clearly believes that in the measure that one is obedient to the particular vocation that one receives – whatever the context – one is drawn into the paschal mystery and enabled to see the glory of the Lord: And it is this vision which enables one in turn to see the world, with all its *grandeurs et misères*, as never without grace, though always in need of reconciliation and transformation. Catholic in this sense means perceiving the inexhaustible fullness of the revealed glory, not reducing or foreshortening it. It means then constantly working to recover those aspects of the tradition which have been lost and obscured. And it means ever greater openness to the world, to its beauties and consolations, its terrors and *longueurs*. In this sense the task of theology is never done. It needs constantly to battle against the tendency to foreclose: to absolutize its own particularities.

We have seen that Balthasar's theology of an enrapturing, dramatic, and eventful trinitarian God has the resources to sustain such openness. Indeed, as O'Hanlon has intimated, it has the resources for its own development beyond the realms of art, music, drama, and philosophy, perhaps in order to engage with the realms of economics and politics as well (if such a development is left as a latent potentiality by Balthasar himself then it can be part of the task taken up by those who follow him). As Balthasar depicts them, the central mysteries of the cross and resurrection, of the bearing and overcoming of human enmity by the Lord of glory, claim and challenge all theologies in every context, from the theologies of revolutionary Latin America to those of the Western universities. And for as long as this divine drama exerts its claim, Balthasar's meditations will have strange and compelling insights to offer.

Notes

1 Balthasar, "In Retrospect," in *The Analogy of Beauty*, ed. J. Riches, p. 220.
2 Ibid., p. 204.
3 Ibid.
4 "Supra-" is a translation of the German prefix "*Über-*," which is used with great

frequency in Balthasar's work. As an example of its use, see *The Glory of the Lord*, vol. I, p. 602.

5 Balthasar, "Analogie und Dialektik," in *Divus Thomas*, 22 (1944), p. 196; cited in Medard Kehl, "Hans Urs von Balthasar: A portrait," in *The Von Balthasar Reader*, ed. Medard Kehl and Werner Löser (Edinburgh, 1982), p. 23.

6 Ibid., p. 176; cited in Kehl, "Hans Urs von Balthasar," p. 21.

7 Cf. Balthasar, *The Glory of the Lord*, vol. I, p. 253.

8 Ibid., pp. 44ff., 52, 56.

9 See, for example, Balthasar's essay in *Elucidations*, "A Verse of Matthias Claudius."

10 Kehl and Löser, *The Von Balthasar Reader*, p. 261; taken from Balthasar, *Neue Klarstellungen* (Einsiedeln, 1979).

11 See Balthasar's own study in *The Glory of the Lord*, vol. III.

12 Riches, *The Analogy of Beauty*, p. 220.

13 Balthasar, *The Glory of the Lord*, vol. I, pp. 45–79.

14 Vols 4 and 5 of *The Glory of the Lord* trace the fate of the perception of Being (in its openness to divine glory) through the whole history of Western metaphysics, ancient and modern. The story of modern metaphysics as Balthasar tells it is a story about the danger (exemplified by Hegel) of closing off the realm of the sovereign transcendence in the light of which alone Being can be perceived for what it is (the gift of God).

15 Balthasar, *Theo-Drama*, vol. II, pp. 54–62.

16 Balthasar, *Theo-Drama*, vol. III, p. 149.

17 Balthasar, *Spouse of the Word: Explorations in theology II* (San Francisco, 1991), p. 53.

18 Balthasar, *Theo-Drama*, vol. II, p. 268.

19 Cf. Balthasar, *Theo-Drama*, vol. IV.

20 Balthasar, *The Glory of the Lord*, vol. V, p. 649.

21 Balthasar, *Elucidations*, p. 51.

22 Balthasar, *Theo-Drama*, vol. III, p. 119.

23 Ibid., p. 159.

24 Ibid., p. 325.

25 Balthasar, *Theo-Drama*, vol. IV, p. 323.

26 Cf., for instance, the ideal of creaturely cooperation as presented in Balthasar, *The Glory of the Lord*, vol. V, p. 105, and its exemplification in Mary (e.g., in Balthasar, *First Glance at Adrienne von Speyr*, p. 52).

27 Riches, *The Analogy of Beauty*, p. 4.

28 Balthasar, "Christlicher Universalismus," in *Verbum Caro* (Einsiedeln, 1960), p. 262.

29 English translation *The Moment of Christian Witness*.

30 Riches, *The Analogy of Beauty*, pp. 19ff.

31 R. Bultmann, *The Gospel of John* (Oxford, 1971), p. 69.

32 For an example of the tendency to see clear resolution in drama, see Balthasar on Shakespeare in *Theo-Drama*, vol. I, p. 478. It is questionable whether the darker ambiguities of this most subtle of playwrights allow one to say with Balthasar that "all the time he is utterly certain that the highest good is to be found in forgiveness."

33 Balthasar, *The Glory of the Lord*, vol. I, p. 562.

34 Cf. Balthasar's speculations about the quasi-mathematical structure of the communion of saints and its capacity to configure the fullness of the Church's sanctity in *First Glance*, pp. 82–5.

35 Kehl and Löser, *The Von Balthasar Reader*, p. 233; taken from Balthasar, *Neue Klarstellungen*.

36 Cf., for example, Balthasar, *The Glory of the Lord*, vol. VII, p. 111.

37 Balthasar, *Mysterium Paschale*, p. 259.

38 Cf. especially Balthasar, "Tragedy and Christian faith," in *Creator Spirit: Explorations in theology III* (San Francisco, 1994).

39 Balthasar, "Christlicher Universalismus," p. 269.

40 Balthasar, *The Way of the Cross*.

41 Riches, *The Analogy of Beauty*, p. 167.

42 O'Hanlon, "Theological dramatics," in *The Beauty of Christ: An introduction to the theology of Hans Urs von Balthasar*, p. 109.

43 Jakob Laubach, "Hans Urs von Balthasar," in *Theologians of Our Time*, ed. Leonhard Reinisch (Notre Dame, IN, 1964), pp. 146–7.

Bibliography

Primary

Balthasar, H. Urs von, *Heart of the World* (San Francisco, 1979; first published 1945).

—— *The Theology of Karl Barth* (San Francisco, 1992; first published 1951).

—— *A Theology of History* (New York, 1963; first published 1959).

—— *The Glory of the Lord*, 7 vols (Edinburgh, 1982–91; first published 1961–9).

—— *Love Alone: The way of revelation* (London, 1968; first published 1963).

—— *The Way of the Cross* (London, 1969; first published 1964).

—— *The Moment of Christian Witness* (New York, 1968; first published 1966).

—— *First Glance at Adrienne von Speyr* (San Francisco, 1981; first published 1968).

—— *Mysterium Paschale* (Edinburgh, 1990; first published 1970).

—— *Elucidations* (London, 1975; first published 1971).

—— *Theo-Drama*, 5 vols (San Francisco, 1988– ; first published 1973–83).

—— *The Christian State of Life* (San Francisco, 1984; first published 1977).

Secondary

McGregor, B. and Norris, T. (eds), *The Beauty of Christ: An introduction to the theology of Hans Urs von Balthasar* (Edinburgh, 1994).

Oakes, E. T., *Pattern of Redemption: The theology of Hans Urs von Balthasar* (New York, 1994).

O'Donnell, J., *Hans Urs von Balthasar* (London, 1992).

O'Hanlon, G. F., *The Immutability of God in the Theology of Hans Urs von Balthasar* (Cambridge, 1990).

Riches, J. (ed.), *The Analogy of Beauty: The theology of Hans Urs von Balthasar* (Edinburgh, 1986).

Edward Schillebeeckx

Robert J. Schreiter, CPPS

Introduction

The Flemish Dominican Edward Schillebeeckx may certainly be described as a genuinely twentieth-century theologian. He was born at the time of the outbreak of the First World War, and his career and thought have been shaped by events and movements typical of the twentieth century. Moreover, his continuing preoccupation as a theologian has been the expression of the gospel and Christian tradition in categories intelligible to twentieth-century Western Christians. His first published articles in 1945 dealt with the challenge of humanism to belief in postwar France, and his concern since the latter 1980s has been for defining how people experience the salvation coming from God in Jesus Christ in their personal lives and in their societies.

Schillebeeckx was born on November 12, 1914, the sixth of 14 children, to a middle-class accountant and his wife in Antwerp. The family had been evacuated to Antwerp from their home in Kortenberg before the advancing German army. After the war, they returned there. Schillebeeckx received his secondary education at a Jesuit boarding school in Turnhout. Upon leaving school, he entered the Dominican Order at Ghent in 1934. His philosophical and theological training for ordination took place at the Dominican house of studies in Louvain, where he came under the influence of Dominicus De Petter, a philosopher who combined the Neo-Thomism of the day with an interest in contemporary phenomenology. Schillebeeckx was mobilized briefly at the beginning of the war, but then returned to Louvain and was ordained a priest in 1941. His superiors appointed him to teach dogmatic theology to the seminarians, since the outbreak of the Second World War made the continuing of his theological education impossible.

After the war he was sent to Paris to study at the Dominican faculty Le Saulchoir, working especially with Yves Congar and M.-D. Chenu. He also attended lectures at other major institutions in Paris, and met Camus and Merleau-Ponty. In Paris, he was schooled in the *nouvelle théologie* with its emphasis on historical research as a counterbalance to the deductive and propositional approach to theology still prevalent in the scholasticism of the time. The discussions about existentialism and personalism also influenced him profoundly.

He returned to Louvain in 1947 and completed his dissertation, a patristic and medieval study of the sacraments as a basis for a renewed understanding of them, in 1951. It is now seen as a major study in that area, but its publication only in Dutch limited its circulation.

In 1957 Schillebeeckx was called to the chair of dogma and the history of theology at the University of Nijmegen in the Netherlands, a position he was to hold until his retirement in 1983. He quickly came into prominence as an advisor to the Dutch bishops, and accompanied them as their advisor to the Second Vatican Council. He was denied the status of *peritus* to the Council by the Roman Curia (the Dutch were already suspect at that time), but exercised influence through the theological lectures he gave outside the sessions to the bishops. Through this he gained international attention. Schillebeeckx has been closely identified with the reform movement inaugurated by the Second Vatican Council since that time. In 1965 he launched, along with others, the journal *Concilium* as a forum for continuing the dialogue which had been begun at the Council.

His first trip to the United States came immediately after the Council, and this experience coincided with a decided change in the style of his theology. Before this he had been concerned especially with the sacraments; now he moved into larger issues of Church and world. To deal with these more adequately, he schooled himself extensively in Heideggerian hermeneutics, Anglo-American philosophy of language, and the social critical theory of the Frankfurt School.

Schillebeeckx's career has been marked by honors as well as challenges to his thought. He has received honorary doctorates from universities in the United States and Europe, and is the only theologian ever to have won the Erasmus Prize for promoting European culture. He also won the quinquennial prize of the Flemish Council of Culture in 1979. He has come into conflict with the officials of his Church: In 1968, 1976, and 1981, the Vatican Congregation of the Doctrine of the Faith raised questions about his orthodoxy. All three occasioned protracted exchanges, but none has resulted in a condemnation of any part of his theology.

Survey

An abiding interest of Schillebeeckx throughout his career has been how the Church relates to the world. He had originally hoped to write his doctoral dissertation in this area, but more pragmatic considerations led to a work on the sacraments. In the first part of his career, from the time of the completion of the dissertation until the end of the Vatican Council, the "Church" part of the equation received primary attention. Central to this was the appearance in 1957 of his *Christ the Sacrament of the Encounter with God* (translated into English in 1963). In this work, Schillebeeckx developed a more personalist and existentialist approach to the sacraments, seeing them as a personal encounter with Christ, the primordial sacrament of God. His intent was to move away from the more mechanistic models for approaching sacraments and grace which had dominated scholastic theology. Following that book, he prepared a long study on marriage, published as *Marriage: Human reality and saving mystery* in 1963. Later, too, came a study on the eucharist (*The Eucharist*, 1967). His theological essays from this period reflect a common tone and style; questions are discussed within the framework of the renewed Thomist theology of the time, but those discussions are enriched with insights flowing from contemporary philosophy, especially phenomenology and existentialism.

The experience of a wider world during and after the Council led to a change both in style and in content in Schillebeeckx's writings. His work from that period onward relied little on scholastic vocabulary and showed the greater influence of contemporary philosophy. One of the things that has made Schillebeeckx's thought difficult for some readers has been the wide range of philosophical traditions he draws upon to frame his theology. Prior to 1965, one had to understand something of Thomism, phenomenology, French existentialism, and personalism to follow his thought. All these influences were still present after 1965, albeit in a minor key, but they were joined by the hermeneutical work of Hans Georg Gadamer, research into the philosophy of language by Ian Ramsey and Ludwig Wittgenstein, and the social critical theory of Max Horkheimer and Jürgen Habermas – to name only the major figures. No twentieth-century theologian (except perhaps Wolfhart Pannenberg) ranges so widely over the philosophical territory.

Schillebeeckx studied these additional figures most intensively in the years 1965–70 (essays on his researches have been collected in *The Understanding of Faith*, 1972; English translation, 1974). This combination of resources continues to shape the philosophical underpinnings of his theology. The thorough philosophical training Schillebeeckx received at the hands of De Petter has given his theology a decided epistemological cast. A number of years ago, Schillebeeckx recalled that he had originally hoped to become a philosopher rather than a theologian, but had acquiesced in the wishes of his superiors in the Order. The concern for philosophical questions remains very much in evidence in his work.

The other element from his background which has shaped his theology throughout his career is the *ressourcement* advocated by the *nouvelle théologie*. His work on marriage in the 1960s, and his work in christology and ministry in the 1970s and 1980s, all bear this clear commitment to exploration of the historical resources for developing a contemporary theology. This has been most widely noted in the first two volumes of the trilogy on christology, *Jesus* (1974; translated 1979) and *Christ* (1977; translated 1980). In these works he attempts (and largely succeeds in presenting) an exhaustive account of New Testament research into Jesus and the early Christian movement. And in the book on ministry (*Ministry*, 1979; reissued in an expanded and revised form as *The Church with a Human Face*, 1985) he explored the first 1,500 years of the history of priesthood in considerable detail.

Schillebeeckx has come to even wider attention through these last two projects, dealing with christology and ministry. In the christology project he has tried to lead contemporary men and women to faith in Christ by allowing them to follow the same path to faith and confession of Christ as did the earliest disciples. He does this through an extensive reconstruction of the life of Jesus and developments in the Jesus movement up to the redaction of the books of the New Testament. The Jesus who emerges is the eschatological prophet announcing the imminent breaking out of the Kingdom of God. He is a figure deeply rooted in an experience of God as *abba*. Already in *Jesus*, but increasingly so in subsequent writings, Schillebeeckx has emphasized the Jewishness and Jewish context of Jesus. Jesus' message was the "praxis of the Kingdom of God," i.e., both Jesus' words and his actions point to what the Kingdom of God will be like.

The second volume, *Christ*, moves especially to a soteriological focus in the christology, exploring how salvation is experienced by those who follow Christ. After an introductory reflection on experience and how it relates to revelation, Schillebeeckx explores the New Testament understanding of grace. Toward the end of the volume he turns especially to the social dimensions of salvation in the world, and develops outlines of a social ethics.

The Jesus who emerges from the first two volumes can be summed up in a favorite formulation of Schillebeeckx, Jesus as "the parable of God and the paradigm of humanity." Who Jesus is and who God is cannot be captured in propositions. One must tell the story of Jesus and live out that story in one's own life, following the praxis of Jesus, to come to know the God to whom Jesus witnesses. Jesus' life, as a parable of God, becomes for us the clearest revelation of the reality of God. Likewise, Jesus' praxis becomes paradigmatic for the achievement of our own humanity. Schillebeeckx is much preoccupied with the suffering taking place in the world. Humanity is a state toward which we aim. The struggle for the *humanum* (the term is Horkheimer's) means that we anticipate our fullness; we do not now participate in it. This insight was first developed in Schillebeeckx's reflections on eschatology in the late 1960s, and has remained part of his thought to this day.

The third volume of the christology took a slightly different direction from what had been planned. Entitled *Church: The human face of God* (1989, English translation 1990), it represents Schillebeeckx's articulation of the heart of the Gospel and of Christian faith. As such, it is a compendium of his thought on revelation and experience, God, Christ, and the Church.

The work on ministry grows out of a pastoral concern created by the shortage of priests, a shortage which is depriving communities of the eucharist. Schillebeeckx's basic argument is that Christian communities have a right to the eucharist, and if present ordination requirements deprive believers of realizing that right, then that right has priority over the requirements. This has been widely misinterpreted (even in Rome) as Schillebeeckx's advocating eucharistic presidency by the non-ordained. His point has been that eligibility for ordination to priesthood should be expanded, and that emergency situations may have to be dealt with in the interim (as was the case at earlier moments in history). He supports his case with an extensive historical study, showing that there was a significant strand in the first millennium of Christianity that placed the needs of the community before the exigencies of church order. He pleads for a reconsideration of this part of the tradition as a way out of the current impasse about the shortage of priests.

Content

The thought of a theologian who has been active for 40 years with more than 400 works published in fourteen languages is not described easily. It was noted above that the relation of the Church to the world has been a continuing preoccupation of Schillebeeckx. Yet he has not written a major work on ecclesiology nor a treatise of any length on the Christian understanding of the world. Rather, the Church–world problematic has been the arena in which many themes have been played out: how the sacramental life of the Church relates to the broader situation, the meaning of salvation in a secularized society, the role of eschatology in understanding human history, and how Christians should conduct themselves in light of the gospel.

It is possible, though, to delineate three insights which weave through the fabric of his thought and give it a coherence through the many themes Schillebeeckx has treated in the course of his career. These insights have to do with the role of experience in belief, the place of suffering in history, and the unbounded love of God.

For Schillebeeckx, human experience is not to be contrasted with divine revelation; it is the vehicle through which such revelation is communicated. Experience is understood here as wider than rationality or even language. It encompasses the full range of human perceptions and activities, and also embraces events. All revelation is mediated to us through the channels of our experience. This does not reduce revelation to another category of our experience, however. Schillebeeckx is at pains to point out that revelation offers its critique of our experience and ends up standing in a dialectical relationship to it. But by putting the discussion of revelation within the context of human experience, Schillebeeckx is able to open up the understanding of revelation as being more than words or propositions. It also allows him to lay the groundwork for showing how events can be revelatory. All of these revelatory experiences come to be mediated by language but are never exhausted by language and concepts.

The root of this insight can be found in Schillebeeckx's early work with De Petter. Like other Thomists of the time, De Petter struggled with how to link reality and concepts in light of Kant's *Critique*. De Petter's response came by way of the influence of phenomenology: We make the link between reality and language by an intuition based on an act of faith. By stressing intuition, De Petter moved beyond the rationalist impasse which dogged so much of the neo-Thomism of that time, but he did so without falling into the voluntarist abyss. Intuition seemed a category that could respect and include the complexity of the perceptual and cognitive processes yet transcend the mind–will dichotomy.

How does this work itself out in Schillebeeckx's own thought? First of all, it is evident in his deep reverence for the nature of experience and especially that which is experienced. From his early writings, Schillebeeckx has emphasized how experience ultimately cannot be captured in concepts and rationality, however much concepts and rationality are keys to understanding experience. A favorite word of his for describing that before which humans stand is "mystery." Mystery is used in the double sense of the unknown and also of the Greek *mysterion*, a path to knowledge that transforms the subject who undertakes it.

This reverence is fundamental for his understanding of God, and the language he employs about the encounter with Christ in the sacraments. It also appears in his eschatology with its emphasis on God's proviso, i.e., that God is still the ultimate transformer in the face of all human efforts to bring about justice and a more humane society. It is especially evident in the perspectival approach that runs through his theology: Every perspective contributes to our understanding, but no human perspective can claim absoluteness. Because of that he has been drawn to employ a wide variety of different philosophical frameworks to interpret Christian history and experience. It has also led him to relativize the place of the Church in the world when seen in light of the Kingdom of God. This profound sense of the perspectival character of knowledge was a major sticking point in his conflict with the Roman Curia over his christology: They misunderstood his denial of any absolute language as a denial of Nicaea and Chalcedon.

Another major consequence of placing experience so centrally in his thought is a commitment to the concreteness of history. "Concrete" is one of Schillebeeckx's most used adjectives. It was concrete experiences in his environment which led to the little books on the eucharist, clerical celibacy, and ministry: People's experiences seemed to be contradicting Church teaching and discipline. It has also led to his formulation of "orthopraxis" as a key concept: Rightness of belief must be expressed in a dialectic of theory and action and not just in theory alone.

To commit oneself to the concreteness of history means that one must come face to face with human suffering, sin, and injustice. And this leads to the second fundamental insight in Schillebeeckx's thought. Beginning in the late 1960s, the theme of human suffering emerged as a major motif in his thought. Schillebeeckx speaks of what he calls "contrast experiences," the experience of events falling short of the ideal of human life, the *humanum*. These contrast experiences are the most revelatory of human experiences in that suffering questions all our assumptions about how the world should be. They provide the basis for developing a critical view of the world that does not succumb to one or other ideology, nor to a naively optimistic view of reality that might be deduced from his respect for human experience. That critical view is called by Schillebeeckx at one point a "critical negativity," emphasizing the need to question any promise of fulfillment ideologies might bring.

Because of their revelatory power, the contrast experiences of those who suffer provide a privileged view of the world. The results of that view become the engine for the struggle for justice and a fuller revelation of the *humanum* in the world. This struggle is joined by all who share these sentiments; it is how Schillebeeckx explains the ability of differing ideologies to work together for the common good of humanity. The *humanum* has not yet been realized; it will be revealed in the coming of the Kingdom of God when that paradigm of humanity, Jesus Christ, is once again among us.

The contrast experience is expressed most acutely in the life and death of Jesus. Jesus went about doing good, yet came to an untimely and violent end. Thus for a Christian to turn to the contrast experience as the basis for critical thought and critical action has its roots in the contrast experience of Jesus.

Reflection on human suffering has led to a greater concentration in Schillebeeckx's later work on the meaning of salvation. He wishes to explore more closely what impact the presence of God has on the suffering world. This leads to the third fundamental insight moving through Schillebeeckx's work.

Throughout his theology, Schillebeeckx emphasizes the primacy of God in all things. Even as his theology has become more anthropological (but not reduced to

157

an anthropology) he has stressed at the same time the importance of maintaining the mystery of God and the sovereignty of God's activity in human history. God is not a human projection. But that sovereign God is also a loving God, a "God mindful of humanity," a phrase that appears often in *Christ* and in later works. This is the God of unbounded love, who has made humanity's cause a divine cause. God wishes the "well-being of humanity," to use another of Schillebeeckx's favorite phrases. Schillebeeckx never tires in his later works of emphasizing how close God is to humanity's struggles and sufferings. Jesus, of course, in his ministry and death, is a parable of that closeness. God is present to us in a "mediated immediacy," i.e., mediated through human history and through creation in such a way as to be made immediate or directly present. This says something about God and about God's creation. God uses the medium of creation and history to be more present to humanity rather than employing it as a barrier to that presence. This implies that creation is an adequate, though not comprehensive, vehicle for divinity. It is this conviction which has not only permitted Schillebeeckx to take human experience seriously, but also allowed a closer connection between communion with God and action for the world, areas Schillebeeckx designates as the mystical and the political. Christians are called to a "political holiness" that does not separate the inner life of prayer from the worldly liturgy of betterment of humanity's cause.

The three insights, then, depend on one another: Experience is grounded in a God who wishes to communicate, the contrast experiences draw us closer to that God, and the experience of God "mindful of humanity" affirms that act of intuition and faith by making a mediation of the paradoxical experience of the immediate. In doing this, Schillebeeckx achieves a great deal in his hope of making the Christian message of God and the experience of salvation offered in Jesus Christ more available to a secularized society.

Debate

A theologian who has written as widely and as creatively as Schillebeeckx is bound to find himself in controversial areas. His position on experience and its role in theology has been perhaps the most controversial of his positions, although it has usually met questioning on one or other specific point rather than on the entire project. Protestants often hear nineteenth-century liberalism when Schillebeeckx begins to speak of experience. That movement (especially as represented in the Erlangen School) ended up succumbing to the culture and diluting the gospel message by its uncritical acceptance of contemporary experience as the frame of reference for theological discourse. Schillebeeckx is well aware of this tradition and would emphasize the critical edge in his theory of experience, represented especially in his understanding of critical negativity.

From the Roman Catholic side, the emphasis on experience seems to undermine authority and some doctrinal formulations. The Vatican Congregation's objections to Schillebeeckx's christology centered on this concern: Must certain things not be maintained dogmatically rather than subjected to the test of experience? His attempt to understand the resurrection faith of the first disciples by proposing how their experience of the Lord was shaped has seemed to some to reduce the event of the resurrection to one interpretation among many. And Schillebeeckx's accentuation of the pneumatological tradition in the development of Church ministry seemed to undermine the dominant christological tradition that sees the priest as the *alter Christus* ruling the community.

Schillebeeckx has responded to challenges of this type by noting the importance of linguistic analysis of formulations, and by reminding his opponents of what it means to take history seriously. One cannot profess being historical in orientation if history must give way to dogmatic statement whenever the situation becomes slightly problematical. This was most evident in the conflict over his book on ministry. There some opponents insisted upon a dogmatic formulation about the origins of ministry – that Christ intended a certain form of ministry for the community and instituted it in that fashion – as the point of departure for reading the historical data, when exegetes have long questioned such a formulation as historical.

But all of this does raise an important issue: What indeed is the relation between history and dogma? History is always informed by theory and interpretive frameworks, and so does not in itself occupy a higher ground than dogma. Schillebeeckx has not answered this thorny question to the satisfaction of his opponents.

In another area of debate, theologians have objected that his *Jesus* and *Christ* are not a christology – they do not deal adequately with the classical questions in this area. Exegetes, on the other hand, have generally applauded his use of their research into the New Testament as an instance of a theologian actually paying attention to what is happening in the exegetical field. The latter do object to some of his interpretations (notably on his use of the Q source, his understanding of the *abba* experience, and aspects of his treatment of the resurrection), but on the whole they have been more supportive of his project than many of his colleagues. Schillebeeckx has responded that his critics are reproving him for a book he has not yet written. *Jesus* and *Christ* are intended as prolegomena to a christology, not the christology itself. What Schillebeeckx has written may appear to call into question how christology as an area in theology is to be organized, but it is difficult to assess to what extent those fears are warranted.

One other area where his project has met criticism is in his use of the concept of praxis. He does not always seem to be consistent here, at times equating praxis only with action rather than the theory–action dialectic. Nor has he worked out in a level of detail satisfactory to some of his critics what he actually means by praxis and by orthopraxis.

On the whole, however, Schillebeeckx's work has been received with great seriousness. The historical depth of his work is widely appreciated, and his attempts to articulate Christian faith in frameworks intelligible to contemporary men and women have gained him a wide readership among theologians and Christians in general.

Achievement and Agenda

It is dangerous to assess the achievement of a theologian who is still alive and quite active, but certain features of the theology of Edward Schillebeeckx suggest aspects of enduring achievement, whatever may still come from his pen. He has proposed, particularly in his work since the 1960s, a kind of modern apologia for Christian faith. This apologia is not of a polemical variety that tries to demonstrate the validity of the Christian faith in the face of an indifferent or hostile secularism. Nor does it address itself primarily to the nonbeliever in the hope of bringing about a conversion. This apologetic is aimed at those who struggle to believe, who strive to be faithful to the gospel and its Lord in a world that cannot immediately make sense of the Christian message in its traditional formulation. That has been the clear intent behind the monumental christology project. As he said in his defense of that project before the Vatican Congregation, he saw his christology not so much as providing the crisp answers believers are supposed to have as a *vade mecum* in their own journey toward their confession of Christ. There is an intent on Schillebeeckx's part to walk with the struggling believer. This accounts in some measure for the style of his writing, which often looks as though it is a transcription from an oral medium where he is trying to explain – often passionately – his point of view. The long, sometimes meandering sentences are attempts to gather in the many perspectives that are needed to see a complex picture fully.

As a theologian, Schillebeeckx has made a significant contribution in showing how he and his colleagues should utilize the results of biblical exegesis. This is an area still not explored as it might be by theologians, who often continue to adhere to biblical positions long since abandoned by their exegetical colleagues.

As a theologian, too, Schillebeeckx's use of a wide range of philosophical hermeneutical systems is a contribution to the field. He has been a leader in emphasizing the importance of epistemological and interpretive categories in Roman Catholic theology. He still intends to prepare a systematic treatise on this area after completion of the christology project.

And for the general believer, especially the Roman Catholic, his achievement has been to allow them to take their own experience of faith more seriously. This was especially evident in the outpouring of sentiment at the time of his difficulties with Rome in the late 1970s. A recurring motif in the correspondence he received was that people appreciated how he had liberated them to think more for themselves and not to dismiss their own experience of God outright when it seemed to be contradicting official formulations. To the extent that this is the case, Schillebeeckx is achieving his project of bringing Church and world into closer conversation with each other.

Bibliography

Primary

Schillebeeckx, E., *Christ the Sacrament of the Encounter with God* (London and New York, 1963).

—— *God the Future of Man* (London and New York, 1968).

—— *The Understanding of Faith* (London and New York, 1974).

—— *Jesus: An experiment in christology* (London and New York, 1979).

—— *Christ: The experience of Jesus as Lord* (London and New York, 1980).

—— *Ministry: Leadership in the community of Jesus Christ* (subtitled in the UK *A case for change*) (London and New York, 1981).

—— *The Church with a Human Face: A new and expanded theology of ministry* (London and New York, 1986).

—— *Church: The human story of God* (London and New York, 1990).

—— *The Schillebeeckx Reader*, ed. Robert J. Schreiter (New York, 1984, and Edinburgh, 1988). Contains a complete bibliography of Edward Schillebeeckx to 1983.

Secondary

Bowden, John, *Edward Schillebeeckx: Portrait of a theologian* (London and New York, 1983).

Kennedy, Philip, *Schillebeeckx* (London and Collegeville, MN, 1993).

Schreiter, Robert and Hilkert, Mary Catherine (eds), *The Praxis of Christian Experience: An orientation to Edward Schillebeeckx* (San Francisco, 1989).

Hans Küng

Werner G. Jeanrond

Introduction: Life and Influences

Hans Küng is a unique phenomenon in twentieth-century theology: No other theologian has been published, translated, and read so widely in this century; no other theologian has been the focus of such a major controversy; no other contemporary theologian has covered such a broad spectrum of theological themes. Virtually all important theological topics discussed in our time have been addressed by Küng at some stage in his career. His bibliography includes major works on God, Jesus Christ, the Church, eternal life, the Christian tradition, theological method, world religions, global responsibility, and the contribution of the arts to religion. Yet it was Küng's challenge to post-Vatican II ecclesiology and Church management which brought him into lasting conflict with the authorities of his Roman Catholic Church. One effect of this controversy has been that Küng's contribution to modern theology has sometimes been perceived to be of a mainly ecclesiological nature and that his other achievements in theology have not been adequately appreciated. Moreover, the conflict between the Roman Catholic priest Küng and some of the members of the Roman Catholic episcopate has occasionally concealed Küng's important contribution to his own Church before, during, and since the Second Vatican Council.

In this survey of Küng's theological development it will not be possible to discuss all aspects of his rich contribution to contemporary theology; instead I shall concentrate on his major works, and above all discuss the development of his theological methodology more closely.

Hans Küng was born in 1928 in Sursee, Switzerland. His studies at the Pontifical Gregorian University in Rome (1948–55) brought him not only into intellectual contact with important philosophers and theologians, but also into personal contact with some of the leading theological and ecclesiastical figures of the time, such as Joseph Lortz, Hans Urs von Balthasar, Yves Congar, and Augustinus Bea. After his ordination to the priesthood in Rome, Küng studied in Paris, where he earned his theological doctorate in 1957 with his now famous dissertation on Karl Barth's doctrine of justification. This work and its ecumenical spirit made Küng known very quickly. His active participation in the preparation and his presence at the Second Vatican Council (1962–5) as an officially appointed *peritus* brought Küng to the center of the conflict between reformers and traditionalists in the Roman Catholic Church and directed his theological attention to questions of ecclesiology. At the young age of 32, Küng was appointed to the chair of fundamental theology at the Roman Catholic Faculty of Theology at the University of Tübingen.

Since the 1970s, Küng's theological work has concentrated on the major articles of Christian faith without, however, neglecting the theme of ecclesiology. His public image has been influenced to a large extent by the discussion of his book *Infallible? An Enquiry* (1970).[1] It has been mainly this book and Küng's refusal to revoke the challenge to Roman Catholic Church authority expressed in this book which, after nine years of controversy, led to the withdrawal of Küng's Roman Catholic *missio canonica* (the Roman Catholic teaching permission which every teacher of Roman Catholic Christianity needs in Germany) by Pope John Paul II, and his subsequent move out of his faculty and into the new independent Institute for Ecumenical Research at the University of Tübingen. Thus Küng has been teaching theology in the University, but he is no longer considered an officially authenticated representative of Roman Catholic theology by the Vatican authorities.

Survey of Küng's Theological Development

Küng's theological development to date may be roughly divided into four periods: (1) his concentration on ecclesiological questions until 1970; (2) his treatment of major articles of Christian faith (God, Jesus Christ, and Eternal Life) during the 1970s; (3) his reflection on theological method and the dialogue between Christianity and other world religions and between religion and culture since 1983; and (4) from 1990 onward his two related projects on global responsibility and on the religious situation of our time, which are connected with all his previous concerns.

All these periods are inspired by a strong commitment both to dialogue with all current religious, political, and cultural forces in the world in general and to Christian ecumenism in particular. Küng's commitment to Christian and even global ecumenism must not be confused with a new kind of essentialism, according to which all Christian traditions or even all religious traditions are essentially the same.[2] Rather, Küng wishes to bring Christians of all backgrounds and the different religious traditions of humankind into a mutually critical conversation.

Beginnings in ecclesiology

Already in his first book, *Justification: The doctrine of Karl Barth and a Catholic reflection* (1957), Küng investigated the foundations for such an inner-Christian conversation. He examined the common ground of Protestant and Roman Catholic doctrine on this central aspect of Christian faith which has divided both traditions for centuries. But he remained critical of Barth's "dangerous inclinations," such as his denigration of the ontic-creaturely aspect and his overemphasis on human sinfulness, and the resulting anti-Catholic polemics. Küng's study concluded that on the whole there exists a fundamental theological conformity between what Barth and the Roman Catholic Church teach on justification. This insight shaped Küng's further questioning of how all Christian churches will have to change in order to promote the process of Christian unity and of what especially the Roman Catholic Church ought to be doing in order to respond more adequately to the gospel in a new ecumenical age.

In the 1960s, the Vatican Council inspired all leading Roman Catholic theologians to reflect very thoroughly on the nature and structure of the Christian church. Thus, it need not surprise us that 15 of Küng's first 20 books deal with ecclesiological questions, most prominent among these publications *Structures of the Church* (1962), *The Church* (1967), and *Infallible?* (1970). *Structures of the Church* was written in response to Pope John XXIII's call for a renewed theological concentration on this topic with reference to the Council; *The Church* offered a systematic study of the nature of the Christian church on the basis of modern biblical exegetical knowledge; and *Infallible?* represented a first critical study of the Roman Catholic Church in view of the increasing disenchantment among Catholics' with the slow process of structural renewal in their Church after the Council.

Perhaps Küng's approach to ecclesiology may be best characterized by his insistence on the need for a critical biblical foundation of all ecclesiology and the resulting insight into the essential difference between the church and the Kingdom of God. The church's mission is to serve the gospel of Jesus Christ, to respond to God's call in Christ, but not to produce God's reign. Moreover, God's reign is proclaimed to sinners as good news. Thus the church, itself a community of sinners, is called to preach the good news to the world, but not to rule the world.[3] Like the Reformers in the sixteenth century, Küng retrieved the biblical image of the priesthood of all believers. Christ's community no longer needs a mediation between the people of God and God, it no longer requires a priestly sacrifice of expiation. *All* Christians are called to proclaim God's word. Accordingly, Küng demands that any consideration of offices in the church must be inspired by this New Testament heritage. This heritage rules out the establishment of a clergy–laity divide in the Christian movement. Therefore, Küng criticizes the formalism which has emerged in the post-biblical church, and he calls for a redefinition of ministry in the church as a service of love. This is not to rule out the special services of priests and bishops, rather it is to describe the proper theological basis of such a service.

The question of authority in the Church was to receive yet further prominence in Küng's theological work when, in 1968, Pope Paul VI issued his encyclical *Humanae Vitae* against all forms of artificial birth control. Together with a great many Christians within and beyond the Roman Catholic Church, Küng protested against this encyclical. But he went further and criticized the entire Roman Church system, which he saw "still characterized by a spiritual absolutism, a formal and often inhuman juridicism and a traditionalism fatal to genuine renewal that are truly shocking to modern man."[4] On the basis of his ecclesiological principles, Küng questioned the infallibility of both the Pope and the Roman teaching office, pointed out past errors of both institutions, and described the peculiar context of the First Vatican Council (1869–70) which had formulated the doctrine of papal infallibility. Finally,

Küng proposed a reappraisal of the traditional belief that the Church as a whole is maintained in the truth in spite of the possibility of errors. He also emphasized that there is no formal guarantee that even a council is infallible. "Councils do not have authority over the truth of Christ. They can strive to attain it. It is for this that the Spirit of Christ is promised to the bishops and all participants, as it is also to every Christian."[5]

Although Küng's primary theological attention shifted then to the central theological questions of God and Jesus Christ, he never lowered his commitment to the renewal of the Roman Catholic Church in particular, and the Christian church in general.

Major articles of Christian faith

Küng's turn to christology did not begin with his famous work *On Being a Christian* (1974) as is generally assumed; rather, this turn was already prepared in his less-known work *The Incarnation of God* (1970; translated into English only in 1987). In this work Küng had already pursued the most crucial theological question, namely how God could be encountered in history and how God is related to the process of history. Here Küng also offered a comprehensive introduction to Hegel's philosophy and theology. His main interest in Hegel derived, however, from this thinker's critique of the traditionally static concept of God. Using this critique, Küng wished to explore the foundations of a future christology.

Over against the classical concept of God influenced by Greek metaphysics, Küng – following Hegel – demands a new theological perspective. "Hegel's philosophy begins by teaching us not to separate God from man and ends by teaching us not to confound them."[6] Küng, however, does not follow Hegel's lead all the way. Rather, he reinterprets Hegel's speculative identity between the process of history and God as, in fact, not a totally closed system by pointing out that "[a]t the level of religion – not of philosophy – Hegel himself, for all his unmistakable emphasis on unity, stoutly maintained that there is an ultimate difference."[7] On this basis of both identity and difference between God and the world, Küng sets out his prolegomena for a future christology. He calls for a christology "from below" which is "interested in the Jesus who meets us today, within the horizon of the world, humankind and God, as the challenge to faith which he personally embodies."[8] This renewed concentration on historical Jesus research is not seen by Küng as a means to present Jesus as he really was; rather it is understood as a critical tool which enables the theologian to scrutinize and verify the faith which has been handed down to us.[9]

Thus methodologically prepared, Küng constructed his christology in *On Being a Christian*. As the title of this book already indicates, Küng's primary concern in christology is not a theoretical one; he wishes to establish what it means to respond to Jesus Christ *today*. Therefore he places his christology in the carefully analyzed context of the contemporary challenges presented by both modern humanism and the world religions. In answering the question of what is special to Christianity in this context, Küng states that Christianity must not be equated with everything true, good, beautiful, and humane in this world. "Christianity does not exist wherever inhumanity is opposed and humanity realized . . . Christianity exists only where the meaning of Jesus Christ is activated in theory and practice."[10]

In the main part of this work, Küng examines the dimensions of the Christian program. He discusses Jesus' life and death in the context of religion and culture at the time, Jesus' proclamation of God's cause, and Jesus' own identification with the human cause, the conflict which led to the death of Jesus, and the reactions to his life and death by the emerging Christian communities. The book concludes with reflections upon contemporary Christian praxis in the light of the christological dimensions presented earlier.

As indicated by Küng in *The Incarnation of God*, any adequate theological approach to God will need to examine the relationship between God and human history. Thus it was only appropriate that Küng should treat christology before presenting his thoughts on the concept of God in *Does God Exist?* (1978). The title of this book is somewhat misleading. Küng does not wish to follow the particular tradition of proving whether or not God actually exists. His answer to that question is yes, but in this book he examines the rationality of the Christian belief in God today.

The book takes the reader through the history of the contemporary understanding of God. It analyzes the contribution to this understanding by the atheistic critique, while it demonstrates at the same time that none of the leading atheists (Feuerbach, Marx, Freud, and Nietzsche) would have been able to disprove God's existence, as indeed none of the leading theists would ever be able to prove it. Instead Küng begins with the question of how the modern person relates to reality as such.

Since there is no one absolute standpoint, our perceptions of the world can never be purely objective. Nor is any perception the exclusive product of a lonely subjectivity. Rather when we speak of "reality," we always mean "something that combines and embraces subject and object, consciousness and being, self and world."[11] The decision which every human being faces, then, is a decision between two basic attitudes to reality: fundamental mistrust or fundamental trust. Moreover, this decision is a lifelong task and it concerns all aspects of our living, research, and activity in this world. Although Küng calls for a clear distinction between this "fundamental trust" on the one hand and "faith in God" on the other,[12] he concludes "that the fundamental trust in the identity, meaningfulness and value of reality, which is the presupposition of human science and autonomous ethics, is justified in the last resort only if reality itself – of which man is also a part – is not groundless, unsupported and aimless."[13]

On the basis of these insights, Küng examines the traditional Christian approaches to God. He also notes the increasing interest in the question of God in our time. He forcefully rejects any attempt to divide reality into two spheres, a divine and a human. Rather he insists that God can be assumed "only in a confidence rooted in reality itself."[14] This in turn means: "If someone affirms God, he knows why he can trust reality."[15] Accordingly, there cannot be any outward rationality able to produce an assured security. "There is not first a rational knowledge and then confident acknowledgment of God." But there is an "inward rationality which can offer a fundamental certainty."[16] Moreover, Küng stresses that belief in God must be considered "a matter not only of human reason but of the whole concrete, living man, with mind and body, reason and instinct, in his quite particular historical situation, in his dependence on traditions, authorities, habits of thought, scales of values, with his interests and in his social involvement."[17]

This need to consider the historical and social context of any belief in God brings Küng back to the specific Christian faith in God. After assessing the history of the Jewish and Christian traditions of believing in God, Küng concludes that the biblical faith in God "is in itself coherent, is also rationally justifiable and has proved itself historically over many thousands of years."[18] Finally, the God of the Bible also has a cosmic dimension, that is to say that the history of the entire universe is the area of this God's presence, not only the history of the individual believer. God operates "in the world process: in, with and among human beings and things. He is himself source, center and goal of the world process."[19] It is this God which Jesus of Nazareth proclaimed in his life, death, and resurrection. Here, Küng's theological and christological reflections merge again.

Although Küng had begun his christology and his examination of the rationality of faith in the Jewish–Christian God by analyzing the horizon of the modern person who is searching for meaning, in 1982 he paid particular attention to this search for meaning in every individual life: His book *Eternal Life?* addressed the whole complex of questions related to the human hope for an eternal future. Küng interprets the various Christian eschatological symbols, such as heaven, hell, eternity, and judgment, in the light of the Christian belief in the resurrection of Jesus of Nazareth. "Jesus did not die into nothingness. In death and from death he died into that incomprehensible and comprehensive absolutely final and absolutely first reality, was accepted by that reality, which we designate by the name of God."[20] Thus, to believe in eternal life does not mean hoping to continue living forever. But it does mean "to rely on the fact that I shall one day be fully understood, freed from guilt and definitely accepted and can be myself without fear; that my impenetrable and ambivalent existence, like the profoundly discordant history of humanity as a whole, will one day become finally transparent and the question of the meaning of history one day be finally answered."[21]

This book concludes Küng's second period of theological work. In this period he attempted to address the major aspects of Christian faith and to correlate them critically with his interpretation of the contemporary cultural and intellectual horizon of theology. This outline can only deal with the most significant publications of this period. The interested reader will, however, be amazed at discovering a much greater number of theological publications which deal with other issues of Christian faith, such as liturgy, sacraments, and, of course, the church.

Methodology and dialogue

The third period of Küng's theological work shows two distinct though related moves: (a) Küng's reflection on theological method and (b) his studies of the relationship between Christianity and other world religions, and of the relationship between religion and the arts. Both of these moves are in response to a changed awareness among many contemporary theologians, namely that the world with its plurality of religious and cultural traditions and movements, with its wealth of human insight and scientific knowledge, and with its ambiguous history demands a new paradigm for theology.

Accordingly, in his book *Christianity and the World Religions* (1984), Küng calls for a global understanding of ecumenism. Ecumenism must no longer be limited to an inner-Christian conversation, but it ought to include a conversation between all great religions if *ecumene* is understood in its original sense as the whole inhabited earth.[22] For Christian theology, this implies that the traditional Christian self-understanding marked by exclusivity and superiority must be overcome by an admission that none of us possesses the full truth, and that we are all on the way to an always greater truth. Such an understanding of truth demands, of course, that Christians broaden their knowledge and understanding of the other great religious traditions of humankind. Therefore, in this book Küng presents introductions to Islam, Hinduism, and Buddhism in cooperation with leading historians of religion. Each of these introductions is followed by Küng's response from a Christian perspective. A dialogue with a Jewish scholar had already been published in 1976,[23] and Küng's dialogue with the major Chinese religious traditions appeared in 1988.[24]

The search for a new paradigm of theology demands the close cooperation of scholars of different backgrounds and expertise. Thus, it is characteristic of this third period of Küng's work that many of his publications are produced in cooperation with other scholars: his dialogues with other world religions, his dialogues with literature,[25] and the results of an international conference on the subject matter of the paradigm change in theology.[26] In addition, Küng presented a collection of his reflections on theological method in his book *Theology for the Third Millennium* (1987), to which we shall turn later.

Global responsibility and the religious situation of our time

In the fourth and continuing period of his theological work, methodological reflection on the demands of a postmodern paradigm for theology and experiences in dialogue with the various spheres of human creativity led Küng's attention to the global context of present-day human existence. Here he is concerned to bring together reflections on religious, cultural, social, political, economic, and ecological experiences in a large-scale project, the program for which was outlined in his manifesto *Global Responsibility* (1990, German title *Projekt Weltethos*). The German title clearly indicates the ethical concentration in Küng's thought. His program displays a rather pragmatic orientation linking the Christian approach to the world with a multidimensional interpretation of the present.

Küng's political interest, which previously was expressed only indirectly, now becomes explicit.[27] Human action needs ethical criteria in a global dimension. However, over against this need stand forms of religion which tend to be more provincial. So Küng's reform program makes self-criticism within each religion a presupposition of worldwide inter-religious dialogue. Such self-criticism should also be applied by all non-religious trends of thought which seek to take part in the global quest for a new ethic. The criticism of every ideology becomes the starting point for Küng's ethical manifesto. His various analyses aim at "a holistic view of the world and human beings in their different dimensions. For along with the economic, social and political dimension there is also the aesthetic, ethical and religious dimension of human beings and humanity."[28] However, "holistic" is not to be confused with "uniform." Rather, the postmodern paradigm calls for an affirmation of the overall pluralistic constellation.

The goal and criterion of the new world ethic is the *humanum*: "human beings must become more than they are: They must become more human!"[29] However, the *humanum* only comes really into view when all the dimensions of existence, i.e., the most humane society possible and an intact environment, are also included. Küng rightly stresses that an analysis of the time which brackets out the religious dimension is deficient. In addition he points out that the categorical nature of the ethical claim, the unconditional nature of the "ought," cannot be grounded in human beings, who are conditioned in so many ways, but only in an unconditional: "an Absolute which can provide an over-arching meaning and which embraces and permeates individual, human nature and indeed the whole of human society. That can only be the ultimate, supreme reality, which while it cannot be proved rationally, can be accepted in a rational trust – regardless of how it is named, understood and interpreted in the different religions."[30] In this sense religion within the context of postmodernity receives new opportunities which ought to be explored.

Küng cannot conceive either a survival without a global ethic or a stable world peace without religious peace. However, this presupposes an honest, critical dialogue between the religions, above all one which is based on self-criticism. The criterion of this dialogue remains the truly human, the *humanum*.[31] Such readiness for dialogue, though it must also be coupled with self-critical steadfastness, already furthers the capacity of religion for peace.

This is the point at which Küng's most recent research program begins; he understands it as a necessary complement to his project on global responsibility. His prime concern is to study the religious situation of our time, in order to locate basic insights into the possibility of inter-religious dialogue. Here his aim is, "as far as possible to obtain the view of the whole of a religion . . . However, the whole of a religion shows not only developments, historical sequences and dates but also structures, patterns of believing, thinking, feeling and acting. A religion is a living system of religious convictions, liturgical rites, spiritual practices and institutions of very different kinds, which develop further and which are highly complex."[32] So this research program envisages a multidisciplinary study of religion, in order "to do as much justice as possible to religions like Judaism, Christianity and Islam in their riches, their many levels and their many dimensions."[33] Above all Küng wants to cover the epoch-making shifts in these (and later perhaps other) religions, so that in each case he can identify their various periods and their structures, and offer prognoses.

So far, in his comprehensive studies of *Judaism* (1991) and *Christianity* (1994), Küng has already succeeded in achieving a substantial part of his project on *the religious situation of our time*. A study of Islam will follow soon. Although I cannot go into a detailed discussion of these two monumental studies here, a brief evaluation of these unique works should be attempted.

Judaism is the first major study by a Christian theologian to take Judaism seriously as a living religion and seek to grasp its own development as a whole.[34] The various paradigm shifts in the history of Judaism are clarified without reference being made to the Christian understanding of salvation, as had been customary in 2,000 years of usually hostile Christian studies. Of course, Küng also investigates the tradition of this ideological approach and the annihilation of countless Jews which is at least connected with it, coming to a horrific culmination in the Holocaust and unfortunately still not at an end. Küng's attempt to inform, to develop an understanding of the other religion as other, and thus to perform a service for religious and world peace, sets standards for future dealings with religious movements.

In *Christianity* Küng attempts a comprehensive reading of the major developments within the Christian tradition.[35] His aim is clearly stated at the beginning of the book: Küng undertakes this major critical, historical account of 20 centuries of Christianity in order to establish criteria for a radical reform of Christianity. "Christianity should become more Christian – this is the only possible perspective for the third millennium, too."[36] What he is interested in here "is not the past as such but how and why Christianity became what it is today – with a view to how it could be."[37] Therefore Küng considers the question of the essence of Christianity as of the utmost importance, though he is not naively trying to distill a pure essence once all perversions have been exposed. Rather he states that "the real essence of Christianity comes about in its perversion."[38] Moreover, the essence of Christianity can only be located in changing historical forms. It is neither an eternal idea, nor a dogma, worldview, or principle. At the center of Christianity stands a living figure, Jesus of Nazareth, and the scandal of his cross. Jesus Christ is the basic figure and the basic motif of Christianity. "The name of Jesus Christ, which had already become a proper name in New Testament times, is thus the abidingly valid, constantly obligatory and simply indispensable element in Christianity."[39] Küng stresses many features which Christianity has in common with Judaism and Islam, but he emphasizes also the distinctiveness of Christian faith: "what is distinctively Christian is this Christ himself, who was crucified and yet is alive."[40] And discipleship "distinguishes Christians from other disciples and adherents of great teachers of humankind, in so far as Christians are ultimately directed to this person, not only to his teaching but also to his life, death and new life."[41] In what follows Küng assesses the different forms of Christian discipleship which have emerged throughout Christian history in terms of the adequacy of their response to the center of Christian faith, namely Jesus the Christ. Thus, in *Christianity* Küng deals much more with the development of the Christian movement in history, while in *On Being a Christian* he concentrated on discussing the center of Christian faith exegetically and systematically.

Applying "paradigm" theory as a heuristic instrument, Küng now identifies five paradigms in Christian history: (1) the Jewish apocalyptic paradigm of earliest Christianity; (2) the ecumenical Hellenistic paradigm of Christian antiquity; (3) the Roman Catholic paradigm of the Middle Ages; (4) the Protestant Evangelical paradigm of the Reformation; and (5) the paradigm of modernity, orientated on reason and progress. Küng attempts to identify in each of these paradigmatic constellations of Christian discipleship both authentic and inauthentic developments. His predilection clearly lies with the much neglected theological initiatives of the early Jewish Christian movement within the first paradigm. "Jewish Christian theology is a critical corrective to an all-too-remote christology which is exposed to the dangers of docetism and spiritualization!"[42] Moreover, a reappraisal of early Jewish Christian theology has much to offer to the dialogue between Christianity, Judaism, and Islam.

Küng's concerns for the ecumenical conversation (both with regard to inner-Christian ecumenics and with regard to inter-religious dialogue) and for his project of working toward a global ethic provide challenging perspectives for his constructive rereading of Christian history in *Christianity*. They form the background for his call for an ongoing reform of Christianity and its ecclesiastical structures.[43] "Today being a true Christian means being an ecumenical Christian."[44]

Key Issues

This extensive survey of Küng's work has been necessary in order to draw appropriate attention to the wide range of his theological interests, developments, and contributions and to offer an initial discussion of his major works. There are at least four unifying constants in Küng's theological work in the four periods described above: (1) his ecumenical interest (originally from an inner-Christian ecumenism toward a global ecumenism); (2) his continuing ecclesiological reflection; (3) his concern with the christological and theological foundations of Christian faith and with the rationality of that faith; and (4) his search for an adequate theological method for today. Let us consider these in reverse order.

Theological methodology

Küng's theological method can be studied both by distilling the implicit methodology operative in his major works and by discussing his explicit discussion of theological method, especially in *Theology for the Third Millennium*. Both his implicit and explicit methodology reveal the same strong commitment to the Bible as the source and ultimate norm of Christian theology, a commitment which has been characteristic of most contemporary Roman Catholic theologians (cf. those discussed in this volume, i.e., Rahner, Congar, Schillebeeckx, and von Balthasar). For Küng, the second source of Christian theology is the wealth of human experiences in the world in which we live today. Both sources, Bible and contemporary world, need to be interpreted, and both interpretations need to be critically correlated.[45] A similar model of critical correlation can also be found in E. Schillebeeckx and D. Tracy's approach to theology. While promoting this model in principle, Küng does, however, point out that this correlation between both sources may at times lead to confrontation, namely when biblical and contemporary experiences contradict one another. In such a situation of conflict, Küng attributes ultimate normative significance "to the special Christian experiences or, rather, the Christian message, the Gospel, Jesus Christ himself."[46]

In *On Being a Christian* Küng had shown how he understands this ultimate norm to work. There he reminds us that "narrative presentation and critical reflection ... must be united in Christian theology and proclamation,"[47] and offers his own critical narrative and interpretation of Jesus' life, death, and resurrection. There, and in *Theology for the Third Millennium* as well as in *Christianity*, Küng emphasizes that his own interpretation of the principal norm of Christian theology, Jesus Christ, is informed by historical-critical scholarship which he considers to be essential for any appropriate theology today. He warns us, however, not to confuse historical-critical exegesis with a responsibly constructed historical-critical dogmatics. The latter ought to include a systematic reflection on the (occasionally conflicting) results of modern biblical exegesis.[48]

The dimensions of the particularly systematic task in theology are clearly outlined by Küng: As already indicated in our survey of Küng's work, for him good theology must be (1) ecumenical (in the global sense indicated above), (2) truthful (that means not opportunistic), (3) free (that means not authoritarian), and (4) critical (not traditionalist).[49] Any candidate for an adequate paradigm for contemporary theology must respect these four essential dimensions.

Fundamental issues in christology and theology

In this context, however, Küng does not make totally explicit all the dimensions which are operative in his systematic theology. Against the mediaeval-neoscholastic paradigm he insists that faith is not simply above reason; against the dichotomies of dialectical theology he emphasizes that faith is not against reason; and against the modern Enlightenment dichotomy he stresses that reason is not against faith. For Küng, all our thinking and doubting, our intuitions and deductions are grounded on an "a priori act of trust" of which we might not always be aware, but which, once we are, we may consciously affirm or reject.[50]

As we have seen, Küng's approach to God in *Does God Exist?* is based on this fundamental insight. Although Küng is critical of Rahner's theology because it was still part of the neoscholastic paradigm,[51] Küng's "a priori act of trust" does bear some resemblance to Rahner's transcendent experience.[52] However, there is also a fundamental difference between the two approaches to God: While for Rahner the transcendental experience of any human being is always related (though not always thematically) to God, the God of Jesus Christ, Küng's a priori act of trust is not simply identified with belief in God. But there exists an essential connection between trust in reality and belief in God. "If someone denies God, he does not know why he ultimately trusts in reality." And respectively: "If someone affirms God, he knows why he can trust reality."[53] The precise nature of this connection needs to be clarified further by Küng.

Like Rahner, Küng owes a lot to the Cartesian starting point, namely the individually thinking subject. While it is, of course, correct that any decision to believe in the Christian God is ultimately a decision made by an individual, it does not automatically follow from this that the concept of God operative in the Christian movement must be exclusively grounded on individual trust. Rather it seems, and here Küng would agree, that there is a rich but naturally ambiguous heritage of philosophical attempts which ontologically relate God, Christ, the human being, and the universe. Many of these philosophical models are certainly inappropriate, as Küng himself has documented in *The Incarnation of God* with reference to the static concept of God in Greek metaphysics. Yet Küng does not sufficiently discuss his own use of ontological language which may lead to misunderstandings, particularly in christological thinking which has to wrestle with adequate expressions of the relationship between Jesus and God. When Küng writes "[f]or me, Jesus of Nazareth is the Son of God,"[54] he makes (if not only a value judgment) some kind of an ontological claim, though existentially qualified. But even a qualified ontology is still an ontology. Similarly, his reference to "reality" as the object of human trust has ontological implications.

Reality is always encountered through particular perspectives. These perspectives are always conditioned by the various dimensions of human experience, including the religious dimensions. Therefore the hermeneutical implications of the method of critical correlation between biblical message and human world would need to be discussed in more detail along the following lines: The contemporary human world is already present, of course, in perspectives which guide our reading of the Bible, as indeed the history of the effects of biblical texts is always present in our Western interpretations of the world. Therefore Küng's "fundamental trust in reality" is already socially, linguistically, and religiously conditioned, a fact which Küng has not yet explicitly treated.[55]

For Küng, the norm of Christian theology is Jesus Christ. He is the center of Scripture. Yet he can only be reached through interpretations of the different early Christian interpretations of his life, death, and resurrection. This hermeneutical situation causes a double pluralism: the contemporary pluralism of readings and the pluralism of early Christian "readings" of Jesus as Christ. Coping with this double pluralism and the heritage of Christian interpretations in a responsible manner must include the risk of saying who Jesus Christ is in relation to God to the best of our knowledge. We have to make tentative ontological statements. Here Küng does implicitly agree. "Jesus of Nazareth in fact has, in the last resort, no decisive meaning for me unless he is proclaimed as the Christ of God. Nor, anyway, does the divine Christ mean much to me unless he is identical with the man Jesus."[56] Even the necessary critical re-examination of old Hellenistic dogmas in the light of the best available exegetical insights into the Bible[57] does not free the Christian theologian from the necessity to say how she or he sees the connection between God and Jesus.

Therefore, tentative ontological statements must have a place in the new paradigm of theology in order to help us to express our particular faith in God, both in terms of our own inner-Christian understanding of truth and in terms of contributing meaningfully to the much wider search for truth in the conversation among different religious traditions.

The need for church reform

Küng has constantly kept to his demand for a thoroughgoing reform of the Roman Catholic Church, despite all the hostility and criticism from the Church authorities which need to be reformed. His collaboration in the conciliar process of reform has permanently shaped his ecclesiology. His criteria for an appropriate ecclesiology, developed at that time, have remained a norm for him. For Küng, the Christian church is and remains a community of free men and women, who respond to God's call as disciples of Christ. He himself sees his ecclesiological thought as shaped by three characteristics: Christian radicality, constancy, and coherence.[58] In the face of all the despondency and depression which affect many committed Christians because of the present climate in the Catholic Church, Küng constantly calls on them to maintain hope and to reflect on the authentic calling of the Church as the trustee of Jesus Christ. "I am staying in the Church because I have been convinced by Jesus Christ and all that he stands for, and because the Church-community, despite all its failures, pleads the cause of Jesus Christ and must continue to do so."[59]

In keeping with his ecumenical position, he constantly calls for recognition of existing Church pluralism.[60] Such a recognition of course presupposes that a clerical minority no longer claims to direct Church people, as it were, "from above." All Christians are called to apostolic discipleship.[61] All Church members therefore have reciprocal obligations.

> [T]he shepherds have the duty and the task to proclaim the Christian message to the congregation again and again, even when it is uncomfortable for the congregation. The congregation, on the other hand, has the duty and the task of retesting again and again whether the shepherds are remaining true to their commission, whether they are acting according to the gospel. For there are not only false prophets, but also faithless shepherds.[62]

Küng's ecclesiology of reform naturally includes the call for a fundamental revison of the role of women in the Church. "In order that the Catholic Church, whose power structure and ministry are completely dominated by men, might become a Church of all human beings, women should be represented in all decision-making bodies and at all levels – the parish, diocesan, national, and international."[63]

In contrast to many of his colleagues, Küng has not allowed himself to be driven into either resignation or cynicism by the conservative Church policy at present being put forward by the Vatican. Rather, he is working with unbroken energy on his vision of a better Church. This is all the more amazing when we reflect how attempts have been made to reduce Hans Küng's vision of the Church to the "Küng case." This "case" reached its sorry "climax" with the withdrawal of his teaching license by the Church in 1979. Here above all, three ecclesiological concepts were a matter of dispute between the self-appointed guardians of Catholic "orthodoxy" and the Tübingen theologian: the question of the freedom of the theologian in the Church, the concept of papal infallibility, and the clash of two different paradigms of theological thought.

However, Küng has never absolutized the freedom of theology. Rather, he constantly stresses that theology has its creative ground and its life in the Word of God, to which human beings bear witness.[64] Küng's theological approach and above all his criterion for judging forms of Church authority and organization, which is grounded in the gospel, make it a priori impossible for him to accept a dogma of papal infallibility. In this connection Küng also points to the great difference between the paradigm of theology still defended by Rome and the paradigm of a critical and self-critical theology come of age which is represented by critical Christians and theologians today. While some Catholics still cling to a neoscholastic paradigm, numerous others have long been living and thinking in a new paradigm. One of the tasks of critical theology must therefore be to encourage communication between the defenders of both paradigms without simply claiming that the more recent paradigm is better because it is later. Its appropriateness may not just be asserted, but must be constantly tested afresh in public discourse.[65]

Global theological strategies

With his book *Global Responsibility*, Küng once again emphasized his global understanding of theological work. At the same time, with this project he has also brought out the impossibility of separating practical theological work from systematic theological work. Whereas contemporary theology often makes a tripartite division of theological work into fundamental, systematic, and practical theology,[66] Küng implicitly emphasizes a twofold division, namely a distinction between fundamental and systematic-practical theological thought. The aim of fundamental theology is to reflect methodologically on theology in the interdisciplinary context of present-day thought. Küng's paradigm theory belongs in this sphere. By contrast, the aim of systematic-practical thought in theology is to demonstrate a vision of Christian existence in the context of the present pluralism of religion and to develop strategies for Christian existence in the present global context. For Küng, the development of such strategies is always already ethical work. This concept of theology allows him always to understand Christian ecumenical theory and practice dialectically, and thus to avoid the tiresome discussion of burdensome theory on the one hand or the dominance of theology by praxis on the other.

The one criticism that must be made in this connection is of Küng's hesitation to enter into the discussion of the concept of the human self in the framework of this global discussion. For most of those taking part in discussion of the postmodern paradigm, the traditional self-understanding of human beings has become questionable. The Cartesian approach to the assessment of the self is no longer any use, since it largely ignores the interdependence on the one hand between human beings and on the other between the individual and the environment. Moreover, it is necessarily still uncritical of all the strategies of suspicion which meanwhile have been advanced against the simple assertion of an independent human will or a trustworthy human reason.[67] But as Küng attributes central importance in his theological approach to both trust and reason, it seems appropriate that he should explicitly enter into this discussion today. It would also give his ethical and political perspective a much stronger foundation and an appreciation of the challenges of otherness which emerge from all angles of the relational nature of Christian existence, namely the Christian's relationship with God, with other human beings, with nature, and with his or her own fragile self.

Hans Küng's Theological Achievement

Hans Küng has not only discussed all essential areas of Christian theology, reflected on necessary changes in theological method today, and opened many doors toward an ecumenical Christian self-understanding, but has also expressed his thoughts in such a way that every intelligent reader can follow them and thus receive the necessary information for entering into the discussion. Küng cannot be praised enough for the attention he has given to the presentation of theological thoughts. Countless people around the world have thus been allowed to nurture their theological interest and transform their lives.

Perhaps Küng's most important contributions to theological method so far have been (1) his proposal for a global theology which is aware of the many facets of human life in this world and of the different and often conflicting religious and cultural interpretations of reality; and (2) his reconsideration of the nature of truth claims in the context of such a global theology.

Küng's call on all human beings to enter into the discussion about the meaning and truth in our lives and to respect the open-endedness of such a discussion is inspired by his understanding of God's revelation in Jesus Christ. The resulting self-understanding of theology must therefore conflict with any theological paradigm which advocates a privileged access to truth for only some people. Genuine conversation about truth cannot tolerate such privileged participants. This applies not only to the Roman Catholic Magisterium, but to all human bodies in and outside Christianity which claim such a special status and access to God and truth. Küng's vision of the global conversation about truth is based on his understanding of God's call in Christ that all people are called to relate to God without intermediary institutions.[68]

Küng's most significant contribution to the discussion of the central articles of Christian faith lies in his effort to demonstrate the rationality of this faith and to reflect upon the implications of this faith for human praxis today. Küng does not only wish to interpret the world, he wishes to help in transforming it by critically retrieving the radical humanism of the Christian faith.[69] Even though Küng has not yet clarified all the philosophical presuppositions of his work, he has already contributed a lot to the radical transformation of the nature of theology in the twentieth century.

But he would be the first to admit that much more is still to be done. His work on the *Global Responsibility* project and the critical survey of the religious situation of our time which is connected with this project has already produced very impressive results. Through this work he has helped many contemporary people to enhance their understanding of the potential and the perversions of Christianity and of Christianity's relationship with other religions. Küng's work has already given rise to much critical thought and transformative action. What more could any theologian work and hope for?

Notes

1   The dates given in parentheses in the text refer to the first German edition of Küng's works. Citations are from the editions listed in the bibliography. All works cited in the notes are written by Küng unless stated otherwise.

2   Cf. *Christianity*, p. 1: "Only the ignorant can claim that all religions are the same."

3   *The Church*, pp. 96ff.

4   *Infallible?* p. 22 (I have corrected the English translation).

5   Ibid., p. 170.

6   *The Incarnation of God*, p. 462.
7   Ibid., p. 428.
8   Ibid., p. 491.
9   Cf. ibid., p. 492.
10 *On Being a Christian*, pp. 125f.
11 *Does God Exist?* p. 432.
12 Cf. ibid., p. 473.
13 Ibid., p. 476.
14 Ibid., p. 570.
15 Ibid., p. 572.
16 Ibid., p. 574.
17 Ibid.
18 Ibid., p. 626.
19 Ibid., p. 649.
20 *Eternal Life?* p. 145.
21 Ibid., p. 287.
22 Cf. *Christianity and the World Religions*, p. xiv.
23 H. Küng and P. Lapide, *Brother or Lord? A Jew and a Christian talk together about Jesus* (London, 1977).
24 H. Küng and J. Ching, *Christianity and Chinese Religion* (New York, 1989).
25 See e.g., W. Jens and H. Küng, *Literature and Religion* (New York, 1991); W. Jens, H. Küng, and K.-J. Kuschel (eds), *Theologie und Literatur. Zum Stand des Dialogs* (Munich, 1986); W. Jens and H. Küng, *Anwälte der Humanität: Thomas Mann, Hermann Hesse, Heinrich Böll* (Munich, 1989).
26 H. Küng and David Tracy (eds), *The New Paradigm in Theology* (Edinburgh, 1989).
27 Cf. Küng's book *Die Schweiz ohne Orientierung: Europäische Perspektiven* (Zurich, 1992).
28 *Global Responsibility*, p. 21.
29 Ibid., p. 31.
30 Ibid., p. 53.
31 Cf. ibid., p. 91. Already in *On Being a Christian*, pp. 554ff., Küng had claimed that Christianity should be rightly understood as radical humanism.
32 *Global Responsibility*, pp. 110f.
33 Ibid., p. 120.
34 Franz Mussner's excellent work *Tractate on the Jews* (Philadelphia, 1983), of course, also takes the ongoing life of Jewish religion seriously, but is primarily interested in a Christian theological approach to Judaism. By contrast, Küng is attempting to understand the religious situation of our time.
35 In connection with his rereading of Christianity Küng also published *Credo: The Apostles' Creed explained for today* (London, 1993).
36 *Christianity*, p. xxii.
37 Ibid., p. xxiv.
38 Ibid., p. 9.
39 Ibid., p. 26.
40 Ibid., p. 39; see also pp. 45f.
41 Ibid., p. 51.
42 Ibid., p. 104.
43 These concerns are also evident in Küng's book *Great Christian Thinkers* (London, 1994), esp. pp. 213–16.
44 *Christianity*, p. 793.
45 *Theology for the Third Millennium*, pp. 118ff.
46 Ibid., p. 122.
47 *On Being a Christian*, p. 418.
48 Cf. *Theology for the Third Millennium*, pp. 113ff.
49 Cf. ibid., pp. 161f. and pp. 203f. See also *Great Christian Thinkers*, pp. 213f.
50 Cf. ibid., p. 201.
51 Cf. ibid., pp. 186ff. For Rahner's concept of transcendental experience see K. Rahner, *Foundations of Christian Faith* (London and New York, 1978), pp. 75–81.
52 Cf. *Does God Exist?* pp. 571ff.
53 Ibid., pp. 571f.
54 Ibid., p. 688.
55 For a discussion of the significance of hermeneutics in theological thinking see Werner G. Jeanrond, *Theological Hermeneutics: Development and significance* (London and New York, 1991 and 1994).
56 *Does God Exist?* p. 687. See also *Credo*, p. 61.
57 Cf. *Christianity*, p. 195.
58 *Reforming the Church Today: Keeping hope alive*, p. 3.
59 Ibid., p. 10.
60 Cf. ibid., p. 41.
61 Cf. ibid., pp. 79ff.
62 Ibid., p. 86.
63 Ibid., p. 103. See also *Christianity*, pp. 752–61.
64 Cf. *Freiheit des Christen*, 3rd edn (Zurich, 1980), p. 143.
65 Cf. *Theology for the Third Millennium*, pp. 203–6.
66 See e.g., D. Tracy, *The Analogical Imagination: Christian theology and the culture of pluralism* (New York and London, 1981), pp. 54–82.

67 Cf. here D. Tracy, *Plurality and Ambiguity: Hermeneutics, religion, hope* (San Francisco and London, 1987).

68 Cf. *On Being Christian*, pp. 481f.
69 Cf. ibid., p. 31.

Bibliography

Primary

Hans Küng, *Justification: The doctrine of Karl Barth and a Catholic reflection* (London and New York, 1965).
—— *The Church* (London and New York, 1967).
—— *Infallible? An enquiry* (London and New York, 1972, 1980).
—— *On Being a Christian* (London and New York, 1977).
—— *Does God Exist? An answer for today* (London and New York, 1980).
—— *Eternal Life? An enquiry* (London and New York, 1984).
—— *The Incarnation of God: An introduction to Hegel's theological thought as prolegomena to a future christology* (Edinburgh, 1987).
—— *Christianity and the World Religions: Paths of dialogue with Islam, Hinduism, and Buddhism* (New York, 1986, and London, 1987).
—— *Theology for the Third Millennium: An ecumenical view* (New York, 1988, and London, 1991).
—— *Reforming the Church Today: Keeping hope alive* (Edinburgh and New York, 1990).
—— *Global Responsibility: In search for a new world ethic* (London and New York, 1991).
—— *Judaism.* (*The Religious Situation of Our Time.*) (London and New York, 1992).
—— *Credo: The Apostles' Creed explained for today* (London and New York, 1993).
—— *Christianity: Its essence and history.* (*The Religious Situation of Our Time.*) (London and New York, 1995).

Secondary

Häring, Hermann and Kuschel, Karl-Josef (eds), *Hans Küng: His work and his way* (London, 1979).
—— *Hans Küng: New horizons for faith and thought* (London, 1993).
Kiwiet, John, *Hans Küng* (Waco, TX, 1985).
LaCugna, Catherine, *The Theological Methodology of Hans Küng* (Atlanta, GA, 1982).
Nowell, Robert, *A Passion for Truth. Hans Küng: A biography* (London 1981).
Swidler, Leonard (ed.), *Küng in Conflict* (Garden City, NY, 1981).

History and Eschatology

In the 1960s Wolfhart Pannenberg and Jürgen Moltmann introduced new ideas and programs to continental European theology. History and eschatology were their common themes, though with very different styles, methods, and conversation partners. They are now senior international and ecumenical theologians, both in the scale of their influence and the range of their interests and dialogues.

Pannenberg challenged both Barth and Bultmann on the issue of faith and history. For him the integrity of Christian theology requires that faith be grounded in knowledge which can be rationally established outside faith. It also requires an understanding of the totality of reality that can match atheist and other worldviews. Since Pannenberg completed his three-volume *Systematic Theology* in 1993, Christoph Schwöbel is able to give an overview of his life's work from the standpoint of that outstanding work. He shows how in it Pannenberg not only continues his previous theology but both responds to criticisms and innovates. Above all, he offers a thoroughgoing integration of theology through his doctrine of the Trinity, pivoting around God as Infinite and as love. He also carries further his understanding of Jesus Christ, of creation, and of the church, and the grand finale is a fresh statement of his eschatology. Schwöbel is especially attentive to Pannenberg's way of relating theology and philosophy, offering as an aid an account of the crucial discussion in *Metaphysics and the Idea of God*. He concludes with some probing questions.

Pannenberg's main contribution is in relating faith to reason; Moltmann's is rather in relating faith to the modern world in a series of major works which have often acutely discerned "the signs of the times." Richard Bauckham describes the basic themes of cross and resurrection and the Trinity, the distinctive orientation of Moltmann's theology toward both praxis and doxology, and the way in which it embodies a structural openness in dialogue. The content of his theology is portrayed under the headings of eschatology, theodicy, God, creation, politics, Christ and Spirit, some of the many criticisms of it are discussed, and our appetite is whetted for the future volume on theological method.

Wolfhart Pannenberg

Christoph Schwöbel

Introduction

In 1961 a slim volume of essays published by a group of younger academics created a considerable sensation in the somewhat static situation of Protestant theology in Germany. The title of the collection, *Offenbarung als Geschichte* (*Revelation as History*), was correctly understood by the theological public as the programmatic statement of a new theological conception. The group of essayists soon became known under the name of their editor as the "Pannenberg Circle."[1] It was Wolfhart Pannenberg, the systematic theologian of the group, whose "Dogmatic Theses on the Doctrine of Revelation" contributed significantly to the programmatic character of the volume. He was soon identified with this theological conception, which was widely considered to be a genuinely new approach to fundamental issues of modern theology.

Revelation as History not only provided the basis from which Pannenberg developed his systematic conception; it can also be regarded as the provisional conclusion of his earlier development in which he gradually achieved an independent position. Born in 1928 in Stettin (now in Poland), Pannenberg grew up in the atmosphere of the totalitarian regime of National Socialism, before he began his studies after the war at the University of Berlin.[2] After spending some time in Göttingen and after a short interlude in Basel, where he encountered Karl Barth, Pannenberg continued his theological studies at the University of Heidelberg. There he wrote his doctoral dissertation *Die Prädestinationslehre des Duns Scotus* (published in 1954) under the supervision of the Lutheran Barthian Edmund Schlink, and in 1955 completed his *Habilitationsschrift* with an analysis of the role of analogy in Western thought up to Thomas Aquinas.[3] After a few years of academic teaching at Heidelberg as *Privatdozent*, in which he discovered the significance of Hegel's thought for the formation of modern theology, Pannenberg was called to become professor at the Kirchliche Hochschule in Wuppertal, where Jürgen Moltmann was his colleague. In 1961 he was appointed to the chair in systematic theology at the University of Mainz.

Although Pannenberg has always attributed the seminal idea of God's indirect self-revelation in history to Rolf Rendtorff (who later abandoned it),[4] his own systematic exposition of this basic idea soon led to the identification of the program of *Revelation and History* with Pannenberg's own theological conception. Even if this is not entirely correct with regard to the initial program, it is perhaps justified to say that Pannenberg's own theological conception developed in his attempt to hammer out the full implications of the basic ideas contained in *Revelation as History* and to find sufficient strategies for substantiating its claims in response to its critics. The "working circle" discontinued its regular meetings in 1969 and since then other members have presented theological conceptions, whether in biblical or systematic theology, which are notably different from that of Pannenberg.

In the course of Pannenberg's development the new conception has been influenced by theological insights from quite different contexts from those of the initial program. Pannenberg's encounter with North American theology is one of the factors that have shaped the systematic structure of his thought. Beginning with an invitation as a guest professor to the University of Chicago in 1963, Pannenberg has lectured widely at most centers of theological learning in the United States, and his continuing dialogue with the leading exponents of process thought has contributed significantly to the development of his theology. Today he is at least as widely recognized as a leading contemporary theologian in the United States as in Germany. Pannenberg's involvement in ecumenical theology, which acquired increasing importance after his move in 1967 to the chair in systematic theology at the University of Munich, where he was also director of the Ecumenical Institute until 1993, has led to new areas of theological reflection in which he attempts to demonstrate the relevance and comprehensiveness of his theological approach. This expansion of themes in Pannenberg's thought reflects the ongoing systematic development of his conception, as well as the reception of his theological ideas in different contexts of theological reflection. From 1988 to 1993 Pannenberg published the three volumes of his *Systematische Theologie*, which presents the synthesis of the various strands of his theological development in a comprehensive dogmatic conception.

Survey

What are the main elements of the new approach in *Revelation as History* which provide an outline for the further development of Pannenberg's theological conception? In his analysis of the structure of the concept of revelation Pannenberg starts from the assertion that revelation cannot be adequately understood as the disclosure of truths about God. It has to be interpreted strictly as the self-revelation of God.[5] This assumption, which shows the measure of Pannenberg's agreement with Barth, is traced back to Hegel, who is seen as the one who established this principle in modern theology and first recognized its full implications.[6] Divine self-revelation entails that, if there is only one God, there can only be a single and unique revelation in which God is at the same time author and medium of revelation. It constitutes genuine, though not necessarily exhaustive, knowledge of God. The next step

– and here Pannenberg parts company with Barth – is the thesis that according to the biblical traditions God does not reveal himself directly (e.g., in his "Word"), but *indirectly* through his acts in history. On the basis of the strict understanding of revelation as God's self-revelation, this cannot refer to specific historical events or series of events. It can only be applied to the end of history from which every preceding event, and indeed the whole of reality, is illuminated. This eschatological perspective constitutes the universality of revelation.

It is for Pannenberg the distinctive claim of Christian faith that God's eschatological self-demonstration is proleptically actualized in the destiny of Jesus of Nazareth, more precisely in his resurrection. The preceding history of Israel has to be understood as a gradual universalization of the understanding of God's action in history, reaching its final stage in Jewish Apocalypticism, where the end of history is expected as the complete revelation of God. From the end the course of history – now understood in its entirety – can be seen as God's indirect self-revelation. The universality of God's self-revelation as it is pre-actualized in the resurrection of Jesus has the important corollary that it can be accessible not only for a specifically privileged group of people. Since it happens for "all flesh," it is in principle open for all who have eyes to see.[7]

The crucial point of this rudimentary program is the claim that the end of history as the final self-revelation of God is proleptically realized in the resurrection of Jesus. Pannenberg tackled the task of substantiating this claim in a comprehensive christological conception published in 1964 as *Grundzüge der Christologie* and translated into English in 1968 under the (somewhat unfortunate) title *Jesus – God and Man*. Because of its impressive synthesis of exegetical and historical research and systematic exposition, the book was celebrated as one of the most comprehensive treatments of christology in this century and soon became one of the standard textbooks in academic theology.

The distinctive and much debated feature of this christological conception is its methodology, which follows from Pannenberg's understanding of the task of christology as that of *establishing* the true significance of Jesus as the Christ of God from his history.[8] For this reason – Pannenberg claims – christological reflection must go back behind the New Testament *kerygma* to the historical reality of Jesus himself and start "from below." Pannenberg uses this somewhat ambiguous metaphor to designate the difference of his method from the approach "from above," starting with the incarnation of the second person of the Trinity which presupposes what it seeks to establish, i.e., the divinity of Jesus Christ. In Pannenberg's view it also neglects the historical particularity of the man Jesus in the religious and cultural context of his time and adopts a humanly impossible epistemic stance.[9] Furthermore, Pannenberg rejects the approach to christology from the question of the significance of Jesus Christ for us, which, in his view, implies that christology becomes, in effect, a "function of soteriology" (P. Tillich). This procedure runs the risk of being dominated by soteriological interests which all too easily turn into the christological projection of human desires for salvation. What Jesus *means* for us must be grounded in what he is, and what he *is* can only be established by starting from the past reality of the historical Jesus.[10]

The starting point "from below" does not mean, however, that Pannenberg's christology remains below. Knowledge of the divinity of Jesus is grounded in the resurrection in which his unity with God is established in such a way that the claim implied in his pre-Easter appearance is vindicated. Only on the presupposition that the resurrection is understood against the background of apocalyptic expectation as the proleptic actualization of the end of history is it possible to see Jesus in his person as God's self-revelation, because the vindication of his unity with God in the resurrection extends retroactively to the pre-Easter life of Jesus.[11] This does not mean that the distinction between Jesus and God the Father is blurred at any point in this conception. In the framework of the revelational unity of God and Jesus the divinity of Jesus has to be understood as the unity of the Son with the Father, which leads directly to the Christian understanding of God as Trinity.[12] More recently Pannenberg has worked out in detail what this self-differentiation in the triune life of God, implied in the cross and resurrection of Jesus, would suggest for a fully-fledged doctrine of the Trinity.[13]

The resurrection, which Pannenberg attempts to establish as a historical event whose probability is stronger than any alternative explanation,[14] is not only the crucial point for the validation of the claims of Jesus' divinity; it is also the foundation for understanding the true humanity of Jesus as the fulfillment of human destiny. From this anthropological perspective Pannenberg explores the soteriological content traditionally presented as the work of Christ, before turning to the relationship of humanity and divinity in Christ. In *Jesus – God and Man* Pannenberg remained sceptical about the adequacy of the traditional Two-Natures Doctrine, conceived in terms of a metaphysics of substance which he sees as inevitably trapped in the dilemma of having to choose between a "unification" and a "disjunction" christology,[15] Pannenberg explores the possibility of asserting that the identity of Jesus with the Son of God is established indirectly through his relationship of absolute obedience to God the Father.[16] In this sense Jesus' eternal Sonship is interpreted as dialectically identical with his humanity, insofar as the relationship of Jesus to God the Father in the historical aspect of his existence mediates the relationship of the eternal Son to the Father. This involves the inversion of the order of knowing and the order of being. While the dialectical identity of Jesus with the Father can only be known from the particularity of Jesus' historical human existence, it is grounded in the ontologically prior relation to divine Sonship as the ground of the existence of Jesus.[17] In this approach Pannenberg sees the possibility of reappropriating the *particula veri* of the Logos christology.[18]

At a number of crucial points the validity of this christological conception rests on the justifiability of its *anthropological* presuppositions. The appeal to the resurrection as the foundation for christological statements about the unity of Jesus with God and about the fulfillment of human destiny in him presupposes that the apocalyptic expectation of the end of history as the disclosure of the totality of meaning can be justified on general anthropological grounds. And Pannenberg's thesis that the identity of Jesus and the eternal Son is established indirectly through his humanity presupposes that the openness for God which is the hallmark of Jesus' obedience to the Father is the determinative feature of the human condition. In his writings on theological anthropology, beginning with a published series of radio talks (*What is Man?* 1970; German edition, 1962) and coming to a preliminary conclusion in his magisterial work *Anthropology in Theological Perspective* (1985; German edition, 1983), Pannenberg has combined the more specific aim of providing the foundational principles for his exposition of Christian faith with the general task of elucidating the anthropological foundation for Christian truth-claims. After the atheistic critique of religion in the modern era, anthropology has become for him the battlefield on which theology has to demonstrate the validity of its claims to universality.[19]

The decisive thesis which has been extensively developed over a period of more than 20 years is already introduced in the first chapter of *What is Man?* The fundamental openness to the world which has been interpreted by modern philosophical anthropology as the key to the understanding of what it means to be human has to be interpreted as a fundamental openness for God.[20] God is the infinite horizon which is implicitly presupposed in every act of human self-transcendence. This fundamental relatedness to God constitutes the irreducible dimension of human religiousness which, according to Pannenberg, underlies all structures of human culture.[21]

Although the universality of all theological claims has to be substantiated by reference to these general anthropological considerations, they do not provide a sufficient platform for developing the specific insights of Christian anthropology. For this task, it is necessary for Pannenberg to distinguish between the actuality of human existence and the final destiny of humanity.[22] Actual human existence is characterized by the universality of sin, evidence of which is given in the egocentricity of human behavior which denies the fundamental *exocentricity* of human life. This consists in the fact that human life receives its center from outside itself.[23] In contrast to actual human existence, what it means to be human has to be understood as the destiny of humanity which was essentially realized in Jesus but is not yet effectively actualized for all humankind. The term "human nature" should therefore be understood as designating the history of the realization of the human destiny.[24]

The claim that the destiny of humanity has been actualized in Jesus and specifically in his resurrection is the ground for the hope that our future resurrection will realize our true being as communion with God in the divine kingdom in which even "the last enemy," death, is overcome. From this basis Pannenberg offers a theological explanation of the reality of freedom as well as of the communal destiny of humanity. Jesus' resurrection as the foundation of our future resurrection is seen as the warrant for the conviction that the individual human person, as the obedient object of God's love, has infinite value and dignity. This is the ground of freedom which cannot be inferred from the actual existence of humanity. It can only be communicated by reconciliation with God in Christ.[25] On the other hand, Christ's sacrificial devotion to God in giving himself to the world, which is vindicated in the resurrection, pre-actualizes the communal destiny of humanity in the kingdom of God. The eschatological community of humankind in the Kingdom of God finds its anticipatory actualization and symbolic representation in the church, which expresses its character most cogently in the eucharist.[26] With this attempt Pannenberg tries to point to the mediation of freedom and community in the Kingdom of God and develops on this basis the constructive task of the church in representing the true "global village" of the Kingdom of God and its critical task of resisting every denial of freedom in the name of penultimate communities and authorities. This perspective not only provides a basis for the description of the role of the church in society, it also illuminates the motivation for Pannenberg's ecumenical activity. If the symbolic representation of the community of humankind in God's kingdom is the primary character of the church from which all other tasks are to be determined, the separation of the churches must seem theologically scandalous.[27] The awakening of a new eucharistic piety which expresses what Pannenberg sees as the true character of the church appears from this viewpoint as the most decisive sign of hope for ecumenism.

The way in which Pannenberg has tried from the outset to integrate different theological disciplines and to relate theological reflection to various non-theological sciences raises many questions concerning the scientific status of theology and its methodology. Pannenberg addressed these questions in his *Theology and the Philosophy of Science* (1976; German edition, 1973) against the backdrop of a detailed description of the development of the philosophy of science and an exposition of the different historical attempts to determine the scientific character of theology.

Starting from the traditional definition of theology as the science of God, Pannenberg immediately qualifies this definition by asserting that God as the subject matter of theology must be understood as a hypothesis if one is to avoid the twofold pitfalls of religious subjectivism and dogmatic positivism.[28] If the word "God" can meaningfully refer only to the reality that determines everything, God cannot be directly experienced like an object in the world, but can only become indirectly accessible in the subjective anticipation of the totality of meaning which is presupposed in all particular experiences. Since the experience of reality as a whole finds symbolic expression in the historic religions, a theory of the history of religions is the place where the indirect co-givenness of God in all experience has to be analyzed.[29] The specific claims of Christian theology to a specific revelation of God have to be substantiated against the background of this general reflection which Pannenberg now calls *fundamental theology*.

On the basis of this understanding of the nature of theology, Pannenberg characterizes theological statements as *hypotheses*. While their complete verification can only be expected from the *eschaton*, there are nevertheless specific criteria for their substantiation. Theological hypotheses purporting to state the implications of Christian faith are to be considered as *not* substantiated, if they cannot be shown to present implications of the biblical traditions; if they are not related to the whole of reality in a way that can be validated by present experience and substantiated against the background of contemporary philosophical reflection; if they are not capable of being integrated with the relevant area of experience; and if they are deemed to be inadequate in relation to the present stage of theological debate.[30]

This comprehensive conception of the status of theological theory and of the criteria regulating theological practice summarizes on a metatheological level some of the main elements which have been present in Pannenberg's theological work from the early stage of *Revelation as History*, and which continue to determine the working out of his conception in new areas of theological reflection.

In all Pannenberg's writings there is a thoroughgoing engagement with the classical themes and theories of the Western philosophical tradition. His theology has also often been criticized as the theological articulation of an underlying philosophical theory, such as the Hegelian metaphysics of history. Pannenberg has consistently rejected such criticisms while insisting that Christian theology must engage with philosophical reflection in order to secure its intelligibility and give a rational account of its claims to universality. Moreover, in many of Pannenberg's writings it becomes apparent that he holds philosophical views which cannot simply be identified with a given philosophical position. In the same year as the first volume of the *Systematic Theology* appeared, Pannenberg also published a book on *Metaphysics and the Idea of God* (1988, English translation, 1990). This book not only offers a comprehensive account of Pannenberg's main philosophical ideas, it also explains his views on the historical and systematic dependence of philosophical reflection in the Western tradition on the Christian idea of God. It also presents Pannenberg's reasons why Christian theology would be well advised to take philosophical criteria of speaking about God into account.

Against the background of a renewal of interest in metaphysics Pannenberg starts by examining theories about the end of metaphysics and its alleged consequences for philosophy and theology. Pannenberg argues that, historically, philosophy developed from a critique of the gods of Greek religion in their depiction by the poets. Systematically, he claims, there will always be a convergence of themes between philosophy and theology, if philosophy transcends the natural consciousness of our everyday experience and raises questions about the totality and unity of our pluriform experience of the world and of ourselves.[31] Conversely, theology will always have to engage with philosophical thinking if it attempts to validate its claims that the one God is the ultimate horizon for the unity of the world and our experiences of it.

Pannenberg investigates this convergence further in an analysis of the problem of the Absolute. If the unity of reality is the central theme of metaphysics, metaphysical reflection will lead logically to the exploration of the relationship between the experience of finite objects to the idea of the Infinite as the horizon in which all finite objects are grasped. Pannenberg follows Descartes in claiming that the idea of the Infinite must have priority in our consciousness and that the Infinite is to be understood as the highest perfection. However, he challenges Descartes's view that the idea of highest perfection is identical with the idea of God, since the idea of God implies in a Christian context the ascription of personhood and will to God.[32] Nevertheless, the idea of the Infinite can function as a criterion for discourse about God. This applies even more to Hegel's conception of the Infinite, which is based on a distinction between the metaphysically Infinite and the mathematically infinite. The concept of the truly (metaphysically) Infinite must exclude dependence from anything else and is therefore to be conceived as truly self-sufficient, as the Absolute. However, if the Infinite is thought of as limited by the finite, it cannot be truly infinite. Therefore the Infinite must comprehend the finite as its opposite within itself. This expands the function of the concept of the Infinite for theological discourse: A truly monotheistic conception of God must understand God as being both transcendent and immanent in relation to the world. Hegel attempted to bring these aspects together in the concept of the Spirit. For Pannenberg, Hegel's view of the Spirit and his conception of the Trinity remains, in spite of all its achievements, theologically insufficient, because it does not succeed in offering a complete conceptualization of the representation of the religious consciousness.[33] This shows for Pannenberg that the philosophical conception of the Absolute can offer criteria for the interpretation of the understanding of God in the Christian religious tradition, but it cannot replace a theological concept of God.

In his considerations of the relationship between consciousness and subjectivity, Pannenberg questions the Kantian view that the consciousness of the identity of the ego is the condition for the possibility of our experience of objects in the world. If the Kantian view is correct, the question of the Absolute turns into the question of the constitutive ground of subjectivity. This, however, implies that human subjectivity must be thought of as positing the idea of its ground, which seems to lead directly to Feuerbach's theory of projection.[34] In contrast, Pannenberg follows suggestions made by William James and developed by George Herbert Mead and Erik H. Erikson that the consciousness of the unity of the ego is mediated through our experience of the world so that the self can be understood as constituted in social and spiritual interaction.[35] Pannenberg then presents it as one of the tasks of a renewed metaphysics of the Absolute to show that both the experience of the world and self-consciousness in their mutual relationship have their foundation in the relationship to the Absolute.[36]

For Pannenberg the basis for such a reconstruction of metaphysics is the relationship of being and time, presented as the central problem of a fundamental ontology in Heidegger's *Being and Time* in 1927. Drawing on such diverse sources as Plotinus, Dilthey, and Heidegger, and correcting what he sees as their shortcomings, Pannenberg argues that the totality of finite being should be thought of as participation in eternity so that the future is conceived as the origin of the totality of finite beings and their being understood as the anticipation of their future.[37]

The implications of this view for our understanding of knowing and being are developed in a discussion of the relationship between concept and anticipation. All concepts are for Pannenberg anticipations of the reality they denote, all factual statements anticipate the appearance of the state of affairs they express. The relationship between the form and the content of all our experience therefore reflects the relationship between the act of anticipating and what is being anticipated by it. Furthermore, Pannenberg claims, here we can see the relationship of identity and difference of our concepts with what they designate. The conceptual anticipation is *not yet* identical with the reality it anticipates. However, since this reality will be fully disclosed in the future, it is *already*, albeit fragmentarily, present in its conceptual anticipation.[38] For Pannenberg this applies not only to our knowing, but also to the being of everything. The identity of whatever there is is not yet completely actualized at any point in the process of time. The essence of everything can only become fully actual at the end of the process of time so that everything has its essence in anticipation of its completion in the future. For Pannenberg, this is the foundation of a new understanding of substance, since things would be *what* they are (as substances) retroactively from the result of their becoming, but the mode of their being what they are (the *how* of their being) is that of an anticipation of the completion of the process of their becoming.[39] If the end of time is eternity, then the essence of everything anticipates eternity in this way. Ontologically and epistemologically, Pannenberg's philosophy can be characterized as a *realism of anticipation* which corresponds to and is part of the *eschatological realism* of his theology.

With this exposition of the basic outlines of his philosophy Pannenberg has provided a useful aid for the interpretation of his thought. Although there is a mutual dependence between philosophy and theology, Pannenberg has warned his readers not to interpret his theology as the religious expression of an independently established philosophical system. Philosophical reflection has in his view primarily not a foundational but a criteriological function for theology in providing critical and constructive criteria for the adequate exposition of the view of reality of religious faith in the realm of thought. However, it is theology which is based on the revelation of God in history that completes the philosophical enterprise of grasping the unity of reality in the One by presenting all reality as grounded in the reality of God. That is the unifying theme of the three volumes of his *Systematic Theology*.

Systematic Theology

In the spring of 1988 Pannenberg published the first volume of his *Systematische Theologie*, comprising the prolegomena to dogmatics and the doctrine of God. In 1991 and 1993 followed the second and third volumes. Compared to Pannenberg's earlier writings, one distinctive difference becomes immediately obvious. While the earlier works can, at least to a certain extent, be seen as successive steps in the development of the theological conception that was programmatically introduced in *Revelation as History*, this conception is now presented in its full systematic *Gestalt*. The systematic balance that is achieved in this comprehensive presentation also leads to a number of important clarifications concerning some of the more contentious aspects of Pannenberg's earlier work.

Truth and God

Pannenberg starts with a discussion of the truth of Christian doctrine as the organizing theme of systematic theology. This has a number of important corollaries. First of all, Pannenberg rejects the notion that theology can be adequately understood as the expression of human notions about the Divine. It must be grounded in the divine mediation of God in revelation.[40] The dependence of all knowledge of God on God as the ground of its possibility necessitates, secondly, understanding dogma not primarily as an expression of the consensus of the church, but as an "eschatological concept" (K. Barth), referring to the final disclosure of truth at the end of history which is nevertheless proleptically present in God's self-revelation in Christ as it is presented in Scripture.[41] This implies, thirdly, that dogmatic theology has to presuppose the truth of the tradition of faith grounded in revelation without claiming that this is an already established and self-evident truth. In order to overcome this apparent dilemma Pannenberg suggests that the fact that God's reality and the truth of his revelation remains contentious before the *eschaton* must itself be understood as grounded in God, if God is indeed the creator of heaven and earth.[42]

In a theological conception where the relationship of "truth" and "God" is made the unifying focus of the exposition of the contents of Christian faith, the questions surrounding the concept of God and the possibility and actuality of knowledge of God are – not surprisingly – of central importance. Pannenberg argues against all attempts to analyze "God" as a proper name and insists that the expression has to be understood as a general designator. The metaphysical concept of God which is expressed by this use of "God" functions in his view as a general condition for understanding Christian God-talk. It has to be presupposed in order to assert the claim that the God of the philosophers really exists as the God of the Bible.[43]

It was, according to Pannenberg, the original intention of "natural theology" to examine the adequacy of religious ways of talking about God in any given religious tradition by formulating criteria for assessing whether God-talk is in accordance with a philosophically coherent conception of the "nature" of the Divine. However, neither the theistic proofs nor the theological critique of natural theology, exemplified by Barth, seem to offer a reliable foundation for the justification of theological claims. Is there a possible resolution to this dilemma? Pannenberg thinks that such a solution can be found, if we hold fast to the underlying conviction of natural theology that God has to be conceived as the ground of the possibility of the existence of the world and humanity. Although this does not offer firm ground for developing a *natural theology* by means of reason alone, it nevertheless indicates the possibility of conceiving of *natural knowledge* of God, not as a human capacity, but as a factual characteristic of human life. Pannenberg thereby shifts the ground of the discussion from the *cognitio Dei naturalis acquisita*, the acquired natural knowledge of God that forms the basis of the formal theistic proofs, to the *cognitio Dei naturalis insita*, the innate knowledge of God. For Pannenberg there is such an awareness of God, a claim that can in his view be substantiated from anthropology, and which is discussed in the history of religious thought with reference to concepts such as "conscience," "immediate awareness," and "basic trust." These notions express, according to Pannenberg, the fact that human beings live in virtue of the "excentric openness" of their existence in an unthematic awareness of their own life as being posited into the whole of reality and dependent on the divine ground of reality. Although this awareness is unthematic and can only be identified as awareness of God from the perspective of a reflective interpretative framework, it is nevertheless not a human possibility that awaits actualization; it is fully actual in the very fact of human existence.[44] In Pannenberg's view it is this feature of the human condition which Paul refers to in Romans 1: 19ff.[45] and which provides an essential *Anknüpfungspunkt* (point of contact) for all Christian claims to universality.

However, Pannenberg emphasizes that every attempt at finding a universal foundation for religious claims has to be based on the interpretation of reality in the concrete religions. Therefore Pannenberg interprets the history of religions as the history of the appearance of the unity of God. This is the way, he claims, in which God discloses his truth. In Pannenberg's view, Israel's understanding of history as the sphere of the appearance of God's unity provides the key for the theological interpretation of the history of religions. It provides a possibility for resolving the thorny problems of particularity and universality in their manifold forms, because the mediation of particularity and universality is an essential characteristic of divine self-demonstration in history itself.[46] Within the framework of this conception the concept of revelation denotes the origin and basic criterion of knowledge of God.

Within the Judaeo-Christian tradition revelation is therefore also seen as the criterion for the adequacy of a religious relationship. The fundamental ambivalence of this relationship is rooted in the fact that human beings become aware of the divine ground of being in the context of human experience of the world. This produces the danger that the divine mystery itself is identified with its sphere of manifestation so that the Infinite is turned into something finite. Pannenberg claims, however, that in Christianity the reduction of the Infinite to a finite entity is sublated by the event of revelation, which creates the possibility that the fundamental ambivalence of the religious relationship is healed in faith grounded in revelation.[47]

Pannenberg's analysis of revelation is in many ways the center of the exposition in the first volume of the *Systematische Theologie*. First of all, it is the place where it has to be shown that human knowledge of God has its origin and foundation in God's self-disclosure. Secondly, it has to be demonstrated how the unthematic awareness of the divine ground of reality receives a definite content in revelation. And thirdly, it is here that the justification of the claim that the notion of God's self-demonstration in history can mediate particularity and universality in the history of religions has to be developed. At the same time these considerations are also the turning point for the structure of the argument in the *Systematische Theologie*. Pannenberg turns from the external perspective where the conception of God and the claims of the history of religions are phenomenologically introduced and analyzed with regard to their function for the view of reality, to the internal perspective of Christian revelation from which a systematic reconstruction of Christian doctrine is developed. This shift of perspective is possible because the concept of revelation appears from the external perspective as the foundational notion for the validation of religious claims.[48]

After a detailed survey of the biblical conceptions of revelation Pannenberg introduces his own conception of God's indirect revelation in history as an attempt at overcoming the various difficulties that have riddled the discussion of revelation in the modern era. He furthermore claims that the notion of God's indirect self-revelation in history provides a possibility for integrating the pluriform conceptions of revelation in the biblical writings and offers a systematic framework for the clarification of the notion of the Word of God.[49]

Throughout the discussion it is Pannenberg's aim to integrate the legitimate emphases of the Word of God theologies in his own conception and to correct overstatements in his original program. This is especially apparent in the discussion of the thesis that had elicited much criticism when *Revelation as History* was first published, that God's revelation in history is open to everyone who has eyes to see. Pannenberg explains that the thesis of the universal epistemic accessibility of God's revelation refers primarily to God's universal self-demonstration in his kingdom. Only insofar as this is pre-actualized in Jesus Christ can the accessibility of revelation be extended to history.[50] It is precisely this notion of the anticipatory disclosure of God's ultimate purpose in Jesus which leads to the understanding of Jesus Christ as the Word of God in the full sense developed in the doctrine of the Trinity.[51]

Pannenberg's conception of the doctrine of the Trinity is perhaps the most interesting aspect of his dogmatic synthesis, since he introduces trinitarian reflection as a new approach to the solution of some of the crucial problems of the traditional conception of the doctrine of God. The result is a reversal of the traditional structure for the exposition of the doctrine of God which started from the existence of

God, proceeded to the discussion of the essence and attributes of the one God and then added the doctrine of the Trinity. Instead, Pannenberg starts from the doctrine of the Trinity and employs this as the interpretative key for the conception of the being and attributes of the triune God.

Pannenberg's proposal is to develop the doctrine of the Trinity from the way in which the relationship of Father, Son, and Spirit is disclosed in revelation.[52] This approach from Jesus' relationship to the Father and the Spirit has a number of important consequences for the conceptuality of the doctrine of the Trinity. The classical Western distinction between the processions of the Son (*generatio*) and the Spirit (*spiratio*) from the Father, which constitute the persons of the immanent Trinity, and the sending of the Son and the gift of the Spirit in the divine economy can no longer be seen as adequate to the witness of Scripture where such a distinction between immanent and economic relations cannot be made. Therefore the mutual self-differentiation of Father, Son, and Spirit in the divine economy must be seen as the concrete form of the immanent trinitarian relations.[53] For Pannenberg, the key to an adequate description of these relations is the fact that Jesus distinguishes himself clearly from the God he calls Father, but in renouncing himself completely he makes room for the action of the Father and the coming of his kingdom. In this way God as he eternally is discloses himself in his relationship to Jesus and this reveals an "aspect" in the humanity of Jesus which is the eternal correlate to the Fatherhood of God: the eternal Son.[54] The way in which Jesus distinguishes himself from the Father discloses, when it is interpreted as the self-revelation of God, that there is an eternal relationship of Father and Son in God. The self-differentiation of the Son from the Father corresponds to the self-differentiation of the Father from the Son which consists in the fact that the Son receives all power in heaven and on earth from the Father (Matthew 28: 18) until God's rule has become universally victorious, when the Son will return the power to the Father (cf. 1 Corinthians 15: 24 and 28). Since God's Godness is not independent of the exercise of his rule, this *motif* enables us to see a mutuality in the relationship of Father and Son which is absent from the traditional language of the "begetting" of the Son.[55] The mutuality of the relationship of the Father and the Son is for Pannenberg the key for the correct interpretation of the cross of Christ so that an alternative between the view of the death of God on the cross and the suffering of the human nature of the Son which does not affect the eternal trinitarian relationship can be found.[56]

The resurrection is in Pannenberg's view the access to an adequate understanding of the Third Person, because it depicts the dependence of the Father and the Son on the Spirit as the medium of their community. And from this perspective the whole work of the Son in the glorification of the Father can be assessed on the basis of his dependence on the Spirit. From this approach it is not surprising that Pannenberg rejects the addition of the *filioque* to the Nicene–Constantinopolitan Creed by the Western church. The reason is not simply that this one-sided step was uncanonical, but more important, that it rests on the mistaken Augustinian view of all relations of the Trinity as originating relations, which overlooks the pluriform character of the trinitarian relations and cannot do justice to the Spirit as the medium of the community of the Father and the Son.[57]

The conception of the Trinity that is developed in this way implies with its dialectic of self-differentiation and mutuality that the three persons cannot be understood as three modes of beings in one subject. They have to be understood as three centers of activity. They cannot be reduced to a single relation, but each of them is a focus of a network of relationships. The mutuality of their active relationships furthermore implies for Pannenberg that the *monarchia* of the Father has to be understood as the result of the cooperation of all three persons. The full realization of the *monarchia* of the Father is the kingdom. From this perspective the world as a whole can be seen as the history in which it will be finally demonstrated that the trinitarian God is the only true God. This claim about the eternal Trinity can, however, not be asserted apart from the dynamics of the divine economy in which it finds its eschatological validation.[58]

In the last chapter of the first volume of the *Systematic Theology* Pannenberg turns to the issues of the unity of the divine essence and the divine attributes. Following his approach of using the doctrine of the Trinity as the framework for the whole doctrine of God, he connects the trinitarian question of the unity of the divine essence with the fundamental questions about God's existence and attributes that are commonly treated before the doctrine of the Trinity. He first identifies the central area where the respective problems of both approaches overlap. For the traditional approach the problem consists in the difficulty of reconciling the unity of the divine essence with the pluriformity of the divine attributes. From the perspective of trinitarian theology the question is how the three persons of the Trinity can be understood as presenting one divine essence without reducing them to moments or aspects of the one essential Godhead and without positing the divine essence as a fourth subject lurking behind the persons of Father, Son, and Spirit. As Pannenberg emphasizes, this is to a large extent a question that is related to the eschatological resolution of the tension between the persons of Father, Son, and Spirit in revelation and the hiddenness of the unity of God in the world.

Pannenberg approaches these problems from the question of the relationship of divine essence and existence. The concept of essence is in Pannenberg's view always relative to an indeterminate something that is determined *as* something by applying an essence concept. In the same way God's existence has to be understood first as the indeterminate Infinite that underlies our knowledge of finite objects which we gain by restricting and qualifying the notion of the Infinite. The essence of something appears in distinct moments of existence, but only the complete range of the appearance of something is sufficient for the determination of its essence. We can only speak of the disclosure of essence if we know the complete appearance of something or have a singular appearance that can be seen as constitutive for the full range of appearances. If we apply this conception to the Christian understanding of God we can say that Father, Son, and Spirit are the forms of existence (*Gestalten des Daseins*) of the one divine essence that make it possible to give the notion of the divine essence a distinctive and determinative content.[59] It is, however, crucial for the universality of Christian claims that the determinative forms of the existence of God as Father, Son, and Spirit are ultimately identical with the whole range of his non-thematic and indeterminate presence in his creation.

This reformulation of the traditional problem of the relationship of God's *essentia* and his *existentia* forms the background for Pannenberg's reflections on the doctrine of the divine attributes. Pannenberg sees many of the difficulties in this field as rooted in the underlying understanding of God as *nous* and he attempts to solve these problems by pointing to the analogies of the biblical notions of God as Spirit with the scientific concept of a universal field of force that is manifested in particular corpuscular constellations. This move enables Pannenberg to retain the notions of energy, dynamic effects, and life without ascribing them to a self-conscious subject. His bold proposal is to understand the divine essence and life on the analogy of the field-model and not in terms of the *nous*-model. The Godhead is in this way understood as the divine Spirit or life that is manifested in the three persons of Father, Son, and Spirit.[60] Nevertheless, Pannenberg insists that the three persons of the Trinity are the primary and immediate subjects of divine activity. At the same time he rejects the view that the three persons are first individually constituted and are only then united by *perichoresis*. Since the three persons have to be seen as the forms of existence of the one divine life they are eternally constituted and correlated by its overflowing energy which is mediated through the inner-trinitarian relations.

With this conception Pannenberg still faces two problems. First of all, it must be shown that there is a connection between the relatedness of the divine Triunity and the relationship of the Trinity to the world. The concept of action is in his view eminently suitable for expressing this relationship between the immanent Trinity and the divine economy. In his actions the agent relates to what is outside himself, but in doing so he also relates to himself. In this way God's active presence as Father, Son, and Spirit in his creation is acutely relevant to the eternal identity of the Trinity.[61] Secondly, Pannenberg has to show that it is possible to find a coherent conception of the unity of divine action, because otherwise the ascription of attributes to God would be questionable. He achieves this by reinterpreting the traditional notion of the *monarchia* of the Father in such a way that one can avoid the subordinationist connotations of the traditional view of the Father as source and origin of the Trinity. The *monarchia* has to be related to the Kingdom of God as the ultimate "objective" of God's action, but this *monarchia* is mediated through the Son who becomes incarnate to make the participation of God's creatures in the kingdom possible and through the Spirit who enables them to participate in the relationship of Father and Son. The *monarchia* of the Father in the kingdom is the unitary focus of all divine activity in creation, redemption, and salvation, and of the interrelationship of the three trinitarian persons.[62] Pannenberg emphasizes that divine action should not be understood as satisfying a deficiency in God's eternal being. Rather, God's action in relation to the world has to be seen as "repetition," or perhaps better a re-enactment of his eternal Godhead in relation to his creation.[63] The correlation of "other-directedness" and self-determination in the notion of action and the interpretation of the *monarchia* of the Father in the kingdom as the unitary focus of the immanent and the economic Trinity are the two essential presuppositions of Pannenberg's attempt at reconciling the view of the three persons as primary subjects of all divine activity with the ascription of divine attributes to the one divine essence.

The divine attributes are divided into two groups by Pannenberg: The first set comprises those attributes (like infinity, eternity, omnipotence, and omnipresence) that identify the being who is the subject of further predications. Their function is to make sure that these attributes are indeed attributes of *God*. The attributes of the second set (like righteousness, faithfulness, wisdom, mercy, patience, etc.) are predicated of the being that conforms to the minimal conditions for talking about God laid down by the first set of attributes. Here as in other parts of the *Systematic Theology* it is Pannenberg's intention to show that the different perspectives of a philosophical conception of God and of a Christian theological understanding of God are ultimately capable of being integrated without losing their respective emphases.

In accordance with the reflections in other parts of the work, the concept of the Infinite is presented as the fundamental notion that regulates the entire conception of the divine attributes. It is, however, only capable of performing this regulative as well as integrative role if it is not understood along the lines of the quantitative notion of the mathematically infinite. Drawing on Hegel's understanding of the Infinite, Pannenberg insists that the truly Infinite cannot simply be understood in contrast to the realm of finitude because that would produce the contradictory notion of a limited infinity. The truly Infinite must comprehend everything finite within itself without blurring the initial contrast of infinity and finitude. In order to underline the religious significance of such a conception of God as infinite Pannenberg refers to the biblical understanding of God's holiness which sees holiness as opposed to the profane, but also comprehends the profane through its inclusion in the sanctifying dynamic of God's truly infinite holiness.[64]

This pattern of opposition and inclusion also determines the conception of the other divine attributes. God's eternity cannot be understood only in contrast to time; it must also be thought of as including time in its totality. In contrast to his temporal creatures, God is not confronted with a future that is different from his present. God is his own future and this implies perfect freedom, a freedom that is not restricted by being bound to a temporally limited present.[65]

Pannenberg's treatment of divine omnipresence follows from his understanding of God's eternity, interpreted as the way in which everything that was, is, and will be is present for God who is his own future. It also shows that his notion of the Infinite as including its opposite corresponds to one of the main implications of the trinitarian conception of God: the mediation of transcendence and immanence. This can be achieved, because the trinitarian conception reconciles the transcendence of the Father with the presence of the Son and the Spirit for the believers which, by virtue of the co-equality of the persons and their *perichoresis*, also extends to the Father.[66]

Omnipresence is a condition for divine omnipotence. Perfect omnipotence can only be predicated of God the creator. Seeing God as the creator would imply that God's omnipotence cannot be understood as opposed to the being of his creation. The perfect exercise of omnipotence therefore consists according to Pannenberg in the divine activity that overcomes the alienation between the creator and his creation. For this reason the incarnation of the Son must be understood as the highest expression of God's omnipotence.[67]

This thought already leads to the treatment of the divine attributes that are predicated of God on the basis of his trinitarian action. Here the notion of divine love has the same integrative and regulative function as the notion of the Infinite for the "metaphysical" attributes of God. On the basis of God's revelation in the story of Jesus, love has to be understood as the concrete form of the unity of the divine essence which is manifested in the relationship of the trinitarian persons. Pannenberg therefore presents God's goodness, grace, mercy, righteousness, faithfulness, patience, and wisdom as aspects of the all-encompassing reality of divine love.[68] In this way the trinitarian conception of love becomes the coping-stone of Pannenberg's dogmatic synthesis..

Pannenberg's exposition of the divine economy in the subsequent two volumes of the *Systematic Theology* presents the unfolding of his conception of God as trinitarian love in the history of salvation which concludes with the ultimate revelation of God's love in the Kingdom of God.[69] This account has two closely related aspects: On the one hand, it is the application of Pannenberg's conception of the immanent Trinity on the divine economy which structures the development of the doctrines of creation, reconciliation, and consummation of the world. On the other hand, it represents the application of the account of the divine economy to the trinitarian doctrine of God which can only be completed when God's relationship with creation has reached its goal. It is one of the major achievements of Pannenberg's *Systematic Theology* that it is a consistently trinitarian theology in which everything that can be said in dogmatics must be seen in the framework of an understanding of God as Trinity.

Creation and Christ

The theological possibilities that are opened up by such a consistently trinitarian account are clearly demonstrated in Pannenberg's exposition of the doctrine of creation.[70] It follows from this approach that the relationship of God to what is not God is seen as rooted in the immanent relations of the Trinity. Pannenberg follows the Western trinitarian tradition of describing the immanent Trinity in terms of immanent *actions* which are the ground of God's action in relation to the world.[71] It is the emphasis of God's creating as a free and sovereign act which leads in Pannenberg's view to the understanding of creation as *creatio ex nihilo*.[72] God's freedom in creating, however, must be understood as the freedom of love if God grants creation its own relatively independent being and its own relative permanence. Since love as the character of God's relationship to creation is to be seen as grounded in the Trinity, God's immanent being as a relationship of love must also include difference and community. Like Hegel, Pannenberg sees the Son as the principle of difference in the Trinity and so as the generative principle of created reality existing in relative independence from God. Unlike Hegel, Pannenberg does not interpret the Son as a logically necessary stage in the history of the Absolute, but sees the free self-distinction of Jesus from the Father as the *ratio cognoscendi*, the foundation of knowing, of the eternal Sonship of Jesus, and this as the basis for the claim that the corresponding eternal self-distinction of the Son from the Father is the *ratio essendi*, the ground of being, for the existence of creation.[73] The Son is therefore the structural archetype of the destiny of creation to achieve communion with God. This, however, can only be achieved through the Spirit who is the principle of communion in the immanent Trinity and so the medium of the participation of created life in the divine trinitarian life.[74] Following Augustine, Pannenberg sees creation as an eternal act which comprehends all stages of the divine economy and so forms the background of concepts such as the conservation and the divine governing of the world, which express the form of God's creativity in relation to a temporal creation.

It is for Pannenberg an essential aspect of the task of a theology of creation to relate its assertions to the findings of the scientific investigation of the world. If it fails to do so, it falls short of its theological task to give a rational account of the sovereignty and exclusiveness of God the Creator. For Pannenberg the conceptuality of a trinitarian doctrine of creation, which focuses on the relations between plurality and unity, particularity and universality, and order and spontaneity, provides the resources for a critical theological appropriation of central scientific concepts.[75] His own proposals for a dialogue between theology and the sciences concentrate on his understanding of the Spirit and the Spirit's activity in terms of a field of force. Other convergences between a theology of creation and scientific theories emerge when Pannenberg rejects the idea that the "beginning" can be conceived as the fundamental concept for understanding the totality of the world. His proposal, that only the end of the history of the world can be understood as the basis for notions of totality, corresponds with the views of "eschatological" cosmologies such as the one proposed by Barrow and Tipler.[76]

The trinitarian framework also shapes Pannenberg's anthropological reflections.[77] In contrast to the mainstream of tradition which identified *pneuma* and *nous* Pannenberg distinguishes them. This means that human reason just as much as the material existence of humans depends on the life-giving Spirit.[78] While reason with its capacity for discerning differences reflects the self-differentiation of the Son from the Father as the ground of all difference, the unity of consciousness, located in the imagination, and the unity of personhood, the disclosure of the totality of a personal life in its existence, are both mediated by the Spirit, the principle of unity in its eschatological fulfillment. From this trinitarian perspective Pannenberg recommends a hermeneutic for the interpretation of the *imago Dei* which combines the statements in Genesis 1: 26f. with the Pauline emphasis on Christ as the image of God. It follows that both the notions of an original perfection of humans and of the Fall as the loss of the image of God must be rejected. The image of God becomes a dynamic notion for the human destiny to live in communion with God which is realized in the Incarnation.[79] However, human beings can only achieve their destiny in conformity with the self-distinction of the Son from the Father. Sin is therefore defined as the refusal of humans to accept their created finitude by distinguishing themselves explicitly from God. In this way they attempt to assume the place of God.[80] Since the character of sin is the separation from God as the source of all life, death becomes the natural consequence of sin. For Pannenberg, however, mortality is not identical with finitude since Christian hope affirms for finite created beings a life where sin and death as its consequence have been overcome.[81]

In his christology in the *Systematic Theology*[82] Pannenberg offers an extensive discussion of the relationship of a christology from "below" to a christology "from above." Christology from below attempts to offer a reconstruction of the development of dogmatic assertions of Jesus Christ from Jesus' history and destiny. In the context of the *Systematic Theology* which interprets the history and destiny of Jesus as the action of the trinitarian God for the salvation of humankind, christology "from below" and "from above" are complementary insofar as the former offers a reconstruction of the foundation of the statements the latter develops systematically.[83] The starting point of christology in the framework of his trinitarian theology of creation is for Pannenberg the distinctive humanity of Christ in which the destiny of humanity to live in communion with God becomes reality in Jesus' filial relationship to God. It is rooted in his self-distinction from the Father by becoming obedient to him. The divinity of Jesus is therefore not a foreign element added to the reality of Jesus' humanity, but the reflection from Jesus' relationship to the Father on his being and on the eternal being of God.[84] Jesus' claim that the future reign of God begins with the acceptance of his message confronted his contemporaries with a stark alternative: Either he assumes the unique authority of God which is the supreme form of blasphemy, or his claim to authority derives from his filial obedience to God the Father. The resurrection is in Pannenberg's interpretation the justification of Jesus by God the Father and in this way validates Jesus' message.[85] This implies that God is eternally as Jesus proclaimed God to be: God is eternally the Father revealed in the Son and therefore the Son is eternally in relation with the Father and in this sense pre-existent.

In *Jesus – God and Man* Pannenberg demonstrated that a christology which attempts to describe Jesus' unity with God in the conceptuality of two natures understood in two separate substances leads to an uneasy impasse between a unification christology and a christology of disjunction. In the *Systematic Theology* he comes to a far more constructive trinitarian account of the doctrine of the Incarnation. In this trinitarian framework humanity is conceived to be essentially in relation to God because it is a specific expression of the Son as the generative principle of difference and of created independence. It therefore has the capacity of becoming the medium for expressing the self-distinction of the Son from the Father and so their communion-in-difference. Since living in communion with God is the created destiny of humanity from the beginning, the Incarnation is not an alien intrusion into humanity but the actualization of its destiny. However, this is only possible where the Spirit elevates humanity ecstatically above its finitude and so enables it to accept its finitude and so to become the medium of the expression of the relationship of Father and Son.[86] Conversely, the Incarnation is the self-actualization or self-fulfillment of God in his relationship to the world, though not – and here Pannenberg differs from Barth – in the eternal immanent trinitarian relations.[87]

For Pannenberg soteriology is a function of christology.[88] The reconciliation of God and the world in Christ is exclusively God's work. Nevertheless, it has the "form" of representation since humanity participates in this process by being represented in Christ.[89] Jesus' death discloses this representation, since he dies for those who condemned him and so brought God's judgment upon themselves. Jesus' representation of humanity, not only through the cross but in his whole history and destiny, has an inclusive significance for all humankind, though only in an anticipatory sense which is worked out through the apostolic ministry of the church. Therefore Pannenberg discusses the theological significance of the Gospel and the doctrine of the inspirations of Scripture in the context of the doctrine of reconciliation.[90] The authority of the Gospel consists in the fact that it represents the authority of Christ over against the church which is called by it to become the sign and anticipatory representation of the community of reconciled humanity in the Kingdom of God. Through the Gospel Christ continues his representation of humanity by employing the ministry of the church for its complete actualization in the Kingdom of God.

The Church and the Kingdom of God

The third volume of the *Systematic Theology* comprises Pannenberg's ecclesiology and his eschatology. His treatment of the church documents his commitment to the ecumenical process. His specific aim is to offer a reassessment of the doctrinal differences between Protestantism and Roman Catholicism in order to examine and, if possible, to overcome the doctrinal obstacles for achieving greater visible unity of the church. This ecumenical emphasis follows from Pannenberg's view that the church is to be interpreted as the anticipation and sign of the community of humankind in the Kingdom of God. This eschatological horizon for discussing the church as the "sacrament of the Kingdom"[91] relativizes all exclusive claims that might be made for any historical ecclesial community, and it forms the background for Pannenberg's ecumenical hermeneutic for ecclesiology which is designed to show that apparently contradictory doctrinal positions can be seen as complementary aspects of a more comprehensive truth.

Pannenberg combines traditional Western and Eastern emphases by arguing that the church is constituted by the Son and the Spirit together.[92] The perichoretic relationship between the Son and the Spirit is reflected in the divine economy in the way in which the Spirit enables believers to participate in the eternal life of God by including them in the filial relationship of the Son to the Father. This trinitarian approach also shapes the systematic structure of Pannenberg's ecclesiology. Pannenberg gives priority neither to the appropriation of salvation by the individual believer nor to the communion of saints. Both are integrated in an ecclesiological perspective which sees individual and communal aspects of salvation as related dimensions of the work of the Spirit. The personal communion of believers is mediated through participation in the sacraments as the means of grace. Eucharistic communion demonstrates that for Pannenberg most clearly: Membership in the body binds the relationship of believers with Christ inextricably together with their relationship with one another. The Spirit is interpreted in this way as the focus of various relationships that make up the church, enabling the immediacy of every individual Christian to God and joining them together in the communion of the body of Christ where they receive in the Spirit their fundamental orientation toward the Kingdom of God.[93]

Pannenberg's discussion of the salvific effects of the Spirit follows the Pauline triad of faith, hope, and love. Here we encounter many of Pannenberg's earlier views on the nature of faith, although they are now integrated into the trinitarian framework of the *Systematic Theology*. If faith is seen as self-grounding and self-authenticating, Pannenberg argues, it cannot be distinguished from mere subjectivism. Faith, therefore, must be seen as having its ground in God's revelation in Israel and its eschatological fulfillment in Jesus.[94] However, if the person, message, and history of Jesus are interpreted as the self-revelation of the trinitarian God, an appropriate notion of the ground of faith must include reference to the trinitarian God.[95] Before God's complete and universal self-disclosure in the Kingdom of God the "thoughts of faith," attempting to give expression to the ground of faith, will remain provisional. Hope is therefore based on faith.[96] Since it is directed toward the fulfillment of the promise of Jesus' history, it is necessarily universal in character so that the hope of and for the individual person must be included in the universal hope of the renewal of humankind in the Kingdom of God. Love is in a similar way related to faith. Faith, as Pannenberg interprets it, is directed toward the inclusion into Jesus' filial relationship with God the Father and must therefore be interpreted as participation in the trinitarian communion of love. Here both love of God and love of a neighbor have their foundation. Love of a neighbor is the inclusion of believers in the movement of God's love to the world which is the point of the divine economy.[97] Pannenberg's theology of prayer has its place in the crucible of faith, hope, and love.[98]

Pannenberg's discussion of the doctrine of justification is shaped by the ecumenical intention of his ecclesiology.[99] He offers a thoroughgoing critique of the forensic understanding of justification which interprets the sinner's being declared righteous as the foundation of the righteousness of faith. Pannenberg argues that the Pauline treatment of the notion of righteousness of faith shows that being declared righteous must have its basis in the righteousness of faith; it does not constitute it. Righteousness of faith, he argues, is to be understood as living in communion with Christ by participating in his death and resurrection through baptism. From this perspective the doctrinal differences in the treatment of justification between the Reformers and the Council of Trent can no longer be seen as fundamental differences that could be allowed to serve as a justification for the continuing division between the Protestant churches and the Roman Catholic Church. The confessional difference is relativized as a difference between two theological schools whose views are both in need of being corrected by scriptural exegesis.[100] One cannot miss the critical point this argument contains against Protestant confessional theology. Pannenberg argues, in fact, that if Protestantism takes the principle *sola scriptura* seriously and sees Scripture as the ultimate criterion of doctrine, it cannot maintain the doctrine of justification as the decisive point of divergence in relation to Roman Catholic theology. This is an implication of Pannenberg's ecclesiology which seems sure to provoke controversy among his fellow Protestant theologians.

With his interpretation of justification Pannenberg has brought baptism and justification closely together: The point of baptism is to be found in the participation of the believer in the death and resurrection of Christ.[101] The celebration of the eucharist is for Pannenberg the symbolic anticipation of the coming reign of God in the presence of the risen Lord.[102] This is the basis for asserting the ecclesiological primacy of the local church: Wherever the eucharist is celebrated, there is the church.[103] Pannenberg follows the approach of recent ecumenical eucharistic theology by stressing that the real presence of Christ cannot be exclusively located in the elements of bread and wine. It must be seen as being mediated in the whole act of eucharistic worship.[104] The link between anamnesis and epiclesis requires a consistently trinitarian interpretation. The Spirit as the transforming power of the world is at work where we are drawn into the movement of Christ's self-giving love. The symbolic act of eucharistic worship presents reality, insofar as the transformation of creation, aimed at the inclusion of creation in the filial relationship of the Son and the Father, has already begun in Christ. Because the sacraments are indications of the mystery of salvation in Christ, and since the sign indicates the presence of the reality signified, Pannenberg can argue for a wide notion of sacramentality. If the character of a sacrament depends exclusively on whether something can be shown to be included in or ordered toward the mystery of salvation in Christ, as Pannenberg argues, it follows that the files on the case of the recognition of the seven sacraments of the Roman Catholic Church by the Protestant Churches must be reopened.[105]

A similar ecumenical thrust can be found in Pannenberg's discussion of church leadership.[106] Church leadership in all its forms is in his view rooted in the notion of apostolic leadership which is called to serve the unity of the church. Since unity is for Pannenberg the first and foremost of the essential attributes of the church, he attempts to correlate different levels of leadership with different levels of church unity, from the local church to the worldwide church.[107] It is consistent with this approach that Pannenberg's reflections conclude with a call for the recognition of the historic function of the bishop of Rome to act as the representative for the whole of Christianity. However, for Pannenberg this is not to be justified by appealing to divine right. It is a matter of historic authority.[108] This is a point where one may wonder whether this form of ecclesiological reflection actually serves the achievement of greater visible unity of the whole church. Many Protestant theologians will feel that Pannenberg is conceding too much to Roman claims in pleading for a special office of unity for the whole church and sacrificing too much in the process, like the ecclesiological significance of the priesthood of all believers as the basis for any special ministry in the church. Many Roman Catholic theologians, one may suspect, will feel that reference to the historic authority of the bishop of Rome does not give a convincing theological justification of papal primacy.

The doctrine of election is for Pannenberg the link between ecclesiology and eschatology.[109] He rejects what one may call the classical view of election as it is developed by Origen and Augustine for its abstract character which results in a highly individualistic notion of election, unable to account for the particular, historical character of election in the biblical traditions.[110] For Pannenberg the biblical image of the "people of God" is the central term of the doctrine of election. It is systematically displaced, he finds, if it is employed only in the context of the church. The notion of the "people of God" helps to see election in its concrete historical circumstances as God's call to particular people to be the church and so to be an anticipatory representation of the universal character of God's will of salvation for the whole of humankind. Pannenberg sees this mediation of particularity and universality as the basis for a comprehensive theology of history which attempts to develop a theological interpretation of church history.[111] While it would be hard to deny the significance of the theological task of interpreting history, the difficulties of Pannenberg's particular approach will be indicated, at least for some of his readers, by the fact that he sees the recognition of the significance of Rome for the whole of Christianity as one of the historical tendencies that are uncovered in such a theological interpretation.[112]

Throughout his theological career Pannenberg has highlighted the significance of eschatology for the whole enterprise of Christian theology. The *Systematic Theology*, which concludes with a discussion on "the perfection of creation in the Kingdom of God," is no exception.[113] For Pannenberg Christian doctrine depends for its content and for its truth on the coming of God to consummate his rule over creation.[114] The Kingdom of God thus becomes the organizing center of his eschatology. Pannenberg relates three aspects.[115] The Kingdom of God is, first of all, the consummation of the community of humankind, and this, radically conceived, includes the resurrection of the dead. Secondly, it is the end of history which in the context of Christian faith cannot mean its abolition and transition into nothingness, but can only mean the inclusion of history in God's eternity. Therefore the Kingdom of God is, thirdly, the entering of eternity into time. This last aspect has central significance for Pannenberg: Everything in eschatology revolves around the relationship of time and eternity.[116] Pannenberg's own account of this relationship is based on his ontology.[117] The present reality of everything is constituted from its eschatological future. Therefore the essence of something can only be understood as the simultaneous totality of its appearances which must be conceived as being "located" in eternity. The process of time is therefore both the form of the appearance and the process of becoming of any essence. If eternity is understood as the future perfection of everything, then this future is present in the processes occurring in time as the aim of these processes. Everything that occurs and perishes in time, Pannenberg claims, is preserved in God's eternity which includes all temporal events. Pannenberg rejects an understanding of the resurrection of the dead and of the restoration of the world which is focused on the continuation of temporal existence beyond death. Rather, the resurrection of the dead and restoration of worldly being must be understood, he argues, as the act through which God returns to the creatures their independent form of existence. The identity of every created being is preserved by their being included into God's eternity and it is reconstituted after their death in the resurrection.[118]

The metaphor of the "Last Judgment" in Pannenberg's interpretation expresses that the participation of created beings in God's eternity requires their radical transformation. The point of divine judgment is therefore not the annihilation of the world but its purification by the light of God's glory to enable its participation in God's eternal life.[119]

Apart from the traditional topics of the doctrine of the Last Things, eschatology has in Pannenberg's *Systematic Theology* an overall function for his theological conception. Right from the outset Pannenberg has emphasized time and again the provisionality of our knowledge of God which remains a matter of controversy before the *eschaton*. Like every other concept the Christian concept of God is an anticipation of the reality it denotes.[120] It is therefore only the eschatological consummation of the reign of God which will provide definite proof of God's existence and essence. Eschatology is therefore the place in the systematic structure where the question of theodicy must be answered.[121] Pannenberg emphasizes with Hegel that all theoretical attempts at offering justification of God in view of the evil in the world remain pointless unless there is a real history of reconciliation, of the overcoming of evil by the rule of God.[122] This history of reconciliation culminates in the eschatological perfection of creation. However, the ultimate perfection of creation is for Pannenberg already present in the time of creation, because the whole of the divine economy reflects the self-prevenience of the future of God in the time of creation.

In this way divine love is seen by Pannenberg as the ground for the distinction of the immanent and the economic trinity and the foundation of their unity. God's love goes beyond the immanent trinitarian life to recreate, to reconcile, and to bring the created world to perfection. Conversely, in the economy of salvation the created world is taken beyond itself in order to be included in the unity of God's own trinitarian life. The distinction and the unity of the immanent and the economic Trinity, which will be fully disclosed in the *eschaton*, is therefore for Pannenberg the heartbeat of divine love, the ground and destiny of the created world.[123]

Achievement and Debate

Pannenberg's theology has from the beginning provoked both criticism and approval. After the publication of *Revelation as History* the two dominating groups of German postwar theology, the Barthian and the Bultmannian schools, reacted vigorously against the criticism of the "Theology of the Word of God" implied in the new theology of history. While the Barthians emphasized the necessity of interpreting the concept of divine self-revelation as God's *direct* revelation in his threefold Word and rejected Pannenberg's conception as a new version of theological rationalism,[124] Bultmann's followers complained about the misunderstanding of the relationship of Christian *kerygma* and the historicity of human existence and accused Pannenberg of reconstituting an obsolete speculative metaphysics of history.[125] Both schools accused Pannenberg of making Christian faith dependent on the results of historical investigation and of sacrificing the autonomy of theological reflection in an attempt at establishing its foundations. In contrast, the close relationship between theology and historical research was one of the reasons why Pannenberg's work was greeted with enthusiasm by more conservative Christians who saw in his arguments for the resurrection as a historical event a decisive refutation of modern skepticism concerning the historical foundations of Christian faith.

There can be no doubt that Pannenberg's theological conception is one of the major contributions to twentieth-century Protestant theology which has also stimulated considerable debate in Roman Catholic theology. Pannenberg's attempts to provide the dogmatic bases for an ecumenical consensus embracing Roman Catholic, Protestant, and Eastern Orthodox churches are being widely discussed in ecumenical circles. However, his endeavor to demonstrate that dogmatic positions which seemed contradictory can be seen as complementary aspects of a more comprehensive truth has been greeted with considerable skepticism by Protestant theologians. They question whether it is possible, or indeed necessary, to seek some sort of doctrinal synthesis as the basis for ecclesial unity. Could a model of reconciled diversity which respects remaining doctrinal differences but does not see them as obstacles for a communion of churches not be a better way of witnessing to the promise of unity?

Although firmly rooted in the intellectual traditions of German theology and philosophy, Pannenberg's theology has influenced theological debate in various other intellectual and religious contexts and has, in turn, been influenced by a variety of intellectual currents and traditions in the Western world. It is thus an example of theological reflection under the conditions of cultural contact and scholarly communication after the Second World War.

When one attempts to summarize the achievements of Pannenberg's theological conception three characteristics seem to be most notable. First of all, Pannenberg's theology is an attempt to meet the challenge of the atheistic critique of religion in the modern era without seeking refuge in strategies of intellectual immunization, and on the reflective level that is required by the intellectual standard of the critique and by its pervasive influence in contemporary culture. Secondly, Pannenberg seeks to realize this aim by developing his theology in close contact with the findings of biblical exegesis and against the background of a comprehensive analysis of the Christian tradition. Thirdly, one of the distinctive marks of Pannenberg's theological reflection is the awareness of the necessity for interdisciplinary cooperation with the human sciences and, to a certain extent, with natural science, in which Christian theology interacts with the intellectual efforts of its time. All three characteristics illustrate the conviction underlying Pannenberg's entire conception that Christian theology will only be able to fulfill its task adequately if it develops a comprehensive view of reality that is authentically Christian as well as intellectually plausible, and that provides ethical orientation in the complexities of the modern situation.

It is precisely this view of the task of theology which can provoke a number of critical questions with regard to the conceptual framework in terms of which Pannenberg attempts its execution. The development of a comprehensive view of reality in Christian theology seems to require some kind of ontology which explains what there is and how it is to be interpreted. If the activity of determining how something is to be interpreted is to be capable of resulting in genuine truth-claims, it is necessary to establish that it can correspond to the determination of what there is. Especially in Pannenberg's earlier writings, we encounter at this point a twofold *indeterminacy* in Pannenberg's conception: What something *is* is only established in what it *becomes* in the future; and every act of determining how what there is is to be interpreted has an irreducibly hypothetical status. Is this a necessary corollary of Christian eschatology or does it introduce an unnecessary element of indeterminacy into the Christian view of reality which would have to be seen as self-defeating? This problem is further illustrated by Pannenberg's proposal of comprehending both God's creation and his self-revelation in the concept of the futurity of God. If the existence and nature of God are finally determined and made evident only in the eschatological self-demonstration of God's kingdom, it would seem that God's relation to the world remains – at least penultimately – indeterminate.

The *Systematic Theology* does not only document Pannenberg's awareness of these difficulties, it also demonstrates his attempt to overcome their problematical consequences. This is illustrated by the determinative role of the doctrine of the Trinity, not only for the understanding of God but for the entire dogmatic conception. If everything that is is ultimately grounded in God's trinitarian relation to his creation and if God's relation to the world is the repetition or re-enactment of his eternal being as Father, Son, and Spirit, then the apparent indeterminacy has its limit precisely in the eternal identity of the triune God. What something is and how it is to be interpreted will only be ultimately established in the Kingdom of God where the relationship of creation to the trinitarian God will be evident for all in the self-demonstration of his rule. But since this is the "repetition" in the relationship to creation of what God is eternally in his triune being, this ultimate disclosure is far from indeterminate.

It does, however, seem questionable, whether the conception of God as Infinite is indeed the most adequate model for understanding the divine essence. One could ask whether this does not reintroduce an element of indeterminacy into the conception of God which the careful description of the relationship of the economic and the immanent Trinity attempted to overcome. It could furthermore be questioned whether the concept of "the Infinite" is indeed a key model for describing the divine essence or whether it does not function as a "qualifier" for other models for the description of the God–world relationship and for the concepts employed to express the divine attributes. Pannenberg's own attempts to give content to this purely formal concept by adapting the Hegelian notion of the "truly Infinite," which comprehends the contrast of finite and infinite in itself, and by developing the analogy with the biblical notion of God's holiness, would seem to point in the same direction. The general question that seems to arise at this point is whether the strong emphasis on God as the Infinite is (in spite of its venerable theological ancestors) really demanded by the contents of Christian faith or whether it is not primarily required by Pannenberg's own conception of the non-thematic awareness of the Infinite which plays such an important role for Pannenberg's religious epistemology.

This leads to the second problem that seems to underlie many of the crucial and much debated features of Pannenberg's theological methodology. Pannenberg has from the outset attempted to find a middle way between the Scylla of a "dogmatic" exposition of Christian doctrine based on revelation which fails to offer sufficient reasons for its assertions and the Charybdis of a "rationalist" treatment of theology which only allows such statements as can be justified by means of reason alone. The *Systematic Theology* presents his most developed attempt to mediate between the internal perspective of faith and the external perspective of reason. His approach, to start from the description of religious and theological claims and to identify within this framework the concept of revelation as the irreplaceable foundation of all theological claims from which the reconstruction of the contents of revelation can then proceed, is certainly one of the most interesting proposals for the solution of this thorny problem in modern theology. It documents Pannenberg's insistence that faith is not grounded in itself and can therefore not be treated as self-justifying, and it illustrates the determined effort to give reasons for the assertions of faith that are intelligible and rationally plausible within the framework of reason. But at least some would disagree with the conclusions which Pannenberg draws from this for the conception of Christian theology. For Pannenberg it is essential that the theologian can establish certain foundational principles outside the perspective of faith that would support the claims to universality made within that framework. Therefore he attempts to reconstitute the traditional insights of natural theology in his conception of the non-thematic awareness of the Infinite that is given in the factual constitution of humanity. The fundamental problem connected with this approach is not the thesis that there is a universal awareness of the Divine which is the basis for the culpability of humanity's attempt at ignoring the reality of God. This thesis only becomes problematical when it is employed as a foundational principle for securing the universality of Christian truth-claims. The use of anthropological and epistemological reflections as a modern *praeambula fidei* would seem to provoke the danger that these considerations are made subject to far-ranging theological reinterpretations that would reduce philosophy to an ancillary role for the constructive theological task. But as the complex history of the relationship of faith and reason documents, this strategy not only threatens the autonomy of philosophical reflection which, after all, would not have to be the primary concern of the theologian. It would also appear that if the theologian employs non-theological considerations as foundational principles for theology the categories developed from the perspective of reason would have a determinative effect for the conception the theologian develops in the reconstruction of the contents of faith from the perspective of faith. Again, the central role of the concept of the Infinite would seem to provide evidence for this danger. However, Pannenberg's insistence that philosophical reflection has primarily a criteriological function for Christian theology, elaborated in *Metaphysics and the Idea of God*, seems to counterbalance some assertions in his earlier work, perhaps most evident in his *Anthropology*, where philosophy and the human sciences seem to acquire a foundational role for Christian theology.

The problems of Pannenberg's attempt at combining the perspective of reason and the perspective of faith in his theological conception could be summarized in the following question: Is it necessary to try to establish the basis for the claims to universality in Christian faith from the perspective of reason, before one turns to the explication of the contents of faith as they are grounded in revelation, or would it be more adequate to treat the universality of theological truth-claims as an implication of the Christian revelation that can only be developed in terms of a rational reconstruction of its contents from the perspective of faith?

Is Pannenberg's theology the type of theology that will determine the future of theology? With regard to its conception of the task of theology in presenting an authentically Christian and intellectually plausible view of reality, developed in intradisciplinary theological cooperation and tested in interdisciplinary dialogue with other sciences, it is to be hoped that many theologians will follow the inspiration of Pannenberg's enterprise. The intellectual rigor of Pannenberg's theological thinking and the willingness, documented in the development of his thought, to subject his arguments to constant re-examination require to be taken so seriously that one should not hesitate to criticize the execution of this program in Pannenberg's own work. However, Pannenberg's work has set standards which his critics also should attempt to meet.

Notes

1   The original group of Rolf Rendtorff and Klaus Koch (Old Testament), Ulrich Wilckens and Dietrich Rössler (New Testament), which was later joined by Martin Elze (church history) and Trutz Rendtorff (social ethics), represented together with Pannenberg almost a complete faculty, and this interdisciplinary cooperation

constituted an effective counter-move against the growing alienation of dogmatic, exegetical, and historical theology.

2 For a biographical portrait see R. J. Neuhaus, "Pannenberg: Profile of a theologian," in W. Pannenberg, *Theology and the Kingdom of God*, ed. Neuhaus, pp. 9–50.

3 For a short description of the formative influences on Pannenberg's early theology see E. Frank Tupper, *The Theology of Wolfhart Pannenberg*, pp. 19–44.

4 See "Epilogue to the second edition," in *Revelation as History*, Supplement 1 to *Kerygma and Dogma*, 2nd edn (Göttingen, 1963), pp. 132–48, p. 132 n. 1.

5 See "Dogmatic theses on the doctrine of revelation," in *Revelation as History*, pp. 125–58.

6 In *Jesus – God and Man*, pp. 127ff. Pannenberg argues for the assumption that Hegel's concept of revelation was mediated to Barth through the Hegelian dogmatician Ph. H. Marheineke.

7 Cf. thesis 3 of the "Dogmatic theses" and the response by the Lutheran theologian Paul Althaus, "Offenbarung als Geschichte und Glaube Bemerkungen zu Wolfhart Pannenbergs Begriff der Offenbarung," *Theologische Literaturzeitung*, 87 (1962), cols 321–30. Pannenberg replied to Althaus's critique in his paper "Insight and faith," in *Basic Questions in Theology*, vol. II, pp. 28–45.

8 See *Jesus – God and Man*, p. 30.

9 Ibid., pp. 33–7.

10 Ibid., pp. 38–49.

11 Ibid., pp. 53–114.

12 Ibid., pp. 115–87.

13 Cf. his essays "Die Subjektivität Gottes und die Trinitätslehre. Ein Beitrag zur Beziehung zwischen Karl Barth und der Philosophie Hegels" and "Der Gott der Geschichte. Der trinitarische Gott und die Wahrheit der Geschichte," *Grundfragen Systematischer Theologie*, vol. II, pp. 96–111 and pp. 112–28.

14 Cf. *Jesus – God and Man*, pp. 88–106, and the essay "Dogmatische Erwägungen zur Auferstehung Jesu," *Grundfragen Systematischer Theologie*, vol. II, pp. 160–73.

15 See *Jesus – God and Man*, pp. 283–96.

16 Cf. ibid., pp. 334–49.

17 Cf. esp. ibid., p. 337.

18 Cf. ibid., pp. 166ff. and the "Postscript to the Fifth German Edition," ibid., pp. 409ff.

19 See the introduction "Theology and Anthropology" in *Anthropology in Theological Perspective*, pp. 11–23.

20 See *What is Man?* pp. 1–13: cf. also the detailed exposition in *Anthropology*, pp. 43–79.

21 See *Anthropology*, pp. 473–84.

22 See *Human Nature, Election, and History*, pp. 23ff.

23 See *Anthropology*, pp. 60–74 (esp. p. 64, n. 61) and pp. 80–6.

24 See *Human Nature*, p. 24.

25 Ibid., pp. 24ff.

26 See "Eucharistic piety – a new experience of Christian community," in *Christian Spirituality and Sacramental Community*, pp. 31–49, esp. 38ff.

27 See also "The Kingdom of God and the Church," in *Theology and the Kingdom of God*, pp. 72–101.

28 See *Theology and the Philosophy of Science*, pp. 297ff.

29 Ibid., pp. 310ff. and pp. 358ff.

30 Ibid., pp. 326–45, esp. pp. 344ff.

31 See *Metaphysics and the Idea of God*, trans. by Philip Clayton (Grand Rapids, MI, and Edinburgh, 1990), pp. 15ff.

32 Ibid., pp. 25ff.

33 Ibid., pp. 38ff.

34 Ibid., p. 46.

35 Ibid., pp. 48–59.

36 Ibid., pp. 61ff.

37 Ibid., pp. 87f.

38 It is interesting to see that Pannenberg develops this view from the theological discussion on the interpretation of Jesus' message of the Kingdom of God and of his resurrection in modern theology and then applies it to the philosophical problem of concept and anticipation. Cf. ibid., pp. 95ff.

39 Ibid., pp. 107f.

40 See *Systematische Theologie* (Göttingen, 1988), vol. I, pp. 12ff.

41 Ibid., pp. 24ff.

42 Ibid., pp. 59ff.

43 Ibid., pp. 78ff.
44 Ibid., pp. 127ff.
45 Ibid., pp. 121ff. and 131ff.
46 Ibid., pp. 189ff.
47 Ibid., pp. 202ff.
48 Ibid., pp. 214ff.
49 Ibid., pp. 266ff.
50 Ibid., pp. 273ff.
51 Ibid., pp. 288ff.
52 Ibid., pp. 331ff. Pannenberg criticizes Barth, who argued programmatically for the same approach, for not following his own program, since he develops the doctrine of the Trinity from the formal notion of revelation as expressed in the statement "God reveals himself as the Lord." With this approach Barth renews Hegel's conception of describing the three persons of the Trinity as "moments" or "states" of the divine self-consciousness by talking about "modes of being" in the one divine subjectivity. Pannenberg interprets this strategy as a renaissance of Augustine's psychological theory of the *vestigia trinitatis* (which Barth had explicitly rejected), since its interpretative key is the *imago trinitatis* in the human soul. Instead of starting from the formal notion of revelation, Pannenberg proposes to develop his trinitarian conception from the content of God's revelation in Christ.
53 Ibid., pp. 332–5.
54 Ibid., pp. 337.
55 Ibid., esp. p. 340.
56 Ibid., p. 341.
57 Ibid., pp. 342–7, esp. pp. 344ff.
58 Ibid., pp. 359ff.
59 Ibid., esp. p. 388.
60 Ibid., pp. 414ff.
61 Ibid., pp. 418ff.
62 Ibid., p. 421 and p. 455.
63 Ibid., p. 422; Pannenberg adapts here Barth's concept of the divine "self-repetition" in his own theological conception.
64 Ibid., pp. 427ff. and pp. 430ff.
65 Ibid., p. 441 and p. 443.
66 Ibid., p. 449.
67 Ibid., p. 451 and pp. 454ff.
68 Ibid., p. 461 and p. 464.
69 Vol. III, pp. 689–94.
70 Vol. II, pp. 15–201.
71 Ibid., pp. 16–22.
72 Ibid., pp. 28–34.
73 Ibid., pp. 36–46.
74 Ibid., p. 45.
75 Ibid., pp. 83ff. and pp. 99–124.
76 Ibid., pp. 185ff. and 94f.
77 Ibid., pp. 203–314.
78 Ibid., pp. 219ff.
79 Ibid., pp. 241–66.
80 Ibid., pp. 298ff.
81 Ibid., pp. 310ff.
82 Ibid., pp. 315–439.
83 Ibid., pp. 327ff.
84 Ibid., pp. 365ff.
85 Ibid., pp. 385–405.
86 Ibid., pp. 427–33.
87 Ibid., pp. 437f.
88 Ibid., pp. 441ff.
89 Ibid., pp. 461ff.
90 Ibid., pp. 501ff.
91 Vol. III, p. 59.
92 Vol. III, pp. 29ff.
93 See the summary, ibid., pp. 154f.
94 Ibid., p. 175.
95 Ibid., p. 182.
96 Ibid., p. 197.
97 Ibid., p. 218.
98 Ibid., pp. 228–37.
99 Ibid., pp. 238–65.
100 Ibid., p. 263.
101 Ibid., pp. 268–314.
102 Ibid., pp. 321ff.
103 Ibid., p. 324.
104 Ibid., pp. 337–57.
105 See the summary of Pannenberg's discussion of the sacraments, ibid., pp. 398–404.
106 Ibid., pp. 404–67.
107 Ibid., pp. 442 and 452–7.
108 Ibid., pp. 468f.
109 Ibid., p. 475.
110 Ibid., pp. 477–85.
111 Ibid., pp. 523–67.
112 Ibid., pp. 558f.
113 Ibid., pp. 569–694.
114 Ibid., p. 573.
115 Ibid., pp. 625–53.
116 Ibid., p. 641.
117 Ibid., pp. 651ff.
118 Ibid., pp. 652f.
119 Ibid., pp. 663ff.
120 Ibid., p. 678.
121 The problem is raised in the context of belief in God the creator; cf. vol. II, pp.

189–201. It is only possible to attempt an answer in the context of eschatology; cf. vol. III, pp. 679–89.

122 Ibid., pp. 682ff.

123 Ibid., p. 694.

124 Cf. L. Steiger, "Revelation history and theological reason: a critique of the theo-

logy of Wolfhart Pannenberg," *History and Hermeneutic* (Journal for Theology and the Church 4), ed. Robert W. Funk (New York, 1967), pp. 82–106.

125 Cf. G. Klein, *Theologie des Wortes Gottes und die Hypothese der Universalgeschichte* (Munich, 1964).

Bibliography

Primary

Pannenberg, Wolfhart, "Dogmatic theses on the doctrine of revelation," in Wolfhart Pannenberg (ed.), *Revelation as History* (New York, 1968) also in *Human Nature, Election, and History* (Philadelphia, 1977).

—— *Jesus – God and Man* (London, 1968).

—— *Theology and the Kingdom of God*, ed. R. J. Neuhaus (Philadelphia, 1969).

—— *Basic Questions in Theology: Collected Essays*, 3 vols (London, 1970–3). (Vol. III was also published under the title *The Idea of God and Human Freedom*, Philadelphia, 1973.)

—— *What Is Man? Contemporary Anthropology in Theological Perspective* (Philadelphia, 1970).

—— *The Apostles' Creed In the Light of Today's Questions* (Philadelphia, 1972).

—— *Theology and the Philosophy of Science* (London, 1976).

—— *Reality and Faith* (Philadelphia, 1977).

—— *Christian Spirituality and Sacramental Community* (London, 1984).

—— *Anthropology in Theological Perspective* (Edinburgh, 1985).

—— *Systematische Theologie*, 3 vols (Göttingen, 1988–93).

—— *Metaphysics and the Idea of God* (Edinburgh, 1990).

—— *An Introduction to Systematic Theology* (Edinburgh, 1991).

Secondary

Braaten, Carl E. and Clayton, Philip (eds), *The Theology of Wolfhart Pannenberg: Twelve American critiques, with an autobiographical essay and response* (Minneapolis, 1988). This contains an excellent bibliography.

McKenzie, D., *Wolfhart Pannenberg and Religious Philosophy* (Washington, DC, 1980).

Tupper, E. F., *The Theology of Wolfhart Pannenberg*, postscript by Wolfhart Pannenberg (London, 1974).

A complete bibliography of primary and secondary works up to the year 1988 can be found in:

Vernunft des Glaubens. Wissenschaftliche Theologie und kirchliche Lehre. Festschrift zum 60. Geburtstag von Wolfhart Pannenberg. Mit einem bibliographischen Anhang herausgegeben von Jan Rohls und Gunther Wenz (Göttingen, 1988).

Jürgen Moltmann

Richard Bauckham

Introduction: Life and Influences

Jürgen Moltmann, born in 1926, and from 1967 to 1994 professor of systematic theology at Tübingen, first became widely known for his *Theology of Hope* (1964). This and his subsequent works have made him one of the most influential of contemporary German Protestant theologians, in the non-Western as well as the Western world, and in wider church circles as well as in academic theology.

Moltmann himself finds the initial source of his theology in his first experience of the reality of God when he was a prisoner of war in the period 1945–8. This was an experience both of God as the power of hope and of God's presence in suffering: the two themes which were to form the two complementary sides of his theology in the 1960s and early 1970s. Moreover, his sense of involvement, during and after the war, in the collective suffering and guilt of the German nation, set him on the road to his later theological involvement with public and political issues, not least the legacy of Auschwitz.

As a student at Göttingen after the war, Moltmann imbibed the theology of Karl Barth and it was some time before he saw any need to move beyond it. The new directions in which he was to move, while remaining indebted to Barth, were inspired in the first place by his teachers at Göttingen: Otto Weber, Ernst Wolf, Hans Joachim Iwand, Gerhard von Rad, and Ernst Käsemann. From Weber and the Dutch "apostolate theology" of A. A. van Ruler and J. C. Hoekendijk, to which Weber introduced him, he gained the eschatological perspective of the church's universal mission toward the coming kingdom of God. Moltmann was one of the first theologians seriously to study Bonhoeffer's work, from which, as well as from Ernst Wolf, he developed his concern for social ethics and the church's involvement in secular society. The influence of Hegel reached Moltmann in the first place through Iwand: Both Hegel and Iwand contributed significantly to the development of Moltmann's dialectical interpretation of the cross and the resurrection. Finally, von Rad and Käsemann helped to give his early theology its solid grounding in current thinking about biblical theology.

The catalyst which finally brought together these converging influences and concerns in Moltmann's theology of hope was the work of the Jewish Marxist philosopher Ernst Bloch. He conceived his *Theology of Hope* as a kind of theological parallel to Bloch's philosophy of hope, and has kept up a continuing dialogue with Bloch throughout his career. Since it was possible for Moltmann to see Bloch's work as, from one point of view, a kind of Marxist inheritance of Jewish messianism, it is not surprising that several important subsequent influences on Moltmann's thought from outside Christian theology were Marxist and Jewish. In the 1960s he was involved in the Christian-Marxist dialogue and, especially in the early 1970s, he took up important concepts from the critical theory of the Frankfurt School. The influence of Jewish theologians such as Franz Rosenzweig and Abraham Heschel can be found at many points in his work. The influence of Marxism later gave way to other political concerns, such as the peace movement and the Green movement.

While Moltmann remains a recognizably Protestant theologian writing in the German context, his work has become increasingly open to other traditions and movements: Roman Catholic theology, Orthodox theology, and the liberation theologies of the Third World. His experience of the worldwide church – including the sufferings, the charismatic worship, and the political commitment of churches in many parts of the world – has also affected his ecclesiology in particular.

Survey: Works, Key Ideas, Method

Moltmann's major works comprise two distinct series. In the first place, there is the early trilogy: *Theology of Hope* (1964), *The Crucified God* (1972), and *The Church in the Power of the Spirit* (1975). These represent three complementary perspectives on Christian theology. *Theology of Hope* is not a study of eschatology so much as a study of the eschatological orientation of the whole of theology. *The Crucified God* is a "theology of the cross" in Luther's sense, i.e., an attempt to see the crucified Christ as the criterion of Christian theology. *The Church in the Power of the Spirit* complements these two angles of approach with an ecclesiological and pneumatological perspective. The three volumes can be read as complementary perspectives in a single theological vision.

Moltmann regards this trilogy as preparatory studies for his second series of major works. This comprises studies of particular Christian doctrines in a planned order, which will resemble a "dogmatics," but which Moltmann prefers to call a series of "contributions" to theological discussion. There are five volumes: *The Trinity and the Kingdom of God* (1980); *God in Creation* (1985); *The Way of Jesus Christ* (1989); *The Spirit of Life* (1991); and *The Coming of God* (1996).

The most important controlling theological idea in Moltmann's early work is his dialectical interpretation of the cross and the resurrection of Jesus, which is then subsumed into the particular form of trinitarianism which becomes the overarching theological principle of his later work. Moltmann's dialectic of cross and resurrection is an interpretation of the cross and resurrection together which underlies the arguments of both *Theology of Hope* and *The Crucified God*. The cross and the resurrection of Jesus are taken to represent opposites: death and life, the absence of

God and the presence of God. Yet the crucified and risen Jesus is the same Jesus in this total contradiction. By raising the crucified Jesus to new life, God created continuity in radical discontinuity. Furthermore, the contradiction of cross and resurrection corresponds to the contradiction between what reality is now and what God promises to make it. In his cross Jesus was identified with the present reality of the world in all its negativity: its subjection to sin, suffering, and death, or what Moltmann calls its godlessness, godforsakenness, and transitoriness. But since the same Jesus was raised, his resurrection constitutes God's promise of new creation for the whole of the reality which the crucified Jesus represents. Moltmann's first two major books work in two complementary directions from this fundamental concept. In *Theology of Hope* the *resurrection* of the crucified Christ is understood in eschatological perspective and interpreted by the themes of dialectical promise, hope, and mission, while in *The Crucified God* the *cross* of the risen Christ is understood from the perspective of the theodicy problem and interpreted by the themes of dialectical love, suffering, and solidarity. (These themes will be explained below.) Finally, it is possible to see *The Church in the Power of the Spirit* as completing this scheme: The Spirit, whose mission derives from the event of the cross and resurrection, moves reality toward the resolution of the dialectic, filling the godforsaken world with God's presence and preparing for the coming kingdom in which the whole world will be transformed in correspondence to the resurrection of Jesus.

The dialectic of cross and resurrection gives Moltmann's theology a strongly christological center in the particular history of Jesus and at the same time a universal direction. The resurrection as eschatological promise opens theology and the church to the whole world and to its future, while the cross as God's identification in love with the godless and the godforsaken requires solidarity with them on the part of theology and the church.

In *The Crucified God* Moltmann's theology became strongly trinitarian, since he interpreted the cross as a trinitarian event between the Father and the Son. From this point he developed an understanding of the *trinitarian history* of God with the world, in which the mutual involvement of God and the world is increasingly stressed. God experiences a history with the world in which he both affects and is affected by the world, and which is also the history of his own trinitarian relationships as a community of divine Persons who include the world within their love. This trinitarian doctrine dominates Moltmann's later work, in which the mutual relationships of the three Persons as a perichoretic, social Trinity are the context for understanding the reciprocal relationships of God and the world. The dialectic of cross and resurrection, developed in a fully trinitarian way, now becomes the decisive moment within this broader trinitarian history, which retains the eschatological direction of *Theology of Hope* and the crucified God's suffering solidarity with the world but also goes further in taking the whole of creation and history within the divine experience. Increasingly, Moltmann has sought to overcome the subordination of pneumatology to christology, and instead to develop both christology and pneumatology in mutual relationship within a trinitarian framework.

In addition to these controlling theological ideas, two methodological principles of Moltmann's theology should be mentioned. The first is that it is orientated both to praxis and to doxology. From the beginning a strongly practical thrust was inherent in Moltmann's theology. His understanding of theology's task not merely to interpret but to change the world, to keep society on the move toward the coming kingdom, produced Moltmann's early political theology. But already with *Theology and Joy* (1971) he became dissatisfied with seeing theology purely as "a theory of a practice," and began to inject elements of contemplation, celebration, and doxology into his work. Praxis itself is distorted into activism unless there is also enjoyment of being and praise of God, not only for what he has done but also for what he is. And if praxis is inspired and required by the eschatological hope of new creation, contemplation anticipates the goal of new creation: enjoyment of God and participation in his pleasure in his creation. This rejection of the *exclusive* claims of praxis in theology enables Moltmann also, in his later work, to distinguish theological knowledge from the pragmatic thinking of the modern world in which the knowing subject masters its object in order to dominate it, and to reinstate, by contrast, that participatory knowledge in which the subject opens himself to the other in wonder and love, perceives himself in mutual relationship with the other, and so can be changed. Such an emphasis fits easily within Moltmann's later trinitarianism, in which reality is characterized by mutual, non-hierarchical relationships – within the Trinity, between the Trinity and creation, and within creation.

Secondly, Moltmann's theology is characterized by its openness to dialogue. He resists the idea of creating a theological "system," as a finished achievement of one theologian, and stresses the provisionality of all theological work and the ability of one theologian only to contribute to the continuing discussion within an ecumenical community of theologians, which itself must be in touch with the wider life and thinking of the churches and the sufferings and hopes of the world. His theology is also in principle open to dialogue with and input from other academic disciplines. This openness is a *structural* openness inherent in his theology from the beginning, since it results from the eschatological perspective of his theology of hope. Theology is in the service of the church's mission as, from its starting point in the cross and resurrection of Jesus, it relates to the world for the sake of the future of the world. The genuine openness of this future ensures that theology does not already know all the answers but can learn from others and from other approaches to reality. At the same time the christological starting point, in the light of which the future is the future of Jesus Christ, keeps Christian theology faithful to its own truth and so allows it to question other approaches and enter *critical* dialogue with them. In later work, this structural openness is reinforced by the principle of relationality which becomes increasingly important to Moltmann: To recognize that one's own standpoint is *relative* to others need not lead to relativism but to productive relationship.

Content: Eschatology, Theodicy, Church, God, Creation, Politics, Christ, Spirit

Eschatology

One of the most important achievements of Moltmann's early theology was to rehabilitate future eschatology. This was in part a response to the demonstration by modern biblical scholarship that future eschatology is of determinative significance for biblical faith. Whereas Schweitzer, Bultmann, and many others had thought biblical eschatology unacceptable to the modern mind unless stripped of reference to the real temporal future of the world, Moltmann, along with some other German theologians in the 1960s, saw in future eschatology precisely the way to make Christian faith relevant in the modern world. He wished to show how the modern experience of history as a process of constant change, in hopeful search of a new future, need not be rejected by the church, as though Christianity stood for reactionary traditionalism or withdrawal from the world. Rather, the orientation of biblical Christian faith toward the future of the world requires the church to engage with the possibilities for change in the modern world, to promote them against all tendencies to stagnation, and to give them eschatological direction toward the coming kingdom of God. The Gospel proves relevant and credible today precisely through the eschatological faith that truth lies in the future and proves itself in changing the present in the direction of the future.

Christian hope, for Moltmann, is thoroughly christological since it arises from the resurrection of Jesus. His famous claim that "from first to last, and not merely in the epilogue, Christianity is eschatology, is hope" (*Theology of Hope*, p. 16) was possible only because it was a claim about the meaning of the resurrection of Jesus. Since the God of Israel had revealed himself to Israel by making promises which opened up the future, his act of raising the crucified Jesus to new life is to be understood as the culminating and definitive event of divine promise. In it God promises the resurrection of all the dead, the new creation of all reality, and the coming of his kingdom of righteousness and glory, and he guarantees this promise by enacting it in Jesus' person. Jesus' resurrection entails the eschatological future of all reality.

When this concept of the resurrection as promise is related to Moltmann's dialectic of cross and resurrection (see above), important aspects of his eschatology emerge. In the first place, the *contradiction* between the cross and the resurrection creates a *dialectical* eschatology, in which the promise contradicts present reality. The eschatological kingdom is no mere fulfillment of the immanent possibilities of the present, but represents a radically new future: life for the dead, righteousness for the unrighteous, new creation for a creation subject to evil and death. But secondly, the *identity* of Jesus in the total contradiction of cross and resurrection is also important. The resurrection was not the survival of some aspect of Jesus which was not subject to death: Jesus was *wholly* dead and *wholly* raised by God. The continuity was given in God's act of new creation. Similarly God's promise is not for *another* world, but for the new creation of *this* world, in all its material and worldly reality. The whole of creation, subject as it is to sin and suffering and death, will be transformed in God's new creation.

Christian eschatology is therefore the hope that the world will be different. It is aroused by a promise whose fulfillment can come only from God's eschatological action transcending all the possibilities of history, since it involves the end of all evil, suffering, and death in the glory of the divine presence indwelling all things. But it is certainly not therefore without effect in the present. On the contrary, the resurrection set in motion a historical process in which the promise already affects the world and moves it in the direction of its future transformation. This process is the universal mission of the church. This is the point at which Moltmann's *Theology of Hope* opened the church to the world as well as to the future. Authentic Christian hope is not that purely other-worldly expectation which is resigned to the unalterability of affairs in this world. Rather, because it is hope for the future of this world, its effect is to show present reality to be *not yet* what it can be and will be. The world is seen as transformable in the direction of the promised future. In this way believers are liberated from accommodation to the status quo and set critically against it. They suffer the contradiction between what is and what is promised. But this critical distance also enables them to seek and activate those present possibilities of world history which lead in the direction of the eschatological future. Thus by arousing *active* hope the promise creates anticipations of the future kingdom within history.

Theodicy

It was characteristic of Moltmann's theology from the beginning to give prominence to the question of God's righteousness in the face of the suffering and evil of the world. In the first phase of his response to the problem, in *Theology of Hope*, he proposes an eschatological theodicy. Innocent and involuntary suffering must not be justified, as it would be if it were explained as contributing to the divine purpose. The promise given in the resurrection of Jesus gives no explanation of suffering, but it does provide hope for God's final triumph over all evil and suffering, and thereby also an initiative for Christian praxis in overcoming suffering now.

In *The Crucified God*, this approach to the theodicy problem is deepened by the additional theme of God's loving solidarity with the world in its suffering. When Moltmann turned from his focus on the resurrection to a complementary focus on the cross, he was concerned to extend the traditional soteriological interest in the cross to embrace "both the question of human guilt and man's liberation from it, and also the question of human suffering and man's liberation from it" (*The Crucified God*, p. 134). He uses the double expression "the godless and the godforsaken" to refer to the plight both of sinners who suffer their own turning away from God and of those who are the innocent victims of pointless suffering. This is the plight of the world, in the absence of divine righteousness, with which Jesus was identified on the cross.

In *The Crucified God* Moltmann's thinking moved back from the resurrection as the event of divine promise to the cross as the event of divine love. In this movement he was asking the question: How does the promise reach those to whom it is addressed, the godless and the godforsaken? His answer is that it reaches them through Jesus' *identification* with them, in their condition, on the cross. His resurrection represents salvation *for them* only because he dies for them, identified with them in their suffering of God's absence. The central concept of *The Crucified God* is love which suffers in solidarity with those who suffer. This is love which meets the involuntary suffering of the godforsaken with another kind of suffering: voluntary fellow-suffering.

To see the cross as God's act of loving solidarity with all who suffer apparently abandoned by God requires an incarnational and trinitarian theology of the cross. By recognizing God's presence, as the incarnate Son of God, in the abandonment of the cross, Moltmann brings the dialectic of cross and resurrection within God's own experience. The cross and resurrection represent the opposition between a reality which does not correspond to God – the world subject to sin, suffering, and death – and the promise of a reality which does correspond to him – the new creation which will reflect his glory. But if God is present in the godlessness and godforsaken-ness of the cross, then he is present in his own contradiction. His love is such that it embraces the godforsaken reality which does not correspond to him, and so he suffers. His love is not simply active benevolence which acts on humanity. It is dia-lectical love which in embracing its own contradiction must suffer. Of course it does so in order to overcome the contradiction: to deliver from sin, suffering, and death.

If Jesus the divine Son suffers the abandonment of the godforsaken, as the cry of desolation shows, the cross must be a trinitarian event between the incarnate Son and his Father who leaves him to die. Moltmann interprets it as an event of divine suffering in which Jesus suffers dying in abandonment by his Father and the Father suffers in grief the death of his Son. As such it is the act of divine solidarity with the godforsaken world, in which the Son willingly surrenders himself in love for the world and the Father willingly surrenders his Son in love for the world. Because at the point of their deepest separation, the Father and the Son are united in their love for the world, the event which separates them is salvific. The love between them now spans the gulf which separates the godless and the godforsaken from God and overcomes it.

In Moltmann's understanding, the cross does not solve the problem of suffering, but meets it with the voluntary fellow-suffering of love. Solidarity in suffering – in the first place, the crucified God's solidarity with all who suffer, and then also his followers' identification with the suffering – does not abolish suffering, but it over-comes what Moltmann calls "the suffering in suffering": the lack of love, the aban-donment in suffering. Moreover, such solidarity, so far from promoting fatalistic submission to suffering, necessarily includes love's protest against the infliction of suffering on those it loves. It leads believers through their solidarity with the suf-fering into liberating praxis on their behalf.

The church

Moltmann describes his ecclesiology alternatively as "messianic ecclesiology" or "relational ecclesiology." Both terms serve to situate the church within God's trinitarian history with the world, more specifically within the missions of the Son and the Spirit on their way to the eschatological kingdom. In the first place, Moltmann's ecclesiology is rooted in his eschatological christology. The church lives between the past history of Jesus and the universal future in which that history will reach its fulfillment: The former directs it in mission toward the latter. But this also means that Moltmann's ecclesiology is strongly pneumatological. For, in Moltmann's understanding of the trinitarian history, it is the Holy Spirit who now, between the history of Jesus and the coming of the kingdom, mediates the eschatological future to the world. If the church is an anticipation of the messianic kingdom, it is so because it is created by and participates in the mission of the Spirit. Its defining characteristics are not therefore its own, but those of the presence and activity of Christ and the Spirit. At every point ecclesiology must be determined by the church's role as a movement within the trinitarian history of God with the world.

If "messianic ecclesiology" characterizes the church as orientated by the missions of Christ and the Spirit toward their eschatological goal, "relational ecclesiology" indicates that, because of its place within the trinitarian history, the church does not exist in, of, or for itself, but only in relationship and can only be understood in its relationships. It participates in the messianic history of Jesus, it lives in the presence and powers of the Spirit, and it exists as a provisional reality for the sake of the universal kingdom of the future. Since the mission of the Spirit on the way to the kingdom includes but is not confined to the church, the church cannot absolutize itself, but must fulfill its own messianic role in open and critical relationship with other realities, its partners in history, notably Israel, the other world religions, and the secular order.

Within this context, the church can only adequately fulfill its vocation if it becomes a "messianic fellowship" of mature and responsible disciples. Here Moltmann, with his eye especially on the German Protestant scene, proposes radical reform and renewal of the church. His criticism is of the extent to which the church is still the civil religion of society, a pastoral church *for* all the people, unable to take up a critical stance in relation to society, unable to foster real community and active Christian commitment. The ideal is a church *of* the people, a fellowship of committed disciples called to responsible participation in messianic mission. Membership of the church must therefore be voluntary (from this follows Moltmann's critique of infant baptism) and characterized not only by faith but by discipleship and a distinctive lifestyle. The messianic fellowship will also be a free society of equals, since the Spirit frees and empowers all Christians for messianic service (from this follows Moltmann's critique of traditional doctrines of the ministry). Its life of loving acceptance of the other, however different, Moltmann is fond of characterizing as "open friendship," since friendship is a relationship of freedom and the church's life of friendly relationships is always essentially open to others. Finally, the church's open friendship must be modeled on that of Jesus and therefore take the form especially of solidarity with the poor. Unlike the pastoral church, with its inevitable tendency to accept the *status quo* in society, the church as a voluntary fellowship of committed disciples is free to be a socially critical church, identified with the most marginalized and the most needy.

Doctrine of God

Moltmann's mature doctrine of God, as it developed from *The Crucified God* onwards, could be said to hinge on a concept of dynamic relationality. It understands the trinitarian God as three divine subjects in mutual loving relationship, and God's relationship to the world as a reciprocal relationship in which God in his love for the world not only affects the world but is also affected by it. God relates to the world as Trinity, experiencing the world within his own trinitarian experience, and so his changing experience of the world is also a changing experience of himself. The trinitarian history of God's relationship with the world is thus a real history for God as well as for the world: It is the history in which God includes the world within his own trinitarian relationships. All this Moltmann takes to be the meaning of the Christian claim that God is love.

Moltmann's distinctive development of the doctrine of God was initiated by his interpretation of the cross in *The Crucified God*. There he took three crucial steps. In the first place, as an event between the Father and the Son, in which God suffers the godforsakenness that separates the Son from the Father, the cross required trinitarian language of a kind which emphasized intersubjective relationship between the divine persons. (The Spirit, however, is less clearly personal at this stage.) Secondly, it also necessitated a doctrine of divine passibility, not only in the narrow sense that God can suffer pain, but in the broader sense that he can be affected by his creation. In rejecting the traditional doctrine of divine impassibility, Moltmann is careful to make clear that not every kind of suffering can be attributed, even analogically, to God. But suffering which is freely undertaken in love for those who suffer Moltmann claims to be required by God's nature as love. Divine love is a genuinely two-way relationship in which God is so involved with his creation as to be affected by it. Moreover, because his experience of the world, on the cross, is an experience between the Father and the Son, it is in his own trinitarian relationships that God is affected by the world.

The third step follows: Moltmann abandons the traditional distinction between the immanent and the economic trinities, between what God eternally is in himself and how he acts outside himself in the world. The cross (and, by extension, the rest of God's history with the world) is *internal* to the divine trinitarian experience. Because God is love, what he is for us he is also for himself. The doctrine of the Trinity is thus not an extrapolation from the history of Jesus and the Spirit: It actually is the history of Jesus and the Spirit in its theological interpretation. It can really only take narrative form as a history of God's changing trinitarian relationships in himself and simultaneously with the world. In his later work Moltmann elaborates this narrative in various forms, eventually including creation.

In all this, Moltmann found himself talking of God's experience. If it is as love that we experience God, then in some sense in experiencing God we also experience his experience of us, and if it is as trinitarian love that we experience God, then in some sense we experience even his threefold experience of himself in our history. On this basis, especially in *The Trinity and the Kingdom of God*, Moltmann develops his fully social doctrine of the Trinity. Significantly, for this to be possible, Moltmann had to recognize an activity of the Spirit in which the Spirit acts as subject in relation to the Father and the Son: This is the Spirit's work of glorifying the Father and the Son. This makes it clear that the divine Persons are all subjects in relation to each other. It also makes clear that there is no fixed order in the Trinity: The traditional, "descending" order Father–Son–Spirit is only one of the changing patterns of trinitarian relationship in God's history with the world. Behind and within these changing relationships is the enduring trinitarian fellowship, in which there is no subordination, only mutual love in freedom.

Moltmann constantly opposes any "monotheistic" or "monarchical" doctrine of God which would reduce the real subjectivity of the three persons. Instead he insists that the unity of God is the unity of persons in relationship. Three points can be made about this. First, it is in their relationships to each other that the three are persons. They are both three and one in their mutual indwelling (*perichoresis*). Secondly, since the unity of God is thus defined in terms of love, as perichoresis, it is a unity which can open itself to and include the world within itself. The goal of the trinitarian history of God is the uniting of all things with God and in God: a trinitarian and eschatological panentheism. Thirdly, Moltmann sees "monotheism" as legitimating "monarchical" relationships of domination and subjection, whereas social trinitarianism grounds relationships of freedom and equality. In himself God is not rule but a fellowship of love; in his relationship with the world it is not so much lordship as loving fellowship which he seeks; and in his "kingdom" it is relationships of free friendship which most adequately reflect and participate in the trinitarian life.

Creation

The doctrine of creation, relatively neglected in Moltmann's earlier work, receives full attention in *God in Creation*. Its explicit context is the ecological crisis, which, as a crisis in the human relationship to nature, requires, in Moltmann's view, a renewed theological understanding of nature and human beings as God's creation and of God's relationship to the world as his creation.

The kind of human relationship to nature which has created the crisis and must be superseded is that of exploitative domination. In its place, Moltmann advocates a sense of human community with nature, respecting nature's independence and participating in mutual relationships with it. Human beings, as the image of God, have a distinctive place within nature, but they are not the owners or rulers of nature: they belong with nature in a community of creation which, as *creation*, is not anthropocentric but theocentric. But in order to ground theologically this emphasis on mutual relationships in nature, Moltmann appeals to his doctrine of God, whose own trinitarian community provides the model for the life of his creation as an intricate community of reciprocal relationships.

Not only is the trinitarian God a perichoretic community and his creation a perichoretic community, but also God's relationship to his creation is one of mutual indwelling. Because God is transcendent beyond the world, it dwells in him, but because, as the Spirit, he is also immanent within the world, he dwells in it. With this dominant notion of the Spirit in creation, Moltmann is able also to take the non-human creation into his general concept of the trinitarian history of God. The whole of creation from the beginning has a messianic orientation toward a future goal: its glorification through divine indwelling. The Spirit in creation co-suffers with creation in its bondage to decay, keeping it open to God and to its future with God. Humanity's eschatological goal does not lift us out of the material creation but confirms our solidarity and relatedness with it. In all of this Moltmann achieves a strong continuity between creation and redemption, and between the creative and salvific activities of the Spirit.

Political theology

Moltmann has never reduced the Gospel to its political aspect, but he has consistently emphasized it. In the years immediately after *Theology of Hope* he developed his thought into an explicitly political theology, in the sense in which that term came into use in Germany at that time, i.e., in the sense of a politically critical theology aiming at radical change in society. Moltmann's praxis-orientated dialectical eschatology was not difficult to translate into an imperative for radical political change, though what appealed to him in Marxism was its vision of a new society of freedom, rather than its economic analysis or its strategy for revolution.

Moltmann's turn to the cross brought with it the requirement of a political praxis of solidarity with the victims, which deepens the praxis of hope. The latter was rescued from the danger of a rather romantic vision of revolution or of confusion with the ideological optimism of the affluent by the requirement that desire for radical change must result from real solidarity with the victims of society and be rooted in their actual interests.

Political concerns continue to feature in his later theology. His social trinitarianism in *The Trinity and the Kingdom of God*, for example, provides a theological basis for democratic freedom in society. But probably the most important later development in his political theology has been the prominence of the notion of human rights, which he grounds in the created dignity and eschatological destiny of humanity as the image of God. It is by means of the concept of human rights that Moltmann's political theology is able to formulate specific political goals. The two earlier themes of revolutionary hope and solidarity with victims gain concreteness especially in this form. Eschatological hope finds its immediate application in striving for the realization of human rights – new dimensions of which can constantly come to light in the movement of history toward the fulfillment of human destiny in the kingdom of God. Solidarity with victims takes political effect in the attempt to secure their rights and dignity as full members of the human community. One could almost claim that human rights came to play the kind of role in Moltmann's political theology that Marxism played in the liberation theology of Latin America. The concept of human rights is a way of specifying the concrete implications of political theology, and a way of doing so which makes contact with non-Christian political goals and activity, thus enabling Christians to join with others in a common struggle for liberation.

Christology

In *The Way of Jesus Christ*, Moltmann returned to christology, which had been at the center of his early work, but was now able to develop a much more comprehensive christology. The dialectic of cross and resurrection is retained from the early work, as is the stress on the Old Testament/Jewish framework of theological interpretation for the history of Jesus. The latter is now developed in a more distinctively messianic rather than simply eschatological form: The Christian dialogue with Judaism must keep christology messianic, looking not only to Jesus' past but also to his future, which is the messianic future of the as yet still unredeemed world. Whereas Moltmann's early theology focused on the way the resurrection of Jesus opened up the eschatological future for the world, but did not especially stress the parousia of Jesus himself, the range of Moltmann's christology is now extended to the coming Christ, as in the Creeds. The metaphor of Jesus Christ "on his way," which is exploited in a variety of ways in the book, indicates, among other things, that Jesus is on his way to the messianic future. Christology therefore is necessarily *Christologia viae*, not fixed and static, but provisional and open to the future.

As well as this more explicit development of the eschatological aspect of christology, there is also much more attention to the earthly life and ministry of Jesus than in Moltmann's previous work – more, indeed, than in most christologies. This has at least two important consequences. In the first place, Moltmann develops a Spirit christology, which stresses that the life and ministry of Jesus, as the messianic prophet, take place in the power of the Spirit. This emphasis belongs within Moltmann's mature view of the trinitarian history of God with the world, in which the trinitarian Persons interrelate in changing and reciprocal ways. The history of Jesus is not to be understood in a narrowly christological but rather in a fully trinitarian way, in which Jesus lives in relation to his Father and the Spirit. The uniqueness of Jesus' trinitarian relationship to the Father and the Son prevents this Spirit christology from being a "degree christology," as other forms of Spirit christology have often been. Secondly, Moltmann highlights, unusually in a christology, the distinctive ethical way of life which Jesus taught his disciples. Christology, he claims, is inextricably related not only to soteriology, but also to Christian ethics; christology must be done in close conjunction with "christopraxis"; and the "total, holistic knowledge of Christ" entails living a life of following his way, in the community of his disciples, in fellowship with him.

Finally, holistic christology requires holistic soteriology, in the sense of a view of salvation which encompasses body and soul, individual and community, humanity and the rest of nature, in a vision of the universal abolition of transience and death and the new creation of all things. This is not new, in Moltmann's theology, but the explicit development of the universal aspect of christology and soteriology as involving the non-human creation is the result both of Moltmann's development of his theology of creation and of his perception of the universal peril in which all creation on this planet now stands. In the situation of nuclear threat and ecological destruction, the world is now in a literally "end-time" situation, in which "the great apocalyptic dying, the death of all things" looms – not, of course, as a fatalistic prophecy, but as an unprecedented peril which puts humanity and the rest of nature in a common danger. In this apocalyptically understood context, Moltmann is easily able to take up again the eschatological dialectic of the cross and the resurrection, which was central to his early theology, and to highlight the contextuality of its soteriological force. In his cross Jesus enters and suffers vicariously the end-time sufferings that threaten the whole creation. He identifies with dying nature as well as with abandoned humans. He undergoes the birth pangs of the new creation, and his resurrection is the eschatological springtime of all nature.

Pneumatology

Moltmann's theology has become more and more strongly pneumatological, a development which culminates in *The Spirit of Life*. This is in part a consequence of his trinitarian doctrine, which stresses the reciprocal and changing relationships of the three Persons, and rejects the subordination of pneumatology to christology. The principle for both pneumatology and christology is that they must be understood in relation to each other within an overall trinitarian framework, rather than that pneumatology should be developed exclusively from christology. This allows Moltmann to give far more attention to the Spirit's role for its own sake than the Western theological tradition has often done. His attention to pneumatology also, however, corresponds to his growing stress on the immanence of God in creation, as his eschatological panentheism (the hope that God will indwell all things in the new creation) has been increasingly accompanied by a stress on the coinherence of God and the world already. As the Spirit, God is already present in his creation, both in suffering the transience and evil of the world and in anticipating the eschatological rebirth of all things.

Moltmann's developed pneumatology understands the Holy Spirit primarily as the divine source of *life*: "the eternal Spirit is the divine wellspring of life – the source of life created, life preserved and life daily renewed, and finally the source of eternal life of all created being" (*The Spirit of Life*, p. 82). This emphasis serves a number of important purposes. In the first place, it breaks out of the narrow association of the Spirit with revelation, which was characteristic of Barth's theology, and so enables Moltmann, in one of his more emphatic rejections of Barthian positions, to give *experience* – the experience of God in the whole of life and of all things in God – a place in theology, not as alternative to but in correlation with the revelatory word of God. The Spirit of life is God experienced in the profundity and vitality of life lived in God. As the Spirit is the wellspring of all life, so all experience can be a discovery of this living source in God.

Secondly, a "holistic pneumatology" corresponds to Moltmann's holistic christology and soteriology. As the Spirit of life, the Spirit is not related to the "spiritual" as opposed to the bodily and material, or to the individual as opposed to the social, or to the human as opposed to the rest of creation. The Spirit is the source of the whole of life in bodiliness and community. Life in the Spirit is not a life of withdrawal from the world into God, but the "vitality of a creative life out of God," which is characterized by love of life and affirmation of all life. This is a relatively new form of Moltmann's characteristic concern for a theology of positive involvement in God's world.

Thirdly, the notion of the Spirit as the divine source of all life highlights both the continuity of God's life and the life of his creation, such that the creatures are not distant from God but live out of his life, and also the continuity of creation and salvation, in that the Spirit is the source both of the transient life which ends in death and of the eternal life of the new creation. The Spirit gives life to all things, sustains all things in life, and brings all things to rebirth beyond death and beyond the reach of death. But finally, this continuity of creation and new creation is not to be understood as excluding the eschatological dualism which has always been a key to Moltmann's thought. Creation is subject to the powers of death and destruction, and the Spirit is the power of the liberating struggle of life against death, the source of life renewed out of death. The continuity of creation and new creation is created by the Spirit's act of restoring the old creation in the eschatologically transcendent new creation. The christological center of Moltmann's theology – the dialectic in which the Spirit raises the crucified Jesus to eschatological life – still holds.

Debate

Some of the issues which have been raised in criticism of Moltmann's work are as follows:

1   Critics of Moltmann's early work frequently complained of one-sided emphasis on some theological themes at the expense of others. This was said especially of the emphasis on the future in *Theology of Hope*, which appeared to deny all present experience of God. However, in retrospect this one-sidedness can be seen to be a result of Moltmann's method, in the early works, of taking up *in turn* a number of complementary perspectives on theology. In the context of the whole trilogy, the one-sidedness of each book is balanced by the others. Present experience of God, polemically played down in *Theology of Hope*, is fully acknowledged in later work, but given an eschatological orientation which preserves the intention of *Theology of Hope*.

2   Much criticism focused on the political implications of *Theology of Hope*, though not always with due attention to the subsequent essays in which these were fully developed. From the liberation theologians of Latin America, themselves influenced by Moltmann, came the criticism that the eschatological transcendence of the kingdom beyond all its present anticipations sanctions the typical European theologian's detachment from concrete political movements and objectives. From some more conservative theologians comes the opposite complaint that Moltmann reduces eschatology to human political achievements. Both criticisms miss the careful way in which Moltmann relates the eschatological kingdom to its anticipations in history, though there is something in the liberationists' charge that Moltmann's political theology is *relatively* lacking in concrete proposals.

3   Criticism of Moltmann's doctrine of God has claimed that, in rejecting the traditional doctrines of divine aseity and impassibility, he compromises the freedom of God and falls into the "Hegelian" mistake of making world history the process by which God realizes himself. To some extent such criticisms provoked Moltmann, after *The Crucified God*, into clarifying his view. He does not dissolve God into world history, but he does intend a real interaction between God and the world. The problem of divine freedom leads him to deny the reality of the contrast between necessity and freedom of choice in God. Because God's freedom is the freedom of his love, he cannot choose not to love and as love he is intrinsically related to the world. A different kind of criticism finds it hard to distinguish Moltmann's social trinitarianism from tritheism, a charge which careful reading of his later trinitarian

work fails to support. The fundamental point – that the trinitarian Persons relate to each other as personal subjects – has, in fact, much more claim to represent the mainstream Christian theological tradition than the modern tendency to conceive God as the supreme individual.

4   Many critics, especially in the Anglo-Saxon tradition, find Moltmann's work lacking in philosophical analysis and logical rigor. This is a question of theological style, and Moltmann's way of doing theology has other merits, such as breadth of vision, which more analytical treatments lack. But it is true that it sometimes obscures conceptual problems in his work which could otherwise come to light and be overcome more quickly. Related to this criticism is the charge that Moltmann is insufficiently aware of the necessarily analogical nature of talk about God, so that his discussion of the divine experience too often becomes unconsciously mythological.

5   Though not often commented on, two related tendencies in some of his later work call for criticism. In the first place, elements of undisciplined speculation appear, and secondly, whereas his earlier work was carefully rooted in current biblical scholarship, his use of biblical material in the later work seems rather often to ignore historical-critical interpretation and to leave his hermeneutical principles dangerously unclear. One reason for both tendencies is that, whereas his earlier work at its best moved between the concreteness of the biblical history and the concrete situations of the modern world, he seems more recently to have been increasingly drawn into the concerns of the theological tradition for their own sake (or, in some cases, such as the *Filioque* issue, by ecumenical discussions).

Achievement and Agenda

Perhaps Moltmann's greatest achievement in the earlier works was to open up hermeneutical structures for relating biblical faith to the modern world. The strength and appropriateness of these structures lie in their biblical basis, their christological center, and their eschatological openness. They give Moltmann's theology a relevance to the modern world which is achieved not only without surrendering the central features of biblical and historic Christian faith, but much more positively by probing the theological meaning of these in relation to contemporary realities and concerns. By recovering a christological center which is both dialectical and eschatological, Moltmann's theology acquired an openness to the world which is not in tension with the christological center but is actually required by the christological center, and which is not an accommodation to conservative, liberal, or radical values, but has a critical edge and a consistent solidarity with the most marginalized members of society.

His later work continues to bring both the biblical history and the central themes of the Christian theological tradition into productive relationship with the contemporary context. In doing so, he has recently become the contemporary theologian who has perhaps most successfully transcended the dominant (theological and non-theological) paradigm of reality as human history, recognized in this a reflex of the modern ideology of domination, and attempted to enter theologically into the reciprocity of human history and the rest of nature as the history of God's creation.

That he has been able to do so by developing and expanding the structures of his earlier thought, rather than rejecting and replacing them, demonstrates the hermeneutical fecundity of his theological vision and its ability to relate illuminatingly to fresh situations and insights.

A very notable feature of the later work is Moltmann's sustained attempt to reconceive the doctrine of God in order to do better justice than the tradition to the Christian perception of God as trinitarian love. In a period when many major theologians, questioning the axioms of metaphysical theism, have recognized the need to envisage God as receptive and suffering as well as active, and have also rediscovered the potential of thoroughgoing trinitarianism, Moltmann's has been one of the boldest and fullest explorations of such a doctrine of God. Its merits lie in the attempt to take utterly seriously those claims about God which lie at the heart of the Christian revelation. The attempt has its problems, but the issues are indisputably important for the credibility of the God of Christian faith today.

Moltmann himself has already stated his agenda for completing his series of systematic contributions to theology (see the survey above), but within this scheme new developments, such as have occurred in all his major works so far, must certainly be expected.

Bibliography

Primary

Moltmann, Jürgen, *Theology of Hope* (London, 1967).
—— *Theology and Joy* (London, 1973).
—— *The Crucified God* (London, 1974).
—— *The Church in the Power of the Spirit* (London, 1975).
—— *The Trinity and the Kingdom of God* (London, 1981).
—— *On Human Dignity* (London, 1984).
—— *God in Creation* (London, 1985).
—— *The Way of Jesus Christ* (London, 1989).
—— *The Spirit of Life* (London, 1991).
—— *History and the Triune God* (London, 1991).
—— *The Coming of God* (London, 1996).

A bibliography of Moltmann's works up to 1987 is in D. Ising, *Bibliographie Jürgen Moltmann* (Munich, 1987), and a further bibliography of Moltmann's works in English translation (together with secondary literature) is in R. Bauckham, *The Theology of Jürgen Moltmann* (Edinburgh, 1995).

Secondary

Bauckham, R., *Moltmann: Messianic theology in the making* (Basingstoke, 1987).
—— *The Theology of Jürgen Moltmann* (Edinburgh, 1995).
Conyers, A. J., *God, Hope, and History* (Macon, GA, 1988).
Meeks, M. D., *Origins of the Theology of Hope* (Philadelphia, 1974).

British Theologies

British theology differs greatly in history, character, and institutional setting from the theologies discussed in Part I, and the three chapters in this section are especially concerned to understand it in its context. Each of the authors is also a significant contributor to the field about which he writes.

Stephen Sykes describes the institutional history of British theology as the background for a discussion of the untypical P. T. Forsyth, followed by analysis of three types of theology through history. In theology through New Testament studies, C. H. Dodd and C. F. D. Moule stand for the essential contribution of historical findings to an orthodox Christian faith, while Dennis Nineham is skeptical about the possibility of any such contribution. In the field of patristics, G. W. H. Lampe and Maurice Wiles are shown arriving through their historical studies at liberal positions on the Trinity and other classical Christian doctrines (positions later contested by the more mainstream orthodox conclusions of Richard Hanson and Rowan Williams, mentioned in the Debate section). In modern history, Norman Sykes recovered the value of the eighteenth century for contemporary ecclesiastical, ecumenical, and political practice; and Herbert Butterfield discerned through more recent centuries the involvement of God and the relevance of Christian faith. Also included is a brief discussion of the controversial volume *The Myth of God Incarnate*. Sykes follows the debates up to the present and sees the main challenge arising out of "the anarchic normlessness of western civilization in the face of desperate poverty and oppression in many parts of the world."

Daniel Hardy traces a number of different ways in which recent British thought has used philosophy on and in theology, arising out of a distinctive tradition of refining and rearticulating both Christian faith and its position in civilization through philosophy. He not only considers the variety of ways in which philosophy is shaped by different norms – for example, those generated within prevailing schools of thought – but also the different ways in which philosophy is used in relation to faith and theology. In some cases there is an explicit attempt to recover the integration of faith with philosophical norms. So Thomas F. Torrance establishes a convergence between scientific and theological thought. John MacQuarrie uses continental existentialism to re-express faith in its connection with human life. Richard Swinburne seeks to extend current analytic philosophy to allow for the meaningfulness and rationality of Christian theology. In other cases, philosophy formed in the analysis of religion (John Hick) or postmodernism (Don Cupitt) is used to transform Christian faith, correcting its alleged errors. In still others, of which Donald MacKinnon is taken as one representative, there is a less predetermined – and more open – engagement between philosophical and theological exploration, in his case by exploring the interface between the two in the dilemmas of life itself. This is seen as deeply influential in contemporary British theology, notably through its further development in the work of Nicholas Lash, but also in many younger theologians. Hardy sees all but the last foreclosing the full possibilities for bringing theology and philosophy together.

Peter Sedgwick introduces a very different cast of characters from the previous two chapters. There is a strong tradition of intensive debate, often closely tied to practical activity, about the complexities of social ethics in modern Britain. Often its practitioners are not academics, and those introduced include economists, politicians, feminists, environmentalists, priests, and sociologists. The four thinkers he concentrates upon embrace two archbishops (one a physiologist), an economics-trained academic, and a radical "grassroots" priest. Sedgwick evokes the liveliness and sensitivity to local context in this tradition, and in the final section surveys a variety of institutional initiatives and also the current agendas. These include the state of the main national institutions and of civil society in contemporary Britain; globalization and postmodernism; and communitarianism and postliberalism.

Theology through History

S. W. Sykes

Introduction: Theology in British Universities

It is a curious fact, worthy of some initial comment, that in a work devoted to modern theologians it has seemed appropriate to group the contribution of British writers into three sections, labeled respectively "Theology through History," "Theology through Philosophy" and "Theology and Society." Why, looking at Part I of *The Modern Theologians*, should it be the case that, whereas there is no shortage of German-speaking theologians of major stature, such as Karl Barth, Rudolf Bultmann, or Karl Rahner, British theology does not have any theologian with a chapter to himself?

One important explanation of this state of affairs has contrasted the favorable philosophical context in German intellectual life with the situation in the British universities. In Germany, from the days of Immanuel Kant (d. 1804), philosophy was the indispensable and highly stimulating conversation-partner for successive generations of theologians. British theologians, who sometimes knew too little German to profit from this literature or who affected to despise it, enjoyed no comparable stimulus from their own context.

A further explanation – or rather excuse – has frequently been offered, namely that what is called "the Anglo-Saxon mind" is inherently disinclined to engage in systematic reflection. For example, a well-known Scottish theologian, Hugh Ross Mackintosh, who wrote an account of *Types of Modern Theology* (posthumously published in 1937), while attributing greater numbers, freedom, and thoroughness to German theological scholarship, offered as a compensation the comforting thought that the "Anglo-Saxon mind" very often displayed sounder judgment.[1] But it is necessary to be skeptical about the existence of national "minds," if only for the reason that, in the past, theories which invoked these entities were often the vehicle of nationalistic prejudice. What these abstractions may amount to is the cumulative impact of a particular pattern of education upon the way in which generations of intellectuals have been taught to think. In the case of British education in theology there have been some very important differences from the way in which theology has been taught and studied on the European continent and in Scandinavia. To these we must give some attention.

Since the nineteenth century, theology of one kind or another has been taught in British universities. In England, the Church of England has been a strong influence upon the content of the syllabuses, and also, especially in Cambridge, Durham, and Oxford, a very high proportion of the teachers of theology have been (until very recently) Anglicans in orders. From the late nineteenth century, however, the virtual Anglican monopoly on the ancient universities was broken, and syllabuses of theology were constructed which were (supposedly) denominationally neutral. That is to say, they were no longer conceived of as programs of study which prepared Anglicans for ordination in the Church of England, but courses which could properly be taken by any interested person. The Church of England from this time onward developed its own independent theological colleges or seminaries, in which specifically Anglican disciplines (liturgical and pastoral studies, for example) were taught. The Free Churches, which under Anglican persecution in the seventeenth century had developed their own sometimes distinguished Dissenting Academies, likewise trained their ministers in their own theological colleges from the late eighteenth century. The (supposed) neutrality of the new syllabuses in theology in both the ancient and the more recent civic universities enabled Methodists, Congregationalists, Baptists, and Presbyterians to participate as both students and teachers, and subsequently, since the ecumenical developments of the 1960s, Roman Catholics have played an increasingly active role. Today both the staff and students of the theological departments of English universities are completely mixed denominationally and, with the exception of certain professorial appointments reserved for Anglican priests in the Universities of Durham and Oxford, academic posts are without denominational (or indeed religious) tie or affiliation.

In this process the key development was the establishment by the Church of England of its own independent theological colleges. By contrast, the Church of Scotland has no such institutions, and the theological faculties of Scottish universities are considered to be ministerial training institutions, many of whose appointments committees have predominantly Church of Scotland representation. Although non-Presbyterians have been, and are, regularly appointed to university teaching posts in the theological faculties in Scotland, the Church of Scotland is obliged to preserve its influence in their syllabuses and staff if its pastoral needs are to be met.

The importance of university curricula to the formation of a national theological tradition will be obvious enough. In Europe and Scandinavia systematic or dogmatic theology is generally understood to be a church-related discipline. All the major theologians considered in Part I have taught in either Protestant or Roman Catholic institutions, and have been subject to the doctrinal norms (and in the case of one theologian, Hans Küng, the ecclesiastical discipline) of their respective denominations. In England, by contrast, the syllabus which is taught and examined is not conceived from the standpoint of the criteria of denominational orthodoxy.

From some points of view freedom from denominational control might well be seen as an advantage; but there have also been costs to be paid. An especially severe consequence has been the failure to promote the study of systematic theology in a university context. (We are speaking now of English and Welsh universities; an exception has to be made in the case of Scotland, where, for the reasons explained above, chairs of reformed dogmatic theology have existed from the sixteenth century.) In England it has not proved possible until very recently to conceive of a non-denominational way of approaching the subject matter of systematic theology. The absence of this discipline has created a vacuum which has not gone unfilled; and a variety of substitutes for systematics can readily be identified. Among these have been "biblical theology," "dogmatic theology," "modern theology," and "philosophical theology." By "biblical theology" one should understand the attempt to construct a theological synthesis of biblical themes, an enterprise which became popular in the 1960s and 1970s and strongly influenced the teaching of New Testament theology. By "dogmatic theology" is meant the study of the formally defined dogmas of the early church, an inquiry which syllabuses of Anglican origin generally terminated in the fifth century. Under "modern theology" the syllabuses generally included the "great names" of nineteenth- and twentieth-century European theology. "Philosophical theology" was a specifically British development of the ancient discipline of "apologetics," applied to the common eighteenth-century topics of God, freedom, and immortality, including such subjects as miracle, prayer, and providence, but generally abstracted from any consideration of the doctrines of creation, election, redemption, or the last things. One major casualty of this more or less unconscious filling of the gap caused by a lack of denominational systematics has been the virtual absence of serious attention to the doctrines of the church and sacraments, which were generally avoided in universities as being either of secondary importance or else too controversial.

It now becomes apparent why it is necessary to treat the contribution of British theologians to modern theology indirectly through the attention given to history and philosophy. The main reason is that the institutional base for the study of systematic theology in the universities, outside Scotland, has been wanting. Nonetheless, both the history and philosophy of theology have been lively disciplines and the contributions made by British theologians to both of these fields have contained some answers to the pressing questions of Christian doctrine.

In the sections that follow I propose to give attention to three doctrinal areas which have been characteristically treated in Britain by those whose training and habit of mind have been historical rather than systematic. These are: christology, especially in the work of three historians of the New Testament period, C. H. Dodd, C. F. D. Moule and D. E. Nineham; trinitarian theology, in the writing of two patristic experts, G. W. H. Lampe and M. F. Wiles; and the doctrine of the church, in the work of two historians of the Reformation and modern eras, N. Sykes and H. Butterfield. But first we must consider the work of a man who, more than any other, deserves to be considered an exception to the account given above, a British systematician of wide influence and importance, Peter Taylor Forsyth.

P. T. Forsyth (1848–1921)

It may come as some surprise that one should include as a modern theologian a man who died in 1921. The explanation lies in the publishing history of his major works.

These, although for the most part written in the decade between 1907 and 1917, were all reissued in the 1950s, a period which also witnessed a flurry of studies of his theological achievement. One reason for the later revival of interest in Forsyth was the discovery that he had earlier articulated many of the themes of Karl Barth's protest against liberalism. Both Barth and Forsyth had reacted vigorously against the dominant Ritschlianism of the early years of the twentieth century, and both had expressed an early appreciation for the thought of Kierkegaard. The similarities between them have led to Forsyth being designated "a Barthian before Barth," a label which needs to be handled with caution.

In the light of what we have said about the tradition of theology in Scotland, it will not come as a surprise to discover that P. T. Forsyth was a Scot, though a Congregationalist and not a member of the Church of Scotland. A classics graduate of the University of Aberdeen, his home town, he first worked as an assistant to the professor of Latin. Forsyth's interest in theology was greatly stimulated by friendship with a brilliant young orientalist, William Robertson Smith, who in 1870, at the age of 24, had become professor of oriental languages and Old Testament exegesis at the Free Church College, Aberdeen. It was at Robertson Smith's suggestion that Forsyth travelled to Göttingen to study theology under Albrecht Ritschl, returning to England to undertake ordination training for the Congregationalist ministry at New College, London. For 25 years, from 1876 to 1901, Forsyth worked in a series of pastorates, in Bradford, London, Manchester, Leicester, and Cambridge. In the light of this experience, it is perhaps unsurprising that in the opening sentence of his first major book, *Positive Preaching and the Modern Mind* (1907), he wrote: "It is, perhaps, an overbold beginning, but I will venture to say that with its preaching Christianity stands or falls." From 1901 until his death in 1921 Forsyth was Principal of Hackney College, a Congregationalist Theological College in London, one of seven (two Anglican, three Congregationalist, one Wesleyan, and one Baptist) which in 1900 had combined to constitute a faculty of theology in the University of London. London University thus became a leading protagonist of the denominationally neutral syllabus of theological study, of which we have spoken. Students would study for the university degree in theology, while at the same time learning in their theological colleges the disciplines and outlook of their own denomination.

Although Forsyth was by every instinct a systematic theologian, rather than a practitioner of theology through history, as were the theologians we are to consider, it is nonetheless instructive to consider his view of the sort of historico-critical biblical study which had set the agenda for so much nineteenth- and twentieth-century theology. Having wholeheartedly abandoned the doctrine of biblical infallibility, Forsyth insisted that the focus of the theologian's attention is on the gospel of God's grace, rather than the mere text of the Bible. It is the communication of the gospel which raises the Bible, he believed, above a mere chronicle of events to be dissected and discussed by scholarly pedants. A genuine historian is distinguished from an annalist by the fact that the former has a theory, hypothesis, or law to advance. In the case of Christian theology the place of theory is taken by an account of God's action, the gospel itself, which he speaks of as God's unique word to man, not man's hypothesis about God.

Forsyth adopted from a contemporary German theologian, Georg Wobbermin

(1869–1943), a distinction between two German words, *Geschichte* and *Historie*. The latter he defined as "history as it may be settled by the methods of historical science"; the former, as "the evolving organism of mankind taken as a moral and spiritual unity."[2] In the records of the events of the New Testament we have to do with both *Historie* and *Geschichte*. The act of God in Jesus Christ is an event conveyed in an inspired (but not infallible) apostolic interpretation emitting its own creative "radiance." Historical study of the life of Christ is not going to provide us with proofs of the propositions of christology, because it is *Geschichte* which supplies us with the tradition in which we stand and which is a larger thing than the sum of individually certain events as established by critical scholarship. The manifestation of the "great fact" of Christ and its self-interpretation are indivisible from the active tradition and experience of the living Church, and it is this integration of Christ, the Lord, and the Holy Spirit which differentiates gospel history from all other history. It is the Holy Spirit who makes of Christ one who is our contemporary. Christian certainty has no foundation in reason or nature, but only points of contact. Religion, Forsyth roundly declared, is natural to man; faith is not. Christianity is not. The common origin of views of this kind, expressed by Forsyth and later by Karl Barth, is undoubtedly Martin Luther.

Biblical criticism is, therefore, no cause for panic among believers whose faith is founded upon grace. Forsyth described how exposure to the historical research of biblical scholars had actually deepened his faith, turning it from "ill-founded sentiment" and "amiable religiosity" to the cross of Christ.

> What was needed before we discussed the evidence for the resurrection, was a revival of the sense of God's judgement – grace in the Cross, a renewal of the sense of holiness and so of sin, as the Cross set forth the one, and exposed the other.[3]

The unity of the Scripture is thus the unity given it by its being the history of redemption.

Forsyth wrote two books on the atonement, *The Cruciality of the Cross* (1909, consisting of revised and expanded papers from the years 1908–9) and *The Work of Christ* (1910). Although the interpretation of the cross was central to his thought, he is widely considered not to have given satisfactory expression to the profundity of what he had to say. Above all else Forsyth wanted to insist on the ethical force of the whole of Christian doctrine, and asserted the need for what he called "the moralizing of dogma." But unlike the Ritschlian school of his day, this methodological proposal did not lead to what has been called the "moral influence" theory of the atonement, the view that God draws humanity to himself by the power of Christ's example of loving self-sacrifice. On the contrary, Forsyth emphasized that God has *done* something for humanity, not merely demonstrated, shown, or said something. Here again we note the priority of the actual. What has been effected is a change of God's practical relation to humanity, carried out by God himself.

The reason for this emphasis lay in Forsyth's retention of the notion of holiness in every use of the idea of divine love. He accepted St Anselm's argument that it is impossible for a holy God to treat sin as though it were not sin. There is a moral necessity for divine judgment. Christ, as God in man, is humanity's representative, a form of anticipated solidarity with the whole of the human race, of which he is Head.

Although Forsyth did not with any clarity espouse any one of the so-called "theories of atonement," one theme is predominant, that of sacrifice. The importance of this traditional idea is apparent in what for many is the most powerful and creative of Forsyth's works, *The Person and Place of Jesus Christ*, also produced in the astonishingly productive year of 1909. Here Forsyth explicitly defended a version of the so-called "kenotic christology," which had flourished in German Protestantism in the second half of the nineteenth century. By 1909, however, this doctrine was, as Forsyth must have known, in eclipse in Germany, having been vigorously opposed by many writers, not least Albrecht Ritschl himself.

The central point of kenotic christology was to speak of the incarnation of the Second Person of the divine Trinity as his self-emptying. It was ostensibly based on Philippians 2: 5–11, especially on the description of Christ as one "who, though he was in the form of God did not count equality with God a thing to be grasped, but emptied himself, taking the form of a servant, being born in the likeness of men." Though the exegesis was disputed, and though the new theory plainly contradicted part of the christology of the authoritative Tome of Leo (AD 451), it proved irresistibly attractive to several British theologians of the early twentieth century, among them a number of Anglicans.

There is no one standard form of kenotic theory, but many of the theories are linked by their receptivity to the idea of sacrifice. In Forsyth's case it is particularly striking that the whole theology of the self-offering of Christ is presented as the paradigm of what he called "priestly religion." The Christian faith, according to this remarkable Congregationalist, is priestly or it is nothing. "It gathers about a priestly cross on earth and a great High Priest Eternal in the heavens." Evangelical Christianity has, he believed, to choose between Christ as an inspiring social reformer and Christ as priestly redeemer. Forsyth laid his stress upon a collective, not merely individualistic priesthood of all believers, and declared:

> The greatest function of the Church in full communion with Him is priestly. It is to confess, to sacrifice, to intercede for the whole human race in Him. The Church, and those who speak in its name, have power and commandment to declare to the world being penitent the absolution and remission of their sins in Him.[4]

This priestly lay religion is founded upon the cross of Christ. Forsyth's program of the moralizing of dogma left him, he believed, with the alternative of conceiving of the incarnation either as the result of a progressive moral growth completed in Christ's sacrificial death, or as the outcome of a great and creative moral decision *before* he entered the world. The latter was Forsyth's preferred course. The act of incarnation, or coming into flesh, must itself therefore be a moral achievement on God's behalf. This is what, he insisted, the doctrine of kenosis, or divine self-emptying, was attempting to express:

> We face in Christ a Godhead self-reduced but real whose infinite power took effect in self-humiliation, whose strength was perfected in weakness, who consented not to

know with an ignorance divinely wise, and who emptied himself in virtue of his divine fulness.[5]

Kenosis is matched by the plerosis, or self-fulfillment, of Christ. Two-nature christology is replaced, in Forsyth's theology, by a two-act christology, an act from the divine side and a corresponding one from the human side. The self-fulfillment he characterized as an appropriation and deepening of the man, Jesus, in a sinless life and holy work. Thus Forsyth allowed a "progressive incarnation," so long as it is seen to have a kenotic basis. In order to explain what he had in mind he deployed the idea of a "mode of being." For one who is infinite omniscience the eternal mode of being will imply an intuitive and simultaneous knowledge of everything. The incarnate Lord, however, will have that mode of being which can have only a dis-cursive and successive knowledge, enlarging itself to greater knowledge under the normal moral conditions of humanity. The entry of the infinite into the temporal and finite therefore involved a "retraction" of the mode of being of the divine attributes from actual to potential; and the history of Christ's growth was corre-spondingly that of the recovery by gradual moral conquest of the mode of being from which he originally came.

The impact of Forsyth upon British theology, and not least of his espousal of a sacrificial-kenotic view of the incarnation and cross, has been considerable. His polemic against the ethical naivety of sentimental Protestantism is still a delight to read. What the writings lack in analytic clarity they gain in rhetorical power, doubt-less the result of his long apprenticeship in the pastoral ministry. His handling of the Bible was brilliantly intuitive and has survived the rise and fall of a number of critical fashions. But it must be said that the aphoristic style of writing which came so naturally to him leaves the student of Forsyth with a large number of puzzles. He was an excellent theologian, but his inheritance needed to be developed more fully and rigorously. Though in his day he had numerous admirers, Forsyth had no obvious successor. Lacking a tradition of systematicians to press further the issues which he so skillfully illuminated, British theology shows his abiding influence in the tradition of critical orthodoxy which has manifestly constituted the core of its theo-logical life.

New Testament Scholars

C. H. Dodd (1844–1973)

We consider now the significance of a group of historians of the New Testament period who have made major contributions to British theology, notably in the area of christology. First among them is C. H. Dodd, a Welshman and a Congregationalist. Dodd won a scholarship to Oxford, where he took a first-class degree in classics in 1907. Like Forsyth he went to Germany for a semester, though in Dodd's case it was at Adolf von Harnack's feet that he sat in the University of Berlin, and the sub-ject of his interest was Roman imperial numismatics. After a period of training for the ministry at Mansfield College, Oxford, he was for three years minister of a

Congregational church in Warwick. He was called back to Oxford in 1915 to a tutorship in his old college, a post which he occupied until his election in 1930 to the Rylands Chair of Biblical Criticism and Exegesis in the University of Manchester. After five years in Manchester he was appointed Norris-Hulse Professor in the University of Cambridge, where he remained until his retirement in 1949. In 1950, however, he was made General Director of the ecumenical group which produced the *New English Bible* (New Testament first edition, 1961; second edition, 1970).

The bare recital of his career somewhat masks its significance in the institutional terms which we have emphasized. C. H. Dodd came up to Oxford a mere 30 years after Oxford and Cambridge had first opened their doors to those who could not in conscience subscribe to the Anglican Thirty-Nine Articles, and at a time when it was still impossible for non-Anglicans to receive higher degrees in divinity. Mansfield College had been founded specifically to enable nonconformists to train for the ministry in the setting of an ancient university and to provide a focus for Congregationalist undergraduates. The college quickly became a magnet for some of the outstanding non-Anglican scholars of the day, who were disbarred from promotion to chairs in Oxford, Cambridge, and London. Dodd's predecessor in the Rylands Chair in Manchester had been the first non-Anglican to become a professor of divinity in an English university, and Dodd's election to the newly merged Norris-Hulse Chair of Divinity in Cambridge was the first occasion on which a dissenter had held a professorship of divinity in one of the ancient universities.[6]

All the more significant, therefore, is the fact that his sustained concern for the historical basis of the New Testament should closely accord with what one might call the critical-orthodox consensus of British theology as a whole. Dodd's writings concerned the central corpus of New Testament books, the letters of Paul, the Synoptic Gospels, and the Fourth Evangelist. But the problem with which he was preoccupied throughout his life was one and the same, the relationship between the theological conviction that God is sovereign over history and the historical particularity of the events surrounding the life of Jesus and the early Christian communities. Dodd is chiefly celebrated as the originator of an influential theory about the character of the primitive preaching of the last things. This is generally known as "realized eschatology," and by it he meant quite simply that the *eschaton* or Age to Come has already broken into history in the ministry, death, and resurrection of Jesus.

In 1905, in an essay devoted to the discussion of evolution, P. T. Forsyth had already insisted that human history does not bear the character of steady evolutionary progress, but rather of progress by crisis. From the standpoint of a Christian philosophy of history, there is a central and absolute crisis in the cross of Christ. In 1920, in Dodd's first complete book, *The Meaning of Paul for Today* (published in a series with the Forsythian title *The Christian Revolution*), "crisis" was the key concept in interpreting Paul's philosophy of history. The fundamental belief of all early Christians, according to Dodd, was their realization that they were living at the crisis of human history, that they were "Children of the Day," and inhabitants of a new world. At first, according to Dodd, Paul had expected a visible return of Christ, but later the apocalyptic imagery with which this thought was clothed grew less central to his way of thinking, and he dwelt more explicitly upon the thought of what Dodd termed "the Divine Commonwealth," a union of humankind deeper than the divisions of nationality, culture, sex, or status.

"Crisis" remained a significant term in Dodd's first major book, *The Authority of the Bible* (1928), a work which contains the most complete statement of his constructive theological position. "The death of Jesus," he affirmed, "was the crisis of religion." The reshaping of human history which was the outcome of the death and resurrection of Christ makes of Christianity a uniquely historical religion; "for the Christian, things and events are a sacramental manifestation of God."[7] This attitude toward history has a natural corollary in relation to research into the life and teaching of Jesus. Plainly such research must be pursued – as, indeed, Harnack had insisted. The difficulty was that Harnack's program had run into trouble from those, such as Albert Schweitzer and Johannes Weiss, who claimed that the New Testament demonstrated both that Jesus believed in the future, coming sovereignty of God, and that this expectation turned out to be unfilfilled. When scholars might arrive at such negative conclusions, was not commitment to historical research intolerably risky for the faith of a Christian?

Dodd's lifelong defense of the necessity for Christian scholars to engage in historical research was of enormous importance for British theology. He maintained it on the grounds of principle, namely that there was no alternative to historical inquiry for a faith which based itself upon a revelation in history. But he did so in persistent and gentle dialogue with a number of prominent movements in biblical research which pointed in other directions. Mention has already been made of those who strongly emphasized the eschatology of Jesus. Other schools of New Testament interpretation had also made an impact. The history-of-religion school, for example, stressed the extent to which early Christianity borrowed ideas from a variety of other religious sources; Dodd accepted many of the school's suggestions, but insisted that, whatever the origins, the assemblage of ideas and practices constituted something new. Later, form criticism hoped to work out the tendencies guiding the transmission of the independent gobbets of Jesus-tradition in the pre-literary period; Dodd believed he could use the same methods to reconstruct a considerable amount of authentic history. In response to Barth's revolt against the dominance of a certain type of theological liberalism which had invested strongly in historical criticism, Dodd acknowledged the value of the idea of the unity of revelation, but maintained that the historical questions needed historical answers. When Rudolf Bultmann declared the impossibility (and undesirability) of all attempts to write a life of the Jesus of history, scholars in Britain taught or influenced by Dodd failed to be impressed. In 1950 Dodd, in a revealing dialogue with Paul Tillich precisely on the issue of the risk of historical research, maintained his characteristic stance. The so-called "New Quest" of the historical Jesus, begun by Bultmann's pupils in the later 1950s, was greeted in Britain with a certain (somewhat smug) satisfaction.

What we find in Dodd is a combination of "crisis theology," according to which the meaning of the whole of history is centered upon the death and resurrection of Jesus, and a cautious and patient commitment to historical research which provides the warrants for relatively conservative conclusions about Jesus' life and teaching. At the end of his career Dodd turned his attention to the Fourth Gospel and argued, after an exhaustive treatment of its major themes in *The Interpretation of the Fourth*

Gospel (1953), for the independent historical value of the traditions which it medi-ates (*Historical Tradition in the Fourth Gospel*, 1963). In particular, and most strik-ingly, he claimed that the Synoptic Gospels' portrait of Jesus is fundamentally in agreement with that of John:

> The synoptic gospels, to sum up, in poetry, parable and vivid dialogue, yield a picture of Jesus as one whose impact on the situation brought men to judgement. Its finality is emphasized through the symbolism of doomsday, but in fact we see the judgement taking place before our eyes. John's method of presentation, in abstract general propositions, is widely different, but the picture lying behind it is essentially the same.[8]

C. F. D. Moule (1908–)

Like C. H. Dodd, C. F. D. Moule was a classicist as a student, who received his theological education in theological college, though in Moule's case in an Anglican institution. In a range of writing, Moule has continued the tradition of critical orthodoxy which we have examined, most notably in his *The Birth of the New Testament* (first edition, 1962; third edition, revised and rewritten, 1981), *The Phenomenon of the New Testament* (1967) and *The Origin of Christology* (1977). Like Dodd, Moule acknowledges the influence of German schools of interpretation, but retains a marked independence of mind and judgment. Over the long period of his tenure of the Lady Margaret Chair of Divinity in Cambridge from 1951 to 1975 he supervised large numbers of research students who have gone on to hold distin-guished appointments themselves.

A major aspect of Moule's work has been the attempt to disprove what has seemed occasionally to be a kind of assumption among scholars, that a "high" christology, which speaks of Jesus as Lord, evolved in the New Testament period out of a more primitive, "low" christology, which treated him as prophet and teacher. Much of the problematic is determined by German scholarship on the significance of the titles used of Jesus in the New Testament. But Moule is centrally interested in the origins of the christology of Paul, for whom Christ is a corporate figure. He argues that from very early days Jesus was interpreted as "one who, as no merely human individual, included persons and communities within him, and upon whom Christians found converging all the patterns of relationship between God and man with which they were familiar from their Scriptures."[9] The purpose of the argument is quite plain. It is to press upon unbelievers the apologetic question of how to account for the earliness of this phenomenon. The same strategy emerges in Moule's characteristic handling of evidence for the resurrection, in which he similarly argues that the story of the empty tomb is part of the earliest tradition, and likewise needs to be accounted for.

D. E. Nineham (1921–)

It would be a mistake to suppose that British New Testament scholarship was committed to forms of "critical orthodoxy" without dissent. The work of D. E.

Nineham is an important indication that more skeptical positions, precisely on the historical issues, also received distinguished representation. Nineham has developed the stance of R. H. Lightfoot (1883–1953), whose early positive reception of form criticism had led to skepticism about the historicity of the Synoptic Gospels. In 1963 Nineham published a commentary on the Gospel of St Mark in which the text is treated as an interweaving of fact and interpretation, an amalgam on which it is simply impossible to deliver a confident historical verdict. A tentative historical outline of a reconstructed life of Jesus might be given, but it would be one which, Nineham increasingly began to feel, would be unacceptable to modern religious taste. In a critical review of C. H. Dodd's last book, *The Founder of Christianity* (1970), Nineham held that the latter's lifelong struggle against the consistent eschatology of Weiss and Schweitzer had been unsuccessful. Nineham's subsequently published lectures, *The Use and Abuse of the Bible* (1976), in which he strongly emphasized the irretrievability of the New Testament past and its unavailability for contemporary Christian apologetic, can best be seen as a sharp reaction to the consensus which we have exhibited.

One of the reasons why the theologians we have discussed were so obdurate about the necessity of persisting with historical inquiry into Jesus' life and teaching may have to do with a fact about their education, namely that many of them were classicists before becoming theologians. A classicist is trained to believe in the possibility of reaching a relatively dispassionate conclusion on historical questions, and we may regard it as a considerable strength in British theology that it has scarcely wavered from the conviction that the truth of certain key historical propositions about Jesus is logically entailed in the theological enterprise of christology. More open to challenge, however, is the supposition that "high" christology needs to be buttressed by a correspondingly large number of secure historical facts. A distinction was not drawn carefully enough between the verification of christological statements and their falsification. It was not frequently enough perceived that the importance of historical research for christology lay in its ability to refute the negative or skeptical historical judgments which would have *falsified* Christian claims about Jesus (for example, that he never existed, that he was a bad man, that he suffered from delusions, and so forth). No facts of a historical kind (for example, that Jesus was crucified, that his disciples at a very early stage believed him to be the final divine intervention in the world) could possibly *verify* the claims of christology. Much of the antagonism which "critical orthodoxy" provoked can be explained by the suspicion, which relatively conservative biblical historians aroused, that they were claiming too much for their conclusions.

Patristic Scholars

G. W. H. Lampe (1912–1980)

We turn now to two British theologians who have pursued their constructive theological interests by writing on the history of patristic theology. They are both

Anglicans, and this fact itself is of significance. Anglican ordinands reared on the Thirty-Nine Articles of Religion, as most were until after the Second World War, would have read there the following affirmation:

> VIII, Of the Three Creeds
> The Three Creeds, *Nicene* Creed, *Athanasius's* Creed, and that which is commonly called the *Apostles'* Creed, ought thoroughly to be received and believed: for they may be proved by most certain warrants of holy Scripture.

Although similar propositions can be found in the writings of most of the continental reformers, and in many of the confessional documents of their churches, Anglicans have been particularly insistent that their reformed episcopalian form of Western Catholicism most closely approximates to the doctrine and order of the undivided church of the first five centuries. The famous words of the Anglican Bishop Lancelot Andrewes (1555–1626) encapsulate this claim with economy and precision: "One canon reduced to writing by God himself, two testaments, three creeds, four general councils, five centuries, and the series of Fathers in that period . . . determine the boundary of our faith." Such a view determined not just the faith of Anglicans; it also governed the implicit priorities of English syllabuses of theology, especially in the Anglican-dominated ancient universities. The supposed denominational neutrality of the syllabuses concealed the fact that they had been drawn up on Anglican assumptions.

It was, then, an Anglican presumption which determined the fact that the close textual study of patristic theology (formerly and significantly known as "dogmatic theology") was compulsory in most theological syllabuses, a state of affairs conditioning the theological formation of non-Anglicans as well as Anglicans, and the atmosphere of the whole of British theology. G. W. H. Lampe was an Oxford-educated patristic historian, whose main scholarly achievement was to oversee the completion of the massive *Patristic Greek Lexicon* (1961–8). In 1951 he wrote a notable work on the doctrine of baptism and confirmation in the New Testament and the fathers, entitled *The Seal of the Spirit*. In this book he challenged an opinion, which had grown popular in Anglican Anglo-Catholic circles, that baptism is no more than a prelude to the sacrament of confirmation. Since this had been argued by means of an appeal to the New Testament and patristic evidence, Lampe's riposte contained a substantial examination of the relevant patristic texts. The work stirred up a considerable discussion which has continued to the present. Lampe himself recognized that the issue in the end devolved upon a theology of baptism; and the sober author of the entry on "confirmation" in the *Oxford Dictionary of the Christian Church* concluded: "The complexity of the evidence is such as to suggest that a final solution will not be reached by an appeal to history."

Lampe's theological pilgrimage took him from his student days, when he was taught a brand of "Barthian neo-orthodoxy," to his participation in a corporate statement of Anglican evangelical convictions, *The Fulness of Christ* (1950), to an increasingly outspoken theological liberalism in the 1960s. From the embracing of a broadly exemplarist theory of the atonement (in "The Atonement: Law and love," contributed to the controversial collected work edited by Alec Vidler, *Soundings*

(1964)), he moved to an attack on the historicity of the narrative of the empty tomb. But it was in the 1970s that he mounted his most explicit and thorough reappraisal of orthodox trinitarian incarnationism, and this too was carried out by means of a reinvestigation of patristic texts.

Lampe, who had himself written the articles on "only" or "only-begotten" (*monogenes*) and "son" (*huios*) in the *Patristic Greek Lexicon*, was in a formidable position to argue the case for the meaninglessness of the trinitarian orthodoxy of the Athanasian Creed. Denying any distinction between dogmas and doctrines, he claimed that all doctrines are more or less tentative and provisional models constructed by Christians with a view to articulating their basic commitment or trust. What is distinctive about Christianity, according to Lampe, is not therefore its doctrines but the response to what has been experienced of God's love in the central and culminating point of Jesus Christ. In Jesus there is the perfect realization and embodiment of the union of the divine Spirit and the Spirit of humanity. The concept of divine Spirit reaching out to human personality and indwelling, inspiring, and motivating it, is Lampe's preferred doctrinal model, for the reason that, so he alleged, it makes possible a full and credible account of Jesus' humanity, a humanness whose autonomy is not violated. A powerful strain of Erasmian humanism thus permeates Lampe's whole approach to the trinitarian incarnationism of orthodoxy.

In his account of how that orthodoxy developed, he built on the fact that there coexisted in the early church's scriptures a variety of models by which Jesus' significance could be interpreted. Divine Spirit, God's son (as Adam, Israel, and the hoped-for Messiah were known), the Wisdom of God, and the Word of God were all terms by means of which the experience of being touched, moved, and inspired by God could be rendered. Unhappily, under the influence of Platonic thought, another possibility arose, that of personifying the word or wisdom of God, which came to be seen as a subordinate agent of God and thus an intermediary between God and humanity. Confronted with the needs to interpret Jesus' own personal presence, early Christian theologians found it irresistible to develop a new interpretative model, that of a pre-existing divine being, God the Son. When the question was asked by Arius in the fourth century whether God the Son was not only distinct, but also different from God, the logic of the initial development compelled the answer given in the Creed of Nicaea. The Son is "one in substance" with the Father, puzzlingly distinguished only by what was called his "mode of subsistence."

Matters were simply made worse, according to Lampe, by the subsequent developments in the theology of the Holy Spirit. Having already asserted the distinct "personhood" of the Son, the Holy Spirit now had also to be seen as a "Third Person," likewise only distinguished in "mode of subsistence." Having stated that the Father only was ingenerate, and that the Son only was begotten, the fathers now fixed on the word "proceed" to describe the Spirit's uniqueness. Lampe regarded it as a sign that the models had somehow been misused that no one has ever ventured to suggest what the difference was between "generation" and "procession." The fathers thus never asked themselves the question, which Lampe puts to their conclusions, whether the theological difficulty about specifying the unique mode of being of the "person" of the Holy Spirit might not be an unreal one.

The importance of retracing the options open to the theologians of the early church lies in the fact that moderns, so Lampe believed, have no obligation to accept either the Platonist theology which undergirded the personification of the Logos or the literalistic exegesis of the proof texts with which they justified their conclusion. In Lampe's view modern theologians should not simply be content to accumulate fresh insights on the basis of those of the past; they must also be prepared to modify or abandon earlier conclusions. Much of the force of Lampe's position derived from his observation, which Friedrich Schleiermacher had made more than 150 years earlier, that Scripture lent itself as readily to a dynamic-monarchian interpretation of the divinity of Christ as to a trinitarian-incarnationalist one. Methodologically (and shockingly for an Anglican), what Lampe disputed was the authority of the orthodox creeds and fathers of the early church. The function of the creeds, he asserted, was less to give answers than to remind us of questions which we must keep on asking.

M. F. Wiles (1929–   )

That last opinion of Lampe's was expressed in an essay in a report produced by the Doctrine Commission of the Church of England in 1976. The chairman of that commission was Maurice Wiles, Regius Professor of Divinity in the University of Oxford, and, like Lampe, a historian of patristic thought. In essays published in the *Journal of Theological Studies* between 1957 and 1962, Wiles had already begun to submit the arguments of previous Anglican theologians for trinitarian orthodoxy to critical scrutiny. The last of these articles, "In Defense of Arius," strove to demonstrate that Arius' teaching was no more logical and unspiritual than was that of Athanasius. Wiles's investigations proposed nothing less than the re-examination of the very heart of Nicene orthodoxy and the article gave rise to a vigorous debate which has lasted some 25 years.

At the time of the publication of the article on Arius, Wiles was a university lecturer in Cambridge, and from here he published a study of the principles of early doctrinal development, *The Making of Christian Doctrine* (1967). It was a brilliantly concise statement of a peculiarly Anglican problem, namely the status of the doctrines and creeds of patristic orthodoxy. Could they remain immune from the kind of critical inquiry which had already disposed of the infallibility of the Scriptures? Wiles held not. Just as it had not proved possible to place a *cordon sanitaire* around the words of Jesus, while submitting the Old Testament and even the epistles of the New Testament to rigorous criticism, so it is impossible, Wiles argued, to protect the conciliar definitions from similar investigation. Modern theologians already hold that the work of the fathers proceeds by the normal fallible processes of argument, and because the official dogmas of the faith are so closely related to the whole pattern of patristic thought it follows that they too cannot be presumed to be free from the possibility of error. Wiles believed that the implications of critical inquiry in the area of patristic theology had not yet been faced with the necessary courage.

Wiles's account of how trinitarian theology developed in the early church anticipated Lampe's by several years and, though it lays its stress differently, it is no less radical in implication. Wiles detects what he believes to be a contradiction between two stages in the development of trinitarian orthodoxy. In the first stage, the second and third centuries, theologians strove to demonstrate the distinctness of Father and Son in order to avoid teaching that the Father himself suffered (the heresy of patri-passianism, otherwise known as modalist monarchianism). Having rejected the idea that there was a single divine monarchy in separate modes, by demonstrating the distinctness of Father and Son, Christian theologians in the next stage of the discussion, in the fourth century, promptly argued for the co-equality of Father and Son (and eventually of the Holy Spirit) by denying all the differences between the three persons, including the very differences which were the initial evidence for their distinctness.

The conclusion of this argument was necessarily negative. For Wiles, as for Lampe, the trinitarian model was in the end less satisfactory for the articulation of basic Christian experience than the unifying concept of God as Spirit. For Wiles, it is of particular importance to stress that trinitarian orthodoxy simply claims too much *knowledge* of God. Increasingly he has posed the issue epistemologically: What may be claimed for the Christian language of God acting? A philosophical argument to the effect that all our language about God is symbolic in character enables Wiles to claim that he is developing, not breaching or destroying the trinitarian tradition. It is important and instructive for us to note that within the approach to Christian doctrine via history certain philosophical issues constantly obtrude.

In 1977, with publication of a sensationally named work, *The Myth of God Incarnate* (edited by J. H. Hick), British theology erupted into a fever of activity which has still not abated.[10] But as many Continental and American critics have noted, the book concerned an intensely British preoccupation, and its authors were predominantly Scripture specialists or patristic scholars (two of the seven were philosophers; two were non-Anglicans). The approach to the question of doctrine was fundamentally to dispute that the evidence of Scripture and early tradition warranted the orthodox conclusion. The specifically philosophical inquiries concerned both the status of the Christian language of incarnation and its effects. The book, however, defies general description because of the contrariety of the viewpoints of its authors. Both Nineham and Wiles were contributors, and Lampe gave the book a warm welcome. Moule, on the other hand, was among its severest critics. One of the failings of the book lay in its unsubtle understanding of the subject matter it purported to question, namely incarnational trinitarianism itself. It assumed that orthodoxy required one to defend the view that propositions about the Trinity had simply *replaced* the Scriptural narrative of God's dealings with humanity, as though, after the Council of Nicaea, we had more knowledge of God than beforehand. Whether some orthodox defenders of the tradition have given that impression or not, this view is simply unintelligible in the light of century upon century of careful debate precisely about the knowledge of God. As we have seen, both Lampe and Wiles found it necessary to supplement their critical treatment of the history of the development of trinitarian orthodoxy with some views about the nature of religious language. Insofar as this aspect of British theology has given rise to a more sophisticated and wide-ranging treatment of the status of talk about God acting, it will have served a useful purpose.

Modern Historians

N. Sykes (1897–1961)

While it will be conceded that historians of the New Testament and patristic periods are likely to make important contributions to constructive theology, the case for so regarding historians of the later church appears at first sight more complex. The importance of the historical disciplines in English academic life has, however, ensured that a long succession of eminent church historians have made major contributions to theology, less by the direct fruit of their particular research than in some of the assumptions and instincts which have motivated and guided their work. The two historians considered here have been chosen because, exceptionally, they have made explicit the connections between their academic labors and the life of the contemporary church.

Norman Sykes was an Anglican priest who held chairs of history successively at Exeter and London before his appointment to the Dixie Chair of Ecclesiastical History in Cambridge in 1944. He was a professional historian who, in a series of major works, *Edmund Gibson, Bishop of London 1669–1748* (1926), *Church and State in England in the Eighteenth Century* (1934) and *William Wake, Archbishop of Canterbury, 1657–1737* (2 vols, 1957), revolutionized the conventional dismissal of the eighteenth-century church. He held a high view of the significance for the church of the profession of ecclesiastical history. Because the Christian faith is based on unique historical events the challenge of historical inquiry could not be evaded. In one of the last of his works, *Man as Churchman* (1960), he made common cause with British New Testament scholars, including T. W. Manson and C. H. Dodd, against the skepticism of the continental form critics. He explicitly endorsed the view, expressed above, that the contribution of historical study to theology might well be limited to the refutation of hostile opinions, rather than the direct verification of Christian doctrines.

Two controversial cases in ecumenical theology exhibit his historical principles at work. A close study of Catholic arguments in favor of Petrine primacy show him ready to accord a providential status of pre-eminence to the Church of Rome, but unable on historical grounds to endorse the dogma of the First Vatican Council concerning the papal magisterium and infallibility. On the other hand, on the basis of the precise terms of the Council of Trent's decree on Scripture and Tradition which requires of authentic traditions a continuity of uninterrupted profession from the days of the Apostles, he claims the dubiety of the Dogma of the Bodily Assumption of the Virgin Mary. The impact of both of these arguments can be seen in the historical cautions and reservations of the documents of the Anglican–Roman Catholic International Commission relating to papal primacy and the Marian doctrines.

In no work is Sykes's major contribution to the instinctive sense of the English contribution to world Christianity plainer than in his brilliant summary, *The English Religious Tradition* (1953, revised in 1961). Here there is an open celebration of "the English genius for compromise," a phrase coined by Butterfield (see below) in *The Englishman and His History* (1944). It was readiness to compromise which had made it possible for established churches both in England and Scotland to coexist with other churches enjoying complete religious liberty and civil equality. Sykes regarded the Butler Education Act of 1944 as an outstanding victory for the spirit of Christian unity and cooperation over denominational differences, an event of major importance because, as he elsewhere argued, educational policy is the central problem in the relations of the church and the modern state. Toleration and the spirit of liberty are, he held with Bishop Mandell Creighton (1843–1901), necessary to the life of the church, and through the contribution of English-speaking Christianity first to the missionary movement and then to the ecumenical movement of the twentieth century their influence can be seen on an international plane.

Though an Anglican, Sykes's view of English Christianity related not just to the Episcopalian, but also to Presbyterian and to independent churches, whose part in the English tradition he fully acknowledged. As a historian of the seventeenth and eighteenth centuries he had noted with approval the precise terms on which leading Anglican theologians of that period had simultaneously defended the episcopate but refused to deny the validity of the ministry and sacraments of the foreign reformed churches. In order to define what he deemed to be the central Anglican tradition he adopted a seventeenth-century distinction between the essence (*esse*) and the well-being (*bene esse*) of the church. An orthodox church with no episcopate may lose nothing of the essence of the church, but may miss something of its glory and perfection. Anglicanism, according to Sykes, has sustained a middle way on the matter of episcopacy. It has contented itself with asserting the historical grounds for its continuance of the threefold ministry. But it has nowhere officially formulated theological grounds for the exclusive dignity of the episcopate. Since the sixteenth century there has been a continuous succession of Anglican theologians who have interpreted the Prayer Book Ordinal and the relevant Articles and Canons specifically so as not to unchurch those who necessarily were deprived of the episcopate. He spoke of these writers as "a great cloud of witnesses" and dismissed suggestions that they were anomalous voices or otherwise merely lax, opportunist, or pragmatic in matters of church order.

Sykes's scholarly career coincided with the discussions which led to the successful launching of the united Church of South India in 1947, an event which he hailed as "the boldest and most promising experiment in ecclesiastical union." For him it reversed what he regarded as a major disaster of English church history, the failure to produce a comprehensive church at the Restoration of the monarchy in 1660, mitigated only by the fact that it led in 1689 to the Toleration Act which perforce recognized in a limited way the existence and right of Dissent. Of Catholicism he wrote in a way which was generous and open, but necessarily more distant, merely anticipating (in 1960!) the need for more unequivocal endorsement of the principle of freedom of conscience as a condition of any Christian discipleship whatsoever. That sound historical scholarship tended to charity in religion was one of his most cherished beliefs.[11]

Sir Herbert Butterfield (1900–1979)

Butterfield, like Sykes, was a Yorkshireman; but his interest in the history of Christianity, unlike Sykes's, which was professional, was almost accidental, the consequence of childhood habits of piety which he never lost throughout his long and distinguished career. Born into a Methodist working-class family, he became a lay preacher at the age of 17, a ministry he continued as an undergraduate at, and later (from 1923) Fellow of Peterhouse in Cambridge. In 1944 he was elected to a chair in modern history; he was Master of Peterhouse from 1955 to 1968, and Vice-Chancellor of the University from 1959 to 1961; he was promoted to the Regius Professorship of Modern History in 1963. From 1948 and for the rest of his active life, Butterfield, in addition to the production of major scholarly works of general history, regularly responded to requests for lectures on the relationship of Christianity and history. His was the outstanding contribution to the theme which we are considering in modern British intellectual history, a voice, somewhat like Dodd's, of maturity and moderation, the more authoritative and persuasive for being, in a certain sense, lay and indirect.

Butterfield's main scholarly works were on Napoleon, Machiavelli, George III, and the origins of modern science. But a highly influential brief treatise on *The Whig Interpretation of History* (1931) made plain his critical interest in the role of presuppositions in the writing of history. The work is a sustained and effective attack on the Protestant and "Whig" view which justified the Reformation on the grounds that it led to liberty. This Butterfield regarded as an illicit abridgement of the complexity of history, an opting for a comfortable distortion of the truth. The book was a plea for more detail, more impartiality, and more imaginative sympathy in a historian. It represented a viewpoint upon humanity which was recognizably postliberal in the tradition of P. T. Forsyth, in that it focused not upon progress, but upon catastrophe and tragedy in human affairs. Though not itself an overtly theological work, it constantly turned to the interpretation of Luther for its examples, and implied a significant degree of scholarly detachment in its verdict on the religious fanaticisms of the sixteenth century.

It was many years later, in 1948, that Butterfield turned to an explicit treatment of Christianity as a historical religion, in a series of open lectures, published as *Christianity and History* (1949). He, like so many of the others we have treated, similarly insists that Christianity is rooted in the ordinary realm of investigation with which the technical student of history is concerned. By "technical history" Butterfield meant a specific discipline of attending to what actually is the case. He linked its origins to the Christian origins of the study of natural science, namely the discovery of a better, because humbler way of studying the ways of Providence. Nonetheless it was, Butterfield believed, a piece of willful forgetfulness when historians suggested that *all* that might be said about the historical process could be said on the basis of "technical history."

By way of explanation of this view Butterfield distinguished between three levels of historical analysis. The first is the biographical, in which human beings are taken as relatively free and responsible for their own decisions. The second is the analysis which seeks to identify deep processes, or even laws within the outworking of historical events. The third level is that of Providence embracing the whole of human history. Each one of these levels is important to the Christian. The Christian historian has to be emphatic about the reality of human freedom, for that is the precondition for seeing humanity in God's sight as sinners. The Christian should be no less responsive to the notion of historical process, which should elicit the response of charity and empathy. Butterfield regarded these apparently lower levels as consequences of the Providential view of history, so that each of them is in fact integral to each of the others.[12]

Butterfield, the Methodist lay preacher, instructively laid great emphasis upon the Old Testament. The people of Israel's contribution to human civilization was precisely the fact that they saw God as the God of history and regarded history as based on his promise. Despair is thus ruled out, despite the intervention of sin, catastrophe, and judgment. Indeed it is precisely catastrophe and judgment which is the setting for the greatest of those symbols or myths which Israel contributed to the Christian church, the ideas of the leaven that leavens the whole lump, the faithful remnant, and the suffering servant. This is the orthodox heart of Butterfield's interpretation of history, the more impressive for being expounded by a technical historian of brilliance:

> Ultimately our interpretation of the whole human drama depends on an intimately personal decision concerning the part we mean to play in it. It is as though we were to say to ourselves: "There is dissonance in the universe, but if I strike the right note it becomes harmony and reconciliation – and though they may kill me for it they cannot spoil that harmony."[13]

Debate

The British theologians whose work we have surveyed do not readily fall into a group identifiable by shared theological convictions; nonetheless they constitute a tradition of theological scholarship which is recognizably British in character. As such they share certain concerns which are unquestionably those of their academic setting. The strong influence of a classical and historical training and the comparative degree of freedom from denominational control has inclined them to a certain impartiality and objectivity in their approach to theological conflicts of the past. It is perhaps fortuitous that each one has responded positively to a greater or lesser degree to the antiliberalism of P. T. Forsyth, but one can sense a marked reserve, even in the absence of explicit discussion, toward the Continental movements of existentialism and dialectical theology. There is evidence of a tradition of "theology of crisis" in the work of such disparate figures as Forsyth, Dodd, and Butterfield, but it lacks the thoroughgoing anthropological perspective which existentialism and depth psychology gave to the Continental movement. The overt celebration of the "English [sic!] genius for compromise" in Butterfield and Sykes reflects not just an understandable nationalism in time of war, but also a quiet satisfaction specifically about certain cultural institutions embodying liberty and toleration, such as the education system, the universities, and the BBC. Each of these reflects a particular settlement of the problem of church and state, with which the British had been wrestling since the sixteenth century. The context of the modern British university unquestionably offered a tolerant, academically serious, and ecumenically significant environment for the work of a theologian.

The areas of scholarship we have considered have continued to be lively fields of research and debate. P. T. Forsyth was the subject of a large-scale colloquium, resulting in the publication of a book of essays on the centenary of his receiving a doctorate of divinity from the University of Aberdeen.[14] The appended bibliography of books, theses and dissertations, and articles about Forsyth confirms the judgment that his achievement remains a powerful and attractive force in modern theology.

Of course, Forsyth did not stop dead in its tracks the kind of theology guilty of what he called "the engaging fallacy of liberalism that Christ is but the eternal God-in-man, supremely revealed and carried to a luminous head in Him, but forming always the spirit of Humanity and looking out in every great Soul." The divinity of Christ (in the sense of the incarnation of the Second Person of the Trinity) remained a difficulty for radical critics. And problematic though optimism about humanity has increasingly become in the light of twentieth-century atrocity, the characteristic social and psychological remedies of non-incarnational theologies have remained self-help and amelioration.

Lines of debate about biblical research diversified after the 1960s. Philosophical hermeneutics exploring the relation of reader to the text and of text to the world made slow progress in Britain. Two works by Anthony Thiselton, *The Two Horizons* and *New Horizons in Hermeneutics*, largely devoted to exposition of Continental and North American thinkers, considerably explained the debates.[15] But British biblical scholars themselves have shown relatively little interest. Social history, on the other hand, has proved an attractive aid to biblical study, and a modest amount of social theory has informed the predominant historical concerns of certain critics.

One of the tasks of the social historian of early Christianity is to illuminate the social context of the New Testament documents in order to shed light on the way in which the early communities held together and interacted with their contemporaries. The world which comes to light is partly strange and partly familiar. But to declare the world of New Testament texts to be either irretrievable or wholly unintelligible turns out to be an exaggeration. The social anthropological themes which inform the study link the contemporary student with antiquity. A certain "fusing of horizons" takes place without benefit of at least much conscious philosophical reflection. That exactly the same tools are used in classical studies to good effect commends them to those brought up in the tradition of historical enquiry we have outlined above.

The debate in the area of patristics has undoubtedly abated somewhat since the publication of two large-scale works on Arianism, by Bishop Richard Hanson and Professor (now Bishop) Rowan Williams.[16] That both authors are Anglicans by denomination is no accident. The future state of patristic studies in Britain is to many a source of some anxiety. Modern reforms of theological syllabuses have marginalized what used to be an integral part of theological education. The formidable linguistic and historical demands of the study of the early church have proved a deterrent to British students. The debate on trinitarian theology, which has continued in a considerable number of publications, has largely ceased to be sustained by arguments from patristic history.[17]

In the nature of the case, modern history is a collection of widely disparate subject areas, any one of which may at any given time prove to be of controversial relevance.

A recent area of theological importance has proved to be the interpretation of the English Reformation. The "Whig view of history," which wisely foresees the inevitability of progress after the event, is said to have characterized a well-informed and long dominant school of A. J. Dickens, author of the standard work, *The English Reformation* (first edition 1964; revised editions 1967 to 1989). A series of studies, some but not all of them from Roman Catholic authors, have tried to show how strong and prevalent was the piety of ordinary English believers on the eve of the Reformation.[18] Was there even one Reformation? Again through the medium of historical study, some important theological arguments are being rehearsed, whose controversial denominational implications are occasionally made explicit.

Agenda

Both the incarnation and the doctrine of the Church require the disciplines of historical study. It has always been tempting to theologians to build a *cordon sanitaire* around sacred history in order to make historical study answer the questions of the contemporary church. Selective blindness to folly and wickedness and romanticism about favored periods or persons need the astringent disciplines of the professional historian and the disputes of a mixed community of scholars. It has been the particular good fortune of British faculties and departments of theology to have had the services of scholars respected in the historical disciplines. Biblical studies have constantly been refreshed by perspectives drawn from the study of Jewish, Greek, and Roman literature. New methodologies in other periods of history have had an impact on the study of the life of ordinary members, as well as the elites of the churches.

The major challenge to the life of the churches in the late twentieth century, which might be termed the anarchic normlessness of Western civilization in the face of desperate poverty and oppression in many parts of the world, has its analogue in professional historical study. It is far from clear according to what interests or norms the historical narratives of the future are going to be written. How is the past history of the church to be remembered, if even moderate compassion and human sympathy are derided as the disposition of a metanarrative? Is there no middle way between the choice of a point of view, which may be partially or wholly partisan according to taste, and a total amoralism? The demands of contemporary politics, including the cry of the oppressed and marginal, coincide with the challenges of the writing of history. Historians who are members of churches may need in future to become more explicit about the theological view of humanity which is implicit in their faith, and which will need justification if it informs their future scholarship, as we have seen it do in the past.

Notes

1 H. R. Mackintosh, *Types of Modern Theology, Schleiermacher to Barth* (London, 1937), p. 4.
2 P. T. Forsyth, *The Principle of Authority*, pp. 112–16.
3 P. T. Forsyth, *Positive Preaching and the Modern Mind*, p. 284.
4 P. T. Forsyth, *The Person and Place of Jesus Christ*, p. 12. The last sentence of the quotation contains words drawn from the Absolution used at Morning and Evening Prayer in the (Anglican) Book of Common Prayer.
5 Ibid., p. 294.
6 See F. W. Dillistone's biography, *C. H. Dodd: Interpreter of the New Testament*.
7 C. H. Dodd, *The Authority of the Bible*, pp. 282, 260.
8 From "The Portrait of Jesus in John and in the Synoptics," in W. R. Farmer, C. F. D. Moule and R. R. Niebuhr (eds), *Christian History and Interpretation: Studies presented to John Knox* (Cambridge, 1967), pp. 183–98; here pp. 191ff.
9 C. F. D. Moule, *The Origin of Christology*, p. 136.
10 See the review of responses by G. M. Newlands in S. Sykes and D. Holmes (eds), *New Studies in Theology* (London, 1980), pp. 181–92.
11 See the preface by G. V. Bennett, in G. V. Bennett and J. D. Walsh, *Essays in Modern English Church History: In memory of Norman Sykes* (London, 1966), pp. v–viii.
12 See the essay "God in history" (1952), reprinted in C. T. McIntyre (ed.), *Herbert Butterfield Writings on Christianity and History*, pp. 3–16.
13 H. Butterfield, *Christianity and History*, p. 86.
14 T. Hart (ed.), *Justice the True and Only Mercy* (Edinburgh, 1995).
15 A. C. Thiselton, *The Two Horizons* (Exeter, 1980), and *New Horizons in Hermeneutics* (London, 1992).
16 R. Williams, *Arius: Heresy and tradition* (London, 1987); R. P. C. Hanson, *The Search for the Christian Doctrine of God: The Arian controversy 318–381* (Edinburgh, 1988).
17 See the following: J. Mackey, *The Christian Experience of God as Trinity* (London, 1983); D. Brown, *The Divine Trinity* (London, 1985); *Modern Theology*, 2 (1986), a special issue on the Doctrine of the Trinity, with contributions from K. Surin, N. L. A. Lash, R. Williams, J. Milbank et al.; *The Forgotten Trinity*, 3 vols, British Council of Churches (London, 1991); C. Gunton, *The Promise of Trinitarian Theology* (Edinburgh, 1991); N. Lash, *Believing: Three ways in one God* (London, 1992).
18 J. J. Scarisbrick, *The Reformation and the English People* (Oxford, 1984); C. Haigh (ed.), *The English Reformation Revised* (Cambridge, 1987); R. Rex, *The Theology of John Fisher* (Cambridge, 1991); E. Duffy, *The Stripping of the Altars: Traditional Religion in England 1400–1580* (New Haven and London, 1992). See also R. O'Day, *The Debate on the English Reformation* (London, 1986).

Bibliography

Primary

Butterfield, H., *Christianity and History* (London, 1950).
—— *Man on His Past* (Cambridge, 1969).
Dodd, C. H., *The Meaning of Paul for Today* (London, 1920).
—— *The Authority of the Bible* (London, 1947).
—— *Historical Tradition and the Fourth Gospel* (Cambridge, 1963).
—— *The Interpretation of the Fourth Gospel* (Cambridge, 1968).
—— *The Founder of Christianity* (London, 1970).
Forsyth, P. T., *Positive Preaching and the Modern Mind* (London, 1901).
—— *The Cruciality of the Cross* (London, 1909).
—— *The Person and Place of Jesus Christ* (London, 1909).
—— *The Work of Christ* (London, 1910).

—— *The Principle of Authority* (London, 1952).

Hick, J. H. (ed.), *The Myth of God Incarnate* (London, 1977).

Lampe, G. W. H., *The Fulness of Christ* (London, 1950).

—— *The Seal of the Spirit* (London, 1951).

—— *God as Spirit* (Oxford, 1976).

McIntyre, C. T. (ed.), *Herbert Butterfield: Writings on Christianity and history* (Oxford and New York, 1979).

Moule, C. F. D., *The Phenomenon of the New Testament* (London, 1967).

—— *The Origin of Christology* (Cambridge, 1977).

—— *The Birth of the New Testament* (London, 1981).

Nineham, D. E., *The Gospel of Mark* (London, 1963).

—— *The Use and Abuse of the Bible* (London, 1976).

Sykes, N., *Man as Churchman* (Cambridge, 1960).

—— *The English Religious Tradition* (London, 1961).

Wiles, M. F., *The Making of Christian Doctrine* (Cambridge, 1967).

—— *The Remaking of Christian Doctrine* (London, 1974).

—— *Faith and the Mystery of God* (London, 1982).

—— *God's Action in the World* (London, 1986).

Secondary

Anderson, Marvin A. (ed.), *The Gospel and Authority. A P. T. Forsyth reader* (Minneapolis, 1971).

Bennett, G. V. and Walsh, J. D. (eds), *Essays in Modern English Church History, in Memory of Norman Sykes* (London, 1966).

Bradley, W. L., *P. T. Forsyth: The man and his work* (London, 1952).

Brown, R. M., *P. T. Forsyth, Prophet for Today* (Philadelphia, 1952).

Dillistone, F. W., *C. H. Dodd: Interpreter of the New Testament* (London, 1977).

Hart, Trevor (ed.), *Justice the True and Only Mercy: Essays on the life and theology of Peter Taylor Forsyth* (with a bibliography by Leslie McCurdy, pp. 256–330) (Edinburgh, 1995).

Moule, C. F. D. (ed.), *G. W. H. Lampe* (London, 1982).

Mozley, J. K., "The Theology of Dr Forsyth," in *The Heart of the Gospel* (London, 1925).

Theology through Philosophy

Daniel W. Hardy

Introduction

From its most ancient roots and through the centuries in which it has been present in Britain, Christian faith has been deeply interwoven with civilization itself. Although there have always been attempts to focus the truth of Christian faith as such, these have normally been accompanied by – even interwoven with – the attempt to Christianize civilization from within. The result has been an integration of faith with its contribution to public life, not usually the separation of faith from its implications for civilization as a whole – except in the case of some of the "free churches."[1] Employing the sociologists' distinction of churches from sects, Christian faith has been perpetuated in Britain by churches deeply immersed in civilization itself.

It is for this reason, probably, that in Britain Christian faith itself has been conceived in close connection with – and even *through* – aspects of human life and understanding which are germinative for civilization itself. There are a few very basic ones: the literary heritage which is germinative for the cultural life of this civilization (closely allied to the determinative role of Scripture), the history of the people and their nation (where the tradition of Christian faith is seen as central), and a unified social life (in which the Church is regarded as co-equal with the state), etc.[2] The identifying features of Christian faith are thus seen in close conjunction with the germinative forces of civilization in Britain, not in contradistinction to them.

This has had a reciprocal effect on the conception of Christian faith, not only in identifying *what* is considered central to faith but also in establishing *how* these features are to be treated. Scripture, tradition, reason, and church are taken without argument to be central to Christian faith; and it is usually accepted that these are to be studied by means of the disciplines which are usual in civilized life, without special pleading. Scripture is to be treated through prevailing modes of thought, whether literary, historical, or cultural; the tradition of Christian faith is to be seen by normal historical methods; and the church is properly to be seen by the approaches normal in sociopolitical life. In each case, of course, there are repeated attempts to identify and proclaim what is particularly Christian, but this is accomplished through or with the disciplines applicable more widely; it is not for long separated from the interwovenness of Christian faith with British civilization. As we shall see, this brings significant difficulties where the "normal" modes for the consideration of civilized life come to be alienated from matters of faith, as has occurred during the twentieth century.

The same is true where "philosophy"[3] is involved. Through the centuries, concentrated thought has enjoyed an important position in Britain, as instrumental to the well-being of the nation, whether theoretical or practical. Far beyond the compass of those who claim the title "philosopher," careful understanding and argument have been seen as valuable in promoting what is best for civilization and refining whatever contributes to this, including Christian faith. As such, philosophy has affected both the contribution of Christian faith to civilization and the conception of faith itself. So far as faith itself is concerned, it has combined with other factors in leading to the conception of faith in concentrated doctrinal terms, and to continued attempts to configure it adequately as such. The chief instrument in such study, reason, has not typically been seen as alien to faith; rather it has been regarded as an endowment given to humanity by God, and therefore well-suited to the articulation of faith in a suitable form – a constructive, not a damaging force.

Where reason is detached from its origin in the creation of God, or seen otherwise than as the gift of the Trinitarian God of Christian faith, however, major difficulties result for Christian faith. Philosophy is then used as an autonomous arbiter and interpreter – or the intermediary for other normative determinants – whose purpose in relation to faith is not only to scrutinize and refresh but also to adjudicate and determine. Where it is used in such a fashion, it can be a means of refashioning faith according to criteria which are at odds with faith itself. And a very powerful force it has proved to be.

Although it has recently become increasingly common to complain of the weakening position of philosophy in academic institutions, the British practice of refining and rearticulating both Christian faith and its position in civilization through philosophy continues to the present day. A distinction can be made between two forms, although this frequently does not hold in practice: One uses philosophy as instrumental to the clarification and reconception of substantial issues in Christian faith, and is called philosophical theology; the other employs philosophy for the critique of religious phenomena, among which are beliefs, and is called philosophy of religion.

In either case, the philosophy employed varies considerably, as do its norms; and the consequences for Christian faith have varied widely. Our purpose here is to attempt to trace characteristic norms and modes of the philosophic mediation of Christian faith in a number of recent representative exponents. Space precludes a more comprehensive account of all those who have made significant contributions, although we shall mention some of them briefly.

Survey: The Dilemma of Philosophical Mediation for Theology

As major eras in the history of theology reveal, it is possible for the re-examination of Christian faith, in the presence of new circumstances rationally (philosophically) understood, to generate a new profundity of insight into faith and its connection with aspects of life, accompanied by the development or enrichment of doctrinal understanding. For several hundred years now, it has been the sifting of human understanding in a realistic – particularly empiricist – framework which has occasioned such a re-examination of faith in Britain. With a few exceptions, this has not resulted in the hardening of philosophically mediated understanding against Christian faith.

More recently, however, the presence of a narrowly empiricist philosophy has brought explicit attempts either to eliminate theology (as meaningless) or to subsume it in alien categories. What produced this was the acceptance of positivistic norms derived from prevailing suppositions about the capacity of the physical sciences to achieve complete understanding of the world – a view which had gained some currency in the sciences around the turn of the century, before passing into the logical analysis of the Vienna School, and from there elsewhere.

It is interesting that this was the same time when neopositivism was emerging within theology, at least on the Continent, whether in the form advocated by Karl Barth or that argued by those intent on delineating salvation history. While scientific positivism did pass into England, however, there was not such a wide reception accorded to theological neopositivism. It was more characteristic of Britain – and this was demonstrably the case in the 1930s – to hope for coexistence between faith and other forms of human understanding.

When "logical positivism" erupted in England in the 1940s and 1950s, however, a variety of strategies were used to deal with this "alien" philosophy. In some cases, theology severed itself from the contaminating force of reason as "the great and mighty enemy of God" (Martin Luther, *Commentary on Galatians*). But others argued that even such theology invoked reason to articulate and clarify theology; and they embraced its use as proper to the task of theology. Still others saw philosophy as an autonomous discipline to which theology should be subject. In view of this series of options, it became a question of how it might be possible to achieve a situation in which theology and philosophy are mutually informed and enriched.

It is not only empiricist philosophy, or the extreme form known as logical positivism, by which recent British philosophy is influenced. There are vestiges of older schools of thought – Kantian and idealist, or Scottish common-sense realism – and also incursions of Continental forms. And there are philosophies developed in special connections, with the natural sciences, sociology, or literature, for example. These provide the matrices within which the strategies mentioned above are employed.

There were those who wished to avoid philosophy (and indeed the natural and social sciences, as well as culture and religion) as if it were somehow contaminating. This, however, was not an option generally favored in the climate we have been tracing; and the following of Karl Barth, seen as its chief advocate, was somewhat despised in mainstream Christian thought in Britain. The positive possibility which a number of leading thinkers – including some who admired Barth's theology but dissented from the view of him as antirational – pursued was to recover the integration of faith with philosophically mediated norms applicable outside it. T. F. Torrance, for example, also a leading scholar of Calvin and Barth, developed the convergence between scientific and theological thought. John Macquarrie, no admirer of Barth, used a sequence of philosophical-anthropological positions (R. Bultmann, M. Heidegger, and K. Rahner) to develop a full theology from his own understanding of religious experience. And Richard Swinburne, also astute in philosophy of science, has used a sophisticated array of modern philosophical theories to re-establish a metaphysically formed theology. But there were also those who insisted that Christian faith should not be privileged, and therefore reversed the tide: Philosophy formed in the analysis of religions (John Hick) or in postmodernism (Don Cupitt)[4] is used to transform Christian faith, correcting its alleged errors. In still others, of which D. M. MacKinnon is here taken as chief representative, the wider tradition of modern philosophy becomes the milieu within which there is a less predetermined – and more open – engagement between philosophical and theological exploration, exploring the interface between the two in the dilemmas of life itself. Although all of these ways of engaging philosophy with theology have made important contributions, all but the last seem to foreclose the fullest possibilities for bringing the two together. For apart from their interest to followers, they have failed in bringing the hoped-for rapprochement between Christian faith and wider intellectual life. It is only the last which seems to offer the greatest promise for rendering Christian faith intelligible in the complexities of current life in Britain.

The Modern Philosophers and Theology

Within the tradition of empiricism which has prevailed in Britain, there was a decisive turn following the Second World War, away from the philosophical idealism (often based in Kant, but frequently Neo-Hegelian) of the previous period and toward the skepticism of logical positivism. This was

> the view that the only real things were sense impressions and (possibly) material objects of a size visible to the naked eye, and that our knowledge was limited to knowledge of how things had been and would be in respect of sense impressions and material objects . . . Talk about anything else was meaningless. This view was codified in the verification principle: the only propositions which are meaningful are those which can (in some sense) be verified by observation. And hence, said the verificationists, all claims about the nature of space and time, about which moral views are true, and of course about God are not false but meaningless.[5]

This began some years of wide-ranging discussion about how it is that assertions are to be construed as meaningful, beginning with the very restrictive conceptions of A. J. Ayer and Bertrand Russell (for whom propositions were meaningful if and only if they could in principle be verified by sense experience), and culminating with the much richer conceptions of meaning advocated by Ludwig Wittgenstein (where meaning is established by attending to the various uses and contexts of words) and "ordinary language" philosophy.

In general, those who sought to respond and advocate the meaningfulness of theological discourse were of two kinds. There were those who directly faced the stringency of current philosophical demands with minimal reference to the content of Christian faith. Ian Ramsey[6] was one example, who sought to show the special kinds of situation – "cosmic disclosure" when "the penny drops" for the hearer, whereby the hearer can anchor what is occurring in personal experience and respond in total commitment. He was criticized both for the vagueness of his approach and for immunizing religious discourse from criticism; his views were said to be symptomatic of "the intellectual crisis of British Christianity" caused by "mushiness" symptomatic of "lack of philosophical competence and insight."[7]

By contrast, there were those who attempted to re-establish a natural philosophy which would be congenial to Christian belief, in particular to argue for the very metaphysics which had been declared impossible by the reigning analytical philosophy. One leading figure among them was Austin Farrer,[8] whose most substantial work *Finite and Infinite* was published in 1943; it was a rigorous attempt to analyze theological statements and the way they are used. He claimed that the experience of finitude – attending to the universal characteristics of finite phenomena (change, motion, contingency, etc.) – would lead to an indirect knowledge of the infinite as the fullness of the being of God. The issue, therefore, was how we rise from the world of interacting finite substances through the scale of being to a God who exists in and of himself, the same God who is the source of our splintered being. Similar arguments were developed by Farrer to show the character of biblical language and human freedom.

Those who were concerned to develop a full Christian response to the prevailing climate met as a group, "the Metaphysicals," at Oxford for some 40 years and included such significant figures as Farrer, Michael Foster, the ethicist Richard Hare, Eric Mascall,[9] and Basil Mitchell.[10] The concerns of those involved proved to be quite different from each other, but they were united by interest in the richness of language (as seen in the use of metaphor and analogy), the value of informal reasoning (as opposed to the restrictions imposed by current philosophy) and the possibility of making a rational assessment of the different assumptions underlying various uses of language. For the most part, the participants were active church people; this and their discussions clearly sustained their awareness of divine presence and the necessity of moral choice and value as grounded in the love of God. They produced the book *Faith and Logic* (1957) as a public demonstration that faith was not philosophically indefensible.[11] The editor, Basil Mitchell, was himself a participant in the "Theology and Falsification" debate of the 1950s, maintaining that belief is not established or refuted by empirical evidence, although it has empirical application. Later, in *The Justification of Religious Belief* (1973), he argued that the Christian view was sustainable cumulatively because of its capacity to make sense of all the evidence.

Although not all British philosophers were so much affected by this tradition of philosophy,[12] the shadow of the controversy generated by it has proved very long, and has produced more than a generation of a theology which is apprehensive of positive claims, especially where particular occurrences are involved. It results in tacitly deist positions which allow for a "continuing relationship of God to the world as a source of existence and giver of purpose to the whole," but disallow "effective causation on the part of God in relation to particular occurrences"[13] – including the

Incarnation. It is this shadow which engulfs many of those we shall now describe, either shaping their strategy in theology or altering their conclusions.

The Integration of Faith with Scientific Thought: Thomas F. Torrance

In this analysis of different strategies by which theology is mediated through philo-sophy, it is most appropriate to start with a man whose work is neither focused on philosophy nor on its mediation of general religious or metaphysical norms,[14] but which is unashamedly theological, Christ-centered, and confessional – T. F. Torrance.[15] Yet it is exactly these concerns which lead him to "think together" theology and the sciences.[16]

It is the "unlimited reality of God in his relations with the universe of all time and space"[17] which requires that theology understand creation itself. And it is be-cause God, the *Logos* through whom everything was made, became incarnate in physical existence in Jesus Christ and fulfilled our redemption in bodily resurrection that we must study the world, not simply – as so much modern thought has supposed – because it is the circumstance for the human relation to God. The study of the natural sciences is therefore necessary to the understanding of God and God's salvation in Christ. But there is also benefit for the sciences; Investigation of the intelligible reality of the triune God in his creation of the contingent and orderly universe, and in the depth of his relation to the universe in his Son, provides for the natural sciences the vertical and horizontal coordinates for the integration of the universe. And from the side of the sciences, the more profound scientific inquiry into the universe becomes, the more it faces cosmological questions and is forced to adopt a fundamental attitude to the universe as a whole.[18] These conclusions support Torrance's concern to anchor dogmatics within the very dynamics of the sciences.

The relation which Torrance finds between the two is both epistemological and ontological. Both theological and natural sciences are objective in the sense that they actively engage with the demands of reality. For theology this is to allow the reality of the divine as it presents itself – and therefore theological truth – to fashion our understanding in accordance with this truth; "true objectivity is to be found only within personal communion or dialogical relation with God."[19] For the natural sciences this is to think in accordance with the real, in this case the given of a reality which is contingent both upon God and in its own structure.[20] For both, therefore, understanding is made possible by reality itself, and the processes of understanding accord with reality. In conventional parlance, this is to say that epistemology must follow ontology, and be constituted by it. Theology and the natural sciences are both therefore a posteriori activities, conditioned by what is given; a priori conceptions are problematic except insofar as they are conducive to this. It is the task of both as sciences to probe as deeply as possible into the constitutive factors of these given realities, to discover what makes each what it is and how the two are related, and not rest content with idealized frameworks which restrict them and their relation.[21]

Hence Torrance – like Barth – places natural theology within revealed theology and – like Einstein – places geometry within physical science; each is made instrumental to the proper content of the reality with which it is concerned. Torrance claims that this opens new possibilities for rational knowledge of God and nature, by displacing the anthropocentricism so widespread in modern theology and the abstractive conceptions so prevalent in the modern sciences. Nonetheless, *as science* theology and the sciences are not to claim the sufficiency of their statements to their objects; they are human endeavors in quest of the truth, subject to refinement through critical investigation, and their value is in their denotation of the realities to which they refer. As "existence-statements," theological statements do not have their truth in themselves but in the divine realities to which they refer.[22]

In accordance with modern quantum physics, Torrance emphasizes the role of the observer. In a fashion reminiscent of Scottish common-sense philosophy, Torrance suggests that knowledge arises through insight shaped by the internal structure of that into which we inquire, and develops "within the structural kinship that arises between our knowing and what we know as we make ourselves dwell in it and gain access to its meaning . . . an intuitive anticipation of a hitherto unknown pattern, or a novel order in things."[23] Hence the human mind has a "tacit power" or unspecifiable skill to discern *Gestalten* (coherent patterns in experience) through a heuristic leap from parts to a whole.[24] As Polanyi argues, this is a personal and informal integrative process, "the insight of a mind informed by intuitive contact with reality."[25] It is not limited to the initial moment of discovery, but persists in scientific work and – through its alternation with analytic and deductive procedures – produces a deepening awareness of the object.[26]

The matrix within which this tacit power operates, whether in theology or the natural sciences, is provided by normative *beliefs*. All forms of scientific activity, whether theological or natural, are sustained by such beliefs. The objectivity of God's truth for humankind in Jesus Christ sustains scientific theological activity, while the objectivity of the truth of nature sustains natural science. Beliefs are "prescientific but fundamental act[s] of acknowledgement of some significant aspect of the nature of things . . . more deeply grounded than any set of scientific evidence, without which scientific inquiry would not be possible."[27] Belief, therefore, is integral to the pursuit of knowledge, although itself irrefutable and unprovable. That is why faith – "the resting of our mind upon objective reality . . . that which really is, the nature and truth of things"[28] – is integral to reason; the two cannot rationally be contrasted,

> for faith is the very mode of rationality adopted by the reason in what it seeks to understand, and as such faith constitutes the most basic form of knowledge upon which all subsequent rational inquiry proceeds.[29]

Beliefs are not "subjective" in the usual modern sense, but personal recognitions of what is objective, which sustain our dialogical relation to what is objective. They are irreducibly personal, although not the less intelligent for that, and as such capable of modification in response to a depth in objective reality ("boundless objectivity") which carries them beyond what the human mind itself can conceive. Therein lies the possibility that the mind can be expanded to meet the fullness of reality, and avoid reducing reality to its own scale.

There are, however, different *kinds of objectivity*, ranging from the objectivity of God (which is the objectivity of a personal subject who is with humankind)[30] to that of natural things to that of human beings. As such, beliefs should be proportioned to the *nature of the truth* of each, ranging from the truth which is God's to the truth of natural things to the truth of human knowledge.

The picture which Torrance draws of the relation between theology and the sciences is one of their common concern with objectivity, knowledge, beliefs, and truth, while they differ in the kinds to which they are dedicated. These kinds differ even in the natural sciences, where there may be some unity within them, but none between them. Ultimately, however, there is a theological basis for a unity of the theological and natural sciences. The different "levels" of truth and objectivity, divine and natural, are both differentiated and unified by God's self-giving action in creation and Jesus Christ.[31] And the belief which responds to this is one which also derives from God's action, the action of the Holy Spirit. Such belief has its ground in its response to God's action, and it cannot therefore be validated "from outside." The task of scientific theology is to unfold this belief in a fashion which is appropriate to the "truth" and "objectivity" to which it is a response, just as the task of natural science is to unfold the belief by which it operates.

For Torrance, the beliefs of theology and the sciences are not free-standing, but have emerged from a long history in which the two have been intertwined. Fully to understand them requires careful hermeneutically guided incorporation of theological and scientific understanding from the past, particularly from the decisive periods of theological and natural-scientific advance in which the two nourished each other. Such advances need to show their truth again, to be coordinated with other theories of later times in which the truth also shines forth, in a unitary view of truth.[32]

Torrance's engagement of the present with the past can be illustrated by two examples. One is his appropriation of the theology of John Calvin and Karl Barth,[33] to whom he is attracted because their approaches exemplify the possibility of a *scientific theology*. In contrast to medieval thought, Calvin saw that knowledge was objectively derived from God as "active," "through modes of knowing imposed on us from the nature of God and from his self-manifestation through the Word"; it was not "factive" through ideas or "images of our own forming." The ideas or language formed by human beings could only be related to such knowledge through the Spirit of God; "the Spirit provides *transparence* in our knowledge and language of God."[34] The great virtue of Barth, as Torrance sees it, was that he recalled theology from "Calvinism," that logicized version of Calvin which is so frequently mistaken for Calvin's own position, to the recognition that knowledge of God comes by the free and graceful activity of God in a dynamic "analogy of grace."

The other illustration comes from Torrance's long-standing concern with patristic theology.[35] Like some members of the Reformed tradition, Torrance finds in fourth-century patristic theology the primary elucidation of "the evangelical and apostolic faith," a theology which is grounded in the constitutive factors of reality itself, following "biblical patterns of thought governed by the Word of God and the obedient hearing of faith."[36] And while letting the fathers speak for themselves, he attempts to "bring to light the inner theological connections which gave coherent structure to the classical theology of the ancient Catholic Church."[37]

This powerful "thinking together" of theology and the sciences, the reappropriation of the past for the present, informed throughout by a realism which suggests that reality affords us the means to know it, and the importance of the personal activity of the observer, is ultimately grounded in active response to the Trinitarian God who created and sustains the intelligibility intrinsic to reality and our capacity to grasp it. It is such an active response, made possible by the grace of God, which makes these things possible, not claims of the sufficiency of the knower.

But how far is this conception of the relation between theology and science sustainable among scientists? Torrance frequently appeals to Einstein, who rediscovered the "sovereign" character of reality, one which transcends all human concepts, *mysterious* but with an infinite *depth of comprehensibility* which precludes any final notion of physical reality of the sort claimed by physicists at the turn of the century. Not only is there an intelligibility in the universe found by the physical and natural sciences, but one which stretches out beyond what we can comprehend.[38] And what is found is a dynamic and open-structured universe far beyond what can be captured in deterministic thought.[39]

So, it appears, Torrance focuses on the dynamic of comprehensibility in a mysterious and dynamic universe as the convergence-point between theology and the sciences. The intelligibility of the universe is invariant and inherent; but as transcendent and mysterious it nonetheless relativizes the concepts through which it is understood.[40] Grasping it requires concentrated, non-deductive thought which also moves in accordance with the contingent order of the universe. That is the role of the natural sciences, which are concerned with the investigation of the ordered, contingent world in its own right. Their interest is in establishing the structures which determine its order, and the vectorial character of its change, including its ultimate origins and ultimate ends. Such investigation is predicated on the two main "ultimates" which are employed in the natural sciences, belief in a universe which is orderly and contingent.

It is no part of the purpose of the natural sciences, however, to establish the source of contingent order, or the rational basis of these "ultimates." But their research does reach "limits set . . . by the initial conditions of nature which, though they cannot be accounted for within the frame of our physical laws, are nevertheless essential to the rational enterprise of science."[41] There are, in other words, theoretical and empirical limits to the enterprise of science; and these are necessary for science to be what it is. They serve to reinforce the contingence of the universe; the openness of the order of the universe does not abolish these limits.

At this point, there comes to light "a hidden traffic between theological and scientific ideas of the most far-reaching significance for both theology and science . . . where [they] are found to have deep mutual relations."[42] It is clear that there is a very close link between the new objectivity of the natural sciences, with the beliefs which sustain it, and the truth and objectivity of the Judaeo-Christian tradition, with the ultimate beliefs which sustain it. The understanding of the order and contingency of the universe is not generated by natural science, but derives from the Judaeo-Christian theological tradition of the West.

Certain features of this tradition make it a more suitable basis for the new scientific understanding: the transcendence of God; his free creation (from nothing) of a world distinct from but fully related to himself; his self-giving in the constitution of its nature and order; his faithfulness in the creation, preservation, and regulation of the world; the matter and form of the world as created out of nothing and pervasively contingent in its rational order; God's deep relation to the actual spatio-temporal structure and dynamic of the universe; the depth of the relation between the inner constitution of the Trinitarian God and the inner constitution of the world as revealed by the Incarnation; and the continual sustenance by this God of the order and contingency of the world. All of this adds up to a "peculiar" interlocking of the independence of the world from God with its dependence upon him, an independence which gives the world its nature and movement (and requires the self-contained attempt of natural science to know it) and yet refers the nature of the world (and natural-scientific understanding) beyond itself to its freely intelligent and creative source (which requires scientific-theological understanding).[43]

So, in Torrance's view, there is a profound coincidence, so far as it may be, of the metascience which clarifies modern natural science with the metascience of Christian theology. This has the effect of directing each to its proper object, natural science to the contingent order of the universe, thereby to grasp its fundamental structure, and theological science to the source of the contingent order of the universe in the self-presentation of the triune God.

Torrance's work is a major attempt to construe the relationship between theology and the natural sciences at the deepest level. For him, insofar as it appears at all, philosophy is employed within theology and the natural sciences to uncover what is normative to each and to relate the two dialogically at this level. It is this normativity which differentiates between the two yet establishes their proper relation.[44]

Yet specters do appear. Norms are difficult to establish in fields so much contested as these; and Torrance's account is inevitably partial to particular views in each, and also at times hardens and extends them beyond their warrant.[45] This seems to be the consequence of his wish always to stay within the actuality of knowledge, which for him is a struggle to purify available knowledge by reference to the inner structure of reality. Correspondingly, it accords a privileged position to those thought to adhere to this actuality, the metascience by which they understand their position and the knowledge which they achieve. Is the line between these and those labeled as "self-willed," "distorting idealisation[s]" so clear?

In the end, Torrance's account – it seems – is a high-level theologically based metascience which coopts tendencies within modern science within a unified view. Dialogical though it claims to be, it arrives prematurely at the synthesis which it claims.

Theology through Anthropology: John Macquarrie

By contrast with Torrance's refusal to operate from general religious experience, or philosophy as such, John Macquarrie's[46] is a theology rooted in experience but drawn toward the (Anglican) Catholic tradition and developed with the assistance of forms of Continental philosophy. It is primarily anthropological – not metaphysical – in focus, and stands outside the empirical tradition of English philosophy.

In opposition to the narrow empiricism dominant in British philosophy, Macquarrie embraced a series of methodologies for investigating the dynamics of human nature, while always seeking also to draw on the Christian tradition. His theology has been developed in critical dialogue with a series of philosophical positions, ranging from the idealists' view of a suprarational absolute (F. H. Bradley), the existentialist Bultmann's understanding of the saving power of events, and Heidegger's dynamic ontology (the act of the existing of being itself), to the transcendental anthropology of Karl Rahner; but he has also drawn on traditional and contemporary theologians, psychologists, modern philosophers, Eastern religions, neo-Marxist thinkers, and scientists. Beginning with the awareness of the holy or the depth and mystery of existence,[47] it was only over the course of time that he found ways of identifying the religious adequately in Christian terms, as he learned to see Christianity as the possibility of an existence to which one is summoned and may respond in faith (Bultmann), and then to enlarge this to a more inclusive ontological view of being in time (Heidegger), and then to develop this still further as a synthesis of transcendental anthropology and Catholicism (Rahner).

Reason and philosophical insight enjoy a special position in Macquarrie's work, as the means of investigating human nature and discerning the patterns and universal structures of human existence, and developing a theological anthropology to which revelation contributes, and for which Scripture and tradition serve as the norms. Hence he develops a profound interconnection between philosophical and theological anthropology whose norms are ultimately derived from God's salvific action.

Chronologically, his first important move was through sharing and refining the position of Rudolf Bultmann, a New Testament critic strongly shaped by the early thought of Martin Heidegger. With that, the "mighty acts" of which Christians speak, but which general religious awareness leaves as optional symbols, are given "practical" import but of a very confined kind: They are seen as a summons to decision through which a new possibility of existence occurs. While they are objective in providing a new possibility of existence, they do so only for those individuals whose existence is transformed by response to the summons. So the objectivity of the new possibility is conditional on its actualization in the existential response of the believer. And the historical record, the New Testament, is to be understood in this way.

The call of Jesus Christ, when preached, mediates God's justification to those in whose existence it is actualized. But speaking of this in historical terms, and preaching of the possibility which is available, both "objectifies" and "symbolizes" it, as we might say, by employing cosmic and cultural notions; this is what occurred in the New Testament. Such "myths" need to be translated, together with the vocabulary in which their significance is stated by writers such as Paul, in such a way as to draw out their fundamental message about human possibilities, a process which requires the use of "viable philosophical concepts" such as those of Heidegger.[48]

Bultmann's position suggests how general religious awareness becomes salvific through a particular call responded to in particular existential decisions. How its mediation in the life, death and resurrection of this man Jesus occurs, and why that is important, and what the particular consequences are for those who respond, are left unclear. Like some of those to whom Macquarrie is attracted, Karl Rahner for example, it seems that the actuality of the human existence of Jesus and that of those who respond to the call are of secondary importance. To put it differently, mediation in materiality seems to make little difference; existential response has taken its place.

The method by which Macquarrie proceeds is that of an "existential ontological theism"; this is to be a philosophical theology (or "new style natural theology") to replace traditional "metaphysical theism." It is to be both more fundamental, tracing the convictions underlying old arguments, and more descriptive (as opposed to deductive); it is a "let us see" approach, for that "brings out into the light the basic situation in which faith is rooted, so that we can then see what its claims are."[49] This avoids the twin temptations of reducing Christianity to the categories of any one individual, culture or philosophy, and of exalting Christianity to a position above all such. But it is to begin from the human being. "This analysis of our own existence will draw attention especially to those structures and experiences which lie at the root of religion and of the life of faith."[50]

Such a method investigates the universal conditions for the possibility of any religion or theology, including those for "God-talk" or particular revelations, as a preparation for the special symbolical theology of Christian faith. So it continues as general, providing for an analytic description of the general conditions for religion and its mediation in particularities. In other words, there is still a question about the importance of mediation in particularities.

Macquarrie employs this philosophical method to discuss human existence, revelation, being and God, the language of theology, and religion. He then moves to an interpretative method (hermeneutics) to discuss the coherent verbal expression of faith in symbolic theology, and considers the major *loci* of Christian theology, the Trinity, creation, God's relation to the world and evil, the person and work of Christ, the Holy Spirit and salvation, and the last things. Afterward, he takes up the expression of faith as guided by reflection in a "quality of life": church, ministry and mission, word and sacraments, worship and ethics. The result is an illuminating defence of Christian faith by description and interpretation, in which material is so used as to give a fair account of modern discussions while also providing a distinctive rationale for theism and for Christianity. In other words, it provides a sophisticated account – at least for those prepared to use this existential-ontological method – of the intelligibility of the claims which Christians make.

The same combination which we have previously noted, of generalism with the claim that it is particularized for those who respond to it, features throughout Macquarrie's account. For example, he allies the question of being and the question of God very closely; and that raises problems about the adequacy of his notion of transcendence. So far as Macquarrie is concerned, the experience of being (the experience that anything can be at all) as present for human beings and the experience of God refer to the same thing. "Being is the *transcendens*, it is already thought with every being, it is the condition that there may be any beings whatsoever."[51] The difference between this general experience of being – which is the business of ontology – is that it may be a matter of indifference or alienation ("this might not have been, but it is"), while the particular experience of being as "holy being" – which is the province of philosophical theology – includes an attitude of acceptance and commitment appropriate to an *"incomparable* that *lets-be* and is *present-and-manifest* . . . strikingly parallel to the analysis of the numinous as *mysterium tremendum et fascinans.*"[52] The difference of the one from the other, the general from the particular, is that between neutrality and positive assent or trust. And Macquarrie suggests that this is not simply a difference of experience, but also a difference in the being which is experienced.

This positivity, as we may call it, comes to concrete theological expression in symbolical theology. Here, where "holy being" is named "God," "primordial Being" is seen as the Father (the "ultimate act or energy of letting be"), "expressive Being" is the Son and "unitive Being" is the Holy Spirit. Likewise, the very nature of "holy being" to "let be" brings it to be present and manifest in created beings, without which it would be indistinguishable from nothing; but it does not lose its nature as holy being by being present in this way. (This is a position which Macquarrie later described as panentheism.) In one of these beings, Jesus, there is a manifest growth toward Christhood which is finally achieved in his death. Jesus is therefore God in the sense that he finally manifests the full possibilities of creaturely beings; and there is a continuity of what he achieves and that which is achieved by Being in other beings.

This positivity also comes to expression in a quality of life which is to be seen in the church. Macquarrie's consideration of humanity emphasizes, much more than do the existentialists, the roots and expression of faith in common humanity. As being is manifest in common humanity, so "holy being" as responded to by Christians is manifest in the common life of Christians; faith must be practiced corporately, brought to expression through the sacramental life of the church:

> Prayer and worship lie at the center of Christian existence, and . . . they build up self-hood, authentic community, and ultimately (such is the Christian hope) the kingdom of God.[53]

The theme which persists throughout Macquarrie's writing is the issue of human self-transcendence. This is intended to unlock the possibilities of human existence, constrained by finitude but open to God. There is a dynamic of spirit in human life, therefore, through which they are always called to possibilities as yet unrealized, to become self-aware and to act creatively and responsibly in a fuller way of life. Such self-transcendence is based in human freedom and self-direction, and extends to the shaping of humanity itself. The source of this freedom is ultimately mysterious, graspable but unobservable.[54] Like Tillich, Macquarrie sees human freedom as requiring that contrary elements in human existence – both individual and social – be kept in a fruitful balance, while also transcending finite limitations. The fact that it can do so is an indication that it is a gift.

The ultimate goal of human self-transcendence is inexhaustible mystery; ordinary human existence – as Macquarrie saw from the beginning– has a religious depth and reference through which it is given overall direction and meaning. Not only apprehended in such a general way, it is also found in particular religious experiences. In

Macquarrie's view, these can be either negative-to-positive in their trajectory, when, for example, brokenness leads to healing, or dynamically positive, when sanctification leads to greater proximity to God. In either case, God is revealed as one who is graciously present in the very dynamic by which people are led to self-transcendence in such experiences. This leads Macquarrie to consider the implications of such views for the transcendence of God.

Set alongside Torrance's tendency to subsume philosophical-scientific understanding within theology and the sciences, Macquarrie's work provides an interesting contrast. Using a wide variety of philosophies – chiefly modern continental European ones – he uses them to elucidate the dynamics of human existence and self-transcendence and therein to ground discussion of the work and nature of God. That, of course, is helpful, but it trades on the likening of general features of being and human life to those of God and Christian life which are considered problematic, and not only by those who begin from revelation.[55] That is, it likens the dynamics of existence to the life of faith in relation to God, and likens the being of God to "being." It also seems to overlook the severity of the problems raised by Heidegger for "ontotheology." In other words, in seeking such a philosophic mediation of anthropology and theology, it underestimates the difficulties inherent in doing so.

Considered as a strategy in the philosophical mediation of Christian faith, Macquarrie's exemplifies a critical openness to a variety of philosophies which does not domesticate them within theology. Rather it attempts to uncover their religious implications and construct from them a dialectical correlation with theism, although not so clearly with central features of Christian faith. The main issue is whether it does not represent an unstable synthesis of the two, to which each will respond by claiming more for itself.

Theology through Metaphysics: Richard G. Swinburne

Swinburne's[56] starting point is Christian conviction maintained in conscious opposition to the anti-Christian worldview which prevails. At the same time, he shows disdain for Christians and for a church indifferent to these challenges, who meet them only through "sloppiness of argument" and unjustified generalizations. Recognizing the value and limitations of the Oxford philosophy in which he had been educated, he saw modern theoretical science as more central to modern understanding. It was this which taught him – *contra* Oxford philosophy – that what made theories regarding matters beyond observation meaningful was not their verifiability but the use of words by analogy with their use for ordinary things. The theories prove "*justified* in so far as (1) they lead us to expect the phenomena we observe around us; (2) those phenomena are such as we would otherwise not expect to find; and (3) the theories are simple theories."[57]

As this suggests, Swinburne is a philosopher concerned with phenomena, and the meaning and justification of theories which explain them. But such theories may include higher-level ones of a metaphysical kind, such as the "Christian theological system." The difference is that scientific theories deal with a limited class of data, while other theories explain these, and a metaphysical theory is the highest level of all, explaining why there is a universe at all, and why it has the character that it does.[58] So Swinburne is a classic case of a philosopher who uses modern natural science, analyzed through modern philosophy, to show the meaningfulness and justification of Christian theology. And unlike some of his predecessors, he is concerned to do so not for theology in some general sense, but for the basic tenets of Christian theology seen in traditional terms. His derision of modern theology leads him to ignore most post-eighteenth-century theological thought, in order to recall theology to a more rational form.

From the first he has been concerned to sustain the main articles of classic metaphysically based theism[59] – as designating one who really exists and can be described. This involves Swinburne in establishing the coherence of statements of this kind and the way in which language is used, as well as the consideration of the particular elements of belief. Setting aside the views that "credal sentences" are the expression of a form of life[60] or incoherent, he develops an inductive and indirect argument, that their coherence derives from their truth – "from known factual premises p, to a non-analytic claim q; evidence for q's truth being evidence that q is coherent."[61]

The basis for Swinburne's consideration of the existence of God derives from his earlier work on confirmation, the relation between evidence and what it supports, an issue for science and metaphysics. Between the two meanings of confirmation, incremental and absolute, where evidence contributes some support and where it provides strong support, Swinburne maintains that arguments for the existence of God (cosmological, teleological, and moral) provide some support, that is, increase the probability of God's existence. When they are accompanied by evidence from providential occurrences and religious experiences, God's existence becomes more probable than not – which, as he says, leaves plenty of room for faith. Hence, from the total range of evidence, Swinburne argues for the probability of God's existence – against the widespread view (deriving from Hume and Kant) that the limitations of reason preclude any justified conclusions beyond immediate experience. Furthermore, the existence of God is justified in the three ways given above, as "a very simple hypothesis which leads us to expect various very general and more specific phenomena which otherwise we would not expect, and for that reason is rendered probable by the phenomena."[62]

A further book in philosophical theology on *Faith and Reason* relates such judgments of probability to religious faith, and another argues for mental states as states of the soul as a separate substance from the body. The trust in and commitment to God which comprises faith appears to require strongly held beliefs about God, from which follows the obligation to travel toward the goals held in such beliefs;[63] these beliefs are true propositions basic to human life, as relative to alternatives, of such a kind as not solely to be made probable by other propositions believed, but which may promote further beliefs.[64] Swinburne's discussion of these issues is general, but applied to Christian faith and "the kind of faith which a Christian Church ought to demand of its members." With his Cartesian defense of the soul, it elucidates the intensive and personal character of religious faith.

Correlative to the issue of faith is that of moral responsibility. In the first of four books devoted to the connection of general considerations with those of Christian religion, *Responsibility and Atonement*, Swinburne investigates not only the tenability of human responsibility and moral obligation and goodness, but also the issues involved in moral life – analyzing notions of merit, guilt, praise, blame, reward, punishment, mercy, gratitude, atonement, resentment, and forgiveness, their logical relations and applicability. This general consideration serves as the basis for considering how they apply between humans and God. Assuming that God is and became incarnate in Jesus Christ and was crucified, Swinburne analyzes Christian doctrines which utilize these notions – sin and original sin, the atoning death of Christ as "the supreme means of human sanctification" through the means of grace provided in the church, eternal punishment and reward. The strategy, which is similar to that seen elsewhere in his work, is to develop an interaction between broadly accepted notions and practices and specifically Christian ones, in such a way as to choose between rival theological accounts of these matters – in favor of what he considers a moderately liberal (mainstream) position.[65]

Swinburne's concern throughout is with the meaning and inner consistency of Christian doctrines, the a priori evidence for and against them, and the criteria which evidence for the historical occurrences involved must meet. Only in a formal sense are the criteria uniform for all; greater or less evidence is required depending on one's basic beliefs. As to whether (for example) God became incarnate and how Jesus behaved, these are matters which also require historical evidence.

The same concerns – for meaning, consistency, evidence, and criteria – predominate in Swinburne's treatment of the grounds for believing the "claim that God has revealed certain truths which it matters that human beings believe," that these truths are found in Scripture, Creeds, and church practice, and are centered on belief in the Trinitarian God incarnate in Jesus Christ for the atonement of human beings. Opposing the "recent" view that revelation does not refer to propositions, he sets out to establish means for determining what the message of revelation is and the issues involved when words convey information – although this does not imply that revelation is only propositional in form. The other major issue is how we recognize something as revealed truth if God provides it. The need is clear for help to understand the deepest reality: "there is some *a priori* reason to suppose that God will reveal to us those things needed for our salvation."[66] But if this is to enable us to choose whether or not to pursue the way to Heaven, we should also have the choice: Revelation should need to be sought and shared. And we would know it, for example, by the fact that it meets internal criteria, the relevance of its content to our deepest needs, its truth and moral content, etc., and meets external ones, such as its authentication by miracle or the quality of its effect on those who follow. Swinburne goes on to show how historical evidence needs to operate to show that Christianity meets these criteria.

Following the same pattern, Swinburne's discussion of *The Christian God*[67] begins again with general metaphysical issues – the nature of substance (material things and immaterial souls with mental events of different kinds), thisness, causality, time, and necessity – before analyzing the divine predicates, which are exactly those discussed earlier in *The Coherence of Theism* but now seen more specifically in Western terms. Now, however, he takes up the issues of unity and individuation in God, and their development in the doctrine of the Trinity, before considering the possibility that such a God could be incarnate. His conclusion is that the weight of evidence leads to the view that "a religion that claims to have a revelation of Trinity and Incarnation is therefore very likely to be a religion with a true revelation, which is to be believed in respect of what else it tells us about the Incarnation – where and when it happened – and other central matters."[68] This gives centrality to the Doctrine of God in Christianity, which makes the Incarnation credible, as opposed to those who on modern humanistic grounds suppose the Incarnation to be unbelievable.

Swinburne's philosophical clarification and defense of Christianity rightly earn great respect. In what sense, however, does he provide a philosophical mediation of Christian faith? By carefully grounding his approach in induction and probability, considering alternatives and arguing that the balance of evidence favors the conclusions he reaches, he provides a carefully reasoned, clear, and elegant presentation of metaphysical theism – in terms of which he then interprets the "Christian system." As such, it both roots Christian belief in a defensible wider conceptual framework and provides a lucid account of traditional theism.

Three questions arise, however. One is whether he has not appropriated a possibility latent in open, inductive reasoning in order to develop the possibility of a metaphysics which most philosophers and scientists would disallow. If that is so, the basis he constructs for the rationality of Christian beliefs is – while possible – not widely shared. So the ground provided for the rationality of Christian faith is not so universal as it might appear. A second is whether the metaphysics he advances – for which he frequently argues from common human suppositions – is rich enough to sustain the profundities of Christian believing. While it suffices for the rudiments of belief, does it allow full scope for the distinctiveness of God and God's work in the world, such as would make them more interesting both to Christians and to others? In the last resort, it may fail to allow for the abundance of God, the Godness of God, and thereby fail as *theology*. Thirdly, it may underrate the potential contribution of the other disciplines to metaphysics and theology. While it may go far to convince "modern secular man" of the value of what Swinburne sees as the moderate liberal position in theology, does it succeed – as in the early Christian centuries others did (Irenaeus, Origen, and Gregory of Nyssa) – in redeveloping Christian theism from the concepts now used in science and philosophy? If not, this will be evidence that it has not engaged with them as deeply as it should for the sake of the credibility of Christian faith today.[69]

Theology through the Philosophy of Religions: John H. Hick

Like Swinburne, John Hick[70] began as an evangelical Christian,[71] and in his subsequent study he engaged primarily with the heritage of Kant and the philosophy of the Anglo-Saxon tradition. Again like Swinburne, this made him dissatisfied with what he considered a simple faith too readily impatient with questioning.

But like Macquarrie, his fundamental conviction was religious rather than directly theological in kind; it was one of the reality of encounter with the transcendent, and this has remained the center of his theology. His understanding of the encounter developed in accordance with his philosophical views, and this gradually modified his theological views from Christocentric to theocentric, from mediating the truth of Christian doctrine to what is taken to be universal truth.

Mediation of the transcendent in experience – in accordance with his own beginnings and with the tradition of Schleiermacher, but unlike Kant – is fundamental for Hick; but his particular interest is with knowledge. He argues that there is a common epistemological pattern which also characterizes religious knowledge, and it has to do with the establishment of significance:

> By significance I mean that fundamental and all-pervasive characteristic of our conscious experience which *de facto* constitutes it for us the experience of a "world" and not of a mere empty void or churning chaos. We find ourselves in a relatively stable and ordered environment in which we have come to feel, so to say, "at home."[72]

And that is not only correlated with the structure of our own consciousness, but also provides appropriate kinds of action. In theistic religion, "the primary locus of religious significance is the believer's experience as a whole . . . a uniquely 'total interpretation'"; therefore, relating oneself to the divine entails a way of being in the world, a way of "directing ourselves within the natural and ethical spheres."[73]

But such an interpretation is "not given to us as a compulsory perception, but is achieved as a voluntary act of interpretation." Such cognitive freedom varies according to whether it operates in sense perception, where it is minimal, or occurs in matters of aesthetic and ethical significance, or in religious cognition of our environment, where it is maximal.[74] Faith is, therefore, a "fundamental expression of human freedom."[75] This explains why people can take such different views in Christianity: These partake of the freedom which characterizes faith.

To suggest that faith is a matter of freedom is ironically to imply that the kinds of faith should be subject to a kind of "quality control." This is often seen in Hick's writing in the form of polarities, after the fashion of some Calvinism. In Hick's case, a contrast is drawn between "two Christianities," that of established orthodoxy which is devotionally strong and confessional but simplistic, objectivistic, and wrongly realistic, and that of truth-seeking liberals who are more cautious, experimental, subjective, and rightly realistic. Later, a similar contrast appears between adherents of "Ptolemaic" and "Copernican" views, those who center their views of other religions on their own and those who are fully theocentric and universalistic. The technique of polarizing serves to sharpen the issue of quality which features prominently in Hick's thought. The choices which he highlights are choices of "quality," for he is concerned above all with the quality of human response to the transcendent. For example, the "orthodox" are wrong in what Hick considers is their kind of realism – the supposition that their faith is simply "given," to be accepted unquestioningly and confessed. The "truth-seekers" are right in their kind of realism, because faith is an interpretative element within religious experience, arising in freedom.

If quality is to be judged both philosophically and historically, by those "master concerns" we noted before, there is a worrisome issue in such polarizing of alternatives. Those included in the alternative groupings are frequently strange partners to each other, alike perhaps in only one feature. The wish to build a case through historical examples leads away from close attention to historical detail and explanation.

Hick's view of faith has profound implications for the question of God, for the position of Christ and Christianity, and for the conception of human life in and beyond this world. Even in Hick's early writing, it was clear that for human beings to be so free, God must conceal himself in an "epistemic difference" to allow us to achieve

> unforced recognition of his presence and free allegiance to his purposes . . . uncoerced growth towards the humanity revealed in Christ, a humanity which both knows God as Lord and trusts him as Father.[76]

The only choices are coercive presence (the option espoused by "orthodoxy") or absence for the sake of human freedom (Hick's view).

How then are human beings actually to be free? For Hick, like Kant, the issue emerges in connection with the achievement of good in the face of evil, and the question of the span within which good is to be achieved.[77] It is unacceptable that evil should be seen in such a way as to provide an insuperable obstacle to the freedom of human beings to achieve goodness through a lived faith, and so he turns away from what he styles the "Augustinian" theodicy with its emphasis on radical evil in humanity which requires direct redemption, to his "Irenean" theodicy, in which evil plays its place in human growth into the likeness of God. So far as the span of life is concerned, he argues for an eternal life through reincarnation in many worlds, as an ascent to goodness comparable with the Christian's growth to the likeness of God. The choice in both issues is between, on the one side, evil and life reckoned as issues of insoluble difficulty and, on the other side, the maximization of the conditions of human freedom by incorporating evil and life in a perspective in which human beings can achieve goodness. The question is intimately related to the issue of God and his actions, and of course, Hick's view of the epistemic distance required of God limits the possibility that God's action actually changes the human situation; God, as he put it, acts by being believed in.

Hick's concern for religious language, provoked by logical positivist criticisms of the meaning of theistic language at the time, reflects much the same strategy. For Hick, it is necessary to accept the empiricist point that for something "to exist" must make an observable difference, lest religious language become non-cognitivist, a "protected discourse, no longer under obligation to show its compatibility with established conclusions in other spheres."[78] And for the transcendent theist, the existence of God does make a difference. Equally, for the humanist, human beings are produced by natural causes, and there is no God to make a difference. Given the freedom of faith, and the ambiguity of the world, each view must be tenable. The issue between these views can only be decided eschatologically, through "our participation in an eschatological situation in which the reality of God's loving purpose for us is confirmed by its fulfillment in a heavenly world."[79] That is not for the believer to beg the question, because – as Hick shows – belief in such a "heavenly world" is at least intelligible.

Such views do not necessitate but open the way for a change in the understanding of human relatedness to God, as well as a progressive limitation of the centrality of Christ. Hick's view of God distances him from particular action in the world, and his views of faith and evil are implicitly universalistic, and the problem is how to reconcile these with the notion of there being one, and only one, true religion. The answer which Hick adopts is to assimilate the notion of the Christ-event to his notion of faith:

> There has to be both divine action in the world and man's appreciation of the occurrence *as* divine action; both God's self-revealing activity and the human response which we call faith. And the Christ-event has these two sides to it. God was acting in human history but acting, as always, in such a way that man remained free to see or fail to see what was happening as God's doing. For religious faith, in its most basic sense, is the cognitive choice whereby we experience events and situations as mediating divine activity.[80]

Correspondingly, the New Testament and subsequent doctrinal formulations of the Incarnation are "interpretations of the meaning of the Christ-event, and not part of the event itself."[81] While cognitive, these are interpretations whereby Christians *experience* Jesus *as* the Christ, finding salvation in him. And modern biblical and philosophical views show that they are not to be read literally, but as metaphorical or mythological expressions of such interpretations; what is more, they vary widely historically.[82] Like the "Ptolemaic" view of the universe, they are extended to explain divergent views (including those of other faiths) by the addition of "epicycles" but without thereby allowing sufficient recognition to other faiths. Also like the Ptolemaic view, they are historically relative.

Recognizing that such Ptolemaic views can be operated by any religion, Hick calls for a "Copernican revolution," in which there is a shift to a theocentric understanding of the religions. In such a case, one begins with the recognition, universal to the religions, that the "ultimate divine reality is infinite and as such transcends the grasp of the human mind":

> From this it follows that the different encounters with the transcendent within the different religious traditions may all be encounters with the one infinite reality, though with partially different and overlapping aspects of that reality. This is a very familiar thought in Indian religious literature . . . in the Bhagavad Gita the Lord Krishna, the personal God of love, says, "Howsoever men approach me, even so do I accept them; for, on all sides, whatever path they may choose is mine."[83]

With this, we may look forward to a future "in which what we now call the different religions will constitute the past history of different emphases and variations within a global religious life."[84] And the person of Christ will be seen to be a "temporal cross-section of God's Agapéing . . . not the entirety of that of which it is a cross-section."[85]

Hick's encounter-centered religious view subordinates Christianity (as well as other religions) and its theology to a universal "critical realism" founded on the freedom of human encounter with a transcendent reality whose nature remains ambiguous. Whether this accords with the truth of the religions as they conceive themselves, or indeed provides for their future in a secular world, remains a question.

Hick's strategy in the philosophical mediation of theology is clearly different from those we have considered so far. While the others are varieties of a strategy which uses philosophy as instrumental to faith, and makes Christian theology or religious experience normative, Hick's approach makes philosophy instrumental to putatively universal religious views, and makes what is claimed to be universal religion normative for Christian theology. As such, it reverses the strategy considered earlier, assimilating Christianity to generic religion. Unlike some who have questioned the legitimacy of religion and Christianity as realistic, such as Don Cupitt, for example, Hick remains sternly realist in such matters, while also demoting those religious views which contradict the universal religion which he advocates; they are "myths" or "metaphors" which show the tendency of religious people to "construct" reality according to a particular worldview. In this respect, he might be called a selective realist.

Theology through Philosophically Mediated Life: Donald M. MacKinnon and Nicholas Lash

In an age when theology has been largely severed from its roots in life and public affairs, a distinctive contribution to their reconnection has been made by the Scottish Anglican philosopher Donald M. MacKinnon.[86] His wide interests spanned philosophy, literature, politics, and theology, and his writings are largely comprised of intensive essays on particular topics. No writer of large systematic treatises, he nonetheless managed to bring these fields and topics into creative contact. Not surprisingly, the same characteristic marked the man: His chief influence was through his long-running interaction with the intellectual life of Britain, as well as his impact on the generations of those who studied or worked with him, who benefited from the intensity of his engagement with them and the breadth and sensitivity of his learning.

Perhaps the most distinctive feature of MacKinnon's work was his "metaphysical-mindedness." For him, this was a preoccupation not so much with basic conceptions detached from their use as with "the kind of metaphysics we often see realized when men half-committed or more than half-committed to particular policies or directions of human life, become articulate and questioning concerning their validity."[87] Metaphysics for him was therefore a phase of the moral pursuit, of the struggle for goodness in life itself. As if to exemplify this concrete struggle, MacKinnon himself always showed an aversion to easy dogmatism and abstractions.

One of the features of a "metaphysical mind" was a "thrust against the limits of language" in such matters as the extended sense in which the concept of fact was used in the logical empiricism of the 1950s to determine truth or falsity. It was not that MacKinnon wished to abandon the notion of fact, but – appealing to its wider use – he thought it needed to be liberalized, without thereby dropping into a "free play of undisciplined inventiveness."[88] While the metaphysician is preoccupied with the transcendent, he or she is never excused from dialogue with the anti-metaphysicians over such matters.

Engaging with those whose convictions are restricted by empiricism, MacKinnon argues for transcendence. For theirs is a simplistic conception of perceptual experience, its objects and its internal structure, which must be deepened and replaced by recognition of the internal complexity of perception. That is important, because MacKinnon is concerned with a metaphysics which moves from the relative to the ultimate, the finite to the infinite, the limited to the absolute. What we discover when we consider this in connection with the New Testament miracles is that the transcendent is also strange and transformative.

Cognition, however, is not the only road to metaphysic: The other is "the approach which sees the metaphysical as something lying beyond the frontiers of intelligible descriptive discourse, yet as something which *presses* on us with a directness and immediacy which requires no argument to convince us of its reality."[89] In that realm, learning from Kant, there is freedom, the capacity for self-determination, the possibility of goodness, and even One who causes them – all of them requiring us to say the unsayable. And MacKinnon, throughout his writing, struggles with these issues.

He was furthered in doing so by a willingness to explore "living discourse" in parables and drama, those forms which inform but are open in texture and by their indirection not only "point to unnoticed possibilities of well-doing, but . . . hint, or more than hint, at ways in which things fundamentally are."[90] In so doing, they illuminate human life by "inducing deeper self-criticism, by puncturing make-believe, by renewing simplicity, etc.,"[91] and opening possibilities for human action which also "orders the world" by reference to moral principles which they convey.[92]

Such considerations are never far from those operative in the public domain. For MacKinnon, it is where people live, think, and pray together that they rely on the transcendent, and where the work of God is present. He never for long loses sight of the "placing" of issues in human life in the world, or the acute dilemmas of modern history.[93]

So far as MacKinnon is concerned, the mediation of the transcendent in the practical is not properly dealt with, either by those who rely on some form of ethical naturalism (the utilitarians or Bentham, for example) or by avant-garde theologians who dispense with the metaphysical. On the one hand, the deep moral insight which is found in the difficulties and tragedies of life (often as expressed in literature) is beyond what can be explained in terms of any form of ethical naturalism.[94] On the other hand, MacKinnon insists on the human "receptivity" of faith "elicited, though not compelled, by external occurrence, and always orientated upon that which lies outside the interior life of the believing subject."[95]

Such remarks show the depth of MacKinnon's interpretation of philosophical tradition up to the present, united to a positive and sensitive reappropriation of the possibilities of metaphysics, morals, and Christian faith as interpenetrating fields within the concrete issues of life. Here there is no quick affirmation of positions, but only the careful sifting of interconnected issues and contributions – even those unsympathetic to his own. Whether in metaphysics, morals, or Christian faith, this sifting takes place through critical reason sharpened by ancient and modern philosophy. And while impatient of all special pleading on the grounds of "authority," it is drawn forward as "the domination of the *mysterium Christi* deepens its almost obsessive sovereignty over my mind."[96] The goal of metaphysics (ontology) is "to give as satisfactory and complete an account as possible of our ultimate conceptual scheme," but in theology this is "bent to new purposes . . . enlarged and stretched in its use." But this "arcane" of the transcendent is no less than the inner reality on which the order of the world is founded, and the most basic point of reference for our moral practice – the depth which is responsible for those profound moral insights evident in great literature.

That makes it a matter of the presence of the transcendent in the factual, of God in the empirical realm, not only in the moral life of people but in *history*. The question of fact is not only a general philosophical one, but one which requires attention to the actual practice of historians, the philosopher freeing the historian from imposing "a restricted inflexible paradigm of what it is to be a fact."[97] There are different sorts of facts, but a genuine difference between what is and what is not factual, and the truth of Christianity rests on the factual.

> Christianity faces men with the paradox that certain events which could have been otherwise are of infinite, transcendent import; and this without losing their character as contingent events . . . We cannot allow any seriousness to Christianity's claim to truth unless we can also claim factual truth in a simple, ordinary sense, for propositions concerning the way [Jesus] . . . approached his end.[98]

And the question of the factuality of the Incarnation and Resurrection of Jesus Christ is one in which history and faith condition each other, and meet their limits in a mystery which "involves and encompasses them."[99] Human understanding reaches its limits in an ontological mystery, the mystery of the conformity of God to the limitations of human particularity, which is precisely where God most fully meets, and discloses himself, to humankind.[100]

The full quality of the transcendent is not altogether fathomable; it is not capable of full explication which is not contingent, and therefore vulnerable. But beyond such contingency (and incompleteness, because MacKinnon recognizes the need to do justice to the world religions), human understanding is problematic and disputable. More than that, it is deeply enmeshed in evil, for which in a genuine sense there is no solution. And one cannot turn a blind eye to these problems, which are empirical, social, metaphysical, and religious in scope, not least because avoiding them is to remain in thrall to them, while at the same time impoverishing human understanding of the fundamental conditions of life.[101] In practical failure, therefore, there is philosophical and theological failure. In a particularly telling comment on current theology, MacKinnon remarks:

> On occasions one notices that a readiness to jettison much that might be thought central to traditional Christian belief goes hand in hand with a tired institutional conservatism. Indeed the former is sometimes invoked to buttress the latter, as if the irreformability of the structures alone provided security against the volatility of faith. But it is by their faithful witness to the *Mysterium Christi*, through word and teaching, through worship and sacrament, that those very structures must be judged, and if found wanting, swiftly rejected.[102]

By what means are things to be improved, then? Implicitly, MacKinnon puts forward the importance of the "master concerns," philosophy and history, to guide public judgment. His work is primarily in philosophy, and is distinguished not only by its deep (but sharply analytical) assimilation of the influence of Immanuel Kant, but also by the deep respect it shows for past and present British philosophy. But his work in philosophy is finely balanced; respect for historical fact disallows full-blown idealism, just as respect for the work of Lenin prevents Christianity from "withdrawing into the securities of metaphysical idealism,"[103] while respect for the transcendent disallows a simple appeal to observation. And the balance is frequently maintained through careful attention to literature and the issues raised there.[104]

It is possible to summarize MacKinnon's philosophy as a combination of "meta-physical-mindedness," critical reason, openness, and ethical realism. Fundamentally, he (like Kant) employs philosophy with the greatest self-consciousness about its assumptions and limits; reason is not to be self-important. He is always preoccupied with the limits of human awareness. At the same time (following his own description of the philosophy of history), philosophy is to operate with "a certain openness of texture or porosity," having "no fixed horizons."[105] If that is so, in his case, such openness is combined with a profound realism, since it is a search for the truth of things, contingently and ultimately; and it is directed to bringing about a corre-spondence between things and their truth.[106]

The ultimate truth to which things are to correspond is the loving will of God. How can one even talk about such a thing, never mind enable human beings to correspond to it? For, as MacKinnon stresses so strongly, theological truth lies at the limits of philosophy, in "the abyss of the unknown, never precisely to be measured but discernibly not altogether fathomless, an infinite resistant to, yet not ultimately alien to, the reach of understanding."[107] After one clears away all the images improp-erly applied to him, God is inexpressible, to be thought "only within the context of the most rigorous discipline of silence."[108]

In that silence, however, MacKinnon finds the possibility of speaking of God, but not through a triumphalist understanding of revelation. God can be spoken of because he himself, in *limiting himself to the finite* in Jesus Christ, has disclosed the basis of his relation to the world. That is why, despite its necessary incompleteness, the doctrine of the Incarnation

> still represents a tremendous effort to do justice to the belief that in Jesus Christ we have to reckon before all else with a quite unique movement from God to man . . . the reality of divine . . . self-limitation, even . . . a wholly unique act of such divine self-limitation that discloses in a way altogether without parallel God's relation to the world he has created. It discloses that relation in a way without parallel because this act of self-limitation is itself the ground of that relationship.[109]

What so many have failed to appreciate is that for God to be accessible to man required not only his coming to man, but his self-transformation in order to come. The relation of God to the world which is shown in the Incarnation is one of loving self-giving, in which are involved Father, Son, and Holy Spirit; and it is that – a factual occurrence in Jesus Christ – upon which all human relation to God depends. It is by that means alone that humanity may be brought into correspondence with the truth of God.

Humanity may correspond to the loving will of God because of the self-limitation of God. But MacKinnon's view is more radical and realistic than that: "If the Christian faith is true . . . its truth is constituted by the correspondence of its credenda with harsh, human reality, and with the divine reality that met that human reality and was broken by it, only in that breaking to achieve its healing."[110] So Christianity does not "deal with the problem of evil by encouraging the believer to view it from a cosmic perspective":

> Rather Christianity takes the history of Jesus and urges the believer to find, in the endurance of the ultimate contradictions of human existence that belongs to its very substance, the assurance that in the worst that can befall his creatures, the creative Word keeps company with those he has called his own.[111]

The fact is that human beings still find such a God with them in the tragedies and tests of their lives. That is why they still believe – despite all opposition and all the alternatives which clever people provide. The presence of God in the perplexities of common practice is the basis of his relationship with them and for the truth by which they are to live. In the end, therefore, the content of Christian faith, and the possibility which it affords for the common practice of life, arise from the activity of God in sharing the conditions and suffering of human life.

MacKinnon's work represents a strategy for the philosophical mediation of Christian faith which is quite different to the others we have considered. It remains within philosophical discussion and within Christian faith, allowing them to interpenetrate in such a way as to challenge the limited vision which prevails in each. He does not, like Torrance, arrive at final views of the meaning and significance of each and provide a systematic synthesis; his considerations of each are more open-textured, explorative, questioning, self-critical, and morally concerned. Nor, like Swinburne, does he open one avenue in current philosophy and science (induction and confirmation through probability) through which a systematic metaphysic-cum-theology can be brought; he is metaphysically minded, continuously engaging with a wide range of ancillary forms of human understanding in a combined effort of philosophy, morality, and theology. Nor, like Hick, does he retreat from that which is particular to Christian faith in order to find a universal religion; for him the "myth of the Incarnation," "in spite of all . . . does justice to the unfathomable paradox of the union of the transcendent and the desperately human . . . that we find in Jesus of Nazareth."[112] What he does do is bring about a mutual indwelling of human life, philosophy, and Christian faith in their full scope.

Both MacKinnon's influence and the strategy exemplified in his work persist today. It is not that MacKinnon has school-followers; the style of his work, thinking from within the thoughts of others and opening them to unrealized possibilities while taking no credit for this himself, precludes a following as such. But this style is what continues in others he taught, as they themselves open fruitful possibilities for theology within the fields of life with which he dealt through an insight informed by philosophical rationality. They are not necessarily informed by such depth of learning in the history of philosophy, because the acumen which they found from contact with him can draw as well from other sources – biblical, patristic, doctrinal, literary, artistic, etc. But they share in the same ability to bring about a mutual indwelling of life and Christian faith in their full scope, while mediating this through the use of different fields.

Who are those who have learned from MacKinnon to do this? They include many of the outstanding figures of British theology today: Sarah Coakley, David Ford, Fergus Kerr, Nicholas Lash, Richard Roberts, Rowan Williams, and Frances Young. And others, although they have learned it elsewhere, follow the strategy exemplified by MacKinnon: Alastair McFadyen, Haddon Willmer, and so on.

One distinguished example is Nicholas Lash, MacKinnon's successor as Norris-Hulse Professor of Divinity at Cambridge.[113] Lash addresses a different situation in which neither the great tradition of Western philosophy nor the pressures of logical empiricism are known so well, and does so from the position of a post-Vatican II English Roman Catholic – and therefore from a tradition challenged within the Church, and from a Church whose presence in the English *intellectual* scene has been marginal until recently.[114] These, and the widespread questioning of theology as an academic discipline, produce in him highly sensitive probing of issues in theology and church. As with MacKinnon, there is no retreat from the issue of truth, but a reappropriation of theology as truthful, performatively tradition-bearing and orienting human life in its concreteness, even within the distortions so much analyzed by the techniques of criticism which abound today – which Lash knows very well.

Lash has derived theological nourishment from a wide variety of sources, particularly in modern philosophy (including pragmatism) and modern Roman Catholicism (Newman and Von Hügel); and he has been accorded a particular hearing in the United States. But most of all, his perception of the possibilities of theology is formed by the transcendental anthropology which has been formative for so much post-Vatican II Roman Catholic theology.

Building from an analysis of human experience in which he engages with William James and others such as Schleiermacher, Newman, and Rahner, Lash tries to show how common human experience and practices – at least in a Christian view – lead to experience and knowledge of the mystery of God, how God is recognized in ordinary events, and what implications this has for the Christian doctrine of God. Unfolding the possibilities latent in the analysis of human experience, with Rahner he finds awareness of incomprehensible mystery to be "the permanent condition of possibility of our (indefinitely extendible) comprehension of contingent particulars."[115] And this puts a question mark over the completeness of all reference points and explanations, much as MacKinnon questioned the sufficiency of reference to "facts" in empiricism. So we must learn to read experience in such a way as to acknowledge our creatureliness, and in that dependence to find freedom. It is precisely in human experience that the question of God is raised. And the Christian community perpetuates the fact that "God has indefeasibly *clarified* the question of the human in one life lived and one death undergone – in a piece of history which, for that reason, we confess to be the incarnation of God's Word."[116]

In a fashion reminiscent of MacKinnon but employing different tools, Lash begins within human experience but implicitly challenges the limitations of the empiricist notion of it, and in its place puts a mystery-laden view which makes God the permanent horizon of all experience, knowledge, and practice. His view shows the same capacity to bring about the interpenetration of human understanding and theology which marked MacKinnon's work, and distinguishes the strategy which he manifested.

Agenda: The Future of Theology Mediated through Philosophy

Where in past centuries it was more natural to conceive Christian faith in close connection with a variety of aspects of human life, and to employ philosophy as a concentrated means of developing this connection, the shaping of philosophy in recent times – often by norms drawn from other disciplines – has made this problematic. We have now reviewed a variety of strategies which have been employed in response to this state of affairs, and considered a variety of people who appear to exemplify these strategies.

Setting aside those who consider that philosophy should be avoided in the consideration of Christian faith, we have found that major emphasis has been given to its use *either* in such a way as to domesticate it in the service of Christian theology *or* as an instrument in subjecting Christian theology to norms drawn from elsewhere. In both cases, the purpose of philosophical inquiry appears to have been preempted, either by the truth of Christian faith or by an alternative, leaving – even strengthening – the impasse between Christian theology and the norms of life in today's world as concentrated in philosophical inquiry. The result is – and will likely continue to be – the perpetuation of division between them, and a jockeying for power.

Another possibility has emerged from our analysis, however. It is where the engagement of theology with the norms of life today – both determined by and determining philosophical inquiry – becomes the proper business of philosophical-theological exploration. In such an engagement, there are no pre-drawn boundaries or limits to the exploration of mutual significance. And there is a readiness for the mutual reinvigoration of theology and other forms of understanding and practice, accompanied by a full critical engagement between them through which the truth of Christian faith and other forms of truth may emerge with full clarity. Along that way seems to lie the achievement of public intelligibility for theology in the future.

The other strategies which we have reviewed continue to have their value, particularly in consolidating and deepening understanding of the tradition which has prevailed in the West and exposing that to critique based in other disciplines and traditions. The steady strengthening of systematic theology in Britain today owes much to Colin E. Gunton,[117] for example. Standing broadly within the Reformed tradition himself, his achievement has derived from a remarkable skill in focusing, analyzing, restoring, and restating fundamental features of theological tradition in an alien climate – and fostering the work of others who do. Unremittingly Christocentric and Trinitarian, his work substantially deepens the perception of what is necessary for Christian belief today, and frequently draws on shrewd assessments of the history of thought. It advocates no metaphysic to mediate between Christian faith and modern conceptions, but restates the crucial elements of faith by correlation with perennial issues of human thought. Whether such an endeavor is as much attuned to the determinants of current thought as it needs to be is the question.

And sensitivity to the vitalities of current thought and life is the virtue of the strategy which we have found in Donald MacKinnon, and others who move in a like direction. Although it still needs to be recognized as a coherent program, it is not simply a hypothetical possibility. It is a reality in the theology which is emerging in Britain today, and one which is true to the mediation of theology through philosophy in past centuries in Britain. It deserves to be more widely known; such theology has a promising future.

Notes

1   So called because they are not established, as is the case with the Church of England and the Church of Scotland. Notable exceptions are the Methodist Church in the North of England and in Wales, which is so widespread as to be established *de facto*.

2   The second and third of these receive particular attention in ch. 13 above and 15 below.

3   In this context, the word must be taken in its more fundamental sense of "love of wisdom," not in the more confined sense which has become usual since the professionalization of academic disciplines in the second half of the nineteenth century.

4   The leading exponent of postmodernism in British philosophy of religion is Don Cupitt. Born in Lancashire in 1934, he studied biology and the history and philosophy of science as an undergraduate at Cambridge; he was supervised by N. R. Hanson, and learned from him both the philosophy of Karl Popper and Hanson's own constructivist position. Then, preparing for ordination at an Anglican theological college, he took Part III of the Theology Tripos at Cambridge before serving an industrial parish for three years (1959–62). He returned to Cambridge as vice-principal of a theological college (1962–6), and became Fellow and Dean of Chapel at Emmanuel College and University Assistant Lecturer, then Lecturer, in Philosophy of Religion in the

Faculty of Divinity until his retirement in 1996.

His influence in England has been wide, partly because in some ways his own progress in religious faith mirrors a sequence of widely held positions with which he has been in dialogue. He has developed from religious conservatism to a radically nonrealist position, eventually dispensing with the objectivity of God and the possibility of grace-given goodness in favor of spiritual development unencumbered by such "controls," and moving even beyond those to a view of faith as creative response to contingency. An account of his position may be found in "British Theology through Philosophy," in David F. Ford (ed.), *The Modern Theologians*, 1st edn (Oxford, 1989), vol. II, ch. 2, and his work is also discussed in ch. 30 below.

5   Richard Swinburne, "Intellectual Autobiography," in Alan G. Padgett (ed.), *Reason and the Christian Religion* (Oxford, 1994), p. 3.

6   Ian Ramsey (1915–72), educated at Cambridge in mathematics, moral sciences, and theology before training for the Anglican priesthood, was Nolloth Professor of the Philosophy of the Christian Religion at Oxford from 1951 to 1966, and afterward Bishop of Durham until his death in 1972. A select bibliography of his publications is given in Jonathan Pye, *A Bibliography of the Published Work of Ian*

Thomas Ramsey (Durham, 1979), and a select bibliography in *Christian Empiricism*, ed. Jerry H. Gill (London, 1974).

7   Ninian Smart, "The intellectual crisis of British Christianity," in Ian Ramsey, *Christian Empiricism*, ed. Jerry H. Gill (London, 1974), pp. 229–36.

8   Austin M. Farrer (1904–68) was educated at Balliol College, Oxford; he was successively Fellow and Chaplain of Trinity College, and Warden of Keble College.

9   Eric Mascall (1905–93) was a mathematically trained Anglican priest and theologian; he was for many years Lecturer and Tutor at Christ Church, Oxford, and afterward Professor of Historical Theology at King's College London. His stance was largely defensive, arguing for natural theology largely along Thomist lines.

10   Basil Mitchell (b. 1917), educated at Oxford, taught at Christ Church and Keble College; following Ian Ramsey, he was Nolloth Professor of the Philosophy of the Christian Religion 1968–84 and Fellow of Oriel. A bibliography of his writing is given in W. J. Abraham and S. W. Holtzer, *The Rationality of Religious Belief* (London, 1987).

11   See the account of this group by Basil Mitchell in Kelly James Clark (ed.), *Philosophers Who Believe* (Downers Grove, 1993), pp. 41–4.

12   Hywel David Lewis (1910–92) was one who was not. His religious upbringing in North Wales, and his education at Oxford under the influence of idealists and realists, made him a defender of metaphysics, a dualist view of mind and body, and personal immortality. A bibliography of his writing is provided in S. R. Sutherland and T. A. Roberts (eds), *Religion, Reason and the Self* (Cardiff, 1989).

13   Maurice Wiles, *The Remaking of Christian Doctrine*, 2nd edn (London, 1978), p. 38.

14   All of these, for Torrance, are products of human consciousness, while in theology we are concerned with God.

15   Thomas Forsyth Torrance, born in China in 1913 and educated at the University of Edinburgh in classics and divinity and at the University of Basel with Karl Barth, is an outstanding churchman and theologian. After two years as Professor of Church History, he was Professor of Dogmatics at the University of Edinburgh from 1952 to 1979, when he retired following the conferral of the Templeton Prize in Religion. A member of the Church of Scotland, he was its Moderator; he has also been much engaged in ecumenical discussions. A full account of his life and work is given in David F. Ford (ed.), *The Modern Theologians*, 1st edn (Oxford, 1989), vol. 1, ch. 3. A bibliography of his writings to 1989, edited by Iain R. Torrance, is in the *Scottish Journal of Theology*, 43 (1990), pp. 225–62.

16   Contrary to the widespread view that Karl Barth was theologically isolationist, Torrance claims Barth's blessing for this project.

17   *Reality and Scientific Theology* (Edinburgh, 1985), p. 67.

18   *Divine and Contingent Order* (Oxford, 1981), p. 1.

19   *Theological Science* (Oxford, 1969), p. 265. This requires regeneration and baptism in the "ontological depth of [the] mind." "The Reconciliation of Mind," *Theological Students' Fellowship Bulletin*, 10/3 (1987), pp. 4–7.

20   *Theology in Reconstruction* (London, 1965), p. 9.

21   Torrance suggests that theological concepts must have an open revisable structure comparable to the unifying worldview and open dynamic field-theories of modern physics. *Zygon*, 23 (1988), pp. 159–69.

22   "The scientific character of theological statements," in *Dialog*, 4 (1965), pp. 112–17.

23   *Transformation and Convergence in the Frame of Knowledge* (Belfast, 1984), pp. 113f.

24   Michael Polanyi, upon whose thought Torrance draws, likened it to looking at a pair of stereoscopic pictures; seeing the two slightly different pictures in a viewer produces a single three-dimensional picture. See Polanyi's *Personal Knowledge, Science, Faith and Society, The Tacit Dimension*, and *Knowing and Being*.

25   Torrance was assisted in the development of his views on belief by Michael Polanyi's

consideration of personally held "fiduciary frameworks" as the basis of scientific activity. Polanyi thought that human beings "indwell" frameworks of belief, and that these frameworks form the "tacit dimension" (which is incapable of full explication) from which they work in intuition and scientific knowledge.

26 *Transformation and Convergence in the Frame of Knowledge*, pp. 116ff., 121.

27 Ibid., p. 133.

28 Ibid., p. 195.

29 Ibid., p. 194.

30 *Theological Science*, pp. 37–43.

31 By analogy with Einstein's account of the history of science, Torrance differentiates levels of theological knowledge in the history of theology: evangelical and doxological; the economic Trinity as three distinctive personal modes of divine activity in space-time; and the "higher theological or scientific level" which transforms the others through conceptual advance in consideration of "the ontological Trinity." *The Ground and Grammar of Theology* (Belfast, 1980), ch. 6.

32 For a consideration of Torrance in the context of other theological engagements with the natural sciences, see ch. 33 below.

33 Cf. *Calvin's Doctrine of Man, The Early Theology of Karl Barth, The Hermeneutics of John Calvin*, and such essays as those included in *Theology in Reconstruction*.

34 *Theology in Reconstruction*, pp. 90–4.

35 The most interesting sustained presentations of Torrance's analysis of patristic theology are *Theology in Reconciliation* (London, 1975), and *The Trinitarian Faith: The evangelical theology of the ancient Catholic Church* (Edinburgh, 1988), but his work in the period started with one of his earliest books, *The Doctrine of Grace in the Apostolic Fathers* (Edinburgh, 1946).

36 *The Trinitarian Faith*, p. 69.

37 Ibid., p. 2.

38 One analogy for this apparent paradox is that of a statue whose front one can see, but whose sides stretch backward out of sight. *Reality and Scientific Theology*, p. 135.

39 Ibid., p. ix.

40 So far as physics is concerned, and indeed so far as Einstein's own theory of relativity is concerned, this means that the more profoundly we penetrate into the ultimate invariances in the space-time structures of the universe, we reach objectivity in our basic description of the universe only so far as relativity is conferred upon the domain of our immediate observations. It is precisely because our thought finally comes to rest upon the objective and invariant structure of being itself, that all our notions of it are thereby relativized. This means that knowledge is not gained in the flat, as it were, by reading it off the surface of things, but in a multidimensional way in which we grapple with a range of intelligible structures that spread out far beyond us. In our theoretic constructions we rise through level after level of organized concepts and statements to their ultimate ontological ground, for our concepts and statements are true only as they rest in the last resort upon being itself. Ibid., pp. 135f.

41 *Divine and Contingent Order*, pp. 27f.

42 *Reality and Scientific Theology*, pp. ix–x.

43 These are matters to which *Space, Time and Incarnation* (London, 1969) and *Space, Time and Resurrection* (Edinburgh, 1976) are devoted.

44 This feature of Torrance's thought has not been fully appreciated by his commentators.

45 Even if we set aside the question of whether he is not developing the implications of this physical science beyond what its practitioners would wish (and there are important questions today about what the implications of modern physical science are), there is still the wider question of whether physical science can be equated with "the natural sciences" as he does. At least, such an approach leaves undecided the question of the productive value of the biological and human sciences for the natural sciences and for theology; it also causes Torrance to sidestep difficult questions about the diversity of creation which appear when one considers the implications of the biological sciences, or

those of human diversity which appear in the social sciences.

46　John Macquarrie was born in Renfrew, Scotland, in 1919, and educated at the University of Glasgow in mental philosophy and theology. After ordination in the Church of Scotland, he served as an army chaplain and then in a parish (during which he began postgraduate study on Heidegger and Bultmann) before becoming a Lecturer in Systematic Theology at the University of Glasgow in 1953. He went to the Union Theological Seminary in New York in 1962 as Professor of Systematic Theology and was soon ordained priest in the American Episcopal Church. In 1970 he was appointed Lady Margaret Professor of Divinity at Oxford, and Canon of Christ Church, and remained there until his retirement in 1986. A bibliography of his writing to 1985 is found in A. Kee and E. T. Long (eds), *Being and Truth: Essays in honour of John Macquarrie* (London, 1986).

47　*Being and Truth*, p. xi.

48　Ibid., pp. 110f.

49　Ibid., p. 50.

50　Ibid., p. 51.

51　*Principles of Christian Theology*, p. 194.

52　Ibid., p. 105.

53　Ibid., p. 443.

54　John Macquarrie, *In Search of Humanity* (London, 1983), p. 13.

55　See Wolfhart Pannenberg, *Systematic Theology* (Grand Rapids, MI, 1991), vol. I, pp. 356f.

56　Richard Swinburne, born in 1934 in Smethwick, West Midlands, was educated in philosophy, politics, and economics, and then philosophy and theology, at the University of Oxford. Research fellowships then allowed him to study philosophy of science. From 1963 to 1972 he was Lecturer and later Senior Lecturer in Philosophy at the University of Hull; from 1972 to 1985 he was Professor of Philosophy at the University of Keele; since 1985 he has been Nolloth Professor of the Philosophy of the Christian Religion at Oxford. Trained in philosophy and the philosophy of science, his early works were mainly in the philosophy of science be-

fore he turned to writing in the philosophy of religion, first by a trilogy on belief in God and then by a tetralogy defending the elements of Christian belief. A select bibliography is found in Alan G. Padgett (ed.), *Reason and the Christian Religion* (Oxford, 1994).

57　"Intellectual autobiography," in *Reason and the Christian Religion*, p. 5.

58　Ibid., p. 8.

59　That is, belief in a personal, spiritual, eternal, free, omnipotent, omniscient, benevolent God, who is creator and sustainer of the universe and worthy of worship and obedience.

60　The view considered is that of D. Z. Phillips in *The Concept of Prayer* (1965).

61　*The Coherence of Theism* (Oxford, 1977), p. 49.

62　"Intellectual autobiography," p. 10.

63　In the lineage of John Locke, Swinburne seems to see faith as added confidence in beliefs judged probable; because of this, he has been called a "psychological foundationalist." William P. Alston, "Swinburne on faith and belief," in *Reason and the Christian Revelation*, p. 24.

64　"Once a proposition has been brought into the belief-corpus, it plays its part in promoting further beliefs, without the extent of its own evidential support very often being brought explicitly into question." *Faith and Reason* (Oxford, 1981), pp. 21–2.

65　His view, however, is decidedly conservative of an unchanged tradition, and shows little tendency to reconceive the tradition through modern patterns of thought – as would most liberals.

66　*Revelation* (Oxford, 1992), pp. 73f.

67　(Oxford, 1994).

68　Ibid., p. 237.

69　It is just this which is advocated by most who call themselves liberals.

70　John Harwood Hick was born in Scarborough, Yorkshire, in 1922, and in 1940 entered the Presbyterian Church in England. He first studied law at Hull University, and after ambulance service during the war, went to Edinburgh University to study philosophy and afterward to complete a D.Phil. at Oxford with H. H.

Price. He then trained for ordination and served as a minister for three years. Two appointments in the United States followed, first at Cornell University (1956–9), then at Princeton Theological Seminary (1959–64), before he became a Lecturer in the Faculty of Divinity at Cambridge (1967–79); he was then appointed H. G. Wood Professor at Birmingham University, an appointment which he later shared with the Danforth Professorship at Claremont Graduate School in California, to which he went full-time in 1982 until his retirement in 1992.

71 This included "the entire evangelical package of theology – the verbal inspiration of the Bible; creation and fall; Jesus as God the Son incarnate, born of a virgin, conscious of his divine nature and performing miracles of divine power; redemption by his blood from sin and guilt; his bodily resurrection and ascension and future return in glory; heaven and hell." *God Has Many Names* (London, 1982).

72 *Faith and Knowledge*, 2nd edn (London, 1967), p. 98.

73 Ibid., pp. 113, 107.

74 Ibid., pp. 123–8.

75 *God Has Many Names*, p. 4.

76 Ibid., p. 135.

77 The one is dealt with in *Evil and the God of Love* (London, 1966), and the other more specifically in the context of Hick's concern with world religions, in *Death and Eternal Life* (London, 1976).

78 *God and the Universe of Faiths* (London, 1973), p. 9.

79 *Faith and Knowledge*, p. 199.

80 *God and the Universe of Faiths*, pp. 111f.

81 Ibid., p. 114.

82 See J. H. Hick (ed.), *The Myth of God Incarnate* (London, 1977), and M. Goulder (ed.), *Incarnation and Myth: The debate continued* (London, 1979).

83 Ibid., pp. 139f.

84 Ibid., p. 146.

85 Ibid., p. 159.

86 Donald M. MacKinnon was born in Oban, a fishing port on the west coast of Scotland, in 1913. He was educated at Winchester College and at New College,

Oxford University, and served for a year as an Assistant in Moral Philosophy at Edinburgh University (to A. E. Taylor) before becoming Fellow and Tutor at Keble College, Oxford, for some ten years, lecturing also at Balliol College in the later years. In 1947 he was appointed Regius Professor of Moral Philosophy at the University of Aberdeen, and afterward (in 1960) became Norris-Hulse Professor of Divinity at the University of Cambridge until his retirement in 1978 to return to Scotland. An Anglican, he was a member of the Scottish Episcopal Church, and was also active politically as a member of the Labour Party. He died in 1994.

87 *The Problem of Metaphysics* (Cambridge, 1974), p. 24.

88 Ibid., p. 44.

89 Ibid., p. 55.

90 Ibid., p. 79.

91 Ibid., p. 94.

92 The way in which we live our lives, even the sharpness with which the question of how we should do so presses on us, imposes a veto on any sort of light-hearted disregard of questions concerning the ways in which things are. Morality is not a matter of arbitrary choice; it is in some sense expressive, at the level of human action, of the order of the world. *The Problem of Metaphysics*, p. 38.

93 It is for this reason that he admires Joseph Butler: "Butler's empiricism is shown in his insistence that we look at the particular elements of our nature, one by one, turning aside from none of them. But it is just when he is doing this that he is most insistently defending the transcendent claims of morality; as if he is sure that only when we see morality as a coming to terms with our actual nature will we esteem it for what it is, something at once quite simple and authoritative, and yet as rich and diverse in content as human life itself." *A Study in Ethical Theory* (London, 1957), p. 178.

94 "It may well be, as I would be prepared to argue, that if we take seriously the sort of moral insight contained in such a work as Shakespeare's *Julius Caesar*, we have already advanced beyond the frontiers

of, e.g., a thorough-going Benthamite ethical naturalism; indeed to take such an insight seriously is one way of advancing beyond such frontiers; to do it *is* so to advance." Ibid., pp. 44f.

95 Ibid., p. 44.

96 *Borderlands of Theology* (London, 1968), p. 31.

97 *Borderlands of Theology*, p. 76.

98 Ibid., p. 87.

99 Ibid., p. 79.

100 Ibid.

101 "It may well be thought that [as regards the significance and role of power in human life] the Churches have all in one way or another failed, either by accepting uncritically the attitudes and standards of the society around them, or of certain strata within it, or else by a kind of half-deliberate aversion from the problems raised, and decisions become necessary, by means of their own involvement with the power-structures around them . . . But in my own personal judgement, we have to reckon with a continuing impoverishment of fundamental theological thought springing from excess reverence for the powers that be as ordained of God." *Themes in Theology* (Edinburgh, 1987), p. 4.

102 Ibid., p. 6.

103 *Explorations in Theology* (London, 1979), p. 22.

104 See, for example, "On the Notion of a Philosophy of History," in *Borderlands of Theology*, pp. 152–68.

105 Ibid., p. 153.

106 *The Problem of Metaphysics*, p. 30.

107 *Themes in Theology*, p. 1.

108 Ibid., p. 19.

109 Ibid., p. 140.

110 *Explorations in Theology*, pp. 21f.

111 *Borderlands of Theology*, p. 93.

112 *Themes in Theology*, p. 143.

113 Nicholas L. A. Lash was born in 1934. After a period in the Corps of Royal Engineers, he was educated for the priesthood at Oscott College, Sutton Coldfield, and at Cambridge before becoming a Fellow of St Edmund's House, Cambridge, in 1969. After serving as Assistant Lecturer, he became Norris-Hulse Professor of Divinity in 1978. His writings include: *His Presence in the World: A study in eucharistic worship and theology* (1968), *Change in Focus: A study of doctrinal change and continuity* (1973), *Newman on Development* (1975), *Voices of Authority* (1976), *Theology on Dover Beach* (1979), *A Matter of Hope: A theologian's reflections on Karl Marx* (1981), *Theology on the Way to Emmaus* (1986), *Easter in Ordinary: Reflections on human experience and the knowledge of God* (1988), *Believing Three Ways in One God: A reading of the Apostles' Creed* (1992), and *The Beginning and End of "Religion"* (1996).

114 For a variety of reasons, Roman Catholics have only recently been able to play a full part in English theology in universities, but they now fill many posts and England is a center of lay Roman Catholic theology.

115 *Easter in Ordinary* (London, 1988), p. 236.

116 Ibid., p. 253.

117 Professor at King's College London, Colin E. Gunton is a prolific writer and lecturer. His major works include: *Becoming and Being* (Oxford, 1978), *Yesterday and Today* (London, 1983), *Enlightenment and Alienation* (Basingstoke, 1985), *The Actuality of Atonement* (Edinburgh, 1988), *The Promise of Trinitarian Theology* (Edinburgh, 1991), and *The One, The Three and the Many* (Oxford, 1993).

Bibliography

Main figures

Hick, J. H., *Faith and Knowledge*, 2nd edn (London, 1967).
—— *God and the Universe of Faiths* (London, 1973).
—— *Death and Eternal Life* (London, 1976).
—— *Evil and the God of Love* (London, 1979).
—— *God Has Many Names* (London, 1980).
Hick, J. H. (ed.), *The Myth of God Incarnate* (London, 1977).

MacKinnon, D. M., *A Study in Ethical Theory* (London, 1957).

—— *Borderlands of Theology and Other Essays* (London, 1968).

—— *The Problem of Metaphysics* (Cambridge, 1974).

—— *Explorations in Theology 5: Donald MacKinnon* (London, 1979).

—— *Themes in Theology* (Edinburgh, 1987).

Macquarrie, J., *An Existentialist Theology: A comparison of Heidegger and Bultmann* (London, 1955–72).

—— *The Scope of Demythologizing* (London, 1960).

—— *Twentieth Century Religious Thought: The frontiers of philosophy and theology, 1900–1960* (London, 1963–81).

—— *Studies in Christian Existentialism* (London, 1966).

—— *Principles of Christian Theology* (London, 1966–77).

—— *God-Talk: An examination of the logic and language of theology* (London, 1967).

—— *In Search of Humanity* (London, 1982).

—— *In Search of Deity* (London, 1984).

Swinburne, R. G., *The Coherence of Theism* (Oxford, 1977, rev. edn, 1993).

—— *The Existence of God* (Oxford, 1979, rev. edn, 1991).

—— *Faith and Reason* (Oxford, 1981).

—— *The Evolution of the Soul* (Oxford, 1986).

—— *Responsibility and Atonement* (Oxford, 1989).

—— *Revelation: From metaphor to analogy* (Oxford, 1992).

—— *The Christian God* (Oxford, 1994).

Torrance, T. F., *Theology in Reconstruction* (London, 1965).

—— *Theological Science* (Oxford, 1969).

—— *Space, Time and Resurrection* (Edinburgh, 1969).

—— *Theology in Reconciliation* (London, 1975).

—— *The Ground and Grammar of Theology* (Belfast, 1980).

—— *Christian Theology and Scientific Culture* (New York, 1980).

—— *Divine and Contingent Order* (Oxford, 1981).

—— *Reality and Evangelical Theology* (Philadelphia, 1982).

—— *Transformation and Convergence in the Frame of Knowledge* (Belfast, 1984).

—— *Reality and Scientific Theology* (Edinburgh, 1985).

—— *The Trinitarian Faith, The Evangelical Theology of the Ancient Catholic Church* (Edinburgh, 1988).

Others

Abraham W. J. and Holtzer, S. W. (eds), *The Rationality of Religious Belief: Essays presented to Basil Mitchell* (London, 1987).

D'Costa, G., *John Hick's Theology of Religions* (Lanham, 1987).

Farrer, A. M., *Finite and Infinite* (London, 1943).

—— *The Glass of Vision* (London, 1948).

—— *The Freedom of the Will* (London, 1958).

—— *Love Almighty and Ills Unlimited* (London, 1962).

—— *Faith and Speculation* (London, 1967).

—— *Reflective Faith*, ed. Charles Conti (London, 1972).

Hebblethwaite, B. and Sutherland, S. (eds), *The Philosophical Frontiers of Christian Theology: Essays presented to D. M. MacKinnon* (Cambridge, 1982).

Kee, A. and Long, E. T. (eds), *Being and Truth: Essays in honour of John Macquarrie* (London, 1986).

Mascall, E. L., *He Who Is* (London, 1943).

Mitchell, B., *The Justification of Religious Belief* (London, 1973).

—— *Morality Religious and Secular* (Oxford, 1980).

—— *How to Play Theological Ping-Pong* (London, 1990).

—— *Faith and Criticism* (London, 1995).

Padgett, Alan G. (ed.), *Reasons and the Christian Religion* (Oxford, 1994).

Ramsey, Ian T., *Christian Empiricism*, ed. Jerry H. Gill (London, 1974).

Sell, A. P. F., *The Philosophy of Religion 1875–1980* (London, 1988).

Theology and Society

Peter Sedgwick

Introduction

In what sense can theology speak about, and witness to, the society which forms the context for that theology itself? In a Christian era there could be a symbiotic relationship between the two, even if the ecclesiastical positions of those who wrote or preached theology may have been in great and enduring tension with those who held ultimate political authority. The twentieth century has posed a very different challenge. At first glance theology may seek to address society because theology has a social conscience. This in turn may be traced back to the ethical idealism which often provided the epistemological foundation for theology, or to the necessity of witness as one stands under the Word of God. An alternative origin may be found in the theological and ethical tradition of ecclesial polity, such as that of Hooker or Coleridge in the Church of England, or Knox and the later Covenanters in the Church of Scotland. Here too theology conceives society as subject to the divine laws or the kingly rule of Christ. And finally theology is an ecclesiastical practice, and if a church is established explicitly, as in their varying ways the Church of England and Church of Scotland are, or implicitly, as was the case for nonconformity in its social dominance at the beginning of the twentieth century in the large northern industrial cities of England, such as Manchester or Leeds, then again theology will express the nature of that establishment of religion by seeking to guide that society.

So far, all this seems straightforward, even if the origins of theology's social engagement are complex and hard to disentangle. However, much more difficult questions press on the relationship of theology and society. Throughout the twentieth century in Britain society was becoming more pluralist, both in the diversity of its religious practice and in its social heterogeneity. At the same time there was a growing belief that society was becoming more secular; whether that was a justified belief is a much-debated question among sociologists of religion. Thirdly, the ethical questions which this pluralist society posed became more intense and of baffling complexity. Few theologians possessed the necessary training to understand

Keynesian economics in depth, or to adjudicate on the biological debates on the distinction between inanimate and animate existence. It is striking that two of the social theologians considered in this article, Ronald Preston and John Habgood, were highly unusual in being trained in these very disciplines – Preston in economics, Habgood in physiology. Yet it would be a mistake simply to construe the ethical task as being that of technical complexity. It was also the intensity of the debates which mattered. There was for a while after 1945 a belief that the endemic tendency of market capitalism to plunge into cyclical depressions, bringing extensive poverty in its wake, and the permanent marginalization of the very poor from any form of security and social well-being had finally been eradicated by a combination of the mixed economy and Keynesian economics. Sadly, by the early 1980s it became clear that poverty and unemployment had returned to Western Europe, and nowhere more so than in Britain. Another, perhaps even more intense issue, which was hardly debated at all when it first appeared in the 1940s, was the totality of modern warfare and the destruction of urban life. Again by the 1970s concern about the growing potential of nuclear destructiveness became a marked feature of church life, especially among young people who were already threatened by rising unemployment and insecurity.

The challenge therefore for Christian social ethics is not simply to witness to society out of a philosophically or theologically developed sense of moral obligation, allied to an appreciation of the tradition of one's denominational heritage and the civic responsibility which it may bear in society as an established religion. This was the situation as it appeared to William Temple in Oxford or John Baillie in Edinburgh before 1914, where the challenge was to break through ecclesiastical introspection and to "win the nation for Christ." By Temple's death in 1944, and far more so by Baillie's death in 1960, the problem of pluralism in social ethics became more acute. Therefore Christian social ethics in Britain (theology and society) has had a different agenda from the mid-century than before. By the last decade of the century the debate was very different from the first. The challenge of the environment, feminism, and the racial issue all combined to accentuate the sense of crisis in theology. Underlying it was the question whether theology wished to find the presence of God in contemporary society, or whether it preferred to abandon that task as hubris and to focus on its proper responsibility of reforming the church as the pilgrim people of God. If there was a consensus among many theologians before 1914 about social relationships, there was very little by the end of the century. Yet much outstanding work had been done on formulating "middle axioms" to enable the theologian to discuss social issues, and there were a substantial number of clergy and laity who had worked in society, and especially industry, as specialist chaplains. A tradition of social witness had been built up by theologians such as Preston, Kane, Atherton, and Jenkins in England, while some university departments in Edinburgh, Manchester, and Cardiff provided a home for bodies concerned with social issues (Centre for Theology and Public Issues, Edinburgh; William Temple Foundation, Manchester; Board for Pastoral Studies, Cardiff). Finally there was the major commitment of the Church of Scotland's Committee on Church and Nation and the Church of England's Board for Social Responsibility.

Survey

Before 1914 the Hegelian strand in British idealism was predominant. Edward Caird, lay theologian and philosopher, spoke of the necessity of understanding "all the ties material and spiritual that bind us to our fellow-men."[1] Among these was the state, and so Caird's love of unity was expressed in lyrical terms. "The national state is still the highest organized whole, the great ethical unity to which our services are immediately owing, and it is in which our services acting with it, or upon it that we can serve humanity."[2] Similar sentiments were felt by another Oxford theologian, R. C. Moberly, at the time of the Boer War. There is a close correlation between morality and imperial dominion.

> Just as the moral qualities which issued in empire had a basis which was of God, so the real purpose and use of the empire when attained, must be God's use and purpose altogether... The administration of justice, incorrupt and inflexible, is in its way a true manifestation of God... So is sympathy, not of heart only but of imagination, the generous appreciation, in personal modesty and meekness, of the ideals of others; and their capacities of development along the proper line of their own ideals.[3]

The Oxford idealism of Caird influenced the young William Temple strongly. He inherited from such theologians as Henry Scott Holland and the Lux Mundi school (including R. C. Moberly and Charles Gore) a concern to extend the influence of Christianity into national life. Education, pacifism, and social reform were part of an overall agenda to change society. In similar vein, the Scottish theologian John Baillie was influenced by A. S. Pringle-Pattison, who argued that moral obligation was the source of all religious faith. Temple wrote a series of philosophical treatises which defended idealism, but his career as a bishop in the Church of England meant that it was the reconstruction of national life which occupied him in the 1920s. By the 1940s three clear schools were beginning to emerge in Britain in social theology. One was associated closely with John Baillie, who chaired a Church of Scotland enquiry ("God's Will in a Time of Crisis") into social reform. Baillie also met with T. S. Eliot and John Middleton Murry in a group organized by J. H. Oldham called the Moot, and also took part in the major 1937 Oxford conference attended by Reinhold Niebuhr, William Temple, and R. H. Tawney. Baillie's theology was moving away from the Kantian outlook which had shaped him as a younger theologian, but ethical theism remained a dominant inspiration. The major school in British social theology was a group loosely associated with William Temple and R. H. Tawney, a lay economic and social historian. Temple's presence at the 1941 Malvern Conference, and his classic paperback *Christianity and Social Order* (1942), gave him unprecedented influence in English society and theology. His early death aged 63 in 1944 was a shattering blow, preventing his participation in the long-awaited construction of the welfare state by the Labour Government of 1945–51. Nevertheless his theology was carefully expounded by the social ethicist Ronald Preston, as well as shaping the views of the Church of England Board for Social Responsibility over many decades. The third school was the Christendom group, who published a journal of Anglo-Catholic sociology with the same name from 1922 onwards.

V. A. Demant was their most prominent theologian, expounding a natural law theology. Demant became Regius Professor of Moral Theology at Oxford in 1949. Demant's theology was extensively criticized by Preston over many years as lacking all relation to economic or social reality, but in recent times there has been a revival of interest in his work from those who themselves reject what is taken to be an unqualified acceptance of sociology by theologians (Milbank, Markham, Northcott).[4]

However, the main emphasis in social theology from the 1940s lay in a welcome to the welfare state, on the one hand, and a small exploration of the working-class estrangement from Christianity on the other. The president of the Methodist Conference in 1953, Donald Soper, declared in his presidential address "I thank God for the Welfare State."[5] Yet the acceptance of a secular society concealed the pluralism latent in an urban Britain where the old ties of class and kinship were being progressively loosened. Nor was there much theological undergirding of this acceptance. It was not until the mid-1960s that R. H. Preston began to develop his position. Much more significant than the acceptance of the welfare state and secularism was the tiny, but deeply committed, group of industrial chaplains who began work in the Sheffield steelworks from the 1940s.[6] They met a world where Marxist class analysis was of more use than the understanding of community as *Koinonia* (participation in the Spirit) offered by contemporary Anglican theologians.

By the last third of the twentieth century there was a rapid change in the understanding of society by theologians. A highly sophisticated defense of the establishment of the Church of England was offered by one of the leading liberals in its ranks, Bishop (later Archbishop) John Habgood. Using Weberian categories to demonstrate the necessity of social cohesion in a pluralist society, he attempted to defend both the privileged position of the Church of England with a vision of an open faith which rested on a liberal catholicism, and to articulate the understanding which science offered of reality in its diverse forms from biology to sociology. Associated with this standpoint were a number of theologians who saw plurality, secularism, and the scientific worldview as the challenge to Christianity (Dyson, Montefiore, Gill, and Baelz, among others).[7] Yet at the same time the decline in churchgoing, the rise of evangelicalism, and the influence of Stanley Hauerwas in the United States led to a very different position, where the primary task of the church is to develop the Christian virtues in a church separate from the pluralist but secular culture. "The Gospel and our Culture" was one umbrella movement for this group.[8] Also allied to Hauerwas, but from a Catholic perspective and (as noted above) appreciative of V. A. Demant and the Christendom group, are a number of younger theologians who would question the sociological "metanarrative" which Preston, Habgood, and liberal theologians have taken as normative.[9]

Pluralism is not, however, the only distinctive division in social theology. A second point of controversy is "the option for the poor." Preston had always been opposed to the liberation theology associated with the World Council of Churches, even if he himself accepted the market as no more than a reluctant necessity. Growing poverty in the bottom quarter of British society, and racial tensions, led to a repudiation of the consensus associated with the welfare state. It is not easy to categorize the different positions under one umbrella. Duncan Forrester in Edinburgh reformulated middle axioms to take account of liberation theology, and explored the breakdown in social cohesion under the impact of successive Conservative governments who were influenced by Hayek and Friedman.[10] His theology united a biblical understanding of justice with contemporary social philosophy (Habermas, Rawls) and empirical work on poverty, criminology, and welfare policy. David Jenkins was another theologian who became a Church of England bishop and used biblical concepts of divine action, correlated with a stringent attack on government policy and market capitalism.[11] Although the Church of England itself, through commissions and reports, was repeatedly critical of the government in power, Jenkins himself seemed nearer to the theology written by Moltmann, African and South American liberation theologians, and European Roman Catholics, where the church was always judged in the light of its commitment to justice and the Kingdom of God. There was a strong tension between Jenkins and the ecclesiastical institution which he represented. Similar tension was found in Margaret Kane's work.[12] A third figure from an Anglo-Catholic perspective, who repudiated the liberalism of Preston and Habgood without accepting the Christendom perspective, was Ken Leech. He drew on a Catholic socialism that was related to Christendom, but was far more explicitly concerned with social transformation and political revolution. Leech was a complex figure, whose writings on spirituality and contemplative prayer drew on the Orthodox, patristic, and Catholic tradition and were highly influential. His choice of where he found his theological inspiration was also very significant. He worked for decades in the impoverished East End of London, with a strong involvement in race relations, youth work, and the drug culture. Although a priest, in recent years he has no longer worked for the institutional church but has become a "community theologian" with his base in a parish church. Finally one should mention the challenge of feminists and environmentalists (sometimes combined) to the consensus established by conservative liberalism in its response to pluralism. Here there is an explicit repudiation of any attempt to establish social cohesion, and a belief that Christianity is about social, environmental, and sexual transformation. Mary Grey, Ann Loades, and Anne Primavesi would all be considered significant theologians.[13] Bishop Peter Selby was another who combined an interest in sexuality and political transformation,[14] as was Elaine Graham.

None of these theologians reflected denominational identities any longer. As British, especially English, society became more fractured and diverse, the tradition of ethical idealism, theological thought going back to the Reformation, and support for the establishment of religion was no longer dominant. Nor, despite its great sophistication, did the conservative liberalism of Preston and Habgood seem to be normative, as it had been from the 1960s to the 1980s. There was a dynamic vitality in British social theology during the last decade of the century, where a variety of analytic tools (neo-Marxism, feminism, and postmodernism) were deployed by theologians who also explored many different forms of spirituality and ecclesial communities. It remained to be seen how these different approaches might be in any dialogue with one another.

A further consideration was that understanding of divine mediation, through the life of the church and the Christian tradition, which each group of theologians sought to articulate. All of them saw the nature of God as deeply concerned with the life of society, with the church as the servant of that task. But for Habgood the question of divine action is to be explored through an awareness of scientific causality, so that the church should seek to interpret how God could be present through an articulation of values and social ideals which are related back to Christianity. For those, primarily but not entirely in a neo-Barthian position, the church expresses the life of Christ as a challenge to the false preoccupations of contemporary society, which has become atomized and concerned with material happiness. Lesslie Newbigin's analysis of the Enlightenment became formative for this movement's analysis.[15] Others, such as Jenkins, Leech, Forrester, and many feminists, found the divine demand for justice and righteousness in Scripture as a judgment on both our contemporary society and church. For them the search for social ideals which might embody Christian truth fails to take account of the transcendent obligation for all ideals to be judged against the flourishing of humanity offered as in Christ, while the return to a church-centered vision as expressive of the life of Christ ignores the importance of finding Christ in secular reality.

The nature of pluralism therefore remained acute for Christian theology as it sought to address society. It increasingly had a less privileged basis from which to speak, but the intellectual ground had shifted as well. One of the most acute critics of British theology, while remaining sympathetic to its aspirations, was the English political philosopher and Labour Party peer Raymond Plant. Plant had himself made a close study of English philosophical idealism at the beginning of this century in relation to the nature of citizenship and political obligation.[16] He drew attention in his Sarum lectures, given in Cambridge in the early 1990s, and in several published articles, to the difficulty of articulating any sense of the common good, drawing on the work both of Alasdair MacIntyre and of the political philosophy of the New Right.[17] Unlike Forrester, he remained sceptical of the possibility of returning to a biblical notion of justice, while not ruling out the insights offered by narrative theology. Plant was very aware of the widening gulf between rich and poor in Britain, but was no longer convinced either that a planned economy would work (thus abandoning the traditional state socialism which earlier theologians such as Temple and Tawney had striven for) or that there could be any unanimity in society on how social transformation could be brought about. Plant, like the Manchester theologian John Atherton, who carried Preston's economic analysis on to the global market of the 1990s, felt that a commitment to the poor must be matched by a dialogue with the values held by those in power, both in government and industry.[18] Could there be an agreed minimum of social morality about which Christian theology and political philosophy might conduct their debate?

Twentieth-Century Theology and Society: Four Cases

It is instructive to examine four theologians in English society who have sought to address the issues of pluralism and social justice. Scotland is a different society, where much greater social cohesion and a growing sense of alienation from the British Parliament at Westminster have combined with a more Barthian approach to theology in a demand for social justice. The four theologians are William Temple (1881–1944); Ronald Preston (b. 1913); John Habgood (b. 1927); and Ken Leech

(b. 1939). Each of these theologians felt that the question of justice was inherent to Christianity, and that the institutional church had an obligation to further that vision of the Kingdom of God. However, they disagree profoundly on the relationship of church, society, and Kingdom in a pluralist society.

William Temple

Born in 1881, Temple was educated at Oxford, where he became a philosophy don, teaching courses on Plato, before becoming ordained in the Church of England. After ordination, he became a headmaster, parish priest of a wealthy and fashionable London church, Bishop of Manchester, and Archbishop of York. He was then only 49. He became Archbishop of Canterbury in 1942 but died two years later, aged 63.

Temple, like every other theologian considered here, was concerned with secularism and pluralism by the time of his death. In his final year he wrote an article entitled "What Christians Stand for in the Secular World."[19] He wanted to be remembered for it, and it showed how far his thought had evolved from Caird's idealism 50 years earlier. While he still maintained a theistic perspective justified from philosophy, especially ethical idealism, and held to the social nature of personality, he now wanted to distinguish between the tasks of the church and society. He recognized the egoistic and power-driven nature of society, where human communities are divided against themselves. Writing in the year in which Fascism and Communism reached their titanic death-struggle, which eventually saw the division of the German nation in which he had as a young philosopher first studied theology, Temple felt that the crisis of the end of his life was a cultural one. Beyond Christian morals, and transcending Christian ideals, there were "the social structures which by their perpetual suggestion form the soul."[20] Moral instruction is impotent against this. Christianity is prone to illusion: Perhaps Temple was reflecting on his early life.

Christianity is thus a movement of personal and social regeneration. This must be a challenge to other creeds with its own interpretation of life. Temple ends by arguing for the importance of hope. Christians must "restore hope to the world through a true understanding of the relation of the Kingdom of God to history, as a transcendent reality that is continually seeking, and partially achieving, embodiment in the activities and conflicts of the temporal order."[21]

Alongside these decisions taken in hope, Temple also argued for principles. In *Christianity and Social Order* he argued for three derivative principles, which were freedom, social fellowship, and service. Temple argues that people are formed by society, and therefore it matters what the nature of that society is. Temple's principles operate as fundamental judgments on society, since he did not feel that society embodied these principles to any true degree. However, there is an ambiguity in Temple at this point.

> The conservative temperament tends to dwell on what is indispensable, that this may be safeguarded. The radical temperament tends to dwell most on the higher ends of life, that these may be facilitated. The world needs both. But wisdom consists in the

union of the two. The great advantage of the conception of Natural Law is that it leads us to consider every activity in its context in the whole economy of life.[22]

Temple could argue that ordinary moral conventions therefore still held authority, even in a cultural crisis. They embody the experience of many generations. They "represent an immense inductive process too vast to be adequately traced out . . . It is the collective reason of innumerable individuals, who all agree (though it may be unconsciously) in the major premise that it is desirable to maintain social life."[23]

In the final section of *Christianity and Social Order* Temple responds to an influential work by Peter Drucker, *The End of Economic Man*. Drucker was trying to end the domination of human life by economic considerations. Temple responds by taking the family, personality, and fellowship as central. It leads him to consider the nature of leisure, of representation in industry and educational reform, and the place of religion in schools.

At this point Temple reveals a limited understanding of pluralism. He moves rapidly from corporate life to individuality and world-fellowship. What is necessary is an allegiance which does not suppress individuality and yet creates bonds with other citizens, including world citizens. "There is only one candidate for this double function: it is Christianity. We must then take steps to secure that the corporate life of the schools is Christian."[24] Temple thus argues for Christian doctrine, worship, and ethos across education.

The presupposition here is that social cohesion is possible and desirable, and can be created by Christianity. While allowing for class conflict, Temple appears to contradict the cultural crisis against which Christianity must strive. At times Temple recognized conflicts of interests as perennial, yet he felt that they could be resolved. Thus Temple remains Platonic, arguing an idealist vision. Truth is there to be found in the sanctity of personality, which Christianity defends in the doctrine of the Incarnation. He remains an ambiguous figure, who developed derivative Christian principles in dealing with society, but who also had a vision of a Christocentric society.

Ronald Preston

Preston was born in 1913, and educated as an economist at the London School of Economics. He worked for the Student Christian Movement as a young man, before being ordained in the Church of England. For many years associated with the University of Manchester, where he became Professor of Social and Pastoral Theology, he also was deeply involved with the church's response to social affairs through conferences, committees, and working parties. His unusually long career spans the famous 1937 Oxford Conference, attended by John Baillie, William Temple, and Reinhold Niebuhr, to an open letter critical of the World Council of Churches in 1992. He published his first major work when he was 66, and has continued to publish five more volumes up to 1994. Many originated from lectures or are collections of articles: like Habgood and Leech, he does not usually write full-length books.

Preston is notable for a number of features. Since his writing began when he was an established scholar, it has a mature, reflective feel, which looks back on a lifetime of church involvement in social affairs. Nor have his views changed much during the 25 years of his publications. A second feature is the way in which his writing has revolved around a few people. He studied under R. H. Tawney in the 1930s, and was deeply influenced by both Tawney and William Temple. He has written about them both throughout his life, while his research student, John Atherton, did his doctorate on Tawney. Atherton's own work is also centered on Manchester, at both the Cathedral and the William Temple Foundation there, while his writing includes a respectful assessment of Ronald Preston, as well as Tawney and Temple. So although Temple died in 1944, and Tawney in 1962, their tradition lives on through their successors (followers would be too confining a term).

Preston is committed to the exploration of middle axioms, the middle ground between general statements and detailed policies. On the one hand there is what Preston calls the Christian understanding of life, an articulated theology based on reflection on Scripture. This understanding "is so far-reaching that it transcends any embodiment in personal life or social structures."[25] On the other hand there is an analysis of the empirical situation. As part of the analysis there should be an understanding of the underlying trends, including "where the Christian understanding of life is particularly being disregarded. A middle axiom is formed to indicate the general direction in which action should be taken to improve the situation." They are not detailed policy formulations, but general, and carry high, informal authority. So they unite Christian and non-Christian, give Christians something to say which is relevant to the concerns of society, and avoid both pietism and absolutism.

Preston rejects both the a priori deductions from alleged maxims of Natural Law, and the two Kingdoms theology of Lutheranism, which allows no guidance in politics from the Christian faith. In his more recent works he has also attacked the World Council of Churches for too great a reliance on the future hope of the Kingdom of God. "The power of expectant hope" is able to ensure a basis for everyday action. He allows for symbolic actions, but only in a restricted way.[26] The legacy of prophecy is a stress on radical transcendence, which takes common morality so much further that it becomes paradoxical. Nevertheless "biblical prophecy is not a direct model for the church today"[27] since it is too easy: It leads to straightforward denunciation, followed by demands for "a totally new social, economic and political order, accompanied by simplistic . . . analyses."[28]

Preston accepts the use of power, and is critical of those who abjure it.[29] Christians live in "two realms," but this Lutheranism should not lead to the isolation of the divine order from the civil one. Equally Preston feels that liberation theology is inadequate, both because of its Marxism and because its biblical exegesis is too conservative. Preston does not advance an alternative exegesis, but there is an implicit skepticism about the historicity of the chronology of Jesus' ministry in the Synoptic Gospels.[30] He respects the vitality of liberation theology, but believes that it needs to be reformulated in a British context.

Preston is concerned that the decline of religion will lead to greater social unrest. In the Industrial Revolution, when Britain became urbanized, evangelicalism provided the internal control for many people, thus enabling rapid social change to happen without much social conflict. Today Britain is becoming harder to govern, because religious practice is much less great. There is therefore less encouragement for public order. "Beyond its perennial evangelistic task, can the church foster, together with any allies she can find among those of other faiths and philosophies, sources of disinterested concern for the common good?"[31]

Evangelicalism increasingly predominates in British church life, as Preston notes, and it is developing a social ethic, although he is suspicious of its interest in the theology of Abraham Kuyper, the early twentieth-century Dutch neo-Calvinist. This tends to cultivate an isolationist spirit in spite of its talk of pluralism, and it is critical of humanism. "Its polemics against humanism ignore the Christian elements latent in the humanism of Western society, which can often be an ally of causes which Christians may wish to promote in that plural society. Its penchant for separate Christian political parties and trade unions is a source of confusion and fissiparousness. It will not do as it stands as a social theology."[32]

Preston thus appeals to a notion of the common good which is a safeguard against possessive individualism. He looks for a political philosophy which nourishes the sense of civic obligation through appropriate structures. It is in the dilemmas of political philosophy that Preston finds the best context to discuss pluralism, and not in contemporary theologies of society. Preston has therefore become increasingly skeptical of other theologians in recent years, finding some far too idealistic (such as Moltmann); others too concerned with local communities as expressions of the Kingdom of God (Hauerwas); and others too involved in a simplistic action/ reflection model.

In his most recent work, Preston appeals again to the theology predominant in the last years of Temple's life: what he calls Christian realism. It is a complex system of Barth, Brunner, Temple, Maritain, Reinhold Niebuhr, and Nygren, but in all this it is Niebuhr who predominates. The dialectic of original sin and original righteousness ensures a hopefulness tempered by realism. Ultimately the question of pluralism is resolved pragmatically by an appeal to experience. His prediction is that all European societies, including Poland and Eire, will cease to be monolithic. It is therefore a matter of living "cheek by jowl with citizens who follow other faiths and philosophies."[33]

But is this enough? It is certainly part of an English common-sense theology, unlike the theologies he criticizes such as Orthodox trinitarianism, liberation theologians, and Roman Catholic teaching epitomized in the most recent encyclical *Veritatis Splendor* (1993). The problem we are left with is how Christianity might function in a pluralist, apparently secular society. Two very different answers, which address the issue in a more intensive way, are given by two other Anglican theologians, John Habgood and Ken Leech. Preston leaves one feeling that the issue of pluralism is an afterthought in his theology, to be handled through political philosophy. With Habgood and Leech, who both began their ministry in the 1950s and not in the 1930s as Preston did, pluralism is the starting point of their social theology.

John Habgood

Habgood was born in 1927, and read physiology at Cambridge. He became a research student there, and after a doctorate on heightened sensitivity to pain, intended to become a scientist. He had, however, converted to Christianity while a student, and finally decided to be ordained rather than pursue his scientific career. He studied for ordination at Oxford and taught for a few years at a theological college in Cambridge, before becoming a parish priest in the Anglican church in Scotland. Subsequently he was principal of a theological college in Birmingham, Bishop of Durham, and finally Archbishop of York.

His books are primarily collections of addresses, sermons, and essays, with the exception of an early book on *Religion and Science*, and his major study, *Church and Nation in a Secular Age* (1983). He is also notable for the extensive contribution he has made to journalism, and for many book reviews and short articles. His public ministry was carried out at a time when there was much greater media exposure than in Temple's day, and so interviews in the press, radio, and television have been a constant feature of his life. This gives his theology a cautious feel, for he is aware that it will inevitably attract much speculation. Yet he has not been afraid to point out the biological weaknesses of a Papal encyclical, the complications of government policy, or even the weaknesses in the state's provision for religious worship in schools, suggesting that this might be counter-productive. He is a clear thinker, who will follow a train of thought to its conclusion whatever the consequences.

Habgood is unusual in that his starting point is that of contemporary pluralism. "We live in a country at least partially divided into different religions and cultures; a country conscious of deep social divisions, divisions made even more apparent by our present economic strains; a country with many uncertainties about its aims and values. We have seen the public dimensions of faith steadily eroded." "Faith" here is ambiguous. It represents both "the public face of the Christian church" and "public faith" – the vision of God's glory in the widest public frame, but also "the foundations; it is about the things which bind us together, and the values we share, and the goals we pursue." It is Habgood's conviction that personal, religious faith is linked (e.g., in Psalm 11) with public values. "If the foundations are destroyed, what can the just man do?"[34]

In many ways this sermon reads as Habgood's manifesto, since he preached it at his enthronement as Archbishop. He speaks furthermore of the possibility of public faith being "critically aware of its limitations." Doubt is an integral part of knowledge, especially in religious faith. Coherence in faith can lead to "complacency, self-sufficiency and intolerance," and only "touches the hem of the robe of the infinite and everlasting God." The necessity of public faith includes radical criticism, "forever building and forever pulling down."[35]

Pluralism is not the same as secularism. Habgood uses Berger as showing the effect of modernization via technology and bureaucracy. Technology creates a private world, by separating work from private life, and by subordinating human relations at work to technical requirements. Bureaucracy equally creates an impersonal world. Religious faith thus suffers a serious crisis of plausibility. Indeed sociological understanding[36] itself makes the community of faith seem a constructed entity and a human phenomenon. Where then is truth to be found?

Habgood turns to Don Cupitt's early work, before Cupitt ceased to affirm the transcendent reality of God. Knowing God is knowledge of pure transcendent spirit. Partly through apophatic theology, partly through the phenomenology of John

Bowker and the awareness that religious traditions can be transformed, Habgood affirms the possibility of theistic faith beyond the reduction of modernism. It is precisely in the problematic nature of religious awareness that true finality is found, belonging to the transcendent.[37]

Nevertheless this sophisticated liberalism is not to be seen as a lack of faith. There is a readiness to accept new truth, since "rational thought about the person of Christ dissolves into a set of paradoxes which serve only to safeguard the mystery."[38] Habgood discusses the difficulties of interfaith dialogue, neither accepting that all religions express the same ultimate truth nor being fully committed to an acceptance of members of other faiths as being anonymous Christians. Habgood argues that a delight in the faith of others, without being threatened, and a love for Christ remain in tension, but can be explored as rich diversity.[39]

This tension is held within an awareness that we begin in thinking about church/ state relationships with the reality of a complex balance of forces. The establishment of the Church of England is part of that complexity. Habgood defends that establishment both on theoretical and practical grounds. Theoretically, the religious/ mythological coordinate makes its presence felt through its grounding of individual morality, the concept of tradition, and the provision of social cohesion. Habgood writes that multiculturalism at least requires the safeguarding of some common values.

> I would myself go further than this and assert the need also for a common language of hope, aspiration and penitence, not necessarily shared by all, but recognized by all as the formal language of the nation in moments when it is important to express some kind of national consciousness. A formal public commitment to religious faith at least provides a basis on which cohesion can be built.[40]

Indeed Habgood cites Hayek as showing the necessity of mythology and moral tradition in a complex society if it is to hold together. However, Habgood also argues that Hayek's justification of mythology as allowing the free market to function is dangerous. A successful society might operate unknowingly on Hayek's principles, "but if it comes to understand itself consciously and exclusively in terms of these principles it runs the risk of destroying the mythology on which it depends." So the mythology has an independent validity, apart from its role in Hayek's arguments.[41]

Finally Habgood justifies the establishment of the Church of England on practical grounds. The existence of an Established Church is a permanent reminder of the religious basis of civil power. It is also the case that the Catholicity of a national church can mean that establishment becomes an effective symbol of the limits of nationalism. Habgood admits that establishment is of little importance in practical politics. It is more of a court of appeal. Yet disestablishment would have a major negative impact: "the nation would appear to be saying that it wished to repudiate its Christian heritage." Secondly, the establishment provides, with the monarchy, a symbolic frame of reference. This extends beyond those who are churchgoers. Thirdly, the Established Church has generally had a broad vision and wide tolerance, which allows for "very different degrees of religious commitment" and provides public access to the pastoral role of Christianity.[42]

Yet, as so often with Habgood, what is given is also qualified. He recognizes, with Stephen Sykes, that Christian doctrine is "an essentially contested concept." Christianity focuses on Jesus Christ, and this generates constantly creative disputes.[43] The worshiping life of the church holds these tensions together. So too the traditions of Christianity must always be in tension, always being held together. Traditions function in a secular society, and there is nothing disreputable intellectually in finding the justification of rationality from traditions which are formed by historical contingency.

So pluralism provides the context for Habgood's thought. Using Berger, MacIntyre, Hayek, and other contemporary thinkers he holds together the traditional *raison d'être* of the Established Church in which he is an Archbishop with a keen appreciation of contemporary sociology and political philosophy. Alongside this there is a sustained debate about such matters as embryology, genetics, and evolution. In accepting pluralism but seeking to justify a position between liberalism and conservatism (his own description is conservative liberal), he provides one of the most eloquently argued standpoints in the contemporary debate. Yet there are many who would doubt its eventual validity. Criticism would be offered by many, including the final theologian considered here, Ken Leech.

Ken Leech

Ken Leech was born in Ashton-under-Lyne in 1939. He came from a working-class background, which was not churchgoing. In 1958 he moved to Cable Street, East London, where he lived while he was studying history at King's College, London. He began to work with the Anglo-Catholic slum priests, and was ordained to an East London parish in 1964. He has returned constantly to the area over 30 years, but his ministry has been both national and international. He has worked for the Church of England as its race relations officer, been the Director of the Runnymede Trust, a research unit on race relations, chaplain at St Augustine's College, Canterbury, and is now a community theologian at St Botolph's, Aldgate, East London. Some of his books originated from talks given in the United States, where he has been a constant visitor over the years, and in Britain.

Leech combines a number of themes in his writing. Originally he began as a church historian, tracing the history of the Anglo-Catholic Socialist movement in the Church of England from a century ago until the present day. Much of that history relates to East London.

Leech's theology is rooted in an incarnational vision, where the materialistic nature of his faith is central. The eucharist gives him a social basis, for the trinitarian basis of the eucharist leads to a struggle for social justice and equality. "The Incarnation presupposes a high and optimistic (though not naive) view of humanity, for it was human nature which Christ assumed."[44] The glory of humanity is best expressed for Leech in the Vatican Council's document *Gaudium et Spes*, where humanity is said to be "the crown and centre of all things." This leads Leech to see all humanity as a solidarity, united in Christ. The new society is inseparable from the new humanity; politics and spirituality are inseparable.

Leech sees much value in the older Anglo-Catholic theology (he wrote a pamphlet on the social theology of Michael Ramsey), but he repudiates the association of European culture with Christianity found in T. S. Eliot, where European civilization depended on the Christian faith. Leech keeps a tension between gospel and culture, both affirming local culture yet seeking to challenge and transform it. It is what he calls critical orthodoxy, which draws on liberation theology, the new evangelical consciousness of Jim Wallis, and the rediscovery of the church in contemporary theology.

Liberation theology provides the overall structure of Leech's thought, and includes a concern for nonviolence, feminism, homosexuality, and racial equality. It is also related to an environmental theology, but this is placed alongside economic slavery and political oppression. The eucharistic offering has a dual emphasis on offering and consecration.

> It is impossible to offer to God the fruits of injustice and oppression, as Irenaeus saw in the second century... The eucharist, however, is not only about offering to God the fruits of labour; it is about the transformation, in Thomist language the transubstantiation, of matter to transform both the material things and the community. A theology which places the transformation of material structures and of human relations at the heart of its liturgy and life should be a theology which is open to the need for such transformation in the economic and political life of society.[45]

This transformation includes the challenge to the "false values of mammon." Anglo-Catholic social vision is utopian, but it is a utopianism which is rooted in the specific and the concrete.

Much of Leech's recent writing has been about how those committed to social change can survive in a rootless, urban culture, with its threats to human dignity and commitment. The answer is found in a disciplined spirituality, where small groups can celebrate their faith and subject illusion and falsehood to rigorous scrutiny. The public role of the theologian or philosopher is a neglected one in Western society. Current spirituality often becomes narcissistic, mirroring the culture of self-cultivation and personal awareness.

Instead of self-cultivation Leech writes about the "desert in the city." "How am I to make creative and redemptive sense of all this anger, despair and pain which surrounds me and all who work in the inner areas? If theological reflection, spiritual renewal, pastoral ministry, all occur within a specific context, then this square mile, east of Aldgate, is my context." Leech rejects for himself any place in academic theology. He chooses an older tradition of theology as rooted in prayer, silence, and specific human communities seeking their freedom.[46]

Leech accepts the end of a Christian culture, believing with MacIntyre that "we remain a society without a metaphysics, without any fundamental beliefs. And it is this combination of private religion and effective nihilism which most of all marks our age."[47] He finds in a desert spirituality of aloneness, stillness, and contemplation the answer to pluralism and social breakdown. He rejects a church which is not open to the world, and interprets Hauerwas's theology as being countercultural.

So Leech's theology unites past and present, local and global, silence and action, in an intriguing way. He places St John of the Cross alongside the Catholic Worker, and Brick Lane (East London) next to the future of capitalism. His focus is on the local, and an embodied spirituality. Two questions may be placed alongside his prolific and influential writings and talks. First, where does his theology relate to the reformulation of christology that has preoccupied academic theologians since Robinson wrote *The Human Face of God*? It is striking that he quotes Robinson's formative work, *The Body*, on the church, but not his questioning christology. To put it differently, Leech allows for doubt, despair, and questions, but that is a subjective process for the person involved in prayer and political struggle. Can Leech's profound account of spirituality speak to the person who finds the Trinity, christology, and the cross either powerful symbols of her or his own life or the expressions of the faith of the early Christians – but on neither account, true and foundational doctrines, but rather provisional expressions of religious faith and therefore open to question? If that theological questioning is allowed, however, can Leech find in his incarnational faith the strength to endure inner struggle and public conflict? Secondly, it is not clear where the institutional church fits into Leech's theology. As he has adopted a prophetic style, a subtle change has occurred. He is not simply the prophet to the Catholic Church embodied in institutional life. The whole vision of the church has become changed into small groups of pilgrims who unite around movements of liberation.[48] It is interesting that Leech writes more easily on the renewal of the sacramental character of priesthood than of the laity.[49] It is sometimes difficult to read Leech and know who are the object of the priest's mediation, illumination, and healing. It is as though the ordinary Christian community has become invisible. This allows Leech to have no problem with the decline of active church membership in British society, but is there a danger that the transition to a holiness which bears the pain of the desert and lives in the rootless world of the modern city has been bought at the cost of giving up the often conservative, traditional, but embodied community that is what remains of the parish church in modern Britain?

One striking exception is Leech's article "Racism and the urban parish," where there is a magnificent description of the local community at worship, preaching, listening, and repentance.[50] There is also reference to the past ministry of the late Stanley Evans and his care of a congregation. Yet what is needed is a further integration of the life of the small, faithful congregation into Leech's theology of struggle and witness against the forces of evil. It is a theology both cosmic and very local, so the question of integration is all-important. Leech needs to develop an ecclesiology which can carry his social ethics, spirituality, and social analysis, related to (but transcending) the fragmentation at the heart of urban life. That is a tall order, but since he is the theologian who has grappled most with pluralism and the collapse of authority, perhaps he can best articulate how *koinonia* and prophecy can coexist in an ever more marginal social institution.

Pluralism and Society

The future of English theology in its involvement with society lacks any clear sense of direction. From 1940 to the 1970s the scene was dominated by a complex

Christian realism which was inherited from William Temple and Reinhold Niebuhr. Since then the strains of pluralism and secularism have made the vision of theology more precarious. It is arguable that it is the appeal of Buddhism and New Age philosophies to young people, or the growing fundamentalism in the midst of religious indifference and apathy, which poses the greatest threat to social theology, far more than the political conservatism of Thatcherism. Poverty causes social harm, but the very credibility of theology is at stake in a pluralist society. John Habgood and Ken Leech offer very different responses to this threat, although a fuller consideration would include the influence of S. Hauerwas from the United States, ecofeminism, and the social theology of John Atherton. What is certain is that the next two decades will increasingly see theology having to argue for its claims to truth and justice in a very different manner from Temple. Temple assumed that Christianity had a central role in society, but had to demonstrate its concern for social change. Contemporary ethicists may take the concept of social reform as inherent to Christianity, but they have to ensure that the Christian faith has any credibility at all in modern British society and politics. In a pragmatic, pluralist, technologically driven world, that is a very considerable challenge.

Debate

Social ethics has remained a peripheral activity among English theologians. A few have embraced it as part of their overall theology, among them David Jenkins (later Bishop of Durham), and it is common to find a social dimension to many other theologians (e.g., Nicholas Lash, Stephen Sykes). Nevertheless the establishing of close intellectual links remains precarious, and the growth of a postmodern epistemology questioned the whole validity of society as an autonomous entity with which theology could engage in dialogue. Preference is given in such theologies to hermeneutical encounters with the Christian tradition, and the foundational nature of doctrine is also an object of suspicion. It followed that the theological method of the majority of English social ethicists would not be accepted, nor indeed would the German confessional school of Moltmann, which paralleled English theology in its concern with social well-being from a different theological perspective.

Another critique comes from those for whom personal existence is more important than social ethics. Although there were theologians who held the two together, especially in feminist circles, there was a strong emphasis on sexuality and personal growth in many recent writings in the last decade, at the expense of social analysis. It often seemed like an inversion of liberation theology, although the reluctance of some social ethicists earlier this century to relate an analysis of society to sexuality meant that the balance needed to be redressed. The resolution of the debate about social and personal existence would require a developed anthropology, which was shown by a few ethicists, such as Elaine Graham.

Although the questions of epistemology and anthropology remain difficult, it remains the case that theology needs to maintain and deepen its interest in its relationship to society. Social ethics ceased to be the amateur pursuit which it often was in preceding centuries, assisted by a proper correlation with sociology and economics, often through the inspiration of such men as R. H. Tawney and J. H. Oldham. The interest in sociology among biblical scholars needs to be taken up again in systematic theology, where a proper account of social structures in the light of divine activity could be given.

Achievement and Agenda

Social ethics came to maturity in English theology during the twentieth century. For the first time since the medieval concept of the just price, theology engaged with economics and with social conditions. Temple's deep concern with unemployment and welfare was neither simply expressed as practical action nor as calls for social change, although he was involved in both. He expressed an intellectually rigorous understanding of the conditions of human well-being, resting on a theological anthropology that informed his judgments. Ronald Preston and later John Atherton carried on a long engagement with economic affairs. The result was a series of impressive social reports, often involving their names, on the world of work. More generalized accounts of social existence (e.g., *Changing Britain*, 1987) were the result of collaboration with John Habgood. The most familiar, and perhaps most influential report was the result of an enquiry into urban life, established by the Archbishop of Canterbury. *Faith in the City*, published in 1985, was a direct attack on government neglect of urban areas, and a plea for a commitment to those areas by the Church of England. It drew an enthusiastic response from all churches, and became a landmark in support by the church for the poor and marginalized. Yet it was only one such report. Lying behind it was a tradition established this century of a theological method that used "middle axioms" to mediate between theology and social analysis, and the vindication of theological judgments on what was conducive to human flourishing. There were also Christians, ordained and lay, who worked ecumenically to implement those judgments both in industry, through industrial mission, and in society, through social responsibility.

It was by no means purely an Anglican phenomenon, although the main theologians were Anglican. Nevertheless the Roman Catholic Church established the Von Hügel Institute in Cambridge, specializing in business ethics and corporate responsibility, and the Catholic Institute for International Relations. Their work on the international debt crisis, exploitation, and human rights was a means of expressing the concerns of liberation theology, while there was a strong Dominican interest both in poverty and nuclear arms (Colin Carr, Timothy Radcliffe, Roger Ruston). An evangelical initiative was the Jubilee Centre in Cambridge, while bodies such as the William Temple Foundation in Manchester (strongly linked with John Atherton) were ecumenical. The Methodist Church worked consistently at issues such as nuclear disarmament (Kenneth Greet) and the welfare state (John Vincent), as did the United Reformed Church. Often this work was channeled through the British Council of Churches. Ken Leech adopted his own style, which was a brilliant mixture of pamphlets, essays, addresses, and sermons, always immersed in the issues he has made himself an expert on: drugs, race, poverty, and the life of East London.

The agenda which remained for social ethics was well addressed by John Habgood in his October 1995 Gerald Priestland lecture. Across British society all social institutions found themselves not merely questioned but often dismissed as irrelevant to personal existence. The law, government, religion, and the monarchy were seen as resting on concepts of authority that were no longer accepted by many individuals. Some social philosophers, such as John Gray (*Enlightenment's Wake*, 1995), espoused a Humean skepticism that would enable us to live in the ruins of the two great faith systems of Christianity and the belief in progress (including the application of science as the instrument of progress). Habgood had much in common with the Chief Rabbi, Jonathan Sacks (*Faith in the Future*, 1995; *The Persistence of Faith*, 1990), in his awareness that a fragmented culture, lack of a moral consensus, and decay of community inexorably lead to a questioning of authority. The other side of the coin is the growing attractiveness of authoritarian truth claims, especially in religion.

Globalization and postmodernism provided the other agenda for social ethics. Many of the contributors to the renaissance of socialism in the 1960s contributed to a slim but trenchant volume *After Socialism?* in 1994. Oestreicher, Lochman, McLellan, Kee, and Davis gathered in Edinburgh to discuss "the future of radical Christianity." Others accepted the impact of the global market. It was the challenge of globalization that forced John Atherton to a more critical, if still deeply respectful, standpoint vis-à-vis Ronald Preston. The global economy must be managed, and the environmental and social challenges met, but it will not go away. A similar theme underlay the 1994 Council for World Mission bicentenary lecture in London by Konrad Raiser, General Secretary of the World Council of Churches.

The final agenda is that of postmodernism, in its communitarian and postliberal perspectives. The communitarianism of MacIntyre, Taylor, and Etzioni found popular echoes in the Christian social democracy of Tony Blair, although the formulation of this philosophy in Christian social ethics was diffused into a presentation of ecclesiology as community. A more political expression of communitarianism in theological ethics remained to be written. The postliberal theology of John Milbank saw the globalized market as the inevitable outcome of secularity. Milbank rejected the refashioning of socialism, in the communicative rationality of the German neo-Marxist philosopher Jürgen Habermas, as the false perpetuation of modernity. For Milbank, the only survival lies in the "universality of love" which is repeated differently across the centuries as the salvific message of Christianity. Yet Milbank's hostility to the market is total, since it dehumanizes social life.

Society remains deeply divided in England. The fragmentation of a social consensus, the globalization of the market, and the advent of postmodernism provide a somber note on which to end. Social ethics in England this century was concerned both to construct a theological method and to participate in building a just society. As the latter prospect seemed more elusive, in spite of greater affluence, the achievement of the former provided a basis for theological debate in refashioning the social critique of English Christianity. Throughout the twentieth century, English theology engaged with social issues with a degree of intellectual rigor not seen for centuries before.

Notes

1. D. MacKinnon, *Themes in Theology: The three fold card* (Edinburgh, 1987), p. 54.
2. Ibid., p. 55.
3. R. C. Moberly, *Christ Our Life* (London, 1902), p. 193.
4. J. Milbank, *Theology and Social Theory* (London, 1990); I. Markham, *Plurality and Christian Ethics* (Cambridge, 1994); M. Northcott in *Theology* (Jan.–Feb. 1993), p. 27.
5. A. Hastings, *A History of English Christianity* (London, 1987), p. 422.
6. L. Erlander, *Faith in the World of Work* (Uppsala, 1991).
7. H. Montefiore, *Christianity and Politics* (London, 1990); P. Baelz, *Ethics and Belief* (London, 1977); A. Dyson, *The Ethics of In Vitro Fertilization* (London, 1994); R. Gill, *Moral Communities* (Exeter, 1992).
8. H. Montefiore (ed.), *The Gospel and Contemporary Culture* (London, 1992).
9. See note 4.
10. D. Forrester, *Theology and Politics* (Oxford, 1988).
11. D. Jenkins, *God, Politics and the Future* (London, 1988).
12. M. Kane, *What Kind of God?* (London, 1986).
13. M. Grey, *Redeeming the Dream* (London, 1992); A. Loades, *Lost Coins* (London, 1992); A. Primavesi, *From Apocalypse to Genesis* (London, 1991).
14. P. Selby, *Belonging* (London, 1991) and *Liberating God* (London, 1983).
15. L. Newbigin, *Foolishness to the Greeks* (London, 1986).
16. *The British Idealists* (with A. Vincent) (London, 1985).
17. *Vision and Prophecy, In Search of a Common Purpose.*
18. *Christianity and the Market.*
19. Reprinted in *Religious Experience and other Essays and Addresses* (London, 1958).
20. Suggate, *William Temple*, p. 71, citing *Religious Experience*, pp. 243–55.
21. Ibid., p. 71.
22. *Christianity and Social Order*, p. 60.
23. Suggate, *William Temple*, p. 129, citing *Mens Creatrix* (London, 1917), pp. 195–8.
24. *Christianity and Social Order*, p. 69.
25. *Explorations*, p. 40.
26. *Confusions*, p. 141.
27. Ibid., p. 151.
28. Ibid., p. 152.
29. Ibid., p. 171.
30. *Future*, p. 193.
31. Ibid., p. 33.
32. *Church and Society*, p. 81.
33. *Future*, p. 127.
34. *Confessions*, p. 8.
35. Ibid., p. 9.
36. *Church and Nation*, p. 67.
37. Don Cupitt, *The Leap of Reason* (London, 1976); John Bowker, *The Religious Imagination and the Sense of God* (London, 1978); Peter Berger, *The Social Reality of Religion* (London, 1969).
38. *Making Sense*, p. 210.
39. Ibid., p. 219.
40. Ibid., p. 144.
41. Ibid., p. 147.
42. Ibid., p. 148.
43. Ibid., p. 163, citing S. W. Sykes, *The Identity of Christianity* (London, 1984), p. 285.
44. *Social God*, p. 29.
45. *Eye*, p. 129.
46. Ibid., p. 194.
47. *True God*, p. 24.
48. *Eye*, p. 89.
49. *Spirituality*, p. 135.
50. *Struggle in Babylon*, pp. 162–95.

Bibliography

Primary

Habgood, John, *A Working Faith* (London, 1980).

—— *Church and Nation in a Secular Age* (London, 1983).
—— *Confessions of a Conservative Liberal* (London, 1988).

—— *Making Sense* (London, 1993).

Leech, Ken, *Soul Friend* (London, 1977).

—— *True Prayer* (London, 1980).

—— *The Social God* (London, 1981).

—— *True God* (London, 1985).

—— *Spirituality and Pastoral Care* (London, 1986).

—— *Struggle in Babylon* (London, 1988).

—— *Care and Conflict* (London, 1990).

—— *The Gospel, the Catholic Church and the world: The social theology of Michael Ramsey* (London, 1990).

—— *The Anglo-Catholic Social Conscience: Two critical essays* (London, 1991).

—— *The Eye of the Storm* (London, 1992).

Preston, Ronald, *Religion and the Persistence of Capitalism* (London, 1979).

—— *Explorations in Theology* (London, 1981).

—— *Church and Society in the late Twentieth Century: The economic and political task* (London, 1983).

—— *The Future of Christian Ethics* (London, 1987).

—— *Religion and the Ambiguities of Capitalism* (London, 1991).

—— *Confusions in Christian Social Ethics: Problems for Geneva and Rome* (London, 1994).

Temple, William, *The Nature of Personality* (London, 1915).

—— *Nature, Man and God* (London, 1934).

—— *Thoughts in Wartime* (London, 1940).

—— *Citizen and Churchman* (London, 1941).

—— *Christianity and Social Order* (London, 1942).

Secondary

Atherton, J. (ed.), *Social Christianity* (London, 1994).

—— *Christianity and the Market* (London, 1992).

Ecclestone, G., *The Church of England and Politics* (London, 1981).

Fergusson, D. (ed.), *Christ, Church and Society: Essays on John Baillie and Donald Baillie* (Edinburgh, 1993).

Hastings, A., *A History of English Christianity 1920–1985* (London, 1987).

Kent, J., *William Temple* (Cambridge, 1992).

Logan, P. (ed.), *In Search of a Common Purpose* (London, 1990).

Markham, I., *Plurality and Christian Ethics* (Cambridge, 1994).

Morton, A. R. (ed.), *God's Will in a Time of Crisis: A Colloquium celebrating the 50th anniversary of the Baillie Commission* (Edinburgh, 1994).

Nicholls, D., *Deity and Domination: Images of God and the state in the nineteenth and twentieth centuries* (London, 1989).

Northcott, M. (ed.), *Vision and Prophecy: The tasks of social theology today* (Edinburgh, 1991).

Peart-Binns, J. S., *Living with Paradox: John Habgood, Archbishop of York* (London, 1987).

Suggate, A., *William Temple and Christian Social Ethics Today* (Edinburgh, 1987).

Theologies in North America

If measured by numbers of academic posts, students, and publications, and by the variety and vigor of the debates, the United States now shares continental Europe's leading role in modern theology. It is helped by its inheritance from many groups of immigrants, its accompanying inner diversity, its vast third-level educational network, and its global involvement, aided by cultural, economic, and political power – and the English language. It is also probable that more Christian theologians from other parts of the world who study or teach abroad do so in the United States than anywhere else. American theology is covered more widely in this volume than in the present section: It appears also in Evangelical and Orthodox Theologies (Part V), Transregional Movements (Part VI), Theology and Religious Diversity (Part VII), and Theology and the Arts and Sciences (Part VIII).

In this Part the five types of theology discussed are highly diverse. William Werpehowski describes a tradition of theological ethics that works within four parameters: the reality of God in full and complex relationship with the world; the narrative and historical particularity yet universal relevance of Christian ethics; a realism about social and political life that avoids both sentimental idealism and despairing cynicism; and a refusal of both cultural Christianity and utter isolationism. He portrays the origins of the tradition in its greatest representatives, Reinhold Niebuhr and H. Richard Niebuhr, its continuation with considerable variations in Paul Ramsey, James Gustafson, Stanley Hauerwas, and Beverly Wildung Harrison, the sharp debates it has sustained, and three leading items on its continuing agenda.

James Buckley brings Edward Farley, Gordon Kaufman, Schubert Ogden, David Tracy, and the movement of process theology into a fascinating debate with each other. Seeing how they cope with the questions of truth, God, persons, and Jesus Christ gives an illuminating way in to one of the liveliest intellectual arenas in contemporary theology, and one in which, as Buckley recounts, the participants are in communication with and about each other. Buckley also suggests a helpful rough criterion for distinguishing revisionists from liberals: Revisionists see Barth and kindred theologians making a permanent contribution to contemporary theology; liberals see the contribution as transient. Buckley both shows the differences between these theologies and also poses a set of basic questions to them.

Postliberal theology first emerged into public prominence in the 1980s, but it had deep roots in relationships of friendship and teaching at Yale over many years. It is now a well-established alternative to those discussed in the previous chapter. William Placher describes the influences that shaped it – Thomas Aquinas, Barth, H. Richard Niebuhr, ecumenical theology, and certain types of literary criticism, philosophy, sociology, and anthropology. It is concerned about the particularity and differences of religious texts, traditions, and communities, is suspicious of the search for philosophical foundations and for a systematic form of apologetics, and has especially focused on scriptural narratives. The two founding fathers, Hans Frei and George Lindbeck, are discussed, together with the ethicist Stanley Hauerwas (also treated in chapter 16) and Ronald Thiemann. Many younger theologians have been inspired by postliberal theology and there has been intensive debate about it; Placher gives an account of its dimensions and some of the issues it faces.

Black, Hispanic/Latino, and Native American theologies have arisen in engagement with the underside of American history: cultural genocide, enslavement, exploitation, and marginalization. Shawn Copeland describes the genesis of each. She traces Black theology through historical phases, stressing its continuing vitality with the emergence of womanist theology and black Catholic theology, and surveying its main thinkers. She then assesses its three main achievements and five key concerns for the future. Hispanic/Latino theology was rooted in the demand for civil rights and for respect in the Roman Catholic Church. Copeland pays special attention to the influence of Virgilio Elizondo and those indebted to him, and to the emergence of *mujerista* theology, before summing up its achievements and agenda. Finally she portrays the very different character of Native American theology, as it engages with a traumatic history, with the natural world, and with the continuing problem of responding to the impact of the modern American economy.

Of all the twentieth-century movements in theology perhaps none has had the pervasive influence of feminism. It has challenged the language and doctrines of Christianity and it has provoked changes at every level – in church structures, participation in ministry, ethics, the interpretation of history, spirituality, social, economic, and political involvement, and fundamental aspects of personal and family life. It is a diverse, worldwide movement, and Ann Loades treats it in that perspective in chapter 29. But its epicenter has been the United States, and Rebecca Chopp gives an account of it there. She offers various meanings of "feminist," describes the changes in the lives of women and the development of women's studies that helped feminist theology to arise, and discusses the diversity of its voices, its critical and reconstructive relation to Christianity, and the main principles of its transformative discourse. She focuses especially on Rosemary Ruether, Elisabeth Schüssler Fiorenza, and Delores S. Williams. Finally she inquires into what is desirable if feminist and womanist Christianity and its theology are to continue to be fruitful.

Theological Ethics

William Werpehowski

Introduction

Christian theological ethics is an intellectual discipline that gives an account of the experience of the reality of God, as decisively disclosed in Jesus Christ, for the purpose of critically describing and commending the kinds of character and conduct that would bear faithful witness to that reality. It is a discipline situated primarily in and for the Christian community. This orientation is not exclusive, however, given the universal reality to which this community answers and the corresponding responsibilities of its members. The "practical import" of theological ethics "is to aid the community and its members in discerning what God is enabling and requiring them to be and to do."[1]

In this essay I will introduce a major tradition of twentieth-century American Protestant theological ethics. Beginning with Reinhold and H. Richard Niebuhr's critical responses to the "social gospel" in the 1930s, the tradition continues in the work of Paul Ramsey, James Gustafson, Stanley Hauerwas, Beverly Harrison, and many others. The representatives I have explicitly identified and will discuss below have disagreed on a number of fronts, and some might even resist this association; nevertheless, their common concerns, training, and professional location remain significant. That they have done their work in critical conversation with one another is itself noteworthy, since a living tradition, as Alasdair MacIntyre has written, "is an historically extended, socially embodied argument, and an argument precisely about the goods which constitute that tradition."[2] The argument that was and is still being conducted concerns the concrete meaning of Christian responsibility to God in the church and in the world.

Survey

The writings of the Niebuhrs in the 1930s were to an important extent a reaction to the vision of the social gospel articulated most powerfully by Washington Gladden and Walter Rauschenbusch. Challenging the individualism of nineteenth-century Protestant social ethics for its inability to respond to the injustices of the Industrial Revolution, the social gospel writers offered the ethic of the historical Jesus as normative for personal and institutional life. That ethic advanced a doctrine of the Kingdom of God, which the social gospel took to be a kind of historical possibility that promised social unity and the overcoming of personal and structural injustice. Adhering to the law of love, valuing the power of education in bringing persons to the path of moral righteousness, and, above all, trusting in God who is at work in history accomplishing the divine purposes, Christians may hope for real and continuing social progress. For Rauschenbusch this progress meant restraining the forces of the capitalist market and moving toward the egalitarianism of social and political democracy.

Neither Reinhold Niebuhr nor his younger brother Richard simply rejected this vision. Both wanted to preserve its commitment to social justice; moreover, the "ethic of Jesus" and the notion of God's dynamic activity in history remain very prominent respectively in Reinhold's and Richard's theological ethics. But these legacies are remarkably revised in the light of some incisive criticisms. In distinct ways, each of the Niebuhrs thought that the social gospel was insufficiently attentive to the reality of God in the fullness of God's work. For Reinhold Niebuhr, the theology of the Kingdom of God was developed at too much of a remove from a careful understanding of the universality of sin in history and God's thoroughgoing judgment of human vice and pretension. Consequently, the call to education and the appeal to Jesus' love ethic could tend toward a naive and moralistic idealism in social ethics that offered little help in a world characterized by social conflict between self-interested groups. H. Richard Niebuhr questioned the social gospel's idea of the Kingdom of God as a moral ideal toward which we make an evolutionary progress. He pointed to the eschatological vision of Jesus, who does not engineer a direct route to some moral goal but who rather prepares for a gift through "repentance, faith, forgiveness, and innocence suffering for guilt" – through, that is, the anticipation of divine judgment and the trust in divine deliverance.[3] For both thinkers, there was great danger in the drift toward identifying some institutional or political scheme, such as "democracy," with the gospel ethic. One may lose thereby a theologically appropriate critical distance from the scheme, or even render the gospel a mere instrument in the realization and preservation of the social system itself.

There emerge from these sorts of challenges four concerns for Christian ethics that characterize the tradition I am describing. First, there is a concern that the content of theological ethics engage the whole reality of God, the unity and distinction of God's creative, judging, governing, and redemptive activities. Second, the method of theological ethics should reflect such content in a fundamental respect. The God in whom Christians believe is disclosed in a particular narrative, the biblical story of Israel and Jesus Christ; yet this very God is trusted as governing and sustaining all of creation with transcendent authority. Hence theological ethics must honor its distinctively storied character while also affirming its universal relevance and legitimacy. Attempting neither a narrow fideism nor a futile rationalism, Christian ethicists must both engage the integral witness and discourse of Christian faith and speak with broader "public" or "universal" purpose.

The other two concerns establish tests for the strategic adequacy of theological ethics as conceived above. So, third, an ethical account should avoid both the sentimental, irrelevant idealism that passes over the facts of human sin in history, and the despairing cynicism that gives up on the objectively binding character of moral norms in social life. Finally, an ethics of the Christian church is to resist both a strictly subordinate accommodation to this or that cultural ethos, and any categorical withdrawal from cultural life in the world. The church's particular historical situation may require a measured identification or a measured withdrawal from a cultural life of unbelief still governed by God; but in principle the church is to be neither strictly "worldly" nor "isolated."

These four considerations have an important place in the ethics of Ramsey, Gustafson, Hauerwas, and Harrison. They may quarrel about how specifically to respond to them, and they will offer alternative interpretations of their meaning; they all, however, operate within parameters set theologically by the entire reality of God, the storied universality of Christian ethics, realism about social and political life, and the refusal of both cultural Christianity and utter isolationism.

Reinhold Niebuhr (1892–1971)

Reinhold Niebuhr is widely regarded as being, after Martin Luther King, Jr., the most influential American theologian and preacher of the twentieth century. Born in Wright City, Missouri, he was raised in the German Evangelical Synod, which later became the Evangelical and Reformed Church. Following two years of study at Yale, his experiences as a pastor in Detroit from 1915 to 1928 brought him face to face with the harshness and disruption of urban industrial life and the seeming irrelevance of his "simple little moral homilies" to it.[4] He left Detroit for Union Theological Seminary in New York City, where he taught until he retired in 1960.

Niebuhr's mature theological ethics carried forward his response to the sentimental idealism of the social gospel through a sustained analysis of human nature and its predicament that owed much to the ideas of Pascal and Kierkegaard. Niebuhr described the human creature as being both finite and free. As finite he or she properly remains dependent upon nature, upon other persons, and above all upon God. As free, the human creature is capable of transcending his or her natural and interpersonal environment, so to evaluate and transform it. The coincidence of finitude and freedom is the condition for the possibility of history; but this also generates in creatures anxiety in the form of uncertainty and insecurity about their dependence and vulnerability. Aware of their freedom, they would be tempted to deny their limitation and dependence through acts of inordinate self-assertion, seeking to set themselves up as laws sufficient unto themselves. When persons sin, their "fall," therefore, is inevitable but not necessary.[5] Thus human history is broken with the activities of prideful persons who seek their own excessively. The basis of their self-elevation is an insecurity that stems from unbelief or the absence of trust in God.

Niebuhr affirms that the law or norm of human existence is the disinterested love of God and neighbor, for only in such love can self-transcendence complete itself. Individual persons retain a capacity for transcending their self-interest in loving regard for the welfare of others. The prospects for large-scale political and economic groups to do the same, however, are comparatively restricted. The causes and ideals of these groups readily become idols for their members, whose moral sensitivities are blunted by their appreciation of the power they hold from interests and resources held in common. They tend to cloak their claims with self-righteous rationales that contain "ideological taint," smugly shielding themselves and their ideals from criticism. Since inordinate self-assertion is magnified in the lives of groups making competing claims upon one another, coercion becomes an irremovable feature of human social life, necessary for preserving order and restraining egoism.

Niebuhr interprets the cross of Jesus Christ to symbolize the merciful love of God in relation to human sin. In perfectly self-giving and suffering love for the sake of others, Jesus refused to participate in the historical patterns of claim and counterclaim. Niebuhr held that the love of Jesus Christ was an "impossible possibility" that can never finally be vindicated in history. Its historical consequence is a life of self-sacrifice that ends tragically, since history is, again, constituted by patterns of competing, self-interested claims. The law of selfless love may correct and complete arrangements for a tolerable social life, but it also judges them all. The Kingdom of God is in an important sense equally distant from all political programs, because all of them involve elements of coercion and resistance which are foreign to a commonwealth of pure mutual love.

At the same time, there are real moral differences between different social and political programs to the extent that they embody, for example, the secure achievement of equality of conditions of life for human creatures. "Equality as a pinnacle of the ideal of justice implicitly points toward love as the final norm of justice; for equal justice is the approximation of brotherhood under the conditions of sin. A higher justice always means a more equal justice."[6] And given the capacities of human self-transcendence, one cannot set in advance any fixed limits on the quality or extent of the mutual fellowship realizable in history. Each new attainment is liable to corruption and criticism.

The quest for justice in the social order stands in tension with the demands for the preservation of order and the maintaining of freedom. Given the inevitable conjoining of justice and power, moreover, that quest must include the realistic conviction that the power of some must be checked by that of others. Niebuhr's argument for democratic dispersal and balance of political power relied on this last point. "Man's capacity for justice makes democracy possible; but man's inclination to injustice makes democracy necessary... If men are inclined to deal unjustly with their fellows, the possession of power aggravates this inclination. That is why irresponsible and uncontrolled power is the greatest source of injustice."[7] Even in this case Niebuhr warned against identifying our democratic ideals with the ultimate values of life.

Reinhold Niebuhr entertained the entire reality of God in his theological ethics by working from an account of human nature and human moral activity that presupposed and reflected the meanings of creation, judgment, and redemption. His method was famously dialectical and confidently "public"; in his most systematic work, *The Nature and Destiny of Man*, features of the Christian "myth" or vision of reality were tested for their adequacy by comparing them to other philosophical positions such as rationalism, romanticism, and naturalism.[8] The "Christian realist" attack on unchastened idealism was unrelenting, but almost as persistent was his attack on any ethic that would jettison moral values from the sphere of political life.

His thought included a prophetic basis for unceasing critique of extant social arrangements, and on that ground he sought to avoid the easy accommodation of Christian ethics to cultural norms. He made much of the necessity of taking on moral responsibilities in history, and chided those who, by his lights, evaded them in the vain and futile quest to maintain moral purity. His challenge to Christian pacifists followed this anti-perfectionist line, which he joined to his familiar charges of irrelevant idealism and the failure to take sin seriously. The pacifists

> merely assert that if only men loved one another, all the complex, and sometimes horrible realities of the political order could be dispensed with. They do not see that their "if" begs the most basic problem of human history. It is because men are sinners that justice can be achieved only by a certain degree of coercion on the one hand, and by resistance to coercion and tyranny on the other.[9]

H. Richard Niebuhr (1894–1962)

H. Richard Niebuhr once wrote that his older brother's projects had more to do with the reform of culture, while his own more nearly addressed the reformation of the church. From that point of departure H. Richard's influence on American Christian ethics was remarkable. During his 31 years of teaching and writing at Yale Divinity School, he developed a deep and multifaceted body of thought, and established himself as an educator of the highest order.

Niebuhr's theology hinged on a belief in the sovereign reality of God – God the slayer who judges and destroys all our idolatrous causes, and God the gracious giver of a new life that we may only receive in repentance and faith. Existence before God is always a matter of response to that prior "reality behind and in all realities," the Absolute One who acts in history.[10] On this matter the theology of Karl Barth appealed to him. Niebuhr also held, with Ernst Troeltsch, that the historically particular and relative shaping of human social life and thought render impossible the attempt to attain a truly "universal view" of reality; there may be only more or less objective "views of the universal." Thus Christians speak about God from the point of view of their particular tradition and faith stance, attending to the distinctive "story of our life" as lived before God in Christ in Christian community. "There is here . . . a metaphysical vision for the fullness of the divine initiative in relation to the created order, but its descriptive force is rendered solely by the given, specific 'life story' of any creature or traditional group."[11]

Niebuhr employed his basic conviction about the sovereignty of God in a critique of the partial and idolatrous faiths present in church and world. Understanding "faith" generally as a confident dependence on a center of value and loyalty to that center's "cause," he distinguished "radical monotheism" from two other faiths in conflict with it: "polytheism", which has many objects of devotion without any unifying center save the arbitrary personal freedom to negotiate between them, and "henotheism," which holds to a single social center of value, be it the "ingroup" of family, church, nation, class, etc. Niebuhr argued powerfully that radical faith in the one God dethrones the henotheisms of both nation and church. Ruled out are not only the nationalisms he saw operating on all sides during and after the Second World War, but also a Christianity that isolates and elevates one as a member of a special group with a special god and a separate existence.[12] Radical faith is "a permanent revolution of the mind and of the heart," a life of turning away from our narrower gods and self-defensive self-loves and toward the apprehension of all beings created of God "with reverence, for all are friends in the friendship of the one to whom we are reconciled in faith."[13]

A Christian with radically monotheistic faith lives "as one who seeks a truth that is true of universal relations and true for all subjects in the universe";[14] but again, he or she carries on only from within his or her particular historical standpoint in the tradition of the church and in allegiance to Jesus Christ. Christian theology must remain confessional. Niebuhr's cautions against "defensiveness" referred both to church-centered henotheisms that magnified the differences between Christians and others, and to forms of apologetics that claimed Christianity's adequacy or superiority on rational, cultural, or other general grounds. He reflected on the ways in which character and moral agency are specifically nurtured in Christian community, and about the fitting social contexts for faithful witness to God in Christ. He wrote of Jesus "as one who forms a new party for the reception of a new dispensation, for the seizure of new opportunities,"[15] and of the church as a distinctive "representative and pioneer" of a new universal humanity promised to all.[16] In a controversy with his brother published in the journal *The Christian Century*, he worried that Reinhold's attempt to relate Christian love, however indirectly, to the web of historical assertion and counterassertion remained a hopeless compromise with one or another cultural ideology. Instead he pleaded for a patient "tilling of the soil so that the Kingdom of God can grow" through a common life of repentance and forgiveness that was made real in and to the world.[17]

By the grace which makes possible these and other practices of reconciliation and radical faith, Jesus Christ may be the converter or transformer of human cultural life. Niebuhr developed this theme in what is perhaps his most important work in ethics, *Christ and Culture*. He presented the conversionist view in a way that highlighted its account of the whole reality of the one God. Human cultural achievements stand always under judgment, but always also under the sovereign rule of God the creator and redeemer. Creatureliness and fallenness are not the same, and all creation, in fact, may be seen to be created in the Word of God. The "Word that became flesh and dwelt among us . . . has entered into a human culture that has never been without his ordering action."[18] In the cultural life of humanity in which fallen human creatures pursue many goods and values held in common, the work of redemption may renew creation without obliterating it in the ever-present possibilities of God's historical action.

H. Richard Niebuhr "trod a delicate path between image- or story-shaped and universal ethics, and between universal and particular story-shaped theology . . . he refused to make a decision between a narrative and . . . a trans-narrative, universal understanding of God's acts in history."[19] The preferred image of human moral agency for this account was that of "responsibility." In general terms, moral action takes place in human interaction with and response to the forces acting upon us in the natural, historical, cultural, and interpersonal worlds. Responses are fitting or not according to the adequacy of our interpretation of "what is going on" in and with these impinging, limiting, and enabling events. Responding as we interpret the meaning of actions upon us, we also respond in anticipation of answers given to our answers within an ongoing community of fellow agents. From the particular stand-point of Christian faith, Jesus Christ empowers us to respond to God, the prior reality acting in and behind all realities, not as the law of our destruction, but as trustworthy, so that we may interpret all that occurs as contained within "a total activity that includes death within the domain of life, that destroys only to re-establish and renew."[20] And this empowerment is the permanent revolution of radi-cally monotheistic faith, in which we break out of the closed circles of self-preservation and defensiveness and relate ourselves to all things as they are of the transcendent God. "Responsibility affirms – God is acting in all actions upon you. So respond to all actions upon you as to respond to his action."[21]

We have seen how H. Richard Niebuhr attended to the first two concerns with his conversionism and the commitment to the "delicate path" between universal and particular story-shaped theology. His moral and political "realism" found expression in the recognition of sin's presence in history, humanity's widespread complicity in subjecting the innocent to great suffering, and the need for constant repentance and the transformation of life in faith. His views on the relation of church and world were historically sensitive and fluid. In the 1930s he argued for the church's withdrawal from its bondage to capitalism and nationalism; but he saw different problems in the 1960s, and at the start of that decade he looked for the church's reformation away from Christian henotheism and toward a new entrance into the world without conformity to it.[22] There was for him a historical rhythm of Christian identification and withdrawal which eschewed both "utilitarian Christianity" and so-called "sectarianism."

Paul Ramsey (1913–1988)

A Methodist who spent most of his career in the Department of Religion at Princeton University, Paul Ramsey studied with H. Richard Niebuhr and, for a brief time in the 1960s, had Reinhold Niebuhr as his university colleague. Both men left their mark on his thought, which covered a wide range of issues in theological, sexual, medical, and political ethics.

Ramsey's Christian ethics is an account of the Christian moral life grounded in the norm to love the neighbor. Christian love or agape defines what is right for the Christian, and what defines that norm is the biblically depicted pattern of God's love for humanity, disclosed in the history of Israel and Jesus Christ. In that history God keeps faith with those with whom a divine covenant has been established. God reaches out in concern for the alien, cares for the vulnerable, loves sinners, and attends to human needs apart from considerations of comparative merit or social status. In short, the pattern of divine love displays fidelity to the well-being of human creatures, cherished for their own sake. Christians are bound to be faithful to the neighbor along the same lines and by this measure, by having their activities correspond and witness to the redeeming divine performance that preeminently identifies God. Moral duties to oneself, while essential to the Christian life, are secondary, being derived from and ordered to the requirement to love the neighbor, who is everyone bearing the human countenance decisively borne by Jesus Christ.[23]

Ramsey participated energetically in public discussions of moral controversies. He attempted to shape the political ethics of his day through a reconstruction and refinement of the Christian theory of a "just war." Applying it to problems such as the Vietnam War, he argued, following Augustine, that loving regard for innocent parties suffering unjust attack warrants a preference for the vulnerable victims. Protecting and defending them by means of violent force to repel injustice was morally justified. At the same time, the love that justified war also limited it because in its name "enemy" noncombatants were always immune from being directly attacked. According to this "principle of discrimination," no constellation of favorable consequences could ever morally justify violation of the neighbor who bears no direct relation to the injustice to be repelled. Ramsey was also a leader in developing moral responses to medical dilemmas concerning human experimentation, genetic intervention, reproductive technology, and care for the sick and dying. He emphasized the importance of protecting persons from violations of their well-being pursued for reasons of greater social utility or lesser "quality of life." The neighbor's worth in the eyes of God is not so ordered. Ramsey argued, for example, that sick, retarded persons should be treated or not treated according to their medical needs and prospects, not according to their limited intellectual capacity; that medical experiments move forward only after subjects have given their free and informed consent; and that children never be allowed to participate in medical experiments of a nontherapeutic nature.[24]

Speaking out in these ways to the secular world, Ramsey believed that Christian discernments could properly be presented as "public ethics"; particular Christian moral insight may resonate with and be relevant to the moral aspirations and ideals of culture. For him the entire world of creation belongs to God and is illumined by the Incarnation of the Word. Structures of "natural law" or "natural justice" in human communities, forged and seemingly sustained at some distance from explicitly Christian deliverances, may yet serve the neighbor well and deserve Christian assent. The same structures, however, are liable to ceaseless challenge and transformation in the direction of agape (cf. Reinhold Niebuhr). Ramsey never tired of reminding his readers of this theme of "love transforming natural justice," and he credited H. Richard Niebuhr for helping him with it.[25] His public ethics called for the protection of persons he took to be especially liable to exploitation and abuse in the name of this or that social cause or for the benefit of this or that preferred person or group. He acknowledged the intractable character of human sinfulness and the dangerous implications of sentimentally expecting too much from the good will and moral ideals of fallen human creatures. It is not surprising or inaccurate to characterize him as a sort of "Christian realist" after the fashion of Reinhold Niebuhr, bent on seeking a more tolerable common life in society and the world through checking with just power the abusive impulses of the prideful human spirit.

James M. Gustafson

The Reformed theologian James Gustafson was also a student of Richard Niebuhr, and with Ramsey he established himself as a leading figure in Protestant ethics from the 1960s onward. He wrote that his major work, *Ethics From a Theocentric Perspective*, was the product of at least 30 years of "homework," which included significant, field-shaping studies in christology, ecumenical ethics, and the moral dimensions of life in the church.

For present purposes, theocentric ethics may be summarized under four points. First, Gustafson thinks that too often theology places God in the service of human beings, rather than doing the reverse. The attack on "anthropocentrism" most clearly marks his thought. To presume that the good of humanity is of paramount concern to God hints at a merely instrumental religious faith, and fails to confront the proper glory of God. Theocentric piety must realize this truth in its readiness to "consent" to the power and powers that sustain and bear down upon us, for our good or ill. From this starting point, and in line with the doctrine of creation, Gustafson relies "more heavily on scientific and other sources of our knowledge of the world . . . than traditional Christian ethics has."[26] This reliance can be tied rather closely to the critique of anthropocentrism, as when scientific investigation raises questions about the possibly instrumental and self-serving character of beliefs in resurrection and personal salvation.

Second, theocentric ethics cannot be understood apart from piety, taken here to be a traditioned religious expression of certain universally perceived human experiences of the world. The condition of faithful consent to God's governance goes along with various human affections, the "senses" of dependence, gratitude, obligation, remorse and repentance, possibility, and directedness. Within the Christian tradition Jesus decisively incarnates such piety. "The only good reason for claiming to be Christian is that we continue to be empowered, sustained, renewed, informed, and judged by Jesus' incarnation of theocentric piety and fidelity." The gospel narratives show what human life "can and ought to be – a life of courage and love grounded in an object of piety and fidelity that transcends the immediate objects of experience."[27]

Third, "since ethics has to do with the interdependence of all things in relation to God," the moral life is founded on God's ordering of the "patterns of interdependence and development within which human activity and life occur."[28] The ways of nature may indicate something of the ways of God's ordering, which is to be interpreted broadly in terms of the proper relations between entities and the "wholes" in which they participate. The good for human persons may be grasped through their relations with one another in families and other units defined socially, economically, politically, nationally, internationally, biologically, and ecologically. There is in piety "a proper incentive to expand the arenas of relationships and interdependencies within which particular entities are explained and understood."[29] "Sin" according to Gustafson is, in fact, a contraction of our commitments, desires, and understandings of the world. The correction of this "human fault" before God lies in an enlargement of the soul and its interests, "and by a more appropriate alignment of ourselves and all things in relation to each other and to the ultimate power and orderer of life."[30] An implication is that persons may direct real concern toward the common good, as variously defined, and be ready for self-denial for that good when warranted by the divine ordering. It is hard not to recall H. Richard Niebuhr's radical monotheism in this connection.

Niebuhr's image of responsibility seems to be linked with the fourth point. For Gustafson, human moral agency is a matter of construing God's relations to the world, and to people as beings who always already interact with but also participate in it in many ways. Neither spectators nor owners nor the lords of creation, human beings are temporary yet responsible stewards of the patterns and processes of interdependence in which they too participate. The basic moral question is "what is God enabling and requiring us, as such participants, to be and to do?" The answer is that "we are to relate ourselves and all things in a manner appropriate to our and their relations to God."[31] Particular moral judgments are made by a keen discrimination or discernment of the necessary conditions for life to be sustained and developed.[32]

James Gustafson has urged his more Christocentric colleagues like Paul Ramsey and Stanley Hauerwas to take nature and the doctrine of creation more seriously, and to that extent the whole reality of God. A Christian ethicist oriented to the life of the academy (currently Emory University), he is careful to consider sources of insight found within the Christian community and in disciplinary inquiries outside of it. His ethics are sensitive to tragic conflicts of value in moral decision-making, and he refuses to paper these over in his accounts of piety and ethical method. A sharp critic of what he once called "the sectarian temptation," he is equally resistant to anthropocentric instrumentalism.

Stanley Hauerwas

Stanley Hauerwas is a Methodist trained in ethics at Yale who sees at least the second fact to be a mixed blessing. Steeped in the tradition of the Niebuhrs, he has been sharply critical of it, allying himself with the thought of the Mennonite theologian John Howard Yoder. He sees Yoder as presenting an alternative to rather than a continuation of that tradition. The author of this essay, however, persists in linking Hauerwas with the other thinkers treated in it, precisely because his criticisms of them appear to be more internal than external to their thought.

The first responsibility of the church, Hauerwas has written, is to be itself.[33] He observes that the dominant moral ethos in contemporary American society is liberalism, which holds that the best or only moral community we can have is based on guaranteeing the freedom of each individual citizen to do as he or she pleases, so long as he or she does not thereby violate the legitimate equal freedom of others. Liberalism celebrates toleration, pluralism, and respect for personal autonomy. The church, however, is devoted to a particular God and a particular way of life that follows Jesus Christ. Its members know themselves not in the first instance as autonomous individuals but as bound to God, to their tradition, and to one another. They know themselves as they are known by the merciful and faithful God, and hence they live in trust, patience, hope, gratitude, hospitality, and forgiveness, seeking not to control history but to witness to God's rule within it as established by Jesus Christ. At least they should know themselves this way. The problem has been that "in our attempt to control our society Christians in America have too readily accepted liberalism as a social strategy appropriate to the Christian story."[34] In doing that, Christians have gone some way in losing the moral skills or virtues that enable a proper description of reality as the Christian narrative of Israel and Jesus presents it. Their moral experience becomes impoverished when what they see is filtered through the dominant value of individual freedom. For example, they might be tempted to view the family as a contractual society rather than as a community in which members learn what it means to live historically in fidelity and responsibility to persons we do not choose to be with. Thus the church needs to recover its distinctiveness and stand as a contrast to liberal society.

Note that Hauerwas prefers to portray the Christian moral life in terms of the virtues that enable Christians to describe and live it truthfully. The pre-eminent virtue is peaceableness. Reading the Gospel narratives in a way that highlights Jesus' political act of refusing recourse to violence, Hauerwas believes that pacifism is the normative mode of witness to God's reign in history. Appeals in the name of love to "just war" need to respond to this biblical reading as well as to pay more attention to the social location of just war discourse. A discerning political realism suggests that such discourse will simply be coopted by nations to rationalize their killing exploits. The issue of social location, and hence of the relationships and virtues that give intelligibility to the moral life, also plays a role in medical ethics. For Hauerwas the practice of medicine is about the faithful refusal to abandon those who are in pain, and health care professionals "are the bridge between the world of the ill and the healthy."[35] In liberal America persons are tempted to adopt strategies that isolate the suffering and insulate the caretaker either in the name of freedom (call this "respecting patient autonomy") or in the name of the power of caretakers (call this "medical paternalism"). In this social context medicine needs the church to offer examples of fidelity and hospitality. "Because of God's faithfulness we are supposed to be a people who have learned how to be faithful to one another by our willingness to be present, with all our vulnerabilities, to one another. For what does our God require of us other than our unfailing presence in the midst of the world's sin and pain?"[36]

Hauerwas's medical ethics presuppose the creaturely goodness of human practices such as healing. He is suspicious, however, of theologies of creation that are separated from the redemptive work of Christ as embodied in the practices of the church, since these typically accommodate the gospel to some cultural or political ideology. He has repeatedly denied that he is a fideist whose ethical method ignores points of contact between the Christian story and more general ethical approaches, just as he has rejected interpretations of his work that have him calling for Christian withdrawal from the world. In both cases his approach is to focus on the significance of Christian practices such as peace-making, baptism, and eucharist. He trusts that the virtues realized in these practices will offer a witness to God that addresses the world with a universal thrust more concrete and effective than any mediating argument, and that displays in contrast the destructive consequences of unbelief in its various expressions. By the same token, he opposes (Reinhold-) Niebuhrian critiques of the irrelevance and irresponsibility of pacifism, since for him pacifists remain free to witness to the state in ways that urge less violence in a world where violence must be employed against itself to protect the innocent. God's providential rule in the "old aeon" of unbelief authorizes this use of the sword, but subordinates it to the evangelical work of nonviolent Christian discipleship.[37]

Beverly Wildung Harrison

An ethicist in the Reformed tradition who teaches at Union Theological Seminary, Beverly Harrison wrote her doctoral dissertation on H. Richard Niebuhr and has been influenced by his discussions of responsibility, human relatedness, and social process. Centrally concerned with feminist ethics and liberation theology, her project is to present a theological critique of the forms of human domination in the light of women's experience.

Harrison sees Jesus as a normative exemplar of radical love, "not in his lust for sacrifice but in his power of mutuality . . . His death was the price he paid for refusing to abandon the radical activity of love – of expressing solidarity and reciprocity with the excluded ones in the community." Christians have "to reach out, to deepen relationship, or to right wrong relations – those that deny, distort, or prevent human dignity from arising – as we recall each other into the power of personhood."[38] Simple self-sacrifice or self-renunciation, historically so destructive of women's flourishing, is rejected as such. She is a sort of "conversionist" in seeing the work of Christian love to be aimed at justice defined as "right relation" in human community. In the fully just community "power would be experienced as reciprocity in relation. In other words, our individual power to act would be nourished and enhanced by mutual regard and cocreativity."[39]

The Christian community obviously fails in achieving justice in its own case, and in response to sexist and misogynist Christian practice Harrison proposes three areas of special concern for feminist theological ethics. First, the language and images describing human relationship with God must be reconceived. God envisioned exclusively as Father, Lord, or King effectively renders women "totally invisible, empty of any connection to God." Second, feminists must overturn a gender-based opposition within Christian tradition between "male" mind or spirit and "female" body which values the former and devalues the latter. Harrison urges women to recover an embodied rationality in which human passion prominently figures as a source of insight and empowerment. Third, the church must jettison another traditional opposition between nature and history, for in these terms men are conceived as historical agents over against a nature that is to serve their needs. Nature-identified women follow suit. Feminist theory defends the truth that all human creatures are "as natural, historical, and cultural creatures . . . profoundly dependent on each other and the rest of the natural/historical/cultural order."[40]

Harrison's political "realism" encompasses her use of Marxian social analysis within a North American context. Her active opposition to sexism and misogyny is the point of departure for responding to realities of human oppression as affected by race, class, and sexual identity. Christian praxis, a total complex of action and reflection in concrete solidarity with the disinherited, affords intimations of a transformed understanding of the relation between human life and divine transcendence. The experience of transcendence "arises in the ecstatic power emergent between those who have connected with each other, intimately engaged with God, in emancipatory praxis. Passion for justice, shared and embodied, is the form God takes among us in our time."[41]

Debate

Critical exchange between these parties may be viewed in a variety of ways. Some recent debates have their origin in disagreements between the Niebuhrs. For example, Reinhold believed that H. Richard's theology, with its stress on repentance and the patient building of communities trained to discern and respond to what God is doing in the world, carried with it the danger of social irresponsibility. H. Richard, in turn, thought that his brother had subordinated Christianity's eschatological vision to the requirements of moral agency for justice in the world, and that this made for a self-defeating compromise of the Christian gospel.[42] One can read Hauerwas's pacifist responses to Reinhold Niebuhr and Paul Ramsey in this light, since Hauerwas stresses how the Christian biblical narrative enables a vision of moral reality and a common life of discipleship that may well be at odds with the call to be "realistic" on the world's terms about the need to seek social justice through methods of coercion and violence. A truthful realism, he might say, is contained in understanding the grip that violence has on all of our lives, and in living as a people that can advance that understanding and present an alternative mode of existence.

Other debates almost seem to be present *within* the thought of H. Richard Niebuhr. Note that Gustafson's revision of radical monotheism is usually seen as opposed to Hauerwas's ethic of the particular, story-shaped character of Christian ethics. Gustafson tends to see Hauerwas as a sort of Christian henotheist and "sectarian," and Hauerwas questions whether Gustafson has succumbed to a universalism that dilutes the integrity of Christian witness by an accommodation to the terms of natural science. Richard Niebuhr, as we have seen, tried to walk "a delicate path" between approaches of these sorts.

The thought of our more contemporary figures may be illumined when we discover how it emerges in each case over against influential predecessors. Here debates rage *between* ethicists *across* generations. Paul Ramsey developed an ethic of unconditional regard for neighbor-need that was a critical response to Reinhold Niebuhr's "impossible possibility" of utterly selfless love, and his focus on the exceptionless principle of discrimination in "just war" theory corrected some consequentialist tendencies in Niebuhr's thought. Harrison's love ethic also distances itself from Reinhold Niebuhr's focus on self-sacrifice. Hauerwas, with Yoder's help, has sought to develop a pacifism that answers Reinhold Niebuhr's criticisms, and he attempts to distinguish sharply his social ethics from H. Richard Niebuhr's (and Ramsey's) conversionism. While it would be too strong to say that Gustafson deems Reinhold Niebuhr's thought anthropocentric, it is clear that he does not want to do theology in the service of ethics in the way Niebuhr did.[43] Harrison takes on Reinhold Niebuhr's critique of Marxist analysis and points out weaknesses in H. Richard Niebuhr's ethics that led him away from fully seizing the gospel's emancipatory potential.[44]

The contemporary debates are legion. In the environment of liberalism, is Ramsey's "public ethics" a legitimate possibility? Does it inevitably compromise theological particularity by forcing an accommodation to the ethos of individualistic freedom, as Hauerwas thinks? Ramsey asked Hauerwas if a responsible Christian pacifism could be defended. What, after all, does "responsible" mean? In our efforts to account for the whole reality of God, how do we interpret the divine activities of creation, preservation, and redemption, and how are these activities ordered in theological ethics? Gustafson asks if Hauerwas's understanding of the locus of redemption in the church tends toward henotheism. Ramsey and Hauerwas ask if Gustafson's appeal to science in his doctrine of creation overwhelms his theology, such that Christian faithfulness becomes merely a matter of reverent and sometimes tragic "consent" to natural world process? Gustafson (and, in a different way, Hauerwas) might wonder if Harrison's identification of the passion for justice and divine transcendence bears a trace of theological functionalism. Harrison strongly challenges the other three, in different ways, to face up to the realities of human oppression, to the complicity of the church in these realities (especially in its treatment of women), and to the need for more telling methods of social analysis and critique.

Agenda

The agenda of theological ethics as grasped through the work of these figures includes at least the following questions.

1 What is the relation between the "church" and the "world"? How does the general answer apply to the specific relation between a distinctive Christian community and American "liberalism," and between the church, as it aspires to a life of nonviolent discipleship, and the violent character of the nation-state? What is the proper description of the bearing of Christian ethics on broader "public" discussions of moral and political matters?

2 How should Christian ethical reflection attend to the interpretations and understandings of nature, history, and culture that are received from nontheological disciplines of inquiry? What specific links should be forged between the Christian moral life and inquiries in natural science, and between the former and critical theories exposing sources of oppression for the poor, African Americans, women, and so forth?

3 How should we gauge the "emancipatory potential" of traditional Christian belief? What is to be made of revisionist proposals regarding talk about God, or about divine transcendence and other theological themes that are argued to legitimate and mask real understanding of an unjust status quo?

These questions will be best pursued in a spirit of vigorous self-criticism, and with keen awareness of the dangers of defensiveness and one-sidedness. With regard to that spirit and that awareness, the Niebuhrs remain worthy exemplars.

Notes

1 James M. Gustafson, *Can Ethics Be Christian?* (Chicago and London, 1975), p. 179.
2 Alasdair MacIntyre, *After Virtue* (Notre Dame, IN, 1984), p. 84.
3 H. Richard Niebuhr, "The social gospel and the mind of Jesus," *Journal of Religious Ethics*, 16 (1933), pp. 115–27 at p. 123.
4 See Larry Rasmussen (ed.), *Reinhold Niebuhr: Theologian of public life* (Minneapolis, 1991), pp. 7–8.
5 Reinhold Niebuhr, *The Nature and Destiny of Man* (New York, 1941), vol. I, p. 251.
6 Ibid., vol. II, p. 254.
7 Reinhold Niebuhr, *The Children of Light and the Children of Darkness* (New York, 1944), pp. xiii–xiv.
8 Robin W. Lovin, *Reinhold Niebuhr and Christian Realism* (Cambridge, 1995), pp. 30–2.
9 In Larry Rasmussen (ed.), *Reinhold Niebuhr*, pp. 243–4.
10 H. Richard Niebuhr, *The Kingdom of God in America* (New York, 1937), p. 88.
11 Hans W. Frei, *Theology and Narrative*, ed. George Hunsinger and William C. Placher (New York and Oxford, 1994), p. 219.
12 H. Richard Niebuhr, *Radical Monotheism and Western Culture* (New York, 1960), p. 60.
13 Ibid., p. 126.
14 Ibid., p. 88.
15 H. Richard Niebuhr, "The social gospel," p. 125.
16 H. Richard Niebuhr, "The responsibility of the church for society," in K. S. Latourette (ed.), *The Gospel, the Church, and the World* (New York, 1946), pp. 126–33.
17 H. Richard Niebuhr, "A communication: the only way into the Kingdom of God," in Richard B. Miller (ed.), *War in the Twentieth Century* (Louisville, KY, 1932), pp. 19–21 at p. 21.
18 H. Richard Niebuhr, *Christ and Culture* (New York, 1951), pp. 192–5.
19 Hans W. Frei, *Theology and Narrative*, p. 229.
20 H. Richard Niebuhr, *The Responsible Self* (New York, 1963), pp. 141–2.
21 Ibid., p. 25.
22 H. Richard Niebuhr, "Reformation: continuing imperative," *Christian Century*, 77 (1960), pp. 248–51 at p. 249.
23 Paul Ramsey, *Basic Christian Ethics* (New York, 1950), pp. 1–23.
24 *The Essential Paul Ramsey*, ed. William Werpehowski and Stephen D. Crocco (New Haven and London, 1994), pp. 60–83, 168–253.
25 Paul Ramsey, *Nine Modern Moralists* (Englewood Cliffs, NJ, 1962), pp. 13, 18.
26 James M. Gustafson, *Ethics from a Theocentric Perspective*. Volume II. *Ethics and Theology* (Chicago, 1984), p. 144.
27 James M. Gustafson, *Ethics from a Theocentric Perspective*. Volume I. *Theology and Ethics* (Chicago, 1981), pp. 276–7.
28 Ibid., vol. II, p. 7.
29 Ibid., p. 15.
30 Ibid., vol. I, p. 307.
31 Ibid., vol. II, p. 146.
32 Ibid., vol. I, pp. 339–40.
33 Stanley Hauerwas, *A Community of Character* (Notre Dame, IN, 1981), p. 10.
34 Ibid., p. 11.
35 Stanley Hauerwas, *Suffering Presence* (Notre Dame, IN, 1986), p. 78.
36 Ibid., p. 80.
37 Stanley Hauerwas, "Epilogue," in Paul Ramsey, *Speak Up for Just War or Pacifism* (University Park, PA, and London, 1988), pp. 167–81.
38 Beverly Wildung Harrison, *Making the Connections* (Boston, 1985), pp. 18–19.
39 Beverly Wildung Harrison, *Our Right to Choose* (Boston, 1983), p. 99.
40 Harrison, *Making the Connections*, p. 229.
41 Ibid., p. 263.
42 Reinhold Niebuhr, "Must we do nothing?" in Richard B. Miller (ed.), *War in the Twentieth Century* (Louisville, KY, 1932); H. Richard Niebuhr, "A communication: the only way into the Kingdom of God" and "The grace of doing nothing," in Miller (ed.), *War in the Twentieth Century*, pp. 19–21, 6–11.
43 Robin W. Lovin, *Reinhold Niebuhr*, p. 34.
44 Harrison, *Making the Connections*, pp. 54–80.

Bibliography

Primary

Gustafson, James M., *Christ and the Moral Life* (New York, 1968).
—— *Can Ethics Be Christian?* (Chicago, 1975).
—— *Ethics from a Theocentric Perspective*, Volume I. *Theology and Ethics* (Chicago, 1981).
—— *Ethics from a Theocentric Perspective*, Volume II. *Ethics and Theology* (Chicago, 1984).
—— "The sectarian temptation: reflections on theology, the church and the university," *Proceedings of the Catholic Theological Society*, 40 (1985), pp. 83–94.
Harrison, Beverly Wildung, *Our Right to Choose* (Boston, 1983).
—— *Making the Connections* (Boston, 1985).
Hauerwas, Stanley, *A Community of Character* (Notre Dame, IN, 1981).
—— *The Peaceable Kingdom* (Notre Dame, IN, 1983).
—— *Against the Nations* (Minneapolis, MN, 1985).
—— *Dispatches from the Front* (Durham, NC, 1994).
Niebuhr, H. Richard, *The Meaning of Revelation* (New York, 1941).
—— *Christ and Culture* (New York, 1951).
—— *Radical Monotheism and Western Culture* (New York, 1960).
—— *The Responsible Self* (New York, 1963).
Niebuhr, Reinhold, *Moral Man and Immoral Society* (New York, 1932).
—— *An Interpretation of Christian Ethics* (New York, 1935).
—— *The Nature and Destiny of Man*, 2 vols (New York, 1941–3).

Ramsey, Paul, *Basic Christian Ethics* (New York, 1950).
—— *War and the Christian Conscience* (Durham, NC, 1961).
—— *Nine Modern Moralists* (Englewood Cliffs, NJ, 1962).
—— *The Patient as Person* (New Haven and London, 1970).
—— *The Essential Paul Ramsey*, William Werpehowski and Stephen D. Crocco, eds (New Haven and London, 1994).
Rauschenbusch, Walter, *A Theology for the Social Gospel* (New York, 1945).

Secondary

Beckley, Harlan A. and Sweezy, Charles M. (eds), *James Gustafson's Theocentric Ethics: Interpretations and assessments* (Macon, GA, 1988).
Diefenthaler, Jon, *H. Richard Niebuhr: A lifetime of reflections on the church and the world* (Macon, GA, 1986).
Fox, Richard, *Reinhold Niebuhr: A biography* (New York, 1985).
Journal of Feminist Studies in Religion, 9 (Spring/Fall 1993). (Special issue in honor of Beverly Wildung Harrison.)
Journal of Religious Ethics, 19 (Fall 1991). (Special issue on the ethics of Paul Ramsey.)
Lovin, Robin W., *Reinhold Niebuhr and Christian Realism* (Cambridge, 1995).
Nelson, Paul, *Narrative and Morality: A theological inquiry* (University Park, PA, and London, 1987).
Ramsey, Paul (ed.), *Faith and Ethics: The theology of H. Richard Niebuhr* (New York, 1957).

Revisionists and Liberals

James J. Buckley

Introduction, History, and Influences

Revisionists and Liberals are a tradition (or so I shall stipulate) of theologians devoted to shaping Christian practices and teachings in dialogue with (revisionists) or on the basis of (liberals) modern philosophies, cultures, and social practices. However, almost all Christian theologians aim to "revise" their Christian heritage in some respects or "liberate it" from its foibles and sin; from this point of view, the labels "revisionist" and "liberals" do not help us carefully discriminate among modern Christian theologians. There is an important lesson here. "Any philosophy [or theology] that can be put in a nutshell," it has been said, "deserves to be there."[1] The labels "revisionist" and "liberal" (like all theological labels) are useful only for some sharply circumscribed purposes.

This essay will concentrate less on the genealogy of the labels "revisionist" or "liberal" than on the stands four representative theologians (Edward Farley [1929–], Gordon Kaufman [1925–], Schubert Ogden [1928–], and David Tracy [1939–]) and one representative movement (process theology) take on four particular issues (truth, God, persons, and Jesus Christ). But readers should know that many figures and movements discussed elsewhere in this volume could also be taken as revisionist or liberal – Bultmann, Tillich, Rahner, Schillebeeckx, as well as many of the newer challenges in theology. Further, the nexus of influences on the theologians selected is quite different and will constantly jeopardize efforts to embrace them under a single label or as a single tradition. They are "Christian," but in very diverse ways: Farley is a Presbyterian at Vanderbilt Divinity School, Kaufman a Mennonite at Harvard Divinity School, Ogden is a Methodist emeritus professor at Southern Methodist University, and Tracy a Roman Catholic at the University of Chicago Divinity School. Process theology, originally centered at the University of Chicago Divinity School and now also at Claremont Graduate School in California, also has representatives from these and other churches and communities. All are committed to liberating Christian tradition or mediating Christian practices and teachings to modern culture, but they focus on different features of modernity. All are committed to critical revisions of this Christian fact and this modern culture, but each locates the key items up for revision in different ways. The following effort to sketch these revisionary and liberal proposals is made even more complicated by the fact that these individual theologians and movements will publish still other works over the next decades. All this suggests just a few of the limits of this effort to sift their proposals. As we work our way through some representative revisionist and liberal theologies, the central aim will be to clarify their theologies, the better to understand their internal debates as well as their external critics.

One crucial issue raised by revisionist and liberal theologies is the character of the story that needs to be told to suggest the need for revisions of the Christian tradition in modernity. On one version, challenged by the rise of modern philosophies and sciences and histories, Christian theologians were pressed to give a new account of the hope that was in them. From one side, orthodox fundamentalists and pietists perceived modernity as a massive threat; from the other side, Christians variously called liberal or modernist endeavored to show that Christian teachings and/or practices were the fulfillment of autonomous humanity. "Mediating theologians" positioned themselves on the boundary of such extremes, arguing Christian faith and modernity can and should live together in peace. Thus, for example, while a "liberal" like G. W. F. Hegel could argue that a faith focused on Jesus Christ could be shown to be "a demonstrable part" of modern science, a "revisionary" mediator like Friedrich Schleiermacher could suggest that the latter "does not contradict" the former.[2] In contrast to these early nineteenth-century European examples, "the Golden Age of liberal theology" in the United States was in the late nineteenth and early twentieth centuries.[3]

However, arguments among liberals and mediators were often overshadowed around the turn of the century by a sort of second stage in modern theology. In the face of cultures largely post-theistic, several novel (neo-)reaffirmations of classic Christianity ("orthodoxy") were recovered or constructed (e.g., Karl Barth, neo-Thomism). In fact, one rough way to distinguish revisionist and liberal narratives of modernity is whether they take this second, "neo-orthodox" stage as making a permanent (revisionist) or transient (liberal) contribution to contemporary theology. Today's revisionaries aim to resolve problems left by the second stage precisely by creating a third stage which sublates the first two. On this reading, neo-Marxists, existential phenomenologists, liberation theologians, and others in the 1970s and 1980s "resume the immanentist, humanist trend of nineteenth century theology, after its interruption by the Barthian period in Protestantism and the Thomist revival in Catholicism."[4] I will not dwell on the early writings of Farley (1960, 1966), Kaufman (1960, 1961), Ogden (1962), and Tracy (1970),[5] but it is important to note that they include a critique of the internal inconsistency of some phase of neo-orthodoxy; in the fourth section below we shall see Barth and Thomas, this time as allies, return at the end of the twentieth century.

Survey

We might characterize the Golden Age of liberal theology in the United States as the age of "naturalism," a broad academic and cultural movement to overcome peculiarly modern bifurcations between nature and spirit, materialism and idealism on modernity's own terms.[6] While it is deceptive to isolate any single academic figure of this era, one of the most important was the British mathematician and philosopher, Alfred North Whitehead (1861–1947). And one way to find a grip on Whitehead's thought is to consider his proposal that "the true method of discovery" is like the flight of an airplane: it begins from the ground of experience, takes off into "the thin air of imaginative generalization," and "again lands for renewed observation rendered acute by rational observation."[7] The theological runway whence the plane takes off is a story indicating the need for a "new reformation" of a theological tradition. A revolution began with Plato (particularly his notion of the divine as persuasive rather than coercive) and early Christianity (particularly the humble power of "the bare manger" and later interpretations of this as the "mutual immanence" of God and world to each other). But this revolution (Whitehead said) failed in its medieval, Protestant, or Catholic forms. God remained too much like an Egyptian or Mesopotamian king, "internally complete."[8] What is the alternative?

Whitehead's personal sympathies were Unitarian.[9] The highest flight of his airplane into the airs of imaginative generalization was his construction of a "categoreal scheme." In this scheme, "God is not to be treated as an exception to all metaphysical principles, invoked to save their collapse. He is their chief exemplification." For example, "analogously to all actual entities, the nature of God is dipolar. He has a primordial nature and a consequent nature." If God is analogous to other actual entities, God must be both similar to and different from them. "Actual entities" (Whitehead stipulates) are the entities that constitute the actual world; "the actual world is a process, and that process is the becoming of actual entities." Further, actual entities have "physical and mental poles." Crudely put, their "physical" pole is how they relate to ("prehend") other actual entities, while their "conceptual" pole is how they relate to that which is not (or not yet) actual (i.e., "eternal objects").[10]

God too is an actual entity, related to other actual entities and eternal objects. Thus God too has a physical and conceptual pole. God's relationship to other actual entities is internal rather than external to God's identity. "It is as true to say that God transcends the world, as that the world transcends God. It is as true to say that God creates the World, as that the World creates God. God and the World are the contrasted opposites in terms of which Creativity achieves its supreme task." And yet it is also important that there are differences between God and other actual entities. Most important, God's conceptual pole (unlike that of other actual entities) is "primordial" (e.g., is prior to God's "physical" pole). "The given course of history presupposes [God's] primordial nature, but his primordial nature does not presuppose it." God's "primordial nature" is conceptual, while God's "consequent nature is the weaving of God's physical feelings upon his primordial concepts."

When Whitehead lands this airplane of imaginative generalization on the ground, the result is the "mutual immanence" of God and the world his "new reformation" sought. "By reason of this reciprocal relation, the love of the world passes into the love in heaven, and floods back again into the world. In this sense, God is the great companion – the fellow-sufferer who understands."[11]

The next generation of liberals included theologians in direct dialogue with Whitehead, as we shall see in the next section. But most of this next generation also carved out its own niche quite distinct from what would become "process theology." The following paragraphs suggest how four common themes are dealt with in different ways by our four individual representatives: Farley, Kaufman, Ogden, and Tracy.

First, all four theologians agree that Christian theology makes truth-claims and provides reasons for its claims. Thus, all reject both the notion that Christian theology makes no truth-claims and simple appeals to "the house of authority" (Farley) to back up the truth-claims they do make. But how can *Christian* theology make *truth*-claims? Here they begin to diverge. Tracy, following Paul Tillich, uses what he sometimes calls a "method of correlation." The point of theology is to correlate our tradition and our situation in ways that are "mutually critical," careful to give neither pole (our tradition or our situation) unequivocal precedence and constantly searching for disclosures of theological truth.[12]

Ogden also speaks of theology as a sort of "correlation of the Christian witness of faith and human existence" subject to "the two criteria of appropriateness [Is x appropriate to normative Christian witness?] and credibility [Does x meet 'the relevant conditions of truth universally established with human existence?']".[13] But Ogden also emphasizes that, since these dual criteria govern distinct aspects of Christian witness, it makes little sense to speak about "correlating" two poles.[14] Perhaps more than Tracy, Farley, or Kaufman, Ogden distinguishes Christian faith and theology (the latter a distinct act of critical reflection and validation).

Farley and Kaufman (for reasons we shall see) resist any talk of correlation or dual criteria but share with Ogden and Tracy a concern with showing that Christian teachings are not only "Christian" but also "true." Farley proposes that the problem of truth is at once "the problem of reality" ("how reality comes forth, occurs, is manifest") and "the problem of criteria" ("how the reality manifesting grounding rises into the judgment"). Because the former is a faith-apprehension of reality, Farley insists that judgments about the latter are "not members of a more general class"; he calls the latter "ecclesial universals" to highlight the way they are different from and similar to more generic universals.[15] For Kaufman, "only criteria of coherence and pragmatic usefulness to human life are relevant and applicable" to large concepts like "world" and "God." He rejects "one-dimensional," authoritarian as well as "two-dimensional," correlational theologies in favor of his "holistic" theology, i.e., one that is a conversation about "the source and ground and meaning of *all that is*"; "(religious) truth should be understood to be specifically dialogical (and thus pluralistic) in character."[16]

Second, all four are concerned with human beings as free *subjects* embedded in a physical and social and historical world, radically threatened by ambiguity and suffering and evil, and seeking ways to overcome this situation. For Tracy, the self is "radical agapic self-transcendence." There are "real and perhaps even irreconcilable ideals of the self," but the self is subject-in-process, "never substance but subject, affected by and affecting both God and the world." The freedom of the Christian, Tracy suggests, is "the real but limited freedom of the prophetic-mystical subject-as-agent-in-process."[17] For Farley, faith-apprehensions "occur pre-reflectively and by means of an enduring participation in a form of corporate historical existence which we are calling ecclesia." Our subjectivity is always a "determinate intersubjectivity" expressed in stories and images, myths and doctrines – the "face" of "the interhuman."

Ogden weaves together the diverse construals of subjectivity (Tracy) and intersubjectivity (Farley) in Wesley, Bultmann, and even liberation theology under a kind of process philosophy for which the self is aware of and responsible for itself as continually becoming, internally related to time and others, an essential fragment of "the integral whole of reality."[18] For Kaufman, human beings are "'biohistorical' beings," organically related to other life-forms and self-reflexive, corrupted by individual anxiety and guilt as well as societal oppression and disorder, and yet somehow participants in "directional movements in a serendipitous universe."

Third, all agree that the monarchical God of classic theism (who acts in history in ways that jeopardize or destroy human subjectivity in nature and history) must be replaced by a God (or other ultimate reality) related to human, religious, or specifically Christian experience. Ogden[19] and Tracy[20] argue on behalf of the God whom we meet in the limit-questions of our experience and who, as soul of the world, is both in and beyond that world. This position is sometimes called "panentheism" (e.g., God is in everything, and everything is in God), although Tracy also insists that "no *ism* . . . is ever adequate for naming and thinking God."[21]

Farley argues for faith's indirect apprehension of God – not a God "represented mythically as thinking, willing, reflecting, and accomplishing in the mode of an in-the-world-being who intervenes selectively in world process" nor simply a general religious "transcendent" but a God for whom "ecclesial process as such *is* the salvific work of God in history."[22] Kaufman argues that "the image/concept of God serves as a focus or center for devotion and orientation" – a focus which must be represented "on a continuum running from highly mythical and symbolical images – God as a personal being who loves and cares – to the more abstract notion of the cosmic ground of all humanity."[23]

Fourth, all agree that life and thought in relationship to the specific figure of Jesus is shaped by the previous issues, although they diverge on exactly how. Of our four figures, Tracy and Farley are the most sympathetic to what Farley calls a kind of "primacy of Christology." For Tracy, the event and person of Jesus Christ – in the immediacy of experience mediated by the tradition (which is normed by the expressions of Scripture), developed and corrected by historical and literary and social criticisms, and correlated with our present situation – is the prime analogue for theological imagination.[24] For Farley, Jesus of Nazareth is "appresented" as historical redeemer in ecclesial existence. One of the tasks, "perhaps the central one," of what Farley calls theological portraiture, is inquiry into the Jesus of Nazareth "[p]roclaimed as the redemption-effecting person – not simply the past Jesus but the present Christ."[25]

But, if Tracy and Farley are the most sympathetic to the primacy of christology, Ogden has devoted the most care to articulating a "revisionary christology." Ogden argues that "the christological question is an existential-historical question about the meaning of Jesus for us." Further, "the subject of the christological assertion is not Jesus in his being in himself, but rather Jesus in his meaning for us"; any appropriate christological predicate is that Jesus Christ is the "decisive re-presentation of God for us" – a re-presentation of something that was there all along and now "becomes fully explicit."[26]

Of our four figures, Kaufman is most critical of traditional christology – although he insists that "the picture and story of Jesus" provides "qualities and potentialities . . . normative for human life." The category of Christ qualifies "in a definitive way" other theological concepts; "Christ crucified" is an appropriate image for a God who "suffers crucifixion in the hope of the resurrection of a new community called to non-violence."[27]

Representatives

Describing our representatives individually will suggest the differences that accompany their common ground on select issues. Whitehead was not a theologian. The theological features of his writing (which I surveyed above) are fragmentary, leaving a host of unanswered questions (e.g., what is the relation between God and Creativity? Is God dispensable to the categoreal scheme? How does God relate to complex societies of actual entities like human beings?). Representatives of what came to be called "process theology" take up these and other issues left by the movement of "naturalism" of which Whitehead was a part.

Process theologians do not agree on how to describe the differences among themselves.[28] In some respects, process theology after Whitehead is like the history of German philosophy after Hegel, dividing into right-wing (revisionary) and left-wing (liberal) branches. I will focus on two central issues in the divide. First, can more (or less) of the Christian tradition be retrieved than Whitehead thought? Second, is Whitehead's "method of discovery" (the metaphor of the airplane's flight) rational or empirical?

Theologians like John B. Cobb (b. 1925) focus on reinterpreting Christian theology in dialogue with Whitehead. Cobb's *A Christian Natural Theology* (1964) does this most explicitly, arguing that a Christian theology ought to assess philosophies not only by their "intrinsic excellence" but also by whether they are or are not "hostile to Christian faith." "The quest for total consensus is an illusion." This "inner tension of Christianity, between its particularism and its universalism" characterizes Cobb's early writing. Despite criticisms, he has tried to maintain this tension as he explores "creative transformation" in Christ, Buddhist–Christian dialogue, and his more recent writing on public policy.[29] Cobb has largely shaped the version of process theology at Claremont Graduate School – a tradition which continues in the work of David Griffin (1977, 1991) and Margorie Suchocki (1989).[30]

On the other hand, Bernard Loomer (1912–1985) was one of the shapers of a different reading of Whitehead at the University of Chicago Divinity School. He proposed that the consistent carrying out of Whitehead's "method of discovery" would yield a "God identified with the totality of the [world]" – a totality which is ambiguous. "An ambiguous God is of greater stature than an unambiguous deity."[31] Henry Nelson Weiman also came to propose radical reinterpretations of both Whitehead and Christianity.[32] If Cobb thinks that more of the Christian tradition can be retrieved than Whitehead thought, Loomer and Wieman think that less can – much less.

Whether these theologians revise Christian theology in the light of something like

Whitehead's brand of naturalism or Whitehead in the light of Christian theology, a second difference emerges in how they go about doing this. Charles Hartshorne (b. 1897) was also at the University of Chicago Divinity School for many years. He shares Whitehead's skepticism on traditional claims about God and Jesus Christ – but he also differs from Whitehead on a number of points. For example, whereas Whitehead thought of God as an actual entity, Hartshorne thinks of God as a series of actual occasions – like a divine person, perfect in transcendence and immanence. He has said that "the whole point of my natural theology is that God is as literally infinite as finite, and vice versa, the union of these contraries . . . being the essence of 'process theology.' "[33] Hartshorne is also known for a version of "the ontological argument" for the existence of God, arguing that God's existence is logically necessary.[34] On the other hand, process theologians like Henry Nelson Wieman and Bernard Loomer argue that this is a "rationalism" which undercuts the priority of Whitehead's Creativity (briefly mentioned in the previous section).[35] Ogden has his criticisms of Hartshorne's philosophical theology; but he (like Cobb) has also spent more time than Hartshorne working not simply on theology's philosophical credibility but also its "appropriateness" to the apostolic witness of Scripture.[36]

It is easier to summarize the particularities of our four other representatives of revisionist and liberal theology. Farley is writing a multivolume interpretation of the major themes of the Christian mythos. The first two volumes are prolegomena. *Ecclesial Man: A social phenomenology of faith and reality* is an analysis of faith's given apprehensions of reality which occurs "in a form of corporate, historical existence which we are calling ecclesia."[37] *Ecclesial Reflection: An anatomy of theological method* internally deconstructs various levels of the "house of authority." Ecclesial reflection is (roughly) an inquiry with three moments: historical and biblical ("theological portraiture"), philosophical and systematic, and practical.[38] We find them applied to theological education in Farley's *Theologia*, where theology is described as a particular sort of *habitus* in the context of ecclesiality.[39] Farley has recently moved from such proposals about theology to his interpretation of "the Christian paradigm," construed as focusing on three themes: redeemed human being, God, and the historical mediations of redemption (Messiah and church). The first installment begins with a "reflective ontology," *Good and Evil: Interpreting a human condition*, in "three spheres of human reality: [individual, personal] agency, the interhuman, and the social." He makes the case that, although each of the three spheres has its own importance, "the interhuman is primary both to agents and the social because it is the sphere that engenders the criterion, the face (Emmanuel Levinas), for the workings of the other spheres."[40]

Gordon Kaufman's *Systematic Theology: An historicist perspective* sought to meet the problem of the irrelevance of Christian faith "by giving at every point a radically *historicist* view of the Christian."[41] The collection of essays in *God the Problem* (1972) deconstructed the concept of God partly begun and partly presupposed in earlier writing, leading Kaufman later to propose a notion of theological method as the "activity of *construction* (and reconstruction) not of description or exposition."[42] Kaufman's later essays develop and apply this new method to a range of topics (1981).[43] In *Nonresistance and Responsibility, and Other Mennonite Essays*, Kaufman displays the ways he has over the years sought "an understanding of Christian faith which is Mennonite but not authoritarian" – which, for all its technical changes, has remained "concerned primarily with forming persons and communities devoted to redemptive love."[44] *In Face of Mystery: A constructive theology* is Kaufman's most thorough articulation of his position to date. Faith proceeds (Kaufman says) by several "small steps." Beginning with a sort of faith that God can be reflected upon in worthwhile ways, theology proceeds to excavate, critically examine, and imaginatively construct this faith by "sketching a picture of the world, and of humanity within the world, based largely on widely accepted modern knowledges and on the modes of experience that ground these knowledges." Theology then proceeds to construct the concept or image of God before re-visioning humanity and world and God in the light of the Christ.[45]

Schubert Ogden's own work[46] reflects his description of theology as critical reflection on Christian witness (see above). The critical reflection initially took the form of a critique of the internal inconsistency of Bultmann's claims that Jesus Christ is act of God and his demand for existential demythologization (1962). *The Reality of God and Other Essays*[47] develops an alternative, using linguistic analysis (Toulmin) and process philosophy (Whitehead and Hartshorne) to support Christian claims about divine agency. *Faith and Freedom: Toward a theology of liberation* is a move from the issues raised by Bultmann's existentialism, process thought, and linguistic analysis to the challenge of liberation theologies on issues of "justice and action."[48] *Is There Only One True Religion or Are There Many?*[49] moves into the world of various religions, arguing against three standard ways of treating religions (exclusivism, inclusivism, and pluralism) in favor of "pluralistic inclusivism."

David Tracy's main project may eventually yield a trilogy on fundamental, systematic, and practical theology.[50] The first volume, *Blessed Rage for Order*,[51] applies a method of correlation to issues of religion, God, and life. *The Analogical Imagination*[52] turns to systematic theology. Systematic theology is hermeneutical, i.e., the interpretation (not repetition) of a tradition given us by our historicity and finitude. The key examples are "classics," especially religious classics. The *Christian* classic is "the event and person of Jesus Christ". *Analogical Imagination* is a paradigm of an analogical imagination which works by picking a primary analogue, showing the unity-in-difference within and between analogues (their order, perhaps harmony, their variety and intensity, including dialectical negations), and risking the self-exposure of putting these similarities and differences in the public forum.[53] More recently David Tracy has "reconceived" (without abandoning) his revisionary methods, arguing that such revisionary methods "must be continually open to critique and revision."[54] More particularly, he has reconceived his method in the light of the neo-Platonic traditions (from Pseudo-Dionysius to Eckhart and especially Ruuysbroec), radical postmodern thought on negativity and difference (Derrida and Deleuze), and "Buddhist – more exactly, Kyoto Mayahana Buddhist – thought."[55]

The Debate

A full description of the debates over revisionary and liberal theologies would require locating these theologians in relationship to all the other chapters of this volume. Here we must be satisfied with more modest remarks. I will distinguish debates "internal" to the revisionist and liberal project and those "external" to the project.

The internal debate is shaped by a sense that the differences (in the third section) override the common ground (in the second section). This applies to the debate among process theologians already sketched – that is, the debates between those who wish to retrieve more or less of the Christian tradition as well as between those who think Whitehead's aeroplane is most helpful on the "empirical" ground or in the "rational" and speculative air. But it applies even more to the forms of revisionist and liberal theologies more prominent in the second half of this century, for they are much more philosophically eclectic than the naturalism which initially spawned process theology. Farley is, shaped by Husserl's phenomenology, Ogden by linguistic analysis and Bultmann's Heidegger (as well as Hartshorne), Kaufman by Kant, David Tracy by Lonergan and Ricoeur.[56]

This sense that the differences override the common ground also accounts for the fragmentary and even infrequently polemical nature of the debate among our four individual figures (e.g., Tracy accusing Kaufman of an uncritical acceptance of modernity, Farley accusing Tracy of pre-revisionary conservativism, and Kaufman accusing both of not carrying through their revisionary proposals to their practical conclusions).

Readers should not let this internal debate fool them into thinking that the differences among our representatives outweigh their common ground; intra-familial debates, to use common wisdom, are often more intense than inter-familial arguments. In any case, these discussions offer clues to the larger controversies. Take, for example, the debate over the possibility and actuality of Christian truth-claims. One way to understand this debate is to range their positions on a spectrum *from* Farley's claim that faith-apprehension yields ecclesial universals *through* Tracy's method of correlation and Ogden's "dual criteria" *to* Kaufman's ultimately pragmatic and humanistic test for truth. (Among process theologians, Cobb and Griffin would stand closer to Farley and Tracy while Hartshorne and Wieman would stand closer to Ogden and Kaufman.)

This spectrum suggests a logic behind the remarks each has made about the others. Thus, Kaufman thinks that Farley's faith-apprehension retains too many vestiges of "objectivist thinking" and is a "version of confessionalism," while Farley wonders how Kaufman's critique of traditional correspondence theories of truth can lead us beyond subjectivism. Farley, let us say, uses a *general* phenomenological framework to show that Christian truth-claims are *specific* to particular communities – while Kaufman requires that specifically Christian claims conform to his pragmatic framework. Tracy and Ogden propose subtle correlations of generality and specificity (and hence belong in the middle of the spectrum). However, both Farley and Kaufman are suspicious of methods of correlation or "dual criteria" – because they can threaten Christian particularity (Farley), because they leave Christian particularity "substantially unquestioned" (Kaufman), or because it is hard to tell whether their revisionary force is central or marginal. The spectrum places Tracy closer to Farley because Farley's "theological portraiture" and Tracy's hermeneutical conversation are more analogous to each other than either is to Ogden or Kaufman. Also,

Farley and Kaufman seem less suspicious of Ogden's dual criteria than of Tracy's locating the correlational task in a philosophically eclectic "hermeneutical" context; Farley and Kaufman worry that Tracy's hermeneutical disclosure experiences avoid rather than confront hard questions about truth (as Farley and Kaufman variously define it). Tracy in turn worries that Ogden does not take into account the "poetic" character of the religious conversation, that Kaufman is too uncritical of modernity, and Farley only implicitly critical.[57] Again, these oppositions should not make us forget their common ground (see the survey above).

The external debate is shaped by a sense that the common ground among revisionists and liberals overrides the differences they perceive in each other. For example, there are both theological and philosophical challenges to revisionist and liberal notions of truth. Thus, Ronald Thiemann proposes a notion of Revelation which enables him to criticize Kaufman (for simply exchanging a divine foundation for a human one) as well as Tracy and Ogden (for steering an unstable middle course between revelation and human imagination).[58] Thiemann's criticisms of Kaufman are similar to Farley's and Tracy's – and his criticisms of Tracy are similar to Farley's and Kaufman's. More important, in at least some respects, Thiemann's proposal is an internal critique of Karl Barth's theology – a "critique" because Thiemann elucidates promissory revelation using Anglo-American "non-foundationalist" philosophy; "internal" because of Thiemann's Barth-like insistence on God's "prevenience" – God has loved us first, prior to our airplane ever arriving on the ground, taking off, or landing.[59]

A philosophical challenge comes from those philosophers of religion less interested in making or justifying Christian truth-claims than in studying them as doctrines of religious communities. Thus, William Christian has argued that there are fewer problems with a community taking its authentic doctrines to be true (Farley) than taking every truth to be a doctrine of their community (Kaufman) – or than "correlating" their own and other truth-claims (Tracy). Christian's stand is more like Farley's than Kaufman's or Ogden's or Tracy's, but his appeal is to the practices and teachings of *particular* communities rather than to Farley's *general* phenomenology (even though Farley's is a phenomenology which centers on faith's positivity and particularity).[60]

Alasdair MacIntyre goes even further in the direction of particularity, contrasting the encyclopedia (especially the "liberal" authors of the ninth edition of the *Encyclopedia Britannica*), the genealogy (Nietzsche), and tradition (Leo XIII) as different and opposed contexts for pursuing rational inquiry. He argues that liberal encyclopedists have not taken seriously the Nietzschean genealogical critique of modernity; this liberal-nihilist impasse generates MacIntyre's rereading of Thomas Aquinas on the rationality of tradition for the pursuit of the true and the good.[61]

Achievement and Questions for the Future

The key achievement of revisionists and liberals has been to challenge our received practices and teachings about truth, human beings, God, and Christ. The key (if not only) questions for the future have to do with the alternatives revisionaries and liberals propose. On this score, certainly revisionists and liberals ought continue to address the issues raised by the debate over "truth" (e.g., is truth correspondence to reality, pragmatic effectiveness, disclosure? Do we need a theory of truth and method?). But both internal and external critics will hopefully not permit this issue to dominate the future agenda; settling issues of truth will not settle issues of who we are, who God is, or who Christ is.

For example, a major achievement of revisionary and liberal visions of humanity (our own and others) is the insistence on the way we are free subjects embedded in a physical, social, and historical world. Yet revisionists and liberals are divided among themselves as to how to do this. Can a categoreal scheme applicable to the whole cosmos (like Whitehead's or Hartshorne's or Kaufman's) do justice to the particular joys and griefs of our human subjectivities? Can probing analyses of the heights and depths of our subjectivities (like Farley's *Good and Evil*) keep us embedded in our physical, social, and historical world? Does Tracy's mystical-political option show a way out, or does it just re-describe the problem? Internal critics of revisionist and liberal theologies offer different answers to such questions.[62] External critics have focused on the secular politics that arises out of revisionist and liberal theologies, arguing from the right or the left that liberal politics is dead. But a different group of external critics (including those dubbed "postliberal" in this volume) has argued that only a church constituted as the Other City can provide the counter-history, the counter-ethics, and the counter-ontology needed to reconcile our violent world.[63]

Another achievement of revisionary and liberal theologies is their insistence that our claims about God be related to the broader world of human religiosity. However, they have thus far paid more attention to the general features of the religious world than to its particularities. For example, all share a great deal if we focus on Kaufman's "formal" notion of God,[64] Ogden's early use of God in a "completely general sense,"[65] or Tracy's case for Ultimate Reality.[66] Yet when it comes to identifying this God, Farley appeals to determinate divine activity, Ogden and Tracy to process theism modified by trinitarian theology, and Kaufman to a non-agential cosmic ground. These are the makings of different religions rather than of a common revisionary or liberal theological project.[67]

Admittedly, revisionists and liberals have entered into careful conversations with Buddhists. Cobb finds Christianity and some kinds of Buddhism complementary, if they can be "mutually transformed."[68] Kaufman seems to go further, finding that a kenotic God (Phillipians 2: 7) is "moving toward" the Buddhist teaching that "everything ought to be understood in terms of 'emptiness.'"[69] On the other hand, Tracy says that Buddhists have helped him understand Christian mystics like Meister Eckhart, although Tracy ultimately stands with Christian trinitarian mystics like Ruuysbroec rather than Eckhart.[70] Ogden, while finding common ground as well as much that is difficult to understand in Buddhism, finds that arguments for analogies between Buddhist emptiness and the kenotic God assume that God can only be "infinitely related" and not also "infinitely unrelated," whereas Christians ought to confess both.[71] Are these different and opposed views of Christian relations with Buddhists symptoms of deep disagreements over Christian theology, or are they simply the result of the young stage of Buddhist–Christian dialogue? Besides Buddhists who might have such questions, another group of external critics of liberals and revisionists on the identity of God includes those who argue that the doctrine of trinitarian *hypostases* is no less unintelligible or inapplicable than dipolar theism, and that the trinity is the best way to account for the transcendence and immanence of God in Christ, church, and world.[72]

Finally, a key debate between liberals and revisionists is whether to continue (like the revisionary tradition from Schleiermacher through Tracy) or discontinue (like the liberal tradition from Whitehead to Kaufman) a broadly christocentric reading of life. "Broadly" is important, for a central challenge to revisionist as well as liberal christologies comes from those like Karl Barth who insist that "there is no question of placing Christ within some allegedly more comprehensive context. Christ *is* the adequate context of Christian theology."[73] Our representatives disagree over what the context ought to be: faith-apprehensions, conversations over texts, the modern world in its historicist-pragmatic complexity, etc. And it is more accurate to describe the revisionary (in contrast to liberal) task as one of relating "context" and "Christ" rather than giving absolute priority to the "event" or "person" (the "context" or "Christ") of Jesus Christ. But *that* the particular figure Jesus requires some prior context to be applicable or intelligible all agree. From this point of view, while revisionists and liberals have made considerable advances over the anthropologies and cosmologies and epistemologies of their mediating predecessors, the christological issue remains much the same.

The comprehensiveness of revisionist and liberal agenda assures that it will be subject to piecemeal critiques on each issue – and that it will withstand them for some time to come. The central challenge to their achievement may come from those who take up issues of truth in the context of attending to divine and human agency in particular narratives, centered on the narratives of Jesus Christ. But this is not the place to pursue that version of the "postliberal" option.

Notes

1 Bernard M. Loomer, "Process theology: origins, strengths, weaknesses," *Process Studies*, 16 (1987), pp. 245–54 (quoting Sidney Harris).

2 John P. Clayton, *The Concept of Correlation: Paul Tillich and the possibility of a mediating theology* (Berlin and New York, 1980), pp. 7–9; Hans Frei, "David Friedrich Strauss," in Ninian Smart, John Clayton, Steven Katz, and Patrick Sherry (eds), *Nineteenth Century Religious Thought in the West* (Cambridge, 1985), vol. 1, p. 221.

3 Sydney E. Ahlstrom, *A Religious History of the American People* (New Haven and London, 1972), p. 763.

4 John Macquarrie, *Twentieth-Century Religious Thought* (New York, 1981; first published 1963), pp. 380, 410.

5 Edward Farley, *The Transcendence of God: A study in contemporary philosophical theology* (Philadelphia, 1960) and *Requiem for a Lost Piety: The contemporary search for the Christian life* (Philadelphia, 1966); Gordon Kaufman, *Relativism, Knowledge, and Faith* (Chicago, 1960) and *The Context of Decision* (Menno Simons Lectures, 1959), (Chicago, 1961); Schubert Ogden, *Christ Without Myth: A study based on the theology of Rudolph Bultmann* (Dallas, TX, 1979; first published 1962); David Tracy, *The Achievement of Bernard Lonergan* (New York, 1970).

6   Loomer, "Process theology."

7   Alfred North Whitehead, *Process and Reality: An essay in cosmology* (Gifford Lectures, 1927–1928), corrected edn by David Ray Griffin and Donald W. Sherburne (London and New York, 1978; first published 1929), p. 5.

8   Alfred North Whitehead, *Adventures of Ideas* (New York, 1967; first published 1933), pp. 167–8; *Process and Reality*, p. 342.

9   Victor Lowe, *Alfred North Whitehead*, ed. J. B. Schneewind (Baltimore, MD, and London, 1990), ch. IX.

10   A. N. Whitehead, *Process and Reality*, pp. 18–30, 239, 343, 345.

11   Ibid., pp. 31, 32, 44, 75, 87, 345, 348, 351.

12   David Tracy, *The Analogical Imagination* (New York, 1981), pp. 59–62, 88 n. 44; *On Naming the Present* (Maryknoll, NY, 1995), p. 75.

13   Schubert M. Ogden, *On Theology* (Dallas, TX, 1992; first published 1986), p. 3.

14   Schubert M. Ogden, "Doing theology today," in John D. Woodbridge and Thomas Edward McComiskey (eds), *Doing Theology in Today's World* (Grand Rapids. MI, 1991), p. 424; see also Ogden's review of Hans Frei's *Types of Christian Theology* in *Modern Theology*, 9 (1993), pp. 211–14 at p. 214.

15   Edward Farley, *Ecclesial Reflection: An anatomy of theological method* (Philadelphia, 1982), pp. xiii, 304–5, 310, 338, 343; *Good and Evil: Interpreting a human condition* (Minneapolis, 1990), p. 3; "Truth and the wisdom of enduring," in Daniel Guerriere (ed.), *Phenomenology of the Truth Proper to Religion* (Albany, NY, 1990).

16   Gordon Kaufman, *Relativism, Knowledge, and Faith*, p. 94; *An Essay on Theological Method* (Missoula, MT, 1979; first published 1975), p. 75; *In Face of Mystery: A constructive theology* (Cambridge, MA, 1993), pp. 29, 467 n. 6.

17   David Tracy, *The Analogical Imagination*, pp. 435–6; *Dialogue with the Other*, (Louvain and Grand Rapids, MI, 1990), pp. 118, 102.

18   Schubert M. Ogden, "Process theology and the Wesleyan witness," *Perkins School of Theology Journal*, 37 (1984), pp. 18–33.

19   Schubert M. Ogden, *The Reality of God and Other Essays* (Dallas, TX, 1992; first published 1966).

20   David Tracy, *Blessed Rage for Order* (New York, 1975).

21   David Tracy, "Approaching the Christian understanding of God," in Francis Schüssler Fiorenza and John P. Galvin (eds), *Systematic Theology: Roman Catholic Perspectives* (Minneapolis, 1991), pp. 131–48; "Literary theory and the return of the forms for naming and thinking God in theology," *Journal of Religion*, 74 (1994), pp. 308–9; *On Naming the Present*, p. 18.

22   Edward Farley, *Ecclesial Man: A social phenomenology of faith and reality* (Philadelphia, 1975), pp. 13, 224, 226; *Ecclesial Reflection*, pp. 156–7; Farley and Peter C. Hodgson, "Scripture and tradition," in Peter Hodgson and Robert King (eds), *Christian Theology* (Philadelphia, 1985), ch. 2.

23   Gordon Kaufman, *The Theological Imagination* (Philadelphia, 1981), pp. 32, 51; *Theology for a Nuclear Age* (Manchester and Philadelphia, 1985), ch. III; *In Face of Mystery*, esp. Part IV and ch. 27.

24   David Tracy, *The Analogical Imagination*, pp. 233–41; *On Naming the Present*, pp. 31, 37, 67, 79, 124–5.

25   Edward Farley, *Ecclesial Man*, pp. 217–19; *Ecclesial Reflection*, pp. xvii, 209, 225.

26   Schubert M. Ogden, *The Point of Christology* (Dallas, TX, 1992; first published 1986), pp. 41, 62, 82.

27   Gordon Kaufman, *The Theological Imagination*, pp. 116, 189–90; *Theology for a Nuclear Age*, ch. IV; *In Face of Mystery*, chs. 7, 25, and 26.

28   Delwin Brown, Ralph E. James, Jr, and Gene Reeves (eds), *Process Philosophy and Christian Thought* (Indianapolis and New York, 1971); John B. Cobb and David Ray Griffin, *Process Theology: An introductory exposition* (Philadelphia, 1976); Kenneth Surin, "Process theology," in David F. Ford (ed.), *The Modern Theologians* (Oxford, 1989), vol. II, pp. 103–14; Delwin Brown and Sheila Greeve Davaney, "Methodological alternatives in process theology," in *Process Studies*, 19 (1990), pp. 75–84.

29 John B. Cobb, Jr, *A Christian Natural Theology* (Philadelphia, 1964), pp. 264–6, 281; *Christ in a Pluralistic Age* (Philadelphia, 1975); *Beyond Dialogue: Toward a mutual transformation of Christianity and Buddhism* (Philadelphia, 1982); *Sustainability* (Maryknoll, NY, 1992). See also David Ray Griffin and Thomas J. J. Altizer (eds), *John Cobb's Theology in Process* (Philadelphia, 1977) and David Ray Griffin and Joseph C. Hough (eds), *Theology and the University: Essays in honor of John J. Cobb, Jr* (Albany, NY, 1991).

30 See note 29 for Griffin references; Margorie Suchocki, *God Christ, Church: A practical guide to process theology*, new rev. edn (New York, 1989).

31 Bernard Loomer, "Process theology," pp. 20–1; see W. Dean and L. E. Axel (eds), *The Size of God: The theology of Bernard Loomer* (Macon, GA, 1987).

32 Cobb and Griffin, *Process Theology*, pp. 177–8.

33 Charles Hartshorne, *The Darkness and the Light* (New York, 1990), p. 227; see also *Man's Vision of God and the Logic of Theism* (Hampden, CT, 1941), *The Divine Reality* (New Haven and London, 1948), and *Creative Synthesis and Philosophical Method* (LaSalle, IL, 1970), as well as Lewis A. Ford (ed.), *Two Process Philosophers: Hartshorne's encounter with Whitehead* (Tallahassee, FL, 1973).

34 Charles Hartshorne, *The Logic of Perfection and Other Essays in Neoclassical Metaphysics* (LaSalle, IL, 1962); *Anselm's Discovery* (LaSalle, IL, 1965).

35 Bernard Loomer, "Process theology."

36 Schubert Ogden, "The experience of God: critical reflections on Hartshorne's theory of analogy," in John B. Cobb, Jr and Franklin I. Gamwell (eds), *Existence and Actuality: Conversations with Charles Hartshorne* (Chicago and London, 1984), pp. 16–37.

37 Edward Farley, *Ecclesial Man*, pp. 127, 29, 57.

38 Edward Farley, *Ecclesial Reflection*, p. 190.

39 Edward Farley, *Theologia* (Philadelphia, 1983); *The Fragility of Knowledge* (Philadelphia, 1988).

40 Edward Farley, *Good and Evil*, pp. xv–xvi, 28–9, 117–18, 287–92.

41 Gordon Kaufman, *Systematic Theology* (New York, 1978; first published 1968), p. 9.

42 Gordon Kaufman, *An Essay on Theological Method*, pp. x, 46.

43 Gordon Kaufman, *The Theological Imagination*.

44 Gordon Kaufman, *Nonresistance and Responsibility, and Other Mennonite Essays* (Newton, KS, 1979), pp. 9–10.

45 Gordon Kaufman, *In Face of Mystery*, esp. chs. 17 and 29.

46 Schubert Ogden, "Faith and freedom," in James M. Wall (ed.), *Theologians in Transition* (The *Christian Century* "How My Mind Has Changed" Series) (New York, 1981); for an Ogden bibliography see Philip E. Devenish and George L. Goodwin (eds), *Witness and Existence: Essays in honor of Schubert M. Ogden* (Chicago and London, 1989).

47 Schubert M. Ogden, *The Reality of God*.

48 Schubert M. Ogden, *Faith and Freedom: Toward a theology of liberation* (Nashville, TN, 1989; first published 1979).

49 Schubert M. Ogden, *Is There Only One True Religion or Are There Many?* (Dallas, TX, 1992).

50 David Tracy, "Defending the public character of theology," in James M. Wall (ed.), *Theologians in Transition*, pp. 113–24. For a Tracy bibliography, see Werner G. Jeanrond and Jennifer L. Rike, *Radical Pluralism and Truth: David Tracy and the hermeneutics of religion* (New York, 1991).

51 David Tracy, *Blessed Rage for Order* (New York, 1975).

52 David Tracy, *The Analogical Imagination* (New York, 1981).

53 Ibid., pp. 62, 99–100, 103, 108, 163, 358; "Theological method," in Peter Hodgson and Robert King (eds), *Christian Theology* (Philadelphia, 1985; first published 1982); *Plurality and Ambiguity* (San Francisco, 1987), ch. 1.

54 David Tracy, "The uneasy alliance reconceived: Catholic theological method, modernity, and postmodernity," *Theological Studies*, 50 (1989), pp. 548–70 at p. 556.

55 David Tracy, *Dialogue with the Other*; "Kenosis, sunyata, and Trinity: a dialogue with Masao Abe," in John B. Cobb and Christopher Ives (eds), *The Emptying God:*

A Buddhist-Jewish-Christian conversation (Maryknoll, NY, 1990), pp. 141–2.

56 For critical appreciations of process theology by this generation see Ogden, "The experience of God"; Tracy, "Theological method" and "Kenosis, sunyata, and Trinity," pp. 136–8; Farley, "Theocentric ethics as a genetic argument," in Harlan R. Beckley and Charles M. Swezey (eds), *James M. Gustafson's Theocentric Ethics* (Macon, GA, 1988), pp. 39–62, and *Good and Evil*, p. xx; Sheila Greeve Davaney, John B. Cobb, Jr, and Gordon Kaufman, review essays on Kaufman's *In Face of Mystery* in *Religious Studies Review*, 20 (1994), pp. 171–81.

57 This paragraph is a summary of discussions and (more often) allusions our representatives make to each other in the texts cited above (see the name indices as well as subject indices under key words like "hermeneutics," etc.), reviews, and a set of unpublished responses of Farley and Kaufman and Tracy to each other's work at a 1982 meeting of the American Academy of Religion. The reviews include Farley, "A [i.e., David Tracy's] revisionist model," in *Christian Century*, XCIII (1976), pp. 371–3; Kaufman, review of Farley's *Ecclesial Man* and Tracy's *Blessed Rage for Order*, *Religious Studies Review*, 2 (1976), pp. 7–12, and "Conceptualizing diversity theologically [a review of Tracy's *The Analogical Imagination*]," *Journal of Religion*, 62 (1982), pp. 392–401. See also Kaufman, *In Face of Mystery* (name index under Farley, Ogden, Tracy, and Whitehead) and the essays in Sheila Greeve Davaney (ed.), *Theology at the End of Modernity: Essays in honor of Gordon D. Kaufman* (Philadelphia, 1991); Philip E. Devenish and George L. Goodwin (eds), *Witness and Existence: Essays in honor of Schubert D. Ogden* (Chicago and London, 1989); and Werner G. Jeanrond and Jennifer L. Rike, *Radical Pluralism and Truth: David Tracy and the Hermeneutics of Religion* (New York, 1991).

58 Ronald F. Thiemann, *Revelation and Theology* (Notre Dame, IN, 1985).

59 Michael Welker, "Barth's theology and process theology," *Theology Today*, XLVII (1986), pp. 383–97.

60 William A. Christian, Sr, *Doctrines of Religious Communities* (New Haven, 1987), esp. ch. 4.

61 Alasdair MacIntyre, *Three Rival Versions of Moral Enquiry* (Gifford Lectures, 1988) (Notre Dame, IN, 1990); see also David Burrell, *Aquinas: God and action* (Notre Dame, IN, 1979), ch. 6; W. Norris Clarke, SJ, "Charles Hartshorne's philosophy of God: a Thomistic critique," in Santiago Sia (ed.), *Charles Hartshorne's Concept of God* (Dordrecht, 1990).

62 David Kelsey, "Human being," in Peter Hodgson and Robert King (eds), *Christian Theology*, ch. 6; Fergus Kerr, *Theology after Wittgenstein* (Oxford, 1986); Charles Taylor, *Sources of the Self: The making of the modern identity* (Cambridge, MA, 1989).

63 John Milbank, *Theology and Social Theory: Beyond secular reason* (Oxford, 1990).

64 Gordon Kaufman, *Theology for a Nuclear Age*, p. 32.

65 Schubert M. Ogden, *The Reality of God*, p. 10.

66 David Tracy, *Plurality and Ambiguity*, ch. 5.

67 Thomas F. Tracy, "Enacting history: Ogden and Kaufman on God's mighty acts," *Journal of Religion*, 64 (1984), pp. 20–36.

68 John B. Cobb, *Beyond Dialogue*.

69 Gordon Kaufman, "God and emptiness: an experimental essay," *Buddhist-Christian Studies*, 9 (1989), pp. 175–87.

70 David Tracy, "Kenosis, sunyata, and Trinity."

71 Schubert Ogden, "Faith in God and realization of emptiness," in John B. Cobb and Christopher Ives (eds), *The Emptying God*, pp. 125–42.

72 For example, William Hill, *The Three-Personed God* (Washington, DC, 1982).

73 Walter Lowe, "Christ and salvation," in Hodgson and King (eds), *Christian Theology*, ch. 8. See also Bruce Marshall, *Christology in Conflict: The identity of a saviour in Rahner and Barth* (Oxford, 1987).

Bibliography

I have included only my own choices of the first texts I would recommend for introductory reading; other texts might be recommended for other purposes. Students interested in further reading can begin with the references in the notes above.

Primary

Cobb, John B., Jr, *A Christian Natural Theology* (Philadelphia, 1964).
—— *Christ in a Pluralistic Age* (Philadelphia, 1975).
Farley, Edward, *Ecclesial Reflection: An anatomy of theological method* (Philadelphia, 1982).
—— *Theologia* (Philadelphia, 1983).
—— *Good and Evil: Interpreting a human condition* (Minneapolis, 1990).
Hartshorne, Charles, *The Divine Relativity* (New Haven and London, 1948).
—— *The Darkness and the Light* (New York, 1990).
Kaufman, Gordon, *Theology for a Nuclear Age* (Manchester and Philadelphia, 1985).
—— *In Face of Mystery: A constructive theology* (Cambridge, MA, 1993).
Ogden, Schubert M., *The Reality of God and Other Essays* (Dallas, New York, and London, 1992; first published 1966).
—— *On Theology* (Dallas and San Francisco, 1992; first published 1986).
Tracy, David, *The Analogical Imagination* (New York, 1981).
—— *Plurality and Ambiguity* (San Francisco, 1987).
Whitehead, Alfred North, *Religion in the Making* (New York, 1926).
—— *Adventures of Ideas* (New York, 1967; first published 1933).

Secondary

There is an abundance of good secondary literature, so that even introductory recommendations are rather arbitrary. Students might also want to read the ongoing discussions and reviews of the above authors in *Religious Studies Review*, *Journal of Religion*, *Process Studies*, and *Theological Studies*.

Ahlstrom, Sydney E., *A Religious History of the American People* (New Haven and London, 1972).
Cobb, John B. and Griffin, David Ray, *Process Theology: An introductory exposition* (Philadelphia, 1976).
Hodgson, Peter, and King, Robert (eds), *Christian Theology: An introduction to its traditions and tasks*, 2nd edn, rev. and enl. (Philadelphia, 1985).
Macquarrie, John, *Twentieth-Century Religious Thought* (New York, 1981; first published in 1963).

Postliberal Theology

William C. Placher

Introduction: The Study of Religion at Yale

In the early 1980s the theologies described in the previous chapter had the broad center of academic theology in the United States more or less to themselves. Evangelicals on the right made few inroads into the faculties of prestige universities, and various forms of liberation theology on the left, while offering much of the intellectual excitement of the time, remained in some degree self-consciously marginal to the academic mainstream. The publication of George Lindbeck's *The Nature of Doctrine* in 1984 therefore marked an important event by bringing a new theological option into focus, a real challenge to liberals and revisionists. The book's last chapter called for a "postliberal theology," and that term, "narrative theology," or "the Yale school," soon came to be widely discussed – though the thinkers so described sometimes felt uncomfortable at being so labeled or indeed at being classified together.

Widely diverse influences lay behind this new approach: the theology of Karl Barth, new ways of reading Aquinas, Thomas Kuhn's philosophy of science, analytic philosophers like Wittgenstein and Gilbert Ryle, sociologists like Peter Berger, anthropologists like Clifford Geertz, and literary theorists like Erich Auerbach. Most of those identified as "postliberals" either taught or had studied at Yale (the thought of the Yale theologian H. Richard Niebuhr lies behind many postliberal themes), and perhaps noting the environment for doing theology at Yale will help to set their context.

In the tradition of scholars like Mircea Eliade of the University of Chicago, many religious studies departments in the United States teach "religion," particularly in their introductory courses, as a universal phenomenon whose themes and symbols manifest the experience of the sacred in different but related ways in different cultures. Christian theology then takes its place as one set of answers to those universal human questions – a liberal or revisionist way of thinking about theology that Paul Tillich stated in classic form.

At Yale the pattern was different, with an emphasis on the study of particular religious traditions, each in its own historical or cultural context. Students studied Christianity or Judaism or Buddhism but not "religion." In Old Testament studies, Brevard Childs developed a "canonical" approach which, in contrast to the sort of biblical scholarship preoccupied with finding the sources behind the texts, paid more attention to the shape of the texts as we have them. Childs (also discussed in chapter 26 below) believed that one important way of understanding texts is to note how they have functioned, and he noted that the Bible has functioned primarily in the context of "the community which treated it as Scripture," not the community of historical-critical scholars.[1] At the same time the New Testament scholar Wayne Meeks was trying to "describe the first Christian group in ways that a sociologist or an anthropologist might," seeking "in social history an antidote to the abstractions of the history of ideas and to the subjective individualism of existentialist hermeneutics."[2]

This milieu therefore provided a context for (1) thinking about the particularities of individual religious traditions; (2) attending to the shape of the biblical texts as we have them, especially the structures of their narratives, utilizing techniques analogous to those of literary critics; and (3) thinking about the relations of biblical texts to the communities that read them – how their narratives shape the identities of those communities, their members, and their understandings of the God they worship. Out of Hans Frei's studies of the history of modern hermeneutics and of Karl Barth in particular, and George Lindbeck's reflections on ecumenical theology in the light of new readings of Aquinas and new styles of sociology and anthropology, postliberal theology emerged.

Survey

The "liberalism" with which postliberal theology contrasts itself refers to the philosophical tradition of Enlightenment liberalism; neither "liberal" nor "postliberal" implies any particular position on the political spectrum. From a postliberal perspective (which may exaggerate the characteristics of its opponents) liberalism seems to seek a foundation for its truth-claims in wider cultural norms or universal human experience. By contrast, postliberal theology has a number of interrelated characteristics: (1) It is non-foundationalist. Like a number of recent philosophers (W. V. O. Quine, Wilfred Sellars, and Richard Rorty, for example), postliberal theologians reject the claim "that knowledge is grounded in a set of non-inferential, self-evident beliefs."[3] They believe that experience always comes already interpreted. The way I experience the pen on the table, let alone the cross on the altar, is shaped by my language and previous experience. Therefore I cannot evaluate my beliefs by checking them against some primordial, uninterpreted experience. (2) It does not engage in systematic apologetics. Postliberal theologians will make *ad hoc* connections with the philosophy or art or miscellaneous experience of the cultures around them, but they do not believe that any non-Christian framework, philosophical or cultural, sets *the* context in which Christian claims must be defended.[4] (3) It attends to the differences among religions, rather than focusing on the things they have in common or trying to argue that they are all saying the same thing. Postliberals believe, in the words of the Yale philosopher of religion William Christian, "in response to the generous impulse which often prompts people to harmonize the doctrines of the world religions, that understanding one another does not always lead to agreement and that respect for one another does not depend on agreement."[5] (4) It emphasizes the scriptural stories or narratives by which Christians identify God and the Christian community and come to understand their own lives. In contrast to approaches which seek to pull a doctrine or moral lesson out of the story as its "real meaning," postliberals insist on the irreducible importance of stories which convey truth and preserve communal identity in a way that gets lost if we try to find what they really mean and then discard the stories.

Hans W. Frei

Everyone associated with postliberal theology owes a great debt to Hans Frei. In *The Eclipse of Biblical Narrative* (1974) he offered an account of how the way Christian theologians read the Bible had gone wrong, beginning in the seventeenth and eighteenth centuries. Before that time, he said, Christians had thought of the grand sweep of biblical narratives as defining the real world. The world is the place created by God, where the Lord rescued Israel from Egypt, Christ came, the church was founded, and Christ will come again; and Christians made sense of their own lives by placing them within that story. But by the eighteenth century, "It is no exaggeration to say that all across the theological spectrum the great reversal had taken place; interpretation was a matter of fitting the biblical story into another world with another story rather than incorporating that world into the biblical story."[6] People took the primacy of the world of their own experience for granted, and theologians felt they had to establish the biblical world's reality by fitting *it* into *that* world – in one of two ways. For John Locke and many others, "The meaning of the stories is their ostensive reference or their failure to refer to certain events."[7] Historical research begins with our experience and tries to move backwards; the stories in the Bible, as with any other ancient text, are "true" if the events they describe can be fitted into this historical framework. Alternatively, the narratives refer to eternal truths which they symbolize. The meaning of a story is not the story itself but some moral lesson or religious truth it illustrates.

These two options have dominated theological hermeneutics ever since. Among the followers of Bultmann, for instance, the right-wing's quests for the historical Jesus represent the first option, and the left-wing's conviction that Jesus only "re-presents" an eternal truth about God's love exemplifies the second. Neither one, Frei argued, permits a faithful interpretation of biblical narratives. As with a realistic novel, the biblical narratives mean what they say: Their meaning lies in the inter-action of character and incident they present, the story they tell. But the first option mentioned above tries to recover historical kernels from the stories, while the second looks for their moral lessons. Either way, the story as story gets lost, just as the story of *David Copperfield* would get lost if one reduced its meaning either to facts about the social history of nineteenth-century England or to general lessons about human nature. This loss will happen inevitably, Frei argued, if theology adopts a systemati-cally apologetic strategy, letting some definition of reality external to Christianity set the rules of the game and trying to defend the biblical narratives in its terms. He therefore argued that a theology faithful to the narrative character of these particular texts must, like Karl Barth's, simply describe the biblical world as "a world with its own linguistic integrity, much as a literary art work is a consistent world in its own right," while insisting "that unlike any other depicted world it is the one common world in which we all live and move and have our being."[8]

Similarly, in *The Identity of Jesus Christ* (1975), Frei considered the concepts of Jesus' *identity* and *presence* and maintained that the logic of Christian faith requires that we begin with identity, not presence. Beginning with "the often nagging and worrisome questions of *how* Christ is present to us and *how* we can believe in his presence" is again a way of letting some extra-Christian definition of the world of our experience set the agenda. It leads to trying either to establish on the historical evidence that Jesus was in fact raised from the dead or else to find Jesus present as an eternal symbol of universal human concerns.[9] Both approaches are unfaithful to the gospel narratives, which are not the stuff of myth but also do not claim to be accurate history. Unlike the timeless, universal symbols provided by myths, they offer the portrait of an unsubstitutable person. We know who he is, as we learn about a character in a novel, by hearing stories about him. Unlike the narratives of critical history, these stories may not be accurate in detail, but they can capture Jesus' identity in the way a good anecdote can do.

Drawing on the philosophy of Gilbert Ryle, Frei argued that a person ordinarily *is* what he or she says and does, not some mysterious inner "ghost in a machine." Therefore theologians should not search for Jesus' essence somehow *behind* the stories but attend to the stories themselves. In any life story, to be sure, there are trivial events and anomalies but also moments when one's identity takes focus. In the gospel narratives, Jesus is most himself in the resurrection. Beginning with questions about Jesus' presence led to a dead end, but in this one unique case beginning with identity can lead to presence, for the story tells us that he is the resurrected one and therefore his identity, properly understood, implies that he is present with us.[10] Just as Anselm's ontological argument (as Barth understood it) states that, if the definition of God makes any sense, then God exists, so, Frei says, if the gospel stories make sense, then the one whose identity they render indeed lives.

As already noted, however, Frei urged theology to eschew systematic arguments for the claim that Jesus lives. Such arguments will make Christian faith dependent on some other starting point and will distort the meaning of the biblical narratives. In lectures given during the last decade of his life and posthumously published as *Types of Christian Theology*, he classified theologians along a spectrum from those (like Kant and Gordon Kaufman) who think of theology purely as an academic discipline, whose rules ought to be defined by the canons of what the Germans call *Wissenschaft*, to those (such as "Wittgensteinian fideists" like D. Z. Phillips) who consider it purely as an activity internal to the Christian community, simply the rules of this particular tribe's language.

Not surprisingly, Frei maintained that theologies which give philosophy a systematic priority inevitably distort Christian faith. But he also thought that those like Phillips who stand at the other end of the spectrum end up doing the same thing by paradoxically offering a philosophical argument for why theology should pay no attention to philosophy. Frei believed that the sort of theology most faithful to the biblical texts as they have been understood down through the Christian tradition would either (like Schleiermacher) try to balance the demands of academic study and Christian community or else (like Barth) would give a modest priority to theology's role in Christian community but engage in a variety of "ad hoc apologetics" to keep in contact with the wider intellectual world. He thought Barth's approach works best of all, but one of the surprises of his typology was to claim that Schleiermacher, often considered a polar opposite, was Barth's methodological near neighbor.

George Lindbeck

George Lindbeck has also described a theology which begins with the world of the scriptural texts: "For those who are steeped in them, no world is more real than the ones they create. A scriptural world is thus able to absorb the universe. It supplies the interpretive framework within which believers seek to live their lives and understand reality."[11] In *The Nature of Doctrine* he considered what such an "intratextual" approach implies about the function of doctrines. He proposed three models of how doctrines work: (1) The *propositionalist* "emphasizes the cognitive aspects of religion and stresses the ways in which church doctrines function as informative propositions or truth-claims about objective realities"; (2) the *experiential-expressivist* "interprets doctrines as noninformative and nondiscursive symbols of inner feelings, attitudes, or existential orientations"; (3) on Lindbeck's own *cultural-linguistic* or *rule* model, "the function of church doctrines that becomes most prominent . . . is their use, not as expressive symbols or as truth-claims, but as communally authoritative rules of discourse, attitude, and action."[12]

Consider the doctrinal assertion, "We are saved by grace alone." The propositionalist will take this as a *factual* claim about the mechanism of salvation. The experiential-expressivist will understand it as the *symbolic expression of an experience* of the power of God in salvation. On Lindbeck's view, the meaning of the doctrine can best be expressed in a *rule* like, "Christians should always speak and act about their salvation in a way that expresses gratitude to God, not pride in their own accomplishment."

From his long experience as a Lutheran participant in ecumenical discussions, Lindbeck noted one problem with the propositionalist model: It cannot explain cases where participants in ecumenical conversations find that their communities can now agree on a point where they formerly disagreed, without either side admitting to having changed its position. On the propositionalists' model, if Lutheran and Catholic doctrines were in contradiction in 1541, then they must still be. But on a regulative model, rules could apply in one circumstance but not another. They could thus still disagree on what it was essential to the health of the church for Christians to say in 1541, while agreeing on what needs saying in the different circumstances of today.

Lindbeck devoted most of his argument, however, to a critique of experiential-expressivism. He argued the implausibility of claiming that all Christians – much less all religious people – share some common experience which religious language seeks to articulate. Indeed, he denied that we can have pre-linguistic "religious experience."

Cases like Helen Keller and "supposed wolf children . . . illustrate, that unless we acquire language of some kind we cannot actualize our specifically human capacities for thought, action, and feeling."[13] We cannot have the kind of experience Christians or Buddhists or Muslims have without having the linguistic framework to structure and articulate that experience. One simply could not have the "experience" of "being saved by faith in Christ," for instance, without a language that included ideas like "salvation," "faith," and "Christ."

Therefore we cannot judge a religious language by measuring it against some prelinguistic experience. Nor can we judge it primarily as to factual accuracy. Lindbeck turns to the standard of "categorial adequacy." Doctrinal systems are in this respect like languages. We do not judge a language "true" or "false." "But one language may in the long run open up all the riches of human history . . . while the other, the better a child learns it, imprisons him more tightly in his little tribe or village."[14] People who grow up in the language of a tribe unaware of modern science do not say false things about particle physics – they lack the vocabulary to talk about it at all. Similarly, a religious system may lack the grammar and vocabulary that engage us to lead richer lives more faithful to God. Thus,

> As actually lived, a religion may be pictured as a single gigantic proposition. It is a true proposition to the extent that its objectivities are interiorized and exercised by groups and individuals in such a way as to conform them in some measure in the various dimensions of their existence to the ultimate reality and goodness that lies at the heart of things.[15]

Lindbeck acknowledges, to be sure, that some religious utterances will make truth-claims or even express experiences.[16] But if the fundamental function of doctrines is to establish the framework of language for a community's conversation, then the adherents of a religion should not concentrate on the search for universal human experiences to express or independently established facts to report but rather on perfecting their own "language" from within. Drawing on the work of scholars like Victor Preller and David Burrell, Lindbeck sees a parallel to his own understanding of religious language in Aquinas. Aquinas wrote that the language Christians use about God is true (in its signification) but that they do not understand *how* it is true (its way of signifying).[17] God does love us, for example, but God is so beyond our imagining that we cannot at all grasp what love would be like for God. Therefore, since we cannot probe behind them to check them out, we should work within the rules our community provides for talk about God.

Stanley Hauerwas

Stanley Hauerwas, a Methodist, did his graduate work at Yale and taught for a number of years at the University of Notre Dame before taking his present position at Duke University. He is discussed elsewhere in this volume in chapter 16 on ethics, but, since he has been the most widely read advocate of postliberal theology in church circles and among ethicists, he deserves some attention in this chapter too. Hauerwas thinks that most contemporary Christian ethics presupposes Lindbeck's experiential-expressivist model: It assumes that "there is some universal experience that all people have that can be characterized as religious. The particular religions and their doctrines are but manifestations of that experience." In contrast, Hauerwas holds that "by our becoming members of a particular community, formed by Christian convictions, an experience not otherwise available is made possible. From this perspective Christian ethics does not simply confirm what all people of good will know, but requires a transformation both personally and socially if we are to be true to the nature of our convictions."[18]

Frei talked about "narratives"; Hauerwas tends to talk about "stories," but the idea is the same, and the category is central to his thought in at least two ways. First, he thinks that too much contemporary ethics takes the form of "quandary ethics." It discusses difficult moral choices in isolation from what goes before or after them and assumes that either some universal moral principle can be brought to bear or else we face moral chaos.[19] Hauerwas believes that we receive moral guidance from stories more than from principles. If we see someone who needs help, the story of the Good Samaritan may be more use to us than any abstract ethical principle. Stories help us imagine what sort of person we think we ought to be. They point to the importance of virtue and character in ethics, for these are formed, not in an isolated moral decision, but in the shape of a good life.

Second, stories function in shaping communities. A nation, a tribe, a school, or any social group defines itself in part by telling a common story. Yet in Hauerwas's view, significantly shaped by his reading of the philosopher Alasdair MacIntyre, too much contemporary ethics seeks to free us from tradition, so that we can guide ourselves by some universal standard of rational ethics: "The story that liberalism teaches us is that we have no story."[20] But we can make thoughtful moral decisions only in the context of the traditions of some community, shaped by communal narratives and inculcating virtues by the ways those narratives help us think about the stories of our own lives. Just as Lindbeck insisted that a religious language creates possibilities of religious life and experience, so Hauerwas says that stories create possibilities for different forms of virtuous life.

The task of Christian ethics, then, is not to establish universal moral principles but to call Christians to preserve a community that tells the stories that make Christian virtues possible:

> The church's social task is first of all its willingness to be a community formed by a language that world does not share . . . the church's social ethics is not first of all to be found in the statements by which it tries to influence the ethos of those in power, but rather . . . is first and foremost found in its ability to sustain a people who are not at home in the liberal presumptions of civilization and society.[21]

As a pacifist, Hauerwas has been particularly concerned to call the church to offer "a political alternative to every nation, witnessing to the kind of social life possible for those that have been formed by the story of Christ."[22]

Ronald Thiemann

Ronald Thiemann, a Lutheran who went from graduate work at Yale to teaching at Haverford College to his present position as Dean of Harvard Divinity School, has brought similar concerns about narrative and community to bear on the doctrine of revelation. A good many theologians, he argues, have gone wrong by associating revelation with a foundationalist epistemology. Thiemann agrees with recent anti-foundationalist philosophers that there is no experience prior to interpretation, no starting point not already embedded in assumptions. He shows how a search for foundations has led a long line of theologians on a doomed quest for some absolutely certain theological starting point – whether miraculous evidence or religious intuition, something so certain it just could not be questioned.

In reaction, some contemporary theologians have proposed giving up the doctrine of revelation altogether. But Thiemann shows how talking about revelation safeguards God's *prevenience*, the conviction that a divine initiative precedes all our speaking and acting and responding. Given his own non-foundationalist principles, Thiemann cannot try to "prove" prevenience from indisputable premises. Instead, he offers a "holist justification" as an example of the kind of argument he thinks theologians ought to make.[23] He shows how much of Christian life and liturgy would have to be sacrificed if we abandoned prevenience and says that our speaking and acting about God come before any divine initiative. If prevenience seems so central to Christian life and thought, and revelation protects prevenience, then a Christian theologian has good reasons for wanting to rescue a doctrine of revelation. Thiemann thinks we can do so if we free it from its association with foundationalism. He proposes an understanding of revelation as "narrated promise." The idea of "promise" preserves the priority of God's initiative, for one can respond to a promise only after it has been made. For Thiemann, we learn of the promise through Scripture's narration of the identity of God as the one who promises. In a careful reading of the Gospel of Matthew, he does not try to penetrate behind the narrative to some moral or experience but shows how the shape of the narrative itself begins with divine initiative and opens up to invite our response. He thus refuses to try to "found" theology either on religious intuition or on revelation itself but treats revelation as a part of the doctrine of God, one implication of God's narrated identity, to be defended by showing its coherence with other aspects of Christian life and teaching.

Debate and Agenda

"Postliberal theology" is still very new, and its boundaries and directions remain in important ways undefined. It has generated strong opposition, but it is often unclear whether criticisms represent real disagreement, misunderstanding, or the identification of points where postliberals have not yet sorted out their views or disagree among themselves. At this stage, one can only note some of the issues on which discussion seems liveliest.

Truth   In *The Nature of Doctrine* Lindbeck defended what he called a "modest cognitivism" such as he finds in Aquinas: While in important ways we do not understand what we mean when we speak about God, still, Christians believe that what we say is true. Similarly, while Frei emphasized the looseness of the gospel narratives to historical detail and the difficulty of *any* positive description of what happened at Jesus' resurrection, he admitted, "About certain events reported in the Gospels we are almost bound to ask, Did they actually take place?"[24] On the other hand, much of the polemical force of Lindbeck's book depended on the contrast between "propositionalists," who hold that doctrines make truth-claims about matters of fact, and his own "regulative" view, in which doctrines (*only?*) describe the rules of discourse within a community. And Frei sometimes criticized "meaning as reference" in a way that seemed to imply that the biblical narratives do not refer to any reality outside themselves.

Perhaps the most common criticism of postliberalism is thus that it is a form of relativism which does not claim the truth of Christian faith but only reports the stories told within a particular community. Overall, this seems a misinterpretation, but one can see how it might arise; postliberals need to be clearer on these issues than they have sometimes been. Frei responded in a particularly interesting way: Of course, he said, given a choice between saying "yes" or "no," he believed that language about God refers, and in the historical reality of Christ's death and resurrection. But he found philosophers unable to agree on the meaning of terms like "reference" and "historical reality," and he did not want to tie Christian faith to any one philosophical theory. So he resisted trying to define such terms too precisely in a theological context (a danger he found at least as common among evangelical theologians as among liberals and revisionists), thereby keeping a kind of eclectic theological independence.[25]

Texts and communities of readers　Frei's early work claimed that reading the Bible as realistic narrative was simply more faithful to the meaning of these texts than the alternatives. In later essays, particularly "The 'Literal Reading' of Biblical Narrative in the Christian Tradition: Does It Stretch or Will It Break?"[26] he put the emphasis elsewhere: Reading the Bible this way is most faithful to the way the Christian community down the centuries has read it. "Early Frei," influenced by literary theorists like Erich Auerbach and the then prominent "New Critics," was making a claim about the texts themselves; "later Frei," influenced by deconstructionist and reader-response critics, was less inclined to say that the texts had one "correct" meaning and instead appealed to how the principal community of their readers has rather consistently understood them. The later position had more in common with David Kelsey's argument that the authority of Scriptures lies in the way a community uses them, not in some feature of the texts themselves,[27] and with Lindbeck's appeals to communal rules.

Claims about the "correct" meaning of a text have certainly gone out of fashion. But there is still something to be said for Frei's earlier position. Long traditions within Christianity have read the Bible in ways that defended slavery or were very oppressive to women. Can there not be some way, by appealing to the texts themselves, to challenge misguided interpretations even when those interpretations are solidly embedded in the church's traditions? Such an effort might recover important insights in the Reformation appeal to *sola scriptura*. Postliberals continue to debate the issue.

The coherence of narratives Many new approaches to biblical scholarship, from feminism to deconstructionism, have shown how there are many different, some-times conflicting, narratives within Scripture. "Postmodern" novelists and many contemporary literary critics challenge the whole idea of a clear, coherent narrative. Readers have learned to regard the omniscient, impartial narrator of earlier realistic novels with considerable suspicion. Part of the force of postliberal theology lies in its appeal to contemporary suspicion of grand claims about universal rationality, its celebration of the stories of a particular community. But those same contemporary forces raise doubts about appeals to "*the* Christian community" or "*the* biblical narrative." Postliberal theologians need to sort out how far they want to celebrate pluralism, in contrast to what claims they need to make for narrative and communal coherence.

Sectarianism? Hauerwas acknowledges his great debt to the Mennonite theologian and ethicist John Howard Yoder, who values the separated Christian community characteristic of the Anabaptist tradition. *Resident Aliens,* the popular book Hauerwas co-authored with William Willimon, dramatically describes a contemporary Ameri-can society in which Christians find themselves outsiders to the dominant cultural values, and argues that this is all to the good for the church's integrity. Lindbeck has suggested that the church may have to foster a kind of "sociological sectarian-ism,"[28] developing the kind of "close-knit groups . . . needed to sustain an alien faith."[29] Critics have too quickly dismissed such conclusions as a withdrawal from social concerns.[30] Communities of Christian pacifists, socialists, or the early Quaker opponents of slavery, after all, have helped shape the consciences of their societies by clearly affirming their own religious convictions – perhaps far more effectively than mainline Protestant denominations which pass resolutions on issues of national importance. Yet Christianity is not yet, anyway, a small minority in the United States. National leaders and ordinary citizens still widely claim allegiance to Chris-tian faith, and that would seem to imply some "non-sectarian" social responsibilities for the Christian community. Addressing such concerns while remaining faithful to its insights into distinctively Christian witness remains a challenge for postliberal theology.

Achievement

A theological approach sometimes has its widest impact by the "classical" texts it brings back into current discussion and the mistakes it warns everyone to avoid. Thus, Frei's work in particular reintroduced Karl Barth's theology into contem-porary conversations, not (as Barth had often been perceived) as a churchly voice of "neo-orthodoxy," but as a postliberal theologian of particular interest in a time of non-foundationalist philosophies. Postliberal discussions of "foundationalism" and "experiential expressivism" may have oversimplified opponents' positions, but they have created a new sensitivity to the dangers of appeals to universal religious experi-ence. Contrasting David Tracy's recent *Plurality and Ambiguity* with his earlier *Blessed*

Rage for Order, for instance, makes it clear that, while he is not becoming a postliberal, he is self-consciously trying to avoid mistakes postliberalism has identified.

Postliberals have also changed the debate within Christian theology about other religions. In the early 1980s pluralists like John Hick and Paul Knitter could plausibly present themselves as the wave of the future in thinking about such matters. The world's religions have a common core, they said, and offer different ways of expressing those universal truths.[31] Lindbeck's critique of experiential-expressivism showed the dangers of such approaches, and, often under his influence, a new generation of scholars like Gavin D'Costa, Paul Griffiths, and J. A. Di Noia have argued that different religions offer different models of reality and urge their adherents to different ways of life.[32] The pluralists defended their views as a corrective to the imperialistic conviction that only Christianity has the truth, but postliberal theologians of religion argue that it is the pluralist claim that all religions are at some deep level saying the same thing, definitively articulated by a Western-trained philosopher of religious dialogue, which constitutes the real intellectual imperialism.

Kathryn Tanner's work has led to a postliberal rethinking of divine transcendence. While most other postliberals have been in debate with liberals and revisionists, she has more explicitly challenged the process theologians. Tanner studied and then taught at Yale before moving to the University of Chicago. In *God and Creation in Christian Theology*[33] she argued that most modern theologians have simply assumed a "contrastive" notion of transcendence. "Transcendence" meant that God is distant and separated from creation, so that the more transcendent God is the less immanent, and vice versa. Process theologians and some feminist theologians then attack divine transcendence as the enemy of God's engagement in the world and the foundation of a hierarchical, patriarchal model of God. Tanner, however, argues that both pre-modern theologians like Aquinas and postliberal theologians like Barth have had a more radical notion of transcendence. For them, God's transcendence meant that God is not one agent among the others in the world, but operates on a completely different dimension of agency, so that events can be both the results of creatures' activities and the acts of God. Transcendence/immanence is thus not a zero-sum game: A transcendent God can be fully engaged in every moment of creation, and the affirmation of divine transcendence turns out to be a good way to challenge the idolatrously absolute claims of human hierarchies. As a postliberal theologian, Tanner refuses to locate divine acts in some larger narrative of what is happening in creation, but insists on the primacy of God's activity, but she sees such an account as "empowerment" of quests for social justice rather than "tyranny."[34]

The impact of postliberal theology in discussions of biblical narrative and of story in ethics is harder to measure. In the 1960s, when Frei was writing the articles which later became *The Identity of Jesus Christ*, the form-critical method developed in classic form by Bultmann – analyzing individual biblical passages and trying to identify the circumstances in which they were originally told or written – was *the* dominant way of reading the Bible among biblical scholars and even most theologians. So many writers now draw on narrative theory and other forms of literary criticism in biblical interpretation that it is hard to judge the impact of Frei's attention to narrative, or to grasp its boldness at the time he wrote it. On the other hand, Frei's *theological* point – the priority for Christian theology of the biblical narratives over the narratives we tell of our lives, and the resulting suspicion of systematic apologetics – gets lost in many current discussions of narrative. Frei himself was always nervous about the term "narrative theology," and postliberal theologians need to emphasize that they are not advocating just any use of narrative categories.

Similarly, discussions of "virtue" and "narrative" have become increasingly prominent among Christian ethicists, but these developments probably owe more to the philosophical work of MacIntyre and to rediscoveries of "virtue ethics" in Aquinas and Aristotle than to the specific impact of postliberal theology. The relations of natural law (increasingly prominent in MacIntyre's most recent work) to distinctively Christian ethics, and of biblical narratives to the narratives we tell of our own lives, remain often unclear, and here too postliberalism distinguishes itself by its insistence on a priority of the Christian perspective.

Hauerwas in particular has certainly made a strong appeal to pastors in many mainline Protestant denominations. The sense of living in a post-Christian society where Christians need to foster the telling of the particular stories that define their communal identity has struck a deeply responsive chord. The impact of postliberal theology in the academic world remains less clear. A model of "religious studies" which is suspicious of theology in general and especially of a theology that emphasizes Christianity's distinctiveness seems if anything to be growing more dominant in colleges and universities in the US. Postliberal theology challenges assumptions that, in some contexts, seem to make religious studies more intellectually respectable among academic colleagues and more appealing to students in a milieu where, as Lindbeck has put it, "religions are seen as multiple suppliers of different forms of a single commodity needed for transcendent self-expression and self-realization."[35] With Frei's death, Lindbeck's retirement, and Tanner's departure, Yale itself is no longer clearly a center of postliberal theology.

Postliberals often find it frustrating to be criticized for retreating into a theological ghetto, away from the intellectual debates of contemporary culture. They think of themselves as not only more faithful to the Christian tradition but, as it happens, in more lively conversation with interesting developments in contemporary philosophy and social science. Still, those who attack the submissiveness of theology to cultural and academic norms are presumably not in a position to complain if their welcome in culture and academy remains a bit uncertain.[36] Indeed, the nervousness of some of their critics may at least be a sign that the postliberals are asking hard and important questions.

Notes

1 Brevard S. Childs, *Introduction to the Old Testament as Scripture* (Collegeville, MN, 1992), pp. 40–1; for Childs's response to "the new Yale theology" see *The New Testament as Canon: An introduction* (Philadelphia, 1984), pp. 541–6.

2 Wayne A. Meeks, *The First Urban Christians* (New Haven, 1983), p. 2.

3 Ronald F. Thiemann, *Revelation and Theology: The Gospel as narrated promise* (Notre Dame, IN, 1985), p. 158.

4 William Werpehowski, "Ad hoc apolo-

getics," *Journal of Religion*, 66 (1986), pp. 282–301.

5 William A. Christian, Sr, *Oppositions of Religious Doctrines* (New York, 1972), p. 5.

6 Hans W. Frei, *The Eclipse of Biblical Narrative* (New Haven, 1974), p. 130.

7 Ibid., p. 99.

8 Hans W. Frei, *Types of Christian Theology* (New Haven, 1992), p. 161.

9 Hans W. Frei, *The Identity of Jesus Christ* (Philadelphia, 1975), p. 4.

10 Ibid., p. 146.

11 George A. Lindbeck, *The Nature of Doctrine: Religion and theology in a postliberal age* (Philadelphia, 1984), p. 117.

12 Ibid., pp. 16–18.

13 Ibid., p. 34.

14 Ibid., p. 60.

15 Ibid., p. 51.

16 Ibid., pp. 68–9.

17 Ibid., p. 66.

18 Stanley Hauerwas, *Against the Nations* (Minneapolis, 1985), p. 2.

19 Stanley Hauerwas, *A Community of Character* (Notre Dame, IN, 1981), p. 134.

20 Ibid., p. 84.

21 Stanley Hauerwas, *Against the Nations*, pp. 11–12.

22 Stanley Hauerwas, *A Community of Character*, p. 12.

23 Ronald F. Thiemann, *Revelation and Theology*, pp. 171–2.

24 Hans W. Frei, *The Identity of Jesus Christ*, p. 132.

25 Hans W. Frei, *Theology and Narrative: Selected essays* (Oxford, 1993), pp. 210–11.

26 Ibid., pp. 117–52.

27 David H. Kelsey, *The Uses of Scripture in Recent Theology* (Philadelphia, 1979), pp. 136–7.

28 George A. Lindbeck, "The sectarian future of the church," in Joseph P. Whelan (ed.), *The God Experience* (New York, 1971), pp. 226–43.

29 George A. Lindbeck, *The Nature of Doctrine*, p. 78.

30 See, for instance, James F. Gustafson, "The sectarian temptation: reflections on theology, the church, and the university," *Proceedings of the Catholic Theological Society*, 40 (1985), pp. 83–94.

31 John Hick, *God Has Many Names* (Philadelphia, 1982); Paul Knitter, *No Other Name?* (London, 1985).

32 Gavin D'Costa, *Christian Uniqueness Reconsidered* (Maryknoll, NY, 1990); Paul Griffiths, *An Apology for Apologetics* (Maryknoll, NY, 1991); J. A. Di Noia, *The Diversity of Religions: A Christian Perspective* (Washington, DC, 1992).

33 Kathryn Tanner, *God and Creation in Christian Theology: Tyranny or Empowerment* (Oxford, 1988).

34 For an interesting critique see Thomas F. Tracy, "Divine action, created causes, and human freedom," in Thomas F. Tracy (ed.), *The God Who Acts* (University Park, PA, 1994), pp. 77–102.

35 George A. Lindbeck, *The Nature of Doctrine*, p. 22.

36 George Hunsinger, "Where the battle rages: confessing Christ in America today," *dialog*, 26 (1987), pp. 264–74; William C. Placher, *Narratives of a Vulnerable God* (Louisville, KY, 1994).

Bibliography

Primary

Buckley, James J., *Seeking the Humanity of God* (Collegeville, MN, 1992).

Di Noia, J. A., *The Diversity of Religions: A Christian perspective* (Washington, DC, 1992).

Frei, Hans W., *The Eclipse of Biblical Narrative* (New Haven, CT, 1974).

—— *The Identity of Jesus Christ* (Philadelphia, 1975).

—— *Types of Christian Theology* (New Haven, CT, 1992).

—— *Theology and Narrative: Selected essays* (New York, 1993).

Hauerwas, Stanley, *A Community of Character* (Notre Dame, IN, 1981).

—— *The Peaceable Kingdom* (Notre Dame, IN, 1983).

—— *Against the Nations* (Minneapolis, 1985).

—— *Dispatches from the Front* (Durham, NC, 1994).

Lindbeck, George A., *The Nature of Doctrine: Religion and theology in a postliberal age* (Philadeiphia, 1984).

Tanner, Kathryn, *God and Creation in Christian Theology: Tyranny or empowerment?* (Oxford, 1988).

—— *The Politics of God: Christian theologies and social justice* (Minneapolis, 1992).

Thiemann, Ronald F., *Revelation and Theology: The Gospel as narrated promise* (Notre Dame, IN, 1985).

Wood, Charles M., *The Formation of Christian Understanding* (Philadelphia, 1981).

Secondary

Green, Garrett (ed.), *Scriptural Authority and Narrative Interpretation* (Philadelphia, 1987).

Kelsey, David H., *The Uses of Scripture in Recent Theology* (Philadelphia, 1979).

Marshall, Bruce D., "Aquinas as postliberal theologian," *Thomist*, 53 (1989), pp. 353–402.

Marshall, Bruce D. (ed.), *Theology and Dialogue: Essays in conversation with George Lindbeck* (Notre Dame, IN, 1990).

Placher, William C., *Unapologetic Theology* (Louisville, KY, 1989).

—— *Narratives of a Vulnerable God* (Louisville KY, 1994).

Vanhooger, Kevin J., *Biblical Narrative in the Philosophy of Paul Ricoeur: A study in hermeneutics and theology* (Cambridge, 1990).

Wallace, Mark I., *The Second Naiveté: Barth, Ricoeur, and the new Yale theology* (Macon, GA, 1990).

Werpehowski, William, "Ad hoc apologetics," *Journal of Religion*, 66 (1986), pp. 282–301.

Black, Hispanic/Latino, and Native American Theologies

M. Shawn Copeland

Introduction

When confronted by the brutal history of misery to which the masses of human persons are subjected, theology would not go unmoved. It turned from philosophical hermeneutics to dialectics and ideology critique, to social (i.e., political, economic, and technological), liberative, and emancipatory priorities. With this conversion, theology has assumed critical, interrogative, and emancipative modes of discourse that take up a range of questions put forward by religiously, intellectually, and morally differentiated consciousness; that uncover just how any symbol, idea, or social system may become ideological; that strive to overcome the alienations of modernity, i.e., secular from sacred, private from public, objectivity from subjectivity, thought from feeling, theory from praxis; and that contest cooptation by structures of domination and resist the destructive experience of being dominated. This conversion constitutes a shift in paradigm: Theology embraces a commitment to the historical as well as spiritual emancipation and liberation of oppressed, marginalized, and poor peoples in their particular cultural and social situations. In the United States, this commitment has been expressed primarily, although not exclusively, in Black, Hispanic/Latino, and Native-American theologies.[1]

There are at least four ways to account for the irruption of these theologies, whether Black and womanist, Hispanic/Latino and *mujerista*, or Native American. *First*, all theology is critical cognitional praxis – reasoned disciplined asking and answering of questions. Black, Hispanic/Latino, and Native American theologies are particular instances of understanding, of theology's critical mediation of Christian faith in multiple cultural contexts. Yet these theologies are never merely socially located knowledges. Black, Hispanic/Latino, and Native American theologies are critical epistemic rejections of the equation of concepts with reality, of the reduction of knowledge to merely subjective or sense experience, of the attempt to ground knowledge in or on a priori first principles. These theologies expose not only the Western idealization of reason, but the modern liberal romanticization of emotion as characteristic of Black, Hispanic/Latino, and Native American communities and cultures. *Second*, many scholars would concede that the worldview or mentality shaped and mediated by classical Greek philosophy and science has collapsed. While the consequences of this breakdown for Christian theology remain ambiguous, it has provoked the insight that theology is not only a matter of faith, but also of culture. Black, Hispanic/Latino, and Native American theologies instantiate the transition from a classical worldview to historical mindedness.[2] These theologies recover, critique, and engage cultural meanings and values that have been assaulted or suppressed or coopted under white supremacist rule. *Third*, in their efforts to retrieve, interpret, inculturate, and transmit Christian faith, Black, Hispanic/Latino, and Native American theologies may be apprehended as irruptions of the Spirit. These theologies stand as forms of prophetic judgment on Christian witness and praxis of the past, the present, and the future. Still, Black, Hispanic/Latino, and Native American theologians must be humbly and self-critically attuned to their own cognitive, religious, and moral praxis, lest unconsciously they appropriate the attitudes, spirit, sensibility, and tools of domination.[3] *Fourth*, since these theologies mediate between African, Hispanic/Latino, and Native American Christian communities of word and witness and their cultures, they must come to terms with the ways in which these cultures have been exploited, rendered dependent, and marginalized within the US social order. Insofar as these theologies articulate a social praxis rooted in Gospel imperatives, they cooperate in the healing and creative work of the Spirit in history and in society.

While there are important differences, the most general features which Black, Hispanic/Latino, and Native American theologies share include: (a) a point of departure in protracted historical and structural oppression, i.e., spiritual and cultural and psychological domination, racism, sexism, political repression, and economic exploitation; (b) commitment to articulate and engage the experiences and conditions of flesh and blood oppressed, marginalized, and poor children, women, and men; (c) critical appropriation of the religious experiences of the people – the Black religion of the "hush arbors," the popular religion of the masses, the symbol performances of Native American dance, pipe, and mask; (d) ideology critique, hermeneutics of suspicion, and social analysis as a tool for understanding history and underlying structures of social oppression; (e) a concern to develop strategies and plans for concrete social transformation; and (f) a drive to self-determination and self-actualization in church and society along with a common refusal to be objects of paternalistic care.

This discussion of Black, Hispanic/Latino, and Native American theologies in the United States departs from the format established for contributions to this volume. This essay begins with a characterization of the shared psychological, cultural, social, and historical location of Black, Hispanic/Latino, and indigenous peoples in relation to the "American experience." In the "discovery" and "invention" of America, these peoples were rendered "the other." Next, each of the three theological programs is presented, occasionally compared with one another, and appraised. Finally, a word on the method of approach. This essay could easily be misread as a static exposition in which important shifts are reduced to linear stages and temporal arbitrary phases are imposed on robust vital movements. But, written by someone who is a theologian and a participant in the Black theology movement, the essay intends nothing of the kind. Rather, it is best understood as a rhetorical strategy for a more or less orderly introduction to dynamic shifts in theological thinking.[4]

A Characterization of the Shared "Location" of Black, Hispanic/Latino, and Native American Theologies

Black, Hispanic/Latino, and Native American theologies come out of communities which have survived the brutish hegemony of white supremacist rule in the Americas. Each of these theologies arises from communities which have been betrayed by a Christianity deeply implicated, not only in the conquest and colonization of the Americas, but also in its invention.[5] Each of these theologies can draw upon legacies of vigorous historical armed and negotiated resistance to cultural genocide, enslavement, exploitation, and marginalization.

Immigration and exile, invention and discovery, conquest and colonization, wilderness and progress: these familiar tropes are employed to characterize the "American experience." But tropes twist and turn and cloak the meanings of words. For Native American, Black, and Hispanic/Latino peoples these tropes signify twisted realities, "master narratives." For the indigenous peoples, the "American experience" has been mediated by US government policies of paternalism and of dependency. The Indians and their descendants were dispossessed by Europeans and their descendants; the land which they cherished and had inhabited for nearly 40,000 years was subdued and degraded in the name of progress.[6] The Africans experienced "America" as rupture, as involuntary, as enslavement, as alienation.[7] For 440 years the enslaved peoples and their progeny have sojourned in the diaspora; for only slightly more than 100 of those years have they been free under law. For Hispanic/Latino peoples, conquest, violation, and the "double rejection" of the *mestizaje* shape their experience of "America." The offspring of sadistic erotic violence, cultural and political subjugation, Hispanic/Latino peoples are forever forced to incarnate loss, displacement, and periphery.[8]

Black Theology

Development

The most obvious provocation for "Black theology" is the ferment agitated by the political and cultural movement of Black consciousness in the mid to late 1960s in the United States. The term seems to have cropped up in the preparation of a 1968 report by the Theological Commission of the National Conference of Black Churchmen (NCBC), a predominantly Protestant group then known as the National Committee of Negro Churchmen. It is likely that a member of the NCBC, perhaps, Albert Cleage, Jr, who promoted a controversial Black Christian nationalism, was the first to articulate and introduce the phrase Black theology. However, no author or theologian has claimed to have used the term prior to the publication of James H. Cone's *Black Theology and Black Power*.[9] For nearly 30 years under Cone's creative intellectual leadership, demanding teaching, and zealous mentoring, theologians of the Black theology movement have sustained one of the more innovative and fertile streams of thought in Christianity in North America.[10]

Although formal, self-conscious articulation of Black theology emerges in the twentieth century, the religious and political resistance of Black women and men in the eighteenth and nineteenth centuries to slavery and white supremacist rule constitute its hermeneutical antecedent. Black theology strives to discern, understand, interpret, and impart the word of God and its meaning for the historical, religious, cultural, and social life of the Black community. Black theology is a complex phenomenon in which several phases can be distinguished: the first, from 1964 to 1969; the second, from 1970 to 1976; the third, from 1977 to 1989; the fourth, from 1990 to the present.[11]

The *formative phase* of Black theology lies in the civil rights movement of the 1950s which grew on the religious faith and activism of the masses of Black Christians. However, by the mid-1960s many Black pastors and clergy had grown increasingly disenchanted with the demand of the Reverend Dr Martin Luther King, Jr, for absolute commitment to nonviolent protest and suffering love. King's strategy was stretched thin by the "weakness of the moderate centrism of the Black Church," the social critiques of Malcolm X, and the protracted police and FBI probes of the Black Panther Party.[12] Finally, the demand for "Black power" by members of the Student Non-violent Coordinating Committee (SNCC or "Snick") polarized and splintered the precarious harmony and fragile compromise that King had forged between Blacks and whites.[13] When the NCBC issued a formal statement in the *New York Times* to affirm and clarify "Black power," they set the stage for a new religious and social perspective – Black theology.

Black theology emerged during a period of intense ecclesial, cultural, and social activism. Black and white clergy and laity demonstrated for programs to redress the effects of anti-Black racism and, in predominantly white churches, Blacks formed caucuses or congresses (e.g., Black Methodists for Church Renewal, the National Office for Black Catholics) for mutual support and strategies for ecclesial change. But the *second phase* of Black theology is marked chiefly by its academic appropriation in North America and Europe. Black theology met serious scrutiny from a small group of Black and white seminary and university professors who questioned its aims and agenda, especially in relation to violence, reconciliation, and ideology. During this period, Black scholars organized the Society for the Study of Black Religion (SSBR) which, under the leadership of Shelby Rooks, resumed the dialogue begun by the NCBC with African theologians in the 1960s. In addition to James Cone, the most provocative Black theologians of this phase were Cecil Cone, Vincent Harding, Major Jones, William Jones, C. Eric Lincoln, Charles Long, J. Deotis Roberts, and Gayraud Wilmore.

There were two challenges that pushed Black theology out of this academic phase and into a third. The first shove came from those Black scholars who called attention to a crisis of identity and sources in the work of the major proponents of Black theology, especially James Cone and J. Deotis Roberts. Cecil Cone, in particular, pointed up the tensions. On the one hand, Black theology had begun to display an impulse for "white academic" legitimation and a "universalism" that clouded its interpretation of the black religious experience. On the other hand, Black theology displayed an uncritical acceptance of Black power; this left it vulnerable to reproach from the centrist wing of the Black church.[14] The second shove came from the participation of Black theologians in Theology in the Americas (TIA). TIA was an ecumenical organization and process for theological reflection directed by an exiled Chilean priest, Sergio Torres, and a Filipino Maryknoll Sister, Virginia Fabella. In August 1975, TIA facilitated a conference of theologians, church workers, social theorists, and activists from Latin America, North America, and Africa, in Detroit. However, the Detroit meeting was dominated by white North American religious leftists who were most eager to dialogue with the Latin Americans. They concentrated discussion on (Marxist) economic analysis and stepped away from any critique of white racism. US minority-group participants formed a caucus to contest both the conference program and process. In this way, TIA was redefined by the cultural, political, economic, and theological concerns of marginalized US peoples and its analysis of injustice in the United States was sharpened. Through their affinity groups (the Black Theology Project, the Hispanic Theology Project, and the Indigenous Peoples Theology Project) Black, Hispanic/Latino, and Native American theologians achieved a new level of collaborative action and theological praxis.[15]

The *third phase* of Black theology lasted more than a decade and has proved quite fertile. Within a year of "Detroit I," the Black Theology Project (BTP) began to prepare for the first national ecumenical consultation on Black theology. Charles S. Spivey, Jr, the first executive director of the Programme to Combat Racism of the World Council of Churches, served as chair of the Project. A core of Black professional theologians and social scientists, including James Cone, Gayraud S. Wilmore, Herbert Edwards, and Howard Dodson, assisted the program staff, Baptist minister Muhammad Kenyatta, and me to design a process for the 1977 consultation, "The Black Church and the Black Community." Participants included not only pastors, priests, church executives, bishops, and Roman Catholic sisters, but also grassroots activists and representatives of progressive as well as left-wing political organizations. The chief aim of the consultation was to determine national and international issues pertinent to the Black community and to reconnect Black theology to the mission and self-understanding of the Black Church. In the keynote address to the conference, James Cone outlined some fresh priorities. His analysis showed the influence of Cone's Union Theological Seminary colleague, philosopher Cornel West, who used Marxist categories to thematize Black theology as a critique of capitalist civilization, and that of Cone's student Jacquelyn Grant, who called attention to the absence of any critique of sexism within male-dominated Black theology. In adverting to global economic and political imperialism and in acknowledging the corrosive sexism of Black male theologians, Cone complexified and extended the scope of Black theology's agenda.

Two instances of Black theology's vitality should be singled out – the emergence of womanist theology and the reception of Black theology by Black Catholics. As early as 1970, some Black women had begun to expose and contest the "double, even triple" jeopardy of their position.[16] But it was not until the 1980s that Black women ethicists, theologians, and sociologists of religion began to differentiate explicitly their theologizing from that of Black male theologians and white (liberal) feminist theologians. James Cone, in *Black Theology and Black Power*, had acknowledged the equality of men and women in the order of divine creation, but he neither investigated nor elaborated the ways in which society and church frustrated women in realizing that equality. In the early 1980s, Katie G. Cannon, Delores S. Williams, Jacquelyn Grant, Toinette M. Eugene, and Cheryl Townsend Gilkes drew explicitly on Black women's religious, cultural, and social experience as data for theological analysis.[17] They named this theology womanist after Alice Walker's creative treatment of the African American cultural epithet, "womanish" (meaning audacious, daring, acting grown, etc.). Walker's controversial definition of womanist is not primarily religious, although it does advert to the centrality of the Spirit as the "operative manifestation of God in everyday [African-American] life."[18] An excellent example of theology in womanist perspective is *Sisters in the Wilderness: The challenge of womanist God-talk* by Delores Williams. Williams exposes Black theology's failure to confront sexist practices in the Black community and the bifurcation of its biblical hermeneutics along gender lines.

The reception of Black theology in a Catholic context is another distinctive feature of this third phase. After more than ten years of adapting their liturgical and pastoral situation to their African-American culture, Black Catholics began to address their theological situation. In the fall of 1978, under the auspices of the National Black Catholic Clergy Caucus, a small group of Black priests led by Thaddeus Posey, OFM Cap., and in consultation with (Sister) Jamie T. Phelps, OP, organized the first meeting of the Black Catholic Theological Symposium (BCTS). Two years later, members of the symposium established the Institute for Black Catholic Studies, a graduate interdisciplinary pastoral theology program at Xavier University of Louisiana.

Despite its fertile expansion, with very good reason, Black theology remained fixed in a critique of anti-black racism in society and in church; its creativity all but monopolized. A "second generation" of Black theologians (to use George Cummings's denotation) broke this impasse not by abandoning critique of anti-black racism altogether, but by shifting their attention to both their enslaved ancestors and to their children. These scholars initiated retrieval of the significance of Africa as a complex historical reality and religious image, of the multifaceted cultural consequences of the "middle passage," and of the foundational stature of the Hebrew Bible for the religion of the enslaved peoples. Thus, by simultaneously looking to the past and the future, these women and men, many of whom were James Cone's students, pointed Black theology toward new sources and directions and ushered in its current *fourth phase*.

Survey

The following survey maps the current terrain of the Black theology movement and presents the work of some of the more prominent theologians of this fourth phase. When Cummings refers to these men and women as "second generation" Black theologians, he is signifying not only new priorities in Black theology, but also the fact that, for the first time, Black students who wished to study theology now had a discipline that emerged from within their own religious and cultural horizon and teachers with whom they might study.

An early criticism of Black theology was its distance from African and African-American culture and sources. When, in the 1970s, Charles H. Long questioned the very possibility of Black theology, he did so because he was skeptical of the adequacy of theology as a European-derived discipline to examine and interpret Black religious experience and expression. Long also argued that existential and psychological analyses of anti-Black racism were equally impoverished for this task. In this fourth phase, Black theologians have given considerable attention to African and African-American sources and Long's position now seems proleptic.[19]

While scholars may dispute his conclusions regarding the death of the Africans' gods, in *Slave Religion: The "invisible institution" in the ante-bellum South*, Albert Raboteau presented a historical study that helped lay the ground for investigations of African retentions in the religious and cultural practices of the slaves. But the most remarkable departure from Black theology as protest against racism came from the collaborations of Dwight Hopkins, George Cummings, and Will Coleman. In *Cut Loose Your Stammering Tongue: Black theology in the slave narratives*, these scholars used interdisciplinary methods to examine the rhetorical strategies, folk culture, music, religious rituals, and interpretative traditions of the enslaved peoples. *Shoes That Fit Our Feet: Sources for a constructive Black theology* is a "five-finger exercise" in which Hopkins mines indigenous religious and cultural sources for Black theology. The basic project of both these books is to ground the praxis of liberation on the political and economic front in the critical discursive, imaginative, and emancipative practices of the enslaved peoples. Other examples of the these interdisciplinary studies include *"A Peculiar People": Slave religion and community-culture among the Gullahs* by Martha Washington Creel, *Dark Symbols, Obscure Signs: God, self and community in the slave mind* by Riggins R. Earl, Jr, and *Conjuring Culture: Biblical formations of Black America* by Theophus H. Smith.

James H. Evans, Jr, in *We Have Been Believers: An African-American systematic theology*, outlines the first formal self-conscious systematic account of the faith that emanates from Black people's encounter with the message of the Gospel. Evans considers theology a churchly task. His project is concerned less with the excavation of cultural sources than with showing how those sources mediate African-American Christian faith. Josiah Young III is another constructive theologian whose work demonstrates the vitality of cultural and political sources. Young's *A Pan-African Theology: Providence and the legacies of the ancestors* explores the emancipatory and liberating aspects of the work of early Pan-Africanists Alexander Crummell and Edward Blyden in order to facilitate the liberation praxis of Black churches in Africa and the Americas.

The notion of Jesus of Nazareth as the "Black Messiah" or the "Black Christ" is recurrent in African-American religious thought. In the formative and first phases of Black theology, Albert Cleage, Jr, James Cone, Vincent Harding, J. Deotis Roberts, and Gayraud Wilmore all wrestled with it. Kelly Brown Douglas reassesses their treatment of the blackness of Jesus in *The Black Christ*. She argues that because the idea of "the Black Christ" is grounded in racial critique, it is inadequate and impotent for the present historical and theological moment. Douglas spells out a version of Black christology that goes beyond the positions of the Black male theologians and of womanist theologian Jacquelyn Grant's *White Women's Christ and Black Women's Jesus*. Douglas achieves this in two ways: First, her starting points are what she calls a "religio-cultural analysis" that identifies the sustaining and liberating dimensions of Black religion and culture and a "social analysis of wholeness" that explores the implications of the intersection of gender, race, class, and sexual orientation. She opens up the three-dimensional category of oppression to include the neglected experience of lesbians and gay men. There is another difference between her view and Grant's formulation of womanist theology. Grant's christological analysis identifies the Christ of Black women's experience with Black women: Hence, Christ *is* a black woman. Douglas, on the other hand, out of "wholeness" affirms Christ's real presence in the entire Black community's collaborative struggle toward wholeness.

The contributions of womanist ethicist Katie Cannon are important for at least two reasons: First, before other Black ethicists and theologians, she pioneered the use of literature, literary theory, history, cultural resources, and narrative style in Black theology; and second, hers was the first extended essay in womanist ethics and theology. In *Black Womanist Ethics*, Cannon clarifies the problematic of Black women's agency by formulating their moral situation as an egregious historical one. By placing Black women's experience at the center of her reflection, Cannon derives "womanist virtues" from Black women's life-giving, sustaining, and liberating practices. The work of womanist ethicists Marcia Y. Riggs (*Awake, Arise and Act: A womanist call to Black liberation*) and Emilie M. Townes (*In a Blaze of Glory: Womanist spirituality as social witness*) extends the path Cannon charted. In their work, Riggs and Townes incorporate social theory, make explicit the transformative character of Black women's voluntary associations, and delineate womanist spirituality as social witness.

George Cummings and Darryl Trimiew have shown ecumenical theological sensitivity to the idea of the "preferential option for the poor." Cummings's interpretative essay, *A Common Journey: Black theology (USA) and Latin American liberation theology*, promotes appreciation of the "thematic universe of the poor" and the use of hegemony as a theoretical framework for understanding the dynamics of domination. Trimiew's book, *Voices of the Silenced: The responsible self in a marginalized community*, is especially notable in its rejection of passivity or victimization as neither an acceptable nor a tolerable moral response for the poor and oppressed to their condition.

The "first generation" of Black theologians continue to contribute to the movement. Cone's *Martin & Malcolm & America* reconstructs the social horizon of Martin Luther King Jr and Malcolm X, both to clarify their responses and to glean wisdom for the future. In *The Prophethood of Black Believers*, J. Deotis Roberts refines his treatment of Black theology as a political theology for ministry. Finally Peter Paris's most recent work, *The Spirituality of African Peoples: The search for a common moral discourse*, thematizes the moral life through historical, religious, and anthropological sources that focus on the African experience in America. These works show how Black theologians and ethicists can assist the church in thinking through its identity and mission.

Achievement, Assessment, and Agenda

Three major achievements of Black theology can be identified. *First*, Black theology has moved beyond racial critique, *without forsaking* children, women, and men oppressed and marginalized by anti-Black racism. By retrieving the religious and cultural experiences of the enslaved peoples, Black theology has begun to illumine the relation of religious and cultural strategies for economic and political liberation and to do so in a way that obviates the constraints of modernity. A *second* achievement is Black theology's use of interdisciplinary research methods. In its retrieval of indigenous sources, Black theology has not hesitated to appropriate and apply the methods of history, anthropology, ethnography, as well as cultural, literary, and aesthetic theory. This extends Black theology's range of interpretative, systematic, and critical operations. *Third*, in its scholarly rigor, Black theology contributes substantively to the debates about Afrocentrism. Through application of interdisciplinary methods, Black theology has rejected any uncritical and rhapsodic image of Africa, thus sniffing out its own potential to ideologization or romanticization. This move insinuates Black theology's regard for theory and this regard is crucial. For oppressed, marginalized, and poor people, withdrawal to theory can never be *merely* an end in itself, but rather for the sake of the lives of the oppressed, the marginalized, the poor – and the life of truth.

Still, Black theology must come to terms with several issues; here are *five* concerns. Black theologians have shown an uncritical attitude toward the Bible. The Hebrew and Christian Scriptures were of paramount importance to the enslaved peoples because they apprehended their own experience in it. Biblical language, imagery, and events became so integral to Black culture and self-expression that Black people came to understand themselves as biblical people. But the intellectual climate generated by Eurocentricism forced Black biblical scholars to contest the prevailing notion that the primary relation of Black people to the Bible is postbiblical. They began to insert Blacks in the Bible and "to recapture the ancient biblical vision of racial and ethnic pluralism as shaped by the Bible's own universalism."[20] More recently, however, Black biblical scholars, including Randall C. Bailey, Obrey Hendricks, Clarice Martin, Vincent Wimbush, and Renita Weems, have recognized the limitations of this project. They have redirected their exegetical skills to disturb several points that, heretofore, Black theology had taken for granted. These questions include, among others, biblical authority, the ambiguous experience of women in the Bible, the status of land in the Bible, and the relation of the chosen people to other peoples they encounter in the Bible. Engagement with critical Black biblical scholarship is indispensable for Black theology's future.

Another shortcoming of Black theology is its lack of taste for the metaphysical. Some Black theologians have argued that such an urgent mediation of Christian faith must conserve its intellectual energy for critiques of the condition of oppressed Black people. These theologians have been suspicious that metaphysics was a "smoke screen to divert attention away from an action oriented theology."[21] Yet, this position is short-sighted. It limits Black theology's horizon to the immediate, to short-term problems, and undermines its regard for theory. Black Catholics have raised this concern on the level of doctrines: How is Black theology to tease out more adequately the soteriological implications of the Nicene/Chalcedonian formulation? How is Black theology to overcome theodicy without a sufficiently grounded notion of God that explicates, rather than describes the "Black experience of God"? The need for a critically derived metaphysics also may be raised on the level of dialectics: With the enigmatic arrival of postmodernity, new questions present themselves, e.g., identity and subjectivity, history and positionality, objectivity and knowing, being and reality. How can Black theology resolve these concerns without becoming mired in relativism? How is it to thematize and critique its own metaphysical assumptions?

Since its inception Black theology has been in more or less regular dialogue and collaboration with other liberation theologies, whether in the Caribbean, South Africa, Brazil, Peru, Korea, or the Philippines. However, the condition of the US social order and the deep anxieties it has spawned call Black theology to more intense dialogue and collaboration with US Hispanic/Latino, Asian, and Native American theologies.

Black women comprise at least half of the Black community and nearly two-thirds of the Black church. Black theology must take seriously sexism and sexist practices in the Black community and the Black church. Black theology must correct its oversight – Black women endure oppression not only in the dominant white racist patriarchal order, but also in the Black community and in the Black church. Black theology must expunge the myth that feminist concerns are white women's concerns.

Finally, homophobia in any Christian community is inimical to the Gospel. Except for the work of Elias Farajaje-Jones, Black male theologians have dodged this issue; womanists, on the other hand, have had to confront it because of the very complexity of Alice Walker's definition. The second of Walker's four-part definition of womanist refers to a woman who sometimes loves other women sexually or nonsexually. In a 1989 round-table discussion in the *Journal of Feminist Studies of Religion* Cheryl J. Sanders charged that the term womanist conveys the connotation of Black lesbian and puts forward a lifestyle that is incompatible with Christian theological and ethical principles. Implicitly, Sanders questioned the relation of sexual orientation to womanist theology. While several womanists responded, they did not directly meet Sanders's characterization of gay and lesbian lifestyles. Kelly Brown Douglas has challenged womanist and Black theologians to break their silence about homosexuality. Indeed, Black and womanist theologies must begin to prosecute a vigorous critique of homophobia in the Black community and the Black church.

The current phase of Black theology coincides with the most shameful political and economic predicament which has trapped the masses of Black and poor people in the United States. This predicament must dominate the agenda for Black theology. Given the spiraling decline of the US social order, Black theology must turn to politics. Moreover, since political thought about the meaning of the good is itself in a dilemma, a Black political theology will need first to clarify the nature of the good then articulate an explanatory account of the cultural and social matrices which comes to terms with the interaction and conditioning of racism, sexism, class exploitation, homophobia, anti-semitism, and capitalist imperialism. At the same time, this theology will meet the psychological and spiritual needs that are related to the suffering and despair brought about by dominative biased social relationships and structures.

Hispanic/Latino Theology

Development

From its beginning, US Hispanic/Latino theology has had to struggle to establish its own identity over against subordination to Latin American theologies of liberation. Although influenced by its Latin American counterpart, US Hispanic/Latino theology is distinct in standpoint, thematic content, and context or *realidad*. In doing theology, Hispanic/Latino theologians begin by reflecting on their own experience within their communities. One of their central concerns is the survival of Hispanic/Latino people as a people in the United States, hence this theology resists the "assimilatory pressures and prejudices of US life."[22] Hispanic/Latino theology objects to the intrusion of values and practices harmful to the survival of its peoples and their cultures. Finally, Hispanic/Latino theology is a "border theology."[23] In its critical mediation of faith, Hispanic/Latino theology simultaneously bridges arrival and departure, transgresses geography and cosmology, contests the restructuring of consciousness by language while creating new consciousness, and privileges oral memory even as it writes and theorizes. At the same time, Hispanic/Latino theology has had to wedge its way into the bipolar (white–black) arrangement of the US situation which in itself presupposes the hiddenness, if not erasure, of Native Americans, the indigenous nations. Thus, Hispanic/Latino theology emerges in forced alterity to mediate the Gospel of the "Other," the "Co-Sufferer" whose life and ministry, death and resurrection inaugurates a new and paradoxical order of beauty and justice.

It is possible already to discern three phases in the development of Hispanic/Latino theology: the first, from the 1950s to the mid-1960s; the second, from about 1968 to 1979; and the third, from 1980 to the present.

The *staging ground* for Hispanic/Latino theology is rooted in the Hispanic *movimiento* for civil rights in society and for respect in the Roman Catholic Church. Hispanic/Latinos had to fight to gain the obligations and benefits already conferred by their US citizenship. In less publicized, but no less arduous campaigns to realize equal treatment and justice before the law, the League of United Latin American Citizens won school desegregation lawsuits in 1945 in California, and in 1948 in Texas before *Brown vs the Board of Education*. Hispanic/Latinos enacted lawsuits for equal access to education, employment, public services and facilities.[24]

Hispanic/Latinos also found themselves fighting for acceptance in their Church.[25] Sensitive to the recurrence of anti-Catholic bias, the hierarchy promoted "Americanization" over against the maintenance of parishes centered around the languages and cultures of European immigrants. This attempt at deculturalization was also directed toward Hispanic/Latinos. While Hispanic/Latinos were to relinquish their language, religious devotions, and cultural customs, the bishops and clergy also urged them to accept gradualism in the face of social injustice. Inevitably, the Church itself became a "target of the *Movimiento*."[26]

During this period, Mexican-American César Chávez came to embody the struggle of Hispanic/Latinos, especially poor and marginalized men and women in society and Church. Inspired by Catholic social teaching, Chávez organized exploited Chicano migrant agricultural workers into the United Farm Workers Union (UFW). But, when the Catholic hierarchy buckled under intimidation by wealthy growers and landowners, Chávez challenged their lack of pastoral care for these poor. Through his radical and unselfish simplicity of life, fierce honesty, and commitment to non-violence, Chávez evangelized his Church. Not only did the hierarchy begin to shed its neutrality, several bishops and clergy joined picket lines and supported boycotts.

While Chávez cannot be credited with the founding of PADRES and *Las Hermanas*, national organizations of Hispanic/Latino priests and vowed religious women respectively, his example galvanized and animated them to radical ministry on behalf of their peoples.[27] Moreover, in his use of religious symbols, precisely the insertion of representations of Our Lady of Guadalupe into sites and moments of political action, Chávez tapped into the peoples' popular devotions and linked their protest to that "first critical and prophetic cry . . . on behalf of *los indos* against the colonialist exploiters."[28] César Chávez planted the seeds for contemporary theological reflection on the condition of Hispanic/Latinos in the United States.

The formative and *second* phase of Hispanic/Latino theology begins with Virgilio Elizondo and extends throughout the decade of the 1970s. While the work of Virgilio Elizondo does not exhaust Hispanic/Latino theology, it would be unimaginable without his creative intellect. Elizondo anticipated nearly all the major analytical categories of Hispanic/Latino theology. He grasped the theological ability of the notion of *mestizaje* or miscegenation to project a theological anthropology that accounted for the peoples' grim experience of divine grace in the midst of erotic violence, cultural and political and economic hegemony. Elizondo was one of the first theologians to grasp the potential of popular religion as a *locus theologicus*. Moreover, Elizondo's deep regard and love for the masses and their devotional practices allowed for an invaluable contribution to theological method by taking culture seriously. Finally, his appropriation and reinterpretation of the story of Our Lady of Guadalupe as myth leads to the very heart of Mexican and Mexican-American culture and identity.[29]

From the outset, Elizondo's work was set in a pastoral and catechetical context. In 1968, he published "Educación religiosa para el México-Norte Americano," in which he pointed out how Catholic catechetical and liturgical materials ignored the faith traditions of Mexican-Americans.[30] With the support of Francis J. Furey, the archbishop of San Antonio, Texas, and Patrico Flores, the first Hispanic/Latino to be named a bishop in the United States, in 1971 Elizondo established the Mexican American Cultural Center (MACC). MACC began as a language institute to teach and promote the Spanish language, especially among non-Spanish-speaking priests and religious who served Hispanic/Latino communities. However, the institute soon developed courses in Scripture, the history and cultures of Latin American and Hispanic/Latino peoples, and pastoral theology. Members of PADRES and *Las Hermanas* served as faculty members and MACC became a model for research, study, writing, reflection, and conversation in support of Hispanic/Latinos and pastoral ministry with them.[31] For the next five years, Elizondo was tireless in lecturing, conducting workshops, and meeting with hundreds of individuals and groups in order to learn about "the actual problems, needs, aspirations, and expectations of [Hispanic/Latino] peoples." The more Elizondo confronted the pastoral situation of Mexican-Americans, the more he found it necessary to gain a deeper and more comprehensive understanding of the "historical process" that gave birth to the *mestizos.*[32]

In its preparation of Hispanic/Latinos and conscientization of Anglo-Americans, MACC engaged the dialectic of theory and praxis concretely. PADRES, *Las Hermanas*, MACC, and other pastoral centers were crucial in upholding the resistance of Hispanic/Latinos to any second-class membership in the Church. Their advocacy and analysis paved the way for the *encuentro* movement which aimed to work out a national pastoral plan for ministry with Hispanic/Latinos. The underlying theme of the *encuentros* was to bring the Church to ever deeper engagement with Hispanic/Latino cultures in evangelization, education, and religious formation. If the results of the *encuentro* movement remain ambiguous, the process invited a wide spectrum of Hispanic/Latino peoples to express their ideas, frustrations, and hopes openly and gave them valuable organizational and theological training. These various experiences instigated a real thirst for Hispanic/Latino theology grounded in the "American experience." The work of Gustavo Gutierrez and the TIA process would stimulate its emergence.

1968 marked the appearance of *Hacia un teología de la liberación* by Gustavo Gutiérrez.[33] This talk, given to priests and laity at Chimbote, Peru, was a first outline of a new theological response to the domination and oppression of the poorest peoples of Latin America. Here, Gutiérrez grasps theology as "a progressive and continuous understanding" and makes the distinction between theology and action. Theology, he declares, is "a second act, a turning back, a reflecting that comes after action. Theology is not first; the commitment is first and theology is the understanding of the commitment, and the commitment is action."[34] These ideas were expanded in a monograph that appeared in Spanish in 1971 and two years later under the English title, *A Theology of Liberation.*[35] This book, like no other, shook the world of theology. It called into question the very nature of theology's epistemological and praxial relationship to the poorest of peoples who clung to the Crucified Jesus. Virgilio Elizondo, according to Allan Figueroa Deck, was the first Hispanic/Latino to personally know Gustavo Gutiérrez. The many lectures and courses that Gutiérrez has presented at MACC not only affirm their friendship, but indicate the impact Gutiérrez has had, not only on Elizondo himself, but on the theological development of MACC.[36]

Hispanic/Latinos participated, along with Blacks and Native Americans, in the 1975 TIA Detroit conference. As part of the preparation for this meeting, participants were assigned to working (later affinity) groups in which they reflected on their histories and concrete situations in the US. After describing the situation, participants reflected on it in light of the Gospel, Christian tradition, and theology; in a third moment in this process, they proposed action for change.[37] The Chicano Reflection Group was led by members of *Las Hermanas* and PADRES, including

Sister Mario Barron, Roberto Peña, Juan Romero, and Edmundo Rodríguez; nearly all of them had been associated with MACC. Their presentation most fully interrogated the religio-cultural dimension of Chicano/a experience, while addressing the danger of immersion *en la lucha* – ignoring the oppression of others in the "third world."

In his analysis of the Detroit conference, Gregory Baum captured the disappointment of Chicanos with the white Catholic theological community's concentration on Europe and European theological traditions. Catholic theologians, they asserted, overlooked the conditions and gifts of "the forgotten" people of the barrios and borders. One of those gifts was their own authentic Catholic religious heritage which they have defended against the Anglicized spirit of US Catholicism with its "demanding efficiency and mastery even in religious matters." Chicano conference participants also protested the tendency of black theologians to divide the United States into the white oppressor and the black oppressed. Such bifurcation, they argued, only inhibits the collaborative struggle of blacks and browns, while the dominant group plays one critique off against the other.[38] Finally, the Chicanos intentionally distanced themselves from attempts by those from outside their situation to speak for them; this was especially true of the Latin American theologians. These Chicano men and women insisted on intellectual independence; they would think for themselves.

The *current* and third phase of Hispanic/Latino theology can be marked by the 1980 founding of the Hispanic/Latino theological journal *Apuntes* and by the 1981 meeting of Hispanic/Latino doctoral students and recent degree recipients at MACC. *Apuntes* is a journal of Hispanic/Latino theology edited by the Methodist historian Justo González and published at the Perkins School of Theology at Southern Methodist University. Until the 1993 appearance of the *Journal of Hispanic/Latino Theology*, this was the sole organ devoted exclusively to the theology of Hispanic/Latino peoples. These events, the publication of *Apuntes* and the meeting of doctoral students, disclose the two most basic tensions of contemporary Hispanic/Latino theology – the academic and the pastoral. Happily, however, these forces have resulted in the dynamic unfolding of creativity in the past 15 years. For, if that gathering of Hispanic/Latino doctoral students intimated the academic impulse, the fact that they met at MACC inserted them in the reality of their people. This creativity is also disclosed in the emergence of *mujerista* theology, the organization of the Academy of Catholic Hispanic Theologians in the United States (ACHTUS), and the founding of the *Journal of Hispanic/Latino Theology*.

From its beginning, Hispanic/Latino theology has been informed by the insights of women and roughly 25 percent of Hispanic/Latino theologians are reported to be women. The first US Hispanic woman to take a doctorate in theology is Marina Herrera and María Pilar Aquino is the first woman to attain a doctorate in theology from the Pontifical University of Salamanca, Spain. Herrera and the Cuban American Ada María Isasi-Díaz have been writing since the mid-1970s. Other outstanding Hispanic/Latino women theologians include María de la Cruz Aymes, Yolanda Tarango, Jeanette Rodríguez, Ana María Pineda, Gloria Inés Loya, and Rosa María Icaza.[39] The originary, thoroughgoing, critical participation of women in the formulation of nascent Hispanic/Latino theology distinguishes it from Black theology and Latin American theologies of liberation at a similar stage.

The chief characteristics of *mujerista theology* as Ada María Isasi-Díaz and Yolanda Tarango develop it in *Hispanic Women: Prophetic voice in the Church* are: *first*, attentiveness to the complex cultural rootedness of Hispanic/Latina women since their peoples include many different national groups; *second*, refusal to be determined by sexism and patriarchy; and *third*, commitment to change oppressive social structures that cripple the survival of Hispanic/Latino peoples, and Hispanic/Latina women specifically. *Mujerista theology* is the critical reflective and liberating praxis of Hispanic/Latina women who, in probing their religious experience, engage four, open-ended, "interwoven and interfacing" movements: sharing their stories, analyzing their situation, liturgizing, and strategizing. In this process, the theologian listens, evokes conversation and dialogue through questions, then assembles the data and presents it. The theologian is a kind of "technician" placing highly specialized skills and competencies (e.g., biblical exegesis, languages, social sciences, archaeology, etc.) at the service of the community in order to enhance its self-determined praxis.[40]

While there is no precise account of the origin of ACHTUS, Allan Figueroa Deck thinks that the idea for such a group surely must have surfaced during the *encuentros*. ACHTUS can be traced more directly, however, to conversations between Figueroa Deck and Arturo Bañuelas while they were doctoral students in Rome. The two were alarmed at the absence of a "more critical and theologically grounded" analysis of the situation of US Hispanic/Latinos. Back in the States, in 1987 Figueroa Deck and Bañuelas identified other theologically trained men and women who shared their concerns: María Pilar Aquino, Roger Luna, Roberto Goizueta, C. Gilbert Romero, Orlando Espín, and Virgilio Elizondo. This group met in January 1988 at the Jesuit School of Theology at Berkeley. They quickly organized themselves and began to canvass for a membership that mirrored the national cultural diversity of Hispanic/Latino peoples. The first annual meeting of ACHTUS took place in June 1989 at the Graduate Theological Union in Berkeley, California.[41] ACHTUS has been a forum in which new initiatives, questions, and issues in Hispanic/Latino theology may be raised for conversation and debate. Moreover, it has been a structured opportunity for crossing borders to dialogue with Hispanic/Latino Protestant and Black Catholic theologians. In October 1991, ACHTUS co-sponsored an ecumenical conference on Hispanic theology at Union Theological Seminary in New York City. Considering the affinity between popular religion and evangelical/pentecostal Christianity, the need for sophisticated sociological analysis and serious dialogue between Catholic and Protestant Hispanic/Latinos cannot be underestimated. The first joint meeting of ACHTUS and BCTS explored points of contact between Hispanic/Latino and African-American communities. The effort of Hispanic/Latino and black Catholic theologians to forge an "ongoing articulation of *teologías de conjunto*" reaches across their Church's attempt, whether conscious or not, to rank in order the plight of their peoples.[42]

During the 1980s the population of Hispanic/Latino peoples in the United States increased by more than one-third. Figueroa Deck has called this a new "second wave" of immigration and it prompts several pastoral challenges for Hispanic/Latino ministry and theology.[43] These include the stiffening of US immigration policies with regard to Mexicans, Central and Latin Americans, as well as discrimination against Hispanic/Latino citizens and green-card holders because of their race and presumed ethnicity; increased hostility toward bilingual and multicultural education; and the growth of evangelical/pentecostal Christianity among Hispanic/Latino Catholics. These pastoral issues insinuate themselves in the ongoing formulation of Hispanic/Latino theology.

Survey

This essay has privileged Catholicism's historic and ironic mediation of the religious experience of Hispanic/Latino peoples and their theology, yet the presence and contribution of Hispanic/Latino Protestantism ought not be discounted. This brief survey will introduce some of the more outstanding Protestant as well as Catholic US Hispanic/Latino theologians who are writing at present.

According to Enrique Dussel, the results of the *desencuentro* between the peoples of Mesoamerica and Spain provoke a Copernican revolution in cultural and historical hermeneutics.[44] On this basis, Justo L. González, the most prominent Hispanic/Latino Protestant theologian, has been excavating the complex religious, historical, and cultural context that is the point of departure for Hispanic/Latino theology. In *Mañana: Christian theology from a Hispanic perspective* González bridges the Protestant–Catholic divide with two dramatic assertions: that "the Spanish American Roman Catholic Church is part of the common background of all Hispanics" and that the Guadalupe event "is indeed part of the gospel message."[45] These claims foreground the subtle, mutual, enduring, and paradoxical saturation of the religious ethos and cultural practices of both *los indos* and the Spanish *conquistadores*. They also reiterate the appearance of the "little Virgin of Guadalupe" as a liberating force for *los indos*, not only in her *mestiza* embodiment, but also in her explicit critique of the collusion of the Church in the oppression of the poor. González clears the ground for theological praxis that is intrepid in both its ecumenicity and decentering of Western European religious and social history.

The impact of the historical analysis González has made is felt especially in evangelization. The late Protestant theologian Orlando Costas, like Virgilio Elizondo, was alert to the pastoral needs of Hispanic/Latinos and was able to translate this concern into strategic responses in Protestant seminaries. In *Liberating News: A theology of contextual evangelization*, Costas, like Elizondo, appropriates the historical situation of Jesus as a Galilean – an outsider to the dominant religious, cultural, and social order – to express the marginalization of Hispanic/Latino peoples. This work is a constructive and contextual theological reflection on evangelization as a prophetic and apostolic task and in light of Scripture as a prophetic and apostolic text.

Protestant pastoral theologians Ignacio Castuera and Roberto Gómez have been developing appropriate strategies in pastoral counseling for Hispanic/Latinos. Jorge Lara-Braud, Jill Martínez, Luis N. Rivera-Pagán, and Harold Recinos have been especially concerned with the interaction of theory and praxis and with cross-cultural dynamics.

Orlando Espín is another Catholic theologian indebted to the generative theological work of Virgilio Elizondo. He has appropriated Elizondo's insights regarding the significance of the popular religion of the people. Espín's theological work is best understood as radically foundational. He retrieves the practices, ethos, and sensibilities of popular religion among Hispanic/Latinos as a privileged *locus* for theology. At the same time, Espín argues a continuity between popular religion and the *sensus fidelium*, which refers to the intuitive grasp on truth that ordinary Christians affirm both in assent to the teachings of the Church and to their own discernment and knowledge of truth by virtue of their living and lived witness of faith. This is a kind of "supernatural sixth sense" that denotes the inner presence and working of God as Spirit in a person of faith. Popular religion, Espín asserts, is the cultural expression of the *sensus fidelium*. This has a bearing on his theology of grace: Since the *sensus fidelium* signifies the pneumatological character of the community of faith, then the concrete experience of grace may be explicated more adequately. One other feature of Espín's theological program is important. Espín's doctoral studies in Brazil have given him intimate access to the lineaments of popular religion that respond to the Spanish and Portuguese disruption of African cultures. Thus, in Espín's work, the *mestizaje* as hermeneutical category is enlarged and complexified.

Allan Figueroa Deck and Arturo Bañuelas bridge the pastoral and the theoretical in their work. Figueroa Deck engages the complexity of the social and pastoral situation in *The Second Wave*. Building from demographic, economic, and historical interpretation, he outlines eight ministerial priorities: sacramentalization, conscientization and empowerment, the formation and nurture of base ecclesial communities, parish renewal, preparation and promotion of lay leadership, youth ministry, and coordinated pastoral planning. For Figueroa Deck the realization of these initiatives also requires the evangelization of a materialistic, individualistic, hedonistic North American culture. Moreover, since the Church is present at the heart of this culture, which is so destructive to the survival of Hispanic/Latino peoples, it has become an ambiguous sign. Figueroa Deck's work demonstrates how Hispanic/Latino theology can provide a critique of the Church's secularization and assimilation of North American culture. While Figueroa Deck incorporates social analysis in his work, he overcomes the dogmatic tendencies in Marxist analysis as well as social science functionalism to adopt a nuanced method – *investigación-acción participativa*.

Bañuelas is Director of the Tepeyac Institute, a lay ministry formation center, and a pastor in El Paso, Texas. Bañuelas's ACHTUS colleagues have been pushing him to thematize a "border epistemology," since he is situated on a geographic as well as a (fundamental) theological border. Bañuelas's ministry positions him to meet the poor who cross into the US from Mexico and Central America seeking survival; his training in fundamental theology will allow him to delineate a critical epistemology that travels back through language and culture to reconstruct a new (metaphysical and epistemological) ground for the liberation of these new migrants.

In *En la Lucha*, Ada María Isasi-Díaz elaborates the proposals she and Tarango put forward in that first work, *Hispanic Women: Prophetic voice of the Church*. In this essay, Isasi-Díaz reflects systematically on theological method and explicitly names sources that enrich and complicate *mujerista theology* – ethnic diversity, popular religion, social location, and the function of Spanish language.

Not all Hispanic/Latina women identify themselves or their theological work as *mujerista*. Both Jeanette Rodríguez and María Pilar Aquino have taken other paths to illumine the theological questions of Hispanic/Latinas. Rodríguez has employed a method of analysis and conversation not unlike that promoted by Tarango and Isasi-Díaz, while adding demographic and associative questionnaires as well as a written reflection by the participant. Her study, *Our Lady of Guadalupe: Faith and empowerment among Mexican-American women*, explores the influence of this powerful female icon of Mexican culture on the everyday lives of Mexican-American women. Rodríguez conjectures a correlation between women's activism and their appropriation of the Guadalupe. Rodríguez concludes that Our Lady of Guadalupe challenges Hispanic/Latina women to transcend the limited roles and tasks assigned to them by home and culture. A Mexican national, María Pilar Aquino has become deeply inserted in the fabric of US Hispanic/Latino theology. Her work is sharply focused by the tensions inherent in working out a theology of liberation in the angular cultural and social context of the United States. Aquino shapes her theological project in the concrete multidimensional matrices of Hispanic/Latino historical and social oppression, thus her work sniffs out unconscious sexist, racist, and classicist presuppositions that crop up even in theologies of liberation. Finally, Aquino's *Our Cry for Life: Feminist theology from Latin America* radically inscribes the option for the poor onto US Hispanic/Latino theology and is singular for its comprehensive attention to social analysis and social location.

In his work, Roberto Goizueta attends to broad foundational (epistemology and aesthetics) and methodological (theory-praxis) questions. He works out in *Caminemos con Jesús: Toward a Hispanic/Latino theology of accompaniment* implications of the popular Catholicism of US Hispanic/Latinos as starting points for a *theology of accompaniment*. What is of special interest here is the way in which Goizueta rethematizes an organic Hispanic/Latino understanding of the human person and human action in the context of a history of the Western notion of praxis. Thus, he not only engages but decenters influential Western philosophical notions in confrontation with the reality of US Hispanic/Latino life. Once Goizueta clears the ground, the Hispanic/Latino apprehension of praxis grounds a *theology of accompaniment* that is itself grounded in the *preferential option for the faith of the poor*.

Achievement, assessment, and agenda

The most conspicuous achievement of US Hispanic/Latino theology is its own liberation. It has established and detached its identity from Latin American theologies of liberation, while continuing to dialogue with these theologies and support their critiques. *Second*, Justo González in *Mañana: Christian theology from a Hispanic perspective* proposes "reading the Bible in Spanish," that is, reading the Bible in light of the Hispanic/Latino experience of massive oppression. Hispanic/Latino biblical scholars including Fernando Segovia and Gilbert Romero early on developed a biblical hermeneutic attentive to the dynamics of historical, religious, cultural, and social oppression. Segovia especially has been working out a hermeneutics of otherness and a literary methodology of intercultural criticism. *Third*, the early engagement of the intellectual discoveries of women gives Hispanic/Latino theology an edge in relation to Black theology, white feminist theology in the US, and Latin American theologies of liberation. *Fourth*, from the beginning, Hispanic/Latino theology has been quite unafraid of theory and metaphysics. It has taken on dialectical readings and critique of Western European philosophy that both utilize and decenter that philosophy to offer a seriously differentiated theology. And *finally*, like Black theology, Hispanic/Latino theology celebrates its spirituality with élan and is unafraid to grasp it as resource for theological praxis.

These "new" theological movements in the US have often been criticized out of hand; sometimes, it is best that criticism come from within. However, there are some issues to be raised. Male chauvinism or sexism is not absent from the Hispanic/Latino community, but it has been sorely misunderstood. Indeed, the very word *machismo* has been construed by those outside the Hispanic/Latino community to convey meanings that are extrinsic to that community. Ada María Isasi-Díaz has pointed out that white women often project their own experience of misogyny onto Hispanic/Latinas. This means that Hispanic/Latinas must both protest the disguised racism that white women direct toward Hispanic/Latino men and the racist cultural and social class elitism that white women direct toward them. Nonetheless, Hispanic/Latino male theologians will need to give deeper attention to sexist oppression of Hispanic/Latinas in the home, the community, the Church, and the larger US society.

The condition of the US social order and the deep anxieties it has spawned call Hispanic/Latino theology to more intense dialogue and collaboration with Black, Asian, and Native American theologies.

Hispanic/Latino theology is deeply impacted by the notion of *mestizaje*; indeed, as a theological category, this notion signifies marginalization, struggle for acceptance and belonging, as well as an assumptive identity of the Crucified Jesus. Yet Hispanic/Latino theology is not sufficiently analytical of the egregious and debilitating white racist supremacy of the United States. Concrete social analysis as well as interrogation of the fabrication of US racist culture would provide Hispanic/Latino theology an opportunity for thoroughgoing solidarity with Black theology. Because Hispanic/Latino peoples are multiracial, such analysis may have the dissonant impact of conversion of life and theological work, making that solidarity all the more exacting and necessary. How can Hispanic/Latino theology claim and celebrate its African heritage, while overlooking those who bear Africa's most indelible mark – skin color?

Hispanic/Latino theology has evaded any discussion of homophobia, but it will have to begin to oppose this form of consciousness in the Hispanic/Latino community. Hispanic/Latino theology will have to meet the pastoral and psychological situation of gays and lesbians. Moreover, it will have to confront and engage ambiguous Catholic attitudes toward sex, sexuality, and sexual expression.

Finally, the basic tension between the pastoral and the theoretical or academic fertilizes Hispanic/Latino theology, yet it can evoke discontinuity. On the one hand, there is the danger that Hispanic/Latino theology will become increasingly identified with academic discourse; on the other hand, theoretical insights are necessary for adequately differentiated pastoral praxis. But, without engaged pastoral praxis, Hispanic/Latino theology risks apolitical religious reflection.

Native American Theology

Development

The attempt of this essay to present and discus the theological work of Native American Christians calls for a different framework. There are several reasons. *First*, there are many indigenous peoples or Native Americans in North America. Each tribe has its own history, its own language, its own sacred traditions, beliefs, and practices, its own cosmology. *Second*, the terms "religion," "theology," and "liberation" mediate concepts more at home in the Western cultural horizon. It is difficult to find words in Native American languages that accurately pin down these meanings. While these words are used here, they are used advisedly and carefully. *Third*, the early Protestant missionaries of North America did not attempt to evangelize the indigenous peoples as did the Roman Catholics in southern and central America. Rather, they tried to bring the indigenous peoples under the rule of Anglo-Saxon law. Later, Christian missionization would be an agent of cultural assault and violence against the peoples and their way of life. *Fourth*, for nearly 400 years, the indigenous peoples have been dehumanized by arbitrary definitions and stereotypes. Not only have the peoples been unnamed (Indians), they have been reduced to "terms" or "objects" in relation to discoverers, Puritans, colonists, missionaries, soldiers, settlers, citizens. *Fifth*, the indigenous peoples have been rendered a "social other": That is, *politically* the sovereign indigenous nations of North America have been subjugated, forcibly removed from their lands, suppressed, and marginalized to reservations; *economically*, treaty rights have been manipulated and disguised as welfare benefits; *technologically*, the indigenous peoples have been relegated to service and recreational labor. Hidden from view, the indigenous peoples have been reduced to quaint historical memories for other Americans; erased from historical texts, they are voices in the margin of history. Still, even this purchase of critical distance may insinuate a type of romantic hermeneutics, allowing evasion of the complexity of the modern Indian context.

In order to clarify the participation of indigenous peoples in liberation theology projects, at least a cursory understanding of their struggle for sovereignty and self-determination on the North American continent is necessary. Once the extent of indigenous resistance is clarified, the possibilities and limitations of the liberation paradigm as a mediator of Native religious life can be evaluated.

From the arrival of the very first settlement of European colonists, the indigenous peoples had to fight to defend their sovereignty and self-determination, to maintain their way of life, to protect the land. Tecumseh, Pontiac, Utsala, Black Kettle, Red Cloud, Sitting Bull, Crazy Horse, or Big Foot: Each indigenous leader adopted peaceful negotiation with whites, only to be driven to self-defense, then armed resistance. Shawnee, Miami, Sauk, Potawatomie, Chippewa, Illinois, Cherokee or Sioux: Thousands of children, women, and men were starved, infected with disease, and killed. This bitter and powerful legacy was a kind of sacred medicine to the modern Native American movement.

While there had been "fish-ins" in Washington state in 1964 and 1965, the first significant Indian protest in North America in the twentieth century occurred in Canada. Indians blockaded the Cornwall Bridge, claiming officials violated the Jay Treaty (1794) which exempted them from tolls and customs taxes. But it was the 1969 "invasion" and occupation of Alcatraz, the abandoned federal high-security prison in San Francisco Bay, that galvanized the attention of Indians and non-Indians. Isolated, without fresh running water or adequate sanitation, oil or mineral rights, industry and employment, or educational facilities for the indigenous peoples, Alcatraz symbolized the insidious conditions of the reservations.[46] This seizure sparked others in Seattle, Sioux Falls, Chicago, and New York. For the next four or five years, Indians protested local and regional infringements on their land, water, and fishing rights. During this period, the indigenous peoples resisted the looting of their burial grounds. In Washington, Minnesota, Iowa, Illinois, Pennsylvania, and New York, Indians disrupted digs conducted by white archaeologists for various museums and reburied the bones of their dead.[47]

But perhaps the two most conspicuous moments of the modern Indian protest were the "Trail of Broken Treaties," which led to confrontation with the Bureau of Indian Affairs (BIA), and the occupation of Wounded Knee, South Dakota. These nonviolent actions were the work of several tribes, but these, as well as others mentioned above, were most often coordinated by the American Indian Movement (AIM). This intertribal group originated among Indians in Minnesota and spread to reservations throughout North America. AIM had a twofold agenda – political activity and protest for Indian sovereignty and the reinstitution of the traditional religious life.

The Indian caravan known as the "Trail of Broken Treaties" intended to bring a documented list of treaty violations to Washington, DC, and demand enforcement. The BIA response was lukewarm and somehow a "scuffle broke out between younger Indians and the federal building guards."[48] All too familiar with police brutality and afraid of mass arrest, the Indians seized the BIA building. Threatened with forcible removal, in desperation and anger the Indians destroyed furniture and BIA files. Through the intervention of the Nixon White House, after about a week, they were persuaded to leave.[49]

The 1973 occupation of Wounded Knee was symbolically charged for Indians and non-Indians alike. Wounded Knee was the site of the December 1890 massacre of nearly 200 unarmed Sioux, mostly women and children. Americans had become aware of this tragedy through the 1971 publication of Dee Brown's *Bury My Heart at Wounded Knee*.[50] For two months, under the charismatic leadership of AIM activists Russell Means and Dennis Banks, the Indians held Wounded Knee. Again, the Nixon White House intervened and the Indians surrendered. But, while the president kept his promise to send a delegation to discuss the violations of the 1868 Sioux treaty, nothing tangible came of these discussions.

Yet, after these protests, no one could doubt the seriousness of the Indians' purpose or ignore the unbearable suffering of the peoples under the reservation system. There are at least three measurable results of this decade of protests and occupations. *First*, because of the militant activism of AIM, the Bureau of Indian Affairs was dismantled and reorganized and Congress authorized a two-year study of the conditions of Indians. *Second*, AIM had invited medicine men, including Leonard

Crow Dog and Frank Fools Crow, to perform traditional religious ceremonies for them during protests. This created an upsurge of interest in Indian religions and customs. *Finally*, this decade of determined Indian protest had reinscribed on the minds and hearts of the indigenous peoples – particularly the youth – the legacy of more than 350 years of struggle for sovereignty and self-determination. Indians now had a "different sense of Indian identity."[51]

In 1975, when Native Americans met Blacks, Hispanic/Latinos, whites, and Latin Americans at the TIA gathering in Detroit, they were animated by their immediate and remote past. But the process of the conference gave Native Americans little room to present their new thinking. The published proceedings of the TIA conference include a paper by the Franciscan Sister Jeanne Rollins, who worked on a Swinomish reservation in Washington state. It is unclear whether this paper was actually presented to the assembly, but it does open a window on the historical and social experience of Native Americans. Entitled "Liberation and Native Americans," this piece situated the indigenous peoples in relation to the oppressive disruption of their relationship to the land and the social and cultural devastation that has followed. These reflections affirmed the indigenous peoples' desire to reestablish their traditional religious life, to reject Western expressions of competition and progress, and to maintain respectful and responsible ways of living with the land.[52] Herb Barnes, Chairman of the National Association of Blackfeet Indians, was among the group who challenged the adequacy of TIA's articulation of the "conditions, experiences, and theological reflections of the nonwhite racial and national minorities living within the United States."[53] Like other members of TIA "reflection groups," Native Americans reorganized as the Indigenous Theology Project (ITP), bringing together native peoples who follow the traditional religious way of life and native peoples who were Christians.

With the conclusion of its first conference, almost immediately Torres and a new Steering Committee began preparations for a second meeting in 1980. In the five years between these gatherings, Torres, Fabella, and the national staff absorbed the critiques of the process, goals, and participant composition of the 1975 meeting. While this boded well for ITP, the very meaning of liberation theology for indigenous peoples was called into question by one of the foremost Native American intellectuals and activists, Vine Deloria, Jr. In an article written two years after the first TIA effort, Deloria expressed his skepticism. Liberation theology, he wrote, "was an absolute necessity if the establishment was going to continue to control the minds of minorities. If a person of a minority group had not invented [liberation theology], the liberal establishment most certainly would have created it." For if liberation theology, he argued, "does not seek to destroy the roots of oppression," then it is a specious liberal "gimmick" to keep oppressed peoples occupied while the oppressors "change the manner in which the oppression manifests itself."[54] Deloria was calling for critical activism for real change, not another conversation or dialogue. Perhaps the words sovereignty and self-determination, rather than emancipation and liberation are more expressive of the indigenous peoples' basic struggle.

The 1980 presentation of the Indigenous Theology Project was given by Brian "Mike" Meyers, of the Seneca Nation. An early member of ITP, Meyers was former

editor of *Akwesasne Notes*, an international journal of indigenous peoples; this association gave TIA a worldwide introduction to dispossessed indigenous peoples.
Moreover, from his position as coordinator of the Haudenosaunee Self-Sufficiency
Center, Meyers organized and facilitated dialogues between Indians from around
the world and non-Indians. Speaking for the Indigenous Theology Project, he set
out the critical vision of the indigenous peoples and the basic themes for any
theological reflection on their struggle for religious, cultural, and political self-
determination. Simply put, the indigenous people were committed to honor life.
Native Americans understood themselves as fighting for life – the very life of the
earth, the life of all living things, their own lives, even the lives of their oppressors.
Thus the ecological integrity of the earth was deemed an absolute and sacred
necessity, but not for the sake of "the two-leggeds" or human beings, rather because
the earth is life, the mother of all that lives. They insisted that any talk of liberation
had to include liberation of the land. To express the peoples' vision and commitment to honor and fight for life even more concretely, Meyers introduced the
notion of family and relatives. In a most exquisite gesture of solidarity and forgiveness, the indigenous peoples went far beyond notions of "coalition" and "alliance"
to embrace *all* the beings of the world as *relatives*. Whatever indigenous theology
would develop must flow organically from this vision.

ITP had prepared an outline of specifics. *First*, the indigenous peoples rejected
any designation of themselves as "third world peoples." Drawing on their historic,
intimate, and deep communion with the land, they named themselves peoples of the
"natural world." *Second*, because many white leftists avowed atheism, the indigenous
peoples rejected their social analysis. To the Indians, atheists lacked any authentic
sense of respect for life and creation, any authentic spirituality. They concluded that
atheism made white leftists "dangerous," not only to themselves, but to creation,
the earth, all that is living. *Third*, the indigenous peoples sharply distinguished their
understandings and practices of "economic development" and "work" from those
of white Americans. Speaking from their historical experience of US oppression, the
indigenous peoples made a connection between "economic development" and "work"
and the ideas of "manifest destiny" and "progress" that had despoiled the land and
displaced their ancestors. The indigenous peoples called for "non-exploitative [and]
non-extractive technologies" that would place people over profit and apprehended
work as recreative participation in the development of life. Finally, the indigenous
peoples opposed their *way of life* to that of the "white way." The indigenous peoples
affirmed women's equal and differentiated share of power in tribal structures; life in
community with a high degree of accountability and mutuality; and celebration of
people and nature.[55]

Even as members of the Indigenous Theology Project collaborated in the TIA
process they challenged the worldview Christianity had mediated. The indigenous
peoples repudiated the split of human beings from nature, matter from spirit, mind
from body, vision from theory, fact from value. But, perhaps, it was not so much
that they rejected Christianity out of hand, but rather wished for a Christianity less
imposing and more attuned to their way. ITP also decentered the theological assumptions of liberation theology. Perhaps a Native American theology might be
most properly expressed in terms of survival and self-determination.

Survey

What follows is a discussion of some of the indigenous peoples involved in working out the theological situation of Native Americans. This brief survey begins with the work of Vine Deloria, Jr. As a college student, Deloria became conscious of the importance of Native traditions to the Indian future; as a seminary student at the Lutheran School of Theology, he "came to a critically antagonistic relationship with Euro-American Christian culture."[56] In questioning the liberation paradigm, Deloria sought to subvert it. He reformulated liberation as "the destruction of the whole complex of Western theories of knowledge and the construction of a new and more comprehensive synthesis of human knowledge and experience."[57] He reasoned that only by changing the very way in which Western peoples think would authentic liberation be possible. Deloria rejected the notion that time is uniform and continuous, that finite descriptions of nature yield absolute and certain knowledge, that the subjective and objective can be divided, that reason is the primary means of knowledge and can be divorced from feeling. Deloria's articulation of these concerns anticipated by more than a decade many of the critiques that Black and Hispanic/Latino theologians would bring against modernity. His evaluation revealed a deep concern for metaphysics and this was the subject of an extended essay, *Metaphysics of Modern Existence*.[58]

Deloria's most extensive theological discussion is *God is Red*, in which he works out "the importance of regaining a sense of space and environment in the midst of time."[59] Here he elucidates the incompatibility of Indian tribal religions with certain Christian notions – fear of fallen nature, concentration on time, and a concern for the interpretation of experience rather than the experience itself. Deloria reinforces the indigenous peoples' relationship to nature, their regard for place over time, and experience over interpretation. He is, as Robert Allen Warrior comments, "overcoming" a theological assumption that, without these Christian notions and their translation into society, "tribal people live an ossified existence." But Deloria is able to open up "continuity between American Indian experience before contact with Europeans and after," thus displacing any notion of fallen nature. Moreover, he presents the tribal religious traditions in such a material way that textured experience is made available.[60] Deloria's work advances, by example, sovereignty and self-determination in the intellectual sphere.

Like Deloria, Robert Allen Warrior has critiqued the adequacy of liberation as a model for Native American theologies. Warrior declared that liberation theologies, in their preoccupation with the biblical narrative of Exodus, employed uncritical biblical hermeneutics. "The covenant," Warrior asserted, "has two parts: deliverance and conquest." To read Native American oppression off the biblical narrative and its paradigm is to grasp that Native Americans are the conquered Canaanites. Warrior's reading problematizes Black and Hispanic/Latino theologies, which find inspiration for their struggle in God's option for the oppressed Israelite slaves. The upshot of this reading for Black and Hispanic/Latino theologies is to "differentiate between the liberating god and the god of conquest." Moreover, Warrior urged all Christians struggling for liberation to "learn [how] to participate in the struggle without making their story the whole story."[61] This thesis dramatically illumines the ambiguity of the liberation paradigm for indigenous peoples. Recently, Warrior has published a book, *Tribal Secrets*, which retrieves and interrogates American Indian intellectual praxis through the work of John Joseph Matthews and Vine Deloria, Jr.

George Tinker's *Missionary Conquest* interrogates American Indian mission history to uncover two basic patterns of missionary dynamics. One pattern perceived America as the New Israel and supplied a theological basis for the doctrine of manifest destiny; the other, even though it opposed military conquest, subdued and suppressed the values, practices, and structures of traditional culture. Tinker discloses the historic as well as continuing collusion of Christianity with military, political, and economic strategies of conquest. Commenting on the Euro-American interest in native peoples' spirituality, Tinker contends that the situation has shifted *from* intentional efforts by Euro-Americans to impose their culture on Indians *to* indiscriminate attempts by Euro-Americans to appropriate and reproduce the spirituality and ceremonies of the indigenous peoples.

Several Native American women, including Rosemary Maxey, Mary C. Churchill, Michelene Pesantubbee, Inés M. Talamantez, and Inés Hernández-Ávila, have begun to contribute to analysis of the indigenous peoples' situation. Maxey was a member of the editorial committee of the TIA-sponsored journal, *DTUS*, and her essays often reflected on the priority of the land in the spirituality of indigenous peoples.[62] In conversation with feminist and womanist thinkers, but from their own independent stances, Churchill, Pesantubbee, and Hernández-Ávila have been probing questions of Native women's identity, positionality, and spirituality. Talamantez has given critical attention to the discipline of Native American religious studies. She resists the dominant theories put forward to explain Native peoples' religious lives, but which do so in categories extrinsic to Native peoples' spirituality.

Achievement, assessment, and agenda

It is, perhaps, much too soon to present any detailed analysis of the development of Native American theology. However, a few points can be offered. *First*, in problematizing the liberation paradigm, Native American theology has made a crucial contribution to the formulation of liberation theologies. The critical reading of the Exodus narrative and the challenge to Western metaphysics are instances of the clarification of ideology, even among those who struggle for liberation. *Second*, by committing itself to the survival of the land, Native American theology fights for the survival of all life. At the same time, Native American theology must contest eco-theological essays that either ignore or crudely manipulate Indian wisdom. *Third*, in affirming the traditional religious life of the indigenous peoples, Native American theology assumes an integrity and authority that can direct an authentic and humble encounter between the message of Jesus and the peoples of the Great Spirit.

Native American theology as read here has had little to say about homophobia, about gays and lesbians; perhaps these concerns will surface in the near future. Further, Native American theology has begun to probe Native women's experience, but whether Native men are misogynist remains to be determined. Finally, the US social order and the deep anxieties it has spawned call Native American theology to more intense dialogue and collaboration with Black, Asian, and Hispanic/Latino theologies.

Conclusion

No peoples have been so divided by suspicion, mistrust, and hostility than the so-called minority groups in the United States. The readiness with which each of these groups, on more than one occasion, has betrayed or frustrated the interests of the others in order to enter into coalitions with the dominant (white) population is more than unseemly. Such behavior signifies the profound self-alienation that these marginalized communities have endured. A first step for these communities toward healing and creating in the future is to intensify their dialogue. Only in this way can each community become more attuned to the histories, experiences, questions, and concerns of the others. A second step for the future is a critique of the intellectual horizon or basic worldview projected by the United States. Black, Hispanic/Latino, and Native American theologies must marshal differentiated critiques of the social surd that the United States has become – that is to say, a critique of vicious values, orders, relations, institutions, meanings, and practices that uphold the oppression of marginalized poor peoples, the suppression of women, the degradation of the earth. The formulation of such critiques will entail not only a shift in the way of thinking about and doing theology, but a radical conversion of the woman and man the theologian is. Yet, while the formulation and mediation of such critiques are necessary and practically intelligent steps for the future, these theologies cannot abandon their witness to the absolute power of the cross of Christ to heal and create, to restore the earth.

Notes

1 There is little consensus regarding the nomenclature used to designate these peoples and their theologies. Many Black scholars use the cultural term "African American," but here I have used "Black" to keep the political struggle of Black theology in the foreground. With the term Hispanic/Latino, I am following a convention employed by a significant group of theologians in the United States who have Central American, Cuban, Latin American, Mexican, and Puerto Rican origins, although some may have European or European-American heritage as well. The peoples of the indigenous nations of what is now the United States sometimes call themselves Indians and sometimes Native Americans; I do so here as well.

2 Bernard Lonergan, "The transition from a classicist world-view to historical-mindedness," In *A Second Collection by Bernard J. F. Lonergan, S. J.*, ed. William F. J. Ryan and Bernard J. Tyrrell (Philadelphia, 1974), pp. 1–9.

3 Audre Lorde, "The master's tools will never dismantle the master's house," in *Sister Outsider* (Trumansburg, NY, 1984), pp. 110–13.

4 I want to thank Professors Jamie T. Phelps, OP, Roberto Goizueta, and Timothy Matovina for sound advice at some crucial moments in this project.

5 See Enrique Dussel, *The Invention of the Americas: Eclipse of "the Other" and the myth of modernity*, trans. Michael D. Barber (New York, 1995), Hans Konig, *Columbus: His enterprise* (New York, 1976), Tzvetan

Todorov, *The Conquest of America*, trans. Richard Howard (New York, 1984; first published 1982), Bartolomé de Las Casas, *The Devastation of the Indies: A brief account*, trans. Herma Briffault (New York, 1974; first published 1552), Miguel Leon-Portillo, *The Broken Spears: The Aztec account of the conquest of Mexico* (Boston, 1962), Bernal Díaz del Castillo, *The Conquest of New Spain*, trans. J. M. Cohen (Baltimore, MD, 1963; first published 1560), Eric Williams, *From Columbus to Castro: The history of the Caribbean, 1492–1969* (New York, 1984), Robert Conrad, *Children of God's Fire: A documentary history of black slavery in Brazil* (Princeton. NJ, 1983).

6   See Francis Paul Prucha, *The Indians in American Society: From the Revolutionary War to the present* (Berkeley, CA, 1985), Francis Jennings, *The Invasion of America: Indians, colonialism, and the cant of conquest* (Chapel Hill, NC, 1975), Roy Harvey Pearce, *Savagism and Civilization: A story of the Indian and the American mind* (Berkeley, CA, 1988; first published 1953).

7   See Philip Curtin, *The Atlantic Slave Trade: A census* (Madison, WI, 1969); Joseph E. Holloway (ed.), *Africanisms in American Culture* (Bloomington and Indianapolis, IN, 1990).

8   Dussel, *The Invention of the Americas*, especially pp. 19–57, 123–38.

9   James H. Cone, *Black Theology and Black Power* (New York, 1969).

10   Here I am thinking of the work of Katie G. Cannon, James H. Evans, Jr, Jacquelyn Grant, Charles H. Long, J. Deotis Roberts, Cheryl Sanders, Cornel West, Delores S. Williams, Preston N. Williams, Gayraud S. Wilmore. For a relatively comprehensive bibliography of global Black theology up to 1985, see James H. Evans, Jr, *Black Theology: A critical assessment and annotated bibliography* (Westport, CT, 1987).

11   Wilmore, "Introduction" (Part I: The End of an Era: Civil rights to Black power) in *Documentary History*, 1–21; Cornel West, *Prophesy Deliverance! An Afro-American revolutionary Christianity* (Philadelphia, 1982), ch. 4, esp. pp. 101–27.

12   Wilmore and Cone (eds), *Documentary History*, p. 69.

13   The term "black power" may have originated with Adam Clayton Powell, who in an address at Howard University on May 29, 1966, declared: "Human rights are God given . . . to demand these God-given rights is to seek black power, the power to build black institutions," cited in Floyd B. Barbaus, *The Black Power Revolt* (Boston, 1968), p. 189; see also Nathan Wright, Jr, *Black Power and Urban Unrest: Creative possibilities* (New York, 1967), pp. 2–3, 13; Stokely Carmichael and Charles V. Hamilton, *Black Power: The politics of liberation in America* (New York, 1967); James H. Cone and Gayraud S. Wilmore (eds), *Black Theology: A documentary history. Volume 1. 1966–1979* (Maryknoll, NY, 1993).

14   Cecil W. Cone, *The Identity Crisis of Black Theology* (Nashville, TN, 1975).

15   TIA formed affinity groups also included the Asian-American Project, the Women's Project, the Church and Labor Dialogue, the (white) Theologians' Task Force, and the Alternative Theology Project.

16   See Toni Cade (ed.), *The Black Woman: An anthology* (New York, 1970), esp. Frances Beale, "Double jeopardy: to be Black and female," pp. 90–100, and Kay Lindsey, "The Black woman as a woman," pp. 85–9.

17   See Delores S. Williams, "Women's oppression and lifeline politics in Black women's religious narratives," *Journal of Feminist Studies in Religion*, 2 (Fall 1985), pp. 59–71, idem, "The color of feminism: or speaking the Black woman's tongue," *Journal of Religious Thought*, 43 (Spring/Summer 1986), pp. 42–58; Katie Geneva Cannon, *Black Womanist Ethics* (Atlanta, GA, 1988), idem, "Hitting a straight lick with a crooked stick: the womanist dilemma in the development of a Black liberation ethic," *The Annual: The Society of Christian Ethics* (1987), pp. 165–77. Jacquelyn Grant was not the first to raise the issue of sexism in the Black church, but she may be the first to raise this issue in Black theology in "Black theology and the Black woman," in Wilmore and Cone (eds), *Black Theology: A documentary history, 1966–1979*, pp. 418–33, idem, "Womanist theology: Black women's experience as a source for doing theology, with special reference to

Christology," *Journal of the Interdenominational Theological Center* 13 (1986), pp. 195–212, idem, *White Women's Christ, Black Women's Jesus: Feminist christology and womanist response* (Atlanta, GA, 1989). See also the work of the sociologist of religion Cheryl Townsend Gilkes, "The role of women in the sanctified church," *Journal of Religious Thought*, 43 (1986), pp. 24–41, idem, "The roles of church and community mothers: ambivalent American sexism or fragmented African familyhood?" *Journal of Feminist Studies in Religion*, 2 (1986), pp. 41–59.

18 Gilkes, "Roundtable Response," *Journal of Feminist Studies in Religion*, 5 (1989), p. 106; see also in this issue responses by Katie G. Cannon, Emilie M. Townes, M. Shawn Copeland, and Bell Hooks to the essay, "Christian ethics and theology in womanist perspective," by Cheryl J. Sanders.

19 Charles H. Long, "Perspectives for a Study of Afro-American Religion in the US," *History of Religions*, 2 (1971), pp. 54–66.

20 Cain Hope Felder (ed.), *Stony the Road We Trod: African American biblical interpretation* (Minneapolis, 1991), idem, *Troubling Biblical Waters: Race, class, and family* (Maryknoll, NY, 1989); Charles B. Copher, "Egypt and Ethiopia in the Old Testament," in Ivan Van Sertima (ed.), *Nile Valley Civilization* (New York, 1985), idem, "3,000 years of biblical interpretation with reference to Black peoples," *Journal of the Interdenominational Theological Center*, 13 (1986), pp. 225–46.

21 Rufus Burrow, Jr, *James H. Cone and Black Liberation Theology* (Jefferson, NC, and London, 1994), pp. 196–7.

22 Yolanda Tarango and Timothy Matovina, "US Hispanic and Latin American theologies: critical distinctions," *Catholic Theological Society of America: Proceedings*, 48 (1993), p. 128; see also Arturo Bañuelas, "US Hispanic Theology," *Missiology*, 20 (1992), pp. 275–300, and Allan Figueroa Deck, *Frontiers of Hispanic Theology in the United States* (Maryknoll, NY, 1992), esp. pp. ix–xxvi.

23 Ibid.

24 Moises Sandoval, *On the Move: A history of the Hispanic Church in the United States* (Maryknoll, NY, 1990), pp. 62–5.

25 One of the chief analytical tools for understanding the Catholic Church in the predominantly Protestant United States has been the notion of immigration. However, this notion is limited in its ability to illumine the experiences of Black and Hispanic/Latino Catholics for at least two reasons. First, not only does immigration deny the capture and enslavement of the Africans, it omits the US military conquest and annexations of Texas and New Mexico and California respectively. Neither Blacks nor Chicanos were immigrant Catholics in the ordinary sense of the nineteenth-century immigrant Irish or Germans or Polish. Enslaved African Catholics arrived in St Augustine's (Florida) in 1565 and in the late nineteenth century, Mexican-Americans had a 250-year-old history of Catholicism. Second, while the notion of immigration can accommodate cultural and linguistic differences, it does not account for anti-black and anti-brown racism in the Catholic Church. Until the push for "Americanization" in the 1940s, national parishes catered to cultural and language groups, but the Church early on tried to suppress the devotions, cultural distinctiveness, and language of Hispanic/Latinos.

26 Sandoval, *On the Move*, p. 96.

27 PADRES is an acronym for Priests Associated for Religious, Educational, and Social Rights, which was founded at a meeting of 50 Mexican-American priests, October 7–9, 1969, in San Antonio, Texas. The first assembly of *Las Hermanas* was held April 2–4, 1971, in Houston, Texas. By creating an organization, the sisters were determined to be of "more effective and active service [to] the Hispanic peoples by using the expertise, knowledge, and experience of religious women in the fields of education, health, pastoral work, and sociology" (Sandoval, *On the Move*, pp. 66–8).

28 Rosino Gibellini, *The Liberation Theology Debate* (Maryknoll, NY, 1988; first published 1987), p. 1.

29 See Bañuelas, "US Hispanic Theology," pp. 275–80, 291–5, and Figueroa Deck, *Frontiers of Hispanic Theology in the United States*, pp. xii–xiii.

30 Virgilio Elizondo, "Educación religiosa para

el México-Norte Americano," *Catequesis Latinoamericana*, 4 (1972), pp. 83–6.

31 Sandoval, *On the Move*, pp. 69–71.

32 Virgilio Elizondo, *Mestizaje, The Dialectic of Cultural Birth and the Gospel: A study in the intercultural dimension of evangelization*. This is the final working draft of Elizondo's thesis for a doctorate in theology, which was presented under the official title: "Mestissage, Violence Culturelle, Annonce De L'Evangile, La dimension interculturelle de l'évangélisation," (PhD dissertation, Institut Catholique de Paris, 1978), pp. vii–viii.

33 Gustavo Gutiérrez, *Hacia un teología de la liberación lineas pastorales de la iglesia en América Latina* (Lima, 1968). The English translation, "Toward a theology of liberation," appears in Alfred T. Hennelly (ed.), *Liberation Theology: A documentary history* (Maryknoll, NY, 1990).

34 Gutiérrez, "Toward a Theology of Liberation," p. 63.

35 Gutiérrez, *A Theology of Liberation: History, politics, and salvation*, trans. and ed. Sister Caridad Inda and John Eagleson (Maryknoll, NY, 1973).

36 Figueroa Deck, *Frontiers of Hispanic Theology*, p. xiv; see also Virgilio Elizondo, *Galilean Journey: The Mexican-American promise* (Maryknoll, NY, 1983), p. 3, idem, "Mestizaje as a locus of theological reflection," pp. 358–60, in *The Future of Liberation Theology: Essays in honor of Gustavo Gutiérrez*, ed. Marc H. Ellis and Otto Maduro (Maryknoll, NY, 1989).

37 Sergio Torres and John Eagleson (eds), *Theology in the Americas* (Maryknoll, NY, 1976), pp. 14–19.

38 Gregory Baum, "The Christian Left at Detroit," in *Theology in the Americas*, pp. 411–14, esp. p. 412.

39 Deck, *Frontiers of Hispanic Theology*, p. xvii.

40 Ada María Isasi-Díaz and Yolanda Tarango, *Hispanic Women: Prophetic voice in the Church* (Minneapolis, 1992; first published 1988), pp. 96, 98–103, 105–6.

41 Deck, *Frontiers of Hispanic Theology*, pp. xxi–xxiv.

42 Ibid.; see also Figueroa Deck, *The Challenge of Evangelical/Pentecostal Christianity to Hispanic Catholicism in the United States* (Working Paper Series 24, no. 1) (Notre Dame, IN, 1992). Four of the eight papers given at the joint meeting of ACHTUS and BCTS were published in the *Journal of Hispanic/Latino Theology*, 3 (1996). In his remarks, associate editor Jean-Pierre Ruíz introduced an excerpt from the synthesis statement developed by participants.

43 Figueroa Deck, *The Second Wave: Hispanic ministry and the evangelization of cultures* (Mahwah, NJ, 1989).

44 Dussel, *The Invention of the Americas*, pp. 63–90.

45 Justo L. González, *Mañana: Christian theology from a Hispanic perspective* (Nashville, TN, 1990), pp. 55, 61. Bañuelas makes this same point in "US Hispanic theology," p. 281.

46 Renny Golden et al. (eds), *Dangerous Memories: Invasion and resistance since 1492* (Chicago, 1991), p. 129.

47 Deloria, *God is Red: A native view of religion* (Golden, CO, 1993; first published 1973), pp. 6–21.

48 Ibid., p. 19.

49 Prucha, *The Indians in American Society*, p. 82.

50 Dee Brown's *Bury My Heart at Wounded Knee: An Indian history of the American West* (New York, 1971).

51 Deloria, *God is Red*, pp. 23–4; see also Prucha, *The Indians in American Society*,

52 Sister Jeanne Rollins, "Liberation and the Native American," *Theology in the Americas*, pp. 202–5.

53 "Statement from the Coalition of US Nonwhite Racial and National Minorities," *Theology in the Americas*, p. 359.

54 Vine Deloria, Jr, "A Native American perspective on liberation," p. 262, *Mission Trends No. 4, Liberation Theologies in North America and Europe*, ed. Gerald H. Anderson and Thomas F. Stransky (New York and Ramsey, 1979).

55 Mike Meyers, "The Native Americans and Western Christianity," pp. 85–9, *Theology in the Americas: Detroit II Conference Papers*, ed. Cornel West, Caridad Guidote, and Margaret Coakley (Maryknoll, NY, 1982).

56 Robert Allen Warrior, *Tribal Secrets: Recovering American Indian intellectual traditions* (Minneapolis, 1994), p. 32.

57 Deloria, "A Native American perspective on liberation," p. 269.
58 Deloria, *Metaphysics of Modern Existence* (San Francisco, 1979).
59 Warrior, *Tribal Secrets*, p. 70.
60 Ibid., pp. 79–80.
61 Robert Allen Warrior, "Canaanites, Cow-

boys, and Indians: deliverance, conquest, and liberation theology today," *Christianity and Crisis*, September 11 (1989), pp. 261–5.
62 *DTUS* was a journal published jointly by TIA affinity groups. DTUS was an acronym for Doing Theology in the United States.

Bibliographies

Black Theology: Primary

Bailey, Randall C. and Grant, Jacquelyn, *The Recovery of Black Presence: An interdisciplinary exploration: Essays in honor of Dr Charles B. Copher.* (Nashville, TN, 1995).

Baker-Fletcher, Garth Kasimu, *Xodus: An African-American male journey* (Minneapolis, 1995).

Baker-Fletcher, Karen, *A Singing Something: Anna Julia Cooper and the foundations of womanist theology* (New York, 1994).

Cannon, Katie, *Black Womanist Ethics* (Atlanta, GA, 1989).

—— *Katie's Cannon: Womanism and the soul of the Black community* (New York, 1995).

Cleage, Albert J., *The Black Messiah* (New York, 1969).

Cone, James H., *Black Theology and Black Power* (New York, 1969; reprint 1986; 20th anniversary edn Maryknoll, NY, 1990).

—— *A Black Theology of Liberation* (Philadelphia, 1970; reprint 1986; 20th anniversary edn Maryknoll, NY, 1990).

—— *The Spirituals and the Blues* (New York, 1972; reprint Maryknoll, NY, 1991).

—— *God of the Oppressed* (New York, 1975).

—— *For My People* (Maryknoll, NY, 1984).

—— *Speaking the Truth* (Grand Rapids, MI, 1986).

—— *Martin, Malcolm, and America: A dream or a nightmare?* (Maryknoll, NY, 1992).

Cone, James H. and Wilmore, Gayraud S. (eds), *Black Theology: A documentary history.* Vol. 1, *1966–1979*, 2nd rev. edn; Vol. 2, *1980–1993* (Maryknoll, NY, 1993).

Copeland M. Shawn, "Difference as a Category in Critical Theologies for the Liberation of Women," in *Concilium: Feminist Theologies in Different Contexts*, ed. Elisabeth Schüssler Fiorenza and M. Shawn Copeland (1996/1), pp. 141–51.

—— "The Exercise of Black Theology in the United States," *Journal of Hispanic/Latino Theology*, 3 (1996), pp. 5–15.

Creel, Martha Washington, *"A Peculiar People": Slave religion and community-culture among the Gullahs* (New York, 1988).

Davis, Cyprian, *The History of Black Catholics in the United States* (New York, 1990).

Douglas, Kelly Brown, *The Black Christ* (Maryknoll, NY, 1994).

Earl, Riggins R., Jr, *Dark Symbols, Obscure Signs: God, self, and community in the slave mind* (Maryknoll, NY, 1993).

Eugene, Toinette, *Lifting as We Climb: A womanist ethic of care* (Nashville, TN, forthcoming).

Evans, James. *We Have Been Believers: An African American systematic theology* (Minneapolis, 1993).

Felder, Caine Hope, *Troubling Biblical Waters: Race, class, and family* (Maryknoll, NY, 1989).

—— (ed.), *Stony the Road We Trod: African American biblical interpretation* (Minneapolis, 1991).

Gilkes, Cheryl Townsend, "The 'loves' and 'troubles' of African-American women's bodies: the womanist challenge to cultural humiliation and community ambivalence," in Emilie M. Townes (ed.) *A Troubling in My Soul: Womanist perspectives on evil and suffering* (Maryknoll, NY, 1993) pp. 232–49.

—— "The roles of church and community mothers: ambivalent American sexism or fragmented African familyhood?" *Journal of Feminist Studies in Religion*, 2 (1986), pp. 41–59.

Grant, Jacquelyn, *White Women's Christ, Black Women's Jesus* (Atlanta, GA, 1989).

Hayes, Diana L., *Hagar's Daughters: Womanist ways of being in the world* (Mahwah, NJ, 1995).

Hood, Robert E., *Must God Remain Greek? Afro cultures and God talk* (Minneapolis, 1990).
—— *Begrimed and Black* (Minneapolis, 1995).
Hopkins, Dwight, *Shoes that Fit Our Feet: Sources for a constructive black theology.* (Maryknoll, NY, 1993).
Hopkins, Dwight and Cummings, George (eds), *Cut Loose Your Stammering Tongue: Black theology in the slave narratives* (Maryknoll, NY, 1992).
Jones, Major, *Black Awareness: A theology of hope* (Nashville, TN, 1971).
—— *The Color of God: The concept of God in Afro-American thought* (Macon, GA, 1987).
Jones, William R., *Is God a White Racist? A preamble to Black theology* (Garden City, NY, 1973).
King, Martin Luther, Jr, *Testament of Hope: The essential writings of Martin Luther King, Jr*, ed. James M. Washington (New York, 1986).
Long, Charles H., *Significations: Signs, symbols, and images in the interpretation of religion* (Philadelphia, 1986).
Paris, Peter J., *The Social Teachings of the Black Churches* (Philadelphia, 1985).
—— *The Spirituality of African Peoples: The search for a common moral discourse* (Minneapolis, 1995).
Phelps, Jamie T. (ed.), *Black and Catholic: The challenge and gift of Black folk: Contributions of African American experience and world view to Catholic theology* (Marquette, WI, forthcoming).
Posey, Thaddeus (ed.), *Theology: A portrait in black* (Proceedings of the Black Catholic Theological Symposium, vol. 1) (1978).
Raboteau, Albert, *Slave Religion: The "invisible" institution in the antebellum South* (New York, 1978).
Riggs, Marcia Y., *Awake, Arise, Act: A womanist call for Black liberation* (Cleveland, OH, 1995).
Robert, J. Deotis, *Liberation and Reconciliation: A Black theology* (Philadelphia, 1971).
—— *A Black Political Theology* (Philadelphia, 1974).
—— *The Roots of a Black Future* (Philadelphia, 1980).
—— *Black Theology Toady* (Lewiston, NY, 1983).
—— *Black Theology in Dialogue* (Philadelphia, 1987).
—— *The Prophethood of Believers: An African American political theology for ministry* (Maryknoll, NY, 1995).

Sanders, Cheryl J., *Empowerment Ethics for a Liberated People: A path to African-American social transformation* (Minneapolis, 1995).
Smith, Theophus H., *Conjuring Culture: Biblical formations of Black America* (New York, 1994).
Townes, Emilie M. (ed.), *A Troubling in My Soul: Womanist perspectives of evil and suffering* (Maryknoll, NY, 1993).
—— *Womanist Justice, Womanist Hope* (Atlanta, GA, 1994).
—— *In a Blaze of Glory: Womanist spirituality as social witness* (Nashville, TN, 1995).
Weems, Renita, *Battered Love: Marriage, sex, and violence in the Hebrew Prophets* (Minneapolis, 1995).
West, Cornel, *Prophesy Deliverance! An Afro-American revolutionary Christianity* (Philadelphia, 1982).
Williams, Delores, *Sisters in the Wilderness: The challenge of womanist God-talk* (Maryknoll, NY, 1993).
Wilmore, Gayraud S., *Black Religion and Black Radicalism*, 2nd rev. edn (Maryknoll, NY, 1983).
Young, Josiah, *A Pan-African Theology: Providence and the legacies of the ancestors* (Trenton, NJ, 1992).

Secondary

Burrow, Rufus, Jr, *James Cone and Black Liberation Theology* (Jefferson, NC, and London, 1994).
Hayes, Diana L., *And Still We Rise: An introduction to Black liberation theology* (Mahwah, NJ, 1996).
Hopkins, Dwight, *Black Theology: United States and South Africa* (Maryknoll, NY, 1989).
Witvliet, Theo, *The Way of the Black Messiah* (Oak Park, IL, 1987).
Young, Josiah, *Black and African Theologies: Siblings or distant cousins?* (Maryknoll, NY, 1986).

Hispanic/Latino Theology: Primary

Aquino, María Pilar, *Our Cry for Life: Feminist theology from Latin America* (Maryknoll, NY, 1993).
Bañuelas, Arturo (ed.), *Mestizo Christianity: Theology for the Latino perspective* (Maryknoll, NY, 1996).

Costas, Orlando, *Liberating News: A theology of contextual evangelization* (Grand Rapids, MI, 1989).

Deck, Allan Figueroa, *The Second Wave: Hispanic ministry and the evangelization of culture* (New York, 1989).

—— *The Challenge of Evangelical/Pentecostal Christianity to Hispanic Catholicism in the United States* (Cushwa Center for the Study of American Catholicism, series 24, no. 1) (Notre Dame, IN, 1992).

—— (ed.), *Frontiers of Hispanic Theology in the United States* (Maryknoll, NY, 1992).

Deck, Allan Figueroa and Dolan, Jay P., *Hispanic Catholic Culture in the US: Issues and concerns* (Notre Dame, IN, 1994).

Elizondo, Virgilio P., *Christianity and Culture: An introduction to pastoral theology and ministry for the bicultural community* (Huntington, IN, 1975).

—— *Galilean Journey: The Mexican-American promise* (Maryknoll, NY, 1983).

—— *The Future is Mestizo: Life where cultures meet* (Bloomington, IN, 1988).

—— *Worship: Touching God* (Laurel, MD, 1995).

Elizondo, Virgilio P. and Boff, Leonardo (eds), *1492–1992: The Voice of the Victims*. London: SCM Press, 1990.

Espín Orlando O., "Popular Catholicism among Latinos," in Jay P. Dolan and Allan Figueroa Deck (eds), *Hispanic Catholic Culture in the US: Issues and Concerns* (Notre Dame, IN, 1994), pp. 308–59.

—— "Pentecostalism and popular Catholicism: the poor and *Traditio*," *Journal of Hispanic/Latino Theology*, 3 (1995), pp. 14–43.

Goizueta, Roberto, *Liberation, Method, and Dialogue: Enrique Dussel and North American theological discourse* (Atlanta, GA, 1988).

—— (ed.), *We Are a People: Initatives in Hispanic American theology* (Minneapolis, 1992).

—— *Caminemos Con Jesús: Toward a Hispanic/Latino theology of accompaniment* (Maryknoll, NY, 1996).

González, Justo L. *Mañana: Christian theology from a Hispanic perspective* (Nashville, TN, 1990).

—— (ed.), *Out of Every Tribe and Nation: Christian theology at the ethnic roundtable* (Nashville, TN, 1992).

—— (ed.), *Voces: Voices from the Hispanic Church* (Nashville, TN, 1992).

Isasi-Díaz, Ada María, *En la lucha: In the Struggle: A Hispanic women's liberation theology* (Minneapolis, 1993).

Isasi-Díaz, Ada María and Tarango, Yolanda, *Hispanic Women Prophetic Voice in the Church: Toward a Hispanic women's liberation theology* (San Francisco, 1989).

Rodríguez, Jeanette, *Our Lady of Guadalupe: Faith and empowerment among Mexican-American women* (Austin, TX, 1994).

Villafañe, Eldin, *The Liberating Spirit: Toward an Hispanic American pentecostal social ethic* (Grand Rapids, MI, 1993).

Secondary

Bañuelas, Arturo, "US Hispanic theology," *Missiology*, 20 (1992), pp. 275–300.

Tarango, Yolanda and Matovina, Timothy, "US Hispanic and Latin American theologies: critical distinctions," *Catholic Theological Society of America: Proceedings*, 48 (June 10–13, 1993), pp. 128–30.

Native American Theology: Primary

Deloria, Vine, Jr, *Custer Died for Your Sins* (New York, 1969).

—— *God is Red: A Native view of religion* (Golden, CO, 1993; first published 1973).

—— *Metaphysics of Modern Existence* (San Francisco, 1979).

—— *Red Earth, White Lies: Native Americans and the myth of scientific fact* (New York, 1995).

—— *Tribal Secrets: Recovering American Indian intellectual traditions* (Minneapolis, 1994).

Tinker, George E., *Missionary Conquest: The Gospel and Native American cultural genocide* (Minneapolis, 1993).

Warrior, Robert Allen, "Canaanites, cowboys, and Indians: deliverance, conquest, and liberation theology today," *Christianity and Crisis*, 49 (1989), pp. 261–5.

Secondary

Peelman, Achiel, *Christ Is a Native American* (Maryknoll, NY, 1995).

Steinmetz, Paul B., *Pipe, Bible, and Peyote among the Oglala Lakota: A study in religious identity* (Knoxville, TN, 1990).

Feminist and Womanist Theologies

Rebecca S. Chopp

Theology is the Christian community's language about God and world. *Feminist* theology shapes Christian language about God and world in and through the voices of women in the community, the struggle over the role of women and the nature of gender, and the desire to speak truly of a God who works for and with all persons. The term "feminist" signifies at least three interrelated but distinguishable realities: (1) the historical reality of women speaking publicly; (2) a theoretical investigation into the centrality of gender for the construction of subjectivity, language, and politics; and (3) a reinterpretation of Christianity as an emancipatory praxis of transformation.

In the United States feminist theology as a late twentieth-century discourse arises in the context of two important developments: rapid changes in the lives of women (especially middle-class women) and the development of women's studies and feminist theory in the academy. A brief review of both these areas is necessary to understand feminist theology.

In the latter half of the twentieth century, dramatic cultural and political changes in the US provide the context for women to define themselves and their communities in new ways. Though not all the cultural changes can be listed, the ones directly affecting many women's lives must at least be identified. These areas of change include the areas of employment, reproductive practices, sexual practices, family structures, and rising rates and awareness of violence against women and children.

Shifts in employment practices affect women unequally. African-American women have always worked outside their homes (usually in white women's homes) as well as inside their own homes. In 1880, for instance, roughly 50 percent of African-American women were in the labor force as compared to about 15 percent of Euro-American women. The particularities of African-American women's work as paid (often domestic) and unpaid (in extended family networks) mean that their work has often been overlooked in dominant modes of social analysis using social class models focusing on social attainment or class conflict.[1] Euro-American middle-class and working-class women entered the work force in massive numbers during the Second World War. By the 1950s economic forces in the US pressured women to work outside the home in increasing numbers. Today at least 78 percent of adult women are employed, at some time or another, in the work force. Though the jobs are often what Nancy Fraser has called feminized and sexualized jobs, women work outside the home for economic reasons.[2]

The second area of change is the development of sophisticated reproductive technologies, especially the emergence and popularity of the birth control pill in the 1960s. This technological revolution impacts the lives of women who can afford the pill since these women can now control whether or not to have children, when to have children, and how many children to have. As compared to women throughout history and in many parts of the world, reproduction does not define parameters of a woman's life, at least for those women who can afford the pill.

The third area of change has to do with sexual practices, by which I mean sexual activity, sexual partners, and sexual identity. Heterosexuality is no longer the only option represented for women's sexuality. Growing numbers of lesbians and bisexual women lead the culture (and the church) to examine the practices of sexuality and the nature of sexual identity. Sexuality both can and has to be thought about as a deliberate choice and as a realization of one's identity.

The fourth area of cultural change directly affecting women's lives in the US has to do with changing family practices. The divorce rate in the US hovers at around 50 percent, dramatically affecting the lives of the many women who believed their destiny to be primarily wife, mother, and homemaker. In addition to a high divorce rate, contemporary American culture contains a broad variety of family patterns. Changing family identity is greatly influenced by new family forms among gays and lesbians as well as new familial patterns among single persons. The nuclear family ideology – the functions assigned to the nuclear family since the nineteenth century – of the formation of identity, the nurturing of intimacy, the development of children, and the propagation of moral values has begun to shift and change.

Rising rates of violence in relation to women and children in the US are the final area of change. Rita Nakashima Brock states quite pointedly: "In the United States suicide is the second most common form of death among teenagers; one in every five children grows up in poverty; one in every three women will be raped as an adult, one in every four daughters and one in every eight sons are molested by the age of eighteen; and every thirty-nine seconds a woman is battered in her own home."[3] The Center for Disease Control in Atlanta, Georgia, has listed violence against women as a leading health threat for women in the US. As the American poet Adrienne Rich has observed, home is the most dangerous place for women in American society.[4]

These dramatic factors of change affect the lives of women and men in the US. The dominant narratives and representations of women in the domestic sphere no longer work for all women. To say it differently, it is now quite rare for a woman to have the option of being the suburban housewife who raises the children and keeps the home fires burning. This narrative of a woman's life never really fitted all women and the women it did represent may well have pushed at its seams and edges. But the dramatic cultural, economic, and technological changes force the fractures of the narrative to rupture even further. Women and men are required to form new narratives and practices for the basic realities of reproduction, work, family, sexuality, and safety/security. And in relation to the need for new narratives and practices, women's studies and feminist theory developed in the academy.

Women's studies draws upon a variety of disciplines to consider a range of questions and issues about women in areas such as the representation of women in literature, the specificity of women writing, the role of women in various historical eras, and the presence and treatment of women in the professions. Women's studies and feminist theory developed as women, and sometimes men, began to analyze the complex identities, roles, and practices of women and men.

Feminist theory, at least for our purposes, considers the construction of gender. By the word "gender" I mean the definition of what it is to be a man or a woman, but also how these definitions are used to distribute power and value in culture. For instance, feminist theory might consider how aggression receives a positive value when it applies to actions usually accomplished by men, and how aggression takes on a negative value when used to qualify female behavior. For a man to be aggressive means he is self-confident and strong; for a woman to be aggressive means she is insecure and irrationally angry. Aggression is assigned a kind of positive, masculine value when it is used to describe the raw strength and winning attitude of armed defense and of professional athletics. But aggression receives a negative, feminine value when military opponents are described as irrational and insecure or when the women's movement is often described as full of unhappy, angry, and crazed women.

Feminist theory has been applied to good effect in textual studies, in history, in cultural studies, and, of course, in economics. The very existence of women's studies and feminist theory signifies the changing realities of women's lives and has contributed significantly to understanding how social institutions and structures have been organized through gender divisions. Feminist theology draws upon women's studies and feminist theory as it works within the context of changed realities for women in the US in order to fashion new narratives and practices for women and men, including new narratives and practices of Christianity.

Survey

A survey of a movement that is itself diverse and emerging cannot by necessity argue the development of a central idea or perspective. Given that feminist theologies exist within the context of vast cultural changes, and that feminist theories tend to function as critical theories of change and transformation, a survey can best be undertaken through describing a constellation of notions around which feminist theologies tend to cluster. A constellation does not survey integrated, interrelated elements for a unity of thought but identifies juxtaposed notions that tend to connect, collide, intersect. According to the critical theorist Theodor Adorno, a constellation is "a juxtaposed rather than integrated cluster of changing elements that resist reduction to a common denominator, essential core, or generative first principle."[5] The "changing elements" I want to describe are: (1) a diversity of voices; (2) a critique of Christianity; (3) productive discourses of transformation with the attending leading principles of embodiment, connectedness, and anticipatory freedom.

A diversity of voices In the 1960s feminist theology emerged within academic malestream circles of Jewish and Christian theology. The feminist theologies written by Christian and Jewish women shared many class and race privileges with their male counterparts. The early feminist theologians identified "woman's" experience as different from man's experience. They criticized the assumption that male experience was all experience and explored what it might mean to do theology from a woman's experience.

At the same time that feminist theology was raising questions about the limits of theology developed out of only "man's" experience, Black and Latin Americans were also criticizing theology as done from a white perspective. Within feminist theology the questions of a hegemonic approach to even "woman's" experience soon exploded. Are all women's experiences the same? What about African-American women who bear the triple jeopardy of race, class, and sex? What about Spanish-speaking women who do not share the heritage of Western, Enlightenment Christianity? What about the diversity of lesbian and bisexual women for whom being man's "other" has not been quite the same looking-glass phenomenon as for heterosexual women?

Feminist theology as reflecting the experiences of white, middle-class women was called to question by the "experiences" of African-American women, of lesbians, of Hispanic-American women and of Asian-American women. Jacquelyn Grant, in *White Women's Christ and Black Women's Jesus,* examines various white women's christologies, showing that despite the differences between biblical, liberationist, and radical feminist christologies, all share a common assumption of white women's experiences of Christ. The works of Carter Heyward and Mary Hunt explore the distinctive experiences of lesbians, revealing the heterosexism of much of feminist theology, and use the experience of lesbian relationships to create new theological symbols and metaphors. Chung Hyun Kyung names the experiences of Korean women and narrates their meaning within the theological symbols of christology, Mariology, and spirituality.

This rich diversity of voices forces the recognition there is no "woman's" experience. The notion that all women share is some essence called "woman" is limiting, narrow, and even dangerous to the health of all! Yet the terms "woman" and "women" are heuristically helpful, as they remind us that women must speak and be heard, and that gender continues to influence not only our personal lives but how culture, knowledge, and politics are organized.

This element of feminist theologies continues to stress the importance of women's experience, but now represents the diversity of experiences. Experience itself is communal, formed by the shared traditions and practices in which persons participate. Experience or identity is changing and diverse: One may be a Spanish-speaking lesbian, a liberal Reformed Jewish woman, an evangelical feminist. Indeed experience is not so much an essence that one uncovers but an identity that one continually constructs and shapes.

Given the vast cultural changes that impact women's lives and the rich resources of feminist theory, experience as an element in feminist theology assumes a kind of narrative quality: Women compose their lives. The naming of experience is the activity of constructing an agent who is responsible for her reflection, her practice, her spirituality. Women name their experiences and thus narrate the meaning of these experiences in new ways.

Critiques of Christianity   As women, in a variety of voices, raise questions about how their communities and culture treat and represent women, so women in Christianity began to raise questions about gender and Christianity. Mary Daly provocatively pursued the interrelationship of men and God as intrinsic to Christianity. Her quite famous adage, "If God is male, then the male is God" expresses the blunt fact that Christianity has elevated men as superior to women, and used religion to express misogynist practices against women.[6] The nearly singular representation of God as male has resulted in the fact that women have not been permitted to become official theologians, and in some churches, not even allowed to teach boys and men. This belief in God as male has to be criticized for a kind of idolatry within the church of elevating the power of men over women.

If the symbol of God as male has functioned within the church to create a two-caste system, in relation to the spirituality of women it has led to narratives that too often create selves with little dignity or respect. This image of the maleness of God is filled in with values of judgment without love, of distance and transcendence without intimacy and immanence. As Carter Heyward observed, many of the central images of God in theology deny or displace God's relatedness to the earth, images such as "being itself" or "wholly other."[7] At its worst, as Susan Brooks Thistlethwaite has observed, patriarchal images contribute to abuse of women and to women's acceptance of such abuse.[8] The critique of Christianity has to do not only with the maleness of God and its idolatrous manifestations in the abuse of women, but also with how other interrelated concepts, images, and narratives have functioned to belittle, restrict, and oppress women.

That feminist theology cast a critical eye on Christianity does not make it distinct. Theological systems almost always are developed in opposition to other visions and forms of Christianity. Christian tradition, at least in its classical form, might be interpreted as debates and conflicts and various voices of critique and reconstruction of Christianity. Furthermore, feminist theologians do not share one particular strategy of critique. For some feminists the critique of Christianity is internal, that is, the places of critique and transformation are already in the classical sources. For others, critique comes from the perspective of how the discourse actually has been used within political and cultural communities, while for still others, critique arises from new voices and new possibilities as a kind of utopian vision.

Productive discourses of transformation   As feminists criticize the limitation of some Christian ideas, as well as the dysfunction and distortion of Christian practices, so feminists offer ideas and practices that seem either more true to a projected Christian idea or that provide ways to promote new forms of flourishing. The production of discourses of transformation cover three fundamental areas: (a) reinterpreting Christian symbols and doctrines; (b) reconstructing the nature of the church; and (c) developing a feminist ethics.

The richness of feminist theologies within the symbolic content of Christianity is immense. While many theologies reduce themselves to dry methodological debates, feminist theologians continue Christianity's long practice of revising its symbols to create, express, and expand Christian language about God. Rita Nakashima Brock in *Journey's By Heart* images a Christ community in which persons are healed. In *Black Womanist Ethics* Katie Cannon draws upon the work of Zora Neale Hurston, Howard Thurman, and Martin Luther King Jr to develop a black womanist ethic. Catherine Keller spins through the founding myths of Greek, Hebrew, and Christian culture, as well as secular anthropologies, to offer new relational images of the self in *From a Broken Web*. Envisioning the body of God, world, and oneself together encourages a new ecological vision and praxis, as Sallie McFague in *The Body of God* interprets the body of God as "not a body, but all the different, peculiar, particular bodies about us."[9]

As a liberation theology, feminist theology is peculiar because women do not share a distinct culture, as in dominant culture or African-American culture. And yet there is a sense in which in any culture there is something that might be called a women-church, the spaces of women in the church, making the meals, active on boards, going into homes when needed, composing the majority of worshipers on Sunday morning. What is the meaning of church as one looks at it from the point of view of those who do the domestic work of congregations instead of those of the clerical knowledge class? Women-church names a reality – women's presence in the church – as well as an ideal – the vision of a flourishing and just Christian community. Ecclesiology as formed through women-church has been interpreted as *ekklesia*, the community of equals, by Elisabeth Schüssler Fiorenza, and in the work of Rosemary Radford Ruether as the true church in which the Spirit of God moves. Rebecca Chopp has spoken of church as places where sin is denounced through lamentations of suffering, critiques of oppression, and resistance against the depth order of patriarchal and phallocentric idolatry. Theologically the church, according to Chopp, is where grace is named: the grace of a new vision of community, a new spirituality, and new practices of justice.

Central to almost all feminist theology is a concern for ethics, in relation to claims of justice, the nature of ethics, and specific ethical topics. Feminists opposing the injustice and inequities of patriarchy pay specific attention to theories of justice and visions of the just community. As feminists have probed the resources and limits of modern ethical theory, they have also come to question the self-imposed limits of ethical theory, especially criticizing the well-accepted separation of the public and the private and the political and the personal in modern ethical theory. In the midst of rethinking the meaning of the term "justice" and the nature of ethics, feminist theologians address countless ethical topics including violence against women, racism, anti-semitism, environmental destruction, and abortion.

The reinterpretation of basic symbols, the new shape of ecclesiology, and the primacy of ethics in US feminist theology share some common ideas and values which I will identify as "leading principles." The notion of leading principles comes from the pragmatist John Dewey and is a kind of hypothetical guide for understanding experience in a general fashion. Leading principles function as guides for deliberation but can themselves be revised as demanded by continued inquiry. Not as static as an ontological structure and not as formal as methodological rules, leading principles combine the substance of values with the guiding character of orienting principles. Leading values that run through feminist theologies include: embodiment or corporeality; connectedness or mutuality; and openness to transformation or anticipatory freedom. These leading principles function both as moral values and core ideas of new narratives of God and world. As moral values, leading principles can be expressed in such phrases as: "We ought to be about transformation"; "we should be attentive to embodiment"; "we must care for the connections between earth, each other and all forms of life." Leading principles also serve as the core ideas around which narratives get formed and contested. Embodiment becomes a core idea to develop the doctrine of God and a way to explore what is viewed as normal and disabled. Connectedness serves as a leading principle in a new anthropology and doctrine of creation and a conflict over who and how these connections get named. Openness to transformation becomes a primary notion in the nature of theology as itself a transformative praxis.

Embodiment calls attention to the fact that human beings have bodies; corporeality draws attention to the fact that the physical realm contains both suffering and flourishing. The term "embodiment" emphasizes the personal and anthropological while the term "corporeality" stresses the materiality of creation. Both terms draw our eyes to the physical in all its complexity and ambiguity. For many women to speak of the physical is to speak not only of liberation and transformation but of survival. Women who suffer physical abuse stand in a symbolic center of feminist critique against patriarchal abuse of women: Their bodies matter. And all the women who have listened to the misogynist messages about their bodies being ugly, all-encompassing, too much and too little, care deeply that we attend to bodies.

Embodiment, traditionally assigned to women in some dominant discourses, becomes a way to retrieve a part of assigned women's nature and use it as normative for all persons. Since women's physical nature has been attributed as inherently sinful, it has been important for feminist theologians to affirm physical nature, including women's bodies, as a part of the "good" creation.

The value of embodiment stresses attentiveness to, but not a romanticization of the body. The body can hurt and be hurt, it can curtail our activities and limit our thought and even our prayers; it forms our world. The value of embodiment means that we attend to all bodies in their differences and that we attend to embodiment as a locus of God.

The second leading principle has to do with connectedness or mutuality. The term "connectedness" signifies the interconnected matrix or web of reality in which we always already exist. The term "mutuality" suggests that to be connected, to seek connections, to build communities, is a transformation of suffering into flourishing, of evil into good.

To explore the interconnectedness of creation is to affirm the good of created order. Indeed connectedness becomes the center and the central value of Christian spirituality. In *The Body of God* Sallie McFague argues that it is the reality of connectedness that leads both to a natural piety and to ethical response, which in turn is rooted in an appreciation of creation. "It is finally, at a deep level, an aesthetic and religious sense, a response of wonder at and appreciation for the unbelievably vast, old, rich, diverse, and surprising cosmos, of which one's self is an infinitesimal but conscious part, the part able to sing its praises."[10]

Connectedness also is used to speak about how sin itself is structural and relational, not simply individual and personal. Feminist theologians explore the various levels and dimensions of the sin of sexual violence: the history of enslaving women to men's desires, linguistic structures for defining women as an object or animal, a legal system that protects the victimizer and punishes the victim, and moral and cognitive systems that distinguish and devalue the personal from the public, the practical from the theoretical.

The notion of mutuality carries the explicit connotation of being in relationship with others and with God. The value of mutuality has sometimes been considered a feminine trait: Women's ability to care and nurture has been understood as biologically, psychologically, and socially determined. Feminists are critical of assigning care of others only to women, and seek to make mutuality a foundational value in human nature. For many feminist theologians, mutuality is a basic value for understanding God's relationship to the world, and God is experienced and worshiped as being in solidarity with the world as a friend.

The third leading principle in feminist theology is that of openness to transformation, or anticipatory freedom. Feminists interpret the central symbols of Christianity to both describe and call for a transformation for justice. Feminists claim that such transformation is in fact necessary for the survival of women and children, and the survival of the earth. To speak about transformation shifts the temporality of Christianity to a kind of open future: Christianity is not just a past tradition we try to maintain, a present experience we feel or speak about, but Christianity is about an open future, a future in which creation flourishes.

Anticipatory freedom becomes a way to speak about the very nature of Christianity. Justice and friendship, spirituality and liturgy all lead us toward a future. The already and the not yet become cast as transfigurative practices in feminist theology. The eucharist is not only memory and participation but an anticipation of a time when there is a place for everyone to eat at a common table.

Figures

Central to many feminist theologies is an insistence on the communal context of all theology and a decentering of the individual theologian. Feminist theology is cautious about the great theologians model – a model that assumes a few good men hand out the truth for all other Christians to follow. Thus, when considering individual feminist theologians, it is important to read them within the context of the community of feminist theologians, and as representatives of their particular communal context. I will identify three different feminist theologians: Rosemary Radford Ruether, Elisabeth Schüssler Fiorenza, and Delores S. Williams.

Rosemary Radford Ruether

Rosemary Radford Ruether is perhaps the most widely read feminist theologian in the US, having written the only thorough presentation of Christian symbols in her *Sexism and God-Talk: Toward a feminist theology*. Ruether's theological method is boldly iconoclastic in the constant correlation of what she calls the prophetic principle of Christianity and the critical principle of feminism. Methodologically Ruether turns feminist theology into an ideology critique, constantly unveiling the distortions of Christian symbols through the positing of a prophetic principle.

Sexism and God-Talk treats the major doctrines of traditional Christian theology: God, cosmology, anthropology, christology, creation, sin, eschatology, etc., bracketed at the beginning and end by two examples of quite different types of theological genres: a feminist midrash on the gospel and a poetic postscript entitled "Women/Body/Nature: the icon of the divine." Within the various doctrines, Ruether continues her radical iconoclastic critique. For instance, in her chapter on anthropology Ruether criticizes patriarchal anthropology which, despite its equality of male and female in the *imago dei*, has become "perilously close" to seeing women as unique bearers of sin.

Ruether has always maintained that systems of social alienation and oppression must be considered together: feminism, racism, anti-semitism, and environmental destruction are all interrelated. In Ruether's *To Change the World* she identifies the fundamental difficulty for Christian theology in the pivotal symbol of christology. The question of the systems of alienation and oppression force us to ask if christology merely contributes to the problem or if it can become a symbol of liberation and transformation.

While Ruether has addressed the problems of oppression and injustice, she also continues to address issues of church and ministry concerns. Her writings on ecclesiology take a variety of different positions on the possibility of transformation within the institutional church. In recent years Ruether has advocated a women's church as an exodus church that embraces a liminal religiosity. "As Women-Church we claim the authentic mission of Christ, the true mission of church, the real agenda of our Mother-Father God who comes to restore and not to destroy our humanity, who comes to ransom the captives and to reclaim the earth as our Promised Land. We are not in exile, but the Church is in exodus with us. God's Shekinah, Holy Wisdom, the Mother-face of God has fled from the high thrones of patriarchy and has gone into exodus with us."[11]

Elisabeth Schüssler Fiorenza

Elisabeth Schüssler Fiorenza is a trained biblical scholar and theologian. Her biblical work focuses on the Book of Revelations and equalitarian movements in early Christianity. Her work in feminist theology covers the authority of the Bible, ecclesiology, theological education, and recently, christology. Fiorenza's work is characterized both by a historical argument about the nature of early Christianity and a revisioning of the nature and norms of theology.

Fiorenza argues that theology ought not to be drawn from women's experiences or some essential notion of what it is to be Christian or human. To base theology on experience, contends Fiorenza, is to tempt making archetypes normative or models of behavior. Fiorenza shapes her theology as a new vision of Christian praxis – one that she contends is already present (and has been present) if only in an emergent form. The center of this movement is what Fiorenza calls the *ekklesia*. As a biblical scholar Fiorenza contends that there was from the beginning a Christian attempt to create the church as a discipleship of equals. Fiorenza argues in *In Memory of Her* (the book that established her as a leading feminist theologian) that one important strand in the New Testament is the vision and reality of the church as a discipleship of equals.

For Fiorenza the *ekklesia* must be distinguished from the women-church position of someone like Ruether. Women-church, for Fiorenza, is problematic in that it sounds exclusionary and separatist. Fiorenza wants to develop new categories for ecclesiology. For Fiorenza the *ekklesia* is both present and to come; the *ekklesia* speaks of longings for a new future. Fiorenza envisions the ideal of the *ekklesia* as a democratic community, with men and women engaged in their own self-determination.

Fiorenza's theological position is that of a pragmatic critical theory – an attempt to let theology name the sufferings and the desires of people in the midst of Christian emancipatory praxis. Theology is not primarily a debate about ontological or epistemological categories, but rather fashions discourses and practices of living justly. As such theology is contextual, using the images, concepts, and symbols involved in a situation to move against distortion and destruction and to envision new ways of flourishing.

Delores S. Williams

Delores Williams is a womanist theologian. As defined by Alice Walker a womanist is a Black feminist or a feminist of color. Womanist theologians have a long history in the lives of African-American women active in church and culture. Drawing upon the complex and diverse lives of African-American women in the US, womanist theologians attempt to speak of God in the context of black women's lives and in so doing relate and distinguish womanist theology from black theology on the one hand and feminist theology on the other. With the emergence of womanist theory and Black feminist theory, womanist theology has a theoretical basis in African-American women's social history, epistemology, and literary criticism. Womanist theologians join womanist theorists in developing a written record of Black women's intellectual tradition, drawing upon sources in music and oral tradition as well as the theology, philosophy, fictional and anthropological writings of African-American women.

In *Sisters in the Wilderness*, Delores Williams offers a reading of the biblical story of Hagar to speak of the distinctiveness of Black women and to develop womanist God-talk. Williams argues that Hagar's story represents how African-American women have struggled to survive in the US and how they turned to God for company, solace, and strength. Black women suffer the interplay of oppression on account of race, sex, and class. The trials and tribulations of Hagar in the wilderness is a story that Black women in the US have lived out in many ways. Under the conditions of slavery Black women were forced to mother white children as well as their own. Under the legal and cultural system of slavery, it was the woman that often protected the family, as well as resisting the conditions of slavery and working for liberation. In the post-bellum period, African-American women had some selected control over forced surrogacy, though poverty and the type of jobs available still forced many Black women into surrogacy roles. In present-day US culture, Black women are forced into new forms of surrogacy. Like Hagar, many Black women at present and in the past have their lives dominated by poverty, exploitation, surrogacy, violence, hopelessness, ethnicity, as well as by "meetings with God."

Williams uses Hagar's story to symbolize the resistance, faith, and strength of Black women in a hostile world. Williams suggests a female-centered tradition of African-American appropriation that she calls "survival/quality-of-life tradition of African-American biblical appropriation." Defiance, risk-taking, independence, endurance, stamina to hold things together for the family, ability in poverty to make a new way, courage to initiate political action in the public arena, and a close personal relation to God are all symbolized in the story of Hagar in the wilderness.

In one of her most provocative theological interpretations, Williams maintains that Jesus, like Black women, gets cast in a surrogacy role in much of traditional christology. Williams questions whether the "image of a surrogate-God has salvific power for black women or whether this image supports and reinforces the exploitation that has accompanied their experience with surrogacy."[12] For Williams, theology is about God-talk, not in abstract or formal ways, but in and through the lives of African-American women, past and present, for whom God "makes a way out of no way."

Debate

Within the notion of constellation, it is also important to speak of some of the leading debates, tensions and conflicts within feminist theologies. Because this survey is figured as a constellation, even the image of debate should not be posed in an either/or, winner or loser, right or wrong way; but as many-sided, ongoing, and constantly changing. These two central debates within feminist theology have to do with the role of tradition and the notion and construction of patriarchy.

The first area of debate or conflict has to do with the deconstruction and construction of "tradition." Certainly in Christianity various historical periods construct the tradition quite differently, both in terms of who counts as the tradition and in how traditional thinkers are read. One example is how Protestants and Catholics read Augustine on grace, or, to take another example, how differently Jesus has been interpreted and portrayed in various historical periods. Feminist theology, like any other theology, has to choose and argue for what it means by tradition and what hermeneutical principles will be employed to interpret the tradition. But, in addition to this normal activity of reconstructing tradition, feminist theology has a peculiar task since the tradition – even in the Scriptures – says so many negative things about women, casts the female gender as the negative side of a binary opposition, and so often condones or ignores the physical and psychological abuse of women.

Feminist theologians have paid a great deal of attention to what the Scriptures say about women and how the Scriptures have been used against women. Attention has been drawn to patriarchal translations, as when Phoebe's title *diakonis* is translated "deaconess" or "servant" when it is applied to her and "minister" or "deacon" when it is used to describe a male leader. Likewise feminist theology examines patriarchal interpretations (as when Eve is simply blamed for sin rather than noted for enabling Adam, the generic human, to become a particular man) and patriarchal oversights (as when the Samaritan woman in John 4 is not the focus of the call to mission, or when the rape of a woman in Judges 19 is ignored or belittled in the commentaries). And within the broader tradition of Christianity women such as Teresa of Avila, Margery Kempe, Juana Ines de la Cruz, Anna Julai Cooper, and Jarena Lee are all claimed as voices of the tradition.

But the internal debate within feminist theology has to do not so much with finding forgotten or neglected women nor with uncovering the patriarchal interpretation, translations, and constructions of the tradition. The internal debate has to do with the possibility of both deconstructing and reconstructing Christianity in order to answer the question: How is tradition normative? For those who find a kind of essential Christianity, represented by Ruether and Daly, the question has to be answered by arguing first what the essentialist position is – will the true form of Christianity please stand up? The other way to frame it is a more historicist position, that Christianity is always a matter of continual reinterpretation and what one historical period or group may count as normative, another will not.

For purposes of clarification, the debate can be identified with three sides. A "tradition friendly" group of feminist theologians argues that, though the tradition has patriarchal texts and constructs, the tradition also has plenty of additional non-patriarchal resources. Indeed the internal critique of patriarchy can be argued on a basis of theologians who at the same time are some of the worst proponents of patriarchy! One good example of a "tradition friendly" theologian is Elizabeth Johnson. Johnson, using a version of traditional analogical argument, argues that feminist language represents the logic of traditional theological argument far better than patriarchal language of God. Feminist theology, like traditional language, affirms many names of God rather than narrowing language to a non-analogical referent. Like the classical tradition, feminist theology opposes idolatrous ways of naming God.

The second position about the nature of tradition simply argues that Christianity is just too patriarchal. Mary Daly, no longer a Christian theologian, suggests that Christianity, with its fundamental message of a male God, is about the oppression of women. Though feminist theologians arguing this position often provide the most thorough critique, they also remove themselves from being feminist *theologians*. To say it differently, this position has little to contribute to revisioning the church, providing new interpretations of symbols, or doing ethics from a Christian position. But it is a position that many feminists find themselves moved to by the power of their own critical arguments.

The third position begins by questioning the question itself: How and why is tradition normative? This position locates feminist theology not first in a set of texts but within the context of a contemporary Christian movement that assumes its responsibility as interpreter of the tradition. These theologians, such as Elisabeth Schüssler Fiorenza, Rebecca Chopp, and Sheila Greeve Davaney, contend that the other two positions tend to argue a kind of essentialist Christian tradition, which gives far too much power to the patriarchal tradition. Instead feminist theology flows out of a living community for which tradition is one empowering source.

The second internal debate also uses the language of essentialism in relation to the nature of patriarchy. As we have already seen, this internal debate is, at least in part, about the class and race privilege assumed in so much of white feminist theology. Women of color, lesbian women, and women of different faith communities question the assumptions behind white feminist theology. This question can also be asked: What is the nature of patriarchy? Is patriarchy the cause of all evils, the first cause out of which all flow? Is patriarchy the same in various historical constructs? How does patriarchy relate to other forms of oppression?

The positions around this debate can be organized around three rubrics. These are not either/or positions, not even "debates" in the contemporary sense, but, as in a constellation, juxtaposed elements which conflict at one point and intersect at another point. The first position refuses to give any primacy to patriarchy and emphasizes the analysis of the interstructuring of oppression. This position is represented by thinkers such as Ada María Isasi-Díaz, Delores Williams, and Susan Brooks Thistlethwaite, who stress the interstructuring of oppression. Ada María Isasi-Díaz, for instance, argues that adding Hispanic women to feminist is not like baking a cake, not just one more ingredient to add. Rather, white feminists must learn about Hispanic culture and learn to define experience in light of relation to Hispanic culture and thus "to assume responsibility for the systematic analysis of ethical prejudice and racism."[13]

The second position includes those feminists who try to think through oppression and patriarchy as itself historically constructed. Does the very construction of patriarchy and even gender itself vary in historical periods? Is patriarchy a shifting historical construct? For feminists deeply attuned to the positive role religion has often played in women's lives, it is necessary to talk about patriarchy and oppression as not necessarily totalistic and even changing. *Changing the Subject* by Mary McClintock Fulkerson is an excellent example of a work by a feminist theologian deeply sensitive to patriarchy and oppression as a cultural construct.

The third position is the one that would indicate or state that sexism is in some sense the base or representative of oppression. Certainly the theological writings of a figure such as Mary Daly could be characterized as arguing that patriarchy is the origin of all evil. Few feminists today would argue this kind of patriarchy as the origins of oppression approach. Instead, for many white feminists patriarchy becomes a kind of representation and symbolization of sin. So, for instance, Rebecca Chopp speaks of how rape symbolizes sin. Viewed through sin, rape is seen as a complete distortion of relationship, a mockery and devastation of what religiously "relationship" might mean. But if sin helps name the reality of rape, the reality of rape also helps us to symbolize sin. Rape reminds us of the doublesidedness of so much sin: Rape is an individual act of violence, but it is also cultural and structural and, in the United States, a cultural epidemic. This position maintains that, while there is not an "essence" to patriarchy, the notion of patriarchy provides us with a way to analyze a powerful reality that must be described and resisted.

These three positions are not either/or positions of the nature of patriarchy. To a certain extent they are different ways to interpret the reasons for feminist theology. What is it critical of, what is it hoping for? Within these positions, there are some elements in direct conflict: The position that Christianity is inherently opposed to women and cannot be retrieved is in conflict with Christian feminist theologies' various attempts to conceive of feminist theology as a living language for Christian faith communities. But in another way these positions about patriarchy and "woman" can be juxtaposed: The historical construction of patriarchy may now have to be read through interstructuring of oppression.

Achievement and Agenda

Feminist theology can be accessed in terms of its contributions to the varied realities of which it speaks: women's voices, gender analysis of Christianity, and a productive religious discourse of emancipatory praxis. In terms of women's voices, feminist theologies continue to express new voices and new concerns. In terms of how the broader US culture constructs groups and movements such as African-American, Spanish-speaking, Asian-American, and lesbian, feminist theology hopes to be inclusive. Though this inclusivity in feminist theology is full of conflict, conversation, and difference, it is an inclusivity of diverse voices to which most feminist theologians are at least committed. But will the diversity of these voices become incorporated in the theologies done by men, or are they for and by women only? Is feminist theology a special language only for a few, or is it an important language for all Christians? This is, I think, still to be seen in the US theological scene.

The answer to the broad influence of feminist theology in the US will be in part related to how successful feminist theology is in using gender analysis as an illumination of theological traditions and religious practices. Certainly the contribution of feminist theology to biblical scholarship and historical studies is one of the most important landmarks in the last 20 years of scholarship in and on Christianity. Constructive feminist theologians have contributed new readings of Christian symbols and doctrines, including the doctrine of God and ecclesiology. And these symbolic visions of God as nurturing and the church as democratic have had widespread influence in the US theological scene. Yet, on a deep structural level, more work remains in front of feminist theology. The analysis of sexuality and gender has barely begun. How does Christianity regulate and produce sexual identity or meaning? The insights of feminist theology about the construction of gender need to move in two basic directions: the construction of masculinity and the deconstruction/reconstruction of gendered forms of power. The investigation of masculinity is starting to be done by male theologians such as Mark Taylor and Phil Culbertson. The depth analysis of gendered forms of power, touched upon by theologians such as Elisabeth Schüssler Fiorenza, Delores Williams, and Mary Daly, requires continued work.

The third achievement is in feminist theology's ability to form and shape Christianity as a transformative praxis. There is, it seems to me, an emergent movement of a new type of Christianity in the US today. Feminist theology is an important element in this emergent movement. Not only has feminist theology contributed to a basic vision of new ways of being Christian, but new interpretations of symbols and new shapes of practices have been shaped by feminists. Feminist theology has also contributed a distinct form of theology as a type of critical theory of emancipatory praxis in and through religious communities. The future agenda will be to lead this emergent movement into a stable form of Christian witness, with due influence in the ongoing institutions and practices. For this feminist theology will have to develop more systematic and comprehensive discourses of transformation.

Notes

1 Patricia Hill Collins, *Black Feminist Thought: Knowledge, Consciousness, and the Politics of Empowerment* (New York and London, 1990), p. 45.

2 Nancy Fraser, "What's Critical about Critical Theory?" in Seyla Benhabib and Drucilla Cornel (eds), *Feminism as Critique on the Politics of Gender* (Minneapolis, 1987), pp. 42–3.

3 Rita Nakashima Brock, *Journeys By Heart: A christology of erotic power* (New York, 1988), p. 3.

4 Adrienne Rich, *Of Woman Born* (New York, 1976).

5 Quoted in Richard J. Bernstein, *The New Constellation: The ethical-political horizons of modernity/postmodernity* (Cambridge, MA, 1993), p. 201.

6 Mary Daly, *Beyond God the Father: Toward a philosophy of women's liberation* (Boston, 1973), p. 19.

7 Carter Heyward, *The Redemption of God: A theology of mutual relation* (Washington, DC, 1982) and *Touching Our Strength: The erotic as power and the love of God* (San Francisco, 1989).

8 Susan Brooks Thistlethwaite, "Every two minutes: battered women and feminist interpretation," in Letty M. Russell (ed.), *Feminist Interpretation of the Bible* (Philadelphia, 1985), pp. 96–110.

9 Sallie McFague, *The Body of God: An ecological theology* (Minneapolis, 1993), p. 211.

10 Ibid., p. 112.

11 Rosemary Radford Ruether, *Women-Church: Theology and practice of feminist liturgical communities* (San Francisco, 1985), p. 72.

12 Delores S. Williams, *Sisters in the Wilderness: The challenge of womanist God-talk* (Maryknoll, NY, 1993), p. 162.

13 Ada María Isasi-Díaz, "Toward an understanding of *Feminism Hispano* in the U.S.A.," in Barbara Hilkert Anderson, Christine E. Gudorf, and Mary A. Pellauer (eds), *Women's Consciousness, Women's Conscience: A reader in feminist ethics* (Minneapolis, 1985), p. 59.

Bibliography

Primary

Fiorenza, E. Schüssler, *In Memory of Her: A feminist theological reconstruction of Christian origins* (New York, 1983).
—— *But She Said: Feminist practices of biblical interpretation* (Boston, 1992).
—— *Jesus: Miriam's child, Sophia's prophet* (New York, 1994).
Ruether, R. Radford, *To Change the World: Christology and cultural criticism* (New York, 1981).
—— *Sexism and God-Talk: Toward a feminist theology* (Boston, 1983).
—— *Women-Church: Theology and practice of feminist liturgical communities* (San Francisco, 1985).

Williams, D. S., *Sisters in the Wilderness: The challenge of womanist God-talk* (Maryknoll, NY, 1993).

Secondary

Brock, R. N., *Journeys by Heart: A christology of erotic power* (New York, 1988).
Cannon, K., *Black Womanist Ethics* (Atlanta, GA, 1988).
Chopp, R., *The Power to Speak: Feminism, language, God* (New York, 1989).
—— *Saving Work: Feminist practices of theological education* (Louisville, KY, 1995).
Davaney, S., "Problems with feminist theory:

historicity and the search for sure foundation," in *Embodied Love*, eds. Cooey, Farmer, and Ross (San Francisco, 1987), pp. 79–98.

Eisland, N., *The Disabled God: Toward a liberatory theology of disability* (Nashville, TN, 1994).

Fulkerson, M. F., *Changing the Subject: Women's discourses and feminist theology* (Minneapolis, 1994).

Grant, J., *White Women's Christ and Black Women's Jesus: Feminist christology and womanist response* (Atlanta, GA, 1989).

Heyward, C., *Touching Our Strength: The erotic as power and the love of God* (San Francisco, 1989).

Hunt, M., *Fierce Tenderness: A feminist theology of friendship* (New York, 1991).

Isasi-Díaz, A., *En La Lucha/In the Struggle: A Hispanic women's liberation theology* (Minneapolis, 1994).

Johnson, E., *She Who Is: The mystery of God in feminist theological discourse* (New York, 1992).

Keller, C., *From a Broken Web: Separation, sexism, and self* (Boston, 1986).

Kyung, C. H., *Struggle to be the Sun Again: Introducing Asian women's theology* (Maryknoll, NY, 1990).

McFague, S., *Models of God: Theology for an ecological, nuclear age* (Philadelphia, 1987).

—— *The Body of God: An ecological theology* (Minneapolis, 1993).

Procter-Smith, M., *In Her Own Rite: Constructing feminist liturgical tradition* (Nashville, TN, 1990).

Russell, L., *Household of Freedom: Authority in feminist theology* (Philadelphia, 1987).

Taylor, M., *Remembering Esperenza: A cultural-political theology for North America praxis* (Maryknoll, NY, 1990).

Thistlethwaite, S., *Sex, Race, and God: Christian feminist in black and white* (New York, 1989).

Latin American, African, and Asian Theologies

Latin America, Africa, and Asia together embrace the majority of the world's Christians and, especially in the second half of the twentieth-century, they have generated an immense amount of theology. Part IV can make no claim to comprehensiveness but, in line with the principles and limitations described in the preface of the book, it attempts a survey and introduces some of the leading themes and representatives. Theology from these regions is also treated in Parts V, VI, and VII of this volume.

Liberation theology has been the main way in which Latin America has affected theology, churches, and politics outside that continent. Rebecca Chopp describes the ways in which Latin American liberation theology was influenced by Vatican II, political theology, and Marxism, and she defines clearly what is meant by praxis and liberation. She portrays a vigorous new genre of theology that expresses a fresh transformation of the Christian faith itself. She offers an interpretation of the development of the theology of Gustavo Gutiérrez, from a primary focus on the transformation of history through the praxis of the poor to a centering on the God of faithfulness and love, who is manifested also in captivity, suffering, and exile, and she discusses the importance of Gutiérrez's 1993 biography of Las Casas. She then outlines the theology of José Miguez Bonino, before entering into controversies about liberation theology and finally suggesting how it calls most modern theologies fundamentally into question and threatens them with rupture. In addition, at the opening and conclusion of her chapter she faces the problem of how those who are not poor might genuinely receive this theology.

The rapid expansion of Christianity in Africa, from under 10 million Christians at the beginning of the twentieth century to well over 200 million now (and still rapidly growing) has turned it into a new heartland of the faith. Kwame Bediako, himself a leading current contributor to the developments he describes, sees African Christianity and theology having a universal vocation, and is especially concerned to indicate how Western Christianity, modern and postmodern, can learn from a theology that has entered deeply into an encounter with traditional African religion and culture. He describes the range of responses to the pre-Christian heritage and discusses the work of John Mbiti in particular. He sums up the achievement of African theologians in working through the impact of the West to the point of no longer being dominated by it, and he outlines some of the main items on the future agenda, stressing the importance of a theology that is rooted in a rich oral, vernacular, religious culture still in touch with primal religion.

John de Gruchy is a leading participant in the South African theological world, which he describes in the aftermath of black majority rule. He identifies five types of theology born in the struggle against apartheid: confessing theology inspired by Barth, Bonhoeffer, and the struggle of the German Confessing Church in Nazi Germany; Black theology, liberation theology, womanist/feminist theology, and prophetic or kairos theology. Finally, he suggests an agenda as the nation is reconstructed. Many theologians are seeking forms of critical solidarity with the new regime, and other issues which were neglected under the pressures of fighting apartheid are being attended to, such as ecumenism, various ethical problems, religious and cultural pluralism, dialogue with African theology, and reconnecting critical theological reflection to "popular theology."

George Gispert-Sauch offers a panoramic view of Asian theology, briefly recounting the three main families of Christian tradition there and surveying the varied influences on its theology. It is treated in clusters: India and Sri Lanka; Korea; China, Taiwan, Japan, and Thailand; the Philippines; and Indonesia. The main specific theologians discussed are Raimundo Panikkar, M. M. Thomas, Swami Abhishiktananda, and Aloysius Pieris. In conclusion, the main features of Asian theology are summarized.

Latin American Liberation Theology

Rebecca S. Chopp

Introduction: Character, Origins, and Influences

Latin American liberation theology is a reflection on God's activity and God's transforming grace among those who are the victims of modern history. To read and really hear this logos of the theos, if one is not a member of the despised masses of the poor, one must begin with an attitude of respect and care in order to be open to the voice of the others of history. In this attitude of respectful care Latin American liberation theology will not be received as an interpretation, a second-level reflection on common human experience, but rather an interruption, an irruption of how God is active, life is lived, and Christianity is practiced among the poor. This chapter assumes that its readers are not the poor, the subjects of Latin American liberation theology, and hence attempts to let Latin American liberation theology speak in its voice, but to do so with an interpreter who stands ever ready to say again and again that this knowledge of God is not directly equitable or commensurable with the modern theology of the First World bourgeoisie. We must hear the voice of Latin American liberation theology, and we must try to listen closely before we can understand; but we must also accept, at the beginning, the integrity of a different voice, a different experience, a different genre of theology that belongs to the same God, the same church, the same Christ of which we speak.

Latin American liberation theology speaks of God as manifest in the poor of history. It must speak of this, for it arises out of the poor's experience of God, an experience that is dependent, as Gustavo Gutiérrez has insisted, upon God's choosing to reveal God's self in the poor.[1] Like many other theologies, this one grows out of and reflects back upon faith itself; it is not laid upon faith by well-meaning theologians, nor is it arrived at by a few radical revolutionaries. Liberation theology seeks to speak of this faith and thus to speak of God; in so doing it seeks to give voice to liberation, which involves not only freedom from oppression but also freedom to become new subjects in history. Liberation theology and the faith upon which it reflects does not try to make the poor the rich, or the rich the poor, or some intermediary in between: Rather the experience of and reflection of God and the poor seek to guide the transformation of all human beings into new ways of being human, ways not dependent upon structures of division between rich and poor, the common and the despised, the persons and the nonpersons of history.[2]

Many factors contribute to the distinctive voice of Latin American liberation theology. The first, and most important factor, is its context in the concrete situation of massive poverty, a context that can only be hinted at by terms such as poverty, starvation, and oppression. The masses of Latin America struggle to survive in severe poverty, severe enough for two-thirds of the population of Latin America to live with hunger as their constant companion. Most of the land and nearly all of the business are in the hands of a wealthy minority. The masses suffer frequent unemployment and, when they do find work, the wages are not enough to provide what we in the First World might call a decent standard of living. The poor see their children starve and often watch them die from lack of food, health care, and proper sanitation. In the midst of this massive poverty, many of the poor live under repressive regimes and have few, if any, political rights.

This present context grows out of the "modern" history of Latin America, a history which, since the "discovery of the New World" has been marked by oppression and colonization.[3] Spain and Portugal settled the New World through the devastation of native cultures in order to make slaves for the conquerors and to Christianize the "heathens" en masse. Even with the emergence of many Latin American nations in the beginning of the nineteenth century, neocolonialism, a system of economic dependency and exploitation, existed between nations and First World countries, first with Great Britain and later with the United States. The 1950s and 1960s saw international commitments to develop dependent countries to be like First World nations such as the United States, but this movement created more and more dependent relations, this time through military oligarchies and multinational corporations.[4] The "modern" history of Latin America, the modern history we know as named by terms such as progress, science, freedom, has been best characterized in words such as exploitation, poverty, and oppression.

A major factor in the development of Latin American liberation theology was the positions on justice and peace that Roman Catholicism and Protestantism began to take in the 1950s and 1960s. Most important among the stances taken was the social teaching of Vatican II concerning human dignity and the need for structural change. Latin American bishops met in Medellin, Colombia, in 1968 to discuss the impact of Vatican II for Latin America; the papers adopted by the bishops became the founding documents of liberation theology.[5] At this conference the struggle for change that would guide liberation theology was invoked, a struggle against the institutionalized violence of the rich against the poor. A new vision of faith was articulated in the view of the poor as human subjects active in history. This vision was located in small grass-roots communities where the poor could determine their own destiny and express their faith as they participated in conscientization or consciousness-raising.

Besides these historical events and contexts, three other influences must be noted: first, that of political theology, second, that of Marxism, and the third that of popular religion. Political theology arose in West Germany as a critique of modern Christianity's concern for the ahistorical authenticity of the bourgeois subject and a reformulation of Christian theology in light of events of massive suffering, such as the Holocaust, in progressive, modern nations. The works of political theologians such as Jürgen Moltmann and Johann Baptist Metz suggested new theological terms such as privatization, oppression, ideology, and liberation. Metz offered a new anthropology that was social and political, while Moltmann constructed an understanding of God in and through the reality of suffering. Both Metz and Moltmann spoke of Christianity as a critical witness in society.[6]

As both a theoretical tool of social analysis and a philosophy of history, Marxism has influenced liberation theology.[7] As a tool of social analysis, Marxism has supplied a dialectical analysis rather than a functional one, an analysis focusing on the relations of power and force in a society instead of covering such forces up in an ideology of society as an organism needing balance. As a philosophy of history, Marxism has contributed, along with other philosophies, toward a view of the human subject as socially or historically constituted, history as open to change and transformation, and oppression and alienation structured through the productive relations of society. Latin American liberation theologians, especially in the early years, critically adopted some of the language and insights from Marxism; but they did so only by transforming these insights and language into their own theological reflections.

A quite different influence from either the first-world-based political theology or Marxist theory is the influence of popular religion in the more recent years of liberation theology. As Latin American liberation theologians focused more and more on the "option for the poor" as a way of life, the importance of popular religion came to the fore. Popular religion takes seriously the cultural specificity of various Latin American peoples and requires a reflection on the particularities of Amerindians, blacks, women, and others who may have distinctive religious practices. Attentiveness to how the ideas and rituals of Christianity settled in among native religious practices is also required when attending to popular religion. Latin American liberation theologians, in general, came to a growing appreciation of how the people's religions included indigenous practices, Afro-American religions, animistic traditions, the practice of magic, and various synchristic blends of religious traditions. Finally, popular religion provides an understanding not only of survival practices among the poor, but also of potential resources for transformation. Devotion to Mary, for instance, includes prayer to the popular female figures Morentia of Guadalupe, the black Aparecida, Purisima, and the Virgin of Charity, to whom persons pray for survival. Theological reflection and praxis also make these manifestations of the mother of the redeemer a symbol of hope for all. As María Clara Bingemer has observed, "What is new about this work is that it reveals a Mary no longer considered individualistically, in terms of a model of ascetic virtues to be imitated, but as a collective symbol, a type of the faithful people within which the holy Spirit of God finds fertile ground to raise up the new people, the seed of the kingdom, which will inaugurate the new creation."[8]

Survey

Latin American liberation theology is not primarily academic discourse for academic debate; it is, rather, church theology coming out of and aimed toward its ecclesial context in basic Christian communities. Basic communities are grass-roots communities among the masses, in which Christians seek to form and live out their Christian witness in their historical situation. Thus the locus of Latin American liberation theology is the church, not the academy, and its genre of liberation theology can be characterized as a reflection on and guide to praxis rather than a second-level hermeneutical reflection on the theoretical meaning of Christianity. Latin American liberation theology is first of all a practical, theological discourse on the reality of the poor. But the poor do not just happen, they are created by structures and institutions, and thus liberation theology is a critique of the structures and institutions that create the poor, including modern Christianity which has identified with the rich. In order to do this, liberation theology engages in dialogue not only with philosophy but also with the social sciences. As a theological discourse of critique and transformation in solidarity with the poor, liberation theology offers a theological anthropology that is political, an interpretation of Christianity that may be characterized through the term liberation, and a vision of Christianity as a praxis of love and solidarity with the oppressed.

The image of human existence (and theological anthropology is always guided by an image) in Latin American liberation theology is the poor. The bishops of Latin America meeting at Puebla in 1979 identified the faces of the poor, the subjects of liberation theology:

> the faces of young children, struck down by poverty before they are born . . . the faces of indigenous peoples, and frequently that of the Afro-Americans as well, living marginalized lives in inhuman situations . . . the faces of the peasants; as a special group, they live in exile almost everywhere on our continent . . . the faces of marginalized and overcrowded urban dwellers, whose lack of material goods is matched by the ostentatious display of wealth by other segments of society; – the faces of old people, who are growing more numerous every day, and who are frequently marginalized in a progress-oriented society that totally disregards people not engaged in production.[9]

These faces are not isolated as individual expressions of some "common" human existence or made objectively real only in God's action; rather, they are the reality of human existence in Latin America.

This human reality, the reality of what it is to be the poor, the despised, the scourged of the earth, is understood, in Latin American liberation theology, through the term "praxis," which has three distinguishable meanings. First of all, praxis means that human beings are constituted through political-historical reality. Where one lives, the status of the socioeconomic class, what kind of power is available, must all be clear considerations for understanding human reality. Secondly, praxis means that human reality is intersubjective, that human beings are not first ahistorical "I"s that express their unique essences in relations to others through language, but that all subjectivity arises out of intersubjective relations between human beings. Finally, praxis as the understanding of human reality means that humans must and can intentionally create history, transforming and shaping reality for the improvement of human flourishing.

This understanding of human reality through praxis is joined by an interpretation, a re-formation, of Christian symbols through the central theme of liberation. The key term "liberation," like any key term functioning as a material norm in theology, is a tensive metaphor, naming the reign and nature of God, the normative vision of history, the work and person of Christ, the witness and mission of the church.[10] It is with the centrality of this term, and many rich readings of the Bible and Christian tradition, that Latin American liberation theology is most clearly understood as not merely a form of ethics or social witness, but as a systematic theology, a radically new interpretation and transformation of Christian faith itself. Sin, for instance, in liberation theology is reflected on not merely through individual moral acts or existential separation and despair, but primarily in terms of social structures. Sin results in suffering, whose burden is carried, time and time again, by the poor of history. Sin is radical distortion, not of some private relation with God, but of all reality, especially of the historical-political world that God gives us to live in. Redemption, correlatively, must relate to liberation, though, of course, it cannot be merely identified with any one liberating act; if redemption has to do with the reconciliation of humanity to God and salvation from sins, then it must be related, tensively and expressively but nonetheless realistically, to our present historical reality. Indeed, among the many readings of Christ in liberation theology – Christ as political rebel, Christ suffering as the scourged of the earth, Christ in solidarity with the poor and oppressed – Christ as liberator, as one who actually effects transformation, as one who brings new ways of being human, is central.

Within the locus of this understanding of human reality and interpretation of Christian symbols, Christianity becomes a praxis of solidarity and liberation; the point of Christianity becomes an activity that is for and of the poor, working for liberation and transformation for all. Christianity represents the witness of freedom: It does not necessarily supply a new political ordering, and it definitely does not offer a new theocratic state; rather it testifies to freedom and liberation, taking sides where God takes sides with the poor and the despised of the earth. Christianity follows God, and as Gustavo Gutiérrez has suggested, "The love of God is a gratuitous gift . . . Loving by preference the poor, doing that, God reveals this gratuity. And by consequence as followers of Jesus Christ, we must also do this preferential option for the poor."[11] In this way, for Christians, faith and love are not separable, indeed may not be distinguishable from justice. Christianity must neither conform itself to culture nor be a radical separatist sect: Rather, Christianity must discern God's activity amid the poor and work for radical transformation of the structures of society in order that all persons may become new human subjects.

It is best, therefore, to think of Latin American liberation theology as a new way or a new genre of theology based on a specific praxis of faith. Though liberation theology shares some common resources with other theologies, its way of organizing, its criteria for reading scriptures and traditions, its tasks, purpose, and intent are specific to Christian praxis amid the poor. This allows, also, the realization that liberation theologians, while sharing common themes of the option for the poor, God as liberator, and the liberation of theology, make their own individual contributions. Latin American liberation theologians write on issues such as christology and ecclesiology, work on how to use the resources of the social sciences, investigate the relation of popular religion to liberation theology, or interpret biblical themes and narratives.

It is, of course, difficult to survey Latin American liberation theologians since liberation theology is a young enterprise, and many of the figures who have written in Spanish or Portuguese have yet to be translated into English. But a brief survey, by alphabetical order, of some figures and their books that are available in English may indicate the range of issues and interests in Latin American liberation theology. In the survey below the theologians mentioned, like most Christians in Latin America, are mainly Roman Catholic. Latin American liberation theology has arisen primarily in the context of the Roman Catholic Church in Latin America, though there has been a parallel movement in the Protestant churches. After this overview of the major figures and works in liberation theology, we will consider an individual Roman Catholic theologian and then a Protestant theologian for a deeper interpretation.

Hugo Assmann has taught in his native Brazil, Germany, and Costa Rica. Assmann's *Theology for a Nomad Church* considers the practical and theoretical nature of theological method in a liberation context. Like other liberation theologians, Assmann's work draws on sociology as a major source for theological reflection and formulates the basis of theological method not through eternal absolutes but through a critical engagement with and interpretation of historical praxis. Also concerned with the nature and method of theological reflection is Clodovis Boff, a Brazilian theologian, whose *Theology and Praxis: Epistemological foundations* serves as the most thorough treatment at present of the epistemological presuppositions in liberation theology. Also attentive to popular religion, Clodovis Boff has published *Feet-on the-Ground Theology: A Brazilian journey*, a diary of his missionary work with the church of Acre and Purus in northwestern Brazil. Clodovis's brother, Leonardo Boff, is well known for his christology, *Jesus Christ Liberator*. Boff's christology is based on the situation of oppression in Latin America and stresses the priority of orthopraxis instead of orthodoxy and the anthropological instead of the ecclesiological element in christology. In recent years, Boff's work has been directed to conversation, and controversy, with the institutional Church. His book *Church: Charism and power: Liberation theology and the institutional Church* seeks not only to address the concerns of the institutional Church in relation to liberation theology but to offer a new model of the Church. This new model is a pneumatic ecclesiology, recalling the primitive elements of community, cooperation, and charism in Christian life. Boff has written another book on ecclesiology entitled *Ecclesiogenesis: The base communities reinvent the Church* in which, drawing on articles written since 1977, he offers a new vision of the Church, based on the experience of basic Christian communities. Another theologian who has interpreted the Church in the present situation is José Comblin, whose book entitled *The Church and the National Security State* attends to the present condition of the Roman Catholic Church in Latin America and offers an interpretation of the present political situation in terms of the failure of developmentalism and the emerging cooperation between oligarchies and multinational corporations.

If the present and the future of the Church is a basic concern for liberation theology, so is interpreting the past. Certainly the history of the Church in the Latin

American context has usually been neglected, or when addressed, read only from the eyes of the victors. Enrique Dussel's *A History of the Church in Latin America* has made a major contribution to a reinterpretation of the Church in Latin America. Dussel, an Argentinean layman in the Roman Catholic Church, also has sought to develop philosophical categories for Latin American liberation theology that focus on "otherness" and an ethics focused on the liberation of the oppressed. Along with ecclesiology, the Scripture has been a major concern for liberation theologians, both as they seek to interpret the concerns of poverty, oppression, and liberation in the Bible and as they reflect on the power of reading the Scriptures as a liberating activity. Books such as José Miranda's *Marx and the Bible: A critique of the philosophy of oppression* and his *Being and the Messiah* suggest a new way of reading the Bible, as well as a new interpretation of topics such as sin and redemption in the Bible.

A theologian concerned with the use of Scripture in theology is Juan Luis Segundo. Segundo's *The Liberation of Theology* reinterprets the hermeneutic circle in theology, addressing how the Bible is to be interpreted in a manner that does not simply repeat past doctrines, but speaks to and transforms the present historical situation. Uruguay's Segundo is one of the most prolific writers in liberation theology, and one who has had many books translated into English. Segundo also represents many theologians who, in the course of their careers, have "become" liberation theologians, moving from a form of theological reflection in a European style to reformulating theological reflection in the Latin American situation. In fact, Segundo's series entitled *A Theology for Artisans of a New Humanity*, written as liberation theology began to emerge, can be read as transitional pieces between the older European model of theology and the concerns and impulses that lie behind liberation theology. This series has five volumes: *The Community Called Church, Grace and the Human Condition, Our Idea of God, The Sacraments Today*, and *Evolution and Guilt*. Segundo's newest series is entitled *Jesus of Nazareth Yesterday and Today*. It continues the methodological work of *The Liberation of Theology* in the first volume of this series, entitled *Faith and Ideologies*, and in the next four volumes develops a christology for today. Segundo's work in this series and in his more recent *Signs of the Time: Theological reflections* suggests the richness and the breadth of Latin American liberation theology. The work of Jon Sobrino of El Salvador indicates the radical reformation of Christianity and of theology that liberation theology represents. Sobrino's *Christology at the Crossroads* offers a christology that combines a rereading of the historical Jesus (contending that Jesus was on the side of the oppressed) against the background of exploitation, injustice, and oppression in Latin America. Sobrino argues, in this widely read text, that we can come to know Jesus only by following Jesus, which means following Jesus into the struggle against oppression and for liberation. An equally radical treatment of ecclesiology is offered in Sobrino's *The True Church and the Poor*, which begins by tracing the differences between liberation theology and European theology and goes on to consider such ecclesiological issues as the practice of justice as essential to the gospel, the experience of God in the church of the poor, the theological significance of the persecution of the Church and evangelization as the mission of the Church. And in his *The Principle of Mercy: Taking the crucified people from the cross*, Sobrino presents the existence of a "crucified people" and urges a theology of mercy. Elsa Tamez, a Protestant, continues the reinterpretation of basic Christian doctrines within the context of the option for the poor in her *The Amnesty of Grace: Justification by faith from a Latin American perspective*. Tamez reinterprets justification as displaying God's affirmation of life for all human beings and thus meaning, in contemporary reality, a humanization that stands in opposition to the condemnation of human beings through poverty, oppression, and marginalization.

Sobrino, Tamez, the other theologians mentioned in this survey, and many other Latin American liberation theologians left unmentioned here have embarked on a bold, new interpretation of Christian witness in Latin America in the present context. Because of the breadth of issues considered, because of the many different approaches used, and because of the reformulation of theology itself, it is important for us to look at two specific theologians and to trace the development of their particular concerns, resources, issues, and theological methods. We will look, then, at Gustavo Gutiérrez, a Roman Catholic from Peru, and José Miguez Bonino, a United Methodist from Argentina.

Two Liberation Theologians

Gustavo Gutiérrez

Gustavo Gutiérrez's work is written from the perspective of the poor; his translated books in English such as *The Theology of Liberation*, *The Power of the Poor in History*, *We Drink From Our Own Wells*, and *On Job* interpret the Bible, Christian faith, history and subjectivity through the eyes of the oppressed, the victims of history.[12] Gutiérrez, perhaps the most influential of all Latin American liberation theologians, has made his theology the language of God from the perspective of the poor in two somewhat distinguishable stages. In the first stage, the poor were the center of theological reflection based on an argument about the irruption of the poor into history. In this stage Gutiérrez offered a philosophy of history as the basis of theological reflection: Modern history was characterized by historical praxis relying on individualism and rationalism to create the industrial, progressive first world. But this historical praxis was built upon massive social and economic contradictions, contradictions which again and again rest on the backs of the poor. In this first stage, Gutiérrez argues that historical praxis is irrupted by liberating praxis of the poor. This dialectical overturn of history, similar to Marx's reliance on the class revolution of the proletariat, occurs, in Gutiérrez's work, with a reliance on the symbols of Exodus and Promise, as well as an interpretation of history and politics in light of redemption and liberation.[13] Gutiérrez argues that liberation and redemption are related on three levels: particular acts, the project of history, and final redemption. This stage of Gutiérrez's theological reflection centers on present possibilities for radical transformation and understands "history" itself as carrying along this tide. Gutiérrez also offers, in this stage, a rereading of the Church and of poverty based on spirituality and an evangelical life. The Church is a sacrament of God's grace in Gutiérrez's theology, and as a sacrament the Church provides a prophetic witness in Latin America. But the Church is also the locus of basic Christian communities, wherein, Gutiérrez suggests, a spirituality of gratuitousness flourishes: a spirituality based on the presence of God amid the poor, combining the scandalous condition of poverty with the gratuitous love of God.

It is this third theme, the gratuitous love of God, that comes to the center of Gutiérrez's second stage. Displaced is the objectivization of liberating praxis as an autonomous force to change the world. Now, or so it seems to this author, captivity, suffering, exile are more dominant themes in Gutiérrez's theology: What Gutiérrez sees from the perspective of the poor is the love and presence of God in their long-suffering struggle to survive. God, faithfulness, and love among poor people now become the center of theological reflection instead of a particular philosophy of history.[14] The poor are still the subjects of theology; but they are the real subjects of theology, not because they express or bear a certain inevitable historical force but because of God's presence. Gutiérrez's argument is worth underscoring at this point: The option for the poor depends not on an interpretation of history but on God's own choice. This second stage is more radical and constructive: More is called into question here about the constitution of modernity and Christianity, more about what it is to be a human subject, more about what it is to experience the love of God, more about what it is to really hear the other of history speak than in the first stage, which can be interpreted as a corrective of a modern philosophy of history. The emphasis on popular religion and spirituality is especially strong in Gutiérrez's works *The Power of the Poor in History*, *We Drink From Our Own Wells*, and *The Truth Shall Make You Free*.

Gutiérrez's insistence on doing theology not simply for the poor but from solidarity with the poor and the correlative insistence on the particularities of the poor of popular religion in Latin America has also resulted in a massive historical study of Bartolomé de Las Casas. Gutiérrez's *Las Casas: In search of the poor of Jesus Christ* is a reading of not only the life of a heroic figure for liberation theology, but also an interpretation of history from and through solidarity with the poor. Las Casas's stress on evangelizing concern to the aboriginal populations, his linkage of salvation and justice, and his insistence on difference and otherness as a way to understand humanity, all are themes of Latin American history and its present reality. Las Casas worked against the systemic injustices and the oppressive cultural practices against the "others" of history. For Gutiérrez, to understand Las Casas is not only to claim a "tradition" behind liberation theology but to name the present reality: "Las Casas's witness is particularly important for the self-discovery that the peoples of Latin America must make today."[15] Gustavo Gutiérrez has been, for good reason, one of the primary interpreters of liberation theology. Gutiérrez's work moves in the direction of a radically new interpretation of Christianity; Gutiérrez has taken the basic symbols of Christian experience, and radically reworked them amid the experience of God's presence in the poor, but likewise, he has used the classical symbols of Christianity to give voice to the experience of the poor in history. In so doing, Gutiérrez has uncovered, for many of us, the presuppositions of power, dominance, and injustice in our basic theological beliefs. What does it mean for modern theology to be so concerned about the nonbelievers in history that it simply ignores the masses of poor? What does it mean for a progressive theology to be so committed to isolating an ahistorical religious dimension that it overlooks historical structures that divide human beings into the rich and the poor, keeping most of God's created subjects as nonpersons in history? Both critically and constructively, Gutiérrez offers, by way of a continual journey, a new language of God that denounces sin and announces grace.

José Miguez Bonino

José Miguez Bonino's work, in books such as *Doing Theology in a Revolutionary Situation*, *Room to be People*, and *Toward a Christian Political Ethics*, exemplifies Latin American liberation theology's understanding of history as the arena of God's action.[16] History has its locus neither in individual historicity nor in the worldly progressive realization of the bourgeoisie, but in the total sociopolitical-economic context in which humans live and in which God continually acts. Miguez Bonino's work illustrates that history has sociopolitical determinates based not only on sociological analysis, but also on theological and scriptural warrants that God acts in history. Indeed, Miguez Bonino suggests that Scripture be understood as a narrative account of God's acts in history and be analogically applied to the present situation. Though God acts in history in different manners and ways at different times, Miguez Bonino suggests, God always acts in love to transform history into the Kingdom of God.

The relation of history to the kingdom is central, according to Miguez Bonino, because in the Scripture this is how God is revealed. We do not relate kingdom to history for our own political ends, but because in the Bible God is constantly transforming history into the kingdom. This important and tensive relationship is, unfortunately, frequently misunderstood. There is a tendency to separate the kingdom and history, a position Miguez Bonino characterizes as dualism, which denies the basic biblical thrust of God in history. There is also a tendency merely to reduce the kingdom to history, or better yet a particular time and place in history, the monist solution, which denies the mission of Christianity and threatens to destroy the nonidentity between Christianity and the world. Rather the relation of history and the kingdom must be held to as a process of transformation, a process that might be compared to the resurrection of the body which does not deny or negate but fulfills and perfects.[17] Miguez Bonino also relates history to the Kingdom of God with a future twist; like the Pauline doctrine of works, history takes on its fullness and meaning as it anticipates the Kingdom of God. History here has not a merely philosophical meaning nor a materialist one; it is decidedly theological. We act in history because God acts, or better said, God acts in history through love to bring the kingdom, and, in our obedience, we act through Christ's love to bring the kingdom.

It is this praxis of obedience which calls out for theology, since the praxis of obedience must continually interpret God's action in history based on biblical themes and must understand the Bible in light of experiencing God's activity of history. This "hermeneutical" activity, that is, the activity of discerning, interpreting, and appropriating God's activity in history into the praxis of Christian obedience, must begin by realizing its own concreteness: that is, it too is historically bound, and cannot reflect outside of the historical categories and conditions available in a particular historical situation. All theology is therefore situated and political: situated because it is done in a particular historical situation, and political because all reflection, like all other aspects of life, grows out of the full sociopolitical reality. Yet theologians must not merely mirror the sociopolitical context; rather, they must position themselves in light of their obedience of Christian praxis, or, as Miguez Bonino says, "we are situated in reality to be sure – historically, geographically, culturally, and most of all groupwise and classwise – but we can also position ourselves differently in relation to the situation."[18] Thus theology must learn to dialogue carefully with the social sciences, in order to analyze, critique, and transform the historical situation in light of God's liberating activity.

Miguez Bonino's work demonstrates the centrality of history in Latin American liberation theology, and the sociopolitical understanding of history. It is important to underscore that sociopolitical history is central to understanding not only because of sociological arguments, that is, that all knowledge is historically conditioned, but also because of scriptural arguments: History is the arena of God's action, action which is the transformation of history through love. Miguez Bonino's theology therefore calls human beings to be responsible for history: responsible both in responding to God's love and responsible for their ever-present involvement in history.

We cannot opt out of history; we always advocate a particular strategy, ethics, position; but as Christians we must position ourselves with God, a God who in our own situation acts with the oppressed of the earth. Miguez Bonino also shows us that liberation theology has a decidedly sociopolitical cast: It advocates historical transformation, it discerns God's liberating activity, and it uses social sciences for analysis, interpretation, and appropriation.

Debate

Latin American liberation theology has been received with a great deal of debate among theologians living in the First World countries. Some theologians have responded by rethinking the basic contours and commitments of their own theological and political positions, while others dismiss liberation theology as inadequate theological reflection or a form of politics using religion. Among the theologians of the First World countries the debate about Latin American liberation theology has been centered in three broad areas: Latin American liberation theology's equation of liberation and redemption, its turn to the political as the primary locus of human life, and its theoretical arguments in relation to ethics and social theory.

For many First World theologians the equation of redemption and liberation tempts a kind of temporal messianism, a heralding of the reign of God on the side of one political cause.[19] This is, to many First World theologians, too reminiscent of totalitarian movements. It is also, for many, unbiblical as it poses God on the side of the poor, a claim which many read as God opposed to the rich.[20] Of course, other formulations are varied, some advocating an existentialist theology with implications to move into political realms, while others advocate a more realist power basis, noting that even Jesus said that the poor will always be with us. To some extent, these arguments also touch a disagreement within liberation theology over how redemption and liberation are related, and correlatively, what is the status of the option for the poor. As we have already seen, Miguez Bonino criticizes some liberation theologians for monist solutions, arguing for a position that distinguishes, while Gutiérrez advocates a three-level relation between redemption and liberation. The option for the poor is, as Gutiérrez suggested, a statement about God's gratuitousness and not, first of all, a romanticization of the poor. This also touches upon a debate among liberation theologians about the role of popular religion, whether or not it is a mystification of consciousness or authentic religious praxis.

Related to this criticism is often the second that religion is not simply politics, and that liberation theology has reduced human life to the political realm.[21] For many years Roman Catholic theologians, for instance, distinguished between two realms, one political and one religious, that should be separated without interference. The response of liberation theologians depends upon a broad understanding of the political as the basis of life. Politics now has to do not merely with the managing of the state, but how our lives are organized and expressed, how we as human beings express and fulfill our subjectivity. That is, politics is now intrinsic to the definition of the human subject, not merely a secondary expression. The gospel, then, is not political in offering a particular theory of political management, but is political in terms of its promise and demand for the fulfillment of human life. Liberation theologians also respond that theology, like all other forms of thought, is always political, advocating a particular view of life and implying a vision of human flourishing.

But even if one grants that in some manner redemption and liberation must be related, and that politics is a necessary dimension of understanding religion, questions can still be asked about liberation theology's theoretical formulations, more specifically, the relative adequacy of its ethical theory and its social theory. Ethicists and theologians in the First World frequently have voiced concern for the lack of ethical concepts and theories to mediate the relation between theological concepts and social reality.[22] Likewise, despite the intrinsic claims of liberation theology to begin in the broadest possible sense of the sociopolitical, liberation theology has yet to offer a fully adequate social theory of the relation between human consciousness and social structures.[23] Both of these theoretical issues can be addressed and worked, yet we may assume that liberation theologians will not be able to adopt simply the theories of social change and concepts of ethical mediation from the First World.

Achievement and Agenda: "Even the Poor have a Right to Think"

The phrase "even the poor have a right to think" is from Gustavo Gutiérrez and suggests the beginning point for even a tentative evaluation of the "achievements" of liberation theology. For any and all accomplishments must be measured by the intent and promise of his theology, that is, the intent to be a voice of the poor and to speak of God's presence and God's power among the victims of history. Concerns such as liberation theology's methodological rigor or its theoretical sophistication are, of course, important but they are secondary in terms of the voice and the rupturing presence of this theology. Throughout this chapter I, a North American woman, have asked that the reader attempt to hear the integrity of the voice of liberation theology. This is a question of rhetoric: Can we suspend the measurement internal to our own theologies long enough to hear and receive others? Rhetoric is not, theologically speaking, "mere" rhetoric, for it has to do with the persuasiveness of language and how we are constituted as communities and persons in linguistic frameworks which themselves are always malleable, rupturable, changeable. In this light, liberation theology has ruptured much of the discourse, purpose and intent of modern theology, even as it has intensified and changed many of its concepts. Freedom, long a concern for the subject of modern theology, becomes intensified in liberation theology to include the historical freedom to become a person having to do with social systems, political rights, economic survival and not merely the freedom of the authentic individual to say yes to God no matter what the historical circumstances. Likewise, modern theology's turn to the subject has been used in liberation theology to concentrate on the subject of the poor. And, where modern theology once assumed the bourgeois subject as a given, and God was the ultimate referent for the already assumed subjectivity, Latin American liberation theology establishes the nonpersons of history through the gratuitous action of God. For us, the readers of liberation theology who are not poor, surely the first accomplishment is hearing the voice of the poor, as the irruption of this voice calls our own into question, rupturing our values, beliefs, commitments, language and displaying our control, manipulativeness, power, and repression of others.

This is the accomplishment we receive, but it is not, I trust, the accomplishment liberation theology has for itself. That is, liberation theology's first and foremost commitment is not to convince the rich of the poor, but to speak from the poor for the poor. Therefore, liberation theology must also be understood as a new vision, ordering, and interpretation of liberation. Liberation theology has for the poor given voice to new understandings of sin, God, love, grace, Jesus Christ. With the new interpretation of these symbols, liberation theology gives new ways to name the world: the reality of structures, the possibility of the future, the meaning of community, love, and justice, and the fact of human subjectivity.

There is a third accomplishment that it is important to mention, having to do with the methodological importance of liberation theology. Latin American liberation theologians, together with Black and feminist liberation theologians, have made a convincing case for the situatedness of all knowledge. This achievement has three dimensions: (a) the situatedness of all knowledge; (b) the inclusion of ideology critique in theology; and (c) the argument for the positionality of theology, or, to state it formally, the rhetorical commitments of knowledge. Latin American liberation theologians, such as José Miguez Bonino, have achieved a political and theoretical clarity about how knowledge itself is related to power, class, and ideological interests. This basic insight has led liberation theologians, in a variety of ways, to include ideology critique as intrinsic to the theological task, that is, intrinsic to Christianity and Christian theology in the uncovering of distortions of knowledge, interest, and power in social systems. Some years before poststructuralist claims about the relations of knowledge, interest, and power became popular in First World academic circles, Latin American theologians argued that reason itself is always a product of history. To be critical, to be able to uncover and reveal the distortions necessitates, of course, also an ability to position oneself and speak constructively, to show a way of being in the world. Indeed, it is in this aspect that the work of Latin American liberation theology continues as the theologians pursue (in a way the poststructuralists often do not) a constructive vision, a world envisioned from the new subjectivity of the poor, a new relation between human consciousness and social structures. The future agenda of liberation theology continues this critical uncovering of the distortions in economic, political, social, linguistic structures; it must, as well, continue pursuing the concreteness of its vision and then begin tracing the possibilities of change and transformation. The influence of popular religion and its stress on cultural practices and spirituality must find a way to combine with socioeconomic critique and the insistence on structural transformation. As Latin American liberation theology pushes further to examine its own diversity, its own mosaic of culture and practices, its future will have to extend more and more to include the voices, and not merely the faces, of women, of blacks, of Amerindians, and others who have not yet spoken even within Latin American liberation theology.

Notes

1 Gustavo Gutiérrez, "Theology and spirituality in a Latin American context," *Harvard Divinity Bulletin*, 14 (June–August 1984).

2 Though a common objection to liberation theology is that it will result in making the poor the rich, and thus simply exchange one group of oppressors for another, liberation theologians, from their earliest works on, have advocated a transformation of social structures to rid the world of the massive disparities between the poor and the rich and have offered anthropologies of transformation stressing new ways of being human for all persons.

3 For good introductions to the history of Latin America see: George Pendle, *A History of Latin America* (New York, 1963); Hubert Herring, *A History of Latin America from the Beginnings to the Present* (New York, 1961) and Enrique D. Dussel, *A History of the Church in Latin America: Colonialism to liberation (1492–1979)* (Grand Rapids, MI, 1981).

4 See José Comblin, *The Church and the National Security State* (Maryknoll, NY, 1979) and Robert Calvo, "The Church and the doctrine of national security," in Daniel H. Levine (ed.), *Churches and Politics in Latin America* (Beverly Hills, CA, 1979).

5 Joseph Gremillion (ed.), *The Gospel of Peace and Justice: Catholic social teaching since Pope John* (Maryknoll, NY, 1976).

6 Representative works by these two theologians are: Jürgen Moltmann, *Theology of Hope: On the grounds and implications of a Christian Eschatology* (New York, 1967); *The Crucified God: The cross of Christ as the foundation and criticism of Christian theology* (New York, 1973); Johann Baptist Metz, *Theology of the World* (New York, 1969) and *Faith in History and Society: Toward a practical fundamental theology* (New York, 1980).

7 For examples of the critical uses of Marxism in liberation theology see: José Miguez Bonino, *Christians and Marxists: The mutual challenge to revolution* (Grand Rapids, MI, 1976) and Juan Luis Segundo, *Faith and Ideologies* (Maryknoll, NY, Melbourne, and London, 1984).

8 María Clara Bingemer, "Women in the future of the theology of liberation," in

Marc H. Ellis and Otto Maduro (eds), *Expanding the View: Gustavo Gutiérrez and the future of liberation theology* (Maryknoll, NY, 1990), p. 185.

9   John Eagleson and Philip Scharper (eds), *Pueblo and Beyond: Documentation and commentary* (Maryknoll, NY, 1979), pars 32–9.

10   I use the term tensive metaphor as a way to suggest the multiple meanings and yet systematic center of this theology in the term liberation. This is a metaphorical way of stating Tillich's notion of the material norm of theology. Paul Tillich, *Systematic Theology* (Chicago, 1951), vol. 1, pp. 47–50.

11   Gutiérrez, "Theology and spirituality in a Latin American context," p. 4.

12   Gustavo Gutiérrez, *A Theology of Liberation: History, politics and salvation, The Power of the Poor in History: Selected writings,* and *We Drink From Our Own Wells: The spiritual journey of a people.*

13   This is developed in Gutiérrez, *A Theology of Liberation.*

14   This notion of two stages in Gutiérrez's writings should not be taken to mean a major break in Gutiérrez's theology; rather, it suggests a certain shifting of the center of his theological reflection from a philosophy of history to an argument about God.

15   Gustavo Gutiérrez, *Las Casas: In search of the poor of Jesus Christ,* trans. Robert R. Barr (Maryknoll, NY, 1993), p. 456.

16   José Miguez Bonino, *Doing Theology in a Revolutionary Situation, Room to be People: An interpretation of the message of the Bible for today's world* (Philadelphia, 1979) and *Toward a Christian Political Ethics.*

17   Miguez Bonino, *Doing Theology,* pp. 136–43.

18   Miguez Bonino, *Toward a Christian Political Ethics,* p. 44.

19   See, for instance, the charge by Dennis McCann that liberation theology "politicizes" the gospel: "Practical theology and social action: or what can the 1980s learn from the 1960s," in Don S. Browning (ed.), *Practical Theology: The Emerging Field in Theology, Church, and World* (San Francisco, 1983), pp. 105–25.

20   For instance, the famous "Ratzinger Letter" (actually "Instruction on Certain Aspects of the Theology of Liberation") criticizes liberation theology for its faulty biblical hermeneutics, as well as its reductionism and uncritical use of Marxism.

21   Schubert Ogden, for instance, has criticized liberation theologians for equating redemption and emancipation in his *Faith and Freedom: Toward a theology of liberation* (Nashville, TN, 1979).

22   See, for instance, the criticism of James Gustafson, *Ethics From a Theocentric Perspective* (Chicago, 1981), vol. 1, p. 73.

23   See, for instance, Rebecca S. Chopp, *The Praxis of Suffering: An interpretation of liberation and political theologies,* pp. 144–8.

Bibliography

Primary

Alves, Ruben, *Tomorrow's Child: Imagination, creativity, and the rebirth of culture* (New York, 1972).

Aquino, María Pilar, *Our Cry for Life: Feminist theology from Latin America.* (Maryknoll, NY, 1993).

Assman, Hugo, *Theology for a Nomad Church* (Maryknoll, NY, 1976).

Boff, Clodovis, *Theology and Praxis: Epistemological foundations* (Maryknoll, NY, 1987).

—— *Feet-on-the-Ground Theology: A Brazilian journey,* trans. Phillip Berryman (Maryknoll, NY, 1987).

Boff, Leonardo, *Jesus Christ Liberator* (Maryknoll, NY, 1978).

—— *Church: Charism and power: Liberation theology and the institutional Church* (New York, 1985).

—— *Ecclesiogenesis: The base communities reinvent the Church* (Maryknoll, NY, 1986).

Comblin, Joseph, *The Church and the National Security State* (Maryknoll, NY, 1979).

Dussel, Enrique, D., *Ethics and the Theology of Liberation* (Maryknoll, NY, 1978).

—— *A History of the Church in Latin America:*

Colonialism to Liberation (1492–1979) (Grand Rapids, MI, 1981).

—— *Philosophy of Liberation* (Maryknoll, NY, 1985).

Gutiérrez, Gustavo, *A Theology of Liberation: History, politics and salvation* (Maryknoll, NY, 1973).

—— *The Power of the Poor in History: Selected writings* (Maryknoll, NY, 1983).

—— *We Drink From Our Own Wells: The spiritual journey of a people* (Maryknoll, NY, and Melbourne, 1984).

—— *On Job: God-talk and the suffering of the innocent* (Maryknoll, NY, 1987).

—— *The Truth Shall Make You Free: Confrontations,* trans. Matthew J. O'Connell (Maryknoll, NY, 1990).

—— *The God of Life* (Maryknoll, NY, 1991).

—— *Las Casas: In search of the poor of Jesus Christ,* trans. Robert R. Barr (Maryknoll, NY, 1993).

Miguez Bonino, José, *Doing Theology in a Revolutionary Situation* (Philadelphia, 1975).

—— *Toward a Christian Political Ethics* (Philadelphia, 1983).

—— *Faces of Jesus: Latin American christologies* (Maryknoll, NY, 1984).

Miranda, José, *Marx and the Bible* (Maryknoll, NY, 1974).

Munoz, Ronaldo, *The God of Christians* (Maryknoll, NY, 1990).

Segundo, Juan Luis, *The Community Called Church* (Maryknoll, NY, 1973).

—— *Grace and the Human Condition* (Maryknoll, NY, 1973).

—— *Our Idea of God* (Maryknoll, NY, 1973).

—— *The Sacraments Today* (Maryknoll, NY, 1974).

—— *Evolution and Guilt* (Maryknoll, NY, 1974).

—— *The Liberation of Theology* (Maryknoll, NY, 1976).

—— *Jesus of Nazareth Yesterday and Today,* Vol. I, *Faith and Ideologies* (Maryknoll, NY, Melbourne, and London, 1982).

—— *Signs of the Times: Theological reflections* (Maryknoll, NY, 1993).

Sobrino, Jon, *Christology at the Crossroads: A Latin American approach* (Maryknoll, NY, 1978).

—— *The True Church and the Poor* (Maryknoll, NY, 1984).

—— *The Principle of Mercy: Taking the crucified people from the cross* (Maryknoll, NY, 1994).

Tamez, Elsa, *The Amnesty of Grace: Justification by faith from a Latin American perspective,* trans. Sharon H. Ringe (Nashville, TN, 1993).

Secondary

Berryman, Phillip, *Liberation Theology* (Oak Park, IL, and New York, 1987).

Brown, Robert McAfee, *Theology in a New Key: Responding to liberation themes* (Philadelphia, 1978).

Candelaria, Michael. *Popular Religion and Liberation* (Albany, NY, 1990).

Chopp, Rebecca S., *The Praxis of Suffering: An interpretation of liberation and political theologies* (Maryknoll, NY, 1986).

Eagleson, Jon and Scharper, Philip (eds), *Pueblo and Beyond* (Maryknoll, NY, 1979).

Ellis, Marc H. and Maduro, Otto (eds), *Expanding the View: Gustavo Gutiérrez and the future of liberation theology* (Maryknoll, NY, 1990).

Fabella, Virginia and Torres, Sergio (eds), *Irruption of the Third World: Challenge to Theology* (Maryknoll, NY, 1983).

Fierro, Alfredo, *The Militant Gospel: A critical introduction to political theologies* (Maryknoll, NY, 1977).

Freire, Paulo, *Pedagogy of the Oppressed* (New York, 1970).

Gibellini, Rosino (ed.), *Frontiers of Theology in Latin America* (Maryknoll, NY, 1974).

Gottwald, Norman (ed.), *The Bible and Liberation: Political and social hermeneutics* (Maryknoll, NY, 1983).

Greinacher, Norbert and Mette, Norbert (eds), *Popular Religion* (Edinburgh, 1986).

Lamb, Matthew, *Solidarity with Victims: Toward a theology of social transformation* (New York, 1982).

Lernoux, Penny, *The Cry of the People: The struggle for human rights in Latin America – the Catholic Church in conflict with US policy* (New York, 1980).

Metz, Johann Baptist, *Theology of the World* (New York, 1969).

—— *Faith in History and Society: Toward a practical fundamental theology* (New York, 1980).

—— *The Emergent Church: The future of Christianity in a postbourgeois world* (New York, 1981).

Moltmann, Jürgen, *Theology of Hope: On the grounds and implications of a Christian eschatology* (New York, 1967).

—— *The Crucified God: The cross of Christ as the foundation and criticism of Christian theology* (New York, 1969).

Sigmund, Paul E., *Liberation Theology at the Crossroads: Democracy or revolution* (New York, 1990).

African Theology

Kwame Bediako

Introduction: African Christian Thought in the Post-missionary Era

Liberation and integration

Two principal trends emerged in African Christian thought in the post-independence and post-missionary era, from the late 1950s to the late 1980s. One was the theological dimension to the struggle for the social and political transformation of the conditions of inequality and oppression in South Africa, and it produced "Black theology," a theology of liberation in the African setting, and in response to the particular circumstances of southern Africa. The other was the theological exploration into the indigenous cultures of African peoples, with particular stress on their pre-Christian (and also pre-Islamic) religious traditions. This trend became more closely associated with the rest of Tropical Africa, where political independence seemed to have taken away a direct regular experience of the kind of sociopolitical pressures which produced Black theology in South Africa. In this second trend, the broad aim was to achieve some integration between the African pre-Christian religious experience and African Christian commitment in ways that would ensure the integrity of African Christian identity and selfhood.

This essay will focus on the second of these "trends", which is what is generally meant by the designation "African theology." The first, together with other strands in South African theology, is treated by John de Gruchy in the second part of this chapter. It needs to be pointed out, though, that the two are by no means to be regarded as mutually exclusive. Rather, they may be described as "a series of concentric circles of which Black Theology is the inner and smaller circle."[1]

An early concern: the African religious past as a Prime theological issue

The predominant concern with the pre-Christian religious traditions of Africa in the early literature of African theology was seen by some observers as an unhealthy, inward-looking preoccupation with an imagined African past. Among such critics was Adrian Hastings, who saw greater possibilities in the more politically-attuned *theologia crucis* of Black theology.[2] At the same time, African non-Christian critics vehemently rejected what they have regarded as African theology's attempt to "Christianize" and hence to distort African tradition. For them, the effort to seek an integration of the pre-Christian religious tradition and African Christian experience was misplaced and unwarranted, being the search for the reconciliation of what were essentially and intrinsically antithetical entities.[3] However, it is significant that it is a practitioner of Black theology, Desmond Tutu, who has made one of the most positive evaluations of African theology and of its achievements. According to Tutu,

> African theologians have set about demonstrating that the African religious experience and heritage were not illusory, and that they should have formed the vehicle for conveying the Gospel verities to Africa . . . It was vital for the African's self-respect that this kind of rehabilitation of his religious heritage should take place. It is the theological counterpart of what has happened in, say, the study of African history. It has helped to give the lie to the supercilious but tacit assumption that religion and history in Africa date from the advent in that continent of the white man. It is reassuring to know that we have had a genuine knowledge of God and that we have had our own ways of communicating with deity, ways which meant that we were able to speak authentically as ourselves and not as pale imitators of others. It means that we have a great store from which we can fashion new ways of speaking to and about God, and new styles of worship consistent with our new faith.[4]

While Tutu's observations are a strong affirmation that the effort made in African theology to "rehabilitate Africa's rich cultural heritage and religious consciousness" has been valid, it still remains important to appreciate why this effort was made as a self-consciously theological endeavor, and in a specifically Christian interest.

Writing on the early developments in African theology in his *African Christianity – An essay in interpretation*, Adrian Hastings drew attention to the fact that "the chief non-Biblical reality with which the African theologian must struggle is the non-Christian religious tradition of his own people," and that African theology early became "something of a dialogue between the African scholar and the perennial religions and spiritualities of Africa."[5] For Hastings this was rather frustrating, since it meant that "areas of traditional Christian doctrine which are not reflected in the African past disappear or are marginalised." He was particularly concerned about the absence of serious discussion on christology.[6]

It is not hard to see what had happened: the very religious traditions – the primal religions of Africa – which had been generally deemed unworthy of serious theological consideration in missionary times, now occupied "the very centre of the academic stage" in African theological reflection.[7] It is worth recalling at this point that in 1910 the Edinburgh World Missionary Conference, operating under the prevailing European value-setting of the Christian faith, had concluded that Africa's primal religions – more often referred to in African theological writing as African traditional religions – "contained no preparation for Christianity."[8] Accordingly, it becomes crucial to understand the reasons for this heightened theological interest in the primal religions of Africa if one is to interpret correctly the pioneer writers of African theology, to recognize their achievement appropriately and to discern accurately the trends and directions which they set.

African theology: shaping a method – theology as the hermeneutic of identity

To the extent that African theology's effort at "rehabilitating Africa's cultural heritage and religious consciousness" has been pursued as a self-consciously Christian and theological activity, it may be said to have been an endeavor at demonstrating the character of African *Christian* identity. For, looked at from the standpoint of the context of the writers themselves, the primal religions of Africa belong, strictly, to the African religious past. However, this is not so much a chronological past as an "ontological" past. The point of the theological importance of such an ontological past consists in the fact that it belongs together with the profession of the Christian faith in giving account of the same entity, namely the history of the religious consciousness of the African Christian. It is in this sense that the theological concern with the African pre-Christian religious heritage became an effort aimed at clarifying the nature and meaning of African Christian identity. Involved in such an effort was the quest for what Kenneth Cragg has described as "integrity in conversion, a unity of self in which one's past is genuinely integrated into present commitment, so that the crisis of repentance and faith that makes us Christian truly integrates what we have been in what we become."[9] It is the same notion which E. W. Fasholé-Luke had in mind in his statement that "the quest for African Christian theologies amounts to attempting to make clear the fact that conversion to Christianity must be coupled with cultural continuity."[10]

Therefore, from the perspective of modern African Christian identity, the missionary presumption of the European value-setting for the Christian faith, which led to the exclusion of any "preparation for Christianity" in African primal religions, could only produce the *problematik* of what John Mbiti meant when he wrote of the post-missionary church in Africa as a "Church without theology and without theological consciousness,"[11] This could only result from not allowing, in the first place, for the existence of a pre-Christian memory in African Christian consciousness. For theological consciousness presupposes religious tradition, and tradition requires memory, and memory is integral to identity: Without memory we have no past, and if we have no past, then we lose our identity. Andrew F. Walls, commenting on the early literature of African theology, rightly, in my view, identified what lay at the heart of the theological investigation of the religious past:

> No question is more clamant than the African Christian identity crisis. It is not simply an intellectual quest. The massive shift in the centre of gravity of the Christian world .which has taken place cannot be separated from the cultural impact of the West in imperial days. Now the Empires are dead. and the Western value-setting of the Christian faith largely rejected. Where does this leave the African Christian? Who is he? What is his past? A past is vital for all of us – without it, like the amnesiac man,

we cannot know who we are. The prime African theological quest at present is this: what is the past of the African Christian? What is the relationship between Africa's old religions and her new one?[12]

Perhaps, it is not surprising, therefore, that "the central theme of this literature" became "the nature of the traditional religion of Africa and its relationship of continuity rather than discontinuity with Christian belief."[13] Whereas this theme of continuity would be pursued with varying degrees of vigor by different writers, nonetheless it could only become a common concern because there existed a number of equally common factors which in turn helped to shape African theology itself. These factors included: the need to make some response to the sense of the theological *problematik* in African Christianity produced by the widespread and much-publicized perception that the Western value-setting of the Christian faith in the missionary era had also entailed a far-reaching underestimation of the African knowledge and sense of God; the unavoidable element of Africa's continuing primal religions, not as the remnants of an outworn and "primitive mentality," but, in terms of their worldview, as living realities in the experience of vast numbers of African Christians in all the churches, and not only in the so-called "independent churches"; and the intellectual struggle for and the feeling after a theological method in a field of enquiry which had hitherto been charted largely by Western anthropological scholarship, and in terminology which the African writers themselves came to regard as unacceptable. Terms like "fetish," "animist," "polytheistic," "primitive," "uncivilized," and "lower" – these were the Western intellectual categories devised to describe and interpret African religious tradition; each of these, African theology would reject. In this respect, it is significant how virtually all the writers of the formative period of African theology, though trained in theology on Western models, in their actual academic and intellectual careers in Africa, became engaged in areas of study and writing for which "no Western theological syllabus had prepared them, being forced to study and lecture on African Traditional Religion . . . and each one writing on it."[14]

It is extraordinary, therefore, that the practitioners of African theology did in fact take on the challenge of reinterpreting African primal religions, approaching the subject, "not as historians of religion do, nor as anthropologists do, but as Christian theologians"[15] and arriving at some startling conclusions. Thus when African theologians came to describe African primal religions, using terms like "monotheism" or "diffused monotheism," as Bolaji Idowu did with regard to Yoruba religion (1962), or when John Mbiti, reversing the verdict of the 1910 Edinburgh World Missionary Conference, called the African pre-missionary religious experience a *praeparatio evangelica*,[16] these writers are simply to be understood as drawing on their sense of belonging within Christian tradition and using categories which, to them, described their understanding of *their* pre-Christian heritage when related to *their* Christian commitment. The failure in some of the criticisms expressed of African theology may be related to a misconception held about what the tasks of these African Christian writers ought to have been. When John Mbiti's *Concepts of God in Africa*[17] is objected to for its "primary theological purpose," in that it "is attempting to lay the basis for a distinctively African theology by blending the African past with the

Judeo-Christian tradition,"[18] or when his collection, *The Prayers of African Religion* (1975) is judged to be "unsatisfactory" because "it tends to blur the distinctiveness of African spirituality by seeking a *praeparatio evangelica* rather than the integrity of the cult-group,"[19] such criticisms have the effect of obscuring the contributions which these African theologians were, in fact, making toward the understanding of what was, after all, their own religious heritage, which is indeed a proper task of theology. In both of these instances, the critics, in my view, rightly interpreted the intentions of the African theologian; only they did not approve of what they discovered. And yet, if it is the case that an underlying motivation of the quest for an African Christian theology in the first place was an endeavor "to draw together the various and disparate sources which make up the total religious experience of Christians in Africa into a coherent and meaningful pattern,"[20] then African theology is more accurately judged by its own "primary theological purpose" than by any extraneous criteria.

Once it is granted that African theology's investigations into African primal religions were qualitatively different from the observations of anthropologists, then it becomes possible also to appreciate how, by its fundamental motivation, African theology, in fact, was charting a new course in theological method. It is not that this course had no parallel in the totality of Christian scholarship; in any case, the categories were being derived from Christian tradition, as much as from the African experience and realm of ideas. Rather, this new theological approach had no counterpart generally in the more recent Western theological thought as it had been forged within the context of the notion of Christendom. At the heart of the new African theological method was the issue of identity, which itself came to be perceived as a theological category, and which therefore entailed confronting constantly the question as to how and how far the "old" and the "new" in African religious consciousness could become integrated into a unified vision of what it meant to be African *and* Christian. The issue of identity in turn forced the theologian to become the *locus* of this struggle for integration through a dialogue which, if it was to be authentic, was bound to become personal and so infinitely more intense. A far cry from "the clinical observations of the sort one might make about Babylonian religion," the African Christian theologian was quite often "handling dynamite, his own past, his people's present."[21] Hence the development of theological concern and the formulation of theological questions became linked as the unavoidable by-product of this process of Christian self-definition. Here, in fact, is the clue to Adrian Hastings's apt observation about African theology becoming early "something of a dialogue between the African Christian scholar and the perennial religions and spiritualities of Africa," but also the answer to his complaint that "areas of traditional Christian doctrine which are not reflected in the African past disappear or are marginalised." African theology, in fact, was being true to its own sense of direction, seeking its own responses to its own questions.

Survey: Indigenizers, Biblicists and Translators

Against this background of common concerns, there emerged, nevertheless, divergences and differences, some of which were considerable.

While the theme of continuity was manifestly central, the terms in which the argument for it was pursued differed among its protagonists. The pace-setter in the argument for a radical continuity was, quite clearly, Bolaji Idowu. Idowu's argument, founded on the continuity and the unity of God (1962), was coupled with an equally strong case made for a "radical indigenisation of the Church" (1965) on the grounds that the Church in Africa, as a result of its peculiar historical connection with Western cultural dominance, was failing to develop its own theology, churchmanship, liturgy, or even discipline. In order to remedy this "predicament of dependence" the African Church needed to build its bridges to the "revelation" given to Africans in their pre-Christian and pre-missionary religious traditions of the past (1965). Ostensibly intended to connect the "old" and the "new" in the African religious experience, this argument, based on the fundamental postulate of the "foreignness of Christianity," tended to lead toward a minimalist reading of the newness of Christianity in Africa at the specific level of religious apprehension. Accordingly, African Christian experience emerged as not much more than a refinement of the experience of the "old" religion[22] and the vindication and the affirmation of African selfhood, which, at the start, had been conceived as the task of the Church, later came to be entrusted to the revitalization of the "old" religions, with their "God-given-heritage of indigenous spiritual and cultural treasures."[23]

The kind of perspective which Idowu exemplified found an echo in later writers, such as Gabriel Setiloane, Samuel Kibicho, and Christian Gaba[24] among others.

A less radical form of the same concern with continuity was exemplified in the work done by another pace-setter and vindicator of claims to a specific African religious consciousness, especially among the francophone, and predominantly Roman Catholic theologians, the Zairean scholar Mulago, and in the school of thought which grew from his researches at the Centre d'Études des Religions Africaines in Kinshasa.[25] While he retained a firm conviction regarding the relevance of the Christian message for Africa, Mulago insisted nonetheless that the process of forging the new integration "cannot be solid and viable except as it remains faithful to ancestral traditions and as it manages to be judicious in its contact with the civilisations of other peoples and with revealed religion."[26]

In its more radical forms, this perspective, with its fundamental postulate of the *foreignness* of the Christianity that had been transmitted in Africa, as well as its minimalist view of the *newness* of the Christian faith in relation to African religious tradition, was always in danger of leading African Christian reflection into an impasse. In other words, if the Christian Gospel brought little that was essentially new to Africa, in religious terms, then in what lay the value and the rationale of the quest for a specifically *Christian* theological thought in Africa? The writings of Bolaji Idowu represent, in my view, an acute form of this dilemma.

At the other extreme of the spectrum was the postulate of radical discontinuity stoutly championed by Byang Kato, then representing the thought of those Christian churches and groups linked with the Association of Evangelicals of Africa (and Madagascar, as it was then called), and who trace their spiritual heritage, in the main, to the missionary work of Western conservative evangelical Faith Missions in Africa. Basing himself on a radical biblicism, Kato stressed the distinctiveness of the experience of the Christian Gospel to such an extent that he rejected all positive evaluations of any pre-Christian religious tradition, considering such efforts as a distraction from the necessary "emphasis on Bible truth."[27] Kato's insistence on the centrality of the Bible for the theological enterprise in Africa must be reckoned a most important contribution to African Christian thought. On the other hand, his outright rejection of the understanding of theology as a synthesis of "old" and "new" in a quest for a unified framework for dealing with culturally rooted questions meant that Kato's particular perspective could not provide a sufficient foundation for a tradition of creative theological engagement of the sort which the African context seemed to require. Before long, other Evangelicals, without denying their commitment to the centrality of the Bible for the theological enterprise, were already seeking more positive ways in which the Christian Gospel might encounter African tradition.[28]

However, the largest portion of the literature of African theology has been in the middle ground between the two radical positions. In other words, as well as a widespread consensus that there does exist an African pre-Christian religious heritage to be taken seriously, there has also been the realization that it is important to recognize the integrity of African *Christian* experience as a religious reality in its own right. The view here is that Christianity as a religious faith is not intrinsically foreign to Africa. On the contrary, it has deep roots in the long histories of the peoples of the continent, while it has proved to be capable of apprehension by Africans in *African* terms, as is demonstrated by the vast, massive, and diverse presence of the faith in African life. In other words, the eternal Gospel has already found a local home within the African response to it, demonstrating that Christ had effectively become the integrating reality linking the "old" and the "new" in the African experience. This perspective, therefore, seemed to offer the most hopeful signs for the development of a sustainable tradition of an African Christian thought into the future. Underlying this view was the critical notion that the Christian faith is capable of "translation" into African terms without injury to its essential content. Consequently, the task of African theology came to consist, not in "indigenizing" Christianity, or theology as such, but rather in letting the Christian Gospel encounter, as well as be shaped by, the African experience; and this task could proceed without anxiety about its possibility, but also without apology to Western traditions of Christianity, since the Western traditions did not enshrine universal norms. The overall goal of African theology then, was to seek to show that there were genuinely and specifically *African* contributions – derived from the twin heritage of African Christianity, namely, the African pre-Christian primal tradition and the African experience of the Christian faith itself – to the theology of the Universal Church.

Some of the best-known exemplars of this perspective became Harry Sawyerr, John Mbiti, and Kwesi Dickson,[29] among others.

John Mbiti

The development of the thought of Mbiti is particularly significant in this regard. Like Idowu, Mbiti also early deplored the lack of sufficient and positive engagement by Western missions with African cultural and religious values. He saw the result of this in an African Church which had "come of age *evangelistically*, but not *theologically*"; "a church without theology, without theologians and without theological concern."[30] However, Mbiti soon came to make a distinction between "Christianity" which "results from the encounter of the Gospel with any given local society" and so is always indigenous and culture-bound, on the one hand, and the Gospel, which is "God-given, eternal and does not change" on the other.

> We can add nothing to the Gospel, for this is an eternal gift of God; but Christianity is always a beggar seeking food and drink, cover and shelter from the cultures it encounters in its never-ending journeys and wanderings.[31]

But Mbiti had already given an indication of this trend of thought elsewhere.

> We cannot artificially create an "African theology" or even plan it; it must evolve spontaneously as the Church teaches and lives *her* Faith and in response to the extremely complex situation in Africa.[32]

But the definitive break came when Mbiti later rejected the very idea of the quest for the indigenization of Christianity or of theology in Africa. In a response to a study of his theology by John Kinney (1979), Mbiti wrote:

> To speak of "indigenising Christianity" is to give the impression that Christianity is a ready-made commodity which has to be transplanted to a local area. Of course, this has been the assumption followed by many missionaries and local theologians. I do not accept it any more.[33]

Mbiti, therefore, came to regard the Gospel as genuinely at home in Africa, as capable of being apprehended by Africans in African terms at the specific level of their religious experience, and that in fact this was how the faith had been received through the Western missionary transmission of it. The Western missionary enterprise, from this perspective, came to have a place within a religious history which properly belongs to African tradition. Since God is One, Mbiti maintained, "God, the Father of our Lord Jesus Christ is the same God who has been known and worshipped in various ways within the religious life of African peoples" and who therefore, was "not a stranger in Africa prior to the coming of missionaries." They did not bring God; rather God brought them, so that by the proclamation of the Gospel through the missionary activity, Jesus Christ might be known, for "without Him [Jesus Christ] the meaning of our religiosity is incomplete."

> The Gospel enabled people to utter the name of Jesus Christ . . . that final and completing element that crowns their traditional religiosity and brings its flickering light to full brilliance.[34]

By this approach, Mbiti in effect "exorcized" the "Westernism" and "foreignness" in the Western transmission of the Gospel. By the same process, he affirmed the missionary endeavor, but without making the missionary central; for the whole operation began with God and was carried through by God. The encounter was, at its deepest levels, not the meeting of Western ideas and African traditions; rather it was the meeting of the African people in their religiosity with Jesus Christ, whose "presence in the world is not a historical [i.e., chronological] but a geographical presence in the world made by Him and through Him."[35]

By the 1980s, Mbiti's theological approach had established him as "the leading African theologian,"[36] and the mainstream developments in African theology have since remained within the terms in which Mbiti directed the discussion.

Achievement and Agenda

Toward the 1990s – into new directions

But perhaps one must consider the decade of the 1980s as a period of transition, as a number of the earlier writers appeared to bring their major work to a close (some, such as Idowu, seemed to have begun to do so even in the 1970s) and a new generation was emerging to continue from where the earlier had left off. While the broad concerns of the relationship of the primal religions to Christianity still retained some interest, all the indications were that a watershed had been passed, and that the fortunes of African Christianity had ceased to be beholden to Western assessments and interpretations of Africa. Not what Western missionaries and observers did or said (or failed to do or say), but what African Christians would do with *their* Christian faith and commitment was now seen to provide the determining factors in the development of African Christian thought.[37]

Furthermore, an indication that the early concentration on the theological meaning of the pre-Christian primal heritage had been appropriate was the fact that a later generation of African theologians, while exploring other themes, were able to do so by taking off from genuinely African categories. This was most markedly so in relation to christological discussion, which had been conspicuously minimal or absent in earlier writings. It was interesting, however, that much of the new concern with christological explorations began around categories such as Christ as Healer, as Master of Initiation, and as Ancestor – all of which were derived directly from the apprehension of reality and of the Transcendent as experienced within the worldviews of African primal religions.[38] Apart from christology, the new African theology was also seriously engaging with subjects such as African Christian theological discourse and methodology,[39] soteriology, and conversion,[40] as well as the broad sweep of the history of Christian expansion and diffusion[41] and historical theology, in which issues in contemporary African Christianity were being related to the Christian tradition as a whole.[42] It seemed as though the growing realization that Africa, in the late twentieth century, had become one of the heartlands of the Christian faith itself,[43] had substantially registered in African scholarship. In an innovative investigation of West African Christian history, Lamin Sanneh felt able to conclude:

> No one can miss the vitality of the [Christian] religion in much of the continent . . . African Christianity may well have entered upon a universal vocation in the onward march of the people of God in history, a destiny comparable to that of Gentile Christianity in the early Christian centuries.[44]

It is no mean achievement, then, that African theology, by the sort of agenda that it set for itself from the start, as well as by the method it evolved, managed to overturn virtually every negative verdict passed on African tradition by the ethnocentrism of the Western interpretation of Africa; and it is a mark of that achievement that African theology has succeeded by and large in providing an *African* reinterpretation of African pre-Christian religious tradition in ways which have ensured that the pursuit of a creative, constructive and perhaps also a self-critical theological enterprise in Africa is not only viable, but in fact distinctly possible, as is evident in the current "theology of reconstruction" associated particularly with the writings of the Zairean theologian, Kä Mana.[45]

African theology – a feeling after new languages?

The era of African theological literature as reaction to Western misrepresentation is past. What lies ahead is a critical theological construction which will relate more fully the widespread African confidence in the Christian faith to the actual and ongoing Christian responses to the life experiences of Africans. Here, academic theological discourse will need to connect with the less academic but fundamental reality of the predominantly *oral* theologies found at the grassroots of many African Christian communities,[46] where, in the words of John Mbiti, "much of the theological activity in Christian Africa today is being done as oral theology, from the living experiences of Christians . . . theology in the open, from the pulpit, in the marketplace, in the home as people pray or read and discuss the Scriptures."[47] This may well validate Adrian Hastings's early observation that:

> It is in vernacular prayer, both public and private, both formal and informal and in the spirituality which grows up from such experience that the true roots of an authentic African Christianity will most surely be found.[48]

In this regard, it may well be that it is in modern Africa where Christianity's essential character as an "infinitely culturally translatable"[49] faith has been most notably demonstrated in more recent Christian history. For unlike, say, in Islam, where the word of Allah is fully heard only through the medium of Arabic, in Christianity the perception of the word of God is achieved in our own mother tongues (Acts 2: 11). This recognition and its impact on missionary action had the effect of loosening the grip of any Western possessiveness of the faith that there may have been in the process of its transmission.[50] Whenever Western missionaries made the Scriptures available to an African people in that people's own language, they weakened, by the same token, whatever Western bias might have characterized their presentation and prescription of the faith. African Christians, with access to the Bible in their mother tongues, could truly claim to be hearing God speak to them in their own language. It amounts to the awareness that *God speaks our language too.*

The significance of this has been far-reaching. For, as Lamin Sanneh has graphically put it, the import of Scripture translation and its priority in missionary work is an indication that "God was not so disdainful of Africans as to be incommunicable in their languages."[51] This not only "imbued African cultures with eternal significance and endowed African languages with a transcendent range"; it also "presumed that the God of the Bible had preceded the missionary into the receptor-culture." As, through the very process of Scripture translation, the central categories of Christian theology – God, Jesus Christ, creation, history – were transposed into their local equivalents, suggesting that "Christianity had been adequately antici-pated,"[52] they created, in indigenous languages, resonances far beyond what the missionary transmission conceived.

Through these local equivalents, Jesus Christ the Lord had shouldered his way into the African religious world, and could be discovered there through faith by all those who "approach the spiritual world with requests for guidance and help in difficulties," even where these requests are "formulated in traditional terms."[53] This process is entirely consistent with what is reported to have taken place in New Testament times as in Acts 14: 15–18. For the centrality of Scripture translation points to the significance of African pre-Christian religious cultures, as a valid car-riage not only for the divine revelation, but also for providing the medium of Christian apprehension. Thus, the possession of the Christian Scriptures in African languages, probably the single most important element of the Western missionary legacy,[54] ensured that an effectual rooting of the Christian faith in African conscious-ness took place. This, in turn, provided the conditions in which an authentic dia-logue would ensue between the Christian faith and African tradition, authentic insofar as it would take place, not in the terms of a foreign language or of an alien culture, but in the categories of the local language, idioms, and worldviews.

At this point, one may, perhaps, express a concern as to why African theologians have not followed the logic of the translatability of their faith into a full-blown recourse to African indigenous languages.[55] John Pobee showed awareness of the problem in his *Toward an African Theology* (1979). Though written in English, Pobee's book nevertheless made ample use of Akan wisdom concepts and proverbial sayings, and he felt it necessary to remark:

> Ideally, African theologies should be in the vernacular. Language is more than syntax and morphology; it is the vehicle for assuming the weight of a culture. Therefore, this attempt to construct an African theology in the English language is the second best, even if it is convenient if it should secure as wide a circulation as possible.[56]

And perhaps it is the same problem to which the Cameroonian theologian Engelbert Mveng attempted to respond, though somewhat polemically:

> When the objection is made that this theology is not written in native languages, we reply that it is *lived* in native languages, in the villages and in the neighbourhoods, before being translated into foreign languages by its own rightful heirs, the African theologians.[57]

Mveng's observation is useful as a pointer to the impact that a "translatable faith," apprehended by and large through the medium of mother tongues, has had in Africa. It arises from the realization that the emergence of a significant African theological tradition in the twentieth century, even if it is articulated predominantly in "foreign languages," is itself an indication that in African Christian life there is a substratum of vital Christian consciousness, and a sufficiently deep apprehension of Jesus Christ at the specific level of religious experience, itself of a theological nature, which alone can be the real basis for a viable activity of academic and literary theology. In that sense, the translated Bible has provided in Africa an essential ingredient for the "birth of theology."[58]

The fact still remains that the seriousness with which African theology will treat African mother tongues as a fundamental medium in its theological discourse may well become an important test of the depth of the impact, not only of the Bible, but also of the Christian faith itself, in African life, and so determine the directions in which African theology too will grow.

Conclusion: African Theology – A Relevance Beyond Africa?

Since African theology developed also as an African response to Western interpretations of African pre-Christian religious traditions, it may be worth exploring whether the African Christian thought that has emerged may, in turn, have any relevance for the same process of the engagement of the Christian faith with culture beyond Africa. The issue may hold some special interest for the present task of theology also in Western society.

It is worth mentioning that when the 1910 Edinburgh World Missionary Conference concluded that the primal religions of Africa contained no "preparation for Christianity," the realization that "it is the primal religions which underlie the Christian faith of the vast majority of Christians of all ages and all nations" in the twenty centuries of Christian history, including the Christians of Europe, still lay in the future.[59] In this connection one may recall Paul Bohannan's observation that "African culture shares more of its traits, its history, its social organisation with Europe than Asia shares with Europe, and certainly more than the North American Indians share with Europe."[60] In relation to our present discussion, what is important is the fact that Europe shares with Africa a pre-Christian primal religious heritage. But it is in Africa (as in some other parts of the non-Western world) that the significance of the primal religions in the history of Christianity has been seen for what it is. In the case of Europe, Christian mission on the basis of substitution appears to have been pursued to such an extent that the primal traditions were virtually completely wiped out.

What this – together with the fact that there was no sustained interest in the use of indigenous European languages and their pre-Christian worldviews for Christian purposes for a long time – has done to the total Western religious memory may probably never be fully recovered. In the light of the European story, one might be forgiven for thinking that the old primal religions of Europe quickly became a spent force. Yet the fact that Christians continued to name the days of the week after pre-Christian deities, that pre-Christian elements and notions made their way into the celebration of Christian festivals, and in several other ways too, must be indicators that the old beliefs had not entirely lost their hold upon people's minds. It may well be that in Africa, the opportunity which was lost in Europe, for a serious and creative theological encounter between the Christian and primal traditions, can be regained.

Curiously, the fact that African theology at its formative stage in the immediate post-missionary era focused on the theological interpretation of the African pre-Christian religious heritage may be the sign that such an encounter is possible; and it could be argued that in the process, African theology has gained rather than lost. For, having been forced to do theology in the interface of their Christian faith and the perennial spiritualities of the African primal traditions of their own backgrounds, as well as having to internalize that dialogue within themselves, African theologians have recaptured the character of theology as Christian intellectual activity on the frontier with the non-Christian world, and hence as essentially *communicative, evangelistic*, and *missionary*. It is this character of African theology which the Dutch theologian, Johannes Verkuyl, recognized.

> African theology does all the things which theology in general does, but in African theology (as in Asian) all these other functions are embraced in the missionary or communicative function. It is not primarily an intra-ecclesiastical exercise, but a discipline whose practitioners keep one question central: How can we best do our theology so that the Gospel will touch Africans most deeply?[61]

But, perhaps even more significant in this African effort has been the underlying argument that space had to be made for a positive pre-Christian religious memory in the African Christian consciousness, on the basis that "religion informs the African's life in its totality."[62] For Dickson, the theologian who fails to

> recognise the structures of religion as revealed by the historian of religions . . . may not notice the absence of religion from his theology. In the context of Africa, Christian theology must of necessity take account of that understanding of religion which bears the stamp of an authentic African contribution [that means the primal religions].[63]

To the extent that the African endeavor has achieved a measure of success, it may hold promise for a modern Western theology which is now also asking seriously how the Christian faith may be related, in a *missionary* sense, to Western culture.[64]

It is this relocation of African primal religions "at the very center of the academic stage" which may prove a benediction to Western Christian theology as it also seeks to be communicative, evangelistic, and missionary in its own context. For the African vindication of the theological significance of African primal religions, if it has validity, also goes to affirm that the European primal heritage was not illusory, to be consigned to oblivion as primitive darkness. The nature of the meeting of Christianity with European primal religions may hold more significance for understanding the modern West than might have been assumed. A serious Christian theological interest in the European primal traditions and in the early forms of Christianity which emerged from the encounter with those traditions, could provide a fresh approach to understanding Christian identity in the West too, as well as opening new possibilities for Christian theological endeavor today. And the primal worldview may turn out to be not so alien to the West after all, even in a post-Enlightenment era.

For the signs of what appears to be a *postmodernist* rejection of the Enlightenment in the West, which can be seen partly in the resurgence of the phenomenon of the occult as well as in the various quests for spiritual experience and wholeness – even if without explicit reference to God – all bear the marks of elements of a primal worldview. These are sufficient indicators that a primal worldview which becomes suppressed rather than encountered, redeemed, and integrated, rises to haunt the future. In this connection, the viability of a Christian consciousness which retains its sense of the spiritual world of primal religions, as well as the theological encounter between the primal worldview and Christian faith that is evident in African Christianity, constitutes an implicit challenge to the notion that humanity can be fully defined in exclusively post-Enlightenment terms.

It seems then, that the world's primal religions – in Europe as in Africa and elsewhere – the religious traditions which have been most closely associated with the continuing Christian presence historically in the world so far, may yet again point the way into the Christian future, and specifically, the future of the Christian theological enterprise.[65] If this expectation proves right, the African contribution will have been an important one. For the questions that African theology has had to wrestle with have not been exotic; they form part and parcel of the consistent development of Christian thought in all ages and in all climes.

Notes

1 Desmond Tutu, "Black Theology and African Theology: soulmates or antagonists?" in John Parratt (ed.), *A Reader in African Christian Theology* (London, 1987), pp. 54–64 at p. 54.

2 Adrian Hastings, *African Catholicism: An essay in discovery* (London, 1989), pp. 30–5.

3 Okot p'Bitek, *African Religions in Western Scholarship* (Kampala, 1970); Ali Mazrui, *The African Condition: A political diagnosis* (London, 1980).

4 Desmond Tutu, "Whither African theology?" in E. Fasholé-Luke et al. (eds), *Christianity in Independent Africa* (London, 1978), pp. 364–9.

5 Adrian Hastings, *African Christianity: An essay in interpretation* (London, 1976), p. 50.

6 As an indication that Hastings was not alone in this concern, I recall that about 21 years ago, at an international theological conference, a Western missionary theological educator working in Africa admitted to me his bewilderment at having to teach "African theology" when virtually all the African theological literature he came upon seemed to be discussing and interpreting "African traditional religions." "Where is the theology in that?" he asked.

7 Hastings, *African Christianity*, p. 183.

8 See *The Missionary Message in Relation to Non-Christian Religions: The World Missionary Conference 1910*, report of Commission IV (Edinburgh and London, 1910), p. 24.

9 Kenneth Cragg, "Conversion and convertibility with special reference to Muslims," in John R. W. Stott and Robert Coote (eds), *Down to Earth: Studies in Christianity and culture* (Grand Rapids, MI, 1980), p. 194.

10 E. Fasholé-Luke, "The quest for an African Christian theology," *Ecumenical Review*, 27 (1975), p. 267.

11 John S. Mbiti, "Some African concepts of christology," in Georg F. Vicedom (ed.),

Christ and the Younger Churches (London, 1972), p. 51.

12 Andrew F. Walls, "Africa and Christian identity," *Mission Focus*, 6/7 (1978), p. 12.

13 Hastings, *African Christianity*, p. 50.

14 Andrew F. Walls, "The Gospel as the prisoner and liberator of culture," *Faith and Thought*, 108 (1981), p. 49.

15 Ibid., p. 50.

16 John S. Mbiti, "The future of Christianity in Africa (1970–2000)," *Communio Viatorum: Theological Quarterly*, 13 (1970), p. 36.

17 John S. Mbiti, *Concepts of God in Africa* (London, 1970).

18 Benjamin C. Ray, *African Religions: Symbols, ritual, and community* (Englewood Cliffs, NJ, 1976), p. 15.

19 P. R. McKenzie, review of John Mbiti's *The Prayers of African Religion*, *Expository Times*, 87 (1975), pp. 220–1.

20 E. Fasholé-Luke, "The quest for an African Christian theology," p. 268.

21 Andrew F. Walls, "The Gospel as the prisoner and liberator of culture."

22 Bolaji Idowu, *Olódùmarè: God in Yoruba belief* (London, 1962), p. 202; *Towards an Indigenous Church* (London, 1965); "The predicament of the church in Africa," in C. G. Baëta (ed.), *Christianity in Tropical Africa* (London, 1968), pp. 415–40; *African Traditional Religion: A definition* (London, 1973), p. 209.

23 Ibid., p. 205.

24 Gabriel M. Setiloane, *The Image of God among the Sotho-Tswana* (Rotterdam, 1976); "How the traditional world-view persists in the Christianity of the Sotho-Tswana," in E. Fasholé-Luke et al. (eds), *Christianity in Independent Africa* (London, 1978), pp. 402–12; Samuel B. Kibicho, "The continuity of the African conception of God into and through Christianity: a Kikuyu case study," in *Christianity in Independent Africa*, pp. 370–88; Christian Gaba, "Sacrifice in Anlo religion. Parts I–II," *Ghana Bulletin of Theology*, 3/5 (1968), pp. 13–19 and 3/7 (1969), pp. 7–17; *Scriptures of an African People* (New York, 1977).

25 For a useful survey of the earliest of the francophone Catholic "responses" see the collection of essays published as *Des Prêtres noirs s'interrogent* (Paris, 1957). Mulago alone contributed two essays.

26 Gwa Cikala Musharhamina Mulago, *La Religion traditionelle des bantu et leur vision du monde*, 2nd edn (Bibliothèque du Centre d'Études des Religions Africaines, 5), (Paris, 1980), p. 7.

27 Byang H. Kato, *Theological Pitfalls in Africa* (Kisumu, 1975), p. 169.

28 Tite Tiénou, "Biblical foundations for African theology," *Missiology*, 10 (1982), pp. 435–48.

29 Harry Sawyerr, *Creative Evangelism: Towards a new Christian encounter with Africa* (London, 1968); John S. Mbiti, *New Testament Eschatology in an African Background: A study of the encounter between New Testament theology and African traditional concepts* (London, 1970); Kwesi Dickson, *Theology in Africa* (London and New York, 1984).

30 John S. Mbiti, *African Religions and Philosophy* (London, 1969) and "Some African concepts of christology."

31 John S. Mbiti, "Christianity and traditional religions in Africa," *International Review of Mission*, 59 (1970), pp. 430–40.

32 John Mbiti, "Ways and means of communicating the Gospel," in C. G. Baëta (ed.), *Christianity in Tropical Africa* (London, 1968), p. 332.

33 John Mbiti, response to the article of John Kinney, *Occasional Bulletin of Missionary Research*, 3/2 (1979), p. 68.

34 Ibid.

35 Ibid.

36 Adrian Hastings, *A History of African Christianity, 1950–1975* (Cambridge, 1979), p. 232.

37 K. Appiah-Kubi and S. Torres (eds), *African Theology en route* (New York, 1979).

38 See John S. Pobee, *Toward an African Theology* (Nashville, TN, 1979); Kwame Bediako, "Biblical christologies in the context of African traditional religions," in Vinay Samuel and Chris Sugden (eds), *Sharing Jesus in the Two-Thirds World* (Grand Rapids, MI, 1984), pp. 81–121, and *Jesus in African Culture: A Ghanaian perspective* (Accra, 1990); Anselme T. Sanon and René Luneau, *Enraciner l'Évangile:*

Initiations africaines et pédagogie de la foi (Paris, 1982); Charles Nyamiti, *Christ as our Ancestor: Christology from an African perspective* (Gweru, 1984); Bénézet Bujo, *African Theology in its Social Context* (New York, 1992); Robert Schreiter (ed.), *Faces of Jesus in Africa* (London, 1991).

39 T. Tschibangu, *La Théologie comme science au XXième siècle* (Kinshasa, 1980); O. Bimwenyi-Kweshi, *Discours théologique négro-africain* (Paris, 1984).

40 C. C. Okorocha, *The Meaning of Religious Conversion in Africa: The case of the Igbo of Nigeria* (Avebury, 1987).

41 Lamin Sanneh, *Translating the Message: The missionary impact on culture* (New York, 1989).

42 Kwame Bediako, *Theology and Identity: The impact of culture upon Christian thought in the second century and modern Africa* (Oxford, 1992).

43 David Barrett, "AD 2000 – 350 million Christians in Africa," *International Review of Mission*, 59 (1970), pp. 39–54; Andrew F. Walls, "Towards understanding Africa's place in Christian history," in J. S. Pobee (ed.), *Religion in a Pluralistic Society* (Leiden, 1976), pp. 180–9.

44 Lamin Sanneh, *West African Christianity: The religious impact* (London, 1983), p. 250.

45 Kä Mana, *L'Afrique va-t-elle-mourir? Bousculer l'imaginaire africain* (Paris, 1991); *Foi chrétienne, crise africaine et reconstruction de l'Afrique* (Nairobi, 1992); *Christ d'Afrique: Enjeux éthiques de la foi africaine en Jésus-Christ* (Nairobi, 1994).

46 For an example from Ghana see Afua Kuma, *Jesus of the Deep Forest: The praises and prayers of Afua Kuma*, compiled and translated from the original Twi by Fr John Kirby (Accra, 1981).

47 John S. Mbiti, *Bible and Theology in African Christianity* (Nairobi, 1986), p. 229, and "Cattle are born with ears, their horns grow later: towards an appreciation of African oral theology," *Africa Theological Journal*, 8 (1979), pp. 15–25.

48 Adrian Hastings, *African Christianity*, p. 49.

49 Andrew F. Walls, "The Gospel as the prisoner and the liberator of culture," p. 39.

50 Kenneth Cragg, *Christianity in World Perspective* (London, 1968).

51 Lamin Sanneh, "The horizontal and the vertical in mission: an African perspective," *International Bulletin of Missionary Research*, 7/4 (1983), p. 166.

52 Ibid.

53 P. Jenkins, "The roots of African church history: some polemical thoughts," *International Bulletin of Missionary Research*, 10/2 (1986), p. 68.

54 Kwame Bediako, "The missionary inheritance," in Robin Keeley (ed.), *Christianity: A world faith* (Tring, 1985), pp. 303–11; Lamin Sanneh, *Translating the Message*.

55 Kwame Bediako, "The roots of African theology," *International Bulletin of Missionary Research*, 13/2 (1989), pp. 58–65, and "Cry Jesus! Christian theology and presence in modern Africa," *Vox Angelica*, XXIII (1993), pp. 7–25.

56 John S. Pobee, *Toward an African Theology*, p. 23.

57 Engelbert Mveng, "African liberation theology," in L. Boff and V. Elizondo (eds), *Third World Theologies: Convergences and differences* (Consilium 199), (Edinburgh, 1988), p. 18.

58 Daniel von Allmen, "The birth of theology: contextualization as the dynamic element in the formation of New Testament theology," *International Review of Mission*, 64 (1975), pp. 37–52.

59 Andrew F. Walls, "Africa and Christian identity," p. 11; Harold W. Turner, "The primal religions of the world and their study," in Victor Hays (ed.), *Australian Essays in World Religions* (Bedford Park, 1977), pp. 27–37.

60 Quoted in Robin Horton, "Philosophy and African studies," in David Brokensha and Michael Crowder (eds), *Africa in the Wider World* (Oxford, 1967), p. 263.

61 Johannes Verkuyl, *Contemporary Missiology: An introduction*, trans. Dale Cooper (Grand Rapids, MI, 1978), p. 277.

62 Kwesi Dickson, *Theology in Africa*, p. 29.

63 Ibid., p. 46.

64 See especially Lesslie Newbigin, *Foolishness to the Greeks: The Gospel and Western culture* (Geneva, 1986); "Can the West be converted?" *International Bulletin of Missionary Research*, 11 (1987), pp. 2–7; *The Gospel in a Pluralistic Society* (Grand Rapids,

MI, 1989); (ed.), *Mission and the Crisis of Western Culture* (Edinburgh, 1989); *Truth to Tell: The Gospel as public truth* (Grand Rapids, MI, and Geneva, 1991).

65 Andrew F. Walls, "Structural problems in mission studies," *International Bulletin of Missionary Research*, 15/4 (1991), pp. 146–55.

Bibliography

Appiah-Kubi, K. and Torres, S. (eds), *African theology en route* (New York, 1979).

Baëta, C. G. (ed.), *Christianity in Tropical Africa* (London, 1968).

Barrett, David, "AD 2000 – 350 million Christians in Africa," *International Review of Mission*, 59 (1970), pp. 39–54.

Bediako, Kwame, "Biblical christologies in the context of African traditional religions," in Samuel Vinay and Chris Sugden (eds), *Sharing Jesus in the Two-Thirds World* (Grand Rapids, MI, 1984), pp. 81–121.

—— "The missionary inheritance," in Robin Keeley (ed.), *Christianity: A World Faith* (Tring, 1985), pp. 303–11.

—— "The roots of African theology," *International Bulletin of Missionary Research*, 13/2 (1989), pp. 58–65.

—— *Jesus in African Culture: A Ghanaian perspective* (Accra, 1990).

—— *Theology and Identity: The impact of culture upon Christian thought in the second century and modern Africa* (Oxford, 1992).

—— "Cry Jesus! Christian theology and presence in modern Africa," *Vox Angelica*, XXIII (1993), pp. 7–25.

Bimwenyi-Kweshi, O., *Discours théologique négro-africain* (Paris, 1984).

p'Bitek, Okot, *African Religions in Western Scholarship* (Kampala, 1970).

Bujo, Bénézet, *African Theology in its Social Context* (New York, 1992). [First published in German as *Afrikanische Theologie in ihrem gesellschaftlichen Kontext*, Düsseldorf, 1986.]

Cragg, Kenneth, *Christianity in World Perspective* (London, 1968).

—— "Conversion and convertibility with special reference to Muslims," in John R. W. Scott and Robert Coote (eds), *Down to Earth: Studies in Christianity and culture* (Grand Rapids, MI, 1980), pp. 193–208.

Dickson, Kwesi, *Theology in Africa* (London and New York, 1984).

Dickson, Kwesi and Ellingworth, Paul (eds), *Biblical Revelation and African Beliefs* (London, 1969).

Fasholé-Luke, E., "The quest for an African Christian theology," *Ecumenical Review*, 27 (1975), pp. 259–69.

Fasholé-Luke, E. et al. (eds), *Christianity in Independent Africa* (London, 1978).

Gaba, Christian R., "Sacrifice in Anlo religion: Parts I and II," *Ghana Bulletin of Theology*, 3/5 and 3/7 (1968–9), pp. 13–19 and 1–7.

—— *Scriptures of an African People* (New York, 1977).

Hastings, Adrian, *African Christianity: An essay in interpretation* (London, 1976).

—— *A History of African Christianity, 1950–1975* (Cambridge, 1979).

—— *African Catholicism: An essay in discovery* (London, 1989).

Horton, Robin, "Philosophy and African studies," in David Brokensha and Michael Crowder (eds), *Africa in the Wider World* (Oxford, 1967), pp. 261–91.

Idowu, Bolaji, *Olódùmarè: God in Yoruba Belief* (London, 1962).

—— *Towards an Indigenous Church* (London, 1965).

—— "The predicament of the church in Africa," in C. G. Baëta (ed.), *Christianity in Tropical Africa* (London, 1968), pp. 415–40.

—— "God," in Kwesi A. Dickson and Paul Ellingworth (eds), *Biblical Revelation and African Beliefs* (London, 1969), pp. 17–29.

—— *African Traditional Religion: A definition* (London, 1973).

Jenkins, P., "The roots of African church history: some polemical thoughts," *International Bulletin of Missionary Research*, 10/2 (1986), pp. 67–71.

Kä Mana, *L'Afrique va-t-elle mourir? Bousculer l'imaginaire africain* (Paris, 1991).

—— *Foi chrétienne, crise africaine et reconstruction de l'Afrique* (Nairobi, 1992).

—— *Christ d'Afrique: Enjeux éthiques de la foi africaine en Jésus-Christ* (Nairobi, 1994).

Kato, Byang H., *Theological Pitfalls in Africa* (Kisumu, 1975).

Kibicho, Samuel G., "The continuity of the African conception of God into and through Christianity: a Kikuyu case study," in E. Fasholé-Luke et al. (eds), *Christianity in Independent Africa* (London, 1978), pp. 370–88.

Kinney, John, "The theology of John Mbiti: his sources, norms and method," *Occasional Bulletin of Missionary Research*, 3/2 (1979), pp. 65–7.

Mazrui, Ali, *The African Condition: A political diagnosis* (London, 1980).

Mbiti, John, "Ways and means of communicating the Gospel," in C. G. Baëta (ed.), *Christianity in Tropical Africa* (London, 1968), pp. 329–50.

—— *African Religions and Philosophy* (London, 1969).

—— "Christianity and traditional religions in Africa," *International Review of Mission*, 59 (1970), pp. 430–40.

—— *Concepts of God in Africa* (London, 1970).

—— *New Testament Eschatology in an African Background: A study of the encounter between New Testament theology and African traditional concepts* (London, 1970).

—— "The future of Christianity in Africa (1970–2000)," *Communio Viatorum: Theological Quarterly*, 13 (1970), pp. 19–38.

—— "Some African concepts of christology," in Georg. F. Vicedom (ed.), *Christ and the Younger Churches* (London, 1972), pp. 51–62. [First published in German in P. Beyerhaus et al. (eds), *Theologische Stimmen aus Afrika, Asien und Lateinamerika III* (Munich, 1968).]

—— "African indigenous culture in relation to evangelism and church development," in R. Pierce Beaver (ed.), *The Gospel and Frontier Peoples* (Pasadena, CA, 1973), pp. 79–95.

—— *The Prayers of African Religion* (London, 1975).

—— "Response to the article by John Kinney," *Occasional Bulletin of Missionary Research*, 3/2 (1979), p. 68.

—— "Cattle are born with ears, their horns grow later: towards an appreciation of African oral theology," *Africa Theological Journal*, 8 (1979), pp. 15–25.

—— *Bible and Theology in African Christianity* (Nairobi, 1986).

Mulago, gwa Cikala Musharhamina, *La Religion traditionnelle des bantu et leur vision du monde*, 2nd edn (Bibliothèque du Centre d'Études des Religions Africaines, 5) (Kinshasa, 1980).

Mveng, Ethelbert, "African liberation theology," in L. Boff and V. Elizondo (eds), *Third World Theologies: Convergences and differences* (Concilium 199) (Edinburgh, 1988), pp. 15–27.

Newbigin, Lesslie, "Can the West be converted?" *International Bulletin of Missionary Research*, 11/1 (1987), pp. 2–7.

—— *The Gospel in a Pluralistic Society* (Grand Rapids, MI, 1989).

—— *Truth to Tell: The Gospel as public truth* (Grand Rapids, MI, and Geneva, 1991).

Newbigin, Lesslie (ed.), *Mission and the Crisis of Western Culture* (Edinburgh, 1989).

Nyamiti, Charles, *Christ as our Ancestor: Christology from an African perspective* (Gweru, 1984).

Okorocha, C. C., *The Meaning of Religious Conversion in Africa: The case of the Igbo of Nigeria* (Avebury, 1987).

Pobee, John S., *Toward an African Theology* (Nashville, TN, 1979).

Ray, Benjamin C., *African Religions: Symbols, ritual, and community* (Englewood Cliffs, NJ, 1976).

Sanneh, Lamin, "The horizontal and the vertical in mission: an African perspective," *International Bulletin of Missionary Research*, 7/4 (1983), pp. 165–71.

—— *West African Christianity: The religious impact* (London, 1983).

—— *Translating the Message: The missionary impact on culture* (New York, 1989).

Sanon, Anselme T. and Luneau, René, *Enraciner l'Évangile: Initiations africaines et pédagogie de la foi* (Paris, 1982).

Sawyerr, Harry, *Creative Evangelism: Towards a new Christian encounter with Africa* (London, 1968).

Schreiter, Robert (ed.), *Faces of Jesus in Africa* (London, 1991).

Setiloane, Gabriel M., *The Image of God among the Sotho-Tswana* (Rotterdam, 1976).

—— "How the traditional world-view persists in the Christianity of the Sotho-Tswana," in E. Fasholé-Luke et al. (eds), *Christianity in Independent Africa* (London, 1978), pp. 402–12.

Tiénou, Tite, "Biblical foundations for African theology," *Missiology*, 10 (1982), pp. 435–48.

Tschibangu, T., "The task of African theologians," in K. Appiah-Kubi and S. Torres (eds), *African Theology en route* (New York, 1978), pp. 73–9.

—— *La Théologie comme science au XXième siècle* (Kinshasa, 1980).

Turner, Harold W., "The primal religions of the world and their study," in Victor Hayes (ed.), *Australian Essays in World Religions* (Bedford Park, 1977), pp. 27–37.

Tutu, Desmond, "Whither African theology?" in E. Fasholé-Luke et al. (eds), *Christianity in Independent Africa* (London, 1978), pp. 364–9.

—— "Black Theology and African Theology: soulmates or antagonists?" in John Parratt (ed.), *A Reader in African Christian Theology* (London, 1987), pp. 54–64.

Verkuyl, Johannes, *Contemporary Missiology: An introduction*, trans. Dale Cooper (Grand Rapids, MI, 1978).

Von Allmen, Daniel, "The birth of theology: contextualisation as the dynamic element in the formation of New Testament theology," *International Review of Mission*, 64 (1975), pp. 37–52.

Walls, Andrew F., "Towards understanding Africa's place in Christian history," in J. S. Pobee (ed.), *Religion in a Pluralistic Society* (Leiden, 1976), pp. 180–9.

—— "Africa and Christian identity," *Mission Focus*, 6/7 (1978), pp. 11–13.

—— "The Gospel as the prisoner and the liberator of culture," *Faith and Thought*, 108 (1981), pp. 39–52.

—— "The translation principle in Christian history," in Philip C. Stine (ed.), *Bible Translation and the Spread of the Church: The last 200 years* (Leiden, 1990), pp. 24–39.

—— "Structural problems in mission studies," *International Bulletin of Missionary Research*, 15/4 (1991), pp. 146–55.

African Theology: South Africa

John W. de Gruchy

Introduction: A Theology Come of Age

Christianity first came to South Africa as the religion of European colonists in the seventeenth century. Each new wave of settlers brought with them those forms of ecclesial life, piety, and belief which were peculiar to their place of origin and basic to their identity – Dutch and French Calvinism; German Lutheranism; Roman Catholicism: and the whole range of British Christianity, from Protestant Non-conformity to Anglo-Catholic Tractarianism. Most significant, however, for the future of Christianity in the region was the new dynamic created as a result of the nineteenth-century European missionary movement. While the missionaries repre-sented European confessional traditions, the interaction between their project and African culture reshaped the way in which Christianity developed. Even before the turn of the century, African Christians had begun to express their faith in ways, both written and oral, which reflected their own unique reception of the gospel. More-over, Christianity, which had given ideological support to colonialism, was in the process of becoming a religion of an emerging African nationalist resistance against colonialism.

During the twentieth century, most theological currents in the northern hemi-sphere found their way into South Africa in one form or another.[1] Depending on confessional bias, social and cultural variables, and the training or personal inclina-tion of theological educators, they have variously impacted upon Christian thinking and the life and witness of the churches. As a result, contemporary South African theology has become eclectic in character, appropriating with varying degrees of understanding a range of insights from diverse Christian traditions, movements, and seminal theologians. At the same time, the struggle against apartheid led to the emergence of a distinctly South African set of theologies which reworked much of what was received from elsewhere in a way which resonated with our own context and experience. These theologies together comprise a theology which has "come of age" in the latter decades of our present century.[2]

Doing theology[3] became a fundamental necessity for Christian existence and witness during the struggle against apartheid.[4] It was not simply a subject to be studied for ordination, but a necessity for the survival of faith, the maintenance of hope, and the struggle for justice and liberation. Much of this theology found expression in workshop papers, synodical reports, submissions to magistrates and judges, letters to government ministers, and more formal confessions of faith. These "irregular dogmatics," to use Karl Barth's term, provided the indispensable raw material for those who sought to do theology in a more systematic and academic manner, relating contextual issues both to the legacy of Christian tradition and the contemporary ecumenical theological debate.

Some who are engaged in more traditional theological discourse may well question whether the theology we shall describe is, in fact, correctly labeled. But that is to misunderstand what has occurred. Most of us engaged in doing theology in South Africa are, by training, systematic theologians. But our experience is that many of the traditional distinctions made between dogmatics, ethics, church history, and hermeneutics, are artificial and often unhelpful. Moreover, in doing theology in South Africa, we have come to the conclusion that such a task is inescapably interdisciplinary, straddling not only the theological disciplines[5] but also the social and historical sciences. The work of Klaus Nürnberger, a systematic theologian, in many ways pioneered this interdisciplinary approach in his study of ideologies and economics in South Africa,[6] but many others have engaged in the task, albeit from different perspectives.

In particular, critical theological reflection on the social history of South Africa, and especially on the role of the church within that history, has been fundamental to the development of a distinctly South African theology. Several works may be mentioned in this regard. My own *Church Struggle in South Africa* (1979) was the first attempt at this task. Subsequently, Mokgethi Motlhabi's *Challenge to Apartheid: Toward a moral national resistance* (1984) located the history of Black political struggle within a Christian ethical framework. Charles Villa-Vicencio in *Trapped in Apartheid* (1985) focused on the social history of the English-speaking churches, emphasizing the extent to which they, and not only the Afrikaner churches, were responsible for apartheid. In like manner, James Cochrane in his *Servants of Power* (1986) engaged in a penetrating theological critique of the extent to which the Anglican and Methodist churches in South Africa gave legitimation and support to the development of racial capitalism in South Africa. Johan Kinghorn's *Die NG Kerk en Apartheid* (1986) provided an internal critique of Afrikaner Calvinism and the role of the Dutch Reformed Church in its formation and implementation.

Survey: Theologies born in Struggle[7]

As intimated, the first distinctly South African theology was undoubtedly African theology whose origins lay in the struggle against European hegemony, both colonial and missionary. Ironically, however, African theology was largely sidelined during the apartheid era except among those missiologists, such as G. C. Oosthuizen, who focused specifically on the African Independent Churches. The major reason for this lacuna was the way in which the ideologists of apartheid turned culture into a tool of repression. If the missionaries had previously spurned African culture as pagan, apartheid ideologists argued that each cultural group should develop separately. This was rightly perceived by Black theologians as a stratagem for racial domination. Hence African theology as developed in the rest of the continent in the postcolonial period had few exponents. An important exception in this regard is Gabriel Setiloane.[8]

Five types of theology born in the struggle against apartheid may be identified, namely confessing, black, liberation, womanist/feminist, and prophetic or kairos theologies. The labels indicate that these theologies are not uniquely South African but are related to similar types of theology elsewhere which also gestated in the struggle against injustice and oppression. It is not surprising, then, that each of these types has borrowed extensively from sources beyond the country's borders. Yet the way in which these theologies have developed and been expressed in South Africa is distinct.

Confessing theology, as distinct from confessional theologies, drew its inspiration from the Confessing Church struggle in Nazi Germany. The German *Kirchenkampf* motivated the formation of the Christian Institute of Southern Africa under the leadership of Beyers Naudé in the mid-1960s. It provided a theological basis for attacking apartheid in much the same way as Karl Barth's theology and the Barmen Declaration sought to counter Nazi ideology in the life of the German church. Apartheid, so confessing theologians argued, created a *status confessionis* in South Africa.[9] Noteworthy in this regard has been the work of Douglas Bax, especially his exegetical and theological demolition of Dutch Reformed documents defending apartheid[10] and Wolfram Kistner of the South African Council of Churches, who provided much of the theological direction for the SACC at the height of the struggle.[11] The endeavors of Charles Villa-Vicencio and myself in trying to relate the theologies of Karl Barth and Dietrich Bonhoeffer to the South African situation also fit within the confessing theology category.[12]

Confessing theology found significant expression in a series of anti-apartheid confessions of faith beginning with the *Message to the People of South Africa* (1968), which condemned apartheid as a "false gospel."[13] One of these was the celebrated *Kairos Document* which we will consider below; another was the *Belhar Confession of Faith* formally adopted by the Dutch Reformed Mission Church in 1986 as a standard of faith and practice (the first additional confessional standard for any Dutch Reformed Church since the post-Reformation period).[14] The *Belhar Confession* thus made unity with the white Dutch Reformed Church contingent on the rejection of apartheid as a heresy.[15]

Black theology emerged in South Africa in the late sixties. Just as confessing theology found a role model in the Confessing Church and the theologies of Barth and Bonhoeffer, so Black theology in South Africa drew inspiration from the Civil Rights Movement in the United States, the prophetic voice of Martin Luther King, Jr, and the pioneering theological work of James Cone. Within South Africa, however, Black theology was specifically rooted in the Black Consciousness Movement associated with Steve Biko, and its antecedents may be traced back to earlier African protest against European hegemony in the church and society more broadly. The pioneering work, which included the papers of the first Consultation in Black Theology, was edited by Basil Moore (1973). The original edition, published in South Africa the year before, was banned by the authorities as subversive literature. Louise Kretzschmar's overview *The Voice of Black Theology in South Africa* (1986) remains a helpful introduction, and two comprehensive studies by non-South Africans, Per Frostin (1988) and Dwight Hopkins (1989), relate Black theology in South Africa to the broader international debate.[16]

Several of the first generation of Black theologians in South Africa attempted to develop Black theology in relation to their confessional traditions. For example, Manas Buthelezi, now a bishop in the Evangelical Lutheran Church, integrated Luther's anthropology and "theology of the cross" with the Black experience of suffering and hope. Desmond Tutu, later to become Anglican Archbishop of Cape Town, focused much of his attention on the relationship between Black theology and African spirituality, finding a necessary critical connection between them and his own Anglican incarnational tradition.[17] Allan Boesak, who became President of the World Alliance of Reformed Churches, likewise related his confessional heritage to his reading of Black theology.[18] Church and public responsibilities largely prevented their participation in the second stage of the development of Black theology in South Africa. Those Black theologians who did take the project further, such as Takatso Mofokeng, Buti Tlhagale, Simon Maimela, Bonganjalo Goba,[19] and Itumuleng Mosala, have also, with the exception of Mofokeng, subsequently become involved in positions of church or public leadership. To some extent, this has taken them out of the academic discussion. Mosala's *Black Hermeneutics and Black Theology in South Africa* (1989) has been widely recognized as the most significant text on Black theology in South Africa in recent years.

During the struggle against apartheid, Black theology fulfilled a critical and empowering role for Black Christians both within the church and in the broader society. But ideological divisions began to surface in the 1980s which mirrored those within the liberation struggle. Those Black theologians who identified more with the non-racialism of the African National Congress moved beyond the parameters of Black Consciousness and became engaged in what is now known as Kairos or prophetic theology. Numbered among these are Frank Chikane and Barney Pityana. Those who have remained committed to the ideological presuppositions of Black Consciousness, notably Mosala and Mofokeng, developed a more Marxian social and cultural analysis. Strictly-speaking, Black theology in South Africa now refers to this latter group rather than the former, and there is considerable debate about its future in the new political dispensation. How this will be resolved remains to be seen, but it is of particular significance that the gap between Black theology and African theology is being bridged with the development of new theological paradigms in which African culture is a primary source for doing theology.[20]

As elsewhere, women have played a vital role in the daily life of the churches in South Africa, as well as in the struggle against apartheid, yet by and large they have been excluded from centers of power and influence. Signs of change have begun to emerge in recent years, not least due to the pressure and critique emanating from women theologians.[21] *Women's theology* in South Africa has also drawn inspiration and insight from elsewhere, chiefly North America, but also increasingly from other

Third World theologians such as Mercy Oduyoye and Elsa Tamez. Yet it too has taken on a distinctly South African character. Initially, the focal point was the ordination of women where this was not possible, but the focus has shifted more to a new way of envisaging the church and its social responsibility, especially with regard to the rights of women. As in North America, some of the debate has centered around the relationship between Black women's position in society (womanist theology) and the role of white women (feminist theology). Black women in South Africa have a particularly onerous and oppressive status, and their concerns have, until recently, not found expression even within Black theology itself. This has unearthed a range of issues which are not only ethically ambiguous (for example, abortion) but also culturally problematic, (for example, lobola, polygyny) issues which have been debated since the first encounters between European Christianity and African culture.

Much women's theology in South Africa is done in seminars and workshops sponsored by organizations such as the Institute for Contextual Theology (Johannesburg), the Pastoral Institute (Grahamstown), or Diakonia (Durban). Key theologians include Bernadette Mosala, Roxanne Jordaan, Emma Mashinini, Louise Kretzschmar, and Denise Ackermann. Few women are on the full-time faculties of seminaries and university theology departments, and there have been, as a consequence, few major publications. There are signs that a new generation of feminist theologians is emerging as South Africa struggles to break free from its traditionally patriarchal past.

While it is possible to distinguish between confessing, Black, and women's theology, in certain respects they are three streams which have critically engaged each other, and sometimes merged in response to common challenges. My *Liberating Reformed Theology*,[22] for example, sought to relate confessing theology to liberation and prophetic theology in a systematic way. Indeed, the antecedents as well as many of the exponents of *prophetic theology* came up through the ranks of these theologies and were signatories to the *Kairos Document* in 1985. Prophetic theology may be described as South Africa's theology of liberation. Yet, although South African theologians have drunk deeply from the wells of Latin American and other forms of liberation theology (Gustavo Gutiérrez, Juan Luis Segundo, Leonardo Boff, and others), prophetic theology remains distinctly South African.

The publication of the *Kairos Document* was a major moment of truth for South African theology and the churches, coming at a time when the country entered into the final decade of apartheid repression and resistance. Widely heralded around the world, the *Kairos Document* engendered much heated debate even among those committed to the liberation struggle.[23] At the heart of the *Kairos Document* was the distinction made between "state theology," a theology which legitimizes apartheid; "church theology," a theology which is formally against apartheid but incapable of engaging in transformative praxis; and "prophetic theology," a theology of critical engagement which recognizes the "signs of the times" and the demand which this makes upon the life and witness of the church. While the *Kairos Document* may not be polished, it spoke a concrete prophetic word in the South African context when it was published in 1985, a word which many claim had a decisive impact on the struggle against apartheid. It also challenged and stimulated some conservative evangelical theologians to take a more critical and courageous stance.[24] Tony Balcomb's study of the issues from an evangelical perspective is particularly noteworthy.[25]

Although the *Kairos Document* was a communal project, several leading theologians were instrumental in developing its stance and message. Frank Chikane,[26] who at the time of its publication was Director of the Institute for Contextual Theology, and Albert Nolan, a Dominican priest, also on the staff of the ICT, are particularly important in this regard. Nolan's *Jesus before Christianity* (1977) was very influential in the development of prophetic theology, and has become something of a classic in its field. His *God in Africa* (1988) was the first major attempt at developing a systematic or constructive theology within this paradigm. The more recent publication of *The Road to Damascus: Kairos and conversion* has extended the Kairos debate even further. As a joint statement by theologians from several Third World countries which shared similar concerns to those facing "the Kairos theologians" in South Africa at the time, it demonstrated the extent to which South African theology was increasingly in dialogue with other Third World theologians.

Agenda: Reconstruction and Transformation

The theologies we have surveyed derived their cutting edge from the struggle against apartheid. But South Africa has undergone remarkable changes since 1994 when the first nonracial democratic government was elected with Nelson Mandela as President. These changes have already had an impact on the doing of theology within our context. Understandably, then, the question has been raised as to whether theology will now lose its prophetic significance, and whether those theologians whose theology was shaped by the struggle will be able to develop in new directions.

Yes indeed, theology now faces fresh challenges. But it is also important to recognize continuities. The struggle against statutory apartheid is over, but the struggle for a just and democratically transformed society continues. As long as racism and other forms of oppression (economic, gender) endure, prophetic critique will remain central to doing theology. Nonetheless, the theological task in tandem with the responsibility of the church has undoubtedly shifted from protest and resistance to *critical solidarity*. Doing theology in critical solidarity with the government's agenda of national reconstruction and democratic transformation means enabling the church, as well as Christians in places of public responsibility, to contribute to that urgent task, but from perspectives informed by Christian faith and critique. The church has to keep on reminding the state of its responsibility toward the poor and other social victims. Thus theology has to grapple more positively with the problems of the responsible exercise of power, but always in the awareness that a change in power relations does not mean that power loses its ability to corrupt. Hence the development of programs of critical theological reflection on public policy.[27] The church also has a special responsibility in enabling society to deal with its past in ways which lead to genuine repentance, reparation, and reconciliation, and therefore the healing of the nation. Church leaders and theologians have helped establish the government Commission on Truth and Reconciliation, with Archbishop

Tutu as chair, and will undoubtedly continue to play an important constructive and critical role.

Alongside these tasks, South African theology also has to deal with a host of issues which were previously left on the back burner for strategic reasons. For example, many of the *ecumenical issues* associated with Faith and Order debates within the World Council of Churches have been ignored to the detriment of the unity and witness of the church. There is much catching up to do in this regard, but also a contribution which can be made from a South African perspective. Of paramount significance is our conviction, widely shared throughout the *oikumene*, that ecclesiological issues cannot be separated from ethical concerns. Hence the insep-arable connection between *theology* and *ethics* will remain central to doing theology in South Africa.[28] Another range of issues has to do with the fact that South Africa has broken with its Constantinian past of Christian privilege and is embarking upon becoming a genuinely multicultural, religiously plural, and secular state. The chal-lenge of a distinctly South African form of *democratic transformation and secularization* – one in which religion and traditional culture still play vital roles – is clearly central to the present task of doing theology. And central to this task is the building of a human rights culture which will ensure the future of our fledgling democracy. Both Charles Villa-Vicencio's *Theology of Reconstruction* (1992) and my own *Christianity and Democracy* (1995) are attempts to contribute to these debates.

The liberation of South Africa has reconnected it with the rest of Africa, and therefore opened up fresh possibilities for constructive *dialogue with African theology* unencumbered by the struggle against apartheid. How this will develop is not yet clear, though steps have already been taken in this regard. What is clear, however, is that it is now possible to take culture far more positively in doing theology. Barney Pityana's *Beyond Transition* (1995), which seeks to overcome the past dicho-tomy between African and Black theology by proposing *a cultural approach* to doing theology in building a new nation, is indicative of this development. Along similar lines, in the spirit of democratic transformation, is the way in which theo-logians are beginning to listen more carefully to the subaltern voices within the Black church. Indeed, perhaps the most creative edge emerging in South African theology today has to do with *reconnecting critical theological reflection to "popular theology,"* the incipient theologies of people of faith expressed in liturgy, song, and grass-roots community action. This is evident in Willa Boesak's *God's Wrathful Children* (1995), which reworks Black theology by listening to indigenous voices in relation to post-apartheid retribution and reconciliation; Robin Petersen's *Time, Resistance and Reconciliation* (1995), which rethinks Kairos theology in relation to the African Independent Churches; and James Cochrane's most recent work, which develops a model for recovering incipient lay theologies. Taken together, these theo-logical projects help us discern some of the possible contours of the next generation of South African theology. They suggest that South African theology has not lost its creative ability, but is rising to the challenges of the post-Kairos era without surrendering the prophetic insights of the past.

Notes

1 Due to the variety of confessional backgrounds and confessional identities of the colonial churches in South Africa, its theology has been influenced by theologies from Europe (especially Holland and Germany); Britain, both English and Scottish; and North America.

2 See an earlier discussion in John W. de Gruchy, "South African theology comes of age," *Religious Studies Review*, 17/3 (1991).

3 The phrase "doing theology" refers explicitly to theological reflection which arises out of Christian witness and social praxis as distinct from, but in critical dialogue with, the production of more academic systematic theologies.

4 John W. de Gruchy and Charles Villa-Vicencio (eds), *Doing Theology in Context: South African perspectives* (Cape Town and Maryknoll, NY, 1994).

5 The contribution of South Africans in such cognate fields as biblical studies, science of religion, missiology, and church history is not inconsiderable. Much of the creative theological work in South Africa has been done by those whose special field is not what is normally designated *systematic* theology. We may refer, for example, to the work of the late David Bosch, one of the foremost missiologists of our times; see especially his *Transforming Mission: Paradigm shifts on theology of mission* (Maryknoll, NY, 1991).

6 Klaus Nürnberger, *Ideologies of Change in South Africa and the Power of the Gospel* (Durban, 1979) and *Power and Beliefs in South Africa* (Pretoria, 1988).

7 Our survey excludes Afrikaner Calvinism which, though uniquely South African, provided theological legitimation for apartheid. Afrikaans Reformed theologians who have rejected this distortion of their tradition and have made significant contributions to theology in South Africa include J. J. F. Durand, W. D. Jonker, Adrio König, and D. J. Smit. Also excluded from our survey is the work of theologians such as the Roman Catholic Brian Gaybba, who has done much creative work on medieval theology, and Felicity Edwards, who has focused on feminist spirituality, modern science, and ecology. A good overview of systematic theology in South Africa, as well as a more detailed discussion of each type of theology described in this survey, may be found in John W. de Gruchy and Charles Villa-Vicencio (eds), *Doing Theology in Context*.

8 Gabriel Setiloane, *African Theology* (Johannesburg, 1986).

9 *Journal of Theology for Southern Africa*, no. 47 (June 1984), a special issue on the significance of the Barmen Declaration for the church struggle against apartheid.

10 John W. de Gruchy and Charles Villa-Vicencio (eds), *Apartheid is a Heresy* (Grand Rapids, MI, 1983), pp. 112–43.

11 Wolfram Kistner, *Outside the Camp* (Johannesburg, 1988).

12 Charles Villa-Vicencio (ed.), *On Reading Karl Barth in South Africa* (Grand Rapids, MI, 1988); John W. de Gruchy, *Bonhoeffer and South Africa: Theology in dialogue* (Grand Rapids, MI, 1984).

13 John W. de Gruchy, *The Church Struggle in South Africa*, 2nd edn (Grand Rapids, MI, 1986) and "Listening to South African voices: critical reflection on contemporary theological documents," in *Proceedings of the Annual Meeting of the Theological Society of Southern Africa* (Port Elizabeth, 1990).

14 The DR Mission Church (NG Sendingkerk), originally established for "coloreds," united with the Black NG Kerk in Africa in 1994 as the Uniting Reformed Church in South Africa.

15 G. D. Cloete and D. J. Smit (eds), *A Moment of Truth: The confession of the Dutch Reformed Mission Church* (Grand Rapids, MI, 1982).

16 Per Frostin, *Liberation theology in Tanzania and South Africa: A First World interpretation* (Lund, 1988); Dwight N. Hopkins, *Black Theology USA and South Africa: Politics, culture, and liberation* (New York, 1989).

17 Desmond Tutu, *Hope and Suffering* (Johannesburg, 1983).

18 Allan Boesak, *Black and Reformed: Apartheid, liberation and the Calvinist tradition* (New York, 1984).

19 Takatso Mofokeng, *The Crucified among the Crossbearers: Towards a black christology* (Utrecht, 1983); Buti Tlhagale and Itumuleng Mosala (eds), *Hammering Swords into Ploughshares: Essays in honour of Archbishop Mpilo Desmond Tutu* (Johannesburg, 1986); Simon Maimela, *Proclaim Freedom to My People* (Johannesburg, 1987); Bonganjalo Goba, *An Agenda for Black Theology in South Africa: Hermeneutics for social change* (Johannesburg, 1988).

20 Barney Pityana, *Beyond Transition: The evolution of theological method in South Africa – a cultural approach* (unpublished PhD thesis, University of Cape Town, 1995).

21 D. Ackermann, J. Draper, and E. Mashinini (eds), *Women Hold up Half the Sky: Women in the church in Southern Africa* (Pietermaritzburg, 1991).

22 John W. de Gruchy, *Liberating Reformed Theology* (Grand Rapids, MI, 1990).

23 Desmond Tutu, for example, refused to sign the *Kairos Document*.

24 See *Evangelical Witness in South Africa*, which was similar to the *Kairos Document* but approached the issues from a more conservative evangelical perspective.

25 A. O. Balcomb, *Third Way Theology: Reconciliation, revolution and reform in the South African church* (Pietermaritzburg, 1993).

26 Frank Chikane, *No Life of my Own* (Johannesburg, 1989).

27 The Research Institute on Christianity in South Africa (RICSA) at the University of Cape Town, for example, has recently instituted a program on theology and public policy.

28 Charles Villa-Vicencio and John W. de Gruchy (eds), *Doing Ethics in Context: South African perspectives* (Cape Town and Maryknoll, NY, 1994).

Bibliography

Ackermann, D., Draper, J., and Mashinini, E. (eds), *Women Hold up Half the Sky: Women in the Church in Southern Africa* (Pietermaritzburg, 1991).

Balcomb, A. O., *Third Way Theology: Reconciliation, revolution and reform in the South African Church* (Pietermaritzburg, 1993).

Boesak, Allan, *Farewell to Innocence* (New York, 1976).

—— *Black and Reformed: Apartheid, liberation and the Calvinist tradition* (New York, 1984).

Boesak, Willa, *God's Wrathful Children* (Grand Rapids, MI, 1995).

Chikane, Frank, *No Life of My Own* (Johannesburg, 1988, and Grand Rapids, MI, 1989).

Cloete, G. D. and Smit, D. J. (eds), *A Moment of Truth: The confession of the Dutch Reformed Mission Church* (Grand Rapids, MI, 1982).

Cochrane, James, *Servants of Power: The role of the English-speaking churches in South Africa* (Johannesburg, 1986).

—— *Incipient Theologies and the Integrity of Faith in a Post-Colonial Age* (forthcoming).

De Gruchy, John W., *Bonhoeffer and South Africa: Theology in dialogue* (Grand Rapids, MI, 1984).

—— *The Church Struggle in South Africa*, 2nd edn (Grand Rapids, MI, 1986).

—— in G. Loots (ed.), "Listening to South African voices: critical reflection on contemporary theological documents," in the *Proceedings of the Annual Meeting of the Theological Society of Southern Africa* (Port Elizabeth, 1990).

—— *Liberating Reformed Theology* (Grand Rapids, MI, 1990).

—— *Christianity and Democracy: A theology for a just world order* (Cambridge, 1995).

De Gruchy, John W. and Villa-Vicencio, Charles (eds), *Apartheid is a Heresy* (Grand Rapids, MI, 1993).

—— *Doing Theology in Context: South African perspectives* (Cape Town and Maryknoll, NY, 1994).

Evangelical Witness in South Africa (Dobsonville, 1986).

Frostin, Per, *Liberation Theology in Tanzania and South Africa: A First World interpretation* (Lund, 1988).

Goba, Bonganjalo, *An Agenda for Black Theology in South Africa: Hermeneutics for social change* (Johannesburg, 1988).

Hopkins, Dwight N., *Black Theology USA and South Africa: Politics, culture, and liberation* (New York, 1989).

Journal of Theology for Southern Africa, no. 47 (June 1984): a special issue on the significance of the Barmen Declaration for the church struggle against apartheid; no. 55 (March 1986): articles on the Kairos Debate; no. 66 (March 1989), a special issue on women's theology in South Africa.

The Kairos Document: Challenge to the church (Johannesburg, 1985; 2nd edn, 1986).

Kistner, Wolfram, *Outside the Camp* (Johannesburg, 1988).

Kretzschmar, Louise, *The Voice of Black Theology in South Africa* (Johannesburg, 1986).

Kretzschmar, Louise (ed.), *Christian Faith and African Culture* (Umtata, 1988).

Maimela, Simon, *Proclaim Freedom to My People* (Johannesburg, 1987).

Mofokeng, Takatso, *The Crucified Among the Crossbearers: Towards a black christology* (Utrecht, 1983).

Moore, Basil (ed.), *The Challenge of Black Theology in South Africa* (Atlanta, GA, 1973).

Mosala, Itumuleng, *Black Hermeneutics and Black Theology in South Africa*, Grand Rapids, MI, 1989).

Mosala, Itumuleng, and Tlhagale, Buti (eds), *The Unquestionable Right to be Free* (Johannesburg and Grand Rapids, MI, 1986).

Motlhabi, Mokgethi, *Challenge to Apartheid: Toward a moral national resistance* (Johannesburg, 1984 and Grand Rapids, MI, 1988).

Nolan, Albert, *Jesus before Christianity* (Cape Town and Grand Rapids, MI, 1977).

—— *God in South Africa* (Cape Town and Grand Rapids, MI, 1988).

Nürnberger, Klaus, *Ideologies of Change in South Africa and the Power of the Gospel* (Durban, 1979).

—— *Power and Beliefs in South Africa* (Pretoria, 1988).

Petersen, Robin, *Time, Resistance and Reconstruction: Rethinking Kairos theology* (unpublished PhD dissertation, University of Chicago, 1995).

Pityana, Barney, *Beyond Transition: The evolution of theological method in South Africa – a cultural approach* (unpublished PhD thesis, University of Cape Town, 1995).

Setiloane, Gabriel, *African Theology* (Johannesburg, 1986).

The Road to Damascus: Kairos and conversion (Johannesburg, 1989).

Tlhagale, Buti and Mosala, Itumuleng (eds), *Hammering Swords into Ploughshares: Essays in honour of Archbishop Mpilo Desmond Tutu* (Johannesburg, 1989).

Tutu, Desmond, *Hope and Suffering* (Johannesburg, 1983).

Villa-Vicencio, Charles, *Trapped in Apartheid* (New York, 1988).

—— *A Theology of Reconstruction: Nation-building and human rights* (Cambridge, 1992).

Villa-Vicencio, Charles (ed.), *On Reading Karl Barth in South Africa* (Grand Rapids, MI, 1988).

Villa-Vicencio, Charles and de Gruchy, John W. (eds), *Resistance and Hope: Essays in honour of Beyers Naudé* (Cape Town and Grand Rapids, MI, 1985).

—— *Doing Ethics in Context: South African perspectives* (Cape Town and Maryknoll, NY, 1994).

Asian Theology

George Gispert-Sauch, SJ

Introduction

In the last half-century, Asia has emerged as a fertile field for Christian theology. Though Christians are a tiny minority in the continent of Asia, numbering less than 5 percent, they are rich in tradition. In this essay we shall not consider Middle Eastern Christianity, surviving as it does in a largely Muslim world. Looking to the rest of Asia, we can distinguish three main families of Christian witness.[1] According to the oldest tradition, the Apostle Thomas evangelized the Middle East and the western and southern coast of India. This tradition derived largely from the vitality of the ancient Syrian Church which in the first millennium had a visible presence in Asia, even in towns of central Asia and China, but which now survives only in India among Keralites in the form of vibrant and well-organized churches. The second tradition arose with the missionary enterprise subsequent to the European discovery of the sea route to India and the rest of Asia toward the very end of the fifteenth century. It derived mostly from south European Christianity and was Roman Catholic in affiliation. This tradition has spread throughout Asia thanks to the joint missionary activities of various European countries, as also of America. The third form of Asian Christianity is closely linked to the later colonial enterprise, especially of the eighteenth and nineteenth centuries, and is north European and American in origin, and Protestant in inspiration.

Today, the denominational differences between the theologies of these churches have diminished considerably. Ecumenism has influenced a great part of Asia and has borne fruit. The Ecumenical Association of Third World Theologians (EATWOT), founded in 1976, has fostered much-needed interaction in a theological community concerned mostly with themes of liberation and interreligious dialogue. The evangelical wing of the churches, however, has largely kept apart from this trend and has formed its own "ecumenical movement" around the concern for evangelization and the spread of the Christian message.

Somewhat earlier, the World Council of Churches (WCC) with the Christian Council of Asia (CCA), started in 1973, and the Roman Catholic Federation of

Asian Bishops' Conference, begun in 1970, had established common platforms of action and discussion with theological agendas that varied considerably in subsequent decades. Initially, the WCC mobilized Protestant churches, but after the Third Assembly in Delhi, in 1961, the Oriental churches (except those in communion with Rome) also contributed to the common discussion.

The centers of theological learning of the Western world, whether Roman Catholic or Protestant, have been important workshops where Asian theologians have tested and refined their ideas, absorbing or reacting to the theological trends of the West. Centers in Italy (especially Rome), Belgium (e.g., Louvain), the UK, France, Germany, the US, and Latin America, to name but a few, provided forums for Asian theologians to encounter various trends of thought, including neoscholasticism, liberal theology, crisis theology, Christian existentialism, liberation theology, and so on. Modern Asian theology has certainly not been an inbred venture. Indeed, one dares to affirm from the vantage point of New Delhi, an important crossroads of East and West, that apart from showing a growing interest in Indian religions as such, Western theologians have expressed considerably less desire to dialogue with Asian theology than Asian theologians have shown toward dialoguing with Western theology. The dialogue between Third World and First World theologians held in Geneva in 1983 at the initiative of EATWOT was no great success and had no follow-up. In the area of Christian theology, the east–west dialogue has been rather one-directional.

In speaking of Asian theology, we refer chiefly to the professional thinking that has been articulated especially from the mid-nineteenth century onward mainly in India, Ceylon (now Sri Lanka), and various other countries such as Korea, Japan, and China. This thought has been formulated largely in Western languages, predominantly in English and to a lesser extent in other colonial tongues such as French, Dutch, and Portuguese. There *was* some pre-nineteenth-century output in local languages. One can mention the work of de Nobili in Tamil, of Desideri in Tibetan, of Ricci in Chinese, and more remarkably, because it was the work of an indigenous thinker, of the Korean Yi-Piek (1754–86) in his native tongue.[2]

It would be wrong to assume, however, that the only training ground of Asian theologians has been the academia of the West. They have drawn from deeper sources. The most important has been the interaction of their Christian faith with the history and culture of their own peoples, including the great religions of Asia, which have their own vast resources of exegetical and theological reflection. These ancient Asian traditions have not been uninfluential in the emergence of Asian theology. But the overwhelming and well nigh all-encompassing experience of colonialism in nearly all of Asia has resulted in an impoverishment in many ways of a large proportion of the population. With the exception of the Philippines, Christians have generally been a tiny minority in this situation and have lacked social power and influence. Perhaps in keeping with I Corinthians 1: 26f., this has contributed to the authenticity of Asian theology.

It is interesting to note that in India a christology was first formulated by Hindus who encountered Christianity through the colonial enterprise. They reacted to what Western education and the missionaries had to offer by an acceptance of Christ but by a rejection of the various churches. In other words, there was a "reception" of the message of Christ but in Hindu terms. Already in 1820, "Raja" Ram Mohan Roy (1772–1832) had written *The Precepts of Jesus: The guide to peace and happiness.* Keshab Chandra Sen, Swami Vivekananda, M. K. Gandhi, Sri Aurobindo, Akhilananda, Abhedananda, and to a lesser extent Rabindranath Tagore, all left their comment-aries on the figure of Jesus. In a few cases, their interest in Christ resulted in a conversion to a church (e.g., K. M. Banerjee, Brahmabandhab Upadhyay, and Maneklal Parekh), but this was the exception rather than the rule. In some cases the reaction to Christ was negative and polemical (e.g., Debendranath Tagore, Rabindranath's influential father, and Swami Dayananda Sarasvati and his followers). Generally, however, representatives of Indian (mainly Hindu) culture assimilated and articulated the meaning of Christ in various ways in the context of a renascent or reformed Hinduism and the movement for national self-affirmation.[3] Much as they rejected the various churches, generally perceived as allies of the colonial regime, they retained a fascination for the figure of *The Oriental Christ*.[4] This Christ is a sage, a Vedantin, a satyagrahin or apostle of nonviolence, a guru. His similarity with the Buddha, and even with Confucius, was noted. This early Asian perception of Christ was not without influence in the birth and growth of Asian theology. Perhaps it should not surprise us that the beginnings of an indigenous Asian christology should be found in the testimony of people of other religions. In a similar manner, the Gospels too record the earliest imperfect professions of a "faith" in Christ, e.g., that of the centurion (Mark 15: 39), various popular views (Matthew 16: 14), even the confessions of "demons" (Mark 1: 24).

Survey

The map of Asian theology resembles a number of countries grouped in clusters. The most important of these is, I think, India and Sri Lanka, thanks probably to the more or less uniform tradition of English education that prevailed among a large proportion of the upper classes, and to the long indigenous traditions of commentarial and theological texts. A much smaller center, though very much alive, would be Korea, squeezed between two powerful cultures, in constant danger of being over-whelmed, and whose Buddhist spirituality was overlaid by a simmering *han* or frustration/anger; this resulted in *minjung* theology (see below). Another cluster is more diffused, comprising countries under not only Buddhist but also Confucian and Taoist influence. China, Taiwan, Japan, and Thailand would figure here. The Philippines, of course, stands in a separate category. There is little original Asianness reflected in its theology, though there, as in Malaysia and in India, the indigenous peoples have awakened to the contribution they might make, and have begun to express the wish to interpret the Christian message according to their own experi-ence.[5] Indonesia is much more difficult to classify, for its culture and politics have been greatly influenced not only by Islam, but also by Hinduism and Buddhism, and by Iberian and Dutch colonization.

There is also the pan-Asian movement of feminist theology which has been articu-lated in the last decade and a half. This movement has sought to use many Asian myths about the divine Feminine in reflecting upon the Christian mystery. In this connection, the Indonesian theologian Marianne Katoppo published her book *Compassionate and Free*[6] in 1979. Again, those who attended the WCC Canberra Assembly in 1991 will remember the stirring plenary address given by the South Korean theologian, Professor Chung Hyun Kyung, in which the Holy Spirit was seen in the image of Kuan Yin, the Chinese female bodhisattva symbol of compassion, who is revered not only in China, but also in Japan, Korea, Singapore, and Vietnam.[7] The address was well received by most Asians, though the puzzlement it caused many Westerners indicates the way Asian theology can and does still disturb. Over the last two decades or so much thinking and writing has been done by Asian Christian women who have their own feminist theological journal, *In God's Image*.[8] Virginia Fabella of the Philippines, Korea's Sun Ai Lee-Park, and India's Jessie B. Tellis-Nayak are among the other leading names of Asian feminist theology. Let us now look a little more closely at certain centers of Asian theology, or at least of theology in Asia.

India

Fairly detailed surveys of Indian theology exist and one may consult the select bibliography given at the end of this essay. The nineteenth century was the period of the pioneers. Apart from the Hindu contribution mentioned earlier, one must recall the writings of the converts noted above.[9] We must also mention the highly influential work of the Scottish "fulfillment" theologian J. N. Farquhar, *The Crown of Hinduism*.[10] As E. Sharpe says, "[By] the inter-war years . . . [this work] had long been a standard text-book for Protestant missionaries in India."[11] On the Catholic side, early in the 1920s, what has been called the "Calcutta School" of Indological theologians developed. This Catholic group, like their Protestant counterparts, consisted largely of foreign-born missionaries. One of the earliest and best known works of this school was *To Christ through the Vedanta* by P. Johanns, SJ (1882–1955). This was a collection of articles that were first published in Calcutta in a pioneering monthly journal entitled *The Light of the East*,[12] edited by G. Dandoy, SJ, with the help of Johanns. This school played a seminal role in shaping the positive approach to other religions, especially Hinduism, of many of the country's Catholic clergy between the twenties and the fifties,[13] and was instrumental in influencing the Declaration on the Relationship of the Catholic Church to non-Christian Religions of Vatican II, through the presence at the Council of a number of Indian bishops and theological experts from India whose theology had been shaped by the school. The original inspiration for this school was the "fulfillment theology" of the early Church Fathers (rather than that of the contemporary Protestant thinkers), who used the thought of the ancient philosophers of Greece and Rome as the matrix for formulating their Christian faith in a theology of *chresis* or "use." What the early Fathers had done for ancient and medieval Christendom the Calcutta School dreamt of doing for Indian culture. In fact, there was hardly any emphasis on (Indian) Muslim, Buddhist, and Jain thought (not to mention the tradition of the indigenous peoples of the subcontinent) in this vision. Another key influence for this way of thinking had been the life and work of Brahmabandhab Upadhyay (mentioned earlier).

An outstanding missionary theologian was the Anglican C. F. Andrews (1871–1940), who was a close friend of M. K. Gandhi and whose pietistic attachment to Christ did not prevent him from embracing a theology whose politics required a distancing of the institutional Church from the British Raj. Andrews was sympathetic to the hopes and ideals of the Indian National Congress.[14] The American Methodist E. Stanley Jones (who died in 1973) was more of an evangelist; nevertheless, he wished to preach *The Christ of the Indian Road* (1926), the title of his most important book, which had a number of sequels.[15]

In the 1920s and 1930s, the influence of the "crisis theology" of Karl Barth subsequently allied to the missiology of the Dutch theologian H. Kraemer was felt in the Indian Protestant world, since many of its leaders were trained in European or American centers where Barthianism was strong. Soon, however, a new generation of Indian Protestant theologians reacted to the eurocentrism of crisis theology. They formed a school of thought which derived its name from a book entitled *Rethinking Christianity in India* (1938), which set out their objectives.[16] D. Chenchiah, V. Chakkarai, A. N. Sundarisanam, and D. M. Devasahayam are the best-known names of this school. It reacted strongly to the eurocentric position espoused by Kraemer at the World Missionary Conference at Tambaram near Madras in 1938, subsequently taking the offensive in the Indian Protestant theological field. Many present-day Protestant theologians would acknowledge a debt of gratitude to this school. The theology it propounded underpinned the desire to make the Indian church more self-governing, self-supporting, and self-expanding. In other words, they wished to indigenize the church institutionally in the current climate of the Indian freedom movement, then at its height.[17]

The second half of the twentieth century has seen a rich harvest of Indian theologians. Rather than simply listing names, let us mention the main foci of theological thinking in the country with their chief characteristics. We may start with the Christian Institute for the Study of Religion and Society (CISRS), established in 1957 and based in Delhi and Bangalore (where it works closely with its neighbor the United Theological College). Both institutions are basically Protestant in inspiration but ecumenical in spirit. The main concern of the CISRS, first formulated by its founder Paul Devanandan and embraced subsequently by his successor M. M. Thomas, is the impact of the Gospel on the Indian political and social scene. Through a series of seminars over the years, numerous publications, and in particular its quarterly journal *Religion and Society*, the Institute has initiated much reflection on the Christian contribution to nation-building.[18] In recent years it has also contributed significantly to the emergence of *dalit* theology (the theology of "the oppressed"), and to the first stirrings of indigenous theological thinking among tribal peoples.

A generation later there has emerged a significant movement, mostly Roman Catholic in inspiration, which has formed around the journal *Jeevadhara*, started in 1971. This was intended as a "progressive" theological journal for the people and theologians of the state of Kerala in south India, and was greatly influenced by the new generation of theologians of the Syro-Malabar Church (an Oriental rite in communion with Rome). *Jeevadhara* took its cue from the post-Vatican II journal *Concilium*, and keeps a similar policy of separate editors for each of its six yearly themes taken from six different branches of theology. It is issued in English and Malayalam in alternate months. The first collaborators of the journal formed the original nucleus of the Indian Theological Association (ITA), founded in 1977, which meets every year and which has expanded to include many Roman Catholic teachers of theology in India. It has effectively replaced the older Indian Christian Theological Association started by Protestant churches in the middle of the century and now defunct. Dharmaram College, a Roman Catholic theological foundation, is the most important theological center of the Syro-Malabar Church, and is closely associated with the *Jeevadhara* group and the ITA.

Also of importance are the Jesuit theological colleges around the country, especially Jnana Deepa Vidyapeeth in Pune, and Vidyajyoti College of Theology in Delhi. Perhaps the best known among the Pune theologians was George Soares-Prabhu (1929–95), a scripture scholar whose writings contain a passionate call for solidarity with the poor, and a strong critique of colonialism, various policies of the Catholic Church, and capitalist culture. Samuel Rayan of Vidyajyoti, a systematic theologian who has been involved in EATWOT, adopts a similar stance, writing on various topics with great suggestive power.

Two other important but somewhat diffuse movements must be mentioned. The first derives from the existence of Christian (mainly Roman Catholic) ashrams and dialogue centers specially set up to interact with the Hindu tradition. Two very well-known leaders of this initiative have been Swami Abhishiktananda (about whom more presently) and Bede Griffiths (1906–93), who succeeded Abhishiktananda (and his collaborator J. Monchanin) in Saccidananda Ashram near Tiruchirapalli in Tamilnadu state. We shall consider the work of the ashram in due course. The Jesuit, Ignatius Hirudayam (1910–95), from Aikya Alayam, his center in Madras, actively fostered dialogue with the Saiva Siddhanta school of devotional Hinduism, and wrote a Tamil treatise on Indian Christian spirituality[19] in which he drew from Saiva Siddhanta teaching. D. S. Amalorpavadass (1932–90), a priest from Pondicherry, opened Anjali Ashram in Mysore. He wrote prolifically during his tenure (1967–82) as founder and Director of the (Roman Catholic) National Biblical, Catechetical, and Liturgical Centre (NBCLC) at Bangalore. The main characteristic of his thought, which did much to promote a renewal of the Indian Catholic Church, was a synthesis of aspects of modern thought and the theology of mission.[20] Sisters Vandana and Sara Grant, both members of the ecumenical and recently reconstituted Krista Prema Seva Ashram in Pune, have also written substantially about dialogue with the Hindu tradition. Sister Grant has focused on the thought of Shankara, the great eighth-century Hindu monist thinker, while Vandana has concentrated on contemplation and its techniques. To these names one should add the following important ones who have dialogue in mind: Ignatius Puthiadam, now in Varanasi; Felix Wilfred of Madras; Eric Lott (now retired to England), who spent many years writing and teaching at United Theological College; and the best known of all perhaps, Raimundo Panikkar (see below). Here we may also mention Jyoti Sahi, who has sought to blend reflection on his Christian faith with his work as a painter, from his art school near Bangalore.[21] Sahi's visual and verbal statements are receiving increasing notice both in his own country and abroad.

The second movement is that of *dalit* theology. It stems from a new consciousness of the depressed classes (the "untouchables"), from whom a large proportion of Indian Christians derive. Dalit Christians protest against the fact that the churches have always been controlled by the upper classes and castes, and that their own experience of pervasive oppression has not found adequate representation and expression in the life of the church. This movement takes its cue from the so-called Dalit Panther movement among Hindu outcasts (especially in Maharashtra state), which itself was inspired by the Black Panthers of America of the sixties. Dalit theology draws significantly from liberation theology but focuses not so much on economic poverty as human dignity and equality for all. In traditional Hindu society, the outcast and the low caste have been considered as ritually polluted and polluting. Dalit theology in this context – a form of liberation theology – means liberation from the false consciousness of pollution in the above sense, and protests against the social system that has created it.

Some Indian Theologians

Though we cannot be exhaustive in this section, it will be useful to illustrate the concerns and range of this branch of Asian theology.

Raimundo Panikkar (1918–)

Few Asian theologians have been so prolific in their output or have touched so extensive an area of human and Christian self-understanding among a variety of cultures and peoples as Raimundo Panikkar. Born of a Keralite father and a Spanish mother, Panikkar (who now lives in Spain) was raised as a Roman Catholic. He came into living contact with the Indian tradition in the early fifties and has since promoted a rich interaction, especially between the Indian traditions and Western expressions of Christian faith. Both as writer and speaker, he has played on many different keyboards in the organ of human thought – oriental, Western classical, medieval, and modern.

Not only biologically but also personally, Panikkar lives the fusion of horizons that he demands of theology. He describes himself as a Christian–Hindu–Buddhist, where each faith exists authentically by itself without denying the others space for expression. He believes that the theology of the future will also be similarly hyphenated: Christian–Hindu–Buddhist–secular–primeval . . . He does not advocate a syncretic amalgamation of the various faiths, but the coexistence and cross-fertilization of all faiths in an authentic dialogue with each other. But the *intra*religious dialogue demands an interreligious dialogue. There must be no room for homogenizing or imperialistic solutions, whether political, cultural, or religious. The world must become, not a global village or city, but an interactive cluster of hamlets united by a network of communicational links. These links must not be an excuse or means for a kind of cultural or religious tourism, but must enable a real interpenetration of cultures and faiths while allowing each to remain unique in its contribution to human self-understanding and salvation.[22]

In common with other Asian theologians, Panikkar not only tolerates religious pluralism but also welcomes it as an expression of the inexhaustible divine richness. Whereas the plurality of religions is a fact, pluralism is a theological position. Pluralism must also apply to the church. The Hebrew–Greek–Latin–Frankish–Germanic–medieval church is only one model, one expression of the church universal that admits of different cultural modes of living the Gospel, whether these be Indian, Chinese, Korean, or others.

Panikkar does not hyphenate only his personal identity. For him the universe, as a plural reality inclusive of the absolute Being, is also hyphenated. Reality is relational, interlocked; to use one of the neologisms that he loves to coin, it is "cosmotheandric." In other words, the cosmic, the divine, and the human form jointly one total reality. This idea is very Hindu. If at first sight this seems to smack of pantheism, Panikkar would probably reply that he deals in relations, not in essences. With an ontology as comprehensive as this, his vision can accommodate many metaphysical views without any obvious sense of contradiction.

If contradiction is felt, this should lead us to analyze our forms of knowledge. Panikkar plays the two modes he identifies as characterizing traditional knowledge – *logos* and *mythos* – off against each other. One represents left-brain thinking: the realm of reason and analysis; the other represents right-brain thinking: the domain of the symbolic, the heart, intuition, the inner reality of things. *Mythos*, so characteristic of Hindu tradition, is believed to reach deeper than *logos*, and to be more comprehensive.

Panikkar relates the great themes of contemporary theological exploration to the themes of classical theology. Thus Buddhism, with its silence about God and its stress on all things as interdependent and interactive (the teaching of *pratityasamutpada*), is revelative of the "unknown reality" that is the Father. The Son is, of course, manifested in the religion of the followers of Jesus, while Hinduism is particularly conducive to the revelation of the Spirit. No doubt things are not as simple as this may sound: There is a great deal of theological density and sophistication in Panikkar's thought. If the Hindu concept of *Isvara* or "Lord" corresponds to Christ as the second person of the Trinity, one cannot say simply that Christ is Jesus. One can say, as Christians do, that Jesus is Christ, not the reverse. For Christ is more than Jesus. In more recent writings, Panikkar prefers to speak in terms of the cosmotheandric principle as constitutive of the universe rather than of the Christic principle.[23] There is a tendency in his theology to interpret the Pauline Christ in terms of the Johannine *logos*, with a consequent relativization of the Jesus of history.

M. M. Thomas (1916–)

In a sense, M. M. Thomas stands at the opposite end from Panikkar in the Asian theological spectrum. This is not so much because Thomas may be seen to represent a more traditional theological position than Panikkar's more daring approach, but from the point of view of method and focus of interest. A layman of the Marthoma Church of southern India, Thomas has imbibed the Christ-centered Oriental piety of his tradition, an Anglican love for the Bible, and a contemporary concern for the social problems of our times. A Marxist in his youth, Thomas has retained leftist leanings for the rest of his life; he came into contact with the ecumenical movement and was impressed by P. Devanandan's concern for the social implications of the Gospel. He succeeded Devanandan as Director of the CISRS (see above), and was Moderator of the Central Committee of the WCC at Geneva from 1968 to 1975.

Perhaps his central thought is best captured in the title of one of his books, *Salvation and Humanisation* (1971).[24] Without quite identifying the biblical message of salvation with secular advancement and growth, he stresses that one's understanding of salvation cannot bypass what he calls "humanization," the becoming more human through modes of secular development, educationally, socially, politically, and culturally. Humanization, in fact, is the visible expression of some of the implications of salvation, salvation being the inwardness of true humanization. Humanization is inherent in Christ's message of salvation. Theologizing for Thomas is a faith commitment to explore the political message of the Cross. Another title of his prolific bibliography makes this point: *The Secular Ideologies of India and the Secular Meaning of Christ* (1975).

Thomas's political theology seems to follow the same line as that of the Niebuhr brothers (see chapter 16 above), except that it was directly focused on the process of nation-building in India after independence till contemporary times. He expressed "prophetic" opposition to Indira Gandhi's political absolutism during the years of Emergency rule in India (1975–7), and he has sought to challenge various hegemonic trends that have appeared on the Indian political scene since. He was appointed Governor of Nagaland in eastern India in 1990, but his term was short-lived since he resigned rather than succumb to central Government pressures in dealing with various individuals. Thus Thomas's last political act was an act of defiance against the political establishment. He now lives in semi-retirement and continues to write in Malayalam, his mother tongue, and in English. His impact on the world scene was perhaps most striking when as Moderator of the Central Committee of the WCC he persistently championed WCC support for what was described as the "freedom struggle" in various countries of Africa.

Swami Abhishiktananda (1910–1973)

Abhishiktananda was a French Benedictine (Henri Le Saux) whose long stay in India (from 1948 till his death), adoption of the *sannyasi* or renouncer way of life, and deep commitment to and creative reflection on the Upanishads make him an influential figure not only of Indian and Asian theology but also in a wider context. He arrived in an India still celebrating its recent independence from colonial rule, and by 1950 had founded with Fr Jules Monchanin (Swami Parama Arubi Anandam, 1895–1957) the Saccidananda Ashram near the small village of Tannirpalli, not far from the city of Tiruchirapalli.

The Ashram was meant to be an Indian adaptation of the Benedictine rule of *Ora et Labora*, contemplation and physical and intellectual work. But ever closer contact with the Advaitic (i.e., non-dualist) saint Ramana Maharshi (1879–1950) living at the holy mountain of Arunachala, south of Madras, and with other Hindu monks in the vicinity, e.g., Swami Gnanananda, convinced him that attempting an Indian adaptation of the Benedictine rule was ill-advised, and that it was necessary to enter fully into the spiritual world of India with special reference to the experience of

Advaita, which the Upanishads and later tradition spoke of so eloquently. This required initiation into the tradition of the solitary renouncer rather than of the coenobites. This led Abhishiktananda to abandon the Tannirpalli establishment in South India and move north to Gyansu, near Uttarkashi in the foothills of the Himalayas, where he built a hut and spent long periods in solitary meditation and writing. In tune with his *sannyasi* vocation, he was more attracted to Saivite religious symbolism than to Viashnavite devotionalism or to the *sanatani* (orthodox) Brahminic tradition.

As a result of many hours of solitude spent meditating on the Upanishads and in the practice of yoga, and of the continuing dialogues he had with Hindu monks and spiritual practitioners, Abhishiktananda wrote copiously, first in French (most of which has been translated) and then in an original "Frenglish" (this too has been translated!), recounting his thoughts and experiences. His language is effusive, picturesque, and suggestive rather than analytical. He had a good knowledge of the Fathers of the Church (a subject he taught briefly at his monastery in France before setting out for India) and of the Christian mystics. He played a key role in a series of meetings between Hindus and Christians to reflect on the Upanishads and the New Testament, which were organized by the then Swiss Ambassador to India, Dr Albert Cuttat. Out of these meetings came two of his most important books, *La Rencontre de l'hindouisme et du christianisme* (1965),[25] and *Sagesse hindoue mystique chrétienne* (1965).[26] In the latter years of his life he revised the last book which has been re-edited in both English and French.

In the last period of his life, although he spent most of his time at Gyansu, Abhishiktananda continued to be involved in the life of the Church through meetings and seminars (some ecumenical) which had issues of inculturation and the relationship between religions on their agenda. He never tired of lamenting the fact that the Christian churches in India had not presented or developed a contemplative dimension in their spirituality although they lived in a culture that was noted for its interior search for the Absolute. He desired a contemplative Church, and hoped that he would have Indian disciples. But it was not to be in the way he had envisaged, though his influence in Christian circles has been considerable. He has left behind a rich store of writings on themes of the Hindu spiritual quest and its relation to the Christian faith which continue to inspire many people in India and abroad. There is an Abhishiktananda Society[27] that keeps his dialogic spirit alive and is responsible for preserving his manuscripts and related material.

For Abhishiktananda the first thing that the Christian must realize is the *ultimate* nature of the Upanishadic experience as interpreted especially by the Vedanta of Shankara. The Upanishads are true, Abhishiktananda declared; that is, only the Absolute is real. The individual, the human being, can be spoken of as real only in the measure that the Absolute is realized as one's very self. The world of history, of events, is *maya*, false reality, or at least not the autonomous reality it pretends to be. The world and the Absolute, therefore, are not two *separate* entities. Advaita or non-duality is at the heart of all existence.

In his work mentioned above, *Sagesse hindoue mystique chrétienne*, Abhishiktananda sought to integrate the Advaitic apophatic experience with Trinitarian faith. In becoming aware of the fact that God alone – the Atman – is real, one must paradoxically go through the crisis of an apophatic experience of self-renunciation at the very level of being. This "ontological" self-denial, a true kenosis, is essential to arrive at the higher plane of Truth. But when we hear the evocation "Today I have begotten You" addressed to the eternal Word, and constitutive of the reality of the second Person of the Trinity, as addressed also to us in the depth of the Christian experience, we too are rescued from our nothingness and experience the Advaita of the mystery of the Absolute, the One without a second (*Chandogya Upanishad* 6.2.1). For Abhishiktananda, the mystery of the divine Spirit consists precisely in Its being the affirmation of the non-duality of Father and Son, and thus of the universe with God.

In the later edition of this work and in other late writings, Abhishiktananda distances himself from earlier ideas where he appears to have subordinated the Advaita of the Upanishads to the Trinitarian experience, for theology for Abhishiktananda operates only at the level of *namarupa* (name and form, the phenomenon; he makes fun of his own theologizings which he called "conceptual games"). This Hindu-Christian monk is now driven by the quest for direct experience of the Infinite, beyond all concepts. The Upanishadic experience of Advaita and christological faith remained in him in a state of unresolved but creative tension. Till the very end he received comfort and experienced deep joy in celebrating the mystery of the Mass. It is in this context that we must strive to understand his final "illumination" as an awakening to the reality of Christ within when he was struck down by a heart attack in Rishikesh a few months before his death. This was an awakening not to Christ as the "Word of God" but to the Christ of the "I am," which the Swami identified with the Upanishadic experience. In a note written to his disciple after this experience he says:

> Marc,
> Siva's Column of Fire
> Brushed against me
> Saturday midday
> In the bazaar at Rishikesh,
> And I still do not understand
> Why it did not carry me off.
> Joy, the serene One,
> Om tat sat.
> Ekadrishti (single vision!),
> Ekarshi (single Rishi),
> Oh
> The crowning grace,
> Om.

In a letter to a friend he says of this event:

Really a door opened in heaven when I was lying on the pavement. But a heaven which was not the opposite of earth . . . but simply "being", "awakening" . . . beyond all myths and symbols . . . I have really been deeply moved by my life with the poor and with poor sadhus of the old tradition . . . If my message could really pass, it would be free from any notion . . . The Christ I might present will be simply the I AM of my (every) deep heart, who can show himself in the dancing Shiva or the amorous Krishna! And the Kingdom is precisely the discovery . . . of the inside of the Grail! . . . The awakening is a total explosion. No Church will recognize its Christ or itself afterwards.[28]

S. J. Samartha

S. J. Samartha is another Indian thinker who makes Advaita an important hermeneutical key of his theology. Ordained in the Church of South India and involved in theological teaching in his earlier years, Samartha has acquired authority especially among Indian Protestants as a result of ten years as Director of the WCC Dialogue Programme which he in fact initiated. His earlier christocentric but nondogmatic stance has been well described by K. Koyama in the first edition of this work. In the years after that study, however, Samartha's theology moved toward a pluralistic model similar to that of Hick and Knitter. When called theocentric by some of its proponents, this theological position becomes ambiguous since it may be argued that by definition all "theology" is "theocentric." The real question is whether one's "theocentrism" includes the affirmation that Jesus Christ "sits at the right hand of the Father," to use a traditional expression. The later Samartha of *One Christ – Many Religions: Toward a revised christology* (1991), proposes that christocentrism is the spirituality proper to the Christian believer, but by no means expressive of all the ways to the divine Mystery; as such it cannot be the norm by which the various religious traditions are evaluated. All approaches to the divine have their validity. The Incarnation is therefore somehow reduced to the level of a symbol of the divine rather than being an expression of God's eschatological action in the world. The death and resurrection of Christ are indeed revelatory of the divine, says Samartha, but the divinity of Christ must no longer be seen as a universally valid paradigm; in fact, it is considered nonbiblical. Theology should enable the Christian to cooperate with members of other religions in the tasks of the Kingdom. A "helicopter Christology" from above is not likely to do so. Rather, a "bullock-cart Christology," closer to the Synoptic Gospels, will show that Jesus is indeed human and divine, but not that he is God, for "an ontological equation of Jesus Christ and God would scarcely allow any serious discussion with neighbours of other faiths or with secular humanists."[29]

Sri Lanka

Aloysius Pieris (1934–)

What Abhishiktananda attempted for Hinduism, this Sri Lankan Jesuit has sought for Buddhism. He has sat at the feet of monks of the Theravada tradition not only to learn their philosophy but also to undergo a spiritual training under their direction. As he himself puts it, it has been his intention to have "a humble participation in the non-Christian experience of liberation." Further, unlike Abhishiktananda,

Pieris has been in close touch with the Marxist movement, especially in the painful decade of the seventies in Sri Lanka.

Pieris unambiguously criticizes the presence of the Christian Church in Asia as an extension of Western Christendom. The Asian Church has no theology of its own, but dresses itself up in the borrowed clothes of classical (capitalist) theology, and in recent times, in the Latin American garb of liberation theology. Liberation is indeed a central theme in the thought of Pieris, but as invested with the resonances of the ancient Asian search for liberation. These are much more comprehensive than the connotations of Western or Latin American theology. In Asia liberation starts in the heart, in the consciousness of the seeker. But this does not mean that its scope is purely spiritual, for it is in relation to mammon that Asian monks and nuns seek liberation. In their voluntary poverty, Pieris contends, is implied a commitment to the liberation of the poor from the poverty imposed on them by feudalistic or capitalist societies (note Abhishiktananda's reference to the poor in the final paragraph describing his "awakening" experience).

From his study of the respective soteriologies Pieris affirms that Buddhism is basically gnostic in its search for wisdom, while Christianity is primarily agapeic in its commitment to the Kingdom of God. However, each tradition contains as secondary traits the primary tendencies of the other: Buddhism has a long tradition of compassion that has informed the cultures of Asia with a spirit of friendship, goodwill, and love, while Christianity has also sought a higher wisdom, especially in its mystical tradition. Pieris proposes that the secondary traits of each tradition can be strengthened by an authentic mutual dialogue.

The Buddhist seeks a new consciousness of reality which enables one to realize the origin of suffering and therefore to eliminate it. A necessary condition for this new vision is precisely detachment from all that ties us to the mammon of our world. In Christianity, especially in the goal of liberation which Pieris believes lies at the very heart of the tradition, evil has to be combated by overcoming not only the personal attachments that enslave us to the world, but also the structural causes that give rise to situations of injustice. With its stronger sense of history, the Christian tradition can give a social and organized response to injustice based on greed, while with its stress on detachment and inner purification, Buddhist ascetic tradition can guarantee the evangelical purity of the Christian response.

According to Pieris, rather than a dialogue between "East" and "West," theology needs a dialogue between cosmic and metacosmic religion. Cosmic religion, which has often been pejoratively called animist, thinks in terms of the elements of nature – earth, fire, water, trees, rivers, mountains. This is generally the religion of tribal and village peoples. Metacosmic religion, on the other hand, is to be found in the "great" traditions of Hinduism, Buddhism, (to some extent) Taoism, in the Stoicism of ancient Rome and the gnostic movements, and in the theologies that draw from these traditions. Pieris thinks that the Bible, rooted as it is in values of the concrete and historical, is more allied to cosmic religiosity than to metacosmic. Latin American liberation theology has recovered the primacy of the historical, i.e., cosmic, over the metacosmic aspects of classical theology. This explains why, in the Catholic Church, there is a tension between Rome, which has traditionally stressed the metacosmic dimension, and liberation theology. Our task today is not to allow the metacosmic so to dominate theology that no space is left for the concrete perceptions and experiences of the common people. This is why it is so important to encourage the existence of grassroots communities, *dalit*, tribal and *minjung* theology, and so on.

Korea: *Minjung* Theology

As we pass from South Asia to Korea, we do more than traverse thousands of kilometers; we enter a different cultural world. This is a world that has been shaped by the great civilizations of China and Japan, but which nevertheless manifests a distinct historical and cultural identity. The people of the tiny peninsula of Korea were hard put to it to survive the pressures that came from China and Japan, and from colonists further afield. This long history of colonial presence has produced *han*, a repressed anger that accounts for the special power of the Korean people.

Christianity has a unique history in Korea which one must recall to understand the country's theologizing. In a sense, the Christian faith in Korea was "self-preached." The seed of faith was planted not directly by missionaries but indirectly, through the Chinese works written by the Jesuit Matteo Ricci and his companions, which visitors to Beijing brought to Korea together with other Chinese works during regular visits to Beijing in the seventeenth and eighteenth centuries. The first reaction of the Korean intellectuals was to criticize these new writings. However, when Yi Piek (1754–86), the son of a military functionary, and some of his friends discussed them in the middle of the eighteenth century, they were convinced of their teachings, and decided to become Christians.[30] No doubt, later missionary and colonial influences shaped the growth of the seed planted in this extraordinary way. Indeed, part of the Korean theological struggle has been to resist the invasion of foreign theologies in the manner in which the country has sought to resist the invasion of foreign arms. Yi Piek had been able to articulate his Christian faith on the basis of a Confucian worldview.

Korean history has left the Korean people with a strong desire to assert themselves, which has been denied to them by the powerful of the world. They have tended to regard themselves as the *minjung*, the powerless people, those on the periphery, often politically oppressed and economically deprived. According to *minjung* theology, Jesus himself was the victim of dominant powers. He continues even today to be disfigured by the power-brokers. In a poem entitled "The Golden-crowned Jesus,"[31] Kim Chi Ha presents Christ crowned with gold pleading with a person suffering from leprosy, a beggar, and a prostitute, to help him be free. The leper is honest: "I am helpless (pointing to his ravaged body); I cannot even take care of myself. How can I help you?" To which Jesus replies: "It is for this exact reason that you *can* help me. You are the *only* one who can do it . . . It is your poverty, your wisdom, your generous spirit and, even more, your courageous resistance against injustice that makes all this possible."

Thus the Cross is the irony of God's wisdom on the powerful. The cross painted on Christian ballet masks in Korea represents the *minjung*, angry and sad, ironic and laughing. Because of the Cross, the people can laugh both at their own suffering and at the rich, just as Jesus derided the Pharisees (see Matthew 23).

The Philippines

A product of Malay Asia, Iberian Christianity, and Western culture, the Filipino is in the process of constructing an identity. This is the only country in Asia where Christians are in the majority and where the Church represents a sociopolitical power. Filipino theologizing is probably closer to that of Latin America than of Asia. Colonization in the Philippines was longer and fiercer than in most other Asian countries, and as a result the indigenous cultures all but disappeared. However, there has been a resurgence in recent times.

Carlos H. Abesimos (1934–   )

Carlos H. Abesimos is a Jesuit who studied theology in Innsbruck and the Bible at the Pontifical Biblical Institute in Rome. He is involved in the grassroots movements of his country and develops from that perspective a biblical catechesis imbued with liberation theology, though he finds the Latin American brand too unconcerned with the culture of the people. Like other liberation theologians he focuses on the this-worldly meaning of God's Kingdom and stresses that the experience of the poor is essential to understand theology. In fact, the real theologians are the poor who live their Christian life in the midst of a daily struggle for existence. Professional theologians are but technicians equipped with better linguistic skills to help the poor articulate their experience. But their role is subsidiary.[32]

This idea has been expanded in what is now characteristic of Filipino theology, a "theology of struggle," which claims to view reality from the viewpoint of the poor and struggling people, in contrast to a theology that supports the status quo. There is no doubt that the experience of the anti-Marcos agitation in the eighties and the establishment of the Corazon Aquino democracy have inspired the shaping of this theology of struggle. One of its main symbols is Jesus' action of protest in the cleansing of the Temple.

This thought pivots on the one hand on the *suffering* of the people, and on the other on the *hope* which the Christian faith engenders. The aim is to articulate a dialectic between the two poles such that "struggle" is not a passive acceptance of injustice, while "hope" does not become a kind of futuristic escape. "Only by struggle can the oppressed forge a better tomorrow; only by struggle can the memory of the dead be resurrected; only by struggle can parents truly love their children and future generations," says Eleazar S. Fernandes, another theologian in this mould.[33] Other names of note in this respect are Karl Gasper and Feliciano Cariño, not to mention some bishops who support the movement both actively and theologically. Among these we may mention Roy Sano, Francisco Claver, and especially Julio Xavier Lebayen, who is critical of Western theological models and who believes that traditional perceptions of conflicts between the "East" and the "West" hide the real problem of a fundamental disparity between the northern and southern hemispheres.

China, Taiwan, and Japan

In the early part of the twentieth century, Chinese theology was especially concerned with affirming its own identity and with defending Chinese nationalism against attack from foreigners. This affirmation of Asianness is also strong in the work of the Taiwanese theologian, *Choan-Sen Song*.[34] Song is one of the most influential theologians of Asia. He has held important academic and ecumenical positions in his own country, the USA, and the WCC. He sees the Bible as a model text of the way God saves peoples. But salvation is multicentered, and each nation, each people, has to tell its own story and discern God in its own name. Song is impressed by the second Isaiah, where God achieves his purposes through the Persian "messiah," Cyrus. This contrasts with the theological centrism of the Deuteronomistic school where all salvation flows from Israel. Song's is a theology from below. In fact, he has served as Dean of the Programme for the Theology and Culture of Asia (PTCA), "a program set up to encourage Asians to use their histories, cultures, religions, social and political struggles as the data for doing theology."[35] As a consequence, his language is more imaginative than conceptual, using the stories of common people more than most theologians do. Song is essentially a theologian of inculturation. For a fuller treatment, see the first edition of this work (volume II, chapter 11, by K. Koyama).

Later in the twentieth century another tradition, more a spirituality than a theology, developed among Christians in China, Japan (and India), which sought to assimilate oriental modes of contemplation, including Zen, Yoga, and Vipassana. Roman Catholics have been the main exponents of this trend. Here we may mention Enomiya Lasalle in Japan, Yves Raguin in Taiwan, and Swami Abhishiktananda, Sebastian Painadath, and, with his own blend of Asian wisdom and western psychology, Tony de Mello, in India. These and others have encouraged many to discover a new mental and spiritual equilibrium by practices that rid the mind of unnecessary conceptual baggage and lead to a deeper level of consciousness and being.[36]

Raguin, who is well versed in the various traditions of China – Buddhism, Confucianism, and Taoism – believes that in entering the depths of our humanity through meditative and other practices, one engages in the search for God, and that this is a valid path of prayer. For the Asian Christian, this cannot be ignored in seeking to encounter God. He does not deny the validity of other paths: that of approaching God in the acknowledgement of his transcendence and historical revelation, or the encounter with God through human relationships of various sorts. But he insists that the path of interiority, of plumbing the human spirit, is vital for our times. This approach is not unrelated to the loss of trust in conceptual theology by some in the West following the death of God theologies of the sixties. He says:

> The three great Chinese traditions are, each in its own way, humanisms – even Buddhism, which teaches the non-consistency of the person when compared with the absolute of *nirvana*. The three images of the perfect man they bring, give their own answer to the secularizing world. Through each we can discern one facet of the spiritual core of the human. Where Buddhism seeks for a humanity "liberated" from all illusions and the weight of *karma*, Taoism looks for human "liberation" from

excessive constraints and the return to the state of simple nature. Confucianism, in its turn, wants a "liberated" humanity, but through acceptance of an order that expresses the harmony between heaven and earth.[37]

To some this search may seem to be more characteristic of the seventies and eighties than of the late nineties. Yet it continues in Indian ashrams, Zen centers, various retreat movements, and attempts to participate in the spirituality of other traditions. Indeed, in international forums of religions, e.g., the World Conference on Religion and Peace, this theme of spirituality beyond theology and even beyond the religions is becoming more prominent. We may be beyond theology here, but perhaps this entails pointing to a goal at which all theology should aim.

The theological dialogue with the Confucian traditions was already present in Yi Piek, the first Korean Christian and theologian (see above). In more recent times, the encounter between Confucianism and Christianity has been studied by Julia Ching,[38] by journals like *Ching Feng* published from Hong Kong, and the *Asia Journal of Theology* (Bangalore, India). In a recent article in the latter, Professor Heup Young Kim works toward a "Confucian Christology" by comparing *jen* ("the Confucian paradigm of hermeneutics") and *agape*.[39] *Jen* may signify humanity or benevolence through a pictographic character that represents the human being and two strokes which signify human togetherness, "co-humanity." In other words, to be human is to be co-human, to be related in humanness. The idea of *jen* has been expanded to embrace a cosmic togetherness:

> Heaven is my father and Earth is my mother, and even such a small creature as I finds an intimate place in their midst. Therefore that which fills the universe I regard as my body and that which directs the universe I consider as my nature. All people are my brothers and sisters, and all things are my companions.[40]

Kim concludes his long article with a section on the Tao and Jesus Christ, which he seeks to integrate into his Confucian christology. For Kim, Tao is self-direction with a sapiential character, and can thus describe Jesus as Sage better than other terms. As Sage, Jesus cannot be separated from the human family. He embodies *jen*. He is with everyone else. He is with the universe. This sense of relatedness at the core of Chinese theology is also found in the thought of Abhishiktananda and R. Panikkar. As such, we can reckon it an Asian perception. In Kim's work, Christ the Sage is envisioned as the root-paradigm of humanity as cosmic, reconciled being-in-togetherness. The Confucian model of reciprocity and mutuality liberates humanity and nature from the models of domination and exploitation deriving from Western dualism.[41]

With *Kosuke Koyama* (b. 1929) we come closest, perhaps, to an Asian theology of history and to political theology. Renowned for his *Waterbuffalo Theology* (1972), which drew upon his experience of teaching theology in Thailand, this Japanese theologian has been consistently intrigued by the diverse ways in which Buddhism and Christianity have dealt with the subject of history, in particular with the problem of greed, itself a form of idolatry. Rooted though he is in a strong biblical sense of God, Koyama finds much to learn from the ascetical and ethical teachings of the

Buddhist tradition. Its ideal of tranquility seems to stand in contrast to the biblical wrath of God. Yet both are ways of dealing with the historical and must learn from each other. In an essay entitled "Forgiveness and Politics," written for a Festschrift in honour of S. Rayan,[42] Koyama reflects on the political history of Japan and the way Japan has tried to cope with its own history in the postwar years. The essay ends with more questions than answers. "What kind of forgiveness are we talking about? Is forgiveness always creative and healing? Is it possible that forgiveness is incompatible with politics as we know it? In the long run, might it damage the quality of human civilization?"

In spite of the complexity and ambiguity of history, Koyama finds in the theme of forgiveness a glimpse of the moral spark that lies in the depth of human civilization. The deeper the understanding and application of forgiveness in the concrete historical contexts becomes, he believes, the more meaningful the life of humanity as a whole is. David Ford concludes his more complete presentation of Koyama with these words: "Koyama's achievement is to have attempted a consistently cross-centred and strongly social and ethical theology in relation to the realities of Asia."[43]

Conclusion: Achievement and Agenda

In any summary of the main features and agenda of Asian theology, heterogeneous though it is, the following points should be included:

1 An affirmation of the interrelatedness of the universe, of a kind of cosmic compactness in which God is in some way present. These are characteristics chiefly of *jen* and a Christian Advaita.

2 The sense of the mystery of the Absolute or supreme reality, which always lies beyond conceptualization or formulation even when faith is professed in the Trinity or in the Father of the Lord Jesus Christ. In fact, *mythos* is preferred to *logos* as the instrument of authentic theology.

3 A conviction about God's revelation to the whole human family, covering the whole of history, and manifesting "in many and various ways," especially in the religious traditions of humanity.

4 Without denying the saving action of Jesus Christ, a stress on a Sage and/or Guru christology, where Jesus is compared in some way to Confucius, the Buddha, etc.

5 An awareness that religions need and complement each other, and that the future of Christian theology depends on the depth and seriousness of an ongoing interreligious dialogue. "In the beginning was the Logos," St John tells us. But Asia tends to interpret this as follows: "In the beginning there is dia-logos."

6 A conviction that the privileged forum for such dialogue is the struggle for justice. Thus there will be an affirmation of the dignity of the *dalits* (oppressed), of the power of the *minjung* (the powerless), of the value of tribal, local or national cultures and identities, etc.

7 An awareness that the eschatological affirmations of the Christian faith cannot remain as simply futuristic or irrelevant to the historical realities of the day, especially

among the poor and dispossessed. A "justice eschatology" must be implemented in the here and now. Only then will we be true to the full teaching of the Gospel.

Notes

1 With special reference to South Asian theology, I am grateful to Dr Julius Lipner, of the Faculty of Divinity, University of Cambridge, for commenting on an earlier draft of this paper.

2 See his "The Essence of Sacred Doctrine," which contains a short summary of biblical history – largely the life of Christ – and an anthropology and ethic derived from Confucianism reinterpreted in the light of the Gospel. It also includes a section on theodicy or natural theology. In recent times it has been translated into French and commented upon by Jean Sangbae Ri (Beauchesne, Paris, 1979).

3 See, e.g., M. M. Thomas, *The Acknowledged Christ of the Indian Renaissance* (Bangalore, 1970); D. Kopf, *The Brahmo Samaj and the Shaping of the Modern Indian Mind* (Princeton, 1979); J. Lipner, "A modern Indian Christian response," in H. G. Coward (ed.), *Modern Indian Responses to Religious Pluralism* (Albany, NY, 1987).

4 The title of a well-known work by the Hindu, Pratap Chandra Majumdar, published in 1883.

5 On the Philippines, see below. Here I am referring directly to the theology rooted in the indigenous consciousness. See, for instance, José de Mesa, *And God said, "Bahala na"* (Maryhill Studies, 2) (Quezon City, 1979). For Malaysia, see M. Fung, SJ, *Shoes-off Barefoot We Walk: A theology of the shoes-off* (Petaling Jaya, 1992). In India one of the most representative spokespersons for tribal theology is the Lutheran Bishop, Nirmal Minz, whose writings and speeches await collation. An important organ for Catholic tribal thought is the annual *Sevartham*, published by St Albert's College, Ranchi. In similar vein but in quite a different context, one may consult *Faith and the Intifada: Palestinian Christian voices*, ed. Naim S. Ateek, Marc H. Ellis, and Rosemary Radford Ruether (Maryknoll, NY, 1992).

6 This work was first published in the RISK book series of the WCC. Orbis brought out an edition in 1980.

7 The full text can be found in the official Assembly Report, *Signs of the Spirit*, ed. M. Kinnamon (Geneva, 1991), pp. 37–47. The invocation and concluding section of the address is given in U. King (ed.), *Feminist Theology from the Third World: A reader* (London, 1994), ch. 38.

8 Published quarterly by the Asian Women's Resource Centre for Culture and Theology, P. O. Box 16, Seoul 120–650.

9 On Krishna Mohan Banerjea, see T. V. Philip, *Krishna Mohan Banerjea, Christian Apologist* (Madras, 1982). On Brahmabandhab Upadhyay, see B. Animananda, *The Blade* (Calcutta, 1946); J. Lipner and G. Gispert-Sauch, SJ, *The Writings of Brahmabandhab Upadhyay*, vol. 1 (Bangalore, 1991). Vol. 2 is in preparation. Lipner is also completing a major study on the life and thought of Upadhyay.

10 The copy available to me was published by Oxford University Press in 1919, although the preface is dated 1913. There is no indication that this was a reprint except possibly the information that it was printed in Bombay. Sharpe (see next note) affirms that the book was published by OUP in 1913, and reprinted in New Delhi in 1971.

11 *Faith meets Faith: Some Christian Interpretations of Hinduism* (London, 1977), p. 123.

12 The first issue appeared in 1922 and the journal was wound up in 1946.

13 I still recall the impression made on me when I was a student of theology in the early sixties by Mgr V. Dyer, then Archbishop of Calcutta, as he described the avidity with which he and his fellow seminarians read *The Light of the East*.

14 See D. O'Connor, *Gospel, Raj and Swaraj: The missionary years of C. F. Andrews 1904–1914* (Frankfurt am Main, 1990).

15 See R. Taylor, *The Contribution of E. Stanley Jones* (Madras, 1973).

16 D. M. Devasahayam and A. N. Sundarisanam, *Rethinking Christianity in India* (Madras, 1938). See also P. Chenchiah, V. Chakkarai, and A. N. Sundarisanam, *Ashrams Past and Present* (Christo Samaj Series no. 2), (Madras, 1941). `

17 For an account of the times by a churchman with evangelical leanings active at the time in the South, see L. Newbigin, *Unfinished Agenda: An autobiography* (London, 1985).

18 See R. W. Taylor, *Essays in Celebration of the CISRS Silver Jubilee* (1983).

19 Entitled *Christava Inthiya Gnana Vazhvu*, in 3 vols (Madras, 1987–92).

20 See J. A. G. Gerwin van Leeuwen, *Fully Indian, Authentically Christian* (Bangalore, 1990).

21 For an idea of Sahi's outlook, see his article "The Ultimate Vision of the Living Seed," in M. Forward (ed.), *Ultimate Visions: Reflections on the religions we choose* (Oxford, 1995), which also has an autobiographical article by Lott. More developed formulations of Sahi's vision may be found in *The Child and the Serpent: Reflections on popular Indian symbols* (London, 1980), and in *Stepping Stones: Reflections on the theology of Indian Christian culture* (Bangalore, 1986).

22 See, e.g., Raimundo Panikkar, *The Intrareligious Dialogue* (New York, 1978). Other works include *The Unknown Christ of Hinduism* (London, 1964; rev. edn, 1981); *The Trinity and World Religions* (Madras, 1970); *Myth, Faith, and Hermeneutics* (New York, 1979); *Blessed Simplicity* (New York, 1982); *The Silence of God* (Maryknoll, NY, 1989). See also the issue of the journal *Cross Currents* devoted to Panikkar: "Panikkar in Santa Barbara," XXIX/2 (1979).

23 See, e.g., his contribution "The Jordan, the Tiber, and the Ganges," in J. Hick and P. Knitter (eds), *The Myth of Christian Uniqueness* (London, 1988).

24 The CLS Bookshop, Tiruvala, Kerala, published a booklet in 1988 entitled *A List of the Published Writings of M. M. Thomas, 1936–1987*; it also records in an appendix eight doctoral dissertations on his thought.

25 English translation: *Hindu-Christian Meeting Point: Within the cave of the heart* (Delhi, 1969).

26 English translation: *Saccidananda: A Christian approach to Advaitic experience* (Delhi, 1974).

27 Registered Office: Brotherhood House, 7 Court Lane, Delhi 110054. The Society's "Abhishiktananda Library" is located at the adjacent Vidyajyoti College of Theology.

28 *Swami Abhishiktananda: His life told through his letters*, ed. James Stuart (Delhi, 1989), pp. 349–50.

29 "The Cross and the Rainbow: Christ in a Multireligious Culture," in J. Hick and P. Knitter (eds), *The Myth of Christian Uniqueness* (Maryknoll, NY, and London, 1987). For an impressive study of S. J. Samartha, see E. Klootwijk, *Commitment and Openness* (Zoetemer, 1992).

30 A study of the beginnings of Christianity in Korea and the work of Yi Piek is found in the book by the Korean priest, Jean Sangbae Ri, cited in note 2. See also its bibliography.

31 In David Kwang-sun Suh, *The Korean Minjung in Christ* (Hong Kong, 1991), pp. 168–9. A good account of *minjung* theology and of the theologian Hyun Young Hak in particular is found in the first edition of the present book. For a detailed study of the theologian Abu Byung-Mu see F. J. Balasundaram, *The Prophetic Voices of Asia* (Colombo, 1994), pp. 60–83.

32 See his *Salvation: Historical and total* (Quezon City, 1978), and *Where are we Going: Heaven or new world?* (Manila, 1983).

33 *Toward a Theology of Struggle* (Maryknoll, NY, 1994), p. 71.

34 See C. S. Song, *Third-Eye Theology* (Maryknoll, NY, 1979); *The Tears of Lady Meng: A parable of peoples' political theology* (Geneva, 1981); *The Compassionate God* (Maryknoll, NY, 1982); *Tell Us Our Names* (Maryknoll, NY, 1984); *Jesus the Crucified People* (New York, 1990).

35 R. S. Sugirtharajah (ed.), *Asian Faces of Jesus* (Maryknoll, NY, 1993), p. 267.

36 This trend continues a long history of Christian assimilation of Yoga begun in the West in the mid-fifties if not earlier. The classical work here is J.-M. Dechanet, CSB, *La Voie du silence* (Paris, 1956) translated as *Christian Yoga* (London, 1960). Indian contributions to this tradition

include Pearl Drego, *Pathways of Liberation* (New Delhi, 1974); Brahmachari Amaldas, *Yoga and Contemplation* (Trichy, 1974); V. F. Vineeth, CMI, *Yoga of Spirituality* (Bangalore, 1995).

37　*The Depth of God* (Hertfordshire, 1979), p. 14.

38　See her *Confucianism and Christianity: A comparative study* (Tokyo, 1977).

39　See the *Asia Journal of Theology*, 8/2 (1994), pp. 335–64.

40　From Chang Tsai, *Western Inscription*,

quoted by Kim, *Asia Journal of Theology*, p. 342.

41　Ibid., p. 360, where Kim also refers to Tu Wei-ming's *Centrality and Commonality: An essay on Confucian religiousness*, rev. edn (Albany, NY, 1989).

42　*Bread and Breath* (Gujarat Sahitya Prakash, 1991), pp. 139–67.

43　*The Modern Theologians: An introduction to Christian theology in the twentieth century*, vol. II (first edn), ed. D. F. Ford (Oxford, 1989), p. 229.

Bibliography

Asian theology: surveys and works of composite authorship

Anderson, G. H., *Asian Voices in Christian Theology* (Maryknoll, NY, 1976).

Arokiasamy, S. and Gispert-Sauch, G. (eds), *Liberation in Asia: Theological Perspectives* (Anand, 1987).

Athyal, J. (ed.), *Keeping Hope Alive: Theological insights from the past for today* (Madras, 1993).

Balasundaram, F. J., *The Prophetic Voices of Asia*, in *Logos, Colombo*, 33 (1994), nos 1–4 in two fascicles, pp. 188f.

——— *Contemporary Asian Christian Theology* (Bangalore and Delhi, 1995).

Batumalai, S., *Asian Theology* (Delhi, 1991).

Elwood, D. J., *Asian Christian Theologies: Emerging themes* (Philadelphia, 1980).

England, J. C. (ed.), *Living Theology in Asia* (London, 1981).

Fabella, V. (ed.), *Asia's Struggle for Full Humanity* (Maryknoll, NY, 1980).

Hargreaves, C., *Asian Christian Thinking: Studies in metaphor and its message* (Delhi, 1972).

King, U. (ed.), *Feminist Theology from the Third World: A reader* (London, 1994).

Samuel, V. and Sugden, C. (eds), *Sharing Jesus in the Two-Thirds World* (Grand Rapids, MI, 1983).

Sugirtharajah, R. S. (ed.), *Asian Faces of Jesus* (London, 1993).

Indian theology: surveys and works of composite authorship

Aleaz, K. P., *The Gospel of Indian Culture* (Calcutta, 1994).

Amaladoss, M. et al., *Theologizing in India* (Bangalore, 1981).

Boyd, R. H. S., *An Introduction to Indian Christian Theology* (Madras, 1969; rev. edn Delhi and Trivandrum, 1975).

Burkle, H. and Roth, W. M. W., *Indian Voices in Today's Theological Debate* (Delhi, 1972).

Gerwin van Leeuwen, J. A. G., OFM, *Fully Indian Authentically Christian: A study of the first fifteen years of the NBCLC (1967–1982)* (Bangalore, 1990).

Job, G. V. et al., *Rethinking Christianity in India* (Madras, 1938).

Klootwijk, E., *Commitment and Openness: The interreligious dialogue and theology of religions in the work of Stanely J. Samartha* (Zoetemer, 1992).

Massey, J. (ed.), *Indigenous People: Dalits*, dalit issues in today's theological debate (Delhi, 1994).

Nirmal, A. P. (ed.), *A Reader in Dalit Theology* (Madras, ca. 1991).

Prabhakar, M. E. (ed.), *Towards a Dalit Theology* (Delhi, 1988).

Sugirtharajah, R. S. and Hargreaves, C. (ed.), *Readings in Indian Christian Theology*, vol. 1 (Delhi, 1993).

Sumithra, S., *Christian Theology from an Indian Perspective* (Bangalore, 1990).

Thomas, M. M., *The Acknowledged Christ of the Indian Renaissance* (Madras, 1970).

Thomas, M. M. and Thomas, P. T., *Towards an Indian Christian Theology* (Tiruvalla, 1992).

Vetakanam, M., *Christology in the Indian Context: An evaluative encounter with K. Rahner and W. Pannenberg* (Frankfurt am Main, 1986).

Wilfred, F., *Beyond Settled Foundations: The journey of Indian theology* (Madras, 1993).

Other

de Mesa, J. M., *And God said, "Bahala na!": The theme of providence in the lowland Filipino context* (Quezon City, 1979).

Drummond, R. H., "A new history of Japanese theology," in *Mission Studies*, X-2 (22), 1994.

Fernandez, E. S., *Toward a Theology of Struggle* (Maryknoll, NY, 1994).

Furuya, Y. (ed.), *Theologiegeschichte der Dritten Welt, Japan* (Munich, 1991).

Lam, Wing-hung, *Chinese Theology in Construction* (Pasadena, CA, 1983).

Moon, C. H. S., *A Korean Minjung Theology* (Maryknoll, NY, 1985).

Ri, J. Sangbae, *Confucius et Jesus Christ: La première théologie chrétienne en Corée d'après l'oeuvre de Yi-Piek* (Paris, 1979).

Stuart, J. (ed.), *Swami Abhishiktananda: His life told through his letters* (Delhi, 1989).

Suh, D. Keang-sun, *The Korean Minjung in Christ* (Hong Kong, 1991).

Evangelical and Orthodox Theologies

Evangelical and Orthodox theologies are best understood first of all in relation to their respective church traditions. Ray Anderson carefully defines what is meant by evangelical theology, gives its historical background, and tells how it relates to the evangelical movement in contemporary Protestantism. He discusses three diverse examples of its theology in G. C. Berkouwer, Helmut Thielicke, and Carl F. H. Henry. He shows how they dealt with the core evangelical concerns of Reformation orthodoxy, biblical authority, and personal experience of salvation, and also how they have responded variously to the challenges of modernity. The revival in the United States during and after the 1950s of an evangelicalism which is not fundamentalist and is concerned for high academic standards is given special attention, the achievement of the whole tradition is assessed, some leading current thinkers indicated, and an agenda for the future suggested.

Orthodox Christianity has been in considerable turmoil since the post-1989 collapse of Communist rule in the Soviet Union and Eastern Europe. Rowan Williams describes twentieth-century Orthodox thought and the ferment of recent years, though it is too early for substantial theological work to have been produced in the post-Communist period. He begins with the nineteenth-century Russian background, including the major figures of Kireevsky, Soloviev, and Khomyakov. He then discusses three theologians: S. N. Bulgakov, the Marxist economist turned philosopher and theologian, whose unified theological metaphysic and thoroughgoing kenotic approach to God are described; V. N. Lossky, with his more hermeneutical, patristic approach and influential "negative theology"; and G. V. Florovsky, who was likewise oriented to patristics, and pursued a program of "re-Hellenizing" Christianity in reaction against much modern thought. The conclusion is a brief survey of recent Orthodox thought in many places – Greece, the United States, France, and Eastern Europe, with a glance at India – accompanied by suggestions about its agenda and encouragement to Western theologians to engage more fully with it.

Both evangelical and Orthodox theologians have been more at home in churches and their seminaries than in universities and are in close relationship with traditions representing hundreds of millions of Christians. They have not yet been done justice to by academic theologians, and Anderson and Williams open the way for this to happen with benefit and challenge to all sides.

Evangelical Theology

Ray S. Anderson

Introduction: The Meaning of "Evangelical"

No Christian theologian has a proprietary claim on the phrase "evangelical theology." As it pertains to the gospel of God's act of saving grace through Jesus Christ, the word "evangelical" is rooted in the earliest traditions of the church's theology including, most certainly, the Pauline and Johannine theology of the New Testament itself. A theology which is not "evangelical" in this fundamental sense may have betrayed both the formal and material reality of its claim to be a "Christian" theology.

It would be naive, however, to ignore the history of theology which has invariably witnessed a polarity of one form or another between theologians who view the "evangel" from quite different perspectives. As a result, theologians of the early Christian era who sought to defend the historical and philosophical truth of the gospel as located in the person and work of Jesus Christ constructed an orthodox formulation of the "evangel" as opposed to what they considered to be a heterodox or even heretical theology. Thus began the association of the word "evangelical" with "orthodox," and later with "reformed," "conservative," or even "fundamentalistic," as opposed to "modern" or "liberal."

Survey

Theology in the Protestant tradition, by its very nature, sought to define its stance over and against other theological traditions. In so doing, it has given rise to a variety of nuances to the word "evangelical" which provide a broad context for the specific purpose of this chapter. While the Reformed (Calvinistic) theological tradition assumed an implicit evangelical and christological orientation, the European Lutheran tradition often carried an explicit evangelical confessional designation. In this way, both attempted to overcome what was perceived as a "non-evangelical" theory and experience in their medieval theological and ecclesial antecedents.

The essence of the saving message for Luther was justification by faith alone through grace received freely where the gospel is proclaimed. Erasmus, Thomas More, and Johannes Eck denigrated those who accepted this view and referred to them as "evangelicals."[1] Luther himself was uncomfortable with the term "evangelical" applied to his followers precisely because he felt that the evangel was essential to all Christianity. Notwithstanding, in Europe the term "evangelical" did become virtually synonymous with Lutheran and even Reformed Protestantism. In 1648 the Peace of Westphalia recognized the Reformed as evangelicals, and in 1653 the *Corpus Evangelicorum* appeared, including Reformed as well as Lutheran creeds.

The eighteenth-century revival in Great Britain led by John Wesley (1703–91) is often referred to as the "evangelical revival." The Evangelical Alliance was formed in London in 1846 with almost 800 participants, including the German F. Tholuck, the Swiss Merle D'Aubigne, and the American S. S. Schmucker. The evangelical movement in Great Britain has its source in two main streams: the Congregationalists with their roots in the old Puritan heritage, and the Evangelicals of the Church of England shaped by a moderate Calvinism and Puritan devotionalism. Unlike the modern Puritans, the Anglican Evangelicals are not separatists. But like the Puritans, they reacted against an Enlightenment rationalism and tended to de-emphasize "High Church" liturgics. The Puritan movement was strongly influenced by the Reformed tradition and its emphasis on covenant, while at the same time it drew upon Pietist leanings toward conversion and sanctification.

Along with the Congregationalists and the Anglican evangelicals, the Baptists and Methodists contributed to the informal "Evangelical Alliance" which was taking shape in Great Britain. Methodism, with its roots in the eighteenth-century revivals of Wesley, continued to place strong emphasis on sanctification as the basis for the renewal of nominal Christianity.

In North America, the New England evangelical awakening began in 1734 as a direct result of the preaching of Jonathan Edwards, who emphasized the saving grace of God received by faith which was itself a sovereign gift of God. The dark, Calvinist view of human nature was illuminated by the sheer splendor and transcendence of divine sovereignty, attracting men and women through its powerful message of saving grace. This form of orthodox theology was especially pronounced in what came to be called the "Old School" Presbyterian theology. This "Old School" theology was ground in the Protestant Orthodoxy of the seventeenth century, holding to an Augustinian view of human nature as totally depraved, and to Calvin's view of the sovereignty of divine grace as the only basis for salvation. Central to this orthodox theology was a view of the Bible as inerrant and the source of divine revelation deductively discerned as objective truth from the factual statements of Scripture.

In the 1820s, under the influence of Nathaniel Taylor at Yale Divinity School, a "New Haven Theology" emerged which emphasized the positive side of human nature and a God more friendly than the "angry God" of Edwards's day. Taylor considered himself to be orthodox, Calvinistic, and evangelical. The Princeton theologians, however, recognized as the nineteenth-century standard-bearers of evangelical orthodoxy, held a different view of him. His positive view of human nature placed him on the side of Pelagius and not Augustine, in their opinion.

By the middle of the nineteenth century the evangelical consensus had moved away from the pessimistic view of human nature found in the tradition of Luther and Calvin, as expressed most vividly by Jonathan Edwards. This more positive theology of the human situation opened the door to a new revivalism which presumed human freedom to respond to the gospel, along with a more "common-sense" approach to theological formulation.

The popular American evangelist, Charles Finney, an ordained Presbyterian minister, broke with the "Old School Calvinism" in favor of a gospel which appealed to the free moral agency of sinners. Finney's pragmatic approach became popular among the evangelical churches which wanted results and found them in applying his methods. Evangelicals like Finney were not content to produce personal reformation alone. Concern for the human social environment was taken to be a consequence of having received the grace of salvation. While evangelism was always primary, the nature of the Christian life entailed social responsibility as well as moral perfection. The revivalism which characterized the "New School" Presbyterians carried a powerful evangelical theology of redemption, liberation, and transformation. This was abhorrent to the Princeton "Old School" theologians on the ground of deeply held theological convictions.[2]

Despite the attack on Finney and other revivalists of this period from "Old School Calvinists" such as B. B. Warfield, the grassroots surge of evangelical experience found its way into the mainstream of American life. This vital and motivating force of evangelicalism spawned a proliferation of Bible colleges, evangelistic campaigns, and swelled the Protestant churches with new and eager converts to the faith.

It was in this context that the theological concerns of evangelicals were eventually to be forged in North America. Evangelical revivalism on the one hand stood in contrast to evangelical orthodoxy on the other. Confronted by the inroads of liberalism and the breakdown of the older evangelical consensus, evangelicals struggled to defend the Bible and the basic beliefs which served as the foundation for the gospel. The orthodox theologians of the "Old Princeton" school viewed with alarm the erosion of biblical authority under the onslaught of liberalism and modernism. The efforts of Princeton Seminary professors Charles Hodge, B. B. Warfield, and others led to a series of pamphlets called *The Fundamentals: A testimony to the truth* (1910–15). The movement took on a more organized form in May of 1919 with the convening of the World Conference on Christian Fundamentals in Philadelphia. The departure of J. Grescham Machen from Princeton Theological Seminary in 1929 over the issue of theological liberalism in the faculty marked the new lines of conservative theology over and against liberalism. Henceforth, "evangelicals" could only be trusted if they adhered to the "fundamentals" of the faith. These fundamental doctrines were used as a touchstone to identify denominational leaders and theologians who were suspected of modernist tendencies.

Dispensational theology, imported from the Plymouth Brethren movement in England through the teaching of John Nelson Darby, found ready soil in the American revivalist movement, where it quickly flourished. The theology of the fundamentalist movement was largely developed out of dispensational theology, leading to a blending of revivalism, evangelicalism, and orthodoxy in a movement which lacked connection to the mainline denominational churches.[3]

In the middle part of the twentieth century, some younger American theologians whose experiential roots were sunk deep into the pietism of the revivalist movement and whose theology was shaped by the dispensationalism of the fundamentalist movement, sought to recover a new form of evangelical theology. Bypassing their experiential roots in revivalism, they looked back to the older Princeton orthodoxy in an attempt to discover their "evangelical heritage." In an effort to shed the image of fundamentalism, they called themselves "new evangelicals."[4] Carl Henry set the agenda for the new evangelical theology with his ground-breaking critique, *The Uneasy Conscience of Modern Fundamentalism* (1947).

In the face of the earlier Puritans they thought they had found a reflection more to their liking than in their pietistic contemporaries. In the stern countenance of the "Old School" Presbyterians they found the unyielding will of divine sovereignty and transcendence which seemed more congenial than the intractable and contentious spirit of their fundamentalist neighbors. In the rediscovery of the christology of the Reformers, along with their liberating and transforming doctrine of grace, they rediscovered what seemed to them the authentic "evangel," a gospel of good news which was rooted in classic orthodoxy and proclaimed with evangelistic fervor by Billy Graham. The theologian Donald Bloesch was to call this an *Evangelical Renaissance* (1973). Bernard Ramm looked in another direction and termed it *The Evangelical Heritage* (1973).

The effect of this movement was to narrow the focus of evangelical theology to the virtual exclusion of other forms of evangelical experience and theology in the North American scene. While the "new evangelical" theologians valued the existential piety of their spiritual ancestors in the revivalist movement, they looked elsewhere for their theological heritage and their place in the ecclesiastical spectrum. They looked across the great divide which fundamentalism had created between the mainline churches with their theological institutions and the independent churches and Bible colleges and determined to establish continuity with what they considered to be the roots of evangelical theology in the magisterial orthodoxy of the Reformers.

No treatment of the emergence of evangelical theology in North America can ignore the fact that the word "evangelical" refers more to a family or mosaic rather than to one single form of several varieties. Robert Johnston, along with Donald Dayton, cautions us against using the term evangelical in too narrow a sense. Dayton, whose own roots are in the Wesleyan (holiness) tradition, prefers not to use the term evangelical at all, as it has come to represent only one strand of the broader mosaic of evangelical theology and experience.[5]

Contemporary Evangelical Theology

The focus of this chapter is narrower and more selective than this broad and general use of the term "evangelical." We are using the phrase "evangelical theology" in a way that is more contemporary than historical. Rather than thinking of "evangelical" as descriptive of a specific denomination or theological tradition, we intend here to depict by the phrase more a theological ethos than a school of thought. In this way, the representative theologians presented here transcend denominational, geographical, and confessional boundaries. On the other hand, it will be shown that there is an identifiable cluster of concerns and commitments which are common to the ethos of evangelical theology as a contemporary phenomenon.

The distinctive features which set contemporary Protestant evangelical theology apart from other theologies can be expressed by three concerns. There is a concern for orthodoxy in doctrine which is rooted in the Reformation confession of *sola scriptura* and *sola gratia*; a concern for biblical authority as an infallible guide to faith and practice; and a concern for a personal experience of salvation through Jesus Christ as proclaimed in the gospel and received by faith through the power of the Holy Spirit.

Christian theology is a broad continuum where these same concerns might be found in diverse forms and differing degrees. What marks evangelical theology as unique is not an exclusive claim to orthodoxy, biblical authority, or Christian experience. Rather, what evangelical theologies hold in common is an expressed concern for these as essential elements of the gospel of Jesus Christ as a confession of faith, a standard for teaching, and a mandate for evangelization and mission to the world.

Evangelical theologies of this sort tend to be developed as movements within or between ecclesial traditions rather than out of a particular confessional or scholarly community. Thus, while representative evangelical theologians may themselves be strongly identified with a tradition or confessional statement, their students and followers form a constituency which cuts across sectarian and denominational boundaries.

Three theologians will be presented in this chapter as representative of three significant and contrasting evangelical theologies. From continental Europe, two theologians will be considered as representative of contemporary evangelical theory. G. C. Berkouwer, Professor of Dogmatic Theology at the Free University of Amsterdam, stands within the Dutch tradition of Bavinck and Kuyper. His 14 volumes in the series *Studies in Dogmatics* offer one of the most comprehensive and systematic expositions of theology from an evangelical perspective available in the English language. Helmut Thielicke, a distinguished Lutheran pastor and Professor of Theology at the University of Hamburg, has produced more than 50 books. Many of these are now available in English, including several volumes of published sermons, theological explorations of contemporary issues, a multivolume work on *Theological Ethics*, and a three-volume theological dogmatics, *The Evangelical Faith*.

In North America, the development of a distinctively evangelical theology in the twentieth century followed a period of conservative fundamentalism which was noted for its vigorous apologetic for orthodoxy in the face of a liberal theology which was perceived as capturing the major centers of theological training and denominational leadership. This "new evangelicalism" was marked by a vision for scholarship combined with evangelical zeal with the express purpose of recapturing the intellectual and ecclesial leadership for the future of the church. As a product of this movement, and as one of its most distinguished scholars, Carl F. H. Henry has made the most systematic attempt to write an evangelical theology in his six-volume work *God, Revelation and Authority*. In presenting the work of Carl Henry, discussion will also include mention of other evangelical theologians with somewhat different emphases, but each within this distinctive movement.

Each of these three theologians shares the three concerns which have been used to identify the distinctive ethos and characteristics of a contemporary evangelical theology. At the same time, it will be shown that each represents a contrasting emphasis and approach to theology from within the broader context of the evangelical movement. It should also be noted that the criteria for the selection of representative evangelical theologians are quite arbitrary. The chief criterion is publication of significant scholarly theological works which make accessible to the larger theological and ecclesial community a systematic formulation of what has been defined above as evangelical theology. Within the various evangelical movements and constituencies there are other significant theologians and leaders who represent their own movement's theology and distinctives.

Gerrit Cornelis Berkouwer (1903–1995)

G. C. Berkouwer has served as pastor and theologian in the Gereformeerde Kerken in Holland for his entire life. He received his theological education at the Free University of Amsterdam. After serving as a pastor for 18 years he was appointed to the chair of dogmatics at the Free University in 1945, where he spent the remainder of his career.

Berkouwer's theological orientation continues in the tradition established by the Dutch Calvinists Abraham Kuyper and Herman Bavinck. Kuyper (1837–1920) was the founder of the Free University in 1880 and its first professor of theology. Bavinck (1854–1921) was professor of theology at the small seminary of the Christelijke Gereformeerde Kerk in Kampen from 1883 to 1902, and then succeeded Kuyper at the Free University in 1902, serving there until his death. Kuyper's main emphasis was the common grace which made possible the organic connection between knowledge of the empirical world and knowledge of God. True knowledge of God is only possible through the Holy Spirit and regeneration, and yet, knowledge of God leads to a knowledge of the world and human society as an integrated whole. It is Bavinck, however, to whom Berkouwer refers most often in his own dogmatic studies, though he never studied under him or met him personally. Bavinck rejected both idealism and empiricism, and held that there is a correspondence between an object and its representation in the experiencing subject. God's creative wisdom, the logos, has been implanted in the human mind as the divine image. All knowledge is ultimately revealed knowledge, and not ascertainable through direct empirical observation or through independent mental activity. Thus, for Bavinck, all knowledge rests on faith.

When Berkouwer began his theological studies, the same issues as preoccupied Kuyper and Bavinck prompted his attention. Modernistic theology, influenced not only by Jacob Arminius but by Descartes, who lived in Holland for 20 years (1629–49), continued to set the agenda with regard to the relation of theology to science and culture. Under the Cartesian influence, the Reformation in Holland began to stress more the rational autonomy of the human mind rather than the response of the believer. Reformed theology appeared to capitulate the truth of divine revelation to the critical and rational human mind. Pietists retreated to the safe world of religious experience and religious values with largely a negative response to the effect of the Enlightenment. Berkouwer speaks approvingly of Bavinck's response: "Bavinck became a model of how theology could be done with commitment to the truth combined with openness to problems, and carefulness in judgments against others."[6] In the end, however, Berkouwer did not follow Kuyper and Bavinck in two ways. Kuyper's "organic relationship" between human understanding and the physical world, and Bavinck's "Logos theory" both pointed toward the fact that God must himself provide the necessary connection between the human mind and natural knowledge as well as the human mind and religious knowledge. Berkouwer did not employ this analogy and reacted strongly against the parallel between natural faith and Christian faith. Secondly, Kuyper and Bavinck both stressed the corporate aspect of the witness of the Holy Spirit. In his book *Holy Scripture* Berkouwer did not pick up this emphasis. He laid great stress on the relation of the Spirit to the words of Scripture, but not on the witness of the Spirit to the corporate church body. On the matter of the nature of biblical authority, however, Berkouwer clearly follows the pathway of Kuyper and Bavinck in stressing the saving purpose of Scripture. The authority of Scripture is affirmed by the inward testimony of the Holy Spirit rather than by the principle of external evidence. Thus, Berkouwer is open to the full humanity of Scripture and accommodation to its historical context. Textual problems do not present a contradiction to the truth of the Word of God as received through the witness of the Spirit in the text itself.

Berkouwer began his theological career with the same concern which was to remain with him throughout his life: the relationship between faith and revelation. The liberal theologians, concluded Berkouwer, had moved toward the subjective side of this issue, with the experiencing human subject the criterion for divine revelation. Orthodox theology, on the other hand, he saw as moving toward the objectivity of revelation as an abstract construct of doctrinal formulations or, as in the case of Barth, a concept of divine revelation as "divine objectivity" and "totally other" than human experience. It is the very nature of divine revelation as Word of God spoken and heard in Holy Scripture, argued Berkouwer, which provides true correlation, or correlation, between faith and knowledge, between faith-subject and revelation-object.

Berkouwer carried through this theme of correlation in the titles of his first three volumes in his *Studies in Dogmatics: Faith and Justification; Faith and Sanctification;* and *Faith and Perseverance.* Faith has no value in and of itself. The value of faith comes entirely from its object, and it is only in correlation with its object – salvation in Jesus Christ – that faith has reality. Faith is not only response to the Word of God which is revealed to us through Holy Scripture, but faith has epistemological significance in that it is only through faith that true knowledge of God and his revelation comes to us.

Berkouwer acknowledged the ambiguity of this concept of "correlation." The concept is open to abuse, he admits, where the subjective axis of faith could be construed as determinative at the expense of the sovereignty of divine grace. On the other hand, he will not surrender the decisive character of personal faith in the act of correlation by which the objective knowledge of God is apprehended. He puts it this way:

> Faith in the correlation bespeaks the working of the Holy Spirit directing man to God's grace . . . it is faith, true faith, which honors the sovereignty of grace. And this is what the reformers and the confessions meant by speaking of faith as an instrument, as well as by the emptiness, the vacuity, the passivity of faith. Such concepts in no way deny the activity of faith, its grasp of its object, or its working itself out in love. Faith is still a human act.[7]

The human act of faith is never merely a human act, however; it is always a gift of God, a result of the working of the Holy Spirit.

Three components of Berkouwer's theology demonstrate his standing as an evangelical theologian. First there is his commitment to the absolute authority of Scripture as the source of divine revelation which faith grasps in a knowing way. The Bible serves as the "boundary" which qualifies both existential faith and rational knowledge. Second, there is a salvific content of Scripture which summons one to faith and personal involvement. Without this correlation between faith and revelation, revelation would either have a purely external authority subject to critical reason, or a purely inward authority subject to human experience alone. Third, the Word of God is decisive as a criterion by which all of humanity is to be seen as under condemnation due to sin and through which the gospel of salvation in Christ is offered to all. Thus, the mission of the church is bound up in its own hearing of the gospel, for the salvation of Christ is not for the sake of the church but for the world.

Through the correlation of faith and revelation, with Scripture as the boundary, Berkouwer attempted to avoid the speculations which plagued scholastic theology. Speculation, argued Berkouwer, attempts to pierce through into the shades of eternity. This is why true faith is content to confess God's revealed truth as the content of his eternal nature and purpose. His concern was for a theology which spoke directly to the need for faith as a personal experience which had practical results in human lives. "For my way of thinking," he once wrote, "theology never seeks a knowledge of the things of faith that transcends the faith of the common people. Theology never seeks to unravel mysteries."[8] Theology must serve revelation and faith, not theology itself as an independent discipline of study. Berkouwer summons the church to listen to the Word of God, to subject its creeds and confessions to the normative criterion of Scripture, and to be the church of the living Word in its worship and its mission to the world.

Helmut Thielicke (1908–1986)

Helmut Thielicke studied philosophy and theology at Greifswald, Marburg, Erlangen, and Bonn. Upon ordination, he spent the first years of his ministry as a pastor and theological teacher in Württemberg. As a Lutheran pastor in Nazi Germany during the church struggle and resistance movement against Hitler, Thielicke was one of the few men in the church who clearly saw the fateful consequences of the merging of romantic nationalism with a theology of the glory of the human spirit under the guise of a "German Christian Theology." In the theological and political chaos of postwar Germany, Thielicke stood with one foot in the pulpit and one in the classroom, and sought to reconstruct the theological foundations for faith, hope, and ethics, grounded in the free and yet historically relevant Word of God. Following a postwar faculty appointment at the University of Tübingen in systematic theology, in 1954 he assumed the chair of systematic theology at Hamburg, where he served until his retirement in 1974. There he began to reconstruct an evangelical theology which was both a return to the essentials of Reformation theology based on "Christ alone," as well as a way forward into the future based on the "Spirit with us." In his sermons, many given during the terrible days of the collapse of Germany, he proclaimed a message of God's creative and liberating Word. So powerful were these in setting forth a theology of God's creative judgment and grace that several volumes were translated into English as some of the first exposure of Thielicke's theology outside of Germany.

Thielicke firmly believed that proclamation must precede theology. The gospel is the answer to the crises of life as well as the critique of human attempts toward self-justification. The final confidence for the theologian as well as for the believer is the self-evident truth of the message of Christ as the Holy Spirit speaks and applies it to the hearer. The ethical task for the theologian begins with the light of the gospel and the primary relationship with God to which the problems of life ultimately must answer. Ethics, therefore, forms the primary link between proclamation and theology proper.

His *Theologische Ethik* (1958–64) builds upon a theological foundation carefully laid in the primacy of Jesus Christ over all areas of Christian thought and life. A monumental four-volume work in German, it has been translated into English in the form of three volumes, *Theological Ethics* (1966). This work stands as a landmark in theological ethics from a self-conscious evangelical commitment to the christological and spiritual priority of God in human affairs as the only way out of the nihilism and fatalism which pervades contemporary society. As with Karl Barth, who clearly has exercised some influence on Thielicke, the foundation for his ethics is a trinitarian structure where the being of God "for us" is identical with the being of God in and of himself. Because he views the trinitarian being of God as personal, relational, and historically relevant, his ethics assume that same orientation. The human person, as a psychological, social, and historical self, is an authentic locus of personal responsibility whose justification in Christ provides the basis for responsible life in the world for and with others.

Publishing his first volume of dogmatic theology in 1968 (*Der evangelische Glaube*, translated into English as *The Evangelical Faith*, three volumes, 1974–7), Thielicke began with a radical critique of the theological task itself. Using the Cartesian principle of the priority of the human subject, he divided contemporary theological approaches into two categories. Theology A he termed "Cartesian theology." Under this category he placed all theologies which took in some form the priority of the human person as a criterion to which the Word of God must be "appropriated." He linked in this way not only the older liberal theology of Schleiermacher and Ritschl with the primacy of self-consciousness as the criterion for revelation, but the more recent existential theology of Rudolf Bultmann, with the primacy of the existing self as criterion. In the category of Cartesian theology, to the consternation of many, he placed the conservative orthodox theologian for whom the objective truth of revelation was determined by the criterion of human rationality. All such approaches to theology, argued Thielicke, are Cartesian in that they seek to appropriate the Word of God to the primacy of the human subject, whether through an intuitive principle, an ethical principle, an existential principle, or a rational principle.

Theology B, countered Thielicke, is a theology which is directed by the Holy Spirit through which the human subject is appropriated to the Word of God. This is evangelical theology, for it preserves the sovereignty and freedom of God in creating faith as response, both experientially and rationally. In taking this approach, Thielicke is clearly following in the Lutheran tradition of "justification by faith alone." In this case, however, this does not become a "principle" or distinctive by which a dialectic is maintained between law and gospel as a soteriological structure. Rather, in Thielicke's approach, justification by faith is a christological structure of reality by which the structures of human thought and action are radically judged as inevitably idolatrous and nihilistic and in need of redemption through grace. For Thielicke, one cannot separate justification and sanctification nor theology and ethics. The Word of God reaches into every nook and cranny of human life and exposes the stubborn and perverse spirit of resistance to God, often concealed in a system of religious, political, and ethical structures viewed as essentially good and valuable in and of themselves.

God's incarnational work is viewed as the solution to the separation between God and the world, with the continuing ministry of the Holy Spirit the source of fellowship with God as well as the criterion for a theological interpretation of moral, social, and political structures of human life. The incarnation means solidarity between God and humanity. The ministry of the Holy Spirit means the use of human instruments and encounters with the problems, struggles, and aspirations of human life.

Unlike Barth, Thielicke does not eschew apologetics, but rather seeks to address the contemporary person in his or her own cultural and existential situation with the ethically relevant message of the gospel. While Thielicke takes with full seriousness the contemporary situation, he none the less brings it radically under the judgment and then the transforming grace of God. His theology is evangelical in the sense that he sees in the Bible God's authentic Word, focusing his attention on *the* Word incarnate, Jesus Christ, in whom God makes our existence his, and in whom he is crucified and raised for our salvation. The cruciality of Christ for faith is not only a theme for his sermons, but is the evangelical foundation of his ethics and theology.

Carl F. H. Henry (1913–   )

In 1978 the American theologian Carl Henry was named by *Time* magazine as evangelicalism's "leading theologian." Henry, the son of a Roman Catholic mother and a Lutheran father, was baptized and confirmed in the Episcopal Church. At an early age he began a career in journalism, but at the age of 20 experienced a radical conversion experience through the witness of a friend. Enrolling in Wheaton College, a Christian liberal arts college in Illinois, he completed his college work in 1938 and promptly enrolled in Northern Baptist Seminary in Chicago, where he graduated and was subsequently ordained as a Baptist minister. After some parish experience, he completed a PhD at Boston University in 1949, having already accepted in 1947 an appointment to the faculty of the newly founded Fuller Theological Seminary in Pasadena, California.

The academic setting for Henry whetted his appetite for scholarly work, and with his strong journalistic skills, he completed nine books during his career of nine years at Fuller Seminary. In 1956 he became the first editor of the newly created evangelical fortnightly journal, *Christianity Today*, where he served until 1968. Through his leadership, the journal, devoted to scholarly articulation of evangelical theology, grew to a circulation of more than 160,000. Leaving the journal after 12 years of service, he became "professor at large" at Eastern Baptist Theological Seminary, and began a career of teaching, writing, and speaking on some of the United States' most prestigious campuses and in countries on every continent. He has written 27 books (some translated into Korean, Norwegian, German, and Spanish), and has contributed numerous articles to a variety of publications. His most ambitious project in systematic theology was the publication of a six-volume work titled *God, Revelation, and Authority* (1976–83). One of his most recent books is the story of his own life, *Confessions of a Theologian: An autobiography* (1986).

The theological career of Carl Henry must be placed within the context of the collision between theological fundamentalism and liberalism during the early part of this century, and particularly in its second quarter.

Through his gifts of scholarship, an insightful theological mind, and his ability to articulate the new agenda for these evangelical leaders, Henry soon rose to the forefront of the movement. Positively, Henry and the "new evangelicals" sought to affirm traditional evangelical theology (Protestant orthodoxy linked with American revivalism) and negatively to reject fundamentalism with its provincial, separatist, and often obscurantist approach to biblical and theological scholarship. Years later, looking back on the origins of this movement, Henry would write:

> What distressed the growing evangelical mainstream about the fundamentalist far right were its personal legalisms, a suspicion of advanced education, disdain for biblical criticism per se, polemical orientation of theological discussion, judgmental attitudes toward those in ecumenically related denominations, and an uncritical political conservatism often defined as "Christian anti communism" and "Christian capitalism" that, while politicizing the gospel on the right, deplored politicizing it on the left.[9]

In a way that was typical of Henry's theological insight and critical analysis, his book published in 1947, *The Uneasy Conscience of Modern Fundamentalism*, set the agenda for the new evangelical theology. Here he called for a renewed concern for social issues, serious interaction with science and culture, and above all, a renewed commitment to biblical theism as the basis for an apologetic which focused on the theological essentials on which evangelicals could unite, not on secondary issues on which they tended to divide.

The distinctive motif of Carl Henry's approach to evangelical theology is clearly seen in what he calls "evangelical theism."

> The strength of evangelical theism lies in its offer of religious realities that human unregeneracy desperately needs and cannot otherwise provide. In a time of spiritual

rootlessness Christianity proclaims God the self-revealed heavenly Redeemer. In a time of intellectual skepticism, it adduces fixed truths about God's holy purpose for man and the world. In a time of ethical permissiveness, it offers moral absolutes and specific divine imperatives. In a time of frightful fear of the future, it presents a sure and final hope. In a time when daily life has turned bitter and sour for multitudes of humans, it offers life-transforming dynamic.[10]

This concept of biblical or evangelical theism constitutes the formative basis for Henry's most substantial work, *God, Revelation, and Authority.* Far from being a comprehensive systematic theology, with equal treatment of the basic loci of theology, this work is based on two major theological themes – the nature of revelation as truth, and the nature of God as the foundation for theological reflection upon creation, human life, and ethics. With his strong commitment to philosophical and analytical method, Henry is basically an apologist, not a biblical scholar. His analysis of the contemporary situation is that the "modern mind" has succumbed to relativism with a loss of absolutes in moral values and of certainty with regard to truth. Christian faith must be rationally defensible in terms of the criteria by which all truth is verified. Otherwise, Henry argues, claims for faith fall back on the slippery slope of existential and subjective experience, with no basis for certainty. Strongly dependent upon his chief intellectual mentor, Gordon Clark, philosopher and theologian, Henry sees the theological task as one of defining and defending faith in terms of truth rather than in personal relationship to God. Influenced also by Edgar Brightman, a personalist philosopher with whom he did doctoral studies at Boston University, Henry argues that faith has its own ontology which is grounded in the objective reality of personal being open to but also critically interacting with nonrevelational world views.

Henry is basically a presuppositionalist with regard to the foundations of theology. Philosophically, his presupposition is the Aristotelian principle of the law of noncontradiction. Both Christians and non-Christians use logic as a test for truth. Theologically, his presupposition is the principle of biblical theism. "From a certain vantage point, the concept of God is determinative for all other concepts; it is the Archimedean lever with which one can fashion an entire world view."[11] The basis for biblical theism is the assumption that God has revealed the truths which determine all rational knowledge and make it certain. "Divine revelation is the source of all truth, the truth of Christianity included; reason is the instrument for recognizing it; Scripture is its verifying principle; logical consistency is a negative test for truth and coherence a subordinate test. The task of Christian theology is to exhibit the content of biblical revelation as an orderly whole."[12]

The structure of Henry's six-volume work is thus organized around two fundamental principles. First, revelation is the ground and authority for faith, and second, the existence and being of God are the answer to the contemporary concern for stability and certainty as the ground for faith and hope. Volume I consists of preliminary considerations, setting forth the basic assumptions for true knowledge of God. Volumes II, III, and IV deal broadly with the subject of revelation and religious epistemology under the heading, *God Who Speaks and Shows.* Volumes V and VI set forth a Christian doctrine of God under the heading, *God Who Stands and*

Stays. In each of the volumes, Henry deals with a broad range of contemporary theologians and issues, critically examining each by the epistemological and theological criteria which he has established.

For Henry, the question of authority is the key issue for evangelical theology. Authority must be grounded in absolute certainty. The means of knowing this certainty must be logically verifiable and rationally accessible to every person, otherwise, the commitment of faith which constitutes a saving relation to God will be liable to doubt and question. Divine revelation is given to us in Holy Scripture in propositional form. This means that the truth which grounds Christian belief in certainty must be univocally related to the human mind, not merely analogical or certainly not equivocal. The finite and the infinite are comprehended in one and the same logicality, Henry has stated.[13]

God is the proper subject of a Christian theology, Henry argues, and from this axis flow all discussions of soteriology and eschatology, as well as social ethics. Christ is the means by which God has provided for salvation through his atonement. The Holy Spirit is the means by which God continues to regenerate and renew individuals on the basis of the revelation given in the Bible and communicated to us in propositions which can stand the test for truth. Human logic and reason have been created as a basis for knowing and testing the truth of divine revelation. Henry's theology is evangelical not only in that it attempts to restate the tenets of orthodoxy as an apologetic, but in that it seeks the conversion of the individual through a personal relationship with Jesus Christ. At the heart of his theology is the passion of his own conversion experience, and the aim of his theology is to authenticate Christian conversion and the Christian life as a viable and intellectually credible alternative to modern secularism and humanism with its inevitable existential despair.

Debate

The differences between the three evangelical theologians presented above are quite obvious, despite their common commitment to the tenets of Protestant orthodoxy, their appeal to biblical authority as a source of divine revelation, and their concern for a personal experience of salvation through Jesus Christ. Berkouwer would sharply disagree with Henry's insistence that human reason can grasp and even validate divine revelation apart from the work of the Holy Spirit and the presence of faith. Thielicke has already, in principle, placed Henry's "rational theism" in the category of Cartesian theology with its claim that the human mind is on the same continuum as the Logos of God. For his part, Henry is suspicious of the "correlation" between revelation and faith which Berkouwer espouses, fearing that it undermines the objective reality of revelation itself as a cognitive construct. Thielicke as well comes under the critical eye of Henry as compromising the authority of Scripture in favor of a "spiritual hermeneutic" which shifts the criterion for truth from revelation to faith itself.

At the same time, Bernard Ramm, perhaps the most significant American evangelical theologian alongside Henry, and a colleague in the development of the new evangelical front in the United States, faults Henry for failing to provide a paradigm of evangelical theology which does not "gloss over" the critical perspectives gained through the Enlightenment. He rates Berkouwer and Thielicke as offering better options for evangelical theology in its interaction with the Enlightenment.[14]

Some conservative Lutheran theologians, however, wonder if Thielicke has not "abandoned the orthodox theology of the ancient church as well as of the Reformation." They are concerned that he has taken a psychological approach to christology, and also to his hermeneutic which, they argue, is closer to Schleiermacher than to Luther. In the end, these critics say, his personalistic approach abandons the objective reality of God as an object of faith, and makes faith itself more of a feeling than a fact.[15] From this perspective, some would not call Thielicke an evangelical theologian. It is true that Thielicke regards the classic creedal formulations (such as Chalcedon) as too abstract and impersonal to "capture" the person of Christ himself. Yet, it is clearly the reality and the person of Christ of whom these formulations speak that Thielicke holds to be the criterion of faith. What makes faith evangelical, says Thielicke, is not faith as an object of reason, but Christ as the Lord of reason, bringing it into captivity to his own true order of reality.

The lines of the debate within evangelical theology, as might be expected, are more sharply drawn between American evangelical theologians. We have already mentioned Bernard Ramm as one who has now called for a new paradigm for evangelical theology, and suggests that the theological approach of Karl Barth, or even Berkouwer or Thielicke, will serve better than that of Carl Henry. Harold Lindsell, a former colleague of Carl Henry at Fuller Seminary, and the editor of the journal *Christianity Today* following Carl Henry, is charged by Ramm with providing a polemical rallying point for fundamentalists and evangelicals with his book on biblical inerrancy (*The Battle for the Bible*, 1976).[16] Ramm's own view is that evangelical theology must be grounded on a solid biblical theology rather than biblical theism. He is concerned that evangelical theology, if it follows the lead of Carl Henry, will fail precisely at the point where he wishes it to make its mark – that is, its rational system of apologetics will appeal only to those who accept the philosophical epistemology on which it is built. If this is true, as many critics of Henry feel it is, then orthodox doctrine rather than a vital and compelling experience of God himself will become the bastion of evangelical theology's defense, and a further retreat from creative encounter with contemporary society.

Donald Bloesch, who has himself made a significant contribution to the literature of contemporary evangelical theology, echoes these concerns. "The method of Gordon Clark and Carl Henry is deductive, deriving conclusions from given rational principles," writes Bloesch. Revelation remains mysterious even in its openness to us through the living Word of God. "We *intend* the truth in our theological statements, but we do not *possess* the truth, since reason is always the servant and never the master or determiner of revelation."[17]

To the credit of Carl Henry, in surveying the evangelical scene from the perspective of more than 40 years of involvement as one of its key leaders, he pleads for a new spirit of openness and unity among evangelical theologians: "Just when the world-press publicly conceded 'the year of the evangelical'," Henry wrote, the evangelical dialogue became focused on "epistemological differences that depicted evangelicals as openly at odds with each other."

An opportunity existed of rallying the whole evangelical enterprise to socio-cultural engagement in which even a crippled soldier might somehow serve the cause of faith. Instead, exulting in their evident public gains, evangelicals indulged in the luxury of internal conflict and channeled theological energies into the controversy over biblical inerrancy... While scriptural authority must be part of any authentic evangelical renewal, evangelicals will affirm it to their own reproof apart from the cry, "Let my heart be broken" and filled with the truth and grace of God.[18]

Achievement and Agenda

The achievements of evangelical theology are modest when viewed from the perspective of academic theology. The work of Berkouwer will certainly survive and be read by future generations of students as part of the Dutch Neo-Calvinist tradition begun so ably by Kuyper and Bavinck. Despite a certain provincialism in Berkouwer's interaction with other theologians and movements, his work has provided and will continue to provide a substantial resource for theological students and pastors who especially appreciate the distinctives of the Reformed tradition. Thielicke will perhaps be read more for his profound contribution to ethics than for his systematic theology. His wide-ranging and penetrating commentary on contemporary issues provides a refreshing challenge to be contemporary in both theological preaching and practical theology. Henry's work will more than likely be viewed as a mandatory research assignment for anyone wishing to evaluate the finest attempt by twentieth-century evangelicalism to argue its case before the bar of modern reason. It will be less likely to be found on the pastor's study shelf and even less satisfactory as a programmatic exercise on which future evangelical theologians can build.

From the perspective of the evangelical movement as a whole, however, evangelical theology has made significant achievements. Not least of these has been its success in breaking free from the theological tragedy of fundamentalism without capitulating to the theological fads of postliberal radicalism. The heavy investment, often at great cost, personally and financially, in establishing first-rate evangelical schools, is already beginning to pay rich dividends. The major mainline Protestant denominations are beginning to experience spiritual and theological reinvigoration through a flood of pastors and leaders trained under the influence of these evangelical faculties. Theologians with evangelical commitments as defined above are finding their way into university faculties and denominational schools, where they are creating a new dialogue between the Scripture as a relevant and revealed Word of God and the contemporary issues and needs of modern society.

If these contributions are to be conserved and expanded, however, issues currently on the agenda of evangelical theology need to be addressed and constructively resolved. The issue of biblical authority and the nature of biblical revelation, particularly with regard to the relation of the text of Scripture to the Word of God, cannot be avoided. There yet remain to be established the grounds for a theological consensus among evangelical theologians on this vital issue.

Evangelical theology has not yet answered effectively the challenge from the larger theological community, not to mention society at large, that it is more concerned for the spiritual and intellectual aspects of salvation than for the social and physical needs of people. With evangelization of the world and the intended conversion of every person to Jesus Christ as a fundamental imperative, evangelical theology has yet to articulate a theology of mission and evangelism which does not tend to be culturally and ethnically imperialistic. The "particularism" of Jesus Christ as the driving force for evangelical mission to the world has not yet dealt with the theological and religious pluralisms which confront the contemporary mission task of the church. In the face of rising challenges to this christological particularism inherent in the theological paradigm of evangelicalism, theologians have yet to restate the case for conversion to Christ in compelling and convincing terms.

While evangelical theologians continue to make significant contributions in the area of biblical studies, little has been produced by way of standard theological texts. One exception is Donald Bloesch, who has published the first two volumes of a projected seven-volume work in systematic theology.[19] With the emergence of the highly pragmatic strategies in church growth theory, the rapidly expanding phenomenon of "seeker sensitive" mega churches, and the growing emphasis on lay-oriented ministry, once again the grassroots renewal of evangelical experience has left its theologians behind. Deeply entrenched in the fortress of accredited academic faculties, evangelical theologians are busy rewriting the theology of their ancestors rather than, like the apostle Paul, revisioning a theology rooted out of the praxis of the Holy Spirit.[20]

Where liberation is the code word as well as the creative force behind much of the most vigorous and exciting theology coming out of the "two-thirds world," evangelical theology has tended to retreat from a praxis-oriented theology into a theory-laden defense of orthodoxy. Contextualization is largely an unknown and basically untried theological method for evangelical theologians. The viability of evangelical theology rests with its willingness to venture into the future, rather than to reside in the present and to take comfort from the past. In a generation, there will be new names in the books written about evangelical theologians. That is as it should be, for evangelical theology is a living and creative continuum, leaving behind its theologians, with gratitude and respect.

Notes

1 See Erasmus, *Epistola contra quosdom, qui se falso iactant Evangelicos*, published in 1529. Cited in *The Evangelicals: What they believe, who they are, where they are changing*, ed. David F. Wells and John D. Woodbridge (Nashville, TN, 1975).

2 For a discussion of Taylor's and Finney's influence on American evangelicalism, see Douglas W. Frank, *Less Than Conquerors: How Evangelicals entered the twentieth century* (Grand Rapids, MI, 1986); and Donald W. Dayton, *Discovering an Evangelical Heritage* (New York, 1976).

3 For additional reading on this period see Ernest Sandeen, *The Roots of Fundamentalism: British and American Millenarianism: 1800–1930* (Chicago, 1970); George Marsden, *Fundamentalism and American Culture: The shaping of twentieth-century evangelicalism: 1870–1925* (New York and Oxford, 1980); George Marsden, *Reforming Fundamentalism: Fuller Seminary and the new evangelicalism* (Grand Rapids, MI, 1987).

4 Among these young scholars were such persons as Carl F. H. Henry, George E. Ladd,

Kenneth Kantzer, Merrill Tenney, Bernard Ramm, Edward John Carnell, and Harold John Okenga, who, in 1957, first coined the phrase, "new evangelicals."

5 Donald W. Dayton and Robert K. Johnston (eds), *The Variety of American Evangelicalism* (Knoxville, TN, 1991). See also George Marsden, "The Evangelical Denomination," in *Evangelicalism and Modern America*, ed. George Marsden (Grand Rapids, MI, 1984). For other attempts to define evangelicalism as a contemporary phenomenon see: Alister McGrath, *Evangelicalism and the Future of Christianity* (Downers Grove, IL, 1995); Mark Noll, David Bebbington, and George Rawlyk (eds), *Evangelicalism: Comparative studies of popular protestantism in North America, the British Isles, and beyond, 1700–1900* (Oxford, 1994); George Rawlyk and Mark Noll (eds), *Amazing Grace: Evangelicalism in Australia, Britain, Canada and the United States* (Grand Rapids, MI, 1994); Walter A. Elwell (ed.), *Handbook of Evangelical Theologians* (Grand Rapids, MI, 1994); James Davison Hunter, *American Evangelicalism* (New Brunswick, NJ, 1983); George Marsden, *Fundamentalism and American Culture: The shaping of twentieth-century evangelicalism, 1870–1925* (New York and Oxford, 1980); John D. Woodbridge, Mark A. Noll, and Nathan O. Hatch (eds), *The Gospel in America: Themes in the story of America's evangelicals* (Grand Rapids, MI, 1979); Robert E. Nether, *Common Roots: A call to Evangelical maturity* (Grand Rapids, MI, 1978); Kenneth S. Kantzer (ed.), *Evangelical Roots* (New York, 1978); David F. Wells and John D. Woodbridge (eds), *The Evangelicals: What they believe, who they are, where they are changing* (New York and Nashville, TN, 1975); Richard Quebedeaux, *The Young Evangelicals* (New York and London, 1974); Bernard L. Ramm, *The Evangelical Heritage* (Waco, TX, 1973); Donald G. Bloesch, *The Evangelical Renaissance* (Grand Rapids, MI, 1973); Ronald H. Nash, *The New Evangelicalism* (Grand Rapids, MI, 1963).

6 G. C. Berkouwer, *A Half Century of Theology*, p. 11.

7 G. C. Berkouwer, *Faith and Justification* (Grand Rapids, MI, 1954), p. 178.

8 G. C. Berkouwer, "Review of Current Religious Thought," in *Christianity Today*, December 22, 1961, p. 39.

9 Carl F. H. Henry, *Evangelicals in Search of Identity*, pp. 30–1.

10 Carl Henry, *Confessions of a Theologian*, p. 389.

11 Carl Henry, *Remaking the Modern Mind* (Grand Rapids, MI, 1946), pp. 232, 171.

12 Carl Henry, *God, Revelation and Authority*, vol. I, p. 215.

13 Ibid., vol. III, pp. 221–2.

14 Bernard Ramm, *After Fundamentalism: The future of Evangelical theology* (San Francisco, 1983), pp. 26–7. Other books by Ramm include: *Offense to Reason: A theology of sin* (San Francisco, 1985); *An Evangelical Christology: Ecumenic and historic* (Nashville, TN, 1985); *The Evangelical Heritage* (Waco, TX, 1973).

15 As an example of such criticism, see Richard Klann, "Helmut Thielicke appraised: a review essay," in *Concordia Journal*, 6 (July 1980), pp. 155–63.

16 Ramm, *After Fundamentalism*, p. 45.

17 Donald Bloesch, *Essentials of Evangelical Theology*, vol. II (San Francisco, 1979), p. 268. In addition to his two-volume *Essentials of Evangelical Theology*, other publications by Bloesch include *Theology of Word and Spirit* (Downers Grove, IL, 1992); *Holy Scripture, Revelation and Interpretation* (Downers Grove, 1994); *Freedom for Obedience: Evangelical ethics for contemporary times* (San Francisco, 1987); *The Future of Evangelical Christianity: A call for unity amid diversity* (Garden City, NY, 1983).

18 Carl Henry, *Confessions of a Theologian*, p. 389.

19 *Theology of Word and Spirit* (Downers Grove, 1992); *Holy Scripture, Revelation and Interpretation* (Downers Grove, IL, 1994);

20 See, "Memo to Theological Educators," in *Ministry on the Fireline: A practical theology for an empowered church*, Ray S. Anderson (Downers Grove, IL, 1993), pp. 197–209.

Bibliography

Primary

Berkouwer, G. C., *Studies in Dogmatics*, 14 vols (Grand Rapids, MI, 1952–76).
—— *Modern Uncertainty and Christian Faith* (Grand Rapids, MI, 1953).
—— "Review of current religious thought," in *Christianity Today* (December 22, 1961).
—— *The Triumph of Grace in the Theology of Karl Barth* (Grand Rapids, MI, 1965).
—— *A Half Century of Theology* (Grand Rapids, MI, 1977).
Henry, Carl F. H., *The Uneasy Conscience of Modern Fundamentalism* (Grand Rapids, MI, 1947).
—— *Giving a Reason for Our Hope* (Boston, 1949).
—— *Christian Personal Ethics* (Grand Rapids, MI, 1957).
—— *Evangelicals at the Brink of Crisis: Significance of the World Congress on Evangelism* (Waco, TX, 1967).
—— *Evangelicals in Search of Identity* (Waco, TX, 1976).
—— *God, Revelation and Authority*, 6 vols (Waco, TX, 1976–83).
—— *The Christian Mindset in a Secular Society: Promoting evangelical renewal and national righteousness* (Portland, OR, 1984).
—— *Confessions of a Theologian: An autobiography* (Waco, TX, 1986).
—— *God of This Age or . . . God* (Nashville, TN, 1994).
Thielicke, Helmut, *Nihilism: Its origin and nature, with a Christian answer* (New York, 1961).
—— *The Freedom of the Christian Man: A Christian confrontation with the secular gods* (New York, 1963).
—— *Theological Ethics*, 3 vols (an abridgement and translation of *Theologische Ethik*), ed. William H. Lazareth (Philadelphia, 1966).
—— *The Evangelical Faith*, 3 vols (Grand Rapids, MI, 1974–7).
—— *Living with Death* (Grand Rapids, MI, 1983).
—— *Being Human – Becoming Human: An essay in Christian anthropology* (Garden City, NY, 1984).

Secondary

Anderson, Ray S., "Memo to Theological Educators," in *Ministry on the Fireline: A practical theology for an empowered church* (Downers Grove, IL, 1993).
Baker, Alvin, *Berkouwer's Doctrine of Election* (Phillipsburg, NJ, 1964).
Bloesch, Donald G., *The Evangelical Renaissance* (Grand Rapids, MI, 1973).
—— *Essentials of Evangelical Theology*. Vol. II (San Francisco, 1979).
—— *The Future of Evangelical Christianity: A call for unity amid diversity* (Garden City, NY, 1983).
—— *Freedom for Obedience: Evangelical ethics for contemporary times* (San Francisco, 1987).
—— *Theology of Word and Spirit* (Downers Grove, IL, 1992).
—— *Holy Scripture, Revelation and Interpretation* (Downers Grove, IL, 1994).
Bromiley, Geoffrey, "Helmut Thielicke," in *A Handbook of Christian Theologians*, enlarged edn, ed. Dean G. Peerman and Martin E. Marty (Nashville, TN, 1984).
Dayton, Donald W., *Discovering an Evangelical Heritage* (New York, 1976).
Dayton, Donald W. and Johnston, Robert K. (eds), *The Variety of American Evangelicalism* (Knoxville, TN, 1991).
De Moore, J. C., *Towards a Biblically Theological Method: A structural analysis and a further elaboration of Dr C. G. Berkouwer's hermeneutic-dogmatic method* (Kampen, 1980).
Elwell, Walter A. (ed.), *Handbook of Evangelical Theologians* (Grand Rapids, MI, 1994).
Fackre, Gabriel, "Carl F. H. Henry," in *A Handbook of Christian Theologians*, enlarged edn, ed. Dean G. Peerman and Martin E. Marty (Nashville, TN, 1984).
Frank, Douglas W., *Less Than Conquerors: How evangelicals entered the twentieth century* (Grand Rapids, MI, 1986).
Higginson, Richard, "Thielicke: preacher and theologian," in *Churchman*, 90 (July/September 1976), pp. 178–92.
Hunter, James Davison, *American Evangelicalism* (New Brunswick, NJ, 1983).

Kantzer, Kenneth S. (ed.), *Evangelical Roots* (New York, 1978).

Klann, Richard, "Helmut Thielicke appraised – a review essay," in *Concordia Journal*, 6 (July 1980), pp. 155–63.

McGrath, Alister, *Evangelicalism and the Future of Christianity* (Downers Grove, IL, 1995).

Marsden, George, *Fundamentalism and American Culture: The shaping of twentieth century evangelicals: 1870–1925* (New York and Oxford, 1980).

—— "The Evangelical Denomination," in *Evangelicalism and Modern America*, ed. George Marsden (Grand Rapids, MI, 1984).

—— *Reforming Fundamentalism: Fuller Seminary and the New Evangelicalism* (Grand Rapids, MI, 1987).

Nash, Ronald, *The New Evangelicalism* (Grand Rapids, MI, 1963).

Noll, Mark et al., *Evangelicalism: Comparative studies of popular Protestantism in North America, the British Isles, and beyond, 1700–1900* (Oxford, 1994).

Patterson, Bob E., *Makers of the Modern Theological Mind – Carl F. H. Henry* (Waco, TX, 1983).

Quebedeaux, Richard, *The Young Evangelicals* (New York and London, 1974).

Ramm, Bernard L., *The Evangelical Heritage* (Waco, TX, 1973).

—— *After Fundamentalism: The future of evangelical theology* (San Francisco, 1983).

—— *Offense to Reason: A theology of sin* (San Francisco, 1985).

—— *An Evangelical Christology: Ecumenic and historic* (Nashville, TN, 1985).

Rawlyk, George and Noll, Mark (eds), *Amazing Grace: Evangelicalism in Australia, Britain, Canada, and the United States* (Grand Rapids, MI, 1994).

Rogers, Jack B., "A third alternative: scripture, tradition and interpretation in the theology of G. C. Berkouwer," in Ward Gasque and William LaSor (eds), *Scripture, Tradition and Interpretation* (Grand Rapids, MI, 1978), pp. 70–91.

Sandeen, Ernest, *The Roots of Fundamentalism: British and American millenarianism: 1800–1930* (Chicago, 1970).

Smedes, Lewis B., "G. C. Berkouwer," in *Creative Minds in Contemporary Theology*, 2nd edn, ed. Philip Edgecumbe Hughes (Grand Rapids, MI, 1969), pp. 63–98.

Timmer, John, "G. C. Berkouwer, theologian of confrontation and correlation," in *Reformed Journal*, 19 (1969), pp. 17–22.

Wells, David F. and Woodbridge, John D., *The Evangelicals: What they believe, who they are, where they are changing* (Nashville, TN, 1975).

Woodbridge, John D. et al., *The Gospel in America: Themes in the story of America's evangelicals* (Grand Rapids, MI, 1979).

Eastern Orthodox Theology

Rowan Williams

Introduction: Background

For most of the twentieth century, the story of Orthodox theology is the story of Russian theology, both in Russia itself before 1917 and in the emigration afterwards (especially in Paris). The exceptional vitality of Russian intellectual life in the later nineteenth century was without parallel in any other historically Orthodox society – partly for the simple reason that no other such society had enjoyed real cultural independence for centuries. Even when Greece finally emerged as a nation after throwing off the Ottoman yoke, it was to be many years before it could begin to boast an intellectual ethos of its own. But Russia, accustomed to be the standard-bearer of the Orthodox world, was the setting for the first serious encounters between traditional Eastern theology and Enlightenment and post-Enlightenment thought; and it is as if three centuries of development in Western Christian thinking had to be telescoped in Russia into a few decades. If Russian religious thought appears at times bizarre, naive and extravagant to Western eyes, we should remember that it is a response to an unprecedented intensity of new impressions, social and intellectual stimuli crowding in over a relatively brief period.

One crucial factor in understanding modern Russian religious thought is the role of Hegel and, even more, of Schelling in the formation of systems. Hegel's work became known in Russia first by way of the theological schools of the Ukraine; it has been very plausibly suggested that Hegel's interest in the late Neoplatonism of Proclus resonated with a theology that accorded great authority to the Pseudo-Dionysius' writings, also deeply marked by the influence of Proclus. But two other factors should be borne in mind as well. German idealism arrived in Russia in close connection with German mysticism – both the Catholic mysticism of the medieval and post-medieval Rhineland and the quasi-hermetic Protestantism of Jakob Böhme. In the early decades of the nineteenth century, the new philosophical ideas coming from Germany appeared as simply another form of the new images of religious interiority offered by German hermetism and eclectic pietism. In other words, idealism was, from the first, received in Russia as a religious philosophy, which, though ambivalent from the point of view of Orthodoxy, might yet be put to work for the traditional faith. The combination of Böhme with Schelling and Hegel seemed to open the way toward a metaphysic of the world as organism, a participatory and intuitive account of knowledge, and a certain relativization of the ideas of an auto-momous and finite ego. It is fair to say that one problem that has *not* beset Russian religious thought is an excess of dualism.

In addition to this, however, it may be that Russian history itself helped to make Hegel attractive. It had been a history of violent alternations – from the Byzantine and European civilization of the Kievan period to the increasing cultural isolation of the Mongol and Muscovite centuries to the Francophile and Francophone culture of the governing class in the eighteenth century; and the war against Napoleon had involved a deep emotional retrieval of the Muscovite ideal of "Holy Russia." Culturally and politically, Russia was eager to find an identity that would resolve the contradictory heritage of the past and heal the injuries caused by the massive disruptions of that history. Thus much of Russia's intellectual history up to 1917 (and since) has to do with the variety of conflicting "bids" to define the nation. Was its destiny to resolve its tensions by joining the history of the European "mainstream," or was there a quite different kind of polity and politics to which it could witness? Nehru or Gandhi? One of the most striking things about revolutionary Marxism in Russia is that it succeeded in blending these two opposing impulses. But for a society with this kind of agenda in the early decades of the nineteenth century, the appeal of a historically oriented metaphysic is obvious. Hegel confirmed the characteristic Russian tendency to fuse together the religious, the philosophical, and the political, and the whole of the enterprise of Russian religious philosophy reflects this fusion.

There were those, however, who, accepting this program, still believed that Hegel was to be left behind. Ivan Vasilievich Kireevsky (1806–56) published, in the year of his death, an essay on "The Need for New Foundations in Philosophy," which argued that Hegel represented the decisive end of one particular style of philosophy, that originating with Bacon and Descartes – i.e., a philosophy whose fundamental problematic was "What is it to *think*?" and which dealt with this in terms of analyzing the processes of observation and argumentation. Kireevsky turned instead to the alternative tradition represented by Pascal (and was also impressed by Schleiermacher), and to the anthropology of the Eastern Fathers, especially the monastic writers, searching for a perspective neither intellectualist nor voluntarist, for a doctrine of the formation of historical persons in action and relation, an integral view of the human. Reasoning, in such a perspective, is concrete and committed, not ahistorical, and we are delivered from the absolute dominance of a "tragic" vision of the relation between spirit and nature. Kireevsky's literary remains are fragmentary and slight, but the reader will catch startling glimpses of something like Kierkegaard as well as something like Heidegger, hermeneutics set against a logos metaphysic.

Vladimir Sergeevich Soloviev (1853–1900) represents most dramatically the opposite approach, a passion for metaphysical construction and systematization. His importance is chiefly in his elaboration of a quasi-mythological cosmology centered upon the figure of "Sophia," the divine Wisdom, the Eternal Feminine. For Soloviev, the Absolute exists both as being and as becoming, as a transcendent unity and as the totality of modes in which that unity can express itself and relate to itself; and this latter form of the Absolute, insofar as it always preserves a movement toward unity, is an organic whole. This is "Sophia" – fragmented in the empirical universe, but still at one in God. In this perspective, the incarnation of the divine Word is the central act of *reintegration* in the cosmos; in the Church, in which the fruits of the incarnation are realized, human personality is united to the cosmic whole (*vseedinstvo*, "total unity"), and delivered from its finite limitations, its alienation from matter and from other subjects. The Orthodox Church does not operate by external and legalistic systems of authority, as does the Roman communion, nor does it countenance the individualism of the Protestant; it is therefore uniquely qualified to be the bearer of the promise of "sophianic" humanity, of *bogochelovechestvo*, "divine humanity" (or "Godmanhood," as it is often rendered). In Orthodox societies, the aim should be a "free theocracy," not legally imposed but organically evolving, which will draw other nations into a universal Christian communion, both church and state.

Soloviev develops some of the ideas of the earlier writer Alexei Stepanovich Khomyakov (1804–60), especially in the use of organic models for the Church and in the elaboration of the concept of *sobornost'*, the Russian word for "catholicity," as a special designation for the supra-individual consciousness of the (Orthodox, especially Slavic) Church. But the vision of Sophia is new, as is the passionate insistence on a universal perspective. Soloviev is without doubt the single most influential Russian religious writer of the age (his impact upon Dostoevsky is clear), and nearly all major Orthodox thinkers up to the Revolution are in one way or another in dialogue with him. However, his system gives very sharp focus to the problems hinted at by Kireevsky: What is the role of history in this, real, *contingent* history? And what can be said about individual identity and liberty in so comprehensive and near-deterministic a scheme? Soloviev's last works include a strange piece of apocalyptic fiction ("A Story of Antichrist") suggesting that he recognized the presence of irresoluble tensions in his metaphysics, and the possibility of tragic revolt and discontinuity. His legacy proved to be as controversial and many-sided as that of Origen; much of the work of his admirers is an attempt to restate a "sophiology" without the elements of pantheism and determinism that pervade a great deal of his writing.

The history of Russian theology in the twentieth century is largely one of debate between those who have, broadly speaking, felt comfortable with the legacy of Soloviev and those who have repudiated it in favor of a more consciously traditional and Church-focused style, seeking to derive general principles for a theological anthropology from the interpretation of the Fathers of the early centuries. Generally, the rejection of Soloviev has been accompanied by a suspicion of Khomyakov's theology as well. The appeal to a distinctive kind of corporate consciousness in the church, analogous to that typical of premodern, especially Slavic, societies has been seen as a naturalistic reduction of the supernatural reality of communion in the Holy Spirit. Twentieth-century Russian theology is thus, in its most creative period (ca. 1925–55) deeply marked by polemic. The rejection of Soloviev and others by a younger generation has some parallels with the rejection of liberal Protestant conventions by the new theologies of the Word in Germany. In both, there is an attempt to shed the legacy of idealism in philosophy, and to break free from what was seen as a psychologizing or moralizing or "naturalizing" of faith, so as to recover a sense of the givenness, the historical and punctiliar character, of a revelation that reconstructs the whole of human knowing and relating. What is different of course is the persistent Orthodox attempt to pursue a theology of the historical *mediation* of revelation, a theology of tradition. For many students of the field, this remains one of the most abidingly interesting and fruitful contributions of the Orthodox vision in contemporary theological discussion.

In what follows, three theologians, Bulgakov, Lossky, and Florovsky, will be discussed in some detail, before surveying and assessing the wider field of Orthodox theology today.

Three Orthodox Theologians

S. N. Bulgakov

Foremost among those who sought to rework Soloviev's themes in more acceptable form was Sergei Nikolaevich Bulgakov (1871–1944). Alienated from the Orthodox Church as a student, he had become a Marxist teacher of economics, with a considerable international reputation, before drifting away from dialectical materialism, first toward a Kantian moralism, then toward Hegel. He finally made his peace with the Church in the early years of this century, and was ordained a priest in 1917; after expulsion from Russia in 1923, he spent most of his remaining years in Paris, as Dean of the newly formed Institut Saint-Serge, a seminary for *émigré* Russians – and also as a deeply loved pastor and director of souls. He was a prolific writer, whose dense and florid style conceals a surprising conceptual boldness which sets him apart from most of his fellow-Orthodox theologians, and occasioned a minor ecclesiastical *cause célèbre* in the Russian emigration when, in 1935, he was denounced to the Patriarchate of Moscow as a heretic, and his theology was condemned by the Patriarchal *locum tenens*, Metropolitan Sergii. He was, however, supported by his own ecclesiastical superiors (whose relations with Moscow at this time were hostile anyway). His work attracted some interest outside the Orthodox world partly because he had become a well-known figure in the ecumenical movement, but a great deal of his writing remains available in Russian only.

Bulgakov's rejection of Marxism had a great deal to do with a theme that he explores in several essays between 1903 and 1911 – the inadequacy of *homo economicus* as a basis for social and political ethics. An account of human needs in terms of economically determinable factors leads – paradoxically – to an alienation from the historical and the material, since it seeks a way out of *personal* struggle and growth, out of the risks of creativity. It sets up a mechanical opposition of economic interests, to be settled either by the logic of history (Marxism) or by the laws of the market (capitalism); but both resolutions sidestep the specifically human task of transfiguring the material world in and through the creation of community. Artistic and economic activity are equally indispensable in this – art as the gratuitous expression of an "eschatological" change in things, matter charged with meaning, economics as the functional harnessing of the world to human need. Either of these in isolation is destructive.

It is Bulgakov's interest in the *work* of humanizing the world that sets him apart from Soloviev, as well as from pure Hegelianism (he remarked once that no one who had ever taken Marxism seriously could accept abstract or passivist versions of idealist dialectic). Hence his assimilation of the Sophia myth represents a considerable qualification of Soloviev's version (and in this he was much influenced by the work of his spiritual mentor, Fr Pavel Florensky, a brilliant and eccentric polymath who finally disappeared in the Gulag), and is continually being revised and refined throughout the whole of Bulgakov's work. Sophia *is* the divine nature, God's own life considered under the aspect of God's freedom to live the divine life in what is not God. God as Trinity is an eternal movement of "giving-away," displacement, so that God's very Godhead presupposes the possibility of there being an object of love and gift beyond itself. Bulgakov is careful to clarify (especially between 1917 and 1925) the point that Sophia is not a "hypostasis" (correcting both Florensky and his own earlier work), and to purge out any residual pantheism: divine Sophia is not an objectified World-Soul, but the impulse in things toward harmony and order, toward complex unity of organization. Bulgakov speaks of this impulse as the world's "eros"; and such language should remind us that Bulgakov's sophiology is far more a sustained metaphor than a theory.

Bulgakov rejects a matter–spirit dualism; but the nature–hypostasis dualism with which he often works introduces some of the dangers he wishes to avoid. When he says that the hypostasis of a human subject, the uncategorizable core of personal identity, is "uncreated" or "absolute," his concern is chiefly to deny that personal identity is an observable determinate *thing*; but the language is redolent of the Germanic hermetism which Bulgakov found both intensely attractive and theologically unsatisfactory. He constantly seems to be implying that there is in human psychology a level or dimension of direct *natural* participation in God – a view which Orthodox theological tradition has normally regarded with hostility. Thus his account of human liberty oscillates between an impressive seriousness about freedom as constituted in historical relation and creativity, and a more monistic notion of a universal divine *Urgrund* of liberty, the image of God residing in a mysterious hinterland of transcendence common to all personal beings.

However, when he addresses the question of the divine image in his later and explicitly theological work, it is more often the *active* role of the human subject that is to the fore. Human being is the agent of meaning in the universe; when distorted self-love breaks the "sophianic" whole into mutually excluding fragments, the redemptive work of God as Word and Spirit is to enable us to be once again capable of revealing the wholeness of things, in work, art, and sacrament. This cannot be simply a matter of injunctions to be obeyed, programs to be followed: Redemption actually effects a change in spiritual self-awareness, so that we know we can exist as selves *only* in communion with other selves. Here the nineteenth-century theme of "catholic" consciousness, *sobornost'*, reappears: The church, Bulgakov was fond of saying, is the fact of human "consubstantiality," not merely a society; it is "Sophia in the process of becoming." The language used about the church as ideal form of creation can, however, mislead. Bulgakov is quite clear that the empirical church is flawed, its work incomplete, its decisions provisional and risky, its existing limits "pragmatic not absolute" – which explains why he has little on the theology of ministerial or hierarchical authority, and was an enthusiastic advocate of intercommunion in certain circumstances. The church is essentially the fellowship of the Spirit, held together by the ontological bond of God's love as figured in the eucharist; the rest is a matter of conditioned historical decisions and policies.

Not surprisingly, perhaps, he is critical of certain kinds of christocentrism in ecclesiology. If the identity of the church is made to reside solely in its relation to Christ rather than in the quality of its consubstantial and catholic life in the Spirit, the church will tend to look for Christ-substitutes – an infallible Pope, an inerrant Bible – or to encourage people to concentrate on an *individual* relation to the Savior. But the work of the Trinity is fundamentally characterized by *kenosis*, a central theme in all Bulgakov's work, but especially in the theological writings of the 1920s and 1930s: Christ therefore acts in the church not as an omnipresent individual, focusing attention on himself, but through the Spirit's formation of the new consciousness – which in turn works "kenotically," directing us to the Father and working always with and never against created freedom. Thus Bulgakov's suspicion of christocentrism does not mean that christology does not have a central and normative place: Here, in the life and death of Jesus, the kenotic pattern is spelled out. The divine self of the Word, unchanged as such, is the subject for which the human self of Jesus now becomes an object: The Word is the "I," the consciousness, for which the humanity of Jesus is the "me," the material of self-consciousness. This is a complex idea, which Bulgakov fails to work out in full detail, but which shows signs of rather more conceptual sophistication than some forms of English kenoticism. Here his doctrine of the "uncreated" hypostasis in all human beings serves him well: He can identify the ultimate subjectivity of Christ with the Word of God while avoiding downright Apollinarianism. But this whole area of his thinking is abstruse and unclear. His main concern in christology, however, is to show how Christ is the place where uncreated and created Sophia are united: The divine life of unconditional self-forgetting generates a created, historical life of the same quality, in which the mutual isolation and refusal of fallen creation is overcome. The incarnate Word as incarnate selflessness is open to *universal* relation, universal accessibility: As that relation becomes ours in the Spirit, our isolation is ended, and the *sobornost'* of the new creation is established.

Bulgakov's achievement is remarkable. His work is sprawling, repetitive, unsystematic, and often appallingly obscure, but it is a rare attempt at a unified theological metaphysic. Many of his insights on the nature of the church became the common currency of the ecumenical movement, and were specially influential for Anglican writers of a certain generation. But other aspects of his work have remained almost unknown. He is one of the first theologians to use and develop the term "panentheism," to distinguish his doctrine of the world's ideality in God from pantheism; he is clearly fascinated by feminine imagery for the Godhead, although he works with an uncritical male/active, female/passive-or-receptive disjunction; he is certainly the only theologian of the century to use kenosis as a pivotal and normative concept for *all* language about God, in creation as in redemption; and in this as in other ways, his use of Jewish Cabbalistic imagery (the myth of *zimzum*, God's self-withdrawal in the creative act) is deeply suggestive. He has yet to be taken fully seriously by Western theology, and yet, of all the major Orthodox thinkers of the century, he is probably the one most consciously and extensively engaged with post-Enlightenment thought (and Western biblical scholarship). Among non-Orthodox writers, it is probably Hans Urs von Balthasar who stands closest to him – in the themes touched upon, but also in densely metaphorical idiom.

V. N. Lossky

The fierce debate over Bulgakov's work in 1935 and 1936 brought into prominence a young historian, Vladimir Nikolaevich Lossky (1903–58), son of a well-known (vaguely idealist) philosopher. Lossky had already begun work on Meister Eckhart (work which was to occupy him intermittently for the rest of his life), and had been instrumental in establishing the "Brotherhood of Saint Photius" in Paris, a group highly critical of Slavophil particularism and the mystique of Holy Russia, but also loyal to the canonical authority of the Patriarchate of Moscow, in contrast to the more aggressively anti-Soviet elements in the emigration and the liberal group (including philosophers like Nikolai Berdyaev and philosophical theologians like Bulgakov), gathered around Metropolitan Evlogii and linked to the Patriarch of Constantinople. The Brotherhood had been active in the denunciation of Bulgakov, and Lossky wrote a substantial (90-page) pamphlet on the whole issue in 1936. In this, he attacked Bulgakov's eclecticism and identified various errors and imbalances in his theology: He criticizes the crypto-Apollinarian strand in Bulgakov's christology, his failure to get rid of the determinist or monist heritage of Soloviev, and above all his confusion of person, will, and nature. Kenosis cannot be "natural," cannot *be* the nature of God, since it is always a free act, in God and in us. If love is nature, it is not innovative or creative, it does not belong to the realm of the personal.

The distinction between person and nature is central in the whole of Lossky's work; but the important point to notice in the 1936 essay is Lossky's strong commitment to an "authentic," patristically based Orthodoxy, freed from the philosophical dilettantism, as he saw it, of the Russian tradition (he had a deep aversion for Dostoevsky). The rest of his sadly brief career as a theologian was devoted to the building-up of a patristic synthesis – classically expressed in his vastly influential little book of 1944, *Essai sur la théologie mystique de l'église d'Orient* (translated into English as *The Mystical Theology of the Eastern Church* in 1957). Digests of the lectures he gave in the last years of his life were published posthumously, edited by his pupil, Olivier Clément. Throughout his work, Lossky's major impulse is hermeneutical – in the tradition of Kireevsky rather than Soloviev. His project is to uncover in patristic tradition the kind of central and normative strand that can allow Orthodoxy to offer a resolution to the tensions of Western Christianity. This leads him into some slightly questionable historical judgments, and to what appears in his earlier work as a persistent unfairness to the Thomist approach (though his mature writing, especially the great book on Eckhart, goes far toward redressing this balance), and to many aspects of Western spirituality. Yet his unpublished wartime journal shows how deep was his affection for French Catholic culture, medieval and modern, and he was on friendly terms both with Thomist scholars like de Gandillac and Gilson and with the great names of the *nouvelle théologie*, de Lubac and Daniélou. His influence on Bouyer and Congar is manifest; and he also enjoyed warm relations with Anglican scholars of the day, notably E. L. Mascall. His polemical vigor was not exercised in the cause of Byzantine, let alone Slavophil, particularism, but in defense of deeply held convictions about what was authentically *Christian*.

His earliest theological work, prior to the controversy with Bulgakov, dealt with the theme of "negative theology" in Pseudo-Dionysius, and this forms the basis for much of the 1944 *Essai*. Negative theology is not, for Lossky, primarily a verbal technique, a dialectical move to qualify positive affirmations about God en route for a developed theory of analogy; it is the *primordial* theological moment, the moment of stripping and renunciation. Theology begins in a kind of shock to, a paralyzing of, the intellect – not by propositions that offend the intellect, but by an encounter with what cannot be mastered. The dialectical imagery of "light" and "darkness," as used by both Dionysius and his precursors, the Cappadocian Fathers, is designed to take us beyond both agnosticism (the being of God is ultimately inaccessible) and intellectualism (the being of God is akin to the finite mind and so its proper and natural object): the reality underpinning apophatic theology is "ecstasy" – not a particular brand of individual mystical experience, but the sober acknowledgement that we must let go of the control of conceptual analysis when we are touched by God and advance to a stage beyond the life of conscious "natural" individuality, closed upon itself. It is in this encounter, this recognition, that *personal* being is brought to birth. The life of an individual of a certain nature is not in itself the life of a person: individuality is a particular configuration of *repeatable* natural features. The person, on the other hand, emerges in and only in the act of spiritual creativity which is response to the self-gift of God – in *ekstasis* and *kenosis*, self-transcending and self-forgetting, the overcoming of the boundaries of mutual exclusion that define individuals over against each other.

It is in this context that Lossky claims that the doctrine of the Trinity is the cardinal point of "negative theology." It is a "cross for the intellect" not in merely providing a logical conundrum but in presenting to us an image of the source of all reality that overturns our understanding of individuality as the most basic category. God is neither an individual nor three individuals: God is the supreme paradigm of the personal, a life wholly lived in *ekstasis* and *kenosis*, since the divine hypostases which are God are wholly defined by relations of love, gift, response. It is from the paradigm of the divine hypostases that we come to grasp our own vocation to personal being.

Thus Lossky attacks all theologies that concentrate on the level of "nature" – what can be grasped and objectified. His fierce criticisms of Western scholasticism are motivated by a conviction that the Western theological tradition separates the divine essence from the divine persons (and so elevates an abstract divinity over the living God), and operates a juridical and external morality based on an artificial concept of human nature, to which grace is added as an extra *thing*. His critique of the *filioque* in the Western creed assumes that post-Augustinian trinitarian theology makes the source of the Spirit's life not the person of the Father but the abstract nature shared by Father and Son (in this critique, he goes further than most of his Orthodox predecessors, but has a special debt to the work of V. Bolotov on the *filioque* at the turn of the century, and to the patristic and medieval studies of L. P. Karsavin, one of his teachers). However, Lossky also insists that the reaction against scholastic Catholicism is just as unbalanced: Here is "person" without "nature," voluntarism and subjectivism. The Protestant error is to turn away from the real ontological transformation effected by encounter with God. So, as Christian trinitarianism mediates between two misguided forms of monotheism, Hellenic abstract monism and Hebraic anthropomorphism and voluntarism, Orthodoxy mediates between Catholic essentialism and Protestant existentialism.

The critique of the West also draws in Lossky's interest in the speculations of the fourteenth-century theologian and mystic Gregory Palamas. Palamas had distinguished between the "essence" and the "energies" or "activities" of God, so as to insist that God was authentically known and "participated" through his activities while remaining incomprehensible in essence. Lossky believes that the absence of this distinction leads back to the unacceptable choice of intellectualism or agnosticism; either God is known in essence, in *definitions*, or he is not known at all. The doctrine of the "energies" allows both real and ultimate unknowing and a real share in the divine life. Lossky was not the first to revive interest in Palamas: Bulgakov had used him, and, in the 1930s, the Russian Basil Krivoshein and the Romanian Dumitru Staniloae had both published important scholarly studies. Lossky's work, however, established Palamas as a focal figure in Byzantine theology, and did much to stimulate the striking development of Palamas scholarship in Europe and the United States in the past 30 years.

There is a Kierkegaardian streak in Lossky (it is not surprising that he thought highly of the French Kierkegaardian scholar Jean Wahl), but it is balanced by a carefully worked out ecclesiology. The church exists at *both* "natural" and "personal" levels, human nature objectively restored in Christ, human persons each uniquely transformed by the Spirit. Thus institutional and canonical regularities matter (Lossky's stubborn loyalty to the canonical authority of the weak and almost discredited Patriarchate of Moscow through many difficult decades expresses this eloquently); but they are not there to impose centralized despotism or unified models of spiritual growth. The institutional and the charismatic are bound together as inseparably as the Word and the Spirit in the Trinity. "Tradition" in the Church is not just a process of narrowly doctrinal transmission, but the *whole* of the Spirit's ecclesial work, realizing in each, in a unique way, the heritage of all, by way of Scripture, ministry, sacraments, iconography and the disciplines of holiness. And catholicity is more than a sentimental *sobornost'*, a deep and emotional sense of solidarity: It is the capacity in each believer and each congregation to receive and live the fullness of God's gifts.

Lossky remains probably the best known and most influential of all modern Orthodox writers. His polemic can be wide of the mark at times, and he remains more firmly within the nineteenth-century Russian tradition than he might have cared to admit, but his originality and imagination in interpreting the Eastern Fathers should secure him a firm place among twentieth-century theologians, and practically all Eastern Orthodox ecclesiology in the past few decades has taken his scheme as a starting point.

G. V. Florovsky

Lossky was not alone in combating the influence of Slavophil mystique in Russian theology, and in trying to rescue the doctrine of the church's catholicity from edifying rhetoric about Slavic *sobornost'*. Georgii Vasilievich Florovsky (1893–1979) pursued the same course in search of a "neo-patristic synthesis," though he did so in more direct and conscious engagement with philosophical questions: His earliest essays (after he had abandoned studies in the natural sciences) addressed fundamental issues of metaphysics and epistemology. In these pieces, he repudiates absolute idealism, insists on the impossibility of affirming or denying anything about objects of cognition in themselves, since they enjoy an inaccessible presence to themselves, and argues on this basis for a radical causal underdetermination in the universe, a kind of "free will" in the material order. He saw very clearly the connection between idealist epistemology (each particular proposition entailing and being entailed by the ensemble of true propositions) and a certain sort of determinism, and his later opposition to Bulgakov's sophiology has its roots in these essays of the prewar period and the early 1920s. In the 1920s, he was also involved in the "Eurasian" controversy among the Russian *émigrés*, a debate (once again) about where Russia was to be culturally "located"; his anti-Slavophil stance in this was pronounced and he was already looking to the ideal of a "Christian Hellenism," with patristic and Byzantine roots.

In the early 1930s Florovsky worked for a while alongside Bulgakov in Paris (he was ordained in 1932), but his disagreements became sharper – and may have been further sharpened by contact with Barth in 1931. His theological papers in these years show both an aggressive insistence on the priority of revelation, and a growing use of patristic categories and argument. In 1931 and 1933, he published his two magisterial surveys of Eastern theology up to the eighth century, and, in two important papers in 1936 and 1938, he castigated the bondage of Russian theology to post-Enlightenment philosophy and announced his program of "re-Hellenizing" the Christian faith, arguing that Christian theology could only recover itself by deepening its commitment to the baptized Hellenism of the Fathers and the Byzantine world. He never wavered in this loyalty to the Greek character of theology, in opposition both to Western religious and secular thought and to the ethnic religiosity of many Russians. In 1937 he published *Ways of Russian Theology*, a brilliant and encyclopedic history of Christian thought in Russia that elaborated a relentlessly hostile account of Slavophil Christianity and concluded with a clarion call to return to the Fathers.

As much of his work shows, Florovsky's patristic enthusiasm was not as naive or as positivist as might appear (though one Russian reviewer in 1931 described an essay of Florovsky's on the atonement as "talmudic" in its use of the Fathers). Florovsky's radical indeterminism disposed him to emphasize the central significance of *history* in knowledge – the encounter with a complex of contingent acts in which we encounter persons. In historical knowledge, above all, we must recognize the impossibility of "objective" mastery: Historical inquiry brings a personal, a committed, agenda, and looks for personal records, unique points of view. There is no historical source that is not a point of view, and no historical research that is not done from a point of view. Historical "events" are acts, mediated by further acts of interpretation (Collingwood and Dilthey are invoked on this); and the meaning of history is an eschatological projection. As against pre-emptive efforts to settle the issue of meaning (Hegel, Marx, Nietzsche), Christianity takes seriously the unfinished and unfinishable character of historical activity, and thus the unique and unfathomable character of the acting *person*. But this also means that Christianity is irreversibly committed to what has as a matter of contingent fact been constructed in its history: We cannot pretend that we can free ourselves of "Hellenism," or that the kerygma is directed from and to a timeless interiority. Hence the priority of patristic methods and themes – though this does not mean that we can do no more than parrot slogans or imitate the style of a distant culture; simply that *these* are our starting point, *this* is how Christian language has concretely taken shape. If we wish to go on speaking a Christian language at all, we cannot ignore or try to dismantle this set of determinations.

As some Russian critics more sympathetic to Bulgakov noted, Florovsky did less than justice to the turbulently dialectical nature of patristic theology, and tended to treat as a finished whole what could only be part of a conversation (comparison with some recent theological uses of Gadamer is instructive). But Florovsky's sophisticated discussion of historical knowledge (most accessibly set out in an article for the 1959 Tillich Festschrift) is of great interest, the most detailed exposition of what we have been calling the "hermeneutical" alternative voice in Russian religious thought, suspicious of metaphysics divorced from doctrinal and ascetical tradition. The emphasis on historical creativity, history as a pattern of free acts, leads naturally to a critique of all theologies that undervalue the historical Jesus: For Florovsky, the category of *podvig* (roughly equivalent to "achievement," even "exploit," and common in speaking of ascetic saints) is central in understanding Christ, as in understanding all human action. Jesus' *whole* existence must be the triumph of freedom in the world if we are to be liberated for proper historical action. Thus his death must be, in some sense, his *act* – and not only contingently so. Florovsky startlingly revives the late patristic notion that Jesus, as possessing a sinless and unfallen humanity, did not *have* to die. And in that Jesus thus brings death itself within the scope of created freedom, the possibility of incorruptible life is implanted in humanity. Necessity, in the form of mortality and disintegration, is shown to be conquerable by freedom – the fusion of divine and human freedom in Christ. We shall die, but we know now that our human nature is still "free" beyond death, as it has been taken through death into resurrection by the man Jesus, whose glorified humanity is given to us in the eucharist.

The eucharist is thus also the foundation of true, ecclesial *sobornost'*. In it, we come to share fellowship not only with one another, but with the whole company of heaven and the entire cosmos; we do so because we here make contact with a humanity free from the limits of ordinary individuality, a humanity belonging to our history yet not sealed off in the past by death. And in the eucharistic fellowship, as "human impermeability and exclusivity" are overcome, human community becomes the image of the divine: The Church (not the individual) is *imago Trinitatis*. Florovsky makes much in this context of the Farewell Discourses in the Fourth Gospel, though patristic evidence is harder to come by; following the lead of a very different kind of theologian, Antonii Khrapovitsky (Metropolitan of Kiev before the Revolution), author of treatises on the "moral idea" of various dogmas, he alludes to Cyril of Alexandria and Hilary of Poitiers. But the notion of the church as imaging the plurality-in-unity of the divine life owes more directly to the nineteenth-century Russian ethos than to the Fathers. It may be a legitimate development of patristic themes, but Florovsky, as much as Lossky, cannot but read the Fathers through spectacles faintly tinged with Slavophil interests.

Florovsky's range of skills and erudition is impressive, though the work overall is more uneven than Lossky's much slighter *oeuvre*. Considerable philosophical sophistication and originality stand side by side with what can sometimes be an archaizing and inflexible theological idiom. His insistence on freedom gives a rather voluntaristic flavor to some of his writings, and there is no clear category unifying the work of divine and human love to compare with the striking use of kenosis in both Bulgakov and Lossky. Methodologically, however, he is much the most lucid and systematic, and his work in this area deserves far more serious attention.

Survey and Assessment of Current Orthodox Theology

The Russian emigration produced many other significant figures, not least Nikolai Afanasiev, author of a major work on ecclesiology that developed many of the themes emerging in Lossky and Florovsky (the *imago Trinitatis*, the centrality of the eucharist), and Pavel Evdokimov, a prolific and eloquent writer of books on the interrelation of liturgy, theology, and spirituality, indebted equally to Lossky and to Bulgakov, as well as to Jung and Eliade. But as the first generation of *émigrés* died, the impact of the Russian theological revival spread beyond Slavic Orthodoxy. Greek-speaking theologians increasingly took up the challenge; until the 1950s, Greek theology had tended to be cast in a rather scholastic mode – doctrinal *capita* with patristic catenae added – but the impact of Lossky and Florovsky has transformed this situation in some areas at least of the Greek Church. John Romanides has developed a fiercely anti-Augustinian theology, and has been an important presence in ecumenical discussions. Christos Yannaras studied Heidegger in Germany and produced a remarkable series of books uniting Lossky's theology with Heidegger's metaphysics. He must be counted as one of the most outstandingly creative voices in Orthodoxy today; his reworking of the essence–energies distinction in terms of *ousia* as *parousia*, "being" as "presence," and his elaboration of the category of *eros* as fundamental in understanding the personal represent an important assimilation of major European philosophical concerns into a consciously but critically traditionalist theology. Yannaras has also made a considerable name as a writer on ethics, politics, and ecology. John Zizioulas's work on ecclesiology links Afanasiev's themes (not without some criticism and refinement) to a whole metaphysic of relation, centered on the trinitarian image of being as *essentially* relational: The great philosophical error is to look for isolated ahistorical substances, since the source of all reality is not "a" substance but a relational system. Zizioulas's doctoral thesis, on eucharist, episcopate, and unity, has been seminally important in ecumenical theology.

In the United States Alexander Schmemann and John Meyendorff transmitted the

Russian *émigré* heritage to new generations, Schmemann with a number of works on liturgical and sacramental theology (above all that small classic, *The World as Sacrament*), Meyendorff with several books on Palamism and Byzantine Christianity in general, and essays on ecclesiology. Both the major Orthodox seminaries in the United States, St Vladimir's and Holy Cross, produce substantial periodicals. The Institut Saint-Serge continues in Paris, and several Orthodox groups there publish theological journals. Orthodoxy in France is now overwhelmingly Francophone, and its leading constructive theologian, Olivier Clément, is of French birth. A friend and pupil of Lossky, he has developed Lossky's critique of the abstract foundations of Western theism, and written of the dialectical necessity of European atheism as a step to recovering the vision of a living God. He has succeeded in constructing an Orthodox theology very deeply engaged with the mainstream of Western European culture, and free from either Byzantinist or Slavophil nostalgia. The role of converts like Clément is of increasing importance in Orthodox intellectual life; one other distinguished instance is (Bishop) Kallistos Ware in England, author of several works on Byzantine spirituality, and an important interpreter of the Orthodox theological style to British academic theology.

Up to 1969, theological work in the Communist countries of Eastern Europe was largely limited to historical scholarship, with a few outstanding exceptions. Foremost among these was Fr Dumitru Staniloae in Romania, a major interpreter of the patristic tradition (he wrote substantial studies of Gregory Palamas and Maximus the Confessor) and of classical monastic spirituality (he edited the Romanian edition of the Philokalia), as well as a constructive theologian of great stature. He has much in common with Lossky and Florovsky – notably in his concern for an ecclesiology based on the living communion of persons; but he criticizes the over-schematic model he finds in Lossky, and has far more eagerness to engage with modern non-Orthodox thought than Florovsky. His most original contributions probably lie in his development of Maximus the Confessor's insights on the theology of creation, the world depending upon the "words" of God conceived as dynamic determinative actions of God, so that the world is a vehicle of divine agency, an agency brought to light and completion in the life of Christ and the Church. Staniloae's *Dogmatic Theology* (of which an English translation is in preparation) discusses very fully many modern ideas about revelation, christology, and so on, and has some penetrating observations on Barth.

Since the great changes in Eastern Europe began, theological education has developed rapidly (if unevenly), and there is more vitality in some areas than there has been for centuries. In Russia, the extraordinary influence of Archpriest Alexander Men (murdered in 1989) has marked a whole generation of Russian intellectuals, especially those from a "dissident" background. His many books represent less a contribution to constructive theology than a program of orientation for theology, laying out basic principles for a critical but faithful reading of the Bible, for a theologically informed encounter with other faiths, and a vision for ecclesiology deeply indebted to the Russian speculative tradition of Soloviev and his disciples, but anchored in a robust sacramental doctrine. In the early 1990s, his influence was decisive in the formation of a number of study circles and "Institutes" for religion and theology in Russian cities. The "Higher School of Religions and Philosophy" in Saint Petersburg has been especially active, and has produced outstandingly interesting work in its journals. Here you will find essays on patristics alongside translations into Russian of Levinas and Voegelin and discussions of phenomenology and postmodernism, as well as literary-critical papers and studies in cultural history. The whole enterprise is a worthy successor to the work of the great Russian thinkers of the pre-Revolutionary period, whose significance for modern Russia has not been overlooked. Whether the leadership of the Russian churches will be able to respond to this resurgence of intellectual creativity in a constructive way remains to be seen; but there are some signs of new life in the larger seminaries.

The constraints and tensions of modern ecumenical dialogue have not, on the whole, encouraged exploratory or creative theology in the Orthodox world in the past couple of decades (with some outstanding exceptions); but there are many encouraging signs, in the Third World as well as in Europe and the United States. Orthodox theology has lately had a considerable impact on Western theology (Congar on tradition and the Holy Spirit, Moltmann on the Trinity, various writers on the church), and is increasingly studied with academic seriousness. Many connections – historical and systematic – wait to be made. Zizioulas's recent work suggests the possibility of useful interaction between this kind of ecclesiology and various Western attempts at "postmodern" or "postliberal" schemes, in its critique of a metaphysic of unrelated substances and an epistemology based on the myth of a detached or neutral subjectivity. Orthodox theologians have shown some willingness to engage with Heidegger, but it is perhaps time for a comparable engagement with Gadamer on the one hand and Wittgenstein on the other (the Romanian novelist Petru Dumitriu has testified eloquently to the importance of Wittgenstein in his own recovery of Christian commitment, but his is not a voice heard at all clearly within "mainstream" Orthodox theology).

For this sort of development to go forward, Orthodox theology at large has to overcome a certain suspicion of (at worst, contempt for) the world of Western philosophy, a suspicion that is part of the inheritance of the debates in the Russian emigration earlier in this century. The impressive examples of Clément and Yannaras, and (from the non-Chalcedonian world) Metropolitan Paulos Mar Gregorios of New Delhi, have shown what can be achieved by confronting the mainstream of European intellectual life, scientific and political as well as philosophical, with perspectives formed, but not restricted, by the Greek patristic vision. And it may be that, if this is to flourish, there needs also to be a new appreciation – however critical it may still be – of the contribution of the Russian religio-philosophical tradition, a reclaiming and reworking of some of the themes of Soloviev and Bulgakov. There are relatively few signs of this as yet (though it is worth noting a recent surge of interest in Florensky, Bulgakov's mentor); but Orthodox thought in the past hundred years has repeatedly surprised Western observers by its self-renewing energy.

Bibliography

Primary

Bulgakov, S. N., *The Wisdom of God* (London, 1937).
—— *Du verbe incarné* (Paris, 1943).
—— *Le Paraclet* (Paris, 1946).
Florovsky, Georges, *The Collected Works of Georges Florovsky* (Belmont, MA, 1972–9).
Lossky, V. N., *The Mystical Theology of the Eastern Church* (Cambridge, 1957).
—— *Orthodox Theology: An introduction* (Clément's digest of Lossky's lectures) (Crestwood, NY, 1959).
Pain, James, and Zernov, Nicholas (eds), *A Bulgakov Anthology* (London, 1976).
Stanilae, Dumitru, *Theology and the Church* (Crestwood, NY, 1980).

Secondary

Blane, Andrew (ed.), *Georges Florovsky: Russian Intellectual and Orthodox Churchman* (Crestwood, NY, 1993).
Clément, O., *Questions sur l'homme* (Paris, 1972).
Dumitriu, P., *To the Unknown God* (London, 1982).
Evdokimov, P., *L'orthodoxie* (Neuchâtel, 1965).
Gregorios, Paulos Mar, *The Human Presence* (Geneva, 1978).
Lelouvier, Y. N., *Perspectives russes sur L'Église. Un théologien contemporain: Georges Florovsky* (Paris, 1968).
Nichols, Aidan, *Light From the East* (Edinburgh, 1995).
Read, C., *Religion, Revolution and the Russian Intelligentsia, 1900–1912* (London, 1979).
Roberts, E. and Shulman, A. (eds), *Christianity for the Twenty-First Century: The life and work of Alexander Men* (London, 1996).
Schmemann, A., *The World as Sacrament* (London, 1966).
Ware, K., *The Orthodox Way* (London, 1979).
Williams, G. H., "Georges Vasilievich Florovsky," *Greek Orthodox Theological Review* (1965), pp. 7–107.
Williams. R., "The Via Negativa and the Foundations of Theology. An Introduction to the Thought of V. N. Lossky," in *New Studies in Theology I*, ed. Stephen Sykes and Derek Holmes (London, 1980), pp. 95–117.
Yannaras, Christos, *Elements of Faith* (Edinburgh, 1991).
—— *The Freedom of Morality* (Crestwood, NY, 1984).
Zernov, N., *The Russian Religious Renaissance of the Twentieth Century* (London, 1963).
Zizioulas, J., *Being as Communion: Studies in personhood and the church* (Crestwood, NY, and London, 1985).

Transregional
Movements

As a global faith, Christianity produces transregional movements in theology as in other aspects of its life. Some are treated in other parts of this volume. The five covered in this part are by no means the only additional ones but are selected because of their academic interest, their influence, and their variety among themselves.

The Bible, the world's most widely disseminated book, is perhaps the most significant thing that Christians have in common. Interpreting it is essential to all Christian churches and movements. Anthony Thiselton describes the distinctively modern influences on biblical interpretation originating in eighteenth- and nineteenth-century Europe. He tells the twentieth-century story both of biblical theology, focusing especially on Eichrodt, von Rad, Childs, Bultmann, and Cullmann, and of hermeneutics, with special attention to Gadamer and Ricoeur. He finally surveys the ongoing agenda with its bewildering array of methods, and questions of history, semantics, the unity of Scripture, truth, manipulation, domination, and self-deception. This is largely a European and American story and can be complemented by the three following chapters and also by Part IV.

The impetus for the Ecumenical Movement, by contrast, came largely from outside Europe and America, as the younger churches questioned the divisions inherited from Western missionaries. Michael Root defines ecumenical theology as a practical and ecclesial theology of Christian identity. It tries to articulate common faith in a reconciling and mutually enriching way, it engages with every major theological topic, and at its best, as he shows, it has inspired considerable theological creativity. It is largely a group activity, and has been a strand in the formation of many of the theologians covered in this volume. Root discusses a selection of major ecumenical texts, he explores in some detail the question of the church as communion and the achievements in the dispute about justification, and he probes the dangers, temptations, debates, and current crisis in ecumenism and its theology.

Mission is intrinsic to Christianity, and one of the most striking phenomena of recent centuries has been its missionary expansion to become a worldwide religion. Viewed globally, its missionary energies have never been greater than in the late twentieth century, and Lamin Sanneh examines the theological dimension of this.

He gives a thorough historical survey of the missionary practices of Christianity from the earliest centuries to the present. He notes the distinctive features in the approaches to mission of each period, and in the twentieth century he builds his story around the contrast between the two World Missionary Conferences. That in Edinburgh in 1910 encouraged ecumenism and envisioned the rapid evangelization of the world. That in Jerusalem in 1928 played down evangelization and claims for the uniqueness and finality of Christ and encouraged involvement in secular transformations as a form of mission. A leading advocate of the latter approach was William Ernest Hocking, who is discussed at length, and his failure to do justice to the differences and particularities of religions and cultures is described. He is contrasted with Hendrik Kraemer who stressed the truth-claims of Christianity and argued for radical discontinuity between Christianity and other faiths. Lesslie Newbigin, the third theologian treated, is seen as doing fuller justice both to the particularity of the Gospel and to its involvements in specific cultures. In conclusion, the vitality of the new phenomenon of world Christianity is affirmed, no longer weighed down by the negative aspects of its missionary past.

Feminist theology has already been introduced in Part III as it has developed in the United States. Ann Loades puts that into a global perspective, surveying in addition feminist theological literature in other continents. (John de Gruchy introduces South African feminist theology at greater length in chapter 22.) Among her special concerns are biblical scholarship, the use of historical scholarship (especially in Britain), and the ways in which feminist theology transforms many conventional boundaries in the field, such as those between doctrine, liturgy, pastoral practice, ethics, and spirituality, as well as divisions between lay and ordained, and, above all, between women and men. She concludes with an agenda for the future, including attention to the unease in Christianity about associating the feminine with the divine, and the importance of expanding further the engagement with justice issues to embrace the young and the fragile.

What is postmodernism? Graham Ward offers a vivid image from Deleuze and Guattari: the subterranean complexity of the rhizome, which is neither one nor many, has neither beginning nor end, has neither one direction nor detectable regularity, constantly spills over from its *milieu*, and is an alternative to such modern forms as the circle, cube, spiral, double helix, or the arrow of progress. He surveys (though that is the sort of word to which postmodern thinkers tend to be allergic) the pluralism of what is called postmodernism in both theology and other areas. When it comes to classifying the theologians there is irony (itself a characteristic of much postmodern discourse) in his refusal to allow as genuinely postmodern those theologians who have been most widely associated with the label. These, the "liberal postmoderns," include Mark C. Taylor, Thomas J. Altizer, Robert P. Scharlemann, Charles Winquist, David Ray Griffin, and Don Cupitt. He describes them in their diversity, and sees all as developments of liberal theology. They fail to see how their own projects are undermined by the five crises to which they variously respond: the crisis of representation, and the end of metaphysics, of history, of the human subject, and of humanism. By contrast, the "conservative postmoderns," represented by George Lindbeck (see also chapter 18 above), John Milbank (see also chapter 15 above), Rowan Williams, Edith Wyschogrod, Ward himself, and above all by Jean-

Luc Marion and Michel de Certeau, are seen as opening up religious questions through postmodern thought and rethinking distinctively Christian (or Jewish) doctrines and concepts. Ward challenges the common assumption that postmodernism is antireligious and suggests how it can lead to a new dissemination of theological questions and discussion.

Biblical Theology and Hermeneutics

Anthony C. Thiselton

Background and Origins

Biblical theology and hermeneutics achieved the status of independent subject-disciplines at roughly the same time. Biblical theology became established as a subject in its own right largely as a result of a programmatic inaugural lecture in 1787 by Johann P. Gabler (1753–1826) at Altdorf. Gabler entitled his lecture "A Discourse on the Proper Distinction between Biblical Theology and the Correct Delimitation of Dogmatic Theology." Friedrich D. E. Schleiermacher (1768–1834) began to establish hermeneutics as a theory of interpretation and of understanding which stood fully on its own feet in his *Aphorisms on Hermeneutics* (1805) and more fully in his *Compendium on Hermeneutics* (1810–28).

In contrast to dogmatic theology, Gabler insisted that biblical theology constituted a *historical* discipline. Dogmatics remained concerned with the different task of exploring conceptual coherence. Within biblical theology, however, Gabler also allowed for a further subdistinction. A "true" (*wahre*) biblical theology restricted itself to the *pure description* of historical data and developments. It must not cover up the tensions and differences which different historical periods or cultures generate in material which may relate to similar themes. On the other hand, Gabler allowed, "pure" (*reine*) biblical theology entailed evaluation also. As theologians rather than only historians of religion, exponents of "biblical theology" might also attempt to sift what they judged to be of permanent value for theology and ethics from the historical variables which might be relevant only to some given culture or historical era. This supposed duality between "description" and "evaluation" persists in the twentieth century, most notably in Krister Stendahl and Heikki Räisänen.[1]

Schleiermacher's fundamental work on the independent status of hermeneutics arose initially from his reflection on the inadequacies of previous work, including J. A. Ernesti's writings (1761). Previous writers seemed to appeal to "hermeneutics" only when "difficulties" emerged. In other words, Schleiermacher rightly perceived, they presupposed that interpretation and understanding somehow took care of themselves until some supposed meaning conflicted with their own prior expectations.

But this gave the game away. They tended to invoke "hermeneutics" to legitimate some prior understanding which they had already reached. Thereby they turned hermeneutics into an instrumental service-discipline. It *served* someone's prior theology, or someone's assumptions about classical texts, whereas in Schleiermacher's view the whole subject should be disengaged from what he called "regional" concerns.

As an independent discipline, hermeneutics could engage fully with its proper task. Kant had formulated a transcendental philosophy which addressed not simply issues of reason, but the very basis on which reason might function, as well as its limits. Schleiermacher insisted that hermeneutics had to explore the basis on which understanding texts (or human life) became possible at all. Hence, he urged, "Hermeneutics is a part of the art of thinking, and is therefore philosophical."[2] It demands both "linguistic competence" and "ability for knowing people."[3] "In interpretation it is essential that one be able to step out of one's own frame of mind into that of the author."[4]

Because this discipline now entailed philosophical issues about the nature of human understanding, linguistic questions about texts, theological enquiries about biblical texts, and social concerns about interpersonal communicative action, hermeneutics after Schleiermacher became in principle inevitably an *interdisciplinary* or *multidisciplinary* subject, as Paul Ricoeur (b. 1913) rightly confirms. Yet it also resists being absorbed into any of the disciplines on which it draws. This would equally lead to its destruction as an effective subject.

Survey

From 1919 to 1959

Gabler and Schleiermacher had made programmatic proposals. Nevertheless initially each discipline tended to collapse back into old paths. In biblical theology many writers accepted Gabler's point about historical enquiry. But his "true" biblical theology tended to become subsumed under the less theological category of "the history of Israelite religion." On the other hand a minority of more conservative writers tended still to impose prior conceptual or dogmatic categories onto biblical material. The situation was similar in hermeneutics. Perhaps only W. Dilthey (1833–1911) fully appreciated the potential of Schleiermacher's hermeneutics, and even he stressed the social, interpersonal, or "psychological" rather than the linguistic side. From 1919 onwards Karl Barth (1886–1968) raised important hermeneutical questions, but it was only with the work of Rudolf Bultmann (1884–1976) and his former pupil Ernst Fuchs (1903–83) that hermeneutics steadily re-emerged as a subject in its own right in theology. Since 1960 it has been reborn in philosophy, in literary and critical theory, and in social studies, as well as in theology.

The turning point for biblical theology arose from an exchange of views on method which took place between Otto Eissfeldt and Walther Eichrodt.[5] Eissfeldt's approach was broadly similar to that of Gabler. Eichrodt, by contrast, believed that a theology of the Old Testament could offer a significant degree of structural coherence without historical distortion. In the first volume of his monumental *Theology of the Old Testament* he organized his theology around the central focus of "covenant." This, he believed, avoided imposing on the Bible some modern dogmatic schema. It permitted the theologian to trace a historical basis for revelation which offered more than a mere "history of Israelite religion." Eichrodt's work is generally regarded as opening the era of "biblical theology" in the twentieth century.

The publication in 1919 of Karl Barth's commentary on Romans (with a second edition in 1921) similarly moved forward both biblical theology and hermeneutics by challenging the adequacy of a purely "historical" exegesis and also of a "history-of-religions" approach. In his preface to the first edition Barth allowed that "critical historical method of biblical research has its validity," but saw it as no more than "the *preparation*" for understanding. Understanding, Barth insisted, entails more than scrutinizing a text as a supposedly value-neutral "object." To understand Romans we ourselves must become the object of address. The text actively engages with the reader, shedding light upon the reader's own stance.

Some dismissed Barth's approach. But in line with his own work on form criticism, Rudolf Bultmann endorsed Barth's view that the New Testament texts did not serve primarily as objects of value-neutral historical enquiry. They "speak" as *kerygma* (proclamation) to readers who are *engaged* with the issues posed by the text. Following Dilthey, Bultmann agrees that an interpreter "is *governed always by a prior understanding of the subject.*"[6] Elsewhere he writes: "*There cannot be any such thing as presuppositionless exegesis.*"[7]

Hans-Georg Gadamer (b. 1900), one of the two greatest theorists of hermeneutics in the twentieth century, observes from the standpoint of philosophy that "Barth's *Romans* is a kind of hermeneutical manifesto,"[8] and adds that Bultmann has contributed explicitly to the problem of hermeneutics.[9] He recognizes affinities between his own philosophical approach and that of Ernst Fuchs in theology. Fuchs shares Heidegger's concern to overcome "the modern entanglement in the subject-object schema."[10] Fuchs writes: "The texts must translate us [*uns übersetzen müssen*] before we can translate them."[11] "*The truth has ourselves as its object*" (his italics).[12] Fuchs published his *Hermeneutik* in 1954 (with a fourth edition in 1970).

In biblical theology Eichrodt owed much to the work of his teacher Otto Procksch (1874–1947), although Procksch's own Old Testament theology was not published until 1949. Procksch also influenced the work of Gerhard von Rad (discussed below). During the war years Ethelbert Stauffer published his *Theology of the New Testament*.[13] Stauffer rejected the kind of history-of-religions approach which drove a wedge between Jesus and Paul. Paul, in his view, was not "the originator of a turn to hellenism."[14] Jesus was aware of his own vocation as Son of Man "to give his life a ransom for many" (Mark 10: 45). He perceived himself as "sent to reveal and accomplish the *gloria dei* in a world intoxicated with its own self-glorification."[15]

The most influential *Theology of the New Testament* was that of Rudolf Bultmann. We include a brief discussion on his work later, together with the distinctive contribution of Oscar Cullmann. Two Roman Catholic works on New Testament theology may also be noted. In 1950 Max Meinertz argued that biblical theology should not be distorted by imposing upon it later dogmatic or structural categories. Jesus Christ constitutes a "center" seen from multiple "points of view." He is like the white light which may be split into the colours of the rainbow.[16] Unity and variety must be held together. J. Bonsirven placed greater emphasis on the New Testament's continuity with the Old Testament, and with the apostolic church as an extension of the ministry of Jesus.[17]

Theodore C. Vriezen (b. 1899) of Utrecht published *An Outline of Old Testament Theology* in 1949 (English translation in 1958). He devotes his first hundred pages to method. He rejects equally an exclusively historical approach, which risks collapsing theology into a quasi-secular "history of Israelite religion" and an exclusively theological approach, which risks collapsing historical diversity and tension into some quasi-churchly dogmatic system. In contrast to each, Vriezen seeks to trace how "through the history of Israel God has entered history as the living Living God who seeks communion with men."[18] Here we may speak of a "line," but one which cannot be "copied by any man." For it does not take the form of a unidirectional line of "development" which can at all points be "observed" as such. It follows twists, turns, hidden periods, surprises, even apparent tensions. "The truth of faith can only be expressed in antinomies."[19] It is profoundly historical. Yet it is more than secularized history; for its mainspring and thread is that of personal interaction between God and the world which constitutes revelation in history.

A parallel in America emerged in G. Ernest Wright (1909–74), in his *God Who Acts: Biblical theology as recital* (1952). Wright stressed the unity of the Old and New Testaments, as a continuing revelation of God in history. Hence he writes: "The Church is the heir to the election of Israel . . . The events of the Exodus, wilderness wanderings and the conquest are as important for the New Testament as for the Old."[20] Revelation entails more than mere "statement"; "recital" is self-involving confession, praise, memory and hope. A response to its question "what precisely has God done?" can be discerned in "the Biblical confessions of faith."[21] These are more than value-neutral reports.

Similarities of approach in New Testament studies can be found in the English theologian Alan Richardson of Nottingham (1905–75). Like Vriezen, he rejects an exclusively historical approach as verging on secular positivism. This method "cannot tell us whether in fact God acted in history or not."[22] But Richardson also published work in philosophical apologetics, and examined the role of rationality and coherence in testing historical and theological reconstruction. Yet, as for Wright, faith and confession retain their role. In the earthly Jesus the power of God was "hidden but manifest to eyes of faith."[23] He follows Stauffer in emphasizing the role of the Son of Man for Jesus, as corporate, suffering, and awaiting vindication.[24] Like Bonsirven he sees the church as "apostolic" and continuing the work of Jesus.[25] Through baptism the verdict of the last judgment may be anticipated, so that the baptized may "be brought past . . . the final judgment . . . into the life of the Age to Come."[26]

With the notable exception of Bultmann's work, however, the work of virtually all of these writers came to be viewed, in spite of their intentions not to ignore historical diversity, as overemphasizing the unity of one or of both Testaments. By the close of the 1950s, biblical theology had passed its peak and it began to decline under the weight of criticisms identified below under "Debate." From 1960 onward "biblical theologies" began to take greater account of historical and theological diversity, but declined as a "movement." By contrast, hermeneutics acquired a new energy and sense of direction from Gadamer's work (1960).

From 1960 to 1995

The story of "biblical theology" since 1960 is brief. The momentum of the 1950s became lost. Hans Conzelmann of Göttingen (1915–89) produced *An Outline of the Theology of the New Testament* (1968; English translation, 1969), in which he made a conscious attempt to differentiate between five distinct strands of New Testament thought. He assigned different sections of his volume to the early community, to the synoptic tradition, to Paul, to post-Pauline material, and to Johannine theology. He is careful, however, not to exaggerate unduly some supposed contrast between a "simple" Jesus and a "complex" Paul.[27]

One year after Conzelmann, Werner G. Kümmel (b. 1905) published his *Theology of the New Testament* (1969; English translation, 1974) from Marburg. He distinguished firmly between the three "main witnesses" Jesus, Paul, and John. But he also allowed for lines of continuity. He writes: "Jesus and Paul are witnesses to the same historical truth, but Paul only points backwards and forward to the salvation brought by Jesus."[28] "*The experience of God's love* in the encounter with Jesus" (Kümmel's italics) can be found in the ministry of Jesus, in Paul, and in John.[29] Others continued the task of writing theologies of the New Testament. Joachim Jeremias (1900–79) published only the first of three projected volumes before his death, namely *The Proclamation of Jesus* (1971). G. E. Ladd produced a *New Testament Theology* in America (1974). B. S. Childs's work (1992) is discussed below. George B. Caird of Oxford, before his untimely death in 1984, was working on material which was edited and published in 1994.[30] Caird expounds salvation in its "three tenses" as a major theme; Jesus, as the bringer of salvation; and the need for and experience of salvation in the purposes of God.

Meanwhile, hermeneutics first became firmly established as a discipline from 1960 to the late 1970s and then exploded into a vast eruption of literature reaching huge proportions in the late 1980s and in the 1990s. Gerhard Ebeling (b. 1912) of Zurich produced a much-used survey "*Hermeneutik*" (1959) and in his inaugural lecture at Tübingen in 1947 he had argued that church history could be perceived as "the history of exposition of holy scripture." This derives part of its force from the principle that how a person or a community expounds and interprets Scripture may reveal as much about themselves as about the biblical writings. With Fuchs, he asserts: "*The text . . . becomes a hermeneutical aid in the understanding of present experience.*"[31] He follows Schleiermacher in insisting that hermeneutics constitutes a "theory of understanding"; it is not "a collection of rules."[32] It is a philosophical equivalent to a theory of knowledge.[33]

Gadamer and Ricoeur (discussed below) strongly influenced thought in America as well as in Europe. In America Robert W. Funk brought the approach of Ernst Fuchs to general notice in his *Language, Hermeneutic and Word of God* (1966). His linking of Fuchs with related issues in narrative theory and literature also recalled claims by Heidegger and Gadamer about projected "narrative worlds." Funk demonstrated the value of these approaches for interpreting the parables of Jesus.

From the early 1950s to the late 1960s many French intellectuals reacted against the subjectivism of existentialist perspectives, and explored a tradition in linguistics (mainly from Saussure) and in anthropology (largely from Lévi-Strauss) that came to be known as structuralism. Some, like F. Bovon, over-hastily saw this as an "objective" approach to meaning. Meaning appeared to be generated by forces of "difference" within a linguistic structure or anthropological system. For example, "brother" draws its meaning from its "difference" from "sister" within a kinship structure. Through the 1970s much energy was devoted by a group of biblical specialists to applying structural "grammar" (especially a grammar of narrative drawn from A. J. Greimas) to Hebrew narratives and to the parables of Jesus.[34]

At first in several respects these approaches were not "hermeneutics," but explanatory hypotheses about language *systems* (Saussure's *la langue*) rather than interpretations of language *uses* or *choices* (Saussure's *la parole*). But by the late 1960s, with the work of Roland Barthes (1915–80) and Jacques Derrida (b. 1930), structuralism had developed its own self-critique. As "poststructuralism" it showed that these "structures" transmitted social interests which made them far from "objective" or innocent. This in turn invited a new, more sophisticated hermeneutic. Some writers now described Derrida as the most important exponent of "radical hermeneutics" in the post-Gadamerian era. Barthes pointed out that such "structural systems," for example, as furniture or clothes generated coded signals about class, status, or power which invited "interpretation" at several levels.[35] Derrida's work entails "hermeneutics" in the sense that meaning is never "closed" but stands under "erasure" as each interpretation becomes deconstructed by fresh readings. Texts are incomplete textures which may be "undone."[36]

To some, biblical texts appeared also to embody structures which were far from politically neutral. Norman Gottwald explored the political and social subtexts which he claimed to detect behind what had hitherto often been viewed as merely "historical" in the reflecting ordinary processes of cause and effect.[37] Michel Foucault (1926–84) and Derrida underlined the part played by social power interests in literary texts. Claims to truth often represented disguised bids to legitimate power over others.[38] The Bible may readily be pressed into the service of such manipulative strategies. Hence behind the rise of the hermeneutics of Latin American liberation theology of the 1970s and behind the feminist hermeneutics of the 1980s lies the suspicion that power interests on behalf of a class or a gender permeate the language of texts and traditions of interpretation.

At first Latin American Liberation theologians restricted their attention to issues about "pre-understanding" (*Vorverständnis*) as these had been raised by Dilthey, Heidegger, and Bultmann. Gustavo Gutiérrez (b. 1928, Peru; *The Theology of Liberation*, 1971) and Juan Luis Segundo (b. 1928, Uruguay; *A Liberation of Theology*, 1975) stressed that no biblical interpretation is value-neutral. Only a pre-understanding already driven by a concern for justice could read liberating texts with transformative effect. Academic neutrality, they believed, is an illusion inherited from the Western Enlightenment. They found a need for a "preliminary" understanding confirmed in Freire's notion of the need for "consciousness-raising" (*concientización*).[39]

This set the stage for a second move. If Bultmann had argued that "myth" might obstruct the true intention of New Testament texts, might not the same be said of "ideology"? A program of "de-ideologization" was proposed, parallel to Bultmann's notion of "demythologizing." By the 1970s they could also draw on Paul Ricoeur's notion of a "hermeneutic of suspicion." Interpretation of texts which appeared superficially "innocent" might hide the real wishes and aims of interpreters to legitimate their power over against claims of others. Leonardo and Clodovis Boff, Severino Croatto, and Hugo Assmann, among others, explore these issues further.

Initially feminist hermeneutics drew little from serious hermeneutical theory. One of the earlier works, Phyllis Trible's *God and the Rhetoric of Sexuality* (1978), explored female imagery relating to God in biblical texts, and the gender-inclusive character of "image of God." Her later *Texts of Terror* (1984) examined narratives of exploited women, such as Hagar and Tamar.

A more explicit "hermeneutic of suspicion" and criticism of ideology may be found in Elisabeth Schüssler Fiorenza's well-known *In Memory of Her* (1983). Here she sets in contrast a willingness of the Johannine tradition to acknowledge the role of Mary Magdalene as the first witness of the resurrection, and therefore "the apostle of the apostles" and tendencies which she believes she finds in Luke and Paul to suppress the role of women in these traditions.[40] Feminists, she urges, must "apply content-criticism (*Sachkritik*) as well as suspicion, to rank and to select women's texts."[41] She endorses the theme found in many feminist writers that biblical scholarship is not, and cannot be, "value-neutral"; since both biblical author and the overwhelming majority of biblical interpreters have been men.[42] They produce or read texts through male eyes, but assign to the texts and readings a gender-neutral status. A flood of literature has now appeared which finds gender issues everywhere. But it should be noted that varying aims, varying hermeneutical strategies, and varying theologies may all go under the misleadingly uniform term "feminist hermeneutics," which conceals their fundamental difference.[43]

Hermeneutical theory and practice in the mid-1990s has become marked by a radical pluralism of goals, assumptions, and methods. The success or failure of a given attempt to meet a specific goal cannot be assessed in terms of criteria formulated in relation to some other goal. Some perceive this as a new hermeneutical freedom, others as verging on hermeneutical anarchy. Limits of space prohibit an exposition of W. Pannenberg's powerful attempt to hold together hermeneutical understanding with an emphasis on the unity of rationality and human knowledge. His work is innovative and masterly.[44]

Specific Writers on Biblical Theology

Walther Eichrodt and Gerhard von Rad

Walther Eichrodt (1890–1978) became a professor at Basel in 1933, and followed the first volume of his *Theology of the Old Testament* with a fifth revised edition in 1957, and a second volume in 1964 (English translations 1961 and 1967). Covenant, he argued, provides the theological basis for a defined relationship between God and his people. He writes: "The fear that constantly haunts the pagan world, the fear of arbitrariness . . . in the Godhead, is excluded. With this God, men know exactly where they stand; *an atmosphere of trust and security* is created."[45] This offers a line of continuity with the New Testament. Jesus trusts God as "Abba" and Paul speaks of a defined relationship of "adoption" (Mark 14: 36; Romans 8: 16, 17). In Eichrodt's view, this is different from any "naturalistic" relationship which depends on divine immanence. It expresses "*personal communion between God and man*"[46] and has "a moral basis."[47]

This covenantal structure makes possible "*sacral communion.*"[48] In this relationship "gift" sacrifices become significant but "*atonement or expiation*" also has a place[49] since God is both "*the creative power of love*" and yet also "*the wholly 'other.'* "[50] God promises an "ultimate goal of history . . . the messianic consummation."[51] He gives his Spirit "to actualize the will of God in all forms of human existence."[52] His purpose thus extends beyond Israel to all creation. Family, friendship, peace, and prosperity indirectly witness to God as the giver of all that is good.

Gerhard von Rad (1901–71) published the two volumes of his influential *Old Testament Theology* in 1957 and 1960 (English translations, 1962 and 1965). He taught at Jena, Göttingen, and Heidelberg. Like Eichrodt, he saw Israel's faith as based on historical events, interpreted as acts of God. Old Testament theology springs from successive reinterpretations of past history in the light of new events in a dialectic of continuity and novelty.

Gunkel's form criticism (especially on the Psalms) influenced Gerhard von Rad. Changes in a psalm's setting (its *Sitz im Leben*) suggested reinterpretations of its earlier meaning and function. The Deuteronomist, similarly, "retells" the narrative of Moses from the vantage point of the Deuteronomist's own setting in history. Deuteronomy and Chronicles offer examples of "the most varied forms of the presentation of God's history with Israel in its different strata."[53] Yet this diversity of "reinterpretation" does not eclipse a thematic unity. Thus in the Hexateuch "God's promise of the land" remains a recurrent theme at all levels. On the other hand, "Israel reflected on this saving act in very diverse ways."[54]

To reinterpret an already interpreted history from various vantage points brings us close to the concept known as "effective history" (*Wirkungsgeschichte*). This assumes importance in the hermeneutics of Gadamer and Wolfhart Pannenberg (b. 1928). One example comes from Israel "historicizing" agrarian festivals. Gerhard von Rad insists that this reflects "a unique understanding of the world . . . Israel's belief that she was not bound primarily to the periodic cycle of nature but the definite historical events . . . [constituted] entering into the saving event itself."[55] This understanding of history as "linear," or as moving toward an end, became for Pannenberg an essential condition for interpreting the meaning of the present within history. Only in the light of the end does the present have meaning. "The eschatological events . . . bind history into a whole."[56] This "linear" view of history gives rise to "expectation" and in Pannenberg's theology this offers an essential clue for christology. "Jesus stood in a tradition that expected the coming of this God." Yet, in a changed setting this also invites reinterpretation. Israel's tradition also became "transformed from within by the appearance of Jesus."[57] This view affirms "an intertwining . . . of words and of events", a "unity of facts and their meaning."[58] The influence of the biblical theology of Gerhard von Rad can scarcely be exaggerated.

Is Brevard Childs an exponent of "biblical theology"?

Brevard S. Childs (b. 1923) of Yale is associated in his earlier work with a critique of "biblical theology" rather than with an exposition of it, in his *Biblical Theology in Crisis* (1970). Yet he has recently published a volume under the title *Biblical Theology of the Old and New Testaments* (1992). The key to Childs's work lies in his approaching the theology of the Bible as a content disclosed by the canonical text of the Bible as the sacred Scripture of the Christian Church, rather than as the end-process of a more primary history which lies behind it. The "context" for inter-pretation is the role of a chapter or book within the larger canonical text, not the process of retracing history back to some "earliest source." This shift of focus from processes *behind* the text to *the text itself* marks off what many call "canon criticism" in contrast to "biblical theology." Childs's proximity to the Yale school of literary theory with its earlier emphasis on the text alone may be thought to play a part.

In his *Biblical Theology in Crisis* Childs accused the biblical theology school of a compromise with the older liberal "history-of-religions" school, in spite of their claims on behalf of "theology." Nevertheless Childs shares with Wright the notion of biblical theology as self-involving confession. Henning Graf Reventlow places him among those biblical theologians for whom theology is "related to faith" and "the descriptive task was included in the theological task."[59] As against Stendahl and Räisänen, Childs approaches the biblical text "from within a community of faith, rather than from a neutral phenomenological reconstruction."[60] Thus his commen-tary on Exodus (1974) includes some account of the "reception" of interpretations among communities of readers.

Rudolf Bultmann and Oscar Cullmann

Bultmann (1884–76) receives attention in a separate chapter. Hence we offer only a brief account of his *Theology of the New Testament* (1948–53; English translations 1952 and 1955) and some notes on his hermeneutics. The message of Jesus is in Bultmann's view not a part of New Testament theology. It is only "a presupposition for the theology of the New Testament."[61] Jesus did proclaim the reign of God and call people to decision.[62] But only retrospectively after the rise of the Easter faith was the "proclaimer" then "proclaimed."[63] Only retrospectively can it be said that Jesus' call to decision implies a christology.[64]

Only in the pre-Pauline hellenistic church did the confession of Jesus as "Lord" and "Son of God" emerge.[65] With the theology of Paul, an appreciation of the message of the cross as pure grace emerged explicitly and the cross perceived as "the judgment of God . . . upon all human accomplishment and boasting."[66] A radical contrast emerges between humankind prior to faith and humankind under faith. "Flesh" (*sarx*) in its most explicitly theological usage denotes "trust in oneself as being able to procure life . . . in one's own strength."[67] Under faith, however, God may pronounce a verdict in advance of the judgment as "rightwised."[68] "The decision of faith has done away with the past," although it must be daily renewed.[69] Humankind may become liberated from bondage to the cause–effect chain of past decisions (law, sin, and death) to experience the freedom of the Holy Spirit as "the power of futurity."[70]

How much of this language, however, can be interpreted as describing states of affairs? Bultmann's proposals about "demythologizing" put forward in other writings make this problematic. Especially in Paul and in John, any quasi-historical language needs to be interpreted as existential language which addresses the hearer or reader in terms of his or her own present. Language which might appear to describe future judgment, for example, may be interpreted without remainder as a summons to responsibility in the present. Supposedly "objective" language in Paul about atonement or resurrection is a "primitive mythology" designed to call the self to self-renunciation and obedience. These issues are discussed fully elsewhere.[71]

Oscar Cullmann (b. 1902) taught at Strasbourg, Basel, and Paris. In his foreword to *Christ and Time* (1945) he asks: "In what does the *specifically Christian element* of New Testament revelation consist?"[72] He rejects the answers of Barth, Bultmann, and Martin Werner. Werner had argued that virtually the whole of New Testament and early Christian theology depended on a conscious reorientation away from eschatology when an expectation of an imminent end did not materialize.

Cullmann recovers the principle that "Primitive Christian faith and thinking do not start from the spatial contrast between the Here and the Beyond, but from the time distinction between Formerly and Now and Then . . . Thus the author of the Epistle to the Hebrews in his famous definition of faith (11: 1) names first of all the 'assurance of things *hoped for*,' that is, things which are future."[73] Cullmann does not deny that a contrast between "above" and "below" exists within the New Testament. But it is not "the essential thing." Even the reference here to faith in "things not seen" refers primarily to what is not yet seen because it has *not yet visibly occurred*. Noah, Abraham, and the people of faith act in the present *on the basis of promise concerning the future* which is yet to become visible, because it is yet to occur.

Purposive time embodies moments of opportunity.[74] Linear time demands the concepts of a "beginning" and an "end."[75] Cyclical notions of time by contrast remain foreign to distinctively biblical perspectives. In contrast to gnosticism and docetism, "primitive Christianity knows nothing of timelessness."[76] The experience of the Holy Spirit does not remove the believer from time. "The Holy Spirit is nothing else than the anticipation of the end in the present."[77] "Man *is* that which he *will become* only in the future."[78] Yet Christians still sin and still die. "The time tension is manifested in the Church through the continuance of sin, which nevertheless has already been defeated by the Spirit."[79] "The decisive battle in a war may already have occurred . . . and yet the war still continues."[80] Thus time may be perceived as a "history of salvation" or "salvation-history" (*Heilsgeschichte*). Within this process Christ represents "the central point." "*For the believing Christian the midpoint, since Easter, no longer lies in the future.*"[81] Judaism and Christianity do not tell different histories, but they differ decisively "in *the division of time.*"[82] Yet expectation of a decisive end still remains in the New Testament. Here Cullmann convincingly attacks the views of Schweitzer and Werner.

The groundwork laid out in *Christ and Time* informs Cullmann's later work *The Christology of the New Testament* (1957; English translations, 1959 and 1963) and *Salvation in History* (1965; English translation, 1967). In his *Christology* Cullmann refuses to underestimate the continuity between the Old and New Testament. As against Bultmann's view that the confession of Christ as "Lord" (*kyrios*) arose first in hellenism, Cullmann refers to the unavoidable "memory" that "*Adonai* was certainly the characteristic Jewish designation for God."[83]

In *Salvation in History* Cullmann argues that Christian apostles, like the Jewish prophets before them, witness to and interpret God's saving activity in history. Like Gerhard von Rad, Cullmann sees each new interpretation as a reinterpretation (often in the light of new events) of already interpreted events. Nevertheless salvation-history remains a single history, of which Christ's coming in redemptive work constitutes the "mid-point." Christian existence draws its distinctive character from its part in the tension between "already fulfilled" and "not yet completed."

Cullmann includes a brief section on hermeneutics. He comments: "It is surely correct that an exegesis without presuppositions is an illusion."[84] His view is not to be equated with Stendahl's. But he warns his readers not to abuse this principle. He stresses the need for *"special effort"* to become aware of our own prejudices, and to engage in *"a simple listening."*[85] More seriously still, he warns against Bultmann's proposals to reduce meanings of texts to the level of the existential present. This would destroy salvation *as history*. Faith, in Paul, means "believing that someone else has already accomplished the saving work *for me*, precisely because it has been done completely *independently of me and my believing.*"[86]

Specific Exponents of Hermeneutical Theory

Hans-Georg Gadamer

Hans-Georg Gadamer (b. 1900) studied under Heidegger and published work on Plato in the 1930s. After difficult war years he became Rector of Leipzig University, and then professor at Frankfurt and Heidelberg. His monumental *Truth and Method* (1960; fourth edition, 1975; English translation from fifth edition, 1989) has entirely reshaped twentieth-century hermeneutics. It led to reappraisals of reason in philosophy, of texts in theology and literary theory, and of understanding in social sciences. His *Collected Works* amount to ten volumes in German.

Gadamer sees "method" as a hindrance to truth. Following too closely the generalizing techniques of science, "method" tends to determine *in advance* the terms on which truth should be understood. Deceived by method in science, an interpreter tries to "master" texts, life, or art, rather than letting them confront him or her on their own terms. Except for his correct exemption of morality, Descartes in effect promoted "the total reconstruction of all truths by reason."[87] But this Enlightenment "method" is misconceived. We must return with Vico to "old truths . . . to the *sensus communis* . . . to elements present in the classical concept of wisdom."[88] Wisdom goes deeper than knowledge and draws on tradition for transmitting reinterpretations and actualizations of truth in events. It does not merely "subsume the individual under a universal category."[89]

Like a game, or like a work of art, truth becomes disclosed in a variety of eventful "performances," none of which is identical in every way with another, or it would not be a game. Art is never "exhausted" by cashing it out as a series of "aesthetic concepts." In play, the game projects a "world" which enfolds the player in its own network of objectives and criteria of success. It provides the horizons within which players think and act. Here we see "the primacy of play over the consciousness of the player."[90] Against the false trail initiated by Enlightenment rationalism, Gadamer traces the hermeneutical tradition from Schleiermacher through Dilthey, Husserl, and Yorck to Heidegger. In Heidegger, the horizon of a pre-given "world" provides the starting point for understanding. But Gadamer has a more positive view of tradition and its "history of effects" (*Wirkungsgeschichte*) than Heidegger. A tradition which, along with its prejudices, also transmits wisdom allows for a "formation" (*Bildung*) which "builds." In particular, this process is achieved through a mutual respect between those who stand within different horizons, through a genuine "listening," each to the other, in dialogue. If neither tries simply to impose assertions onto the other, "something new" may "emerge," in which truth becomes "actualized" in an event of meeting. The key is not "asserting one's view," but "being transformed . . . We do not remain what we were."[91]

In theology this invites a renewed understanding of what it is to listen to the text and to listen to others (or to God) without imposing our own terms as the "grid" or "method" which we ourselves choose to use. This has profound consequences for reappraisals of reason. Reason alone is not enough; but credulity alone would not be "wisdom." Like Hegel and Wittgenstein, Gadamer's creative genius treads a razor edge from which it can fall into either of two opposite difficulties. Some see Gadamer as upholding tradition; others see him as legitimizing a move toward contextual relativism and postmodernism. Both responses are partly true and partly false, and demand that we read Gadamer with care.

Paul Ricoeur

Paul Ricoeur (b. 1913) studied at the Sorbonne with Marcel, and has been a professor at Strasbourg, Paris, and Chicago. Behind his earlier works on the human will (1950) and human fallibility (1960) lay Marcel's interest in human personhood. But during the years of war, in which he both won the Croix de Guerre and was a prisoner in Germany, Ricoeur used the opportunity to undertake a close study of Jaspers, Husserl, and Heidegger. Jaspers's dual interest in philosophy and psychiatry informed Ricoeur's work *The Symbolism of Evil* (1960; English translation, 1969). Sharing Jaspers's positive view of symbols, Ricoeur argued that symbols operate with power not least because they embrace two levels of meaning. Guilt, for example, draws on the "double meaning" of burden, bondage, and stain. Far from being inferior versions of conceptual thought, "the symbol gives rise to thought."[92]

We noted above why French intellectual life turned first to structuralism and then to its own self-critique in poststructuralism. Ricoeur cautiously utilized aspects of these approaches for "explanation" or "critique," as a check against uncritical "understanding." His first genuinely "double" hermeneutic, of critical "suspicion" and postcritical "retrieval," comes in his masterly volume *Freud and Philosophy* (1965; English translation, 1970). The argument turns on "relations between desire and language."[93] Freud had shown that dreams could be expressions of hidden desire, but were "disguised . . . expressions."[94] Deception and disguise operate at several levels, so that even the self is deceived about its true wishes. People "tell" dreams (the "dream-text") which differ from the dream-content ("dream-thoughts"). Hence the interpreter needs "a hermeneutic of suspicion" to try to understand them. In a key comment Ricoeur asserts: "Hermeneutics seem to me to be animated by this double motivation: willingness to suspect, willingness to listen; vow of rigor, vow of obedience."[95] Ricoeur concludes: "*The idols must die – so that symbols may live.*"[96]

Ricoeur pays particular attention to metaphor, where he draws on the interactive theory of Max Black. As tensive "double-meaning" expressions which entail "split reference" they operate with creative force. However, the climax of Ricoeur's work, after a series of other volumes, appears first in his three-volume *Time and Narrative* (1983–5; English translation, 1984–8) and then in his *Oneself as Another* (1990; English translation, 1992). He begins *Time and Narrative* by discussing Augustine's reflections on time. The human experience of time makes possible an experience which becomes differentiated into expectation (future), attention (present), and memory (past). Hence, "through the experience of human time (memory, attention, hope) I come to understand the world, its objects, and my own present."[97] But Augustine considers human time both as a series of moments and as a whole, as a part of creation. "It is true of the whole history of mankind."[98] "Temporality" (in Heidegger's sense of the "possibility" of "human" time) constitutes the necessary condition for narrative and for the intelligibility of texts, life, and action. This is complemented by Aristotle's theory of "plot" (*muthos*). "Plot" *organizes* narrative events into a *coherent whole*, through "*poiésis*" or "making" (*faire*). "To make up a plot is . . . to make the intelligible spring from the accidental, the universal from the singular."[99] In temporal terms it projects "a world that the reader appropriates."[100] This readily applies to biblical texts. Some argue, for example, that the Gospel of Mark uses changes in the speed of "human time" to depict a hastening toward a goal which turns out to be the Passion portrayed as if in slow motion. Thus "plot" "organizes" the action by *poiésis*.

Ricoeur's complex volume *Oneself as Another* exceeds even *Time and Narrative* in depth and power. He draws on earlier themes to vindicate a concept of personhood as identity-within-temporal-change that does much to restore human selfhood against the skepticism not only of Hume and positivism but more especially of the shifting quicksands of postmodernity.

Debate, Achievement, and Agenda

The "biblical theology" movement

The central item of controversy surrounding the classical exponents of biblical theology in the 1950s concerned their emphasis on the unity of the Old or New Testament, and often also the unity between them. Did this serve negatively to flatten the rich diversity of distinct theological and historical traditions? Or did it reflect positively the coherent outworking of divine purposes which lead toward a promised goal? Such unity need not be "timeless" nor uniformly "linear." As Vriezen argued, it may allow for twists and turns, for relative discontinuities, tensions and surprises. On the other hand, a new emphasis on theological diversity arose from redaction criticism in the late 1950s and this weakened the hold of "biblical theology."

A more difficult clash of method arises from a recurring debate about the possibility of a purely descriptive approach to historical phenomena (Stendahl, Räisänen) and those who believe that this standpoint proves to be inadequate for theology or impossible for hermeneutics (Bultmann, Wright, Childs, Gadamer). Childs sees no way of accommodating the contrast between a liberal or secular "history-of-religions" approach and the role of the biblical writings as texts for Christian theology. Reventlow traces how this *impasse* emerges again and again in the history of the subject. Nowadays it has come to be perceived as an explicit issue within hermeneutics[101] where it becomes transposed into issues about the difference between report and descriptive propositions and the logic of self-involvement or of speech-acts. Stendahl and Räisänen fail to address these issues adequately, but on the other side we must note Pannenberg's comments (below).

In his rightly influential work *The Semantics of Biblical Language* (1962), James Barr attacks tendencies among exponents of biblical theology from the 1930s to the 1960s to exaggerate the supposed distinctiveness of "Hebraic thought-forms" on the basis of accidents of grammar and lexicography. This tendency is present in the first four volumes edited by Gerhard Kittel of the *Theological Dictionary of the New Testament* (in German, 1933–42), even if it is less pronounced in later volumes edited by G. Friedrich (in English, 10 volumes, 1964–76). Such arguments often rested on dubious evidence. They also exaggerated differences from the modern world. However, these generalizing claims should not be countered merely by equally sweeping claims in the opposite direction. A "linear" rather than cyclical view of time and history, for example, does indeed characterize Hebrew-Christian traditions. Barr perceived that part of the problem arose from overestimating the importance of histories of words. He observes: "the etymology of a word is not a statement about its meaning but about its history."[102]

The specific approach to history worked out by Gerhard von Rad maintains a strong influence on contemporary systematic theology. This plays a major part in Pannenberg and in Moltmann, and has affinities with Gadamer's hermeneutics. Cullmann's recovery of the importance of the temporal dimension for understanding salvation and God's acts also has far-reaching effects. It avoids dualist distortions of biblical Christianity. Nevertheless Pannenberg resists the notion of what he perceives as "a ghetto of redemptive history" which is found too readily in "biblical theology."[103] If God is one, history is one, and knowledge is one. Creation and eschatology point to this.

Hermeneutics

Gadamer's epoch-making work has placed a permanent question mark against the privilege accorded by Enlightenment rationalism to the centrality of the individual self and to the "method" of reason alone. All human life, including action, art, and texts, invites understanding on its own terms, not in terms of some prior method predetermined in advance of engaging with the material. Nothing is value-neutral in the sense of failing to reflect some prior horizon of understanding. From within that horizon, an advance can be made only by respecting fully the otherness of other horizons, and undergoing an open process of listening which may result in the transformation of the self and its prior horizons. Horizons may then move and become enlarged.

The strengths of Gadamer's work for biblical studies include a recognition on grounds other than theology of "the primacy of the text," and for pastoral theology they encourage respect for the other and "listening." Wisdom is rightly perceived to transcend mere knowledge. This is especially relevant to our age of information technology. Nevertheless Gadamer's work may also lead in a less constructive direction. It may also encourage a contextual pragmatism which offers no criteria to determine what would count as a "valid," "appropriate," or even "edifying" (cf. *Bildung*) performance of a text or work of art outside its own context. Hence his work may be interpreted either in a more conservative direction (with G. Warnke) or in a postmodernist direction (with R. Rorty).

A fine balance is achieved by Ricoeur between the need for a hermeneutic of suspicion which "destroys idols," and a hermeneutic of retrieval which seeks to recover the creative power of symbol, metaphor, and narrative. He recognizes and counters the attack of postmodernism on the human self as a responsible agent; but with equal balance rejects Enlightenment rationalism which places the self at the center. Rightly, he draws on the interdisciplinary resources of philosophy, semiotics, literary theory, social studies, and at times theology to offer a constructive way forward. Perhaps only his account of the relation of certain texts to history and his over-ready acceptance of notions of "the death of the author" call for serious hesitation.

Hermeneutics has now given birth to a wide plurality of goals, methods, criteria, and approaches. Even supposedly single named movements (e.g., feminist hermeneutics) cover a multitude of approaches, some incompatible with others. Some view this as positive liberation, others as negative anarchy. The latter see this trend as reducing biblical and Christian claims to truth to the status of textual forces, or worse, to bids for power by sub-traditions or guilds. A massive agenda has been set for theology which raises profound issues of language, meaning, truth, manipulation, domination, and self-deception.

Notes

1 Krister Stendahl, "Biblical theology, contemporary," in *Interpreter's Dictionary of the Bible* (Nashville, TN, 1962), vol. 1, pp. 418–31, and "Method in the study of biblical theology," in J. P. Hyatt (ed.), *The Bible in Modern Scholarship* (Nashville, TN, 1965), pp. 196–209; Heikki Räisänen, *Beyond New Testament Theology* (London, 1990).

2 F. D. E. Schleiermacher, *Hermeneutics: The handwritten manuscripts* (Missoula, MN, 1977), p. 97 (manuscript from 1819).

3 Ibid., p. 101.

4 Ibid., p. 42 (manuscript from 1805).

5 Eissfeldt and Eichrodt published their essays respectively in *Zeitschrift für die alttestamentliche Wissenschaft*, 44 (1926), pp. 1–12, and 47 (1929), pp. 83–91.

6 Rudolf Bultmann, "The problem of hermeneutics," in *Essays Philosophical and Theological* (London, 1955), p. 239; Bultmann's italics.

7 Rudolf Bultmann, *Existence and Faith* (London, 1961), p. 344.

8 Hans-Georg Gadamer, *Truth and Method*, 2nd English edn (London, 1989), p. 509.

9 Ibid., p. 521.

10 Ibid., p. 527.

11 Ernst Fuchs, "The hermeneutical problem," in J. M. Robinson (ed.), *The Future of Our Religious Past* (London, 1971), p. 277; published in German in E. Dinkler (ed.), *Zeit und Geschichte* (1964), p. 365.

12 E. Fuchs, "The New Testament and the hermeneutical problem," in J. M. Robinson and J. B. Cobb, Jr, *New Frontiers in Theology II: The New Hermeneutic* (New York, 1964), p. 143.

13 Ethelbert Stauffer, *Theology of the New Testament* (London, 1955). First published in German in 1941, with a revised edition in 1948.

14 Ibid., p. 75.

15 Ibid., p. 28.

16 M. Meinertz, *Theologie des Neuen Testament*, 2 vols (Bonn, 1950), vol. 1, p. 3.

17 J. Bonsirven, *Theology of the New Testament* (London, 1963).

18 Theodore C. Vriezen, *Outline of Old Testament Theology* (Oxford, 1958), p. 17.

19 Ibid., pp. 125, 76,

20 G. Ernest Wright, *God Who Acts: Biblical theology as recital* (London, 1952), pp. 62–3.

21 Ibid., p. 66.

22 Alan Richardson, *An Introduction to the Theology of the New Testament* (London, 1958), p. 11.

23 Ibid., p. 63.

24 Ibid., p. 139.

25 Ibid., p. 291.

26 Ibid., p. 341.

27 H. Conzelmann, *An Outline of the Theology of the New Testament* (London, 1969), pp. 157–70.

28 W. G. Kümmel, *The Theology of the New Testament* (London, 1974), p. 254; cf. pp. 249–54.

29 Ibid., p. 55.

30 G. B. Caird, *New Testament Theology*, ed. L. D. Hurst (Oxford, 1994).

31 Gerhard Ebeling, *Word and Faith* (London, 1963), p. 33; Ebeling's italics.

32 Ibid., p. 313.

33 Ibid., p. 317.

34 A typical exponent is D. Patte, *What is Structural Exegesis?* (Philadelphia, 1976)

and *The Religious Dimensions of Biblical Texts* (Atlanta, GA, 1990).

35 R. Barthes, *Elements of Semiology* (London, 1967) and *Mythologies* (London, 1972).

36 J. Derrida, *Speech and Phenomena, and Other Essays on Husserl's Theory of Signs* (Evanston, IL, 1973) and *Of Grammatology* (Baltimore, MD, 1975); cf. Hugh J. Silverman, *Textualities: Between hermeneutics and deconstruction* (New York and London, 1994).

37 N. Gottwald, *The Tribes of Yahweh* (New York, 1979).

38 M. Foucault, *The Order of Things* (London, 1970) and many other works.

39 Gustavo Gutiérrez, *A Theology of Liberation* (New York, 1973, and London, 1974), p. 156; cf. pp. 6, 11, 216–25.

40 Elisabeth Schüssler Fiorenza, *In Memory of Her* (New York and London, 1983), pp. 315–34; cf. p. 52.

41 Elisabeth Schüssler Fiorenza, "The will to choose or to reject," in Letty M. Russell (ed.), *Feminist Interpretation of the Bible* (Oxford, 1985), pp. 125–46.

42 Ibid., p. 130.

43 Anthony C. Thiselton, *New Horizons in Hermeneutics: The theory and practice of transforming biblical reading* (London and Grand Rapids, MI, 1992), pp. 430–70; cf. 379–409.

44 Wolfhart Pannenberg, *Basic Questions in Theology*, 3 vols (London, 1970–3), vol. 1, pp. 96–210; cf. Thiselton, *New Horizons in Hermeneutics*, pp. 331–8.

45 Walther Eichrodt, *Theology of the Old Testament*, 2 vols (London, 1961–7), vol. 1, p. 38; Eichrodt's italics.

46 Ibid., p. 43; Eichrodt's italics.

47 Ibid., p. 61.

48 Ibid., p. 154; Eichrodt's italics.

49 Ibid., p. 138.

50 Ibid., p. 281.

51 Ibid., pp. 478–9.

52 Ibid., vol. 2, p. 63.

53 Gerhard von Rad, *Old Testament Theology*, 2 vols (Edinburgh, 1962–5), vol. 1, p. v.

54 Ibid., pp. 296–7.

55 Ibid., vol. 2, p. 104.

56 Wolfhart Pannenberg, "The revelation of God in Jesus of Nazareth," in J. M. Robinson and J. B. Cobb, Jr (eds), *New Frontiers*

in *Theology III: Theology as history* (New York, 1967), p. 122; cf. 101–33.

57 Ibid., pp. 102, 108.

58 Ibid., pp. 120, 127.

59 Henning Graf Reventlow, *Problems of Biblical Theology in the Twentieth Century* (London, 1986), p. 8.

60 Brevard S. Childs, *Biblical Theology of the Old and New Testaments* (London, 1992), p. 100.

61 Rudolf Bultmann, *Theology of the New Testament*, 2 vols (London, 1952–5), vol. 1, p. 3.

62 Ibid., p. 9.

63 Ibid., pp. 48–9.

64 Ibid., p. 43.

65 Ibid., pp. 121–33.

66 Ibid., p. 188.

67 Ibid., p. 239.

68 Ibid., pp. 270–9.

69 Ibid., p. 322.

70 Ibid., p. 335.

71 Anthony C. Thiselton, *The Two Horizons: New Testament hermeneutics and philosophical description* (Carlisle and Grand Rapids, MI, 1980 and 1993), pp. 205–92.

72 Oscar Cullmann, *Christ and Time* (London, 1951), p. 12.

73 Ibid., p. 37.

74 Greek *kairos*; ibid., pp. 39–44.

75 *Arché* and *telos*; ibid., pp. 51–60.

76 Ibid., p. 62.

77 Ibid., p. 72.

78 Ibid., p. 75.

79 Ibid., p. 155.

80 Ibid., p. 84.

81 Ibid., p. 81; Cullmann's italics.

82 Ibid., p. 82; Cullmann's italics.

83 Oscar Cullmann, *Christology of the New Testamant* (London, 1959), p. 200.

84 Oscar Cullmann, *Salvation in History* (London, 1967), p. 66.

85 Ibid., p. 67; Cullmann's italics.

86 Ibid., p. 69; Cullmann's italics.

87 Hans-Georg Gadamer, *Truth and Method*, 2nd English edn (London, 1989), p. 279.

88 Ibid., p. 19.

89 Ibid., p. 21.

90 Ibid., p. 102.

91 Ibid., p. 379.

92 Paul Ricoeur, *The Symbolism of Evil* (1969).

93 Paul Ricoeur, *Freud and Philosophy: An essay on interpretation* (New Haven, 1970), p. 5.

94 Ibid.

95 Ibid., p. 27.

96 Ibid., p. 531; Ricoeur's italics.

97 Paul Ricoeur, *Time and Narrative*, 3 vols (Chicago and London, 1984–8), vol. 1, p. 16.

98 Ibid., p. 22.

99 Ibid., p. 41.

100 Ibid., p. 50.

101 Francis Watson, *Text, Church and World: Biblical interpretation in theological perspective* (Edinburgh, 1994), pp. 1–77; Thiselton, *The Two Horizons*, pp. 53–114, 314–26, and *New Horizons in Hermeneutics*, pp. 272–313, 558–619.

102 James Barr, *The Semantics of Biblical Language* (Oxford, 1961), p. 109.

103 Wolfhart Pannenberg, *Basic Questions in Theology*, vol. 1, p. 41.

Bibliography

Primary: biblical theology

Bultmann, Rudolf, *Theology of the New Testament*, 2 vols (London, 1952–5).

Childs, Brevard S., *Biblical Theology of the Old and New Testaments* (London, 1992).

Cullmann, Oscar, *Christ and Time* (London, 1951).

—— *Salvation in History* (London, 1967).

Eichrodt, Walther, *Theology of the Old Testament*, 2 vols (London, 1961–7).

Rad, Gerhard von, *Old Testament Theology*, 2 vols (Edinburgh, 1962–5).

Richardson, Alan, *An Introduction to the Theology of the New Testament* (London, 1958).

Vriezen, Theodore C., *Outline of Old Testament Theology* (Oxford, 1958).

Wright, G. Ernest, *God Who Acts: Biblical theology as recital* (London, 1952).

Primary: hermeneutics

Bultmann, Rudolf, "The Problem of Hermeneutics," in *Essays Philosophical and Theological* (London, 1955), pp. 234–61.

Ebeling, Gerhard, *Word and Faith* (London, 1963).

Gadamer, Hans-Georg, *Truth and Method*, 2nd Eng. edn (London, 1989).

Pannenberg, Wolfhart, *Basic Questions in Theology*, 3 vols (London, 1970–3), vol. 1, pp. 96–181 and vol. 3, pp. 192–210.

Ricoeur, Paul, *Freud and Philosophy: An essay on interpretation* (New Haven, 1970).

—— *Essays on Biblical Interpretation* (Philadelphia, 1980).

—— *Time and Narrative*, 3 vols (Chicago and London, 1984–8).

—— *Oneself as Another* (Chicago and London, 1992).

—— *Figuring the Sacred: Religion, narrative and imagination* (Minneapolis, 1995).

Schleiermacher, Friedrich D. E., *Hermeneutics: The handwritten manuscripts* (Missoula, MN, 1977).

Secondary or critical

Barr, James, *The Semantics of Biblical Language* (Oxford, 1961).

Childs, Brevard S., *Biblical Theology in Crisis* (Philadelphia, 1970).

Fodor, James, *Christian Hermeneutics: Paul Ricoeur and the refiguring of theology* (Oxford, 1995).

Grondin, Jean, *Introduction to Philosophical Hermeneutics* (New Haven and London, 1994).

Harrington, Wilfrid, *The Path of Biblical Theology* (Dublin, 1973).

Hayes, John H. and Prussner, F. C., *Old Testament Theology: Its history and development* (London and Atlanta, GA, 1985).

Jeanrond, Werner G., *Theological Hermeneutics* (London, 1991).

Morgan, Robert, with Barton, John, *Biblical Interpretation* (Oxford, 1988).

Mueller-Volmer, Kurt (ed.), *The Hermeneutics Reader* (Oxford, 1986).

Räisänen, Heikki, *Beyond New Testament Theology* (London, 1990).

Reventlow, Henning Graf, *Problems of Biblical Theology in the Twentieth Century* (London, 1986).

Schneiders, Sandra M., *The Revelatory Text: Interpreting the New Testament as sacred Scripture* (San Francisco, 1991).

Smart, James D., *The Past, Present and Future of Biblical Theology* (Philadelphia, 1979).

Stendahl, Krister, "Biblical theology, contemporary," *Interpreter's Dictionary of the Bible* (Nashville, TN, 1962), vol. 1, pp. 418–31.

—— "Method in the study of biblical theology," in J. P. Hyatt (ed.), *The Bible in Modern Scholarship* (Nashville, TN, 1965), pp. 196–209.

Thiselton, Anthony C., *The Two Horizons: New Testament hermeneutics and philosophical description* (Carlisle and Grand Rapids, MI, 1980 and 1993).

—— *New Horizons in Hermeneutics: The theory and practice of transforming biblical reading* (London and Grand Rapids, MI, 1992).

Warnke, Georgia, *Gadamer: Hermeneutics, tradition and reason* (Cambridge, 1987).

Watson, Francis, *Text, Church and World: Biblical interpretation in theological perspective* (Edinburgh, 1994).

Ecumenical Theology

Michael Root

Introduction

"Ecumenical" is a characteristic virtually all theology would claim for itself. Who today would want to be anti-ecumenical? In the course of the twentieth century, however, "ecumenical theology" has come to refer to a specific branch of theological work, with its own distinctive goal, style, and central texts. Most often "ecumenical theology" refers to theology produced with the conscious intent of contributing to the recent movement toward a greater or more visible unity of the church.

Ecumenical theology is thus defined by a *goal* and a *context*. The *goal* is the visible unity of the church. Theologians have always sought to understand and witness to the church's unity (and, of course, to its holiness, catholicity and apostolicity). In the twentieth century, however, this pursuit has taken a new turn. The experience and perception have grown that the unity of the church is deeper and more resilient than its divisions. Catholics, Anglicans, Lutherans, Orthodox, Baptists, all belong to the one Church of Christ. That the churches nevertheless exist in division, refusing each other fellowship or communion in the Eucharist, has come be seen as a contradiction of the church's true nature. After all, Christ came "that all might be one" (John 17: 21).

In addition, the perception has grown that the divisions of the churches have impoverished their lives and their theologies, their understandings of themselves and of the Christian faith. An important force behind ecumenical theology has been the perception that in exploring together the shared foundations which make Christians one, we learn from each other and find new ways of expressing the fullness of Christian faith and life. At its best, ecumenical theology has sought not just unity, but renewal in the foundations and fullness of unity.

The *context* that has defined ecumenical theology has been the modern ecumenical movement. During the first decade of this century, experiences of unity across church divisions and of the difficulties created by the disunity of the churches, especially in the mission fields of Africa and Asia, led to the creation of international organizations dedicated to cooperation among the churches. In the interwar years, the foundations were laid for the World Council of Churches (WCC), whose war-delayed first assembly occurred in 1948. During this early phase of the ecumenical movement, the involvement of the Orthodox churches, while significant, was limited and the attitude of the Roman Catholic Church was officially negative. In the early 1960s, however, the full range of Orthodox churches joined the WCC and the Second Vatican Council marked the enthusiastic entrance of the Catholic Church into the ecumenical movement. Within this movement, ecumenical theology has sometimes been the work of individual theologians writing books and essays under their own names, but it has more centrally been the product of dialogues between churches or of groups within churches or ecumenical organizations (e.g., the Faith and Order Commission of the WCC).

A survey of ecumenical theology thus cannot focus on individual theologians. As will be seen, it is characteristic of ecumenical theology that it breaks with the pattern of the virtuoso individual theologian and substitutes a more communal or ecclesial mode of doing theology. The focus will thus fall on the sorts of groups carrying out ecumenical theology and the kinds of texts they have produced. Out of this survey some characteristics of ecumenical theology will emerge.

Survey: Types of Ecumenical Texts

At least three kinds of ecumenical texts can be distinguished on the basis of the sort of group that produces them.

Texts from single churches

First, some texts come from a single church, laying out its convictions about and commitments to the unity of the church. The greatest example of this sort of text, both in historical importance and theological depth, is the 1964 Roman Catholic *Decree on Ecumenism* of the Second Vatican Council, known by its first two Latin words *Unitatis Redintegratio* (The Restoration of Unity). Here a full theology of ecumenical activity is laid out.

A typical and ground-breaking early example of this sort of text is "An Appeal to All Christian People," issued in 1920 by the Lambeth Conference, the once-each-decade gathering of Anglican bishops from around the world. The Appeal acknowledged "all those who believe in our Lord Jesus Christ, and have been baptized into the name of the Holy Trinity, as sharing with us membership in the universal Church of Christ which is His Body."[1] For this Church "God wills fellowship" and "it is God's purpose to manifest this fellowship, so far as this world is concerned, in an outward, visible, united society, holding one faith, having its own recognized offices, using God-given means of grace, and inspiring all its members to the world-wide service of the Kingdom of God."[2] The "visible unity of the Church" involves the "whole-hearted acceptance" of the Bible as "rule and ultimate standard of faith"; of the Nicene and Apostles' Creeds; of the sacraments of Baptism and Holy Communion; and of "a ministry acknowledged by every part of the Church as possessing not only the inward call of the Spirit, but also the commission of Christ and the authority of the whole body."[3] The Appeal then argues that some form of episcopacy holds the greatest promise of being so acknowledged by every part of the church and the text then lays out very tentatively how the churches might come together on the basis of the four elements outlined with "mutual deference to one another's consciences" and without anyone repudiating their own past.

The Lambeth Appeal is typical of many ecumenical texts in its explicit affirmation of an already existing unity, its explication of the essential characteristics of a united church, and some tentative proposals for how such visible unity could be realized.

Multilateral texts

A second group of ecumenical texts are produced by groups of churches gathered together in ecumenical organizations, such as the WCC or national councils of churches. (Since they involve groups of churches, such texts are called multilateral.) These texts are extremely varied, addressing virtually every sort of topic, theological, political, economic, and cultural. Sometimes they are the product of large assemblies and are little more than resolutions expressing a certain theological standpoint with little supporting argumentation. The more important texts have been carefully worked out by groups of theologians from various traditions. Some relate to social and political questions. Their concern is less directly to overcome church-dividing differences than to find a way for the churches to work and witness together socially and politically. From its beginnings, an important impetus for the ecumenical movement was the sense that the challenges of war and peace, of capitalism and communism, and of the economic injustices of the North–South gap could only be met by the churches together. A series of international ecumenical assemblies addressing social challenges met in Oxford (1937), Geneva (1966), and Seoul (1991). Especially since the late 1960s, such social and political work has been controversial as churches from the southern hemisphere have made their voices heard on subjects of racism, liberation, and exploitation.

Multilateral theological work directly aimed at addressing church divisions has been taken up at the world level by the Faith and Order Commission, created in Lausanne, Switzerland, in 1927 and since 1948 a part of the WCC. Unlike the WCC itself, however, its membership includes the Roman Catholic Church. In its early years, the work of Faith and Order was extensively one of comparative doctrine, seeking to establish the precise doctrinal commonalities and differences that joined and divided the churches. In the early 1950s, it became clear that progress could only be made by pressing beyond comparison and attempting to state together the shared foundations of faith. On this basis, one could then seek a framework in which traditional difficulties could be seen in a new light. As the 1952 Lund (Sweden) Conference on Faith and Order said, "as we seek to draw closer to Christ we come closer to one another."[4]

The fruit of this approach can best be seen in two complementary Faith and Order texts, *Baptism, Eucharist and Ministry* (1982) and *Confessing One Faith* (1991). The former, usually referred to by its initials, *BEM*, sought to summarize the result of decades of discussion on these ecumenically difficult topics. The claim was not that the text represented a *consensus*, i.e., "that experience of life and articulation of faith necessary to realize and maintain the Church's visible unity."[5] Only a *convergence* was claimed, a movement of the churches toward a common understanding. The text was sent to the churches with the request that each church "at the highest appropriate level of authority" respond to a series of questions about the text, the most important of which asked "the extent to which your church can recognize in this text the faith of the church through the ages."[6] The churches' responses to *BEM*, published in a series of six volumes, eventually numbered more than 160 and provide a comprehensive survey of contemporary official thinking on ministry and the sacraments.[7]

While *BEM* addressed issues that have traditionally divided the churches, *Confessing One Faith*[8] seeks a common and extended (about 100-page) explication of the apostolic faith which the churches share. Perhaps because it does not focus on controversial questions, *Confessing One Faith* has not received the same attention as *BEM*. Nevertheless, it forms *BEM*'s necessary complement. If they are to be one, the churches must do more than overcome differences; they must witness to the recognizably same Christian message.

Three aspects shared by *BEM* and *Confessing One Faith* are typical of much recent ecumenical theology. First, both are relentlessly Trinitarian, not just in their discussions of God, but in their entire exposition of the Christian faith and especially in their ecclesiology. As God is a unity in diversity, so must the church be. (See the discussion below of the church as communion.)

Second, each text (but especially *BEM*) makes extensive use of the concept of sacramental sign. On the one hand, the sacraments and even the church are not *empty* signs, but *sacramental* signs which realize or communicate what they signify. Baptism, the Lord's Supper, ordination, and the total life of the Christian community are means by which God brings to pass what is symbolized. Ordination is a sign of a gift of the Spirit and the Spirit is at work in the sign, giving the gift; the church is a sign of the eschatological Kingdom in such a way that it is also a foretaste of that Kingdom. On the other hand, a sign implies a distinction between the sign and what it signifies. The presence of Christ in the Eucharist remains a mystery, not a matter-of-fact presence at our disposal; the church is a sign of the Kingdom, but not itself the Kingdom. A crucial point of division in the debate about *BEM* was whether the link between signifier and signified was too close or not close enough. This division related not just to traditional differences over the sacraments, but pointed to the larger question of how one understands the relation between, on the one hand, the church and its concrete structures and, on the other, both the final Kingdom and the present working of the Holy Spirit.

Third, while not using such language, both texts seek what has been called an "internally differentiated consensus."[9] In relation to any topic, an internally differentiated consensus differentiates between the level or sort of agreement needed for a common life within a single church and the diversity or disagreement which can continue to exist without destroying that unity. The pursuit of unity implies the pursuit of that consensus the church needs if it is to witness clearly to the one faith. But that unity permits, even in some cases should encourage, diversity of opinion within the limits set by a common life and confession. Ecumenical texts must seek only that consensus the church needs to manifest its unity. To demand more would risk imposing a greater uniformity than is needed and thus risk compromising the freedom which is also a necessary aspect of the church's life. (An example of such an internally differentiated consensus is given below in relation to justification.)

Bilateral texts

A third group of texts still needs to be noted. Not only do churches come together in bodies such as the WCC; they also enter direct, usually one-to-one, discussions with each other about the issues that have divided them. Since they usually involve only two churches, such dialogues are referred to as bilateral. Over the last 30 years, virtually every combination of churches has had its dialogue: Catholic–Anglican, Lutheran–Orthodox, Anglican–Reformed, Lutheran–Methodist, Catholic–Pentecostal, and so on.

Bilateral discussions have their own distinctive characteristics. They are at once more esoteric and more practical. Because only two churches are involved, the discussion can be far more detailed. The particular issues raised by the separation of the two churches can be explored. Since the majority of the dialogues have dealt with the traditional issues that have divided the churches, the dialogues have produced a wealth of historical-theological work; historical because the historical roots of the disputes cannot be ignored; theological because the history is done with an eye to its relevance to the contemporary relations between the churches. The bilateral dialogues have thus become one of the most important contexts for a theology of *ressourcement*, of a renewal of a narrow and thin church life by a reappropriation of the richness and variety of the past. The focus on traditional subjects of controversy, however, has also exposed the dialogues to the accusation of being inherently conservative in their method and effect.

Unlike *BEM* and most multilateral discussions, bilateral dialogues are sometimes highly practical in making explicit proposals for unity or fellowship between the churches involved. The stakes in bilateral dialogues can thus be relatively high and success or failure is measured not just conceptually but also in terms of whether the churches involved are or are not brought together. Some striking breakthroughs have occurred. The Leuenberg Agreement of 1973, based on dialogues going back to the 1950s, brought the Lutheran and Reformed churches of continental Europe into full fellowship, ending (at least in Europe) the division that went back to the confrontation of Luther and Zwingli at Marburg in 1529. Perhaps even more remarkable, but little noticed, has been the series of agreements between the Oriental Orthodox churches, i.e., those ancient Eastern churches (e.g., the Coptic, Syrian, and Armenian churches) which rejected the definition of the two natures in the one person of Christ given by the Council of Chalcedon in 451, and both the Orthodox and Roman Catholic Churches. Here churches which could not easily be accused of an easy doctrinal relativism agreed that, despite their disagreement over the traditional doctrinal language, neither wished to deny what the other wished to affirm. The oldest dispute still dividing major churches is thus perhaps at the brink of resolution.

If bilateral dialogues have paved the way for such ecumenical successes, they have also led to bitter disappointment when the churches involved have found the proposals inadequate. Ecumenical relations help to define a particular church's identity and ecumenical proposals can thus stir intense debate.

No full survey can be given here of the vast range of theological work within the dialogues both internationally and nationally. Besides those already mentioned, three examples can show the present state of discussion and some of the underlying problems.

The *Lutheran–Anglican* dialogue faced only one issue, the nature and importance of episcopacy and episcopal succession (i.e., the succession of bishops, each consecrated by other bishops, in a succession going back to the earliest church). This issue can seem trivial, yet it is important for Catholics, Orthodox, and Anglicans (if in subtly different ways). The Lutheran–Anglican dialogues, especially the international *Niagara Report*,[10] sought to place the issue in the context of the underlying concern which has fueled the debate, the nature of the church's continuity, i.e., its identity over time. It is essential that the church today be the same church called forth by the Spirit at Pentecost. But what does "same" mean in this context? Is identity simply a matter of preaching the same message? Or must there be some continuity in structure? The *Niagara Report* addressed these questions with an emphasis on the faithfulness of God to the church as the foundation of the church's continuity and on the need for a comprehensive judgment about continuity rather than a focus on the simple presence or absence of certain marks or elements. Unlike some dialogues, the Lutheran–Anglican discussions have led to concrete actions leading to closer relations in Europe and Africa and proposals for new relations in North America.

The *Anglican–Roman Catholic* dialogue, carried out at the international level by the Anglican–Roman Catholic International Commission (ARCIC), has addressed a wide range of topics: Eucharist, ministry, authority, justification, the nature of the church, and ethics.[11] The dialogue has demonstrated the difficulty of specifying the kind of agreement ecumenical discussions should be seeking. On the Eucharist and ministry, ARCIC claimed to have reached "substantial agreement," by which they clearly understood an agreement sufficient for unity. As the reactions from the Anglican and Catholic Churches made clear, however, disagreement existed between and within the churches on the degree of agreement unity requires.

More ground-breaking and controversial has been ARCIC's work on authority. It has addressed one of the most difficult of all topics, the papacy and its infallibility. Claiming only convergence, not consensus, it has sought to place the differing concerns and commitments of the two traditions in a conceptual context that would at least allow meaningful discussion and perhaps future reconciliation. This context is the shared commitment to the church's *indefectability*, the belief shared by almost all traditions that, since it is promised that the true Church of Jesus Christ will continue to exist until Christ's return (Matthew 16: 18), that church will never so err that it would fail to proclaim the gospel and thus would cease to be the church. In this context, ARCIC asked what was the role of the reception or acceptance by the entire church of a dogmatic decision pronounced by a council or pope. Can such reception or nonreception potentially distinguish matters on which the church has not erred from those in which a truly final decision is still to be awaited?[12] The dialogue itself was tentative in answering this question and the Anglican and especially the Catholic churches hesitant in their official responses. Nevertheless, the dialogue indicated a set of concepts that promise to be helpful for further discussion of a topic that cannot be avoided.

The dialogues between the *Roman Catholic and Orthodox* churches show the importance and limitations of dialogues and dialogue texts. The texts, addressing questions of sacraments, ministry, and church, are conceptually rich and make significant contributions toward a form of theological speech in which East and West could speak to one another and perhaps with one voice to the world. From its beginnings in the mid-1960s under the influence of the Second Vatican Council, however, emphasis has fallen more on the "dialogue of love," a growing together in church life and practice, than on dialogue on more abstract theology. Even the theological dialogue was forced to turn to more practical matters following 1990 when the fall of the communist regimes of Central and Eastern Europe changed the context in which Catholic and Orthodox relate in some of the countries with the largest Orthodox populations.

This survey, rapid as it has been, allows us to draw some conclusions about the general character and dangers of ecumenical theology. Above all, ecumenical theology is *a practical and ecclesial theology of communal Christian identity*. The identity of the Christian community, of the church, is the background issue that is always present in ecumenical theology, for it is this identity which determines the basis, character, shape, and limits of unity in the church. The ever present background question is "What is it to be the Church of Jesus Christ?" Individual questions about the Trinity, the sacraments, ministry, or ethics are asked with an eye to their relevance to this background question and with a particular goal in mind: the realization of a greater or more visible unity among the presently divided churches. In this sense, ecumenical theology is practical or even instrumental. Moreover, since this goal requires that the theological conclusions and reasoning both represent and be accepted by the churches, the theological work is oriented ecclesially. The paradigm is not the creativity that seeks the new and distinctive as much as the creativity that can articulate the common faith in a reconciling way so that divergent traditions can recognize their oneness and be enriched by it.

With this character come certain dangers and temptations. The constant presence of the ecclesial question means that ecumenical theology runs the risk of furthering the churches' self-absorption. The details of arguments about the nature of the church can become isolated from the mission the church should be carrying out. A deeper danger is one ecumenical theology shares with some forms of liberation theology, the danger of the instrumentalization of theology in a way that subverts a concern for truth. The conviction that the churches are truly one can become a warrant for ignoring differences of conviction that should not be glossed over, a warrant for accepting whatever arguments would justify greater visible unity, regardless of the cogency or validity of those arguments. The underlying question is the relation between the practical character of ecumenical theology, its orientation toward a particular goal, and the more general commitment of all theology to truth. Herein lies the importance of the interrelation of the pursuit of unity and of theological renewal. The pursuit of unity must be a part of the pursuit of greater faithfulness and of a richer grasp of the faith. When the pursuit of unity remains an aspect of this larger pursuit, the danger of an instrumentalization of theology is at least diminished.

Themes and Debates in Ecumenical Theology

After this survey, a closer examination of certain themes and debates can give a more precise picture of the present state of ecumenical discussions.

The nature of the church as communion

A difficulty in any discussion between traditions which have developed in some isolation from one another is the lack of a common language and conceptual context within which to carry out a fruitful debate. A particular difficulty in ecumenical discussions has been the lack of a common language to discuss the pervading background question of the church. An unavoidable question for ecumenical discussions is: What sort of unity should the church possess? What institutional forms would be the appropriate realization or expression of the unity of all Christians in Christ? Or is unity in Christ something strictly spiritual in a sense that excludes any institutional realization? Are these questions ones we are free to answer according to our best theological lights, or are some aspects of church unity divinely given, to be thankfully accepted rather than subjected to theological debate?

A major development in ecumenical theology over the last 35 years has been the emergence of a set of widely used concepts which frame a common language for discussing these foundational ecclesiological questions. These concepts have become widely used both in explicitly ecumenical discussions and in the churches' own self-understandings.

Central to this development has been the concept of the church as a communion. Every Christian has simultaneously communion with God in Christ and the Spirit and also communion with all others who are in Christ. This communion is rooted in, in fact it is a participation in, the communion of the Father, Son, and Holy Spirit which is the life of the Trinity. The concept of communion thus indicates the Trinitarian basis of the church and also the essentially social character of Christian life in which the individual's relation with Christ is always inseparable from his or her relation with all others who are in Christ.

An ecumenical attraction of the concept of the church as a communion lies in its ability to reconcile emphases on both unity and diversity. As the Father, Son, and Spirit remain distinct yet perfectly one in the life of the Trinity, so the communion which is the church should respect differences even while living a life in which these differences come together in true unity. An emphasis on the character of the church as communion thus permits a more detailed elaboration of an assertion made from the beginning of the ecumenical movement, that unity must not mean uniformity.

This understanding of the church as a communion, however, does not represent an agreement on the substantive questions that have separated the churches. It represents only a language within which the debate can be carried out in a more fruitful way, with a greater confidence that we are in fact addressing one another.

545

The differing ways the concept can be filled out can be seen by looking at some aspects of its recent development.

Within the WCC, a debate on the nature of the unity has gone on from its founding. From the late 1950s to today, one can trace a steady development of an understanding of unity which in recent years has explicitly made use of the concept of communion. The first product of this development was a statement from the 1961 WCC Assembly in New Delhi which is of such importance that it should be quoted at length:

> We believe that the unity which is both God's will and his gift to his Church is being made visible as all in each place who are baptized into Jesus Christ and confess him as Lord and Saviour are brought by the Holy Spirit into one fully committed fellowship, holding the one apostolic faith, preaching the one Gospel, breaking the one bread, joining in common prayer, and having a corporate life reaching out in witness and service to all and who at the same time are united with the whole Christian fellowship in all places and all ages in such wise that ministry and members are accepted by all, and that all can act and speak together as occasion requires for the tasks to which God calls his people.[13]

This statement lays out what are still widely regarded as the essential elements of unity. Note that here the emphasis falls on the unity "of all at each place," that is, on unity at the local level.

At the 1975 WCC Assembly in Nairobi, the unity of the local churches with one another was more fully addressed in a statement on "What Unity Requires," which began: "The one Church is to be envisioned as a conciliar fellowship of local churches which are themselves truly united."[14] The idea of "conciliar fellowship" was widely discussed in the 1970s. Local churches, each understood to be a full realization of the one church, still have a duty to counsel with other churches (if need be, in the early church) and reach binding conclusions for the sake of witness and mission.

This picture of local churches in conciliar fellowship was further developed by the 1991 WCC Assembly in Canberra by means of the concept of communion. This concept rooted earlier developments more clearly in understandings of both God and the mission of the church. "The purpose of the church is to unite people with Christ in the power of the Spirit, to manifest communion in prayer and action and thus to point to the fullness of communion with God, humanity and the whole creation in the glory of the kingdom."[15]

While this development has found widespread acceptance, it has also raised questions. Does the notion of unity as the "committed fellowship" of "all in each place" mean the disappearance at the local level of the distinct traditions and forms of Christian life that have developed in history? If, say, Catholics, Orthodox, Reformed, and Methodist could remove all obstacles to their unity, would Christian life and mission in fact be served if the distinct local congregations were simply to merge into some new local reality? Or should the distinct traditions continue to exist *as distinct* in some form of "reconciled diversity"?[16] Or would that be only a way of preserving division, but calling it unity?

Questions also remain to be answered about the nature of the church as communion at the worldwide level. What are the concrete links that tie the local churches together into a worldwide communion? In a much discussed 1992 letter to the bishops of the Roman Catholic Church on "Some Aspects of the Church Understood as Communion," the Vatican's Congregation for the Doctrine of the Faith adopted significant aspects of the ecumenical discussion of the church as communion and then used them as a framework for an understanding of the papacy as one necessary link binding the local churches together.[17] The local churches are bound together by (among other things) the unity of their leaders, the bishops. The bishops are in turn bound together by (among other things) their common relation to the head of the community of bishops, the bishop of Rome, the successor of Peter, the first among the apostles. This connection with the worldwide church is not something external to the life of the local church, but part of its essential nature. Thus a local church without this connection, a church without this relation to the bishop of Rome, is "wounded" in its very nature as a church.

What this controversial letter demonstrated was that the understanding of the church as communion provides a common language for a debate about the church and its unity, but does not solve the traditional problems that have stood at the center of the debate. Whether further discussion of the church as communion can foster a debate which can lead to resolution only the future will tell.

Is agreement possible? The example of justification

But how can churches come to agree on matters which in the past led to disagreements so basic that division was judged to be necessary? Is the only possibility that one group or the other confess that they and their forebears were simply wrong? How is ecumenical agreement possible without a simple repudiation of one's own specific tradition?

A good example of consensus without self-repudiation is offered by the ecumenical discussions of justification by faith. Disagreements over justification, the righteousness of the Christian before God, stood at the center of the Reformation. Lutheran theologians came to speak of the conviction that the Christian is justified before God solely through the righteousness of Christ, given by grace and received by faith, as "the article by which the church stands and falls." Reformed and Anglicans, while less vehement, were committed to similar understandings of justification, which the Roman Catholic Church solemnly rejected at the Council of Trent in the mid-sixteenth century.

Or so it had appeared. Careful historical study has shown that mutual misunderstanding was rife during the Reformation period. The Reformers rejected popular beliefs widely held in the late Middle Ages, some of which were never official Catholic teaching and some of which were stated in a far more careful and less problematic way when Catholic teaching on justification was formalized by the Council of Trent. The Council, on the other hand, worked to a significant extent with a list of quotations from the Reformers and thus without the context needed to understand what they were saying. In a significant number of cases, each side was rejecting positions the other side did not in fact hold.

With misunderstandings removed, a significant fund of shared belief becomes evident. The North American Lutheran–Catholic dialogue sought to summarize this common basis:

> Our entire hope of justification and salvation rests on Christ Jesus and on the gospel whereby the good news of God's merciful action in Christ is made known; we do not place our ultimate trust in anything other than God's promise and saving work in Christ. This excludes ultimate reliance on our faith, virtues, or merits, even though we acknowledge God working in these by grace alone (*sola gratia*).[18]

At the level of such a fundamental description, Lutherans and Catholics are in agreement. Differences appear when one turns from this general assertion to a variety of more specific topics: the role of human cooperation in the reception of the gift of salvation, the sense in which the Christian remains a sinner even while justified, and, most importantly, the sense in which grace works merit in the believer or simply communicates the merit of Christ.

The remaining differences are closely related to differing underlying concerns and fears. Roman Catholic theology and practice has wished to stress the importance of Christian life and discipleship. In the Christian life, grace is working merit in the Christian, even if this merit is not the foundation of our ultimate trust. The Reformers wished to stress the constant and confident dependence of the Christian on the all-sufficient merit of Christ and thus rejected the application of the concept "merit" directly to the Christian. These seemingly detailed differences are part of much wider differences in styles of piety and Christian life. Each sees in the language and practice of the other a significant danger: The Catholic worries that the Lutheran solution undermines the pursuit of holiness; the Lutheran worries that the Catholic solution turns attention away from the good news of what has been given us in Christ. Yet neither would reject the underlying concern of the other. As a German dialogue put it in speaking about justification: "Catholic doctrine does not overlook what Protestant faith finds so important, and vice versa; and Catholic doctrine does not maintain what Protestant doctrine is afraid of, and vice versa."[19] Both the German and the North American dialogues have argued that *if* this quoted sentence is true (and it has been vehemently debated), then the differences that distinguish the two traditions on justification need not continue to divide the Catholic from the Lutheran (and, by extension, from other Protestant or Anglican) churches.

The dialogues on justification display a typical ecumenical method in addressing past differences. Careful historical and biblical work seeks to lay out a common fundamental belief, often stated in language other than that in which the original debate was carried out. This common fundamental belief can then provide a framework for considering the nature of the particular opposed beliefs. Within this framework it might (but only might) turn out that the opposed beliefs need not be seen as requiring division but can be seen as a diversity permissible within the one church.

Decisive for such a method is that its success need not depend on anyone abandoning what they had earlier thought to be central to Christian faith. It *does* depend on both sides being willing to place their traditions in a wider context that will allow one-sided emphases to be corrected. Here again, unity and theological renewal go together. The ecumenical discussion of justification has enriched both Catholic and Protestant teaching. Both have come to see how polemic has distorted theology. Differences remain but each has been enriched.

Debate and crisis in ecumenical theology

Already in 1932, a major ecumenical conference heard an address titled: "The Crisis of the Ecumenical Movement," the first of many speeches and essays on such a theme. The ecumenical movement and ecumenical theology seem peculiarly prone to a sense of crisis, to a sense that matters are stagnating or that developments are moving in a radically wrong direction. One reason for this recurrent sense of crisis is the goal-oriented character of ecumenism: It seeks results. Unfortunately, depending on how one judges the present situation, the ecumenical movement can plausibly seen either as a smashing success or as a near total failure.

The goal-oriented character of ecumenical theology also contributes to an internal tension within ecumenical theology. On the one hand, ecumenical work seeks to change the churches. It is unhappy with things as they ecclesially are. On the other hand, ecumenical theology must work with and (in ecumenical dialogues) even represent the churches as they presently exist. Ecumenical theology has attracted two different theological mindsets: a prophetic mindset, attracted to criticism and social engagement, and a more confessional mindset, attracted to the open yet profoundly traditional theological content of, e.g., the bilateral dialogues. To a degree, this tension is typical of the reformist vs. revolutionary division within many movements for change. The sometimes uneasy cohabitation of these mindsets in the larger ecumenical movement has led to intense debates within ecumenical institutions and theology. Some of the most biting critiques of the course of the ecumenical movement have come from leaders of the movement. Typically, one of the most thorough critiques of some forms of ecumenical theology can be found in Konrad Raiser's *Ecumenism in Transition: A paradigm shift in the ecumenical movement?* (1991), published shortly before Raiser himself became General Secretary of the WCC.

While debate and criticism have been a part of ecumenical theology throughout its life, the discussion has become sharper in recent years. While the arguments and positions are rarely altogether new, changes in the wider theological and ecclesial scene have given them an added edge. Ecumenical theology is finally concerned with communal Christian identity and the changes and conflicts in communal Christian identity since the late 1960s have necessarily had their effect on the ecumenical debates. Whether the criticisms are of particular forms of ecumenical work and theology or of the ecumenical enterprise as a whole is often hard to determine. Criticisms have come from various angles. Because this chapter has stressed the more confessional or reformist side of ecumenical theology, those criticisms that come from the more prophetic or revolutionary mindset will be stressed. Three large questions will be noted: Should we be seeking unity? Should we be seeking theological consensus? Is theological discussion the way to the unity?

Should we be seeking unity? As noted above, the nature of the unity we are seeking has always been a matter of debate in the ecumenical movement. More recently, however, the search for church unity, however understood, has itself been criticized. In its weaker form, the argument is for a replacement of the term "unity" with terms such as "fellowship" or "federation," terms which imply a looser institutional form of unity. Oscar Cullmann, a leading New Testament scholar and Protestant observer at the Second Vatican Council, has described this more minimal goal as a "community of harmoniously separated churches."[20]

Some arguments, however, are more far-reaching. Unity can be and (the argument runs) usually has been oppressive. The roots of the ecumenical movement lie in early twentieth-century internationalism and in evangelical-liberal elements in the missionary movement. Both of these, it is argued, for all their high-mindedness, were expressions of Western hegemony. The desire for church unity is part of an outlook which is not ready to accept difference and the Other. However often ecumenical leaders may insist that unity does not imply uniformity, the dynamic of the ecumenical movement is toward suppression of legitimate diversity.

Or, if we should be seeking unity, should we be so concerned with the unity of the *church*? Since the late 1960s, some have argued that the ecumenical movement must primarily be about the unity of *humanity* and thus primarily address the racial, political, sexual, and economic divisions within the wider world. After all, it is argued, the church exists to serve the world or, more carefully put, to serve God's healing mission to the world. When church divisions contribute to larger human divisions (as in Ireland or the former Yugoslavia), a concern for greater unity among the churches is appropriate. Otherwise, such a concern is a luxury the churches in a suffering world cannot afford.[21]

Should we be seeking theological consensus? Similar to the criticism of unity as the social or institutional goal is a criticism of consensus as the conceptual or theological goal. In reaction to the many dialogue documents of the early 1980s, especially to *BEM*, a criticism has developed of "consensus-ecumenism." Aspects of this criticism repeat the arguments about unity. Is the pursuit of consensus an expression of intolerance of difference and the Other? Certain arguments, however, are distinctive. On the one hand, does the pursuit of consensus undermine rather than support theological renewal? If one thinks that renewal will come from a renewed sense of the breadth and fullness of the faith, then the linkage of dialogue and renewal is plausible. But has renewal really come in that way historically? Did the great theological renewers – Augustine, the Cappadocians, Aquinas, Luther, Barth – seek consensus? Is theology and the clear proclamation of the gospel better served by open, even polemical debate, as long as that debate is objective and non-violent?[22] When Paul said "dissensions are necessary if only to show which of your members are sound" (I Corinthians 11: 18; NEB), was he speaking a deeper theological truth than he knew?

On the other hand, is modern theology so disagreement-prone that the pursuit of consensus is illusory? The modern academic theologian is a trained arguer with a professional self-interest in disagreement. Besides, in light of the authorities and criteria appealed to within theological debate, is there any hope of reaching true consensus? Do the Bible (the only authority accepted by everyone in the ecumenical discussions) and minimal rules of reasoning provide a sufficient basis to reach agreement on the controverted topics?

The pursuit of theological consensus, it is argued, harms theology and will result in unity being endlessly postponed as theologians find yet something else to argue over.

Is theology the way to unity? The critique of the pursuit of theological consensus is usually accompanied by an understanding of unity which downplays the importance of such consensus. Do we need consensus beyond an agreement on the basic outlines of the life of Christ and on propositions widely accepted in the church, e.g., Jesus is Lord? The plausibility of such proposals depends on a shift of weight onto something else as central to Christian unity. For example, some would argue that what matters is a common experience of fellowship or unity with Christ. All who have this experience are one in the only sense in which they need to be one. That they speak about this experience in different, even contradictory ways, should not be a problem. It can even be evangelically fruitful, since different ways of describing the experience may appeal to different persons.

Important within the ecumenical movement from its beginnings has been the view summarized in the slogan: "Doctrine divides; service unites." Here the emphasis falls on common service to the neighbor as the tie that binds. In its less radical forms, this argument is simply pragmatic. Doctrinal differences may prevent our coming together in the Lord's Supper, but they do not hinder common engagement to meet the needs of the world. Cooperation in common service would create an atmosphere of mutual trust and affection within which theological discussions might be carried on in a more accommodating and fruitful way.

In its more radical form, this argument emphasizes common service of the neighbor as itself the needed form of common discipleship of Christ. In fact, such common engagement for the needy neighbor can produce a profound community among persons. As a community in common discipleship, it is already a form of community in Christ and not something merely preliminary. Especially if the true ecumenical goal is the unity of humanity, it is argued that such unity in discipleship, even including some who do not explicitly confess Christ, may be of greater theological significance than doctrinal consensus.[23]

No attempt will be made here to discuss these criticisms in either their more or less radical forms. Obviously, how they are addressed will shape the future of ecumenical theology.

Achievement and Agenda

Ecumenical theology has not produced texts with the individuality and conceptual brilliance of those of Barth, Pannenberg, or Rahner. It has had a different goal: direct service to the ecumenical activities and hopes of the churches. Ecumenical texts must be assessed by the standards that apply to all theology, but also assessed in relation to their contribution to these activities and hopes.

The most significant achievement of ecumenical theology has been its challenge to the mutual isolation of the churches' self-understandings. Catholic, or Anglican, or Presbyterian self-identity is today more often specified in positive relation to other churches rather than in a polemical relation. In the process, ecumenical theology has given a model of a critically constructive attitude to tradition. It has held up an ideal of a communally loyal creativity, even if it has sometimes failed to be sufficiently loyal or creative.

The future agenda of ecumenical theology is a function of the course of ecumenical developments. It is widely said that the task of the immediate future is reception, i.e., the movement of the results of the ecumenical discussions into the minds and lives of the churches. Most immediately, reception implies an official response by the churches to the texts and proposals, but reception must also involve the transformation of wider attitudes and practices and not just decisions by synods. Reception places at least two tasks before ecumenical theology. First, more careful thought needs to be given to the criteria by which ecumenical texts and proposals are judged. What degree and kind of agreement is being sought? How should the text of an agreement compare to the language and concepts that have been the official doctrine of the involved churches? Second, we need a more subtle understanding of the significance and nature of the churches as they actually exist. What is the relation between the Body of Christ and the mutually exclusive institutions through which the churches live? How do we relate the chapters on the church in theology textbooks to the mundane and divided realities of everyday ecclesial life?

Ecumenical theology as a distinct theological genre is a recent creation and its future existence is not certain. If the ecumenical movement were to achieve total success, there would be no need for a distinct ecumenical theology. If the ecumenical movement were to be abandoned as hopeless, ecumenical theology might return to its more pessimistic roots in comparative dogmatics and "polemical theology." Both extremes seem unlikely in the near future. The tasks that ecumenical theology has taken up will probably be with us for some time. Some means of addressing them will need to be found. If ecumenical theology didn't exist, we would have to invent something much like it.

Notes

1 Lambeth Conference 1920 in R. Davidson (ed.), *The Six Lambeth Conferences: 1867–1920* (London, 1928), Appendix.
2 Ibid., p. 27.
3 Ibid., p. 28.
4 Lukas Vischer (ed.), *A Documentary History of the Faith and Order Movement 1927–1963* (St Louis, MO, 1963), p. 85.
5 Faith and Order Paper 111, *Baptism, Eucharist and Ministry* (Geneva, 1982), p. ix.
6 Ibid., p. x.
7 Faith and Order, *Churches Respond to BEM*, ed. Max Thurian (Geneva, 1986–8).
8 Faith and Order Paper 153, *Confessing One Faith* (Geneva, 1991).
9 Harding Meyer, "What kind of consensus is necessary for church unity?" in Eugene Brand (ed.), *Communio and Dialogue* (Geneva, 1992), p. 54.
10 Anglican-Lutheran International Continuation Committee, *The Niagara Report* (London and Geneva, 1987).
11 Christopher Hill and Edward Yarnold, *Anglicans and Roman Catholics: The search for unity* (London, 1994).
12 Ibid., pp. 70–5.
13 Günther Gassmann, *Documentary History of Faith and Order 1963–1993* (Faith and Order Paper 159) (Geneva, 1993), p. 3.
14 Ibid., p. 3.
15 Ibid., p. 4.
16 Harding Meyer and Günther Gassmann, *The Unity of the Church: Requirements and structure* (LWF Report 15) (Geneva, 1983).

17 Congregation for the Doctrine of the Faith, "Some aspects of the Church understood as communion," *Origins*, 22 (1992), pp. 108–12.

18 H. Anderson et al. (eds), *Justification by Faith: Lutherans and Catholics in Dialogue VII* (Minneapolis and Augsburg, 1985), p. 16.

19 Karl Lehmann and Wolfhart Pannenberg (eds), *The Condemnations of the Reformation Era: Do they still divide?* (Minneapolis, 1990), p. 53.

20 Oscar Cullmann, *Unity through Diversity* (Philadelphia, 1988), p. 31.

21 Agnes Abuom, "Discerning the signs of the times," in T. Best and W. Granberg-Michaelson (eds), *Costly Unity* (Geneva, 1993), p. 51.

22 Erich Geldbach, *Ökumene in Gegensätzen* (Bensheimer Hefte 66) (Göttingen, 1987).

23 Bert Hoedemaker, "Introductory reflections on JPIC and koinonia," in T. Best and W. Granberg-Michaelson (eds), *Costly Unity* (Geneva, 1993), p. 6.

Bibliography

Note The texts cited give an overview of much of the most important ecumenical literature. The standard *History of the Ecumenical Movement* through 1968 is in two volumes published in 1986, the first covering 1517–1948 and edited by Rouse and Neil, the second covering 1948–68 and edited by Fey. International dialogues through 1982 are included in *Growth in Agreement* (1984), edited by Meyer and Vischer. A forthcoming second volume will include documents through 1990. *A Bibliography of Interchurch and Interconfessional Theological Dialogues* (1984) by Puglisi and Voicu contains a comprehensive bibliography of texts from ecumenical dialogues and literature discussing them through 1984. This bibliography has been regularly updated in the *Bulletin* of the Centro pro Unione (Rome).

Texts from individual theologians discussing ecumenical issues are almost innumerable. Two of great historical importance are *Divided Christendom* (1939), by Yves Congar, and *The Nature of Doctrine* (1984), by George A. Lindbeck. The student just beginning with this material might first look at *BEM*, the *Decree on Ecumenism* of the Second Vatican Council, and Konrad Reiser's *Ecumenism in Transition* (1991). These three texts, quite different in form and content, introduce the most important tendencies in recent ecumenical theology. Lindbeck's book and Robert Jenson's *Unbaptized God* (1992) are the most insightful recent secondary studies of ecumenical theology; both are difficult but will reward careful reading if one has looked at a few of the primary documents.

Abuom, Agnes, "Discerning the signs of the times," in T. Best and W. Granberg-Michaelson (eds), *Costly Unity* (Geneva, 1993), pp. 44–51.

Anderson, H. George, Murphy, T. Austin, and Burgess, Joseph A. (eds), *Justification by Faith: Lutherans and Catholics in Dialogue VII* (Minneapolis and Augsburg, 1985).

Anglican-Lutheran International Continuation Committee, *The Niagara Report* (London and Geneva, 1987).

Congar, Yves M.-J., *Divided Christendom: A Catholic study of the problem of reunion* (London, 1939).

Congregation for the Doctrine of the Faith, "Some aspects of the Church understood as communion," *Origins*, 22 (1992), pp. 108–12.

Cullmann, Oscar, *Unity through Diversity: Its foundation, and a contribution to the discussion concerning the possibilities of its actualization* (Philadelphia, 1988).

Decree on Ecumenism (Second Vatican Council) in Norman P. Tanner (ed.), *Decrees of the Ecumenical Councils* (London and Washington, 1990), pp. 908–20.

Faith and Order, *Baptism, Eucharist and Ministry* (Faith and Order Paper 111) (Geneva, 1982).

Faith and Order, *Churches Respond to BEM: Official responses to the "Baptism, Eucharist and Ministry" text*, ed. Max Thurian, 6 vols (Geneva, 1986–8).

Faith and Order, *Confessing One Faith: An ecumenical explication of the Apostolic Faith as it* is confessed in the Nicene-Constantinopolitan Creed (381) (Faith and Order Paper 153) (Geneva, 1991).

Fey, Harold E. (ed.), *The Ecumenical Advance: A history of the ecumenical movement*, vol. 2 (1948–68), 2nd edn (Geneva, 1986).

Gassmann, Günther, *Documentary History of Faith and Order 1963–1993* (Faith and Order Paper 159) (Geneva, 1993).

Geldbach, Erich, *Ökumene in Gegensätzen* (Bensheimer Hefte 66) (Göttingen, 1987).

Hill, Christopher and Yarnold, Edward, *Anglicans and Roman Catholics: The search for unity* (London, 1994).

Hoedemaker, Bert, "Introductory reflections on JPIC and koinonia," in T. Best and W. Granberg-Michaelson (eds), *Costly Unity* (Geneva, 1993), pp. 1–8.

Jenson, Robert, *Unbaptized God: The basic flaw in ecumenical theology* (Minneapolis, 1992).

Lambeth Conference 1920, in R. Davidson (ed.), *The Six Lambeth Conferences: 1867–1920*, (London, 1928), Appendix.

Lehmann, Karl and Pannenberg, Wolfhart (eds), *The Condemnations of the Reformation Era: Do they still divide?* (Minneapolis, 1990).

Lindbeck, George A., *The Nature of Doctrine: Religion and theology in a postliberal age* (Philadelphia, 1984).

Meyer, Harding, "What kind of consensus is necessary for church unity?" In Eugene Brand (ed.), *Communio and Dialogue* (Geneva, 1992).

Meyer, Harding and Gassmann, Günther, *The Unity of the Church: Requirements and structure* (LWF Report 15) (Geneva, 1983).

Meyer, Harding and Vischer, Lukas (eds), *Growth in Agreement: Reports and agreed statements of ecumenical conversations on a world level* (New York and Geneva, 1984).

Puglisi, J. F. and Voicu, S. J., *A Bibliography of Interchurch and Interconfessional Theological Dialogues* (Rome, 1984).

Raiser, Konrad, *Ecumenism in Transition: A paradigm shift in the ecumenical movement?* (Geneva, 1991).

Rouse, Ruth and Neill, S. C. (eds), *A History of the Ecumenical Movement 1517–1948*, 3rd edn (Geneva, 1986).

Vischer, Lukas (ed.), *A Documentary History of the Faith and Order Movement 1927–1963* (St Louis, MO, 1963).

Theology of Mission

Lamin Sanneh

Introduction

"The church lives by mission as fire lives by burning." That was the vivid way the twentieth-century theologian, Emil Brunner, once described mission. This statement could be understood in several senses. First, Christianity is a missionary religion in the sense of mission being its living essence, even though it may require a favorable climate to spark interest in it. Second, the Christian religion requires personal faith for its identity and vocation, and mission is the expression of that. Third, mission is the motive spring of Christianity, the force animating its life and thought. Fourth, mission effects the inner transformation of Christianity by exchanging one cultural and historical mode of it for another, and in the process creating something new. Finally, mission is Christian self-expenditure, an enterprise in which Christians illuminate their heritage by consuming it. God has entrusted the church with the gift of faith and required for the saving of it the losing. The church lives for others, or it dies. Mission is the acting out of the fundamental convictions of faith and in turn the testing and refinement of those convictions in the light of the experience and consequences of mission practice. There is involved a form of destruction, some of it willful and unnecessary, as well as constructiveness. Thus, however Brunner intended his remark, the thought he expresses brings mission into all the dimensions of Christianity. We should now explore what those dimensions involve.

One of the first things to say about mission is that it is as old as Christianity itself: The church was born in mission and lives by it. When the apostles and disciples embarked on mission, they were convinced that they were following the direction of Jesus' own teaching as well as the explicit command of Scripture to "go and teach all nations, baptizing them in the name of the Father, and of the Son, and of the Holy Ghost" (Matthew 28: 19; also Mark 16: 15). Whether these Gospel passages directly represent the exact, original words of Jesus, there is little debate about the fact that when the disciples decided to define their responsibility for the message of Jesus, they did so in terms of preaching and of receiving converts into the church by having them "baptized in the name of the Lord Jesus" (Acts 8: 16). The overwhelming sense of faithfulness to Jesus' preaching and teaching carried this missionary obligation as something fully consistent with the mind and intention of Jesus whom God has now vindicated as the exalted Christ and the soon expected Messiah. Mission was witness to the Kingdom Jesus had already inaugurated, not a means to bring the Kingdom.

It was that unshakable conviction that impelled the disciples to contemplate the otherwise unusual action of targeting Gentiles, considered unclean, as legitimate candidates for baptism and membership in the church. We can be certain that nothing else freed the disciples to contemplate what would be a flagrant breach of existing racial and ritual interdiction in the form of mixed Jewish–Gentile congregations than that Jesus willed it so (Acts 10: 28). And so in the ensuing conflicts, controversies, uncertainties, pleas, assurances, and directives about the rightness of Gentile inclusion, the first Christians adopted the path of faith-filled openness as the irrevocable logic of mission, with all the dangers and risks of opening the church to people with little preparation in the millennia-old Jewish traditions. There was a cost to this, such as would be involved in a journey into the unknown (Galatians 2: 1–15), but all of that would be put in the shade by the convincing demonstration of God having acted decisively in Christ and thereby called all people to accept the message when the disciples presented it to them (Galatians 3: 28–9; Acts 8: 27–39; Acts 10; 11: 18; 14: 27; 15: 14). As they set about organizing the task of preaching and ministering to new communities of converts, with little precedent to go by except Jewish practice and Roman order, the early Christians felt confirmed in their religious conviction that this was what God had planned for them from the beginning. They expressed themselves in the language of the Bible, with Peter, Stephen, Mark, and Paul, for example, claiming that the evidence of lives transformed, souls saved, the lowly and the outcast embraced, men and women and slave and free reconciled, diseases cured, broken spirits recovered in a living, growing church, all of that had been attested to by Scripture and was proof that Jesus had not lived in vain or abandoned them. From that intimacy of Scripture, the person of Jesus, and the ministry of the sacraments, the disciples arrived at a powerful sense of imminent eschatological judgment, and hence of the urgency of mission to prepare for it. In that important sense, mission was first and last the work of Jesus. From the logic and the growing momentum of mission, the church would come to know that Jesus as the coming Messiah was indeed Jesus the Messiah come and, as the commandment of Jesus' mission was thus also the assurance of his abiding faithfulness. To abandon it was to abandon the whole edifice on which Jesus built his career and reputation.

In depicting the origin and nature of Christian mission this way, we should flag the point that mission involved setting out on a cross-cultural course, such as that involving Jew and Gentile, Jerusalem and Antioch, Asia and Europe, Athens and Damascus, Ethiopia and Rome, Cyprus and Libya. At the heart of that cross-cultural vocation is the redeemed, emancipated person as the dwelling place of God's Spirit. The freedom the early Christians felt about there being no requirement to tie mission to the original language of Jesus enabled them to embrace other languages, such as Greek and Latin, or Coptic and Armenian. Second, the willingness to identify mission with the Gentile movement in the church freed the disciples from any obligation to observe Jerusalem as an exclusive geographical center or the

Jewish ritual code as definitive of the religion of Jesus. That allowed numerous centers to grow and proliferate as believers assimilated the Pauline teaching that God's temple, like circumcision, is no longer an external, physical structure or attribute, but the believer's body duly consecrated to the Spirit (1 Corinthians 3: 16–17; 6: 19). This new conception of religion as fixed in no single revealed language or culture and as bound by no exclusive geographical frontier but rather as truth abiding with believers, whoever and wherever they happen to be, was constitutive of the identity of Christianity as mission from the very beginning, however much later generations of Christians would deviate from it or abandon it entirely.

Historical Survey

Early opportunity and setback

If Christianity was born in mission, it was also in mission that Christianity would emerge with the diversity and pluralism that have culturally and historically distinguished it. From the experience and example of the disciples mission generated a vigorous multicultural movement. In a matter of a few centuries, mission had taken Christianity into such different and diverse worlds as Athens, Alexandria, Meroë and Axum in Upper Egypt, Rome, and Armenia. By the ninth century the missionary movement had gained permanent footholds from Moravia in the East to England and Ireland in the West, and from North-Rhine Westphalia in the Carolingian Empire to Abyssinia in East Africa.

Yet, by a curious turn of fortune, the missionary tide that stirred in Christianity in its early formative centuries and crested with the conversion of the so-called northern barbarians ebbed, and from about A.D. 900 to 1350 the religion turned moribund. The work of translation and interpretation went on in several important sectors of the church, but the vision of a missionary drive to plant the church in new lands was no longer dominant. Christians at the time understood their task to be one of consolidation, partly as a response to a militant Islamic resurgence on the doorstep of Western Europe, particularly in Constantinople, Spain, and Sicily, and partly as a reflection of the pressures of the recently established Holy Roman Empire. Christianity became absorbed in the inward-looking policies of imperial territoriality, with Rome often scrambling to hold its footing in the rapidly changing political situation.

It is difficult to say which was the greater influence on Christianity: its transformation into political territoriality, with the consequence of the Gospel becoming subordinate to its cultural setting, or its preoccupation with a militant Islam which appeared to be succeeding in checking Christendom's triumphant march into the eastern and southern Mediterranean and beyond.

Whether in its territorial form or in its preoccupation with Islam, Christianity became fixed on the idea of an exemplary, devout, and sanctified prince or ruler, much in the pattern of Charlemagne, as the supreme model of a Christian society. Consequently, in the period, say, between 1350 and 1500, mission was understood as the project to convert political rulers and the aristocracies, and from that position of power and privilege to subsume the rest of society into the church. Even after 1500, this understanding of the missionary task of the church was predominant in the Spanish and Portuguese missions to the New World, Asia, and sub-Saharan Africa. It led to the formula that evangelization was the same as colonization, and vice versa. As practical policy the formula was fraught with the difficulties typical of cross-cultural transplanting, and it produced Fortress Christianity as small communities of practicing Christians were collected and quarantined inside fortresses and castles in Africa, Asia, and elsewhere, to be defended by cannon and gunboats, scarcely a promising way to pursue mission. It created for sensitive and thoughtful missionaries, such as Las Casas in the New World and Francis Xavier in the East, the grounds for protest, and thus arguments against the territorial status quo, or at any rate against that status quo as an exportable arrangement.

Matters might have remained thus suspended in that moribund state had not a new climate of opinion ushered in change of a momentous nature. It was signaled by the sixteenth-century Protestant Reformation and the related Catholic Reformation, and the consequences of these two movements pushed mission in a totally new direction. The explosion of maritime exploration, led by Spain and Portugal, and later joined by England, made for the shift from land-based power to sea-based power. Whereas before Vasco da Gama in 1415 the dominant world powers were those which controlled the land routes, from the Tell Atlas on the Atlantic rim to the silk depots of Samarkand, now the dominant powers would be those with un-challenged suzerainty over the sea lanes, from Lisbon and Genoa, or Plymouth and Dover, to Goa and Shanghai. The social revolution attendant on such a major shift of power arrangements brought into play a new mercantile class whose entrepreneurial spirit sent them looking for wealth and profit in hitherto unknown or unexplored lands. As one such adventurer expressed it, they crossed the seas "to serve God and His majesty, to give light to those who were in darkness," but most emphatically "to grow rich, as all men desire to do."[1]

With that new-found wealth pouring into Europe and feeding the engine for social change, the ranks of the new middle class and urban populations were enlarged, allowing for a corresponding degree of social and gender mobility. It was in these conditions of a global shift in power relations and of internal social change that the machinery of the new missionary movement was assembled, at first haphazardly and clumsily, often unrealistically and at enormous personal cost, but in the end decisively and with unforeseen but irrevocable consequences for the emergence of world Christianity. When we speak of modern missions, then, we have in mind not merely a simple chronological change but a fundamental alteration of worldview from the religious territoriality characteristic of the Middle Ages to the social buoyancy conducive to the emergence of a new middle class and gender mobility, and of a rising sense of risk-taking and personal responsibility, attributes that became central to the culture of the modern missionary enterprise.

The Missionary Strategy: Cause and Consequence

A close study of the results of the modern missionary movement would warrant the conclusion that mission was the exception to the rule of the survival of the fittest.

The change in emphasis from looking to princes, political rulers, and the members of the aristocracy, the fittest of the fit, for creating a truly Christian society to focusing on ordinary persons who might be trained and equipped to lead useful, industrious lives opened the door to people at the bottom of the social heap, those normally marginalized or otherwise excluded in their own societies. In one sense Christian missions took advantage of situations of social crisis to attract members, but in another sense Christian missions offered a crucial alternative to ultimate despair and disenchantment, and thus a safety valve and at the same time a boost for peaceful social change.

Let us characterize the change in tone and strategy as follows. Under religious territoriality, mission attempted to outwit history by bypassing the normal religious channels and looking to the political instrument to establish the church. Religious territoriality raised the stakes by taking faith as the conviction of scattered individuals and groups and moving it to the visible level of a recognized, formative agency at the center of national life. Thus converts were "pacified" tributary natives who could be absorbed as colonial dependents or vassal subjects of Ferdinand and Isabella, King and Queen of Spain. Evangelization was colonization, and colonization was evangelization, with the identification expressed in territorial power, economic exploitation, and communal cohesion. In this view Christianity was inescapable. The next stage in the missionary strategy was to abandon territorial conquest as the guarantee of missionary success and to look for indigenous institutions that might thus be reclaimed to create milder versions of Christendom, such as missionary "spheres of influence," with missionary societies creating their own identities free of church or denominational connections. Missions would be transformed into native fiefdoms, each securing its future by making provision for its self-perpetuation.

In many places the power of missionary societies prevented or discouraged the emergence and growth of churches, and where such churches eventually emerged, there was a legacy of distrust of the missions from which they sprang. Only indigenous exigencies, and the unviability of continued foreign control, ultimately overcame the reluctance to merge mission and church.

Another strategy was to fix on the individual, not necessarily in the existential isolation with which we are familiar today, but in terms of the risk-taking and responsibility we noted above. So individuals were presented as facing the danger of eternal damnation without faith in Christ and required to take personal responsibility for their own souls. This infused a sense of urgency into the task of evangelization and conversion, so that the millions being confined to the flames of damnation might be rescued before all was lost. The dark residue of medieval piety that had concentrated people's minds on the cult of the dead and on the macabre had survived and was stirred to infuse mission with somber purpose as it set about its statistical rescue plan to save the lost from impending doom. There was but one way to truth and salvation, and Christ was that way. There was need for haste.

Fortunately, that view of conversion was overtaken early on in the missionary enterprise by a more realistic assessment of field possibility and challenge, but at the point of organizing the missionary effort in Europe and North America the older view produced the rhetoric of a harmful triumphalism. So many of the so-called missionary hymns are burdened with heathen savages needing to be snatched from the blaze by heroic missionaries. In reality, much of the effective work of missions, in both Catholic and Protestant areas, was accomplished by local agents such as catechists, teachers, exhorters, class leaders, nurses and elders. It was individual risk-taking and personal responsibility expressed in terms of building structures of agency, community, and communication.

However, the distortions and caricatures aside, there is a valid theological premise about the sense of urgency in mission, and that has to do with salvation as God's intention for the whole world, not just for the so-called heathen. Jesus is savior of the whole world, not merely of one portion of it or of one preferred group or caucus. Wherever and whoever they may be, men and women are prey to physical and spiritual ill, what Shakespeare in *Macbeth* called "minds diseased and memories burdened with rooted sorrow," and in that condition they ache for a savior who can heal and assure and fill their hearts with good things. It is this universal human condition that the Gospel addresses and to which mission has attempted to speak and minister. In the sense, then, of the teaching of Jesus about the mission of the church, no one is so wholly evil, or so wholly pure, as to be beyond the need and possibility of salvation, and where missionary motives denied this for whatever reason, whether for reasons of white racial superiority or political expediency, then the results of mission incriminated the whole enterprise.

The understanding of mission as preaching and teaching on the one hand, and as healing and building community on the other, has defined the main task of the modern missionary enterprise. Individuals were presented with the message of the Gospel, with its irreducible demand for repentance and faith in the living God through Jesus. It assumed that people are free and unconstrained in their acceptance or rejection of the Gospel, and that no distinction of tribe, race, nationality, color, gender, or economic status be allowed to pre-empt, undercut, or in any way circumvent that fundamental choice. Yet that supreme personal responsibility entailed paying attention to the physical, political, and material conditions of life, so missionary organizations became involved in geographical and scientific exploration and discovery, in cultural and linguistic research and documentation, in education, in medical and public health work, in the cure, control, and eradication of disease, in the institution of proper methods of quarantine and hygiene, in suppressing the slave trade and encouraging in its place lawful trade and general economic development. Through these wide-ranging projects missions promoted the enterprise culture as the natural setting of the Gospel. These missionary projects saw personal salvation and God's righteousness as two aspects of the one truth, believing that grace and justice belonged together. All of that left mission with a vast agenda and excited correspondingly high expectations. It turned out that evangelization as the work of God and social work as meeting human needs made superhuman demands on mere human instruments. Consequently, in several accounts of the missionary enterprise, observers were unable to avoid the twin traps of spiritual idealization and political vilification, even though the reality was more complex than that. Thus was the missionary enterprise subjected to stringent censure in line with its high ideals and world-scale ambition, a censure for which the facts and records of mission itself provide ample fodder.

Mission as Expansion

In the critical literature on the theology and history of the missionary movement, the first major emphasis was on mission as expansion. The historical engine for this was the maritime expansion of Europe in the era of Columbus, when territorial acquisition accompanied commercial exploitation of the non-Western world. In his Bull of 1493, *Ceteris Partibus*, the pope accorded recognition to Portugal and Spain in their overseas dominions. The classic expression of this expansion was colonialism in New Spain in the Western hemisphere and in the East Indies and West Africa, regions into which mission penetrated under the terms of the *Padroado* which by papal authority vested in Portugal rights and privileges in Africa, Asia, and Brazil.

The fifteenth- and sixteenth-century missions of Spain and Portugal set the tone for much of the succeeding centuries until well into the eighteenth century when several influences coalesced into the worldwide evangelical revival. New movements are often old themes placed at an acute angle with otherwise scarcely discernible tilts of habit and routine, so that men and women catch a reflection of familiar ideas at their elevated intersection with the new circumstances, and the evangelical revival was no exception. In its missionary dimension, the evangelical revival hinged the old themes of conquest and expansion on a new sense of personal heroism to draw native populations into the church, with its place firmly secure within the European sphere. As pioneers and pathfinders, the new breed of evangelical missionaries went forth into the world to reduce strange and different cultures to the familiar and comprehensible, to usher in the enterprise culture, with progress and enlightenment replacing fatalism and superstition. New advances in science and technology allowed the West to extend its control over the natural world and its physical resources, and to increase confidence in the perfectibility of human beings and social institutions, whatever the cultural differences or alternative religious systems.

A few examples of such confident thinking among the leaders of the missionary movement include the head of the London-based Church Missionary Society, Henry Venn (d. 1873),[2] Rufus Anderson of the American Board of Commissioners for Foreign Missions, and J. H. Oldham. The leading figures of the movement spoke confidently of conquest, of struggle against, of taking a stand against surrender and compromise, of marching forward, of an aggressive errand into the world.

World Missionary Conferences: Edinburgh and Jerusalem

An epoch-making conference was convened at Edinburgh in 1910, called the World Missionary Conference. The conference was important in at least two distinctive ways. In the first place it marked the beginning of the modern ecumenical movement which attempted a scheme of church unity among the various Protestant churches and denominations. This emphasis on church unity struck a chord with the leaders of the younger churches of Africa and Asia, who felt increasingly that the word "mission" had a bad odor as it represented European domination and financial control, while the focus on church unity rightly drew attention to indigenous leadership and responsibility.

The second distinctive theme of the conference was the role of Christianity in a new global environment, such as nationalism in the emerging nations of China, India, and Japan, the challenge of non-Christian religions, particularly Islam, and the challenge of secularism. For instance, in his book *The Decisive Hour of Christian Missions* (1910) John R. Mott took up the challenge of Islam, warning that Africa would become a Muslim continent if present trends continued. To respond to that challenge, Edinburgh spoke grandiloquently of the need for a "comprehensive plan for world occupation," an echo of the late nineteenth-century American Student Volunteer Movement's slogan, "the evangelization of the world in this generation."

These two currents of church unity and missionary extension and conquest in time diverged, and when the ecumenical movement was eventually institutionalized as the World Council of Churches, the Commission on World Mission and Evangelism as the continuation of the missionary impulse at Edinburgh was absorbed, and finally dissolved. Signs had already been apparent at Edinburgh of the tension between church and mission, and several delegates commented specifically on it. Even as sympathetic a figure as the Indian churchman, V. S. Azariah, urged the advocates of mission to commend not just self-sacrifice but Christian friendship, in other words, to counsel a shift from missionary heroism and unilateral transmission to indigenous appropriation and mutual solidarity.

As a watershed, Edinburgh 1910 was followed by a series of missionary consultations and ecumenical conferences, all of which produced further refinements in thinking about the mission of the church in the twentieth century. However, the spirit of optimism and positive resolve that was sounded in such a din at Edinburgh was much more muted in subsequent meetings. The reason was obvious. In the aftermath of the 1914–18 World War, a certain sobriety, a self-conscious realism, perhaps even a sense of Christian defensiveness began to dominate contemporary thinking. Among serving missionaries, there was a crisis of confidence about the value of the Gospel in the light of the destruction and upheaval of the Great War. This forced a sharp question on such missionaries, namely if evangelized, Christian countries of Europe could make war on each other, then what was the use of evangelizing non-Western societies? Why should people give up their own imperfection for the imperfection that Christianity was? One missionary at the time concluded: Either Christ has failed, or we have failed!

Thus at the second World Missionary Conference, held in Jerusalem in 1928, a revisionist understanding of the mission of the church was put forward. In its essential outlines, this revisionist view was that the Christian claim about the uniqueness and finality of Christ was no longer tenable in view of the reality of other faiths. In this thinking there could be no exclusive salvation through Christ alone, for other religions provided equally valid salvific vehicles for their followers. The most reasonable outcome for all religions, it was argued, was for them to arrive at an enlightened synthesis in which all their offensive, exclusive claims are set aside and the truth of all subsumed in a progressive, global unity. In the meantime, the mission of the church was for Christianity to lead the way into that future by specifically abjuring any claim to mission and conversion as unwarranted intrusions into the traditions of others, and committing itself to economic and social structures of national life and the new international order.

This line of thinking had radical theological implications for Christianity and the church, as was eventually to be demonstrated by the 1960 conference of the World Student Christian Federation at Strasbourg, whose theme was "The Life and Mission of the Church." Thus the shift now afoot assumed that the church is not the repository of unchanging truths but the center of a new activism, that religious virtues like faith and hope are not a charter for resignation and fatalism but a warrant for self-improvement, that the Last Judgment is not the end of the world but the summons to social justice, and everlasting life not a blissful, deathless existence beyond time and space but a free, prosperous, and happy life here and now. This mood ripened into a radical call for flexible, mobile, Christian social groups to set out to desacralize the church, and thus to replace primacy of doctrine with the duty of social engagement.[3] As a study report of the World Council of Churches put it, it is the world, not the church, that now writes God's agenda.[4] If we could write a motto for this kind of thinking, it would be, in Longfellow's words, "Life is real, life is earnest, and the grave is not its goal."

Two figures were prominent in this revisionist shift, and their influence was to endure well beyond their time. One was William Ernest Hocking (1873–1966) who chaired a commission of inquiry into the nature and future of Christian missions, and we shall return to him more fully presently; the other was R. H. Tawney (1880–1962), the author of the celebrated and influential *Religion and the Rise of Capitalism*, and a major architect of the post-1945 social welfare state in Britain. Tawney's acute analysis of Christian social responsibility turned the searchlight on a this-worldly pragmatism, proclaiming that this world was indeed part of God's Kingdom, even if the Kingdom of God was not of this world. Tawney held up the idea that God's honor was at stake in the welfare of human beings, and consequently, economic prosperity must be accompanied by a strengthening of the institutions which provide moral stamina. He inveighed against what he saw as the false separation of a change of heart from a change of social order, arguing that the distinction that some Christians preferred between the life of the spirit and the fabric of society was a false antithesis and had no "foundation either in the teaching of the New Testament or in that of the church in its most vigorous periods." Not for him the rigors of Christian monasticism. The mission of Christians was to overcome this false dualism. His purpose, he concluded, was to make clear "that the churches are neglecting an essential part of their mission unless they foster the zeal for social righteousness and disseminate the knowledge by which such zeal may be made effective."[5]

The Jerusalem conference adopted this revisionist point of view as the charter for the new mission of the church, a mission to be undertaken on the basis that "man is a unity: his spiritual life is indivisibly rooted in all his conditions, physical, mental and social." Missionary work "must be sufficiently comprehensive to serve the whole man in every aspect of his life." That became the new liberalism in which the secular state and agencies would be the engine of social progress and the guarantee of equality and justice. Such a social vision would also set the limits of state power in the sense that no government should be allowed to defeat the personal development of its citizens. The conference embraced that liberalism and called attention to the importance of industrial society for the church's responsibility, charging the churches with the task "both to carry the message of Christ to the individual soul and to create a Christian civilisation within which all human beings can grow to their full spiritual stature." Thus was set up in 1930 the Bureau of Social and Economic Research within the International Missionary Council. The outcome of this shift for classical mission was predictable, for, with the new claimants for the pre-eminence of the social gospel being empaneled in decision-making bodies, Christians were being served notice that mission was only a supernumerary avocation, an appendage to the main business of building the Kingdom here and now.

William Ernest Hocking

We should now return to William Ernest Hocking, himself the child of a Congregational home who experienced conversion in his youth. He became a professor of philosophy at Harvard. Hocking approved of the thinking of the Jerusalem conference to which he had contributed in no small measure. He echoed the conference when he said that ministry to the secular needs of people in the spirit of Christ *is evangelism* (his emphasis), and that the human condition in society "is an express object of God's concern." Hocking was subsequently appointed to chair the commission set up by the American Laymen's Foreign Missions Inquiry between May 1930 and September 1931 to inquire into the whole purpose and justification for Christian mission, and for that task the members of the commission traveled extensively in Africa and Asia, the continents with the highest concentration of missionaries, to gather data, record observations and trends, and glean insights about the present conduct and (unlikely) future of the enterprise. The inquiry, in effect, was to serve notice on mission as a continuing legitimate enterprise of the church, as became clear in the report subsequently drawn up and published in seven volumes, with the first three consisting of regional accounts, and the rest the findings of the inquirers themselves. Much of its observations, insights and conclusions were distilled in the chairman's single-volume account, *Re-Thinking Missions.*[6]

Re-Thinking Missions is a lucid, astringent, and in parts a moving probe into the practice and justification of mission. In his fair-minded way, Hocking went straight to the heart of the issue. Christian mission, he said, displayed the loftiest of ideals, which made it difficult to assert the rest of the truth of demonstrated weakness and mediocrity in several areas of practice. Mission was the victim of its own rhetoric, and admiration for it should carry the obligation of recognition of its failures. Its impressive scope and zeal, its taking human dedication to the limits of endurance, must reveal limits of the less impressive kind. Potential goodness is also potential harmfulness. As such, the missionary is no exception to the rule of human weakness, and the desire to transmit God's gift of life may mask "the predatory temper," the will to power. Yet it would be an error to think that with the drift in the direction of philanthropy, the missionary can remedy the loss of a clear-cut spiritual vision. "Uplifters and social betterment experts easily fall into the vain supposition that by simply improving the economic basis of life or by cleverly reshuffling human relationships they can produce the happy world of their hopes. All proposals for cure through philanthropy alone miss the point of central importance, namely, that there must be *first of all a new kind of person as the unit of society if there is to be a new social order.*"[7]

Hocking frames his interpretation of mission with the observation that Christian expansion was related to expansions of the military, geographical, and commercial kind: The expansion of Christendom up to the tenth century was essentially the violent military and political expansion of the northern Germanic tribes; the expansion in the sixteenth century that of Catholic explorers and *conquistadors*; and the expansion in the nineteenth century that of Protestant commercial exploiters and prospectors. So the association of mission with conquest or gainful adventure discredits the sincerity of missionary motives. Missionaries were tools or dupes of Western self-interest, what the nineteenth-century slogan called "philanthropy and 6 percent."

In admitting all of this, however, Hocking returns to the issue of motives because of its undoubted evident centrality in the missionary enterprise, but also because it is crucial to Hocking's own philosophical idealism, about which more later.

Hocking concedes that, in the nature of the modern missionary enterprise, it is inadequate to explain it by selfish or imperialist motives alone. "No movement so far-reaching, so persistently renewed during two thousand years, can be supposed to spring from an impulse essentially fallacious or quixotic or selfish," he testified. It would be necessary, he went on, to examine not just the originating motives but also what those motives brought to pass in the field and at home, and in turn what the effects on missionary motives were of changes in theology and the global scene.

Consequently, the motives of conversion on the basis of rescue and redemption have been affected by alterations in the metaphysical system. Christianity in its Western form abandoned a negative view of religion and substituted a gospel of beneficence for that of fear and retribution. In its accommodation with science, Christianity gave up its insistence on biblical accounts of creation and miracles and embraced a free, modernized version of religion as a complement of science. Furthermore, from its encounter with other religions and cultures, Christianity accepted coexistence with them rather than requiring their dissolution.

The world context itself has changed fundamentally. The gulf between East and West, between Western science and Eastern philosophy, has narrowed considerably, and in several sectors where it matters the gulf has been bridged. We now live with accumulating evidence of common traffic in a common idiom shaped by literacy, science, technology, trade, art, and literature. That common idiom is in effect the unifying ascendancy of secularism. This, Hocking affirms, has affected the religious motives of mission and produced the corresponding secularization of the terms of religious life. Hocking did not think that secularism would completely replace religious traditions, but he was of the mind that the secular impact would raise human religious consciousness to a new level. This new consciousness he called "the religion of the modern man," whose chief characteristic is an inclusive openness to all truth-claims, and, by implication, a willingness to relinquish the claims to uniqueness and finality of any one religion, beginning but not ending with Christianity. It is this new kind of consciousness that is "the religious aspect of the coming world-culture." Hocking's use of the singular demonstrates his conviction of an emerging universal self-propagating world-culture of which secularism is the unifying engine, with religion as a safety switch against disenchantment.

Mission has contributed immensely to the project of a unified human experience, to the general raising of human consciousness on a global scale, but other agencies of an increasingly secular nature are now far more effective in advancing this project without the hazard of religious sectarianism or cultural partisanship. It is necessary, Hocking insisted, to separate Christianity from Western culture and agency and "to present it in its universal capacity," that is to say, in its capacity of responsiveness to the insights of a unified human experience.

The goal remains one: the unity of human religious consciousness. The paths are many. Christianity as one such path needs to make common cause with others rather than plan their demise or seek their dishonor. If Christianity has a mission, Hocking counseled, then that should be it. "So far from taking satisfaction in moribund or decadent conditions where they exist within other faiths, Christianity may find itself bound to aid these faiths, and frequently does aid them, to a truer interpretation of their own meaning than they had otherwise achieved." The future for Christian mission is not to tie itself to the sinking hulks of an exclusive triumphalist theology, but to "hold itself clear and give a distinctive version of what religion, in its purity, may mean." This requires making the most of what is genuinely religious, not the least. For Hocking, religion is a quality of the human mind, and religious systems may be graded on their attainment of this quality. The uniqueness of Christianity is its simplicity, its system of symbols, ritual, patterns of observance and fellowship, and its founder and his life and teachings.[8] However, when it is all said and done, in Hocking's view there is nothing that God can do for us that we cannot do for ourselves, including thinking thoughts!

In the nature of the case, Hocking would forbid preaching and proclamation. He wrote: "We believe, then, that the time has come to set the educational and other philanthropic aspects of mission work free from organized responsibility to the work of conscious and direct evangelization. We must be willing to give largely without any preaching; to cooperate with non-Christian agencies for social improvement; and to foster the initiative of the Orient in defining ways in which we shall be invited to help."[9]

The issue of motives was important for Hocking for his own philosophical project. The controlling principle of Hocking's assessment of Christianity in general and of missions in particular is the idea of a ruling unity in life and world affairs. The thrust of all human striving and world events, the grand motive force of history and humanity, is toward the clarification of this ideal, and with its attainment we shall be able to escape that groping and stumbling after truth imposed on us by the inconveniences of difference, particularity, pluralism, and uniqueness. In Hocking's scheme particular cultures, languages, and religions are imperfect pointers and inadequate representations of the universal ideal, and apart from saying that it is an attribute of the human mind, Hocking gives the impression of the universal ideal as a formal abstraction. When he grasps the social concreteness and wholeness of human life, he does so with the tendency to sift and systematize toward a universalized ideal so as to fit in with his scheme of unity. The historical concreteness of religious life and thought may thus be detached from the unthematized essence of religious truth. So the thematic representation of religion does not participate except by accident in the essence of religion as a universal human quality. Like the eighteenth-century Enlightenment rationalists, Hocking believes that knowledge of the universal ideal is possible because of our identical natures. The unitary nature of knowledge and the unitary nature of humanity belong together. Although Hocking is critical of mission as the forcing of ourselves and our ideas on others, he is less shy about prescribing for universal humanity from premises that are his own, and those premises are singularly inhospitable to the historical variety of human experience and culture. If we ask where is the universal blueprint of which religions and cultures are temporal and diversionary representations and hypostases, Hocking would answer that it is identical with his own mind and spirit, and since human beings have identical natures, then one Western systematic instantiation of it may stand for all humanity.

In assessing the contribution of Hocking to a theology of mission, two facts need special mention. One is his assumption, shared with Tawney and others, that religion may be reduced to its social usefulness, which suggests that religions are better seen as social projects than as belief systems. The second is that Christianity's claim of the uniqueness and finality of Christ is the cause of Christianity's mischief and intolerance, so that abandoning such uniqueness and finality would change the religion into a force for good and for genuine acceptance of others. Yet these two facts stand in contradiction. The idea that belief in uniqueness and finality is the cause of mischief and bigotry is weakened by the claim that religions are social projects rather than belief systems. So Hocking turns his back on doctrine only to find himself forced back to it in wishing to prescribe for tolerance and goodness. His dilemma is the postmodern dilemma: how to justify social change and moral reform without drawing on the reserves of religious doctrine and ideals already deemed at fault for impeding change and reform. Furthermore, Hocking's diagnosis of mischief and intolerance draws explicitly on Christianity's uniqueness and distinctiveness, which prompts the thought that, if Christian uniqueness can be used validly to diagnose, then presumably it may also contribute commensurably to the prescribed remedy. Perhaps Christian uniqueness, and religious uniqueness generally, is congruent with universality. In any case, the difference between Hocking's conception of universal truth and mission is that mission sought to extend God's affirmation of a diverse humanity not so much in humanity's self-abstracted essence as in its variegated, Christ-filled, mother tongue particularity.

Be that as it may. Hocking was the gadfly that perturbed the conscience of his generation. He commenced a wide-ranging debate in church and missionary circles about how Christians should henceforth understand their responsibility for faith and witness. Many felt he had cut the ground from under the feet of missions. In the main, he put into words the general feeling in many of the mainline Protestant churches, which were reeling from the Great Depression and from the effects of the 1914–18 War. Hocking was the theological equivalent of the League of Nations, and his ambition was similarly to minimize national and religious differences in the interests of global interdependence and solidarity. It would be fair to say that with him Protestant liberalism wrote its verdict on missions.

Hendrik Kraemer

Yet Hocking did not go unchallenged, especially for what in retrospect appears as his glib optimism. In response to his criticisms and controversial reconception of Christian missions, the Dutch theologian, Hendrik Kraemer (1888–1965), wrote in 1938 his equally influential work, *The Christian Message in a Non-Christian World*. Kraemer was conscious that he was writing under the darkening shadows of impending tragedy, for a year after his book was published a war broke out in Europe that was eventually to engulf the whole world. Even at such close historical proximity to those events, Kraemer could not have foreseen the scale of the disaster nor its permanent repercussions.

Kraemer was sent out to Java, Indonesia, as a lay missionary of the Netherlands Bible Society, serving from 1922 to 1928. At first reluctantly, and then with great energy, he stepped forward boldly to take up the challenge of the new thinking required for mission. He wrote confidently of the church as an apostolic body under commission from her Lord to bear "witness to God and His decisive creative and redeeming acts and purposes" in both the Christian and non-Christian worlds.

Kraemer accepted Hocking's working premise that the world is becoming one, saying that "everybody is forced to think and live in terms of the world, and not only in terms of his own country or community. There is no sphere of life in which different peoples all over the world are not interrelated to each other."[10] Yet the technological and material unity of the world "has intensified disorder, enmity and destruction. Universalism is replaced by militant antagonisms." Also, Kraemer criticized Hocking's weakening of the apostolic mandate for mission.[11]

The root of modern disenchantment Kraemer traces to relativism and secularism which together as self-made absolutisms banished God from our operative universe. That opened the way for the ideologies of Communism, Fascism, and National Socialism which were propagated with religious fervor.

Mission in these circumstances must not accommodate but confront, challenge, and rebuke. The liberal contention that mission is a violation of the sacredness of personality, echoing Gandhi's objection to Christian missions in India, is an accommodation with religion as a product of the national soil, and thus of the Chosen People ideology.

In his theological reflections on the mission of the church, Kraemer echoes many of the voices current in his age. For example, he accepted the need for a new realism in the light of global changes. He pointed out how humanity has an aversion to being deceived, but felt that we should take that not as a prescription but as a symptom of a profound disillusionment whose remedy lies in the divine realism of the Gospel. In that divine realism human beings are affirmed in their high origin and destiny as well as in their capacity for evil and evasion. The Gospel offers as remedy a God who is equally radical in His rejection and condemnation of human sin as well as in His indomitable faithfulness and saving grace. The mission of the church is the witness to that kind of God. Kraemer felt that by the nature of the enterprise mission is always a minority calling, but that it is necessary to the life of the church that rank-and-file Christians catch its vision and be infused with its calling.

The old theological structures of mission need recasting because of the new changes. Political changes in Asia and Africa, for example, indicate that those societies are in a stage of rapid transition and social change. Their traditional institutions and ideas are undergoing fateful change. Theology as a datum is inadequate in those circumstances. Thus, mission must furnish itself with new tools and a fresh understanding. It must develop an "anthropology of change" as well as a "'missiology' of change," and normative criteria to deal with the race question, nationalism, the rise of the autonomous secular state, and the reconstruction of traditional societies. Ultimately, however, the justification for Christian mission is not its success in addressing the otherwise vital concerns of the day but its faithfulness through Scripture to the sovereign will of God who acted decisively in Christ and now rules in the world through the Spirit.

Kraemer wrote that the central issue facing Christianity in general, and mission in particular, is theological in nature: the truth-claim of religion. He distinguishes truth-claim from value-judgment by saying that value-judgment seeks only to pronounce on cultures, religions, and other aspects of the human enterprise as a valuable asset of historic human life. As a function of human self-understanding, the value-argument as such does not deal with truth-claims, with the affirmation of revealed truth that has its source in a realm transcending the natural sphere. Kraemer has been accused of a certain unhelpful anti-naturalism, but it is fair to say that he conceded at least a preparatory role for natural theology by arguing that in their natural state people are moved to seek that imperishable truth which is in harmony "with man's deepest and noblest instincts."[12] It is when he comes to the issue of the criteria for truth that Kraemar is sceptical of what he calls "the subjectively-motivated superiority of religious truths, experiences and values" which can never by themselves substantiate the claim for truth. That truth for him is to be found in God's revelation of "*the* Way and *the* Life and *the* Truth in Jesus Christ" and in willing this to be known throughout the world.[13]

This distinction between natural theology and revelation was fundamental to Kraemer's conception of the role of Christianity among the religions of the world and of the missionary task of the church. As a religious system, Christianity is no different from other religions and cultures. It is all too human, "often as degrading as the baser elements in the other religions . . . a combination of sublime and abject and tolerable elements."[14] No one who knows this can speak glibly of the superiority of Christianity, and such knowledge should undermine "the unchristian intellectualistic and narrow-minded arrogance towards other religions."[15] The same thing, however, can be said of other religions – their gander deserves the same sauce as the Christian goose.

In one crucial respect, however, Christianity stands above all the other religions of the world, and that is in its possession of the Christ who "as the ultimate standard of reference, is the crisis of all religions, of the non-Christian religions and of empirical Christianity too."[16] This requires that we judge all religions in the light of the revelation of Christ. Yet how do we make this judgment unless God has revealed Himself in the other religions? How can we judge the shortcomings of others unless we also know their strengths, and besides, how is such knowledge valid without a bond?

Kraemer's answer to that question is a surprising one, and one that has caused much controversy ever since. The Christian revelation is *sui generis*, restricted to Jesus Christ and unrepeated in the other world religions. It is by that unique revelation that we must judge and evaluate human religiosity as falling short of the truth of God. We are not permitted, Kraemer insisted, to consider the glimpses of truth and revelation in the intuitions of other religions as in any way connected to the full revelation in Christ. There is no possibility of fulfillment in other religions, of the bringing to perfection what may naturally be found of truth and goodness in them.[17] There is thus a dialectical condition in the break between religion and revelation, between natural theology and Christ. "To indicate systematically and concretely where God revealed Himself and wrestled and wrestles with man in the non-Christian religions is not feasible."[18] The reason for this is that there are no bridges from human religious consciousness to the reality in Christ who stands unimpaired in his divinely appointed exclusiveness, the dialectical "no" of the revelation in Christ to all religious life everywhere.

This is a surprising conclusion because it postulates that, while there is an absolute discontinuity between the Christian revelation and the other religions, there is nevertheless a continuity of tradition and human quest which allows for proximity at that level but repudiates any continuity in terms of knowledge of truth. We may thus counter that religious truth-claims are always and everywhere thematized in historical and cultural traditions, those of Christianity not excepted, and to exclude those traditions from a share in the truth-claims they mediate and transmit is to shut the door on the possibility of knowing any truth-claim at all. If Kraemer intended his views as a rebuttal to Hocking's philosophical liberalism, then he has unwittingly made Hocking appear attractive and reasonable.

Similarly, Kraemer's position has caused controversy because it has seemed to undervalue all efforts at genuine interfaith and intercultural understanding and solidarity. In an age when Christianity was poised to make unprecedented strides in non-Western cultures and societies, Kraemer's stand here was a liability for missionary apologetics as such. As for "cradle" Christianity in the West, his dialectical system made it easy to historicize him as out of date in a pluralist world. His failure to accord a place in his system to that pluralism, in both its secular and religious temper, has not aided the cause of mission, which was his declared aim.

Lesslie Newbigin

With Lesslie Newbigin (b. 1909) we have some continuity with Hendrik Kraemer's theology of mission. Like Kraemer, Newbigin is insistent on God's unique and matchless revelation in Christ, and the obligation to proclaim that in mission and service.

Newbigin served as a missionary in India, where he became a bishop of the Church of South India from 1947 to 1957. He was then appointed as general secretary of the International Missionary Council, before returning to India for the final time as bishop from 1965 to 1974. He retired to England, where he went on to publish a number of studies on mission to Western culture.

Whatever his theological affinity with Kraemer, whom he knew personally, Newbigin has argued for a rational conception of Christian truth that is in harmony with the objective rational claims of science. His aim is not to surrender the Gospel to the superior claims of science, but to commend the Gospel as an objectively valid source of knowledge about God and the world, the sort of knowledge, besides, that can remedy the defects and inadequacies of an atomized science and its individualist culture. According to him, there is no disembodied rationality; all knowing, whether of the religious or scientific kind, involves personal risk and commitment. Newbigin sees the postmodern West as a missiological emergency. Michael Polanyi had written that the incandescent confidence of secular autonomy, in its break with medieval irrationalism, "had fed on the combustion of the Christian heritage in the oxygen of Greek rationalism, and when this fuel was exhausted the critical framework itself burnt away."[19] Newbigin agrees,[20] and says the answer is to recover the Christian heritage in its original missionary form. Mission, Newbigin argues, is like science in being self-consistent with its logic: the acting out of a conviction in the process of which that conviction itself is reconsidered and readjusted in the light of new experience and evidence, though only within scope of its own idiom.[21]

On the matter of other religions, Newbigin is adamant that it is not our business to say who can or cannot be saved. "I confess that I am astounded at the arrogance of theologians who seem to think that we are authorized, in our capacity as Christians, to inform the rest of the world about who is vindicated and who is to be condemned at the last judgment."[22] This leaves Newbigin free to explore human religiosity in both its historical and intellectual expression, something that Kraemer rejected. Drawing on his Indian experience, for example, Newbigin writes of Tamil piety and its important cultural underpinnings.

> Anyone who has lived within the Tamil churches knows there are rich resources of living Christian faith and experience embodied in the continuing stream of Tamil Christian lyrical poetry, a stream which has flowed for a century and a half and is still flowing strongly. The people who write and read and sing these lyrics do not take any part in the work of the ecumenical movement. Their lyrics cannot be translated into a European language without losing their power and beauty. The world of thought, the concepts through which they capture and express the deepest Christian experiences, are not those which appear in the documents of ecumenical meetings . . . It is almost impossible for them to communicate in these meanings what is most vital and powerful in the life of the churches from which they come.[23]

Newbigin's most decisive theological break with Kraemer is to recognize a fact of incalculable importance, namely that the Bible as a missionary text has adopted without qualification the name for God of other languages and cultures. He says that, in translating the Bible into the languages of non-Christian peoples of the world, missionaries adopted the name for God of those peoples, the name by which indigenous Christians who use these languages worship "the God and Father of Jesus Christ . . . The name of the God revealed in Jesus Christ can only be known by using those names for God which have been developed within the non-Christian systems of belief and worship. It is therefore impossible to claim that there is a total discontinuity between the two."[24] This leads Newbigin to a general point about the Gospel and the particularity of culture. He states:

Wherever the gospel is preached it is preached in a human language, which means the language of one particular culture; wherever a community tries to live out the gospel, it is also part of one particular human culture. Wherever and whenever missionaries have gone preaching the gospel, they have brought not an ethereal something disinfected of all human cultural ingredients; they have brought a gospel expressed in the language and life-style of a particular culture.[25]

Conclusion: World Christianity Comes of Age

The modern missionary movement has produced many consequences, both in theological appraisals of Christianity and the church as well as in indigenous religious forms and practices. But one crucial global dimension is the emergence in our day of world Christianity, of Christianity as a world religion. Not only has Christianity become a world religion, it has taken on the national and cultural characteristics of its new adopted home cultures. The religion has lived transformed into forms and habits that have but the remotest resemblance to the forms and habits of the originating European cultures. Something new about the nature of faith was thus brought to light by the very process of transmission that sought to impose an unalterable truth in foreign garb.

Thus through setback and opportunity, through numerous vicissitudes, the apostolic heritage has become a genuinely multicultural world religion, thriving profusely in the forms and habits of other languages and cultures, marked by a lively cross-cultural and interreligious sensibility, unburdened by the heavy artillery of doctors and councils, and otherwise undaunted by the scandalous paucity of money, trained leadership, infrastructure, and resources. In all of this nothing better demonstrates the newness of world Christianity than the fact that it has ceased, or is ceasing, to be weighed down by its missionary past. In the churches and congregations we find fresh energy and intelligence being devoted to the production of new hymns, music, artistic and liturgical materials, to the creation of fresh categories for doing theology, to the retrieval of threatened cultural resources, to the application of faith to public agenda issues, and to the promotion of ecumenical sharing and partnership.

Such activity, lamentably sluggish or timorous in some threshold areas, exhilarating and galvanizing in others, has, in all its variegated forms, signaled a crucial shift from Christianity's external relations, from its inflammatory missionary burden and controversy, to insights pertinent to local potential and possibility. We sense in all of this the dawn of a new dispensation, a fresh, if sometimes uneven, point of departure for the Apostolic heritage, a galvanizing hope born of proven confidence that we can move beyond Day One of the missionary landing to enter new fields and spheres with our hearts and minds fixed on the right things. All things considered, it represents a landslide change in the old order, an axial shift of mass and direction, a fact to which Stephen Neill, in his own appraisal of the subject, has called attention.[26]

Notes

1 J. H. Parry, *The Age of Reconnaissance* (New York, 1964), p. 33.
2 Wilbert R. Shenk, *Henry Venn: Missionary statesman* (Maryknoll, NY, 1983).
3 Arendt T. van Leeuwen, *Christianity in World History: The meeting of the Faiths of East and West* (London, 1964).
4 World Council of Churches, *The Church for Others* (1963), pp. 20–3, quoted by L. Newbigin in *The Open Secret*, p. 10.
5 J. D. Gort, "Jerusalem 1928: Mission, Kingdom, Church," *International Review of Missions*, 67 (July 1978), pp. 249–72.
6 William Ernest Hocking, *Re-Thinking Missions: A layman's inquiry after one hundred years* (New York, 1932).
7 Ibid., p. 63.
8 Ibid., pp. 50, 51, 55.
9 Ibid., p. 70.
10 Hendrik Kraemer, *The Christian Message in a Non-Christian World* (London, 1938), p. 2.
11 Ibid., p. 36.
12 Ibid., p. 107.
13 Ibid.
14 Ibid., p. 108.
15 Ibid.
16 Ibid., p. 110.
17 Ibid., pp. 123–4.
18 Ibid., p. 127.
19 Michael Polanyi, *Personal Knowledge* (Chicago, 1958), p. 265.
20 Lesslie Newbigin, *Foolishness to the Greeks* (Geneva and Grand Rapids, MI, 1986), p. 109.
21 Lesslie Newbigin, *The Open Secret* (Grand Rapids, MI, 1978), p. 31.
22 Lesslie Newbigin, *The Gospel in a Pluralist Society* (Grand Rapids, MI, 1989), p. 177.
23 Newbigin, *The Open Secret*, pp. 170–1.
24 Ibid., p. 192.
25 Newbigin, *The Gospel in a Pluralist Society*, p. 189.
26 Stephen Neill, *A History of Christian Missions* (London, 1964), p. 559.

Bibliography

Allen, Roland, *The Spontaneous Expansion of the Church and the Causes which Hinder it* (London, 1956).
—— *Missionary Principles* (Grand Rapids, MI, 1964).
Beaver, R. Pierce (ed.), *To Advance the Gospel: Selections from the writings of Rufus Anderson* (Grand Rapids, MI, 1967).
Bosch, David, *Transforming Mission: Paradigm shifts in the theology of mission* (Maryknoll, NY, 1991).
Burrow, William R. (ed.), *Redemption and Dialogue: Reading* Redemptoris Missio *and* Dialogue and Proclamation (Maryknoll, NY, 1993).
Gort, J. D., "Jerusalem 1928: mission, kingdom, church," *International Review of Missions*, 67 (July, 1978), pp. 249–72.
Hocking, William Ernest, *Re-Thinking Missions: A layman's inquiry after one hundred years* (New York, 1932).
—— *Living Religions and a World Faith* (London, 1940).

Hocking, William Ernest et al. (eds), *The Church and the New World Mind* (St Louis, MO, 1944).
Kraemer, Hendrik, *The Christian Message in a Non-Christian World* (London, 1938).
Leeuwen, Arendt T. van, *Christianity in World History: The meeting of the faiths of East and West* (London, 1964).
Mott, John R., *The Decisive Hour of Christian Missions* (Edinburgh, 1910).
Neill, Stephen, *A History of Christian Missions* (London, 1964).
Newbigin, Lesslie, *Honest Religion for Secular Man* (London, 1966).
—— *The Open Secret: Sketches for a missionary theology* (Grand Rapids, MI, 1978).
—— *The Other Side of 1984: Questions for the churches* (Geneva, 1984).
—— *Foolishness to the Greeks: The Gospel and Western culture* (Geneva and Grand Rapids, MI, 1986).
—— *The Gospel in a Pluralist Society* (Grand Rapids, MI, 1989).

Parry, J. H., *The Age of Reconnaissance* (New York, 1964).

Sanneh, Lamin, *Translating the Message: The missionary impact on culture* (Maryknoll, NY, 1989).

Shenk, Wilbert R., *Henry Venn: Missionary statesman* (Maryknoll, NY, 1983).

Yates, Timothy, *Christian Mission in the Twentieth Century* (Cambridge, 1994).

Feminist Theology

Ann Loades

Introduction

Feminist theology continues to flourish as a diverse field of enterprises, both context-dependent and crossing boundaries of ecclesiastical allegiance and cultures. There is no one thing meant by "feminism," "theology," or "Christian," and within feminism there is increasing sensitivity to complexities of race and class, to "grass roots" and "lay" as well as "academic" feminism. "Feminist theology" remains a convenient way of referring to the movement as a whole, so long as these sensitivities are constantly held in mind. No one group presumes to speak for another, but what is held in common is the central conviction that women's perspectives are to be taken seriously in theology. The point is that since being female is as much the predominant human experience as being male, the insights and experiences of women are as valuable as those of men. The challenge from feminist theology within the Christian tradition as it continues to develop is to come to terms with this reality in a way it has not done before, because it simply has not had to do so. The importance of transregional contact for feminist theologians is that by means of it they are able most readily to learn from the experiences of other women in order to shed light on their own, and to aid in the evaluation of their own work. The activities and publications of the World Council of Churches will no doubt continue to be invaluable in this regard.

The central focus of feminist theology is on gender relations, arising from biological, social, and cultural conditions which vary over time, and the interaction of gender with how human beings understand and relate to God.[1] Feminist theologians are notably preoccupied with the impact of theological convictions on the lives of women, and this gives feminist theology a very wide agenda. Feminist theology seeks a reintegration of areas of theological discipline too often kept apart, such as liturgy, pastoral practice, ethics, and spirituality[2] as well as with theology construed as doctrine. Such a reintegration could in time have a major impact on the way these varied disciplines are treated in "academic" contexts.

Now that it is approximately a century from the publication of Elizabeth Cady

Stanton's *The Woman's Bible*[3] feminist theologians both continue their preoccupation with the interpretation of Scripture but are also turning their attention to the re-evaluation and possible transformation of central Christian doctrines, and to ecclesiology. But to begin with, it is essential to be alert to the impact of feminist criticism in respect of the biblical canon, allowing here for ecclesiastical differences about its limits. It is no accident that feminist theology may be said to have begun in the last century in conjunction with women's access to education in general, and to theological education in particular, and to the use of biblical texts to circumscribe women's lives. To this we now turn in our survey of the movement before attending to possible future dimensions of feminist theology.

Survey

Feminist theology sharpens debate about how to relate to and use the biblical tradition, and the weight to be accorded to reason and experience, as well as participation in a believing community, in the human effort to respond to God. There is no inherent reason why feminists should bear a major share of the burden of insisting on the multifaceted character of biblical interpretation, though in fact they do, and are inevitably concerned with women's contribution to the past history of such interpretation. Feminist theology is a powerful source of stimulus to look again at "sacred texts" of all kinds, beginning with the biblical "foundation" documents.[4] Outstanding contributions have been made by writers of North American origin, most notably by Phyllis Trible and Elisabeth Schüssler Fiorenza.[5] Both of them have consistently given a very strong lead in thinking hard both about the texts they reconstrue in relation to women now, and to the strictly theological import of such texts, the former in exploring female/feminine imagery for God, the latter in attending to God/Sophia. Phyllis Trible's *Texts of Terror* of 1984 has provoked hitherto unparalleled attention to material on women in appalling circumstances.[6] To give only one example, the Tamar of 2 Samuel 13 has become a focus of reflection for those concerned about heterosexual rape and incest, both arguably inherent in "patriarchal structures," patriarchy meaning the web of connections which have developed in which *some* male experience is specially privileged, and in which those men who embody a certain construction of what it is to be male/masculine hold a great deal of the power in terms of which reality is both comprehended and ordered. After the work of Phyllis Trible, a major example of "terror-texts" is a book by J. Cheryl Exum[7] and we may note in passing the crucial importance of certain publishing houses in making feminist biblical scholarship available worldwide, for instance, Sheffield Academic Press's series, "The Feminist Companion to the Bible."

The major achievement in feminist New Testament work remains Elisabeth Schüssler Fiorenza's *In Memory of Her* of 1983, and she has now edited *Searching the Scriptures: A feminist introduction*, with its companion volume of *Feminist Commentary*[8] both of which reveal the inescapably transregional character of this part of the feminist theological movement. The first, for instance, includes essays by the very distinguished historian Elisabeth Gössmann of Tokyo and Munich in the history of biblical interpretation by and the work of writers from Nigeria, Münster, Brazil,

Berlin and Nijmegen/Heerlen. Between them they cover a wide spectrum of discussion, as one would hope and expect. As a whole, this pair of volumes constitutes one of the most exciting collections of essays on Scripture currently available, and, it must be said, it is entirely appropriate to the very diverse ethnic and cultural origins of the biblical texts themselves, a point we have somehow forgotten to take seriously. Insofar as it is possible to discern a consensus in such a collection, it is to the effect that we need not suppose that the biblical canon is hopelessly patriarchal or "kyriarchal," despite sensitivity to the androcentrism of some of the very texts themselves. Some of the writers want to transgress the boundaries of the biblical canon in order to refuse the risk of reinstatement of canonical authority. And there is clear determination to learn from those who inhabit other religious traditions (most notably Judaism and Islam) about the relationships their adherents have with specially sanctioned texts.[9] Some want to stay with the canon, as it were, and look at it again. All will find it uncomfortable to learn that in some parts of the world the interpretation and use of the biblical text cemented patriarchy, and that in others it greatly diminished the status and freedom of women.[10]

Moving on from preoccupation solely with the biblical canon, though certainly not dispensing with it, again one can find much refreshing theology from a variety of quarters. A rapid introduction to the whole "Third World" dimension can be found in a volume edited by Ursula King[11] to which one may add Chung Hyung Kyung's *Struggle to be the Sun again*[12] and its remarkable exploration of the search for liberation from spiritual and physical affliction through the shamanistic tradition to illuminate christology.[13] Interestingly, despite its association with "liberation," it has taken some time for liberation theology as a movement explicitly to find a focus on women, despite its preoccupation with the poor, who are, transregionally, predominantly female, and despite the crucial importance to the Roman Catholic tradition of the doctrines and symbols associated with Mary, the mother of Jesus.[14] A cynic might of course comment that it is precisely because "Mary" has been construed "patriarchally" that the use of symbolism associated with her might as readily obscure the fate of many "real" women as illuminate it.[15] There are signs that this form of theology may become of particular importance for the development of feminist theology in South Africa.[16]

Returning to mainland Europe and to the Netherlands, key figures in the development of feminist theology in this region were Catharina Halkes, and (until she returned to England) Mary Grey.[17] Most recently Els Maeckelberghe's book on Mary[18] and Julie Hopkins on christology "from below"[19] tackle the problems presented by certain doctrines and their associated symbolism for women.[20] It is certainly the case that feminist theologians from the Netherlands have played an important role in sustaining the European Society of Women in Theological Research, whose multilingual yearbooks are invaluable sources of information about what is going on. As Sheffield Academic Press, SCM, and SPCK in the UK have fostered feminist theology by being willing to publish it, so credit is also due to Kok Pharos of Kampen.[21]

The single outstanding work of scholarship from Scandinavia is undoubtedly Kari Elisabeth Børresen's critique of the nature and role of women in the work of Augustine and Aquinas,[22] and for convenience's sake we may link discussion of these two figures by Genevieve Lloyd of Australia in another book which has now become a classic, on "the man of reason."[23] Survey articles on the development of feminist theology in German-speaking Europe reveal what one both expects and finds elsewhere, which is translations of the major works of feminist theology from North America into German, although so far, relatively little material has been translated out of it. The names of Elisabeth Gössmann (already mentioned) and Elisabeth Moltmann-Wendel represent the pioneer generation, with some of the latter's works long available in English.[24] However, the work of Luise Schottroff, who works as a social-historical feminist theologian, is available,[25] as is the work of Susanne Heine,[26] who is both constructively critical of obsession with what may be imagined about an allegedly matriarchal past in relation to women's well-being, and offers a constructive proposal about biblical covenant as summoning human beings toward the future.

In France, feminist theology again largely relies for major treatment of its topics on work in translation, some of it mediated through French-speaking Canadian theologians, and it is evident that a lively discussion and assimilation of feminist theology is being conducted through French-language journals. French-speaking feminist theology is likely to take a very distinctive turn, given the presence of some French feminist writers with theological interests, such as Julia Kristeva. However, there are three significant works of interest for feminist theology, two of them historical, and the third an exercise in beginning feminist theology within the Orthodox tradition. Aline Rousselle is a specialist in the history of ideas of the Greco-Roman and early Christian period, and her work on how bodies were construed is both controversial and fascinating.[27] Aimé Georges Martimort's work on deaconnesses scrupulously attends to the way in which an ancient institution was encumbered with ambiguities, and in any case is of doubtful significance in our own time.[28] Elisabeth Behr-Sigel's work on the ministry of women is an attempt to consider some of the questions raised particularly, of course, by movements for the ordination of women in other denominations from within the Orthodox tradition, while being utterly faithful to her own tradition. Those who have read only the most misogynistic elements from the "Fathers" of the Church need carefully to peruse this book as offering a more resourceful approach, not least in relation to Orthodox Mariology.[29]

To turn finally to the United Kingdom, one must acknowledge with immense gratitude the work, here as elsewhere, of laywomen such as Monica Furlong, Susan Dowell, Linda Hurcombe, Sarah Maitland (whose novels are of outstanding importance), Janet Morley[30] and Lavinia Byrne.[31] It is arguable that in the UK there are some distinctive features of feminist theology. In the first place, there seems to be a willingness to attend to the extremely important work of professional historians. This enables feminist theologians to avoid simplistic categorization and judgment of what gender roles have necessarily been like in a whole range of circumstances.[32] It is particularly noteworthy that the 1996–7 program of the Ecclesiastical History Society[33] is focused on "Gender and the Christian Religion," an agenda which must certainly be of interest to feminist theologians, as it is intended to tackle the complex theme of the interaction between gender relations and Christian practice and experience over 20 centuries of recorded human history. There are three themes in particular. The first has to do with the question of how the masculinity of those who have almost entirely led, organized, and administered Christian churches and sects has influenced the patterns and styles of public and private Christian life. The point is that it is at last being recognized that gender relations are a matter for both sexes/genders and not just for feminists. The second theme is concerned with the matter of how women, within whatever constrictions, found space to express themselves and their spirituality. And the third theme has to do with the way in which the experience and articulation by women of their Christian faith has played a part over the centuries in the rise of feminist consciousness. It is wisely acknowledged that gender, in some way or another, enters into all of life's transactions and relationships, to cite the words of the 1996–7 President of the Ecclesiastical History Society, Anthony Fletcher.[34]

Second, there are works of "freelance" writers which have been, and continue to be important, such as Marina Warner's book on the Virgin Mary, and, to take the other "female" and Christian paradigm, Mary of Magdala, the recent tome by Susan Haskins.[35] By exploration of the multiform traditions connected with both these figures, feminist theologians can learn much about the twists and turns of what it has sometimes meant to be female and feminine in Christian history. Another, very different tradition is explored in Catherine Wilcox's book about seventeenth-century English Quakerism, and the christology which enabled the Quakers, at least for a time, to challenge traditional views of women.[36]

Third, if it accepted that men can be feminist in the sense at the very least of wanting to be part of a movement for change for the better in terms of justice for women, the male perspective on and contribution to feminist theology can be extremely helpful. Excellent examples may be found in essays evaluating feminist biblical criticism as well as parts of the Christian tradition in a book edited by Janet Martin Soskice[37] and in another by male authors.[38] Truly, feminist theology can be humanly inclusive in a most illuminating way.

Fourth, it is fair to say that so far as "professional" theology is concerned in the "academy," feminist theology is likely to be taught by theologians who happen to be female and feminist. It is improbable as yet, or indeed for some time to come, that feminist theology will be deemed to be so central to theological study that it becomes a major subject in its own right, with appointments made specifically with this movement in mind. Feminist theology is most likely to continue to thrive when taught by theologians who integrate it with the rest of what they do. And they are likely to have to go on depending on the work of feminist scholars from outside theology, not least, given the dearth of feminist scholarship in patristics, on the work of feminists among the classicists and ancient historians.[39] So far, there are some notable achievements, such as Grace Jantzen's work on Julian of Norwich,[40] and her study of the interweaving of power and gender in medieval mysticism.[41] Her work on feminist philosophy of religion is also likely to be of importance to feminist theology.[42] In feminist theological ethics Anne Borrowdale's book about work tackles a major "justice" issue for women,[43] and Susan Parsons's book on feminism and Christian ethics[44] is a major contribution to the agenda of Christian ethics. A very distinctive "voice" is likely to be that of Janet Martin Soskice, a Canadian who now teaches in the UK. First published in a collection entitled *Women's Voices* her essay

"Can a Feminist Call God Father?"[45] is an outstanding example of fidelity to a tradition combined with a refreshing capacity to reappropriate it. Here Janet Martin Soskice brings to bear insights from Ricoeur, and more tentatively from Julia Kristeva, and finds "the heart of religion in hope," despite her knowledge of patristic and later opinions of female deficiency. She is well aware of the association of "maleness" with being powerful, dominant, implacable, distant, and controlling, but hopes that the language of divine fatherhood can be detached from the male idol of patriarchal religion which underwrites the social and ecclesiastical patterns which privilege men over women. As President of the Catholic Theological Association of Great Britain she gave an address on trinitarian theology and the feminine "other" about being related in "difference," which indicates some of her developing thought.[46] Her determination to value human experience includes, in her case, finding God in the messiness of child-rearing. We can do without "carved stone monuments" if we can find something "inchoately graced" in our dealings with the very young.[47]

Influence, Achievement, Agenda

It is not to be supposed that feminism or feminist theology will enlighten every issue, any more than there can be a feminist point of view on an equilateral triangle, but over a period of time, feminist theology will undoubtedly have an effect on the churches, as well as on the "academy." It is, however, both recent and still rare for women to be permitted to teach theology, but since they now teach in contexts where few may have a vocation to the ordained ministry, they have considerable opportunities in the long run to transform the self-understanding of the laity. With the existence of the Britain and Ireland School of Feminist Theology, as well as of the European Society of Women in Theological Research, there are now two useful organizations to link up teachers and taught, ordained and lay who are interested in the development of a humanly inclusive theology in the future. For some, it will become an acute question as to whether they should part from the Christian tradition for their own well-being. They may well feel, at least for some time, that by continuing to associate themselves with it they are betraying other women and their needs by staying, and incidentally, doing little if anything to transform relationships between women and men for the better. The critics may well be right, or at least, women may be continuing to incapacitate themselves by opting for "reformist" feminist theology, rather than for a radical feminist one which repudiates any religious inheritance.

The core issue is the unease in the Christian tradition about the association of the female and the feminine with the godlike and the divine. This is why it is arguable that feminist the*o*logy is a contradiction in terms, whereas feminist the*a*logy would not be. The suggestion could then be made that theology needs to be qualified as "masculinist" to make clear that it is not deemed to be humanly inclusive. On the other hand, the phrase "feminist theology," somewhat paradoxical though it is, may be used to indicate the hope that God is given to us and can be imaged/symbolized in gender-inclusive ways, although the fundamental rubric that God transcends both sex and gender must always be kept in mind. Some feminist theologians may well want to argue for a kind of intellectual and spiritual asceticism here, at least for a kind of "negative way" which constantly recalls us to the incomprehensibility and mystery of God. Others may wish to use a proliferation of names to indicate the mystery of God, each name acting as a corrective against the tendency of any particular one to become reified and literal. Such a move could help us make the shift we need, which is to acknowledge that the female/feminine can of and by itself image God in as full and in as limited a way as God is imaged by the male/masculine. This is not a matter of simply adding a "feminine" dimension to a God basically imaged as "masculine," nor of dislodging the mainstream tradition, but of enriching it. It is by no means evident, however, that to overcome the unease about the association of the female/feminine with God will in, of, and by itself dislodge disabling gender constructions for women, nor that such gender constructions could not be dislodged without making such a theological shift. The way in which the symbolism of religious traditions works, and both reflects social assumptions and shapes and reshapes those assumptions, is a complex matter indeed. In any event, the agenda cannot be to obliterate sex/gender differences, but at the very least it ought to be possible to find ways of avoiding associating all those deemed to be "masculine" with the top of our hierarchies of value, and locating those deemed to be "feminine" at the bottom. Those currently associated with femininity are just as important aspects of being human as those associated with masculinity, for members of both sexes.

A particular focus of feminist theology is likely to remain on "justice" issues, not only in the interests of women and men, but in respect of their shared responsibilities for the young and for the fragile. At present, feminist theological ethics typically attends to those values of which women are culturally the bearers, such as care, connectedness, relationality, interdependence, and so forth. Feminist theological ethics needs to find some social and political cutting edge to its agenda, both to tackle immediate problems, such as sexual abuse and violence against women, as well as working for long-term social change. At the moment, it is too inchoate as a movement to be clear about a possible political agenda, though the following might well be found on such an agenda: issues about pregnancy termination in contexts of economic injustice (notably at work); what is euphemistically referred to as "fetal tissue use"; the burdens associated with developments in artificially assisted human reproduction; and new ethical issues arising from developments in human genetics, especially in respect of socially constructed attitudes to the "disabled." Were such matters to become part of the agenda of feminist theology, it might even be the case that other feminists might think that theology and the Christian tradition have something to offer them too, instead of the tradition being almost wholly ignored by most self-respecting feminists. Insofar as women have found themselves to be positively affirmed by the Christian tradition, despite the ways in which they can also find themselves diminished by it, they have developed very strong convictions about the value of what they have to offer one another and their ecclesiastical institutions. If their institutions could take them seriously in terms of feminist theology and what it has to offer, they could find themselves to some degree re-equipped to offer themselves beyond their institutional life, to the many and varied societies of which they are inescapably a part, invigorated and transformed by the debate which feminist theology continues to endeavor to precipitate.

Notes

1 Ursula King (ed.), *Religion and Gender* (Oxford, 1995); Elaine Graham, *Making the Difference: Gender, personhood and theology* (London and New York, 1995) – essential bibliography.

2 Ursula King, *Women and Spirituality: Voices of protest and promise* (London, 1989) – essential bibliography.

3 Ann Loades, *Searching for Lost Coins: Explorations in Christianity and feminism* (London, 1987) and *Feminist Theology: A reader*, ed. Ann Loades (London and Louisville, KY, 1990).

4 For a survey of feminist biblical interpretation see Anthony Thiselton, *New Horizons in Hermeneutics* (London, 1992).

5 See Ann Loades, *Feminist Theology*, for introductions to both.

6 See, for instance, F. van Dijk-Hemmes, "Tamar and the limits of patriarchy: between rape and seduction," in Mieke Bal (ed.), *Anti-Covenant: Counter-reading women's lives* (Sheffield, 1989), pp. 135–56.

7 J. Cheryl Exum, *Fragmented Women: Feminist (sub)versions of biblical narratives* (Sheffield, 1993).

8 E. Schüssler Fiorenza (ed.), *Searching the Scriptures I: A Feminist Introduction*; II: *A Feminist Commentary* (London, 1994–5).

9 Kari Elisabeth Børresen and Kari Vogt (eds), *Women's Studies of the Christian and Islamic Traditions: Ancient, medieval and Renaissance foremothers* (Dordrecht, Boston, and London, 1993); Jeanne Becher (ed.), *Women, Religion and Sexuality: Studies on the impact of religious teachings on women* (Geneva, 1990); Jean Holm, *Women in Religion* (London, 1994).

10 Nam-Soon Kang, "Creating 'dangerous memory': challenges for Asian and Korean feminist theology," *Ecumenical Review*, 47 (1995), pp. 21–31; N. K. Gottwald and R. A. Horsley (eds), *The Bible and Liberation: Political and social hermeneutics* (Maryknoll, NY, and London, 1993); Hisako

Kinukawa, *Women and Jesus in Mark: A Japanese feminist perspective* (Maryknoll, NY, 1994).

11 Ursula King (ed.), *Feminist Theology from the Third World: A reader* (Maryknoll, NY, 1994).

12 Chung Hyung Kyung, *Struggle to be the Sun again* (Maryknoll, NY, 1990).

13 For an African perspective see Maercy Amba Oduyoye, "Feminist theology in an African perspective," in Rosino Gibelli (ed.), *Paths of African Theology* (Maryknoll, NY, 1994), pp. 166–81.

14 Ivone Gebara and Maria Clara Bingemer, *Mary, Mother of God, Mother of the Poor* (London, 1989).

15 See Ana María Tepedino and Margarida L. Ribeiro Brandao, "Women and the theology of liberation," in Ignacio Ellacuría and Jon Sobrino (eds), and Jon Sobrino (eds), *Mysterium Salutis: Fundamental concepts of liberation theology* (Maryknoll, NY, 1993), pp. 222–31; María Pilar Aquino (ed.), *Our Cry for Life: Feminist theology from Latin America* (Maryknoll, NY, 1995).

16 See Jordaan and Mpumlwana in Ursula King (ed.), *Feminist Theology from the Third World*, pp. 150–69; Christina Landman, *The Piety of Afrikaans Women* (Pretoria, 1994); Devarakshanam B. Govinden, "Woman-searching in South Africa," *Journal of Theology for Southern Africa*, 89 (1994), pp. 3–18.

17 Mary Grey, *Redeeming the Dream: Feminism, redemption, and Christian tradition* (London, 1989) and *The Wisdom of Fools? Seeking revelation today* (London, 1993).

18 Els Maeckelberghe, *Desperately Seeking Mary: The feminist reappropriation of a religious symbol* (Kampen, 1991).

19 Julie Hopkins, *Towards a Feminist Christology: Jesus of Nazareth, European women and the christological crisis* (Kampen, 1995).

20 See also Athalya Bremme and F. van Dijk-Hemmes (eds), *Reflections on Theology and Gender* (Kampen, 1994); Hedwig Meyer-

Wilmes, *Rebellion on the Borders: Feminist theology between theory and praxis* (Kampen, 1995).

21 For feminist theology in Europe as a whole to date see Annette Esser and Luise Schottroff (eds), *Feminist Theology in a European Context* (Kampen, 1993).

22 Kari Elisabeth Børresen, *Subordination and Equivalence: The nature and role of women in Augustine and Thomas Aquinas* (Kampen, 1968; reprinted 1995).

23 Genevieve Lloyd, *The Man of Reason: "Male" and "Female" in Western philosophy* (London, 1984; reprinted 1993).

24 Elisabeth Moltmann-Wendel, *The Women around Jesus* (New York and London, 1982) and *A Land Flowing with Milk and Honey* (London, 1986).

25 Luise Schottroff, *Let the Oppressed Go Free: Feminist perspectives on the New Testament* (Louisville, KY, 1993) and *Lydia's Impatient Sisters: A feminist social history of early Christianity* (Louisville, KY, 1995).

26 Susan Heine, *Matriarchs, Goddesses, and Images of God* (Philadelphia, 1989).

27 Aline Rousselle, *Porneia: On desire and the body in antiquity* (Oxford, 1988); for more on late antique asceticism see Gillian Clark, "Women and asceticism in late antiquity: the refusal of status and gender," and Averil Cameron, "Ascetic closure and the end of antiquity," both in V. L. Wimbush and R. Valantasis (eds), *Asceticism* (New York and Oxford, 1995), pp. 33–48 and 147–61.

28 Aimé Georges Martimort, *Deaconesses: An historical study* (San Francisco, 1986).

29 Elisabeth Behr-Siegel, *The Ministry of Women in the Church* (Wheathampstead, 1991).

30 Janet Morley, *All Desires Known* (London, 1988).

31 Lavinia Byrne, *Women Before God* (London, 1988; reprinted 1995) and *Women at the Altar: The ordination of women in the Roman Catholic Church* (London, 1994).

32 Derek Baker (ed.), *Medieval Women* (Oxford, 1978); Diana Wood and W. J. Sheils (eds), *Women in the Church* (Oxford, 1990).

33 See the Society's *Proceedings*.

34 Anthony Fletcher, *Gender, Sex and Subordination in England 1500–1800* (New Haven and London, 1995).

35 Marina Warner, *Alone of all Her Sex: The myth and cult of the Virgin Mary* (London, 1976); Susan Haskins, *Mary Magdalen* (London, 1993).

36 Catherine Wilcox, *Theology and Women's Ministry in Seventeenth-Century English Quakerism: Handmaids of the Lord* (Dyfed, Lewiston, NY, and Queenston, Ontario, 1996).

37 Janet Martin Soskice (ed.), *After Eve: Women, theology and the Christian tradition* (London, 1990).

38 R. Holloway, *Who Needs Feminism? Male responses to sexism in the church* (London, 1991).

39 Gillian Cloke, *"This Female Man of God": Women and spiritual power in the Patristic Age, AD 350–450* (London, 1995).

40 Grace Jantzen, *Julian of Norwich: Mystic and theologian* (London and Mahwah, NJ, 1987).

41 Grace Jantzen, *Power, Gender and Christian Mysticism* (Cambridge, 1995).

42 Grace Jantzen, *Exploring the Female Divine: A feminist philosophy of religion* (Oxford, 1996).

43 Anne Borrowdale, *A Woman's Work: Changing Christian attitudes* (London, 1989).

44 Susan Parsons, *Feminism and Christian Ethics* (Cambridge, 1996).

45 Janet Martin Soskice, "Can a feminist call God Father?" in Teresa Elwes (ed.), *Women's Voices: Essays in contemporary feminist theology* (London, 1992), pp. 15–29; also in A. F. Kimel (ed.), *Speaking the Christian God: The Holy Spirit and the challenge of feminism* (Grand Rapids, MI, and Leominster, 1992), pp. 81–94.

46 Janet Martin Soskice, "Trinity and 'the feminine Other,'" *New Blackfriars*, 75 (1994), pp. 2–17.

47 Janet Martin Soskice, "Love and attention," in M. McGhee (ed.), *Philosophy, Religion and the Spiritual Life* (Cambridge, 1992), pp. 59–72.

Bibliography

Primary

Børresen, Kari Elisabeth, *Subordination and Equivalence: The nature and role of women in Augustine and Thomas Aquinas* (Kampen, 1968; reprinted 1995).

Cloke, Gillian, *"This Female Man of God": Women and spiritual power in the Patristic Age, AD 350–450* (London, 1995).

Graham, Elaine, *Making the Difference: Gender, personhood and theology* (London and New York, 1995).

Jantzen, Grace, *Power, Gender and Christian Mysticism* (Cambridge, 1995).

King, Ursula (ed.), *Feminist Theology from the Third World: A reader* (Maryknoll, NY, and London, 1994).

Loades, Ann (ed.), *Feminist Theology: A reader* (London and Louisville, KY, 1990).

Parsons, Susan, *Feminism and Christian Ethics* (Cambridge, 1996).

Soskice, Janet Martin (ed.), *After Eve: Women, theology and the Christian tradition* (London, 1990).

Secondary

Aquino, María Pilar (ed.), *Our Cry for Life: Feminist theology from Latin America* (Maryknoll, NY, 1995).

Becher, Jeanne (ed.), *Women, Religion and Sexuality: Studies on the impact of religious teachings on women* (Geneva, 1990).

Ecumenical Review, "Churches in solidarity with women: a mid-decade assessment," 46 (1994), pp. 133–212.

Exum, J. Cheryl, *Fragmented Women: Feminist (sub)versions of biblical narratives* (Sheffield, 1993).

Grey, Mary, *Redeeming the Dream: Feminism, redemption and Christian tradition* (London, 1989).

Schottroff, Luise, *Lydia's Impatient Sisters: A feminist social history of early Christianity* (Louisville, KY, 1995).

Soskice, Janet Martin, "Trinity and 'the Feminine Other,'" *New Blackfriars*, 75 (1994), pp. 2–17.

Postmodern Theology

Graham Ward

Varieties of Postmodernism

If thinking in modernity (a period roughly inaugurated by the rapid development of capitalism, technology, and the cult of the individual in the late sixteenth century) is dominated by highly determined forms such as the circle, the cube, the spiral, even the double helix, then postmodernity (not a period, as we shall see, but more a condition) finds expression in indeterminate forms such as Deleuze and Guattari's thinking about the rhizome. As a form the "rhizome is reducible neither to the One nor the multiple . . . It is composed not of units but of dimensions, or rather directions in motion. It has neither beginning nor end, but always a middle (*milieu*) from which it grows and which it overspills."[1] The dreams of order – Newtonian, Leibnizian – the economies of evolutionary progress – Hegelian and Darwinian – the aesthetics of pure color and geometrical forms – in Kandinsky and the Bauhaus – collapse into the subterranean complexity of the rhizome: a root-stock growing in no particular direction and without detectable regularity. Words like development, progression, advancement, meaning, profundity, and depths are supplanted by other words like dissemination, indeterminacy, deferral, aporia, seduction, and surface. Meaning is local, community is tribal, society is pluralistic, and economics is the pragmatics of the marketplace. This is the age of the sign.

In such a cultural space it is to be expected that there is not one postmodernism. There is the eclecticism of postmodern architecture in which classical columns and architraves are mixed with multicolored bricks or polychromatic ironwork. The newly opened building for the Judge Institute of Managerial Science, in Trumpington Street, Cambridge, is a good example of such architecture. Then there is the ironization of the aesthetic medium in the paintings of Anselm Kiefer, who employs materials like sand, earth, ash, straw, and charred photographs in compositions which play on a tension between spatial emptiness, burnt edges, blistered textures, and religious titles. A series of sixteen paintings of stark desert landscapes made up of multilayered images is entitled *Departure from Egypt.*[2] There is a similar ironization (and irony is always iconoclastic) in the novels of Thomas Pynchon, in which characters are flat and cartoon-like and the narration endlessly turns in upon itself in a self-conscious "this-fiction-writer-is-writing-fiction" gesture. Obsessed to the point of paranoia by a symbol of a horn and the company WASTE for which it is the logo, one Oedipa Mass in Pynchon's *The Crying of Lot 49* attempts to decipher the gathering heaps of hieroglyphics around her by visiting Mr Thoth. Mr Thoth shows her a ring cut by his grandfather from the hand of a man disguised as an Indian who had attacked him one night. On the ring is the symbol of WASTE. Surprised, once again, Oedipa

> looked around, spooked at the sunlight pouring in all the windows, as if she had been trapped at the centre of some intricate crystal, and said, "My God."
> "And I feel him, certain days, days of a certain temperature," said Mr Thoth, "and barometric pressure. Did you know that? I feel him close to me."
> "Your grandfather?"
> "No, my God."[3]

Then there are the French intellectuals – Foucault, Lacan, Derrida, Levinas, Baudrillard, among others – whose work details radical critiques of history, rationality, representation, and self. Frequently, the poststructuralism and deconstruction they represent is seen as a post-1968 phenomenon. But several of these popular thinkers – like Blanchot, Bataille, Lacan, and Levinas – produced significant critical work much earlier.[4] All these postmodern projects are not easily made analogous. Besides, art theorists like Charles Jencks, Clement Greenberg, and Rosalind E. Krauss, philosophers like Jürgen Habermas, Jean-François Lyotard, and Gianni Vattimo, and social theorists like Zygmunt Bauman and Frederic Jameson still argue (frequently with each other) about the characteristics of various shades of modernism (in itself and then prefixed with "late" or "post").[5] In the *Zeitgeist* of postmodernity, there can only be postmodernisms.

Similarly, there is not one postmodern theology; there are (to quote the title of one of David Ray Griffin's books) *Varieties of Postmodern Theology*. Even so this essay, while outlining this variety, nevertheless would wish to argue that some of these theologies are more thoroughly postmodern than others. It will argue for a distinction to be drawn between liberal and conservative postmodern theologies, pointing out that early espousals of postmodernism were simply continuing liberal theology's concerns with apologetics, correlation, and local expressions of a universal condition. Some practitioners of postmodern theology are therefore seen to be dreaming of a bacchanalian nihilism in what George Steiner terms the garden of liberal culture.[6] These thinkers can only advocate freedom through abandoning oneself to the effervescent flux because of the leisure society to which they belong (and which provides them with employment and an income). If liberalism promotes the politics and economics of *laissez-faire*, then their work is an expression of such a culture, not a critique of it.[7] Of course, among these theologians, some are more liberal than others; but all of them are idealists (and to use what is now a quaint term, bourgeois). As for the conservative postmodern theologians, they tend to employ the insights and analyses of postmodern thought to reread foundational Christian texts and, with reference to the Scripture, liturgies, and creeds, construct new Christian theologies in, through, and at the margins of postmodernism. These theologians locate themselves in the place of faith and the Christian tradition prior to the secondary, postmodern reflections upon that tradition which their work explores. Rather than interpreting poststructuralism or deconstruction as the final nail in theology's coffin, the work of these theologians opens up the theological horizons within postmodern thought itself. These theologians also recognize that postmodernism does not delineate an epoch at the end of modernism, beginning in the 1960s, say. Rather, postmodernism is a moment within modernism; the moment modernism pushes into the margins and represses in order to construct its circles of development, its linear progressions and its harmonies of part and whole. In this sense, postmodernism, described in terms of Freudian psychoanalysis, marks the return of the repressed. It is the repressed "other" of modernism. This is postmodernism as understood and described by Jean-François Lyotard: "postmodernism is not modernism at its end, but in a nascent state, and this state is recurrent."[8] "The postmodern would be that which in the modern invokes the unpresentable in presentation itself, that which refuses the consolation of correct forms, refuses the consensus of taste permitting a common experience of nostalgia for the impossible, and inquires into new presentations – not to take pleasure in them, but to better produce the feeling that there is something unpresentable . . . *Postmodern* would be understanding according to the paradox of the future (*post*) anterior (*modo*)."[9]

The postmodern moment, then, is composed of that which is excluded from or excess to the discourses of knowledge or the orders governing various sciences, and the authorities which police them. The University, with its *Geist-* and *Naturwissenschaften* and the division of faculties, is one example of authority. In this way postmodern thinking forces open a new space for theological thinking by paying attention to the pre-emptive foreclosures of systems (philosophical, institutional, and political). With profound philosophical and psychological investigations into an unerasable instability, uncertainty, agnosticism, skepticism, even nihilism, theological questions have begun again to surface and permeate contemporary thought. It is not surprising then to find Derrida writing eloquently about Eckhart and negative theology in relation to his own notion of *différance*.[10] Not only does Kristeva distinguish the critical difference "love" in Christian discourses makes to primary narcissism in psychoanalytic discourses, but a *theologia crucis* operates at the center of her thinking on the need to reintegrate the abjected, chaotic other, what she terms the *khora*.[11] Levinas, as a Jewish philosopher working out of the tradition which produced Hermann Cohen and Franz Rosenzweig, cannot separate God from his account of our primordial responsibility for the wholly other, what he terms *illeity*. The Good, the ethical God, lies beyond Being, but elects us all to an endless responsibility for the other.[12] Irigaray's work on sexual difference has repeatedly called for a feminine symbolics of the divine and a more developed notion of what it is to be incarnate ("bringing the god to life through us, in a resurrection or transfiguration of blood and flesh").[13] In Lyotard's more recent work, his concern with waging war on totality and bearing witness to the unpresentable has drawn him into detailed analyses of the sublime, its experience, its characterization.[14] Cixous has advocated we rethink our understanding of "soul," announces a radical ethics of love and kenosis, and refers throughout her work to the face of God, the Bible and our immortality.[15]

Three particular theological (and ethical) horizons are opened up by this postmodern thinking. First, the role of the unsayable and unpresentable as it both constitutes and ruptures all that is said and presented. Secondly, the self as divided, multiple, or even abyssal, and therefore never self-enclosed but always open onto that which transcends its own self-understanding (rather than simply being an agent and a *cogito*). Thirdly, the movement of desire initiated and fostered by the other, that which lies outside and for future possession, the other which is also prior and cannot be gathered into the rational folds of present consciousness. The place in which these three horizons interlace is the "body." That is, these horizons can never be abstracted from the texts, the social practices, and the institutions which configure or give expression to them. As such, postmodernism's critique of body/soul, body/mind, form/contents, sign/signified divisions demands new understandings and imaginings of what it is to be embodied, incarnate. And although "the cross," "resurrection," the "soul," "immortality," and the "divine" are always employed rhetorically in these philosophical discourses, nevertheless they show themselves profoundly indebted to (if not heavily dependent upon) the Judeo-Christian tradition. Furthermore, they would question what is being meant when theologians seek for these words a literal reference. It is on the basis of these horizons that the sociologist Zygmunt Bauman has emphasized how "postmodernity can be seen as restoring to the world what modernity, presumptuously, had taken away; as a *re-enchantment* of the world that modernity tried hard to *dis-enchant*."[16]

Liberal Postmodern Theologies

Until recently, postmodern theology's most popular and well-known exponents in North America were Mark C. Taylor, Thomas J. J. Altizer, Robert P. Scharlemann, Charles Winquist, and David Ray Griffin. Its most popular and well-known exponent in Britain was Don Cupitt. Significantly for all these writers, their projects issue from a radicalization of an older liberal theology that previously engaged them. The existential concerns of Paul Tillich and Rudolf Bultmann and the process philosophy of Alfred Whitehead remain as important as Nietzsche's pronouncements about the death of God and truth as a mobile army of metaphors. The projects of these postmodern theologians are not identical.

David Ray Griffin has been concerned to reread process theology in the light of certain characteristics of postmodernity – particularly the critique of Enlightenment rationalism and the decentering of the Cartesian *cogito*. He develops, through an examination of quantum mechanics, a notion of postmodern animism in which everything in the world from rocks to human beings embodies creative energies. A postmodern naturalistic theism emerges.[17] There are certain aspects of this project which connect with the more recent work of Don Cupitt, who, in outlining the philosophy which informs his thinking, describes it as a *Lebensphilosophie*. Cupitt too is arguing for an "outlook that is monistic and naturalistic"[18] and appeals to the flux of life which is both biological and sociocultural. Where Don Cupitt differs from David Ray Griffin (and draws closer to Mark C. Taylor and Charles Winquist) is in the support he elicits from French postmodern philosophers like Jacques Derrida, Michel Foucault, and Gilles Deleuze. The writings of these thinkers provide the philosophical analysis and argument for the antifoundationalism and the antirealism that Don Cupitt and Mark C. Taylor both wish to endorse and the bases for the a/theology they both advocate. In particular, the work of Don Cupitt and Mark C. Taylor develops the consequences for theology of a linguistic idealism they believe Derrida and others expound.[19] The burden of Mark C. Taylor's apocalyptic chapter "The Empty Mirror" (in his book *Deconstructing Theology*) is that we do not find but construct reality. We are not only caught up within but constituted by nets of shifting signifiers endlessly deferring identity. We deal not with meaning but interpretations. He, like Don Cupitt, encourages us to enjoy the cavalcade of tropes and metaphors, the endless stream of simulacra, which represent to us our world. We are advised to stop mourning for defunct authorities (the authority of God, Truth, and Self) and embrace the creativity of play and plurality. For "one who has gazed into the empty mirror can never regard God or self as he did before."[20] The death of God is the death of a transcendental signifier stabilizing identity and truth. It is the death of identity, *telos*, and therefore meaning in anything but a local and pragmatic sense. That death has led to a new emphasis upon the immanent flux, the material, the body and its desires – all of which deny there is anything "higher" or "out there." With Griffin, Cupitt, and Taylor whatever is religious issues from a profoundly nihilistic ontology.

It is with the consequences of the death of God that Thomas Altizer's project is concerned, which, in the wake of Tillich, examines the relationship between contemporary culture and the Christian faith. Subsequently, Altizer reverses Tillich's priorities – judging God in the darkness of modern culture rather than culture by the ultimate revelation of God. Tillich and the death of God are also important orientating foci in the theological project of Charles Winquist. In his most recent volume, *Desiring Theology*, he speaks explicitly about extending rather than abandoning the theological work of Tillich.[21] Winquist's project is indebted to Altizer's. He considers Altizer to have made one of the most important statements of what it means to think theologically in the closing years of this century.[22] To a large extent, Winquist's form of deconstructing the pretensions of theology by reminding theologians they are only writing, is providing the fundamental theology Altizer's project lacks. For Winquist's work draws attention to the textual body of theology: to language as a dialectic of meaning and desire; to the endless deferral of truth that issues from theology's necessary dependence upon representation and tropes; to the wounds and fissures in logical argumentation which proliferate rather than delimit ambiguity and hinder rational progression. His is a navel-gazing theological investigation. He does not think theologically himself, rather (as he himself observes) "deconstruction in theology resembles a second-order critique looking for the conditions that make theological thinking possible."[23] Nevertheless, though the textual surface of theological discourse is broken up and raked, the Tillichian and liberal emphasis upon the primacy of "religous experience" remains. The gaps and aporias – what remains unsaid and unthought in what is said and thought in the textual body of theological discourse – point to "epiphanies of darkness" and the God of the gaps.

It is significant, with respect to the distinction drawn between liberal and conservative postmodern theology, that these theologians understand their French philosophical support to be advocating absence, nonidentity, and the unbearable lightness of a being in which all is rhetoric and surface. It is also important that the relationship of postmodern philosophy to the projects of these radical theologians is epiphenomenal. Their work does not issue from postmodern philosophy, its insights and methodologies; postmodern philosophy (as they interpret it) substantiates their theses concerning contemporary culture. Altizer's theological project, for example, and Cupitt's, were underway several years before Derrida or Foucault, Lyotard or Deleuze were writing their poststructural philosophies. Nevertheless if these thinkers represent for Mark C. Taylor and others the postmodern experience they wish theology to address and they are not representatives and purveyors of nihilism in the way Mark C. Taylor and others believe, liberal postmodern theology may have to think again. For the moment it is sufficient to outline that all these postmodern theological projects are united in attempting to construct, in Mark C. Taylor's words, "a radically new theology, a secular, post-ecclesiastical theology."[24] Each is aware that, in doing this, theology and anthropology become indistinguishable, religious studies becomes a subset of cultural studies, even aesthetics, and transcendence issues only within immanence. Hence Mark C. Taylor's neologism: "a/theology."

While these theologians dissolve the specificity of Christianity into a world-spirit, the work of Robert P. Scharlemann does not go so far. Scharlemann's theology is still trading off the inheritance of Schleiermacher, Tillich, and Bultmann, but for him the specificity of the Christ-event remains uniquely paradigmatic. His work relies heavily on the existential analyses of Martin Heidegger. Soteriology is worked out in terms of selfhood, in terms, that is, of developing the notion of the "exstantial I." This I is the resurrected I, the I which is drawn out of the interiority of the *cogito* by the process of what Scharlemann calls "acoluthetic reason" – reason which follows after, follows in the wake of Christ. Christ himself instantiates, as archetypal example, the exstantial I as someone living beyond himself for the other, emptying himself out for the other.[25] As Scharlemann writes "If the exstantial I is a symbol of God . . . then it is *as* that exstantial I that God (who is not I and not the world but not nothing either) exists. The exstantial I is not *what* God is but *where* God is."[26]

Scharlemann's work is densely analytical and philosophical, and he permits (possibly like Winquist) a transcendence missing from Taylor, Altizer, and Cupitt. His is a repristination of Logos christology and his central appeal to the ethics and theology of discipleship gives weight to ecclesiology. But his analyses and philosophy owe much to the projects of modernity rather than postmodernity. He, more than the others, illustrates the fact that these "postmodern theologians" are really theologians of modernity. Their work is not the deconstruction of the liberal tradition (however much they employ the term "deconstruction"), it is the apotheosis of the liberal tradition. Most of these figures have, at times, wished to emphasize they are not postmodern all the way; but the work of all of them has been characterized by a preoccupation with that most postmodern of all themes, the crisis of representation.

We need to return to the liberal roots of these theologies for a moment and reflect upon them in the context of the poststructural and deconstructive philosophies to which they frequently appeal. Each theologian, in his way, is continuing to write theological apologetics based upon the liberal notions of correlation, a primary monism, and the exponential pursuit of human emancipation. For what each assumes is a major cultural shift, what Altizer describes as the dawn of "a wholly new historical era,"[27] that can be described as "postmodern" and, like their liberal forebears, it is with relation to this new culture that theology must radically transform itself. What is significant is that the epithet "postmodern" is here being used as a period concept, frequently an apocalyptic concept denoting a culture at the "end of history," "the end of the autonomous person," the "end of representation," and the mortal wounding of rational argumentation. Altizer makes this explicit in his book *History as Apocalypse*. Our postmodern culture, he argues, is what the development of history has brought us to. Hence our new situation calls for a revolution in our thinking. The old texts have to be rewritten for them to speak again in contemporary society. Postmodernism, as such, becomes interchangeable with postmodernity (i.e., the sociological concept describing the character of the age in which we live). But as Lyotard has pointed out concerning this use of "post" in postmodernism, "this idea of a linear chronology is itself perfectly 'modern.'"[28] Connotations of "progress," "development," and "evolution" – the basis for the liberal dream for the emancipation of humanity – lie concealed about the body of "post"modernism as it is employed by these theologians. Let me delineate this further, for it is central to my argument. These theologians, in fact, are continuing the crisis of theology characteristic of "modernism," where it was believed that a clean break from theology's past was possible and necessary for a new liberation and new humanism. Their iconoclasm is only in the name of a more foundational monism – what Altizer terms a "new totality of bliss."[29] They are indissolubly linked, therefore, to a certain conception of history (a profoundly unpostmodern part-and-whole metanarrative). And this is the direct legacy of the historicism, romantic idealism, and neo-empiricism of the nineteenth century. Altizer writes: "Contemporary radical theologians inherit the C19th Catholic and Protestant theological conceptions of the evolutionary development of Christianity, but recognizing that the forward historical movement of Christianity has led to the eclipse or silence of God."[30]

There is, significantly for these liberal theologies, a difference between *deus absconditus* and *deus mortuus*. It is the death of God in history, not (as with Karl Barth and Hans Urs von Balthasar) God's hiddenness that is being foregrounded in their work. The death of God, as such, is part of the ever-deepening movement of the Incarnation. Hegel and a kenotic christology emphasizing negativity and emptying are fundamental reference points. Christ merges with creation. As Altizer puts it: "the movement of secularization is finally a consequence of faith, and of faith in the Christ who lies in our future, the radical theologian is concerned with opening the corporate and communal body of faith to the new and more universal body of Christ."[31] Creation, not the Church, is now the body of Christ. Institutions such as the Church, bodies of historical tradition like its teaching and liturgies, find no room in such liberal "postmodern" theologies. The more profound the death of God, the more Christ is broken and poured out to perfume the mundane. The theological, stripped of any transcendence, becomes the incarnational to the point at which a Christian atheism emerges.

My question is whether this work can accurately be described as postmodern theology at all. To varying degrees each of these thinkers appeals to sets of ideas associated with postmodernism. We can distinguish five such sets. The first (and of primary importance to Cupitt, Taylor, and Winquist) is the way the linguistic turn in the early decades of this century has been transformed into the extended surface of ubiquitous textuality. On to this crisis of representation are grafted four other crises – the end of metaphysics, the end of history, the end of the subject, and the end of humanism. But significantly, with these five postmodern crises the end of liberalism itself is forcefully announced. Fundamentalism and postliberatlism characterize the splintered culture of postmodernism. The isolation and construction of local, non-apologetic identities, of faiths radically opposed to Western globalization – these are the characteristics of postmodernity emphasized by sociologists such as Ernest Gellner[32] and Akbar S. Ahmed.[33] Hence there are cultural (if not ethnographic) and philosophical tensions between these self-ascribed postmodern theologies and postmodernism itself. Each theology aims to eradicate difference or otherness because of the philosophical monism of their commitment to a general "life-force."[34] They each interpret Nietzsche's Eternal Recurrence as the dissolution of identity and difference[35] and this flies in the face of postmodernism, where difference is lionized. Nihilism, as such, is indifference; and joyful affirmation for these theologians issues from embracing the sheer contingent meaninglessness of existence.

Where do we look then for "postmodern theology" if the work of self-described postmodern theologians is not postmodern at all? We have seen that one possibility is to reject postmodernism as a period concept. Another is to recognize that for these theologians postmodernism is a given and emphatically a secular given. In other words, these thinkers do not examine the theological horizons of postmodernism, but rather the secular implications (in terms of critique) such postmodernism will have for the task of theology. Again the "modern" character of their projects becomes increasingly manifest. For the various projects of Feuerbach, Durkheim, and Freud were all involved in the same program – the secularization of theology by means of developing more rational and comprehensive explanations: neo-Kantian anthropology, sociology, and psychology respectively. As such, "postmodernism" provides these theologians with yet another grand explanatory narrative within the framework of which theology has to defend and adjust its thesis. And what happens is that theology, as such, is made bankrupt, its metaphors dispersed, its sacred space converted into a theme-park. But we can reverse the logic of this liberal analysis. Rather than postmodernism summoning theology to its judgment seat, we can explore the limits of the philosophical and the limits of explanatory narratives to which postmodernism draws attention. Theology then summons postmodernism to declare its own theological character. In fact, the theological horizons beyond philosophy (which postmodernism opens up) can be read as the theological fissuring and refiguring of the human, the mundane and the metaphysical which it has consistently been the task of theology to investigate. What is then brought to our attention in the work of Derrida, Kristeva, Irigaray, Levinas, Lacan, and others can be read back into the theological tradition, beginning with such readings as their own. It is here that we can locate conservative postmodern theologies, which, I suggest, are more accurately entitled postmodern.

Conservative Postmodern Theologies

Among Anglo-American works, we could list here the postliberalism of George Lindbeck's influential volume *The Nature of Doctrine*,[36] building as it does on a cultural-linguistic model of religion owing much to the social anthropology of Clifford Geertz and Wittgenstein's notion of meaning issuing from specific linguistic practices or games. More recently, there has been the postmodern Augustinianism of John Milbank,[37] given significant expression in his book *Theology and Social Theory*. The task of theology is rendered more questioning and complex by Rowan Williams,[38] Edith Wyschogrod's work on sainthood,[39] and my own postmodern Barthianism.[40] But conservative postmodern theologies are much more developed by French thinkers indebted to the Catholic heritage this century of Étienne Gilson, Henri du Lubac, and Jean Daniélou, and indebted also, more directly, to poststructural and deconstructive philosophies as they issued out of existential phenomenology. Of these theologies two names are becoming increasingly prominent in English and North American theological academies – Jean-Luc Marion and Michel de Certeau. Much of de Certeau's important work is now translated and, following in the wake of the intellectual stir caused by the translation of Marion's *God Without Being*, several of Marion's books are now in the process of being translated into English. It is with the work of these theologians that a more "authentic" postmodern theology appears.[41]

Jean-Luc Marion

Jean-Luc Marion, a professor of philosophy at the University of Nanterre, established his academic reputation on analyses of Descartes's work. With Marion a more nuanced Descartes emerges than the philosopher frequently cited as one of the primary craftsmen of modernity. Seen as the harbinger of our modern world, what is emphasized in Descartes's work is his notion of the self-determining *cogito*, the I which determines the nature of any object through its consciousness and the creation of ideas. As such, we are on the road to anthropology via atheism. But Marion's Descartes is haunted by questions of God and eternal truths. Marion's work points out that the gaze of the *cogito* in Descartes exists both in harmony and in conflict with a second gaze – the gaze of God. In harmony, the *cogito* is a reflection of *causa sive ratio* of God. In conflict, it is independent. An irreducible ambivalence emerges in Descartes's analysis of the *cogito*, for Descartes refuses to reduce the operation of consciousness upon the world either to anthropology or theology. Descartes, then, opens up *the question* of epistemological and ontological foundations, "a question concerning infinity and the unknown."[42]

It seems that Marion's project is to return to the philosophical origins of modernity and point up its ambivalences. Like his friend and colleague, the philosopher Jean-François Courtine, Marion has wished to distinguish between theological and metaphysical thinking. Metaphysical thinking about God is recognized as a product of modernity, issuing from the work of the Spanish Renaissance philosopher Francisco Suarez on Aristotle. With Suarez God, Being, and Reason are conflated, leading to the project of onto-theology as it subsequently developed through Leibniz,

Hegel, and finally Heidegger. What has been forgotten here – which was never, forgotten by Anselm and Aquinas, for all their emphasis upon theology as seeking understanding – is the priority of faith and a God beyond both Being and human reason. Marion reaffirms that theological thinking proceeds along a different track and according to another logic. It is the logic of theology beyond the logic of philosophy which Marion attempts to elucidate in his theological books.[43] Marion was engaging with theology prior to and throughout his early researches into Cartesianism. His first published works were articles on Bultmann and Augustine, Maximus the Confessor and Pseudo-Dionysius, revelation and liturgy for the conservative French Catholic journal *Résurrection*. He was to go on to become a regular contributor to the *Revue catholique internationale Communio*.

In his theological researches, Marion draws heavily upon Patristic thinkers. He is following here in the footsteps of those Catholic neo-Patristic theologians Jean Daniélou, Henri du Lubac, and Hans Urs von Balthasar. He refers repeatedly to the work of Pseudo-Dionysius and the Cappadocian Fathers. He has, on the basis of his philosophical interest in consciousness and the construction of the object, consistently attempted a phenomenology of the icon, or more generally, visibility.[44] On the basis of this phenomenology he then proceeds to the theological implications of what he discerns as a gift of the invisible in the visible.

We can observe the intellectual moves he makes in *God Without Being*. In that book he begins by sketching phenomenological accounts of the idol (which simply reflects its creator and is self-determinately visible) and the icon which provokes a vision of the invisible and infinite (whose visibility is a gift of the other). This gift or revelation of the infinite as it crosses through the finite and visible Marion reads as cutting across the metaphysics of modernity. We are drawn by the icon beyond a world created in the human consciousness by human ideas corresponding to the condition of reality "out there." The icon presents a different mode of being which stands in antithesis to the way human consciousness makes the world present to itself. An ontological difference is opened up by this crossing of the finite by the infinite. Here Marion is indebted to Heidegger; though he believes his own work goes much further than Heidegger's.[45] This radical difference is read theologically. The gift crossing Being is the crucifixion of the Word in the world. The Cross is read as the unperceived watermark of the real. In the crisis of representation, when idolatry is struck through by the iconic, the visible by the invisible, there issues a revelation of divine distance, a revelation beyond Being and philosophy of consciousness. Marion reads this mode of revelation as having its origin in the Son's self-abandonment on the Cross. With the crucifixion of Christ there opens up in the world the space for seeing the kenotic love of the Father revealed in the Son. The crucifixion becomes the site for God's revelation of Himself. Marion develops his theological understanding of this crossing through Being and finitude – and the agapaic giving it reveals – through biblical exegesis of passages in the Old and New Testaments in which Being is recognized as questioned by the God beyond Being, the God who loves. "Only love does not have to be. And God loves without being."[46] Ecclesiastically, the eucharist becomes the privileged site for Marion's theology of the icon – the site where God gives Himself and where the Word is therefore spoken in the breaking of the visible elements. Rather ironically, given that Marion is not a cleric, he advocates that the priest and bishop are the primary expositors of such a theology insofar as they participate in the sacramental practice as icons of Christ themselves.

The postmodernism of such a theology lies both in its ecclesiological conservatism and in its theological exploration of such postmodern themes as the crisis of representation and identity, the other, the unnameable, the aporetic, and the deconstruction of metaphysics. In his early work, *L'Idole et la distance*, Marion advances his thesis of the principle of love (*charité*) and the kenotic, unthinkable abandonment of the Father through the Son, on the basis of Heidegger's concept of *Ereignis* and withdrawal, Levinas's analysis of the infinite distance which both surpasses and provides the condition for Being, and Derrida's notion of *différance* which sketches the economy of a trace beyond absence and presence. Marion's thesis situates his own project in relation to these postmodern thinkers, positing the Trinitarian God as conceived by certain Partistic writers, in the distance, the absence, the aporia, the anarchy which other postmodern thinkers have read as nihilism (though not Levinas or Derrida and, possibly, not Heidegger either). Postmodern critique therefore provides access to or is framed by a Christian faith which is never argued for; it is assumed. In *God Without Being*, on the basis of a distinction (first declared by Heidegger) that the logic of philosophy and the logic of faith are irreconcilable, Marion simply affirms "the field of revelation that the Johannine *Logos* opens to faith"[47] with the Bible and the eucharist as the two sites in which this revelation manifests itself. Postmodern insights and approaches are employed within theological discussions concerning ontology and analogy.

Michel de Certeau

Like Marion in his early work on Descartes, Michel de Certeau returns us to the instauration of the modern in the sixteenth and seventeenth centuries. As a Christian thinker concerned with history and the forces which create and sustain particular communities, Certeau analyses the mystical writings of that Counter-Reformation period in terms of the way in which the West opened itself (through travel and the economies of empire-building) to what was foreign or other only to colonize it. He points to disruptions, ambiguities, and the excesses of otherness as they infest the early evolution of modern thinking and rationalism. These were all eventually to be suppressed by a developing scientism and the politicization of the religious in the name of an economic, technological, and political progress: "a capitalist and conquering society."[48] With a rather idealistic notion of the medieval period, Certeau observes that in the seventeenth century the churches began to receive "their models and their rights from the monarchies, even if they represent a 'religiousness' that legitimizes the temporal powers."[49] As the seventeenth and eighteenth centuries develop, the temporal powers gradually transfer to their own account the religious values, kudos, and mystique once the exclusive property of the Church. It is with this transference that secular reason announces itself. A new spatialization appears – the spatialization of knowledge with the advance of the different sciences, a spatialization of the world with cartography. This spatialization – corresponding to the new colonialism and imperialism of the West – aims at the conquest and subjugation of what is other.

This spatialization in terms of the developing bodies of knowledge is founded upon the proliferation of writing (and texts). Modernity, for Certeau, is the "scriptural age," the age of writing. Prior to this age the sacred text is a voice and so "this writing (Holy Scripture) speaks."[50] The modern age is formed by discovering "this Spoken Word is no longer heard, that it has been altered by textual corruptions and avatars of history."[51] Now, hearing and assimilation become working and the will to power. Certeau recognizes that "the only force opposed to this passion to be a sign is the cry, a deviation or an ecstasy, a revolt or flight of that which, within the body, escapes the law of the named."[52] This deviation or rupture of the logic of the written is the postmodernist moment which, for Certeau, is paradigmatically evident in the mystical manner of speaking.

In the closing pages of Michel de Certeau's last work *The Mystic Fable* (first published in 1982, four years before Certeau's death in 1986), we find: "We must, then, move through *mystics* once more, no longer exploring the language it invents but the 'body' that speaks therein: the social (or political) body, the lived (erotic and/or pathological) body, the scriptural body (like a biblical tattoo), the narrative body (a tale of passion), the poetic body (the 'glorious body'). Inventions of bodies for the Other."[53] With these words the distinctive characteristics and significance of Certeau's work are evident. They announce what he himself calls "a poetics of the body."[54] The body here is not an object out there, nor the subject possessing his or her own body. Any body is disseminated across several fields (religious, psychological, socio-anthropological, political, ecclesiastical, literary, liturgical). Each field traffics in symbols and patrols its own self-legitimating discourse. For Certeau the fields of these discourses gravitate around desiring to locate the impossible body of the Other, impossible because always the Other is absent, excluded, abjected from the symbolic code constructed to describe and define it, which, in effect, substitutes for it. *Mystics* (understood not as a collection of spiritual people, but as a collection of spiritual texts displaying a new epistemological form and announcing a new field of knowledge),[55] reveals for Certeau "how that 'difference' manifests itself socially, and also how it sallies forth from its repression to go elsewhere."[56] He is concerned in his work to excavate not only what is believed but how what is believed becomes believable. Therefore, he examines the relationship between religious representations and the organization of society which gives or denies them credence. The theological (and ecclesiological) examination is undertaken by means of a hybrid methodology which draws the psychoanalysis of Freud and Lacan into the orbit of Bourdieu's social anthropology and Foucault's analyses of the politics of knowledge. He will also, though not uncritically, adopt some of the insights on the philosophical character of the spoken and the written developed in the early work of Derrida. On the basis of the critical histories which emerge, Certeau then constructs a picture of the differences and gaps between beliefs and doctrines, experience and institutions. "Reference to what is *experienced* (illuminating or devastating) endlessly opens up the problem of its relation to what is *represented* (official, received, or imposed)."[57]

The experience of the divine Other is at the heart of Certeau's understanding of language as the product and promoter of desire. The Other calls. It "echoes in the body like an inner voice that one cannot specify by name but that transforms one's use of words."[58] For Certeau the Jesuit, "vocation" and "obedience" are as important for him as that other Jesuit theologian, von Balthasar. He traces the linguistics and politics of vocation in what constitutes a theology of the Spirit, a pneumatology read through psychoanalytical accounts of desire. "Whoever is 'seized' or 'possessed' by it begins to speak in a haunted tongue. The music, come from an unknown quarter, inaugurates a new rhythm of existence . . . It simultaneously captivates an attentiveness from within, disturbs the orderly flow of thought, and opens up or frees new spaces. There is no *mystics* without it."[59] Mystic utterance becomes paradigmatic of an Other, an Unnameable, which appears in language which is consciously attempting to subvert its own logic. "Mystics is the anti-Babel, the quest for a common speech after its breakdown, the invention of a language 'of God' or 'of the angels' that would compensate for the dispersal of human language."[60] As such, knowledge is a product of language as desire. True knowledge of the other (which, after Lacan, Certeau calls the *réel*) is, following Augustine and Anselm, situated in the field of prayer. Mystics speak from a different place and attempt to translate this into an acceptable parlance. The means by which that parlance is acceptable, while not completely domesticating the otherness from whence it receives its authority, involves it in a cultural politics, a writing and therefore a history. The body, therefore, any body of knowledge, every social institution, is "informed" by this call of the Other which it either suppresses of encourages. The body of Christ as the Church has to weave a problematic way between its founding experience and its social reality, but there is a *sacramentum mundi* for those able to read it. Incarnation is a love song established by the call of the Other as the initiator of desire. And yet what Certeau, the historian, charts is the policing of this Other throughout the development of modernity. He explores the borderlands of the sixteenth and seventeenth centuries as new sciences and knowledges establish themselves independent of the "unitary architecture of theology"[61] in the medieval period. Hence the "vital role mysticism plays in the historian's relation with writing."[62] For with mysticism the hegemony of a specific culture is critiqued.

Historiography here is operating within a developed and explicit theology of history. But it is not a unified history, a Hegelian notion of history in which all time is swept up into the grand expression of the Absolute *Geist*. This is a broken history, a history of resistances to what is uniform and global, a history opening up to us other pasts, other options concerning the meaning of history.[63] It is based not in chains of causes and effects, but the fields of symbolic production and the relations of power which operate between and within these fields. Aporias are opened in theories of history. Events, which preoccupy the science of history, are understood as inextricably caught up in our projections, politics and ideologies. They take place within fields of symbolic relations. Events are therefore highly coded texts which frame and obscure what psychoanalysis terms "the other scene." The scene of the other is Lacan's *réel* – the world unmediated by representations, that which is the raw material of experience prior to being filtered through systems of knowledge. This "scene of the other" can be glimpsed when the cultural is ruptured, and this occurs when the Spirit speaks. Mystic discourse is forever asking the question who is speaking and from whence.[64] The glimpse of the *réel* in the everyday Certeau calls *ravissement*. This is a word with mystical connotations, but which also has many affinities with Barthes's poststructural "bliss" and the *jouissance* of Lacan, Foucault,

Irigaray, and Kristeva. There are affinities here also with Lyotard's analysis of the sublime.[65]

The postmodernism of Certeau's theological project lies again in developing the horizons of the Other, examining what Derrida has recently described as, "a certain aporetic experience of the impossible."[66] In doing this he employs the postmodern methodologies of Lacan, Bourdieu, and Foucault to advocate a neomedieval ecclesiology. As he emphasizes in his lecture "How is Christianity thinkable today?": "The Christian faith has no security other than the *living* God discovered by communities which are alive and which undergo the experience of *losing* objective securities . . . That is the first question: no longer to know whether God exists, but to *exist* as Christian communities."[67] From this emphasis Certeau develops a theology of desire and praxis, a pneumatology, based in the mystical experience. If Marion's postmodern theology can be termed a fundamental theology (in the Catholic sense of a theology embracing both dogmatics and the philosophy of religion), Certeau's work inscribes a historical theology which does not simply handle religious practices and religious societies as subjects for historiography, but also develops a theology of history. The text of history is a complex mapping and movement of praxes which no one explanatory principle can embrace. The meaning of history therefore must always remain open, excessive, to the writing of history. Like Certeau's description of *Abbas* Daniel in the street of sixth-century Alexandria, "This seems to be his 'theological' task: to trace, in the symbolic institutions, an otherness already known to the crowd and that they are always 'forgetting'."[68]

Conclusion

Postmodernism has been thought by some to be profoundly anti-religious. Partly, this is based upon a misreading of postmodern concerns with the deferral of meaning and the endless plurality of forces, political, cultural, physiological, economic, and psychological. Postmodernism popularly invokes fears of relativism, nihilism, and linguistic idealism (there is nothing that is not the construct of language). Liberal postmodern a/theologies do nothing to counter this popular conception. In fact, they have helped create it with their own emphases upon the death of God, an ontology of violence, and the untameable flux of existence. With Marion and Certeau postmodern theology portrays how religious questions are opened up (not closed down or annihilated) by postmodern thought. The postmodern God is emphatically the God of love, and the economy of love is kenotic. Desire, only possible through difference, alterity, and distance, is the substructure of creation. It makes transcendence both possible and necessary. In specific Christian communities – communities defined and created by the narratives of Christ's life and work, the creedal teachings of the Church and liturgical practices – the operation of this love provides a redescription of the Trinitarian God and the economy of salvation. Postmodernism, read theologically, is not the erasure of the divine. Rather, it defines the space within which the divine demands to be taken into account. The divine arrives with the endless institution of the question – Levinas's "enigma," Cixous's "mystery." Hélène Cixous, Jewish by origin, pupil of Derrida, co-founder of *Écriture feminine*,[69] confesses: "When I have finished writing, when I am a hundred and ten, all I will have done will have been to attempt a portrait of God. Of the God. Of what escapes us and makes us wonder. Of what we do not know but feel. Of what makes us live."[70]

Notes

1 *A Thousand Plateaus: Capitalism and schizo-phrenia*, trans. Brian Massumi (Minneapolis, 1987), p. 21.

2 See Mark C. Taylor's essay "Reframing Postmodernism" in Philippa Berry and Andrew Wernick (eds), *Shadow of Spirit: Post-modernism and religion* (London, 1992), pp. 11–29.

3 *The Crying of Lot 49* (London, 1979), p. 64.

4 Jacques Lacan's *Écrits* was first published in 1966 and consists of lectures given between 1948 and 1960, and Emmanuel Levinas's *Totality and Infinity* was published in 1969. Thomas Pynchon's *The Crying of Lot 49* was first published in 1966.

5 For an excellent summary of the arguments waged among theorists and art critics over what postmodernism is and its relationship to modernism and high modernism, see Ingeborg Hoesterey (ed.), *Zeitgeist in Babel: The post-modernist controversy* (Bloomington, IN, 1991).

6 *In Bluebeard's Castle: Some notes towards a re-definition of culture* (London, 1971), p. 14.

7 For the association of liberalism and with the doctrines of *laissez-faire*, see David Thomson's account of the development of the ideas of Adam Smith and Jeremy Bentham in Victorian Britain in *England in the Nineteenth Century* (London, 1950).

8 *The Postmodern Explained*, trans. Don Barry et al. (Minneapolis, 1993), p. 13.

9 Ibid., p. 15.

10 See "How to avoid speaking: denials," trans. Ken Frieden in Stanley Budick and Wolfgang Iser (eds), *Languages of the Unsayable: The play of negativity in literature and literary theory* (New York, 1989), pp. 3–70.

11 See Kristeva's books *Tales of Love*, trans. Leon Roudiez (New York, 1987) and *In the Beginning Was Love*, trans. Arthur Goldhammer (New York, 1988).

12 Levinas's epic works are *Totality and Infinity: Essay on exteriority*, trans. A. Lingis (Pittsburgh, 1969) and *Otherwise than Being or Beyond Essence*, trans. A. Lingis (The Hague, 1981).

13 See Irigaray's books *An Ethics of Sexual Difference*, trans. Carolyn Burke and Gillian C. Gill (London, 1993) and *Sexes and Genealogies*, trans. Gillian C. Gill (New York, 1993).

14 See Lyotard's books *The Inhuman*, trans. Geoffrey Bennington and Rachel Bowlby (Cambridge, 1993) and *Lessons on the Analytic of the Sublime*, trans. Elizabeth Rottenberg (Stanford, CA, 1994).

15 See Cixous's books *"Coming to Writing" and Other Essays*, trans. Sarah Cornell et al., ed. Deborah Jenson (Cambridge, MA, 1991) and *Reading with Clarice Lispector*, trans. Verena Andermatt Conley (Hemel Hempstead, 1990).

16 *Intimations of Postmodernity* (London, 1992), p. x. Bauman is arguing for post-modernity as a sociological movement away from what Max Weber saw as the disenchantment of the world.

17 David Ray Griffin's book *God and Religion in the Postmodern World: Essays in post-modern theology* (Albany, NY, 1989).

18 Don Cupitt, *The Last Philosophy* (London, 1995), p. 63.

19 Derrida himself has always countered the idea that he is advocating linguistic idealism. See here his interview entitled "Afterword" in *Limited Inc.*, trans. Samuel Weber (Evanston, IL, 1988), pp. 111–54, and my book *Barth, Derrida and the Language of Theology* (Cambridge, 1995).

20 *De-constructing Theology* (Chicago, 1982), p. 103.

21 *Desiring Theology* (Chicago, 1995), p. 63.

22 Ibid., p. 108.

23 Ibid., p. xi.

24 *De-constructing Theology*, p. xix.

25 The concept of kenosis has an important place in death-of-God theologies. It is the concept rather than the traditional doctrine based upon the *carmen Christi* of Paul's letter to the Philippians which is reworked. God's complete absence from the world is understood in terms of Christ's final identification with the world which has been worked over through the historical development of Christianity as a religion. Christianity itself dissolves here. Kenosis is employed as a metaphor for this historical development and final eclipse of Christianity and the transcendent God.

26 *The Reason of Following: Christology and the ecstatic I* (Chicago, 1991), p. 198.

27 Thomas J. J. Altizer (ed.), *Towards a New Christianity: Readings in the death of God theology* (New York, 1967), p. 315.

28 *The Postmodern Explained*, p. 76.

29 *Towards a New Christianity*, p. 318.

30 Ibid., p. 12.

31 Ibid., p. 13.

32 See *Postmodernism, Reason and Religion* (London, 1992).

33 See *Postmodernism and Islam* (London, 1992).

34 This is Don Cupitt's term.

35 *Towards a New Christianity*, p. 315.

36 *The Nature of Doctrine: Religion and theology in a postliberal age* (London, 1984).

37 See the final chapter of *Theology and Social Theory: Beyond secular reason* (Oxford, 1990).

38 See the final chapter of *Arius: Heresy and spirituality* (London, 1987).

39 See *Saints and Postmodernism: Revisioning moral philosophy* (Chicago, 1990).

40 See *Barth, Derrida and the Language of Theology* (Cambridge, 1995).

41 By "authentic" here I am simply wishing to suggest that the work of Marion and de Certeau takes up and is situated within the theological horizons and philosophical methodologies of French poststructural thinking. Neither of these thinkers explicitly call themselves postmodern.

42 *Sur la théologie blanche de Descartes: Analogie, création des vérités éternelles, fondement* (Paris, 1981), p. 23.

43 The distinction between the logic of philosophical thinking and Christo-logic is fundamental to the work of Hans Urs von Balthasar, whose influence on Marion's work is considerable.

44 Marion's phenomenological accounts of visibility and invisibility owe much to the work of the French philosopher Maurice Merleau-Ponty.

45 Marion's understanding of Heidegger is a vexed one. See my essay "Theology and the Crisis of Representation," in Gregory Salyer and Robert Detweiler (eds), *Literature and Theology at Century's End* (Atlanta, GA, 1995), pp. 131–58 and Laurence Hemming, "Reading Heidegger: Is God Without Being?" *New Blackfriars*, 76 (July/August 1995).

46 *God Without Being*, trans. Thomas A. Carlson (Chicago, 1991), p. 138.

47 Ibid., p. 63.

48 *The Practice of Everyday Life*, trans. Steven Rendall (Berkeley, CA, 1984), p. 136.

49 *The Mystic Fable*, trans. Michael B. Smith (Chicago, 1992), p. 182.

50 *The Practice of Everyday Life*, p. 137.

51 Ibid.

52 Ibid., p. 149.

53 *The Mystic Fable*, p. 293.

54 Ibid., p. 295.

55 Ibid., p. 16.

56 Ibid., p. 242.

57 *The Writing of History*, trans. Tom Conley (New York, 1988), p. 129.

58 *The Mystic Fable*, p. 297.

59 Ibid.

60 Ibid., p. 157.

61 Ibid., p. 104.

62 Ibid., p. xiv.

63 *The Writing of History*, p. 141.

64 *The Mystic Fable*, p. 178.

65 See note 14 for Lyotard's work on the experience of "presence" as the experience of the sublime.

66 *Aporias*, trans. Thomas Dutoit (Stanford, CA), p. 15.

67 "How is Christianity thinkable today?" *Theology Digest*, 19 (1971), pp. 344–5.

68 *The Writing of History*, p. 43.

69 For a brief introduction to this movement and what it stood for see Toril Moi, *Sexual/Textual Politics: Feminist literary theory* (London, 1985), pp. 108–26.

70 *"Coming to Writing" and Other Essays*, p. 129.

Bibliography

Primary

Altizer, Thomas J. J. (ed.), *Towards a New Christianity: Readings in the death of God theology* (New York, 1967).
—— *History as Apocalypse* (Albany, NY, 1985).
Certeau, Michel de, *The Mystic Fable*, trans. Michael B. Smith (Chicago, 1992).
Cupitt, Don, *The Long-Legged Fly* (London, 1987).
—— *Last Philosophy* (London, 1995).
Griffin, David Ray, *God and Religion in the Postmodern World: Essays in postmodern theology* (Albany, NY, 1989).
Marion, Jean-Luc, *God Without Being*, trans. Thomas A. Carlson (Chicago, 1991).
Scharlemann, Robert P., *The Reason of Following: Christology and the ecstatic* (Chicago, 1991).
Taylor, Mark C., *De-constructing Theology* (Atlanta, GA, 1982).

—— *Erring: A postmodern a/theology* (Chicago, 1984).
Winquist, Charles, *Epiphanies of Darkness: Deconstruction in theology* (Chicago, 1986).
—— *Desiring Theology* (Chicago, 1995).

Secondary

Berry, Philippa and Wernick, Andrew (eds), *Shadow of Spirit: Postmodernism and religion* (London, 1992).
Hoesterey, Ingeborg (ed.), *Zeitgeist in Babel: The post-modernist controversy* (Bloomington, IN, 1991).
Lyotard, Jean-François, *The Postmodern Explained*, trans. Don Barry et al. (Minneapolis, 1993).
Vattimo, Gianni, *The End of Modernity*, trans. Jon R. Snyder (Cambridge, 1988).

Theology and Religious Diversity

The encounter between religions was part of the early formation of Christianity, but for many centuries most of Christendom was religiously uniform and its relations with other faiths often took the form of polemics, persecution (especially of Jews), or imperialism. That has now changed for many reasons, such as different power relations, partial secularization, increased global communication and interaction, population shifts which have brought religious communities into new situations, an explosion in the study of religions, and changes in the churches (such as the Second Vatican Council and the World Council of Churches). Many theologians in earlier chapters have treated the theology of religions, notably Tillich (at the end of his life), Rahner, Küng, Pannenberg, many of the revisionists, liberals, postliberals and feminists, Africans, Asians, and theologians of mission.

The Christian engagement with Judaism has been especially intensive, agonized, and fruitful in the last half of the twentieth century. Peter Ochs, himself a Jewish scholar, philosopher, and theologian who is deeply involved in current discussions, sees the central dialectic in Christian theologies of Judaism pivoting around two poles: a Barthian critique of liberal or Enlightenment-based theological projects united with a postcritical return to the study of the Bible, community and tradition; and an encounter with the shock of the Shoah (Holocaust), resulting in a radical re-thinking of Christianity. Ochs therefore sets the current relationship between the two faiths in the context not only of the aftermath of the Shoah but also of "the demise of the great conceptual systems of modernity." He surveys the radical response to the Shoah and, at greater length, the postcritical theologies in their American, English, and German versions. He gives some account of the main processes of dialogue between Jews and Christians, especially Roman Catholics, and mentions the contributions of biblical studies, Holocaust studies, and Israel studies. He gives more detailed attention to Barth, Ruether, Eckardt, van Buren, Protestant state-ments about Judaism, and Pawlikowski. In conclusion he sums up the debate be-tween postcriticals and radicals and underlines key questions about Israel and the church, about christology, about the land and state of Israel, about the study of Judaism and the historical-critical study of the Bible.

Gavin D'Costa maps the field of the Christian theology of religions by first giving some historical and contemporary statistics and then discussing the typology of pluralism (John Hick), exclusivism (George Lindbeck), and inclusivism (Karl Rahner). He then conducts a debate which covers objections to each approach and also objections to the whole typology. D'Costa himself sees the limitations of the three types and goes beyond them in his description of the emerging agenda. In particular he stresses the ways in which encounters between particular religions may produce their own theologies, and even raises the fascinating possibility that theology arising in this way might deserve priority over, or even invalidate, theology of religions.

Judaism and Christian Theology

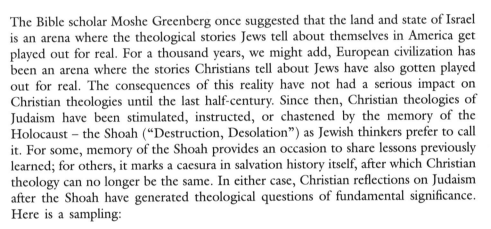

Peter Ochs

The Bible scholar Moshe Greenberg once suggested that the land and state of Israel is an arena where the theological stories Jews tell about themselves in America get played out for real. For a thousand years, we might add, European civilization has been an arena where the stories Christians tell about Jews have also gotten played out for real. The consequences of this reality have not had a serious impact on Christian theologies until the last half-century. Since then, Christian theologies of Judaism have been stimulated, instructed, or chastened by the memory of the Holocaust – the Shoah ("Destruction, Desolation") as Jewish thinkers prefer to call it. For some, memory of the Shoah provides an occasion to share lessons previously learned; for others, it marks a caesura in salvation history itself, after which Christian theology can no longer be the same. In either case, Christian reflections on Judaism after the Shoah have generated theological questions of fundamental significance. Here is a sampling:

- What are Christians to make of the persistence of the Jewish people?
- Is the Church the new Israel? If so, who are these people? If not, what happens to the doctrines of promise and fulfillment, law and grace?
- Is Jesus of the people Israel? For whom is he Messiah?
- What of Israel's sins? In the shadow of the Holocaust, will the "wandering Jews" and the "Synagogue blindfolded" still serve as marks of disobedience and unbelief?
- What of Israel's land and state?
- What role should historical-critical scholarship play in responding to these questions? What are the limits of such scholarship as witness to the demands of the Gospel?

Survey

Of the many contemporary Christian theologians who have responded significantly to these questions, I offer here a sampling of those whose work contributes to what

I believe is the central dialectic animating recent Christian theologies of Judaism. One pole of this dialectic is a Barthian critique of liberal or Enlightenment-based theological projects and a correlative return to the study of Bible and community (for Protestants), or Bible and tradition (for Catholics). The other pole of this dialectic is an encounter with the historical events of the Shoah and, secondarily, of the birth of the new State of Israel. From out of this encounter come rejections, reaffirmations, or revisions of the Barthian critique: what I label "radical," "post-critical," and "Catholic varieties of postcritical" theologies of Judaism.

This survey begins, then, with *Karl Barth*. His dialectical and ambivalent theology of Judaism displays to a modern reader the classical sources of both Christian supersessionism and Christian love of the people Israel. Addressing the scriptural word that speaks both to Jews and Christians, Barth's theology also provides the most productive basis for fruitful and ingenuous theological exchange between Judaism and Christianity. (See a detailed study below.)

For many Christians, however, the memory of the Shoah makes certain implications of traditional scriptural reading intolerable. For some, this memory erodes their faith in the Gospel tradition itself, drawing them to seek extrascriptural grounds for modern Christian theology. For others, this memory drives a more tempered reform or rereading of scriptural categories and claims.

In the shock of memory: the radical theologians Here are Christian theologians for whom the Shoah culminates a 1900-year history of Christian anti-semitism, calling Christians not only to refashion their relation to Jews and Judaism, but also to make radical reforms in the basic tenets of their faith. For these theologians, the anti-Jewish side of Barth's theology represents the ineradicable core of the Gospel witness itself. One of the more radical examples is Rosemary Ruether. In *Faith and Fratricide*, she argues that anti-Judaism is inseparable from central doctrines of the New Testament read in its plain sense, that the horrible events of this century are among the fruits of that anti-Judaism, and that Christians can therefore no longer afford to perpetuate those doctrines without serious revision. In her more recent work, she has argued that Israel, too – the state and the people – must apply prophetic judgment to itself as well as to others. Her work is linked in this way to more recent liberation theologies. Another radical theologian is Roy Eckardt. Since his first book-length study in 1948, he, along with his wife Alice Eckardt, has pioneered the radical Christian response to the Shoah. While his recent work overlaps in many ways with the work of liberationist theologies, his critique of Christianity has not spawned a comparably radical critique of Israel's classical faith.

Memory that reforms: the postcritical theologians Another, increasingly large collection of theologians is shocked by the Holocaust, but in a way that prompts them to reread rather than rewrite the scriptural witness to their faith. They believe that their very capacity to recognize the ills of any scripturally based Christian practice rests in intimacy with the witness to Christ presented in those scriptures. They conclude that neither God, nor Christ, nor Jesus, nor Paul is the problem. The problem rests instead in the way in which the Gospel witness is received and transmitted. They label this problem variously, "constantianism," "supersessionism," "onto-theology," or "mediating theology," corresponding to reformatory studies of "primitive or semitic Christianity," "the voice of the Jewish Jesus," or "the Bible interpreting itself." Along with Barth, the postcritical theologians thus appeal to the classic Reformers' spirit of revitalization through scriptural reading. Their reading is informed, however, by modern historical research on the Bible, as well as by a postmodern sensitivity to the limits of historical-critical scholarship. According to the central teachers of postcritical theology, George Lindbeck and the late Hans Frei, modern Christian theology fails when it seeks to reduce interpretations of the biblical accounts of God and Jesus Christ to the terms of "being" (*ontos* or *esse*) or, therefore, of human reasoning. One reason that Lindbeck and Frei have found classical rabbinic thinking attractive is that, from late Second Temple times on, proto-rabbinic scholars and rabbis presented their nonliteral biblical hermeneutic in opposition to what they termed "Greek," or essentializing allegory. An emergent school of Jewish philosophers, drawing on the work of Franz Rosenzweig, Martin Buber, Emmanuel Levinas, and their more recent students, has sought to redefine Jewish philosophy, non-rationalistically, as a way of reflecting on the patterns of classical rabbinic scriptural interpretation. While wary of any philosophic vocabulary for theology, Lindbeck, in particular, has maintained a productive dialogue with the Jewish philosophic theology generated out of this reflection, as have other postcritical theologians, such as Stanley Hauerwas, the Catholic philosopher David Burrell, and such colleagues and students of Frei's and Lindbeck's as Garrett Green, William Placher, Bruce Marshall, Kathryn Tanner, Gary Comstock, Robert Cathy, editors of the journal *Modern Theology* (Gregory Jones, Steven Fowl, James Buckley), the literary theologian Wesley Kort, and many others.

Another reason that Lindbeck, Frei, and others have found classical rabbinic thinking attractive is that it offers a model for the Church after the demise of its Constantinian epoch. Frei writes,

> [T]he most fateful issue for Christian self-description is that of regaining its autonomous vocation as a religion, after its defeat in its secondary vocation of providing ideological coherence, foundation, and stability to Western culture. Beyond that, however, the example of Judaism in the modern Western world might be a beacon to a reconstituted Christian community.[1]

Or, in Lindbeck's terms,

> [I]t may not be too far-fetched to suggest that, in order to survive, mainstream Christianity will become more concerned about developing distinctive and encompassing forms of minority communal life than it has been since Constantine.[2]

> Some of the more impressive examples of such communities are to be found in rabbinic Judaism in its creative periods.[3]

In a discussion of "Martin Luther and the Rabbinic Mind," Lindbeck surveys features of rabbinic Judaism that are particularly instructive for contemporary Christians. He argues that, while Luther's *Kontrovers-theologische* writings include anti-semitic vitriol, "the catechetical Luther [was] the authoritative one," and the *catechetical* writings depict a *rabbinic*-like Christianity:[4] "Like the rabbis, [the catechetical] Luther viewed religious texts as practical guides which shape the total form of life of whole communities."[5]

Paul van Buren, the most energetic postcritical theologian of Judaism, is also the most radical. For this reason, his work mediates among the postcritical, liberation, and Barthian theologies mentioned thus far. Van Buren portrays Rabbinic Judaism and Christianity as the two Ways of walking after the God of Israel that emerged out of the first century religion of Israel. One Way is traced by the Apostolic writings, the other by the rabbinic writings; neither Way separates faith and works, and neither Way tolerates secularization or spiritualization. Van Buren's notion of "walking in God's Way" implies that his theology must itself display a performative dimension – a "way of walking" in which its words are "known by their fruits." A primary illustration is his participation in the Shalom Hartmann Center in Jerusalem – an institute for Talmudic study in the postcritical style. He co-directs the Center's annual study sessions for Jewish and Christian theologians. Other postcritical theologians perform their theologies in comparable forms of institutionalized dialogue.

English analogues to postcritical inquiry   In both his writings and his institutional work at the Center of Theological Inquiry in Princeton, the American and English theologian Daniel Hardy has forged links among contemporary Jewish theologians, American postcritical theologians, and a less self-consciously collected group of theologians in Great Britain, including Rowan Williams, John Milbank, Lewis Ayres, David Ford, Alisdair McFadyen, Haddon Wilmer, and others. This group shares many of the features of postcritical theology mentioned above, including a positive relation to Barth's scriptural theology, but without the allergy to philosophic inquiry. In fact, in addition to concerns raised by their response to the Shoah, the group engages Judaism primarily through dialogues with Jewish philosophers. In recent essays, for example, Ford (1994) writes about Levinas's philosophy of "the other"; Williams and Ayres (1995) write about Gillian Rose's work in metaphysics and Jewish postmodernism; and Milbank (1995) writes about Derrida. These theologians appear to believe that recent Jewish philosophy offers disciplined reasoning without rationalism, served by a metaphysics that is "beyond being" (*au delà de l'être*) – a notion shared by Levinas and the French Catholic philosopher Jean-Luc Marion.[6] Here Levinas draws on a Jewish tradition that links recent Jewish thinkers to Maimonides to the Talmudic sages to the heritage of Sinai. For each of these, God's commanding word comes from beyond the created order, and thus beyond being, to enjoin humans to care for one another and for the creator.

German analogues to postcritical inquiry   A group of German Protestant theologians of Judaism (including Johan Goud, Bertold Klappert, Martin Stöhr, and others) displays many of the traits of postcritical theology: with Friedrich Marquardt exemplifying the more centrist tendencies (corresponding to Lindbeck and Frei) and Peter von der Osten-Sacken exemplifying the more radical tendencies (closer to van Buren). Marquardt attempts to break the link between Christianity and anti-Judaism. Offering a close study of Jesus' life as *part* of Jewish history, he describes Jesus' uninterrupted loyalty to Torah and the many continuities as well as discontinuities between Jesus and the Pharisees. According to the Jewish scholar Michael Wyschogrod, Marquardt's greatest contribution is his understanding of Israel, in von Balthasar's terms, as "formal Christology."[7] This is to display the continuities of major Christian theological categories with the biblical history of Israel, showing, for example, how incarnation is itself a Jewish notion, displayed in God's indwelling in the people Israel. Marquardt argues that, by saying no to Jesus, Israel draws attention to the fact that the world is not yet redeemed and that there is a waiting in creation to which Israel witnesses. Von der Osten-Sacken reclaims Israel's "no" in a comparable way, claiming that "God adheres to his election of Israel . . . even if it says no to Jesus Christ."[8] "With their 'no' to the gospel, the Jewish people exhibit not rebellion but an obedience which is determined by their zeal for God (Romans 10: 2)."[9] This "no" thereby "results in the extension of salvation to the Gentiles and in no way implies the rejection of the Jewish people."[10] Guided both by historical-critical study and a pragmatic concern to obviate anti-Jewish readings of the New Testament, von der Osten-Sacken concludes that Jesus' uniqueness does not lie in his piety, which is Jewish, but in his mediatory role. Jesus is Messiah as the one who reconciles Jews and Gentiles; bringing Gentiles into fellowship with God and thereby bringing Jews into fellowship with Gentiles – but *"without* becoming Christians."[11]

Performance: dialogue and doctrine   The new theologies of Judaism are *performed*, in part, in the many Jewish–Christian dialogues that have been institutionalized, particularly in the United States and Germany. One example is the dialogue that Leonard Swidler initiated in 1984 among American Jewish and Christian theologians and East German Lutheran theologians.[12] Another example is the regular series of theological dialogues sponsored by Richard Neuhaus, Director of the Center for Religion and Society, along with Avery Dulles and others. *Crosscurrents, the Journal of the Association for Religion and Intellectual Life* also sponsors regular dialogues, under editors William Birmingham, Joseph Cunneen, and Nancy Malone, OSU. A final illustration, among many others, is the newsletter *Explorations: Rethinking Relationships among Jews and Christian,* edited by James Charlesworth.

These new theologies are *measured*, in part, by their influence on church doctrines. From 1948 to today, for example, the Assemblies of the World Council of Churches moved from acknowledging "the special meaning of the Jewish people for Christian faith" (1948) to removing general Jewish culpability for the death of Jesus (1967), to recognizing Jesus' context among Pharisaic Jews (1982). The Council's theology of the land and state of Israel has been more complex.[13] Denominational assemblies have been more varied, but also more radical.

Memory and tradition: Catholic–Jewish dialogue   The most direct insight into Catholic theologies of Judaism is gained by looking, first, at official statements of the Vatican, of which the most revolutionary has been paragraph 4 of *Nostra Aetate: Declaration on the Relationship of the Church to Non-Christian Religions* (1965). Edward Flannery, President of the National Christian Leadership Conference for Israel, writes that, "despite flaws and diminutive stature, [paragraph 4] looms large on the pages of religious history . . . Terminating in a stroke a millennial teaching of contempt of Jews and Judaism and unequivocally asserting the Church's debt to its Jewish heritage, it represents. . . . a leap into a new dimension of Jewish-Christian relations" – performed, as he explains, not in its words alone, but in the "remarkable flowering" they have stimulated in Jewish–Christian dialogue.[14] According to this document, "the Jews still remain most dear to God because of their fathers, for He does not repent of the gifts He makes nor of the calls He issues (Rom. 11: 28–9)."[15] In 1975, the Vatican added to *Nostra Aetate* expanded "Guidelines and Suggestions for Jewish-Christian Relations." These encourage Christians to engage in joint study with Jews and, most significantly, to recall "the following facts" – for example, that the same God speaks in both covenants, that Jesus and his apostles were Jews, and that the history of Judaism continued after the destruction of Jerusalem. In 1985, to provide guidance for teaching those facts, the Vatican Commission for Religious Relations with the Jews published "Notes on the Correct Way to Present Jews and Judaism in Preaching and Catechesis in the Roman Catholic Church."[16] The Notes teach, *inter alia*, that Jesus' "ministry was deliberately limited 'to the lost sheep of the house of Israel' (Matt. 15: 4)," that "he wished to submit himself to the law (cf. Gal. 4: 4)," that "the Son of God is incarnate in a people and a human family (cf. Gal. 4: 4; Rom. 9: 5), [taking] away nothing . . . from the fact that he was born for all men," that there is thus "a unity of biblical revelation," even if, "in light of the event of the dead and risen Christ . . . there is a Christian reading of the Old Testament which does not necessarily coincide with the Jewish reading."

Against the backdrop of these Vatican documents, contemporary Catholic theologians, such as Franz Mussner, Hans Küng, Clemens Thoma, and John Pawlikowski, emphasize a variety of different perspectives on Judaism. In *On Being a Christian*, Küng maintained, in the words of John Pawlikowski,

> that after the Nazi Holocaust Christians must clearly admit guilt for the centuries of anti-Judaism within the Church that helped make Auschwitz possible . . . He also stresses the significance of the re-emergence of the modern State of Israel. He calls this rebirth the most important event in Jewish history since the destruction of Jerusalem and its Temple . . . Küng maintains that Judaism is the indispensable content of Christian theology. Without Judaism there would have been no Christianity.[17]

In *Judaism*, Küng goes further, offering a historical-theological reading of the major contributors to Jewish civilization, from Abraham to the postmodern Jewish thinkers. Beyond the limits of his earlier work, Küng calls for a "critical solidarity of Christians with the state of Israel" – clear diplomatic recognition of the state, but without "uncritical identification" with all of its policies.[18] Situating Jesus in the context of first-century Judaism, Küng concludes that Jesus had contacts with Pharisees but was no mere "love Pharisee": however many of his teachings parallel Pharisaic teachings, Jesus remained outside "the Jewish establishment," seeking "to deepen, concentrate and radicalize the law of God" in a way no Pharisee did or could.[19]

John Pawlikowski articulates his Catholic variety of postcritical theology through discussions and arguments with other theologians, claiming, for example, that Küng's effort remains incomplete, since he has not reinterpreted his christology itself in light of Jesus' Jewishness. In his own reinterpretation, Pawlikowski situates Jesus' work as an extension of the Pharisees' and of Jesus' unique "Abba experience."[20]

A return to history The single most significant concern of Catholic theologians after the Holocaust is a *return to history*. Pawlikowski writes that

> the philosopher Frederich Herr has spoken of [a] "rehistorication" of the church in extremely blunt terms. For him, Catholicism's failure to challenge the Nazis in any effective way is symptomatic of how the Roman church has dealt with other manifestations of evil . . . What is demanded by the Auschwitz experience is the creation of a theological vision in which the church is clearly seen as immersed in history despite its transcendental dimensions.[21]

Sharing this concern, Clemens Thoma has sought to base his *Christian Theology of Judaism* on a "sound knowledge of Judaism and past Jewish-Christian history" that "could no longer be the cause of, or furnish an alibi for, clichés about Judaism or disdain and persecution of Jews."[22] Thoma understands Jesus and Paul as deeply embedded in Pharisaic tradition and closer to rabbinic Judaism than to Jewish hellenism or non-Jewish movements.[23] He notes that the early Christians' messianic faith was Jewish as was their incarnationalism; apart from its historical realization, "a christological perception of God . . . is not unjewish!"[24] In this regard, Thoma cites supportive comments from Wyschogrod, with whom he has also collaborated on several book projects for Paulist Press. Paulist Press's contributions to the Christian theology of Judaism exemplifies the historical turn in Catholic theology.[25]

Biblical studies is now one of the foci of Christian self-understanding in light of Jewish–Christian dialogue, drawing increasing attention to the Jewishness of the early Christian communities and of what were previously thought to be exclusively Christian texts, such as the *Parables of Enoch*.[26] Among many leading Catholic contributors to this study have been Lawrence Boadt and Jorge Mejia; among many leading Protestants have been Christiaan Beker, James Charlesworth, W. D. Davies, John Gager, Lloyd Gaston, E. Käsemann, E. P. Sanders, Krister Stendahl, and Robert Wilken.

Holocaust studies remains another major area of Catholic contribution to a theological return to history. John Metz has stated the case most strongly:

> Christians can protect their identity [now] only . . . together with the history of the beliefs of the Jews . . . But this means that we Christians for our own sakes are from now assigned to the victims of Auschwitz – assigned, in fact, in an alliance belonging to the heat of *saving history*, provided the word "history" in this Christian expression is to have a definite meaning and not just serve as a screen for a triumphalist metaphysics of salvation which never learns from catastrophes nor finds in them a cause for conversation.[27]

Franklin Littell is one of many Catholics whose theological responses to the *Holocaust* and *antisemitism* are both historical and practical and whose *practical theologies* are *performed* in dialogic work with Jews.[28] Among these theologians, some are known first through their writings (such as Edward Flannery) and others through their institutional as well as literary work (such as John Oesterreicher and Rose Thering).

Israel studies remains a new and undeveloped area of Catholic – and of Protestant – response to recent history. Evaluating the significance of the Second Vatican Council for relations with Israel, Flannery observes, "If Israel's participation in the election and covenant is still valid for the Jewish people, the covenant and promise should be understood in their original meaning... They should, in other words, include Israel as a land."[29] The most developed statement on this issue comes from Marcel Dubois, the Dominican philosopher who served for many years as chairman of the Hebrew University Department of Philosophy. He writes that, "If Christians feel so ill at ease in interpreting the peculiar brand of Israeli nationalism, it is because they are not yet capable of accommodating in their faith the complex elements which, for the Jewish consciousness, are absolutely fundamental. Election, and the Jewish people's link with the land are... the most important of these."[30] Dubois labels the consequence of this election "positive solitude" – a national solitude in service to "a universal destination," fulfilling God's commands "to keep to the true God, to keep to the tradition, and to keep to the cohesion of the people chosen by God."[31] "This paradox of singularity and universality... comes to very topical... expression in the return of the Jews to Zion."[32] For Dubois, the Jews' return to Jerusalem remains the central symbol of their paradoxical service to God: It is only an *earthly* city of human beings that serves as symbol of the celestial city, the golden Jerusalem. For Christians, the "sacramental meaning of Jerusalem" is comparably paradoxical. To encounter their golden city, Christians must come as pilgrims to the earthly city that symbolizes it. "In this spirit, Israel and Jerusalem will be... the place where Jews and Christians can meet one another... 'In a single movement of hope which will be a promise for the whole world.'"[33] The Christian theologians who reflect today on the heavenly Jerusalem tend to do so from out of institutions built in the earthly one – among them, the Ratisbonne Center for Studies and Documentation on Judaism; and the Maison Saint Isäie, a Dominican *maison d'études* founded by Father Bruno Hussar, who later established Neve Shalom, a community for indigenous Jews and Arabs. Tantur, the Ecumenical Institute for Theological Research, also houses such itinerant theologians of Israel as the Catholic David Burrell.[34]

More Detailed Studies

Karl Barth

Wyschogrod captures Barth's importance this way: "Because he reads Scripture obediently, [Barth] becomes aware of the centrality of Israel in God's relation with man and with the very message that Christianity proclaims to the world."[35] Because he does not substitute humanity's word for the word of God, Barth learns of Israel's role in sacred history the way the traditional Jew learns it, thus acknowledging the enduring election of Israel. "Without any doubt, the Jews are to this very day the chosen people of God in the same sense as they have been so from the beginning, according to the Old and New Testaments."[36] "A Church that becomes antisemitic or even only asemitic sooner or later suffers the loss of its faith by losing the object of it."[37] On the other hand, Barth cannot understand Israel's commitment to the commandments the way the traditional Jew understands it. For Barth, the law is fulfilled in Christ; Israel's persistence in it remains a mark of its sinfulness. In *Church Dogmatics*, Barth may thus also refer to the Synagogue as "the disobedient, idolatrous Israel of every age," "the Synagogue of death," which "hears the Word and yet for all its hearing is still unbelieving," "with no party now in the fulfillment of the promise given it."[38]

For Wyschogrod, Barth therefore remains not only a critic but also a proponent of a kind of theological anti-semitism, intermixed with his own personal distaste for Jews. While noting Barth's ambivalence toward the people Israel, Marquardt offers ways to reform the Barthian position and find a positive role for Israel's "no" to Christ. Against Marquardt, however, Katherine Sonderegger concludes that Barth's ambivalence is irremediable. Barth holds that, although Jesus Christ is "an Israelite out of Israel," the Jews rejected Christ and therefore "have only the transient life of a severed branch, and the sure and immediate prospect of withering away."[39] Thus, "the solidarity between Christians and Jews that Barth so vigorously advocates is based upon the quiet assumption that Judaism does not exist."[40] Taking Barth's work as a model, Sonderegger concludes that, "In my judgment, a positive Christian theology of Judaism must begin by acknowledging the irreconcilable and ineradicable differences . . . Christian theology must recognize in Judaism an order and an organization of biblical idiom and response that evokes but competes with its own."[41]

Rosemary Ruether and the liberation theologians

Ruether's work begins with a challenge to the Church on behalf of Israel and ends with a challenge to Israel on behalf of the Church. She writes "that the anti-Judaic myth is neither a superficial nor a secondary element in Christian thought. The foundations of anti-Judaic thought were laid in the New Testament. They were developed in the classical age of Christian theology in a way that laid the basis for attitudes and practices that continually produced terrible results . . . [A]s long as Christology and anti-Judaism intertwine, one cannot be safe from a repetition of this history in new form."[42] Since "the end of Christiandom means Christianity must now think of itself as a Diaspora religion,"[43] Ruether offers the following remedies within the context of a post-Constantinian Christianity. *On Judgment and Promise*: "By applying prophetic judgment to 'the Jews' and messianic hope to 'the Church,' Christianity deprived the Jews of their future."[44] Now, the Church must apply this prophetic judgment to itself, by rereading the Gospels through methods of historical criticism, "demythologization" and "a concerted hermeneutical training of the preacher in the seminary." The goal is to criticize the "hypocrisy" and "legalism" of one's own people and Church leaders, and not to characterize the "nature" of another people with whom the Church no longer identifies."[45] *On Letter and Spirit*: "Christian anti-Judaic exegesis used the language of both Jewish and Hellenic dialectics to express its belief in its supersession of Judaism."[46] In this way, the early Church subsumed Philo's dialectical, platonic dualism of spirit and letter "into a messianic sectarian dualism between the old historical and the new messianic humanity." Since history had been fulfilled, this dialectic became static; Judaism was reduced to the "old" and "outward," over against the "new" and "inner" or "spiritual." *On Christology*: Claiming Jesus as the Messiah whom the Jews "awaited" is "an illegitimate historicizing of the eschatological." "As the recent Theology of Hope has put it, the Resurrection is not the final happening of the eschatological event, but the proleptic experiencing of the final future."[47]

In her more recent work, Ruether expresses her concern that Israel, too – the state and the people – applies prophetic judgment to itself as well as to others.[48] Her work is linked in this way to more recent liberation theology. With some exceptions, Judaism is not a central concern for liberation theologians and, when it is, the established institutions of Judaism, the state of Israel in particular, tend to be introduced as subjects of criticism, often couched in prophetic terms and at times replaying supersessionist discourses of the early Church. For example, Gustavo Gutiérrez has written that, "when the infidelities of the Jewish people rendered the Old Covenant invalid, the Promise was incarnated both in the proclamation of a new Covenant, which was awaited and sustained by the 'remnant,' as well as in the promises which prepared and accompanied its advent."[49] Leonardo Boff writes that liberation theology adopts "the Exodus as a paradigm of all liberation," with liberation from (the oppression of Pharaoh) and liberation to (entry into the Promised Land). But the agency of liberation has now been given to a new Israel: "God is no longer the old God of the Torah," but "a God of infinite goodness . . . He draws near in grace, going far beyond anything prescribed or ordained by the law."[50] This discussion thus belongs to a theology that is political in the senses both of relating to issues of lived power relations *and* of advocating particular political alliances. Ruether has thus advocated "a Jewish recovery of its prophetic voice vis-à-vis the world Zionist establishment and government of Israel,"[51] hoping for "a renewed confidence in the ultimate grounding of Jewish peoplehood, which does not need the 'good works' of the state of Israel to justify its 'right to exist' or to protect it from annihilation . . . Any new annihilation that would seriously endanger the Jewish people would take the whole planet with it . . . The Holocaust, as a specially Jewish tragedy, cannot be repeated. The next holocaust can be a holocaust of us all."[52]

Roy Eckardt

Over the years, Eckardt has been one of the most prolific contributors to the Jewish–Christian dialogue, maintaining "the position that Christianity has not replaced Israel in the drama of human salvation . . . God's design, according to Eckardt, preordained that a majority of the people of Israel would say 'no' to the Christ event."[53] While Eckardt's theologies have been fluid, John Pawlikowski notes that he has tended to favor a single-covenant theology:

> Eckardt sees Israel and the Church standing in dialectical tension to each other within the one covenant . . . Israel's primary role remains to turn inward to the Jewish people, while Christianity is outer-directed toward the Gentiles. The corresponding

temptations are that the Jews may allow their election to produce self-exaltation. The Church's reliance on grace as given, on the other hand, may lead to a false sense of freedom from all duties prescribed by the Torah.[54]

More recently, Eckardt writes that "The Christian crime of today is that of an ongoing antisemitism and anti-Judaism that refused to end when the Holocaust took place."[55] Eckardt's own search for God's presence after the Shoah lies in reclaiming the Jesus of history as the peripatetic "Jewish *hasid* from the town of Nazareth" through whom the Gentiles are brought to covenant with the God of Israel. This Jesus is, *inter alia*, "the champion of Israel," the "one through whom God humbles Godself," liberator of the wretched, and redeemer of women.[56]

Viewing Christianity in this way "as essentially Judaism for the Gentiles,"[57] Eckardt criticizes theologians whose christologies are not changed by their studies of Judaism. In his earlier work, he argued, for example, that Pannenberg's maintaining a doctrine of resurrection despite Auschwitz "points up the way in which the teaching of an achieved resurrection can lie at the center of the Christian opposition and hostility to Judaism and the Jewish people. For only with that teaching does Christian triumphalism reach fulfillment."[58] More recently, he has "come at least tentatively to the view that a moral-theological remedy for Christian resurrection supersessionism . . . is to apprehend the resurrection of Jesus in the frame of reference 'Spirit of God' within the special and continuing history of Judaism and the Jewish people. It is within the reality of Israel that the all-decisive meeting or convergence of religious faith and historical event takes place"; "For is not Jesus, the Jewish *hasid* . . . loose (again) in the social world, amidst all the anguish and all the joy of human events?"[59]

Paul van Buren

While influenced by his earlier work with Barth, van Buren made his first reputation as a "death of God" theologian, turning later to Wittgenstein and the analytic philosophy of religion and only after that, in the 1970s, to the kind of systematic theology for which he is now known. He recalls that this last step was stimulated by his encounter with living, Jewish theologians and thus the continued life of Judaism.

> The Christianity I knew said that [the living Judaism] I was coming to see so clearly simply did not exist, had not existed since Jesus Christ . . . It was but a ghost of ancient Israel, kept alive in the world as only a shadow of something else. What I was coming face to face with, however, was no shadow . . . If Christian theology said that this did not exist, then Christian theology, at least on *this* point, was simply wrong . . . What would Christian theology look like if it were corrected at so central a point?[60]

In his resulting *Theology of the Jewish-Christian Reality*, van Buren offers what, following Pawlikowski, we might call a theory of "one covenant" with two Ways: Jesus, sent only to save the lost sheep of Israel, has become the One who gathers Gentiles to the God of Israel. Unlike Eckardt, van Buren identifies this One as the Christ, Son of God, who was crucified and resurrected. This resurrected Christ is no impediment to philo-semitism; rather, the very "mystery of the Trinity is the mystery of a historical event – the gathering of a Gentile church into the worship of Israel's God."[61] "God so loved the world that He gave . . . Only His peculiar people, Israel, seemed to have an inkling of what this involved – a life of thanksgiving that turned in love to the neighbor. So in order that this might be for Gentiles as well, God gave His Son, the embodiment of His purpose and love in one faithfully Jewish son."[62] The teachings and the life of Jesus are new events in the life of Israel: not because they change Israel's covenant, but only because they bring the Gentiles into their own Way with God. The relationship between the Jewish and the Christian Ways of God became problematic only in the Christian writings that succeeded the Apostolic writings. As illustrated in Justin Martyr's *Dialogue with Trypho*, "the original denial to the Jews of the right to their own interpretation of their own book . . . led to the denial of the Jews' basic civil rights, once the church was able to influence and then write laws of the Empire."[63]

Against Barth, van Buren argues that biblical revelation "is scarcely ever divine *self*-revelation," but is rather revelation *to* Israel, taking "therefore the form primarily of Torah, as the path for Israel . . . and of Jesus . . . for the Gentile church."[64] While acknowledging Israel's Scripture as its canon, the Church failed, however, to recognize Israel's enduring election. While Barth corrected this error, he did not also correct the Church's overlooking Paul's enduring Jewishness, misrepresenting the rabbis' Torah as "legalism" rather than as love of walking in God's Way, spiritualizing the chosenness of the land of Israel, and denying that "Israel in its covenant is the fundamental context of Jesus Christ."[65]

Church doctrines: statements of the Protestant denominations

In a recent review of church statements, Rolf Rendtorff notes that, over the last two decades, denominational assemblies have mostly done away with the traditional doctrine that Israel's election has been transferred to the church. According to the Texas Conferences of Churches (1982), "Jews and Christians share a common calling as God's covenanted people . . . Both . . . are called to the covenant as they understand it."[66] Traditional Christian prejudices against "Jewish legalism" have also been moderated, if not obliterated: "Every Jew is under obligation to participate actively in [the] covenant by living according to the will of God as expressed in the Torah. Christians should realize that this Jewish understanding is not necessarily legalistic but may lead to a life in the presence of God."[67] As for contemporary issues, van Buren notes that as yet "the churches have had difficulty in accounting for th[e] new phenomenon [of the State of Israel]."[68] The Central Board of the Swiss Protestant Church Federation said, in 1977, "We consider it the duty of the Christian churches and all Christians to intervene in defence of the right to existence of the Jewish people . . . and to stand by Israel in her growing isolation." In 1978, the General Assembly of the Presbyterian Church stated, more cautiously, "The establishment of the State of Israel in our day has been seen by many devout Jews as the fulfillment of God's divine promise. Other Jews are equally sure that it is not . . . Still other Jews interpret the State of Israel in purely secular terms. Christian opinion is equally diverse. As Reformed Christians, however, we believe that no government at any time can ever be the full expression of God's will . . . The State of Israel is a geopolitical entity and is not to be validated theologically." The General Assembly added, in another document, "Both Christians and Jews are called to wait and to hope in God. While we wait, Jews and Christians are called to the service of God in the world."[69]

John Pawlikowski

In *Christ in the Light of the Christian-Jewish Dialogue*, Pawlikowski criticizes what he considers the two different tendencies in Christian theology after the Shoah. "In the first place, he criticizes Pannenberg, Moltmann, Küng, Gutiérrez, Sobrino, Boff, and Bonino for succumbing to the traditional Christian temptation to render the identity of Jesus – and hence the distinctiveness of Christianity – by employing stereotypical, negative contrasts with Judaism . . . In the second place, Pawlikowski rejects those theologians who have gone to the other extreme by surrendering too much of the distinctiveness of Jesus. These include Ruether, van Buren, Eckardt, Schoenveld, and Hellwig."[70] Pawlikowski argues, for example, that Küng's sensitivity to the Jews "has not really found its way into the core of his Christology . . . Gregory Baum has written that Küng's emphasis on the Law/Gospel conflict leads him to a Christological formulation 'little apt to improve the Christian-Jewish dialogue.'"[71] On the other hand, Pawlikowski fears that an approach like van Buren's or, all the more so, Ruether's, "leaves little rationale for the continued existence of Christianity as an independent religion and that it undercuts any claim that Christianity constitutes a major world religion in its own right."[72] The Pharisees offered a "fundamentally new perception of the God-human person relationship." Jesus' personal sense of identification with the Father "represents an extension, albeit of quantum proportions, of the new consciousness . . . experienced by the Pharisees."[73]

Debate and Assessment

Christian theologies are written today not only after the Shoah, but also after the demise of the great conceptual systems of modernity. For this reason, Christian theologies of Judaism may serve not only as responses to the Shoah, but also as instruments of theological attempts to replace modern, conceptual systems *either* with scripturally based and context-directed readings *or* with new, "radical" systems. To clarify differences among the theologies collected in this survey, I have found it more helpful to ask how they respond to modernity than how they respond, alone, to the Shoah. From this perspective, there is a more significant divide between postcritical and radical theologies than there is between theologies that "leave traditional christologies intact" and those that refashion them. Whether more conservative or reformatory in their christologies, the postcritical theologians (along with their Catholic cousins) tend to let text or tradition speak before reason. This reduces the "clarity and distinctness" of their categories of reasoning, but it allows them to reason *from* the text in more pluralistic and context-specific ways. In this sense more like the modern system-builders, the radical theologians tend to let their reasoning, even if it concerns specific political issues, speak before text or tradition. This lends their reasoning greater clarity and determinacy, but it limits the subtlety and range of their interpretations of text and tradition. Debates among these theologians cluster around the series of questions listed at the outset of this survey:

Questions about the people Israel and the Church: Among radical theologians, Ruether and Eckardt reject early Church tendencies to describe the Old Covenant as fulfilled in the New, while Latin American theologians, until very recently, tend to reaffirm those tendencies. Barth maintains the general typological distinction of Old and New, while postcritical theologians – Barthian, Catholic, and other – tend to do away with them, while asserting other ways of maintaining distinctions that still lend enduring merit to Israel's separate covenantal or shared-covenantal life.

Questions about Christology: Ruether and Eckardt reject the plain-sense christologies of the New Testament as inherently oppressive to Jews and others, while other liberation theologians simply delimit the application of these Christologies to issues of liberation from poverty and political oppression. Postcritical theologians tend to respect these christologies, while taking pains not to overdetermine their meanings a priori and to interpret and practice them in context-specific and non-oppressive ways. Theologians outside the postcritical practice, such as Küng and Pannenberg, tend to define their christological doctrines a priori, taking pains to guard the *applications* of these doctrines from oppressive use.

Questions about the land and state of Israel: With the strong exception of Eckardt, radical theologians tend to identify the people Israel's assertion of a geopolitical life with the disobedience of Israel as portrayed in early Church doctrines. In the words of Julio de Santa Anna, liberation theologians need, furthermore, to "challenge the theology of the Holocaust," the force of which has been to "defend . . . [the] reactionary attitude of the state of Israel."[74] According to Ruether, liberationist arguments like these are political. They are offered to counter "a collaboration of the Jewish and Christian establishments . . . a kind of right-wing ecumenism, in which each helps to repress the critics and dissenters in the other community."[75] Exhibiting the positions of many postcritical theologians, Pawlikowski argues that this liberationist critique is supersessionist, conceptually overdetermined, and inattentive to the historical contexts both of first-century Judaism and of the emergence of the state of Israel.[76]

Questions about the study of Judaism and historical-critical study of the Bible: Christian theologians of Judaism may be distinguished by the relative authority they grant to historical-critical as opposed to other modes of study. Except for the Latin American liberationists, radical theologians tend to grant authority to the scriptural texts and traditions only when the meanings of those texts can be verified through historical-critical scholarship, and when the behavioral consequences of those meanings are judged of value to the contemporary community. The liberationists have tended to make limited use of historical-critical method in their studies of Judaism. The postcritical theologians tend to grant overall behavioral authority to the scriptural text, as interpreted by a given church community in the context of its tradition history. The interpretation is informed by textual scholarship of all kinds, without privileging any single one. Among these approaches, radical Christian theologians will most likely have more fruitful dialogues with modern and radical Jewish thinkers, with whom they may share theological style and hermeneutical method. The postcritical theologians will have more to discuss with classical rabbinic scholars and with those recent Jewish thinkers who re-engage scriptural and rabbinic texts as first premises for their "postmodern" reasonings. Both groups of Christian theologians engage in dialogues and debates whose liveliness and irrepressibility will please any Jewish thinker still animated by the tradition or at least the style of Talmudic argumentation.[77]

Notes

1   Hans Frei, "The 'literal reading' of the biblical narrative in the Christian tradition: Does it stretch or will it break?" in Frank McConnell (ed.), *The Bible and the Narrative Tradition* (New York and Oxford, 1986), pp. 73–4.

2   George Lindbeck, *The Nature of Doctrine: Religion and theology in a postliberal age* (Philadelphia, 1984), p. 164.

3   George Lindbeck, "Toward a postliberal theology," in Peter Ochs (ed.), *The Return to Scripture in Judaism and Christianity* (New York, 1993), p. 100.

4   George Lindbeck, "Martin Luther and the rabbinic mind," in Peter Ochs (ed.), *Understanding the Rabbinic Mind: Essays on the hermeneutic of Max Kadushin* (Atlanta, GA, 1990), pp. 156f.

5   Ibid., p. 163.

6   Emmanuel Levinas, *Otherwise than Being or Beyond Essence* (The Hague, 1981); Jean-Luc Marion, *God Without Being* (Chicago and London, 1991).

7   Michael Wyschogrod, review of Friedrich-Wilhelm Marquardt, *Das christliche Bekenntnis zu Jesus, dem Juden. Eine Christologie*, in *Journal of Ecumenical Studies*, 29 (1992), pp. 275–6.

8   Peter von der Osten-Sacken, *Christian-Jewish Dialogue: Theological foundations* (Philadelphia, 1986), p. 163, also quoted in Matthew Comer Hawk, *Root, Branch, and Rhetoric: Judaism and Christian self-understanding after the Holocaust* (PhD dissertation, Yale University, 1992), p. 150.

9   Peter von der Osten-Sacken, *Christian-Jewish Dialogue*, p. 765; Matthew Comer Hawk, *Root, Branch, and Rhetoric*, p. 153.

10   Ibid.

11   Peter von der Osten-Sacken, *Christian-Jewish Dialogue*, pp. 58, 83.

12   Leonard Swidler (ed.), *Breaking Down the Wall: Between Americans and East Germans – Jews and Christians through dialogue* (Lanham, NY, and London, 1987).

13   World Council of Churches, *The Theology of the Churches and the Jewish People* (Geneva, 1988).

14   Roger Brooks, *Unanswered Questions: Theological views of Jewish–Catholic relations* (Notre Dame, IN, 1988), pp. 128–9.

15   Ibid., pp. 20–1.

16   Ibid., p. 15.

17   John Pawlikowski, *Christ in the Light of the Christian–Jewish Dialogue* (New York, 1982), pp. 47–8.

18   Hans Küng, *Judaism* (New York, 1995), pp. 563–4.

19   Ibid., pp. 313ff.

20   M. C. Hawk, *Root, Branch, and Rhetoric*, p. 135.

21   Richard W. Rousseau, *Christianity and Judaism: The deepening dialogue* (Scranton, PA, 1983), pp. 102–3.

22   Clemens Thoma, *A Christian Theology of Judaism* (Ramsey, NY, 1980), p. 23, and M. C. Hawk, *Root, Branch, and Rhetoric*, p. 120.

23   Clemens Thoma, *A Christian Theology of Judaism*, p. 66.

24   Ibid., pp. 127ff.

25   Cf. on biblical studies, Lawrence Boadt et al. (eds), *Biblical Studies: Meeting ground for Jews and Christians* (New York, 1980); Clemens Thoma and Michael Wyschogrod (eds), *Understanding Scripture: Explorations of Jewish and Christian traditions of interpretation* (Mahwah, NY, 1987); on liturgy,

Eugene Fisher (ed.), *The Jewish Roots of Christian Liturgy* (Mahwah, NY, 1990); on anti-semitism, Edward Flannery, *The Anguish of the Jews* (Mahwah, NY, 1985); on dialogue, Eugene Fisher (ed.), *Visions of the Other: Jewish and Christian theologians assess the dialogue* (Mahwah, NY, 1984); Eugene Fisher and Leon Klenicki (eds), *In Our Time: The flowering of Jewish–Catholic Dialogue* (Mahwah, NY, 1990).

26 James H. Charlesworth, *The Old Testament Pseudoepigrapha and the New Testament* (Cambridge, 1985–7) and *Jews and Christians*, edited by James H. Charlesworth (New York, 1990).

27 Johannes Metz, *The Emergent Church* (New York, 1981), pp. 19–20; also Eugene Fisher (ed.), *Visions of the Other*, p. 43.

28 Franklin Littell, *The Crucifixion of the Jews* (New York, 1975).

29 Cited in Marcel J. Dubois, "Israel and Christian self-understanding," in David Burrell and Yehezkel Landau (eds), *Voices from Jerusalem* (Mahwah, NY, 1992), p. 71.

30 Ibid., pp. 69–70.

31 Ibid., p. 79.

32 Ibid., p. 80.

33 Ibid., p. 90, citing a document of the French bishops.

34 Cf. Burrell and Landau (eds), *Voices from Jerusalem*.

35 Michael Wyschogrod, "Why was and is the theology of Karl Barth of interest to a Jewish theologian?" in *Footnotes to a Theology: The Karl Barth Colloquium of 1972*, ed. Martin Rumscheidt: SR Supplements (1972), p. 111.

36 Karl Barth, "The Jewish problem and the Christian answer," in *Against the Stream* (London, 1954), p. 200, cited in M. Wyschogrod, "The theology of Karl Barth," p. 105.

37 Karl Barth, *Church Dogmatics* (Edinburgh, 1936), vol. II.2, p. 234.

38 Ibid., pp. 195ff., cited in M. Wyschogrod, "The theology of Karl Barth," pp. 110–11.

39 Karl Barth, *Church Dogmatics*, vol. II.2, pp. 224–5, 287; cited in Katherine Sonderegger, *That Jesus Christ was Born a Jew: Karl Barth's "Doctrine of Israel"* (University Park, PA, 1992), pp. 66, 99.

40 Ibid., p. 142.

41 Ibid., p. 179.

42 Rosemary R. Ruether, *Faith and Fratricide: The theological roots of anti-semitism* (New York, 1974), p. 226.

43 Ibid., pp. 226–7.

44 Ibid., p. 230.

45 Ibid., p. 231.

46 Ibid., p. 239.

47 Ibid., p. 249.

48 Rosemary R. and Herman J. Ruether, *The Wrath of Jonah: Religion and nationalism in the Israeli-Palestinian conflict* (San Francisco, 1989).

49 Gustavo Gutiérrez, *A Theology of Liberation* (Maryknoll, NY, 1973), p. 161, cited in Otto Maduro (ed.), *Judaism, Christianity, and Liberation: An agenda for dialogue* (Maryknoll, NY, 1991), p. 6.

50 Leonardo Boff, *Jesus Christ Liberator* (Maryknoll, NY, 1978), p. 284, cited in John Pawlikowski, *Christ in the Light of the Christian–Jewish Dialogue*, p. 72.

51 Rosemary R. Ruether, "False Messianism and prophetic consciousness," in Otto Maduro (ed.), *Judaism, Christianity, and Liberation*, p. 91.

52 Ibid., p. 93.

53 John Pawlikowski, *Christ in the Light of the Christian-Jewish Dialogue*, p. 15.

54 Ibid.

55 A. Roy Eckardt, *Collecting Myself: A writer's retrospective* (Atlanta, GA, 1993), p. 274.

56 Ibid., pp. 229, 209, Part II passim.

57 John Pawlikowski, *Christ in the Light of the Christian-Jewish Dialogue*, p. 17.

58 A. Roy Eckardt, "Christians and Jews: along a theological frontier," *Encounter*, 40 (1979), pp. 106–8.

59 A. Roy Eckhardt, *Reclaiming the Jesus of History: Christology today* (Minneapolis, 1992), pp. 214, 217.

60 Richard W. Rousseau, *Christianity and Judaism*, pp. 58–9.

61 Paul van Buren, *A Theology of the Jewish–Christian Reality. Part 1. Discerning the Way* (San Francisco, 1980), p. 92.

62 Ibid., p. 118.

63 Ibid., p. 141.

64 Ibid., *Part 2. A Christian Theology of the People Israel* (1983), p. 7.

65 Ibid., pp. 76, 279; *Part 3. Christ in Context* (1988), p. 65.

66 World Council of Churches, *The Theology of the Churches and the Jewish People*, p. 135.

67 Ibid., p. 161, from a consultation of the Lutheran World Federation.

68 Ibid., p. 170.

69 Ibid., p. 179.

70 M. C. Hawk, *Root, Branch, and Rhetoric*, pp. 130–1.

71 Gregory Baum, "Küng and Kasper on Christ," *Ecumenist*, 14 (1977), p. 20, cited in John Pawlikowski, *Christ in the Light of the Christian–Jewish Dialogue*, pp. 47–50.

72 Ibid., p. 14.

73 Ibid., pp. 88, 93; also M. C. Hawk, *Root, Branch, and Rhetoric*, p. 139.

74 Julio de Santa Anna, "The Holocaust and liberation," in Otto Maduro (ed.), *Judaism, Christianity, and Liberation*, p. 49.

75 Rosemary R. Ruether, "False Messianism," in Otto Maduro (ed.), *Judaism, Christianity, and Liberation*, p. 90.

76 John Pawlikowski, *Christ in the Light of the Christian–Jewish Dialogue*, p. 69.

77 My thanks to the following scholars who contributed to the research for this survey: Eugene Borowitz, Robert Cathy, Todd Driskil, Catherine Keller, Bruce Marshall, Olga Sirgurdson, Michael Wyschogrod.

Bibliography

The following sources help amplify the preceding discussions.

On Barth and Judaism: Goud, 1992; Marquardt, 1967; Smith, 1983; Ward, 1995; Wyschogrod, 1986.

On German theologies of Judaism: Flothkötter, 1990; Harder, 1986; Marquardt, 1985; Moltmann, 1993; von der Osten-Sacken, 1982.

On the dialogue with Judaism: Comstock, 1990; Rahner, 1987; Klenicki and Neuhaus 1989; Marshall (forthcoming).

Historical and biblical studies: Gager, 1983; Gaston, 1987; Manuel, 1992; Sanders, 1985.

On Jewish responses to the Christian theologies: Borowitz, 1980; Heschel; Klein, 1978; Novak, 1989; Ochs, 1993; Rothschild, 1990.

General bibliographies on Judaism in Christian theology: Charlesworth, 1990; Fisher, 1990.

Ayres, Lewis, "Representation, theology and faith," in L. Gregory Jones and Stephen Fowl (eds), *Rethinking Metaphysics* (Oxford, 1995), pp. 23–46.

Barth, Karl, *Church Dogmatics*, trans. G. W. Bromiley, T. F. Torrance, et al. (Edinburgh, 1936–69).

—— "The Jewish problem and the Christian answer," in *Against the Stream* (London, 1954).

Baum, Gregory, "Küng and Kasper on Christ," *Ecumenist*, 14 (1977), p. 20.

Boff, Leonardo, *Jesus Christ Liberator* (Maryknoll, NY, 1978).

Borowitz, Eugene, *Contemporary Christologies: A Jewish response* (Ramsey, NY, 1980).

Brooks, Roger, *Unanswered Questions: Theological views of Jewish–Catholic relations* (Notre Dame, IN, 1988).

Burrell, David, and Landau, Yehezkel (eds), *Voices from Jerusalem: Jews and Christians reflect on the Holy Land* (Mahwah, NY, 1992).

Charlesworth, James H., *The Old Testament Pseudoepigrapha and the New Testament* (Cambridge, 1985–7).

Charlesworth, James H. (ed.), *Jews and Christians: Exploring the past, present, and future* (New York, 1990).

Comstock, Gary, "Christian value concepts," in Peter Ochs (ed.), *Understanding the Rabbinic Mind: Essays on the hermeneutic of Max Kadushin* (Atlanta, GA, 1990), pp. 113–40.

de Santa Anna, Julio, "The Holocaust and liberation," in Otto Maduro (ed.), *Judaism, Christianity, and Liberation: An agenda for dialogue* (Maryknoll, NY, 1991).

Dubois, Marcel J., "Israel and Christian self-understanding," in David Burrell and Yehezkel Landau (eds), *Voices from Jerusalem* (Mahwah, NY, 1992), pp. 63–90.

Eckardt, A. Roy, *Christianity and the Children of Israel* (New York, 1948).

—— "Christians and Jews: along a theological frontier," *Encounter*, 40 (1979), pp. 89–127.

—— *Collecting Myself: A writer's retrospective*, ed. Alice J. Eckardt et al. (Atlanta, GA, 1993).

—— *Reclaiming the Jesus of History: Christology today* (Minneapolis, 1992).

Fisher, Eugene (ed.), *The Jewish Roots of Christian Liturgy* (Mahwah, NY, 1990).

—— *Visions of the Other: Jewish and Christian theologians assess the dialogue* (Mahwah, NY, 1994).

Fisher, Eugene and Klenicki, Leon (eds), *In Our Time: The flowering of Jewish–Catholic dialogue* (Mahwah, NY, 1990).

Flannery, Edward, *The Anguish of the Jews: Twenty-three centuries of anti-semitism*, rev. edn (New York, 1985).

Flothkötter, Hermann and Nacke, Bernard (eds), *Das Judentum – eine Wurzel des Christlichen, Neue Perspektiven des Miteinanders* (Würzburg, 1990).

Ford, David, "Hosting a Dialogue: Jüngel and Levinas on God, self and language," in John Webster (ed.), *The Possibilities of Theology: Studies in the theology of Eberhard Jüngel in his sixtieth year* (Edinburgh, 1994).

Frei, Hans, "The 'literal reading' of the biblical narrative in the Christian tradition: Does it stretch or will it break?" in Frank McConnell (ed.), *The Bible and the Narrative Tradition* (New York and Oxford, 1986), pp. 36–69.

Gager, John G., *The Origins of Anti-semitism* (New York and Oxford, 1983).

Gaston, Lloyd, *Paul and the Torah* (Vancouver, 1987).

Goud, Johan, *Emmanuel Levinas und Karl Barth: Ein religionsphilosophischer und ethischer Vergleich* (Bonn and Berlin, 1992).

Gutiérrez, Gustavo, *A Theology of Liberation* (Maryknoll, NY, 1973).

Harder, Günther, *Kirche und Israel, Arbeiten zum christlich-jüdischen Verhältnis* (Berlin, 1986).

Hawk, Matthew Comer, *Root, Branch, and Rhetoric: Judaism and Christian self-understanding after the Holocaust* (PhD dissertation, Yale University, 1992).

Klein, Charlotte, *Anti-Judaism in Christian Theology* (Philadelphia, 1978).

Klenicki, Leon, and Neuhaus, Richard, *Believing Today: Jew and Christian in Conversation* (Grand Rapids, MJ, 1989).

Küng, Hans, *Judaism, Between Yesterday and Tomorrow* (New York, 1995).

Levinas, Emmanuel, *Otherwise Than Being or Beyond Essence*, trans. A. Lingis (The Hague, 1981).

Lindbeck, George, *The Nature of Doctrine: Religion and theology in a postliberal age* (Philadelphia, 1984).

—— "Martin Luther and the rabbinic mind," in Peter Ochs (ed.), *Understanding the Rabbinic Mind: Essays on the hermeneutic of Max Kadushin* (Atlanta, GA, 1990), pp. 141–64.

Littell, Franklin, *The Crucifixion of the Jews* (New York, 1975).

Maduro, Otto (ed.), *Judaism, Christianity, and Liberation: An agenda for dialogue* (Maryknoll, NY, 1991).

Manuel, Frank E., *The Broken Staff: Judaism through Christian eyes* (Cambridge, MA, and London, 1992).

Marion, Jean-Luc, *God Without Being*, trans. Thomas A. Carlson (Chicago and London, 1991).

Marquardt, Friedrich-Wilhelm, *Die Entdeckung des Judentums für die Christliche Theologie, Israel im Denken Karl Barths* (München, 1967).

—— *Die Gegenwart des Auferstandenen bei seinem Volk Israel* (München, 1985).

—— *Das Christliche Bekenntnis zu Jesus, dem Juden. Eine Christologie*, 2 vols (München, 1990–1).

Marshall, Bruce, "The Jewish people and Christian theology," in *The Cambridge Companion to Christian Doctrine* (forthcoming).

Metz, Johannes, *The Emergent Church* (New York, 1981).

Milbank, John, "Can a gift be given? Prolegomena to a future Trinitarian metaphysic," in L. Gregory Jones and Stephen Fowl (eds), *Rethinking Metaphysics* (Oxford, 1995), pp. 119–61.

Moltmann, Jürgen, "Christology in Jewish–Christian dialogue," in *The Way of Jesus Christ: Christology in Messianic dimensions* (Minneapolis, 1993), pp. 28–37.

Mussner, Franz, *Tractate on the Jews: The significance of Judaism for Christian faith*, trans. Leonard Swidler (Philadelphia, 1979).

Novak, David, *Jewish–Christian Dialogue: A Jewish justification* (Oxford and New York, 1989).

Ochs, Peter (ed.), *The Return to Scripture in Judaism and Christianity: Essays in postcritical scriptural interpretation* (Mahwah, NY, 1993).

—— "Pragmatic conditions for Jewish–Christian theological dialogue," *Modern Theology*, 9 (1993), pp. 123–40.

Oesterreicher, John, *The New Encounter Between Christians and Jews* (New York, 1986).

Pawlikowski, John, *Christ in the Light of the Christian–Jewish Dialogue* (New York, 1982).

Rahner, Karl and Lapide, Pinchas, *Encountering Jesus – Encountering Judaism*, trans. Davis Perkins (New York, 1987).

Rothschild, Fritz A. (ed.), *Jewish Perspectives on Christianity* (New York, 1990).

Rousseau, Richard W. (ed.), *Christianity and Judaism: The deepening dialogue* (Scranton, PA, 1983).

Ruether, Rosemary R., *Faith and Fratricide: The theological roots of antisemitism* (New York, 1974).

—— "False Messianism and prophetic consciousness," in Otto Maduro (ed.), *Judaism, Christianity, and Liberation: An agenda for dialogue* (Maryknoll, NY, 1991).

Ruether, Rosemary R. and Ruether, Herman J., *The Wrath of Jonah: Religion and nationalism in the Israeli-Palestinian conflict* (San Francisco, 1989).

Sanders, E. P., *Jesus and Judaism* (Philadelphia, 1985).

Smith, Steven G., *The Argument to the Other: Reason beyond reason in the thought of Karl Barth and Emmanuel Levinas* (Chicago, 1983).

Sonderegger, Katherine, *That Jesus Christ was Born a Jew: Karl Barth's "Doctrine of Israel"* (University Park, PA, 1992).

Swidler, Leonard (ed.), *Breaking Down the Wall Between Americans and East Germans – Jews and Christians Through Dialogue* (Lanham, New York and London, 1987).

Thoma, Clemens, *A Christian Theology of Judaism*, trans. Helga Croner (Ramsey and New York, 1980).

Thoma, Clemens and Wyschogrod, Michael (eds), *Understanding Scripture: Explorations of Jewish and Christian traditions of interpretation* (Mahwah, NY, 1987).

van Buren, Paul, *A Theology of the Jewish–Christian Reality. Part I. Discerning the Way* (San Francisco, 1980).

—— *Part 2. A Christian Theology of the People. Israel* (1983).

—— *Part 3. Christ in Context* (1988).

von der Osten-Sacken, Peter, *Grundzüge einer Theologie im christlich-jüdischen Gespräch* (München, 1982).

—— *Christian–Jewish Dialogue: Theological foundations*, trans. Margaret Kohl (Philadelphia, 1986).

Ward, Graham, *Barth, Derrida and the Language of Theology* (Cambridge, 1995).

Williams, Rowan D., "Between politics and metaphysics: Reflections in the Wake of Gillian Rose," in L. Gregory Jones and Stephen Fowl (eds), *Rethinking Metaphysics*, (Oxford, 1995), pp. 3–22.

World Council of Churches, with Allan Brockway et al., *The Theology of the Churches and the Jewish People: Statements by the World Council of Churches* (Geneva, 1988).

Wyschogrod, Michael, "Why was and is the theology of Karl Barth of interest to a Jewish theologian?" in *Footnotes to a Theology: The Karl Barth Colloquium of 1972*, ed. Martin Rumscheidt, SR Supplements (1972), pp. 95–111.

—— "A Jewish perspective on Karl Barth," in Donald K. McKim (ed.), *How Karl Barth Changed My Mind* (Grand Rapids, MI, 1986), pp. 156–61.

—— Review of Friedrich-Wilhelm Marquardt, Das Christliche Bekenntnis zu Jesus, dem Juden. Eine Christologie. *Journal of Ecumenical Studies*, 29 (1992), pp. 275–6.

Theology of Religions

Gavin D'Costa

Introduction

Christianity was born into a religiously pluralist world and has remained in one ever since. At different times in its history it has been especially sensitive to this context. The mandate to go preach the gospel to the corners of the earth as well as its own socioeconomic political position in society has resulted in a complex range of relations and responses to other religions. In the modern period, and especially in the West, it stands unsure of its own distinct nature and deeply aware of its implication in various imperialist exploits. Christians in the modern world cannot ignore the existence of other religions. Global communications, extensive travel, migration, colonialism, and international trade are all factors that have brought the religions closer to each other in both destructive and creative ways.

A brief look at some statistics may help, although their reliability is a problem, no less than their interpretation. Compare, for instance, the difference between 1491 and 1991. In 1491 roughly 19 percent of the world's population was Christian and while 2 percent of the non-Christian world was in contact with Christianity, 79 percent remained entirely ignorant of its existence. Some 93 percent of all Christians were white Europeans. Compare these figures with 1991, when 33 percent of the global population were Christians, with 44 percent of the non-Christian world being aware of Christianity, while only 23 percent had no contact with Christians and the gospel. The ethnic basis of Christianity has also radically shifted so that the largest Christian community is now to be found in Latin America, only then followed by Europe, with Africa third (and growing much faster than Europe), followed by North America and then South Asia.

To get a sense of the broader picture, it will be helpful to briefly survey the figures for 1991 regarding the numerical strengths of world religions. After Christians (roughly $1\frac{3}{4}$ billion), Muslims are the largest religious group (962 million), followed by Hindus (721 million), with Buddhists then forming less than half the number of Hindus (327 million). New religions, notoriously difficult to classify, number some 119 million, followed by another amorphous classification, tribal religions which

constitute roughly 99 million. Finally, and in Western consciousness far more prominent, come Sikhs with nearly 19 million and Jews with nearly 18 million.[1]

Christians cannot ignore the existence of other religions. Furthermore, with the
awareness of their existence a host of theological, philosophical, methodological,
and practical questions are raised. Should, for example, Buddhist meditation groups
be allowed the use of church halls? How should religious education be taught? What
kind of social and political cooperation or opposition is appropriate with people of
other faiths? There are also fundamental theological issues at stake. If salvation is
possible outside Christ/Christianity, is the uniqueness of Christ and the universal
mission of the church called into question? Or if salvation is not possible outside
Christ/Christianity, is it credible that a loving God would consign the majority of
humankind to perdition, often through no fault of their own? Can Christians learn
from other faiths? Can they be enriched rather than diluted or polluted from this
encounter? Clearly, other religions in varying degrees have also undergone their own
self-questioning in the light of religious pluralism, but that is another subject.[2]

There have been many different Christian responses to the world religions. To
limit ourselves to the modern period only makes things slightly easier. No set of
categories is adequate to analyze and deal with the complexity of the topic, but it
may help to label three types of theological response to other religions for heuristic
purposes only. There are of course considerable differences between theologians
belonging to the same "camp" and many features of overlap between different
approaches. I shall call these approaches: *pluralism* (that all religions are equal and
valid paths to the one divine reality and Christ is one revelation among many equally
important revelations); *exclusivism* (only those who hear the gospel proclaimed and
explicitly confess Christ are saved); and *inclusivism* (that Christ is the normative
revelation of God, although salvation is possible outside of the explicit Christian
church, but this salvation is always from Christ). Various presuppositions undergird
each approach, often revolving around Christology and the doctrine of God and the
doctrine of human beings.

Survey

Pluralism

Pluralism is almost entirely a recent phenomenon within Christianity and this kind
of approach has many supporters within what is sometimes called "liberal Christianity." Although it has been prominent in Anglo-American circles, there are an
increasing number of theologians in Asia that support this kind of position. However, the manner in which theologians arrive at this outcome is various and at times
incompatible. Some argue that all religions have a common core or essence that can
be historically identified, often within the mystical traditions of the world religions.[3]
This emphasis on mysticism is also shared by what is termed the "perennial philosophy," which has followers in different religions. Here it is argued that a straightforward historical comparison of the religions will not show this common essence,

which is only found among "esoteric" believers who have penetrated the mystical depths of their own tradition to discover the non-duality of God and the soul, a unity that transcends all formulations. "Exoteric" believers absolutize their symbols and creeds and fail to penetrate to the transcendent unity of religions. Hence, exoteric believers hold that Christ and/or the Church become the only way to salvation.[4]

Another form of pluralism begins from a consideration of historical relativity and it is argued that all traditions are relative and cannot claim superiority over other equally limited and relative ways to salvation.[5] Others argue that all religions have important and substantial historical differences and the view of a common essence is in danger of compromising the integrity of each particular tradition by emphasizing only one aspect of that tradition. The real unity of religions is found not in doctrine or transreligious experience and esoteric doctrines but in the common experience of salvation or liberation.[6] This latter emphasis has often developed in dialogue with liberation theology and other religions. Others, such as the English philosopher of religion, John Hick, have developed their position mainly in dialogue with traditional Western philosophy and the world religions. It will be instructive to look in detail at Hick, who combines many of the emphases in the above approaches.

John Hick's pluralism

Initially, Hick argued that the *solus Christus* assumption (that salvation is only through Christ) held by exclusivists is incompatible with the Christian teaching of a God who desires to save all people. There are many millions who have never heard of Christ through no fault of their own, before and after the New Testament period – the *invincibly ignorant*. It is therefore un-Christian to think that God would have "ordained that men must be saved in such a way that only a small minority can in fact receive this salvation."[7] Hick argued that it was God, and not Christianity or Christ, toward whom all religions move, and from whom they gain their salvific efficacy. Hick therefore proposed a *theocentric* revolution away from a *Christocentric* or *ecclesiocentric* position that has dominated Christian history. But what then of Christ? Hick argued that the doctrine of the incarnation should be understood mythically – as an expression of devotion and commitment by Christians, not as an ontological claim that here in this particular place and in this particular man God has chosen to reveal himself uniquely and definitively, in what was later called the "God-man": Jesus Christ.[8] Hick stressed the doctrine of an all-loving God over that of the *solus Christus* principle.

An important later development in Hick's position came in response to the criticism that his theological revolution was still theocentric and thereby excluded non-theistic religions. Pluralist positions, typically, must account for problems such as this if their claims are to be taken seriously. Hick developed a Kantian-type distinction between a divine noumenal reality "that exists independently and outside man's perception of it" which he calls the "Eternal One," and the phenomenal world, "which is that world as it appears to our human consciousness," in effect the various human responses to the Eternal One.[9] These responses are then seen as both theistic and non-theistic (e.g., God or Allah, and Nirvana or Nirguna Brahman). In this way Hick tries to overcome any underlying theistic essentialism.

The above arguments cumulatively suggest that Christians can fruitfully view the history of religions as a history of the Eternal One's (God's) activity without making any special claims for Christianity. Christian attitudes to other religions need not be characterized by a desire to convert, or claims to superiority, but a will to learn and grow together toward the truth. Mission should be jointly carried out to the secular world by the religions, rather than towards each other. Hick suggests that exclusivism and inclusivism cannot provide such fruitful conditions for interreligious dialogue.

Hick's philosophical approach to religious pluralism could be contrasted with the very pragmatic approach taken by those deeply influenced by liberation theology, such as Paul Knitter or the Asian Roman Catholic theologian, Aloysius Pieris. Pieris emphasizes the overcoming of the theocentric, Christocentric and ecclesiocentric problems that bedevil this debate by emphasizing the liberative power of religion as the only criteria for authenticity. In this respect, he finds that Buddhist monasticism (with its voluntary, rather than imposed poverty) and its commitment to the cessation of suffering through gnosis allows "an engagement in a positive and practical programme of psychic-social restructuring of human existence here on earth in accordance with the path leading to nirvanic freedom."[10] Hence, the religions must work together in this common cause and Pieris renounces claims for Christianity's uniqueness and his own Church's fulfillment theology as forms of Western imperialism.[11]

Exclusivism

Some argue that the rape of cultures and civilizations has often been justified in the name of Christianity armed with an exclusivist missionary theology.[12] Furthermore, racism and colonial imperialism are often closely identified with Christian mission. This chequered history cannot be denied, although it is a complex and ambiguous one. Hence, we should note the persuasive arguments that much missionary work was not in fact pursued in tandem with empire-building, but actually resisted it.[13] Others have defended the rich cultural contributions made by missionaries in terms of the issue of "translation" and criticized the "western guilt complex" in relation to mission work.[14]

I have highlighted these issues to show the ways in which theological attitudes are so closely related to practice. Nevertheless, there are serious theological issues underlying exclusivism. No major systematic theologian holds a rigorist exclusivism, so in this part I will outline a position without close reference to a single named theologian. The exclusivist position (most often found in Lutheran and Calvinist circles) is fundamentally concerned to affirm two central insights. The first is that God has sent his Son, Jesus Christ, to bring salvation into the world and that this salvation is both judgment and mercy to all human beings who are deeply estranged from God. Salvation therefore comes from faith in Christ, and in this alone – *solus*

Christus. In this respect, many inclusivists share this affirmation. Secondly, this salvation won by Christ is only available through *explicit* faith in Christ which comes from hearing the gospel preached (*fides ex auditu*), requiring repentance, baptism, and the embracing of a new life in Christ. It is in the context of this second axiom that inclusivists partly differ from exclusivists – as we shall see later.

Concerning the first principle, most exclusivists regard human nature as fallen and sinful. Hence, men and women are only capable of idolatry, for all their attempts to reach God are precisely that: human attempts at capturing the living God.[15] While I cite Barth, Barth overturns these categories by being both an exclusivist, inclusivist, and universalist! More of this later. Herein lies the judgment of God upon all acts of idolatry for all human actions ultimately (in subtle and not so subtle ways) usurp God's power in creating gods of their own making. However inspiring, intelligent, and humane a religion may be, such religions are never more than the products of fallen persons, who in their very attempt to reach out and upwards, compound their own situation, for they blind themselves to the way in which God has reached down and inward to humanity in the person of Christ. In fact, the extent of sinfulness is such that human beings are incapable of truly recognizing their own situation of radical fallenness and it is only in the light of Christ that sin is seen most clearly and fully for what it really is.[16]

Given the predicament of humankind, the logic of this type of theology requires that salvation is an utterly gratuitous gift, entirely unmerited by us. Rather than be indignant at the particularity of God's action (as are pluralists), the exclusivist is awed and grateful at God's gratuity. His mercy and redemption are not something merited by us, and this gift's particularity is nevertheless universal in import and offer, so that the exclusivist can only humbly proclaim this truth rather than question it. Hence, mission and evangelism are more appropriate than dialogue. Doctrinally, the *sola fide* and *fides ex auditu* principles are paramount, for anything less compromises the incarnation and atonement and God's salvific action toward his creatures.[17]

No exclusivist would usually wish non-Christians ill or that they be lost. Rather, they would no doubt emphasize the urgency and necessity of worldwide evangelization, rather than spend time and energy on improper speculation about the possibility of salvation occurring in the non-Christian religions. However, some tend to state baldly the apparent consequences of this approach, as found in the proclamation of the Chicago Congress on World Mission in 1960: "In the years since the war, more than one billion souls have passed into eternity and more than half of these went to the torment of hell fire without even hearing of Jesus Christ, who He was, or why He died on the cross of Calvary."[18]

Others, it must be said, refuse to speculate on the outcome and destiny of the non-Christian for a variety of reasons. The first is to suggest that we cannot know the fate of non-Christians and must simply trust in the mercy and justice of God.[19] Hence, such exclusivists are willing to acknowledge that salvation may be offered to the invincibly ignorant although they refuse to speculate further about how this will happen. On the other hand, George Lindbeck, who emphasizes that becoming a Christian is a process of being included into a cultural-linguistic practice, argues that if Christianity is a learned form of life then it follows that "there is no damnation

– just as there is no salvation – outside the church. One must, in other words, learn the language of faith before one can know enough about its message knowingly to reject it and thus be lost."[20] Lindbeck (and this recalls our earlier comment on Barth's breaking of the typologies) in fact holds out on theological grounds a hope for the salvation of all and suggests a post-mortem confrontation with Christ (thereby satisfying the *fides ex auditu* principle) to account for non-Christians.[21] A Roman Catholic pupil of Lindbeck's, Joseph Di Noia, has given this possibility a developed formulation in terms of employing the doctrine of purgatory (a process of cleansing also undergone by the Christian) as a means whereby the non-Christian who has already responded positively to God in their lives will be purified in anticipation of the trinitarian beatific vision.[22] A third and somewhat novel (some might say heretical) strategy has been suggested whereby reincarnation is posited to solve the problem of the invincibly ignorant who will therefore have a chance to hear the gospel at least once before they "properly" die.[23]

It is clear then, that the boundary lines between these latter forms of exclusivism and some forms of inclusivism are thin and grey. So it is to inclusivism that we now turn.

Inclusivism

Inclusivism has a lineage in the Christian tradition, in so much as grace has been acknowledged to operate outside the confines of the visible church. Quite a number of Roman Catholics, Orthodox, and Protestants share this approach with varying differences. The main differences revolve around the question as to whether non-Christian religions can be said to have salvific structures;[24] and whether, finally, a person can come to salvation apart from explicitly confessing Christ. In respect to the latter point, there is a very unclear line between inclusivists and exclusivists. Inclusivists tend to be united on the main point that whenever and wherever non-Christians respond to grace, this grace is the grace of the triune God. In this respect, inclusivism has often been related to theologies of fulfillment, drawing on the ancient tradition of a *preparatio evangelica*.

Karl Rahner's inclusivism

Karl Rahner, a German Jesuit, is probably the most influential inclusivist theologian of the twentieth century. Rahner's theological anthropology shapes his brand of inclusivism, although he argues his case from Catholic doctrine. Rahner argues that the precondition of finite (categorial) knowledge is an unconditional openness to being (*Vorgriff*), which is an unthematic, prereflective awareness of God – who is infinite being. Our transcendental openness to being constitutes both the hiddenness of grace and its prethematic presence at the heart of our existence. Men and women therefore search in history for a categorial disclosure of this hidden grace. In Jesus' total abandonment to God, his total "Yes" through his life, death, and resurrection, he is established as the culmination and prime mediator of grace. Therefore Christian revelation is the explicit expression of grace which men and women experience implicitly in the depths of their being when, for example, they reach out through the power of grace in trusting love and self-sacrifice, or in acts of hope and charity.

Rahner (1966) attempts to balance the *solus Christus* principle with the doctrine of the *universal salvific will of God*, so as to maintain that Christ is the sole cause of salvation in the world, but that this salvific grace may be mediated within history without an explicit confrontation with Christ. Such is the case in the history of Israel which Rahner calls a "lawful religion" prior to the time of Christ. Rahner maintains it remains a lawful religion for those who have never been confronted historically and existentially with the gospel. By this he means that, although a person might hear the gospel being preached historically (say by a person whose life is dissolute and dishonest) that person may not have existentially been addressed for all sorts of reasons (the difficulty of making sense of this message in terms of the medium of presentation – and so on). Hence, this person cannot really count as having "heard" the gospel and rejected it. To return to the argument: If Israel in a certain context had a "lawful religion," may it not in principle be the case with other religions of the world?

Rahner argues that if salvific grace exists outside the visible Church, as he believes it does in the history of Israel, and in creation and through conscience, then this grace is both causally related to Christ (always and everywhere – as prime mediator) and his Church. Rahner argues that christology and the doctrine of God cannot be separated from the Church as Christ is historically mediated through the Church. This means that Rahner must reconcile membership of the Church as a means of salvation and the possibility that salvific grace is mediated outside the historically tangible borders of the Church. He does this along the lines of the traditional Catholic teachings regarding the *votum ecclesiae* (a wish to belong to the Church), and the related notion of implicit desire. (See the beginnings of Rahner's thought on this matter in relation to Pius XII's *Mystici Corporis Christi*.)[25] Furthermore, given the sociohistorical nature of men and women, grace must be mediated historically and socially. The incarnation is paradigmatic of this. Hence, if and when non-Christians respond to grace, then this grace must be mediated *through* the non-Christian's religion, however imperfectly. Hence, non-Christian religions may be "lawful religions" with the same qualifications registered regarding Israel. Rahner thus coins the term "anonymous Christian" (this refers to the source of saving grace that is responded to: Christ), and "anonymous Christianity" (this refers to its dynamic orientation toward its definitive historical and social expression in the Church).[26]

Because God has already been active within the non-Christian religions, the Christian can be open to learning about God through her non-Christian partner. Furthermore, the Christian is also free to engage in active social and political co-operation when appropriate. Hence, the inclusivist has a firm theological basis for fruitful dialogue. Given Rahner's notion that grace must seek to objectivize itself, mission is clearly important. Hence, Rahner is able to affirm that Christianity is the one true religion, while at the same time holding that other religions may have a provisional salvific status.

The debate

Objections to pluralism

There have been a number of objections specifically to Hick's thesis, some of which indicate more general problems with pluralism.[27] First, there are objections to the way in which the centrality of Christ seems to be bypassed. It is argued that Hick's initial theocentric revolution is based on a shaky premise. He rejects the *solus Christus* for he thinks it leads to the a priori damnation of non-Christians. We have seen above that it need not. Furthermore, when Hick proposes to emphasize God rather than Christ, he is in danger of severing christology from ontology and introducing a free-floating God divorced from any particular revelation. In fact Judaism, Christianity, and Islam have all tended to center on revelatory paradigms for their discourse and practice. Hick's theocentrism pays little attention to the importance of historical particularity and the grounding of theistic discourse. In fact, the theological basis of his proposal (that of an all-loving God) is undermined if Hick cannot give normative ontological status to the revelatory event upon which this axiom is grounded – originally for Hick, that of the revelation of God in Christ. And even if he responds, as he has done, that "an all-loving God" is to be found in Judaism and Islam, it is certainly problematic to base this claim in Buddhism or Confucianism.

A related objection follows from Hick's response to precisely this seeming prioritization of theism. Critics maintain that if the meaning of "God" lacked specificity in Hick's theocentrism, it seems further relativized in his more recent works as the personal, loving, creator "God" is seen as one aspect of the "Eternal One" that apparently can also be characterized by non-personal, non-creator, non-theistic predicates. As all such predicates are from the human side, Hick argues, they are thereby not properly applicable to the Eternal One in any literal way. Hence, replies the critic, "God" cannot be said to be personal or loving in any proper ontological sense. The Kantian noumenon encountered a similar problem in not providing for a correspondence between phenomena and things-in-themselves. Hick seems to be close to a transcendental agnosticism (i.e., affirming a transcendence without any qualities).[28] Despite Hick's stress on soteriocentrism in a liberated lifestyle, can he properly address the question of the nature of God (or the Eternal One) who actually saves and liberates people, or is his doctrine of "God" in danger of avoiding all particularities so as to accommodate every particularity? Again, Hick's response is on the lines that we can never properly describe the Eternal One "in himself," only in "relation to us." Clearly, the outcome of these debates remains unresolved, but highlights the theological centrality of christology and the doctrine of God in the discussion about other faiths.

Pieris's attempt to bypass problems of Christocentrism, theocentrism, and ecclesiocentrism is admirably motivated by a desire for justice and righteousness in Asian society – and not least, peace between the Asian religions. However, critics have argued that Pieris cannot really address the question of liberation without the categories of Christ, God, and the church.[29] It is precisely in Christ and the trinitarian revelation therein that the decisive meaning of liberation is to be found. The further Pieris tries to get away from such specification the closer he gets to another but unstated set of assumptions. From where does he derive the meaning of "liberation"? Why should such a meaning be privileged and exalted above all religions and used as a judge of them? Is this not a new form of imperialism? Fundamental to this debate is the understanding of action. The critique cited derives from the argument that all action is always emplotted within a narrative form which both shapes and informs it, so that one cannot simply parallel similar actions (feeding the poor) as if they did not occupy different narrative spaces. Stanley Hauerwas raises this pointed criticism at Gutiérrez's liberation theology.[30] Clearly, within this political perspective, one can see a similar role for a type of feminist theology of religions which focuses specifically on the question of the liberation of women within the world religions.[31]

The debate will clearly continue and one can see the complex interrelations of a number of issues.

Objections to exclusivism

The type of exclusivism I outlined faces a number of difficulties. Hick has criticized this position for being incompatible with the God of love disclosed at the heart of Christianity. Quoting the statement of the Congress on World Mission (see above), Hick argues that such an outcome is theologically unacceptable, especially when one considers the invincibly ignorant.[32] There are two important points in the exclusivist response. First, for some exclusivists Hick presumes too much in questioning the ways of God as being unjust! Rather, given human sinfulness, we should start from being amazed that God saves anyone at all. The issue at stake here concerns human nature. Secondly, a number of exclusivists have taken seriously the problem of the person who through no fault of his or her own has never heard the gospel. And these developments have been outlined above.

Another criticism aimed at exclusivists is that grace, within the Christian tradition, is not limited purely to an explicit confrontation with Christ.[33] This contention is based on a number of arguments. In traditional Christian theology, Judaism up to the time of Christ was certainly accorded revelatory status. Hence, a Christian exclusivist who denied any revelation outside Christ would be hard-pressed to explain the use of the Old Testament as part of Christian scripture. Besides the history of Israel testifying to salvific grace outside the particular event of the historical Jesus, there are also a number of passages within the New Testament that highlight the importance of right living. If, for instance, a person's courageous self-sacrificing love is due to certain demands within their religion, can these acts of *responding to grace* be divorced from the mediators of such grace? Or, can the humanist's self-sacrificial love for another, so powerfully portrayed in Camus's *The Plague*, have nothing to do with Jesus' implied teaching that "as you did it to one of the least of my brethren, you did it to me" (Matthew 25: 40)?

The exclusivist may respond in a number of ways. First, pointing out that the revelation Israel received was always directed toward Christ and was not properly salvific in itself, except by virtue of its teleological completion in Christ. Hence, the real question here is whether implicit faith in Christ is alone sufficient for salvation, or whether it requires at some stage explicit faith. It is interesting to note that the major inclusivist theologian, Rahner, also held in his earlier writings on death that a post-mortem meeting with Christ was essential for the completion of our lives and in preparation for the beatific vision.[34] Furthermore, if salvific grace is available through creation and history, apart from explicit faith, does this not call into question the necessity of Jesus Christ for salvation? Exclusivists might also respond that any resort to arguments from virtuous actions is to depart from the *sola fide* principle, and concede to Pelagianism. Clearly, the arguments will rage on, but again we find the central questions revolving around christology, God, practice, human nature, and the church.

Objections to inclusivism

Rahner is criticized by both pluralists and exclusivists. Pluralists argue that the term "anonymous Christian" is deeply offensive to non-Christians and creates a stalemate in dialogue with each side calling the other names (anonymous Hindus, anonymous Muslims, and so on).[35] Hans Küng has accused Rahner of creating a terminological distinction to sweep a resistant non-Christian humanity into the Christian church through the back door.[36] Rahner has made it very clear that his theory is for internal Christian consumption only, i.e., it is a question within dogmatic theology and not a reflection meant for interfaith dialogue. He is simply reflecting on the possibility that the non-Christian may already have encountered God and, if this is so, then "God" must be the same God as disclosed by Christ. Of course, pluralists respond that this is still an imperialist assertion, always claiming to know more about God than anyone else, and it also sees others purely in terms of their reflection of Christianity.[37] Pluralists also criticize the way in which Rahner wants to secure all grace as christologically mediated when he in fact acknowledges that it is mediated within other religions where Christ is not known. This, they want to argue, amounts to a verbal ownership of God, which practically acknowledges the opposite. Rahner would no doubt respond that his argument is one regarding ontological causality, not particular historical mediation.

Rahner also faces severe criticism from those who oppose pluralism and see in his theology certain pluralist tendencies. For instance, it is argued that Rahner compromises the *solus Christus* principle in a fundamental manner. Salvation is made possible without surrender to Christ and this inevitably renders Christ unnecessary in the economy of salvation.[38] If salvation requires no explicit faith at all then this dangerously obscures the way in which the church claims to form and nourish genuine faith within a historical-social community. From his cultural-linguistic approach, Lindbeck accuses Rahner of operating with a very defective view of the relationship between experience and interpretation. Put crudely, experience is seen as prior to all interpretation, which leads to what Lindbeck calls "experiential expressivism"; the notion that expression must follow experience. This is contrasted with the cultural-linguistic model, which argues that experience is in large part shaped by the interpretative tradition of the experiencer. Hence, in Rahner's view Christianity is thereby seen as just a better interpretation of the same experience of grace in different religions. But surely Christian faith is more than this? It is the being shaped in a specific Christoformic fashion by involvement within the specific community of the church. Hence, the question posed to Rahner: What would the difference be between an anonymous and an explicit Christian in terms of faith? Rahner's invisible Church, it is claimed, is unbiblical and also detracts from the importance of explicit confession as a criterion for membership.[39] The very foundations of Rahner's theology which undergird his theology of the anonymous Christian have also been called into question by his Roman Catholic colleague, Hans Urs von Balthasar, who has seen in Rahner's transcendental anthropology the danger of the conflation of nature and grace and the reduction of revelation to a predetermined anthropological system.[40] Balthasar is concerned that, by viewing supernatural grace as being part of the very nature of men and women, Rahner minimizes both the transforming power of the glory of the Lord that shines forth in Christ and the character of sin and of tragedy, which also explains Rahner's impoverished theology of the cross.

Rahner has responded to these criticisms and I cannot follow the complex debate here, except to briefly say that he has maintained against his more conservative critics that there is no compromise on the basic tenet (shared with exclusivists) that salvation comes exclusively through faith in Christ; and that Christ's life, death, and resurrection have ontologically (not chronologically) brought salvation irrevocably into the world. Rahner claims he is simply offering one explanation of a teaching maintained by the church that salvation is available to invincibly ignorant non-Christians and he is not unconditionally theologically endorsing the value of non-Christian religions per se.

Objections to the threefold typology

There are some who have either claimed a fourth option or there are those who are unhappy with this threefold classification altogether (and therefore, also with any fourth option). Regarding those who propose a fourth option,[41] Di Noia restricts the definition of exclusivism to stipulating that only those who explicitly confess Christ *in this life* will be saved. Hence, his purgatorial option allegedly constitutes a fourth option. In Ogden's case his fourth option rests on the distinction that pluralists claim that other religions *are* salvific means, while he wishes to claim that they *may be* salvific means. Ogden claims this to be a new fourth option between inclusivism and pluralism, but it perhaps questionably presumes that all pluralists are committed to an a priori affirmation of other religions as salvific means.

Challenges to the whole enterprise have been put forward most forcefully by Kenneth Surin and John Milbank, both primarily reacting against pluralism but finding problems with the entire project.[42] Surin's criticism is essentially political and genealogical (deriving from Michel Foucault), suggesting that rather than serve up theories about religious unity in an abstract, ahistorical, and apolitical fashion, real attention should be paid to the social, political, and power relationships between religions in their particular locality. Theological talk has usually served to obscure rather than identify the real terrain in which the exercise of power in the materialist order is the key to understanding the superstructure where legitimating theologizing is produced. Hence, pluralist theologies perpetuate the existing status quo by distracting attention away from the real problems. While Surin's criticisms are powerful and incisive, there is a danger that he redescribes the territory so radically that there are no valid theological questions left. While this materialist reductionism is insightful, ultimately it surrenders theology entirely into the hands of social and political theorists, reducing all theological discourse to genealogical origins.

Milbank, while sharing much in common with Surin, proposes quite a different role for theology. Milbank is deeply suspicious of the notion of "religion," as well as the belief that dialogue provides a privileged access to truth. Rather he urges that Christianity must simply proclaim its vision through its particular form of practice within the church. The church can do no other than this, nor ought it to try. What both Surin and Milbank do so clearly is alert us to the fact that all theology is also tied up within a political and social nexus. We will return to this point later.

Finally, I must declare certain reservations with the threefold paradigm, despite my having employed it heuristically in this chapter. We have already seen the thin dividing lines between strong forms of inclusivism and weak forms of exclusivism, and likewise with weak forms of inclusivism and certain forms of pluralism. The typology is constantly inadequate. Furthermore, typologies can easily harden into Procrustean beds, forcing diverse materials into easily controlled locations. All this should keep us on our guard. But most seriously, it might be the case that in using the depictions (pluralism, inclusivism, and exclusivism) we disguise the fact that what we are really dealing with are different forms of exclusivism! Pluralism often claims the high ground in being more tolerant, more liberal, more affirmative of truth in other religions, etc. This typology rhetorically reaffirms this false self-description. Pluralism, as I have argued elsewhere, has its own intolerant, illiberal shadow-side, for if it is to be effective at all, then it must operate with criteria to discern truth, "God," and salvation.[43] And in so doing, it will naturally exclude all that is not in keeping with these criteria. So in this respect, it is no different from exclusivism. The difficult *criteriological* questions that underlie this debate are therefore not always highlighted via this typology, although, as has been seen above, it is the choice and use of such criteria that dictate the differences within this schema.

Achievement and Agenda

The achievement of the modern debate is that the question of other religions is here to stay with Christian theology into the twenty-first century. This can be regarded as an achievement in the sense that the credibility of Christianity will partly depend on the way in which it can respond to the bewildering plurality that characterizes the modern world. This works in at least two ways. If Christianity is not able to see itself as distinct and unique in any sense at all it will probably be assimilated and absorbed by traditions that do feel they have a special vision for the world. People are not particularly interested and challenged by nothing at all! On the other hand, if Christian theology denigrates the rich heritage of millions of women and men it will fail to respect the goodness of creation affirmed within its own creed and foolishly turn its back on the many riches and glories found within other religions. By facing up to the difficult theological issues raised by the presence of other religions, one can only hope that various churches will be able to deal more constructively with the complex reality facing them.

The modern debate has raised an agenda, which will expand and be reshaped as time progresses, ranging from questions regarding the nature of religion, the socio-political context of religious encounters, the person of Jesus Christ, the nature of God, the character of the church and its mission. It would be fair to say that at the heart of the matter lies the question: "Who do you say that I am?" The way in which Christians relate to other religions is deeply shaped by the way in which they relate to Jesus Christ, thereby showing that the future agenda is both intra-Christian and extra-Christian. By intra-Christian I mean that the various developments in theology will substantially affect the question of other religions. This relates both to questions of method and theological content. For example, within "liberal" Christian circles, especially where there is a strong emphasis on "God" and sociopolitical liberation, we are likely to find a certain pattern in responding to other religions which is predictable prior to interreligious encounter. On the other hand, theologies that are strongly Christocentric, utilizing categories such as story or narrative, are more likely to emphasize the particularity of the Christian message and its power to shape people in terms of a specific narrative. Such theologies are likely to be more suspicious of liberal approaches, although they will not necessarily result in negative assessments of other religions. Furthermore, the recent recovery of trinitarian theologies is also likely to give the debate a new injection of life, for it gives a richness to christology that is often neglected.[44] We have seen to some extent the way in which liberation theology has affected the debate, and in the future feminist, ecological, postmodern, Asian, Latin American, African, and very many other types of theology will all bring their own distinctive insights to bear more fully on the matters of christology, God, the church, and other religions. It is difficult to predict the outcome of such theologies but it is also difficult to see how Christ, God, and the church can be bypassed in any serious attempt to grapple theologically with the question of other religions.

By extra-Christian I want to register an issue, among many others, that could not be dealt with in such a short space. We have had no time to deal with the dynamics of specific encounters where the theology of religions may take on all sorts of encounter-specific characteristics. For example, in the Jewish–Christian dialogue, the antisemitism within traditional christology comes to the fore in a most painful and disturbing manner; as well as the nature of God's promises regarding his "covenant."[45] Also, and less aired, is the question regarding Messianic Jews and Hebrew Christians, who have often been shunned and rejected by both Jews and Christians. Clearly, the issues in this latter arena are quite different to ones raised when Christianity encounters a profoundly non-theistic tradition like Buddhism, where it has not had the same fratricidal relationship, although here the context of colonialism is deeply relevant and often painful. Hence, the debates with Buddhism have ranged over very different issues such as: the relation of apophatic theology to the apparent non-theism of Buddhism; the meditative techniques within Buddhism that bring about a freedom to act in charity and love; and the question of the portrayal of Buddhism in the West, for example, the Victorian construction of Buddhism.[46] Hence, extra-Christian presence in the debate is likely to create all sorts of unforeseen developments. Furthermore, these specific encounters also raise the question of the relationship between a theology *of* religions and a theology arising *out of* specific encounters. Some argue that the latter should have priority over the former, and some would go further to suggest that the latter even invalidates the exercise of the former altogether.

We have also not touched on the question of inculturation which is closely linked with our theme, as the culture for so many churches, especially in Asia and Africa, is formed by various non-Christian religions. Hence, as we saw with Pieris above, the question of a truly Asian church may call for an entirely different attitude to Buddhism and Hinduism than has been traditional in Western theologies. There are already churches in Asia where readings from the sacred scriptures of the Hindus such as the *Bhagavad Gita* or *Upanishads* are incorporated into the liturgy (usually prior to the Old Testament and sometimes instead of the Old Testament – thereby reflecting a fulfillment theology of inclusivism). And in such churches one can often find a liturgy and lifestyle which Western Christians may find hard to recognize due to its deeply Indian roots. There are also individuals such as Brahmabāndhab Upādhyāy who considered themselves Hindu-Christians, which raises all sorts of new and interesting questions. When I mentioned that the different developments in theology are likely to shape the way this question is approached, it is clear that theologians from churches often faced with this dramatic religious plurality are likely to be the main practitioners of future theology of religions. There are also issues of the relationship of theology of religions to systematic theology and the study of religions within the church and within the academy. While some see this area as integral to systematic theology with institutional repurcussions,[47] others have argued for a more ambitious nondenominational global or world theology which has radical and far-reaching implications.[48] This whole issue raises the question which has remained implicit throughout this exploration: Will our theological method significantly determine our answer to the question concerning other religions? Might it be the case that a theology of religions must ultimately pay as much attention to the "Other" as well as the manner in which we deal with the gracious and holy "Other" who is made known in Father, Son, and Spirit?

Notes

1 D. Barrett, "The status of the Christian world mission in the 1990s," in G. Anderson, *Mission in the Nineteen Nineties* (New Haven and Grand Rapids, MI, 1991), pp. 72–3.

2 See, for example, P. Griffiths (ed.), *Christianity through Non-Christian Eyes* (New York, 1991) and H. Coward, *Pluralism: Challenge to world religions* (New York, 1985).

3 William James, *The Varieties of Religious Experience* (London, 1960; first published 1902).

4 Aldous Huxley, *The Perennial Philosophy* (New York, 1945); H. Smith, *Essays on World Religions*, ed. M. Darrol Bryant (New York, 1992).

5 E. Troeltsch, *The Absoluteness of Christianity and the History of Religions* (London, 1972) and, most recently, G. Kaufman, "Religious diversity, historical consciousness, and Christian theology," in John Hick and Paul Knitter (eds), *The Myth of Christian Uniqueness* (London, 1987), pp. 3–15.

6 Paul Knitter, *No Other Name? A critical study of Christian attitudes towards the world religions* (London, 1985); "Towards a liberation theology of religions," in John Hick

and Paul Knitter, *The Myth of Christian Uniqueness*, pp. 178–200; and "Dialogue and liberation," *Drew Gateway*, 58 (1987), pp. 1–53; A. Pieris, *An Asian Theology of Liberation* (New York, 1988); F. Wilfred, *Sunset in the East? Asian challenges and Christian involvement* (Madras, 1991).

7   John Hick, *God and the Universe of Faiths* (London, 1977), p. 122.

8   Ibid., pp. 165–79.

9   John Hick, *An Interpretation of Religion* (Basingstoke, 1988), pp. 233–52.

10 A. Pieris, "Black flags for the Pope" cited by Robert Crusz, *Tablet* (14 January 1995), pp. 36–7.

11 A. Pieris, *An Asian Theology of Liberation* (New York, 1988), pp. 35–40, 47, 60.

12 Jan Morris, *Heaven's Command: An imperial progress* (London, 1973).

13 B. Stanley, *The Bible and the Flag* (Leicester, 1990).

14 Lamin Sanneh, *Encountering the West* (London, 1993) and "Christian mission and the Western guilt complex," *Christian Century* (8 April 1987), pp. 330–4, respectively.

15 Karl Barth, *Church Dogmatics* (Edinburgh, 1970), vol. I.2, p. 17.

16 Karl Barth, *Church Dogmatics* (Edinburgh, 1956), vol. IV.1, p. 60.

17 H. Lindsell, *A Christian Philosophy of Religion* (Wheaton, PA, 1949); A. Fernando, *The Christian's Attitude towards World Religions* (Wheaton, PA, 1987).

18 J. Percy (ed.), *Facing the Unfinished Task* (Grand Rapids, MI, 1961), p. 9. See also the Frankfurt Declaration in *Christianity Today* (19 June 1970), pp. 844–6 and the Lausanne Statement, *Christian Witness to the Jewish People* (Illinois, 1980).

19 L. Newbigin, "The basis, purpose, and manner of inter-faith dialogue," in R. Rousseau (ed.), *Interreligious Dialogue* (Montrose, 1981), p. 20; J. Stott, response to D. L. Edwards, in D. Edwards (ed.), *Evangelical Essentials* (Illinois, 1988), p. 327.

20 George Lindbeck, *The Nature of Doctrine: Religion and theology in a postliberal age* (Philadelphia, 1984), p. 59.

21 G. Lindbeck, "Fides ex auditu and the salvation of non-Christians," in V. Vajta (ed.), *The Gospel and the Ambiguity of the Church* (Philadelphia, 1974).

22 J. A. Di Noia, *The Diversity of Religions: A Christian perspective* (Washington, DC, 1992).

23 O. Jathanna, *The Decisiveness of the Christ Event and the Universality of Christianity in a World of Religious Plurality* (Berne, 1981).

24 For, see Karl Rahner, "Christianity and the non-Christian religions," in *Theological Investigations* (London, 1966), vol. 5, pp. 115–34; against, see M. Ruokanen, *The Catholic Doctrine of Non-Christian Religions* (Leiden, 1992) and H. van Straelen, *The Catholic Encounter with World Religions* (London, 1966).

25 Karl Rahner, *Theological Investigations*, vol. 1 (1963), pp. 1–89.

26 Karl Rahner, *Theological Investigations*, vol. 5 (1966), ch. 5; vol. 6 (1969), chs 16, 23; vol. 12 (1974), ch. 9; vol. 14 (1976), ch. 17; vol. 16 (1979), chs 4, 13; vol. 17 (1980), ch. 5.

27 For critical debate on Hick see G. Carruthers, *The Uniqueness of Jesus Christ* (Lanham, 1990); G. D'Costa, *Theology and Religious Pluralism* (Oxford and New York, 1986), pp. 22–51 and *John Hick's Theology of Religions* (Lanham, MD, and London, 1987); C. Gillis, *A Question of Final Belief: John Hick's pluralistic theory of salvation* (London, 1989); K. Surin, "A politics of speech," in G. D'Costa (ed.), *Christian Uniqueness Reconsidered* (New York, 1990), pp. 192–212; G. Loughlin, "Prefacing pluralism: John Hick and the mystery of religion," *Modern Theology*, 7 (1990), pp. 29–55 and "Squares and circles: John Hick and the doctrine of the incarnation," in H. Hewitt (ed.), *Problems in the Philosophy of John Hick* (London, 1991), pp. 181–205. Hick responds to his critics in "Straightening the record: some responses to criticism," *Modern Theology*, 6 (1990), pp. 187–95, and "Responses," in H. Hewitt (ed.), *Problems in the Philosophy of John Hick*.

28 G. D'Costa, "John Hick and religious pluralism: yet another revolution," in H. Hewitt (ed.), *Problems in the Philosophy of John Hick*, pp. 102–16.

29 G. D'Costa, "Nostra aetate. Telling God's story in Asia," in M. Lamberigts and L. Kenis (eds), *Vatican II* (Leuven, 1997). On Knitter, who develops similar arguments,

see G. D'Costa, "The reign of God and a trinitarian ecclesiology," in P. Mojzes and L. Swidler (eds), *Christian Mission and Interreligious Dialogue* (New York, 1990); Hans Küng and J. Moltmann (eds), *Christianity among the World Religions* (Edinburgh, 1986), p. 123; J. Milbank, "The end of dialogue," in G. D'Costa (ed.), *Christian Uniqueness Reconsidered* (New York, 1990), pp. 174–91.

30 S. Hauerwas, "Some theological reflections on Gutiérrez's use of liberation as a theological concept," *Modern Theology*, 3 (1986), pp. 67–76.

31 M. O'Neill, *Women Speaking, Women Listening* (New York, 1990); Rosemary R. Ruether, "Feminism and Jewish-Christian dialogue," in John Hick and Paul Knitter (eds), *The Myth of Christian Uniqueness*, pp. 137–48.

32 John Hick, *God and the Universe of Faiths* (London, 1977), pp. 121–2.

33 G. D'Costa, *Theology and Religious Pluralism*, pp. 52–79.

34 Karl Rahner, *Theology of Death* (London, 1965).

35 John Hick, *God and the Universe of Faiths*, pp. 131–2; A. Race, *Christians and Religious Pluralism* (London, 1983), pp. 45–62; A. Pieris, *Love Meets Wisdom* (New York, 1988), pp. 3–4, 131.

36 Hans Küng, *On Being a Christian* (London, 1976), pp. 77–8.

37 G. D'Costa, *Christianity and Distorted Visions of World Religions* (Birmingham, 1995).

38 H. van Straelen, *The Catholic Encounter with World Religions*; J. A. Di Noia, *The Diversity of Religions*; George Lindbeck, "Fides ex auditu," and *The Nature of Doctrine*.

39 Lindbeck, "Fides ex auditu," and *The Nature of Doctrine*, pp. 30–46.

40 See Hans Urs von Balthasar, *The Moment of Christian Witness* (New York, 1969); R. Williams, "Balthasar and Rahner," in J. Riches (ed.), *The Analogy of Beauty* (Edinburgh, 1986), pp. 11–34.

41 S. Ogden, *Is there only One True Religion or are there Many?* (Dallas, TX, 1992); J. A. Di Noia, *The Diversity of Religions*.

42 K. Surin, "A politics of speech," and J. Milbank, "The end of dialogue."

43 G. D'Costa, "The impossibility of a pluralist view of religions," *Religious Studies*, 32 (1996), pp. 223–32.

44 See, for example, C. Schwöbel, "Particularity, universality, and the religions," in G. D'Costa (ed.), *Christian Uniqueness Reconsidered*, pp. 30–48; R. Williams, "Trinity and pluralism," in *Christian Uniqueness Reconsidered*, pp. 3–15; R. Pannikar, *The Trinity and the Religious Experience of Man* (London, 1973); N. Smart and S. Konstantine, *Christian Systematic Theology in a World Context* (Minneapolis, 1991); G. D'Costa, "Christ, the Trinity, and religious plurality," in *Christian Uniqueness Reconsidered*, pp. 16–29.

45 See John Pawlikowski, *What are they Saying about Jewish–Christian Relations?* (New York, 1980) and *Christ in the Light of the Christian–Jewish Dialogue* (New York, 1982); Rosemary R. Ruether, *Faith and Fratricide: The theological roots of anti-semitism* (New York, 1974); G. D'Costa, "One covenant or many covenants? Towards a theology of Christian–Jewish relations," *Journal of Ecumenical Studies*, 27 (1990), pp. 441–52; see also chapter 31 of this book on Jewish–Christian relations.

46 See R. Pannikar, *The Trinity and the Religious Experience of Man*; A. Pieris, *Love Meets Wisdom* (New York, 1988); and P. Almond, *The British Discovery of Buddhism* (Cambridge, 1988) respectively.

47 See G. D'Costa, "The end of systematic theology," *Theology*, no. 767 (1992), pp. 324–34 and "The end of 'theology' and 'religious studies,'" *Theology* (forthcoming, 1996); see also N. Smart and S. Konstantine, *Christian Systematic Theology*.

48 See John Hick, *An Interpretation of Religion*; L. Swidler, *After the Absolute* (Philadelphia, 1990); W. C. Smith, *Towards a World Theology* (Philadelphia, 1981).

Bibliography

Almond, P., *The British Discovery of Buddhism* (Cambridge, 1988).

Balthasar, Hans Urs von, *The Moment of Christian Witness* (New York, 1969).

Barrett, D., "The status of the Christian world mission in the 1990s," in G. Anderson, *Mission in the Nineteen Nineties* (New Haven and Grand Rapids, MI, 1991).

Barth, K., *Church Dogmatics* (Edinburgh, 1956–70), vols I.2 (1970) and IV.1 (1956).

Carruthers, G., *The Uniqueness of Jesus Christ in the Theocentric Model of the Christian Theology of World Religions: An elaboration and evaluation of the position of John Hick* (Lanham, MD, 1990).

Coward, H., *Pluralism: Challenge to world religions* (New York, 1985).

D'Costa, G., *Theology and Religious Pluralism* (Oxford and New York, 1986).

—— *John Hick's Theology of Religions: A critical evaluation* (Lanham, MD, 1987).

—— "The reign of God and a trinitarian ecclesiology: an analysis of soteriocentrism," in P. Mojzes and L. Swidler (eds), *Christian Mission and Interreligious Dialogue* (New York, 1990), pp. 51–61.

—— "One covenant or many covenants? Towards a theology of Christian–Jewish relations," *Journal of Ecumenical Studies*, 27 (1990), pp. 441–52.

—— "Christ, the Trinity, and religious plurality," in G. D'Costa (ed.), *Christian Uniqueness Reconsidered: The myth of a pluralistic theology of religions* (New York, 1990), pp. 16–29.

—— "John Hick and religious pluralism: yet another revolution," in H. Hewitt (ed.), *Problems in the Philosophy of John Hick: Critical studies of the work of John Hick* (Basingstoke, 1991), pp. 102–16.

—— "The end of systematic theology," *Theology*, no. 767 (1992), pp. 324–34.

—— *Christianity and Distorted Visions of World Religions* (Birmingham, 1995).

—— "The impossibility of a pluralist view of religions," *Religious Studies*, 32 (1996), pp. 223–32.

—— "Nostra aetate: Telling God's story in Asia," in M. Lamberigts and L. Kenis (eds), *Vatican II* (Leuven, 1997).

—— "The end of 'theology' and 'religious studies.'" *Theology* (1996, forthcoming).

Di Noia, J. A., *The Diversity of Religions. A Christian perspective* (Washington, DC, 1992).

Fernando, A., *The Christian's Attitude Towards World Religions* (Wheaton, IL, 1987).

Frankfurt Declaration in *Christianity Today* (19 June 1970), pp. 844–6.

Gillis, C., *A Question of Final Belief: John Hick's pluralistic theory of salvation* (London, 1989).

Griffiths, P. (ed.), *Christianity through Non-Christian Eyes* (New York, 1991).

Hauerwas, S., "Some theological reflections on Gutiérrez's use of liberation as a theological concept," *Modern Theology*, 3 (1986), pp. 67–76.

Hick, J., *God and the Universe of Faiths* (London, 1977).

—— *An Interpretation of Religion* (Basingstoke, 1988).

—— "Straightening the record: some responses to criticism," *Modern Theology*, 6 (1990), pp. 187–95.

—— "Responses," in H. Hewitt (ed.), *Problems in the Philosophy of John Hick: Critical studies of the work of John Hick* (Basingstoke, 1991).

Huxley, A., *The Perennial Philosophy* (New York, 1945).

James, W., *The Varieties of Religious Experience* (London, 1960; first published 1902).

Jathanna, O., *The Decisiveness of the Christ Event and the Universality of Christianity in a World of Religious Plurality* (Berne, 1981).

Kaufman, G., "Religious diversity, historical consciousness, and Christian theology," in John Hick and Paul Knitter (eds), *The Myth of Christian Uniqueness* (London, 1987), pp. 3–15.

Knitter, P., *No Other Name? A critical study of Christian attitudes towards the world religions* (London, 1985).

—— "Towards a liberation theology of religions," in J. Hick and P. Knitter (eds), *The Myth of Christian Uniqueness* (London, 1987), pp. 178–200.

—— "Dialogue and liberation," *Drew Gateway*, 58 (1987), pp. 1–53.

Küng, Hans, *On Being a Christian* (London, 1976).

Küng, Hans and Moltmann, J. (eds), *Christianity among the World Religions, Concilium* (Edinburgh, 1986).

Lausanne Statement, *Christian Witness to the Jewish People* (Illinois, 1980).

Lindbeck, G. "Fides ex auditu and the salvation of non-Christians," in V. Vajta (ed.), *The Gospel and the Ambiguity of the Church* (Philadelphia, 1974), pp. 91–123.

—— *The Nature of Doctrine: Religion and theology in a postliberal age* (London, 1984).

Lindsell, H., *A Christian Philosophy of Religion* (Wheaton, IL, 1949).

Loughlin, G., "Prefacing pluralism: John Hick and the mastery of religion," *Modern Theology*, 7 (1990), pp. 29–55.

—— "Squares and circles: John Hick and the doctrine of the incarnation," in H. Hewitt (ed.), *Problems in the Philosophy of John Hick* (London, 1991), pp. 181–205.

Milbank, J., "The end of dialogue," in G. D'Costa (ed.), *Christian Uniqueness Reconsidered* (New York, 1990), pp. 174–91.

Morris, Jan, *Heaven's Command: An imperial progress* (London, 1973).

Newbigin, L., "The basis, purpose and manner of inter-faith dialogue," in R. Rousseau (ed.), *Interreligious Dialogue* (Montrose, 1981), pp. 13–31.

Ogden, S., *Is there only one True Religion or are there Many?* (Dallas, TX, 1992).

O'Neill, M., *Women Speaking, Women Listening: Women in interreligious dialogue* (New York, 1990).

Pannikar, R., *The Trinity and the Religious Experience of Man* (London, 1973).

—— *The Silence of God: The answer of the Buddha* (New York, 1989).

Pawlikowski, J., *What are they Saying about Jewish–Christian Relations?* (New York, 1980).

—— *Christ in the Light of the Christian–Jewish Dialogue* (New York, 1982).

Percy, J. (ed.), *Facing the Unfinished Task: Messages delivered at the Congress on World Mission* (Grand Rapids, MI, 1961).

Pieris, A., *An Asian Theology of Liberation* (New York, 1988).

—— *Love Meets Wisdom* (New York, 1988).

—— Black Flags for the Pope (Robert Crusz citing Pieris). *The Tablet*, 14 January 1988, pp. 36–7.

Race, A., *Christians and Religious Pluralism* (London, 1983).

Rahner, Karl, *Theological Investigations* (London, 1963–80), vols 1, 5, 6, 12, 14, 16–17.

—— *Theology of Death* (London, 1965).

Ruether, Rosemary R., *Faith and Fratricide: The theological roots of anti-semitism* (New York, 1974).

—— "Feminism and Jewish–Christian dialogue," in John Hick and Paul Knitter (eds), *The Myth of Christian Uniqueness* (London, 1987), pp. 137–48.

Ruokanen, M., *The Catholic Doctrine of Non-Christian Religions According to the Second Vatican Council* (Leiden, 1992).

Sanneh, Lamin, "Christian mission and the Western guilt complex," *Christian Century* (8 April 1987), pp. 330–4.

—— *Encountering the West: Christianity and the global cultural process: The African dimension* (London, 1993).

Schwöbel, C., "Particularity, universality, and the religions," in G. D'Costa (ed.), *Christian Uniqueness Reconsidered: The myth of a pluralistic theology of religions* (New York, 1990), pp. 30–48.

Smart, N., and Konstantine, S., *Christian Systematic Theology in a World Context* (Minneapolis, 1991).

Smith, H., *Essays on World Religions*, ed. M. Darrol Bryant (New York, 1992).

Smith, W. C., *Towards a World Theology* (Philadelphia, 1981).

Stanley, B., *The Bible and the Flag* (Leicester, 1990).

Stott, J., "Response to D. L. Edwards," in D. Edwards (ed.), *Evangelical Essentials: A Liberal–Evangelical dialogue* (Illinois, 1988).

Surin, K., "A politics of speech: religious pluralism in the age of the Macdonald's hamburger," in G. D'Costa (ed.), *Christian Uniqueness Reconsidered* (New York, 1990), pp. 192–212.

Swidler, L., *After the Absolute: The dialogical future of religious reflection* (Philadelphia, 1990).

Troeltsch, E., *The Absoluteness of Christianity and the History of Religions* (London, 1972).

van Straelen, H., *The Catholic Encounter with World Religions* (London, 1966).

Wilfred, F., *Sunset in the East? Asian challenges and Christian involvement* (Madras, 1991).

Williams, R., "Balthasar and Rahner," in J. Riches (ed.), *The Analogy of Beauty* (Edinburgh, 1986), pp. 11–34.

—— "Trinity and pluralism," in G. D'Costa (ed.), *Christian Uniqueness Reconsidered: The myth of a pluralistic theology of religions* (New York, 1990), pp. 3–15.

Theology and the Arts and Sciences

"Theology and . . ." has become a rapidly expanding aspect of academic theology. Some of the reasons are obvious: The cultural and intellectual world has become more differentiated into a proliferation of disciplines and forms of cultural expression; and at the same time modern education and communications have enabled more people to be at least partly aware of this diversity of imaginative and intellectual life. How might God be conceived as being in relation to that life? What are its consequences for understanding the created world, humanity, institutions, evil and sin, the future, and so on? How can Christian thought be responsibly engaged in the enrichment, critique, and transformation of that life? How can a faith which has always been in conversation with the arts and sciences respond to such an explosion of vitality? The complexity is immense, and it is clear that generalizations, habits of response, and conclusions that had some validity in the past cannot be assumed to be adequate. For theology there is no intellectually responsible alternative to full engagement with the particularities of each area. Part VIII gives just a sample of what is going on at present in four areas. There is no treatment of some vast and relevant themes, such as psychology, information science and technology, economics, management, social anthropology, medicine, education, criminology, literature, theater, film, and dance. Nor is there more than passing reference to the arts outside Western Christianity. The aim is rather to convey a sense of what it is to engage in genuinely theological ways with a few key areas.

The natural and human sciences have engaged deeply in the realities and vitalities of the natural and social world. They focus energy and knowledge in ways that have transformed modern civilization. Ted Peters surveys eight ways in which science and religion are currently related: scientism, scientific imperialism, ecclesiastical authoritarianism, scientific creationism, two-language theory, hypothetical consonance, ethical overlap, and New Age spirituality. He looks at some of the most thorough engagements with theology and natural science by Gilkey, van Huyssteen, Pannenberg, Torrance, Peacocke, Polkinghorne, and Russell. He makes clear his own preference for hypothetical consonance combined with ethical overlap. This allows for both theology and science being affected by their mutual involvement as the consequences of "seeing cosmos as creation" are explored.

Graham Howes looks at aspects of theology and the visual arts in the West, where they have been in a wide variety of relationships as complementary or competitive ways of viewing the world. His survey concentrates on three key areas of interaction: meaning, representation (including a section on architecture) and belief. He takes Dillenberger's typology as the framework within which theological responses to the visual arts are treated, and comments specifically on Barth, Otto, Tillich, Rahner, Küng, Wolterstorff, Balthasar, and others. He concludes with comments on the new audiovisual nature of much modern culture, the threat of the "acids of modernity" and the continuing creative energies generated through involvement with the distinctive reality of the God of Jesus Christ.

Jeremy Begbie explores theology and music. This is an area to which far less theological attention has been paid than to the visual arts, and he speculates on the reasons for this. He was given editorial encouragement to help set an agenda for this undercultivated field by suggesting what might be possible. The result is a stimulating attempt to answer the question: What would it mean to theologize not simply *about* music but *through* music? He takes two themes, time and improvization, and shows the fruitfulness of thinking them through at once musically and theologically. The resonances extend through creation, sin, freedom, patience, hope, "healed temporality," incarnation, contingency, the Holy Spirit, and physicality. He concludes with a quotation from Micheal O'Siadhail, whose poetry is often done "through music" in ways that harmonize with Begbie's theology.

The social sciences have had profound effects on modern worldviews and self-understanding. Theology has made diverse responses to this, and Richard Roberts offers a social historical perspective before suggesting a typology of five strategies of negotiation employed by representative theologians. In fundamentalism theology repels the social sciences but yet often uses them instrumentally for religious ends. A second strategy is that of Ernst Troeltsch, who reductively absorbs theology in sociology. In Dietrich Bonhoeffer sociology is embraced in the service of theology, providing "an enduring theological prototype of critical and responsible reflexivity in the face of modernity." In Edward Farley theology and the social sciences are mutually merged. John Milbank rejects sociology as promoting a secular metanarrative which sponsors an order of violence and proposes instead the Christian metanarrative of peace in relation to the triune God: Roberts characterizes this as "postmodern quasi-fundamentalism." Roberts finds none of the five completely satisfactory, and discusses the problems and possibilities of theology's use of social science, noting that the main issues are all unresolved. He then offers a tentative agenda for a theology which recognizes that it needs to cope with the complex conjuncture of premodernity, modernity, and postmodernity. Traditions, Enlightenment, and critical reflexivity need to be creatively coordinated. Key theological ideas are those of saints, gift, vocation, the subversive emancipation of the Gospel, discipleship, hope, and faith – but all reconceived through engagement with the social sciences. It is a radical vision of the risky reconfiguration of theology; and Bonhoeffer, despite the "archaism" of his sociology "offers most insight . . . Bonhoeffer embodies the supreme adventure of the life of the mind and heart that is theology rightly understood."

Theology and Natural Science

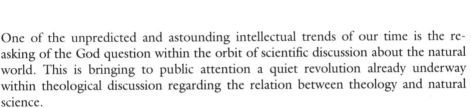

Ted Peters

One of the unpredicted and astounding intellectual trends of our time is the re-asking of the God question within the orbit of scientific discussion about the natural world. This is bringing to public attention a quiet revolution already underway within theological discussion regarding the relation between theology and natural science.

The pre-revolutionary situation can best be described as the assumption that a border should separate what we know about the natural world through science and what religious thinkers say about the transcendent world. Since the Enlightenment we have pretty much assumed that these two represent separate domains of human knowing. We have erected a high wall of separation between church and laboratory. Yet this is increasingly recognized as most unfortunate, because we all are aware that there is but one reality, so sooner or later we will become dissatisfied with consigning our differences to separate ghettos of knowledge. The quiet revolutionaries since the 1960s have been looking for parallels, points of contact, consonance, crossovers, and conflations. The emerging new discipline as yet without a name is studying developments in natural science – especially physics and the life sciences – and is engaging in serious reflection on various loci of Christian doctrine.

Scientists and theologians are engaged in a common search for shared understanding. The search is not merely for a shared discipline. They are not looking merely for rapprochement between separate fields of inquiry. Rather, scientists and theologians are aiming for increased knowledge, for an actual advance in the human understanding of reality. Until a name comes along, we will refer to this new enterprise as "Theology and Natural Science."

In what follows I will briefly outline eight different ways in which science and religion are currently thought to be related. I will note that the dominant view in academic circles is what I label the "two-language theory," but I will go on to point out that the advancing frontier is taking us in the direction of hypothetical consonance. Then I will turn to the central methodological issue, namely the classic concern for the relation between faith and reason. Rather than sharply contrasting what we can know by faith and what we can know by reason, current scholars such as

Nancey Murphy and Wentzel van Huyssteen are maximizing the overlap. Along the way I will briefly introduce the work of some of the more important scholars in the field of theology and natural science: Ian Barbour, Wim Drees, Langdon Gilkey, Philip Hefner, Nancey Murphy, Wolfhart Pannenberg, Arthur Peacocke, John Polkinghorne, Robert John Russell, and Thomas F. Torrance. I will then conclude with my own observations regarding the merits of hypothetical consonance and the value of making a theological interpretation of nature so that we can see the natural cosmos as divine creation.

Survey: Eight Ways of Relating Science and Theology

Not everyone views the relation between science and religion in the same way. If we extend the metaphor of warfare bequeathed us by A. D. White in his notorious book, *A History of the Warfare of Science with Theology*, we can see that relations vary from pitched battle to an uneasy truce.[1]

1   *Scientism*, sometimes called "naturalism" or "secular humanism," seeks war with total victory for one side. Scientism, like other "isms," is an ideology, this one built upon the assumption that science provides all the knowledge that we can know. There is only one reality, the natural, and science has a monopoly on the knowledge we have about nature.[2] Religion, which claims to purvey knowledge about things supernatural, provides only pseudo-knowledge – that is, false impressions about nonexistent fictions.

Some decades ago, the British philosopher and atheist Bertrand Russell told a BBC audience that "what science cannot tell us, mankind cannot know." At mid-century the astronomer Fred Hoyle argued that the Jewish and Christian religions have become outdated by modern science. He explained religious behavior as escapist, as pursued by people who seek illusory security from the mysteries of the universe.[3]

More recently, physicists Stephen Hawking and Carl Sagan have teamed up to assert that the cosmos is all there is or was or ever will be, and to assert that there was no absolute beginning to the singularity that exploded in the Big Bang. Why no beginning? Had there been an absolute beginning, then time would have an edge; and beyond this edge we could dimly glimpse a transcendent reality such as a creator God. But this is intolerable to scientism. So, by describing the cosmos as temporally self-contained, Sagan could write confidently in the introduction to Hawking's *A Brief History of Time* about "the absence of God." God must be absent, because there is "nothing for a Creator to do."[4] In the warfare between science and theology, scientism demands elimination of the enemy.

2   *Scientific imperialism* is scientism in a slightly different form. Rather than eliminating the enemy, scientific imperialism seeks to conquer the territory formally possessed by theology and claim it as its own. Whereas scientism is atheistic, scientific imperialism affirms the existence of something divine but claims knowledge of the divine comes from scientific research rather than religious revelation. "Science has actually advanced to the point where what were formerly religious questions can be seriously tackled . . . [by] the new physics," writes Paul Davies.[5] The physicist Frank

Tipler, claiming that quantum theory combined with the Big Bang and thermo-dynamics can provide a better explanation than Christianity for the future resurrection of the dead, declares that theology should become a branch of physics.[6]

3 *Ecclesiastical authoritarianism* is the defensive tactic followed by some in the Roman Catholic tradition who perceive science and scientism as a threat. Presuming a two-step route to truth in which natural reason is followed by divine revelation, theological dogma is here ceded authority over science on the grounds that it is founded on God's revelation. In 1864 Pope Pius IX promulgated *The Syllabus of Errors*, wherein item 57 stated it to be an error to think that science and philosophy could withdraw from ecclesiastical authority. A century later the Second Vatican Council dropped the defenses by declaring the natural sciences to be free from ecclesiastical authority and called them "autonomous" disciplines.[7] Pope John Paul II, who has a serious interest in fostering dialogue between theology and the natural sciences, is negotiating a new peace between faith and reason.[8]

4 *Scientific creationism*, sometimes called "creation science," is not a Protestant version of church authoritarianism, even though it is frequently mistaken as such. The grandparents of today's scientific creationists were fundamentalists, to be sure, and fundamentalism appealed to biblical authority in a fashion parallel to the Roman Catholic appeal to church authority. Yet there is a marked difference between fun-damentalist authoritarianism and contemporary creation science. Today's creation scientists are willing to argue their case in the arena of science, not biblical authority. They assume that biblical truth and scientific truth belong to the same domain. When there is a conflict between a scientific assertion and a religious assertion, then we allegedly have a conflict in scientific theories. The creationists argue that the book of Genesis is itself a theory which tells us how the world was physically created: God fixed the distinct kinds (species) of organisms at the point of original creation. They did not evolve. Geological and biological facts attest to biblical truth, they argue.

With regard to theological commitments, scientific creationists typically affirm (1) the creation of the world out of nothing; (2) the insufficiency of mutation and nat-ural selection to explain the process of evolution; (3) the stability of existing species and the impossibility of one species evolving out of another; (4) separate ancestry for apes and humans; (5) catastrophism to explain certain geological formations, e.g., the flood explains why sea fossils appear on mountains; and (6) the relatively recent formation of the earth about six to ten thousand years ago.[9]

Establishment scientists typically try to gain quick victory over creationists by dis-missing them. Stephen Jay Gould, the colorful Harvard paleontologist, says the very term "scientific creationism" is meaningless and self-contradictory.[10] Although the battle between scientific creationists and established scientists appears to be all-out war, this is not the case. The creationists, many of whom are themselves practicing scientists, see themselves as soldiers within the science army.[11]

5 *The two-language theory* might appear to be the way to establish a truce with an enduring peace. This is because it respects the sovereign territory of both science and theology and because it is advocated by highly respected persons in both fields. Albert Einstein, for example, distinguished between the language of fact and the lan-guage of value. "Science can only ascertain what *is*, but not what *should be*," he once told an audience at Princeton, "religion, on the other hand, deals only with evaluations

of human thought and action." Note the use of "only" here. Each language is *restricted* to its respective domain.

The neo-orthodox theologian Langdon Gilkey has long argued for the two-language approach. Science, he says, deals only with objective or public knowing of *proximate* origins, whereas religion and its theological articulation deals with existential or personal knowing of *ultimate* origins. Science asks "*how?*" while religion asks "*why?*"[12] What Gilkey wants, of course, is for one person to be a citizen in two lands – that is, to be able to embrace both Christian faith and scientific method without conflict.[13] To speak both languages is to be bilingual, and bilingual intellectuals can work with one another in peace.

The modern two-language theory of the relation between science and theology ought not to be confused with a premodern concept of the two books. In medieval times, revelation regarding God could be read from two books, the *book of nature* and the *book of scripture*. Both science and theology could speak of things divine. Both natural revelation and special revelation pointed us in one direction: toward God. The two-language theory, in contrast, points us in two different directions: either toward God or toward the world.

A problem I have with the two-language theory is that it gains peace through separation, by establishing a demilitarized zone that prevents communication. In the event that a scientist might desire to speak about divine matters or a theologian might desire to speak about the actual world created by God, the two would have to speak past one another on the assumption that shared understanding is impossible. Why begin with such an assumption? The method of hypothetical consonance makes just the opposite assumption, namely that there is but one reality and sooner or later scientists and theologians should be able to find some areas of shared understanding.

6   *Hypothetical consonance* is the name I give to the frontier that seems to be emerging beyond the two-language policy. The term "consonance," coming from the work of Ernan McMullin,[14] indicates that we are looking for those areas where there is a correspondence between what can be said scientifically about the natural world and what the theologian understands to be God's creation. "Consonance" in the strong sense means accord, harmony. Accord or harmony might be a treasure we hope to find, but we have not found it yet. Where we find ourselves now is working with consonance in a weak sense – that is, by identifying common domains of question-asking. The advances in physics, especially thermodynamics and quantum theory in relation to Big Bang cosmology, have in their own way raised questions about transcendent reality. The God question can be honestly asked from within scientific reasoning. Theologians and scientists now share a common subject matter, and the idea of hypothetical consonance encourages further cooperation.

It also asks theologians to view their discipline somewhat differently. Rather than beginning from a rigid position of inviolable truth, the term "hypothetical" asks theologians to subject their own assertions to further investigation and possible confirmation or disconfirmation. An openness to learning something new on the part of theologians and scientists alike is essential for hypothetical consonance to move us forward. Most of the theologians we will look at later in this chapter pursue some form of hypothetical consonance.

7   *Ethical overlap* refers to the recognized need on the part of theologians to speak to the questions of human meaning created by our industrial and technological society and, even more urgently, to the ethical challenges posed by the environmental crisis and the need to plan for the long-range future of the planet. The ecological challenge arises from the crisscrossing forces of population growth, increased industrial and agricultural production that depletes nonrenewable natural resources while polluting air and soil and water, the widening split between the haves and the have-nots around the world, and the loss of a sense of responsibility for the welfare of future generations. Modern technology is largely responsible for this ecological crisis, and theologians along with secular moralists are struggling to gain ethical control over technological and economic forces that, if left to themselves, will drive us toward destruction.

An advocate of hypothetical consonance, I belong also to the ethical overlap camp and I believe that, at root, the ecological crisis poses a spiritual issue, namely the crying need of world civilization for an ethical vision. An ethical vision – a vision of a just and sustainable society that lives in harmony with its environment and at peace with itself – is essential for future planning and motivating the peoples of the world to fruitful action. Ecological thinking is future thinking. Its logic takes the following form: *understanding–decision–control*. Prescinding from the scientific model, we implicitly assume that to solve the ecocrisis we need to understand the forces of destruction; then we need to make the decisions and take the actions that will put us in control of our future and establish a human economy that is in harmony with earth's natural ecology.

In order to bring theological resources to bear on the ecological challenge, most theologians have tried to mine the doctrine of creation for its wealth of ethical resources. It is my judgment that we need more than creation; we also need to appeal to eschatological redemption – that is, new creation. God's redeeming work is equally important when we begin with a creation that has somehow gone awry.

I believe the promise of eschatological renewal can provide a sense of direction, a vision of the coming just and sustainable society, and a motivating power that speaks relevantly to the understanding–decision–control formula. We need to combine creation with new creation. Theologians can make a genuine contribution to the public discussion if, on the basis of eschatological resources, we can project a vision of the coming new world order – that is, announce the promised kingdom of God and work from that vision backward to our present circumstance. This vision should picture our world in terms of (a) a single, worldwide planetary society; (b) united in devotion to the will of God; (c) sustainable within the biological carrying capacity of the planet and harmonized with the principles of the ecosphere; (d) organized politically so as to preserve the just rights and voluntary contributions of all individuals; (e) organized economically so as to guarantee the basic survival needs of each person; (f) organized socially so that dignity and freedom are respected and protected in every quarter; and (g) dedicated to advancing the quality of life in behalf of future generations.[15]

8   *New Age spirituality* is the next and last in our list of parties interested in the science–religion struggle. The key to New Age thinking is holism – that is, the attempt to overcome modern dualisms such as the split between science and spirit,

ideas and feelings, male and female, rich and poor, humanity and nature. New Age artillery is loaded with three explosive sets of ideas: (1) discoveries in twentieth-century physics, especially quantum theory; (2) acknowledgement of the important role played by imagination in human knowing; and (3) a recognition of the ethical exigency of preserving our planet from ecological destruction.

Fritjof Capra and David Bohm, who combine Hindu mysticism with physical theory, are among the favorite New Age physicists. Bohm, for example, argues that the explicate order of things that we accept as the natural world and that is studied in laboratories is not the fundamental reality; there is under and behind it an implicate order, a realm of undivided wholeness. This wholeness, like a hologram, is fully present in each of the explicate parts. Reality, according to Bohm, is ultimately "undivided wholeness in flowing movement."[16] When we focus on either objective knowing or subjective feeling we temporarily forget the unity that binds them. New Age spirituality seeks to cultivate awareness of this underlying and continually changing unity.

By adding evolutionary theory to physics and especially to Big Bang cosmology, New Age theorists find themselves constructing a grand story – a myth – regarding the history and future of the cosmos of which we human beings are an integral and conscious part. On the basis of this grand myth, New Age ethics tries to proffer a vision of the future that will guide and motivate action appropriate to solving the ecological problem. Science here provides the background not only for ethical overlap but also for a fundamental religious revelation. Brian Swimme and Thomas Berry put it this way: "Our new sense of the universe is itself a type of revelatory experience. Presently we are moving beyond any religious expression so far known to the human into a meta-religious age, that seems to be a new comprehensive context for all religions . . . The natural world itself is the primary economic reality, the primary educator, the primary governance, the primary technologist, the primary healer, the primary presence of the sacred, the primary moral value."[17]

Now, I happen to find the ethical vision of New Age inspiring. But I cannot in good conscience endorse its metareligious naturalism. I find it contrived and uncompelling. Nearly the same ecological ethic with an even stronger emphasis on social justice can be derived from Christian eschatology.

Returning to the more theoretical tie between science and theology, I earlier recommended hypothetical consonance as the most viable option for the near future. Hypothetical consonance takes us beyond the limits of the two-language theory without initially violating the integrity of either natural science or Christian theology. Where the leading scholars find themselves, in my interpretation, is with one foot in the two-language theory and the other stretched for a stride to go beyond. In what follows we will look first at the methodological rapprochement between science and theology regarding epistemology; and then we will look briefly at some of the scholars in England and America who are taking this new bold step.

Faith and Reason in Science and Theology

The key development among those scholars who either strive for consonance or are at least in partial sympathy with consonance is the attempt to demonstrate overlap between scientific and theological reasoning. Two insights guide the discussion. First, scientific reasoning depends in part on a faith component, on foundational yet unprovable assumptions. Second, theological reasoning should be recast so as to take on a hypothetical character that is subject to testing. What is a matter of some dispute, however, is whether or not theological assertions refer – that is, is theology a form of realism? Do theological statements merely give expression to the faith of a religious community or do they refer to a reality beyond themselves, such as God? Theologians are asking to what extent *critical realism* in the philosophy of science should be incorporated into theological methodology.

Langdon Gilkey has long argued the point that science, every bit as much as theology, rests upon faith. Science must appeal to some foundational assumptions regarding the nature of reality and our apprehension of it, assumptions which themselves cannot be proved within the scope of scientific reasoning. In its own disguised fashion, science is religious, mythical. "The activity of knowing," he writes, "points beyond itself to a ground of ultimacy which its own forms of discourse cannot usefully thematize, and for which religious symbolization is alone adequate."[18] Scientific reasoning depends upon the deeply held conviction – the passion of the scientist – that the world is rational and knowable and that truth is worth pursuing. "This is not 'faith' in the strictly religious and certainly not in the Christian sense," he observes, "But it is a *commitment* in the sense that it is a personal act of acceptance and affirmation of an ultimate in one's life."[19]

On the scientific side, Paul Davies acknowledges the faith dimension to science in terms of assumptions regarding rationality. Presumed here is a gnostic style connection between the rational structure of the universe and the corresponding spark of rationality in the human mind. That human reasoning is generally reliable constitutes his "optimistic view."[20] Yet he acknowledges that the pursuit of scientific knowledge will not eliminate all mystery, because every chain of reasoning will eventually hit its limit and force on us the metascientific question of transcendence. "Sooner or later we all have to accept something as given," he writes, "whether it is God, or logic, or a set of laws, or some other foundation of existence. Thus 'ultimate' questions will always lie beyond the scope of empirical science."[21]

On the issue of faith at the level of assumption, theologians and scientists, at least philosophers of science, agree. This raises a second related issue: Does theology, like science, seek to explain? If so, then theology cannot restrict itself to individual or even communal subjectivity or to authoritarian methods of justification that isolate it from common human reasoning. This is what Philip Clayton argues: "theology cannot avoid an appeal to broader canons of rational argumentation and explanatory adequacy."[22] Clayton proceeds to argue for inter-subjective criticizability and to view theology as engaged in transcommunal explanation.

If theology seeks to explain, does it also refer? This is the question of critical realism to which we now turn.

Critical Realism and Theological Reference

Wentzel van Huyssteen, professor in the first chair in the United States designated for Theology and Natural Science at Princeton, believes that theological statements about God refer to God. He advocates "critical-theological realism" and a method for justifying theories in systematic theology that parallels what we find in natural science. Justification occurs through progressive illumination offered by a theological theory, not as traditionally done by appeal to ecclesiastical or some other undisputable authority. Van Huyssteen recognizes the relativistic and contextual and metaphorical dimensions of human speech that flood all discourse, theological and scientific alike. Progress toward truth requires constructive thought, the building up of metaphors and models so as to emit growing insight.[23] And, most significantly, theological assertions refer. They refer to God. They are realistic. "Theology," he writes, "given both the ultimate religious commitment of the theologian and the metaphoric nature of our religious language, is scientifically committed to a realist point of view . . . Our theological theories do indeed refer to a Reality beyond and greater than ours."[24]

On the one hand, critical realism should be contrasted with nonliteralist methods such as positivism and instrumentalism, because it recognizes that theories represent the real world. On the other hand, critical realism should be contrasted also with "naive realism," which invokes the correspondence theory of truth to presume a literal correspondence between one's mental picture and the object to which this picture refers. Critical realism, in contrast, is nonliteral while still referential. The indirectness comes from the conscious use of metaphors, models, and theories. Ian Barbour notes that "Models and theories are abstract symbol systems, which inadequately and selectively represent particular aspects of the world for specific purposes. This view preserves the scientist's realistic intent while recognizing that models and theories are imaginative human constructs. Models, on this reading, are to be taken seriously but not literally."[25] Urging the adoption of critical realism by theologians, Arthur Peacocke maintains that "Critical realism in theology would maintain that theological concepts and models should be regarded as partial and inadequate, but necessary and, indeed, the only ways of referring to the reality that is named as 'God' and to God's relation with humanity."[26]

Not all theological voices chime in with harmony here. Nancey C. Murphy recommends that theologians avoid critical realism on the grounds that it remains modern just when we need to move toward postmodern reasoning. Critical realism remains caught in three restrictive elements of modern minds: (1) epistemological foundationalism which attempts to provide an indubitable ground for believing; (2) representational thinking with its correspondence theory of truth; and (3) excessive individualism and inadequate attention to the community. The postmodern elements she lifts up for the theological agenda are (1) a non-foundationalist epistemological holism and (2) meaning as use in language philosophy.[27] What counts for Murphy is the progressive nature of a research program; and this is a sufficient criterion for evaluating theological research regardless of its referentiality. One of Murphy's significant contributions to the field has been to adapt Imre Lakatos's notion of a progressive research program for theological methodology.[28]

Theological Assertions as Hypotheses

Would the tasks of explanation and reference make theology itself scientific? Yes, answers the Munich systematic theologian Wolfhart Pannenberg. Describing theology as the science of God, he contends that each theological assertion has the logical structure of a hypothesis. This makes it subject to verification against the relevant state of affairs it seeks to explain. But how can we confirm or disconfirm an assertion about God? A theologian cannot follow a method of direct verification because the existence of its object, God, is itself in dispute and because God – defined by Pannenberg as the all-determining reality – is not a reproducible finite entity. An indirect method of verification is available, however. Building in part on Karl Popper's procedures for critical verification and falsification, Pannenberg submits that we can test assertions by their implications. Assertions about a divine life and divine actions can be tested by their implications for understanding the whole of finite reality, a wholeness which is implicitly anticipated in the ordinary experience of meaning.

Because of the temporal process in which the finite world is ever changing, the whole, which is an essential framework for any item of experience to have a deterministic meaning, does not exist yet as a totality. If there is a whole at all, then it must be future, so it can only be imagined, anticipated. As anticipation, the very positing of a temporal whole involves an element of hypothesis. Even the reality of God fits into this class. The reality of God is present to us now only in subjective anticipation of the totality of finite reality, in a conceptual model of the whole of meaning that we presuppose in all particular experience. Christians think of the whole temporally and eschatologically. The theological idea of the eschatological Kingdom of God that arises from our historic religious tradition is subject to future confirmation or refutation by what happens. The *direct confirmation* of this eschatological hypothesis is dependent upon the actual coming of that eschatological wholeness. In the meantime, while we await the eschatological fulfillment, our faith in the future takes the form of a hypothesis that can gain *indirect confirmation* by the increased intelligibility it offers to our understanding of our experience of finite reality. It is this openness to confirmation that makes theological assertions hypothetical and hence scientific.

"Science and Religion" vs "Science and Theology"

Whereas Pannenberg believes theology gains its scientific status from its hypothetical structure, Thomas Forsyth Torrance dubs theology scientific because it is objective. Torrance, Professor of Christian Dogmatics at the University of Edinburgh from 1952 to 1979 and 1978 winner of the Templeton Prize, has extended the Barthian heritage into the theology–science interaction.

The first and salient legacy of the Torrance approach is a key distinction: "science and religion" vs "science and theology." These two are not the same. Religion has to do with human consciousness and human behavior. Theology has to do with God. "Whenever religion is substituted in the place of God, the fact that in religion we are concerned with the behaviour of *religious people*, sooner or later means the substitution of humanity in the place of religion."[29] Torrance clearly prefers to take up the distinctively theological task, defining theology as a science. He describes theology (or a philosophy of theology) as a "meta-science of our direct cognitive relation with God. Science and meta-science are required not because God is a problem but because *we* are . . . It is because *our* relations with God have become problematic that we must have a scientific theology."[30] One can see clearly here the influence of Karl Barth in getting beyond religious consciousness as the object of theology and allowing our consciousness to be shaped by the true object of theology, God. "Scientific theology is active engagement in that cognitive relation to God in obedience to the demands of His reality and self-giving."[31]

Torrance stresses that authentic inquiry, both scientific inquiry and theological inquiry, attend to what is, to what is actual, to what is real; and this means that we should guard against superimposing upon reality an a priori or idealistic scheme. To this end we allow our inquiry to be guided by its object, by the reality of the object under study. The transition from the Newtonian worldview to the Einstein revolution could take place only when science was authentic, only when it let nature tell us what nature is like.

In stressing this point, Torrance elegantly moves natural theology from its previous position of prolegomena into positive theology proper. This move parallels Einstein's treatment of geometry. The Euclidian geometry inherited with Newtonian physics provided a context for inquiry that presupposed absolute mathematical space and time with bodies in motion. For Einstein, this constituted an idealized presupposition detached from nature as he was studying it. Einstein's revolution in the theory of relativity consisted of placing geometry into the material content of physics. Rather than treating geometry as an idealized framework, Einstein brought it into the midst of physics, where it became a natural science indissolubly united to physics.

Torrance wants to learn from Einstein's example. Torrance puts natural theology where Einstein had put geometry. "So it is with natural theology: brought within the embrace of positive theology and developed as a complex of rational structures arising in our actual knowledge of God it becomes 'natural' in a new way, natural to its proper object, God in self-revealing interaction with us in space and time. Natural theology then constitutes the epistemological geometry, as it were, within the fabric of revealed theology."[32] By making this post-Barthian move, Torrance denies natural theology any independent status while making it serve as an instrument for unfolding and expressing the knowledge content of Christian theology.

Authentic theology, then, attends to its object, God. It listens to what the Word of God tells us. This form of objectivity – listening to the object of inquiry – makes science scientific and theology scientific.

> Theology is the unique science devoted to knowledge of God, differing from other sciences by the uniqueness of its object [God] which can be apprehended only on its own terms and from within the actual situation it has created in our existence in making itself known . . . Yet as a *science* theology is only a human endeavour in quest of the truth, in which we seek to apprehend God as far as we may, to understand what we apprehend, and to speak clearly and carefully about what we understand. It takes place only within the environment of the special sciences and only within the bounds of human learning and reasoning where critical judgment and rigorous testing are required, but where in faithfulness to its ultimate term of reference beyond itself to God it cannot attempt to justify itself on the grounds occupied by the other sciences or within their frames of interpretation.[33]

Torrance recognizes the finite and perspectival limits of human knowing as it operates in theology and the other sciences; and it is just this perspectival limit that mandates that authentic inquiry attend to its object and learn from its object.

Departing from Barth, for whom theology could be methodologically isolated from other disciplines, Torrance argues that theology should engage the natural sciences in conversation. Torrance affirms *creatio ex nihilo*, noting that the divine transcendence implied here renders the created world contingent. The contingency of the world requires that we study the world directly to unlock its secrets. No idealistic shortcuts or revelations about God can substitute for empirical research. This functions as a sort of theological blessing upon the scientific enterprise.

Torrance wants the theologian to broaden the scope of attention, to get beyond anthropology to include nature around and in us. Theology has been suffering from tunnel vision, he complains, the tunnel vision wherein we have limited theology to the relationship between God and the human race. Theology cannot be restricted to the relationship of God to humanity. "Theology has to do with the unlimited reality of God in his relations with the universe of all time and space."[34] Hence, the sciences broaden our knowledge of God's creation and provide an understanding of the arena within which incarnation and resurrection take place.

This enlargement of the scope of theology to include all space and time provides the framework for specifying just how God can be an object of inquiry and how knowledge of God can be objective. Torrance is a trinitarian theologian, and the finite objectivity of God incarnate grounds the objectivity of theology.[35]

> The framework of objective meaning which concerns the theologian here is bound up with the incarnation of the Son of God to be one with us in our physical human existence within the world of space and time in such a way that through his vicarious life and passion he might redeem human being and creatively reground it in the very life of God himself, and therefore it is also bound up with the resurrection of Jesus Christ in body, or the physical reality of his human existence among us, for it is in the resurrection that God's incarnate and redeeming purpose for us is brought to its triumphant fulfillment.[36]

One of the difficulties any Barthian theologian confronts when engaging in dialogue with the natural sciences is the apparent self-referentiality of the theological circle. The existence of the object of theological inquiry, God, is just what is in dispute in the modern world. To presuppose its truth and then contend that this produces knowledge seems to beg the question. Torrance is aware of the difficulty. He defends the method with a *tu quoque* argument, noting that all theories are circular, striving to establish themselves through coherence because they cannot be derived or justified on any grounds other than what they themselves constitute. In this regard, theology is no worse off than any other discipline.[37]

Science and Systematic Theology

For good or ill, it seems that within the subfields of theology one group, the systematic theologians, have taken the lead in developing a working relationship with the natural sciences. Biblical studies have long employed the investigative techniques of archaeology, to be sure; and historical theology and ethics are coming to rely more and more on methods developed by the social sciences. But it has been the systematic theologians who have examined carefully scientific methods, adopted some into theological methodology, and then proceeded in certain cases to incorporate knowledge gained from natural science into the formulation of doctrinal beliefs.

Significant here is the creative work of Arthur Peacocke. A biochemist turned theologian, Peacocke was Dean of Chapel at Clare College at Cambridge, now directs the Ian Ramsey Centre at Oxford, and is Warden Emeritus of the Society of Ordained Scientists. "Theology needs to be consonant and coherent with, though far from being derived from, scientific perspectives on the world," he asserts.[38] The task for theology is clear: to rethink religious conceptualizations in light of the perspective on the world afforded by the sciences.

This rethinking leads to questions about God. God is mysterious, affirms Peacocke. Natural theology paints a picture of an ineffable and transcendent God beyond human comprehension. The special revelation of God experienced in the person of Jesus Christ only enhances the mystery of the divine. Yet mystery is by no means confined to theology. Twentieth-century science is characterized by a new appreciation of the mystery of existence. Quantum physics, with such things as indeterminacy and vacuum fluctuations, has increased our knowledge while at the same time it has humbled our previous *hubris* for assuming causal explanations would be right around the corner. The foundation of physical reality is more elusive than once thought. "So the mystery-of-existence question becomes even more pressing in the light of the cosmic panorama disclosed by the natural sciences."[39] Also mysterious is human personhood, arising as it does from the biological sphere to that of consciousness and then becoming itself a top-down cause. Peacocke believes that "this recognition of an ultimate ineffability in the nature of the divine parallels that of our ultimate inability to say what even things and persons are in themselves."[40]

What is happening is that Peacocke's rethinking of theological conceptions in light of natural science is leading him to assert certain things about God: Beyond the eternity of the divine *being* God is engaged in temporal *becoming*; beyond *creatio ex nihilo* God is engaged in *creatio continua*; God creates and dynamically "lets be"; God is the ultimate source and ground of both necessity and chance; God has a self-limited omnipotence and omniscience, thereby permitting necessity and chance in the history of nature; the divine act of self-limitation for the good of the creation warrants our saying that *God is love*. These reconceptualizations lead finally to panentheism and theopaschism: "God suffers in, with and under the creative processes of the world."[41]

Peacocke is a hybrid – that is, he is trained in both science and theology. Another hybrid is mathematician-physicist turned theologian John Polkinghorne, now President of Queen's College, Cambridge. Polkinghorne pursues systematic theology with what he calls a "bottom-up" method. The bases with which he begins are scientific data regarding the natural world, historical data regarding the biography of Jesus, the church's threefold encounter with the economic Trinity, and such. The *up* with which he concludes is a high degree of confidence regarding the fundamental commitments of the Christian faith, commitments that are completely compatible with the truths pursued in the field of science.[42]

Steadfast in affirming that epistemology models ontology, Polkinghorne begins methodologically with faith and reason. Faith is not merely a polite expression for unsubstantiated assertion, not an excuse for believing in God as an irrational act. Rather, faith and reason belong together. Both reflect the quest for truth. Truth-seeking is something shared by scientists and theologians alike. "Although faith goes beyond what is logically demonstrable," he writes, "yet it is capable of rational motivation. Christians do not have to close their minds, nor are they faced with the dilemma of having to choose between ancient faith and modern knowledge. They can hold both together."[43]

Polkinghorne is committed to *consonance* – that is, theological reflection on creation must be consonant with what science says about Big Bang and evolution. This by no means requires that theological assertions be reducible to scientific assertions. The scientific worldview is itself subject to interrogation and expansion, and this is pursued through metaphysics.

None of us can do without metaphysics, he observes, and then admonishes us to do metaphysics deliberately. Rejecting Cartesian dualism in favor of what he calls "dual-aspect monism,"[44] Polkinghorne opens biology to the existence of supra-physical consciousness or spirit; and he opens physics to a reality that transcends the world of the Big Bang and the evolution of conscious life. At this point extrapolation and speculation from a scientific basis cease. Polkinghorne then turns to orthodox Christian commitments – such as a theistic understanding of God and *creatio ex nihilo* – and simply defends them against competing positions. For example, he distinguishes his position from the deism implied in the proposals of Stephen Hawking and other physicists regarding the onset of the Big Bang with its possible edge of time at the beginning, the implication of which is that creation becomes limited to a single act at the beginning. From then on God is presumed to let nature take its evolutionary course. But Polkinghorne is a theist who believes in an active God, so he combines *creatio ex nihilo* with *creatio continua* to emphasize God's continuing involvement in nature. Polkinghorne's active God is omnipotent, but is by no means a tyrant. God's power has been withheld to make room for freedom within nature. God still acts in nature without obviating this freedom. "One is trying to steer a path between the unrelaxing grip of a Cosmic Tyrant and the impotence or indifference of a Deistic Spectator."[45]

Then, looking in the other direction, Polkinghorne distinguishes his position from the panentheism of process theology, because the latter fails to provide sufficient grounds for hope. The Whiteheadian God can very well share our suffering, but there is no eschatological guarantee here that evil will be overcome. Being remembered by the consequent nature of God is unsatisfying to Polkinghorne. "I do not want to be just a fly in the amber of divine remembrance," he writes; "I look forward to a destiny and a continuing life beyond death. To put it bluntly, the God of process theology does not seem to be the God who raised Jesus from the dead."[46]

I wonder if this defense of theism, as clear and forceful as it is, actually needs the discussion of science. It seems to me that this classic debate between deists, theists, and panentheists is only occasioned by issues rising out of Big Bang physics. The physics itself does not actually influence the direction, let alone determine the destination of the debate as we find it in Polkinghorne.

Polkinghorne rightly defines his position sharply against panentheistic colleagues in the field such as Arthur Peacocke and Ian Barbour. The strength of Peacocke and Barbour is perhaps that they wrestle more thoroughly with the actual scientific ideas and seek a fuller integration with theological ideas. The strength of Polkinghorne is his confidence that the Christian faith, when subjected to the same rational scrutiny that science exacts upon its data and theories, exhibits an honest pursuit of truth accompanied by a confidence in its rational motivation.

On the other side of the Atlantic we find Robert John Russell, a hybrid physicist and systematic theologian directing the program he founded in 1981: the Center for Theology and the Natural Sciences at the Graduate Theological Union in Berkeley. Methodologically, Russell belongs to the consonance school but in his own way he emphasizes the dialectic between consonance and dissonance. For an example of dissonance, Russell is clear that scientific prognostications regarding the future of the cosmos do not square with Christian eschatology. A projected heat death due to entropy is not consonant with the promise of resurrection and new creation. Here is dissonance that needs to be acknowledged. Inspired by the work of his former student, Nancey Murphy, Russell seeks to embed the consonance–dissonance dialectic more tightly into a theological method that sees itself as a progressive research program.

In careful conversation with physical cosmologists and with theologians such as Ian Barbour and Wim Drees, Russell has pressed for consonance on understandings of the origin of the universe found in Big Bang cosmology and the Christian concept of creation. The orienting question is this: Is the Christian doctrine of *creatio ex nihilo* consonant with the Big Bang? Many answers have been given, all unsatisfying to Russell. The two-language answer is no, because this school believes in principle that no scientific picture of the universe's origin has any conceptual relevance for theology. It precludes looking for consonance at the outset. An alternative answer, a semi-literalist answer, would be: Yes, they are consonant because the scientific discovery of a beginning to the universe corroborates the Christian view that the creation had a beginning boundary, before which there was nothing. Two things make this unsatisfying. First, current conversations regarding quantum theory make it premature to say that the scientific consensus is that the universe – at least the original singularity – had an absolute beginning. Second, the force of the *creatio ex nihilo* idea is that the world is ontologically dependent upon God, and this would be the case even if there were no beginning boundary.

Russell feels the need to find his own answer. Following the Lakatos–Murphy distinction between the inner core commitment and the outer belt of auxiliary hypotheses in a research program, he posits the following as core: *Creatio ex nihilo* means ontological dependence. Then he adumbrates three auxiliary hypotheses: (1) ontological dependence entails finitude; (2) finitude includes temporal finitude; and (3) temporal finitude entails past finitude – that is, going backwards in finite time must take us to a beginning, a $t = 0$ point. This fits with what we know from Big Bang cosmology in which the data of astrophysics, the theory of general relativity, and other factors point us to an initial singularity, $t = 0$. That this singularity may have a quantum life of its own does not stop Russell from tendering a modest conclusion: The empirical origination described by t = 0 in Big Bang cosmology tends to confirm what is entailed in this theory's core, namely *creatio ex nihilo* means ontological dependence. This is not a proof, but it is a partial confirmation.

Russell's contribution to the internal theological debate is the distinction he draws between finitude and boundedness. Traditionally theologians have identified the two. But they are not identical. Ontological dependence upon God requires that the world be finite but not necessarily bounded. The initial singularity may have had a quantum life of its own and hence no temporal boundaries; yet we can still say that the world has a beginning and that it is finite in time. Big Bang cosmology, even in its quantum form, becomes a character witness, even if not an eyewitness, to the creation of the world.

Like Russell, Philip Hefner picks up on the Lakatos–Murphy methodology with its core–auxiliary distinction. He puts God in the hard core, "that to which all terrestrial and cosmic data are related."[47] He adds seven auxiliary hypotheses which I will not enumerate here. He believes that the test of theology is its explanatory adequacy, that it is subject to falsification by experience, and that its relative success should be measured by its fruitfulness. "What is at stake in the falsification of theological theories is not whether they can prove the existence of God," he writes, "but rather whether, with the help of auxiliary hypotheses, they lead to interpretations of the world and of our experience in the world that are empirically credible and fruitful – that is, productive of new insights and research."[48]

Hefner teaches systematic theology at the Lutheran School of Theology at Chicago, edits the journal *Zygon*, and directs the Chicago Center for Science and Religion. His career work in the field has been devoted less to physical cosmology and more to rapprochement between theology and the life sciences, especially evolutionary theory. He has sought to develop an anthropology and even a christology in what he calls a biocultural evolutionary scheme. His is a grand vision, and at the focal center of this vision is the concept of the human being as the *created co-creator*. A basic element embedded within the core rather than located in an outer auxiliary hypothesis, the concept of the created co-creator is Hefner's central contribution to the theology and natural science enterprise. He writes, "Human beings are God's created co-creators whose purpose is to be the agency, acting in freedom, to birth the future that is most wholesome for the nature that has birthed us – the nature that is not only our own genetic heritage, but also the entire human community and the evolutionary and ecological reality in which and to which we belong. Exercising this agency is said to be God's will for humans."[49]

Hefner has been criticized for advocating human *hubris*, for placing humanity on a level with the divine and overestimating the human potential for creativity. Such a criticism might apply to New Age thought, but not to Hefner. Hefner is clear that we human beings are dependent creatures, brought here by God the creator even if God employed evolution to create us. This is what he means by *created* co-creator. Nevertheless, when explicating the biblical concept of the *imago dei*, Hefner wants to include creativity in the divine image and exhort us ethically to take responsibility for creating a future that is more human, more just, and more loving.

Conclusion: Seeing Cosmos as Creation

We in the Christian tradition are used to speaking glibly of the natural world as God's creation. On what basis do we do this? Looking at nature through scientific glasses does not reveal that it is the product of a divine hand or the object of divine care. Since the Enlightenment we have been assuming that no footprints of the divine can be discerned in the sands of the natural world. Western science assumes that if we study natural processes with the intention of learning the laws by which nature operates, what we will end up with is just a handful of natural laws. Nature, when viewed through microscopes and telescopes, does not seem to disclose her ultimate foundation or even her existential meaning. What natural revelation reveals is simply nature, not God. If we want to know more, we have to ask more questions. And we have to go beyond our natural relationship with nature to find the answers.

Christian theologians, seeing the limits to natural revelation in a modern world replete with science and scientism, find they need to go to the historical events of the death and resurrection of Jesus Christ, the events that stand at the heart and center of God's special revelation. Good Friday and Easter do not reveal that God is the world's creator for the first time, of course. But these events do confirm what had already been suspected in ancient Israel, namely that the creation of the world was the necessary first act in God's continuing drama of salvation. The world in which we live is not merely a conglomeration of actualized natural laws. The cosmos exists because it plays a part in the divine scenario of redemption. It is on the basis of what we know about the God who raised Jesus from the dead that St Paul can perceive how creation has been "subjected to futility," that it "has been groaning in travail," and that God has furthermore "subjected it in hope" because it "will be set free from its bondage to decay and obtain the glorious liberty of the children of God" (Romans 8: 18–25).

Special experiences of God reveal special knowledge. We need to know – or at least need to hypothesize – that there is a God with divine intentions before we can see clearly that the world around and in us is in fact a creation with a meaning. It is primarily on the strength of Israel's experience with the liberating God of the Exodus that the Old Testament writers could depict the world as God's creative handiwork. It is on the strength of the New Testament experience with the incarnate Lord that Christians in today's world can say that "God so loved the world" (John 3: 16). The biblical promise of an eschatological new creation tells us something essential about the present creation. Theologically, it is God's promised Kingdom that determines creation, and creation is the promise of that Kingdom. Whether we interpret nature through the symbol of the Exodus, the incarnation, the Kingdom or another similar religious symbol, we find that we are dependent upon some form of revelation of God's purposes if we are to put nature into proper theological perspective – that is, if we are to think of nature as creation.

So, curiously enough, we might consider the possibility of a reversal in natural theology. Traditionally the aim of natural theology has been to ask what our study of nature can contribute to our knowledge of God. But might it work in reverse? Might we ask what our knowledge of God can contribute to our knowledge of nature? To know that God is the creator is to know that the world in which we live and move and have our being is *creation*.

We may not have to choose between the two methods, of course. We could begin with nature and then ask about God; or we could begin with what we think we know about God and then ask how this influences what we think about nature. Or we could do both. Both, I believe, should be on the agenda of those working in the field of theology and natural science.

Notes

1 The lineup of contending forces I offer here is revised from that sketched previously in my preface to *Cosmos as Creation* (Nashville, TN, 1989), pp. 13–17. It is also more nuanced compared to the one offered by Ian Barbour in his Gifford Lectures, *Religion in an Age of Science* (San Francisco, 1990), pp. 3–30, where he identifies four ways: conflict, independence, dialogue, and integration. My categories of scientism and church authoritarianism fit his conflict category; and the two-language theory is a model of independence in both schemes. Yet Barbour's notions of dialogue and integration lack the nuance that I believe is operative under the notion of consonance. Consonance involves dialogue, to be sure, but it acknowledges that integration may be only a hope and not an achievement. Also, Barbour thinks of scientific creationism in terms of "biblical literalism" and thereby places it in the conflict category, overlooking the fact that creationists think of themselves as sharing a common domain with science; they see themselves in conflict with scientism but not with science itself. Mark Richardson (in *CTNS Bulletin*, 14/3 (Summer 1994), pp. 24–5) offers us a three-part typology: (1) integration typified by the work of Lionel Thornton, William Temple, Austin Farrar, Arthur Peacocke, and John Polkinghorne; (2) romanticism typified by the poets Wordsworth or Whitman and by contemporary New Age figures such as Brian Swimme, Thomas Berry, and Matthew Fox; and (3) scientific constraint, where one speaks univocally about the natural and transcendent worlds, typified by Paul Davies, Freeman Dyson, Stephen Hawking, and Frank Tipler.

2 Langdon Gilkey, *Nature, Reality, and the Sacred: The nexus of science and religion* (Minneapolis, 1993), p. 14.

3 Fred Hoyle, *The Nature of the Universe* (New York, 1950), p. 125.

4 Carl Sagan, *Cosmos* (New York, 1980), p. 4; Stephen Hawking, *A Brief History of Time* (New York, 1988), p. 136.

5 Paul Davies, *God and the New Physics* (New York, 1983), p. ix.

6 Frank Tipler, *The Physics of Immortality* (New York, 1994), pp. ix, 10, 17, 247.

7 Second Vatican Council, *Gaudium et Spes* (1964), p. 59.

8 *John Paul II on Science and Religion*, ed. R. J. Russell et al. (Notre Dame, IN, 1990).

9 Duane T. Gish, *The Fossils Say No!* (San Diego, CA, 1973), pp. 24–5; Roger E. Timm, "Scientific creationism and biblical theology," in Ted Peters (ed.), *Cosmos as Creation* (Nashville, TN, 1989), pp. 247–64.

10 Stephen Jay Gould, *Hens' Teeth and Horses' Toes: Reflections on Natural History* (New York, 1983), p. 254.

11 One could describe the war as a battle between atheistic science and theistic science. Langdon Gilkey (*Nature, Reality, and the Sacred*, p. 55) suggests that scientism (what he calls scientific positivism) goes beyond the limits of science to propound an atheistic cosmology, and this initiates the reaction that results in scientific creationism.

12 Langdon Gilkey, *Creationism on Trial* (San Francisco, 1985), pp. 49–52, 108–13.

13 In his more recent work, Gilkey (*Nature, Reality, and the Sacred*, pp. 3, 11, 75, 111, 129) has pressed for a closer relationship – a mutual interdependence – between science and religion. Gilkey attacks scientism

(what he calls naturalism or scientific positivism) when it depicts nature as valueless, determined, and void of the sacred, on the grounds that these are supra-scientific or philosophical judgments that go beyond science itself. Science therefore must be supplemented by philosophy and religion if we are to understand reality fully.

14 Ernan McMullin, "How should cosmology relate to theology?" in Arthur Peacocke (ed.), *The Sciences and Theology in the Twentieth Century* (Notre Dame, IN, 1981), p. 39.

15 Ted Peters, *GOD – The World's Future: Systematic theology for a postmodern future* (Minneapolis, 1992), ch. 12.

16 David Bohm, *Wholeness and the Implicate Order* (London, 1980), p. 11.

17 Brian Swimme and Thomas Berry, *The Universe Story* (San Francisco, 1992), p. 255.

18 Langdon Gilkey, *Religion and the Scientific Future* (San Francisco, 1970), p. 41.

19 Ibid., p. 50.

20 Paul Davies, *The Mind of God* (New York, 1992), p. 24.

21 Ibid., p. 15.

22 Philip Clayton, *Explanatin from Physics to Theology* (New Haven and London, 1989), p. 13; see also Ted Peters, *GOD – The World's Future*, pp. 74–6.

23 The criterion for evaluating the progressive strength of a theory is fertility, and this constitutes the chief argument in behalf of critical realism for Ernan McMullin ("A case for scientific realism," in Jarret Leplin (ed.), *Scientific Realism* (Berkeley, CA, 1984), p. 26.

24 Wentzel van Huyssteen, *Theology and the Justification of Faith* (Grand Rapids, MI, 1989), pp. 162–3.

25 Ian Barbour, *Religion in an Age of Science* (San Francisco, 1990), p. 43; cf. his *Myths, Models, and Paradigms* (San Francisco, 1974), p. 38 and Sallie McFague, *Metaphorical Theology* (Minneapolis, 1982), pp. 133–4.

26 Arthur Peacocke, *Theology for a Scientific Age*, enlarged edn (Minneapolis, 1993; first published in Oxford, 1990), p. 14.

27 Nancey C. Murphy, "Relating theology and science in a postmodern age," in *CTNS Bulletin*, 7/4 (Autumn, 1987), pp. 1–10.

28 Nancey C. Murphy, *Theology in the Age of Scientific Reasoning* (Ithaca, NY, 1990).

29 T. F. Torrance, *Theological Science* (Oxford, 1969), pp. iv–v.

30 Ibid., p. v.

31 Ibid.

32 T. F. Torrance, *Reality and Scientific Theology* (Edinburgh, 1985), p. 39. Karl Barth is reported to have granted full agreement to this new place for natural theology; see Torrance, *Space, Time, and Resurrection* (Grand Rapids, MI, 1976), pp. ix–xiii.

33 T. F. Torrance, *Theological Science*, pp. 281–2.

34 T. F. Torrance, *Reality and Scientific Theology*, p. 67.

35 T. F. Torrance, *Space, Time, and Incarnation* (Oxford, 1969).

36 T. F. Torrance, *Space, Time, and Resurrection*, p. 13.

37 Ibid., p. 15. Wolfhart Pannenberg (*Theology and the Philosophy of Science* (Louisville, KY, p. 45)) would fear that such a *tu quoque* ("you also," says Brutus to Caesar) might become a rational excuse for an irrational commitment.

38 Arthur Peacocke, *Theology for a Scientific Age*, p. 10. Peacocke's early work, *Creation and the World of Science* (1979), is organized somewhat like a systematic theology. More recently, in *Theology for a Scientific Age*, the theological agenda has taken the driver's seat. Distinctively theological commitments are being rethought in light of scientific apprehensions of nature.

Peacocke heads the Society of Ordained Scientists, based in Oxford. This and other research and professional organizations give evidence that a lively and creative worldwide discussion of the mutual interaction of science and faith is taking place right now. Antje Jackelén, of Löberöd, Sweden, heads the European Society for the Study of Science and Theology (ESSAT). In the United States Donald Munro is executive director of the American Scientific Affiliation (ASA). Christopher Corbally, SJ, and Nancy Anschuetz lead the annual Star Island retreats for the Institute on Religion in an Age of Science (IRAS). Philip Hefner directs the Chicago Center for Religion and Science, and edits a leading journal in the field, *Zygon*. At the Graduate Theological Union in Berkeley, California, Robert John Russell is founder and director of the Center for Theology and the Natural Sciences, which publishes a journal, the *CTNS Bulletin*.

39 Ibid., p. 101.
40 Ibid., p. 102.
41 Ibid., p. 126.
42 John Polkinghorne, *The Faith of a Physicist* (Princeton, NJ, 1994), p. 193.
43 Ibid., p. 5.
44 Ibid., p. 21.
45 Ibid., p. 80.
46 Ibid., p. 68.
47 Philip Hefner, *The Human Factor: Evolution, culture, religion* (Minneapolis, 1993), p. 260.
48 Ibid., p. 261.
49 Ibid., p. 264; cf. p. 32.

Bibliography

Barbour, Ian, *Myths, Models, and Paradigms* (San Francisco, 1974).
—— *Religion in an Age of Science* (vol. I of Gifford Lectures) (San Francisco, 1990).
—— *Ethics in an Age of Technology* (vol. II of Gifford Lectures) (San Francisco, 1993).
Bohm, David, *Wholeness and the Implicate Order* (London, 1980).
Capra, Fritjof, *The Tao of Physics* (New York, 1977).
—— *The Turning Point* (New York, 1982).
Clayton, Philip, *Explanation from Physics to Theology* (New Haven and London, 1989).
Davies, Paul, *God and the New Physics* (New York, 1983).
—— *The Mind of God* (New York, 1992).
—— *Are We Alone?* (London and New York, 1995).
Drees, Willem B., *Beyond the Big Bang: Quantum cosmologies and God* (LaSalle, IL, 1990).
Gilkey, Langdon, *Religion and the Scientific Future* (San Francisco, 1970).
—— *Creationism on Trial* (San Francisco, 1985).
—— *Nature, Reality, and the Sacred: The nexus of science and religion* (Minneapolis, 1993).
Gish, Duane T., *Evolution: The fossils say no!* (San Diego, 1973).
Gould, Stephen Jay, *Hens' Teeth and Horses' Toes: Reflections on natural history* (New York, 1983).
Hawking, Stephen, *A Brief History of Time* (New York, 1988).
Hefner, Philip, *The Human Factor: Evolution, culture, religion* (Minneapolis, 1993).
Hoyle, Fred, *The Nature of the Universe* (New York, 1950).
Huyssteen, Wentzel van, *Theology and the Justification of Faith: Constructing theories in systematic theology* (Grand Rapids, MI, 1989).
John Paul II On Science and Religion: Reflections on the new view from Rome, ed. Robert John Russell, William R. Stoeger, and George V. Coyne (Notre Dame, IN, and Vatican City State, 1990).
Lakatos, Imre, *The Methodology of Scientific Research Programmes: Philosophical papers*, vol. 1, ed. John Warrall and Gregory Currie (Cambridge, 1978).
Leplin, Jarret (ed.), *Scientific Realism* (Berkeley, CA, 1984).
McFague, Sallie, *Metaphorical Theology* (Minneapolis, 1982).
McMullin, Ernan, "How should cosmology relate to theology?" in Arthur Peacocke (ed.), *The Sciences and Theology in the Twentieth Century* (Notre Dame, IN, 1981).
Murphy, Nancey, C., "Relating Theology and Science in a Postmodern Age," *CTNS Bulletin*, 7/4 (Autumn 1987), pp. 1–10.
—— *Theology in the Age of Scientific Reasoning* (Ithaca, NY, 1990).
Pannenberg, Wolfhart, *Theology and the Philosophy of Science* (Louisville, KY, 1976).
—— *Systematic Theology*, 3 vols (Grand Rapids, MI, 1991–6).
—— *Toward a Theology of Nature*, ed. Ted Peters (Louisville, KY, 1993).
Peacocke, Arthur, *Creation and the World of Science* (Oxford, 1979).
—— *Intimations of Reality: Critical realism in science and religion* (Notre Dame, IN, 1984).
—— *God and the New Biology* (San Francisco, 1986).
—— *Theology for a Scientific Age*, enlarged edn (Minneapolis, 1993; first published in Oxford, 1990).
Peters, Ted, *GOD – The World's Future: System-*

atic theology for a postmodern era (Minneapolis, 1992).

—— GOD as Trinity: Relationality and temporality in divine life (Louisville, KY, 1993).

Peters, Ted (ed.), Cosmos as Creation: Science and theology in consonance (Nashville, TN, 1989).

Polkinghorne, John, Science and Providence: God's interaction with the world (Boston, 1989).

—— The Faith of a Physicist (Princeton, NJ, 1994).

Richardson, Mark, "Research Fellow's Report," CTNS Bulletin, 14/3 (Summer, 1994), pp. 24–5.

Russell, Robert John, Murphy, Nancey, and Isham, C. J. (eds), Quantum Cosmology and the Laws of Nature (Vatican City State and Notre Dame, IN, 1993).

Russell, Robert John, Stoeger, William R., and Coyne, George V. (eds), Physics, Philosophy, and Theology (Vatican City State and Notre Dame, IN, 1988).

Sagan, Carl, Cosmos (New York, 1980).

Swimme, Brian, and Berry, Thomas, The Universe Story (San Francisco, 1992).

Timm, Roger E., "Scientific creationism and biblical theology," in Ted Peters (ed.), Cosmos as Creation (Nashville, TN, 1989), pp. 247–64.

Tipler, Frank, The Physics of Immortality (New York, 1994).

Torrance, T. F., Theological Science (Oxford, 1969).

—— Space, Time and Incarnation (Oxford, 1969).

—— Space, Time and Resurrection (Grand Rapids, MI, 1976).

—— Reality and Scientific Theology (Edinburgh, 1985).

White, A. D., A History of the Warfare of Science with Theology (New York, 1896; reprinted 1960).

Theology and the Arts: Visual Arts

Graham Howes

Introduction

"Christian theology" and "the arts" are not two discrete entities. They can more fruitfully be seen as media by which the world is interpreted and represented; ways of perceiving and articulating memory, aspiration, community, celebration, loss, the heightened charge that natural or ordinary things can carry to the imaginatively active mind. They speak of the fragility of our perceptions and the need to rehearse and renew these perceptions (perpetually re-establishing a "covenantal" relationship with the things we see, hear, touch, use, and enjoy). They are reminders of that co-inherence of activity and receptivity which is involved in a properly dynamic relationship with the world; the need for openness to being surprised, claimed, and transformed by genuinely new perceptions of things. Both theology and art testify to all this. And they have together testified to even more than this: to the glory of God, revealed concretely yet inexhaustibly in the face of Jesus Christ.

Not surprisingly, then, Christian history has seen multiple, overlapping, shifting patterns of relation between different kinds of theological, as well as different kinds of artistic, perception and articulation. These relations have varied from an intense and intimate community of purpose to a strained hostility. But in virtually no period have they been *uninteresting* relations. The present time in the West is one of the most interesting of all. The extraordinary proliferation and diversity of artistic expression reminds theology of what, at its best, it already knows: that the theologically interesting is not the same as the churchy, and that its interpretative horizons must be the very broadest ones. And the alertness of much recent theology to questions about the relationship of individuals to their shaping communities, and of communities to their memories and hopes, reminds art of what, at its best, it too already knows: An interior vision has never been of any interest except when it is caught and communicated to others.

Moreover, both theology and art stand together, at the present time, in the face of the supremacy of "technique." Both, at their best, resist it. Falsely isolated "technique" is a way, especially in a sophisticated, industrial economy, of getting results without investing the self. Theology and art do not get results in this way. The distinctively modern pressures represented by the dominance of technique help them to rediscover what the medievals knew: Theology finds in art a complement and not a rival in its task of understanding and giving expression to the fullness of created human being. Good theology and art can be agents in the rebirth of a festivity and expressive celebration that is not bound to utility.

Good theology and good art will discipline false dichotomies that stand in the way of such fullness of expression: dichotomies between sacred and secular "realms"; spiritual and material "values"; the intellectual and the affective. Good theology and art may, as William Purdy suggests, find themselves engaged together in what Eliot calls a "raid on the inarticulate," acting "as fellow-strugglers rather than in a master-pupil relationship or one of censor and censored, or one of official and self-assured professional to rather dangerous amateur."[1] They may again find that they have a common vocation: to make "raids" on the weakened and impoverished modern imagination, to break open its hidden resources and equip it for adaptation to change, for celebration, and for the envisioning of alternative futures. When they are properly engaged in this vocation, theology and art may not in fact be two separate things-in-relationship at all, but the *same* thing.

Survey

In early Christianity the icon was regarded as a major form of revelation and knowledge of God. As St John of Damascus (ca. AD 730) put it "icons contain a mystery and like a sacrament are vessels of divine energy and grace . . . through the intermediary of sensible perception our minds are uplifted towards the invisible divine majesty."[2]

Similarly, as Émile Male demonstrated, there was a close connection between the anonymous and iconographical (as opposed to the individual) character of twelfth- and thirteenth-century Gothic art and architecture and the prevailing sacramental conception of the world, especially the conception of humanity as receiver of faith.

Again the dominant aesthetic of the High Renaissance and the Baroque emphasized the spiritual potential of art. As Bernini's patron, the Jesuit Vicar-General Oliva, put it in 1665 "In all our churches both Ignatius our father, and all of us who are his sons, try to reach up to the sublimity of God's eternal omnipotence with such appurtenances of glory as we can to the best of our powers achieve."[3]

Finally, for much of the nineteenth century, in both Europe and the United States, a clear conception of the overtly "religious" functions of the arts (deeply rooted in eighteenth-century notions of "the sublime" and Romanticism's version of "natural" religion) was widely prevalent. As the century's leading art critic, John Ruskin, frequently reminded his many readers, the supreme value of art was that it disclosed spiritual and ethical insights one could not reach in any other way, and could even act as "a new inlet for devotion."[4]

This oversimplified, art-historical outline raises three important questions for twentieth-century theologians. One is how far does art still function as the aesthetic expression of Christian doctrine? As early as 1025 a Synod at Arras had proclaimed that "art teaches the unlettered what they cannot learn from books,"[5] and it is clear that the function of art as a kind of visual theology, especially in detailing, reinforcing and encouraging imaginative participation in biblical narrative, has remained a constant until well into this century. A second question is the precise relationship of the arts to religious institutions. Churches allowed artists considerable leeway in the design of commissioned works, and particular churches encouraged particular emphases, themes, and concerns special to them. The artists – especially we might think of the innovators of the early Renaissance – showed enormous feeling, originality, and distinctive character precisely within the traditional framework which they inherited. It was a model of personal artistry finding its place in a corporate tradition. It continued to function long after it ceased to be taken for granted that most artwork would be religious, and when displaced it was often succeeded by secular variations on it. The question for contemporary Chritianity is how its corporate tradition might appropriately shape art today.

A third theological issue centers upon the profound – and persistent – dichotomy between word and image within Christian aesthetics. The issue is, more specifically, a christological one, namely the idea of humanity as made in the image of God. The classic example is the iconoclastic controversy[6] of the eighth and ninth centuries. The Iconoclasts objected to any attempt to portray Christ on the grounds that to do so would presuppose that he was only a human being. They argued that his divine nature should be ignored (since representation of this was impossible) and so visual portrayals were a most misleading way of presenting the God-man. The opponents of the Iconoclasts, the Iconophiles, defended the practice of painting Christ on the grounds that this was the obvious way of taking the Incarnation seriously. For them, not to seek to embody Christ in a picture or sculpture betrayed a residual disbelief in the genuine historicity and humanity of Christ. In one crucial sense the controversy was supra-aesthetic. It was about something central to Christian belief – the reality of the Incarnation itself. Out of this clash came not only what Ladner has called "two normative approaches to the human body – the incarnational and the spiritualized"[7] – which have remained in tension throughout Christian history, but also two attitudes toward the arts which have played a dominant role in theology, as well as church history and art history, ever since. The Iconophiles in the end won the day, and with it the theology they had developed. It was the Incarnation that legitimated Christian art, making possible the visualization of God through humanity.

The issue both symbolized, and was a product of, those historical realities and deep structural tensions – concerning word and image, and relation of both to liturgy – which lie at the heart of Christian aesthetics. The central question then, as now, was whether art is a way of seeing and knowing which is as truth-bearing as philosophical and scientific method. The core dimensions of the historical relationship between theology and the arts – art as a source of revelation, as sacrament, as symbol of ecclesiastical hegemony, as battleground between word and image – remain historical constants to this day. But to these must be added three other artistic developments of especial significance to twentieth-century theology.

One has been the emergence of a genuinely religious art which does *not* set out to be iconic. "I want to paint man and woman," wrote Van Gogh "with something of the eternal which the halo used to symbolize, but which we now seem to confer through the actual radiance of our colour vibrations."[8] Even more self-evidently, the work of a Rembrandt or Rouault may achieve something of what the icon can achieve, but it functions differently. It may set out to enflesh and communicate a transfigured and transfiguring Christian vision, but the result is not overtly liturgical or ecclesiastical in character. There has been a partial divorce between art and liturgy in the West. The key question, as Rowan Williams has suggested, is whether this has been an unmitigated disaster for the Christian (and secular) imagination in the West.[9]

Second, it is clear that from about the mid-nineteenth century, a period in which many exceptional artists and musicians flourished and in which many of them were intensely religious, there are fewer instances of a great master being asked to decorate or paint for a church. (Notable exceptions are the older Matisse, Rouault, Leger, Chagall, Sutherland, Eric Gill, John Piper, and Stanley Spencer.) Since that time most major aesthetic movements (for example, Impressionism or Surrealism) have developed in opposition to or supposed freedom from organized religion. It would appear that many of the works of greatest interest today from an artistic or religious point of view are works executed by artists independently outside the churches.

Third, it is clear that from about 1750, art, rather than supporting and articulating church-based theology, often began to separate itself from both religious institutions ("art," wrote Goethe in 1804, "has consolidated its status as an independent cult, sometimes more flourishing than the churches themselves")[10] and Christian theology. "Art became," as Max Weber noted, "a cosmos of more and more consciously grasped independent values which exist in their own right . . . taking over the function of a this-worldly salvation," competing directly with religion, and "transforming judgments of moral intent into judgments of taste."[11] In this sense art easily becomes a manifestation, in Tillich's phrase, of "one form of the latent church."

Hence art comes to be treated as a source of truth, including theological truth in its own right. Through art we see not only certain connections with culture and its traditions. We also see aspects of a judgment on that culture which are part of any significant artistic expression. The semantic system of art (like that of theology) offers order and orientation, as all signs do, provided one has learned the conventional responses to them. As Morse Peckham puts it: "From the late nineteenth century . . . art became itself the mythological explanation which subsumed the self. Art becomes redemptive."[12]

In our own day the complex relationship between theology and the arts, although grounded in the historical and cultural preconditions already outlined, is acted out principally in three critical areas – those of meaning, representation, and belief.

Meaning

Modernity, at least thus far, has, according to some interpretations, been relatively antagonistic to dimensions of the transcendent in the human condition and, as Peter Berger and others[13] have argued, there has been a weakening of the plausibility of religious prescriptions of reality among large numbers of people in many Western countries. It is no accident that counter-modernizing trends and movements have frequently been characterized by powerful reaffirmations of transcendence – what

Eliade[14] has called hierophanies or manifestations of the sacred, experienced as the breaking in of another reality into the secular reality of ordinary life. The arts are self-evidently part of this process.

Nevertheless the absence of a shared symbolic order remains a major contemporary cultural characteristic. Even the art critic Peter Fuller,[15] an avowed agnostic for much of his life, looked back to when institutional religion provided just such an order. His belief was that, at certain periods, even when this order was disintegrating, artists supplied consolation for its loss in the form of work whose purpose was imaginatively to transfigure the world of visual experience and thereby reconcile humanity to it.

Yet today there is often an indifference both to the meaning of such art and even more to its historical context. In the twentieth century the stories and institutional practices, the imperatives and texts, which shape artists and their work (even when they suppose themselves to be searching for meaning within themselves) are different or detached from the Christian forms and content that might have shaped them. Their work tends to be individualistic and even autobiographical. There is no communal, let alone liturgical imperative for the use of the Bible as a point of departure. Artists are often capable of expressing religious feelings and religious perceptions without any explicit confessional commitment. As Mark Rothko once put it "the individual who learns to weep before my paintings will have the same religious experience I had when I painted them."[16] It is clear that many artists still search for some spiritual meaning in their work above and beyond the truth of what they see. Some, like Craigie Aitchison, first ask spiritual questions and then find themselves giving religious answers. But even Aitchison warns us specifically against assuming that "any artist who questions the meaning of life is thereby committing a religious act."[17]

One way in which contemporary art has some genuine creedal resonance is indicated by Hans Küng. He asks, "What if in the course of modern development the idea of a pre-existing divine order of meaning has been increasingly shattered and this meaning itself has become more questionable?" Can the work of art still be meaningful when the great synthesis of meaning no longer exists? Küng's answer is that "in a time of meaninglessness, the work of art can symbolize 'meaninglessness' very precisely in a way that is aesthetically completely meaningful – that is to say inwardly harmonious – and does so to a large extent in modern art."[18] If he is right, then the most appropriate role model for today's artist is not necessarily to profess a specific confessional commitment, nor to try to lift the still-dominant aesthetic taboo against explicit narrative content. It might rather be to testify to the complexities, ambiguities, fragmentations, and disruptions that have characterized much modern experience (and also, of course, much traditional and contemporary Christian experience), while allowing for characteristically Christian testimony that that is not necessarily the last word.

Representation

The encouragement of thematically intentional and representational Christian works of art in our own time creates a profound aesthetic dilemma. Historically, as we have seen, Christian art in its many varieties has done more than is commonly recognized in giving form to the Christian consciousness and direction to Christian activity – far more, perhaps, than many statements of theology. But it is also the case that such overtly representational religious art – especially within the Roman Catholic tradition – carries its own crude inner logic. Such art is useful to the Church because it is unambiguously catechetical. This is what Rowan Williams has called the "lightly Platonized aesthetic"[19] which lies behind so many vulgar and banal pictures of Christ now in general circulation, and the cheap icons of Mary that saturate Italy, Spain, and the Americas. Nonetheless, such *bondieuserie* seems to indicate that we continue to live at a time when the normative forms and images of the Judeo-Christian tradition are still accessible to the popular imagination. They can for centuries be media for formative memories which act as fertile soil for new improvisations on Christian faith, as in liberation theology and many forms of Pentecostalism. However, the aesthetic consequences of this may sometimes be what Tillich so caustically called a "sentimental, beautifying naturalism . . . the feeble drawing, the poverty of vision, the petty historicity of our church-sponsored art." This he says "is not simply unendurable but incredible . . . It calls for iconoclasm."[20]

Yet the alternative, for many Western twentieth-century artists, involves deliberately sidestepping any literal depiction of the Gospel. The prevailing aesthetic is usually too narrow to permit it, proceeding, as it does, away from all literary content toward the "universal" art of abstraction. Such abstraction, while it remains the dominant cultural mode, will continue to present to the churches an art without symbols or imagery, and therefore without any specific doctrinal allusion. At the same time, for many lay consumers, much of all abstract art (which can still claim to be regarded as the prevalent religious art of our time in the West) remains psychologically inaccessible. This is not only because we continue to think of art as representation or ornament, but also because, as Rosenberg puts it, "the central language of modern art has entered our consciousness indirectly, by way of the popular arts – advertising, TV, etc. But since it is indirect, and quite detached from those orders of society to which we overtly feel committed – church, politics, class formation, etc. – the great images of modern art are never available for our inner nourishment."[21] Such an argument provides a powerful and pessimistic counterpoint both to facile aesthetic progressivism and the fashionable neo-Jungian notion that the archetypes by which spiritual realities express themselves are available and constantly clothed in the forms of modern art.

Hence, unsurprisingly, a substantial alternative tradition based on the human figure is currently being rediscovered. As a result, explicit thematic content – or even narration – is no longer regarded by younger artists as pure archaism, a retrograde element. This partial lifting of the aesthetic taboo against the figurative and narrative has particular significance so long as Gospel narrative remains the central core of Christianity.

Either way, wherever religion exists, its symbols – mental, visual, dramatic – are in constant use. What symbols do we re-inhabit or appropriate for contemporary religious contexts, and what qualities are necessary to make such symbols fruitful within our own religious experience? Are there still distinctive symbolic forms which serve in human experience to relate humanity to ultimate mystery? Certainly in the

earlier experience of the Christian church symbolic forms of this kind gained recognition and served to bind people to one another within a common relatedness
to God through Christ. It is true that they underwent countless varieties of transformation in the succeeding centuries of the Church's life. But until comparatively
recently they retained a significant place – some would say *the* most significant place
– in the life and culture of Western civilization. The crucial question today is
whether such symbols can any longer configure and refigure reality in the modern
scientific and secular world. Have they lost their focus, power and meaning?

No answer should be given to this question that fails to take account of the
symbolic force and the public role that church architecture continues to play in the
modern world. Religious building has always been one of the most powerful contributions by the churches to the public realm. It is also one of the most visible
forms of Christian testimony at the heart of communities of every kind. Churches
and cathedrals are religious art in themselves. They are symbols of Christian presence, mission, hospitality, rejoicing, and care. They *represent* Christianity to people.

The time since the Second World War has seen a quite unparalleled set of developments in church architecture which have enabled this representational power to
sustain vibrancy and impact. In Europe, the effects of bombing opened opportunities for fresh construction; while in other parts of the world (and especially the
developing world) the growth of Christianity has led to the building of many new
churches and cathedrals. The twentieth century has seen experiments in style ranging
from the curved surfaces and irregular shapes of Le Corbusier's pilgrimage chapel
at Ronchamp to Gaudi's riotous mixture of Gothic and *art nouveau* styles in the
church of the Sagrada Familia in Barcelona, to Philip Johnson's steel and glass
"Crystal Cathedral" in Los Angeles.

These have been made possible by a spectacular extension of technical resources
and materials. Reinforced concrete, steel, and glass have enabled a huge number of
innovations and a breathtaking imaginative renewal. The great virtues of reinforced
concrete structure are its strength (it can hold up great weight and still allow for
the creative and extensive use of glass), its lightness, its cheapness, and a flexibility
which facilitates elegance of line as well as making dramatic shapes possible. These
have often been powerfully symbolic and representational, suggesting, for example,
the crown of Christ the King or the Crown of Thorns, as at the great cathedral of
Brasilia (designed for the new capital of Brazil by Oscar Niemeyer and Joachim
Cardozo) or the Roman Catholic cathedral of Christ the King in Liverpool (conceived by Sir Frederick Gibberd and completed in 1967).

Often, such innovations have been used in the service of a widespread concern
with new liturgical practice. Circular church buildings like that at Liverpool enable
the effective central placing of the main altar, which reflects the contemporary
liturgical concern with the gathering of the people of God (the body of Christ)
around the sacred presence at their heart.

And just as there are now far greater possibilities for the participation of the people
in liturgical activity, so also in the process of choosing church styles. This too is a
significant modern development. The architects of both of the cathedrals in Liverpool
(Anglican and Roman Catholic) were selected in open competition, from a large
number of entries, and this attracted public attention and stimulated widespread

opinion and response. The architect of the Anglican cathedral in Coventry, Sir Basil Spence, was also selected in a competition. Since Coventry Cathedral was completed in 1962, millions of people have queued to visit it. They testify to the way that the project of building a modern church still succeeds in involving people's sympathies and in engaging their interest.

A few examples taken from the rich field of modern church architecture serve to show the continuing symbolic importance and representational power that are focused in contemporary religious buildings. John Piper's use of colored glass in the cylinder above the Liverpool altar, for example, symbolizes continuity with the past together with an outward-looking vision. It is a sign of continuity even as it is innovatory: The effect of the colored lights is compared by some with the jeweling of a sacred reliquary. But when it is dark, the cylinder acts like a beacon: The light from the cathedral shines out across the city, as a sign of its mission to and service in the world. Coventry, too, has a great torrent of John Piper's colored glass in its baptistery, representing the pouring out of the Holy Spirit, and it also has a vast west window of engraved glass by John Hutton, uniting the cathedral interior with the outside world. The city, as a consequence, is viewed through the transparent figures of angels. Once again, the "spiritual" and the "material" are shown to interpenetrate: Theology and art together act as a medium for the viewing of the world.

Belief

One of John Ruskin's strongest convictions was that the supreme value of art lay in its disclosure, through aesthetic contemplation, of spiritual and ethical insights that one could not reach in any other kind of way. Yet the twentieth century is a time when in the West there is some empirical evidence for both the loss of religious beliefs and the apparent paradox of normative agnosticism combined with continuing religious needs. In such circumstances, it is difficult to refashion religious art – whether representational or non-representational – when people often do not have an organic, meaningful relationship with it. There is no overarching symbolic world to inhabit.

More specifically, as John Berger[22] has argued, the cultural changes accompanying the arrival of modernity are not just a question of improved technologies, such as faster transport, quicker messages, a more complex scientific vocabulary, higher accumulation of capital under markets, international organizations, etc. They appear to establish new circumstances, described by George Steiner as "where God's presence is no longer a tenable supposition and where His presence is no longer a felt, indeed overwhelming, weight, certain dimensions of thought and creativity are no longer attainable."[23] How therefore, he asks, can we encounter that real presence which great art ("touched", in his phrase "by the fire and ice of God") has to offer? In general "we must look on the world *as if* created and respond to it *as if* to the 'real presence of the transcendental' and, especially, in an era of secularization, the artist must 'make a wager on transcendence.'" In this sense, movements such as Cubism or Abstract Expressionism might be interpreted more as a creative response to the loss of transcendence rather than a celebration of it, more of an attempt to reopen rather than to close the space in which God and "the spirit" can be recognized. But how to do so without confusing the aesthetic with religion, and making an idol out of art, remains problematic.

Theological Response

As was indicated earlier, the arts, if not always historically interdependent with theology, are most certainly a parallel activity to it and are sometimes indistinguishable from it. Indeed in our own time, when both Christian theology and the arts often pose and present themselves as a series of questions rather than a pattern of answers, both the fundamental character of Christian belief *and* the so-called Western tradition in art are being examined and challenged. One could go further and suggest that theology in isolation from the arts is starved of concrete embodiments of its insights into the fullness of human life. Art can give theology the eyes to see ourselves in all our dimensions, the ears to hear the voice of our inner lives, and the instruments with which to communicate with each other. At the same time the past suggests that the arts may realize their potential most fully within that unifying vision of God which lies at the heart of Christianity.

The languages of theology are themselves a matter of determining the structures by which people have defined their relation to the world and responded to their apprehension of the manifestation of the divine. In this sense to do theology is not to know God in a particularly modern way, but to respond to God through the weight and structure and purpose of a given language. That language should be both verbal and visual, embodying both a theology of the arts and art as an expression of theology.

Karl Barth

It is useful here to categorize the responses of representative twentieth-century theologians to the arts within the threefold typology suggested by John Dillenberger.[24] The first is where *"no relation is seen between the arts and theological work."*

Looking at the theologians in this volume it is hard to argue that any of them fall clearly into this category, though many pay almost no attention to the arts. Karl Barth is an interesting test case. He was intensely musical, writing a monograph on Mozart – who, he says, "although not especially good or especially pious, *heard* the peace which passes all understanding."[25] Barth likened the Kingdom of God to a composition by Mozart which is at once "beautiful play" and "virtually the equivalent of a parable." Jeremy Begbie discusses Barth on music in the second part of this chapter. But Barth's attitude to the visual arts was different, especially in the context of worship. He maintained that "images and symbols have no place *at all* in a building designed for Protestant worship."[26] Yet art could, like John the Baptist in Grünewald's Isenheim altarpiece (a picture that much preoccupied Barth), witness by pointing in the direction of the revelation of God in the person of Jesus Christ. Barth is, however, deeply suspicious of any conception of art which suggested that it might somehow be a human point of contact for experience of God. He was well aware of the temptation to find in the aesthetic sphere a privileged mediation of the divine (especially when, as in modern Western culture, the intellectual and practical significance of God are so often dismissed). When he met this he was vigorously iconoclastic in the interests of the free initiative of God in revealing himself. Robert Jenson in chapter 1 of this volume describes Barth's complex relationship to natural theology, to liberal Protestantism, and especially to Schleiermacher, and it is helpful to remember that Barth saw the arts often being appropriated for such theologies. With regard to Dillenberger's first type, it would be just to say only that Barth found no necessary, intrinsic, or systematic relation between the arts and theological work, though God is of course free to testify to himself through the arts.

Rudolf Otto and Paul Tillich

Dillenberger's second type of relationship between theology and the arts is *"where a positive relation is articulated, sometimes successfully and sometimes not."*

In our own century, the roots of this approach can be found in Rudolf Otto's seminal *The Idea of the Holy* and especially in his comparison between religious experiences of the numinous and aesthetic experience of the beautiful – a relationship which for him was more than mere analogy. He believed, too, in the power of the abstract to convey numinous experience, suggesting that there are, especially in oriental art, very many pictures, especially those connected with contemplation, which impress the observer with the feeling that the void itself is depicted as a subject, is indeed the *main* subject of the picture. Otto argued that this pictorial emptiness was similar to the void spoken of by the mystics. "For void," he wrote, "is, like darkness and silence and rejection, but a negation that does away with every 'this' and 'here' in order that the 'wholly other' may become actual."[27]

Pre-eminent, and perhaps most influential here, is Paul Tillich (see above, chapter 5), for whom the visual, like all aspects of human life, belongs to the world with which theology is concerned. In a suggestive essay entitled "On the Theology of Fine Art and Architecture," Tillich observes that it was natural for a theologian to raise the question "How is the aesthetic function of the human spirit related to the religious function? How are artistic symbols – and all artistic creations are symbols, however naturalistic their styles may be – related to the symbols in which religion expresses itself?"[28] Tillich's answer is that there is no style which excludes the artistic expression of ultimate concern, as the ultimate is not bound to any special form of things or experiences. Indeed "the ultimate is present in experiences in which not only reality is experienced, but in the encounter itself with reality."[29] In practice Tillich does not develop a systematic analysis of the relationship between religion and art. Rather he presents a series of separate studies intended to disclose the way in which particular artifacts can be interpreted as expressions of ultimate concern. "Art," he maintained, "indicates what the character of a spiritual situation is: it does this more immediately and directly than do science and philosophy, for it is less burdened by objective considerations."[30]

Although Tillich's analysis of the relationship between artistic styles and religion in general – in terms of subject matter, form, and style – is clear and persuasive, and his central contention that, when "once more religion is without a home within man's spiritual life, it looks around for another spiritual function to join . . . namely the aesthetic,"[31] is relatively plausible, several difficulties remain. One is that Tillich's discussion of art, especially in his *Systematic Theology*, is limited by the relative restriction of his remarks to the role art plays in the life of the institutional church. More critically, his contention that "the rediscovery of the expressive element in art since about 1900 is a *decisive event* [my italics] for the relation of religion and the visual arts. It has made religious art possible again,"[32] surely overestimates Expressionism, even Abstract Expressionism, at the expense of purely abstract art and other twentieth-century movements? Ironically, as the Dillenbergers have pointed out, Tillich's heavy reliance on "expressionism" in art hindered him from "seeing precisely those facets in contemporary art which accorded with his own viewpoint."[33] The work of Abstract Expressionists like Mark Rothko, Adolf Gottlieb, and Barnett Newman resonates with expressions of the tragic, the sublime, the demonic[34] – all elements familiar to Tillich's cultural analysis. Nonetheless, of all the theologians in our century, he set the primary agenda for the role of the arts in theological work.

Karl Rahner and others

Tillich's approach to art is echoed and developed in at least one theologically antithetical quarter – in the work of Karl Rahner. In an important and somewhat neglected essay, he raises the question of whether or not the visual arts can be left out of theological activity. What shall we do, he asks, about the nonverbal arts, architecture, sculpture, painting, and music? If they are "human self-expressions which embody one way or another the process of human self-discovery" do they not "have the same value and significance as the verbal arts?" If that is the case, and

> if as insofar as theology is man's reflexive self-expression about himself in the light of divine revelation we could propose the thesis that theology cannot be complete until it appropriates these arts as an integral moment of itself and its own life, until the arts become an intrinsic moment of theology itself . . . They communicate something about what the human really is in the eyes of God which cannot be completely translated into verbal theology . . . If theology is simply and arbitrarily defined as being identical with verbal theology, then of course we cannot say that. But then we would have to ask whether such a reduction of theology to verbal theology does justice to the value and uniqueness of these arts, and whether it does not unjustifiably limit the capacity of the arts to be used by God in this revelation.[35]

It is precisely in contending that the nonverbal provides what cannot be totally translated into verbal theology that Rahner assures art's necessary place. For him art and theology, different and related, are both rooted in humanity's transcendent nature.

Other contemporary theologians have extended the argument further. Ray Hart argues that the arts should be taken as seriously as the metaphysical; "they are not an adjunct to the verbal but provide, as do other modalities, fundamental clues as to what we are and what we are becoming."[36] John Cobb too, drawing extensively upon André Malraux's *Metamorphoses of the Gods* (1954), sees in contemporary, especially abstract art "a secular development that can be positively rather than negatively understood" and argues that although explicitly Christian subject matter may have disappeared, "the logos is now hiddenly and immanently present waiting to be named as Christ in a new form.[37] Hans Küng, although primarily focused on art as the expression of estrangement, claims that art functions eschatologically, so that the tree painted beautifully on canvas "is not sealed in its reality, but rouses the hope . . . that the world as it ought to be will at some time actually arise,"[38] a hope, in short, for a new heaven and a new earth.

Finally, Mark Taylor, for all his theological attempts at deconstructive atheism, successfully shows how in the history of art the death of God, followed by the loss of the self and the transition from transcendence to immanence, may be culturally documented. In his most recent work, *Disfiguring*, he clearly shows precisely how religious presuppositions have informed modern artistic theory and also how the visual arts continue to act as a rich resource for the theological imagination. If his conclusion is somewhat bleak, in that the purest expressions of postmodern art and architecture are, for him, no more than "epiphanies of God, a God who is and only is a totally catastrophic abyss,"[39] his identification of the spiritual subtext and creedal coda of much twentieth-century art is convincing, and more traditionally Tillichian than he would probably admit.

Nicholas Wolterstorff and Hans Urs von Balthasar

The third, and final type of theological response to the arts suggested by Dillenberger, and already implied by Taylor, is *where the arts themselves provide paradigms and images that affect the nature of theological methods.* The question is a complex one, involving both the way art functions theologically and in what mode art is relevant to theology. It is clear, of course, that the semantic systems of both the arts and theology offer order and orientation, as all signs do, provided one has learned to participate in them. Thus a painting or piece of music is a visual or auditory exemplification of an elaborate and wide-ranging system of explanation which regresses from the sign through a hierarchical series of stages of explanatory regression to the single terminal explanatory term "God." Theology is a verbal exemplification of the same system of aesthetic apprehension.

Hence Nicholas Wolterstorff argues that aesthetic delight is shared – "a component within and a species of that joy which belongs to the shalom that God has ordained as the goal of personal and communal existence." Therefore, he claims, "it becomes a matter of responsible action to help make available, to ourselves *and others*, the experience of aesthetic delight."[40] It is, in short, a theological as well as a moral imperative.

A more complex approach is to be found in the work of Hans Urs von Balthasar, who develops a highly sophisticated theological aesthetics, which traces analogies between Christian faith and the visual arts. This is aesthetics read theologically, and goes far beyond merely pointing out Christian themes in works of art or showing parallels between theology and painting. It is an attempt to situate our perception of objects – of that which is "beautiful" in created being – in its unfinalizable but real relation to our perception of God's glory, which opens itself to us both in and beyond created being. Von Balthasar shows how, throughout history, aesthetic categories have offered illumination to Christian theologians as they have attempted to describe the cosmos, Christian life, the Kingdom, and the nature and action of God.

Von Balthasar shows that aesthetics draws on what is first a contemplative stance, which is prepared to accord a primacy to the object. Aesthetics is prepared to respect the integrity of the form which is perceived, rather than trying to pull it apart so as to satisfy some alien set of questions or expectations. In other words, it is prepared to let the form of the object discipline and condition its responses. And because divine revelation, too, takes concrete form, von Balthasar sets out to emphasize the analogies between it and an aesthetic object, and the importance of a contemplative stance in *each* case.

Then, in attending to the form, the contemplative person discovers that he or she receives the revelation (or the work of art) not as a mirror reflects an image or a blank surface receives an imprint, but by a kind of imaginative participation. The object of contemplation generates life beyond itself, and the response of the contemplative person can be a medium by which that which is contemplated is transposed into new contexts. As Burch Brown has pointed out, von Balthasar's own writing is itself an example of such transposition: a demonstration "that theology can order its own language and reflection in such a way as to exhibit aesthetic integrity, proportion and a certain *claritas* befitting its objects and actions."[41]

Theology takes up the work of aesthetics at a higher level, according to von Balthasar, and reveals to aesthetics its true vocation. Aesthetic contemplation reveals only fragments of form in the world: It reveals the fact that worldly forms are incomplete, partial, not self-grounding. But the object which commands *theological* contemplation – the revelation of God's most universal and simultaneously most concrete form – gives a center and integrity to the many fragments, and makes the beautiful – rightly perceived – a potential medium of the "glorious."

At times, von Balthasar's sustained exploration of the analogies between faith and revelation on the one hand and aesthetic insights on the other can seem a little forced and over-schematic. Nevertheless, his is a potentially creative theological response to the arts, which is awake to the broad dimensions of the task of the modern theologian. He sees, along with so many other twentieth-century theologians, the importance of going beyond the notion that art is theologically interesting only when it has an explicitly ecclesial function or a didactic purpose.

Conclusion

In a culture in which many artists and their audiences are not interested in explicitly religious themes and there is not a comprehensive religious tradition which the majority of people inhabit and sustain, the way that theology and art interact remains to some extent problematic. This is, arguably, the way things are in many parts of the developed world, and although, as we have seen, Christian theologians and philosophers of religion are taking aesthetics seriously again, the essential interaction between theology and the arts (like the essential exchange between artist and audience) may not be set to take place within an identifiably "religious" frame of reference.

One reason may be that in the West at least we have seen the gradual triumph of the verbal over the visual, of word over image in the process of religious apprehension. In this sense Protestantism not only reified language as a means of communication between humanity and God: Its literal awareness of the word also encouraged a negative theological aesthetic. "There is every reason," says Frank Burch Brown, "to take seriously a claim that . . . the Protestant Reformers, in supplanting the Catholic emphasis on the visual with an emphasis on the aural (verbal and musical) altered a whole religious sensibility at a perceptual level."[42]

Yet today even that sensibility itself shows signs of being altered once again through the sheer superfluity of available sense data. Indeed, a strong case could be made for the dominant imagery of contemporary Western culture being neither primarily visual nor verbal but essentially audiovisual – the singer "Madonna" rather than the Madonna as it were. The result is the contemporary paradox of a highly visual culture in which Christian imagery has itself become increasingly invisible.

It may, of course, be a symptom of postmodern culture itself, one of whose features, as we have seen, is the so-called crisis in representation, that we no longer view artistic form as a repository of perceptual customs and experiences shared by the theologian, the artist, and ourselves. This is not only because of the current critical tendency – which continues to make its impact on theology – to view the form and content of a work of art – or of theology – as essentially structured by its readers and perceivers. It is also because today, as Martin has put it, "all the frameworks of narrative description employed in the history and interpretation of both art and religion as well as all previous identifications of beauty and holiness as categories of interpretation . . . are dissolved in the acids of modernity."[43]

If it is true that we are caught between, on the one hand, a post-Enlightenment predisposition to separate image and reality, and on the other, if the postmodernists are right, an art (indeed all art) purged of its referential forms, then we are faced with the very difficult challenge of restoring the intimate and intricate relation between theology and art that has traditionally characterized theological aesthetics. One way is by the use (the re-inhabiting) of the symbols of Christian self-understanding and self-expression by means of an attentiveness to their history and a disciplined corporate practice (a kind of rehearsal) that reinstates them and enables them to be performed once again in new contexts. This does not mean a return to a crudely didactic or narrative use of art. But it certainly does mean a rejection of the idea that there is such a thing as "generalized religious experience" which is always going to be most at home in the abstract. It means a recognition that faith lives from the *particular*, and that it was with great insight that the Iconophiles in the eighth and ninth centuries defended depiction of the Incarnate One in art, against a false notion of transcendence. The historic, the concrete, and the explicitly incarnational are not the straightforward opposites of the mysterious and the numinous. Rather, as theologians like von Balthasar have done much to show us, finite forms encounter us in infinitely various ways, and can open up unfathomable reaches of meaning. The face of a human being is the medium both of what is familiar and also of what is unknown and still to be discovered: the concrete mediating the transcendent. It is no accident that one of the most traditional Christian symbols of all is the face of Jesus Christ.

Whether accepting this case for the value of representational forms, however, or whether continuing to favor abstract forms of expression, and whether committed to explicitly religious subject matter or not, modern artists reassert through their direct appeal to visual perception (as opposed to the verbal lessons of a text) the primacy of the eye over the word in the sacramental economy. In this they may perhaps be making an affirmation of what Burch Brown calls "the right of any religious tradition to formulate certain aesthetic theories especially appropriate to its own religious understanding."[44] Christianity has the challenge of doing the same thing, which may not in every way be an easy task. For although theological aesthetics have recently begun a modest revival in some circles, there is, as we have shown, as yet comparatively little sustained debate about art *objects* (as channels of grace, as perceptual equivalents of the Real Presence, or even as servants of idolatry), as opposed to *theories* about art itself.

Yet theological and artistic developments remain historically interdependent, if not always integrated, with incarnational theology especially prominent in affirming the validity of aesthetics – and vice versa. In this sense art can continue to enhance our theological understanding. It reminds us that, although the traditional boundaries between the sacred and the profane have become increasingly blurred, and although what Michael Camille calls "our collective repositories of immanence"[45] may be in danger of disappearing altogether, the revelation of God, and our delight in responding to it in the medium of art as in every dimension of life, is not about to vanish away.

Notes

1   William Purdy, *Seeing and Believing: Theology and art* (Dublin and Cork, 1976), p. 118.

2   St John of Damascus, *On the Divine Images* (New York, 1980), pp. 56–7.

3   Francis Haskell, *Patrons and Painters* (London, 1965), p. 86.

4   John Ruskin, *Pre-Raphaelitism* (London, 1906 edition), p. 41.

5   Quoted by M. Camille, *The Gothic Idol* (Cambridge, 1990), p. 112.

6   The controversy is discussed *in extenso* in J. Pelikan, *Imago Dei* (New Haven, 1990).

7   G. B. Ladner, "Origin and Significance of the Byzantine Iconoclastic Controversy," in *Medieval Studies* (1940, no. 2), pp. 128–9.

8   M. Roskill (ed.), *The Letters of Vincent Van Gogh* (London, 1972), p. 151.

9   R. Williams, "Christian art and cultural pluralism," in *Eastern Churches Review*, VIII/1 (1976), p. 42.

10 Quoted in E. Holt, *A Documentary History of Art*, vol. II (New York, 1958), p. 362.

11 M. Weber, *The Sociology of Music* (Illinois, 1957), p. 117.

12 M. Peckham, *Romanticism and Behaviour: Collected essays,* vol. II (Durham, SC, 1957), pp. 94–5.

13 P. Berger and T. Luckmann, *The Social Reality of Religion* (London, 1969), passim.

14 M. Eliade, *Symbolism, the Sacred, and the Arts* (New York, 1992), passim.

15 P. Fuller, *Theoria: Art and the absence of grace* (London, 1988) is an insightful explanation of many of the themes raised in the essay.

16 Quoted in S. J. Barnes, *The Rothko Chapel* (Austin, TX, 1989), p. 25.

17 Interview in *Modern Painters*, 2/1 (1989), p. 69.

18 H. Küng, *Art and the Question of Meaning* (London, 1981), pp. 12–13.

19 R. Williams, "Christian art," p. 39.

20 P. Tillich, *On Art and Architecture*, ed. J. and J. Dillenberger (New York, 1960), p. 133.

21 H. Rosenberg, *Tradition and the New* (New York, 1960), p. 210.

22 J. Berger, *Ways of Seeing* (London, 1972), passim.

23 G. Steiner *Real Presences* (London, 1989), passim.

24 J. Dillenberger, *A Theology of Artistic Sensibilities* (London, 1987), p. 217.

25 K. Barth, *Wolfgang Amadeus Mozart* (Grand Rapids, MI, 1986), pp. 33–40, 55–7.

26 K. Barth, "The architectural problem of Protestant places of worship," in A. Bieler (ed.), *Architecture and Worship* (Edinburgh and London, 1965), p. 93.

27 R. Otto, *The Idea of the Holy* (London, 1959), p. 85.

28 P. Tillich, "On the theology of fine art and architecture," in *On Art and Architecture*, p. 207.

29 Ibid., p. 219.

30 Ibid., p. 80.

31 Ibid., p. 113.

32 Ibid., p. 124.

33 Ibid., introduction by the editors, p. xxv.

34 See David Jasper's perceptive discussion of Abstract Expressionism in "Untitled: Theology and American Abstract Expression," in *Religious Studies and Theology* (April 1995), pp. 21–35.

35 K. Rahner, "Theology and the Arts," in *Thought: Fordham University Quarterly*, 57 (1982), pp. 24–5.

36 R. Hart, *Unfinished Man and the Imagination* (New York, 1979), p. 19.

37 J. Cobb, *Christ in a Pluralistic Age* (Philadelphia, 1984), passim.

38 H. Küng, *Art and the Question of Meaning*, p. 52.

39 M. C. Taylor, *Disfiguring* (Chicago, 1992), p. 114.

40 Quoted in F. Burch Brown, *Religious Aesthetics* (Princeton, NJ, 1989), p. 146.

41 Ibid., p. 17.

42 Ibid., p. 158.

43 J. A. Martin, *Beauty and Holiness* (Princeton, NJ, 1990), p. 132.

44 Burch Brown, *Religious Aesthetics*, p. 186.

45 Camille, *The Gothic Idol*, p. 147.

Bibliography

Primary

Balthasar, Han Urs von, *The Glory of the Lord: A theological aesthetics*, 7 vols (San Francisco, 1982–6).

Barth, Karl, *Wolfgang Amadeus Mozart*, trans. C. K. Pott (Grand Rapids, MI, 1986).

—— "The architectural problem of Protestant places of worship," in *Architecture in Worship: The Christian Place of Worship*, ed. A. Bieler (Edinburgh and London, 1986).

Cobb, John B., *Christ in a Pluralistic Age* (Philadelphia, 1984).

Eliade, Mircea, *Symbolism, the Sacred, and the Arts*, ed. D. Apostolos-Cappadona (New York, 1985).

Hart, Ray L., *Unfinished Man and the Imagination: Toward an ontology and rhetoric of revelation* (New York, 1979).

Küng, Hans, *Art and the Question of Meaning*, trans. E. Quinn (London, 1981).

Rahner, Karl, "Theology and the Arts," in *Thought: Fordham University Quarterly*, 57 (March 1982).

Taylor, Mark C., *Disfiguring – Art, Architecture, Religion* (Chicago, 1992).

Tillich, Paul, *On Art and Architecture*, ed. J. and J. Dillenberger (New York, 1987).

Wolterstorff, Nicholas, *Art in Action: Toward a Christian aesthetic* (Grand Rapids, MI, 1980).

Secondary

Adams, D., and Apostolos-Cappadona, D. (eds), *Art as Religious Studies* (New York, 1987).

Apostolos-Cappadona, D. (ed.), *Art, Creativity and the Sacred*, rev. 2nd edn (New York, 1996).

Baggley, J., *Doors of Perception: Icons and their spiritual significance* (London, 1987).

Begbie, J. S., *Voicing Creation's Praise* (Edinburgh, 1991).

Belting, H., *Likeness and Presence* (Chicago, 1994).

Berger, J., *Ways of Seeing* (London, 1972).

Berger, P. and Luckmann, T., *The Social Reality of Religion* (London, 1970).

Brown, F. Burch, *Religious Aesthetics* (Princeton, NJ, 1989).

Burman, P. and Nugent, K. (eds), *Prophecy and Vision* (Bristol, 1982).

Camille, M., *The Gothic Idol* (Cambridge, 1990).

Cope, G. (ed.), *Christianity and the Visual Arts* (London, 1964).

Dillenberger, Jane, *Style and Content in Christian Art* (New York, 1965).

Dillenberger, John, *A Theology of Artistic Sensibilities* (London, 1987).

Dixon, J. W., *Art and the Theological Imagination* (New York, 1978).

Fuller, P., *Theoria: Art and the Absence of Grace* (London, 1988).

Harned, D. B., *Theology and the Arts* (Philadelphia, 1966).

Harries, R., *Art and the Beauty of God* (London, 1993).

Jasper, D., "Untitled: Theology and American Abstract Expression," in *Religious Studies and Theology* (April 1995).

Laeuchli, S., *Religion and Art in Conflict* (Philadelphia, 1980).

Male, E., *Religious Art: From the twelfth to the eighteenth century* (New York, 1949).

Martin, D., "Secularization and the Arts – the case of music," in *The Religious and the Secular* (London, 1969).

Martin, J. A., *Beauty and Holiness: The dialogue between aesthetics and religion* (Princeton, NJ, 1990).

Martland, T. R., *Religion as Art: An interpretation* (Albany, NY, 1990).

Nichols, A., *The Art of God Incarnate: Theology and symbol from Genesis to the twentieth century* (London, 1980).

Pattison, G., *Art, Modernity and Faith* (London, 1991).

Peckham, M., "Iconography and iconology in the arts of the nineteenth and twentieth centuries," in *Romanticism and Behavior* (Durham, SC, 1976).

Pelikan, J., *Imago Dei: The Byzantine apology for icons* (New Haven, 1990).

Rookmaaker, H. R., *Modern Art and the Death of a Culture* (Wheaton, IL, and Leicester, 1994).

Starkings, D. (ed.), *Religion and the Arts in Education: Dimensions of spirituality* (London, 1993).

Steiner, G., *Real Presences* (London, 1989).

Van der Leeuw, *Sacred and Profane Beáuty* (London, 1963).

Williams, R., "Christian art and cultural pluralism," in *Eastern Churches Review*, VIII/1 (1976).

Yates, W., *The Arts in Theological Education* (Atlanta, GA, 1987).

ARTS (The Arts in Religious and Theological Studies) (Minneapolis, 1988 onwards) is a very useful journal. See especially articles on "Art and the tradition: theology, art and meaning" by Mary Charles Murray (Summer 1993) and "Seeing theologically" by John W. Cook (June 1988).

Theology and the Arts: Music

Jeremy Begbie

Introduction

The interaction between music and theology is a field in which modern theologians are conspicuous by their absence. The visual arts have been tackled extensively by some (as the previous section demonstrates) and the same could be said of literature. But music has received very little sustained attention. There are some notable exceptions, one of the most recent being Frances Young's book *The Art of Performance*, a penetrating essay in musical hermeneutics,[1] and there have been a few courageous forays by musicologists into theology.[2] But in general, very few twentieth-century theologians have seen fit to trace significant connections between, on the one hand, the intriguing world of improvising a blues, tuning a violin, teaching children a song, and on the other, the world of theology with its supposedly limitless interests and scope.

In some respects this is puzzling. The presence of music in virtually all cultures past and present is well attested. Our so-called postmodern context is saturated by a huge range of music. Several theologians in previous centuries have treated music with theological seriousness (e.g., Augustine). Moreover, for large tracts of the church's history, music has had a crucial role as a vehicle of communication and an even more prominent place in corporate worship. Christian doctrine has at times significantly affected the form, content, and development of music, and arguably, this worked in the other direction too: Music is bound to affect our apprehension of that which is articulated through it.

Nevertheless, more often than not, the theologian's stance toward music has been characterized by hesitation and suspicion, with the result that what theological treatment of music there has been habitually gravitates toward ethical matters, the ethical propriety of this or that form of music. A number of factors can be mentioned as contributing to this uncertainty. There are those which apply to virtually all the arts, for example, the church's fear of idolatry, an anxiety about the materiality of the arts, the seeming triviality of the arts compared to more pressing life-and-death issues, the fact that the church is no longer a major agent of artistic renewal, the general wane of explicitly religious symbolism in the arts, and a cast of mind which tends to isolate the arts and marginalize them in favor of other spheres of human endeavor. With regard to music, since at least the time of Plato there have been profound misgivings about the peculiar emotional power of music, and thus, not least in the church, a fear of the capacity of music to manipulate. Combined with this, music's competence in specifically referring to extra-musical objects and states of affairs is generally regarded as very limited, leaving many not only dubious about its ability to be "truth-bearing" but fearful that it will inevitably draw us away from reality. Even more significant is music's evanescence. Where is the symphony when the last chord ceases? While music's transience has endeared it to some theologians, for others it has brought a deep uneasiness, especially if theology is thought to deal primarily with matters which are enduring and stable. Furthermore, rigorous thinking about music is extraordinarily demanding and often leaves a strong sense of inadequacy. Music is stubbornly irreducible to empirical seizure, a matter much dwelt upon by George Steiner and for him of great theological significance.[3] As Hans Keller put it: "There is no art that produces as much comfort for the mind feeling and thinking it, and as much discomfort for the mind thinking about it, as . . . music."[4]

In any case, whatever the reasons for modern theology's "tone-deafness," unlike most of the other chapters in this book, we will have difficulty in providing a "survey" or "debate," let alone an account of "influence" or "achievement," given the relatively paltry quantity of material at our disposal. Nonetheless, as far as "agenda" is concerned, there is much to say. The conversation between theology and music is potentially one of great fruitfulness, and what little interaction there has already been in this century is, in some cases, highly suggestive. The time is especially ripe for such interaction, given the growing literature on the politics, sociology, and psychology of music, the recent emergence of ethnomusicology, and the intriguing deployment of musical metaphors by a number of natural scientists.

Here we attempt to evoke something of the possibilities of the field. The intention will be not so much to situate music in relation to some relatively fixed environment of systematic theology, but to proceed from particular musical phenomena and explore their theological resonances. Jacques Attali declares that "Music is more than an object of study: it is a way of perceiving the world. My intention is . . . not only to theorise *about* music, but to theorise *through* music."[5] Attali's interests are in the socioeconomic aspects of music, but his words prompt the question: What would it mean to theologize not simply *about* music but *through* music? Here we attempt to indicate something of what such an enterprise might entail, in the belief that through it new features of theological truth are apprehended and familiar features apprehended in fresh ways.[6] Because of limitations of space, we shall limit ourselves to two dimensions of music: musical time and improvisation. We shall concentrate on one major tradition of music – the "tonal" tradition, which has dominated Western music for the last 300 years or so. And we shall focus most of the discussion on music without words, since we are keen to bring to light the distinctive features and theological capacities of music in its own right.

Musical Time

To begin with the obvious: Music takes time. But it takes time not only in the sense that it requires duration, but that it enmeshes closely with the patterns of time in which we live our lives. This has not always been appreciated. The capacity of music to offer a measure of distance from the times which command daily life has led some to see in music a means of evoking or approximating to a time*less* condition or state. The twentieth century has seen many such uses of music – Olivier Messiaen[7] and the contemporary English composer John Tavener[8] are two examples. On occasions this has been supported by a theological rationale which acclaims music's ability to suggest the (purported) "timelessness" of eternity. This is sometimes allied to an appeal to what is perceived to be music's freedom from physical things, its insubstantiality – music is the most "spiritual" (i.e., nonphysical) of the arts.[9] By contrast, we shall suggest that music can be most theologically fruitful precisely in and through its ability to interact positively with time, and this is closely bound up with its thoroughly physical character. As such, it has much to contribute in a culture which seems unable to live peaceably with time: We have tended to regard time as enemy or threat, and therefore as requiring either to be controlled (witness, for example, the modern reification of "clock-time") or to be escaped in some manner (as in various contemporary forms of allegedly "time-denying" spirituality). Music shows us that these are not the only options.

To appreciate this we take a step back and note the way in which two doctrinal convictions normative to Christian orthodoxy – the reality of time as intrinsic to God's creation, and its fundamentally positive character as part of God's "good ordering" of the world – have frequently been eclipsed in the history of theology, with damaging consequences. It has often been pointed out, for example, that modern christology has been plagued by various forms of a pernicious dichotomy between time and eternity, appearing as a split between the "accidental truths of history" and "necessary truths of reason," the contingent particular and the universal, the "historical" Jesus and the Christ of faith, and so on, resulting in an inability to come to terms adequately with God's direct engagement with our time in Jesus Christ. It is probable that part of the difficulty lies in a profound suspicion about the reality and goodness of time in much Christian thought and practice.

The seminal work of Augustine (354–430) is as good a place to start as any. "What then is time?" Augustine asks. "Provided that no one asks me, I know. If I want to explain it to an inquirer, I do not know."[10] At the heart of Augustine's intellectual struggle with time lies the problem of temporal extension in the face of the bewildering experience of the nonappearance of the future, the disappearance of the past, and therefore – he presumed – the nonexistence of both. If Gerard O'Daly is correct, behind Augustine's "what then is time?" lies not the search for a definition but the question: How can we measure time given *distentio animi*,[11] the sense of temporality as fractured and dispersed (in contrast to God). Augustine concludes that, despite its being extensionless and having no duration, only the "present" is, in the sense of "exists now."[12] Nevertheless, the past and future are present in the mind, in memory and expectation respectively. So the answer to the question "how can we measure time?" is: in the mind.[13] We measure the effect or "impression (*affectio*)" which perceptions leave behind, like footprints, in the memory.[14]

The two doctrinal issues noted above need to be highlighted here. First, there is the reality of time as intrinsic to God's created order. As Brian Leftow shows,[15] Augustine adopted the Neoplatonic conviction that "true" existence is immutable existence; crudely put, timeless entities exist more genuinely than temporal ones. This goes hand in hand with Augustine's conviction that genuine existence is present existence. The upshot is to render the reality of time itself ambivalent, even within the mind (his notion of past, present, and future all being "at once" in the mind has the paradoxical effect of making time more like eternity). Second, similar things can be said of the goodness of time. Augustine appears dubious about the temporal world as a potential sphere of constructive order. Significantly, Augustine's high regard for music was not principally for what it could achieve *qua* temporal but in what it could effect in relation to that which is utterly beyond the temporal order. His relatively early work, *De Musica*, mediated a modified form of the aesthetics of Plato and Plotinus and was to have an enormous influence on medieval aesthetic thought. Music is able to lead the soul from the world of sense to intelligible reality, by enabling us to delight in the eternal numbers of reason rather than the "lower" numbers of sense, and thus to rise toward God. In the *Confessions*, the attitude to the created order, materiality, and temporality is more affirmative, but the primary orientation with regard to time and music (and, indeed, the other arts) remains essentially intact.[16] God desires to "re-collect" the distended mind, bringing it back from the distracting world of the temporal to that contemplation from which it fell. Music can serve this purpose (although Augustine here considers only the "music" of spoken words). Insofar as music is the bearer of meter and rhythm and as such offers a "time-bridging" glimpse of the unified order of eternity, there is implicitly a positive account of music here. Nevertheless, music's primary significance is not that it can embody temporal order per se, but that it can empower the mind, despite its agonising *distentio*, to apprehend the timeless order of eternity.

What would seem to be required is to follow through more consistently Augustine's own conviction that the world was created not before time or in time but with time, and that therefore there can be no time without the created world.[17] This would be part and parcel of a thoroughgoing doctrine of *creatio ex nihilo* in which time is established as a real and good part of God's good world, and of the incarnation, in which the Creator directly engages with created time as part of his redemption of all things, so confirming both its reality and fundamental goodness.

Music, we would contend, is of considerable assistance here. For it challenges the ambivalence about time's reality which has marred so much post-Augustinian theology, showing not only the conceivability but also the concrete possibility of time as intrinsic to the created world. Of decisive importance here is the work of the Austrian musicologist Victor Zuckerkandl.[18] He observes that the most direct way in which music engages with time is through meter, the pattern of beats, grouped in bars, which underlies most music. These beats are arranged in waves of tension and resolution. They are not simply points on a timeline but dynamically interrelated to one another within a dynamic wave-field. Zuckerkandl proposes that it is time itself which is generative of this dynamic interrelatedness: The beats are related to each other dynamically in and through time. A parallel claim is made about melody: Each note is internally connected to what precedes it and what follows it; in every note there is a carrying of what precedes it and a pointing toward its future. Again, argues Zuckerkandl, it is time which accomplishes this energetic interrelatedness. If Zuckerkandl is correct – and we are having to exclude large portions of the argument – time is disclosed in music not as an absolute receptacle or inert background, nor merely as psychological or cultural construction, but as an integral function of the interrelationship between entities, as an intrinsic dimension of physical realities.

Moreover, music also poses a number of challenges to any assumption of a necessary bond between temporality and fallenness. Three can be noted here. First, and perhaps most obviously, music demonstrates that there can be ordered change, structure and dynamics. Music undermines "the dogma that order is possible only in the enduring, the immutably fixed, the substantial"; music presents us with "the unprecedented spectacle of an order that is wholly flux, of a building without matter."[19] Second, music challenges the assumption that because something takes time to be what it is, it is thereby ontologically inferior to that which is not subject to created time. Music concretely models the profoundly biblical conviction that it need not be regarded as a vice of creation that it can reach its perfection only in and through time. Third, music challenges the assumption that temporal limits or boundaries are necessarily problematic or damaging. A supposed link between transience and futility runs deep in many cultures, including our own. Music is constantly dying, giving way: The next note in the plainsong melody can only come if the last one is not sung. Notes never coagulate, as it were, to form a substantial thing. Music relies more than any other art on the incessant birthing and dying of finite entities. It is the art-form most prone to the supposed destructive effects of time. *And yet*, music can also be ordered, glorious, and enhancing, the very opposite of futile. Music can "sound forth" the theological truth that limited duration can be beneficial, and moreover, can be known as divine generosity. It liberates us from the illusion that we must try to be as God. It is in this light that we should approach Karl Barth's notorious adulation of Mozart's music as a "parable of the Kingdom."[20] Why did Barth believe this composer deserved a central place in theology, "especially in the doctrine of creation and also in eschatology"?[21] Why did he think the angels sang Mozart in heaven? The answer is seen when we recall that in the *Church Dogmatics* the fulsome eulogy on Mozart appears in the midst of a discussion of the "shadowside (*Schattenseite*)" or negative aspect of the universe. Comparison with a later passage[22] makes it probable that Barth is thinking of finitude and all its effects (including death). This is not to be confused with evil (*das Nichtige*) – that would mask the destructive nature of the latter and suggest that finitude was somehow itself evil. The shadowside is the expression of God's "positive will, election and activity."[23] Mozart's music appears as articulating the praise of creation in all its aspects: It sings the praise of the cosmos in its "total goodness," *including its shadowside*. Mozart's music contains its "No" but this is the "No" of the shadowside, not evil.[24] In Mozart's music "the shadow is not darkness, deficiency is not defeat, sadness cannot become despair, trouble cannot degenerate into tragedy and infinite melancholy is not ultimately forced to claim undisputed sway."[25] Even the limit of death is acknowledged by Mozart, but he heard the negative only in and with the positive: God's almighty "Yes" to creation. In Mozart's music, therefore, creation praises God in its very finitude and thus shows what authentic praise truly is.[26] This is what gives Mozart's music its "freedom," its light and effortless quality.[27] It is the freedom of creation liberated to praise God in and through its God-given temporal limitations.

To draw this together, the Christian faith announces that our experience of temporality corresponds to a dimension of created reality with its own integrity established by the Creator. This temporality is a good gift: Our interaction with time need not be characterized by struggle, competition, intrusion, or invasion, nor by retreat, evasion, or escape. Music, in this context, has inestimable potential in demonstrating that these two broad routes do not exhaust the possibilities: Music can provide a concrete means of establishing a more contented "living peaceably with time" than our contemporary existence seems to offer.

When we move from the doctrine of creation to salvation, the temporality of music is found to be no less rich with theological import. In order to see something of this, we should note that the temporal order of Western music has generally, though not exclusively, operated according to teleological principles. That is to say, it typically possesses an integral relational order which in its overall constitution is sensed or perceived as directional, leading to some kind of goal or "gathering together" of the temporal process. This teleological dynamic is generated primarily through the twin elements of tension and resolution: Tensions are established which demand some form of resolution. Configurations of tension and resolution work in many different ways and levels, engaging every parameter of music.

The resonances of this with salvation are varied and fecund and might go at least part of the way toward explaining why music has been so pervasively employed by the church in its celebration of God's saving work. We mention three of these resonances here.

First, music schools us in a concentrated way in the biblical art of patience. One of the crucial skills of any composer is ordering the dynamic "space" between tension and resolution, deferring gratification such that hope in the assured resolution, and thus patience, is sustained. Israel's faith might be characterized as one enormous upbeat spanning the centuries, in a continual though varied state of patient tension. In the New Testament there is a further discernment of incompletion: "For the creation waits with eager longing . . . if we hope for what we do not see, we wait for it with patience" (Romans 8: 19, 25). Yet this waiting, of course, is never described as being empty or void. Music grants us a "meantime" which is not a bland, homogeneous, and inert state of being, nor a period of stoical resigned fortitude, but one which is fulsome and enhancing. At its best – and there is much church music which singularly fails to do this – music invites us to discover a kind of patience which enlarges and deepens us in the very waiting. To put it another way, in the patience proper to salvation something new is learned which cannot be learned in any other way. In effect, music says to us: "There are things you will learn only by passing through this process, by being caught up in this series of relations and transformations."[28]

Second, music can offer the experience of resolution as the intensification of hope. As in Scripture, so in a piece of music, not every resolution is delayed. Otherwise we would simply lose patience and interest. We are given partial resolutions of varying degrees of settledness. These provisional realizations, far from diminishing expectation, serve to intensify it. Music's temporal structure operates chiefly through a hierarchy of metrical waves of tension and resolution. A move toward resolution at one level will increase the tension at a higher level. However strong the sense of resolution may be at any particular level, *there will always be a higher level (or levels) in relation to which every resolution process generates a heightening of tension, giving rise to a stronger reaching out for further resolution.* The correspondences between this and the character of Jewish and Christian hope are remarkable and hardly need to be pointed out. "Fulfillments" both ease tension and intensify it. The coming of Christ is a resolution on the level of the collective hopes of Israel; at other levels, supremely in the overarching purposes of God, it functions as a spur toward yet more fervent longing. It may well be that numerous pseudo-problems in eschatology have arisen because of a failure to think in terms of a multilevel temporal process, and a tendency to believe "fulfillment" can only properly take place at one level in one singular event – the temporality of musical tension and resolution not only provides fresh conceptualities for us here but vividly articulates them in sound.

Third, the dynamic order of music entails an interpenetration of the temporal modes of past, present, and future. The time in which music occurs is subject to a mutual alienation of past, present, and future. Created time is "refracted time, time that has broken loose from God."[29] So, for example, the worst of our past condemns us, and the best (we suspect) is lost for ever, rapidly receding into nothingness. Our future becomes apparently impenetrable, and thus engenders the fear that a step into the future might be a step into nothingness. Furiously filling the future in anticipation is a common but dangerous ploy, pouring energy into hopes likely to be dashed. It is small wonder that the culture of modernity takes refuge in the isolated present, and postmodernity engenders the fragmentation of past, present, and future (witness the welter of discontinuous images of the "screen culture"). Whatever else salvation involves, it entails a reconfiguration of our time in Jesus Christ. The worst of humanity's past is judged and buried in the grave; the glory of the past, especially Israel's past, is not lost but carried forward, renewed, and directed toward a future. In Christ's life, death and resurrection, creation's past, present, and future are re-integrated, made to co-inhere. In the risen and ascended Christ, there is a kind of newness which neither negates time nor grows old. Through the Spirit who binds us to Christ, we share in this healed temporality such that our past can be reoriented to a promised future and thus transfigure our present.

As we have already indicated, music is capable of "sounding forth" a temporality in which the past of a musical occurrence does not retreat into an ever-receding "beyond," but is carried by its constant future orientation, borne along by its waves of tension and resolution. Musical events do not fall backwards into vacuity: They are new in the sense of being *always new*. Similarly, the future of a musical event is not the future of the bleak unknown, but the future whose charge, so to speak, is experienced in the "now" as it bears its past. As musical occurrences anticipate their future they carry their past; as their future is *un*folded, their past – and ours – is *en*folded. This is the dynamic into which we are invited and caught up by music. "To a great extent the problems posed by the old concept of time arise from the fact that it distinguished three mutually exclusive elements, whereas only the picture of a constant interaction and intertwining of these elements is adequate to the actual process [of music]."[30] In this way, therefore, music "takes" our time and "returns it" to us reshaped, and this bears a striking correspondence to the dynamic at the heart of redemption, through which creation's temporal disruption is in some manner amended. It is a correspondence which opens up enormous possibilities for the theologian who seeks to expound the temporal facets of salvation, and not least as they are concentrated in the *anamnesis* of the eucharist.

Improvisation

Improvisation, "the simultaneous conception and production of sound in performance,"[31] despite the flurry of interest in it in recent years by musicologists,[32] is treated by many musicians with suspicion, even disdain. For some it is synonymous with anti-musical randomness, an absence of intellectual rigor, or unbridled emotionalism. Yet the evidence is that not only is there an element of improvisation in virtually all music of all cultures, but that there is scarcely a musical technique or form of composition that did not originate in improvisation or was not essentially influenced by it. Musical notation did not exist until about AD 800, and the notion of a performer adhering strictly to a score is relatively recent. (It is worth recalling that Bach, Mozart, and Beethoven were all as well known in some circles as improvisers as they were composers.) Even with scrupulously notated music, decisions still have to be taken about the exact tempo, phrasing, emphasis, dynamics, timbre, and so forth, and much will depend on the circumstances of the performance. All this might suggest that instead of regarding music which is strictly notated and largely planned as the norm and improvisation as an unfortunate distortion or epiphenomenon, it might be more illuminating to invert that and ask whether improvisation reveals to us fundamental aspects of musical creativity easily forgotten in traditions bound predominantly to the practices of rigorous rehearsal and notation.

If it does, any conversation between theology and music must take improvisation very seriously. Moreover, we quickly discover that striking theological overtones emerge in any study of improvisation. (It is perhaps no accident that some of the most sophisticated and influential forms of musical improvisation have emerged in the church.) Writers such as Arthur Peacocke have already made effective use of the model of improvisation in relation to the doctrine of creation, to illuminate God's free interaction with the world.[33] Here we shall concentrate on three other areas of theological possibility.

First, much of the recent literature on improvisation has highlighted the implicit social and even political provocations it presents. Group improvisation questions many dominant procedures through which music is made, reproduced, circulated, and consumed today. In particular, it disrupts conventional barriers between "composer," "performer," and "audience," for an improviser is (normally) all three concurrently. Without necessarily conceding the more inflated claims about improvisation as an embryonic microcosm of social utopia, there is undoubtedly much to be said for the verdict, common to many writers, that improvisation offers uncommon opportunities for profitable "dialogical interrelations" between musicians.[34] In more formalized concert music-making, communication is interposed by an external agency, the score. By shifting attention to social process rather than the resulting text, improvisation encourages a particular kind of immediacy of personal exchange which is undoubtedly one of its most attractive features.

In this way, improvisation can enable to a significant extent what Alistair McFadyen has described as "undistorted communication." In "monologue" the individual manipulates or is manipulated: One person treats the other as a means to an end, such that the other becomes self-confirmatory, the other's "otherness" becomes "a repetition of a privately co-ordinated understanding."[35] In "dialogue" or undistorted communication, the other's freedom is acknowledged such that one allows for the possibility of one's own expectations and intentions to be resisted: "To recognise and intend the freedom of the other in response is to recognise that the form and content of that response cannot be overdetermined by the address."[36] "There is a readiness to allow the calls of others to transform us in response."[37] This does not entail assuming the "superiority" of the other, nor quantitative equality between dialogue partners. Commenting on McFadyen's work, Francis Watson writes: "Something similar is suggested by the Pauline image of the church as body, where the allocation of varying gifts and roles by the same Spirit establishes a formal [not quantitative] equality... within a diversity of roles which allows for hierarchical elements so long as these are understood in strictly reciprocal rather than monological terms."[38] Very much the same could be said of improvisation, in which there is the constitution of personal particularity through reciprocal musical dialogue. All the skills which promote undistorted communication – which are to characterize the church considered as persons in active communion – are, in the best forms of improvisation, present to a very heightened degree; for example, alertness of the whole person, rigorous discipline and training that can never be entirely formalized into rules, attentive listening and contributing, sensitive decision-making, risking, role-changing, resolving conflict, and (often most important) keeping silent. Moreover, the nonverbal character of musical improvisation means that these skills have to be learned in new ways, and often in more intense ways, given the absence of conventional verbal communication. (This may have much to say about widening music in worship in many churches to include more improvisatory practice by the whole congregation, not least in social contexts where hegemonic power suppresses the contribution of dissident groups.)

Second, improvisation, to a very large extent, entails what the poet Peter Riley has called "the exploration of occasion."[39] Much depends on the particularities of the specific context of performance – for example, the acoustic of the building, the time of day, the number of people present, their expectations and experience, their audible responses as the performance proceeds, and, not least, the music produced by fellow-improvisers. These elements are not accidental to the outcome but constitutive of it. A skillful improviser, in bringing alive the "given" material – whether chord sequence, agreed overall structure, or whatever – endeavors not only to be sensitive to such contextual factors but to incorporate them into the improvisation in some manner, in order that the improvisation is, so to speak, "true" and profoundly authentic to this time and place. Moreover, with its large measure of openness, this particularizing process, it is commonly acknowledged, generates an intense sense of anticipation and hopefulness.

At a time of renewed interest in the doctrine of the Holy Spirit, this dimension of improvisation may have much to contribute to the search for new conceptualities in pneumatology. The Spirit is the Spirit of faithfulness, of fidelity to the givenness of God's self-declaration in Jesus Christ. But, far from merely replicating this "given," the Spirit constantly actualizes it in a way which engages with and brings to fruition the particularities of each time and place. As is often said now – and here much recent pneumatology is attempting to obviate problematic and even harmful aspects of the Western tradition – though it is the work of Spirit to unify, to bind and sustain togetherness, this activity includes in and with it the recognition and promotion of particularity and distinctiveness. On the day of Pentecost, the Spirit did not create one uniform language but liberated people to hear each other "in their own tongues" (Acts 2: 6, 11). Pentecost was a divine "exploration of occasion" if ever there was one. Furthermore, this particularizing activity is a function of the Spirit's eschatological ministry to anticipate here and now in ever fresh ways the Father's final, eschatological desire (2 Corinthians 1: 22; Ephesians 1: 14; Romans 8: 23): The particularizing engenders hope. Life in the Spirit, therefore, involves a combination of faithfulness and particularizing what is received in the present in anticipation of the future. This is the dynamic of musical improvisation. If it is true, as many urge, that we sorely require models of the Spirit's work, which in hermeneutics take full account of the particularities of the present as well as faithfulness to the apostolic witness of Scripture,[40] and which in theologies of mission and ministry avoid over-stressing backward orientation to the career of Jesus and the apostolic church, then improvisation has much to offer, given the way in which its disciplined fidelity to a shared tradition and its concern for singularity of circumstance are interwoven in a dynamic of patient hopefulness.

Third, although all music-making involves a significant amount of physical involvement, improvisation foregrounds this aspect of music to a high degree. When there is no music to read, the relation between performer and instrument becomes especially close. You are more directly aware of the instrument you are playing, its limitations and possibilities. Moreover, improvisation makes one more acutely conscious of the physical sounds themselves: Insofar as improvisation is a thought process, it is not so much imposing a grid of pure thought on acoustic phenomena, it is rather thinking in notes and rhythms; not thinking "before" them, or on to them, or through them but thinking *in* physical sound – notes, melodies, harmonies, meters. You indwell these physical realities, and establish them as you rearrange them. In other words, improvisation is a form of listening to (and shaping) configurations of the material world whose peculiar integrity calls forth from us careful, attentive respect. The "freedom" so celebrated and enjoyed in improvisation is not primarily freedom from the constraint of the physical but a freedom discovered in an attentive "attunement to living sound," a courteous interaction with a rich and multivalent physical sonic order.

Related to this, embodiedness is especially crucial to improvisation, for the embeddedness of music in the physical world is mediated through our own physicality.

In his remarkable book *Ways of the Hand*,[41] David Sudnow gives an account of his struggle to learn to improvise jazz. Most manuals on learning to improvise, he found, treated the hands as no more than instruments subservient to the mind: The books give you "places to go" and then tell you what to do with your hands to get there. Sudnow memorized these devices, but when it came to playing in a trio he found "The music was literally 'out of hand' . . . The music was not mine."[42] The breakthrough into authentic jazz came when he trusted his hands to explore their own relation to the physical peculiarities of the keyboard. He discovered that particular sorts of sound were associated with particular configurations of the hand; in playing blues, for example, one aims, not so much for particular notes or groups of notes, but for a characteristic sound produced by a specific hand-shape. Sudnow realized that because it operates in this way, the hand has all sorts of surprises in store for the pianist. Interestingly, before he made this discovery, he was acutely aware of making mistakes. But now, an unforeseen "mistake" or "error" could be taken up by the hand – the hand could "make the best of things." The hands, then, far from being passive instruments of the intellect, he found to be both intrinsic and essential to the musical process. "To define jazz," says Sudnow, "is to *describe* the body's ways."[43] He made further progress by acknowledging that the movement of the whole body played a crucial part – "finger-snapping, head-bobbing, arm-and-shoulder rotating" all became integral parts of improvisation rather than merely accompaniments to it.[44] Critical also was the place of singing, the most basic bodily form of music-making. "I sing with my fingers," he claims.[45] Musical intention was thus formed through a "mutual jurisdiction" between voice and hand, a "joint knowing of voice and fingers."[46]

Improvisation brings to the foreground these physical dimensions of music-making. The fact that the improviser's freedom is discovered in what we have called a "courteous interaction" might well provide models of divine freedom and creativity which do greater justice than some to the materiality of God's presence to the world in Jesus Christ, in and through whom creation's integrity is neither over-ridden nor ignored but established and renewed. Moreover, a theological account of our own active embodiedness in the physical world at large, which seeks to avoid over-intellectual accounts of what it is to be human, or accounts which suggest patterns of oppressive domination in relation to the nonhuman order, will be greatly served by attentiveness to the practice of improvisation.

Coda

> A beat poised, a crossgrained rhythm,
> interplays, imbrications of voice over voice,
> mutinies of living are rocking the steady
> state of a theme; these riffs and overlappings
> a love of deviance, our genesis in noise.[47]

It remains to be seen how far theologians avail themselves of the opportunities afforded by music, opportunities which we have only hinted at above. But it may well be that the discovery this poet has made about the potential of music to evoke the dynamics of the creation of the cosmos – and he is writing of improvisation – will be repeated in all sorts of ways that will astonish us and make us wonder how it is that so much theology this century has managed to do with so little music.

Notes

1 (London, 1990).
2 E.g., Wilfrid, Mellers, *Bach and the Dance of God* (New York, 1981); *Beethoven and the Voice of God* (New York, 1983); Eric Chafe, *Tonal Allegory in the Vocal Music of J. S. Bach* (Berkeley, 1991).
3 George Steiner, *Real Presences. Is There Anything in What We Say?* (London, 1989).
4 In Christopher Wintle (ed.), *Hans Keller: Essays on Music* (Cambridge, 1994), p. 121.
5 Jacques Attali, *Noise,* trans. Brian Massumi (Manchester, 1985), p. 4.
6 I develop this at length in *The Sound of God: Resonances between theology and music* (Cambridge, 1997, forthcoming).
7 As Messiaen's pupil Robert Sherlaw Johnson comments, "it has always been Messiaen's aim to suspend the sense of time in music . . . in order to express the idea of the 'eternal' – in which time does not exist – as distinct from the temporal." As quoted in Jonathan D. Kramer, *The Time of Music* (New York, 1988), p. 214.
8 Cf. Jeremy Begbie, "Theology through music: Tavener, time and eternity," in David Ford and Dennis Stamps (eds), *Essentials of Christian Community* (Edinburgh, 1996), pp. 23–48.
9 Such was the conviction of the Scottish Congregationalist theologian, P. T. Forsyth, writing at the turn of the last century. Cf. Jeremy Begbie, "The ambivalent rainbow: Forsyth, art and creation," in Trevor Hart (ed.), *Justice the True and Only Mercy* (Edinburgh, 1995), pp. 197–219.
10 *Confessions,* XI: 14.17.
11 Ibid., XI: 23.30; XI: 26.33; cf. also XI: 29.39.
12 Ibid., XI: 17.22–XI: 20.26.
13 Ibid., XI: 27.36.
14 Ibid., XI: 27.36; for the footprints metaphor, cf. XI: 18.23.
15 Brian Leftow, *Time and Eternity* (Ithaca and London, 1991), ch. 5.
16 *Confessions,* Book XI, especially 26.33; 28.38. Augustine could speak in rhapsodic terms about music, and at the same time fear its damaging pleasures. X: 33.49, 50.
17 Cf. *Confessions,* XI: 12.14–XI: 13.15.
18 Victor Zuckerkandl, *Man the Musician* (Princeton, 1973); *Sound and Symbol: Music and the external world* (London, 1956).
19 Zuckerkandl, *Sound and Symbol,* pp. 241f.
20 Karl Barth, *Wolfgang Amadeus Mozart,* trans. Clarence K. Pott (Grand Rapids, MI, 1986), p. 57.
21 Karl Barth, *Church Dogmatics,* III/3, trans. and ed. by G. W. Bromiley and T. F. Torrance (Edinburgh, 1960), p. 298.
22 Ibid., pp. 349f.
23 Ibid., p. 350.
24 Ibid., pp. 297ff.
25 Ibid., p. 298.
26 Later Barth speaks of the difference between shadowside and "nothingness" or *das Nichtige* – when the creature "crosses the frontier" of finitude, "nothingness achieves its actuality in the created world." Ibid., p. 350. This is just what Mozart's music does not do. Nor does Mozart: he does not obtrude himself in some "mania for self-expression" (ibid., p. 298) or in order to convey a message. He does not "will to proclaim the praise of God. He just does it – precisely in that humility in which he himself is, so to speak, only the instrument with which he allows us to hear what he hears: what surges at him from God's creation, what rises in him, and must proceed from him." *Wolfgang Amadeus Mozart,* p. 38. "He simply offered himself as the agent by which little bits of horn, metal and catgut could serve as the voices of creation." Ibid., p. 298.
27 *Wolfgang Amadeus Mozart,* pp. 47ff.
28 Rowan Williams, *Open to Judgement: Sermons and addresses* (London, 1994), p. 247

29 Thomas F. Torrance, *Space, Time and Resurrection* (Edinburgh, 1976), p. 97.
30 Zuckerkandl, *Sound and Symbol*, p. 228.
31 Roger Dean, *Creative Improvisation* (Milton Keynes, 1989), p. ix.
32 Cf. the survey by J. Pressing in "Improvisation: methods and models," in J. A. Sloboda (ed.), *Generative Processes in Music* (Oxford, 1988), pp. 141–5.
33 Arthur Peacocke, *Theology for a Scientific Age* (Oxford, 1993), pp. 175ff.
34 E. Prévost, "Improvisation: music for an occasion," in *British Journal of Music Education*, 2/2 (1985), pp. 177–86.
35 Alistair E. McFadyen, *The Call To Personhood: A Christian theory of the individual in social relationships* (Cambridge, 1990), p. 26.
36 Ibid., p. 119.
37 Ibid., p. 121.

38 Francis Watson, *Text, Church and World: Biblical interpretation in theological perspective* (Edinburgh, 1994), p. 112.
39 As cited in Dean, *Creative Improvisation*, p. xvi.
40 For an expansion of the improvisatory model in biblical hermeneutics, cf. N. T. Wright, *The New Testament and the People of God* (London, 1992), pp. 139ff.
41 D. Sudnow, *Ways of the Hand: The organisation of improvised conduct* (London, 1978).
42 Ibid., pp. 33, 30.
43 Ibid., p. 146.
44 Ibid., p. 104.
45 Ibid., p. 87.
46 Ibid., pp. 95, 150.
47 From "Cosmos," in Micheal O'Siadhail, *Hail! Madam Jazz: New and selected poems* (Newcastle, 1992), p. 149.

Bibliography

Attali, Jacques, *Noise*, trans. Brian Massumi (Manchester, 1985).

Augustine, *Confessions*, ed. Henry Chadwick (Oxford, 1991).

Bailey, D., *Improvisation: Its nature and practice in music* (London, 1992).

Barry, Barbara, *Musical Time: The sense of order* (Stuyvesant: 1990).

Barth, Karl, *Church Dogmatics*, III/3, trans. and ed. G. W. Bromiley and T. F. Torrance, (Edinburgh, 1960).

—— *Wolfgang Amadeus Mozart*, trans. Clarence K. Pott (Grand Rapids, MI, 1986).

Begbie, Jeremy S., *Music in God's Purposes* (Edinburgh, 1989).

—— "The ambivalent rainbow: Forsyth, art and creation," in Trevor Hart (ed.), *Justice the True and Only Mercy* (Edinburgh, 1995), pp. 197–219.

—— "Theology through music: Tavener, time and eternity," in David Ford and Dennis Stamps (eds), *Essentials of Christian Community* (Edinburgh, 1996), pp. 23–48.

—— *Voicing Creation's Praise: Towards a theology of the arts* (Edinburgh, 1991).

Bloch, Ernst, *Essays on the Philosophy of Music* (Cambridge, 1974).

Brown, David, and Loades, Ann (eds), *The Sense of the Sacramental: Movement and measure in art and music, place and time* (London, 1995).

Chafe, Eric, *Tonal Allegory in the Vocal Music of J. S. Bach* (Berkeley, CA, 1991).

Clifton, Thomas, *Music as Heard: A study in applied phenomenology* (New Haven, 1983).

Dean, Roger, *Creative Improvisation* (Milton Keynes, 1989).

Gunton, Colin, *The One, the Three and the Many: God, creation and the culture of modernity* (Cambridge, 1993).

—— "Mozart the Theologian," in *Theology*, 94 (1991), pp. 346–9.

Harvey, David, *The Condition of Postmodernity: An enquiry into the origins of cultural change* (Oxford, 1989).

Kramer, Jonathan D., *The Time of Music* (New York, 1988).

Leftow, Brian, *Time and Eternity* (Ithaca, NY, and London, 1991).

McFadyen, Alistair E., *The Call To Personhood: A Christian theory of the individual in social relationships* (Cambridge, 1990).

Mellers, Wilfrid, *Beethoven and the Voice of God* (New York, 1983).

—— *Bach and the Dance of God* (New York, 1981).

Meyer, Leonard B., *Emotion and Meaning in Music* (Chicago, 1970).

Nattiez, Jean-Jacques, *Music and Discourse: Toward a semiology of music*, trans. Carolyn Abbate (Princeton, NJ, 1990).

O'Siadhail, Micheal, *Hail! Madam Jazz: New and selected poems* (Newcastle, 1992).

Peacocke, Arthur, *Theology for a Scientific Age* (Oxford, 1993).

Pressing, J., "Improvisation: methods and models," in J. A. Sloboda (ed.), *Generative Processes in Music* (Oxford, 1988), pp. 128–78.

Prévost, E., "Improvisation: music for an occasion," in *British Journal of Music Education*, 2/2 (1985), pp. 177–86.

Sloboda, John, *The Musical Mind* (Oxford, 1983).

Smith, F. Joseph, *The Experiencing of Musical Sound: Prelude to a phenomenology of music* (New York, London, and Paris, 1979).

Steiner, George, *Real Presences: Is there anything in what we say?* (London, 1989).

Sudnow, D., *Ways of the Hand: The organisation of improvised conduct* (London, 1978).

Watson, Francis, *Text, Church and World: Biblical interpretation in theological perspective* (Edinburgh, 1994).

Williams, Rowan, *Open to Judgement: Sermons and addresses* (London, 1994).

Wintle, Christopher (ed.), *Hans Keller: Essays on music* (Cambridge, 1994).

Wright, N. T., *The New Testament and the People of God* (London, 1992).

Young, Frances, *The Art of Performance: Towards a theology of Holy Scripture* (London, 1990).

Zuckerkandl, Victor, *Man the Musician* (Princeton, 1973).

——*Sound and Symbol: Music and the external world* (London, 1956).

Theology and the Social Sciences

Richard H. Roberts

Introduction

At first sight, as observed from the standpoint of the social scientist, the relation of theology to the social sciences looks somewhat unpromising. The history of social science presents itself as a narrative of divergence from, and the surpassing of, both religion as such, and of the idea of there being a revealed core to Western culture. Modernity (*Neuzeit*) has witnessed the long and sometimes tortuous relinquishment of the central role of theology in culture and society. Indeed sociology understood in terms of "grand theory" may plausibly be understood in a certain sense as the successor to theology as "queen of the sciences." There is something of a natural progression from the *mentalité* of the once all-knowing theologian to that of the ambitious contemporary social scientist who aims not merely at comprehensive interpretation of human life-worlds, but also to promote the emancipatory role of social science as itself the agent of enlightened modernity. By contrast, the theologian would now seem to occupy a shrunken and marginalized residual territory confronted by a hostile secularized reality; such theology lives on in reduced circumstances. This is, of course, a gross simplification, not least because the theologies of mainline religion now face pluriform postmodern and New Age recompositions of the religious field.

From the early seventeenth century, as scholastic philosophy was confronted by early natural science and philosophy moved in Cartesian and empiricist directions, so the theological residuum was gradually whittled away. Correspondingly, from the early nineteenth century onward, disciplines in the social and human sciences differentiated themselves and this further usurped the territory of theological thought. Kant's magisterial attempt to stave off the nihilistic implications of an abstract juxtaposition of empiricism and idealism has now, some argue, reached the limit of its use. In an era of nihilism, the possibilities for theology seem both extreme and contradictory for, if we are to believe some commentators, there can be no common ground between theology and secular thought. Those who start out from such an uncompromising standpoint regard all mediating and liberal theologies as mistaken, even perverse, and have little regard for much of the theology examined in the present volume.

In the setting outlined above, it is possible to explore the relation of theology and the social sciences along two lines of approach. On the one hand, there are the efforts made by a number of theologians from Ernst Troeltsch and Dietrich Bonhoeffer onward who have sought to take account of sociological insights in their work. On the other hand, however, there is the larger question as to how the divergence of and subsequent relation between two inherently complex and contrasting (and in many respects antagonistic) traditions of reflection should be understood once other factors are taken into account. We therefore adopt the following procedure. First, through a brief survey and typology we outline five strategies of negotiation employed by representative theologians who have attempted to develop relationships between theology and the social sciences. Then second, key issues are drawn out and related to current debates which provide the basis for a more general appraisal of the relation of theology to the social sciences in the light of contrasting responses to modernity. In conclusion, a tentative agenda for theology in relation to the social sciences is proposed. The latter involves the formulation of a framework for the *episteme* of theology conceived as an emancipatory "human science."[1]

The engagement between theology and the social sciences has by and large been relatively one-sided. Some theologians have been committed to the use of socio-scientific insights, whereas social scientists have characteristically resisted normative styles of thought and favored modes of rationality which valorize critical, interpretative, quantitative, and theoretical skills, as opposed to concerns with ultimate or transcendental questions. The sociological imagination as classically deployed under-cuts religious and theological pretensions. Recently, however, the very extremity of twentieth-century history has provoked a number of sociologists into more explicit ethical and normative reflection.[2] Moreover, resurgent religion and religiosities, the ethnic revival, and the all-encompassing character of an "outer-directed" social order have provoked a revived socioscientific interest in religion that goes well beyond the limits of the subdiscipline of the sociology of religion. Other theoretical developments within post-structuralist cultural theory and associated sociological thought invite the posing of questions which, if they are not explicitly theological, certainly have a quasi-theological character. The representation of the human condition as susceptible to interpretation as premodern, modern, and postmodern also has considerable import for the construal of the relation of theology and the social sciences. Entrenched and doctrinaire oppositional stances may no longer be appropriate, but what alternative mode of intellectual cohabitation might now be more fitting is a contested question.

Theologians and the Social Sciences: Survey and Typology

From the side of Christian church and academic theology it has long been recognized by some theologians that they cannot operate effectively without recourse to the social sciences. In "practical" or "pastoral theology" eclectic appropriations of insights and methodology often take place, and pragmatic syntheses are arranged which enhance instrumental insight into the ministerial task and the ongoing life of the church. Moreover, in such areas as Old and New Testament studies, church history, and Christian social ethics the use of material drawn from the social sciences has become increasingly common. Much more difficult issues arise, however, when we consider the role of social science in relation to systematic theology, for it is here that the immanent critique and relativism of sociological thought clashes with the re-enactment (or even the re-creation) of tradition(s) in given sociocultural contexts. Under post-traditional or "de-traditionalized"[3] social conditions the very idea of tradition is regarded as problematic, yet for others it remains indispensable.

The "turn to the subject" initiated by Martin Luther and furthered by later theologians, not least Friedrich Schleiermacher, intensified religious experience while loosening the hold of theological explanation upon the "outer", physical world. Such a development serves as a prelude to the growth of individualism and modern self-identity.[4] While Protestant theology thus willingly ceded sociocultural space in return for an intensification of religious consciousness, its battle with modernity was largely fought out elsewhere, notably in the long struggle with the implications of the historical-critical method and historicism. Having accepted an increasingly individualistic and subjective role in social reality (an option most consistently worked out in the history of Pietism), Protestant theology then had to suffer the virtual destruction of the scripture principle and its chosen textual foundations. Lacking the diachronic stability provided by the institutional hierarchy of Catholicism, German Protestant theologians were nonetheless culturally licensed to provide religious legitimation for a nascent and ascendant Germany. This theological and cultural role was based upon a transmutation of religious consciousness and the evolution of forms of enlightened religious inwardness (pioneered by Schleiermacher) which were compatible with the ethos of progress. In its turn, Protestant liberalism became a fundamental feature of the sociocultural compact between church and state (that as a consequence of Bismarck's *Kulturpolitik* also eventually came to include the Catholic Church), an arrangement which endured until the catastrophic collapse of Germany at the end of the First World War.

The "first postmodernity" of the culture of the Weimar Republic[5] was the seedbed not only of twentieth-century Protestant theology but also of many other strands of thought (and notably of those conducted in dialogue with Marxism). For the intellectuals of Weimar, many of whom were Jews later to be scattered after Hitler's coming to power, it was Marxism which became the bearer of hope. Now, however, in the so-called "postmodern condition"[6] and after the collapse of communism (albeit recognized as an ideology long drained of authenticity), the present state of affairs in certain respects mirrors the inner-European vacuum created by the implosion of Germany after the Armistice of 1919. In both contexts human beings confront rapid economic and technological change and sociocultural instability; now under the conditions of "advanced" or "high" capitalism they are seemingly obliged to shop for lifestyle options[7] in competitive markets of human identity.

As a consequence of the Reformation and the Enlightenment, both Catholic and Protestant theologies retrenched and retreated in distinctive ways. As regards the Catholic Church, the totalizing ambitions of scholastic theology were eventually reborn in reduced form in neoscholastic Thomism underpinned by the authority of

Pope Leo XIII in response to the threat of immanentist thought. Speculative abstract theological reflection within Protestantism underwent a form of revival in German (above all Hegelian) idealism. The Western and Enlightenment aspiration toward the totalization of knowledge (paradigmatically represented in Goethe's *Faust* and its philosophical parallel, Hegel's *Phenomenology of Mind*) was transmitted to Marxism and to social science. In the battle for the *episteme* which took place (and continues) both between and within the disciplines of the emergent human and social sciences, which was mapped out with uncompromising clarity by Michel Foucault,[8] religion and theology have a problematic status. In the most general terms, "religion" and the "sacred" underwent marginalization and migration, and the history of aesthetics and the "sublime" is one point of entry into understanding this process. Significantly, as regards theology, not only did Wilhelm von Humboldt exclude the divinity faculty of the University of Berlin from the faculty of humanities, but this marginalization was repeated in Wilhelm Dilthey's configuration of the human sciences (*Geisteswissenschaften*)[9] in the early twentieth century. Paradoxically (given its extraordinarily well-funded base in Germany), such has been the degree of cultural isolation of theology that the New Testament theologian Ernst Käsemann could write of the status of theological thought as a "nature reserve" in European culture. This is an apt but alarming image.

As noted earlier, the relationship between theology and the social sciences is problematic and as a first step we examine briefly, and in highly simplified terms, a typology of five possible strategies of appropriation enacted by theologians. First, the fundamentalist option involves the repudiation of modernity and comcomitant forms of regression; second, theology can tend toward reductive absorption into the social scientific perspective (Ernst Troeltsch); third, the theologian may draw upon and use sociological categories as part of his or her essentially theological project (Dietrich Bonhoeffer, H. R. Niebuhr); fourth, theological and sociological categories can be regarded as co-inherent aspects of an integral "form of life," "life-world," or "phenomenology of tradition" (Edward Farley) which subsists at a remove from the question of modernity; fifth, the theologian may repudiate sociology as heretical secular thought and posit the persuasive option of commitment to the Christian cultural-linguistic practice (John Milbank). As we shall indicate in the sections that follow, the present writer considers that no one of these strategies should be considered adequate as it stands: Further factors have to be taken into account.

Theology repels the social sciences: fundamentalism

It is a mistake to confuse fundamentalism with premodern thinking as such. Fundamentalism involves in large part the rejection of modernity or its manipulation. Thus in recent studies Gilles Kepel and Martin Riesebrodt have depicted global fundamentalism as attempts at re-conquering the world and patriarchal protest movements respectively.[10] Biblical (and other) scriptural literalism, the creation of consistent subcultures, the imposition of distinctive gender roles for men and women, and so on, are characteristic. It is, however, easier to discern the conflict between fundamentalism and modernity than that between active conservatism and so-called "postmodernity." Under postmodern conditions of fragmentation rational choice gives way to "seduction" by the rhetorics of discourses which recognize no final hegemonies. Thus, curiously, the distinction between naive Protestant fundamentalism and the sophisticated quasi-fundamentalism of our fifth strategist is more a question of consciousness: The former is unaware of the full implications of modernity; the latter certainly is, but persists nevertheless in demanding decisions on the basis of an either–or choice between exclusive alternatives. If and when fundamentalism encounters social science it is most often where this makes instrumental use of social psychological or other techniques in order to facilitate conversion and other religious experience. The functional compatibility between instrumental reason as employed in technology and fundamentalist beliefs is well-documented where (for example) the latter serve as means of social empowerment over against an invasive, Western-dominated modernity.[11] Postmodern or quasi-fundamentalism is, as argued below, altogether more problematic.

Ernst Troeltsch: sociology overcomes theology

Ernst Troeltsch, the polymath sociologist and theologian-historian (and close associate of Max Weber), pioneered the application of sociological method to the study of Christian origins. Thus the history of dogma (as paradigmatically represented by Harnack) became the model for a sociological interpretation of the interdependent relation between the transformed socio-ethical teachings of the church and the changing sociopolitical context of an organization that grew from its status as an obscure religious minority group with strong eschatological beliefs into the state religious monopoly of the late Roman Empire.[12]

Troeltsch's thought was dominated by a prolonged intellectual and personal struggle with historicism. This conception of history asserts the universality of cause and effect in the nexus of events and excludes a priori the "absolute truths" necessary to religious faith from objective historical study. In essence Troeltsch argued that the modern idea of history depended on critical source analysis and psychological analogy and that history was of the development of peoples, cultures, and the components of cultures. According to this approach all dogmas dissolve into the flow of events none of which is accorded a status of priority on the basis of extra-historical presuppositions. The historian works up from appropriate comparison through a combination of material drawn from evidence in order to work toward a comprehensive account.[13]

Troeltsch experienced a severe crisis of faith and then famously exchanged faculties. He was left with a residual and individualistic commitment to Christian values and with the scientific conviction that all historical truth was relative and conditioned. For Troeltsch, there was no escape (as with Karl Barth) from the rigorous constraints of *Historismus* into the dialectics of crisis, and the reappearance of the Word in the supra-historical *Momente* existentially perceived in the interstices of the historical order. As a consequence, many twentieth-century Protestant theologians have faced a dilemma: Should they opt for Troeltsch and the ascesis of historicism, or follow Barth on the dialectical path and renegotiate theologies of the Word.[14] In reality, this dilemma accords too dominant a role to historicism as the mediator of modernity, for, as is argued below, Christian theology has undergone an aborted and unsatisfactory encounter with modernity. This is the product, at least in part, of the institutional arrangements that have compounded the isolation of theology in the Anglo-Saxon world.

Ernst Troeltsch and his friend and colleague Max Weber were jointly responsible for the initiation and development of an organizational typology, the celebrated church–sect distinction, which related the social structure of religious organizations to belief and religious behavior. The dichotomies formulated by Weber and Troeltsch have been employed in systematic study of the whole Western Christian tradition. The further refinement of this theoretical approach proved particularly fruitful in the study of differentiated North American Protestantism, religious sects, and new religious movements. More recently, the church–sect typology and stratification theory have been applied to the study of the New Testament Church.

H. R. Niebuhr[15] took up the Weberian church–sect typology and applied it to the analysis of the growth of denominations in a way typical of the pragmatic appropriations made by theologians. It is significant that Niebuhr's text is repeatedly cited within the theological literature, whereas, by contrast, the later sociological discussion of social movements has largely failed to make a transition to theology. Thus, while this latter discussion has considerable importance for understanding the dynamics of religious group behavior and is thus of relevance to contemporary theology, it has remained largely within the sphere of influence of the sociology of religion. In such particular contexts disciplinary differentiation and the corresponding protective, interest-driven strategies of disciplines (and subdisciplines like the sociology of religion) may distort and fragment what should ideally be a more comprehensive and integrated approach. Such failures of connection have had an impact not only upon the ongoing task of theology, but also the informed study of religion. As a specific example, while the French sociologist Alain Touraine's studies of new social movements and of "post-industrial society"[16] have had important implications for research conducted by, for example, the sociologist James Beckford into new religious movements in "advanced industrial society"[17] the further step of applying such work in the field of theology has proved harder to achieve.

The Weberian influence extends far beyond the much cited "Protestant Ethic" theses and the economic sociology of the first volume of *Economy and Society*. The theoretical work of the American sociologist Talcott Parsons (who did much to transmit Weber's ideas to the United States) and the structuration theory of the English sociologist Anthony Giddens, to take but two examples, both owe a considerable debt to Weber. The sociological tradition of grand theory has until relatively recently had minimal impact upon the practice of theology. Our fourth type, the mutual assimilation of theological and sociological categories, does express a greater measure of appropriation of Parsonian systems theory, but, as will become apparent, this is achieved at the cost of downplaying the substantive content of the theology in favor of phenomenological and systemic description. In reality, confrontation with modernity exacts a higher price, and this is perhaps nowhere more apparent than in Dietrich Bonhoeffer's attempt to relate a theology of the Word to convincing analysis of the social being of the Christian community.

Dietrich Bonhoeffer: theology recruits sociology

Dietrich Bonhoeffer was raised in the elite center of German cultural life and he thus absorbed the major theological and cultural influences of his time. After early experience as a pastor he became convinced that there were profound flaws in a theology which seemingly failed to equip Christians to act effectively and in a distinctive way in a hostile social reality. Worse, this theology later proved incapable of resisting its political abuse by the German Christians. In his doctoral thesis *Sanctorum Communio* (1930) Bonhoeffer engaged with the question as to whether Christianity has a sociologically definable essence. Taking up Ferdinand Toennies's famous categories of community (*Gemeinschaft*) and association (*Gesellschaft*), Bonhoeffer tried to understand how the church might enact itself in the context of a post-organic, associative modernity, and whether, furthermore, it had a sociologically definable essence which Bonhoeffer identified (in debate with K. L. Schmidt) as that of an agapeistic community. *Sanctorum Communio* is a pioneering work, but it was a relatively isolated example of the recruitment of specifically sociological conceptuality in the service of a theology of the Word. In terms of both substance and methodology this text remains an erratic and undeveloped element in Bonhoeffer's curtailed theological achievement. Besides the term "sanctorum communio," others such as "ethics as formation," "presence" in christology, "religionless Christianity," and the "ultimate" and "penultimate" in theological ethics passed into post-Second World War theological reflection in Europe and North America. Bonhoeffer's sensitivity to the all-pervasiveness of totalitarian social systems, which first became apparent in his observation of the German émigré community in Barcelona and was later developed in confrontation with National Socialism, is still of immense relevance. This was demonstrated not least in the struggle against apartheid in South Africa, but now in the post-communist era, when capitalism is without effective critique or constraint, Bonhoeffer's assertion of the penultimacy of all things over against the ultimacy of the divine has gained a new and urgent relevance.[18]

A second important aspect of Bonhoeffer's theological legacy consists in his confrontation with the progressive secularization of Western society and culture, an issue which not only provoked the so-called "secular theology" of the sixties, but provides within theological reflection the major parallel with an issue which dominated much postwar sociological study of religion. In much quoted passages in the *Letters and Papers from Prison*, Bonhoeffer set out an agenda in which he accepted and ingested the implications of secularization, albeit with highly paradoxical consequences for theology. It was apparent to Bonhoeffer that the emergence of the world's autonomy which had origins in science, religion, philosophy, politics, and natural law was an inescapable reality. He concluded that "God as a working hypothesis in morals, politics or science, has been surmounted and abolished."[19] Thus any yearning for a lost golden past in the Middle Ages would be mere despair cloaked by infantile nostalgia. Bonhoeffer takes with absolute seriousness Kant's strictures on maturity as emergence from heteronomy and his injunction: *Sapere aude*, dare to know, is incumbent not least upon Christians. Rather than side with either Barth (whose ontology Bonhoeffer had criticized in *Act and Being*) or with

Nietzsche (and relinquish theological language altogether), Bonhoeffer admits the reality of secularizing modernity and strives to interpret it theologically.

> And we cannot be honest unless we recognize that we have to live in the world *etsi deus non daretur*. And this is just what we do recognize – before God! God himself compels us to recognize it. So our coming of age leads us to a true recognition of our situation before God. God would have us know that we must live as men who manage our lives without him. The God who is with us is the God who forsakes us (Mark 15: 34). The God who lets us live in the world without the working hypotheses of God is the God before whom we stand continually. Before God and with God we live without God. God lets himself be pushed out of the world on to the cross. He is weak and powerless in the world, and that is precisely the way, the only way, in which he is with us and helps us. Matt. 8.17 makes it quite clear that Christ helps us, not by virtue of his omnipotence, but by virtue of his weakness and suffering.[20]

While it would be idle to pretend that Bonhoeffer's response to secularization was to play a large role in the postwar research or theoretical work of mainstream sociologists, his account did set an agenda worked out by theologians who sought further to explore the idea of a so-called nonreligious Gospel and a "secular city" in which thoroughgoing secularity could itself provide the basis of theological *jouissance*. Above all, and despite the relatively outdated character of the sociological theory he used, Dietrich Bonhoeffer provides an enduring theological prototype of critical and responsible reflexivity in the face of modernity. As will be argued further in the conclusion of this chapter, it is the development and reinforcement of such a reflexivity that has to be a central feature of a socioscientifically informed reconstitution of the theological task today. Whereas it is arguable that Troeltsch capitulates to modernity as he understood it and that Bonhoeffer sought to create a dialectical cohabitation which preserved the tensions in the confrontation, our next example, the work of Edward Farley, proposes a mutual absorption which blunts the substantive edges of both theology (as grounded in tradition and authority) and social science (as bearer of modernity).

Edward Farley: theology and social science mutually merged?

It is not our present purpose to analyze or evaluate in detail the theological proposals of Edward Farley. What is of major concern here is how this representative thinker has assimilated socioscientific insights and made them mutual and intrinsic aspects of a method that seemingly overcomes any contested divergence between theology and the social sciences. Farley endorses theological proposals which reverse both the Barthian tendency to polarize "faith" and "religion" and the whole post-Enlightenment predilection for reconstructionist theologies which adhere to and amplify a single category of ethical or affective experience which then becomes the medium of theological construction. In this he is directly assisted by broadly phenomenological methods.

In *Ecclesial Man* (1975) Edward Farley tackled the problem of foundations, the ways in which realities are pre-given to theology, whereas *Ecclesial Reflection* (1982) concerns judgment, the ways in which those realities lay claim to truth. The task of foundations is, according to Farley, "that of describing faith, the faith world, the community of faith (ecclesial existence) as the matrix of reality-givenness."[21] The "criteriology" expounded in *Ecclesial Reflection* begins with an "archaeology" of the "house of faith" which is analogous to Heidegger's critique of the history of ontology. Furthermore, Farley propounds a "phenomenology of tradition," that is, a phenomenology of "ecclesial process and its bearers."[22] The implications of this are spelt out clearly and pertain directly to our interpretation, for,

> the move from foundations and pregivenness to theological judgement is not simply a move into philosophy of religion nor from the determination of faith to the general level of ontology. Theological judgments are made from a historical faith-community which has a determinate corporate memory carried in a determinate network of symbols. The bearers of that determinacy, even written collections from the past, play some role in judgment. And the nature of that role is established not by authority but by the structure of the ecclesial process itself. This is why a phenomenology and even sociology of tradition plays such a central part in this prolegomenon.[23]

This sort of approach emancipates theology from the constraints of historicism and purports to overcome difficulties posed by alternatives principles used by the ancestral "houses" of authority of Protestantism and Catholicism. More seriously, while this approach ostensibly liberates theology from the "house of authority" it thereby sidesteps the critique of power. Theology comes into existence at the point of correlation between the "meaning and proper function" of the literature of the ecclesial community and the "nature of ecclesiality and its duration over time."[24] Thus theological reflection consists in "the depiction of ecclesiality (portraiture), the truth question, and reflective praxis."[25] In effect, the description and analysis of the means of "social duration" (Pitirim Sorokin) of ecclesial bodies replaces the prescriptive role of outdated, unacceptable tradition. It is an open question as to why such an approach should result in a distinctively Christian theology as opposed to the highly general, even reified description of "ecclesial being."

The intention here is not to test the adequacy of this sophisticated sociological and phenomenological synthesis as such, but to raise questions which stem from the broader context of the disjunction of theology and the social sciences. Thus the phenomenological approach exploited by Farley makes full and free use of apposite sociological conceptuality, but as *theology* is it more than a religiously nuanced "portraiture," and thus simply a phenomenology of religion? George Lindbeck's use of the idea of a "cultural linguistic practice" is similar in some ways to that of Farley; both are enabled by their American background of pragmatism. There is a parallel between the phenomenological approach and recent reconstruals of Christian theology through the medium of theories of the origin and nature of language.[26] Both use theory as the basis for constructive proposals that appear to emancipate theological reflection from the Enlightenment critique. Yet can the Enlightenment principle be banished so easily? Is the descriptive phenomenological approach (or indeed the linguistic turn) not in some way an evasion? Our answer to these questions begins with an exploration of some of the wider issues affecting the relation of theology and the social sciences touched upon in the following section.

Postmodern quasi-fundamentalism (John Milbank)

One drastic and influential response to the whole problematic of the relation of theology and the social sciences is that advocated by the English theological thinker John Milbank in his monumental work *Theology and Social Theory*. Milbank provides an extended "archaeology" of the "heresy" of secular (i.e., sociological) thought as it has diverged from Christian truth and then poses an uncompromising either–or. Secular social theory and Christianity in effect stand in contradiction to each other. All the main components of secular social theory have a (usually genetic) relation with Christianity, and the main bulk of Milbank's work is dedicated to exposing these connections. Because there is no ultimate foundational basis in *rationality* for distinguishing between the claims of Christianity and those of secular reason, the project consists in an "exercise in sceptical relativism." Ultimacy is not a matter of rational choice; the Christian *perspective* is *persuasive* and not conveyed through "the apologetic mediation of human reason" (that is, put less ambitiously, through *argument* as such). Correspondingly, in a *Nietzschean* postmodernity the Christian perspective is offered to theologians for their positive appropriation.

Thus according to Milbank, as metadiscourse and cultural-linguistic practice "Christianity" relativizes modern (i.e., "liberal") theology, which is seen to be an immanent idolatry (the "oracular voice of some finite idol" stemming from history, psychology, or transcendental philosophy). Any "liberal" theology construed as an adjunct of secular reason faces a dilemma: It *either* fuses idolatrously with a particular immanent field of knowledge *or* it is effectively alienated and "confined to intimations of a sublimity beyond representation."[27] Taken in the latter sense, theology as a "sublimity beyond representation" negatively affirms (from Milbank's point of view questionably) an autonomous secular realm open to rational understanding.

The situation is, however, further compounded by another complexity. While theology is not to be identified with secular reason it is nevertheless a wholly contingent historical construct embedded in "semiotic and figural codings" (in other words, its horizons are always those of cultural-linguistic practice). This state of affairs is conceded and endorsed: There can be no return to, or restoration of, the premodern position of Christianity. Christianity must *neither* accommodate *nor* adapt itself to the space apparently left to it within social reality. Any such involvement weakens Christianity as *faith* and as radical *praxis* by (mistakenly) searching for common ground.

It is at this juncture that Milbank notes a fundamental conjuncture: the postmodern *necessity of myth*. Nietzsche has shown that all cultural associations are traceable to the will-to-power. Nietzsche further indicates that the basis of *all* social and economic power is "religious" inasmuch as myth masks the will-to-power. Thus social theory and theology subsist on the same ground: To pass *beyond* Nietzsche is to recognize "the necessity and yet the ungrounded character of some sort of metanarrative, some privileged transcendent factor, even when it comes disguised as the constant element in an immanent process."[28]

There can be no significant "sociological" representation of religion and theology precisely because *religion* is the ultimate transcendental. All forms of secular reason (and thus social science) can be traced archaeologically to, and then deconstructed into, their *theological* progenitors. This can be understood as the *inversion* (not merely the reconstrual) of Hans Blumenberg's account of the "legitimacy" of modernity (as opposed to the perverse Christian obstruction of human *curiositas*).[29] Seen thus, secularity and secular discourse are *heresy* in relation to orthodox Christianity, and the archaeological investigations will show that all "scientific" social theories are in fact "theologies or anti-theologies" in disguise.

We hear two "voices" in Western culture. The first is classical and medieval, the voice of an Alasdair MacIntyre speaking in Platonic–Aristotelian–Augustinian–Thomist terms.[30] The second is the nihilistic, Nietzschean voice which historicizes and seeks to show that "every supposedly objective reasoning simply promotes its own difference, and disguises the power which is its sole support."[31] In the final analysis the first, the voice of "Christian virtue" triumphs. In such a setting, a scenario implying a reading of the whole Western tradition, Christianity may reassert its total originality:

> Christianity, however, recognizes no original violence. It construes the infinite not as chaos, but as harmonic peace which is yet beyond the circumscribing power of any totalizing reason. Peace no longer depends upon the reduction to the self-identical, but is the *sociality* of harmonious difference. . . . Christianity . . . is the coding of transcendental difference as peace.[32]

At the very last moment Christianity subverts and exposes the Nietzschean assertion that "difference, non-totalization and indeterminacy of being necessarily imply arbitrariness and violence."[33] In conclusion, Milbank posits a "third voice" which pursues the above "argument," which amounts in effect to a "choice," an effective *seduction* by one encoding as opposed to the other. This is what we might call the ecclesial supersession, a sublation in which a "historicist and pragmatist, yet *theologically* realist" position is advanced, in which

> no claim is made to "represent" an objective social reality; instead the social knowledge advocated is but the continuation of ecclesial practice, the imagination in action of a peaceful, reconciled social order, beyond even the violence of legality.[34]

On the assumption that "truth is social," then a "lived narrative" projects and "represents" the triune God who is "transcendental peace through differential relation."[35] This is the ultimate "social science" and the sole offer that may establish theology, give content to the idea of "God," and impress itself upon the world through practice. The metadiscourse of theology is the "discourse of non-mastery" that may alone save us from nihilism. In the final analysis, this is a *theological* transvaluation of all "theology," myth and "religion" (and the nihilistic human condition that they mask). Social science is at best a signpost to the root from which there has been catastrophic deviation; at worst it is a heretical perversion.

Milbank posits an abstract, quasi-manichaeistic (yet mutually involuted) opposition of false alternatives which entails abuses of both "theology" and "social theory." In effect, both "theology" and "social theory" (equivalent for present purposes to the social sciences) are reduced to the *rhetorics* embedded in and expressive of cultural practices in a way that universalizes Nietzschean perspectivism. But this procedure rules out through a priori occultation the wide variety of rationalities, epistemological strategies (not least induction), and epistemic resolutions that characterize both these areas of intellectual activity. Construed thus, theology becomes the imposition of *stasis*, a rearward-looking construal that has consequences which paralyze theology as embedded, grace-driven reflection entrenched in the real conflict and injustices of the human condition. Active theological thinking *from the future*, the anticipatory consciousness of the Spirit, is excluded. In somewhat extravagant but not altogether misleading terms, John Milbank may be said once more to enact the infinite cunning of reason that extinguishes itself and migrates in order to survive as "theology."

Sociology as a discipline should not be construed *reductively* and *exclusively* in terms of the perverse metanarrative of secular reason. Sociology and the social sciences may also be classically construed as the *critical representation* and *clarification* of the patterns of social organization necessary to the sustenance of humane societies, rather than (as Milbank would have it) the partner in the promotion of an allegedly necessary and totalitarian violence of order. The tasks of theology and sociology are mutual in at least as much as they address the human condition in exploratory and interpretative terms, and do not subsume (in however virtuoso a fashion) *everything* into the dance of death and totalitarian logic of Western secular reason. Moreover, sociology and theology which embody concerns for the other cannot afford to neglect or express contempt for ethnography, that is, the effective representation and interpretation of what is actually happening in human lives. Both theology and the social sciences should be concerned in their distinctive ways with life and with how things are.

On a scale of proximity and modes of negotiation and assimilation between social science and theology, fundamentalism tends to flee modernity (and thus the social sciences) but in so doing it may be tempted to exploit social scientific insights in instrumental ways to facilitate conversion experiences; Troeltsch tended to absorb theological questions into historicism and early social science; Bonhoeffer attempted (not least under the influence of Karl Barth) to maintain a dialectical cohabitation of theological and sociological categories; and Edward Farley has expressed theology in terms of a thoroughgoing appropriation of the phenomenology of ecclesial being. John Milbank drives a wedge between theology and the social sciences and demands that we resist all accommodations and decide upon one or the other in what amounts to a despairing postmodern quasi-fundamentalism of paradoxical sophistication. This depiction of possible ways of configuring the relation of theology and the social sciences is in no way exhaustive, but it is representative of a range of possible strategies in a fraught borderland.

Theology's use of social science: some observations

The exceptionally high profile of Protestant theology in German thought and culture is unique in Europe, if not the world. Moreover, many of the subdisciplines within Christian theology either originated or were given vital impulse in Germany throughout the post-Enlightenment period. The contextual character of this widely disseminated and thereby universalized theological tradition cannot be left out of account.[36] It is only recently that a leading role appears to have passed to the United States and, in consequence, it is reasonable to anticipate the assimilation of distinctively American concerns and insights. The ascendancy of American theology is remarkable as regards both Protestant theology from the North and Catholic liberation theology from the Latin South respectively. This growing, albeit differentiated hegemony is also evident in the proliferation of feminist, and other special interest and communitarian theologies. These developments incorporate societal changes of profound significance. The shift of interest away from the archetypically 'male' paradigm of all-embracing, hegemonic theologies of largely German inspiration toward the contemporary pluralism of *theologies* of gender, race, ethnicity, sexual-orientation, poverty, and so on, is contemporaneous with a major crisis in the ethnic 'melting-pot' of the United States.[37] The responsible use of such theologies is, however, improbable apart from the just and intelligent deployment of social scientific insight which defines the constituencies to which each type of theological reflection primarily relates. In a "glocalized" (Roland Robertson) world, liberal values, conceptions of universal human rights and theologies which imply catholicity are now prone to systemic crisis and readily attacked as postcolonial hegemony, cultural neo-imperialism or regressive patriarchy. Without effective means of representing human universals there is a danger that it will become impossible to represent any interests over and above those of special groups. It is at this juncture that religious and theological insights once more become important resources.[38]

The brief typology presented in the foregoing section of this chapter and the differentiation and pluralism in contemporary theology alluded to above illuminate dimensions of the changing relationship between Christian theology and the social sciences. On a more abstract level what concerns us are the implications of what the English sociologist Anthony Giddens means when he asserts that modernity is intrinsically sociological.[39] In other words, if sociological (that is to say reflexive, as opposed to tradition-dominated) self-understanding is a defining feature of modernity then theology is faced with the requirement that it engage in the comprehensive negotiation of its relationship with the social sciences. While some forms of liberation theology may have attempted this inasmuch as they sought to build contextual theological foundations influenced by Marxist insight (thereby invoking the consequences of a problematic alliance), the Western engagement has been fragmented and incomplete. The mediation of modernity and theology's response to it is, however, a matter of central importance around which cluster many aspects of the relation of theology and the social sciences.

Christian theology remains, and it should rightly so remain, church- or community-related theology. Despite its many ambiguous (and largely successful) attempts to gain and retain academic legitimacy, theological thought often subsists in social and economic contexts which distance it from any need to reckon not merely with secularization but also with the fuller impact of modernization and modernity. "Modernity," itself a much disputed concept, has been opposed to "tradition." For some social scientists the very idea of "tradition" is not merely seen as inherently problematic, but as primary and defining characteristic of a superseded premodern condition.[40] Contemporary culture and society may thus be regarded as post-traditional.[41]

Other sociologists have argued for the continuing force of the idea of tradition[42] in ways which, for example, in part endorse Farley's formulations. What greatly complicates the situation that we now encounter are two further factors. On the one hand, social reality has not remained static: The "sacred" has undergone ambiguous displacements and transmutations in reaching accommodations with modernity in what, for example, George Steiner has suggestively described as the twentieth-century "after-life of religion."[43] On the other hand, the Barthian critique of "religion" and the scission between theology and the academic study of religion has tended to disable the former's ability to come to terms with the resurgence of religion and its ambiguous "afterlife."

A theology uninformed by engagement with the social sciences may well persist as a form of "false consciousness," but it will do so at a dangerous distance from what the German Reformed theologian Jürgen Moltmann once referred to as the "dialectic of the real."[44] This "real" now includes a range of new possibilities and challenges. For example, poststructuralist intimations of theology (or *a*theology),[45] New Age "self religion,"[46] globalized spiritualities,[47] goddess-centered Neo-Paganism,[48] varieties of fundamentalism,[49] and ecological religiosity all tend to outflank a wearied Christian theology often largely concerned with the internal politics of its own decline. Thus Christian theology not only has to face up to its own partially aborted reception of modernity but also its correlative fear and ignorance of new developments which meet human religious needs the world over. In addition, it must also confront and come to terms with acute and profound problems with regard to gender, power, and the status of nature that it will only begin adequately to comprehend if it successfully relocates itself at the conjuncture of premodernity (where its origins lie), modernity (where it underwent crippling damage) and the "postmodern condition" or, less contentiously, "high" or "late" modernity in which new possibilities open up on a daily basis. The idea and the reality of "tradition"[50] have to comprehend and manage these dialectically cohabiting dimensions. If theology fails to achieve this then it may persist as *mauvaise foi* for as long as funding continues, but it will not be answering the challenge posed by the history and present state of the human and social sciences. To these challenges and opportunities we shall shortly return.

The argument pursued so far in this paper does not imply that no effective collaborations between sociologists and theologians have taken place.[51] Our contention is, however, that such collaboration is not only marked more by discontinuity than coherence but that underlying alliance and conflict there are major unresolved issues. These stem from the historic differentiation of disciplines and adjustments which relate to modernization, secularization, and the nature of the Enlightenment project. It will therefore require thoroughgoing methodological renewal within theology (rather than occasional intellectual transfers by unusually energetic theologians) before the disjunctions between theology, the sociology of religion, and mainline social theory are better understood and viable working relationships established.

Theology and the Social Sciences: A Tentative Agenda

The current identity crisis of Christian theology neither lacks precedent nor is it confined uniquely to that necessarily strange discipline. We have already alluded to

Michel Foucault's depiction of the interlinked "deaths" of God and man at the very heart of the evolution of the human and social sciences (*les sciences humaines*).[52] Human identity itself, and the means of grasping and expressing our knowledge of the human, the *episteme*, is not possessed by any one discipline or field of knowledge precisely because of the evolutionary differentiation and changing basic configurations of the disciplines in the absence of overarching means of integration. In even more basic terms, it is of the essence of human being that identity is not predefined. There is, however, no shortage of agencies and powers that queue up and strive to impose their demands upon the human agent; in more formal terms, we are all the victims of social construction. On the other hand, the necessary condition of the sustenance of civilized life demands a degree of willed conformity to agreed norms. The fact that theology or metaphysical philosophy may once have provided the basis of coherent identity and legitimation does not now sanction regressions into a mythic past or the invocation of a utopian futurity when faced with the challenge of secularization and modernity. On the contrary, other means have to be found through which tradition(s), Enlightenment, and critical reflexivity may be creatively coordinated anew.

We have seen how the relation between social science and specifically Christian (besides religious) thought is fraught with difficulties. Humankind now exists in the extremely complex nexus between an invasive world system that transforms ever more effectively all facets of human life into marketable commodities, and, on the other, the resurgence of local identities (ethnic, cultural, gender, national, and so on). Moreover, the interlinked processes of globalization and localization are overshadowed by ecological crisis, a veritable "ecological eschaton." Market choice, informational integration, and global competition have, it is arguable, replaced the struggle of monolithic hegemonies, all the more so since the near-total collapse of Marxist socialism. Yet even this does not fully comprise the difficulties. Theology will require practitioners who, like "postmodern saints" (Edith Wyschogrod), will be able to extinguish themselves in seeking to enter this dialectical complex. There is no easy way forward.

On a pragmatic level, a responsible postmodern theology of integrity must recognize and own new affinities and new allegiances if it is to grapple in effective ways with contemporary orgies of collective tribal power,[53] the manipulation characteristic of marketization,[54] an increasingly divided, yet globalized and ever more powerful world system (Robertson), and the crisis of male gender identity.[55] This involves a re-engagement with the real on every level: We must begin with the effective understanding of human "life-worlds";[56] yet socioscientific analysis informed by critical reflexivity[57] is insufficient on its own. Theological reflection must understand itself in this matrix; yet here it requires the unpredetermined gift, the charisma that comes with a vocation. At the base of this we must seek new and active fusion of the human sciences together with the articulation and admission of the human right, following the example of Bonhoeffer, to express a self-transcending identity. It is ironic that in empirical terms the realization that the human sciences should be employed in inner-directed and emancipatory, rather than outer-directed and hegemonic terms occurs at core points within management theory and practice where it critically differentiates itself from its shadow side, managerialism.[58] In a so-called rationally managed reality (now being uncritically extended to the life of the churches) we may find the paradigmatic societal microcosms in which the theologian might first test his or her renewed skills and vision. This is where the subversive emancipation of the Gospel may be enacted to good effect.

In this brief study of the relation of theology to the social sciences we have argued on the basis that the latter should be understood within the overall conspectus of the human sciences (*les sciences humaines*). At the heart of the human and social sciences there is a combative void from which essential human concerns have been banished. The twofold death of which Foucault writes is one pointed way of characterizing a multiplex crisis of human identity. This crisis has many aspects and it is spread worldwide with the invasive power of global capitalism, before which all cultural particularities would sometimes seem to bend if not break. Religion, and the self-critical reflexive discourses of religion, theology, can provide forms of resistant cultural capital. There are those like the American Catholic theologian Michael Novak, who would, however, wish to use religion as a means of filling the "empty shrine" of the global economic system.[59] According to this view, Christianity and Judaism are supremely well-suited to such a role. Our contention is that assimilation of this kind may well involve a betrayal.

Fundamentalists may react with equal vehemence in favor of such an integration into the aims of the dominant economic system and advocate prosperity theologies.[60] Conversely, quasi-fundamentalists may react against capitalism, advocate political impossibilism, and await revolution in a state of Adornian "hibernation." Correspondingly, the day of the theological reductionist is largely over; liberalism that trades upon the infinite extendability of death by a thousand small cuts holds little attraction in an era of catastrophe. Yet, as Edward Farley has shown, the diachronic continuity of the meaning-systems of ecclesial communities may be understood through phenomenology and a mutual assimilation of theology and social science; but in his case, this may take place without either evincing Christian or other theological particularity, or confronting the full rigors of modernity. Of the strategies reviewed, it is Bonhoeffer, who, despite the archaism of his sociological appropriations, offers most insight. Unflinching in confronting modernity as he experienced it, Bonhoeffer embodies the supreme adventure of the life of the mind and heart that is theology rightly understood. He was prepared to risk the unpredictable consequences that follow any sincere obedience to the command: "Follow me." All truth-seekers take such risks, but Christians and Christian theologians draw upon an identity and hope for a future that is life promised only on the basis of death. The substantive content of Christian traditions (understood in the most comprehensive sense) is a resource, but to regard the future as open, and to act is the supreme test of the resolve of faith.

We inhabit a wilderness, yet somewhere there are rocks that may be touched and from which sustenance will flow. Each person who is aware of such possibilities may seek out sources from within their own faith-tradition; ecumenism must now become an ecumenism of religions, not merely of belief systems within any given tradition. It is not the case that in premodernity the touching places were wholly obvious, nor is it true to think that reflexivity is the sole prerogative of modernity. Nor again should we believe that religion and theology die off on the margins in a secularized modernity; indeed, the resurgence of religion and religiosity precludes such naivety.

The theological task of our day should not consist simply in attempts (however sophisticated) to recapture a lost past; yet "tradition" as a resource is as refunctionable in postmodernity (or "late modernity") as are all other cultural artifacts. How this reappropriation is responsibly to be conducted is a task we are only beginning to learn. The mechanical recapitulation of Christian doctrine merely as items in an inherited belief system, undertaken as though nothing had happened, is indefensible.

The reconfiguration of the theological task requires immersion in the dialectics of identity as they emerge from the history and evolution of the social and human sciences in the transitions of modernity. Religion and the expression of its critical and responsible reflexivity, theology, can become methodologically equipped to address this enigma of identity. They will have to do so, however, while being willing to confront the absolute contrast of the individual and the collective, the relative and the absolute and the immanent and the transcendent. These and other contingencies touched upon in this chapter are inherent in our condition as human beings. This means that all theology should be contextual and should relate to human needs, be it at the level of basic communities or the global condition. It should also be stirred by an articulate hope that things can be other than they are.[61] Anything less is a perversion. Understanding must be grounded in such correlations, but it is misleading to suppose that co-responsibility of this kind implies a contempt for the intellect. As Antonio Gramsci argued for socialism, so for a theology informed by the social and human sciences, the theologian should be an organic intellectual, a risk-taker, a humane entrepreneur of the mind who is willing to withstand the systemic marginality that afflicts all those who are willing to cross boundaries in the borderland that is normative in the contemporary human condition.

Notes

1 The term "human sciences" includes not only the social sciences but also other fields, notably discourse, law, history, literary theory and literature, and so forth. See the introduction to R. H. Roberts and J. M. M. Good, *The Recovery of Rhetoric* (Charlottesville, VA, 1993).

2 Zygmunt Bauman, *Modernity and the Holocaust* (London, 1989) and *Postmodern Ethics* (London, 1993).

3 P. Heelas, S. Lash, and P. Morris, *Detraditionalization: Critical reflections on authority and identity* (Oxford, 1995).

4 Charles Taylor, *The Sources of the Self* (Cambridge, 1989).

5 R. H. Roberts, "Barth and the eschatology of Weimar," in R. H. Roberts (ed.), *A Theology on its Way: Essays on Karl Barth* (Edinburgh, 1991), pp. 169–99.

6 Jean-François Lyotard, *The Postmodern Condition* (Manchester, 1984).

7 Anthony Giddens, *The Consequences of Modernity* (Cambridge, 1990).

8 Michel Foucault, *The Order of Things* (London, 1970).

9 W. Dilthey, *An Introduction to the Human Sciences* (London, 1988).

10 G. Kepel, *The Revenge of God* (Cambridge, 1994); M. Riesebrodt, *Pious Passion: The emergence of modern fundamentalism in the United States and Iran* (Berkeley, CA, 1993).

11 G. Kepel, *The Revenge of God*.

12 E. Troeltsch, *The Social Teaching of the Christian Church* (London, 1931); M. Mann, *The Sources of Social Power*. Vol. 1 (Cambridge, 1986).

13 E. Troeltsch, *The Absoluteness of Christianity and the History of Religion* (London, 1972).

14 For an unmatched account of this crucially important era in the history of modern

Protestant theology, see C. Gestrich, *Neu-zeitliches Denken und die Spaltung der dialektischen Theologie* (Tübingen, 1977).

15 H. Richard Niebuhr, *The Social Sources of Denominationalism* (New York, 1975; first published 1929).

16 A. Touraine, *The Post-Industrial Society* (London, 1974).

17 J. A. Beckford, *Religion and the Advanced Industrial Society* (London, 1989).

18 R. H. Roberts, *Religion and the Resurgence of Capitalism* (London, forthcoming).

19 Dietrich Bonhoeffer, *Letters and Papers from Prison*, 3rd edn (London, 1967).

20 Ibid., pp. 360–1.

21 Edward Farley, *Ecclesial Reflection* (Philadelphia, 1982), p. xiv.

22 Ibid., p. xv.

23 Ibid.

24 Ibid., p. xvii.

25 Ibid., p. xviii.

26 G. Ward, *Barth, Derrida and the Language of Theology* (Cambridge, 1995).

27 J. Milbank, *Theology and Social Theory* (Oxford, 1990), p. 1.

28 Ibid., p. 2.

29 H. Blumenberg, *The Legitimacy of the Modern Age* (Cambridge, MA, 1985).

30 A. MacIntyre, *After Virtue* (London, 1981).

31 J. Milbank, *Theology and Social Theory*, p. 5.

32 Ibid., pp. 5–6.

33 Ibid., p. 5.

34 Ibid., p. 6.

35 Ibid.

36 See R. H. Roberts, "The reception of the theology of Karl Barth in the Anglo-Saxon world: history, typology and prospect," in R. H. Roberts (ed.), *A Theology on its Way*, pp. 95–168, for a cross-cultural account of the reception of one major strand of this tradition.

37 This has been represented in dramatic terms by Samuel P. Huntington in "The clash of civilizations," in *Foreign Affairs* (1993), pp. 22–49.

38 An important countervailing attempt to restate universal values in the context of growing pluralism is the global ethic co-ordinated by the Swiss-German theologian

Hans Küng and promulgated at the Parliament of the World's Religions held in Chicago in 1993. See R. H. Roberts, "Globalized religion? The Parliament of the world's religions (Chicago, 1993) in theoretical perspective," *Journal of Contemporary Religion*, 10 (1995), pp. 121–37.

39 A. Giddens, *The Consequences of Modernity*.

40 Ibid.

41 P. Heelas, S. Lash, and P. Morris, *Detraditionalization*.

42 Edward Shils, *Tradition* (London, 1981).

43 George Steiner, *In Bluebeard's Castle* (London, 1977).

44 J. Moltmann, *The Crucified God* (London, 1976).

45 P. Berry and A. Wernick, *The Shadow of Spirit* (London, 1992).

46 P. Heelas, *The Sacralization of the Self* (London, forthcoming).

47 R. H. Roberts, "Globalized religion?"

48 Monika Sjöö and Barbara Mor, *The Great Cosmic Mother* (San Francisco, 1991).

49 G. Kepel, *The Revenge of God* and M. Riesebrodt, *Pious Passion*.

50 E. Shils, *Tradition*.

51 R. Gill, *The Social Context of Theology* (London, 1975); D. Martin, J. Orme-Mills, and W. S. F. Pickering, *Sociology and Theology* (Brighton, 1980).

52 M. Foucault, *The Order of Things*, pp. 384ff.

53 M. Maffesoli, *The Time of the Tribes* (London, 1995).

54 G. Ritzer, *The McDonaldization of Society* (London, 1993).

55 R. Bly, *Iron John: A book about men* (Shaftesbury, 1991).

56 A. Schutz, *The Phenomenology of the Social World* (London, 1972).

57 P. Bourdieu and L. J. D. Wacquant, *An Invitation to Reflexive Sociology* (Chicago, 1992).

58 W. F. Entemann, *Managerialism* (Madison, WI, 1993).

59 M. Novak, *The Spirit of Democratic Capitalism* (London, 1991; first published 1982).

60 R. H. Roberts, *Religion and the Transformation of Capitalism* (London, 1995).

61 R. H. Roberts, *Hope and its Hieroglyph: A critical decipherment of Ernst Bloch's "Principle of Hope"* (Atlanta, GA, 1990).

Bibliography

Bauman, Zygmunt, *Modernity and the Holocaust* (London, 1989).
—— *Postmodern Ethics* (London, 1993).
Beckford, J. A., *Religion and Advanced Industrial Society* (London, 1989).
Berry, P. and Wernick, A., *The Shadow of Spirit: Postmodernism and religion* (London, 1992).
Blumenberg, H., *The Legitimacy of the Modern Age* (Cambridge, MA, 1985).
Bly, R., *Iron John: A book about men* (Shaftesbury, 1991).
Bonhoeffer, D., *Act and Being* (London, 1962).
—— *Sanctorum Communio: A dogmatic enquiry into the sociology of the church* (London, 1963).
—— *Letters and Papers from Prison*, 3rd edn (London, 1967).
Bourdieu, P. and Wacquant, L. J. D., *An Invitation to Reflexive Sociology* (Chicago, 1992).
Dilthey, W., *Introduction to the Human Sciences: An attempt to lay a foundation for the study of society and history* (London, 1988).
Entemann, W. F., *Managerialism: The emergence of a new ideology* (Madison, WI, 1993).
Farley, Edward, *Ecclesial Man: A social phenomenology of faith and reality* (Philadelphia, 1975).
—— *Ecclesial Reflection: An anatomy of theological method* (Philadelphia, 1982).
Foucault, M., *The Order of Things: An archaeology of the human sciences* (London, 1970).
Giddens, A., *The Consequences of Modernity* (Cambridge, 1990).
Gill, R., *The Social Context of Theology: A methodological enquiry* (London, 1975).
Habermas, J., *The Philosophical Discourse of Modernity* (Cambridge, MA, 1987).
Harvey, Van A., *The Historian and the Believer* (London, 1968).
Heelas, P., *The Sacralization of the Self* (London, forthcoming).
Heelas, P., Lash, S., and Morris, P., *Detraditionalization: Critical reflections on authority and identity* (Oxford, 1995).
Kepel, G., *The Revenge of God: The resurgence of Islam, Christianity and Judaism in the modern world* (Cambridge, 1994).
Lyotard, J.-F., *The Postmodern Condition: A report on knowledge* (Manchester, 1984).
MacIntyre, A., *After Virtue: A study in moral theory* (London, 1981).

Maffesoli, M., *The Time of the Tribes: The decline of individualism in mass society* (London, 1995).
Mann, M., *The Sources of Social Power*. Vol. I: *A History of Power from the Beginning to AD 1760* (Cambridge, 1986).
Martin, D., Orme-Mills, J., and Pickering, W. S. F., *Sociology and Theology: Alliance or conflict* (Brighton, 1980).
Meštrović, S. G., *The Barbarian Temperament: Toward a postmodern critical theory* (London, 1993).
Milbank, J., *Theology and Social Theory: Beyond secular reason* (Oxford, 1990).
Moltmann, J., *The Crucified God: The Cross of Christ as the foundation and criticism of Christian theology* (London, 1976).
Niebuhr, H. R., *The Social Sources of Denominationalism* (New York, 1975; first published 1929).
Novak, M., *The Spirit of Democratic Capitalism* (London, 1991; first published 1982).
Riesebrodt, M., *Pious Passion: The emergence of modern fundamentalism in the United States and Iran* (Berkeley, CA, 1993).
Ritzer, G., *The McDonaldization of Society: An investigation into the changing character of social life* (London, 1993).
Roberts, R. H., *Hope and its Hieroglyph: A critical decipherment of Ernst Bloch's "Principle of Hope"* (Atlanta, GA, 1990).
—— "The reception of the theology of Karl Barth in the Anglo-Saxon world: history, typology and prospect," in R. H. Roberts (ed.), *A Theology on its Way: Essays on Karl Barth* (Edinburgh, 1991), pp. 95–168.
—— "Barth and the eschatology of Weimar," in *A Theology on its Way: Essays on Karl Barth* (Edinburgh, 1991), pp. 169–99.
—— "Globalized religion? The Parliament of the World's Religions (Chicago, 1993), in theoretical perspective," *Journal of Contemporary Religion*, 10 (1995), pp. 121–37.
—— *Religion and the Resurgence of Capitalism* (London, forthcoming).
Roberts, R. H. (ed.), *Religion and the Transformations of Capitalism: Comparative approaches* (London, 1995).
Roberts, R. H. and Good, J. M. M., *The Recovery of Rhetoric: Persuasive discourse and*

disciplinarity in the human sciences (Charlottes-ville, VA, 1993).

Schutz, A., *The Phenomenology of the Social World* (London, 1972).

Shils, Edward, *Tradition* (London, 1981).

Sjöö, Monika and Mor, Barbara, *The Great Cosmic Mother* (San Francisco, 1991).

Steiner, George, *In Bluebeard's Castle* (London, 1971).

Taylor, Charles, *The Sources of the Self: The making of modern identity* (Cambridge, 1989).

Touraine, A., *The Post-Industrial Society: Tomorrow's social history, classes, conflicts and culture in the programmed society* (London, 1974).

Troeltsch, E., *The Social Teaching of the Christian Church* (London, 1931).

—— *The Absoluteness of Christianity and the History of Religion* (London, 1972).

Ward, G., *Barth, Derrida and the Language of Theology* (Cambridge, 1995).

Epilogue: Christian Theology at the Turn of the Millennium

David F. Ford

Scholarly differences about the exact date of birth of Jesus of Nazareth are such that its two thousandth anniversary may well be some years before the year 2000, so at the time of writing in 1996 that millennium may already have arrived. Whenever it might be, what is there for Christian theologians to celebrate? The obvious answer is: Jesus Christ. It is also obviously an answer full of questions. Of those questions, this epilogue takes up just a few to do with the health of the discipline of theology. It is a concern which deserves the attention not only of Christian theologians but of anyone with an interest in the meaning, truth, and practice of Christianity at the turn of the millennium.

Theology and the Abundance of God

One mark of full celebration is a sense of abundance. As the first reader of this expanded second edition of *The Modern Theologians*, that has certainly been my sense. The many-faceted richness and vitality of twentieth-century Christian theology has been overwhelming to the point of bewilderment. It has overflowed the few concepts, types, and historical forms that I offered in the introduction. This phenomenon itself invites theological interpretations.

Such interpretations need to take seriously not only the ways various disciplines (history, sociology, philosophy, and so on) might understand such variety but also to attempt to relate the variety to God. One line of interpretation might stress the contradictions, tensions, and disharmonies between many of these theologies, disturbed to the point of incredulity that a God of truth should be so variously understood even within one (albeit deeply divided) faith tradition. There is justice in that, and it raises a range of perennially perplexing questions about God, providence, freedom, truth, ignorance, sin, faith, revelation, incarnation, history, culture, tradition, and much else. But another line of response is to find, for all the unavoidability of the questions raised by the first line, a hint of the abundance of God.

That the truth and vitality of God are inexhaustible has always been part of

Christian faith. In this century – through such phenomena as a global church, at least one and a half billion Christians in hundreds of denominations, the massive transformations mentioned in the introduction, and unprecedented opportunities for travel, communication, and education – theologians have been faced with an explosion in Christian and other intellectual exchanges. These make the scale of the diversity unavoidable and also invite us into a fuller appreciation of the abundance of God traced through varied testimonies to truth, beauty, and goodness. It is an abundance that overwhelms its students without the possibility of overview. It stretches the mind to do some justice to it, just as it stretches other capacities. In all areas the burgeoning abundance of knowledge and interpretation has shown more clearly than ever the need for collaborative communities of disciplined learning for coping with it. The global upsurge of Christian theologies, as one community or group after another has found its voice, can be read as testimony to the polyphonic abundance of God.[1]

It is no accident that twentieth-century theologians have been especially fascinated by the theme of God as Trinity, which might be seen as the classic expression of the dynamic, differentiated relationality of an infinitely rich God. They have also been deeply concerned with the relation of this God to evil, sin, suffering, oppression, violence, and death. The twentieth century has in many respects been one of excess – in its aspirations, its global changes, and its evils. It has also been called a century of testimony (Elie Wiesel) – a basic, irreducible form taken by truth when faced by the unprecedented and excessive. These theologies attest to a threefold abundance: of God, of culture and creation, and of evil. They also invite the rigorous cross-examination required by any testimony on which a great deal depends.

The Future of Theology: Some Leading Questions

What of the future of theology? The most instructive way into this is through the sections in the chapters of this volume on debates and agendas. That way, justice is done to the pluralism of the discipline and attention is paid to each theology's particularities and implications. Studying these debates and agendas gives a glimpse of the "interrogative field" in response to which a great deal of future theology is likely to be done. There is no substitute for examining those sections in context one by one. I do not intend to review them all now; rather I will suggest a set of leading questions which may help readers to shape their thinking about theology itself in the face of that vast array of particular problems and orientations. I will take for granted the questions raised by those sections, and also the remarks in the introduction about the past and present of theology.

How attest in truth to God and to all else in relation to God?

This is the encompassing question for Christian theology. It involves a willingness to think thoroughly, imaginatively and practically of God. That in turn calls for ontology – inquiry into the being of God and of all creation (although whether and how being can be ascribed to God is a major issue). It embraces epistemology – how we might discover, test and reliably communicate the truth of God. It also, less obviously but perhaps more primarily, involves theological ethics – attestation to God as a matter of responsibility before other people and before God. It is a question that calls for worship, the building up of communities, the shaping of whole lives, and much else besides theology; but at least it does require that: a thoughtful relation to God in communities of learning and teaching.

Christian theology as treated in this volume is just one aspect of that wider theological activity, mostly carried on in universities, colleges, seminaries, research institutions, and a wide variety of courses and study groups, but reaching many more through sermons, books, periodicals, and other media. The quality of its future in all of these forms depends crucially on its response to this first leading question. Nor is it just the future of the discipline that is at stake. Coleridge's aphorism about the fundamental importance of truth to Christianity describes a downward spiral of corruption that affects communities as well as individuals: "He who begins by loving Christianity better than truth will proceed by loving his own sect or church better than Christianity, and end in loving himself better than all."[2]

How can theology distribute its efforts so as to be thoughtfully responsible in many spheres?

Any field's future depends on its lines of inquiry, and the previous chapters of this volume suggest what those lines might be. But how those lines are pursued is influenced by many factors, not least of which are contexts, institutional settings, and commitments. The introduction[3] has sketched the present situation. A key issue was seen to be theology's threefold responsibilities to academy, church, and society. If those responsibilities, with all their tensions and ambiguities, are to be fulfilled better in the future, how does the field need to be shaped?

Perhaps the greatest challenge and opportunity is in relation to responsibility to society. By this I mean many spheres of contemporary life apart from the two places where Christian theology is most visible institutionally, the academy and the churches. If God is conceived as related to all reality and is also to be loved with the mind, then theology cannot avoid being answerable in many different "courts." How can faith engage intelligently in economic activities, culture, education, social welfare, law, politics, government, health care, and other areas? Issues that are labeled "religious" arise in all those spheres, and much world news is about the conflicts and other problems associated with the religions. Yet such issues and problems are only the tip of the iceberg. The deeper matters are to do with the shaping of industries, nations, institutions, professions, cultures, and practices of all sorts. In them questions of the human good, ethical aims, conceptions of public meaning, truth and beauty, the interrelation of human beings and the natural world, envisioning the future, and much else are continually being considered. It is not an option for the religions to avoid such questions: Their members are daily dealing with them. The critical matter is how thoughtful, imaginative, and practical the faith is which informs their dealings.

One new and growing factor for theology in this situation is that this is the first century in Christian history in which considerable numbers of theologians have been educated without specifically church institutional roles in view. Theology has increasingly been "declericalized" and those educated in it are distributed in many roles and careers. They bring new possibilities for the engagement of intelligent faith with the diverse activities of complex societies. With them there are millions of educated lay Christians and also many with other than Christian commitments who are concerned with thinking through questions of faith in relation to the centers of vitality and of suffering in contemporary societies. These are all potential participants in theological inquiry and discussion if that proves capable of being relevant to their own responsibilities in society. There is a growing number of groups, networks, courses, and movements which try to work out understanding and practice that is informed by Christian faith. There is also massive resistance to them, not only from those suspicious of or opposed to Christianity as true or practical, but also from those Christians whose faith is a more "private" or "other-worldly" matter. Enabling far larger numbers to experience thoughtful, collaborative seeking after the wisdom of a God who is complexly involved in all areas of life: That is a task that calls for institutional creativity and improvisation, not least on the part of churches and academic bodies.

Will the academy be a place of genuine theology?

If "genuine" theology is a discipline that pursues questions of meaning, truth, goodness, and beauty raised by, between, and about particular religions, how hospitable to that will our academic institutions prove to be in the future?

It is easy to see how the pursuit of those questions can be curtailed or inhibited. The "guilds" of various specialties (history, scripture, human sciences, philosophy, etc.) can define their fields and "religion" in ways that strictly limit the scope of inquiries. Interdisciplinary methods and categories (such as those which subsume religions under "cultures") can do the same. There is often a bias against full exploration of the normative or the practical dimensions of religions. Whereas in economics it might be taken for granted that an academic could produce constructive theories and practical strategies of relevance to the world's economic practices, a parallel activity in Christian theology may be academically suspect.

Perhaps the most important single issue for many of the institutions in which the theologies in this volume (and the chapters about them) have been produced is that of the distinction between "theology" and "religious studies." One reading of these terms sees theology as confessional and church-affiliated, while religious studies is unaffiliated in that sense and owes allegiance only to the norms of the various academic disciplines that study the religions. That description is, however, highly unsatisfactory as regards what goes on in what I would judge to be the most lively centers of "theology and religious studies." If they are signs of the future, what might the desirable future be like?

If church-affiliated institutions of theology are to follow through the consequences of faith in Coleridge's God of truth then it is hard to see how they can avoid trying to do justice to the range of disciplines that are used in religious studies. There are, of course, many strategies for doing this (the typology used in the introduction to this volume covers the main options; Daniel Hardy in chapter 14 and Richard Roberts in chapter 35 offer alternatives), but from the side of the churches and of Christian theologians it is hard to see good theological reasons for splitting the field between theology and religious studies. The most convincing reasons for a division are prudential – when religious studies in a specific instance seems to be in the service of some ideology intolerant of intelligent Christian faith. But such ideology is not inherent in religious studies, and the churches are also vulnerable to that sort of oppressive intolerance. Indeed, full engagement in a range of disciplines (including many that most religious studies does not embrace, such as economics, politics, medicine, or the natural sciences) can combine with rigorous pursuit of the first leading question about the truth of God to become a healthy way of helping to reverse Coleridge's downward spiral into self-preoccupation which afflicts many churches and many academic disciplines. An irony is that church-affiliated institutions can, even more than other academic institutions, easily become so imprisoned in specialties, inhibited by dominant "guilds," and sensitive to doctrinal and ethical pressures from their own constituencies that they are incapacitated for any adventurous pursuit of the truth questions.

How can those academic institutions that are not church-affiliated cope with a subject as controversial and self-involving as theology and religious studies? One attractive way is to try to separate understanding from faith and evaluation of truth and goodness, so that it matters as little as possible what an academic's faith and values are. The usual form this takes is, as described above, the assimilation of religions into various disciplines without remainder. Theology is seen as intellectual history to be described, analyzed, interpreted, and explained. Religious studies finds it extraordinarily difficult to sustain an engagement with the larger truth questions. It is often distanced from them by a double enclosure: by defining its object as a "phenomenon" and as "religious." This categorizing as "religious phenomenon" easily acts as a strategy of domestication and control, "fixing" the object so as to be amenable to a professional use of the various disciplines. The problem with this is clearest when it comes to the question of God. If this field includes reference to God, and if there is an academic imperative to pursue the truth of God, then faith (which for millions of intelligent people is intrinsic to understanding God truly) cannot be bracketed out. In general terms, it is a matter of the distinctive content of this subject (which includes reference to God) being taken into account in how it is conceived.

More specific to God (or the various ultimates and absolutes which are analogues for "God") is the point that the attempt to confine inquiry into the truth of God within the limits of any discipline is bound to be arbitrary – the question of God transcends the boundaries. Or, if it is not arbitrary, it will be found to appeal to something which in theological terms would be called a faith. Any laying down of boundaries that excludes the aim of understanding the truth of God in appropriate ways must take on itself the burden of proof that the imposed limitation is justified. There should be no presumption that faith is necessarily more of a hindrance than a help in inquiring into the truth of God. It is obvious that faith may be untrue, biased, prejudiced, irrational, infantile, and much else; but faith may also be intelligent, critical, mature, and reliant on sound testimony.

All of this amounts to an argument from the academic side against the division of theology from religious studies. Positively, it suggests a reconstitution of the priorities of theology and religious studies to allow for the full question of truth. In the case of Christian theology this is best tested by the question of the truth of God, but all the other major doctrinal and ethical questions can also function as coping-stones. The best situation is one in which theological questions can be pursued in accordance with the major issues raised by the subject matter and without arbitrary boundaries.

It is not easy to realize this institutionally, but it is better to risk doing so than to continue with a constricted religious studies which is impoverished by its inhibitions in relation to the largest questions of truth and practice raised by its own field. Is it possible for an academic institution which takes religions seriously to avoid ignoring or domesticating the question of God? Is it possible to imagine academic settings in which various particular understandings of God (including atheism) can flourish and can find, through continuing discussion and negotiation, ways of being together and collaboratively cultivating the field? Might it even be that in such settings various conceptions of God can operate iconoclastically against any attempt to impose upon the field an ideological framework which would give priority to something other than understanding God truly? In some institutions it is possible to see signs of affirmative answers to those questions, and they seem to represent the most hopeful centers of vitality for the future. They all transcend the division into theology and religious studies.

Will churches be communities informed by theology?

Churches often do not have an atmosphere conducive to eager learning of the faith and its implications. Yet their members in many parts of the world constantly meet with and have to respond thoughtfully to challenges to their faith. Such challenges may encourage a larger, more intelligent, or more practical faith, or, more frequently, they may be ambiguous, confusing, or negative. They come through the media, through meeting those with different convictions, through the communication and conduct of Christians and of churches, through the explicit and implicit commitments of the institutions they relate to, or through a range of questions or doubts suggested through education and experience. There are many ways in which a church can cope or fail to cope with building up and sustaining faith in such circumstances, including entering on Coleridge's downward spiral of turning away from truth (this can have considerable "success" by some criteria); but it is hard to see any long-term wise alternative to becoming more and more fully a learning and teaching community. This has always been an imperative, but in such an information-laden world as ours it becomes more urgent.

Being a learning community requires far more than theology, and it also makes new demands on theologians, but the embracing requirement is for a church to recognize that its classic "marks" as "one, holy, catholic and apostolic" are each inextricable from its learning.

The quality of church unity is linked to how its members can learn to share in the truth together and relate it all to the one God. If Coleridge is right, there is an intrinsic connection between community and truth-seeking. For a faith which believes in a God of all truth any notion of its own unity must include joint, collaborative learning which is in principle endless. "Speaking the truth in love" is a summary of this dynamism offered in the context of one of the classic statements of Christian unity.[4] Such a conception of unity is non-sectarian in Coleridge's sense, and it has important analogies with other communities. There is the possibility of churches and academic communities having much to learn from each other if they fulfill their respective vocations to unity.

The church's holiness clearly requires it to love God with the mind as well as in other ways. That is not only a matter of amazement, wonder, and awe leading into a passion for seeking God's wisdom. It also has a purifying, disciplining rigor which acknowledges the need to "unlearn" much, to be agnostic about much else, and to avoid time and energy being dissipated on trivia or on what is merely fashionable. Again, there are many analogies with other communities. Academic communities have their own practices of "holiness" in those senses, and some of the deepest convergences and divergences between Christians and others come under this heading. Perhaps the strongest provocation here is to do with understanding through worship and prayer.

The catholicity or universality of a church cannot be sustained unless there is deepening understanding of the full scope of Jesus Christ's reality and salvation as witnessed to by the Bible, various traditions, and contemporary Christians around the world. There are challenges here to seeking truth across boundaries of time, space, race, language, gender, class, education, and religion which also face the worldwide academic community. There are also "scandals of particularity" as Christians relate such boundaries to the difference made by Jesus Christ.

Being apostolic means being sent to spheres of life and truth beyond the boundaries of any church in order to learn, teach, and dispute. That demands endless rethinking, re-imagining, intelligent improvisation and risk-taking. It also embraces taking on responsibilities to society and within the academy as discussed above.

That brief sketch suggests how intrinsic truth-seeking is to church identity. It also shows how radical a question it is whether churches will be communities informed by that aspect of truth-seeking which is called theology.

Who does theology?

The obvious answer to the question "Who does theology?" is: anyone who thinks about the questions raised throughout this volume. In this epilogue I have been especially concerned to define the subject much more widely than academic theology, and have portrayed it being carried on by the most diverse people in all areas of life. But the "who?" question leads further.

It leads first to asking about the formation of the theologian. One common description of theology is that it is "self-involving." So too are other disciplines in various ways: the activities of attending, questioning, understanding, judging, and deciding change the student whatever the topic. But the subject matter of theology also has a specific concern with the radical transformation of selves. To be fully involved in the subject is to be questioned in ways that go to the heart of one's identity. To give oneself to this discipline is to find the whole "ecology of selfhood" at stake. The future of theology is bound up with those who give themselves in this way.

But that is too constricted a description of the interrogated and interrogating identity of the theologian if it does not make explicit that theology is also "world-involving." As the chapters of this volume have exemplified in so many ways, theology can be mediated through all areas of life and knowledge. So the "who" of the theologian is potentially concerned with all of nature and culture: that is the horizon, however narrow the focus of study may be in pursuing a particular question.

Yet even that does not make explicit the main concern of this epilogue: that theology is also "God-involving."[5] Enough has been said above about this, except to pose the most radical and controversial question of all about the future of the field: How will God be involved in the discipline of theology? One possible answer to the question, "Who does theology?" is that God does it; and, if so, then the most important question for a theologian is how God's self-attestation is mediated, discerned, and responded to.

How to Celebrate the Millennium?

Returning to my opening question in the light of this epilogue's questioning about the future of Christian theology, how might Christian theologians appropriately celebrate the millennium? A simple yet rich answer is by being guests and hosts. A theology under the sign of hospitality is formed through its generous welcome to others – theologies, traditions, disciplines, and spheres of life. It has the host's responsibility for homemaking, the hard work of preparation, and the vulnerability of courteously offering something while having little control over its reception. It also has the different responsibility of being a guest, trying to be sensitive to strange households, learning complex codes and risking new food and drink. Ideally, habitual hospitality gives rise to trust and friendship in which exchanges can plumb the depths of similarity, difference, and suffering.

Worthwhile theological thinking is rooted in those relationships in which we are welcomed into other people's thoughts and lives and above all into their communion with God. It can happen in many ways, through family life, church life, books, works of art, and many types of experience. In more formal theological education we think of how teachers have spread the feast before us, of their advice about which invitations to accept and which to reject, of intense conversations and arguments, of the amazing sense of hospitality across time and space as ancient Israel and India feed in, as well as women in South Africa, German academics, and English architects. Then there is the delicate interplay between being guest and being host, as one begins to cook for others, try out new dishes, bring together guests who have never met before, and later have further surprises through meeting them in their homes.

Such hospitality, the literal inextricable from the metaphorical, is a taste of what the theologies in this volume savor as the abundance of God.

Notes

1 For a perceptive philosophical presentation of attestation or testimony as pivotal for a contemporary conception of truth, see Paul Ricoeur, *Oneself as Another* (Chicago and London, 1992). For some of its religious implications see his *Figuring the Sacred: Religion, narrative, and imagination* (Minneapolis, 1995).

2 Samuel Taylor Coleridge, *Aids to Reflection* (London and Princeton, 1993), p. 107.

3 See above, pp. 1–15.

4 Letter to the Ephesians, chapter 4. It is noteworthy how this chapter interweaves with unity the themes of God, faith, growth in knowledge, and growth in love, and diverse callings to communicate the truth.

5 On theology as self-involving, world-involving, and God-involving see Daniel W. Hardy, *God's Ways With The World* (Edinburgh, 1996), ch. 3.

List of Dates

1884	Rudolf Bultmann b.	
1886	Karl Barth b.	
	Paul Tillich b.	
1892	Reinhold Niebuhr b.	
1894	H. Richard Niebuhr b.	
1895		*The Women's Bible* published
1896	Henri de Lubac b.	
1904	Yves Congar b.	
	Bernard Lonergan b.	
	Karl Rahner b.	
1905	Hans Urs von Balthasar b.	
1906	Dietrich Bonhoeffer b.	
	D. M. MacKinnon b.	
1913	Thomas F. Torrance b.	
1914–1918		First World War
1914	Edward Schillebeeckx b.	
1917		Russian Revolution
1919		Karl Barth's *Epistle to the Romans*, first edition
1922	H. W. Frei b.	
1923	Ernst Troeltsch d.	
1926	Jürgen Moltmann b.	
1927		Faith and Order Conference, Lausanne
1928	G. Lindbeck b.	
	Hans Küng b.	
	Wolfhart Pannenberg b.	
1933		Adolf Hitler Chancellor of Germany
1934	Eberhard Jüngel b.	
	Nicholas Lash b.	
1939–1945		Second World War, the Holocaust, atomic bombs dropped on Japan

1945	Dietrich Bonhoeffer d.	
1947		India and Pakistan independent
1948		State of Israel founded
		Nationalist Party in power in South Africa
		World Council of Churches formed
1949		People's Republic of China founded
1962–1965		Second Vatican Council
1962	H. Richard Niebuhr d.	
1963		All-Africa Council of Churches formed
		Civil Rights Movement in USA
1965	Paul Tillich d.	
1968	Karl Barth d.	Meeting of Latin American Bishops at Medellin
1971	Reinhold Niebuhr d.	
1976	Rudolf Bultmann d.	Ecumenical Association of Third World Theologians formed
1977		Ecumenical Association of African Theologians formed
1979		Iranian Revolution, overthrow of Shah
1984	Bernard Lonergan d.	
	Karl Rahner d.	
1988	Hans Urs von Balthasar d.	
	Hans Frei d.	
1989		Opening up of Berlin Wall and other East German borders
1990		End of Communism in Soviet Union
1991	Henri de Lubac d.	Last apartheid law repealed in South Africa
1992		Ordination of women as priests in Church of England
		"Earth Summit" in Rio (UN Conference on Environment and Development)
1994	D. M. MacKinnon d.	
1995	Yves Congar d.	

Glossary

a posteriori Latin phrase referring to thought or knowledge based on or arising consequent to experience.

a priori Latin phrase referring to thought or knowledge which arises from a concept or principle, or which precedes empirical verification, or occurs independently of experience.

absolution Act of releasing a penitent from sins.

absolutism Position which makes one element, text, person, ideology, or reality supreme or absolute in relation to everything; or an understanding of the absolute (ultimate reality) as existing independently or unconditionally.

abstract art Nonrepresentational or nonfigurative art, in which elements of form rather than surface appearance have been emphasized in handling the subject matter.

abstract expressionism Art which makes use of color, form and texture – but not recognizable subject matter; a movement within **abstract art** in the 1940s and 1950s.

actualism Understanding of objects from their manifestation in act, event, and movement (contrasted with **essentialism**), or the view that only the

actual world is real, in contrast with other possible worlds which do not exist.

Adornian Relating to the thought of Theodor Adorno (1903–69), German sociologist and political thinker, and a leading member of the Frankfurt School.

advaita Nondualist school of thought, one of the principal forms of the Hindu **Vedanta**, denying the ultimate reality of everything but the impersonal Brahman.

aesthetics The philosophy of the beautiful, particularly in relation to works of art; also, the study of the feelings, concepts, and judgments related to perception of the beautiful. Theological aesthetics are specifically the aesthetic dimensions of a religious tradition's own thought, worship, and practice.

Afrocentricism Method for cultural, historical, and social research and analysis that places Africa and Africans at the center.

agapeistic See **agapic**.

agapic Having the quality of *agape*, a Greek word for "love" used in the New Testament to describe the love of God expressed in Jesus Christ and commended and enabled between human beings and God, as well as among human beings.

aggiornamento Italian word for renewal, bringing up to date (especially used with reference to the reforms of the Second Vatican Council). See **Vatican II**.

agnosticism Belief that it is not possible to know the truth value of a certain proposition or propositions; often in theology referring to the belief that no one truly knows or can know whether or not God exists.

alienation Estrangement, lack of identification or commitment.

analogia entis See **analogy of being**.

analogy Proportion between things (frequently in terms of a metaphorical comparison) in which the degree of similarity and relative dissimilarity between the things is not a matter for exact measurement or definition, and the similarities cannot be interpreted univocally.

analogy of being The doctrine, associated especially with Thomas Aquinas and vigorously attacked by Barth, that there exists an **ontological** proportion or correspondence between the being of the created order and the uncreated Being of God.

androcentric Male-centered; understanding or implying that the masculine is superior or primary in relation to the feminine.

Anglican Name given to the churches and the members of the churches stemming from Henry VIII's schism from the Roman Catholic Church in 1534 and now members of the Anglican Communion.

anhypostasis Greek term in **christology** after the Council of Chalcedon (AD 451) which understands the human nature of Jesus Christ to have no personal locus of its own independent of the divine Word or **Logos** (see also **enhypostasia**).

animistic Relating to animism, religious belief, and practice involving a complex pantheon of spiritual beings and seeing natural objects as having spiritual life and values.

anthropocentric Referring to a view of life and the universe with humanity at the center, or to an approach whose starting point is humankind.

anthropology Theory or study of the nature of human being or of humankind.

anthropology, theological The theological study of being human.

anthropomorphism Conceiving of some being or beings, especially God, in terms of human attributes and characteristics.

anti-foundationalism Rejection of the supposition that certain universal or normative criteria exist and provide the basis for all philosophical and/or theological truth claims.

anti-metaphysical In opposition to a **metaphysical** understanding of reality; rejecting or lacking interest in overall, general accounts of reality.

anti-realist In opposition to a **realist** philosophical or theological stance.

anti-semitism Term for prejudice against and hostility toward Semites, usually meaning Jews.

apocalyptic Literally, the unveiling of what is covered or hidden; a genre of literature concerning the last things and the end of the world; more widely, revelatory literature concerned with **eschatology**, often containing dreams, allegories, and elaborate symbolism.

apologetic Maintaining a given position; explanation from a given position.

apologetics Branch of theology concerned with defence of **orthodox** doctrine in the face of opposing arguments and points of view, usually attempting to meet critics' questions and objections by looking for shared grounds or criteria for what is reasonable or true.

apophatic Relating to what is beyond expression in speech; more specifically, relating to the method of negative theology which stresses the transcendence of God over all human language and categories, and prefers forms of reference which say what God is not.

aporetic Relating to or having the qualities of an **aporia**.

aporia An irresolvable inconsistency, for example, in the conjunction of individually plausible propositions which are logically incompatible with one another.

apostolate theology Strand of 20th-century Dutch **Calvinist** theology stressing the central importance of mission, especially in the work of converting and transforming secular government and society.

Arian Relating to the teachings of Arius (ca. 250–ca. 336), who believed that Jesus Christ was not eternally divine and whose views were condemned at the Council of Nicea (AD 325).

Aristotelian Relating to the philosopher Aristotle (384–322 BC), or his thought, or that of his followers.

ascesis See **asceticism**.

asceticism Effort in the pursuit of holiness or virtue, often applied to hermits or other religious who strictly exercise themselves in religious devotion and voluntary self-discipline.

aseity The quality of God as completely self-sufficient and independent of all other beings, having his being from himself alone.

Athanasian creed Fifth-century creed, wrongly ascribed to Athanasius of Alexandria (ca. 296–373), which ex-

presses the doctrines of the **incarnation** and **Trinity**.

atheism The belief that God does not exist, that there is no God.

atman The self (in Sanskrit); in some contexts, the inner self or spirit.

atonement Literally, at-one-ment; the work of Jesus Christ on the cross reconciling the world to God; the doctrine of the salvific work of Christ.

Augustinian Of or relating to Augustine of Hippo (354–430), bishop, theologian, and saint.

autonomy State of being self-directing, independent.

beatific vision The soul's immediate knowledge of God, which is the principal joy of heaven.

behaviorism View that the causes and conditioning factors of behavior can be identified and measured, and that human behavior patterns can be modified relatively simply by the manipulation of such causes and conditions.

biblical criticism Use of techniques applicable to other forms of literature to study the Bible, usually focusing on original meaning and context, authorship, form, style, and historical reliability.

biblical theology Theology conceived from and with constant reference to the Bible, especially applied to a movement producing such theology mainly in the 1940s and 1950s.

biblicism Idolatry of the Bible; absolutizing of the Bible.

Big Bang A model for the history of the universe according to which it began in an infinitely compact state and has been expanding ever since.

Black Consciousness Movement originating in black America in the 1960s, calling for black people to act on the basis of organized group power, to promote independent black cultural and educational institutions and political strategies that would propel Black people into positions of social influence.

Black Messiah Christological title; signifies Jesus' identification with the black oppressed.

Black theology Theological movement which seeks to expound the Gospel in the light of the history, experiences, and cultures of Black people.

bodhisattva Specifically Buddhist term referring to an enlightened/spiritually awakened individual expressing effective compassion and saving wisdom toward others.

bondieuserie The ultra-realistic and sentimental religiosity associated by some with certain approved forms of popular ecclesiastical art.

cabbalistic Relating to Cabbalism, or the Kabbalah, the name for various streams of Jewish mysticism and spirituality.

Calvinism Type of Christianity or theology associated with the **Protestant Reformation** leader John Calvin (1509–64) and his followers.

capitalism Economic system in industrialized societies in which the concentration and control of the means of production (capital) is in the hands of private (i.e., nongovernmental) owners; resources and wealth are acquired through the operation of a free market; and the maximization of profit is the key stimulus of economic activity.

Cappadocian Fathers Group of church leaders and theologians from Cappadocia (in modern Turkey), especially Gregory of Nazianzus (329–89), Basil of Caesarea (330–79) and Gregory of Nyssa (330–95). Their theology, especially about Jesus Christ, the Holy Spirit, and the **Trinity**, was supported by the Council of Constantinople (AD 381).

Cartesian Referring to the philosophy of René Descartes (1596–1650), often indicating the separation of subject from object, knower from known, and affirming that the individual thinking self is the best starting point for philosophy.

catechesis Term for the oral teaching or instruction given to those preparing to become full members of a church.

categorial Working with or in the terms of a fixed number of basic categories; relating to or involving categories.

categorial adequacy Within the idiom of a particular religious outlook, the adequacy of certain categories (or "grammar" or "rules of the game") to the construal of reality, the expression of experience, and the ordering of life. A term associated especially with **postliberal** theology.

categorical Asserting absolutely or positively, rather than conditionally, hypothetically, or in a qualified way.

catholic Universal, comprehensive; often used to refer to those churches which affirm continuity of faith with the Christian creeds of the first five centuries.

cenobite Also "coenobite"; a monk or nun who lives in community, in contrast to one whose life is solitary.

Chalcedonian Relating to the Council of Chalcedon (AD 451) and especially to its definition of the person of Jesus Christ which affirmed his full divinity and full humanity.

charismatic Relating to the gifts of the Holy Spirit, such as prophecy, healing, words of wisdom, discernment of spirits, speaking in tongues, interpretation of tongues; also refers to a Christian movement (sometimes called Neopentecostalism) beginning in the 1960s, which encourages the exercise of gifts of the Holy Spirit.

christocentric Centered on Christ.

christocentrism Thought or theology which makes Jesus Christ central.

christology Branch of theology concerned with the doctrine of the person and work of Jesus Christ.

christomonism Generally used pejoratively, to describe a theological system which uses Jesus Christ as an overriding regulative principle, to the relative exclusion of other doctrines.

circumincession Also "*circumincessio*"; see *perichoresis*.

classic theism Understanding of God as absolute, unchanging, and transcending the world, which reached its classical expression in the Middle Ages.

classical Related to the standard accepted formulation of something, or to what became the paradigm for what followed; more specifically, referring to the period, civilization, and thought of ancient Greece and Rome.

classical theology That which is the paradigm for subsequent theology; in Christianity usually referring to **patristic** theology of the first five centuries.

coenobite See *cenobite*.

cognition Intellectual knowledge; the act of knowing.

conciliar Relating to certain church councils, e.g., Nicea, Trent, **Vatican II**.

confessional Referring to a theological position (sometimes called confessionalism) based on a particular confession or statement of faith (usually one of the **Reformation** statements); or, more widely, referring to a stance or position adopted from the inside as distinct from **phenomenology** or observation from the outside.

confessionalism See **confessional**.

Congregationalist Referring to Congregationalism and the Congregational Churches, a **Protestant** denomination in which ultimate powers in matters of church polity lie with each local congregation.

conscientization The process by which a person is converted from being passive or a spectator to being someone who questions, understands, thinks, judges for her/himself.

consequentialism The philosophical doctrine that all actions are right or wrong solely in virtue of their consequences, and that a good action is one which maximizes certain valued consequences.

consubstantial With or of the same substance or being; from a Latin translation of the Greek word *homoousios*, which was incorporated into the creed at the Council of Nicea, AD 325, in order to designate the relationship of Jesus Christ to God.

consummation Fulfillment.

contextual Relating to context, the particular setting of something in history, culture, or other respects.

contextualization Viewing, placing, or considering in a particular setting.

contingency Fortuitous character or non-necessity of an event or being.

contingent Relating to **contingency**.

continuum Something which is continuous, the parts of which are interrelated and pass into each other, rather than being separate components.

conversionism Attitude or practice which advocates or devotes itself to the religious conversion of others.

correlation Literally, one-to-one correspondence; in Tillich's theology (and the thought of those influenced by him), the relating of questions and issues of modernity with answers or symbols from the tradition.

cosmology Study of, and speculative theory about, the cosmos or universe.

covenant Binding agreement; in the Bible, an indissoluble agreement initiated by God between God and his people.

crisis theology See **dialectical theology**.

criteriology Study or discussion of criteria, the standards applied to something to judge it, usually regarding its truth or value.

crypto-Apollinarian Term for theological positions leaning toward the understanding of the **incarnation** associated with Apollinarius (310–90), which denied that Jesus was either fully God or fully human, or was both, and affirmed that he was a mixture of the two.

cultural-linguistic Referring to the description of religion (by analogy with a culture or language) as a system of meaning with its own rules which have to be learnt, thus providing an idiom through which to experience, understand, and act.

cybernetics The theory or study of communication and control mechanisms in machines, complex electronic systems, and living beings (especially humans).

dalit Indian term meaning "oppressed."

deconstruction A destabilizing method of analysis and description which exposes by means of internal critique the arbitrariness, manipulation, or bias in both the composing of texts and the construction of modes of thinking, speech, or behavior, and demonstrates how their logic invites its own refutation.

deductive Relating to deduction, a method of reasoning in which the conclusion is the logical and necessary consequence of the premises.

degree christology **Christology** which asserts that Jesus Christ was a human being like others, whose distinctiveness came from being inspired and empowered by the Spirit to an exceptional degree.

deism Understanding of God as creator, but denying continuing divine participation or intervention in the created order.

demythologization Process of interpreting traditional texts considered mythological (in the sense that they express their meaning in terms of an outmoded or mythological worldview), with the aim of showing that their continuing **existential** or practical relevance can be grasped despite their mythological expression.

denominational Referring to the various self-governing and doctrinally autonomous religious bodies or denominations within Christianity.

determinism The doctrine that all historical events can be understood wholly in terms of some antecedent cause or causes, and are the necessary effects of such causes; theologically, it is sometimes held to be a consequence of the doctrine of the **sovereignty** of God.

detraditionalization The loss or undermining of the shared practices and histories which shape and regulate an individual's concepts, sense of selfhood, emotional responses, etc., in relation to a community or society.

deuteronomic theology Theological development of the Hebrew Torah as seen in the Book of Deuteronomy.

diachronic From the Greek for "through time," describing events that take place successively in time, or states of affairs that are extended in time.

dialectic Method of reasoning (sometimes called dialectical method) in which the conclusion emerges from the tension between two opposing positions; or a force seen as operating in history, moving it through conflict toward some form of culmination. The radical tension between cross and re-surrection is often treated in dialectical terms (by Moltmann, for example).

dialectic (Hegelian) The rational process of reality, uniting object and subject, that which is "in itself" and that which is "for itself," in the unfolding movement of the whole (the "in-and-for-itself"), oriented toward the reconciliation of all in the embracing unity of absolute spirit.

dialectical materialism Marxist-Leninist theory of history in which human activity or **praxis** operates within determinative material conditions, and in which events move toward the progressive resolution of the contradictions of each historical epoch, culminating in the classless society.

dialectical theology Theology of the period after the First World War (initiated mainly by Barth's *Epistle to the Romans*), which radically negated (above all by reference to the crucifixion) all human ways of knowing and relating to God, and stressed the corresponding need for God's initiative in **revelation**; also known as crisis theology because of its stress on God's judgment (Greek *krisis*) on church and world.

diaspora Dispersal of the Jewish people around the Mediterranean world after 586 BC; more widely, any dispersion of a group from an original or established location.

diastasis Originally a Greek word, meaning "separation."

dichotomy Split or division into two, e.g., mind and body, fact and value, sacred and secular.

discourse Any language particular to a group or society, along with the ideas and social outcomes associated with it; understood by Michel Foucault (1926–84) as a tool of social power. Social phenomena are constructed and comprehended from within a discourse.

ditheism Belief in the existence of two gods, usually one good and the other evil, struggling for supremacy.

docetism The belief that Jesus Christ only seemed to be a human being. A view associated with **Gnosticism** and **Manichaeism**.

dogmatics Coherent presentation of the Christian faith through its doctrines.

Dominican Member of, or relating to, the Roman Catholic religious order of preaching friars founded by St Dominic (1170–1221).

double helix The spiral ladder-shape of the molecule which constitutes DNA (the genetic material of most living organisms).

doxology Address of praise to God, especially "Glory be to the Father, and to the Son, and to the Holy Spirit, as it was in the beginning, is now and ever shall be, world without end, Amen"; more widely, the study of praise and worship as theology.

dualism View of the world which holds that there are two ultimately distinct principles or spheres, such as good and evil, matter and spirit, or nature and grace.

ecclesial Relating to the church.

ecclesiology Understanding or doctrine of the church.

eclectic Coming from diverse and varied sources.

economy, divine God's plan for salvation incorporating the whole universe.

ecosphere The sphere (also called the "biosphere") in which the Earth's living organisms interact, both with each other and with the nonliving parts of their environment.

ecumenical Relating to **ecumenism**.

ecumenics Study of **ecumenism**.

ecumenism From a Greek word for the

whole inhabited world; in Christianity it is a movement for worldwide unity among Christian churches; sometimes used of cooperation between religions.

efficient cause The agent or agency which causes something else to be or to change (one of Aristotle's four types of cause, the others being material, formal, and final).

egocentricity Understanding which starts from the ego or self; not to be confused with "egoism" or selfishness (contrast with **exocentricity** below).

eirenicism Peacefulness or absence of crisis in a position (from the Greek word for "peace").

ekstasis Greek term for "standing outside oneself," or being in a state in which one's normal consciousness or capacities are enhanced, often in relation to the divine.

election Doctrine that God chooses people for salvation (and, within some traditions, for damnation).

empirical Approach to knowledge based upon what can be derived from and ratified by sense experience.

empiricism Understanding of sense experience as the source and test of all knowledge.

enhypostasia/enhypostasis Term in the development of **christology** after the Council of Chalcedon (AD 451) which indicates that Christ's human and divine natures can have no existence independently of each other, and that all the attributes of his human nature are included in the Son's divine personhood.

Enlightenment, the Period of European thought (at its height in the 18th century) which typically emphasized human reason and experience and the autonomy of the individual, rather than traditional (religious or other) authority.

epiclesis Invocation of the Holy Spirit upon the bread and wine within the **eucharistic** prayer.

epiphenomenal Accompanying some process or state of affairs in a merely incidental way, and having no effects of its own.

episcopalian Relating to episcopalism or episcopalianism, a form of church government in which ultimate authority resides with a body of bishops rather than with one leader or with the general membership; more specifically, a term for Anglicans and the Anglican Church in Scotland, the USA, and some other countries.

episcopate The bishops of a particular church, or the state of being a bishop.

episteme Greek word for "knowledge"; used to mean any form of knowing which determines the way in which the world is experienced or viewed.

epistemic Referring to the structure of knowledge.

epistemology Theory or study of human knowing, regarding its bases, forms, criteria.

Erasmian humanism Renaissance **humanism** of a moderate, conciliatory, and scholarly nature, concerned with church reform based on New Testament principles, associated with Erasmus of Rotterdam (ca. 1466–1536).

eschatology Understanding or doctrine of the **eschaton**, or ultimate destiny of the world.

eschaton Consummation or end time, the time associated in Christian theology with the resurrection of the dead and with judgment; sometimes used in relation to the end of an individual life, but more generally in relation to the end of world history, traditionally known as the Last Day or Day of Judgment.

essence The basic or primary element in

the being or nature of a thing; that without which it could not be what it is.

essentialism Understanding of objects from their **essence**.

ethical idealism Sometimes used to mark a contrast with the kind of **ethical realism** which stresses ambiguity and imperfection; more usually describes ethics associated with some form of philosophical **idealism** (e.g., in Kant, the distinction between duty and self-interest; or, in Hegel, the locating of individual freedom within the concrete ethos of a community which expresses the **immanent** rationality of Spirit).

ethical naturalism Ethical position grounded in natural or biological principles.

ethical realism Theory of ethics affirming the objective reality of values; or an approach to morality which stresses the ambiguities and imperfection of people and societies, and the limited possibilities of improvement.

eucharist **Sacrament** or celebration of the Lord's Supper (from a Greek word for "thanksgiving").

evangelical Relating to the New Testament Gospel or to the concern for preaching it; also, a term for the large **Protestant** denomination which is focused in Germany and Switzerland; also, a term for a diverse movement, spanning many Protestant churches and groups, with special concern for the final authority of Scripture, evangelism, and personal salvation and holiness.

exclusivism Belief that God will not grant salvation to those outside the Christian church, or outside faith in Christ.

exegesis Detailed and methodical interpretation of a text.

existential Relating to individual existence and subjectivity, describing the way of being that is distinctive of human life, action, and orientation toward the world.

existentialism Movement of thought, most influential in philosophy, theology, literature, and psychotherapy, which focuses on individual existence and subjectivity, affirms that existence precedes essence (especially in the sense that a person's decisions and responses to **contingent** events, rather than his or her supposed essential nature, constitute who that person essentially is), upholds the freedom of the will and its irreducibility to anything else, wrestles with the darker aspects of the human predicament such as anxiety, dread, inauthenticity, meaninglessness, alienation, guilt, anticipation of death, and despair, and is suspicious of generalization, abstraction, rational overview, systematization, claims to objective knowledge regarding human existence, and fixed ethical principles.

exocentricity The receiving of one's center from outside oneself; or an understanding which starts from outside the ego or self (contrast with **egocentricity** above).

Exodus Second book of the Bible, so called after the departure (exodus) of the Israelite people escaping from oppression in Egypt.

exorcism Act of driving out an evil spirit.

experiential-expressivist Relating to experiential expressivism, an understanding of religion as originating in inner experience of the **transcendent**, the various outward aspects of religion being attempts to express this.

expiation Understanding of sacrifice as that which makes amends for past wrongdoings.

expressionism Art in which the emotions of the artist are paramount and take precedence over a rational and faithful-to-life rendering of subject matter. Especially associated with German movements of the early 20th century.

extra-textual   Referring to the location of the meaning or reference of a text outside or independent of the text itself.

extra-trinitarian   Proper to the economic Trinity (see **Trinity, economic**), and to the **missions** of the trinitarian persons in the **economy** of salvation, and their relationship to created realities.

extrinsicism   Understanding of values or attributes as attaching externally to an object rather than belonging internally to it.

fatalism   Belief in the unalterable determination of events in advance, human freedom having no significant role.

fatalistic   Assuming that human destiny and development is predetermined and beyond human control.

feminism   Movement concerned with the dignity, rights, and liberation of women and the implications of this for humanity.

feminist theology   Theology sharing the concerns of **feminism**; in Christianity especially focusing on the critique of the tradition as **patriarchal** and on reconceiving it in nonpatriarchal terms.

fideism   Position that faith is the central and irreducible basis of all theological thought and knowledge; often used pejoratively of a position which appeals to faith and denies the need or possibility of rational justification.

fiduciary   Relating to a position of trust with regard to an object of faith.

filial   Regarding the relationship of son to father; in theology, usually referring to the Son's relationship with the Father within the doctrine of the **Trinity**.

filioque   Latin word meaning "and from the Son," added by the Western Church to the **Nicene Creed** to indicate that the Holy Spirit proceeds not only from the Father, but also from the Son.

finite   Limited, especially to the natural order; unable to transcend certain boundaries.

finitude   Inability of an object or person to transcend the boundaries of their existence; limitation, especially to the natural order.

form criticism   Approach to a text which focuses upon its constituent units and their particular functions for the original audience or readers.

foundationalism   Thesis that valid philosophical or theological truth-claims are founded on self-evident propositions or on truths of experience (or a combination of the two).

functionalism   Understanding of an object or discipline in the light of its purpose or function.

fundamental theology   Branch of theology which tries to ground as comprehensively as possible the whole enterprise of theology, usually with extensive consideration of the contributions of philosophy and other disciplines.

fundamentalism   In Christianity, a varied movement usually affirming a set of basic beliefs by reference to the authority of a literally interpreted, inerrant Bible.

glocalization   Word invented by the contemporary sociologist Roland Robertson, referring to the paradoxical conjunction of processes of globalization and localization.

Gnosticism   Name (derived from the Greek word *gnosis*, knowledge) given to a varied and diffuse religious movement which saw creation as the work of an inferior god, sharply divided the physical from the spiritual, and offered to initiates exclusive knowledge enabling them to escape from the world and physicality to union with the supreme divine being.

hamartiology The doctrine or part of theology which treats sin.

han Anger, frustration, resentment.

Hegelian Referring to the philosopher G. W. F. Hegel (1770–1831), his thought and his followers.

hegemony Leadership or domination; often referring to the domination of one person, class, culture, or idea over others.

Hellenism Greek culture and ideas influential in non-Greek areas in the period after Alexander the Great (356–323 BC).

henotheism Worship of one god in preference to or to the exclusion of other deities.

hermeneutical Interpretative; relating to **hermeneutics**.

hermeneutical theology Approach to theology which concentrates upon issues of interpretation and meaning.

hermeneutics Study of interpretation and meaning.

Hermetism Tradition of thought associated with the mysterious figure, Hermes Trismegistos, and especially with a collection of texts of a generally **Gnostic** character attributed to him and produced in Alexandria between the first and third centuries AD, whose rediscovery in the Renaissance was influential in relation to later esoteric philosophy, magic, and various types of **cosmology** and mystical spirituality.

heterodox Other than the accepted opinion in matters of faith and doctrine; opposite of **orthodox**.

heteronomy State of being governed by, or subject to, outside or alien control (opposite of **autonomy**).

heuristic Approach intended to open up an issue or argument for further questioning and discoveries.

hierophanies As identified by Mircea Eliade (1907–86): manifestations of the sacred or **transcendent** in any particular cultural situation.

historical theology Approach to theology which concentrates upon its development through historical contexts.

historical-critical method Approach to a text which seeks to determine its meaning in the light of what it would have meant in its earliest form and context, and to understand beliefs, institutions, and practices in terms of how they were produced by historical conditions and events.

historicism Approach which tries to describe and explain history purely in terms of the **historical-critical method**.

holism Attitude emphasizing the priority of a whole over its parts.

Holocaust Originally, a burnt offering; more commonly used as a proper noun to describe the mass murder of Jews by the Nazis between 1939 and 1945.

humanism Movement, originating in the Renaissance, to understand human life without recourse to higher (divine) authority; more widely, a worldview cultivating respect for humanity and confidence in its possibilities.

hypostases, divine Members of the **Trinity**.

hypostasis Greek word originally meaning "substance," it came, in relation to Jesus Christ and the **Trinity**, to mean individual reality, the subject of attributes, or person (in the sense of a member of the Trinity).

hypostatic union Definition of **christology** agreed at the Council of Chalcedon (AD 451) which affirms the dynamic union of two natures, divine and human, in the one person or "**hypostasis**" of Christ.

hypothetico-deductive Description of a method which tests the deduced consequences of a hypothesis against experimental data, to see if the hypothesis is thereby falsified.

iconoclasm Literally, the breaking of images; more widely, disrespect for or attack on established beliefs, ideas, or practices.

iconography Illustration or description through visual images and symbols (as distinct from iconology: the study and interpretation of images and symbols).

idealism Philosophical tradition originating with Plato which understands the mind, ideas, or spirit as fundamental to reality. The forms of idealism most influential on modern Christian theology have been Kant's transcendental idealism and the absolute idealism of Fichte, Schelling, and especially Hegel.

idealism, ethical See **ethical idealism**.

idealism, linguistic Position which holds that there is nothing which is not the construct of language.

idealism, romantic Strand of **idealism** emphasizing the unifying power of the imagination, the mind's creative freedom in thought and artistic expression, and the world of nature as mirror of the human soul (both being absorbed in the essential interconnectedness of the totality of things).

ideology Structure of concepts and beliefs governing the action and understanding of a group of people; often used pejoratively to describe beliefs and ideas which are rationalizations justifying vested interests or an oppressive system or practice.

idolatry Literally, worship of idols; more widely, false worship, worship of, or treating as ultimate anything less than or other than God.

immanence, divine Presence of God within the world, including everyday events and situations.

immanent Relating to **immanence**, indwelling presence, usually referring to God's presence in the world; see also **Trinity, immanent**.

immanentism The view that any events or phenomena within the world are explicable in terms of other events or phenomena within the world, thus excluding any direct agency by God or other supernatural powers; or a view of God which stresses his **immanence** or indwelling in the world rather than his **transcendence**.

immutability, divine The divine attribute or aspect which means that God is not subject to change.

impassibility, divine The divine attribute or aspect which means that God cannot suffer.

incarnation Literally, becoming flesh; the event of God becoming a human being.

inclusivism, religious Position which holds that a particular religion offers salvific truth by including rather than denying the truths of other religions.

incognito Unknown or unrecognized.

indeterminacy The view that some events (often specifically **quantum** events) have no causes; they just happen, and nothing in the previous state of the world explains them. In the principle associated with Werner Heisenberg (1901–76), indeterminacy means that it is not possible to know simultaneously and with accuracy both the position and the momentum of a sub-atomic particle.

indigenization Inculturation or expression in local terms of what comes from elsewhere.

individualism Attitude or position favoring the rights, value, or salvation primarily of persons, understood as autonomous and not essentially social.

infallibility Inerrancy, being incapable of making a mistake; more specifically, the Roman Catholic dogma that pronouncements of the Pope made *ex cathedra* are without error.

infinite Unlimited, inexhaustible, without boundaries.

instrumentalism The view that theories are simply tools or calculating devices which enable us to order and anticipate the observable world, and ought not to be regarded as themselves true or false.

integralism Also "integrism", attitude associated with certain strands of Roman Catholicism, holding that the Church is absolutely self-sufficient in all matters connected with faith and morals, and that its teaching is the positive norm in these spheres, on the basis of God-given revelation; often seeks to promote the political power and social standing of the Church as a basis for its exercise of doctrinal and pastoral authority.

interiority A person's subjectivity, especially the capacity for self-consciousness, thoughtful judgment, and decision.

inter-subjectivity Mode of relating between persons, understood as human subjects with **interiority**.

intra-textual Referring to the location of the meaning or reference of a text within itself, without reference to or justification by what is outside it.

intra-trinitarian Proper to the immanent Trinity and its relations (see **Trin**ity, **immanent**), i.e., to what God is "in himself."

ironization Making something ironical; using something ironically.

Isvara Sanskrit term for the supreme being as Lord of all.

jen Chinese term signifying human togetherness.

Jesuit A member of the Roman Catholic Society of Jesus, founded by St Ignatius of Loyola in 1534.

jouissance Notion developed by Jacques Lacan (1901–81), to describe going beyond oneself in relation to the fullness of Being: an ecstasy that does not end in equilibrium.

justification Being pronounced or made righteous; the act of God through the death and resurrection of Jesus Christ, bringing about **reconciliation** between himself and human beings.

justification by faith Justification understood as a free, unconditional gift of God received in faith.

kairos Significant, pivotal time in history; for Tillich, a crisis or turning point which demands decision.

Kantian Relating to the philosophy of Immanuel Kant (1724–1804) and his followers.

karma Sanskrit for "action"; in Hinduism and Buddhism, the metaphysical residue of self-regarding action, expendable through the experiences of repeated birth.

kenosis Greek word for "self-emptying," used in theology to describe Jesus Christ's laying down of certain divine attributes (e.g., glory, **omnipotence**), in order to become fully human. Sometimes used more generally of all analogous self-emptying.

kenotic christology Understanding of the **incarnation** of Jesus as involving *kenosis*.

kerygma From the Greek word for a herald's message, a term used for the proclamation of the New Testament church about Jesus.

Keynesian economics Economic theory which uses the techniques developed by John Maynard Keynes (1883–1946), concentrating on large-scale aggregate concerns rather than individual income and expenditure, and arguing for the effectiveness of varying government expenditure as a means of adjusting total national income and expenditure.

kyriarchical Relating to rule or domination in the form of "lordship."

laissez-faire A doctrine that the (usually economic) affairs of society are best guided by the decisions of individuals rather than by collective or state authority.

laity The members of a church, often distinguished from its clergy.

liberalism Moral or political ethos concerned to guarantee the freedom of each individual to do as he or she pleases (so long as it does not violate the equally legitimate freedom of others) and which celebrates **pluralism** and respect for personal **autonomy**. In theology, a movement attempting to open theology to modern experience, worldviews, and criteria, and especially to the contributions of other academic disciplines; more specifically, nineteenth-century liberal theology tended to stress religious experience, historical consciousness, and the need for freedom from traditional dogma and frameworks in recovering Christianity.

liberation theology Theology originating in Latin America in the 1960s in contexts of political and economic oppression, which seeks to apply the Christian faith from the standpoint of the needs of the poor and exploited.

liturgy Communal worship of God (from a Greek word meaning "action of the people"); more narrowly, a term for the various aspects of prescribed public worship.

lobola In certain Black African cultures, the payment which a man must make to the family or guardians of a woman in exchange for marriage to her.

logico-deductive Referring to a method which holds that the conclusions of an argument or thesis will logically and necessarily follow from its premises.

logos Greek for "word"; more widely, the rational or ordering principle in something or in reality as a whole; in **christology**, used to refer to Jesus Christ as the Word of God, God's self-disclosure.

logos christology Christology whose key concept is Jesus understood as the historical expression of the eternal, divine **logos** through which everything was created.

los indos (Spanish) the Indians; the name Christopher Columbus gave to the inhabitants of the Americas.

Lutheran Referring to churches, traditions, or theologies stemming from the **Reformation** tradition begun by Martin Luther (1483–1546).

Magisterium The Roman Catholic Church's official teaching authority, exercised ordinarily in the instruction of the faithful, and occasionally in solemn declarations of the Pope or councils of bishops approved by the Pope.

managerialism The model of corporate organization (widespread in current government, business, and comparable corporate structures) in which the power of an executive is administered by an elite of professional managers.

Manichaean Referring to some aspect, or an adherent, of Manichaeism, a religion founded in the third century AD which held an extreme form of **dualism**, believing in two ultimate powers, one good and the other evil.

Marian Referring to Mary, the mother of Jesus.

mariology Branch of theology concerning Mary, the mother of Jesus.

marketization Development within **capitalism** of an economic (and more widely, a social) order based on minimal state control in favor of the use of individual or other private resources which compete for custom in the so-called "open" market; in particular, the extension of this ethos to other (professional and/or formerly state-funded) areas, such as education and health care.

Marxism Thought or movement stemming from Karl Marx (1818–83).

materialism Position which asserts the sole and/or ultimate reality of matter.

mauvaise foi French for "bad faith." In the terms of Jean-Paul Sartre's (1905–80) **existentialism**, the denial or avoidance of one's own authorship of one's actions and choices.

mechanistic Understanding the world according to the analogy of a machine, with a special concern for tracing effects to causes.

Mennonites Protestant denomination founded by Menno Simons (1496–1561), stressing believers' baptism, congregational autonomy, pacifism, and nonparticipation in public office.

messianism Hope for the coming of a messiah or savior who will liberate from oppression.

mestizaje (Spanish) racial and/or cultural mixing of Spanish and Amerindian; as a theological category, denotes the dialectic of cultural birth.

mestizo, mestiza (Spanish) a person of mixed blood and/or culture.

metadiscourse Discourse used to describe one or more other **discourses**.

metanarrative Overarching narrative or account which attempts to comprehend, include or explain other narratives.

metaphysics Study of reality in general; the science of being, existence, and knowing, aiming to encompass and understand the basic constituents of reality.

metaphysics, christological A Christ-centered understanding of reality.

metaphysics, classical The **metaphysics** of Plato, Aristotle, and their followers.

metaphysics, idealist The **metaphysics** of Berkeley, Descartes, Kant, Hegel, and their followers.

metatheological Relating to the discussion of theology in general, its nature, bases, methods, and purposes.

Methodist Member of, or relating to, the **Protestant** denomination founded by John Wesley (1703–91).

methodology Reflection on the systematic approach to a topic or field.

middle axioms Term coined in 1937 by J. H. Oldham to describe axioms which mediate in ethics between general statements of goals or principles, and details of application or practice in context.

middle passage Refers to Atlantic slave trade; the area of the Atlantic Ocean between the west coast of Africa and the Caribbean (West Indies); for the captured Africans, chained below deck, the "middle passage" constituted a geographic and psychological boundary of great magnitude.

minjung The powerless.

missions (trinitarian) The two trinitarian missions are the redeeming work of the Son (in his **incarnation**, and through the cross and resurrection), and the **sanctifying**/divinizing work of the Holy Spirit; the missions belong to the economic Trinity (see **Trinity, economic**), and correspond to the differentiating **processions** of **Logos** and Spirit in the immanent Trinity (see **Trinity, immanent**).

modernism, Catholic   Position of some late 19th- and early 20th-century Roman Catholic theologians who sought to come to terms with the intellectual climate of modernity, especially in the adoption of a positive attitude toward **biblical criticism**, alongside a critical attitude to traditional Christian doctrine. It was officially condemned by the Holy Office in 1907.

monarchia   From a Greek word meaning "one origin" or "one rule"; referring in trinitarian theology to the Father as the source of the Son and Spirit; sometimes interpreted heretically to mean that Jesus was not divine, or was divine in a secondary sense.

monarchial   Relating to **monarchia**.

monarchianism, dynamic   A 2nd- and 3rd-century heresy which stressed the unity of the **Trinity** at the expense of the distinction between its members, maintaining that Jesus was God only in the sense that a power of influence (Greek, *dunamis*) from the Father rested on his human person.

monarchical   Relating to **monarchia**.

monergism   Understanding that the Holy Spirit is the sole agent responsible for the regeneration of Christians (contrast with **synergism, synergic**).

monism   Position that one regulative principle governs the universe; also, a position that all reality is one, or is to be explained in terms of one fundamental constituent.

Monophysitism   The heresy condemned by the Council of Chalcedon (AD 451) that there is only one nature in Jesus Christ, his humanity being entirely absorbed by his divinity.

monotheism   Belief in only one God as ultimate reality.

mujerista   (Spanish, from *mujer*, woman) theological reflection done by and emerging from the reality of Hispanic/Latino women; *mujeristas* struggle for liberation, not as individuals, but as members of a Hispanic community.

multiplex   Manifold or multiple; having or involving many individual parts.

mysticism   Strand in many religions stressing the knowledge of God or the **transcendent** through experience, often in the form of immediate intuition or other direct communication or sense of union, and often denying the possibility of adequate linguistic communication of such experience; often contrasted with knowledge of God through indirect means such as reasoning, Scripture, or tradition.

myth   In theology, usually understood as an expression of religious meaning through story or symbol, often using a premodern worldview.

mythology   Study of, or a collection of **myths**.

natural religion   Unrevealed religion; religion arrived at through human reasoning about the world and human existence.

natural theology   Theology attempting to know God and God's relationship to the world through nature and human reasoning without divine **revelation**.

naturalism   Position affirming that the world can be understood (especially through the natural sciences) without reference to any explanatory factor beyond the natural order, which is usually understood in a **materialist** way.

naturalistic   Relating to **naturalism**.

necessitarian   Relating to necessitarianism, a position which views all events as happening by necessity and denies free will; often used synonymously with **determinism**.

negative theology Way of knowing God through negation and silence, indicating his transcendence of all thought and expression.

Neo-Calvinist Relating to a new or modern interpretation of **Calvinism**.

neo-conservatism Term for the theology of Barth and his followers, interchangeable with **neo-orthodoxy**; or a movement in contemporary **Protestantism**, often **fundamentalist** and politically right-wing.

neo-empiricism Movement of new or revived interest in **empiricism**, which is the strand in philosophy which attempts to tie knowledge to what can be observed to be true by sensory experience.

neo-Jungian Referring to revivals of the thought of the Swiss psychoanalyst Carl Gustav Jung (1875–1961).

neo-Kantianism Movement of revived interest in the philosophy of Kant after the decline of **Hegelian idealism**; in theology it especially emphasized Kant's distinction between pure and practical reason as a means to meet scientific challenges to the validity of religion and theology.

neo-Marxism New or modern version of **Marxism**, usually referring to revisions of Marxism relating it to recent developments in capitalist countries.

neo-orthodoxy Term applied to the Protestant theological movement associated with Barth, Emil Brunner, and Reinhold Niebuhr, referring to their attempt to counter the "unorthodox" **liberal** 19th-century theology by re-grounding theology on the principles of **Reformation Protestantism**.

Neoplatonism Religious philosophy of Plotinus (ca. AD 205–69) and his followers, which owed most to Plato and

offered a rational spirituality aimed at union with the One or the absolute which unites all reality.

neo-Protestantism Term interchangeable with **neo-orthodoxy**.

neo-scholasticism 19th- and 20th-century Roman Catholic movement which revived the theology and philosophy of Thomas Aquinas and made it the norm against which all other theology and philosophy are judged.

Neo-Thomism Term interchangeable with **neo-scholasticism**.

Nicene Creed Creed formulated at the Council of Nicea (AD 325), noted especially for its affirmation that Jesus Christ is of one substance, essence, or being (Greek, *homoousios*) with God the Father.

nihilism Belief that all reduces ultimately to nothing, or that existence makes no sense and is purposeless.

nirvana Buddhist (Sanskrit) term for the state of enlightenment.

noetic Referring to the mind or intellect, or to understanding gained through human rational processes.

nominalism Understanding of universal categories as class names which have no reality outside the individual particulars which make them up (contrasted with **realism**).

nonconformist Relating or belonging to nonconformity, the refusal to conform to the doctrines, polity, or discipline of any established church; originally referring to those Presbyterians, **Congregationalists**, Quakers, Baptists, and **Methodists** who refused to conform to the discipline and practice of the Church of England.

non-foundationalism Approach to philosophy or theology which does not require the necessary, prior affirmation of certain supposedly universal or normative truths or criteria.

nontheistic religion Religion that does not include belief in God or gods.

noumenal Relating to a **noumenon**.

noumenon According to Kant's distinction, a thing as it is "in itself" as opposed to a phenomenon (which is a thing as it is "for us," that is, a thing knowable by the senses).

numinous Term applied to those elements in the experience of the holy which are mysterious, awe-inspiring, and fascinating.

objectivism The theory that the world exists in itself independently of our comprehension of it; or that knowledge is based on factual evidence that describes things as they are and is discovered by objective methods of science and reasoning; or that the only true knowledge is that derived from and/or confirmed by sensory experience. In relation to values, the theory that values are independent of our comprehension of them, but can be found and known, and should be used as principles for human judgment and conduct.

objectivity State of being detached from and external to whatever is being perceived or affirmed, often seen as aiding neutrality and therefore accuracy in judgment, but sometimes seen as impossible or inappropriate in matters of religion.

objectivity, primary According to Barth's distinction, God's reality in his triune life (in his **aseity**).

objectivity, secondary According to Barth's distinction, God's reality in the revelation of himself in Jesus Christ.

occasionalist Referring to occasionalism, a position denying all-embracing causal relationships in the natural realm and regarding events as occasions through which God, the sole cause of all, effects change.

occultation The hiding or concealment of something; cutting off from view.

oikumene The whole body of Christian churches, conceived inclusively in terms of what they have in common rather than in terms of their **denominational** divisions.

omnipotence Possession of all or infinite power.

omnipresence Presence everywhere, at all times, to all things.

omniscience Possession of complete knowledge of all things.

ontic Referring to existing reality.

ontological argument, the Argument that when we conceive of God we conceive of that than which nothing greater can be conceived, and that such a concept of God entails his existence.

ontology Branch of philosophy concerned with the study of being, or reality in its most fundamental and comprehensive forms.

onto-theology Branch of theology concerned with being, and with the insights yielded by **ontology**, and identifying questions about God with questions about being.

original sin Doctrine of the radical corruption of all humanity through the sin of Adam and Eve, receiving its classical formulation from Augustine.

orthodoxy Right belief in and adherence to the essential doctrines of a faith as officially defined; or conventional or traditional belief.

orthopraxis Right belief combined with right practice, a term specially used in Latin American **liberation theology**, often in contrast with an **orthodoxy** seen as uninterested in the practical and political content of faith.

Palamism Teaching associated with Gregory Palamas (ca. 1269–1359), especially concerning the form of **mystical** prayer called hesychasm and the distinction between the divine **essence** and the divine operations or energies.

panentheism Understanding of the world as existing in God yet without negating the transcendence of God (God is both in and beyond the world); often also holding that the world and God are mutually dependent upon each other for their fulfillment.

pantheism Understanding that identifies God and the world as one, either without qualification, or with the world as a divine emanation, body, development, appearance, or modality.

papalist Person who sees the Pope as ultimate authority in all matters of dogma and church discipline.

paradigm Model, pattern, ideal type, or basic set of ideas serving to integrate or explain reality.

paralogy Postmodern approach to the analysis of **discourse**, associated with Jean-François Lyotard (b. 1924), which undermines established language use by indicating differences and contradictions, and by constant innovation and experimentation, and which is especially subversive of totalities, general truths, and "metanarratives," stressing instead the **pluralism, contingency,** and local character of all discourse.

parousia Expected appearance of Jesus Christ (the "second coming") before the consummation of history in the **eschaton** or Last Judgment.

particularity What is specific, definite, and distinctive; often implying the primacy of reference to **contingent,** historical reality over general or abstract statements.

paschal Referring to the suffering and death of Jesus Christ.

passibility Capability of undergoing suffering or pain, or of being changed by an external power.

pastoral theology See **practical theology**.

patriarchy Literally, rule by fathers; more widely, the totality of those social, political, and economic relations which assert male authority and influence.

patripassianism Belief that God the Father suffered and died in the death of God the Son.

patristic Referring to the fathers of the church and their period, usually covering the first five centuries AD.

Pelagian Relating to the 5th-century English monk, Pelagius, and his teaching that human beings are autonomously able to do good and contribute to their own salvation, thus denying the doctrine of **original sin.**

penultimate Next before the last or ultimate; referring to the stage immediately prior to the final or ultimate event; in Bonhoeffer, referring to everything prior to God's act of **justification**.

perdition State of damnation or of being lost.

perichoresis Greek term for the mutual indwelling or co-inherence of the three members of the Trinity. (The Latin equivalent is *circumincessio.*)

periphery Denotes relation of cultural, social (i.e., political, economic, technological) marginalization; in relation to the center, at the edge.

personalism Philosophical movement, beginning in the 19th century, stressing the human personality as the ultimate value and key notion in understanding reality.

perspectivism The view that all truth is truth from or within a particular perspective, and that conclusions about truth are as various as the perspectives which yield them.

petrine Relating to the apostle Peter; more widely, relating to the type of church authority represented by the Roman Catholic Church, whose papacy is traced to Peter.

phenomenal Relating to appearances, or to what appears to the human observer.

phenomenology Philosophical movement aiming to ground philosophy in a descriptive and scientific method, which understands religious and other phenomena in non-**reductionist** terms as they reveal themselves to consciousness, and seeks the distinctive laws of human consciousness, especially emphasizing its intentional character.

phenomenology, existential Descriptive philosophy of consciousness, focusing especially on the individual's immediate experience of his or her situation and self, as a thinking, believing, hoping, fearing, desiring being with a need to find purpose and a will that determines action.

philosophical theology Branch of theology that relates theological and philosophical thought, usually concentrating on areas of mutual concern.

pietism Originally, a 17th- and 18th-century Protestant movement reacting against the **rationalism** and rigidity of traditional **Lutheran orthodoxy** with an emphasis on the personal, devotional, and practical aspects of Christianity; more widely, a type of faith combining deep feeling, stress on personal salvation and holiness, and lack of concern for theological elaboration.

Platonism Thought of the Greek philosopher Plato (ca. 427–347 BC), and of the various philosophical and theological traditions stemming from him.

pleroma Fullness or plenitude or completeness, usually referring to the nature of God or Christ.

plerosis Greek word meaning "completeness" or "fulfillment."

pluralism Situation or understanding which embraces a diversity of contrasting cultures, values, ideas, religions, or other major elements seen as independently valid.

pneumatic ecclesiology Understanding or doctrine of the church as created and sustained by the Holy Spirit.

pneumatology Branch of theology dealing with the doctrine of the Holy Spirit.

polemic Confrontational, controversial statement directly challenging an opposing position.

political theology Theology that works out the political implications of faith; more specifically, that project as carried on in the context of a modern **capitalist** society.

polygyny Polygamy in which a man is married to two or more wives.

polymath Person of great and/or varied learning.

polyonymous Having many names or titles.

popular religion The religious understandings, practices, and devotions of the masses, in contrast to the theology and practices of "official" Christianity.

positivism In the 19th century, a movement associated with Auguste Comte (1798–1857), which saw history in terms of inevitable progress culminating in the "positive" stage of scientific knowledge, technology, and an **atheist** religion of reason and humanity; in the 20th century, logical positivism has been a philosophical movement stressing **empirical** verification, natural scientific method, and the rejection of **metaphysics**.

postcritical Related to **postliberalism**, and referring to an approach which tends to let tradition speak before reason, and which responds to texts in context-specific ways.

postliberalism In theology, a movement especially associated with Yale Divinity School and Duke University since the 1980s, which characteristically affirms Christian **orthodoxy**, criticizes the **liberal** reliance on human experience, and reclaims the notion of community tradition as a controlling influence in theology.

postmodernism Position which regards much of the present intellectual and cultural situation, especially in advanced **capitalist** societies, as in discontinuity with modernity, springing from a decline in confidence about the possibility of universal, rational principles, and manifesting itself in skepticism about progress, objective or scientific truth, or fixed meanings. It is often characterized by eclecticism and self-conscious parody.

poststructuralism The view that all perceptions, concepts and claims to truth are indeed constructed in language, as **structuralism** argued, but that they are transient and are the products of contexts (social and psychological) which do not obey structural laws.

practical theology Theology in its application to the work of the church, in particular the ministry of pastoral care.

praeparatio evangelica See *preparatio evangelica.*

pragmatic Practical, aiming at usefulness and effectiveness; in philosophy, relating to **pragmatism**.

pragmaticism In philosophy, a synonym for **pragmatism**.

pragmatics Study of language focusing on the users and the context of language use rather than on the reference, truth, or grammar of what is said.

pragmatism A position stressing knowledge derived from experience and experiment and used to solve practical problems, with truth tested by its practical utility and consequences.

pratityasamutpada Buddhist (Sanskrit) term referring to the causal interdependence of all things in the world of conventional reality.

praxis Greek term for action, practical ability, or practice, used in **Marxism** and adopted by Latin American **liberation theology** to denote a combination of action and reflection aimed at transforming an oppressive situation.

predestination Doctrine of the eternal decision and knowledge of God with respect to the destiny of human beings as regards salvation (sometimes called the doctrine of **election** and rejection).

predestination, double In classical **Calvinism**, the doctrine that God decrees from eternity that some human beings are destined for damnation and others for salvation.

preparatio evangelica Something which prepares or predisposes a person or people to receive the Gospel.

Presbyterianism Reformed church tradition, particularly influenced by **Calvinism**, in which authority is centered upon elders.

prevenience Literally, coming before or first; usually referring to a quality of God or God's grace as having the initiative in relation to human action, and being its prior cause or condition.

primatial Relating to the role of leader or primate among the bishops of a church or communion of churches.

process theism Understanding of God in **process theology**, stressing God's dipolarity, capacity to be affected by creation, and persuasive rather than absolute power.

process theology Theological movement, following the philosophy of A. N. Whitehead (1861–1947), which emphasizes notions of movement and becoming (process), rather than being or substance, and which affirms divine participation in process.

procession (trinitarian) Derivation (proceeding, procession) of the Son and the Holy Spirit within the trinitarian being of God.

progressivism The belief that later times are improvements over earlier times.

projectionism Transfer of an attribute or need of a person or group onto another object; in Feuerbach's (1804–72) thought God is explained as a projection of ideal human nature onto an imagined being.

prolegomena Work of a preliminary, introductory nature, preparing for fuller treatment.

proleptic Of an anticipatory nature; used, for example, of the resurrection of Jesus as an anticipation of the final consummation.

promeity Applied to God, the quality of being "for me" (Latin *pro me*), i.e., in the **economy** of salvation.

propaideutics Set of introductory ideas or principles required for the study of a subject.

propositionalism Method of asserting or proposing statements that are capable of being judged true or false.

Protestant Name for those Christians and churches which separated from the Roman Catholic Church at the **Reformation**, and for other churches and groups descended from them.

purgatory Intermediate condition between death and heaven, where those destined for heaven do penance for sins and are purified.

quantum theory Theory associated with Max Planck (1858–1947) about the discontinuous or disjointed movement at subatomic level of all particles of matter in the physical universe, and the wave properties sometimes associated with the movement of such particles.

racism Systematized or institutionalized oppression of one race by another.

rationalism Position in philosophy emphasizing reason as the primary source of knowledge, prior or superior to, and independent of, sense perceptions, often testing truth by criteria of coherence and logical consistency; more widely, used pejoratively of positions whose appeal to reason is seen as narrow, **reductionist** and unable to do justice to the subject matter.

rationality That which is characterized by conformity with reason, adhering to qualities of thought such as intelligibility, consistency, coherence, order, logical structure, completeness, testability, and simplicity.

realidad (Spanish) reality or context.

realism A philosophical position (in opposition to **nominalism**) affirming that a universal category (e.g., animal) may have a reality outside its individual manifestations (e.g., lion, cow) and independently of human consciousness; or a philosophical position (in opposition to **idealism**) affirming that reality exists independently of the human knower.

realism, ethical See **ethical realism**.

realism, sociological Approach which focuses on the way people in groups actually behave and on how social structures actually function.

realism, theological In the 20th century, usually referring to a position (contrasting with theological **idealism** or **liberalism**) which stresses the reality and initiative of God in **revelation**, and asserting that the God referred to in theological statements exists independently of human experience of or faith in him.

realized eschatology Understanding that the **eschaton** has been actualized in history, especially associated with C. H. Dodd's position that the eschaton was present in the life and death of Jesus.

reconciliation Re-establishment of a state of harmony or good relationship between God and humanity or among human beings; often used interchangeably with **redemption, atonement,** or salvation.

redaction Editorial ordering of material in a text.

redemption Literally, buying back; a financial metaphor (relating originally to ransom payments and slave-buying) for **atonement, reconciliation,** or salvation; the act or process by which liberation from bondage (described variously in Christian theology as sin, death, the law, the devil, the world) takes place.

reductionism Explanation of complex data in inappropriately simple terms; in theology, often referring to the attempt to explain beliefs referring to, e.g., God, in terms that do not assume the reality of God, e.g., in psychological, sociological, philosophical, or other terms.

reflexivity/reflection The idea that a subject does not merely experience events, but comprehends them in a way that is in turn socially constitutive of the situations concerned. The subject and his or her accounts may act to reproduce or transform the social situations to which they refer.

Reformation Movement for the reform of the Roman Catholic Church, beginning in the 16th century, resulting in the formation of independent **Protestant** churches.

reformism The label given to political and social policies whose object is to modify a political practice or aspect of social legislation without changing the fundamental political and social structure.

regression Retreat to some previous phase of development.

reincarnation Return to existence in another form, referring to the belief that human life is one stage in a cycle of existence to be carried on beyond death in a different form.

relativism A position holding the impossibility of attaining final, eternal truth or values, and stressing diversity among individuals, groups, cultures, and periods; sometimes also ruling out the comparison of truth claims and values.

religious socialism Movement, especially strong in continental Europe after the Russian Revolution (1917), uniting socialism with Christianity and especially with the expectation of the Kingdom of God.

representational art Art which tries to depict figures and objects as they appear to the eye (contrast **abstract art**).

ressourcement French word for return to original sources in order to inform modern understanding.

revelation Disclosure of what was previously unknown; in theology, usually the disclosure to human beings by God of his nature, salvation, or will.

revelation positivism Characterization (originating with Bonhoeffer) of Barth's position that no genuine knowledge of God is available apart from God's **revelation** of it, that such knowledge has no ground in human reason or experience but solely in God's giving of the capacity to apprehend it, and that there can be no question of going beyond the limits of what is thus given.

revisionist Relating to revisionism, the questioning and reconceiving of the core of a tradition.

rhetoric The use of language so as to persuade or influence others. The late 20th century has seen a renewal of the belief that all **discourse** and argument contains a political and persuasive core, which articulates itself in rhetoric.

Rishi Sanskrit for "sage, seer."

Ritschlianism Theology associated with the German Albrecht Ritschl (1822–89), which was especially concerned with **justification**, ethics, and the Christian community, and suspicious of **metaphysics** and religious experience.

Roman Index The list of books banned to Roman Catholic readers by the Holy Office. The Index ceased to exist at the time of **Vatican II**.

romanticism Movement, especially in literature, art, philosophy, and theology, which rejected **Enlightenment rationalism**, and duty-centered ethics in favor of a stress on feeling, artistic sensitivity and genius, community, and an ethics that took account of nature, desire and passion; more specifically, a movement in late 18th- and early 19th-century Germany whose leading figures were Goethe, Schlegel, and, in theology, Schleiermacher.

sacrament Action, ceremony, or celebration in which created things become channels and symbols of God's activity and promises (in Roman Catholicism: baptism, **eucharist**, confirmation, matrimony, holy orders, penance, and extreme unction; in **Protestantism**, usually: baptism and eucharist); more widely used to refer to the ways in which God and salvation are communicated through action and material reality.

sacramentum mundi Literally, "the sacrament of the world"; the whole created order seen as a sign of divine blessing and grace.

sadhu Indian term meaning "holy man."

salvation history Those events which the Bible narrates as revealing God's action for the salvation of the world.

sanctification Process of being brought to a state of holiness.

sannyasi (-sa) Renouncer (state of renunciation of/withdrawal from the world).

schism Divergence of opinion between two groups; in relation to the church, a breach of unity on doctrinal grounds, leading to deliberate separation from an ecclesiastical community.

scholastic theology, scholasticism Education, methods, and theology of the 13th-century Christian thinkers often called the Medieval Schoolmen, and of their followers in later times, notable especially for their application of logic to theology and their systematic attempts to reconcile faith and reason.

scientism Usually a pejorative term, describing the view that the methods and objects of enquiry recognized by science are the only proper elements of any philosophical or other enquiry.

scission Division or separation.

sectarianism Position associated with a sect, a religious or other group claiming exclusive possession of some truth or way of salvation, and tending to stress boundaries, division, and oppositions in relation to other groups – usually used pejoratively.

secularism Position advocating the elimination of religious influence in the state, social institutions, and the understanding of reality as a whole.

semantic Relating to semantics, the branch of **semiotics** which studies the meaning of words and the relation of signs to the things they signify.

semiotic Relating to a symbolic system.

semiotics The study of symbolic systems (including language); a tradition of study developed notably by Ferdinand de Saussure (1852–1913).

Semitic Relating to the racial grouping common to most peoples in the Middle East, but particularly referring to Jews.

shamanistic Relating to the belief that good and evil are brought about by spirits who can be influenced by particular individuals with access to the spirit world ("shamans").

Shoah Literally, "calamity"; used to describe the **Holocaust** in World War II.

Siva Name for the supreme Being ("the Gracious One") in some Hindu traditions; name of a Hindu "god."

social gospel Teaching emphasizing the material and sociopolitical implications of the Christian message.

sophiology Study of wisdom (Greek, *sophia*); or a theology or philosophy whose central concept is wisdom.

soteriocentrism Thought or theology which makes salvation or the doctrine of salvation central.

soteriology Branch of theology concerned with the doctrine of salvation (or **reconciliation, atonement**, or **redemption**).

sovereignty Relating to God, an attribute of the divine nature referring to his complete independence, freedom, and power to act in relation to creation.

speculative Referring to speculation: the attempt to project an overall understanding of the truth of a matter using rational thought.

stoicism School of philosophy founded at Athens by Zeno (335–263 BC); a form of **materialist pantheism** which sees God as the energy pervading and sustaining the natural world and as the

rationality or *logos* which orders it, and which emphasizes living in conformity with this natural order; best known for teaching detachment from desires and passions in the interests of self-sufficiency and imperturbability.

structuralism Belief that language, conceptual schemes, and systems of social organization are best described and analyzed in terms of irreducible and underlying structures or structural units; a movement which began in France in the 1960s.

structuration theory Approach adopted by Anthony Giddens (b. 1938) in which neither agency (**voluntarism**) nor structure (**structuralism**) is accorded primacy in sociological explanations, but rather the interrelation of both.

subjectivism Approach to knowledge focusing on the knowing subject rather than the object to be known, emphasizing the contribution to knowledge of the knower's mental constitution and states and denying the possibility of affirming truth objectively; or, an approach to aesthetics and ethics emphasizing values as reflections of the feelings, attitudes, and responses of the individual and as having no independent or objective validity.

subjectivity State of being a self-conscious, thinking agent; or, state of being personally involved so that one's perceptions and understanding are relative to one's individual experience or characteristics.

sublation A term (*Aufhebung* in German) used by Hegel simultaneously to mean "stopping," "preserving," and "raising up"; used to describe the thinking together of two apparent alternatives (or terms of a **dialectical** opposition) within some higher order "Notion" (*Begriff*).

Sublime, the A concept deeply embedded in 18th-century **aesthetics**, describing that which exceeds our perceptual and imaginative grasp, which is vast, exhilarating, majestic, and which arouses pride, awe, and sometimes terror. Linked by Kant with the realization of moral freedom.

subordinationism Trinitarian understanding of the nature of the Son and/or the Holy Spirit, which subordinates one or both to the Father. This can appear to compromise the Son's full divinity.

substitutionary Relating to the death of Jesus, the understanding which sees it as an act through which he took the place of sinful humanity, receiving on humanity's behalf the condemnation and punishment which belonged to it.

supernatural Relating to that which is conceived to be beyond the natural order, or beyond nature unaided by grace.

supernaturalism Thought dealing with that which is conceived to be beyond the natural order.

supersessionism Also "supercessionism"; position which claims, anticipates, or advocates the displacing of one thing by another (often used to describe a Christian attitude toward Judaism).

synchronic Describing two or more concurrent or simultaneous events or states of affairs, without regard to temporal progression.

syncretism Combination of varied or opposing ideas, doctrines, or practices, especially in the realm of religious and philosophical thought.

synergic Referring to synergism, an understanding stressing the cooperation of the Holy Spirit, the word of God, and the human being in the act of regeneration.

synoptic Referring to the Gospels of Matthew, Mark, and Luke; more generally, describing a combined or comprehensive view or presentation of something.

systematic theology/systematics Type of theology seeking to give a rationally ordered, comprehensive account of the doctrines of a religion and their interrelationships.

talmudic Relating to the Talmud, a body of commentary and elaboration on parts of the Mishnah (the Jewish legal and theological system completed ca. AD 200).

Tao(ism) Chinese term for "the way" (a particular philosophical outlook emphasizing inner and outer harmony).

theism Belief in, or set of beliefs about, God.

theocentric God-centered; revolving around the reality of God.

theocracy Literally, rule by God; an institution or society which is governed by its religious authorities.

theodicy Justification or explanation of belief in God in the face of the existence of evil.

theonomous Referring to God being primary or in control or the constitutive reality for an action, person, or situation in accordance with its own nature and integrity; contrasted with both **autonomous** (referring to independence from God) and **heteronomous** (referring to subjection to an alien control or principle).

theopaschite Referring to a 6th-century AD **Monophysite** group which held that the divine nature of Jesus Christ suffered on the cross; by extension, referring to any theology which asserts the suffering of God.

theophorous Bearing or containing the name of a god.

theos Greek word for "God."

thermodynamics Study of the laws

governing the movement of energy within a physical system.

Thomism Term for the theology of, and the schools of thought stemming from, Thomas Aquinas (1226–74).

Tractarianism A name for the earlier stages of the Oxford Movement in the mid-19th century, derived from the *Tracts for the Times* which the movement issued.

traditionalism Position appealing to past forms of a religion, culture, or other form of belief, understanding or behavior; more specifically, a reaction to modernity holding that religious knowledge cannot be derived from human reason or experience but only through faith in divine **revelation** communicated through tradition.

transcendent Existing, going or leading beyond; of God, referring to his being beyond all created reality; of self, going beyond one's present state, often by knowing, willing or some other mode of consciousness.

transcendental philosophy Usually referring to the philosophy of Kant and his followers.

transcendental theology Theology concerned to explore the fundamental conditions of theological knowledge, beyond any particular instances of such knowledge.

transcendental Thomism Movement in 20th-century theology (e.g., Maréchal, Rahner, Lonergan) concerned to marry the theology and philosophy of Thomas Aquinas with the philosophy of Kant and post-Kantian philosophers, and especially focusing on the knowing and willing human subject.

transcendentalism, Kantian Human experiencing and knowing, which go beyond **empirical** experience because they are presupposed by all experience.

transubstantiation The doctrine according to which the substance of the bread and wine (their essential or constitutive reality) is transformed in the **eucharist** into the body and blood of Christ, while their "accidental" properties (those things which are not essential to them, including their appearance) remain intact.

Tridentine Referring to the Roman Catholic Church's Council of Trent (1545–63), and used often to describe the form of the **liturgy** which emerged from the Council.

Trinity Christian understanding of the Godhead as three in one: the Father, the Son, and the Holy Spirit.

Trinity, economic **Trinity** in relation to creation and the revealing of God through history.

Trinity, immanent **Trinity** understood in itself through the interrelationship of its three members.

Trinity, social **Trinity** conceived in interpersonal terms as a society of three.

tritheism Belief in three gods, often referring to doctrines of the **Trinity** in which the unity of God is seen as compromised.

triune Being three in one.

ultramontanist Literally, "over the mountains" (meaning the Alps), and used at different times in European history (especially in 18th- and 19th-century France) to describe Roman Catholics who regarded the Pope as ultimate authority.

unitarianism Understanding and religious movement associated with rejection of the doctrine of the **Trinity**, denying a differentiated understanding of the Godhead and denying the divinity of Jesus Christ and of the Holy Spirit.

universal history The totality of history, with special reference to its unity, purpose, and pattern.

universalism Understanding of the all-encompassing nature of salvation, including the belief that ultimately all will be saved.

Upanishad(s) Text(s) forming chronologically the final part of the Veda or Hindu canonical scripture; also called "Vedanta" (i.e., "end of the Veda").

utilitarianism Version of **consequentialism**, associated especially with J. S. Mill (1806–73), in which the most valued consequence of human action is identified in terms of "happiness" (usually the greatest happiness for the greatest number of people).

vacuum fluctuations Energy fluctuations affecting space which is otherwise totally devoid of matter and energy. The recognition of fundamental fluctuations in empty space (occasionally correlated with the doctrine of creation from nothing) is a distinctive feature of **quantum** mechanics.

Vatican II The Second Vatican Council of the Roman Catholic Church (1962–5), characteristically associated with an attitude of renewed openness to the church's cultural and ecumenical environment, and with a desire to adapt its laws and institutions to the times.

Vedanta "End of the Veda"; see **Upanishad**; also, philosophical-theological school based on teachings of the Upanishads.

vicarious Relating to a state of being or an action which is undertaken on behalf of others, usually referring to the humanity or the death of Jesus Christ.

Vichy The government (led by Marshal Pétain) which ruled that part of France not occupied by the Nazis after the defeat of France in 1940.

voluntarism Understanding of human action focusing on the role of the will in determining action and behavior and stressing human freedom.

womanist theology Reflection on religion and religious experience emerging from the perspective of Black women.

Index